ENCYCLOPEDIA OF WORLD BIOGRAPHY

SUPPLEMENT

29

ENCYCLOPEDIA OF WORLD BIOGRAPHY

SUPPLEMENT

$\dfrac{\text{A}}{\text{Z}}$ **29**

GALE
CENGAGE Learning™

Detroit • New York • San Francisco • New Haven. Conn • Waterville. Maine • London

Encyclopedia of World Biography Supplement, Volume 29

Project Editor: James Craddock

Editorial: Tracie Moy, Jeffrey Muhr

Image Research and Acquisition: Leitha Ehteridge-Sims

Rights Acquisition and Management: Mollika Basu, Jermaine Bobbitt, Jackie Jones

Imaging and Multimedia: Lezlie Light

Manufacturing: Drew Kalasky

For product information and technology assistance, contact us at **Gale Customer Support, 1-800-877-4253.** For permission to use material from this text or product, submit all requests online at **www.cengage.com/permissions.** Further permissions questions can be emailed to **permissionrequest@cengage.com**

Gale
27500 Drake Rd.
Farmington Hills, MI, 48331-3535

ISBN-13: 978-1-4144-3367-7
ISBN-10: 1-4144-3367-0
ISSN 1099-7326

This title is also available as an e-book.
ISBN-13: 978-1-4144-5341-5 ISBN-10: 1-4144-5341-8
Contact your Gale sales representative for ordering information.

Printed in the United States of America
1 2 3 4 5 6 7 12 11 10 09

CONTENTS

INTRODUCTION

The study of biography has always held an important, if not explicitly stated, place in school curricula. The absence in schools of a class specifically devoted to studying the lives of the giants of human history belies the focus most courses have always had on people. From ancient times to the present, the world has been shaped by the decisions, philosophies, inventions, discoveries, artistic creations, medical breakthroughs, and written works of its myriad personalities. Librarians, teachers, and students alike recognize that our lives are immensely enriched when we learn about those individuals who have made their mark on the world we live in today.

Encyclopedia of World Biography Supplement, Volume 29, provides biographical information on 175 individuals not covered in the 17-volume second edition of *Encyclopedia of World Biography (EWB)* and its supplements, Volumes 18, 19, 20, 21, 22, 23, 24, 25, 26, 27, and 28. Like other volumes in the *EWB* series, this supplement represents a unique, comprehensive source for biographical information on those people who, for their contributions to human culture and society, have reputations that stand the test of time. Each original article ends with a bibliographic section. There is also an index to names and subjects, which cumulates all persons appearing as main entries in the *EWB* second edition, the Volume 18, 19, 20, 21, 22, 23, 24, 25, 26, 27, and 28 supplements, and this supplement—more than 8,000 people!

Articles. Arranged alphabetically following the letter-by-letter convention (spaces and hyphens have been ignored), articles begin with the full name of the person profiled in large, bold type. Next is a boldfaced, descriptive paragraph that includes birth and death years in parentheses. It provides a capsule identification and a statement of the person's significance. The essay that follows is approximately 2,000 words in length and offers a substantial treatment of the person's life. Some

of the essays proceed chronologically while others confine biographical data to a paragraph or two and move on to a consideration and evaluation of the subject's work. Where very few biographical facts are known, the article is necessarily devoted to an analysis of the subject's contribution.

Following the essay is a bibliographic section arranged by source type. Citations include books, periodicals, and online Internet addresses for World Wide Web pages, where current information can be found.

Portraits accompany many of the articles and provide either an authentic likeness, contemporaneous with the subject, or a later representation of artistic merit. For artists, occasionally self-portraits have been included. Of the ancient figures, there are depictions from coins, engravings, and sculptures; of the moderns, there are many portrait photographs.

Index. The *EWB Supplement* index is a useful key to the encyclopedia. Persons, places, battles, treaties, institutions, buildings, inventions, books, works of art, ideas, philosophies, styles, movements—all are indexed for quick reference just as in a general encyclopedia. The index entry for a person includes a brief identification with birth and death dates *and* is cumulative so that any person for whom an article was written who appears in the second edition of *EWB* (volumes 1-16) and its supplements (volumes 18-29) can be located. The subject terms within the index, however, apply only to volume 29. Every index reference includes the title of the article to which the reader is being directed as well as the volume and page numbers.

Because *EWB Supplement,* Volume 29, is an encyclopedia of biography, its index differs in important ways from the indexes to other encyclopedias. Basically, this is an index of people, and that fact has several interesting consequences. First, the information to which the index refers the reader on a particular topic is always about people associated with that topic. Thus the entry "Quantum theory (physics)" lists articles on people associated with quantum theory. Each article may discuss a person's contribution to quantum theory, but no single article or group of articles is intended to provide a comprehensive treatment of quantum theory as such. Second, the index is rich in classified entries. All persons who are subjects of articles in the encyclopedia, for example, are listed in one or more classifications in the index—abolitionists, astronomers, engineers, philosophers, zoologists, etc.

The index, together with the biographical articles, make *EWB Supplement* an enduring and valuable source for biographical information. As school course work changes to reflect advances in technology and further revelations about the universe, the life stories of the people who have risen above the ordinary and earned a place in the annals of human history will continue to fascinate students of all ages.

We Welcome Your Suggestions. Mail your comments and suggestions for enhancing and improving the *Encyclopedia of World Biography Supplement* to:

The Editors
Encyclopedia of World Biography Supplement
Gale, a Cengage Learning company
27500 Drake Road
Farmington Hills, MI 48331-3535
Phone: (800) 347-4253

ADVISORY BOARD

Grateful acknowledgment is made to those publishers, photographers, and artists whose works appear in this volume. Following is a list of the copyright holders who have granted us permission to reproduce material in this volume of *EWB*. Every effort has been made to trace copyright, but if omissions have been made, please let us know.

PHOTOGRAPHS AND ILLUSTRATIONS APPEARING IN EWB, VOLUME 29, WERE RECEIVED FROM THE FOLLOWING SOURCES:

ALAMY: Jose Nicolas de Azara, Charles Tilson Bright, Madeleine de Scudery.

AP IMAGES: Arthur Brisbane.

CORBIS: Pietro Aretino, Lauren Bacall, Moe Berg, Alice Stone Blackwell, Dewey Bridgman, Laura Bridgman, Heywood Campbell Broun, Empress Carlota of Mexico, Roy Marcus Cohn, Elisha Gray, Janet Guthrie, Anna Held, Robert W. Holley, Brian Keenan, Mary A. Livermore, Joseph L. Mankiewicz, Giulietta Masina, George Merck, Henry Fairfield Osborn, Sr., Peter Scott, Madame Marie de Rabatin-Chantal, Alice B. Toklas, Lurleen Wallace, John Wanamaker, Yoshinobu.

EVERETT COLLECTION: Leonid Nikolayevich Andreyev, Falloppio, Ned (Edward) Kelly.

GETTY: Anne of Brittany, Italo Balbo, Alfredo Baldomir, Jozef Beck, Carl Bernstein, ''Yogi'' (Lawrence) Berra, Bramwell Booth, Catherine Mumford Booth, Katherine von Bora, Antoinette Bourignon, Max Brod, Anne Bronte, Claire Leer Chennault, Charlotte Corday, Mairead Corrigan, Michael Curtiz, Marion Davies, Vittorio de Sica, Bo AKA Otha Elias Bates or Otha Elias McDaniel Diddley, Sir John Sholto Douglas, Le Duan, Franz Ferdinand, Franz Joseph Gall, Horatio Gates, Sheilah Graham (Westbrook), Jean Harlow, Lorenz Hart, Zellma Henderson, Lou Henry Hoover, Alan Hovhaness, John Hunter, Kon Ichikawa, Hayato Ikeda, Joseph Joachim, Ollie Johnston, Chuck Jones, Hamilton Jordan, Vi Kyuin Wellington Koo, Mary Ann Lamb, David Lean, Lotte Lenya, Carole Lombard, Nol Lon, Glenn L. Martin, William Bradley (or Barclay) ''Bat'' Masterson, Vincent Minnelli, Sir Henry Morgan, Giorgio Moroder, Hermann Julius Oberth, Chukwuemeka Odumegwu Ojukwu, Sir William Edward Parry, Thomas J. Pendergast, Juan Pizarro, Ernst Roehm, Nicolas Konstantinovitch Roerich, Antonio Maria Salieri, Dorothy L. Sayers, Max Schmeling, Norma Shearer, Albert Goodwill Spalding, Erich von Stroheim, Gloria Swanson, Edward L Tatum, Germaine Tillion, Jack Webb, Sunita Williams, Count Ferdinand von Zeppelin.

IMAGE WORKS: Charles Glover Barkla, Giovanni Borelli.

LANDOV: Emile Augier, Carl Bosch, (Abraham) Louise Breguet, Isreal ''Cachao'' Lopez, (Hans) Jurgen Massaquoi, Wilhelm Maybach, Antonin Novotny, Erwin Piscator, Baron Manfred von Richthofen, Ernst Stuhlinger, Charlie Wilson.

LEBRECHT: Zakir Hussein.

LIBRARY OF CONGRESS: Francisco Leon de la Barra.

NEW YORK PUBLIC LIBRARY: George Pierce Baker.

OBITUARIES

The following people, appearing in volumes 1-28 of the *Encyclopedia of World Biography,* have died since the publication of the second edition and its supplements. Each entry lists the volume where the full biography can be found.

ALLEN, PAULA GUNN (born 1939), Native American poet, novelist, activist, and literary critic, died of lung cancer in Fort Bragg, California on May 29, 2008 (Vol. 1).

BEVEL, JAMES L. (born 1936), American civil rights leader, died of pancreatic cancer in Springfield, Virginia, on December 19, 2008 (Vol. 2).

CARLIN, GEORGE (born 1937), American comedian, actor, and author, died of heart failure in Santa Monica, California on June 22, 2008 (Vol. 3).

CHAHINE, YOUSSEF (born 1926), Egyptian filmmaker, died after a cerebral hemorrhage in Cairo, Egypt on March 19, 2008 (Vol. 25).

CRICHTON, MICHAEL (born 1942), American novelist, screenwriter, and director, died of cancer in Los Angeles, California on November 4, 2008 (Vol. 4).

DARWISH, MAHMUD (born 1941), Palestinian poet, died after complications from heart surgery in Houston, Texas on August 9, 2008 (Vol. 4).

DEBAKEY, MICHAEL E. (born 1908), American surgeon, died in Houston, Texas on July 11, 2008 (Vol. 4)

DITH PRAN (born 1942), Cambodian-American journalist and activist, died of pancreatic cancer in New Brunswick, New Jersey on March 30, 2008 (Vol. 18).

FULLER, MILLARD (born 1935), American lawyer and social activist, died near Americus, Georgia on February 3, 2009 (Vol. 18).

GIBSON, WILLIAM (born 1914), American poet, playwright, and critic, died in Stockbridge, Massachusetts on November 25, 2008 (Vol. 6).

HELMS, JESSE (born 1921), American politician, died in Raleigh, North Carolina on July 4, 2008 (Vol. 7).

HIGHTOWER, ROSELLA (born 1920), Native American dancer, died after multiple strokes in Cannes, France on November 4, 2008 (Vol. 26).

KITT, EARTHA (born 1927), African American actress and singer, died of colon cancer on December 25, 2008 (Vol. 26).

MAKEBA, MIRIAM (born 1932), South African singer and activist, died of a heart attack in Castel Volturno on November 10, 2008 (Vol. 22)

MONDAVI, ROBERT (born 1913), American winemaker, died in Yountville, California on May 16, 2008 (Vol. 19).

MORTIMER, JOHN (born 1923), British actor and playwright, died in Chilterns, England on January 16, 2009 (Vol. 11).

MPHAHLELE, EZEKIEL (born 1919), South African author and scholar, died in Lebawakgomo, South Africa on October 27, 2008 (Vol. 11)

NEWMAN, PAUL (born 1925), American actor and humanitarian, died of cancer in Westport, Connecticut on September 26, 2008 (Vol. 18)

PERLE, GEORGE (born 1915), American musician, died of natural causes in Manhattan, New York on January 23, 2009 (Vol. 12).

PICCARD, JACQUES (born 1922), Swiss scientist, died in Lake Geneva, Switzerland on November 1, 2008 (Vol. 12).

PINTER, HAROLD (born 1930), English playwright, died of cancer on December 24, 2008 (Vol. 12).

RAUSCHENBERG, ROBERT (born 1925), American painter and printmaker, died of heart failure in Captiva Island, Florida on May 12, 2008 (Vol. 13).

SAINT LAURENT, YVES (born 1936), French fashion designer, died in Paris, France on June 1, 2008 (Vol. 20).

SINGH, VISHWANATH PRATAP (born 1931), Indian Prime Minister from 1989-1990, died of cancer and chronic renal failure in New Delhi, India on November 27, 2008 (Vol. 14).

SOLZHENITSYN, ALEKSANDR (born 1918), Soviet novelist, died of a hear ailment in Moscow, Russia on August 3, 2008 (Vol. 14).

SUZMAN, HELEN (born 1917), South African politician and activist, died in Johannesburg, South Africa on January 1, 2009 (Vol. 15).

TERKEL, STUDS (born 1912), American author and radio personality, died in Chicago, Illinois on October 31, 2008 (Vol. 15)

UPDIKE, JOHN (born 1932), American author, died of lung cancer on January 27, 2009 (Vol. 15).

WALD, FLORENCE SOPHIE (born 1917), American founder of the hospice movement, died in Branford, Connecticut on November 8, 2008 (Vol. 24).

Ezra Ames

American artist Ezra Ames (1768–1836) captured the likenesses of many early Americans, creating works of both artistic and historical interest. From his beginnings as a craftsman compelled to peddle artistic supplies to make ends meet, Ames rose to success in middle age based on the strength of his depictions of New York Governor George Clinton and other figures of the day. The artist was also a prominent member of the Masonic organization, serving in both state and national leadership. Nearly 575 pieces attributed to Ames are known today.

The fourth child of farmer Jesse Ames and his wife, Bette (Bent) Ames, Ezra Ames was born on May 5, 1768, in Framingham, Massachusetts. Ames seems to have been among the first of the family to use the spelling "Ames" consistently; records show that four generations of Ames's ancestors had preferred the alternatives "Emes" or "Eames." Ames's father served in the militia during the American Revolution, leaving the service after the 1776 deaths of first Ames's mother and, later that year, a younger sister. Ames's father remarried in April 1777, and the still-growing Ames family moved to East Sudbury, Massachusetts, and, around 1790, to Staatsburg, New York.

By this time, Ames was a young man and did not accompany his family. Instead, he remained in Massachusetts, living and working in Worcester, the site of his earliest recorded artistic activity: the painting of a chaise in May 1790. Ames spent the next few years in Worcester, where he painted only a handful of miniature portraits in

favor of decorative projects. His painting graced such diverse items as fire buckets, signs, clock faces, and sleighs. The year 1792 marked the probable creation of Ames's first oil portrait, painted for—but perhaps not of—a Mr. Draper. That same year, the artist painted a rare landscape as decoration on a chaise. As with the majority of Ames's work, contemporary knowledge of the dates of creation and at times decisions of attribution for these pieces rely on the series of account books kept by the artist throughout his career. Because the account books seem to serve as a record only of pieces for which he was owed money, however, Ames presumably produced more works of both decorative art and portraiture than are currently known.

Settled in Albany

In 1793, Ames traveled through parts of New York state, settling in the small but growing community of Albany, New York, sometime before August. Although the remainder of the year produced little work for Ames, the following year proved to be a better one. Writing in *Ezra Ames of Albany*, Theodore Bolton and Irwin F. Cortelyou noted that "[t]he amount of miscellaneous work for which Ames recorded payment due him during 1794 was quite as large and as surprisingly varied as it was in Worcester." This work included both the painting of sundry household items and, despite a significant increase in Ames's prices, a fair amount of portraiture. Two of these portrait miniatures depicted New York Governor George Clinton and his wife—the first of many portraits Ames would produce for the governor's family. The year 1794 brought personal success as well; that fall, Ames traveled to Massachusetts, where he married Zipporah Wood on October 6. The couple had their first child the next year, a daughter named Lucretia who died in infancy. This daughter would be succeeded by another, Marcia Lucretia, in 1798, as well as sons Julius Rubens in 1801 and Angelo in 1803. All of these children survived their father, with Julius following in his father's professional footsteps as a miniature portrait painter, albeit one of less renown.

Toward the end of 1794, Ames began what would be a long and prominent tenure as a Freemason when he joined an existing Masonic Lodge in Albany. The next year, he became a charter member of a new lodge in the town and moved steadily up the organization's ranks; in 1800, he became High Priest of Temple Chapter and from 1802 until 1826, he held the position of Most Excellent High Priest of the Grand Chapter of New York. He also served as Grand Captain General of the Grand Encampment of New York and of the United States during the late 1810s. From the start, this association led to a great deal of artistic work for Ames as he was employed to paint and engrave Masonic regalia, certificates, and medals throughout much of his career.

Based on the records in his account books, during the 1790s Ames seems to have supported himself primarily through the sale of prints and other art-related items; his records show that he painted only about 25 portraits during his first several years in Albany, although other portraits may have gone unnoted. By the turn of the century, Ames was also decorating clock faces for a watchmaker and taking in boarders at his home to bolster his income. He recorded no portraits in his account books between the years 1799 and 1802, when he produced a depiction of a Leonard Gansevoort. The following year, Ames painted a greater number of both oil and miniature portraits, with several of these surviving to the present day. In 1805, Ames painted—among several others—a bust portrait of William Cooper, the founder of Cooperstown, New York, and father of novelist James Fenimore Cooper; the following year, he painted a bust portrait of famed Native American chief Joseph Brant.

Experienced Growing Professional Success

Around this time, the artist seems to have begun enjoying greater financial success, despite remaining known for his artwork only in the Albany area. Although Ames continued to decorate miscellaneous pieces to supplement his income, he turned more decisively toward portraiture, beginning to refine what had been a varied collection of styles into a more distinctive artistic vision that was somewhat influenced by the works of Gilbert Stuart. By the end of the first decade of the 1800s, Ames appears to have acquired a measure of recognition outside of Albany, for a New York publisher requested one of his depictions of Alexander Hamilton as the frontispiece for an edition of Hamilton's writings.

In 1811, Ames submitted an unidentified portrait to the First Annual Exhibition of the Society of Artists of the United States, held in Philadelphia. The acceptance of this work led Ames to create the following year what the Dictionary of American Biography called the "portrait by which he gained the widest reputation"—a view of former New York governor and then-vice-president of the United States, George Clinton. The work was exhibited at the Pennsylvania Academy of Fine Arts as part of the Second Exhibition of the Society of Artists. Ultimately destroyed in

a fire in 1845, the exact form that this landmark piece took is now unknown. Although many believe the portrait to have been a full-length view, Bolton and Cortelyou argued that "it was probably not . . . because the artist's only portraits of this size located so far . . . reveal the artist's ineptitude rather than his ability as an artist." Ames certainly did produce a full-length portrait of Clinton the following year along with a companion portrait of George Washington, both commissioned for the New York state capitol building. This commission seems to mark the point at which Ames firmly considered himself a portrait painter rather than a general artist.

Despite this shift, Ames produced at about this time a handful of landscapes. At least one of these—the so-called "Romantic Landscape"—acted as a forerunner of the works of Thomas Cole and other Hudson River School artists of the mid-1800s. Ames also became a director of the local Mechanics' and Farmers' Bank, an association that would last until his death. These activities did not prevent Ames from painting numerous portraits over the next few years, including a series of nine portraits created for an intended portrait gallery of "Distinguished Americans" in 1818. This set included a depiction of the first wife of then-New York Governor DeWitt Clinton; that same year, Ames also produced portraits of the governor's two sons and three still life works for the governor, as well as completing the official portrait of the governor himself. Two years later, Ames again received commissions from Clinton, painting another still life and a portrait of the governor's second wife. By the beginning of the 1820s and presumably at least in part because of this work for Clinton, Ames's reputation as a painter seems to have spread throughout upstate New York.

In 1823, Ames took part in the opening ceremonies of the Erie Canal at Albany, laying the capstone for the canal as part of his duties as the Masonic Grand High Priest; he also served as part of the second opening ceremony for the fully completed canal in 1825. Professionally, Ames continued to produce mostly portraits, including depictions of Revolutionary War leader Benjamin Tallmadge; Albany businessman William James, long-time patron of Ames and grandfather of novelist Henry James; and, in about 1826, Mrs. Allan Melville, mother of novelist Herman Melville. The American Academy of the Fine Arts elected Ames as a member in 1824, but he did not participate in the organization's exhibitions.

During the second half of the 1820s, Ames—by then in his sixties—began decreasing his activities, perhaps as the result of declining health. He painted at least 35 portraits, however, including one of Mechanics' and Farmers' bank vice-president Samuel Stephenson Fowler that Bolton and Cortelyou describe as "one of Ames's most attractive works." The artist also continued to be active in the Masonic lodge until 1831, despite having retired from the position of Grand High Priest in 1826.

Death and Legacy

In his later years, Ames painted only a few known portraits, recording one in 1831 and another in 1834, this final portrait depicting Albany physician and former New York Secretary of State Charles Cooper. From that year until the time of his death, Ames served as president of the Mechanics' and Farmers' Bank. He died in Albany on February 23, 1836, at the age of 67, and was buried the following day at a now-unknown location. Around 1868, his grave was moved to the Albany Rural Cemetery, where it can still be seen today.

Although not widely remembered in modern times, Ames served an important role in his own era. The *Dictionary of American Biography* argued that Ames "ministered to the esthetic needs of his generation in nearly every field from the painting of carriages to the portraiture of statesmen." Indeed, these portraits have been Ames's most valuable lasting artistic works. Bolton and Cortelyou summed up Ames's contributions thus: "His portraits . . . are important not only as pictorial records of men and women in New York State during the early decades of the 19th century, but also as works of art many of which rank with those of the first painters of his time." Today, many of Ames's portraits are held by the New York Historical Society, as well as by major institutions including the Smithsonian American Art Museum and the Metropolitan Museum of Art.

Books

Bolton, Theodore, and Irwin F. Cortelyou, *Ezra Ames of Albany: Portrait Painter, Craftsman, Royal Arch Mason, Banker, 1768–1836*, New York Historical Society, 1955.

Cortelyou, Irwin F., *A Supplement to the Catalogue of Pictures by Ezra Ames of Albany*, New York Historical Society, 1957.

Dictionary of American Biography, American Council of Learned Societies, 1928–1936.

Online

"Ames, Ezra," *Grove Art Online*, http://www.oxfordartonline. com:/subscriber/article/grove/artT002340 (November 20, 2008). □

Guillaume Amontons

The French physicist Guillaume Amontons (1663–1705) improved the construction of the thermometer, the barometer, and other meteorological instruments, bringing them closer to the form and principles of construction they still display today.

A noteworthy feature of Amontons's career is that he was profoundly deaf (meaning that he could hear only very loud sounds). He refused the medical treatments available at the time for his condition, contending that deafness made it possible for him to concentrate more deeply on his scientific studies. Isaac Asimov, writing in his *Biographical Dictionary of Science and Technology*, pointed out that "this view was much the same as that held two centuries later by [Thomas Alva] Edison, who was similarly afflicted." In addition to his purely technical accomplishments, Amontons had a visionary streak; he anticipated key ideas in physics, perhaps including that of absolute zero, that lay decades or even centuries in the future.

Suffered Deafness Onset as Adolescent

The facts of Amontons's life are known only in outline, but his dates of birth and death have been firmly established. His father was a lawyer from France's Normandy region who moved to Paris, where Amontons was born on August 31, 1663. Amontons grew up during the so-called War of Devolution, an expanionist effort on the part of King Louis XIV to conquer the Spanish-controlled Netherlands. His hearing was apparently normal at birth but deteriorated sharply during his adolescence—whether because of accident or illness is unknown. Little information has survived as to how Amontons communicated with scientific colleagues as an adult, but ordinary interactions were apparently impossible for him: his friend, the writer Bernard le Bovier de Fontenelle, as quoted by Harry G. Lang and Bonnie Meath Lang in *Deaf Persons in the Arts and Sciences,* wrote of "a candor which his infrequent dealings with men had helped to preserve" in Amontons's personality.

Amontons seems to have become interested in science after the onset of his deafness. His family had a negative attitude toward his efforts, which at first were centered on humanity's always futile effort to develop a perpetual motion machine. But he persisted, studying new areas of science that involved precision measurements: architectural drawing, celestial mechanics (the motions of bodies in the sky), meteorology, and optical telegraphy—an early effort to communicate over long distances by means of flashing lights. In 1687 he constructed a hygrometer—a device to measure humidity—consisting of a hard but flexible ball filled with mercury; its size would change along with changing levels in the atmospheric humidity.

At some point between 1688 and 1695 he demonstrated to the king and his family an optical telegraph that involved a series of relay stations manned by operators equipped with handheld telescopes. Nothing came of the idea, but leading French scientists became aware of the young man's originality. In 1690 the astronomer Jean Le Fêvre sponsored Amontons for induction into the Royal Academy of Sciences in Paris. Established by Louis XIV, the Academy facilitated communication among French scientists and kept France near the forefront of technological innovation for much of the next two centuries. It was under the auspices of the Academy that Amontons demonstrated the technological discoveries he achieved as an adult.

Those discoveries centered on improvements in the basic instruments scientists used to measure the qualities of the atmosphere: at first the hygrometer, then the thermometer and barometer. Amontons did not invent these instruments, and key advances in their construction had been made by Galileo Galilei (1564–1642) and other predecessors. The principles that gases expand when heated and that the expansion could be used for the measurement of temperature were both well known, and had been since the time of the ancient Greeks. Galileo constructed an air thermometer in which air in a tube was trapped under water, causing the water level to rise as the ambient temperature increased.

Improved on Galileo's Designs

Amontons improved on Galileo's air thermometer. Instead of water in the tube he used mercury, which expands and contracts more than water under temperature changes. The most serious problem with Galileo's thermometer was that it responded to changes in atmospheric pressure, like a barometer, as well as to temperature changes. Amontons helped to solve this problem by making sure that the mercury was added at a fixed point in the tube, thus ensuring that the volume of air in the thermometer remained constant. The height of the column of mercury was thus altered by changes in the pressure of the air, not simply its volume, which minimized the effects of barometric pressure. Amontons's new thermometer was accurate enough to enable him to establish that the boiling point of water was constant, and it is regarded as an important predecessor to the mercury thermometer of German physicist Daniel Fahrenheit, which in its essentials is still in use today.

Several of Amontons's innovations were intended for use on board ship. A ship, with its constant instability, was a difficult environment for precision measurements involving liquids, but maritime conditions also made such measurements important. In 1695 Amontons wrote a book, *Remarques et experiences physiques sur la construction d'une nouvelle clepsydre* (Remarks and Physical Observations on the Construction of a New Clepsydra), promoting the use of the clepsydra, or water clock, for use at sea as part of a process to determine a ship's location. This idea gained little currency, but the essay also described two more ideas for which Amontons became well known among instrument makers, and for the next century, his new shipboard barometer and thermometer designs were attributed to him by name. They never became standard, but the principles involved once again advanced barometers and thermometers toward their modern designs.

The barometer outlined in Amontons's paper was known as a cisternless barometer. Instead of a pool of mercury that would be forced upward into a wide measuring tube by air pressure (impractical at sea because the whole apparatus would slosh), he suggested an inverted funnel shape, narrow enough that the mercury would be held in place by the walls of the tube, as in a modern mercury thermometer. His ocean air thermometer was, like his earlier thermometers, designed to eliminate the effects of changes in air pressure. It consisted of a closed U-shaped tube one of whose arms was filled with air, while the bottom and the other arm contained mercury that would rise as the air expanded. Amontons was clearly involved in the lines of thinking that led to the invention and refinement of the modern fixed-volume air thermometer, but he is not thought to have actually constructed such a device; Ferdinando II de' Medici, Grand Duke of Tuscany, is generally credited as its pioneer.

Embarked on Visionary Experiments

Later in life, Amontons's research took on a more speculative character. Around 1699, he completed what is thought to be the first study in history of the loss of energy due to friction in the operation of machines, stating for the first time the law that friction is proportional to the pressure placed on

the bodies in contact. His paper titled ''A Commodious Way of Substituting the Action of Fire, Instead of the Force of Men and Horses, to Move Machines'' described a heat-driven motor, powered by an external combustion source, that would turn a rotor directly. In the process of doing this research he noted that the volume of air rising from the freezing point to the boiling point increases by about one third, and he noticed that no matter how hard water is boiled, its temperature does not increase past the boiling point. Newton and other scientists had preceded Amontons in this discovery, but Amontons recognized its general significance. He went on to suggest the boiling point as a fixed point on the thermomenter scale, another advance in the process leading to standardized temperature scales, and he later suggested new ways of graduating—adding a scaled volume indicator to—alcohol-based thermometers.

Amontons also expanded on the research of French physicist Esme Mariotte (c. 1620–1684). Mariotte had established the validity of Boyle's Law, stating that the volume of air increases with temperature. Amontons's experiments showed that any gas would change in volume by a fixed amount when undergoing the same temperature change. In his remarks on this subject, notated in 1699, Amontons (like Boyle before him) hinted at the existence of a temperature so cold that gases would reach a state at which they could not contract any further. His ideas on the subject were skeletal, but they were known to the scientists of the late eighteenth century whose work paved the way for Lord Kelvin (1824–1907) and his discovery of the principle of Absolute Zero. The Swiss physicist Johann Heinrich Lambert (1728–1777), building on Amontons's work long after the French researcher's death, guessed that the theoretical temperature of Absolute Zero was -270.3 degrees Celsius, not far from the actual value of -273.15 degrees.

Amontons also extended his ideas about air pressure into a theory of the causes of earthquakes. In 1702 he suggested that earthquakes might result when air trapped beneath the surface of the earth became so compressed that even a small change in temperature could cause it to increase suddenly in volume. That his idea was incorrect does not minimize its originality in an age when the scientific study of earthquakes was unknown.

Despite his deafness, Amontons participated fully in the scientific life of his time. It is not known exactly how he communicated with others (there was no deaf community or established French sign language at the time), but he kept up a busy schedule of presentations at the Academy, and continued his publications and his work on French governmental civil service projects. Affectionately regarded by his colleagues, he was married and had a new young son in 1705. That year, he demonstrated a principle leading to a new advance in the accuracy of thermometers, showing that the effects of the expansion of the thermometer glass itself under temperature change had to be taken into consideration. His demonstration at the Academy involved the use of a thermometer made from a gun barrel, which expanded less than glass would. Shortly after this triumph, however, he died on October 11, 1705, of an unknown cause. He was only 42 years old, but he had helped lay the foundations for the science that would eventually become known as thermodynamics.

Books

Asimov, Isaac, *Asimov's Biographical Encyclopedia of Science and Technology,* 2nd rev. ed., Doubleday, 1982.

Lang, Harry G., and Bonnie Meath Lang, *Deaf Persons in the Arts and Sciences: A Biographical Dictionary,* Greenwood, 1995.

Middleton, W.E.K., *The History of the Barometer,* Johns Hopkins, 1968.

Payen, Jacques, "Amontons, Guillaume," in Gillispie, Charles Coulston, ed., *Dictionary of Scientific Biography,* Scribner's, 1970.

Online

"Amontons, Guillaume," Galileo Project (Rice University), http://www.galileo.rice.edu/Catalog/NewFiles/amontons.html (Octeober 3, 2008).

"Guillaume Amontons," World of Invention. Online. Thomson Gale, 2006. http://www.galenet.galegroup.com/servlet/BioRC (October 3, 2008). □

Jean-Jacques Antoine Ampère

Literary historian and celebrated man of letters Jean-Jacques Ampère (1800–1864) spent his life traveling and studying, in a relentless pursuit of the origins of language and literature. His treasured presence in some of the period's most exclusive and enlightened literary and philosophical salons allowed him to permeate and enhance the fabric of French society.

Jean-Jacques Ampère was born on August 12, 1800, just northwest of Lyon, France, in the village of Polémieux. His father was André-Marie Ampère (1775–1836), the eminent mathematician and physicist after whom the basic unit of electrical current was named. His mother, Julie Carron, was ill much of her young life, and succumbed to tuberculosis in 1803 when Ampère was four years old. American-born British author Henry James (1843–1916) revealed in his book *French Poets and Novelists* that Jean-Jacques "grew up among all-favouring influences, surrounded by doting grandmothers and aunts, in an atmosphere of learning and morality." Ampère's father took whatever teaching positions became available to him, and married a second time in 1807. This second marriage did not last, and in 1820 Ampère's father took an appointment at the University of Paris. Ampère and his paternal grandmother followed his father, and the young Ampère had the good fortune to be academically and socially educated in the fabled City of Lights.

Education

Described as a quick study but a terrible student, Ampère's excellent memory and strong sense of natural beauty were not accompanied by an aptitude for science, a fact that astonished everyone, considering his paternal heritage. He studied a wide variety of things, from botany, theology, and architecture to history, languages, and literature, but remained uninterested in science and politics. Early on in his career he hoped he might be a poet, and composed verse and tragedies that were respected, if not admired. While he and his father were both undeniably brilliant, they were impractical to a fault and made only enough money to continue doing what they loved to do.

Social Constellations

Ampère's Paris was the birthplace of the literary and philosophical *salons*—gatherings of extraordinary people in the home of an inspiring hostess or host with the aim of entertaining one another, fine-tuning their tastes, and augmenting their knowledge through reading and the fine art of conversation. Madame Récamier, born Juliette Bernard in 1777 and married to banker Monsieur Récamier (30 years her senior) in 1793, was the premier salon hostess of Ampère's time. Her charms were said to be legendary.

A 20-year-old Ampère was introduced into this elite circle by his father on the first of January in 1820, in Récamier's home at the Abbaye au Bois. Ampère spent much of the rest of his life idolizing Madame Récamier and expending significant energy on his efforts to remain close to her. A comprehensive biographical collection titled *Modern Frenchmen,* by Ampère's contemporary Philip Gilbert Hamerton, claimed that the relationship between Madame Récamier and Ampère was always essentially passionless on her side, if not on his.

Seeking Edification, Will Travel

Ampère left Paris in 1826 to study in Germany. Once there, he established himself in Bonn and met renowned literary critic and philosopher Friedrich Schlegel (1772–1829). Ampère attended lectures on German language and literature, as well as German statesman and historian Barthold Georg Niebuhr's (1776–1831) History of Rome lecture series. At the end of his stay in Bonn, he made arrangements to stay at Weimar with legendary *Faust* author Johann Wolfgang von Goethe (1749–1832). Goethe was much impressed with Ampère. According to Robert Nisbet in an article in *Proceedings of the American Philosophical Society,* when Goethe was asked how he explained the "extraordinary richness and maturity of mind of the 24-year-old Frenchman Jean-Jacques Ampère," Goethe replied, "Imagine a city like Paris where the most excellent minds of a great realm are congregated in a single place and enlighten and strengthen each other in daily association, strife and competition...and you will understand how a fine mind like Ampère's can be so advanced at age 24."

In 1827 Ampère took a tour of the Nordic countries and Northern Europe to study folk songs and popular poetry, and in 1830 he returned to France to give a series of lectures on Scandinavian and early Germanic poetry.

The first of these was printed as *De l'histoire de la poésie* (The History of Poetry), remarkable because it was the first time the French public had ever been introduced to Germanic and Scandinavian epics. Ampère served as a professor at the University of Paris from 1830 to 1833, at which time he took a position teaching French literature at the Collège de France (College of France) in Paris, an appointment he held until his death. Ampère found many outlets for the knowledge he so ardently collected, including a teaching position in Marseilles, at the Sorbonne, and contributions to *Library Magazine,* the *Globe,* and the *French Journal,* where he addressed history, literary criticism, and the origins of language and literature.

On June 6, 1836, Ampère's father died from bronchitis complications while inspecting schools in the south of France. Hoping to soothe his resulting grief, Ampère accompanied two friends to Italy in 1838 on a trip guided by the literary works of Dante. His three-volume *Histoire littéraire de la France avant le xii siècle* (Literary History of France Before the Twelfth Century) was published in 1840, and won the monetary Gobert prize two years in a row, which helped sustain him as well as providing funding for more travel. The year 1841 also saw the publication of his *Histoire de la formation de la langue française* (The Formation of the French Language), after which Ampère toured Northern Africa, Greece, and Italy with his colleague, the French dramatist, historian, archaeologist, and writer Prosper Mérimée (1803–1870)—among others. This prompted the publication of Ampère's essay *Voyage dantesque,* published in the 1848 work *Grece, Rome et Dante,* which made the study of Dante very popular among French academics.

Recognition

On April 22, 1847, Ampère was elected to the thirty-seventh seat of L'Académie française (French Academy), the renowned French organization considered the authority on the French language. Support for his election was so great that French writer, politician, and diplomat François-René de Chateaubriand (1768–1848)—the founder of Romanticism in French literature who was in his eighties—had himself brought in by wheelchair to vote for Ampère.

Ampère's private correspondence with his intellectual and social peers provided priceless insight into their lives and works. James featured the two Ampère's, father and son, in *French Poets and Novelists.* James included important correspondents in his study because "letters, after all, reveal character; they also record the manners of the day. And character and manners are the very stuff of fiction." James joked that Ampère traveled so much it was a wonder he found any time to write, and he wrote so much that one might believe he would have had no time for travel.

Friends and "Relations"

Ampère never married, but spent his affection first on Madame Récamier, and finally on a woman identified only as Madame L, whom he met in Rome in 1853. She was a terminally ill young widow with a little daughter. The woman's family, a Madame and Monsieur Cheuvreux, essentially adopted him when Madame L died in 1859.

One of Ampère's greatest colleagues and companions was French political thinker and historian Alexis de Tocqueville (1805–1859). They met in 1835 at Madame Récamier's salon, and Ampère was such a frequent visitor to Tocqueville's home that the scholar had a tower room built specifically to suit Ampère's tastes, calling it *le chambre d'Ampère* or the Ampère Room. Their friendship was based on a mutual intelligence and a belief that travel was the best way to truly develop one's understanding of all things. Their private correspondence provided an additional layer to the published works of both men, affording scholars an additional perspective on the views of these great thinkers. As Sally Gershman explained in an article in *French Historical Studies,* private correspondence and travel diaries were important because they "contained [the authors'] reasons for writing and [their] attitude toward [their] published work."

As Madame Récamier grew old and progressively blind, Ampère cared for her, even avoiding travel to remain close by. She died in 1849 at age 72, of cholera, and soon afterward he traveled to Spain, Portugal, England, London, and Scotland. In 1850 his *Litteraire, voyages et poesies* (Literature, Travels and Poetry) was published. While Ampère made no major discoveries personally, he was the first Frenchman and European to build a solid link between travel and learning. In 1843 he began to study Egyptian hieroglyphics in Italian museums, but went to Egypt after a year to see them in person. While there, dysentery weakened him, but by 1851 he was recovered enough to tour North America—Boston, Quebec, Illinois, and Cincinnati—after which he returned to Rome in 1862. In 1855 *Promenade en Amérique: États-Unis, Cuba et Mexique* (Travels in America: United States, Cuba and Mexico) was released, and his opus, *L'Histoire romaineà Rome* (Roman History in Rome) [1861–1864], made a posthumous appearance.

Last Days

While he was a young man, Ampère had never worried about dying on the road, but he valued his friendships so much at the end of his life that he stopped traveling. In March of 1864 he wrote of having felt pain around the heart, and he died in Pau, France, on March 27, 1864—in bed, his coverlet obscured by books and papers, the pencil just fallen from his hand.

Ampère willed all his literary remains to Monsieur and Madame Cheuvreux, and his private papers to their granddaughter. The surviving correspondence between the famous father and son was published in 1875 as *Correspondence et souvenirs* (Correspondence and Souvenirs), in two volumes that covered the 49 years between 1805 and 1854. This release of their correspondence made Polémieux a mecca for lovers of both literature and science.

Citizen of the World

As Tocqueville wrote to a friend in a 1854 letter quoted on the Alexis de Toqueville Web site, "No one was wittier, or more likable for his wit, than Ampère, whose temperament was as free as a bird's and whose character was adaptable enough that he could, for a time, not only adopt any lifestyle but do so with joy and revel in it.'' Philip Gilbert Hamerton, in his book *Modern Frenchmen: Five Biographies,* identified the three great needs of Ampère's life as ''friendship, imagination, and labor,'' and it was the scholar's admiration for both history and literature that helped him develop his gift for throwing himself and his reader back into the past. It is as one of the first true citizens of the world that Ampère will be remembered.

Books

The Bibliophile Library of Literature, Art and Rare Manuscripts, compiled and arranged by Nathan Haskell Dole, Forrest Morgan and Caroline Ticknor, International Bibliophile Society, 1904.

Biographical Dictionary and Synopsis of Books Ancient and Modern, edited by Charles Dudley Warner, Gale Research Company, 1965.

Hamerton, Philip Gilbert, Modern Frenchmen: Five Biographies, Roberts Brothers, 1878.

James, Henry, French Poets and Novelists, The Universal Library, 1964.

Merriam-Webster's Biographical Dictionary, Merriam-Webster Inc., 1995.

The Oxford Companion to French Literature, compiled and edited by Sir Paul Harvey and J.E. Heseltine, Oxford University Press, 1959.

Story, Norah, The Oxford Companion to Canadian History and Literature, Oxford University Press, 1967.

Periodicals

Journal of the Folklore Institute, Vol. 12, No. 1, 1975.

French Historical Studies, Spring 1976.

Proceedings of the American Philosophical Society, December 17, 1982.

Online

''Alexis de Tocquevill—Portraits,'' *Alexis de Tocqueville,* http://www.tocqueville.culture.fr/en/portraits/p_amis-ampere.html (October 13, 2008).

''Jean-Jacques Ampère,'' *Academie Francaise,* http://www.translate.google.com/translate?hl=en&sl=fr&u=http://www.academie-francaise.fr/immortels/base/academiciens/fiche.asp%3Fparam%3D390&sa=X&oi=translate&resnum=1&ct=result&prev=/search%3Fq%3Djean-jacques%2Bampere%2Bbiography%26start%3D20%26hl%3Den%26sa%3DN (October 13, 2008).

''Jean-Jacques Ampère,'' *Economic Expert,* http://www.economicexpert.com/a/Jean:Jacques:Ampere.html (October 13, 2008).

''Jean-Jacques Antoine Ampère,'' *MSN Encarta,* http://www.encarta.msn.com/encnet/refpages/RefArticle.aspx?refid=762507719 (October 13, 2008).

''October 13th, 2008—Today in History,'' *Spiritus Temporis,* http://www.spiritus-temporis.com/jean-jacques-amp%E8re/ (October 13, 2008). □

Anacletus II

Italian cleric Anacletus II (c.1090–1138) was the main figure in the Papal Schism of 1130 and one of several antipopes in the history of the Roman Catholic Church. Historians argue that Anacletus was actually a legitimately elected pope, and that his rival, Innocent II, was instead the wrongful claimant to the throne of St. Peter. For seven years Anacletus ruled in Rome, the place of his birth and where he had great popular support, with his main ally only Roger II of Sicily, whom he had made king. At ecclesiastical conferences across the rest of Europe, Anacletus was denounced by bishops for his role in the papal schism and for his family's Jewish origins.

A nacletus's actual date of birth is not known but is estimated to be around 1090; he was born Pietro Pierleoni and came from a wealthy family in Rome. Jews had been an integral part of urban Roman life since before the time of Christ, and had settled around the Trastavere area, a section of the city that took its name from its place on the west bank of the Tiber River, which in Latin became *trans Tiberim.* Some sources claim that the Pierleonis were possibly descended from a powerful Roman clan of the classical and early medieval period, the Anicii, but scholars believe such assertions were made to lend an aura of patrician authenticity to newer families who rose to positions of wealth and influence.

Grandfather Converted from Judaism

The actual origins of the Pierleoni family are not known, but the record shows that the first family member to convert from Judaism to Christianity was Benedictus Christianus, who was baptized by no less than Pope Leo IX around 1050. He was likely a wealthy banker who accrued a fortune by loaning money; at the time, charging interest on sums of money loaned to others under contract was forbidden for Christians. That ancestor married a Roman woman, and they named their son ''Leo,'' which became ''Pier Leoni,'' and the figure known as Pier Leoni was the father of Anacletus.

The Pierleoni family allied themselves with the popes during a time of major strife in Europe over who would control the naming of bishops and other high-ranking church officials. Popes claimed it was their right, but the Holy Roman Emperors sought to control this prerogative. This battle became known as the Investiture Controversy, and pitted many of Europe's most powerful hereditary rulers—those who claimed their right to lead was divine, or given by God—against the Holy Father in Rome, who claimed to be God's representative on Earth and to whom all Christians, and even monarchs should submit, according to church law.

Anacletus's father Pier Leoni held the office of consul, a high-ranking government post, and apparently tried to place his oldest son—whose name is not known—as prefect of Rome, another top job, in 1116. Opponents of the family, however, blocked this appointment. Three years later, the historical record notes that Anacletus's brother Gratianus was present at a council in Rheims, France, summoned to forge a peace between Rome and Henry V, the Holy Roman Emperor, and was apparently taken hostage before being released into the custody of Pope Calixtus II. Surviving documents from this council include an account from Orderic Vitalis, an English historian who wrote disparagingly of the Pierleoni family's Jewish background.

Educated in Paris

In many Roman and European noble families, tradition held that one son would inherit, while the second was to enter the service of the Church. That latter role apparently fell to Anacletus, who became a monk of the French Cluniac order after studying in Paris. The Cluniac monks took their name from the magnificent Abbey of Cluny in east-central France, and they became influential scholars and advisors to kings during this period of European history. Anacletus rose to become the papal legate in France, or papal representative, and was called back to Rome by Pope Paschal II, who headed the Church from 1099 to 1118.

Anacletus was appointed cardinal-deacon of the basilica church of Santi Cosma e Damiano (Saints Cosmas and Damian, who were early Christian martyrs), a landmark Roman church dating back to the sixth century that may have also been the site of a temple dedicated to the Roman god Jupiter as far back as the second century BCE. He was said to have fled with Paschal's successor, Pope Gelasius II, to France when the latter's election as pope displeased Henry V, who enjoined the head of another powerful Roman family, the Frangipane, to take the new pope into custody. Riots ensued with that event, and Gelasius was freed and returned, but forced to leave the city once again when attacked while celebrating Mass. He died in January of 1119, almost a year to the day of his controversial election.

Upon the death of a pope, the cardinals of the Church would customarily convene to elect a successor from among themselves. Anacletus did not become a member of this significant body until December of 1120, when Pope Calixtus II promoted him to the rank of cardinal-priest. He may have served as a papal legate to England, too, at some point before becoming embroiled in the 1130 schism.

The controversy that resulted in two competing popes began in early 1130 when the death of Pope Honorius II was imminent. Honorius had also been forced to flee Rome, but had also managed to come to an agreement with Henry V in 1122, which was known as the Concordat of Worms. This compromise permitted kings the right to give bishops secular authority in areas they governed, but not invest them with sacred authority as well. Therefore, the bishops would supposedly remain loyal to the Church, not the king to whom they owed their power.

Papal Conclave Torn by Dispute

There were still factions in Rome that were displeased by the settlement of the Investiture Controversy in an arrangement that seemed to favor the Church, not the Holy Roman Emperor. At the time, some church officials were quite

corrupt, and cardinals' papal votes could be bought. Both of these issues—one European, the other ethical—were major factors in the schism that occurred with Anacletus's election. David Philipson explained the sides and the anti-Semitic character of the battle in *Old European Jewries,* an 1894 tome which traces the lineage of Europe's most prominent Jewish families. "According to contemporary writers, whose testimony, however, must be used with much care," Philipson explained, the Pierleoni "family never entirely lost its Jewish type, either physically or mentally... The ancestor of the family had amassed an immense fortune by money transactions, and the rest followed in his footsteps. His numerous descendants intermarried largely with the Roman grandees. The remainder of the nobility, however, hated them as upstarts."

The pro-Frangipani faction hoped to influence the election, and managed to move the dying pope to a position nearer to the Frangipani stronghold in the city, where Honorius died on February 13, 1130. The cardinals on this side were the minority, but appointed a cleric named Haimeric as the papal chancellor; Haimeric's choice for pope was Cardinal Gregory Papareschi, who did not want the title. He was forced to accept it, however, under threat of excommunication.

Across town, the cardinals who rightfully held the authority to elect the new pope met at the Basilica of San Marco and elected Pierleoni, who took the name Anacletus after Anacletus I, the third pope in the history of the Christian church, who followed the apostle Peter and then Linus. Both popes were consecrated on the same day, February 23: Anacletus's took place in St. Peter's Basilica, while Papareschi became Pope Innocent II in Santa Maria Nuova. The latter is rightfully listed in the chronology of popes, but many scholars view him as qualifying as the antipope, or the one who was not legitimately elected or claimed the title unlawfully.

Derided for Jewish Heritage

The battle between the popes took place mostly outside of Rome: Anacletus and the Pierleoni clan had enough supporters to hold out in the city, while Innocent was forced to flee. He went by boat first to Pisa, then headed over the Alps to meet with Bernard of Clairvaux, a leading figure in the Church and head of the Cistercian monastic order. The French king, Louis VI, summoned a meeting of the French bishops to Etampes, and appointed Bernard to head it. The monk sided with Innocent, and may have organized a subtle campaign against Anacletus because of his Jewish ancestry. He wrote in *De consideratione,* "There is no more disgraceful slavery, none worse than that of the Jews: whithersoever they go they drag the chain, and everywhere displease their masters," according to Mary Stroll's 1987 book *The Jewish Pope: Ideology and Politics in the Papal Schism of 1130.* The current abbot of Cluny, Peter the Venerable, also expressed some anti-Semitic sentiment, as did Archbishop Walter of Ravenna, who called the divisive battle a "heresy of Jewish perfidy" according to Philipson's *Old European Jewries.*

At the time, the Mediterranean maritime trade had bred religious tolerance in places like southern Italy, but soldiers returning from the Crusades in the Middle East in northern Europe harbored intense animosity toward those outside of the Christian flock. There were pogroms in France around this time, such as one at Rouen, where returnees from the First Crusade locked the city's Jews in the synagogue and then set it aflame.

Lothair III became the new Holy Roman Emperor in 1133 and his help was enlisted by the pro-Innocent faction. Lothair and his army escorted Innocent back to Rome, but by now Anacletus had won two influential supporters: Duke William X of Aquitaine, who opposed his own bishops in publicly supporting Anacletus, and Duke Roger of Apulia, the Norman noble. In return for the support, Anacletus named the latter Roger II, King of Sicily. Some sources claim that one of the Pierleoni family was related to Roger by marriage.

Advanced Roger II's Claims

Lothair did not bring any significant military strength when he arrived in Rome with Innocent in the spring of 1133, and Anacletus's side easily repelled the 2,000 cavalry troops outside of his papal fortress, the Castel Sant'Angelo. Lothair was crowned Holy Roman Emperor by Innocent in the Basilica of St. John Lateran, the seat of the pope in his role as Bishop of Rome, before returning to Germany. He came back with a more significant force in 1136 with the intention of ousting Roger in Sicily, whose claims included valuable royal holdings in France thanks to fortuitous but childless marriages in Roger's extended family that made him the rightful heir. Lothair's war against Roger was backed by the Byzantine emperor, John II Komnenos, who hoped to end Norman dominance of the Mediterranean world. After some notable setbacks, Roger prevailed in the spring of 1138.

Anacletus had died by then, on January 25, 1138. His successor as antipope was Victor IV, but Innocent was able to enter Rome and take control. Victor left the city and visited Bernard of Clairvaux to ask formal forgiveness. A year later, the Second Lateran Council was convened by Innocent II, in which nearly a thousand noted ecclesiastical figures were summoned to Rome to decide on important matters, among them healing the Church after the Papal Schism of 1130 and setting a path for its future. Some noted reforms to come out of the Council included firm and final decisions on usury and the marriage of priests.

The Pierleoni family remained powerful in Rome and in Sicily, too, for several more centuries. Their descendants still are titled Italian nobility and can be found in the lineage of the Matelica and Pesaro families of Italy's Marche region and the Città di Castello clan of Umbria.

Books

Philipson, David, *Old European Jewries,* Jewish Publication Society of America, 1894.

Stroll, Mary, *The Jewish Pope: Ideology and Politics in the Papal Schism of 1130,* E. J. Brill, 1987.

Online

Loughlin, J., "Anacletus II," *The Catholic Encyclopedia,* Robert Appleton Company, 1907, http://www.newadvent.org/cathen/01447a.htm (December 17, 2008). □

Anacreon

The ancient Greek poet Anacreon (c. 570 B.C.E.– c. 490 B.C.E.) might be called the party animal of early Greek lyric poetry. Although his poetry touched on various subjects, he favored wine, women (and men), and song above all, and it was for those writings that he was celebrated in his own time and remembered by his successors.

Those successors were numerous, for Anacreon's influence was greater than that of most other Greek writers. The themes of his poetry were so timeless and so characteristically expressed that, for a millennium after his death, imitations of his work were common. These imitations were, until the advent of modern classical scholarship in the nineteenth century, accepted as genuine works by Anacreon, whose actual surviving output consists of a few complete poems and various fragments found on torn pieces of papyrus. The name Anacreon became poetic shorthand for the celebration of the powers of strong drink, a device that even appeared in an English song that was the immediate ancestor of "The Star-Spangled Banner," the national anthem of the United States.

As with other early Greek writers, hard evidence regarding the events of Anacreon's life is scant once one tries to move beyond his places of residence. Much of what is known about him has been gleaned from his writings themselves, which may merely have fit the conventions of the time rather than providing reliable testimony. It seems, however, that Anacreon (pronounced a-NACK-ree-on) was born in the Greek town of Teos, in the province of Ionia (now in western Turkey), near the Aegean Sea, around 570 B.C.E. His origins thus lay in the century before the first great flowering of ancient Greek drama and philosophy, but he grew up in an unstable world. The Greek cities of what is now Turkey were under attack from Persian armies led by Cyrus the Great. Teos fell to a Persian force under a general named Harpagus in the middle or late 540s, B.C.E.

Fled Home City

Nothing is known of Anacreon's childhood other than that his father was named Scynthius, but it can be inferred that he followed other young men from the region in fleeing the advancing Persians and settling in a city they called Abdera, in the region of Thrace (the town is now in eastern Greece). Anacreon's early writings refer directly to Abdera, which was enmeshed in its own military conflicts. One poem (all examples of Anacreon's poetry cited were translated into prose and quoted by C.M. Bowra in *Greek Lyric*

Poetry, unless otherwise noted) recounts that "Strong Agathon, who died for Abdera, was mourned at his pyre by the whole of the city," and other writings clearly refer to the wartime surroundings in which Anacreon spent his early years. "He fell in love with the tearful spear-point," Anacreon wrote of one warrior, suggesting at least a partly skeptical attitude toward the militaristic personality.

Indeed Anacreon's first writings were not all of a heroic quality; the romantic and often erotic qualities for which his writing became known were already in evidence at this stage. One of his poems, perhaps addressed to a young woman with whom he was in love, carries clear sexual double entendres, although it can also be read entirely as a poem about horseback riding. "Thracian filly," Anacreon wrote, "why do you look askance at me with your eyes and cruelly flee from me and think that I have no sense? Know that I could nicely put a bridle on you and hold the reins and turn you about the limits of the course. But now you graze over the meadows and skip lightly; for you have no skilled horseman to mount you."

The elegant artifice of poems like this was something new in Greek poetry, and Anacreon's fame spread. After about a decade in Abdera, Anacreon was brought to the glittering island city of Samos by the Greek ruler Polycrates and installed as a kind of court poet. He was ordered to teach music and poetry, which at the time were closely linked (all of Anacreon's poetry would have been sung, often by the poet himself with his own lyre as accompaniment) to Polycrates's son. A dictatorial ruler, Polycrates loved luxury and supported the arts. Anacreon found himself surrounded by older poets and singers who stimulated his own talents.

Wrote Poem About Romantic Dispute

The relationship between Anacreon and Polycrates occasioned comment from later Greek writers. Clearly, Anacreon was more than a hired employee. The historian Herodotus recounted the story of a messenger who came upon the king and the poet together in a banquet hall. And the two apparently were rivals in love, both pursuing a young Thracian man named Smerdies. At one point, an angered Polycrates ordered that Smerdies's hair be cut off, an event that Anacreon, either seriously or in jest, memorialized in verse. Few of Anacreon's poems from this part of his career have survived, but other writers reported that his poems encompassed not only matters of love and appeals to the gods, but also occasional commentary on court intrigues; one fragment that does survive reads, "In the island, Megistes, the Chatterers hold sway over the sacred town"—the Chatterers probably being a rival faction opposed to the tyrant's reign.

The episode with the messenger who found Polycrates and Anacreon together proved to have dire consequences for the former; Oroetes, a nearby Persian-allied ruler who had sent the messenger, was insulted because Polycrates ignored the herald and continued his conversation with Anacreon. On the pretext of sharing some newfound wealth, Oroetes lured Polycrates to the city of Magnesia, where the king was crucified (or impaled) and his corpse disfigured. Anacreon, therefore, was uprooted for a second time as a result of political events. Fortunately, his reputation by now

preceded him, and he received a royal welcome in Athens. Legend among the ancient Greeks held that the brother duo of Hippias and Hipparchus, sons of the great Athenian king Peisistratus, sent a penteconter—a ship with 50 oars—to pick Anacreon up and bring him to Athens.

In Athens, noted Anthony J. Podlecki in *The Early Greek Poets and Their Times,* "Anacreon behaved...much as he had on Samos: singing, loving, carousing." A statue on the Acropolis depicted the poet in a state of inebriation; the statue is now lost, but it was described by the historian Pausanias in the second century C.E., some 700 years after Anacreon lived. Other images of the poet, on vases, often show the poet singing to a small audience of aristocratic youths, and in one surviving fragment he alludes to his own skills: "Boys would love me for my words; for I sing what is charming and I know how to say what is charming." As with his earlier stay on Samos, there are clues that Anacreon traveled in the highest circles of Athenian society. One of his poems mentions a boy, Critias, a member of a powerful family that later spawned another Critias who was the uncle of the philosopher Plato.

The sensuous life Anacreon lived was reflected in his writings. Sometimes he wrote poems to the gods, but when asked why he did not do so more often he replied, according to a later chronicler quoted by Bowra, "Because our loves are our gods." Often he wrote about the experience of love itself: "Love, like a smith, smote me again with a great axe and soused me in a wintry torrent." But many of his poems were, at least ostensibly, about or directed toward Anacreon's actual lovers. Those lovers included both young men and women; ancient Greek society did not make a strong distinction between heterosexual and homosexual love, and Anacreon addressed both genders in similar terms. One little verse attained immortality in grammar books used in the study of ancient Greek, for it illustrated the way a Greek noun (such as a name) would change as it appeared in different grammatical cases: "Cleobulus I love, for Cleobulus I am mad, on Cleobulus I gaze." Many of his poems are funny or satirical, and he was never above making himself the object of humor.

When Hippias was overthrown around 510 B.C.E., Anacreon was forced yet again to take refuge, this time in the Thessaly region in northern Greece. This time, however, he was soon able to return to Athens. He lived an unusually long time for a citizen of ancient Greece; the Greeks themselves said he lived to be 85, which is not certain, but he apparently lived well into the fifth century B.C.E., long enough to hear and admire the early tragedies of the playwright Aeschylus—who in turn was influenced by Anacreon in the use of certain poetic techniques.

Said to Have Choked on Grape Seed

Anacreon did not welcome the advance of his old age. In several poems he lamented the decline of his appeal to potential romantic partners, writing at one point that "Love, who has seen my chin going white, flies past me on the wind of his wings agleam with gold." In one poem he gave vent at length to his fears of death: "My temples are already hoary, and my head is white; no longer is graceful youth with me, and my teeth are old. No more is a long span of sweet life left to me. Often in the fear of Tartarus I lament this; for dread is the pit of death, and hard the way down to it. For there is no way by which a man who has gone down can come up." Anacreon died in Athens around 490 B.C.E.—according to legend because he choked on a grape seed, but the tale accords a bit too neatly with his reputation as a lover of wine for scholars to have accepted it at face value. Accounts disagree as to whether he was buried in Athens or in his hometown of Teos.

The growth in Anacreon's reputation was hardly slowed by his death. Indeed, his poetry so perfectly represented an ongoing strain of sensual pleasures in Greek culture that numerous later writers, some of them as late as the era of the Byzantine Empire, penned poems in Anacreon's style. Before the chronology of Greek writings was well understood, educated readers, particularly in England, read these ersatz Anacreon poems, collectively known as the *Anacreontea,* with gusto, both in the original Greek and in translations by the Irish poet Thomas Moore and others. Among the features enabling scholars to distinguish real poems by Anacreon from the fakes was the poet's use of a distinctive Ionian dialect of Greek; his imitators either could not or did not bother to reproduce it.

Moore alone translated several dozen of the *Anacreontea* poems, and their net effect was to swell the perceived size of Anacreon's output, and to create the impression that he was almost exclusively concerned with sensual pleasures, for that was the topic of nearly all these imitations. The name of Anacreon was well known among common English readers, and by the 1760s Ralph Tomlinson, the composer of the words to a popular drinking song, "To Anacreon in Heaven" (also known as the Anacreontic Song) could allude to the poet with confidence that listeners would understand the reference: "To Anacreon in Heav'n, / Where he sat in full glee, / A few Sons of Harmony / Sent a petition / That he their Inspirer / And Patron would be; / When this answer arrived / From the jolly old Grecian: / 'Voice, fiddle, and flute, / No longer be mute, / I'll lend you my name / And inspire you to boot.'" The song (whose text appears on a Library of Congress Web site about the history of "The Star-Spangled Banner") served at first simply as the anthem of Tomlinson's club, the Anacreontic Society, but it became well enough known on both sides of the Atlantic that Francis Scott Key's publishers, when they issued his verses describing the British shelling of Fort McHenry in Baltimore Harbor during the War of 1812, could simply direct buyers to sing the words of "The Star-Spangled Banner" to the tune of "To Anacreon in Heaven."

Books

Bowra, C.M., *Greek Lyric Poetry,* 2nd rev. ed., Oxford, 1961.

Grant, Michael, *Greek and Latin Authors, 800 B.C.–A.D. 1000,* Wilson, 1980.

Hornblower, Simon, and Tony Spawforth, eds., *Who's Who in the Classical World,* Oxford, 2000.

Magill, Frank, ed., *Cyclopedia of World Authors,* rev. 3rd ed., Salem, 1997.

Podlecki, Anthony J., *The Early Greek Poets and Their Times,* University of British Columbia Press, 1984.

Rosenmeyer, Patricia A. *The Poetics of Imitation: Anacreon and the Anacreontic Tradition,* Cambridge, 1992.

Online

"To Anacreon in Heaven / John Stafford Smith," Library of Congress, http://lcweb2.loc.gov/diglib/ihas/loc.natlib.ihas.100010464/pageturner.html (October 5, 2008).

"Who Was Anacreon—and Why Do We Care?," Library of Congress, http://www.loc.gov/wiseguide/jun06/anacreon.html (October 5, 2008). □

Leonid Andreyev

Leonid Nikolaevich Andreyev (1871–1919) was considered one of Russia's foremost writers of fiction and plays during his lifetime. His grim, realistic portrayals of life under the Tsar and the hardships endured by the lower classes are judged by critics to be ideal examples of early twentieth-century Russian Expressionist literature and are often compared to the work of Russian novelist Fyodor Dostoevsky. As Andreyev's political ideals grew more conservative later in life, however, he found himself at odds with a growing revolutionary movement, and was forced to flee the country as Russia's imperial era drew to a close. Soviet censorship virtually erased his contributions from the annals of Russian literary history for several decades.

The first of six children, Andreyev was born on June 18, 1871, in Orel, a city in central Russia. His father was a land surveyor and bank clerk, and his mother hailed from a Polish aristocratic family who had lost their fortune by then. The young Andreyev was an admittedly poor student, chafing against the rules and routine of school, but was an avid reader who was particularly entranced by the novels of American writer James Fenimore Cooper, and dreamed of running away to America and exploring the Wild West in which Cooper's stories were set.

Attempted Suicide

Just as Andreyev was finishing his high school education, his father died, possibly in a bar fight. The family's fortunes declined precipitously, but Andreyev's mother took in boarders to their home so that he could attend St. Petersburg University, which he began in the fall of 1891. At times he was penniless to the point of starvation, but supported himself through portrait painting. Like his father, he possessed a rather melancholic personality that was exacerbated by alcoholism, and modern literary scholars posit Andreyev may have suffered from manic depression. Failed romances drove him to attempt suicide, and on one occasion he attempted to shoot himself but was saved by the copper button on his coat. In the fall of 1893, he transferred to Moscow University, where he completed his course in law and passed the bar exam in the spring of 1897.

Andreyev was a practicing attorney only briefly before giving it up altogether to work instead as a police-court reporter for the *Moscow Courier* newspaper. His first published piece of fiction came in early 1898 when he was invited to write the paper's annual Easter story. The title characters in "Bargamot i Garas'ka" (Bargamot and Garas'ka) were a police officer and the town drunk, who put aside their animosity for the religious holiday. Subsequent stories that appeared in the *Courier* attracted the attention of the writer Maxim Gorky, whose own literary career was already underway through his realistic and often grim tales of peasant and urban life in Tsarist Russia. Gorky championed Andreyev's work, which led to the publication of Andreyev's first collection of short stories, *Rasskazy* (Stories) in 1901. The volume sold more than 200,000 copies and launched his literary career.

In 1902 a pair of Andreyev's newest short stories caused a minor scandal in Russian literary circles when they were published. The first was "Bezdna" (The Abyss), in which a couple out for a walk in the countryside meet with a band of robbers, who sexually assault the woman. The trauma turns her previously mild-mannered boyfriend into a sexual deviant. In the second tale, "V tumane" (In the Fog), a university student contracts a venereal disease from an encounter with a prostitute. Both tales were denounced by conservatives as degenerate and unsuitable for publication, but they also won him praise from other contemporary writers.

Gave Up Binge Drinking

Andreyev's private life improved considerably around this same time thanks to his 1902 marriage to Aleksandra Mikhailovna Veligorskaia. The marital union resulted in a drastic curtailment of his alcohol intake, and he publicly credited Veligorskaia for saving him from his own demons. She also provided a sounding board for his writings, which he shared with her while they were in the draft stages.

In 1904, longstanding tensions between imperial Russia and its formidable neighbor in the east erupted into the Russo-Japanese War. Andreyev's short story "The Red Laugh" dealt with the trauma of an entire regiment affected by combat-related psychosis, which they bring back to their home towns and families. In early 1904, Andreyev and the *Courier* came under the scrutiny of the Tsar's internal police when Andreyev's short story "Net proshcheniia" (No Forgiveness) prompted a raid on the newspaper's offices. Censorship authorities objected to the story's portrayal of a bourgeois teacher who harbors fantasies about training to become a domestic spy so that he may have legitimate reason to stalk an attractive woman he believes is involved with the revolutionary movement.

The Russo-Japanese War provided a major impetus to the democracy movement in Tsarist Russia. There was a brief 1905 attempt at revolution, which was suppressed by the Tsar's armies but did result in a few major reforms, including the creation of a legislative body called the Duma. One of the leading voices for change was the Russian Social-Democratic Labor Party (RSDLP), and Andreyev, like Gorky, was an ardent supporter. In February of 1905, Andreyev was taken into custody and spent two weeks in jail for allowing a party meeting to take place at his home.

Forced into Exile

Political revolution was the theme of Andreyev's first play, *K zvezdam* (To the Stars), which was written in 1905 and first performed in Vienna a year later. The drama centers around the son of a prominent astronomer who flees with his fiancé to his father's mountain observatory because of their revolutionary activities. By the time it premiered, Andreyev had fled the country himself after earning the enmity of a pro-tsarist group called the Black Hundred. The secret organization drew up a list of those it marked for political assassination, and Andreyev's name was on it. He and his wife fled to Berlin, and later went to Finland.

Andreyev watched the political events of Russia from a distance, but involved himself when he could: when Tsar Nicholas II dissolved the Duma after just ten weeks, a force of anti-imperialists gathered in Helsinki, Finland's capital, and Andreyev spoke to this crowd of 20,000. His stirring words included the declaration that Russian people were indeed ready for revolution. The demonstration was broken up by force, and Andreyev had to flee to the fjords along the coast of Norway, where he spent two weeks in hiding.

One of Andreyev's most enduring and politically charged works is "Rasskaz o semi poveshennykh" (The Seven Who Were Hanged), a 1908 short story recounting the arrest, trial, and execution of a group who attempt to assassinate a government minister. The work is a strong condemnation of the death penalty, and became one of the key pieces of literature in the anti-capital punishment movement both in Russia and elsewhere in the world with its translation into several languages. The English version appeared in the *New York Times* on November 8, 1908, and was accompanied by a letter from Andreyev. "My task was to point out the horror and the iniquity of capital punishment under any circumstances," he wrote. "The horror of capital punishment is great when it falls to the lot of courageous and honest people whose only crime is their excess of love and the sense of righteousness—in such instances our conscience revolts. But the rope is still more horrible when it forms the noose around the necks of weak and ignorant people."

Beset by Personal Tragedy

Another vital work of Andreyev's from this period is *Zhizn' cheloveka* (The Life of a Man), which was staged at the Moscow Art Theater by director Constantin Stanislavski in 1907. The "Everyman" protagonist rises from early poverty to become a successful architect, but his career is ruined by professional envy, and he sinks into grief over the death of his son. Again, the subject matter aroused the ire of the Black Hundred and was even banned in some cities. The tragedy echoed events in Andreyev's own life: his wife died in Berlin in November of 1906, a few weeks after the birth of their second son. Grief-stricken, he went to stay with Gorky, who was in exile on the Italian isle of Capri, and resumed his prodigious drinking habits once again.

The year 1907 also marked a shift in the political ideas found in Andreyev's writings. In the play *Tsar' Golod* (King Hunger), he takes a more cynical view of the democracy and reform movement. Writing in the *Dictionary of Literary Biography,* Avram Brown described it as an "affecting grotesquerie" in which "a demonic personification of hunger incites urban 'have-nots' to revolt and then betrays them when the 'haves' regain control. The reader's sympathies are confused throughout. The work was published but barred from the stage. The few upstanding proletarians are far outnumbered by the hooligans, pimps, and murderers whom Tsar Hunger heads."

Andreyev remarried in April of 1908 to Anna Il'inichna Denisevich, and had three more children by her in addition to his two sons by Veligorskaia. Because of the unstable political climate in Russia, they settled in Finland permanently, where Andreyev commissioned a small wooden castle to be built on the banks of the Vammelsuu, or Black River. He continued to write plays, but with the outbreak of World War I in 1914 became one of the most enthusiastic supporters of the Russian cause against imperial Germany. The editorial pieces he wrote surprised many of his longtime literary colleagues and RSDLP supporters, most of whom recognized that the battle between the two monolithic powers would bring immeasurable suffering to all Russians with the exception of the elite.

Urged Civil War

The final work of Andreyev's to achieve any literary endurance was the play *Tot, kto poluchaet poshchechiny* (He Who Gets Slapped), which premiered in St. Petersburg in 1915. The tragic story of a circus clown who was once a respected writer before his wife left him for his friend and literary rival, the play's translated editions were still occasionally staged by American and European theater companies nearly a century after its premiere.

Andreyev bitterly opposed the Bolshevik Revolution of 1917, in which the more radical faction of the RSDLP wrested power from moderates, who had overthrown the Tsar several months earlier. In subsequent editorial pieces he wrote from Finland, Andreyev was highly critical of the new Soviet state, and in 1919 issued a pamphlet titled "S.O.S." in which he openly begged the outside world to help oust the Bolsheviks. The 48-year-old writer died not long after this from heart failure in Kuokkala, Finland, on September 12, 1919.

Because of his failure to support the Bolshevik cause, Andreyev was not considered a politically relevant writer in the four-plus decades that followed his death. His name vanished from the official literary history of Russia, and no works of his were published in the Soviet Union until 1956, when the death of longtime leader Josef Stalin occasioned a period of cultural thaw. "Officially," wrote Olga Carlisle in the introduction to her book *Visions: Stories and Photographs,* "he was presented as a minor figure corrupted by early fame and by decadent ideas."

Books

Andreyev, Leonid, *Visions: Stories and Photographs,* edited by Olga Andreyev Carlisle, Harcourt Brace Jovanovich, 1987.

Brown, Avram, "Leonid Nikolaevich Andreyev," *Dictionary of Literary Biography,* Volume 295: *Russian Writers of the Silver Age, 1890–1925,* edited by Judith E. Kalb and J. Alexander Ogden, Gale, 2004, pp. 21–33.

Periodicals

New York Times, September 5, 1908, p. BR487; November 8, 1908, p. SM3; October 4, 1987. □

Anne of Brittany

During her lifetime, Anne of Brittany (1477–1514) was Europe's wealthiest woman and enjoyed the protection of her own private army when she traveled the Continent. In an unusual exception to medieval European laws of succession, Anne had inherited the Duchy of Brittany from her father, but was twice forced into marriages to successive kings of France. As a result, she spent much of her relatively short lifetime fighting to keep the duchy an independent and sovereign state.

Born on January 25, 1477, Anne was a descendant of the house of Dreux-Montfort, which is a branch of Europe's largest royal dynasty and whose members trace their ancestry back to Hugh Capet, the tenth-century French king. Anne's father was Francis II, the ruling

Duke of Brittany. Her mother was Princess Margaret of Foix, the daughter of Eleanor of Navarre, who would go on to become queen of two major Spanish kingdoms, Aragon and Navarre, two years following the birth of her granddaughter.

Heir to Breton Lands

At the time of Anne's birth, Brittany was a distinct area located on present-day France's Armorican peninsula. The duchy was one of numerous feudal princedoms that comprised the map of Europe at the time, and as a result was perennially at risk from becoming subsumed by its larger, more powerful neighbors like France. Brittany had historic ties to England dating back several centuries. The ancient Celts built immense stone megaliths, and probably united and intermarried with the Vikings in the eighth century. Even the Breton language was different from its French counterpart, and is traced by linguists back to the Brythonic branch of the Celtic family; it shared more similarities to Cornish, which was spoken on the southwestern part of England known as Cornwall until the 1700s.

Anne was born in Nantes, which was not the capital of Brittany but was its largest city and the site where the duchy had been founded. She had a younger sister, Isabelle, who died in 1490 in her twelfth year. In 1486, when Anne was nine years old, her mother died, and the possibility that Francis would remarry and produce a male Montfort heir seemed slim. With this in mind, he secured an arrangement

whereby Anne would be permitted to inherit his title and powers upon his death.

That deal was tied to Anne's future marital prospects, however. There were careful diplomatic negotiations to find her a potential mate—one who would not permit Brittany to be taken over by France, nor marry Anne solely to annex her lands to his own holdings. As the future ruler of a prosperous small nation, she was in great demand as a future bride. Among the initial suitors discussed were Edward, the Prince of Wales, who was the son of England's King Edward IV. A tentative agreement for their marriage was made in 1483, but the 15-year-old prince vanished not long after he inherited the throne after his father died that same year, and he was never crowned. His death was thought to have been ordered by his uncle and successor, Richard III.

Wed King of France

Another potential husband for Anne was Louis, the Duc d'Orleans and an heir to the French throne. It was thought that he might be able to have his current marriage annulled by the Church in order to legally wed Anne. The third and best prospect seemed to be Emperor Maximilian of Austria, who was 18 years her senior and widowed. Then, in 1488 Francis's ducal army lost a minor skirmish against France, and the resulting Treaty of Sablé also known as the Treaty of Verger—contained a clause stating that neither Anne nor Isabelle could wed without permission of the King of France, who at the time was Charles VIII. Less than a month later, Francis died after suffering a fall from his horse.

With her father's death in September of 1488, the 11-year-old Anne inherited the titles of Duchess of Brittany, Countess of Nantes, Montfort and Richmont, and Viscountess of Limoges. Two years later, she wed Maximilian, the Holy Roman Emperor, but the marriage was initially done by proxy, or with a stand-in for the husband at the altar—usually a brother of the bride's or close male relative. The marriage treaty, however, had not been approved by France, and Maximilian's Austrian realm was an enemy of France at the time.

That violation of the Treaty of Sablé led to war. Charles and the French army marched through Brittany, whose garrisons fell to the more powerful enemy, and then besieged the capital, Rennes, which held out to protect their ruler. Anne's advisors had hoped that Austria would send reinforcement troops, but Maximilian's armies were involved in other skirmishes far away in Central Europe and Spain and he was unable to provide military aid. Finally, Rennes fell to Charles, and Anne agreed to marry him. By submitting to this arrangement, Anne hoped to secure for Brittany a special autonomy that recognized its ancient roots.

Anne traveled to France for the wedding with her own army. The ceremony took place at the Château de Langeais, a famous medieval castle located on the Loire River, on December 6, 1491, when she was 14 years old. Legend states that Anne brought with her two beds to Langeais, a show of independence from Charles. Her coronation as Queen of France took place at the cathedral of Saint-Denis near Paris on February 8, 1492. In order to become Queen of France, however, she was legally obligated to give up her title as Duchess of Brittany.

Lost Four Children

Not surprisingly, news of this marriage provoked Austria because Anne was still technically married to Maximilian; furthermore, Charles had actually been engaged to Maximilian's daughter, Margaret of Austria, since he was two years old. Charles and France prevailed, however, and Anne was forced into a marriage contract that stated whichever one of them outlived the other would inherit Brittany; however, if there were no male heirs from the union and Charles died first, Anne would have to wed his successor.

Anne became pregnant almost immediately, and a male heir was born in October of 1492. That son was Charles Orland, and he died from a case of the measles just before his third birthday. Another son, also named Charles, died in his first weeks, and two other children—Francis and Anne—each died hours after their births. Anne was reportedly devastated by the loss of her toddler son and subsequent tragedies. It also placed her in a precarious position. When Charles died in April of 1498 at the age of 27, she was 21 years old and, according to her marriage contract, obligated to marry the new French king, Louis XII, who was already married. This was the previous suitor known as the Duc d'Orléans, who had been married to a distant relative, Jeanne, for more than two decades.

Anne agreed to the marriage on the condition that the Pope formally annul Louis's marriage to Jeanne within a one-year period. Reportedly, she believed that Pope Alexander VI might delay the request, or refuse altogether to grant it, but Alexander was the most corrupt of the Borgia popes, and sought to gain favors for his family. The hearing to annul the marriage became the talk of courtiers and church officials between Paris and Rome, for Louis claimed that his marriage to Jeanne should be annulled not on the basis of consanguinity, or the fact that they were related by blood, or because they may have been as young as 11 years old when it took place, but rather because Jeanne had a physical deformity that he said prevented them from physically consummating the marriage. Jeanne, in response, produced witnesses claiming that Louis had bragged about the frequency of their conjugal relations; Louis's rejoinder was that he had been the victim of witchcraft.

Returned in Brief Triumph

Prior to the rather salacious annulment hearings, Anne returned to Brittany to rule in October of 1498, much to the joy of her subjects. Legally she was able to reassert her authority, and used the time to enact several important laws. Less than three months later, however, the Pope granted Louis his annulment, and for a second time in her life Anne wed the King of France. This ceremony took place on January 8, 1499, and for it she wore a white dress instead of the traditional red, and the fashion in the West for white bridal gowns allegedly dates back to this event.

Nine months later, Anne's daughter Claude was born. Exactly a year later, a second daughter, Renée, was born. The two surviving children were not the only difference between this and her previous marriage: this time, Anne had managed to secure a marital contract that did not force her to give up her title as Duchess of Brittany. Therefore, Claude was set to inherit the Duchy of Brittany upon her mother's death, and Anne arranged a marriage for Claude to Charles of Luxembourg in 1501, but Louis negated this. Instead Claude was promised to her cousin and heir to the French throne, the Duc d'Angoulême, Francis, whom she wed in May of 1514. Anne's attempts to pass her title on to Renée were also unsuccessful, and the younger daughter was instead promised to Ercole II, Duke of Ferrara—an Italian noble and member of the Borgia clan—whom she wed in 1528.

Anne was not present at the weddings of either daughter. In the winter of 1513-14 she became ill with kidney stones, and died on January 9, 1514, at the age of 36, at her Château de Blois. She was buried at the cathedral of Saint-Denis, the traditional resting place of the French kings, after a 40-day funeral. Her will specified that her heart was to be excised and sealed inside a magnificent enamel-and-gold reliquary with a crown atop it; it was to be taken to Nantes and placed inside the vault of the Carmelite friars where her parents were both buried. For the next two and a half centuries, it remained a beloved symbol to the Breton people of their former independence and the ruler who had sacrificed herself twice in marriage to ensure their sovereignty.

Anne's Artistic Legacy

In 1792, Anne's reliquary was seized during the French Revolution by order of the National Convention, or legislative assembly. Like other symbols of aristocratic excess, it was to be melted down after its contents were emptied. After the heart was removed, however, the costly artifact was instead hidden inside the National Library. It was returned to Nantes in 1819, where it remained on display in the Dobrée Museum with the inscription: "In this small vessel / Made of pure gold / Rests one of the greatest hearts / A woman had in this world / Anne was her name / She became Queen twice / Duchess of the Bretons / Regal and Sovereign." The reverse side bears these words: "This heart was so generous / Its liberal virtue made good / From the earth to the sky / But Good took back its better part / And this terrestrial part / Remains with us in this significant mourning."

Anne was renowned for her artistic patronage. The Unicorn Tapestries that were donated by the Rockefeller family to the Metropolitan Museum of Art of New York and are thought to have been commissioned by Anne. They are one of the most popular attractions at The Cloisters, the Museum's separate branch for its European medieval holdings.

Books

Hale, J. R., *Renaissance Europe: The Individual and Society, 1480–1520,* Harper & Row, 1971.

Sanborn, Helen J., *Anne of Brittany: The Story of a Duchess and Twice-Crowned Queen,* Lothrop, Lee, & Shepard, 1917.□

Pietro Aretino

**Italian writer Pietro Aretino (1492–1556) was a
prolific and linguistically brilliant creator in nearly
every literary genre of his time. The bawdy spirit
that appeared in the work of many Renaissance
writers reached new extremes with Aretino, resulting in attempts to suppress his writings both during
his own lifetime and for centuries afterward.**

t was not just Aretino's comic erotica and explicit poetry
that stirred the ire of the Catholic Church. He made
enemies in both religious and secular circles (which
overlapped a great deal in Renaissance Italy) because of
the sharpness of his satirical pen. This also contributed to
Aretino's historical eclipse: many of his writings are topical,
full of references and wordplay that would have been clear
to readers of his own time but are difficult to understand
now, and are even more difficult to translate from Italian
into other languages. Nevertheless, as Raymond Waddington observed in 2004 in *Aretino's Satyr,* "It has taken half a
millennium . . . but in the past decade Pietro Aretino . . . has
become respectable." In his own time he had little need for
respectability, for he was extremely successful: an inventory
of 729 books in the stock of one bookseller found 126 by
Aretino, far more than by any other single author.

Various salacious legends surrounded Aretino's life
during the centuries when his books were prohibited to
many readers, arousing curiosity about the person who
wrote them. In reality, though, not much is known about
his origins and early life. He was born on April 20 in the
historic year of 1492 in Arezzo and later took the name
Aretino to indicate his hometown (the name means "man
from Arezzo" in Italian). His father, Luca del Tura was a
shoemaker; his mother, Margherita Bonci, may have lived
for a time with a local nobleman who Aretino sometimes
claimed was his real father. Apparently very beautiful, his
mother sometimes worked as an artist's model. Aretino
probably had little formal education, and it might have
been his mother's modeling activity that first stimulated
his interest in the fine arts.

When he was about 18, Aretino left home for the city
of Perugia, making a living as an artist's apprentice and
house servant. He plunged into the life of the culturally
vital city. Even early in life he had a tendency to stir up
scandal; one story recorded that he and a friend were
arrested for indecently exposing themselves at an open
window. In Perugia Aretino encountered the humanist
movement in full flower, encountering visual artists like
the great Perugino who painted humans realistically; writers who favored compositions with elegant grammar and
rhetoric over those that contained religious dogma; composers of music who created clever secular verses full of
double meanings instead of biblical texts. In 1512 he somehow scraped together money to have a volume of his
poems printed. It was called *Opera nova del fecundissimo
giovene Pietro pictore Arretino* (New Works of the Most
Productive Young Man, the Painter Pietro Aretino). His

brashness and his intention to conquer various artistic fields
were both on display in the title.

Deciding that the way to fame and fortune in Italy was
to attach himself to the rich and powerful, Aretino moved
to Rome in 1517 and looked around for a patron. He
worked as a valet for a lawyer and then as a bookbinder,
and he continued to publicize himself through outrageous
controversy. According to one story, he took a dislike to a
fresco in the Piazza Grande depicting Mary Magdalene at
the feet of Christ, and one night, armed with paint and
brushes, he turned her back into a high-class prostitute,
adding a lute to her hands and altering her facial expression. But he finally found a supporter in the Siena-born
banker Agostino Chigi, who had an interest in the arts.
Working for the Chigi household provided Aretino with
the means to get the attention of people in high places.

Aretino was only a moderately talented painter himself, but he proved to be a keen observer of the art scene,
evolving rapidly under the influence of changes such as
the discovery of perspective. Many of Aretino's early writings were about art, and by some historians he is considered the founder of art criticism. He won the admiration of
painters; Raphael, the greatest Roman artist of the day,
painted a portrait of Aretino that hangs in Paris's Louvre
museum today, and the Venetian painter Tiziano (Titian),
who became Aretino's friend, hailed his ability to break
down the elements of visual art into line, color, light,
and so on—seemingly obvious ideas now, but quite new
at the time.

Aretino did not restrict his choice of subject matter to art, however. Then as now, political satire made news, and Aretino became known as one of its best and most ruthless practitioners. After Chigi's death in 1520, he attached himself to the most powerful patrons of all—Florence's Medici family, whose influence extended to Rome and nearly every other city in Italy through their control over networks of trade, an influence that did not stop at secular matters. Indeed, Giulio de Medici emerged as a leading candidate for Pope in 1521, and Aretino was pressed into service writing pamphlets extolling Giulio's abilities and deprecating the other candidates. When one of those other candidates, Adrian of Utrecht, was in fact chosen as Pope, Aretino had to make a quick exit from the Roman scene. He served with Federico Gonzaga, Duke of Mantua, for two years and returned to Rome when Giulio ascended to the papacy as Clement VII, in 1523.

That did not help Aretino, however, after he became embroiled in his biggest scandal yet. In 1524 artist Marcantonio Raimondi, working from drawings by Giulio Romano, published a set of 16 pornographic engravings called *I Modi* (The Ways) that depicted figures from classical literature and mythology in a variety of sexual positions. Raimondi was imprisoned, but Aretino supported him after a fashion by composing 16 obscene poems, the *Sonneti lussuriosi* or Lewd Sonnets, to accompany Raimondi's engravings. The artist was in fact released, angering the Pope's assistant, Bishop Gian Matteo Gilberti, who ordered Aretino's assassination. He also directed that all the copies of the engravings and poems be collected and burned, and the images survive today only in later reconstructions.

Aretino fled Rome ahead of the bishop's killers, heading temporarily to France. He soon returned to the Eternal City after becoming reconciled to Pope Clement, but he did not change his ways. He wrote comic plays that contained thinly disguised depictions of corruption and hypocrisy in the papal court, and his list of friends in Rome grew shorter. After successfully seducing the mistress of an influential Roman named Della Volta, Aretino again faced the prospect of being killed. He moved first to Mantua, where he enjoyed the protection of the Gonzaga family, and then, in 1527, to Venice. That wide open port city, with its flourishing art scene relatively free from Church restrictions, proved to be a comfortable environment for Aretino, and he continued to live there until his death.

One reason Aretino's situation was so precarious was that he was a skilled and devastating writer of polemical texts. He was something of a hired gun for Italy's political and financial figures, turning out attack pamphlets on demand. Later in his career he used his talents as a freelancer, threatening to spread bad publicity about his targets unless they bought him off. The poet Ariosto dubbed him the Scourge of Princes. Aretino also continued to write pornography. He was certainly not the first writer to compose material of an erotic nature, but he was among the most celebrated writers of the Renaissance era to do so, and he is sometimes considered the father of modern pornography. Another of his notorious texts was a trilogy of dialogues called the *Ragionamenti,* (Conversations), published in English

as *The Ragionamenti: The Lives of Nuns; The Lives of Married Women; The Lives of Courtesans* in 1971 and later appearing in a more contemporary translation as *The Secret Life of Nuns, The School of Wives,* and *The School of Whoredom.*

The *Ragionamenti* were among Aretino's most famous, and later most heatedly condemned, works. They combined advice that would not be out of place in a contemporary sex manual, with raunchy stories about women from all walks of life, including cloistered nuns. Each featured an older woman named Nanna instructing a younger one in the wicked ways of the world. The variety of sexual metaphors Aretino used was nearly inexhaustible. "My husband couldn't care less about honor and decency; he wants to ransack the warehouse and the pantry of that peasant woman of ours," ran one of the more printable passages in *The Secret Life of Wives,* as translated by Andrew Brown.

The sometime pornographer, however, also wrote a number of purely religious works, including a *Life of Christ* (published in 1534, the same year as the *Ragionamenti*) and a series of biographies of saints. Aretino was such a prolific writer of plays, history, art criticism, poetry, topical texts, and material in the other new genres of the Renaissance that he eventually became a wealthy man. In his sumptuous home in the center of Venice overlooking the Rialto bridge, he carried on affairs with both women and men; he had several children but never married. He was one of three leading Venetian citizens chosen to meet the Holy Roman Emperor Charles V in Verona in 1543. Several of his late plays, including *La talanta* and *Lo ipocrito,* both of 1542, are considered among his best works. Even in the midst of his busy schedule he found time to write some 3,000 letters, which are among the most often reprinted of his writings; they give invaluable insight into the political and cultural scenes of the times.

Aretino died on October 21, 1556, in Venice, of what has been speculated to be either pneumonia or an apoplectic fit. Shortly after that, the Catholic Church took a sharp turn to the right, known as the Counter Reformation. Many of Aretino's writings were placed on the church's Index of Forbidden Books. They continued to circulate, however, in underground copies, and the *Sonetti lussuriosi* survived even as Raimondi's original engravings were lost. Critics of the Victorian era, who tended to idolize and idealize the great creators of the Renaissance, struggled with the combination of obvious literary talent and low subject matter in Aretino's writings, but his star began to rise again in the late twentieth century, and several of his writings appeared in new English translations.

Books

Aretino, Pietro, *The School of Whoredom,* intro. and trans. Andrew Brown, Hesperus, 2003.

Aretino, Pietro, *The Secret Life of Wives,* intro. and trans. Andrew Brown, Hesperus, 2006.

Cleugh, James, *The Divine Aretino,* Stein and Day, 1966.

Waddington, Raymond B., *Aretino's Satyr: Sexuality, Satire, and Self-Projection in Sixteenth-Century Literature and Art,* University of Toronto Press, 2004.

International Dictionary of Theatre, Volume 2: Playwrights, St. James Press, 1993.

Online

"Aretino and His Sixteen Postures," ArtArchiv.net, http://www.artarchiv.net/doku/museum/Aretino.htm (October 20, 2008).
"Pietro Aretino," *World Eras, Vol. 1: European Renaissance and Reformation* (1350–1600). Gale Group, 2001. □

Samuel Argall

English mariner Sir Samuel Argall (1580–1626) played an important role in the settlement of the English colony of Jamestown, Virginia. During his relatively brief but influential career, Argall kidnapped Pocahontas, destroyed a number of French settlements in North America, and served as the deputy governor of Virginia. His actions helped support the fragile Jamestown colony and thus paved the way for extensive English colonization of North America.

Background and Early Life

The descendent of a Scandinavian family that had long resided in southeastern England, Samuel Argall was born somewhere around East Sutton, England in 1580; although the exact date is unknown, records show that he was baptized on December 4 of that year. The son of Richard Argall and Mary (Scott) Argall, Samuel Argall was the eighth and final son out of fifteen children had by the couple. Argall's father died when Argall was still a child, and Mary Argall soon remarried; Argall's stepfather, Lawrence Washington, was of the same family as the ancestors of George Washington. The family moved to Washington's home at Maidstone, where the young Argall probably attended school. Writing in *Pocahontas and Her World,* Philip L. Barbour argued that "whatever his educational background...it is clear that his surroundings counted more...all of Samuel's friends and relatives were landowners who were economically tied to the soil in one way or another." Influenced by this environment, Argall developed a practical and somewhat less pugnacious outlook on the world.

Argall does not seem to have attended university, but probably did travel to the Netherlands to fight against Spain on the behalf of the Dutch, who were seeking independence from the Spanish empire. Historical record does not provide any information about Argall's life during the first years of the 17th century, but his later experiences make it likely that Argall acquired experience as both a solider and a sailor during this era.

Ventured to the Americas

In 1606, James I of England had granted settlement charters for areas along the Atlantic coast of North America and the Virginia Company had formed. By 1608, a relation of Argall's had become the head of the Virginia Company, and he turned to the now-Captain Samuel Argall to explore a faster, safer route to the settlement—specifically, one that

avoided the Spanish holdings in the West Indies. The route that Argall selected stretched from the Portuguese Azores islands westward to Bermuda, and then northward to the James River, initially requiring just shy of ten weeks of sailing and skirting potential conflict with the Spanish. Argall believed that the route could be completed in as few as seven weeks. As part of this commission, Argall was also tasked with fishing for sturgeon, a fish prized for their caviar. He also carried a cargo of food and wine that he gave to the hungry settlers at Jamestown, although it does not seem to have been intended for them.

Argall informed the colonists of a large supply fleet en route to the colony under the command of Sir Thomas Gates. The mariner spent the next month fishing and occupying himself about the colony until the arrival of this fleet and subsequent clashes between two factions within the colonial leadership. Argall managed to remain outside of the dispute, however, and set sail for London around the end of August 1609. By November, Argall was back in England, where he informed the Virginia Company both of the success of his own mission and the difficulties faced by the Jamestown settlers.

On April 1 of the following year, Argall captained the ship carrying Virginia's new Royal Governor, Sir Thomas West, Lord De La Warr, on an expedition bringing additional supplies and colonists to the Jamestown settlement. Argall's arrival just over nine weeks later confirmed the course of history; Barbour claimed that "had he been delayed a day or two longer, it is not inconceivable that Jamestown would have followed Roanoke into oblivion and that America, north of Florida, would have been left to the slowly emerging Indian nations who had so successfully fought off Spanish forays." De La Warr appointed Argall to a captaincy, and the mariner, along with Admiral Sir George Somers, soon sailed from Jamestown in the direction of Bermuda in the hopes of obtaining food stores for the colony. The pair was unable to locate Bermuda and turned northward toward Cape Cod; ultimately, Argall lost sight of Somers' ship but did manage to happen across a large bay, which he named after Lord De La Warr.

Soon after Argall's return to Jamestown in the autumn of 1610, De La Warr sent the mariner and a number of others to exact revenge on some Native Americans in the area for the breaking of a (forced) promise to provide supplies to the colonists. The party burned two Native American villages to the ground and destroyed the villages' crops, despite Jamestown's own urgent need for food. The following spring, Argall engaged in peaceful relations with the leader of the Potomac tribe, Iapassus (also known as Japazeus), that resulted in the purchase of a great deal of food for the settlement. Finding De La Warr in poor health upon his return to Jamestown, Argall took the Lord Governor back to England.

Kidnapped Pocahontas

Argall remained in England until July 1612, when he set out on a new mission for the Virginia Company: the discouragement of French settlement in northern lands. Argall's ship, the *Treasurer,* carried 60 men in addition to fourteen guns. Argall first returned to Jamestown, where he helped build the settlement's food supplies in preparation for winter and shore up the colony's navy. Around the end of 1612, Argall traded with Iapassus for food supplies; the following spring, he again reached out to the Native American leader, although this time with a different intent.

The greatest Native American adversary facing the English colonists was Powhatan, a sort of emperor over the Virginia Native American tribes and father to Pocahontas, a Native American youth who had become friendly with Captain John Smith and other Jamestown settlers as a girl. Argall determined that the capture of Pocahontas, whose importance to her father could force him to release several English hostages, turn over a great deal of stolen arms and other goods, and supply the colony with a quantity of corn, could halt Native American hostilities and thus greatly assist the struggling Jamestown settlement.

Argall proposed his plan to Iapassus and asked the Native American for his assistance in luring Pocahontas to the site of her capture. Initially, Iapassus strongly refused, arguing that such an action would bring the not insignificant wrath of Powhatan down on him and his people; however, Argall promised support in that event. After consideration—perhaps influenced by his existing trade relationship with Argall and his limited formal connection to Powhatan—Iapassus agreed. The two men devised a plan using Iapassus' wife to lure Pocahontas onto Argall's ship; once the Native American girl was on board, Argall provided her with food and a place to rest. Soon, Pocahontas became suspicious and asked to leave the ship. Argall refused, explaining the situation and promising Pocahontas that she would be treated as an honored guest in a manner befitting her rank. Iapassus and his wife left the ship and passed word to Powhatan of the capture.

Powhatan agreed to the exchange as demanded, but Argall decided to return to Jamestown so that his actions could be approved by the colony's leadership. At the colony, Pocahontas seems to have been treated well and accorded a fair amount of freedom. In the meantime, Powhatan had been waiting impatiently for Argall. According to David A. Price noted in *Love and Hate in Jamestown: John Smith, Pocahontas, and the Heart of the New Nation*, Powhatan "took the initiative and sent his seven English captives home, along with a handful of tools and broken guns and a canoe filled with corn." The leader explained the absence of the remaining goods by stating that they had been broken or lost, and offered a quantity of corn as a replacement. The current head of the colony, Sir Thomas Gates, rejected this offer. With Pocahontas seeming to be ensconced at Jamestown for the foreseeable future, Argall ostensibly left the settlement on a fishing voyage. (Soon, Pocahontas would famously meet and marry the Englishman John Rolfe.)

Fought Against French Interests

The true nature of Argall's voyage was more complex than mere fishing. His instructions to displace the growing French settlement to the north had not been forgotten but simply delayed, and in June 1613 he set off with that goal. The following month, he arrived at and easily captured a French colony on Mount Desert Island, Maine; pilfering the

royal papers authorizing the colony, he accused the settlers of being pirates. Argall then took a number of the colonists back to Jamestown as prisoners before returning north to destroy more French settlements. Having taken informative papers during his raid in Maine, Argall presumably knew where he was heading; he razed the old settlement of Sainte-Croix before arriving at the completely unsuspecting French settlement Port-Royal. Again, Argall completely destroyed the colony and its crops after taking what animals and loot he desired for Jamestown.

French authorities complained of Argall's attacks to the English government and, upon Argall's return to England in 1614, he discovered that he had to face an inquiry into his actions. Although Argall was ultimately cleared, he was nevertheless annoyed over the situation and considered leaving the employ of the Virginia Company. He did not do so, and in 1616, the Virginia Company elected Argall to the deputy governorship of Virginia.

When Argall assumed his position the following year, he found the colony in disarray and set about establishing order. His actions were not universally popular, however, and accusations of cruelty and theft soon reached London. The *Dictionary of Canadian Biography Online* argued that these "neglect all the evidence which refuted the accusations" and were the result of writings by Sir Edwin Sandys, a strong opponent of Argall's. In spring 1619, Argall appointed a new acting governor and left Virginia for good. Back in England, Argall again faced an inquiry into his activities, and was again found blameless.

Later Career and Death

In 1620, Argall commanded a ship as part of an expedition to oust pirates based around Algiers from the surrounding waters. The mission was cancelled due to renewed hostilities between the Netherlands and Spain, and Argall turned his attention to the creation of an English colony in New England. The council managing this project appointed Argall the Admiral of New England in spring, 1622; on June 26 of that year, King James I knighted Argall in recognition of his services to the English crown. Argall occupied himself with matters of the New England Council over the next several months, becoming acquainted with the politically powerful Duke of Buckingham as a result of this affiliation.

Buckingham supported strengthening the somewhat powerless English navy, and in 1625, Argall received an admiralty and was charged with dispatching a number of privateers off the French coast. He participated in an attack on Puerto Santa Maria in October 1625, returning to England in December of that year. On January 24, 1626, Argall unexpectedly died at the age of 43 while at sea. Having never married, he left his lands and property in Virginia to an Annie Percivall, about whom little else is known. Several years later, London census records show that Argall had a daughter, Anne, whose mother remains unidentified. Although not as famous as others who participated in the early English settlement of North America, Argall nevertheless was vital to the survival of Jamestown, and, ultimately, the English presence that would lead to the formation of the United States 150 years after his death.

Books

Barbour, Philip L., *Pocahontas and Her World,* The Easton Press, 1969.

Price, David A., *Love and Hate in Jamestown: John Smith, Pocahontas, and the Heart of a New Nation,* Alfred A. Knopf, 2003.

The Columbia Encyclopedia, Columbia University Press, 2007.

Online

"Argall (Argoll), Sir Samuel" *Dictionary of Canadian Biography Online,* http://biographi.ca/009004-119.01-e.php?&id_nbr=27 (January 11, 2009). ☐

Émile Augier

French dramatist Émile Augier (1820–1889) wrote witty comedies whose plots skewered the aspirations of the French bourgeoisie and the declining fortunes of the old aristocratic class in mid-nineteenth-century France. For more than thirty years he was one of the most successful playwrights in Paris, with his works regularly staged at the Comédie-Française and other centers of Parisian entertainment of the era. Writing in the *McGraw-Hill Encyclopedia of World Drama,* Joseph E. Garreau assessed Augier as "a committed social dramatist, seriously portraying the life of the Second Empire and realistically analyzing a social crisis of his own time: the disintegration of bourgeois morality under the influence of growing materialism and the efforts of the middle class to merge with the aristocracy."

Augier was born on September 17, 1820, in Valence, a city in the southeastern French department of Drôme. His father was a lawyer who also wrote novels, and the family moved to Paris in 1828 when Augier's father secured an official appointment. Augier's mother was Anna-Honorine Pigault-Lebrun, the granddaughter of a notorious rake of the French revolutionary era. Known fully as Charles-Antoine-Guillaume Pigault de l'Epinoy, Augier's infamous ancestor led a storied life but also had great success as a playwright. Another ancestor of the family's was said to have been one of the famous *Les Bourgeois de Calais* (The Burghers of Calais) in Auguste Rodin's monumental civic sculpture of the same name. Rodin's piece commemorates a fourteenth-century episode in the port city during the Hundred Years' War with England.

Trained as a Lawyer

In Paris, Augier attended the Lycée Louis-le-Grand, one of the most elite schools in all of France. He began writing plays in his teens after becoming enamored with the lavish historical novels of Scottish writer Sir Walter Scott. Following his family's wishes, however, he studied law at the University of Paris in the early 1840s, and worked at a law firm before abandoning this career path forever. His first play, *La Ciguë* (Hemlock), was produced at the Théâtre de l'Odéon in 1844. Like his first several works, it is set in an historical, romantic locale—in this case, the Athens of antiquity—and is written in verse. The story centers around Clinias, who has engaged in so much debauched behavior in his life that he declares himself bored and intends to commit suicide via hemlock, the poisonous plant. He tells his two friends that whoever of the two wins the love of his female slave will inherit the rest of his fortune. Both companions behave abominably in their race for the prize, and in the end the slave declares it is Clinias she loves, who then abandons his suicide plan to run off with her. The play was performed in London in December of 1847, where a reviewer for the *Times* asserted that its plot "is carried on with the greatest elegance, the contests of the rivals are marked by the nicest epigrammatic dialogue, and there is in the work that completeness which must give satisfaction to any one who takes interest in dramatic construction as a peculiar art."

Augier's third play was 1848's *L'Aventurière* (The Adventuress), which was set in 1500s Italy and featured a young pair from noble families hoping to marry. The young woman's father is determined to marry an unsavory woman, however, which will bring the family to certain ruin. When the family's long-lost son Fabrice returns, but in disguise, he exposes the courtesan Clorinde, who "shows depths of self-sacrifice which touch Fabrice, who sees in her attitude toward his father an example of the only real love he has ever witnessed," noted Anthony Levi's *Guide to French Literature: 1789 to the Present*. "It seems that perhaps she really wanted to make the old man happy, and was not just an adventuress after all."

Augier's 1849 play, *Gabrielle*—which, like many, found its way to London audiences in translation; in this case it was produced as *Good for Evil* in 1860—deals with the plight of a young wife who falls in love with an employee of her husband's firm. Writing in the *International Dictionary of Theatre*, David H. Walker marked it as one of the new modern works to come from Augier's pen with its tale of "a feckless wife whose failure to replace a button missing from her husband's shirt is the first symptom of a slide towards marital infidelity in the pursuit of a romantic dream."

Inspired by 1848 Revolution

During this period of his life, Augier held the post of librarian for his childhood friend, the Duc d'Aumale, and also served as co-editor and drama critic for of *Le Specteur républicain*, a new publication whose title reflected the rising movement for reform in France in the late 1840s. In 1848, there was a short-lived revolution that ousted Louis-Philippe, the last king of France. This was a time of immense upheaval in the country, with a rising new middle class who were exerting greater financial control, but until then were not able to vote—only landowners had that right. The 1848 revolution proclaimed universal male suffrage, but its attempt to radically reform the social order disintegrated and the Second Empire was proclaimed and fully in power by 1852.

Augier's plays were contemporary tales reflecting the rise of the new middle class, and they became a great success. He was often compared to Molière, the seventeenth-century dramatist who is considered the French language's greatest playwright, and also to Eugène Scribe, a popular dramatist whose works enjoyed immense success earlier in the nineteenth century but whose prolific career was winding down just as Augier's first works began to appear on the stage of the Comédie-Française.

In his day, Augier's primary rival for the affection of Paris theater-goers was Alexander Dumas the Younger, usually known as Dumas *fils* to distinguish him from his namesake father, who is called Dumas *père* and authored *The Count of Monte Cristo* and *The Three Musketeers*, among other classics. The Anglo-American novelist Henry James, writing in the *Nation* in the final years of Augier's and Dumas *fils*'s careers, noted that "in Paris there is scarcely any event so important as the appearance of a new play by one of these gentlemen, unless it be the production of a piece by the other."

Wrote Retort to *La Dame*

Dumas *fils* had a tremendous success with his 1848 play with *La Dame aux Camélias*, which became the basis for the Giuseppe Verdi opera *La Traviata*. The story of a courtesan who finds true love, the Dumas work prompted a literary response from Augier in the form of *Le Mariage*

d'Olympe, which was produced at the Théâtre du Vaudeville in Paris in 1855. The plot centers around a famed courtesan named Olympe Taverney who has supposedly died of yellow fever in America—but instead she has returned to France under an assumed name, Pauline Morin, and hides her background from a wealthy suitor, Henri de Puygiron. Pauline soon becomes bored by marriage, however, and takes a lover; she then threatens to blackmail her in-laws when she finds a diary belonging to her husband's niece. "Her essential vulgarity of character and moral laxity gradually emerge until the old marquis, who is head of the family, is obliged to shoot her to protect its honour," wrote Christopher Robinson, in *French Literature in the Nineteenth Century*. The Marquis de Puygiron then appears to turn the weapon on himself as the curtain falls. The play, and especially this final scene, caused somewhat of a scandal when it premiered in Paris.

Augier also collaborated with others, including the novelist Jules Sandeau, with whom he authored *La Chasse au roman, La Pierre de touche,* and *Le Gendre de M. Poirier*. This third work, produced at Paris's Théâtre du Gymnase in 1854, was translated as *Monsieur Poirier's Son-in-Law*. The titular characters are an immensely successful draper and the titled wastrel who urges his only daughter to marry in order to advance the family's social standing. Gaston, the son-in-law, treats his father-in-law terribly, and his new wife, too, despite the fact that it is Monsieur Poirier's wealth that supports the household. The situation reaches a crisis point involving a duel and possible jail term, but when Antoinette rallies to Gaston's side, he falls in love with her, and is rewarded for his repentance with a secure job thanks to a family friend.

Marriages and their economic ramifications remained central to Augier's plays for the entirety of his career. In 1858's *Les Lionnes pauvres*, co-authored with Édouard Foussier and translated as *A False Step*, "he wished to demonstrate how an inordinate fondness for luxury could turn a respectable married woman into a predatory kept woman," wrote Judith Graves Miller in the *Dictionary of Literary Biography*, adding that the main character is, "kept, furthermore, by her dear friend's husband. This play's 'impoverished lioness' nearly destroys two families in her hunt for a more elegant hat."

Works Took on Political Overtones

On March 31, 1857, Augier was installed as a member of the esteemed Académie Française, or French Academy, whose role included the safeguarding of the French language in all forms. He was just 36 years old at the time, and to be approved for membership was an impressive honor at such a young age. Duly, his plays began to address more serious themes than love and marriage, though they remained reliant on romance for their plot turns. One example of this is *Les Effrontés* (The Insolent), which was produced at the Comédie-Française in 1861. It centers around a corrupt newspaper publisher and his involvement in the lives of two families. "Clémence Charrier, the rich banker's daughter, eventually marries de Sergine, the aristocratic but impoverished muckraking journalist, after she, too, loses her fortune through her father's noble decision to pay back business debts he has owed for many years," noted Graves Miller in the *Dictionary of Literary Biography*, "What the family loses in money it gains in honor and righteousness."

Another important play from this period was *Le Fils de Giboyer*, which premiered at the Comédie-Française in December of 1862. The story concerns a conservative older aristocrat, the Marquis d'Auberville, who allies with the Roman Catholic clergy to undermine the Liberal Party by pressuring his learned but impoverished friend, Giboyer, to become a speechwriter for the Conservative Party. Giboyer is desperate to educate his son, Maximilien, who does not know that Giboyer is his father, and a complex romantic plot ensues between Maximilien and the daughter of d'Auberville's arch-enemy, a prominent Liberal.

In 1864, Augier's *Maître Guérin* (Master Guérin), skewered the unscrupulous members of the legal profession. This may have been a reflection of some issues in his own life, for he had been embroiled in battles with others that initially played out as duels—one, in 1853, was a response to a scathing attack on one of his plays from a critic, but neither party was injured—and the more contemporary counterpart of the duel, the lawsuit, several of which engaged him throughout the 1860s.

Retired Prematurely

The final play from Augier's pen was *Les Fourchambault*, which was produced at the Comédie-Française in the spring of 1878. The family of the title are wealthy merchants in Le Havre, but their fortunes have declined. A young man who has created a successful shipbuilding business is pursuing a young woman who is a guest of the Fourchambaults, but is stunned when his mother urges him to rescue the Fourchambault firm from financial disaster. The mother may have had a youthful affair with Monsieur Fourchambault, and her son was the result of that liaison.

Augier announced he was retiring in 1878. Five years earlier, he wed Laure Lambert, a stage actor. He stated his reasons in a letter to the German dramatist Paul Lindau, mentioning an incident early in his career when a theater manager avoided a visit from Scribe, who was one of France's most celebrated dramatists at the time. "I have decided to stop too early," his *New York Times* obituary quoted him as telling Lindau. "The theatre does not please me: I noticed it at the opening of 'L'Aventurière.' Rehearsals annoy me, tire me, irritate me, and I cannot work." He died at his home at Croissy-sur-Seine, near Paris, on October 25, 1889.

Books

Hochman, Stanley, editor in chief, *McGraw-Hill Encyclopedia of World Drama*, second edition, McGraw-Hill, Inc., 1984, pp. 225–227.

International Dictionary of Theatre, Volume 2: *Playwrights*, St. James Press, 1993, pp. 49–50.

Levi, Anthony, *Guide to French Literature: 1789 to the Present*, St. James Press, 1992, pp. 39–42.

Miller, Judith Graves, "Émile Augier," in *Dictionary of Literary Biography*, Volume 192: *French Dramatists, 1789-1914*, edited by Barbara T. Cooper, Gale, 1998, pp. 3–11.

Robinson, Christopher, *French Literature in the Nineteenth Century*, David & Charles, 1978.

Periodicals

Nation, June 27, 1878.

New York Times, December 1, 1889.

Times (London, England), December 7, 1847.□

Moses Austin

American pioneer and entrepreneur Moses Austin (1761–1821) is best known to historians for having laid the plans for American settlement of Texas that were carried out by his son Stephen F. Austin, and for having conducted the initial negotiations necessary to bring those plans to fruition.

The elder Austin, however, was a notable figure in American history in his own right. He expanded the industry of lead mining and manufacturing in the young United States, amassing wealth and influence in the Missouri Territory to which he was propelled by a combination of hearsay and pioneer instinct. Austin was a colorful figure who made fortunes and lost them, faced threats to life and limb as he traveled the frontier on horseback and on foot, launched new enterprises as others were playing it safe, and generally exemplified the American pioneer spirit.

Named Home after Hometown

A descendant of early Puritan immigrants to the Massachusetts Bay Colony, Moses Austin was born in Durham, Connecticut, on October 4, 1761. His father, Elias, was a tailor, farmer, and sometime tavernkeeper. When he was 21, Austin moved to the larger city of Middletown and opened a "dry goods" shop selling a miscellany of items that might include cloth, buttons and buckles, tea, eyeglasses, and whatever else he could acquire for resale from the traders that plied Connecticut's waterways. In 1783 he followed his older brother Stephen to the bustling mercantile city of Philadelphia, and never saw Connecticut again. Yet when he built a mansion in Missouri from his lead mining earnings, he named it Durham Hall in homage to the place of his childhood.

Austin and some partners opened another store in Philadelphia, where they flourished despite boycotts of imported goods during the Revolutionary War. About a year after arriving, Austin went to Richmond, Virginia, to open a branch operation and stayed on there, establishing a new store confidently named Moses Austin and Company. By 1785 he was well enough established that he could send for a girl, Mary Brown, whom he had met during his stay in Philadelphia. The two married and had five children, three of whom lived to adulthood. The oldest of those was Stephen Fuller Austin, popularly regarded as the founding father of Texas. By 1789 Moses Austin was doing well in Richmond, had some $25,000 to invest, and was looking around for new moneymaking ventures.

The plan that he finally devised, with financial support from his brother Stephen, was a bold one: he would reopen and refurbish a disused lead mine in Wythe County, Virginia, in the mountains some 250 miles southwest of Richmond, hiring laborers and opening a smelting furnace designed according to the latest techniques from Europe. Austin claimed in a letter to Virginia's governor that he would soon be able to produce enough lead to serve the needs of the entire American lead market, most of which at the time relied on European imports. As part of the early financing of the operation, he won a contract from the Virginia legislature to install a lead roof on Virginia's new state capitol building.

As would happen throughout his career, Austin managed to realize a substantial part of his plan but then overextended himself financially. The mine was productive from the start, and by 1792 a company town, called Austinville and still in existence, boasted stores offering merchandise shipped from Richmond. Austin himself took up residence with his frontier-shocked family as the town took shape. Moses and Stephen Austin purchased the mine outright in 1793, but by that time their financing for the venture was drying up. The roofing scheme, unsurprisingly, was not a success; after repeated attempts by Austin's workmen to stop the leaks that plagued the new building, his contract was apparently revoked.

Austin, in financial trouble by the mid-1790s, responded by once again seeking out new horizons. He heard that in the northern part of the Spanish-controlled Louisiana territory, in what is now Missouri, mining lead was often as easy as picking up chunks of ore deposits lying on the ground. In December of 1796, at the beginning of an unusually cold and snowy winter in Kentucky, he set out on horseback with one man from the Austinville mines and a pack mule, crossing the Cumberland Gap into Kentucky. In a letter quoted by biographer David B. Gracy II, Austin remarked on the desperate conditions faced by some of the early Kentucky settlers he met: "Nor can any thing be more distressing to a man of feeling than to see woman and Children in the Snow passing large rivers and Creeks with out Shoe or Stocking, and barely as maney raggs as covers their Nakedness, without money or provisions except what the Wilderness affords."

Observed Streams to Find Bearings in Storm

Before reaching Missouri, Austin had a desperate winter adventure of his own; misdirected by a local guide, his party lost the road in the snow. They contemplated eating their horses, but found their bearings by observing the direction in which all the small streams around them were running. When he finally reached a lead-rich site that local French miners called Mineà Breton, however, he spotted high-quality ore and immediately realized that his journey had been worth the hazard. He petitioned local officials, asking that he be given a tract of land that included the mines, promising in return (as quoted by Gracy), among other things, to furnish the King of Spain with "all the lead in rolls which he will need for the service of his navel [naval] forces in his colonies." His petition was granted, although for several years Austin still wrangled with the French miners who were established in the area. He also faced armed conflict with hostile Native American tribes.

In 1798, however, near what is now Potosi, Missouri, Austin established the first American settlement west of the Mississippi that was not on the river itself.

At one point, Austin renounced his American citizenship and swore allegiance to the Spanish crown. His nationality changed twice in short order; Spain returned Louisiana to France in 1800, and Austin became an American again with the Louisiana Purchase of 1803. Unimpeded by far-off diplomatic maneuvers, Austin's empire grew. Through a combination of aggressive expansion and technical savvy, he amassed a fortune estimated at $190,000 over the next decade. He established a town called Herculaneum, southwest of St. Louis, and located a new lead smelting operation there (its descendants are still in operation), importing skilled smelter workers from England who were familiar with new reverberatory furnace designs. He had one major rival in the extraction and production of lead, John Smith, who was also based in Missouri. But Austin dominated the industry to such an extent that historians of lead-making refer to the phase of Austin's activity as the Moses Austin Period. Austin cultivated friends in the halls of government, and he was in turn appointed a judge of the Court of Common Pleas and Quarter Sessions by Missouri territorial governor and future president William Henry Harrison.

Once again, however, Austin fell on hard times. Lead sales were hurt by a series of political events several years apart. In the middle of the first decade of the nineteenth century, former Vice President Aaron Burr was arrested and charged with treason after rumors surfaced that he was trying to raise an army to seize much of the new Louisiana Purchase and install himself as king or emperor. The War of 1812 was followed by several bad economic years, and Austin and other Missouri leaders pressed the national government for a freer monetary supply policy. Austin took matters into his own hands by founding the Bank of St. Louis, the first U.S. bank west of the Mississippi River. He moved to Herculaneum, leaving the mining operation in the hands of his son Stephen.

As the bank's finances deteriorated, Austin once again found himself besieged by debt. And, as he had always done under those circumstances, he looked around for new opportunities. He made inquiries about a perpetual motion machine that a Philadelphia inventor claimed to have built. Austin hit rock bottom after the Bank of St. Louis failed during the Panic of 1819, and he began to act on a plan he had been mulling for several years: he intended to petition Spanish administrators for permission to establish a settlement in what was then the sparsely populated and largely unproductive Spanish province of Texas (Mexico had declared independence from Spain in 1810, but the country's war of independence lasted until 1821, and Texas was still under Spanish colonial control.) Austin won over his son Stephen, who had moved to Little Rock, and Stephen agreed to provide financial support for his 59-year-old father's overland trip to San Antonio de Bexar, the modern city of San Antonio. Austin, traveling via Natchitoches, Louisiana, arrived there on December 23, 1820, and presented himself to the provincial governor, Antonio María Martínez.

Found Help After Chance Encounter

The meeting was a disaster. Military tensions between the United States and Mexico were already beginning to rise, and Martínez had been ordered to keep foreigners out of Spanish lands. Austin spoke no Spanish, and the governor no English; they communicated imperfectly in their only common language, which was French. Austin's argument that he himself was a former Spanish citizen had no impact, and the governor ordered Austin to leave the premises. A despondent Austin made immediate plans to begin the grueling thousand-mile winter trip back to Missouri.

Before he left, however, and by sheer coincidence, he encountered a man who called himself the Baron de Bastrop. Bastrop in reality had no noble background but had committed small-time financial crimes in his native Netherlands and made his way to New Orleans, where Austin had met him on a business trip 20 years before. Despite the long interval, the two recognized each other, and Austin explained his situation. Bastrop, who lived in San Antonio, spoke Spanish, and was well acquainted with the Spanish authorities there, agreed to help Austin make a repeat attempt to present his plan to Martínez. He rewrote Austin's petition, adding the rhetorical flourishes and flattery that would be expected by a representative of Spanish royalty. This time the outcome was different: Martínez agreed to forward the plan to colonial authorities.

Elated, Austin once again set out for Missouri. But this was to be his last long journey. Austin and a slave named Richmond acquired a traveling companion who, Austin learned, was a dealer in stolen mules. That in itself threatened the success of Austin's Texas enterprise, but Austin's situation went from bad to worse when he became a victim himself: the mule dealer made off with Austin's own horses, mules, and gear one night while he was sleeping. Austin and the slave continued on foot, living on whatever nuts and berries they could find in midwinter. The slave, unable to continue, left the road when he met someone he knew, and Austin walked for more than a week toward Natchitoches, "undergoing," he wrote in letter quoted by James L. Haley in *Texas: An Album of History,* "everything but death." He finally arrived in Natchitoches and spent several weeks recuperating at an inn there, but his health was permanently ruined.

Back in Missouri, Austin briefly experienced a revival of his flagging spirits when he learned that the Spanish authorities had agreed to permit him to establish his new colony. Pioneer families had already expressed an interest in moving to Texas, and Austin stood to receive thousands of dollars in fees. But he was suffering from pneumonia, likely contracted on his long trek from San Antonio, and as he pushed himself to launch the new venture his health worsened. Realizing that his time was short, he urged his son Stephen to carry on the work he had started. "Raise your spirits," he wrote in a letter quoted by Haley. "Times are changing, a new chance presents itself." He died on June 10, 1821, at the home of his daughter, Emily Bryan, in Hazel Run, Missouri. The state capital of Texas still bears the name of the Austins, father and son.

Books

Cantrell, Gregg, *Stephen F. Austin: Empresario of Texas,* Yale, 1999.

Gracy, David B., II, *Moses Austin: His Life,* Trinity University Press (San Antonio), 1987.

Haley, James L., *Texas: An Album of History,* Doubleday, 1985.

Online

"Austin, Moses," Handbook of Texas Online, http://www.tshaonline.org/handbook/online/articles/AA/fau12.html (October 22, 2008). □

José Nicolás de Azara

The Spanish diplomat, intellectual, and avid collector of Italian art José Nicolás de Azara (c. 1731–1804) served as an ambassador in Rome, Italy, and Paris, France. Azara is known for his aid in the election of Pope Pius VI, as well as for his unfortunate involvement in a treaty which led his home country, Spain, to be manipulated completely by Napoleon and the French alliance. Azara was a great intellect and an astute diplomat.

José Nicolás de Azara was born c. 1731 at Barbunales, Aragon, in Spain. Azara's career began when he was appointed as a Spanish agent and procurator-general in 1765. Another member of Azara's family was also well known. His younger brother, Felix, was considered notable due to the 20 years he spent in South America as a commissioner and naturalist. The Azara brothers communicated by letter while José served as ambassador and Felix worked in South America.

Assisted in Translations

José Nicolás de Azara had many friendships and acquaintances. He was friends with Francisco Antonio Lorenzana y Butron. The two men were prominent personalities during the reign of Charles III and Charles IV, when there were great constraints that surrounded all the Episcopal activities of Lorenzana. Azara was also associated with editor Carlo Fèa's reprint of Johann Joachim Winckelmann's second translation of 'Storia delle Arti del Disegno presso gli Antichi' (1783-86). Azara, considered a scholar by many, assisted and collaborated with Fèa on a translation of the new edition.

Ambassador at Rome

Azara was appointed ambassador at Rome in 1785. He established himself as an active and able diplomat during his long stay there. He also became a collector of Italian antiquities and art.

IOS. NIC. DE AZARA.
CELTIBER.

E.q Ant. Raph. Mengs pinx.   Bonav. Salesa del.   Iac Bossi sculp Roma 1785.

Azara represented the Bourbons of Spain, who sought a pope that would restrain the Jesuits. Spain opposed the Society of Jesus, or the Jesuits, due to their protection of the native people of the Americas against mistreatment caused by Spanish colonizers. Spain took repressive action against the Jesuits in 1767. As Spain's ambassador to Rome, Azara played an important role in the tough and risky mission of trying to eradicate the Jesuits from Spain.

He also played a significant role in the election of Pope Pius VI. Spain, along with Portugal and France, had originally been opposed to the election of Pius VI, who was at first thought to be sympathetic to the Jesuits, due to his educational roots in a Jesuit college. Azara served the Bourbons as ambassador during the appointment of Pius VI.

In 1782, after Pius VI's visit to Joseph II, Azara stepped in to ease the tension between Vienna and Rome regarding church-state relations. The possibility of a break with the pope was discussed by the emperor. During a 1782 winter visit to Rome, Azara helped convince the emperor to put aside the notion of a break with the pope and instead come to an agreement with him. These negotiations showed Azara's aptitude for his position as a diplomat, as well as his loyalty to Rome. Even after the French took control of Rome in 1798 and Azara went to Florence, he continued to act on behalf of the pope, both during the pope's exile and even after his death in 1799.

While Azara served as a diplomat to the pope, he also maintained close relations with the Duchy of Parma. The cities of Parma and Piacenza detached themselves from the Papal states during the 1500s. The Farnese family maintained this area until the family line became extinct, then the area was passed to the Spanish Bourbons in 1731. Entrusted with the responsibility of directing the Parma agency from Rome, Azara made first contact with the duchy in 1771 under orders from the king. Again, Azara acted as a capable diplomat, actively partaking in the cultural life of the duchy and preserving relationships with many of its key cultural figures. In 1801 the duke, Fernando de Bourbon, awarded Azara with the title of marquis of Nibbiano in acknowledgement of the care with which he helped solve the situation brought about by France's hold on the Italian states, and in particular the Duchy of Parma.

Diplomat at Paris

After Pius VI's death at Valence in 1799, Azara was appointed Spanish ambassador at Paris. While he was serving there, the Spanish government required him to carry out the unpleasant negotiations which led to the treaty of San Ildefonso in 1801. As a result of this treaty, Spain had to return the Louisiana territory in America to France. France had given up this territory to Spain in 1763. After this treaty, Azara realized his country was completely subjected to Napoleon. The United States also saw potential disaster due to the treaty and to Napoleon's rule, as the French began to restrict navigational access to the Mississippi River and did not allow trade in New Orleans.

Azara remained pleasant with the French alliance, who found him easy to manipulate, and he was much esteemed by Napoleon. But his vast experience as an ambassador allowed him the presence to realize that Spain was being sacrificed to Napoleon. His fears were first realized when Napoleon agreed to transfer Louisiana to a third party, the United States. President Jefferson asked Robert Livingston to make contact with the French government about the purchase of New Orleans. Napoleon had previously agreed never to transfer the land, but sold the land anyway to the United States. Although Azara's home country filed a protest, Spain was in no position to invalidate the transfer.

Azara's duty in Paris was to guarantee Spanish neutrality. However, he lost his good status with France at the hands of Godoy and Lucien Bonaparte, due to his opposition to the Treaty of Badajoz in 1802 and the Treaty of Neutrality and Subsidies in 1803. Azara considered these treaties to be extremely harmful. Although Azara had remained neutral during his first few years as an ambassador at Paris, his objections to these treaties ended with his obvious retirement. By the end of his life, he was most likely disheartened by his observations of the evils Spain was suffering at the hands of the French alliance. Azara died in Paris in 1804.

Known for Letters

While Azara is known for his diplomatic duties in both Rome and Paris, he is also well known for his written correspondence with Manuel de Roda. His letters, written from Rome between 1768 and 1780, demonstrated Azara's advanced knowledge in Enlightenment thought. While he responded strongly against the overindulgences of the French Revolution, he still admired the libertarian position of the Revolution and thought France was on the brink of a larger social change. Azara demonstrated through his letters his anticipation of the liberation of Spain and Italy. The letters between Azara and Roda were published in 1846 in a three-volume work titled *El Esperitu of D. Jose Nicolas de Azara*. More recent catalogs of bibliographic data from Azara's library continued to demonstrate his international influences and to reflect the eighteenth-century thoughts and ideals that inspired his career as a diplomat.

Books

Gannon, Kevin, *Encyclopedia of the New American Nation,* Charles Scribner's Sons, 2006.

Periodicals

Cuadernos de Arte de la Universidad de Granada, 1996.
Cuadernos de Historia Diplomatica, 1955.
Dieciocho: Hispanic Enlightenment, September 2000.
Estudios de Historica Social, 1986.
Roma Moderna e Contemporanea, 2002.
Suma de estudios en homenaje al Ilmo, 1969.
Zeitschrift fuer Katholische Theologie, 1958.

Online

''Archives, Maryland Province, Society of Jesus Folder Listing,'' www.library.georgetown.edu/dept/speccoll/fl/f119}1.htm, (November 21, 2008).

''Don Jose Nicholas de Azara,'' http://www.1911encyclopedia. org/Don_Jose_Nicholas_de_Azara, (November 19, 2008).

''Duchy of Parma and Piacenza,'' http://www.britannica.com/ EBchecked/topic444343/Duchy-of-Parma-and-Piacenza, (November 22, 2008).

''Pope Pius VI,'' http://www.catholiccity.com/encyclopedia/p/ pius_vi, pope.html, (November 21, 2008).

''Roman Catholicism,'' http://www.britannica.com/EBchecked/ topic/507284/Roman-Catholicism/43756/Suppression-of-the-Jesuits, (December 1, 2008).

''Treaty of San Ildefonso,'' http://www.napoleon-series.org/ research/government/diplomatic/c_ildefonso.html, (November 21, 2008).□

B

Anthony Babington

English aristocrat Anthony Babington (1561–1586) was just 24 years old when he was executed for the political assassination plot that bears his name. He belonged to an underground network of Roman Catholics in England who were driven into secrecy after major religious upheavals related to the onset of the Protestant Reformation. Like his fellow Catholics, Babington wished for a complete restoration of the faith in the British Isles, and his scheme involved the murder of Queen Elizabeth I and the ascension to the throne of the figure whom Catholics considered the rightful heir, Mary I of Scotland, also known as Mary, Queen of Scots or Mary Stuart. Babington's plot was easily foiled, and his actions brought about one of the more ignoble episodes in English history— the execution of Mary on orders of Elizabeth.

Babington was born in October of 1561 in Dethick in the county of Derbyshire. His family may have come across the English Channel during the 1066 Norman invasion with William the Conqueror. Mary, Babington's mother, was the granddaughter of Thomas, Lord Darcy, who in 1538 was executed for his role in a revolt in York known as the Pilgrimage of Grace. The uprising came in protest of sweeping new laws instituted by King Henry VIII that established a new church independent of Rome and the dictates of the Pope, the leader of all Roman Catholics. Henry VIII had wished to have his first marriage to Catharine of Aragon annulled, or formally dissolved by the church, so that he could marry Anne Boleyn. Catharine's Spanish relatives, however, pressured the Pope to resist Henry's demands.

Born into "Papist" Family

England's break with Rome began in earnest in 1533 under Henry VIII, and the York uprising was a response to one particularly harsh measure known by its legislative name, the Dissolution of the Monasteries. Though Babington was born several years after all this turmoil, the English Reformation played a crucial role in his brief life. The Babingtons, like a good number of other English landowning families, had publicly given their support to Henry VIII's establishment of a separate Church of England, but continued to practice Roman Catholicism in the privacy of their homes. Babington's father died when he was ten, and his mother subsequently married Henry Foljambe, who was thought to also have been a secret "papist," as those who still considered the Holy Father in Rome their leader were called.

Henry VIII died in 1547, and the throne passed to his son Edward VI, who was the product of his third marriage to Jane Seymour. Edward ruled just six years, and was succeeded by his half-sister, Mary I, who was not the same Mary who became the focal point of the Babington plot. Mary I had been born during Henry VIII's first marriage to Catharine of Aragon. When she ascended to the throne in 1553, she restored the primacy of the Roman Catholic church, but her measures included an infamous order to burn some 300 Protestants at the stake. Mary I died after just five years on the throne, and was succeeded by the daughter of Henry's marriage to Boleyn, Elizabeth.

The other Mary—Mary Stuart—was the daughter of King James V of Scotland, who died of cholera when she was just a week old. With his death she became Queen of

Scotland—though a regent ruled for her until she reached maturity—and a marriage to the future king of France was arranged. Mary was actually next in the line of succession to the English throne, too, because her late father was a cousin to Elizabeth. English Catholics, however, considered Elizabeth's ascension to the throne to be invalid because Henry's marriage to Anne Boleyn was not recognized by the Roman Catholic church, and therefore she was an illegitimate heir.

Mary Stuart was a devout Roman Catholic, which made her the focus of English Catholics' desire to regain power. She was widowed at 17 and returned to Scotland, but a series of dramatic incidents caused her to lose support among Scottish nobles and incur the wrath of Elizabeth. When Mary fled to England in May of 1568, Elizabeth I ordered her arrested and jailed.

Met Legendary Queen

One of the several manor homes in which Mary was incarcerated over the years belonged to George Talbot, the 6th Earl of Shrewsbury and Waterford. At the age of 15, Babington was sent to the household to serve as a page—a common practice among noble families. It was during this period that he met Mary, whose plight aroused his sympathies. In 1579, the same year that Babington turned 18, he married Margery Draycott of Cresswell, Staffordshire. The couple moved to London, where Babington studied law and was admitted to the bar of Lincoln's Inn, but became involved in the glittering excitement of life at Elizabeth's court instead. By all appearances, he and other well-connected young men at court who were later implicated in the plot to kill the queen were outwardly Protestant and devoted to the Virgin Queen, as the unmarried Elizabeth was called.

Elizabeth's Secretary of State, however, was Sir Francis Walsingham, whom historians often call the founder of modern espionage. Walsingham built up a network of spies and informers to maintain a watchful eye on possible Roman Catholic insurrections, either fomented on English soil or with the help of unfriendly foreign powers. Among his targets were a group of well-born nobles who secretly harbored Roman Catholic priests in their home. Babington's mother and stepfather were members of this group, and thus Babington came under suspicion as well. Babington's visits to the Continent also came to the attention of Walsingham: he first visited France in the early 1580s, and then returned in 1585 and met with Mary's representatives in Paris, Charles Paget and Thomas Morgan. He later went on to Rome, where he had a secret audience with the Pope, and returned to England with documents for Mary from Paget and Morgan.

The plot that bears Babington's name is generally acknowledged to have been devised by John Ballard, an English Roman Catholic who studied for the priesthood in France and was admitted to the Jesuit order; he spent time in England under an assumed name, where he likely roused support among English Catholics for a plot against Elizabeth. Under his plan, Elizabeth was to be killed while Mary was being freed by sympathizers. Ballard told Babington that Spain—an ardently Catholic land and England's arch-enemy at the time—had pledged their military support for the idea.

By this point, Mary had been in English custody for nearly two decades. There had been earlier plots to free her—one, in 1571, was called the Ridolfi Plot for the role a Florentine banker named Roberto di Ridolfi played in the scheme to murder Elizabeth and have Mary wed the Duke of Norfolk, Elizabeth's cousin. Mary escaped formal charges on that one, but after the Throckmorton Plot of 1582 was foiled by Walsingham, Parliament passed the Bond of Association, a law stating that any plot against Elizabeth with Mary as her successor was a capital crime—even if Mary herself had played no role in it.

Enlisted Brewer's Support

Following these failed plots, Mary was placed under stricter watch, and her correspondence was drastically restricted. After 1580 she was imprisoned at Chartley Hall in Staffordshire, where its head of household, Sir Amyas Paulet, accepted Elizabeth's request to serve as Mary's official Keeper. Babington began corresponding with Mary in 1586 with the help of a local brewer who made deliveries to Chartley Hall. They wrote in code, using Greek letters plus numbers and symbols, and the letters were put into a small leather case and inserted into the cork stoppers of the beer barrels.

Babington also began recruiting others to carry out the plan. He selected six men whom he knew from the priest-hiding group, all of whom were of aristocratic birth and had entry into court—and thus access to their target. For the escape part of the plot, Babington recruited ten friends who were to be aided by a hundred or so loyalists. On July 6, Babington wrote to Mary with details of the plot. In her reply, she asked to know more about it, but neither gave her consent nor disapproval. She did note, however, that any plan to free her would be dependant on foreign military assistance if it was to succeed.

One of the friends that Babington recruited was Gilbert Gifford, who had secretly trained to become a priest. Several months before his involvement, however, Gifford was arrested by Walsingham and agreed to become an informant in exchange for his freedom. Thus nearly all of Babington's activities were known to Walsingham, who also managed to intercept the letters in the beer barrels and, with the help of a clever forger, readily decipher their contents. Walsingham actually issued arrest warrants in July of 1586 for Babington and Ballard, but decided to hold them so that he might root out additional conspirators. Ballard was arrested at a London meeting about the plot on August 4, and tortured until he confessed its full scope.

Fled to St. John's Wood

Likely unnerved by the arrest, Babington asked Walsingham for a passport, and told him he would work as a spy during his travels. Walsingham refused, and Babington then hinted he had information about a plot against Elizabeth, but Walsingham remained adamant and refused the request to travel abroad. Only at a dinner party with friends did Babington discover a document hinting at his ultimate fate, and immediately fled to the forest of St. John's Wood in what is the present-day residential district of the same name in north London. His co-conspirators joined him, and they spent three weeks on the run, staying one step ahead of Walsingham's agents by hiding in the homes of Catholic sympathizers. Babington was arrested at a farmhouse in Uxendon, and transported back to London, where he was jailed in the infamous Tower of London.

The trial of the conspirators began at Westminster Hall on September 13, 1586. Babington laid all the blame for the plot on Ballard, who was also on trial, but all were convicted of high treason and sentenced to be hanged, drawn, and quartered—a particularly brutal form of public execution. Babington wrote a letter to Elizabeth on September 19, asking for mercy, which went unheeded. On September 20, the first seven of the 13 men condemned were brought via horse-drawn sledge from Tower Hill to St. Giles, near Holborn for their public execution.

Under orders from Elizabeth—horrified that the charming, handsome young men from her royal court had been prepared to slit her throat—the deaths were to be "protracted to the extremitie of payne" according to Frederick George Lee's book *The Church Under Queen Elizabeth: An Historical Sketch.* "On the first day the hanging of each was by deliberate intention a mere pretence, for they were only half-choked or strangled a little, and then promptly cut down alive. The detailed cruelties of the executioners which ensued, with their savage slowness, and bloody knives, were endured by" Babington and the others, continued Lee, "but the populace, horribly disgusted, became so excited at such deliberate barbarity, that, on the morrow, the others were hung till they were quite dead, and then dismembered, disembowelled, and quartered as usual." Reportedly Elizabeth had heard eyewitness accounts of the deaths and had a change of heart about the manner of the next set of executions.

Elizabeth was more reluctant to sign the death warrant for Mary, who had been tried and convicted for high treason, but finally did so in February of 1587 and was present at her beheading. Some of the events of the Babington Plot were depicted in the 2007 film *Elizabeth: The Golden Age,* which starred Cate Blanchett in the title role and Eddie Redmayne as Babington.

Books

Fraser, Antonia, *Mary Queen of Scots,* Delacorte Press, 1970.

Lee, Frederick George, *The Church Under Queen Elizabeth: An Historical Sketch,* Thomas Baker, 1896.

Online

"Anthony Babington," TudorPlace.com, http://www.tudor place.com.ar/Bios/AnthonyBabington.htm (November 14, 2008). □

Lauren Bacall

American actress Lauren Bacall (born 1924) was one of the most familiar faces on movie screens in the 1940s and 1950s, often paired with that of her lover and then husband, Humphrey Bogart.

Indeed, the 13-year relationship between "Bogey and Bacall" was one of the great Hollywood romances. What set it apart from many of the others was the way it was reflected on screen. Bacall's first film role, in *To Have and Have Not* (1944), drew part of its energy from her developing infatuation with the much older Bogart, and in other classics of American film such as *The Big Sleep* (1946) and *Key Largo* their onscreen chemistry mirrored their personal familiarity. Bacall's career was notable for its longevity and variety; she continued to make new and challenging films well into her ninth decade of life at the beginning of the twenty-first century.

Graduated from High School at 16

Of central European Jewish background (her immigrant mother Natalie spoke German and Rumanian), Bacall was born Betty Joan Perske on September 16, 1924, in New York City. Her parents divorced when she was young, and her mother began using her own mother's family name, Bacal. Bacall began performing early at a summer camp in Maine, where she danced and acted in plays. She attended the all-girls Julia Richmond High School in Manhattan, taking classes at the New York School of the Theatre on the side and graduating at age 16. Bacall met actress Bette Davis, and saw a 1939 production of *Hamlet* featuring the great British Shakespearean actor John Gielgud. Despite warnings from Davis about the difficulties of life as an actress, she was determined to make it her life's work, and enrolled at the American Academy of Dramatic Arts in 1940.

Bacall enjoyed her studies, and showed an early ability to catch the eye of leading men when she went on a few dates with classmate Kirk Douglas. But family finances forced Bacall to drop out after a year—the school's few scholarships were given only to men. She began taking modeling jobs while looking for even small parts in Broadway productions, landing one early in 1942 in a little-known show called *Johnny 2x4* and touring briefly in a comedy, *Franklin Street,* that was directed by George Kaufman. Bacall made a living selling a periodical called *Actor's Cue* on the street outside a restaurant, Sardi's, frequented by show folk, and by ushering and working as a hostess at the Stage Door Canteen armed forces entertainment center.

Her first real breakthrough came not in acting but in modeling: in late 1942 a friend introduced her to editors at *Harper's Bazaar* magazine, where the powerful fashion editor Diana Vreeland took a liking to the still-teenaged Bacall's unusual but perfectly formed face. A picture of her appeared in the January 1943 issue, and there were several more in February, one of which misspelled her name as Betty Becall. In March, Bacall wound up on the magazine's cover, and soon she was fielding offers from Hollywood studios. After passing a nerve-wracking screen test, she signed a contract with director Howard Hawks, who had been advised of Bacall's potential by his wife, Slim. The following year, Hawks would retain the extra "l" in her last name, restore "a" as its initial vowel, and rename her Lauren.

Hawks reportedly had a penchant for taking a young actress and molding her into a star, and he coached Bacall in the finer points of cinema. After he told her to learn to use a low voice even in highly emotional scenes, Bacall drove her newly acquired Plymouth coupé to a quiet spot on Mulholland Drive and practiced. "If anyone had ever passed by, they would have found me a candidate for an asylum," she recalled in her autobiography, *By Myself.* "Who sat on mountaintops reading books aloud to the canyons? I did!"

Evolving Script Mirrored Bogart Relationship

In 1944 Bacall was cast opposite veteran star Humphrey Bogart in *To Have and Have Not,* loosely adapted from a novel by Ernest Hemingway. Bacall concealed her Jewish background from Hawks but later confessed it to Bogart, who was untroubled by it. She played a teenage runaway and pickpocket who brashly asks Bogart to light her cigarette. Sparks fly, along with repartee between the two characters as Bacall delivers the film's most famous line, "You do know how to whistle, don't you? You just put your lips together and blow." Bogart at the time was in the final stages of a dysfunctional and often violent marriage, and soon attraction was building between the two leads, who began spending time together off the set. Several passages in the film were rewritten to take advantage of the intensity Bacall was obviously feeling. At one point, according to biographer Howard Greenberger, writing in *Bogey's Baby,* Bacall, after parting from Bogart in a scene onscreen, said to Hawks, "Boy, that was a dumb move." Asked why, she

said, "If it were up to me, I wouldn't have left. And if I did, I'd go back for a guy like that." "Then do it," Hawks replied, ordering the cameras to keep rolling.

With chronic stage fright complicating her romantic feelings, Bacall found her head shaking during one scene with Bogart. To make it stop, she tucked her head down and looked up at her costar obliquely. Created accidentally, the seductive pose, dubbed "the Look," did much to make Bacall a star. She and her handlers had good instincts for high fashion, and in the later days of World War II her image was often imitated by young female moviegoers. *To Have and Have Not* was followed by a bomb, *Confidential Agent,* in 1945, but she climbed box-office charts once again the following year when she was reunited with Hawks and Bogart in the intricately plotted noir mystery *The Big Sleep.* The two had married on May 21, 1945.

Bacall's output of films was not large by the standards of the time. Sometimes she turned films down because she was picky about roles, sometimes because of family responsibilities: she and Bogart had two children, Stephen and Leslie. Between 1944 and 1950 she appeared in only eight films, four of them with Bogart. In *Key Largo* the pair filmed an epic gangster tale with director John Huston. In 1950 Bacall left the Warner Brothers studio, which had acquired her contract from Hawks. She appeared, independently of Bogart, in the successful comedy *How to Marry a Millionaire* (1953) and the garish melodrama *Written on the Wind* in 1957. Devoted to Bogart to the end, she nursed him in his final days as he died that year of esophageal cancer.

In the late 1950s and 1960s Bacall's screen appearances were even more rare. Partly she was hampered by having been so closely identified with Bogart. "I think the minute I married Bogie I was just considered his wife. My career kind of stopped. Fortunately, I was in some very good movies without him while he was still alive, but after that—boy, I was in some duds," she recalled to Brad Goldfarb of *Interview.* She returned temporarily to the stage, starring in *Goodbye Charlie* in 1959. After a brief engagement to Frank Sinatra, she met stage actor Jason Robards Jr. Bacall and Robards (who, like Bogart, was plagued by alcohol abuse) married in 1961 and had a son, Sam, before their divorce in 1973. In the 1970s Bacall was a frequent presence as a character actress in made-for-television films and on network television series such as *The Rockford Files,* earning two Emmy awards. In 1974 she was seen in the all-star film vehicle *Murder on the Orient Express.*

Starred in Broadway Shows

Bacall's most acclaimed work during this period was accomplished on stage. A 1959 Broadway play called *Goodbye Charlie* bombed financially, but Bacall bounced back with the 1965 comedy *Cactus Flower,* which enjoyed a two-year run on Broadway and was later made into a film. In 1969 Bacall took the role of Margo Channing in *Applause!,* an adaptation of the film *All About Eve* in which the same role had originally been played by Bacall's first cinematic inspiration, Bette Davis. The show became a smash hit and toured nationally and internationally over the next several years. With another successful starring role on Broadway in the musical *Woman of the Year,* also based on a classic Hollywood film, Bacall remained a familiar face to theater audiences for the better part of two decades. She won Tony awards for both shows.

Passed over for a role in the film version of *Applause!,* Bacall offered tart comments to the press. She gained a reputation as a public figure with strong independent opinions. Sometimes those opinions were political; as far back as the 1950s she had lent her public support to the presidential campaigns of Democrat Adlai Stevenson Jr. Bacall came into her own in terms of self-expression with her 1978 autobiography, *By Myself.* Far beyond the usual run of show-business biographies in its perceptive portraits and depth of detail, the book's prose captured Bacall's combative and often humorous personality, and it delved into the supportive role Bacall's mother had played as her daughter's career developed. *By Myself* won a National Book Award in 1980. That book and a later autobiography, *Now* (1994), were written by Bacall herself, in pen, without the aid of ghostwriters.

In 1985 Bacall, who since Bogart's death had divided her time between New York and London, starred in a successful London stage production of the Tennessee Williams play *Sweet Bird of Youth.* But she hungered for major new film roles and was critical of the dearth of opportunities for older actresses in Hollywood films. She appeared in several films under director Robert Altman, including *Health* (1980) and *Ready to Wear* (1994), but it was a female director, Barbra Streisand, who gave Bacall a new shot at the limelight in the acclaimed 1996 drama *The Mirror Has Two Faces.* Continuing to seek out new opportunities, Bacall appeared in 2003 in *Dogville,* a film by avant-garde Danish director Lars von Trier.

In the course of working on that film, Bacall struck up a friendship with costar Nicole Kidman, but Kidman and her former husband Tom Cruise became targets of Bacall's sharp tongue in subsequent interviews. She remained in the public eye, and continued to make new films into her eighties. She had voice parts in several animated films, including *Howl's Moving Castle* (Japan, 2004) and *Scooby Doo and the Goblin King* (2008), and had a starring role in the 2007 thriller *The Walker.* "What is the point of working all your life and then stopping?," Bacall remarked to *Time* interviewer Rebecca Winters. "All right, so you start off when you're a kid, and you make an impression. You can't always be a leading lady. You can't always be a glamour-puss. It all changes, thank God."

Books

Bacall, Lauren, *By Myself,* Knopf, 1979.

Bacall, Lauren, *Now,* Knopf, 1994.

Greenberger, Howard, *Bogey's Baby,* St. Martin's, 1978.

International Dictionary of Films and Filmmakers, Volume 3: Actors and Actresses, 4th ed., St. James, 2000.

Newsmakers, issue 4, Gale, 1997.

Periodicals

Harper's Bazaar, April 2004.

Interview, April 2004.

People, February 12, 1996, p. 140; December 17, 2007.

Time, August 8, 2005.

Online

"Lauren Bacall," *All Movie Guide,* http://www.allmovie.com (October 28, 2008). □

Michael Baius

Belgian theologian Michael Baius (1513–1589) stirred great controversy in the Roman Catholic Church with his ideas about the nature of sin and the means to personal salvation. Like Saint Augustine of Hippo (354–430) before him, Baius raised serious questions about humanity's original nature, and he believed that people could not be saved by good works, but only by the grace of the Christian God. His doctrine, known as Baianism, represented one of the major challenges faced by the Church in the sixteenth century, and inspired generations of theologians and church reformers.

The exact date of Michael Baius's birth is unknown, but he was born in 1513 to Jean de Bay and Andrinette Nve in the town of Melin in what is now Belgium. At the time, this town was located in a province called Hainaut, and the territory of Belgium was part of the Holy Roman Empire, a religious and political entity that dominated most of central Europe. The empire was ruled by a monarch, or king, and the official religion of the empire was Roman Catholicism.

Baius's parents named him Michel de Bay, and he was the third of seven children. Later in life he would change his name to Michael Baius, a Latin form of his birth name. Little else is known about Baius's childhood, but he probably spent his youth and received an early education in Belgium. He would spend most of the rest of his life in Belgium as well as in academia, first as a student and then as an educator.

Baius the Student

Baius must have received some formal or informal education in his early years, because in 1533 he enrolled at the University of Louvain in Belgium. Like most institutions of the time, it was a Catholic university. Baius began by studying the humanities, with a particular emphasis on philosophy and theology. Theology is the study of religious faith, in particular the study of God.

Within two years, Baius earned a master of arts degree. From 1536 through 1541, he focused on the study of theology. At the completion of his studies, Baius underwent ordination, the ceremony to become a priest. Subsequently he received his first appointment as the principal of Standonk College, a member college of the University of Louvain.

Throughout his life, Baius held various positions at the university. In 1544 he became the chair of the philosophy department and taught philosophy until 1550. He also continued his theology studies, becoming a doctor of theology in 1550. At that time, Baius became the president of the College of Adrien and was appointed as substitute to the professor of the Holy Scripture, a highly regarded post.

Around 1550, Baius also met and befriended the theologian Jan Hessels. Together, Hessels and Baius would begin an intense study of Church doctrine. Their interpretations and writings would lead them into direct conflict with the Church, and Baius would spend most of the rest of his life alternately defending and recanting the ideas that would come to be known as Baianism.

Baius's Theology

In 1551, the Holy Roman Emperor Charles V appointed Baius as Regius Professor of Sacred Scripture at the University of Louvain. This was a high honor, and Baius took full advantage of the appointment to pursue his ideas.

Baius both taught and recorded his propositions, some on his own and some in conjunction with Hessels. In matters of the Church, a proposition was a statement of religious belief. Most of Baius's propositions led to immediate controversy.

Baius—and Hessels—drew many of their propositions from their interpretation of Saint Augustine's writings. Augustine was a Church Father. The Church Fathers comprised a group of early scholars, theologians, and writers who had helped established official Church doctrine over time. Highly revered for his religious devotion, Augustine had written extensively of his beliefs. His most renowned works, *City of God* and *Confessions,* remain crucial texts in the study of Christian thought.

Much of Augustine's writing focused on matters of original sin and the fall of humanity. According to Catholicism, Adam, Eve, and all their descendants were stained by sin and doomed to behave in sinful ways. The nature of this original sin, as well as how humanity could be saved, or redeemed, and returned to good standing with God the Creator, had been the focus of centuries of debate within the Catholic Church. Augustine, and later Baius, focused largely on these issues, and both theologians took a fairly critical and pessimistic view of humanity's position.

Like Augustine, Baius believed that only those who accepted God's grace through Christ could be redeemed or saved. No action, however seemingly good, could be good unless done through one's faith in God and Christ. In contrast, the Church believed that humanity, though prone to sin, was capable of finding its way back to God through good works as well as faith, and that Christ had been sent to help guide humanity back to its natural and original path, to accept the gift that Adam had rejected.

Censure and Recantation

Around 1560, the Sorbonne of Paris, another university, censured 18 of Baius's propositions. To censure meant to officially criticize or condemn. Despite this censure, the King of Spain selected Baius in 1563 to represent the Belgian lands at the Council of Trent, a meeting of Church officials from throughout Europe to discuss matters of theology.

The Council of Trent met three times in the mid-sixteenth century with the final gathering occurring in 1562–1563. The Church had convened the council to respond to the Protestant Reformation, a movement that challenged traditional Church doctrines and sought to reform the institution of the Church. The Protestant Reformation led to a major splintering within Christianity. Through the Council of Trent, the Pope and other officials hoped to resolve matters under dispute. The Pope issued a series of bulls, or statements, that clarified the Church's official position on a wide range of doctrines.

Baius arrived late to the council in 1563, so he was unable to participate in most of the debates. Most of his colleagues regarded him with suspicion and did not approve of the propositions that Baius had published prior to attending the council.

Yet Baius kept teaching and writing his ideas. In 1564 he returned to Louvain and published new propositions. These propositions were organized into pamphlets called *obuscula.* In 1566, following the death of his friend Hessels, Baius gathered these propositions into two collected works, "Obuscula omnia" and "M. Baii opuscula theologica." The Universities of Alcala and Salamanca immediately condemned parts of these works, and the Pope soon followed suit.

On October 1, 1567, Pope Pius V issued the papal bull *Ex Omnibus Afflictionibus,* and although it did not identify Baius by name, it specifically condemned many of his propositions. Baius at first accepted this condemnation, but later decided to object.

In 1569 Baius wrote a letter to Cardinal Simonetta that defended his propositions. In the letter, recorded in part in the *Catholic Encyclopedia,* Baius explained, "I endeavored to bring theology back to Holy Scripture and the writing of the Fathers."

Baius also wrote directly to the Pope. He admitted that some of the condemned propositions were wrong and had been censured justly, but he also insisted that many were correct interpretations of the Church Fathers' ideas. He requested an apology for the condemnation not only on his behalf but also on behalf of Saint Augustine.

In the 1570s, the Pope reviewed the propositions and upheld his earlier bull, demanding that Baius submit to the censure and sign an official recantation. Baius apparently submitted unofficially, but did not sign an official recantation at that time.

Baius's submission and reportedly apologetic demeanor earned him a series of new appointments. In 1575 he became the Chancellor of Louvain, the Dean of St. Peter's Collegiate Church, and the conservator of the university's privileges. But Baius could not resist pursuing his own theology.

Not long after his submission, Baius began talking about his ideas again, and the new Pope learned of his conduct. On January 25, 1580, Pope Gregory XIII issued a new bull, *Provisionis nostrae,* again condemning Baius's propositions, even requiring the entire faculty at the University of Louvain to agree to the Papal condemnations in the bull.

On March 24, 1581, Baius signed a document, "Confessio Michaelis Baii," officially recanting the condemned propositions. The document, as quoted in the *Catholic Encyclopedia,* read, in part: "I am convinced that the condemnation of all those propositions is just and lawful. I confess that very many of these propositions are in my books, and in the sense in which they are condemned. I renounce them all and resolve never more to teach or defend any of them."

Baius's Legacy

The remainder of Baius's life seems to have been quiet and without controversy. He stayed at the University of Louvain, teaching theology according to official Church doctrine and serving as chancellor. He did not publish any additional propositions.

On September 16, 1589, Baius died at the university that had been his home for 56 years. Although his works had been condemned and he himself had recanted them, they did not disappear. Students and theologians continued to discuss the ideas that became known as Baianism.

In the early 1600s, a Dutch theologian named Cornelius Jansen picked up Baius's ideas. Jansen wrote another interpretation of Saint Augustine's treatises on original sin and grace. The Church condemned Jansen's work as heretical. Heretical ideas were considered to be in violation of official Church doctrine. Unlike Baianism, however, Jansenism became a significant theological movement, especially in France. The Church found it difficult to quell Jansen and his followers' challenges.

In 1696 a group of French monks called the Maurists, known for their scholarship and their willingness to examine non-traditional ideas, published many of Baius's works. The fame Baius achieved was short-lived and was earned by the controversy that he had caused within the Church. Ultimately, he did not succeed in changing official Church doctrine. However, his propositions were a major contribution to Christian thought. They addressed the most integral ideas of the Roman Catholic faith, issues that are still debated in scholarly and Church circles today.

Moreover, Baius's theology—and his censure—were part of the larger story of the Reformation, a division in the Christian faith that ultimately led to the decline in political power of the Roman Catholic Church, once the most powerful institution in Europe.

Books

Encyclopedia of World Biography, Vol. 8, 2nd ed., Gale Group, 2004 (November 12, 2008).

Kolakowski, Leszek, *God Owes Us Nothing: A Brief Remark on Pascal's Religion and on the Spirit of Jansenism,* University of Chicago Press, 1995.

Online

"Augustine, Saint," *Columbia Encyclopedia,* Sixth ed., http://www.bartleby.com/65/au/AugustnSt.html (November 5, 2008).

"Baius and Baianism." *New Catholic Encyclopedia.* Catholic University of America. 2nd ed. 15 vols. Gale, 2003.

"Baius, Michael," *Columbia Encyclopedia,* Sixth ed., http://www.bartleby.com/65/ba/Baius.html (October 16, 2008).

"Michael Baius," *Encyclopedia Britannica,* http://www.search.eb.com/eb/article-9011837 (October 16, 2008).

"Michael Baius Biography," *Biography Base,* http://www.biographybase.com/biography/Baius_Michael.html (October 16, 2008).

"Michel de Bay," *Speedy Look,* http://www.speedylook.com/Michel_De_Bay.html (January 5, 2009).

"Saint Augustine," *Encyclopedia Britannica,* http://www.search.eb.com/eb/article-9109388 (November 5, 2008).

"Trent, Council of," *Columbia Encyclopedia,* Sixth Ed., http://www.bartleby.com/65/tr/Trent-Co.html (November 5, 2008).

"Ex Omnibus Afflictionibus," *Gale Virtual Reference Library,* http://www.find.galegroup.com/ips/start.do?prodId=IPS (November 12, 2008).

"Michael Baius," *The Catholic Encyclopedia,* Vol. 2., http://www.newadvent.org/cathen/02209c.htm (October 16, 2008). □

George Pierce Baker

American educator George Pierce Baker (1866–1935) instructed and shaped the works of some of the United States' best-known playwrights, including Eugene O'Neill and Thomas Wolfe. Called "the father of modern American playwrights" by contemporaries, Baker inaugurated playwriting as an academic course, teaching at both Harvard and Yale, where he established the institution's drama department. A collection of Baker's lectures published as the *Dramatic Technique* remained the authoritative manual of playwriting for decades after its initial publication in 1919.

Childhood Shaped by the Theater

The only child of Dr. George Pierce Baker and his wife, Lucy (Cady) Baker, George Pierce Baker was born in Providence, Rhode Island, on April 4, 1866. His father's literary interests and his mother's love of popular entertainment helped shape the young Baker's personality and later career; as a child, Baker received a toy theater from his parents, which was later replaced with a real stage in a room of the Baker home. A somewhat sickly childhood led Baker to turn much of his attention to theatrical amusements rather than outdoor play, and Wisner Payne Kinne noted in *George Pierce Baker and the American Theatre* that "the toy theatre and its juvenile drama grew to be a symbol of the boy's happiness." Baker also attended local theater productions as early as the age of six. In addition to his informal theatrical education, Baker attended the private Mowry and Goff's school and, later, Providence High School, where he was active in debate and literary clubs. In 1883, Baker enrolled at Harvard in Cambridge, Massachusetts, beginning a long and fruitful association with that institution.

Baker's father had hoped that his son would follow in his professional footsteps as a physician, and early in his Harvard career Baker combined studies in mathematics and sciences with courses in classics and languages. Socially isolated, Baker turned to the nearby theaters of Boston for entertainment. At this time, Baker's dramatic interests lie in acting; he also enjoyed writing verse. After unsuccessfully

his position and traveled through Europe researching both Elizabethan and contemporary drama. During this time, he was also actively writing plays, primarily one-act comedies, and occasionally appearing onstage. However, his success as both a playwright and an actor was limited, and after 1895— the same year that he received an assistant professorship at Harvard—Baker gave up writing plays completely and acted so rarely that by the time of his death, his activities as both a playwright and actor had been practically forgotten.

In 1893, Baker married Christina Hopkinson, the niece of Harvard's president, Charles Eliot. The couple later had four sons, John Hopkinson in 1894, Edwin Osborne in 1896, Myles Pierce in 1901, and George Pierce Jr. in 1903. Also in 1893, he published his first book, *Specimens of Argumentation,* followed in 1894 by an edition of John Lyly's Elizabethan comedy *Endymion,* and in 1895 by *The Principles of Argumentation.* Baker also turned his attention to the conversion of Harvard's Sanders Theatre into an accurate reproduction of an Elizabethan stage, which Kinne called "perhaps the most revolutionary technical event in the history of the American theatre." In the late 1890s, Baker completed an edition of *A Midsummer Night's Dream* and, around the turn of the century, became the editor of the dramatic works produced as part of a series of classic literature. Throughout the decade and into the 20th century, Baker also gave lectures on the state of American drama, arguing that the dramatic audience needed to be both better educated and more demanding of quality in its homegrown plays.

Inaugurated Playwriting Courses at Harvard and Radcliffe

On sabbatical in Europe during the 1901–1902 academic year, Baker wrote a series of dramatic reviews that were printed in the *Boston Transcript* and formed his first published dramatic criticism. Returning to Cambridge, Baker began informally instructing students in playwriting and increasingly considering the possibility of an academic course in the subject. His first experiment came in 1903, when he offered students in his contemporary drama class at Radcliffe the option of writing a play rather than a thesis as their final project. The success of this experiment led to the establishment of a playwriting course at Radcliffe the following year.

The Radcliffe course served as the model for the now full professor Baker's seminal graduate course in playwriting at Harvard, English 47, inaugurated in 1905. The *Dictionary of American Biography* noted that "[a] brilliant student in this first year, Edward Sheldon, sold his play, *Salvation Nell,* calling wide public attention to the new course." At about this time, Baker delivered a series of lectures at the Lowell Institute later collected as *The Development of Shakespeare as a Dramatist.* The lectures were given at the invitation of A. Lawrence Lowell, who soon replaced Eliot as president of Harvard. Unlike his predecessor, who had always considered Baker's talents to excel in the instruction of argumentation, Lowell urged Baker to focus his energies on dramatic courses.

Returning to Cambridge in 1909 after a stint as the James Hazen Hyde lecturer at the Sorbonne in Paris, Baker resumed

submitting several poems to publications including Harvard's *Lampoon* and the *Atlantic Monthly,* Baker wrote a poem the summer following his freshman year that *Life* magazine accepted for publication. This was soon followed by a comedic play written in verse, *Not Sentimental,* that although unpublished remains Baker's first dramatic work.

Baker turned in earnest to literary studies his sophomore year, supporting dreams of a career as a writer or editor by becoming the editor-in-chief of the *Harvard Monthly* for the 1886–1887 academic year. During his tenure, the magazine expanded greatly from a college publication to a respected literary magazine throughout New England. Baker graduated from Harvard in 1887, and after a year spent traveling in Europe and the American West, returned to his alma mater as an instructor.

First Years as an Instructor

At first, Baker served as an assistant in various speaking courses, but soon began leading his own courses in rhetoric and forensic speaking. During the 1890–1891 academic year, Baker assumed control of a relatively new course dedicated to the early history of English drama, which he would continue to teach practically unchanged until 1921. In this class, Baker espoused the connection between the personal lives of playwrights and their works, as well as his belief that plays were written to be acted rather than to be read. The following year, Baker took a leave of absence from teaching courses in the history of drama as well as playwriting, although this latter course earned the lion's share of Baker's attention after 1913. From the beginning, the playwrights who came out of English 47 were in demand; Kinne argued that "the quality of their product, perhaps, was not quite so important as the novelty and seeming magic of it. For here was something . . . new and fresh in the theatre[.]" The accomplishments of Baker's early students were generally known and served to attract other talented writers to the course.

In 1913, English 47 led to the creation of the 47 Workshop, a joint effort between the playwrights in Baker's class and other interested volunteers to stage the plays written in the course. Baker believed that this workshop allowed playwrights to gain a better understanding of the practical tools of the theatre such as lighting as well as receive useful critical feedback from audience members on the dramatic value of their works. These performances contributed to advances in set design and staging as well as in playwriting. By the mid-1910s, the 47 Workshop was highly respected, gaining funding from private individuals to stay afloat and attracting such students as Eugene O'Neill, George Abbott, and Thomas Wolfe. In 1915, Baker also began teaching an advanced playwriting course for the most talented graduates of his English 47 course. The 47 Workshop inspired other groups around the United States to form little theatres, and in 1918 two volumes of plays edited by Baker—*Plays of the 47 Workshop* and *Plays of the Harvard Dramatic Club*—were published to serve these dramatic companies.

After the United States' entry into World War I in 1917, Baker acted as the head of the Department of Scenarios for the United States Bureau of Public Information as well as overseeing the 47 Workshop, then performing for troops around New England. In 1919, Houghton Mifflin published Baker's *Dramatic Technique,* based on a series of lectures he had given at the Lowell Institute in 1913 and spent years refining. This volume, which Baker declared in the preface was "written for the person who cannot be content except when writing plays," became a standard instructional work in the field of playwriting. At about this time, he also edited a collection called *Modern American Plays* and developed a grand pageant for the Plymouth Tercentennial Celebration, one of many that he oversaw after 1910.

Established Drama Department at Yale

Baker had long hoped for the construction of a new theatre at Harvard, and by the early 1920s his frustration at the unresponsiveness of the college's administration to this dream was substantial. The success of the plays of the 47 Workshop did not persuade the college to provide funds for what Baker considered a necessary facet of his instruction, perhaps because neither the Workshop nor the associated summer courses in stage construction and other technical matters were officially sanctioned university courses. In 1924, a fire destroyed part of the building in which the Workshop had made its home, and the ensuing temporary suspension of the Workshop became permanent when Baker retired from his post at Harvard to become the first director of the new department of drama at Yale.

This post, bringing with it a generous endowment and the promise of the much longed for theatre, took Baker from Cambridge to New Haven, Connecticut, where he remained as both department head and drama instructor until his retirement. At Yale, Baker wished to nurture talents like those he had fostered at Harvard, even naming his playwriting course Drama 47. The department grew quickly, reflecting the increased interest in drama around the country that Baker himself had contributed to earlier in his career. When Baker retired from Yale in 1933, many hailed the event as the end of an era.

Baker seems to have experienced rapidly declining health in the last few months of his life. On January 6, 1935, he died in New York City as the result of heart failure. He was buried soon after at the Swan Point Cemetery in Providence. His death was much mourned among those whose lives and works he had touched, and in 1939 a booklet eulogizing his life, *George Pierce Baker: A Memorial,* was produced to raise funds for the support of future playwrights. In this booklet, a reprint of a letter to the *New York Times* written by Baker's student Eugene O'Neill noted: "Only those of us who had the privilege of membership in the drama class of George Pierce Baker back in the dark age when the American theatre was still, for playwrights, the closed-shop, star-system, amusement racket, can know what a profound influence Professor Baker . . . exerted toward the encouragement and birth of American drama." Certainly, Baker's contributions as an educator molded and supported the growth of his beloved theatre and led to the establishment of playwriting as a serious academic venture, in addition to nurturing the talents that created some of the 20th century's finest works of drama.

Books

Baker, George Pierce, *Dramatic Technique,* Houghton Mifflin, 1919.
Dictionary of American Biography, Supplements 1–2: To 1940, American Council of Learned Societies, 1944–1958.
Kinne, Wisner Payne, *George Pierce Baker and the American Theatre,* Greenwood Press, 1968.
New York City Dramatists Play Service, *George Pierce Baker: A Memorial,* Dramatists Play Service, 1939. □

Léon Bakst

Russian artist Léon Bakst (1866–1924) was a gifted painter whose set designs and costumes for the Ballet Russes dance troupe revolutionized the stage in the early years of the twentieth century. His use of bold colors and motifs borrowed from other cultures added a deeper layer of the exotic to the Ballet Russes productions and were widely imitated in both the decorative and performing arts in the years that followed, and he is generally given major credit for helping to usher in the era of modernism in Western art. "The impact of Bakst and the Ballets Russes was so strong it was impossible to avoid it," noted London *Sunday*

Times journalist Colin McDowell about Bakst's influence. "It made everything else look provincial and dowdy."

Bakst was born Lev Samuilovich Rosenberg on May 10, 1866, in Grodno, Belarus, when the city and surrounding region were part of the Russian Empire. His moderately prosperous Jewish family moved to the imperial capital, St. Petersburg, where he attended the Sixth Gymnasium from 1874 to 1883. At the age of 17, he enrolled in classes at the St. Petersburg Academy of Arts and began taking book-illustration jobs to support himself. The first exhibition of his work was held in 1889, and he began using the name of his maternal grandmother, Bakst, professionally.

Moved to Paris

In St. Petersburg, Bakst fell in with a group of wealthy, well-connected young people who were fascinated by new trends in the arts from Europe. Writing in the *New York Times* in 1977, the art critic John Russell noted this circle "took the best from all over, and mated it with old Russian sources." Russell cited future balletomane Serge Diaghilev and painter Alexandre Benois as key figures among the group, along with Bakst. "They were some of the most truly cosmopolitan people who ever lived," asserted Russell, "and it was thanks in large part to them that Bakst left Russia with enough ideas in his head to last for a lifetime."

Bakst moved to Paris in 1893 to enroll at the Académie Julian art school, and for the next four years divided his time between France and St. Petersburg. In 1898, he became one of the founding members of a new movement based in St. Petersburg known as *Mir Iskusstva,* or "World of Art," after the journal of the same name, which Diaghilev edited and Bakst illustrated. Diaghilev also organized groundbreaking exhibitions that energized young painters in both Russia and abroad, each of whom were fascinated by one another's styles.

During this period of his career, Bakst taught art to the children of Grand Duke Vladimir Alexandrovich, and the duke became an important and influential early patron. Vladimir was also president of the Imperial Academy of Arts, and helped Bakst secure a few notable commissions, including a portrait of the Russian naval admiral, Avellan, and *The Reception of the Russian Sailors in Paris,* which commemorated an historic 1893 diplomatic event between the two nations.

Drawn to Theater

Bakst also gained acclaim as an artist for his portraits of other well-known figures, among them the painter Filipp Malyavin and the writers Vasily Rozanov and Andrei Bely. In a 1906 portrait of symbolist poet Zinaida Gippius, he depicts this iconoclast woman writer in formal male attire, lounging somewhat decadently in repose while gazing frankly at the viewer. Bakst's burgeoning interest in the theater came about through his friend Benois, who knew the operatic director of the Maryinsky Theater, the leading stage for opera and major theater productions in St. Petersburg. They began frequenting its exciting backstage world, which fascinated them.

Bakst's first set designs for the stage debuted in a 1902 production of *Le Coeur de la Marquise* at the Hermitage Theater in St. Petersburg. Over the next decade he became a leading figure in the modernization of ballet as he fell in with a group of young dancers and choreographers discovered by Diaghilev, who established the *Ballet Russes* (Russian Ballet) in 1909. Bakst had already worked with several of its members by then, including the exotic beauty Ida Rubinstein, a dancer and choreographer; dancer Anna Pavlova; choreographer Mikhail Fokine; composer Igor Stravinsky; and Vaslav Nijinsky, considered one of the greatest male dancers in the history of ballet.

Diaghilev and the others were determined to revolutionize ballet, which had changed very little in the previous two centuries. Costumes were invariably simple tutus and leotards, and the sets rarely ventured further afield than a dull flattened landscape as a backdrop. Bakst served as the main designer for the Ballets Russes, whose official opening night in Paris on May 19, 1909, is considered a turning point in dance and the arts. The vitality of the production helped unleash the creative stirrings of modern dance, while Bakst's sets and costumes were part of the fascinating appeal of the avant-garde that began taking hold in these first years of the twentieth century. According to his *Times* of London obituary, Bakst once said that the world was "moving towards the birth of a new and great art. The art of the future seeks the simplest form. The child's design, its movement, synthesis, its colours have become the problem which painters today seek to solve."

Caused Sensation in London

Bakst's design credits for major Ballet Russes productions include *Cléopâtre* in 1909, *Scheherazade* and *Carnaval* from the second season, and *Narcisse* and *Le Spectre de la Rose* in 1911. In the summer of 1911 the Ballet Russes caused a sensation when it made its London debut at the Royal Opera with *Cléopâtre* during the coronation week of King George V. A reviewer for the *Times* of London remarked that Bakst had attained renown in stage design for "scenes of barbaric and fantastic splendour. Tall, orange-coloured columns run around the three sides of the purple-tiled temple, and through them is seen the shimmer of green water with red-roofed houses beyond." In another London performance that same summer, Nijinsky took to the stage in *Le Spectre de la Rose* "dressed in a flesh-coloured silk tricot onto which Bakst had directly pinned dozens of pinky-red and purple silk petals," noted Juliet Nicolson in her 2007 book, *The Perfect Summer: England 1911, Just Before the Storm,* "making Nijinsky wince in the process." Nicolson also noted that "by the end of the week the Knightsbridge store Harvey Nichols had cleared their windows of the white, cream and lilac of summer fashion and filled them instead with hangings in Bakst purple and red."

An essay in the *International Dictionary of Ballet* also singled out the company's production of *Le Martyre de Saint-Sébastien* in Paris later in 1911 as exemplary of Bakst's vision. The ballet dealt with "themes of the hidden and direly forbidden. The shameful lust of Potiphar's wife for Joseph, the shameful lust of the emperor Hadrian for Sebastian, in fact, all the shameful lusts of Bakst's Parisian audience were rendered in these works with exquisite precision and care for historical detail." As Bakst perfected the art of set design over these first few seasons, he revolutionized the theater itself, noted the *International Dictionary of Ballet*. Bakst's "conception of the stage space as a kinetic environment adapted to the scale of its human inhabitants and their actions," the essay noted, "plus his introduction of radical diagonal perspectives, helped to bring stage design into the modern age."

Bakst was internationally famous by 1912 when he was exiled from Russia because of his Jewish roots. At the time, Jews in tsarist Russia needed an official dispensation to live beyond the Pale of Settlement in what is present-day Poland, Ukraine, Lithuania, and other lands in its western region. Even though his works hung in St. Petersburg museums, he was forced to leave the imperial capital quite suddenly. He gave an account of the event to the *New York Times* shortly afterward. "My passport bears the stamp of the Russian police ordering me to leave [St. Petersburg] in twenty-four hours, and even if I were able to reach the capital without mishap no hotel would dream of receiving me under its roof," he told the newspaper, adding that any friends who took him in for the night would be subject to criminal prosecution as well. He cited his 1903 conversion to the Greek Orthodox religion as the root of the problem with authorities; back then, intermarriage between the faiths was prohibited, but reform laws enacted a few years later prompted him to revert to Judaism, which he believed had displeased some officials. In the *New York Times* interview he described his situation as "a huge farce, but I am sorry my country should still allow the existence of laws absolutely incompatible with civilization."

Influenced Women's Fashion

During World War I, Bakst remained in Paris with the Ballet Russes company, and was often cited in the popular press as having had a profound influence on new women's fashions from Parisian designers like Paul Poiret. Turbans, bold graphic prints, and tunic dresses were all credited to Bakst's sensuous designs for Pavlova, Rubinstein, Nijinsky, and other dancers, which seemed to have been created with the goal of displaying the body, not concealing it. McDowell, the *Sunday Times* writer, said that Bakst even influenced jewelry design. "His colours for *Scheherazade*"—the 1910 Ballet Russes masterpiece—were "peacock green and Persian blue [and] impressed Cartier to such an extent that it began to set emeralds and sapphires together, a combination not seen since the Mogul emperors."

Bakst began to spend more time in New York City, and by 1922 had split with Diaghilev and the Ballet Russes entirely. His final theater job was for Rubinstein's company in Paris in a 1924 production of *Istar*. A wealthy American arts patron, Alice Whitridge Garrett, commissioned him to design a spectacular private theater at Evergreen, her Maryland estate, that later became part of the museum holdings of Johns Hopkins University. He died on December 28, 1924, in Paris, from a lung ailment. His seven-year

marriage to Lubov Gritsenko ended in divorce but produced a son, Andrei.

Bakst's daring ballet costumes provided inspiration for successive generations of fashion designers. The slave bracelets and ropes of pearls seen in early Ballet Russes productions were famously adopted by French designer Coco Chanel in the 1920s as part of her signature look, while a later French couturier, Yves Saint Laurent, directly credited Bakst with his 1976 collection *Homage to the Ballets Russes*, which launched a fashion for peasant-inspired blouson dresses and folklore-inspired prints, among other trends.

In the realm of fine art, Bakst also influenced a younger generation of painters. Another Russian Jewish artist, Marc Chagall, was a student of his between 1908 and 1910, and Bakst's exuberant use of color can also be seen in the art of Raoul Dufy and Sonia Delaunay. Later critics appraised Bakst's contribution to modernism more coolly, believing that he, Diaghilev, and others exploited the view of Russia as an exotic, "foreign" land to garner attention. "Bakst presented the bored, pre-1914 middle class of Europe with just the mixture they wanted: barbaric, 'primitive' colour clashes, eroticism barely veiled under a mask of classicism and a loose drape of exoticism," wrote Paul Overy in a *Times* of London piece from 1973. "It was the mixture which popular preconception had led the public to expect from a Russia seen as part medieval, part oriental, part barbarous."

Books

International Dictionary of Ballet, 2 volumes, St. James Press, 1993.

Nicolson, Juliet, *The Perfect Summer: England 1911, Just Before the Storm*, Grove Press, 2007.

Periodicals

International Herald Tribune, February 13, 1996.

New York Times, November 24, 1912; February 6, 1977.

Sunday Times (London, England), January 28, 1996.

Times (London, England), July 8, 1911; December 29, 1924; December 11, 1973. □

Italo Balbo

Italian air marshal Italo Balbo (1896–1940) became an important member and leader of the Fascist party. He built Benito Mussolini an impressive air force and was a leader of the Blackshirt militia. Balbo is also known for introducing intercontinental flights, first to Rio de Janeiro and then to the United States.

Italo Balbo was born on June 6, 1896, in Ferrara, Italy. He was educated at Florence University and the Institute of Social Science in Rome. After completing his studies, he served in World War I as an officer in the Alpine Corps. He was promoted to Captain and earned one bronze and two silver medals for his war service. Early in his career

Balbo worked as a bank clerk; however, he quit this job when he was offered a position as secretary of a local Fascist section. He was a very enthusiastic and effective leader of Fascist gangs; the unit he led was called "Celibano," named after a cherry brandy spirit that Balbo's gang members used to drink.

The "Celibano" were known for their violence. In Copparo, Massa Fiscaglia, Messola, and other areas near Ferrara, the group's hostility was aimed at the communists and socialists, and on seats of democratic parties. In the summer of 1921, Balbo, along with 4,000 gang members, invaded Portomaggiore and opened fire. For two days the group shot, beat, and murdered people, leaving great destruction in their wake. Portomaggiore was not the only city attacked under Balbo's command. He and his troops committed similar atrocities in Bologna, Modena, and Ravenna. However, communists in Parma were able to stop the "Celibano" by using barricades. During this time, Balbo became very well known throughout the Fascist party ranks.

Moved up in the Fascist Party

Because Balbo's reputation as a Fascist leader was well known, he was nominated as the leader of the Blackshirt militia in the March on Rome during October of 1922. Benito Mussolini moved Balbo quickly up through the ranks of the Fascist party. Balbo was appointed general of militia in 1923, undersecretary of state for air in 1926, air

minister in 1929, and air marshal in 1933. He was then appointed as Governor of Libya in January of 1934.

While Balbo moved upward in the party ranks, he faced some severe accusations. In 1923 he was charged with the murder of Father Giuseppe Minzoni. Minzoni was a parish priest in Argenta, near Ferrara. He encouraged local peasants to protect themselves against the Blackshirts. Balbo's trial did not go in his favor, so he fled Ferrara and moved to Rome.

Although a murder charge might have ended another's career, Balbo remained quite successful. Balbo expressed his love of adventure during this period by becoming very involved in the developments in aircraft technology. After he was promoted in 1929 as minister of the Air Force, he organized flights from one continent to another. These flights made the Italian aviator very famous. The first such intercontinental flight took place between December 17, 1930, and January 15, 1931. He led twelve Savoia Marchetti S. 55X planes on a 10,400 Km (more than 6,442 miles) journey to Rio de Janeiro.

Century of Progress Exposition

Balbo's second notable transatlantic flight took off in the summer of 1933 from Orbetallo airfield near Rome, and landed at the Century of Progress Exposition in Chicago, Illinois. Balbo led a flight of more than 20 seaplanes, and received a hero's welcome when he arrived in Chicago. An article in the *New York Times* describing the event, quoted much later in *Design Issues,* called Balbo's flight "the greatest mass flight in aviation history." The *Design Issues* article also quoted the *Chicago Tribune,* which hailed Balbo's arrival on the shores of Lake Michigan as "the most notable landing in America since Columbus."

The Century of Progress Exposition was a way for Chicagoans to look back at the past while celebrating the anticipated progress of the future. Balbo's transatlantic flight to Chicago was a way for Fascist Italy to demonstrate its own modernization. While in Chicago, 7th Street was renamed Balbo Drive, and President Roosevelt invited the aviator to lunch. Later, an ancient Roman column was given to the United States as a gift from Fascist Italy, to commemorate Balbo's flight. The column was placed on the fair grounds near Soldier Field. As noted on the *Encyclopedia of Chicago* Web site, Sioux Indian Chief Blackhorn presented Balbo with a headdress and named Balbo "Chief Flying Eagle." Balbo in turn presented the chief with a Fascist medallion pendant.

Balbo's success was apparent at the fair itself. In the Italian pavilion, a giant airplane wing was incorporated as part of the pavilion's design. Models of the S55 seaplane were featured, and people hung posters celebrating the flight. Other accessories such as paperweights, letter openers, ashtrays, and souvenirs from the fair soon began to circulate both in Chicago and Italy.

Governor of Libya

Upon returning to Italy after his flight to Chicago, Balbo received great honors and a hero's welcome. He and his airmen paraded under Constantine's Arch in Rome. However, at about this time, Balbo's political career in Italy began to decline. It is surmised that Mussolini and other important figures in the Fascist party were jealous of Balbo's reputation and popularity, and envied his achievements. In January of 1934, Mussolini appointed Balbo as governor to Libya.

While in Africa, Balbo led a comfortable life. He ordered the construction of "Balbia," a coast road. He also welcomed Italian families trying to escape poverty, who were welcomed under a state-aided settler colonization in Libya beginning in 1938, under Italy's Quarta Aponda, or Fourth Shore Program. Nearly 32,000 settlers moved there before the outbreak of World War II. There were approximately 110,000 Italians living in Libya by 1939. As governor, Balbo also tried to encourage Muslim support of Fascism under the Fascist Italianization program for Libya. This program allowed Libyan Muslims to become Muslim Italians.

Shot Down Over Tobruk

After Germany invaded Poland, Balbo returned to Rome to express his disappointment with Mussolini and the Fascists. A profile of Balbo posted on the Comando Supremo Web site claimed that Balbo had referred to the Fascists as "the Germans' shoe-shiners." In the same historical profile, Mussolini reportedly responded that Balbo was a "democratic pig." Balbo continued with his opposition even after Italy entered the war. The Web site article related that Balbo had even declared, "It is necessary to get rid of Mussolini before it's too late," and "Hitler will have a bad ending."

Because of Balbo's outspoken behavior at the time, historians have wondered whether his death was an accident or an orchestrated murder. Italo Balbo died on June 28, 1940, when his S. 79 plane was shot down in Tobruk. It was maintained that Balbo was accidentally shot down by Italian guns when he failed to give correct recognition signals, but Balbo's wife, the countess Emanuela Florio, stated that Mussolini had wanted him dead, and conspiracy theories arose. Did Mussolini order his assassination? An investigation carried out for the Balbo family suggested, however, that the poor state of radio communications, along with the poor organization of Italian antiaircraft units in Tobruk harbor, were the most likely cause of his death, and there appeared to be no real evidence supporting a conspiracy theory.

Present Day Controversies

Although welcomed as a hero at the Century of Progress Exposition in Chicago, and with the added honorary name of Balbo Drive and gift of a Roman column, Chicagoans now only remember Balbo's name with a muted awareness. Many are embarrassed the city welcomed a Fascist general with such warmth.

As recently as 2006, a column by Eric Zorn in the *Chicago Tribune* supported politician Tom Allen, who was trying to put an end to such honorary street names as Balbo Drive. The piece went on to suggest that steps should be taken to rename the street after a more worthy person of Italian descent.

Americans were not the only ones questioning the recognition of Italo Balbo. As noted in a *London Times* article, a senior Italian Air Force general, Leonardo Tricarico, faced

pressure to resign after naming a square at a Rome airport in honor of Balbo. General Tricarico was quoted as being "deeply embittered" by protests from Roman Catholic groups and the Centre Left Opposition about naming the forecourt at Ciampino airport Piazza Balbo. Tricarico reportedly stated that the naming was "an act consistent with our tradition, which acknowledges the merits of Italo Balbo in the history of the Italian Air Force." The article also noted that government officials claimed the protests "were absurd, since a statue of Balbo had been erected at the Ministry of Defense during the previous Centre Left Government."

Books

Encyclopedia of the Modern Middle East and North Africa, Philip Mattar, ed. 2nd ed. 4 vols. Macmillan Reference USA, 2004.

Periodicals

Chicago Tribune, March 2, 2006.
Design Issues, Spring 1997, Vol. 13, Issue 1.
London Times, August 1, 2002.

Online

"Chief Blackhorn and Italo Balbo, 1933," *Encyclopedia of Chicago,* http:www.encyclopedia.chicagohistory.org/pages/11277.html (December 2, 2008).
"Italo Balbo," *Britannica Online Encyclopedia,* http://www.Britannica.com/EBchecked/topic/49907/ItaloBalbo (December 2, 2008).
"Italo Balbo," *Comando Supremo,* http://www.comandosupremo.com/Balbo.html (December 2, 2008).
"Italo Balbo," Encyclopedia.com, http://www.encyclopedia.com/doc/1E1-Balbo-It.html (December 2, 2008). □

Alfredo Baldomir

Alfredo Baldomir (1884–1948) was president of Uruguay from 1938 to 1943. Baldomir allowed the United States to use air and naval bases during World War II. He also suspended the South American country's constitution to purge elements of his government that had Nazi ties.

Alfredo Baldomir was born on August 27, 1884, in Montevideo, Uruguay's capital. He joined the army in 1900 and became Montevideo police chief in 1931. Baldomir, who belonged to the Colorado party, became the country's president on June 19, 1938. Four years earlier, Uruguay had overhauled its constitution. The changes were intended to prop up the struggling revolutionary presidency of Gabriel Terra, who had assumed power in a 1933 coup. "The authoritarian and illiberal nature of Terra's rule (1933-8) cannot be questioned: press censorship was introduced, opposition political groups persecuted and political leaders exiled," Leslie Bethell wrote in the *Cambridge History*

of Latin America. Terra's rule followed relative stability under that of Jose Batile y Ordonez. "The system, controlled by Batile up to his death in 1929, thereafter was left to fend for itself," Torcuato Salvador Di Tella wrote in *History of Political Parties in Twentieth-Century Latin America.*

"The regime installed by coup in 1933 legitimized itself by a new constitution in 1934," Bethell wrote. It essentially provided a coalition of factions belonging to Terra and Blanco party leader General Luis Alberto de Herrera. The constitution granted three of nine Cabinet positions and an equal split of senators to the primary opposition party. "The purpose of this arrangement was to avoid the fatal results of party divisions. But it had the side effect of allowing many different bed-fellows to coexist in the same broadly defined party, or 'Lema,'" Di Tella wrote.

The law proved to be "a thorn to the democratically elected government" of Baldomir, *Time* magazine wrote in 1942. By the time Terra left office, Herrera support was also on the wane. "In a massive Colorado victory Alfredo Baldomir, a relatively little figure, was elected to succeed him. There was soon speculation about constitutional reform," Bethell wrote.

The international landscape and its effect on Uruguay had also changed after 1933. Surging Italian fascism had fascinated Terra and German influence had expanded in southeastern South America through contracts for hydroelectric projects awarded to German interests along Argentina's Rio Negro, or "Black River." The country cut diplomatic relations with

the Soviet Union in 1935 and then with Spain's Republican government one year later.

"The outbreak of the second World War further weakened the alliance of the governing Colorado and Blanco factions and further emphasized the isolation of the *herreristas,*" Bethell wrote. "Although Uruguay formally declared neutrality, public sentiment was strongly against the Axis powers, particularly after evidence of Nazi activity in the country was made public, and Alfredo Baldomir's government gave all possible assistance to the Allies. While Britain had every reason to be satisfied with this attitude, relations with the United States grew particularly close."

Baldomir, who survived a coup attempt, had wanted to overhaul the constitution again. He was slow, however, to implement such changes. Early in Baldomir's administration, the opposition, with help from organized labor and the National Party, pressured the president into advocating free elections, a free press, and a new constitution. The election of Baldomir ushered "a new period of reform-oriented rule," DiTella wrote. "However, factional oscillations again left the executive without a congressional majority in 1942, and Baldomir then resorted to the same weapon earlier used by Terra," DiTella added. "Terra's and Baldomir's coups were relatively *blandos* (soft) if judged by continental standards, and were quickly corrected with a return to normality, reminiscent if at all of [Charles] De Gaulle's [ascension] to power in France in 1958." Though the coups reflected internal discord, DiTella wrote, neither involved serious repression. "In contrast to the French case, however, in Uruguay the process was not accompanied by a radical mutation in the party system, which might have helped to channel in a clearer way the existing tensions."

Took Action during World War II

In 1939, Baldomir declared his country neutral, just as World War II broke out. But "Baldomir's administration could not avoid the consequences of World War II or the pressures and interests of the Allied forces," said a writer in *Library of Congress Country Studies.* In December of 1939, during the Battle of the Rio de la Plata, the crew of the German battleship *Graf Spee* blew up the ship rather than leave it in the port of Montevideo, as ordered. That prompted Uruguay to side with the Allies. In 1940, Uruguay discovered Nazi sympathizers within its government and two years later, at a conference in Rio de Janeiro, Brazil, the country announced it had severed all ties with the Axis powers. Brazil, Uruguay's northern neighbor, was already pro-Allied. Only Argentina— separated from Uruguay in southeastern South America by the *Rio de la Plata* (River Plate) estuary—and Chile retained diplomacy with Germany. "Uruguay's foreign policy has been shaped by its democratic tradition, its history of being a victim of foreign intervention, its status as the second-smallest country in South America [after Suriname], and its location between the two rival giants of the region: Argentina to the west and Brazil to the north," Uruguayan President Luis Alberto Lacalle de Herrera said in a speech in September of 1990 to the Organization of American States, which the Library of Congress posted on its *Country Studies* website.

In 1941, one year after further constitutional changes were discussed, the Herrera faction withdrew from the Cabinet. In February of 1942, Baldomir dissolved the legislature. "When a democratic nation scraps democratic processes, it may be because the machinery merely needs overhauling," *Time* wrote. Baldomir acted after the opposition, and in a ten to six vote, censured the government's policy of defending its hemisphere. In addition to suspending Parliament, Baldomir dispatched troops to trouble spots in Montevideo, and postponed the presidential election scheduled for March 29 of that year. Baldomir also declared that a Council of State would govern, and draft changes to the 1934 overhaul, until the presidential election was finally held. He pressured Minister of War Julio A. Roletti to resign, and replaced him with Foreign Minister Alberto Guani, with Guani to investigate whether the army was loyal.

Herrera supporters said operating outside the constitution disqualified Baldomir as president, and they stormed Congressional Hall. After police held them off, a scuffle ensued in which five people, including two bystanders, were injured. Calm, however, prevailed throughout the rest of Uruguay. Baldomir said in a radio address, as quoted in *Time,* that he took harsh measures because the Herra faction "wanted a government with a Nazi attitude." He promised he would not run again for president. The white-collar and laboring classes—his primary sources of support—applauded when he said, according to *Time,* "Uruguay will comply faithfully and honorably with all obligations undertaken, especially in the field of inter-American solidarity."

Granted U.S. Access to Bases

"Traditionally, relations between Uruguay and the United States have been based on a common dedication to democratic ideals," Lacalle said in his Washington speech, recorded on the *Country Studies* website. Uruguay had tried to remain neutral in World War I. The government of Feliciano Viera, however, broke relations with Germany in October of 1917, three-fourths into the war.

Uruguay's rival party, the Blancos, opposed the Colorados' pro-United States stance and tried stubbornly to impede Baldomir's legislative proposals. In contrast, Herrera insisted that Uruguay remain neutral and staunchly opposed the president's decision to allow the establishment of U.S. bases in that country. Baldomir responded by forcing three pro-Herrera ministers to resign; the 1934 constitutional changes had made their presence possible.

After Baldomir appointed a board, sans Herrerists, to examine constitutional overhaul, Baldomir dissolved the General Assembly and replaced it with a *Consejo de Estado* (Council of State), that consisted of Colorados. This involved no newspaper closings, arrests, or deportations. "It was an in-house agreement to overcome the institutional crisis initiated on March 31, 1933, and to avoid enforcement of the existing constitution," the Library of Congress *Country Studies* website wrote. "Battlists and Communists welcomed the new situation, but the Socialists argued that Baldomir had been one of the protagonists of the 1933 coup. Independent Nationalists remained on the sidelines. Herrerism, freely accused of being pro-Nazi, pro-Franco, and pro-Argentine, was the big loser."

"The political base of the 1933 regime was therefore eroded by its inability either to reflect the popular consensus at home or to maintain its coherence in the face of a rapidly changing international situation," Bethell wrote. "That, and the more favorable conditions for the growth of [the] manufacturing industry, under which *battlismo* had traditionally flourished, made change inevitable. By 1940 constitutional reform was under discussion."

National elections were held in November of 1942. Independent Nationalists could participate, despite a 1939 law that impeded groups perceived as a threat to the Colorado-Blanco two-party system. Also in 1942, seventy-seven percent of voters approved the new constitution, which retained the presidency and General Assembly, and called for proportional representation in the Senate. It also abolished the 1934 provision that required co-participation in ministries.

After Baldomir allowed the United States to construct bases in his country, the Americans helped supply the Uruguayan armed forces. After Uruguay broke relations in January of 1942—one month after Japan attacked Pearl Harbor in Hawaii, triggering U.S. involvement in the war—the Americans provided loans. "Uruguay has had strong political and cultural ties with the countries of Europe and the Americas," the Library of Congress wrote. "It has shared basic values with them, such as support for constitutional democracy, political pluralism, and individual liberties."

Baldomir was promoted to a general's rank in the army in 1942. One year later, he resigned as president, with Juan Jose de Amezaga succeeding him. Baldomir died on February 25, 1948, in Montevideo, at age sixty-three.

Baldomir's Legacy

Baldomir's maneuvering was paradoxical. The Uruguayan president subverted democracy with the ultimate goal of reinstating it. He also was instrumental in enhancing the navy and its air service, particularly after the 1939 battle of Rio de la Plata. Military help from the United States throughout the 1940s and 1950s augmented the South American country.

It led to Uruguay in 1959—in conjunction with the United States, Brazil, and Argentina—engaging in the first large-scale joint exercise that involved Latin American countries. U.S. cooperation continued, and in 1990, Uruguay's navy received two cutters decommissioned by the U.S. Coast Guard for coastal control—the country's east coast hugs the Atlantic Ocean—and work under an anti-narcotics program run by the U.S. Department of State.

Books

Cambridge History of Latin America, Vol. VIII; 1930 to the Present, Cambridge University Press, 1984–2008.

History of Political Parties in Twentieth-Century Latin America, Transaction Publishers, 2004.

Periodicals

Time, March 2, 1942.

Online

"A Country Study: Uruguay," Library of Congress Country Studies, http://memory.loc.gov/frd/cs/uytoc.html (December 4, 2008). □

John Ballance

New Zealand Prime Minister, John Ballance (1839–1893), combined the raw honesty of journalism with the steady skepticism of politics to serve as one of New Zealand's boldest and most progressive leaders, gaining significant popularity and respect for the Liberal Party.

John Ballance, the oldest of a large family, was born on March 27, 1839 in Ballypitmave—two miles from the parish of Glenavy, in County Antrim, Ireland. Ballance's father, Samuel Ballance (1800–1879), was a farmer and evangelical protestant and his mother, Mary McNiece, was a liberal Quaker from a wealthy family.

Education

Ballance attended the local national school, followed by a stint at Belfast's Wilson's Academy, during which time he helped his father compose speeches to deliver at local political events. Timothy McIvor's 1984 doctoral thesis, *On Ballance: a Biography of John Ballance, Journalist and Politician* explained how Ballance's "reputation for laziness arose from a dislike of farm work and a remarkable propensity, from an early age, to do nothing all day but read." Ballance left formal school early to seek an apprenticeship with an iron-monger in Belfast, and he moved to Birmingham in 1857 to split his time between a job as a traveling salesman and evening classes in biography, politics and history at the Birmingham and Midland Institute—an institution that embodied what McIvor's thesis described as "a mid-Victorian culture of self-improvement. . . . Ballance joined the ranks of many young men bent on a 'moral and intellectual' development that would form the basis for social and economic improvement . . . he joined a debating society, became secretary of a Birmingham literary society, played chess and wrote articles for the local newspapers. He attended lectures and meetings of well-known figures." Everything was done, it seemed, in the name of self-improvement.

Made a Fresh Start

On June 17, 1863 Ballance married Fanny Taylor. Fanny was in poor health when they met, and it was decided that they would emigrate to Wanganui, New Zealand—where Fanny's brother lived—in part to improve her health, as well as to make a new start in a land that seemed rich with opportunities. Some sources claim that the Ballances emigrated that same year, in 1863, but others maintain that it was two years later, in 1865.

The frontier town of Wanganui was, at that time, about two thousand people strong, and while its progress and development were fairly steady, its overall position remained delicate for many reasons. It was this innate uncertainty that some scholars believe ultimately fueled Ballance's remarkable drive to support and enlarge the small town he had adopted as his home. Others argue that, as a local journalist

and newspaper owner, Ballance's economic security was entirely dependant upon the town and inhabitants of Wanganui, and that it was this dependence that motivated both his personal and political policies.

Started a Daily Newspaper

Ballance initially opened a small jewelry shop, which did poorly, prompting him to quickly turn to journalism as the truest path to lasting change and success. Wanganui had two local papers when Ballance arrived, both bi-weeklies—the *Wanganui Times* and the *Wanganui Chronicle*—and both of which accepted articles written by Ballance. Ambitious, sometimes to a fault, Ballance decided to start a local, daily evening paper called the *Evening Herald* (later changed to the *Wanganui Herald*), and its weekly counterpart, the *Weekly Herald* (later changed to *The Yeoman*). When the *Herald* was founded in 1867, both the other local papers began publishing three times a week, but Wanganui was only big enough to support two publications, and the *Times* was discontinued in 1869.

The years between 1860 and 1865 saw land wars between the native *Maori* (normal) and the *Pakeha* (foreigners). Often called the "Maori Wars" by the Pakeha, and *te riri Pakeha* (white man's anger) by the Maori, the politically correct term for the land wars is now the New Zealand Wars, and Ballance spent these years running his paper, entrenching himself in the local politics, and serving as a member of Wanganui Cavalry Corps—in which he experienced both military action and leadership while combining the roles of field correspondent and soldier to provide a uniquely comprehensive, if not objective view of the fighting.

As Tim McIvor stated in his 2004 *Oxford Dictionary of National Biography* entry on Ballance, "In March, 1868 Fanny Ballance died, at the age of twenty-four. On 19 May 1870, in Wellington, Ballance married Ellen Anderson . . . There were no children from either marriage, but in 1886 Ellen and John adopted Ellen's four-year-old niece [Kathleen]." Ellen, an intelligent and confident woman also originally from Ireland, strongly influenced Ballance's position on women's suffrage throughout his political career, and served as the Women's Progressive Society's vice-president.

Entered Politics

In 1875 Ballance won a Rangitikei parliamentary seat and joined New Zealand's House of Representatives as a member of the Liberal Party. In 1878 he became a member of the ministry of George Grey (1812–1898) when he accepted appointments as commissioner of customs and stamp duties, minister of education and, eventually, even colonial treasurer. In 1879 he won a Wanganui parliamentary seat, which he lost briefly two years later and then regained in 1884 as a member of Sir Robert Stout's (1884–1887) ministry in the role of minister of lands and native affairs. During his five-year hiatus from the parliamentary world, McIvor's *Oxford Dictionary of National Biography* entry states that Ballance kept busy "writing a series of articles (collected in 1887 as *A National Land Policy Based on the Principle of State Ownership*) on land reform and nationalization. A convinced secularist, he [also] formed the Wanganui Freethought

Association in 1883 and brought out the monthly *Freethought Review* (1883–1885)." Stout's ministry was defeated in 1887, and Ballance was elected to lead the liberal opposition. In 1891, Ballance became Prime Minister of New Zealand and appointed British-born Richard John Seddon (1845–1906) as his Minister of Public Works, Defense, and Mines.

As the 2008 *The Rough Guide to New Zealand* explains in its historical summary, "From 1879 until 1896 New Zealand went into the 'long depression', mostly overseen by the conservative 'Continuous Ministry'—the last government composed of colonial gentry.... in 1890, [the liberal party] wrested power from those who had controlled the country for two decades and ushered in an era of unprecedented social change. Its first leader, John Ballance, firmly believed in state intervention and installed... [a radically socialist Minister of Labour who was] instrumental in pushing through sweeping reforms... that were so progressive that no further changes were made to labour laws until 1936."

With gold rushes in the South Island area and a sheep farming platform for the production of wool and the shipping of meat as the country's economical mainstays, it was no wonder that land was of such importance to anyone and everyone that had a say. From his days as a journalist to the short time he spent leading the country, Ballance's maxim was self-reliance—for Pakeha and Maori alike. The progressive land and income tax policies that Ballance pushed to introduce, as well as his ministry's other reform efforts made for a collectively intrepid platform that infused the liberal party with renewed popularity and respect. Ballance was far from beyond censure, however, and his taxes were roundly criticized until 1892, when he reported an extraordinary budget surplus. Lauded for ushering in a time of prosperity, he was as quickly chastised when New Zealand's economic situation deteriorated into a depression.

Last Days

In 1892, Ballance became ill and Seddon picked up the responsibilities of leader of the House. Ballance died April 27, 1893 in Premier House in Wellington—too soon to observe the fruits of his labor. He was the first Premier to die while still in office, and Seddon was immediately asked to form a government. It was during Seddon's much longer term in office that many of Ballance's policies found their way through the red tape and into practical applications. Ballance never saw the introduction of graduated land and income taxes, the abolition of large holdings, the first enforced state arbitration system in the world, an eight-hour work day, or a woman's right to vote (in 1893 New Zealand became the first country in the world to establish full women's suffrage).

Those who heard Ballance speak reported that he may not have been particularly captivating as a public speaker, but his written persona was both compelling and bold, and he inspired immense loyalty among those who knew him. McIvor described Ballance's funeral in his 1984 thesis, *On Ballance:* "The colony had never seen quite such a funeral. The procession began in Tinakori Road, and then crept down to the railway station, to the trains waiting to convey the mourners to Wanganui. The main train carried two hundred persons. As it stopped for water on its way north

crowds greeted it in silence, whilst bands played slow marches. On arrival in Wanganui... special boats had brought another two thousand mourners to the town."

Glenavy restored and established Ballance's birthplace and childhood home in Ballypitmave as the Ballance House—dedicated to the memory of the 19th century Premier. The building has also become Ireland's Honorary Consulate for New Zealand and the site of an annual celebration involving a circus and a local craft fair, with festivities that focus on locally grown raspberries and homemade raspberry tea—a regional focus that one cannot help but believe Ballance would have highly approved of.

Not everyone has embraced a positive legacy for the self-sufficient journalist and politician. Literary reviewer C. J. Woods questioned Ballance's very presence in Henry Boylan's 1998 *Dictionary of Irish Biography.* In a 1979 *Irish Historical Studies* review of Boylan's dictionary, Woods argued, "The other necessary criterion for selection, apart from Irishness, is eminence or distinction.... a very personal choice is exercised with regard to [persons not of primary or secondary importance] (John Ballance...) Ireland still lacks a definitive dictionary of national biography... the result of coordinated efforts by a large number of scholars working from all known sources. Mr Boylan's work is a reminder."

The New Zealand Press Association also reported that "a proposal to reinstate the John Ballance statue in Wanganui's Moutoa Gardens" was overturned on June 27, 2005. The article went on to explain, "The Wanganui District Council today voted that the Moutoa Gardens Historical Reserve Board be responsible for a decision on where to re-erect the statue... The statue was smashed in 1994 by Maori protesters who said the politician intended genocide for their people. Only a pair of feet have remained on the plinth, testimony to some of the feelings that inspired the 1995 occupation of the reserve." While New Zealand Maori continue to feel misrepresented, marginalized and cheated by the original treaty erected between their people and the first settlers of New Zealand, much of the rest of the population perceives their history and government as models of enlightened democracy and evolution. It is Ballance's fate as a pivotal political figure to be at the center of every opinion and judgment, and whether one views his time and energies as having been ultimately good or bad for New Zealand, he clearly championed change in a difficult time.

Books

Boylan, Henry,*A Dictionary of Irish Biography*, Roberts Rinehart Publishers, 1998.

*Encyclopedia of World Biography Vol. 14,*Gale, 2006.

McIvor, Timothy J.,*On Ballance: a Biography of John Ballance, Journalist and Politician, 1839–1893*, Victoria University of Wellington, 1984.

Merriam-Webster's Biographical Dictionary, Merriam-Webster, Inc., 1995.

Oxford Dictionary of National Biography, edited by H.C.G. Matthew and Brian Harrison, Oxford University Press, 2004.

The Rough Guide to New Zealand, written and researched by Laura Harper, Tony Mudd and Paul Whitfield, Rough Guides, 2008.

Periodicals

Asia Africa Intelligence Wire, June 27, 2005.
Asia Africa Intelligence Wire, November 6, 2005.
Europe Intelligence Wire, July 25, 2005.
The News Letter, 1999.
Irish Historical Studies, September, 1979.

Online

"On Ballance: a Biography of John Ballance, Journalist and Politician, 1839–1893", *Victoria Research Archive,* http://research archive.vuw.ac.nz/handle/10063/538?show=full (October 23, 2008). □

Edwin James Barclay

Liberian politician and statesman Edwin Barclay (1882–1955) served in Liberia's government for a number of years before becoming the nation's president. His administration covered nearly 15 years and was marked by a dedication to honest government. As president, Barclay worked to support open international relations and develop stronger ties to the United States, laying the foundation for the Open Door Policy typically credited to his successor, William V.S. Tubman. In 1943, Barclay became the first leader of an African nation to visit the White House.

Edwin James Barclay was born into a prominent Liberian political family on January 5, 1882, in Brewerville, Liberia, a suburb of the nation's capital, Monrovia. Barclay's family traced its roots to North America; conflicting reports state alternately that his grandparents had been enslaved Kentuckians who migrated to Liberia during the Civil War or that they had left the island of Barbados for Liberia as part of the Barbados Colonization Society at about the time same. Regardless of the family's true antecedents, the Barclay descendents fared well in their new home. Ernest Barclay—Edwin Barclay's father—served as Liberia's Secretary of State, and his uncle, Arthur Barclay, had a lengthy political career culminating in a tenure as the nation's 14th President during the years 1904–1912.

Edwin Barclay attended Liberia College (today the University of Liberia), graduating in 1903 with a degree in liberal arts. Barclay pursued legal studies and soon began a career in politics. After serving as County Attorney of Montserrado County, Attorney General of Liberia, and Secretary of Education, Barclay became Secretary of State in the administration of President Charles D.B. King.

Worked in the King Administration

King was inaugurated in January 1920, and during his tenure as Liberia's leader the nation underwent a period of significant change. Under President Theodore Roosevelt, the United States had granted Liberia a significant loan to support the reorganization of its troubled finances; however, early progress on this chore had been derailed by the advent of World War I. At the beginning of his administration, King held talks with black nationalist leader Marcus Garvey, creator and leading proponent of the "Back to Africa" movement. Garvey hoped to develop a strong African homeland for people of African descent to return to, and he proposed significant financial support for Liberian infrastructure to further that end. Although King at first encouraged this plan, political and economic changes later led the administration to ban the movement.

One significant factor leading to this policy change was the interest of the Firestone Tire Rubber Company in Liberia's rubber resources. As Secretary of State, Barclay served as the representative of his country's interests in negotiations between Firestone and Liberia. The talks, which consumed three years, would in 1926 result in Firestone being granted 1,000,000 acres for a rubber plantation on what the *Dictionary of African Historical Biography* characterized as "terms very advantageous to Firestone," including a remission of all present and future taxes. As a result of its participation in this agreement, the nation of Liberia was granted a significant loan from the Finance Corporation of America, a company specifically created for this purpose by Firestone. This loan was somewhat controversial both within and outside of the country; *Liberia: Past and Present* argued that it "turned Liberia de facto into an American protectorate." Despite the objections, the loan allowed Liberia to consolidate its debt and solidify its financial footing for the first time in decades; in 1952, the nation discharged all of its foreign debt for the first time since 1871.

In 1927, King won reelection over the opposition candidate, Thomas J.R. Faulkner, in one of the most blatantly fraudulent elections of all time—although only about 15,000 Liberians had the right to vote, over fifteen times that number of ballots were cast in support of the sitting president. Faulkner responded to this defeat by issuing accusations of forced labor and even slavery in Liberia, claiming that high-ranking government officials were using Liberia's army, the Frontier Force, to forcibly send laborers to Spanish plantations on the island of Fernando Po. King requested an official inquiry by the League of Nations into the matter in 1929, which resulted in the implication of his vice-president, Allen Yancy, in the scandal. Although King had been exonerated of the slavery charges, he was considered to have failed in his duty to protect the rights of his people; both he and Yancy resigned their posts the following year. Under Liberia's constitution, Secretary of State Edwin Barclay—who had not been accused of any wrongdoing—ascended to the presidency.

Faced Problems at Home and Abroad

Barclay took office in 1930 and successfully won election in his own right the following year. He faced a number of both internal and external challenges: Liberia's Kru people staged a rebellion, financial and sanitation woes plagued the nation, and the United States and other Western nations refused to recognize the new government as legitimate due to the lingering slavery scandal of Barclay's predecessors. The Kru rebellion was one of Liberia's bloodiest, and the harsh actions of the Frontier Force drew criticism from abroad.

Barclay strove to resolve many of the nation's problems through diplomatic means. Soon after taking office, he eased restrictions on foreign economic activity in Liberia by repealing an 1846 Ports of Entry law that had brought about a closed-door economic policy for the nation. As part of its investigation into the slavery allegations, the League of Nations had recommended that Liberia place itself under the control of the League for a period of seven years, during which the League could encourage much-needed reform. Barclay refused to do so, arguing that his government was performing the necessary actions on their own. By 1935, the United States has restored diplomatic ties with Liberia, and normalization with other nations quickly followed suit. In the interim, "Barclay embarked on a diplomatic offense in Eastern Europe for assistance, especially in health and related matters," according to Joseph Saye Guannu, writing in the *Daily Observer*. These overtures were well received by the nations of Poland and Czechoslovakia.

Shortly after taking office, Barclay undertook the administrative reorganization of the hinterlands, creating three official provinces—the Western, Central, and Eastern—each headed up by a president-appointed provincial commissioner. Districts were created within each province under the direction of district commissioners, and these districts further subdivided into chiefdoms. The lasting success of this system seems questionable; the *Dictionary of African Historical Biography* noted that "real progress was not made until the administration of [Barclay's] successor," and indeed Barclay's divisions were scrapped thirty years later and replaced with counties. Barclay also tried to reach out to Liberians in the interior of the nation by staging regional conferences and shifting the responsibility for tax collection from the notoriously aggressive army to a Revenue Agent working under the Secretary of the Treasury.

Liberia stood against the Axis powers during World War II, first unofficially and later openly. In March 1941, eleven Nazi supporters in Liberia planned an assassination attempt on Barclay; warned of the plot, Barclay directed members of Liberia's army to round up the conspirators. At about that time, Barclay approved an agreement that granted the United States authority over Liberia's airports and military holdings through the conclusion of the war. (Barclay's successor would officially declare war on Germany as one of his first actions in 1944.)

In 1943, Barclay—accompanied by his soon-to-be successor, Associate Supreme Court Justice William V.S. Tubman—made an official visit to the United States in return for an earlier visit paid by American President Franklin Delano Roosevelt to Liberia. Reporting on the event, *Time* magazine noted that "not since Theodore Roosevelt had invited Booker T. Washington to stay for lunch in 1901 had a Negro been a guest at the White House. Last week the Liberian President and President-elect became the first ever to spend the night there." Barclay also attended sessions of the United States Senate and House of Representatives, becoming the first African or African American to address those assemblies since the days of Reconstruction nearly 75 years previously.

Because Liberia's constitution prevented him from holding the presidency again upon the completion of his second term, Barclay left office in 1944. Prior to the 1943 election in which Liberians selected Tubman as Barclay's successor, *Time* magazine noted that "in times like these, the President's supporters, taking their cue from the great paternal democracy across the Atlantic, were beginning to call able Edwin Barclay indispensable, were talking about Term III and changing the Constitution to make it possible." One of Barclay's last actions as president, enacted on December 31, 1943, was the adoption of the United States dollar as Liberia's sole legal tender. This action paved the way for significant foreign investment and helped usher in the Open Door Policy that came into full bloom under Tubman.

Attempted Return to Politics

Over a decade after his retirement from public life in 1944, Barclay again stood for the presidency against Tubman, a move that Guannu claimed was made "in order to grapple with what he called 'organized corruption, graft and financial irresponsibility.'" Barclay suffered a wide defeat in the election of 1955, and soon afterward Tubman banned the opposition Coalition Reformation and True Whig parties.

Barclay died on November 6, 1955, at the age of 73. A statesman so dedicated to his country that he wrote a patriotic song entitled "The Lone Star Forever" honoring Liberia's singly-starred flag, Barclay stands out as one of Liberia's most honest and influential leaders. F.P.M van der Kraaij commented in *The Open Door Policy of Liberia: An Economic History of Modern Liberia* that "it seems justified . . . to say that: whatever modern Liberia is today, it owes to Tubman although this president could never have been as successful if his predecessors had not done what they did. Specifically meant here are Presidents Artur [sic] and Edwin Barclay." Barclay's long tenure as president saw the nation through the difficulties of the 1930s and into World War II, setting the stage for Liberia's increased involvement in world affairs in later years.

Books

Lipschutz, Mark R. and R. Kent Rasmussen, *Dictionary of African Historical Biography*, Aldine, 1978.

van der Kraaij, F.P.M., *The Open Door Policy of Liberia: An Economic History of Modern Liberia*, 1983.

Periodicals

Guannu, Joseph Saye, *Daily Observer*, August 27, 2008.

Time, May 27, 1935; June 24, 1935; April 7, 1941; December 28, 1941; December 14, 1942; June 7, 1943.

Online

"Liberia," *Encyclopedia Brittanica*, http://search.eb.com/ (January 13, 2009).

"Liberia Past and Present," http://www.liberiapastandpresent.org/ (January 13, 2009). □

Charles Glover Barkla

Charles Glover Barkla (1877–1944) was a renowned English physicist. He made many contributions to science, but his major fame came from his studies revealing the true nature of a form of electromagnetic radiation in X-rays. Through his research on X-rays, his later studies also answered questions regarding the true nature of the atom. Barkla won the Nobel Prize for Physics in 1917 for his discovery of the relationship between atomic structure and X-rays.

Charles Glover Barkla was born on June 7, 1877, in Widnes, Lancashire, England. His father, John Martin Barkla, worked as secretary to the Atlas Chemical Company. His mother, Sarah, was the daughter of a watchmaker. Barkla's middle name, Glover, was his mother's maiden name.

As a young student Barkla was educated at the Liverpool Institute, where he graduated in 1895. After graduation he entered University College, Liverpool. There he majored in mathematics and physics. While at college, he also studied experimental physics under Oliver Lodge. He earned his bachelor of science degree with first class honors in 1898, and completed his master of science degree one year later.

In 1899 Barkla was presented with a research scholarship by the Royal Commissioners for the Exhibition of 1851. This scholarship allowed him to further his graduate studies at Trinity College, Cambridge, where he studied with George Stokes and J.J. Thomson. However, after 18 months Barkla decided to transfer to King's College, in order to become a member of their prestigious chapel choir. Barkla had a magnificent singing voice, noted as either a baritone or a bass according to various biographers. He was known to draw a large audience for his solo performances. Although extremely gifted at music, Barkla decided not to pursue a musical career. After his tenure at King's College, he moved on to accept a position as Oliver Lodge Fellow at the University of Liverpool, where he continued his research on X-rays.

Researched X-Rays

Barkla began his research on X-rays while completing his graduate studies at King's College during the early 1900s. His research yielded more than 70 academic and scientific papers on the subject. Wilhelm Conrad Röntgen, the man who discovered X-rays, observed what is known as secondary radiation. Secondary radiation is the radiation that is formed after a substance is exposed to primary radiation. Röntgen, however, did not continue to research this occurrence, which opened the door for Barkla to pursue that area of study. In doing so, he made many important discoveries. First, he found that secondary radiation is absorbed by a material in almost the same way that primary radiation is absorbed. Second, from this research, Barkla was able to support the hypothesis that X-rays are a type of electromagnetic radiation.

Barkla's first paper on secondary radiation was published in 1903. Through his research, he found that the more massive the atom, the more charged particles it contained. He then concluded that the number of particles in the atom of a specific material was thus accountable for the variation in the way the radiation was scattered. Barkla's research suggested just how important the amount of charge was in an atom to determine an element's position on the periodic table, instead of just the atom's atomic weight. His findings indicated that the higher an element was located on the periodic table, the more penetrating were the rays it created. Barkla's main observation was that the X-ray pattern he studied for an element was related to the number of electrons in the atoms of that element.

A few years later, in 1913, Barkla's work was completed by another English physicist. H.G.J. Moseley. Moseley discovered that X-ray spectra for elements changed in a straightforward and ordinary way as one moved up the periodic table. Like Barkla, Moseley credited these results to the number of electrons in the atoms of each element, and thereby to the total positive charge on the nucleus of each atom. Barkla's initial work with X-rays aided Moseley as he devised his model of giving atomic numbers to the elements in a way that reflected the regular, integral, linear relationship of their X-ray spectra.

Barkla's successful findings and work with X-rays led him to rapid upward advancement in academic circles. He received his doctorate in science from Liverpool in 1904, and continued his research on X-rays from 1904-1907. In this time he found that heavy elements formed secondary radiation of a longer wavelength than that of the primary X-ray beam. This finding was different compared to atomic elements with low atomic weights. He found that the radiation from the heavier elements consisted of two different types. Barkla named the two types the K-series, which had more penetrating emissions, and the L-series, for less penetrating emissions. Later he would hypothesize about a J-series and an M-series of penetrating emissions.

Additional Accomplishments

While in the midst of his scientific research, Barkla married Mary Esther Cowell in 1907. Together they had three sons and one daughter. All of their children eventually graduated from Edinburgh. Michael, Barkla's youngest son, was a flight lieutenant. Like his father, he was also a brilliant scholar. Unfortunately, he was tragically killed in an airplane accident while serving as a surgeon for the Royal Air Force in August of 1943. Barkla lived most of his adult life with his wife and children in rural surroundings at the Hermitage of Braid in Edinburgh. His home is now a tourist visitor center for the Hermitage of Braid nature trail.

After receiving his doctorate, Barkla not only continued with his research but was also appointed demonstrator and assistant lecturer in physics in 1905 at Liverpool. In 1907 he became a lecturer in advanced electricity, a post created specifically for Barkla. Two years later he moved to King's College in London, where he accepted a position as Wheatstone Professor of Physics. Finally, in 1913 Barkla went to the University of Edinburgh as a Professor of Natural Philosophy. He played a significant role at the University of Edinburgh by actively helping to establish degrees in pure science, including an honors degree in physics. He remained in Edinburgh until his death on October 23, 1944.

In addition to his scientific discoveries, Barkla also earned several honorary degrees. He was elected a fellow of the Royal Society in 1912, and later was awarded the Hughes Medal. However, Barkla's most significant accomplishment and the crowning point of his research career came in 1917, when he was awarded the Nobel Prize for Physics for discovering the relationship between X-rays and atomic structure.

Barkla delivered his Nobel lecture on June 3, 1920. In his lecture he decided to discuss two main points of his research. First he discussed the phenomena of scattering. He described his work with X-rays and the results of his experiments as having a bearing on the quantum theory of radiation. He also chose to discuss the potential evidence of the existence of a J-series of radiation. In his lecture he described his recent experiments, which suggested that a characteristic radiation of a higher frequency than the K-series existed, although he did note that evidence for the J-series had proved much more difficult to obtain. Later, his obsession with the J-series would slightly tarnish his reputation.

Although Barkla delivered a very scientific Nobel lecture on June 3, his speech at the Nobel banquet in Stockholm on June 1, 1920, was extremely humble. The Nobel Foundation's Web site posted the banquet speech, in which Barkla declared that "the Nobel Prize is without doubt the highest honour, the most coveted honour, which can be bestowed on a Scientist." He gave credit to the Swedish Academy of Science for giving Nobel awards without discrimination against a person's nationality or social position. Further, Barkla made note of other Nobel winners who had helped him in the field of science, especially Professors Planck and Stark. He particularly thanked Professor Stark, who invited Barkla to publicly deliver his first full account of his explorations on secondary radiation.

Scrutiny of Barkla's Later Work

Most of Barkla's scientific renown was related to the success of his work in the field of X-ray experimentation. However, his aptitude as a theoretical physicist caused doubts among many in his field. As early as 1910, Barkla began to fall behind in the ongoing research and changes taking place in the field of physics. He often rejected new findings, concepts, and research by other scientists. For example, Barkla rejected the work of Albert Einstein and Max Planck, which introduced quantum theory.

Unfortunately, Barkla's later life was spent in almost total isolation. Instead of using new research and theory to teach, he preferred to structure his lectures based on his own previous achievements, and relied only on his own research. After discovering the K-series and L-series in radiation, he had predicted that an M-series and a J-series of emissions might also exist. He had made note of the J-series in his Nobel lecture in 1917. He suspected that these emissions would have different penetrable effects.

Toward the end of his career, Barkla spent the majority of his time committed to finding a J-series of secondary radiation, otherwise known as the "J phenomenon." Although he spent a great deal of time trying to locate the "J phenomenon," his work proved fruitless. However, even though his work in that area resulted in nothing useful for scientists, his predictions about an M-series were fulfilled, as an M-series was later discovered.

Achievements Acknowledged

Although the end of Charles Glover Barkla's life did not produce any new or solid hypotheses in theoretical physics, his earlier experiments and discoveries have become an integral part of the contemporary science community. In 2006 the University of Liverpool held the Charles Barkla Lectures. The 2004 Nobel Prize winner, Professor Frank Wilczek, presented the first lecture of the series in February of 2006. An article describing the event, posted on the University of Liverpool's Web site, described Professor Wilczek's discoveries and explained his findings that "quarks, the fundamental particles that make up 99.9% of ordinary matter, are bound together to form protons and neutrons." The presentation of Wilczek's findings took place at the lecture honoring Barkla.

The Charles Barkla lectures were sponsored by the University's Department of Mathematical Science and the Department of Physics. In the article on the University of Liverpool's Web site, Professor Alon Faraggi commented, "For many years, physicists all over the world have been working to understand the unification of electromagnetic, gravitational and nuclear forces. The Charles Barkla lectures will highlight the importance of new research in this area and welcome some of the most distinguished physicists and mathematicians in the world.''

Barkla's experiments with X-rays and his published papers from the early 1900s earned him a Nobel Prize, and his early discoveries paved the way for his successors in the fields of physics and mathematics to continue to research and provide new theories and experiments which stem from his research in electromagnetic radiation focusing on X-rays.

Periodicals

Physics in Perspective, December 24, 2007.

Online

''Charles Glover Barkla Banquet Speech'' http://www.holiker. narod.ru/four/barkla-speech.html (December 16, 2008).

''The Nobel Prize in Physics 1917,'' Nobelprize.org, http:// nobelprize.org/nobel_prizes/physics/laureates/1917/barkla-lecture.pdf (December 16, 2008).

''Nobel Prize Winner to Deliver First 'Charles Barkla Lecture,''' University of Liverpool, http://www.liv.ac.uk/ news/press_releases/2006/01/barkla_lecture.html (December 10, 2008).□

Józef Beck

Poland's foreign minister from 1932 to 1939, Colonel Józef Beck remains one of the most controversial diplomatic figures of the years leading up to World War II.

Beck faced the task of navigating Polish policy between the threats posed by two powerful and expansionist neighbors, Germany to the west and the Soviet Union to the east. Like the leaders and diplomats of the western European powers, he attempted, with disastrous results, to placate German leader Adolf Hitler by acquiescing in German initiatives that redrew the map of Eastern Europe in preparation for a German invasion. He alternately plotted against neighboring countries and tried to organize them into a cohesive force. In 1939, as the nature of Germany's intentions of conquest became clear, it was Beck who negotiated Poland's mutual defense agreement with Britain—an agreement that immediately preceded the outbreak of war in September of that year. Beck was a figure constrained by forces beyond his control. In the words of Henry L. Roberts, writing in *The Diplomats,* ''The feeling, so apparent in his memoirs, that there were no feasible alternatives, was characteristic of a general European mood which was creating, and was being created by, the approaching catastrophe.''

Joined Underground Fighters

Born on June 6, 1894, in Warsaw, Beck was groomed as an engineer. He attended the Polytechnic University of Lwow (now Lviv, Ukraine), and the *Exportakademie* in Vienna, Austria (now part of the Vienna University of Economics). World War I, however, changed the course of his life. In 1914 he enlisted in the Polish Legion, one of several quasi-official military organizations devoted to the cause of an independent Poland (the country was partitioned into German, Russian, and Austrian sectors at the time). Beck served in the Polish Legion's First Brigade under the man who would become his political mentor, future Polish leader Józef Pilsudski. The brigade dissolved as German and Austrian forces overran Polish territory, but Beck escaped. He made his way to a cell of the Polish Military Organization, an underground group known by its Polish-language initials, P.O.W. In Russia in the chaotic year of 1918 he impersonated an officer and successfully fooled the Red Army into putting him in charge of a battalion of mostly Polish fighters. Beck succeeded in giving many of them passes to return to Poland and in making his own escape as the Russian secret police closed in.

Poland declared its independence in 1918, but the country faced several years of instability after World War I ended. For much of 1919 and 1920 Poland was in a state of war with the new Communist government of Russia as the country tried to reestablish its historical boundaries. With Marshal Pilsudski serving as Poland's top military commander and first head of state, Beck was increasingly chosen as a top-level agent for the emerging Polish government, from the final year of World War I onward. Beck rose through the ranks of the new Polish army, becoming commander of an artillery battery and then a member of the military's general staff. In 1922 and 1923 Beck served as Poland's military attaché in France, departing under murky circumstances about which historians disagree.

Beck returned to Poland and for two years attended the country's War College, graduating with distinction. By that time Poland had fledgling democratic institutions, and Pilsudski had temporarily retired from both the political and military scenes. In 1926, however, he launched a successful military coup and installed himself as premier. After that, Poland had various titular leaders, but the real power resided with Pilsudski almost until his death in 1935. Beck was an active participant in the 1926 coup, and his star rose steadily as Pilsudski consolidated his power. Beck served as Pilsudski's cabinet chief in the late 1920s, and in 1930, when Pilsudski became prime minister, he named Beck as his deputy prime minister.

Became Foreign Minister

According to Roberts, Pilsudski told top military officials that they should not "count on" Beck resuming his military career; "[Monsieur] Beck will go to Foreign Affairs, to be charged with responsibilities of high importance." Pilsudski followed through on those plans, naming Beck Poland's Foreign Minister in 1932. At first he followed Pilsudski's lead in charting Poland's foreign policy, but Pilsudski, suffering from cancer, was in increasingly poor health in the last months of his life. For most of the time after Hitler took power in Germany in 1933, it was Beck who directed the country's international affairs in the face of outside threats.

From Beck's perspective, there were several main actors on the world stage. In addition to Germany and the newly named Soviet Union, there was the League of Nations (a United Nations predecessor fostering international cooperation that also controlled the disputed Polish-German city of Gdansk, or, as it was called at the time, Danzig), the so-called Little Entente alliance among Czechoslovakia, Romania, and Yugoslavia, and the western European powers of France and Britain, who sought alliances in Eastern Europe to counter a possible resurgence of German militarism. Poland had been truly independent for little more than a decade when Beck assumed his position, and it was not at all clear where the country's allegiances should lie. Poland had historically contended with attempts at Russian domination, and had running territorial disputes with Czechoslovakia to the south.

Beck distrusted the League of Nations, partly because of the Danzig issue, partly because the United States had weakened the group by refusing to join, and generally because, as he wrote in his memoirs (quoted by Roberts), small countries were, in an international group like the League, forced by larger powers "to make unforeseen friends and enemies in connection with questions which had nothing in common with their own interests." Accordingly, Beck tried to keep nearly all other nations at arm's length. Some historians believe that he helped plan for a preemptive war against a still rebuilding Germany in the early 1930s, but this is disputed. He refused to consider Polish participation in the deteriorating Little Entente, and generally tried to keep Poland's relations with both Germany and Russia on an even

keel. He relied on Hitler's personal assurances that Germany had no intention of trying to annex Danzig, which at the time was predominantly ethnically German.

The major test of Beck's policies came in 1938, when the series of events leading up to World War II began to intensify. Germany demanded that Czechoslovakia cede another ethnically German area, the province of Sudetenland in western Czechoslovakia, and at the Munich Conference in September of 1938 the western European powers, hopeful of averting wider conflict, agreed to Hitler's demands. A key player in the sequence of events was Poland, which was soon given the go-ahead to annex the Teschen (now Cieszyn) region, itself disputed between Poland and Czechoslovakia. Poland applied heavy pressure on the Czechs during the negotiations. A British diplomatic note (quoted by Roberts, who suggested that "this was not Colonel Beck's finest hour") complained that Poland's relationship with Germany, though officially neutral, was "degenerating into an undignified imitation of the small fish that seek their meat in the wake of the shark." As tensions deepened, Beck still refused to allow Soviet troops into Poland as a counterweight to growing German power. The degree to which Beck's mistrust of the Soviets and his extended attempt to placate Germany worsened the diplomatic situation in the late 1930s are matters of debate among historians.

Signed Pact with British

It did not take Beck long to realize the extent of his mistake, although it remained an open question as to whether he could ultimately have done anything to influence the course of events. Meeting with Hitler in January of 1939, Beck was disturbed by an obvious new belligerence in the dictator's attitude. Germany disregarded the Munich Agreement and overran much of Czechoslovakia in the spring of 1939. In April of that year, Beck turned to the country he saw as his last reliable ally (France had failed to come to Czechoslovakia's aid despite the mutual aid specified in a treaty agreement). He visited London and worked out a military alliance with Britain. On August 23, 1939, he and the entire Polish nation watched with alarm as Poland's two historical enemies, Germany and Soviet Russia, signed a non-aggression treaty, known as the Molotov-Ribbentrop Pact. Beck and his British counterparts quickly formalized the agreement under which Britain agreed to guarantee Poland's security, signing it on August 25.

Those events marked the immediate prelude to World War II. The agreement deterred Hitler for only several days. On September 1, German forces invaded Poland and launched an all-out war that resulted in the deaths of thousands of Polish civilians. Britain and France declared war on Germany, although they offered the Poles only token support; fighting in western Europe did not begin in earnest until Germany undertook new offensives in 1940. Warsaw came under German bombardment, after which Beck and the rest of the Polish cabinet fled, first to the small town of Zaleszczyki and then to the border town of Kuty. After less than three weeks of fighting, Beck saw that resistance was futile. Essentially his last act as foreign minister was to negotiate passage into Romania for most of the top members of the Polish government and military. On the evening of September 17,

1939, Beck and other government members crossed the Czeremosz River by car into Romania.

Once there, some of them eventually succeeded in reaching France, where a government-in-exile was formed, and some made it to Switzerland. But Romania, although not yet under formal German control in the early days of the war, was in no position to resist German pressure to keep close surveillance on the Polish officials. Beck was placed under house arrest in a hotel near the capital city of Bucharest. He was later moved to the village of Stanesti, where he spent the rest of his life, passing much of the time writing memoirs that have proven to be valuable sources of information on the events that led to World War II. Suffering from tuberculosis, he died in Stanesti on June 6, 1944, the ''D-day'' on which the Allied invasion of the German-controlled European continent began.

Books

Biskupski, Mieczyslaw B., *The History of Poland,* Greenwood, 2000.

Davies, Norman, *God's Playground: A History of Poland, Volume II: 1795 to the Present,* rev. ed., Columbia University Press, 2005.

Roberts, Henry L., ''The Diplomacy of Colonel Beck,'' in *The Diplomats, 1919–1939,* Gordon A. Craig and Felix Gilbert, eds., Princeton University Press, 1953.

Watt, Richard M., *Bitter Glory: Poland and Its Fate, 1918–1939,* Simon and Schuster, 1979.

Online

''Beck, Józef,'' http://www.rulers.org, (October 18, 2008).

''Colonel Józef Beck—the Polish foreign minister who negotiated with Neville Chamberlain,'' BBC Radio, http://www.bbc.co.uk/radio4/history/making_history/makhist10_prog9a.shtml (October 18, 2008). □

Moe Berg

Moe Berg (1902–1972) enjoyed two different careers: one as a baseball catcher and the other as a wartime spy for the United States. During the 1930s, Berg, who spoke at least nine languages, was known as baseball's resident intellectual, and was admired for his wit as much as (or perhaps more than) his play on the field. As a spy, Berg traveled Europe, gathering information on Germany's nuclear program, indulging his eccentricities, and embracing his profession's reputation for daring, refined adventure.

Morris ''Moe'' Berg was born on March 2, 1902, in Manhattan, New York. His parents, Bernard and Rose, were Ukrainian-Jewish immigrants. The family moved in 1906 to Newark, New Jersey, where they lived above Berg's father's drug store. Berg began playing baseball at age seven for a church team. He attended Princeton University, where he majored in modern languages, studying

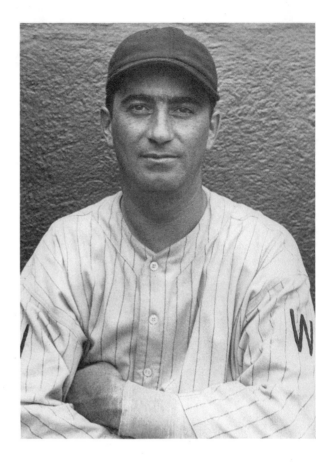

French, Spanish, Italian, German, Latin, Greek, and Sanskrit. He also played shortstop on the school's baseball team, which won 21 games and lost 4 his senior year. On the field, he and a teammate would talk in Latin.

Berg graduated from Princeton with honors in 1923 and was signed the next day by the Brooklyn Robins (later renamed the Dodgers). In his first season, he played in 49 games and had a .186 batting average. He spent the winter studying linguistics and phonetics at the Sorbonne in Paris, paying for the tuition with his $5,000 salary from the baseball season. He returned to the United States in 1924 in time for spring training. While playing baseball in the minor and major leagues, he also studied at Columbia Law School.

Berg joined the Chicago White Sox in 1926. Though a shortstop at first, he switched to catcher in 1927 after three White Sox catchers were injured within a few days. It was a good move for him, and he played the rest of his career behind the plate. Meanwhile, he pursued his legal career in the off-seasons. He passed the New York State Bar in 1929, received his law degree in 1930, and spent the following winter practicing law with a firm in New York City.

In 16 years, Berg played major league baseball for six teams: the Robins, White Sox, Cleveland Indians, Washington Senators, and Boston Red Sox. His best season was 1929, when he appeared in 106 games for Chicago (the most he ever played in one year) and had a batting average of .288. He severely injured his knee in 1930, however, and played only sporadically after that, usually as a second- or third-string catcher.

Teams valued Berg more for his catching than for his hitting. Early in his career, Mike Gonzalez, a scout for the St. Louis Cardinals, coined a phrase to describe him, according to Nick Acocella of ESPN.com, that became a common saying in baseball: "Good field, no hit." When Berg was playing for the Senators, a reporter mentioned to teammate Dave "Sheriff" Harris that he spoke at least seven languages. "Yeah, I know," Harris replied, according to Jonathan Yardley of the *Washington Post*, "and he can't hit in any of them."

But Berg had a strong throwing arm and was gifted at working with pitchers. Teams also enjoyed good publicity while he was on their roster. Sports writers often penned columns about him, counting on him for knowledgeable, thoughtful quotes on slow news days. "Moe was undoubtedly the most scholarly professional athlete I ever knew," sports columnist John Kieran told the *New York Times*. Kieran appeared regularly on the radio quiz show *Information Please,* and Berg joined him on the show three times in 1939, impressing listeners with his encyclopedic knowledge.

Berg loved the wandering life of the ballplayer. "Isn't this wonderful?" he once said, as reported by Dick Teresi of the *New York Times*. "Work three hours a day, travel around the country, live in the best hotels, meet the best people and get paid for it."

In September of 1939, however, after Germany invaded Poland and set off World War II, Berg confided in *New York Times* writer Arthur Daley about how the news affected him. "Europe is in flames, withering in a fire set by Hitler," Berg said. "All over that continent men and women and children are dying. Soon we, too, will be involved. And what am I doing? I'm sitting in the bull pen, telling jokes to the relief pitchers." The comment foreshadowed Berg's wartime service.

After the 1939 season, the Red Sox dropped Berg from their roster and made him the team's bullpen catcher. He ended his playing career with a lifetime batting average of .243 and only six home runs and six triples. During Berg's two years as a coach for the Boston Red Sox, he wrote an article about the sport, a 1941 piece in the *Atlantic Monthly* entitled "Pitchers and Catchers." He left baseball on January 14, 1942, the same day his father died. It was curious timing, since his father had always been opposed to him playing baseball, feeling he was wasting his intellectual talents. Although baseball was his first career, he was about to embark on a new, more exciting career path.

Berg took a job with the federal government's Office of Inter-American Affairs, run by Nelson Rockefeller. He traveled through Central and South America, officially reporting on how conditions could be improved for U.S. troops at military bases. He also collected intelligence about relations between the United States and Latin America and secondhand information about the United States' wartime enemies. In 1943, Berg went to work as an undercover agent for the Office of Strategic Services, the United States spy agency that was a forerunner to the Central Intelligence Agency. He spent much of 1944 and 1945 in Europe, trying to learn some of the secrets of Germany's atomic energy program for the Manhattan Project, the United States' top-secret atomic weapons program.

The OSS was an agency of brilliant eccentrics, so Berg fit right in. He traveled with few restrictions on his time or how much he spent, racking up $21,000 in expenses that he could not account for. He dressed with panache, always wearing a gray fedora. He was hardly the perfect spy, however. On one flight to Europe, his gun fell out of his coat and landed in another passenger's lap. On another flight, someone figured out he was a spy by noticing his wristwatch, issued by the OSS.

His peculiarities did not always impress his superiors. "Confidentially, he is as easy to handle as an opera singer and [it is] difficult for me to find time these days to coddle him along," complained OSS spymaster Allen Dulles in a message he sent from Bern, Switzerland to OSS director William Donovan in Washington (as quoted by Nicholas Dawidoff in *The American Scholar*). "His work is at times brilliant, but also temperamental. When he leaves here this time, I think it preferable that . . . he not return here for the time being."

To learn about Germany's atomic energy program, Berg traveled Europe, convincing physicists to tell him what they had heard about German physicists' work. "Berg provided the first substantial accounts about what the Germans were doing and thinking on a nuclear bomb," Thomas Powers, author of *Heisenberg's War: The Secret History of the German Bomb,* told Matthew Benjamin of *U.S. News & World Report.* After the Allied invasion of Italy, Berg was dropped into territory still held by the Italians, and found an Italian atomic scientist who passed on his knowledge of Germany's nuclear effort.

In December of 1944, Berg attended a lecture in Zurich, Switzerland by Werner Heisenberg, the top physicist in Germany and a leader of its effort to build an atomic weapon. Armed with a revolver, Berg was under orders to shoot Heisenberg if the scientist said anything that suggested Germany was nearly ready to build a nuclear bomb. Berg also carried a cyanide capsule, which he could use to kill himself if captured. However, the lecture, on the subject of matrix theory, did not contain any hints about nuclear weaponry. Heisenberg, it turned out, was not much of a threat. Though a brilliant theoretical physicist, he was a poor engineer and manager. After the war, the United States and its allies determined that the Germans had not come close to creating an atomic bomb.

After the war, in 1946, Berg was awarded the Medal of Freedom for his work. He refused to accept it, however, perhaps because he felt he had spent his time as a spy chasing an exaggerated danger. He accepted a few missions for the CIA, but he did not fit in well at the new agency, which was more professional and bureaucratic than its predecessor. Retired CIA agents have said that Berg performed poorly on missions.

Once he left government service, Berg never again held a steady job. "He was like a ghost," Harvey Yavener, a friend of his, told Dawidoff in *The American Scholar*. "He'd appear and disappear." For 25 years, he wandered the United States, dropping in on friends and asking them to feed him and put him up for a week or six. He could be a difficult houseguest to dislodge. His own brother, Sam, ended one very long stay by sending Berg two eviction notices. Most of his friends took him in gladly, though, because they saw him as a fascinating person, able to talk about philosophy, politics, and baseball history. After his brother evicted him, he lived with his sister in New Jersey between sojourns.

"Berg traveled light, carrying only a toothbrush, a razor, and some old books," Dawidoff wrote in *The American Scholar*. "Clumps of newspapers peeped out of his jacket pockets. On the road, instead of hauling around a change of clothes—which he often couldn't afford—Berg would quietly wash everything before going to bed and hang it over the bathtub." For reasons unknown, Berg almost always wore a single black wash-and-wear suit and a white nylon shirt. He wore the outfit to baseball games, which he went to about twice a week. He attended every All-Star Game and every World Series for years.

No one is sure why Berg avoided work and took on the life of a friendly drifter. "Travel was a salve for Berg, a way for him to sidestep things—and one thing in particular: himself," Dawidoff suggested in *The American Scholar*. "Rather than make commitments of any sort, he traveled or, perhaps more precisely, he fled."

Berg, Dawidoff noted, avoided talking about himself. He would silence questions about his time in the war by putting a finger to his lips and making a hushing noise. So the idea of him on the run from himself and others' questions is very plausible. But Benjamin of *U.S. News & World Report* suggested a simpler possibility. "Just as likely, he feared the dull prospect of settling down after baseball and a good war and so decided to schedule the rest of his life as a series of away games," he wrote.

Berg died on May 29, 1972 in Belleville, New Jersey, of an abdominal aortic aneurysm. He was 70. Even in death, he was a vagabond with an air of mystery. His sister took Berg's ashes to Israel to be buried. The location of his grave is unknown.

Books

Andryszewski, Tricia, *The Amazing Life of Moe Berg: Catcher, Scholar, Spy,* Millbrook Press, 1996.

Periodicals

American Scholar, Summer 1994.
New York Times, June 1, 1972; July 14, 1994; July 24, 1994.
Time, August 15, 1994.
U.S. News & World Report, January 27-February 3, 2003.
Washington Post, July 3, 1994.

Online

"Moe Berg: Catcher and spy," *ESPN.com,* http://espn.go.com/classic/biography/s/Berg_Moe.html (December 14, 2008). □

Carl Bernstein

Carl Bernstein (born 1944), one half of the most famous investigative reporting team in American history, uncovered key parts of the Watergate scandal, the

criminal burglary and espionage conspiracy involving U.S. President Richard Nixon and his aides. After Nixon resigned, Bernstein and partner Bob Woodward became national celebrities, portrayed in film and inspiring countless writers to pursue journalism. After years of public excess and personal difficulties, Bernstein authored three ambitious books, a memoir about his family and biographies of Pope John Paul II and Hillary Clinton.

Son Of Radicals

Bernstein was born on February 14, 1944, in Washington, D.C. His parents, Al and Sylvia Bernstein, were activists for left-wing causes in the 1950s. Al Bernstein, a lawyer, worked as a union organizer and defended government workers accused of political disloyalty, while operating a laundromat to support the family. When Bernstein was a child, his mother often took him along to protests at restaurants in Washington, D.C. that would only serve white people. His parents were also members of the Communist Party USA—a fact that was a family secret until Bernstein published a memoir decades later. His parents were both called to testify before congressional committees investigating suspected Communist organizations. Agents for the Federal Bureau of Investigation even attended Bernstein's bar mitzvah.

The family moved to Silver Spring, Maryland, when Bernstein was 11. At age 16, he began working as a copy boy at one of Washington's daily newspapers, the *Washington Star*. Rebelling against his parents' politics, Bernstein was attracted to journalism's neutrality. "One of the things that attracted me to journalism was its utter absence of absolute belief," he told Walt Harrington of the *Washington Post Magazine*. Bernstein spent two years enrolled at the University of Maryland, but he was not a serious or successful student. He left the *Star* to take a reporting job at a newspaper in New Jersey, and then was hired as a reporter at the *Washington Post* a year later, in 1966, when he was 22 years old.

Helped Break the Watergate Story

At the *Post,* Bernstein gained a reputation as a very talented but unreliable reporter, a peculiar personality, charming but eccentric, with the messiest desk in the newsroom. He wrote long, colorful feature stories, preferring vivid tales of everyday life in Washington to reporting about the Capitol and government agencies. Bernstein became famous, however, as one of the two reporters who revealed key aspects of one of the biggest scandals in 20th century American politics, a criminal conspiracy that included the president of the United States.

In June of 1972, during the presidential election campaign, U.S. President Richard Nixon's re-election committee hired burglars to plant wiretaps inside the Democratic National Committee's headquarters in the Watergate complex in Washington, D.C. The burglars were caught in the act and arrested. *Washington Post* editors assigned the burglary story to Bernstein and fellow reporter Bob Woodward. In the next few months, their stories revealed several ties between the burglars and the Nixon campaign. That October, they reported that the Watergate burglary was part of a larger effort of illegal espionage and sabotage against Nixon's political opponents, directed by senior aides in the Nixon Administration. The *Post's* Watergate coverage won a Pulitzer Prize, journalism's highest honor, in 1973.

Bernstein and Woodward's Watergate reporting became American journalism's greatest modern example of investigative reporting and the use of anonymous sources. "We did not name a single significant source in the first 150 stories that we did in the first year of Watergate," Bernstein told an interviewer for the PBS show *Frontline*. "The only people who were identified by name more often than not were telling lies, because they were spokesmen for the Nixon White House. In terms of real sources of information, they were all confidential, every one."

The two men's talents complemented one another. It was Woodward, not Bernstein, who learned many secrets of the Watergate scandal from his key secret source, FBI associate director Mark Felt. Bernstein's intimate hometown knowledge of Washington, D.C., however, proved extremely valuable on aspects of the story involving local courts and police. His ability to charm people and get them to talk helped him and Woodward gain many sources in the Nixon campaign, who spoke to them at substantial personal risk. Bernstein also obtained the laundered check that showed the Watergate burglars were working for the Nixon campaign.

And it was Bernstein who first correctly suggested that Nixon himself was involved in the conspiracy.

In the fall of 1973, at Bernstein's suggestion, he and Woodward began working on *All the President's Men,* a book that told in dramatic narrative how they had collected their information for the *Post's* Watergate stories. The book, a classic of American political reporting, was released in June of 1974 and made into a 1976 feature film starring Dustin Hoffman as Bernstein. When Nixon resigned in August of 1974 to avoid impeachment on obstruction of justice charges, the two writers took a leave of absence from the newspaper to work on a second Watergate book.

Tempted by Fame

Officially, Bernstein and Woodward collaborated on *The Final Days,* a book about the end of the Nixon Administration. But by then, Bernstein was reveling in the life of a celebrity, spending much of his time in social circles in New York City and dating Nora Ephron, a writer for *New York* magazine. Bernstein did only about 20 of the almost 400 interviews for the book, wrote a small portion of it, and lightly edited about half of it; Woodward and two assistants did the rest. Still, Bernstein was paid $1 million for his part in the project. Furious, Woodward did not speak to Bernstein for more than a year.

Bernstein's Watergate success fed his self-indulgence. "It's something I handled very badly in some ways," he admitted to David Segal of the *Washington Post.* "I hope not as badly as some have said." He spent all of the roughly $3 million he made from Watergate books and movies on travel, home renovations, stylish clothes, and other purchases. He left the *Washington Post,* wrote for publications such as *Rolling Stone,* and spent a year researching a book about his parents, but failed to finish it. He married Ephron in 1976, and they moved to a country house on Long Island, New York.

Unhappy and missing the thrill of daily journalism, Bernstein accepted an offer in 1980 to become Washington bureau chief for ABC News. It proved to be a bad hire, however. He was disorganized, and his personality was unfit for management. In 1981, he became an investigative reporter for the network instead, where he worked until 1984.

Meanwhile, his personal life was a mess. He began to drink heavily, and carried on an extramarital affair with Margaret Jay, wife of the British ambassador to the United States. He and Ephron divorced, and she retaliated by writing a novel, *Heartburn,* published in 1983, with a thinly disguised version of Bernstein as the egotistical, emotionally barren central character.

That year, Bernstein was arrested on a drunken driving charge, then got into an auto accident the next day. Ben Bradlee, the top editor of the *Washington Post,* convinced Bernstein to check into a hospital; Woodward drove him there. Bernstein cut back on his drinking and quit years later. For much of the 1980s, however, he often appeared in tabloid coverage of New York City celebrity nightlife. He was seen accompanying actress Elizabeth Taylor and Bianca Jagger, former wife of rock star Mick Jagger, to Manhattan clubs. A reporter for *Spy,* a snarky pop culture magazine, once tailed Bernstein during an especially ambitious evening of nightclubbing and chronicled his exploits in a feature titled "Nightlife Iron Man Decathlon."

Told His Family's Story

After leaving ABC, Bernstein resumed working on his memoir about his parents and their struggles during the anti-Communist Red Scare of the 1950s. Titled *Loyalties: A Son's Memoir,* it was published in 1989. In it, he revealed that his parents had attended about 12 Communist Party meetings over 5 years, but said the FBI's 2,500-page file about them included no evidence they had attempted to subvert the U.S. government. Instead, they had been activists for racial equality and labor unions. He concluded that his parents had done nothing wrong.

"I feel good," he told Harrington of the *Washington Post Magazine* after the book's release, "because there were two periods of serious pain in my life—and the result of them both is this book. I was trying to do the best work I could, deal with my children, my ex-wife. Was my production as high? Absolutely not. I was trying to hold the roof up."

A year after the memoir was published, Bernstein joined *Time* as a Washington correspondent. In 1996, he co-authored the book *John Paul II and the Hidden History of Our Time* with Marco Politi, a reporter for an Italian newspaper. The book chronicled the ways Pope John Paul II used his influence as head of the Catholic Church to help push for an end to Communism in Eastern Europe, including his native Poland. Bernstein and Politi argued, controversially, that the pope had formed an anti-Communist alliance with U.S. President Ronald Reagan, an idea *Washington Post* reviewer George Weigel dismissed as an exaggeration.

In 2005, Bernstein married Christine Kuehbeck, an executive assistant at the International Longevity Center, a nonprofit organization. The same year, he and Woodward announced that they were selling their papers to the University of Texas for $5 million. Press reports speculated that Woodward agreed to do so because Bernstein needed the money.

More than 30 years after the Watergate scandal, a surprise revelation brought Bernstein and Woodward together to revisit their reporting triumphs. In a 2005 article in *Vanity Fair,* Felt revealed that he had been Woodward's secret Watergate source. Bernstein joined Woodward on several television interviews confirming Felt's account and talking freely, at last, about the man who had become the world's most famous anonymous source. Bernstein wrote the foreword to Woodward's book about Felt, *The Secret Man.* In November of 2008, Bernstein finally met Felt, joining Woodward at lunch with the former FBI official at his California home, only a month before Felt died at age 95. Bernstein told an audience in Walnut Creek, California (according to Carol Pogash of the *New York Times),* that the meeting had been a "closing of the circle."

Successful Biographer

Bernstein spent several years working on a biography of U.S. senator and former first lady Hillary Clinton. He was reportedly paid $750,000 for the rights to the book, which was originally intended for publication in 2003. But it took him much longer to finish it, mostly, he admitted, because he liked to travel and procrastinate. Finally, in 2007, during Clinton's campaign for president, Bernstein's 640-page biography, *A Woman in Charge: The Life of Hillary Rodham Clinton,* was published. He wrote the book in a flurry of activity to meet its well-timed new publishing date. "I worked 18-hour days in the last year," he told Segal of the *Washington Post.* "I was surprised I could work like that at my age."

The book was generally well received. Still, reviewers and profilers often used it as an opportunity to review Bernstein's life. Some offered the backhanded praise that the book was his most serious, sustained effort in a long time. One reviewer even argued convincingly that Bernstein's character flaws gave him useful insight into Clinton's marriage.

"His book suggests that it isn't his executive-scandal bona fides that make him a qualified Hillary biographer; it's his bona fides as a lousy husband," wrote Jennifer Senior, in the *New York Times.* "Like Bill Clinton, Bernstein carried on a very public affair while married to a formidable, high-profile woman, and one of the perverse strengths of his book is his intuitive understanding—a sinner's lament, really—of what happens to a proud woman when she's intimately betrayed and publicly humiliated."

Washington Post writer Segal, meeting Bernstein after the Clinton biography came out, suggested that Bernstein had finally tempered the rewards of fame with self-discipline, while retaining his rakish charm. "Dressed in a dark sport jacket and a white Oxford shirt, Carl Bernstein looks like an aging Italian tycoon," Segal wrote. "He is 63, white-haired and plump. Despite the years, there remains something boyish and irrepressible in his eyes."

Periodicals

New York Times, June 3, 2005; July 15, 2007; November 19, 2008.
Washington Post, May 17, 1984; March 2, 1989; January 12, 1990; September 22, 1996; June 20, 2007.
Washington Post Magazine, March 19, 1989.

Online

"News War: Interviews: Carl Bernstein," *Frontline,* http://www.pbs.org/wgbh/pages/frontline/newswar/interviews/bernstein.html (December 14, 2008).
"Watergate Papers, Woodward and Bernstein Biographical Sketch," *Harry Ransom Center, The University of Texas at Austin,* http://www.hrc.utexas.edu/research/fa/woodstein.bio.html (January 1, 2009).□

Yogi Berra

A top echelon star with the New York Yankees in the 1950s, American professional baseball player Yogi Berra (born 1925) became an icon of American popular culture thanks to his unique way with words.

Berra was a beloved sports personality, famous for his modesty and for his persistence and hard work. But what made him a familiar figure even among Americans with little interest in professional sports were his "Yogi-isms"—unique turns of phrase that were funny and perceptive at the same time, yet slightly off-kilter. Remaining widely repeated even today, and decades after he left the baseball diamond, Berra's comments have been enshrined in quotation dictionaries, and he has published several books in which his recollections and his optimistic view of the world are organized around his aphoristic statements.

Born to Italian Immigrants

Yogi Berra was born Lawrence Peter Berra on May 12, 1925, in St. Louis, Missouri. Future major league catcher and broadcaster Joe Garagiola was raised in the same heavily Italian St. Louis neighborhood, which was called the Hill (or, at the time, Dago Hill), and the two were close friends. Berra's father, Pietro, and mother, Paulina Berra, were immigrants, from the farming community of Malvaglio in northern Italy. Pietro came to the United States, worked in Colorado and California, and then returned to Italy to marry. The couple settled at 5446 Elizabeth Avenue in St. Louis, where Pietro worked in a factory. They had four sons, of whom Lawrence, whom they called Lawdie, was the fourth, and then one daughter. As of 2003, she still lived in the family home.

All the Berra boys played baseball, softball, football (often using rolled-up newspapers or bundles of rags), and other sports. Yogi boxed at a local Italian-American club, winning 14 matches with a purse of five dollars each. All quit school early to help pay the family bills, and Yogi worked as a tack puller in a shoe factory, among other jobs. But his status as the youngest, along with his obvious athletic talent, combined to make it possible for him to pursue his dreams: his siblings ganged up on his father and urged him to let Yogi make a try at playing baseball seriously. The early signs were good when the Stockham Post, a local American Legion-affiliated team Berra played for beginning at age 14, reached the national semifinals in its league championships for two years running. It was during a baseball game that Berra, as a teen, received the nickname Yogi from a friend who had seen a travelogue about India and decided that Berra's contemplative posture while seated on the bench, with arms folded, resembled that of a yogi or Indian yoga specialist.

In 1942 Berra and Garagiola were given a tryout by the St. Louis Cardinals after Garagiola bribed a clubhouse assistant with some of his father's homemade wine. Garagiola signed a contract with a $500 bonus, but Berra was offered either half that, or nothing at all (recollections differ). Cardinals' general mananger Branch Rickey expressed skepticism about Berra's chances of making it into the major leagues, possibly because, at five foot, eight inches tall, Berra was short for a major-leaguer. But Rickey may have been trying to keep Berra available so that he could sign him after his own upcoming move to the Brooklyn Dodgers. "I don't know for sure, but I'd have to say . . . based on all the evidence and how well Yogi did in those tryouts, that Mr. Rickey was trying to stash him for the Dodgers," Garagiola told Phil Pepe, as quoted in *The Wit and Wisdom of Yogi Berra*. The plan, if there was one, did not work, for in 1943 Berra signed with the New York Yankees (receiving a $500 bonus) and was dispatched to the Yankees' Norfolk, Virginia, farm team.

Participated in D-Day Invasion

He advanced to their Kansas City squad in 1944 but, having turned 18, he enlisted in the United States Navy that year and became a gunner. Sent to participate in the D-Day invasion of France, he participated in the fighting for 15 consecutive days. Once back in the United States, Berra played for a Navy squad in Connecticut and became the object of an unsuccessful contract raid by the New York Giants. In 1946 Berra hit .314 for the Yankees' Newark (New Jersey) Bears affiliate and joined the Yankees at the end of the season. Playing seven games in 1946, he notched eight hits in 22 at-bats. The following year, despite a wild swing, he performed solidly, batting .280 with 11 home runs and 54 runs batted in (RBIs). He played in the World Series that year, scoring the first pinch-hit home run in major league World Series history. Throughout his career, Berra was a consistent hitter who very rarely struck out.

It was also in 1947 that Berra first began to attract attention with statements that did not come out exactly as he wanted them to. At a Yogi Berra Night organized in St. Louis, he said (as quoted on the Baseball Library Web site) that he wanted " to thank everyone for making this night necessary." Of an especially popular Italian restaurant in St. Louis where he had once worked as a waiter, he said (as reported by Ted Kreiter in the *Saturday Evening Post*), "Nobody goes there anymore; it's too crowded." Berra married Carmen Short in 1949, and the couple raised three sons. Asked by broadcaster Harry Caray why he had not married an Italian girl from his own neighborhood, he answered, according to Kreiter, "They had their chance."

Some of the turns of phrase that were soon dubbed Yogi-isms were simple malapropisms—mistaken uses of a word in place of another similar word. But most of them (and in this lay their particular charm) were not incorrect as such. ""He doesn't use the wrong words," Joe Garagiola pointed out to Kreiter. He just puts words together in ways nobody else would ever do." When Berra asserted (according to Kreiter) that "90 percent of the game is half mental," he was joining catchphrases that did not fit together quite properly, as if he had learned the English language in phrases rather than single words. Coming to maturity a generation after the great wave of European immigration to America in the 1920s, Berra seemed an endearing figure who spoke in ways that reminded other children of first-generation immigrants of the fractured speech patterns they had heard from their own relatives.

Berra got along well with Casey Stengel, who began a long run as the Yankees' manager in 1949, and his game improved. He became the Yankees' starting catcher that year, holding the position until 1959. Berra hit his stride as a player in the early 1950s, winning the American League's Most Valuable Player award in 1951, 1954, and 1955. In 1952 he set a major league record for catchers, with 30 home runs. With the Yankees ruling baseball during this era, he played in the World Series 14 times and in the All-Star Game 15 times. Beyond his solid accomplishments as a hitter, eclipsed only by the Yankees' fabled stars, Berra made an intangible contribution to the club's performance on the field. He was an acute reader of pitchers' personalities, adjusting his approach to them accordingly, and he was behind the plate for three no-hit games by Yankees pitchers. One of those was among the most famous games in baseball history: the perfect game thrown by Don Larsen in the 1956 World Series. A newspaper photograph distributed around the country showed Berra on the pitcher's mound, leaping into Larsen's arms at the end of the game.

Steered Hapless Mets to Pennant

Berra essentially retired as a player at the end of the 1963 season. His lifetime batting average was .285, with 358 home runs and 1,430 RBIs. The perennially popular Berra was made the Yankees' manager in 1964, steering the team to an American League pennant but losing to the St. Louis Cardinals in a seven-game World Series. Despite this strong performance, Berra was fired. He then rejoined Stengel, who was managing the New York Mets expansion team. Serving as a coach for the Mets from 1965 to 1971, he was elevated to manager in 1972 and again produced a pennant winner in 1973 even though the Mets had finished in the National League cellar the year before. That season produced perhaps the most familiar Yogi-ism of all, "It ain't over till it's over," uttered as the Mets stood nine games out

of first place in the month of September. In the high pressure world of New York sports, Berra's accomplishments were still not enough to carry him through to the end of his three-year contract. After losing his job in 1975, he returned to the Yankees, this time as a coach.

Berra did one more stint as the Yankees' manager, this time under mercurial owner George Steinbrenner in 1984 and the beginning of the 1985 season. His firing that year was finally enough to break the long tie that had linked Berra to New York sports audiences. Not given any reason for his dismissal, he joined the Houston Astros as a coach in the fall of that year, after taking his first summer vacation since entering professional baseball. He stepped down as coach in 1989, remained in Houston as team advisor in 1992, and then retired for good, returning to his longtime home in Montclair, New Jersey, outside New York. The Yankees installed a permanent commemerative Yogi Berra plaque in center field of Yankee Stadium in 1998, soon after which Berra became reconciled with the Yankees' management. Well into his ninth decade he was an informal presence in the Yankees' management structure, traveling with team manager Joe Torre, watching game films, and offering tips.

Although the majority of professional sports stars settle into quiet obscurity after their careers end, Berra remained a popular and marketable figure. A television cartoon figure, Yogi Bear, paid tribute to Berra. With the assistance of co-writers and editors he published a long series of books. Some were autobiographical, while others collected his aphorisms into presentations of homespun wisdom. The series began with *Yogi: The Autobiography of a Professional Baseball Player* in 1961 and continued with such titles as *Behind the Plate* (1962), *Yogi: It Ain't Over* (1989), *The Yogi Book: I Really Didn't Say Everything I Said!* (1998), *When You Come to a Fork in the Road, Take It!: Inspiration and Wisdom from One of Baseball's Greatest Heroes* (2001), *What Time Is It? You Mean Now?: Advice for Life from the Zennest Master of Them All* (2002), *Ten Rings: My Championship Seasons* (2003), and *You Can Observe a Lot By Watching: What I've Learned About Teamwork from the Yankees and Life* (2008). About *Ten Rings*, he told *Publishers Weekly* (according to *Notable Sports Figures*) that "I never realized I always wanted to do a book like this." Berra remained busy as host of the Yogi Berra Celebrity Golf Classic, and as patron of the Yogi Berra Museum and Learning Center at New Jersey's Montclair State University.

Books

Berra, Yogi, with Ed Fitzgerald, *Yogi: The Autobiography of a Professional Baseball Player,* Doubleday, 1961.

Berra, Yogi, with Dave Kaplan, *Ten Rings: My Championship Seasons,* Morrow, 2003.

Berra, Yogi, with Tom Horton, *Yogi: It Ain't Over...,* McGraw-Hill, 1989.

Notable Sports Figures, 4 vols., Gale, 2004.

Pepe, Phil, *The Wit and Wisdom of Yogi Berra,* Hawthorn, 1974.

Periodicals

America, May 2, 1998, p. 2.

Library Journal, July 1, 2008, p. 86.

New York Times, October 1, 1989; March 14 2006.
People, April 8, 1985.
Saturday Evening Post, July-August 2002.

Online

"Yogi Berra," Baseball Library, http://www.baseballlibrary.com/
  ballplayers/player.php?name=Yogi_Berra_1925 (November
  1, 2008). □

Raymond Berry

Raymond Berry (born 1933) had to wear special shoes when he played football, because one leg was shorter than the other, but he went on to a Hall of Fame pro football career. Despite displaying only average speed, Berry, a wide receiver, caught for 9,275 yards and 68 touchdowns over 631 games in 13 seasons with the Baltimore Colts. He played in two National Football League (NFL) championship games, and starred in the Colts' overtime victory over the New York Giants in the memorable 1958 title contest. Berry also coached the 1985 New England Patriots to a Super Bowl appearance.

Berry was born Raymond Emmett Berry on February 27, 1933, in Corpus Christi, Texas. He didn't start for Paris High School until his senior year. His taskmaster father was the head coach. "My dad was a tough man to play for. But it was a small high school and there wasn't anybody else at my position, so that helped," Berry told the *Chicago Sun-Times,* as quoted on the HighBeam Research Web site. Overcoming his foot impediment, Berry went on to Southern Methodist University, where he caught only 33 passes and scored but one touchdown in three varsity seasons. He played mostly defense in college.

The Colts selected Berry as a "future choice" in 1954. "He figured the only reason they brought him to camp was to have him hand out towels," *Football Digest* commented. Berry developed 88 patterns to beat defenders downfield and mastered difficult catches. He also practiced dutifully, staying late on the field to practice his passes, studied footage at the office of NFL Films during the offseason, and used Silly Putty to toughen his hands and wrists.

In 1956, Berry's second year with the team, John Unitas, just released by the Pittsburgh Steelers, arrived as the Colts' quarterback. Unitas overcame a shaky start—an interception return for a touchdown against the Chicago Bears in his first pass—and went on to a Hall of Fame career that included two championships.

Unitas and Berry built a special bond, Berry told *Sporting News*: "Before that 1956 season was over, we combined for a lot of big plays," he recalled. Berry, in fact, finished tenth in the NFL in receptions that year. "It was a real launching for both of us," he added.

Standout in Memorable Title Game

The improving Colts recorded their first winning season in 1957, with a 7-5 record. One year later, they won the NFL's West Division championship at 9-3. After the New York Giants defeated the Cleveland Browns 10-0 in a playoff game to settle the East title, the Colts and Giants were paired for a December 28, 1958, league championship game at New York's chilly Yankee Stadium.

Over the years, players, league officials, and media observers have considered the Colts' 23-17 overtime victory that day to be the game that put pro football on the U.S. sports map. It was the first postseason game to run into overtime, and was one of the earliest telecasts of a pro football title game. Stan Hochman, a columnist for the *Philadelphia Inquirer,* called the game a watershed event "because 45 million watched it and America fell in love with the sudden-death way to avoid a frustrating tie. Fell in love with a crewcut castoff quarterback named Johnny Unitas and a gimpy receiver who ran meticulous patterns named Raymond Berry."

Berry, who had caught a 15-yarder from Unitas in the first half for the Colts' second touchdown, was Unitas's go-to man at crunch time. The Giants, who had trailed 14-3 at the half, took a 17-14 lead in the fourth quarter and had Baltimore pinned on its own 14-yard line with two-and-a-half minutes remaining. Unitas then went to work. He completed four of seven passes in a 63-yard drive to the Giants' 13. His last three passes went to Berry, all completions—of 25, 16, and 22 yards. Steve Myhra kicked a 20-yard field goal with seven seconds remaining to even the score 17-17, and force extra play.

Baltimore won 23-17 on Alan Ameche's one-yard touchdown run in sudden-death overtime—which meant that the first team to score wins the game. Overall that day, Berry caught 12 passes for 178 yards and one touchdown. On the winning drive in overtime, Berry caught a Unitas pass that gave Baltimore a first-and-goal from New York's 8.

The happy Colts were oblivious to the history they and the Giants had made. "At the time, none of us had any real clue about the real significance of the game," Berry wrote in *Football Digest.*

Coached Patriots to Super Bowl

The Colts repeated as champions in 1959, scoring 24 points in the fourth quarter to defeat the Giants in a title-game rematch, 31-16, this time at Memorial Stadium in Baltimore. Berry that year caught a career-high 14 touchdown passes. He was a first team All-Pro from 1958 through 1960, inclusive, and earned second-term honors three other times. He retired in 1967 after appearing in only seven games that season. His 631 receptions were an NFL high at the time. Berry was inducted into the Pro Football Hall of Fame in 1973 and named to the NFL's seventy-fifth anniversary team, announced in 1994. The Colts, who moved to Indianapolis in 1984, retired his jersey number, 82.

Berry served as an assistant coach for the New England Patriots for several years, beginning in the late 1970s. After the Foxborough, Massachusetts, team fired head coach Ron Meyer, New England made Berry its eighth head coach. They split their last eight games of 1984 and missed the playoffs, but Berry had the tools in place for a breakthrough in 1985. During the offseason, he traveled across the United States to consult with players and get to know them better.

In his first full season in New England, Berry guided the Patriots, who began play in 1960 with the old American Football League, to their first Super Bowl appearance. It came the hard way. The Patriots, who finished 11-5 and earned an American Football Conference wild-card playoff berth, won three postseason games on the road. The Patriots used a conservative offense that neutralized the inexperience of quarterback Tony Eason and an opportunistic defense coordinated by assistant Rod Rust—whom Berry's predecessor, Meyer, had fired. In the playoffs, they beat the New York Jets 26-14, the Los Angeles Raiders 27-20, and the Miami Dolphins 31-14, to earn a spot in Super Bowl XXV.

While Berry was self-effacing as his team appeared in the national spotlight, his players praised him as a calming influence. "Raymond comes in and talks to us constantly about playing together as a unit and lifting each other up.... He's made a big difference," defensive back Raymond Clayborn said in the *Sun-Times* article.

The Patriots' joyride derailed, however, in Super Bowl XXV at the Louisiana Superdome in New Orleans. The Chicago Bears routed New England 46-10 in what at the time was the most one-sided Super Bowl ever. New England won the AFC East the following year with another 11-5 record, but dropped a first-round playoff game to the Broncos in Denver.

A downward spiral followed, and the Patriots fired Berry after the 1989 season. Though the team's record that

year may have triggered the firing, Mark Blaudschun of the *Boston Globe,* in an article posted at HighBeam Research, cited disputes between Berry, general manager Patrick Sullivan and owner Victor Kiam over the hiring of assistant coaches and other personnel. "The reasons for Berry's firing were said to involve philosophical differences regarding changes that had to be made in the organization to improve on last year's dismal 5-11 season," Blaudschun wrote. "The situation deteriorated steadily." Rust, who by then had become the Pittsburgh Steelers' defensive coordinator, succeeded Berry.

Berry went into private business in his later years. He briefly returned to pro football in 1991 as quarterback coach for the Detroit Lions. That year they finished 12-4 in the regular season and reached the National Football Conference (NFC) championship game, ending one victory short of a Super Bowl appearance.

Berry also rose through the ranks of the Fellowship of Christian Athletes, joining its board of directors. He spoke frequently at fellowship functions, and to businesses and secular groups. His business interests included endorsements for Pur Air filters. Berry and his wife bought a home in Murfreesboro, Tennessee, and moved there from Colorado in 2003.

The Berry Legacy

Berry overcame a physical handicap and doubts about his football ability to prosper as a player, and continued to succeed as a coach and in business. "I've got two perspectives—one as a player and one as a coach," Berry said, on the PurAir Filters Web site. "As a coach I had to constantly evaluate personnel. So in evaluating myself, I can say objectively that I could catch the ball as well as anyone who ever played the game."

He added, in the same interview: "I'd love to play today. Receivers today, against zone defenses, run to an area. And they seldom get hit before they catch the ball. In my day you had to earn every catch. You could get killed before you even took your first step, and a defender could hit you all the way down field."

Berry is still best known for his star turn in the 1958 title game, which some pundits have called the greatest game ever. "The game captured the collective attention of the nation and as a result, pro football exploded across the country in the following years. By the mid-1960s, professional football became the nation's favorite sport to watch and has remained on top ever since," the Pro Football Hall of Fame wrote on its Web site.

Periodicals

Football Digest, November 2001.
Sporting News, September 23, 2002.

Online

"Colts Shock Giants in Sudden Death, 23-17," *Star Ledger* (Newark, NJ), http://www.blog.nj.com/giantsarchive/2008/01/colts_shock_giants_in_sudden_d.html, (January 25, 2008).
"Greatest Game Ever Played," Pro Football Hall of Fame, http://www.profootballhof.com/hof/release.jsp?release_id=1805

"Patriots Attribute Rebirth to Berry," HighBeam Research, http://www.highbeam.com/doc/1P2-3746066.html, (October 14, 2008).

"Patriots Fire Berry, Look to Hire Rust," HighBeam Research, http://www.highbeam.com/doc/1P2-8162524.html, (October 14, 2008).

"Raymond Berry," Pro Football Hall of Fame, http://www.profootballhof.com/hof/member.jsp?player_id=25, (October 14, 2008).

"Raymond Berry Statistics," Pro Football-Reference.com, http://www.pro-football-reference.com/players/B/BerrRa00.htm, (October 14, 2008).

"Stan Hochman: 50 Years Later, 1958 NFL Title Game Popular on Bookshelves," *Philadelphia Daily News,*http://www. philly.com/dailynews/columnists/20081223_Stan_Hochman__50_years_later__1958_NFL_title_game_popular_on_bookshelves.html, (December 23, 2008).

"When Pro Football Was a Lark," *Baltimore Sun,* http://www.baltimoresun.com/services/newspaper/printedition/sunday/ideas/bal-id.profile21dec21,0,7591882.story, (December 21, 2008).□

Rowland Harry Biffen

Trained in the natural sciences, Sir Rowland Harry Biffen (1894–1949) began his scientific career studying the making of rubber in Mexico. He then pursued studies in botany and agriculture. At Cambridge University in the United Kingdom, Biffen's research led to the development of two resilient hybrid wheat varieties that helped change the nature of food production around the world.

Rowland Harry Biffen was born on May 28, 1874, to Henry John and Mary Biffen in Cheltenham, a small town in southwestern England. At the time of Biffen's birth, his father served as the headmaster of a small public school, Christ Church Higher Grade School, in Cheltenham. Biffen was the eldest child, with one brother and three sisters.

From 1883 through 1893, Biffen attended Cheltenham Grammar School and studied basic subjects such as reading and mathematics. The only science course taught at the grammar school was chemistry. However, under his science instructor's encouragement, Biffen engaged in a great deal of independent study. He also reportedly enjoyed sketching and wandering about the countryside collecting fossils and plants.

A Scientific Education

Biffen led a largely academic life. After finishing his childhood education, he went on to study at Emmanuel College, part of the University of Cambridge. He studied natural sciences at Emmanuel from 1893 to 1896, when he graduated with high marks.

In 1897 Biffen was invited to join a research expedition to South and Central America. He spent several months studying rubber production in Mexico, Brazil, and the West Indies. There he became very interested in the people, climate, and plant life, and developed a wider interest in agricultural botany, or the study of plants used in farming.

Biffen was surprised to learn that little research had been done in the field, and he decided that he could best apply his knowledge to the field of economic botany, or the study of how people use plants to meet their needs. Biffen kept a journal of his studies, which is now held in the Library of the Botany School at Cambridge. He also published two reports on rubber production, the purpose for his journey overseas.

On returning to Cambridge in 1898, Biffen patented a method for handling rubber latex with his colleague E.W. Howard. Latex is a natural substance produced by many plants, including the rubber tree. Biffen was also awarded the Frank Smart Studentship in Botany at Gonville & Caius College, also part of Cambridge University. It was during this time that Biffen began to pursue in earnest his interest in agricultural science. Biffen began conducting independent research, and in particular, he worked on conducting cereal trials in order to identify the best varieties of wheat.

A Lifelong Career

Biffen soon went from attending his university as a student to working at the university as an educator. In 1899 he became a lecturer at Cambridge's newly formed School of Agriculture. That same year, Biffen married Mary Hemus of Worcestershire. He and his wife would remain together at Cambridge for the rest of their lives.

In 1900 Hugo de Vries and Carl Correns unearthed and publicized the genetic research of German scientist Gregor Johann Mendel (1822–1884). Genetics is the study of how living beings pass on certain traits through their genes, or small building blocks of life. Mendel became known as the "Father of Genetics," as noted in an entry on him in *ThinkQuest,* for his studies of genetic traits in pea plants. He concluded that these traits were inherited, or passed on, from one generation of plants to another.

Like other scientists of the time, Biffen was intrigued by Mendel's observations and conclusions. Specifically, Biffen seized on Mendel's laws of inheritance: he wanted to use the principle that traits were inherited, in order to improve plant breeding.

In 1905 Biffen founded the *Journal of Agricultural Science* with four of his colleagues, as a means of sharing information and publicizing their research. In 1908 he became a professor of agricultural botany at Cambridge. He would serve in that position until 1931. During his tenure, Biffen helped set up the National Institute of Agricultural Botany. He also joined the John Innes Centre (JIC), an institution set up to conduct research and training in plant sciences. He served on the JIC Council from 1909 through 1921.

Biffen's obituary, published on the *Royal Society Publishing* Web site, called the scientist a "reluctant teacher" who would much rather be conducting research than lecturing. However, for most of his professional career Biffen would be the only lecturer at Cambridge who specialized in economic botany and plant breeding, and his expertise attracted many students to the university.

Still, the bulk of Biffen's work was in research. He conducted a great deal of research on plant variation and inheritance of traits while at Cambridge. He collected wheat and barley plants from around the world to test, and his studies showed that traits could be inherited in plants. In 1910 Biffen found that a resistance to yellow rust was an inherited trait in wheat. Yellow rust was a plant disease that destroyed wheat and other crops. By breeding wheat varieties that grew well in many soil types and that had a natural resistance to the rust, Biffen hoped to improve the British—and world—food supply. That same year, he released his first wheat variety, Little Joss, to the public.

In 1912 he became the director of the Plant Breeding Institute at Cambridge. This research center was started by the British government to work on improving crop plants. Biffen served as the director of the institute until he retired in 1936. During that time, he developed his most renowned wheat variety—the Yeoman. Like Little Joss, Yeoman was resistant to the yellow rust, and it became the standard for wheat cultivation for decades to come. Yeoman remains one of the most common British strains of wheat produced today.

In 1914 war struck Europe. For the next four years, in addition to his teaching and research duties, Biffen served in the Food Production Department. He fulfilled his service largely by conducting field surveys. Because of his teaching and plant breeding obligations, Biffen was not sent overseas. During World Wars I and II, Biffen's wheat varieties proved especially useful in feeding a struggling population.

Recognition for His Work

Biffen's work with wheat varieties and inheritance soon earned him recognition in his field. In 1914 he was elected as a Fellow of the Royal Society of London for the Improvement of Natural Knowledge. Founded in 1660, the Royal Society had been advancing research, publication, and education in the natural sciences for more than two centuries. Fellows of the Royal Society elected new fellows each year based on their accomplishments and expertise, and fellowship was considered a great honor.

Each year the Royal Society also honored a scientist working in a biological field with the Darwin Medal. Named for Charles Darwin (1809–1882), the English scientist who promoted the idea of evolution, the award was meant to recognize one scientist's excellence in advancing biological knowledge. In 1859, Darwin had published his most renowned work, *On the Origin of Species,* in which he advanced the theory that organic matter such as plants and animals evolve slowly over long periods of time. Darwin's observations and theories were critical to the development of modern biological studies. In 1920 the Royal Society awarded Biffen the Darwin Medal for his work in plant breeding.

Five years later, Biffen was knighted for his contributions to agriculture in the United Kingdom. Thereafter he was referred to as Sir Rowland Harry Biffen. In 1926 the JIC Council unanimously agreed to offer Biffen the directorship of the John Innes Horticultural Institution, although he declined the appointment. In late 1926 and early 1927, Biffen spent several months in Kenya researching wheat rusts.

He studied the soil, vegetation, and climate, looking for ways to expand wheat production in the struggling country.

In 1935 Biffen earned an honorary doctorate in science from Reading University and an honorary membership to the Royal Agricultural Society of England, the Scottish and Highland Agricultural Society, and the Swedish Plant Breeding Station, Svalöf. For years, Biffen served as a botanist with the Royal Agricultural Society, addressing questions and concerns posed by farmers and government official from around the country. Biffen often answered the inquiries of farmers directly and repeatedly gave lectures on agricultural botany to groups of farmers.

Retirement

Although the focus of Biffen's life was his work, he also enjoyed sketching, painting watercolors, walking, and reading. He drew and painted landscapes and other sites that he and his wife found during their jaunts by car through the countryside. Biffen also had a love for photography and printmaking, and he and his wife enjoyed gardening at their home.

Biffen remained at the University of Cambridge until his retirement in 1936. He left his position as a professor and also gave up his directorship of the Plant Breeding Institute. Although he was no longer teaching, Biffen and his wife stayed on in Cambridge. He continued working as an editor for the *Journal of Agricultural Science* until his death.

Biffen and his wife had no children. Mary Biffen died in January of 1948, and her husband died soon after, on July 12, 1949, in Cambridge.

A year after his death, the University Press of Cambridge published Biffen's book *The Auricula: The Story of a Florist's Flower.* In this book, Biffen examined the genetics of the auricula, reflecting his interest in the wider field of botany beyond agriculture.

Biffen's research in plant breeding not only helped advance the modern field of genetics but also improved and increased the world food supply. The varieties of wheat strains he developed based on his discoveries have fed people around the world. Many later scientists have used Yeoman wheat strains as the parents for developing new wheat varieties.

In the obituary on the *Royal Society Publishing* Web site, Biffen was remembered as commenting that plant breeding was "a game of chance played between man and plants," and added that "the chances seemed in favour of the plants." Biffen's work, conducted over the course of his lifetime, helped even those odds.

Books

Cambridge Dictionary of Scientists, Second Edition, edited by David Millar et al, Cambridge University Press, 2002.

Random House Webster's Dictionary of Scientists, Random House Inc., 1997.

Online

"Biffen, Rowland Harry (1874–1949)," *Hutchinson Encyclopedia,* http://www.encyclopedia.farlex.com/Biffen,+Rowland+Harry (October 16, 2008).

"Darwin archive winner 1948–1890," *The Royal Society,* http://www.royalsociety.org/page.asp?id=1761 (January 2, 2009).

"Gifts of Radar and Wheat," *Brits at Their Best,* http://www.britsattheirbest.com/001105.php (January 2, 2009).

"Miss Hemus—Sweet pea breeder in Worcestershire," *National Sweet Pea Society Annual 2008,* http://www.upton.uk.net/events/bloom/2008/sweetpeas.pdf (January 2, 2009).

"The People of Genetics," *ThinkQuest,* http://www.library.thinkquest.org/20465/mendl.html (February 4, 2009).

"Rowland Harry Biffen, 1874-1949," *Royal Society Publishing,* http://www.journals.royalsociety.org/content/3257p6126k321022/ (January 4, 2009).

"Science Timeline, 20th Century, 1900–1930," *Brits at Their Best,* http://www.britsattheirbest.com/ingenious/ii_20th_century_1900-1930.htm (January 2, 2009).

"A short history of the John Innes Centre (1910-2005)," John Innes Centre, http://www.jic.ac.uk/corporate/about/history.htm (January 2, 2009).

"Sir Rowland Harry Biffen," *Answers.com,* http://www.answers.com/topic/rowland-biffen (October 16, 2008).

"Yeomen Wheat," *British Society and Culture,* http://www.bsc2007.blogspot.com/2007/09/yeomen-wheat.html (January 2, 2009). □

Alice Stone Blackwell

An important figure in early American feminism, the American writer and editor Alice Stone Blackwell (1857–1950) was also a pioneer of what would later be called human rights activism.

Blackwell succeeded her mother, Lucy Stone, as editor of Boston's *Woman's Journal,* a key publication in the fight for woman suffrage (voting rights for women) that culminated in the ratification of the nineteenth amendment to the United States Constitution in 1920. As a writer herself, she penned a biography of her mother, a pioneer of the suffrage movement, and she was an indefatigable producer of pamphlets and letters to newspaper editors. Spurred by a close relationship with an immigrant Armenian poet, Blackwell became interested in the plight of the Armenian people, the victims of repeated genocidal attacks from some of the peoples of the Ottoman Empire. She assisted in the translation of the works of Armenian writers into English and later published collections of writing from other politically sensitive parts of the world.

Raised in Suffragist Family

Alice Stone Blackwell was born on September 14, 1857, in Orange, New Jersey. Both parents inspired her to work for women's rights, although she resisted the idea at first. In her biography of her mother, Alice wrote, "In my childhood, I heard so much about woman suffrage that I was bored by it and thought I hated it, until one day I came across a magazine article on the other side and found myself bristling up like a hen in defense of her chickens." Lucy Stone, educated at the abolitionist stronghold of Oberlin College, kept her own name when she married the reform-minded Ohio merchant and speculator Henry Blackwell; women who refused to relinquish their maiden names were for several generations afterward known as Lucy Stoners. A full-time lecturer, she inspired the suffragist Susan B. Anthony among other activists. Several other members of the family took strides forward for women in the United States: Alice's aunt Elizabeth Blackwell was the first female graduate of an American medical school, and another aunt, Antoinette Blackwell, was the nation's first formally ordained female minister.

The family moved around frequently as Alice's parents lectured and met with small groups. An only child, Alice developed into a solitary, serious girl with a strong gift for written expression. Her mother said that she hoped Alice would be able to understand jokes in the next world. The family settled in Boston in 1869, moving into an imposing hilltop house in what was then the suburb of Dorchester. Lucy Stone established the American Woman Suffrage Association and the *Woman's Journal* with offices in Boston, and Alice became an expert latchkey kid, often taking a streetcar into the city to visit her parents' office or to take advantage of Boston's rich cultural institutions such as the Boston Public Library. From 1872 to 1874 she kept a detailed diary, later published as *Growing Up in Boston's Gilded Age;* it provided a wealth of information on the lives of upper middle class families of the time. Alice's growing feminism was also evident in her diaries; in one entry, quoted by Peter Balakian in *The Burning Tigris*, she criticized a book by novelist James Fenimore Cooper because he "disapproved of Womans Rights and called Queen Bess a monster because she was strong minded."

As a teen, Blackwell was something of a spiritual searcher who was drawn to the Unitarian church but also observed with keen interest the intense Catholic and Episcopalian religious lives of the family's household servants. She attended the private Harris Grammar School and then Chauncy Hall School, where she was one of just a few female students. There she was required to participate in an (all-girl) military drill team and learned to handle firearms. She enjoyed Chauncy Hall's demanding academic atmosphere and found herself well equipped to handle the rigors of Boston University, where she was one of two women in the class of 1881. She became class president and was inducted into the Phi Beta Kappa honor society upon her graduation, after which she went to work in the editorial offices of the *Woman's Journal*.

Blackwell started off as assistant editor and proofreader, but it was not long before she was in the thick of the magazine's operations, gathering reviews and writing detailed pro-suffrage editorials. One male anti-suffragist editor grudgingly named her the only woman in Massachusetts who could write a paragraph. Beginning in 1887, she was the author of what would now be called a syndicated column, the "Woman's Column," that was distributed to newspapers around the country. Readership for the *Woman's Journal* grew, and by the time it took on Blackwell's personal stamp it had become arguably the most influential feminist publication in the country.

Worked to Heal Suffragist Split

In the late 1880s Blackwell worked to foster a rapprochement between the country's two leading suffragist organizations, Lucy Stone's American Woman Suffrage Association and the rival National Woman Suffrage Association led by Susan B. Anthony and Elizabeth Cady Stanton. The two groups had split in the 1860s over the question of whether freed slaves should be given the vote if women did not also receive the same right, with Stone's group having argued in the affirmative. Blackwell's efforts were rewarded when the two groups merged in 1890 to form the National American Woman Suffrage Association, with Blackwell as recording secretary. After the death of Lucy Stone in 1893, Blackwell became editor-in-chief of the *Woman's Journal*.

That year her life took a new direction as well. At the summer home of her colleague Isabel Barrows on Lake Memphremagog in the Canadian province of Quebec, just over the border from Vermont, she met Ohannes Chatschumian, an Armenian theology student who had recently arrived in the United States. Chatschumian learned to speak English as he described the glories of Armenian literature to Blackwell, and the two fell in love amid the scenery of the Green Mountains. Blackwell and Barrows persuaded Chatschumian to apply to the Harvard University Divinity School, and Barrows suggested that Blackwell and Chatschumian work together on translating Armenian writings into English.

They began work on a long poem called "The Tears of Araxes" by Raphael Patkanian.

Blackwell also became interested in the problems faced by the Armenian people, who in the mid-1890s were suffering from discrimination and frequent violence at the hands of the Ottoman Empire, under whose rule many of them lived. Blackwell and Chatschumian formed a group called Friends of Armenia, which, according to Balakian, constituted America's first international human rights movement. The group attracted high-profile supporters including Julia Ward Howe, the composer of the text of the "Battle Hymn of the Republic." Howe became the society's president, and Blackwell devoted much of her energy to gathering news of the situation in Armenia and attending and organizing meetings of concerned Bostonians. Many pages of the *Woman's Journal* were given over to articles about violence in Armenia. "Blackwell's coverage of the Armenian massacres strikes one today as astonishingly modern," noted Balakian, "and her focus on gender and violence in the Armenian case seems also prophetic."

The budding romance between Blackwell and Chatschumian was, sadly, put to an end in 1896 when Chatschumian, suffering from tuberculosis, died while studying in Germany. Blackwell and Barrows had set sail for Germany with the intent of taking Chatschumian to Arizona to recover in the healthful climate of the desert Southwest, but en route they received a telegram informing them of the theologian's death. Blackwell completed her Armenian translations with the help of another emigré, Bedros Keljik, and they were published as *Armenian Poems* later in 1896. The first edition sold out within 15 days, and the book went into a second printing. The book was reprinted again in 1917, as the first large-scale act of genocide in the twentieth century was carried out by Turks against Armenians.

Assisted Armenian Immigrants

Blackwell never married or had children. Chatschumian's death did not diminish Blackwell's commitment to the Armenian cause. Her Dorchester home became an informal employment clearinghouse for recent Armenian immigrants, and she became an honored figure in the Armenian community. In 1904 she was feted for her literary work by a largely Armenian gathering of 200, and presented with a portrait of herself by Armenian American artist Carnig Eksergian. Blackwell continued her literary support of the Armenian people with a series of books presenting poems in translation from Russian (*Songs of Russia,* 1906), Yiddish (*Songs of Grief and Gladness,* 1907), Spanish (*Some Spanish-American Poets,* 1929), French, and Hungarian. She also edited *The Little Grandmother of the Russian Revolution* (1917), a collection of writings about Catherine Breshkovsky, known as Babushka, a longtime Russian reformer.

Blackwell's reform instincts also led her into other areas. After the goal of suffrage was achieved in 1920 she became a founding member of the Massachusetts League of Women Voters. She was also active in the pro-Prohibition Woman's Christian Temperance Union (WCTU), the National Association for the Advancement of Colored People (NAACP), the Anti-Vivisection League, the American Peace Society, the Armenian General Benevolent Union, and the Friends of Russian Freedom, as well as several other organizations. Issuing pamphlets on topics ranging from the importance of the vote for teachers to suffrage in New Zealand, she remained as editor of the *Woman's Journal* until 1918 and served for two decades as recording secretary of the National American Woman Suffrage Association.

Much of Blackwell's time in the 1920s was spent working on her mother's biography. *Lucy Stone* was published in 1930 and reissued in 1971. But she continued to throw herself into progressive causes. Somewhat disillusioned by the fact that woman suffrage did not result in widespread social changes, and in fact did not even forestall a swing to the right in American politics in the 1920s, she herself became more radical as she grew older. She supported Progressive third-party candidate Robert M. LaFollette in the 1924 presidential election and flirted with socialist ideas, although she never joined the U.S. Socialist Party. Blackwell was an outspoken defender of the anarchist immigrants Nicola Sacco and Bartolomeo Vanzetti, who many believed were wrongly accused in a robbery-murder case because of their political beliefs. One Boston newspaper refused to print her increasingly controversial letters to the editor.

In the 1930s Blackwell worked on a League of Women Voters campaign to prevent Massachusetts municipalities from firing married women from government jobs in order to create vacancies for men. During the decade she gradually went blind and was swindled out of most of her savings by a dishonest adviser. Supported by friends, she moved into an apartment in Cambridge, Massachusetts, where she lived until March 15, 1950, and occasionally agreed to interviews with young reporters who were guaranteed to come away with a strongly stated opinion on one matter or another. Before Blackwell died, she asked that a copy of her biography of Lucy Stone be placed in the libraries of all the women's colleges in the United States.

Books

Balakian, Peter, *The Burning Tigris: The Armenian Genocide and America's Response,* HarperCollins, 2003.

Blackwell, Alice Stone, *Growing up in Boston's Gilded Age: The Journal of Alice Stone Blackwell, 1872–1874,* ed. Marlene Deahl Merrill, Yale, 1990.

Blackwell, Alice Stone, *Pioneer of Woman's Rights,* Little, Brown, 1930.

Notable American Women: A Biographical Dictionary, Harvard, 1971.

Online

"Alice Stone Blackwell: Biography," Armenian House, http://www.armenianhouse.org/blackwell/biography-en.html (November 5, 2008).

"Alice Stone Blackwell, 1857–1950," Dorchester Atheneum, http://www.dorchesteratheneum.org/page.php?id=38 (November 5, 2008).□

Paul Bomani

Paul Bomani (1925–2005) was Tanzania's ambassador to the United States and Mexico from 1972 through 1983. He held several Tanzanian ministry positions and, at the time of his death, was chancellor of the University of Dar es Salaam. Bomani helped to improve the quality of life for Tanzanians through cooperative efforts, and was instrumental in the development of the Tanganyika African National Union (TANU), a group that lobbied for Tanzania's independence in the early 1960s.

Bomani was born on January 1, 1925, in Musoma, Tanzania. He received his primary education at the Nassa S.D.A. School in Mwanza, and attended Ikizu S.D.A. and Tabora secondary schools, and Ikizu Teacher Training School. Bomani earned his undergraduate degree from Loughborough College in Leicester, England, in 1954, and his master's degree in international relations in 1976 from Johns Hopkins University in Baltimore, Maryland.

He had roots in the Sukuma tribe of northwestern Tanganyika. His involvement with the cooperative movement began in 1950, when he was president of the Lake Province Cotton Growers Association. One year later, Bomani became president of the Sukuma Union, founded to enhance tribal causes. One of its accomplishments was the democratizing of the Sukuma Chiefs, who had ruled through appointed councils when the British ruled the country. The Sukuma Union evolved into the Tanganyika African Association (TAA). Bomani became the TAA chairman for Lake Province and chairman of the region for the Tanganyika African National Union (TANU), a pro-independence organization founded in 1954. Also in 1954, the British governor-general appointed Bomani to the Legislative Council. "My appointment to the [Legislative Council] was a tribute to the work I had previously done to promote the social and economic well being of the people of the Lake Victoria zone," Bomani said on his website.

Bomani was named to the Ramage Constitutional Reform Committee in 1958. Three years after that he joined the Ian Macleod Constitutional Committee, which helped lay the foundation for Tanganyika's independence. Great Britain had previously taken over Tanganyika, situated on the east coast of Africa, from Germany after World War I. Bomani took his first cabinet position in 1960, when he became minister of natural resources and cooperative development. Other ministry positions he held through 1970 included finance for Tanganyika; and for Tanzania, finance and economic affairs; development planning; and commerce, industry, and mining.

During the formative years leading up to independence, Bomani bonded with Julius Kambarage Nyerere, a political philosopher and statesman who became Tanzania's first president. Nyerere had formed the Tanganyika African National Union (TANU) in 1954. "The early years of TANU were difficult ones," Gale Group wrote in its *Encyclopedia of World Biography, Vol. 11.* "Tanganyika's lack of educated

Africans free of government restriction and its poor communications system hindered organizational work. But limited progress was made, spear-headed by a group comprising Nyerere, Paul Bomani, Oscar Kambona, and Rashidi Mfaume Kawawa."

Alexander MacDonald, in *Tanzania: Young Nation in a Hurry,* called Bomani "the able Nyerere lieutenant." He added, "His brilliance in business and economic matters made him the obvious heir to the finance portfolio after the resignation of Sir Ernest Vasey, last of the colonial administrators in the Tanganyika government." MacDonald said Bomani and others around Nyerere had a "sudden and difficult inheritance" in the new Tanganyikan government.

Bomani also chaired a group that served as Tanganyika's new development committee. It based its actions on a report by the World Bank Mission, a nine-member economic team published in November of 1960 that said the country had run itself on a per annum basis and that "any planning had been both confusing and lacking in continuity," MacDonald wrote. The report, entitled *The Economic Development of Tanganyika,* made nearly 300 recommendations that called mostly for improving Tanganyika's peasant agriculture. "Unless the government effectively marshaled the nation's limited resources, the Tanganyika would be in serious trouble," MacDonald noted that the report warned. The group met for weeks, often running late at night. Finally, in May of 1961, the *Developmental Plan for Tanganyika, 1961-64,* came out. Three years later, Tanganyika and Zanzibar, an island in the Indian Ocean, merged to become Tanzania.

In 1968, Bomani was a member of the Philip Commission for the Treaty and the Establishment of the East African Community. The commission, established the previous December and chaired by Danish economics professor K. Philip, consisted of three members from each of the three East African countries. After meeting for eighteen months and conducting interviews, it established a common market, such services as harbors and railways, a joint airline, and social services. In addition, Bomani was a governor of the IRBD (World Bank) from 1962 to 1970, attending general meetings of the International Monetary Fund (IMF) and the IRBD.

Ambassador to United States, Mexico

From 1972 through 1983, Bomani was Tanzania's ambassador to the United States and Mexico. "During this period the freedom of African countries still under colonial rule as well as the fight against white minority rule in South Africa were high on the agenda of Tanzania's forting policy," Bomani said on his website. "My mission was to sensitize U.S. government and congressional leaders to a better understanding of the struggles of the people of Zimbabwe, Mazambique, Angola, and Namibia for political independence and the crusade against apartheid in South Africa." Bomani said he and others had to minimize the perception that decolonization would open the door to communist regimes in Africa.

Speaking in 1974 and quoted in *Jet* magazine, Bomani told the Pan African Congress in Chicago, Illinois, the purpose of such events is "to bring together African people and persons of African descent to discuss the future of

the black world . . . to build cooperation and understanding among black people." The conference at the time attracted roughly 400 to 600 persons. They included scientists, educators, and historians.

In an *Ebony* magazine article that appeared in 1978, Bomani envisioned closer relations between American black persons and Africans. "Young blacks should begin preparing now by learning African history, and by learning about the problems and aspirations of our people," he said as quoted in *Ebony.* "If they are interested in helping us advance technologically, we will need mining engineers, electricians, and English teachers among other professionals."

Bomani returned to Tanzania in 1983. He spent one year each as minister for natural resources and mining, and for lands, natural resources, tourism, and housing. He became agriculture and marketing minister in 1986, and labor and social welfare minister in 1988. After serving one year as minister for local government, marketing, cooperative, and community development, in 1990 Bomani became minister of the president's office, which involved implementing and coordinating cabinet policy. "Apart from serving in the government, Bomani also served as member of parliament for his area and held top ceremonial positions for a number of local and international organizations," the *IPP Media* reported. Bomani served on his country's parliament from 1960 to 1985.

Bomani also spoke stridently about poverty, hunger, and disease on his country and continent. He co-authored *Conquest of World Hunger and Poverty,* published in 1990 with Douglas Ensminger, a sociologist who had overseen Ford Foundation programs in emerging countries. Speaking about the need to educate people about malaria, Bomani said on his website: "Most children who die under five years, especially in remote rural areas with poor access to health care. . . . More than any other diseases, malaria hits the poor. . . . The estimated costs of malaria, in terms of strains on the health system and economic activity, are enormous. In affected countries, as many as 3 in 10 beds are occupied by victims of malaria."

Praised for Brewery Stewardship

Throughout the 1970s and 1980s, Bomani held a variety of ministry positions and belonged to several councils. He left the government in 1990 after serving as the minister in the president's office for the implementation and coordination of cabinet policy. In 1992, Bomani became the chairman of Tanzania Breweries and Tanzania Distilleries. Tanzania Breweries was a joint venture between the government and a private shareholders group led by South African Breweries; Tanzania Distilleries was its subsidiary. The parent company listed on the Dar es Salaam Stock Exchange. When the offering was closed in September of 1998, the public had acquired 20.3 million shares, or 8.6 percent of the company.

In July of 2000, the company opened an $8 million brewery capable of producing 13 million cases of beer annually. Andrew Parker, South African Breweries managing director for Asia and Africa, told the *Africa News Service* the Tanzanian company was "a very sick baby" before it bought a majority stake, but praised the Tanzanians for their role in restoring its vibrancy. ''We are well on our way to achieving our vision of being one of the most successful and best managed commercial enterprises in East Africa by the year 2002,'' Bomani said, also as quoted by the *Africa News Service.* The company became East African Breweries through a 2002 share swap and in 2005 became the first company in the region to achieve a U.S. currency value of $1 billion.

Respected as University Chancellor

Bomani in 1993 took over as chancellor of the University of Dar es Salaam, the country's oldest and largest university. Bomani had been instrumental in its founding. ''In Tanzania there was not a single university or university college, in existence during the whole period of colonial rule,'' Bomani said on his website. He lobbied for better educational funding at a conference in 1963, saying his country was poorly funded. What started as a University of London affiliate in 1961 became the University of Dar es Salaam, in Tanzania's capital and largest city, in 1970. By the end of that decade, enrollment had exceeded 1,000. By 2001, the school and its two constituent colleges— Makerere University College in Uganda and Nairobi University College in Kenya—had a combined enrollment of about 7,500 students.

''Ambassador Paul Bomani was not only the chancellor of UDSM but also the guardian,'' the university wrote in its *Mlimani Newsletter.* ''He considered this institution as part of his life as well as his family. He managed it on the expectation of making UDSM as the best university ever in Africa and he was so close to its executives.''

Bomani spoke of university life on his website: ''It has constantly been emphasized that the universities, especially in Africa in general and in Tanzania in particular, could not for long operate as ivory towers isolated from the societal concerns of the countries in which they were located.... Universities had to persist in their legitimate pursuit of academic excellency [sic] while at the same time incorporating in their curricula the equally legitimate preoccupation of [citizens] of countries in which universities are located.''

Bomani's Legacy

Bomani died on April 1, 2005, at age eighty, in Dar es Salaam after spending six days at TMJ Hospital. The university's *Mlimani Newsletter* called it ''the most sorrowful day,'' adding: ''We were full of hope that he would recover and join us in our endeavors as soon as his health was better. This was not the case. Our hopes were not fulfilled.''

He was buried at Capri Point in Mwanza, transported by ferry from Dar es Salaam after a public viewing at Nyamagana Stadium. Mourners, including former Prime Minister Joseph Sinde, paid last respects at Nkrumah Hall on the university's main campus. Special prayer sessions were held on campus.

Pius Ng'wandu, Tanzania's minister for higher education, science, and technology, cited the former diplomat's years of public service and praised Bomani as a tireless worker who defended faculty and students. Ng'wandu, according to

IPP Media, said: ''The late Paul Bomani was a freedom fighter who led Tanzanians to liberate themselves from abject poverty through cooperative actions.''

Books

''Julius Kamberage Nyerere,'' *Encyclopedia of World Biography, Vol. 11,* Gale Group, 1997.

MacDonald, Alexander, *Tanzania: Young Nation in a Hurry,* Hawthorn Books, 1966.

Periodicals

Ebony, August, 1978.

Jet, November 16, 1978.

Mlimani Newsletter, April-September 2005.

Online

''Hundreds Pay Last Respects to Paul Bomani,'' Kafoi.com, http://www.kafoi.com/news/article.php?id=738, April 4, 2005.

''Late Ambassador Paul Bomani's Web Site,'' http://www.paulbomani.com/galleryleft.htm (December 4, 2008).

''Paul Bomani Dies in Dar es Salaam,'' *IPP Media,* http://www.kafoi.com/news/article.php?id=720, April 2, 2005.

Other

Africa News Service, July 27, 2000.□

Bramwell Booth

British religious leader Bramwell Booth (1856–1929) was the organizational genius behind the Salvation Army, succeeding his father, William Booth, the Army's founder, as its second leader, or General.

I t was Bramwell Booth who conceived the Salvation Army's quasi-military structure. He built the group into an international force, organized the training infrastructure that held it together, and put in place the system of overnight shelters for which the Army is most recognized today. Those shelters came about after his father saw homeless Londoners sleeping on bridges. ''Go and do something!'' William Booth told his son, as he so often did (all quotations here, unless otherwise noted, come from *Bramwell Booth,* Catherine Bramwell Booth's biography of her father). ''Doing something'' about his father's ideas often involved fundraising, an activity for which Bramwell Booth had a rare talent.

Grew Up in Traveling Evangelist Household

William Bramwell Booth was born on March 8, 1856, in Halifax, Yorkshire, England. At that time, the Salvation Army did not yet exist. His father was a touring evangelist and revival preacher, trying to draw adherents to his own unorthodox brand of the Methodist faith (called the Methodist New Connexion) and to recruit lost souls from the ranks of substance abusers and society's downtrodden,

according to an account quoted by Catherine Bramwell Booth, "caught him, head and legs, and bashed him against a tree to bang Salvation out of him." After that, Bramwell was home-schooled.

For a time, Bramwell considered a career in the ministry. But as he grew into adulthood he found himself more and more closely involved with his father's growing mission. From his early adolescence onward he conducted large prayer meetings for children, and among Salvation Army members he would be affectionately referred to as the Young People's General. Beginning at age 15 he addressed crowds of adults, and he often visited the households of new converts to the church, who were often desperately poor, sick, or dying. In 1878 the East London Mission held what it called a four-day War Council concluding with an all-night prayer session. An assistant, preparing a fundraising appeal, called the Mission a "volunteer army," but Bramwell objected, "Volunteer! Here, I'm not a volunteer! I'm a regular or nothing!" William Booth took a pen, crossed out the word "volunteer," and wrote "Salvation."

Became Salvation Army Chief of Staff

Thus was born the Salvation Army, with William Booth as General and Bramwell, as of 1880, as Chief of Staff. One of his first acts was to create the Salvation Army Training Home as a center where the group's corps of "officers" could absorb Salvation Army ideas, techniques, and above all what Bramwell called "the training of the heart." In 1882 Bramwell, who at the time sported a long black beard, married Florence Soper, a young woman who had heard his mother preaching in London's West End and came to the house to visit. An admission fee of one shilling was charged to those attending the wedding. Under Bramwell's direction the Salvation Army evolved into an organization in which women played a significant role largely equal to that of men; preaching by women to mixed-gender groups, still prohibited in some faiths today, was almost unheard-of in Victorian England, but it was practiced in the Salvation Army from the beginning. Bramwell "deplored the tendency to give men precedence in leading positions and to relegate women to posts where their services were more economical than men's." He was also instrumental in promoting new measures to combat child prostitution in England, including an increase in the age of consent from 13 to 16.

Florence herself founded a Salvation Army subdivision called Women's Social Work, later called the Home League. She also kept the home fires burning for the couple's two sons and five daughters, for Bramwell spent almost every night at the Salvation Army's offices and was often on the road. The Booth children were, like Bramwell himself, educated at home, and all became active in the Salvation Army. The organization, under William Booth's inspiration but mostly Bramwell's administration, evolved into an international organization, with missions in most European countries and ambitions toward worldwide penetration. In 1913 he visited the United States, a country whose history fascinated him, and a New York newspaper reported that no Britisher had ever received a similar reception. Later in life Bramwell toured Asia and ministered to a

who were largely ignored by mainstream churches. The rigors of life on the road were mitigated by Bramwell's large group of siblings; he was the oldest of eight children, seven of whom became preachers.

Still, the seriousness of the family's work shaped his childhood. His mother, Catherine Mumford Booth, in the words of daughter Catherine, "lifted him, as it were, up to the windows of life before he was tall enough to reach them, and from her arms he glimpsed the boundless horizons of unsolved problems and mysterious sorrows." In 1865, shortly after the family arrived in London, William Booth took his oldest son on a tour of the bars of London's seedy Whitechapel district, pointing out "men in all stages of intoxication, women with babies at their breasts, children squeezed in between the adults; noise, stench, degradation." "Willie," he said, "these are our people, these are the people I want you to live for and bring to Christ."

In the teeming city, William Booth founded the East London Mission, unconnected with the Methodist church or any other existing faith. It was the direct ancestor of the Salvation Army, which, Bramwell later wrote, was neither Catholic nor Protestant. The young Bramwell showed the boundless energy for which he was later famous, and he had a lifelong enthusiasm for music. He would later directly supervise the compilation of several editions of the Salvation Army's hymn book. Bramwell attended the City of London School for a time, but on one occasion was beaten by schoolmates, who called him Holy Willie, so severely that he started to bleed from the mouth; they had,

group of 300 lepers on what is now the Indonesian island of Sumatra. He stirred controversy during World War I when he refused to sever the home Salvation Army's ties with the Army's large German branch. In his 1915 Christmas message to the Salvation Army faithful he wrote, "Every land is my fatherland, for all lands are my Father's."

By that time Bramwell Booth had become the Salvation Army's second General, named to the post in a sealed letter written in 1890 by his father and opened after his father's death in 1912. After his elevation, he continued to develop the Salvation Army social projects he had established. Those included the homeless shelters the organization has continued to provide. The shelter system was established by Bramwell beginning in the 1880s after William Booth saw homeless people sleeping around a London bridge one night. "Well, yes," Bramwell told his father, "a lot of poor fellows I suppose do that." Told by his father that he ought to feel ashamed that he had done nothing to help them, Bramwell began to enumerate the antipoverty initiatives the Army had already undertaken, but was cut off by a wave of his father's hand. "Go and do something!," William said. "We *must* do something." "What can we do?" Bramwell asked. "Get them a shelter!" "That will cost money," was the long-suffering Bramwell's objection. "Well, that is your affair. Something must be done," his father answered.

Composed Hymns

In the midst of a consistently hectic lifestyle, Bramwell Booth managed to find time for reflection. A prolific letter writer, he also kept detailed journals that touched on spiritual matters as well as daily Salvation Army affairs. A lover of animals who was active in the anti-vivisection cause, he found spiritual inspiration in natural phenomena and was characterized by his daughter as a mystic by temperament. "Walked to Broad—cold wind, but absolutely perfect spring day," he wrote in one journal entry. Blue skies— gentle seas—bold and friendly birds—a sense of unity in the mighty forces surrounding us. These things speak to me in certain moments—call to me and appear to have a language I can interpret to myself—if I cannot speak them to others." Booth continued to enjoy music, and he composed several hymns himself.

As it evolved into an institution, the Salvation Army took on traits largely unlike those of any other religious body. To separate the contributions of father and son, who worked together over much of William Booth's long lifetime, is difficult; in Catherine Bramwell Booth's words, "these two men established a militant Church." She listed some of the main tenets of Salvation Army procedures: the absence of sacraments and of ordination for ministers, the laity's right to preach, equal rights for women members, the requirement that all members renounce gambling and the use of alcohol, tobacco, and drugs, the readiness of members to testify for Christ in public, the wearing of uniforms, an emphasis on social and business enterprises as an integral part of the faith, and an orientation toward internationalism with control maintained at a single center.

Despite his constant engagement with the daily details of Salvation Army life, Booth often addressed the group's huge revival meetings and was thought by many to be his father's equal as a speaker. Photographs taken of Booth addressing hearers in London's Trafalgar Square in 1923, using a microphone for the first time, show a crowd filling the entire space. His international travel schedule only increased in intensity as the Salvation Army grew, taking him as far afield as India and Japan. At home, Booth wrote a book about holiness and two books offering recollections of his career. He contributed frequently to the Salvation Army periodical *War Cry*, and was well known among the British public, sometimes penning essays that appeared in major newspapers. He often spent Christmas day among the homeless the Army served.

The last chapter of Booth's life was not an especially happy one. Supported by Booth's sister Eva, top Salvation Army officers sought to formulate a new constitution that would, among other things, strip Booth of his right to appoint his successor as General in favor of the group's High Council. Booth resisted, but the situation was soon complicated by the deterioration of the 70-year-old General's health. Suffering from cardiac problems, he was asked to resign but insisted that he would shortly recover. In February of 1929 he was stripped of his title by the High Council, and future leaders would be appointed by that group. Before his death on June 16, 1929, he was inducted into the Order of the Companions of Honor by King George V.

Books

Booth, Catherine Bramwell, *Bramwell Booth,* Sears, 1934.

Online

"Bramwell Booth," Salvation Army International Heritage Centre, http://www1.salvationarmy.org/heritage.nsf/36c107e27b0ba7a 98025692e0032abaa/b150026d36fded0b80256952003654b3! OpenDocument (November 10, 2008).

"Founders of the Salvation Army," Bala Keselamatan: Salvation Army Indonesia Territory, http://www.salvationarmy.or.id/ balkes/history.html (November 10, 2008).

"General Bramwell Booth," Salvation Army Collectibles, http:// www.sacollectables.com/postcards_bios/bramwell.htm (November 10, 2008).☐

Catherine Booth

The British evangelist Catherine Mumford Booth (1829–1890) was the co-founder of the Salvation Army with her husband, William Booth. She is sometimes called the Mother of the Salvation Army.

Catherine Booth was not simply a supporter of her husband's spiritual and social enterprises. She shaped some of the large assistance projects for which the group became known, and she campaigned on behalf of women factory employees who suffered in horrendous working conditions. Perhaps Booth's most important contribution came over William Booth's initial objections and in spite of deeply ingrained societal norms: she began to preach,

suffered from poor health as a girl; at 14 she had what Victorian England called a spinal attack (perhaps a sudden onset of spinal curvature), leaving her bedridden for months. She put the time to use by reading theology, and came for herself to a vigorous rejection of the Calvinist doctrine of predestination.

One day when Catherine was 16, she was singing a Methodist hymn whose words she knew well. This time, however (as quoted by Hattersley), she "felt the assurance of Salvation," and the words—"My God, I am thine. What a comfort Divine. What a blessing to know that my Jesus is mine."—"came home to my innermost soul with a force and illumination they had never before possessed, and I no longer hoped that I was saved. I was certain of it." Her faith was soon tested when she was diagnosed with tuberculosis, an ordeal that actually caused her considerable gloom but no outward fear of death.

In the spring of 1852, Catherine Mumford met William Booth, at the time making a living as a pawnbroker's clerk, at a tea party given by a Methodist bootmaker who know them both. Upon hearing that his mother had occasionally given him a glass of port wine when he was not feeling well, she launched into an attack on the consumption of any alcohol whatsoever. Shortly after that, on Good Friday, April 10, 1852, they met again. It was a momentous day in William Booth's life, for it was on that date that he decided to devote himself to preaching full time. William and Catherine fell in love, and by May 15 they were engaged.

Argued for Rights of Women in Church

The marriage did not immediately take place, however, for the young couple had an obstacle to overcome. While Catherine did not reject the subordinate role of the traditional Victorian wife, she believed that in religious matters men and women were equal. She based this belief on the Bible, specifically on a famous passage in St. Paul's Epistle to the Galatians holding that "there is neither male nor female for ye are all one in Christ Jesus." Thus, she concluded, she should be allowed to preach—a virtually unheard-of idea in European Christian churches at the time, and one that for much of her life subjected Catherine to charges of scandal. But she did not back down. She wrote letters of protest to other ministers who made remarks about the spiritual inferiority of women, and she made clear to her fiancé that she believed in gender equality in church and expected to take up preaching herself.

William Booth resisted these ideas strenuously. However, through a series of letters in which Catherine assented to the general idea of women's deficiency in intellectual ability (again, a commonplace idea in Victorian Britain), the couple reached a compromise. "I would not stop a woman preaching on any account," William wrote in a latter quoted by Hattersley. "I would not encourage one to begin. You shall preach if you feel moved thereto, feel equal to the task. I would not stop you if you had the power to do so. Altho I should not like it." Catherine and William Booth were married on June 16, 1855. Similar processes of compromise kept their marriage alive and productive for the rest of Catherine's life, through often difficult circumstances

conducting many of the Army's great open-air revival meetings. It was thanks to Catherine Booth's influence that the Salvation Army adopted the then-radical idea of gender equality.

Mother Welcomed Deaths of Brothers

Booth was born Catherine Mumford on January 17, 1829, in the small town of Ashbourne in central England's Derbyshire region. Although her father, John Mumford was an occasional preacher, it was her mother, Sarah, who inculcated in her a special degree of religious zeal. Catherine was not allowed to read secular books or to play with other children. When Catherine's three older brothers died, according to the Booths' biographer Roy Hattersley (writing in *Blood and Fire*), Sarah Booth said that "it was a positive joy to her to think that they were in heaven," and that she "would not have them back for anything." A Salvation Army legend holds that Booth had read the entire Bible eight times by the time she was 12; even if not literally true the story points to her unusual piety.

The Booth family moved to the larger town of Boston and then to London's Brixton neighborhood, but Catherine was kept largely sequestered from the wider world. She developed strong opinions as a teen, giving up eating sugar as a protest against the colonial exploitation of black Africans. and once she ran out in the street and chased down a charcoal maker whom she had seen hitting a donkey with a hammer, and snatched the hammer out of his hand. Booth

and frequent periods of separation. William spoke at church meetings on their honeymoon.

Catherine's own preaching career began with temperance meetings and addresses to children and to alcoholics, with whom the Booths soon began to work in their London mission. In 1860 she felt moved to rise and speak at Gateshead Bethesda Chapel. To an inner voice that said she would look like a fool, she answered that she had never yet been willing to be a fool for Christ, but that she would be one now. William's mind was completely changed by the power of Catherine's preaching, and as the Salvation Army evolved from a renegade branch of Methodism to a new church with its own formally stated principles, equality for female members became one of them. Catherine designed the Salvation Army's flag and contributed to various aspects of its early organization.

Organized Soup Kitchens

The Salvation Army itself grew out of the Christian Mission the Booths established in London's East End. Catherine Booth was an equal partner with her husband in both the mission's charitable and evangelistic arms, preaching open-air sermons (despite attacks by "skeleton armies" sponsored by breweries and legal harassment from the Church of England) in London's vast new working-class neighborhoods and operating some of the world's first large-scale soup kitchens. At Christmas, the mission would distribute dinners, many cooked by Catherine herself, among London's poor, who at any time could buy, for sixpence, a hot three-course dinner with soup at the Food-for-the-Million Shops she developed. Hattersley's biography credits Catherine Booth with much of the emphasis on social services that continues to characterize the Salvation Army today.

Among the Salvation Army campaigns with which Catherine Booth was especially closely identified was what would now be called anti-sweatshop activism; the Victorian term was "sweated labor." She worked to increase the wages of women factory employees, who were paid a fraction of the wages received by men in comparable jobs, and tried to improve their working conditions. Booth took aim at the match manufacturer Bryant & May, which produced matches tipped with yellow phosphorous. That substance released toxic fumes with terrible effects: the faces of workers (due to bone necrosis) turned green and then black, and many of them died. The company refused to switch to safer red phosphorous, used successfully in other countries, on grounds of cost.

Booth's campaign to force Bryant & May to switch to red phosphorous was ultimately successful; the company gave in after William Booth organized a model factory that used red phosphorous and paid higher wages than Bryant & May did. But Catherine did not live to see that triumph. She died in a small house she and William rented in Clacton-on-Sea, England, on October 4, 1890, after suffering from breast cancer for several years. An important part of her legacy was the group of eight children she and William raised: all of them became involved in Salvation Army activities, and in 1934 Catherine's daughter Evangeline Booth became the fourth General of the Salvation Army, and the first of two women to have held that position as of this writing.

Books

Hattersley, Roy, *Blood and Fire: William and Catherine Booth and Their Salvation Army,* Doubleday, 1999.

Murdoch, Norman H., *Origins of the Salvation Army,* University of Tennessee Press, 1994.

Periodicals

Houston Chronicle, September 24, 2000.

Online

"Catherine Booth," Spartacus Schoolnet, http://www.spartacus.schoolnet.co.uk/Wbooth.htm (January 19, 2009).

"Catherine Booth—Ashbourne's Golden Lady," Bygone Derbyshire, http://bygonederbyshire.co.uk/articles/Booth,_Catherine_-_Ashbourne%27s_%27Golden_Lady%27 (January 19, 2009).□

Giovanni Alfonso Borelli

Known as the "father of biomechanics," Giovanni Alfonso Borelli (1608–1679) was the first scientist to explain human and animal bodily movements as a result of muscular contractions. Borelli contributed innovative ideas to several fields of study during his long career, grounding his research in observations of the natural world and in the testing of hypotheses. His ideas helped lay the foundation for modern mathematics, physics, and anatomy.

Giovanni Alfonso Borelli was born Giovanni Francesco Antonio Alonso on January 28, 1608. At the time, his father, Miguel Alonso, was a Spanish infantryman stationed at Castel Nuevo outside Naples in southern Italy. His mother, Laura Porello, was a local woman. Borelli would later adopt a variation of her name in place of his father's name.

Borelli was the eldest of six children, and the family lived on the outskirts of Naples, though little is known of their early lives and education. He showed an early talent for mathematics and other studies, and whatever education he did receive led him into his first profession as a physician. Sources are uncertain as to whether Borelli attended the University of Naples and received formal medical training or studied informally under Tommaso Campanella, an Italian theologian, scientist, and philosopher.

Although his early education is unclear, Borelli made enough progress to advance quickly. Between 1628 and 1630, he traveled to Rome to study under the respected mathematician Benedetto Castelli. Impressed by his student's abilities, Castelli recommended Borelli to his former teacher Galileo Galilei and to others. Castelli's support helped win

Borelli his first professorship, at the University of Messina. Like Castelli, Borelli began by teaching mathematics.

Shifting Gears

In 1641 the Senate of Messina made Borelli a member and gave him an important mission. Borelli was charged with visiting various centers of learning throughout Italy to recruit scientists, mathematicians, and other scholars, and for the next two years, Borelli traveled throughout the country. He had hoped to meet Galileo, a scientist whom he much admired, but the physicist had died the year before he set out.

Instead, Borelli met Marco Aurelio Severino, a well-known surgeon and scholar of anatomy. He also visited Vincenzo Viviano, a mathematician and former student of Galileo's, and Bonaventura Cavalieri, another respected mathematician. Borelli had already made a reputation for himself in the mathematical fields, but his tour through Italy increased his professional exposure and connections.

At the conclusion of his journey, he returned to Messina to teach mathematics, but he also began branching more into other sciences. In 1656, Ferdinand, the Duke of Tuscany, asked Borelli to accept a professorship at the University of Pisa. He accepted, and remained there for the next decade.

At Pisa, Borelli established his own laboratory and was able to pursue his passions for both astronomy and anatomy when he was not teaching. Astronomy is the study of the stars, planets, and other bodies in space. Anatomy is the study of animal bodies and how they work. Like Galileo, he

went about his research through his observations of the natural world, forming hypotheses and then testing them.

Through his anatomical studies, Borelli befriended the Italian physician Marcello Malpighi. Malpighi had begun studying components of the human body, such as blood and tissue, through a microscope. Together, Borelli and Malpighi helped start the Accademia del Cimento, a research academy dedicated to investigating the sciences, and in particular, anatomy.

Borelli's Work

Through the academy, Borelli undertook the effort that would become a lifelong source of study—that of biomechanics, or the study of how animals move. In 1658 he was asked to investigate a disease epidemic in Sicily. His research led him to conclude that the fever was not caused by changes in the weather or movements among the stars. Borelli determined that this epidemic and other diseases had their origins in the body—in imbalances in the body's chemistry. That year, he published his findings in *Della Cagioni delle Febbri Maligne (On the Causes of Malignant Fevers)*.

While Borelli was investigating and reporting on the epidemic in Sicily, he also continued with his studies in mathematics, and in 1658 he published a revision of Euclid's *Elements,* titled *Euclides Restitutus.* Euclid was an ancient Greek mathematician, and his book had been one of the most important texts in mathematics for centuries. Within the next few years, Borelli also revised sections of Apollonio's *Conics,* another treatise on mathematics. Like Euclid, Apollonio was an ancient Greek mathematician and astronomer. Apollonio examined not only cones but also parabolas and ellipses, two shapes that would prove crucial to Borelli's own astronomical observations.

Borelli worked on many scientific undertakings simultaneously. Even as he taught mathematics and developed his theories about biomechanics, he also looked to the stars and explored astronomy. The *Dictionary of Scientific Biography* noted that Borelli "worked on many problems, contributed significantly to all the topics he touched, and in fact played an important part in establishing and extending the new experimental-mathematical philosophy."

From late 1664 into February of 1665, Borelli tracked the path of a comet. He took careful measurements until it moved past the moon and beyond view, finally concluding that the comet was moving in an elliptical or similarly curved orbit around the sun. These findings went against the accepted scientific theory of the day, which supposed that Earth was the center of the universe.

It was a dangerous time to oppose the approved theories of the Catholic Church, so Borelli published his conclusions under the name Pier Maria Mutoli. In his treatise *Del Movimento della Cometa Apparasa il mese di Dicembre,* Borelli suggested that not only comets but also planets orbited the sun. He claimed that two opposing forces, one attracting bodies to the sun and one pulling them away from it, kept the planets and other bodies in balance.

Later that year, Borelli wrote Duke Leopold de Medici, the head of a powerful Italian family, about his observations.

He explained that comets did not move in straight lines but in curved lines. Soon after, he traveled to Florence to demonstrate his ideas to Medici, even designing a mechanical device to show his theories in action.

Borelli returned to Messina in 1667 or 1668. He published more works, including one on the moons of Jupiter and the forces that kept them in motion. He also became more involved in political matters.

Politics and Exile

In the late 1660s, a political uprising was growing against the Spanish in Italy. Borelli joined the anti-Spanish forces despite his own familial ties through his father. Historians have speculated that Borelli changed his surname from his father's name to a variation of his mother's to hide his ties to the Spanish.

By 1674 the authorities had learned of Borelli's possible involvement in political matters. He was persecuted and eventually exiled from Messina to Rome. There he sought the protection of the former Queen of Sweden, Christina. She had been forced to give up her throne two decades earlier when she became a Catholic, and had been living in Rome ever since. A woman full of intellectual curiosity, Christina had gathered many scholars, philosophers, and scientists around her. Borelli fit into her circle neatly, and she offered him what protection and support she could.

Borelli served as Christina's physician and continued work on his scientific studies. Still, he had few resources, and lived in relative poverty. In 1667 he went to live in the cloister of the Clerks Regular of the Pious Schools, a religious order. He spent his last two years of life teaching mathematics to the women at the convent and working on the two volumes that would earn him long-lasting recognition.

Legacy

Borelli died in Rome on December 31, 1679, of unknown causes. For decades, he had added to the scientific knowledge of Europe, and yet his greatest work remained unpublished.

Within a year after his death, Borelli's patron Christina and other supporters helped finance the publication of *De Motu Animalium* (On the Movement of Animals). The first volume was printed in 1680 and the second in 1681. This tract became the founding text of modern biomechanics.

In *De Motu*, Borelli examined the movement of animals and tried to explain their locomotion in mechanical terms. This school of thought became known as iatrophysics, applying principles of physics to the functions of animal bodies. Borelli proposed that all bodily movements resulted from muscular contractions. Like rubber bands, muscles contracted, or moved, to make a body's bones move. These contractions resulted from chemical triggers.

Borelli also recognized that some bodily movements were geared toward external activities, like walking, while others were geared toward internal tasks, like breathing and blood flow. He was the first to recognize that the heart was itself a muscle that worked like a pump. Like other muscles, the heart responded to chemicals that caused it to contract, and the contractions of the heart caused it to act like a pump, pushing blood throughout the body.

Throughout his life, Borelli looked both inward and outward for answers. He studied human and animal bodies and explored the stars and planets as far as his laboratories would let him. He used mathematical models to record observations, suggest theories, and explain the world's mysteries. Although he began as a physician, Borelli was really a scholar and a researcher. Like other Renaissance scientists, he used the scientific method to propose and test his theories.

Many of Borelli's ideas were considered dangerous because they defied the explanations of the Catholic Church, then the major power in Europe. Although Borelli believed that the Catholic God had designed the human body and its functions, he did not believe that such a god controlled the body's daily movements. He suggested that a divine spirit guided the body and its functions, but that the animal body acted under its own control and ability.

A physician, mathematician, physicist, astronomer, biologist, educator, and writer, Borelli forever changed the human understanding of the natural world and the species' place in it. He was best known for *De Motu*, but he wrote many tracts in other scientific fields.

The *Dictionary of Scientific Biography* noted that "historians have undervalued [Borelli's] place in the development of the sciences in the seventeenth century, and they have paid little attention to his career or his personality.... But he was highly respected by his contemporaries."

Borelli's thorough research, observations, and conclusions helped lay the foundation for much of modern science. In particular, he can be credited with proposing new ways to think about the universe and with helping advance important medical discoveries through his studies of anatomy. Today, many of his early methods and conclusions remain critical to an understanding of the body, the world, and the universe.

Books

Biographical Dictionary of Scientists, Second Edition, edited by Roy Porter, Oxford University Press, 1994.

Gribbin, John, *The Scientists: A History of Science Told Through the Lives of Its Greatest Inventors,* Random House, 2002.

Random House Webster's Dictionary of Scientists, Random House, 1997.

Science and Its Times: Understanding the Social Significance of Scientific Discovery, Vol. 3: 1450–1699, edited by Josh Lauer and Neil Schlager, Gale Group, 2001 (November 12, 2008).

Yeomans, Donald K., *Comets: A Chronological History of Observation, Science, Myth, and Folklore,* John Wiley & Sons, 1991.

Online

"Borelli, Giovanni Alfonso," Bioingegneria.uniba.it, http://www.bioingegneria.uniba.it/borelli.html (October 16, 2008).

"Borelli, Giovanni Alfonso," *Columbia Encyclopedia,* http://www.bartleby.com/65/bo/Borelli.html (October 16, 2008).

"Borelli, Giovanni Alfonso," *Dictionary of Scientific Biography,* http://www.chlt.org/sandbox/lhl/dsb/page.306.php (October 16, 2008).

"Comet," *Columbia Encyclopedia,* http://www.bartleby.com/65/co/comet.html (October 16, 2008).

"Giovanni Alfonso Borelli," *Encyclopedia Britannica,* http://www.search.eb.com/eb/article-9080729 (October 16, 2008).

"Giovanni Alfonso Borelli," *Institute and Museum of the History of Science,* http://www.brunelleschi.imss.fi.it/museum/esim. asp?c=300084 (October 16, 2008).

"Giovanni Alfonso Borelli," *NNDB,* http://www.nndb.com/people/047/000100744/ (October 16, 2008).

"Giovanni Borelli," *Molecular Expressions,* http://www.micro.magnet.fsu.edu/optics/timeline/people/borelli.html (October 16, 2008). □

Mikhail Borodin

Russian diplomat Mikhail Borodin (1884–1951) spent several years in China in the 1920s in an attempt to convert its internal strife into a full-fledged Communist revolution. Borodin's goal was to bring followers of Marxism into China's Kuomintang (KMT), or Nationalist Party, and then foment an organizational coup that would turn the KMT's provisional government into a Communist-led ruling party. His efforts on behalf of the Soviet Union—the world's first Communist state and a dire threat to the rest of the Western, capitalism-driven international economy—might have ultimately succeeded had it not been for the untimely death of the KMT chief, Sun Yat-sen.

"Borodin" was actually an alias used by Mikhail Gruzenberg, who was born on July 9, 1884, in what was known as Yanowitski, Belorussia, at the time. Belorussia—the present-day independent nation of Belarus—was at the time part of the vast Russian empire, and the western area where Borodin was born was in the Vitebsk region, which belonged to the delineated Pale of Settlement. According to tsarist decree, Russia's Jews were restricted to this area, which corresponds to parts of present-day Poland, Lithuania, and Ukraine.

Joined the Bolshevik Cause

Borodin attended a Jewish school and later moved to Riga, the main city in Latvia, where he took night-school courses. In 1901, the year he turned 17, he joined the Bund, a political party more formally known as the General Jewish Labour Union of Lithuania, Poland and Russia. It was a secular party with social-democratic overtones, and some of its members went on to create the Russian Social-Democratic Labor Party (RSDLP), which Borodin is known to have joined in Riga in 1903. The RSDLP split that same year, however, into two important factions. The Bolsheviks were the more radical members, who believed that imperial Russia was ready for a revolution led by the proletariat, or working classes, while the Mensheviks, by contrast, were more moderate in their political goals and did not view the vast majority of Russia's proletariat and rural peasantry as ready to participate in a socialist revolution.

Not surprisingly, the RSDLP was an illegal party in Tsarist Russia and Borodin, like other adherents, was forced into exile. It is known that Borodin was in Switzerland in 1904, where he met the leader of the Bolshevik faction, Vladimir I. Lenin. In 1905, there was an attempt to overthrow the tsarist regime of Nicholas II, the head of the House of Romanov, but it failed. The Tsar did concede, however, to a limited form of parliamentary rule.

Borodin was part of a team of dedicated Bolsheviks who worked to shore up support from abroad. Workers' rights movements had succeeded in several other industrialized countries, with gains made in the United States, Britain, and Germany, and the brutal regime and lack of political rights in tsarist Russia aroused the sympathies of many, not just those of the extreme left. So-called agitators like Borodin, however, were closely watched by authorities, and Borodin's fundraising efforts in England and Scotland for the Bolshevik cause resulted in his arrest and deportation in 1907. Offered a chance to emigrate to the United States, he agreed, and made his way from New York City to the Midwest, where he took courses in philosophy and law at Valparaiso University in Indiana. He met his future wife there, and they eventually moved to Chicago. There, he was active in the American Socialist Party and spent several years as a teacher of English as a second language. He taught classes for immigrants at Hull House, the well-known community center, and later ran his own school.

Arrested in Glasgow

With the 1917 October Revolution in Russia, Borodin was able to return home. This was actually the second revolution that year—earlier, in February, a provisional government had seized power and Nicholas II was ousted, but internal battles between factions over the next several months resulted in the Bolsheviks gaining complete control. Borodin's excellent English skills led to a post as a translator for Lenin, and he also held a post with the new government's foreign ministry—technically, a difficult situation, because few foreign nations formally recognized the new Soviet state.

In March of 1919, Moscow played host to an historic "Communist International," or Comintern conference that was attended by representatives of most of the world's communist parties. Its delegates resolved to work towards the end of the bourgeois state everywhere. Borodin became a Comintern agent, and was dispatched first to Spain and then to Mexico, where he became a key figure in the formation of the Mexican Communist Party. He also traveled in the United States and Britain, but was arrested in Glasgow under the alias "George Brown" in August of 1922 and deported once again, this time to St. Petersburg. A *Times* of London report from 1926 cited his name as "Jacob" Borodin and noted that British authorities regarded him "as a most dangerous person. He was one of the 'underground' agents of the Communist International, and was sent to foster sedition."

With his name and aliases on file with several Western governments, Borodin traveled east on behalf of the Comintern. Many believed that China would be the site of the world's next major revolution, especially following the 1911 overthrow of the Ch'ing dynasty, an event which had been led by Kuomintang founder Sun Yat-sen; in the interim years, the nation had descended into what *New York Times* writer Albert J. Weeks termed "traditional interregnum disarray. Provincial warlords and rival capitals, north and south, grappled for power. From his southern base at Canton, Sun sought to reorganize his political party, the Kuomintang... into a militant revolutionary force backed by a disciplined, well-trained army—to subdue the warlords and spread his form of social-democratic republicanism throughout the mainland."

Headed Comintern Efforts in China

Sun had requested military and financial aid from the United States, Britain, and even Japan for help in quelling the instability, but none were interested. Lenin and the Bolshevik Party, however, seized the opportunity, and Borodin arrived in Canton, China, in September of 1923. This was the seat of the provisional Kuomintang government, and his first task was to remove what the Bolsheviks considered the bourgeois elements of China's uprising, because the KMT was not a genuinely Marxist party. He became an important advisor to Sun and authored the KMT's constitution of 1924. He also contributed significantly to the foreign policy aims of the KMT. "In that capacity he revolutionized Chinese diplomacy," noted another *Times* of London report. "Under his influence the National Government not only assumed from the outset a position of equality with all foreign Powers—arrogating to itself the right, which it certainly did not possess, to speak for China as a whole—but also adopted an aggressive policy which, as military successes followed, led to the gradual abandonment in law of some foreign concessions in China, and in fact of all but the most elementary of foreign rights."

In January of 1924, Sun announced that the KMT and the Communist Party of China (CCP) would join forces; this proved to be a short-lived alliance, but had been the result of Borodin's efforts. In China, Borodin was responsible for the non-military aspect of the Comintern's work; the martial details were handled by General Vasily Blyukher, who had risen to fame as a commander of Bolshevik units during Russia's civil war a few years earlier. In Canton, Borodin led propaganda efforts and posted a young Chinese Communist named Mao Tse-tung as head of the KMT press and propaganda department. Borodin was also said to have been instrumental in installing another Communist, Zhou En-lai, at a high rank in the KMT forces. A final element in the Soviet effort in China was the funding of the Whampoa Military Academy, also known as the Nationalist Party of China Army Officer Academy, near the port city of Guangzhou. The military school would train most of the next generation of Chinese military leaders.

Borodin's work in China fell apart with the death of Sun in March of 1925 from liver cancer. With that, the alliance between the CCP and the KMT disintegrated, and the KMT was forced to relocate to the city of Wuhan. There, Borodin worked to shore up support for a CCP coup, but this was a failure and the KMT began to purge the Communists within its ranks. The Soviet Embassy in Beijing was raided and a cache of top-secret documents discovered. In a series of reports published in the *Times* of London in the spring of 1927, concrete evidence was uncovered of the exact extent of Soviet aid to China, which had only been suspected by Western governments up until that point. Records in the embassy listed financial transfers from Moscow that totaled some £2 million, about £59 million in 2008 numbers or roughly $85 million in U.S. dollars. Another article noted that Borodin's wife had been arrested while aboard a steamer of the Russian Volunteer Fleet which was suspected of "carrying on an illicit trade," according to the *Times*—most likely munitions shipments that were being dropped overboard—and she was jailed at Nanking along with three others, all of whom may have been executed. The *Times* report noted that she had been allowed to telegraph her husband and was being treated cordially.

Died in Labor Camp

Borodin was forced to flee China in a camel caravan. He returned to a Moscow that was much different from the one he left in 1923. Lenin died in 1924, and a coalition of top leaders succeeded him as head of the Soviet Communist Party. One of them was Josef Stalin, who consolidated power by 1927 and began implementing ambitious five-year economic plans. He also eradicated opposition from within by expanding the ranks of the secret police and instilling a climate of fear in which any dissenting opinion was viewed as anti-Soviet and thus counterrevolutionary. Transgressors could be sent to "re-education" camps—actually harsh penal-labor colonies—in the frigid regions of Siberia.

Borodin reportedly underwent a period of interrogation that lasted two years in which he recounted all of his exploits abroad in great detail. Nevertheless, he was blamed for the failure in China and the victory of KMT forces in pushing back the Chinese Communists. Eventually he became deputy commissar for labor, and after 1932 worked as deputy director of TASS, the official Soviet state news agency. He also served as editor of the *Moscow News*, an English language newspaper. He was in his early sixties when the Soviet Union achieved victory—and its first measure of international respect—in an alliance with Great Britain and the United States against Nazi Germany during World War II, but the events of the global strife had repercussions in China, too: in 1949, the KMT were forced into retreat on the island of Taiwan, and CCP forces led by Mao Tse-tung proclaimed the People's Republic of China on the mainland.

In 1949, the year that Borodin turned 65, he was declared an enemy of the state and sentenced to the gulag. Some historians attribute this to the failure, two decades earlier, of Soviet efforts to gain a foothold in China, but the Stalinist era was also known for a number of anti-Semitic purges, when anyone of a Jewish background was viewed as politically suspect. Upon learning that Borodin was destined for one of the infamous Siberian gulags, Mao reportedly sent word to Stalin asking for clemency for Borodin, which was ignored. Borodin died in a labor camp near Yakutsk, Siberia, on May 29, 1951, but his death was not reported until 1953. His name vanished from the historical record for a time, but he was rehabilitated posthumously in the 1960s. The first English-language work to chronicle his life was a 1981 biography, *Borodin: Stalin's Man in China,* by Dan N. Jacobs and published by Harvard University Press in 1981.

Books

''Borodin (Gruzenberg), Michael Markovitsch,'' *Encyclopaedia Judaica,* edited by Michael Berenbaum and Fred Skolnik, Volume 4, Macmillan Reference USA, 2007, p. 91.

Kagan, Richard, C., ''Michael Borodin,'' *Encyclopedia of Asian History,* four volumes, Charles Scribner's Sons, 1988.

Periodicals

New York Times, June 21, 1981.

Times (London, England), December 23, 1926, p. 10; March 11, 1927, p. 14; April 27, 1927, p. 14; April 29, 1927, p. 14; May 28, 1927, p. 12; October 14, 1954, p. 11.□

Stephen Borough

The name of English navigator Stephen Borough (1525–1584) may be a relatively unknown one in the annals of sea exploration, but he was one of a daring group of sixteenth-century English seafarers whose achievements set the stage for Britain's control over the seas in the centuries to follow. Borough is the first explorer on record to have reached Russia from England by sea. The route he mapped out went through the frigid regions of Russia's White Sea—one which Norwegian traders apparently knew, but had kept a closely guarded secret—and opened the door for trade between Britain and Russia.

Borough was the son of Walter and Mary (Dough) Borough and born on September 25, 1525, in Northam, a small town in Devon in the southwest corner of England, where his father had a small manor farm. A younger brother, William, was born in 1536, and would later accompany Borough on some of his historic journeys. Because Northam was near Bideway Bay, an Atlantic port, both boys probably climbed to hilly promontory points to watch the English merchant ships sailing to and from Newfoundland, Iceland, and other points west.

Apprenticed to Uncle

After some rudimentary schooling, the adolescent Borough was likely apprenticed to his uncle, a well-known mariner named John Aborough. When Borough was still a young child, his uncle's name is listed in historical records of having piloted ships to Sicily and Venice in the service of one Lord Lisle, who was a British government official in the French port of Calais. Aborough also received a commission from King Henry VIII to shore up the coastline at Dover, on England's southeast coast, and commanded a navy ship used in attacks on Scotland later in the 1540s.

Borough's name first appears in the public record in 1553 as one of a dozen counsellors of a trade and exploration company formed to discover a new sea route to the East. At the time, the British were eager to exploit trade possibilities with China and other Asian lands—in the late 1490s, a Portuguese sea captain, Vasco de Gama, had been the first to successfully sail from Europe to India and back, and the investors who had put up the original funds for de Gama's voyage reportedly earned back their investment 100,000 times over thanks to the sale of spices, gold, and ivory that came back in the cargo holds. After that, the Spanish Empire began to dominate the maritime trade, and was even making regular jaunts across the Atlantic. Piracy on the seas was rampant, however, and British ships risked great losses if they took the southern route—down and around the coast of Africa—to reach the riches of Asia. The long overland route was fraught with peril, too: between France and China lay scores of smallish kingdoms and principalities, some with allegiance to the Holy Roman Empire, which was hostile to England because of the schism led by Henry VIII; other places were Muslim-ruled, where the abuses of the Christian Crusades a few centuries earlier were still remembered.

In 1551, ''The Company of Merchant Adventurers for the Discovery of Regions, Dominions, Islands, and Places Unknown'' was formed in London by Sebastian Cabot, Richard Chancellor, and Sir Hugh Willoughby to find the northeast sea route to Asia. Cabot was England's first and most famous explorer of the era, but he did not travel with the expeditions; instead his expertise and name were both vital to the success of the venture. Chancellor had extensive seafaring experience and had worked with Cabot previously. Willoughby was an able military commander whose title came from his role in the wartime seizure of Edinburgh in 1544.

Set Sail in May of 1553

The capital raised by the original investors was used to build and outfit the trio of ships that set out on the first expedition in 1553. Willoughby was captain of the *Bona Esperanza,* Chancellor was listed at the helm of the *Edward Bonaventura* and also named as the master pilot of the fleet of three vessels, and a Dutch seafarer named Cornelius Durfoorth captained the *Bona Confidentia.* Borough was listed as the master of the *Edward Bonaventura,* a term that gave him responsibility for the sails, steering, and other navigational matters.

The Vikings had probably made the first journeys by sea to Russia, for they were known to have been settled in the Kiev and Novgorod regions in the 800s, intermarried with the original Slavic tribes, and came to dominate the area as the Varangians. Further north and east of the kingdom of Kievan Rus, however, led to Arctic waters and lands that remained a mystery to the rest of Europe at the time. During Borough's era there were rumors, both of deadly whirlpools that devoured ships and sea monsters.

The fleet set out from the Thames River in London on May 10, 1553, and sailed north along the English coast until East Anglia, at which point the ships set out on a northeasterly route. They reached Rost, the last island in a lengthy archipelago that stretched out from the northern tip of Norway, and left it on July 22. Eight days later, near Senja Island, a fierce storm erupted and Borough's ship lost sight of the other two. The crews of both were never seen again, though years later their tragic fates did become known.

Reached White Sea

The historical data hints that Borough and Chancellor decided to sail eastward and hope that the other two ships would meet up with them at Wardhouse, later known as Vardø, on the other side of the great cape that was called Murmansky Nos but was named by either Chancellor or Borough the "North Cape" (*Nordkapp* in Norwegian), which is considered the northernmost point in Europe. They waited there a week, then headed along the coast until they reached *Beloye More*, or the "White Sea" in Russian. In a small port the English called St. Nicholas but known in Russian as Nenocksa, local records note the arrival of a ship from England commanded by "one named 'Ritzert' [Richard] ... saying he was going to the Great Sovereign the Czar," according to Kit Mayers's book, *North-East Passage to Muscovy: Stephen Borough and the First Tudor Explorations*. The tsar in question was Ivan the Terrible, one of the most notoriously brutal of all Russia's tsars in his later years.

Borough did not make the journey to Moscow, over both land and by smaller boat via the numerous rivers that led to the White Sea, but rather waited with the majority of the crew of the *Edward Bonaventura* in a bay called Unskaya Guba, near Nenocksa and the present-day city of Severodinsk. Chancellor and his party returned in February of 1554 with a letter from Ivan inviting English ships to trade with his realm and promising not to levy customs taxes on any of the goods. That document led to the founding of the Muscovy Company in London in February of 1555. This was the first joint stock company in England. Its investors were wealthy London merchants involved in the cloth trade, but scores of affluent or titled figures contributed £25 to the start-up capital fund.

Borough and Chancellor embarked on a second expedition to Russia in 1556, again in the *Edward Bonaventura*; accompanying this vessel was the *Phillip and Mary* and then a smaller oared ship, called a pinnace and named the *Serchthrift*. Extra men were aboard the two larger vessels, for the two missing ships of the first voyage had been found and brought to Nenocksa, and the extra crew members were needed to sail them back to England. The expedition left London on April 23, 1556, and when they reached Vardø Borough boarded the *Serchthrift* in order to discover the fabled northeast passage.

Reached Novaya Zemlya

In June, near the present-day Russian port city of Murmansk at the mouth of the Kola River, Borough enlisted the services of several local skippers and their *lodyas*, the fishing vessels used for hunting and fishing, to take him and the *Serchthrift* further inland. These people were known as the Pomors and had come to the area, probably from Novgorod, about 500 years earlier. The name of the German-Polish region known as Pomerania is also derived from this word. Chancellor, meanwhile, embarked upon a second 600-mile trek to Moscow to make further arrangements with Ivan.

Borough's journal records indicate that they reached the Pechora River in mid-July, and anchored at Vaygach Island on July 31. Willoughby had actually reached this area, too, but he and his crew later froze to death on the coast of Lapland. All along the way, Borough took careful measurements with the most technologically advanced instruments at the time, which used the North Star and other constellations to triangulate positions.

Vaygach Island was part of a larger archipelago known as Novaya Zemlya. It was the ancestral home of an indigenous group called the Nenets, a Samoyedic people who herded reindeer. Near this point, Borough and his English crew also saw what was probably a Northern Right whale, and were apparently greatly agitated by the sight of so large an animal after reports of sea monsters. In early August, when the *Serchthrift* began to encounter ice, they decided to turn back lest they be frozen in for the winter. Borough and the crew reached the town of Kholmogory on the Dvina River on September 11, 1556, and settled in for the winter.

Became Chief Pilot of Muscovy Company

Borough's original plan had been to reach the Ob River in Western Siberia. By following it and tributaries south, it would have been possible to reach Kazakhstan, Mongolia, and then China. Instead, at Kholmogory he received word that he should locate the two ships missing from the 1553 expedition that had been recovered—the *Bona Confidentia* and the *Bona Esperanza*—along with Chancellor's *Phillip and Mary* and *Edward Bonaventura*, which had also gone missing.

Apparently the last three of those ships had left St. Nicholas on July 20, 1556, but had not reached England. Borough piloted the *Serchthrift* up along the coast of what was called Lappia at the time and consists of the northernmost parts of Russia, Finland, Sweden, and Norway. At the time, the indigenous Sami people—once called Lapps, or Laplanders—were the area's main inhabitants and were reindeer herders like the Nenets.

Near Murmansk, Borough encountered some sailors from Trondheim, Norway, who told him that the *Phillip and Mary* had already sailed for England but that the *Bona Confidentia* had been shipwrecked. The *Bona Esperanza* had apparently been lost at sea. Chancellor and the *Edward Bonaventura*, meanwhile, had made it as far as the coast of Scotland, but were lost at sea in a November storm. In a heroic act, however, Chancellor had ensured the survival of his esteemed Russian passenger, Ossip Nepeja, the first Russian ambassador to England.

Journeyed to Spain

Borough and his crew returned to England in the summer of 1557. With Chancellor gone, he was made the chief pilot of the Muscovy Company, and made several more trips east between 1560 and 1571. In 1558, he made an expedition to Spain at the invitation of the court there, and returned to England with an important book by Martin Cortés, *Breve compendio de la sphera y de la arte navegar,* which was translated into English as *The Arte of Navigation* and became a vital aid in the English dominance of the seas in the next several decades as the British began to trade with and colonize a large part of the globe.

In 1563, Borough was granted a royal appointment as chief pilot of Queen Elizabeth I's fleet on the Medway River. He held this post until his death in Chatham, England, on July 12, 1584, where he had a house called Goodsight. His brother William, who accompanied him on his 1556–57 voyage to Russia, became Controller of the Royal Navy. His son Christopher was also an explorer and ventured all the way from the White Sea to the Caspian Sea. Christopher was his son by his first marriage to Eleanora Smithe of Shropshire, who died in 1562. Borough's second wife was Joanna or Joan Overye, with whom he had five daughters. One of them married John Vassall, thought to have been the builder and original owner of the *Mayflower,* the ship that carried the first permanent English settlers to the Massachusetts Bay Colony.

Books

''Borough, Stephen,'' *Dictionary of National Biography,* edited by Leslie Stephen, Volume V: *Bicheno—Bottisham,* Macmillan and Co., 1886, pp. 402–404.

Mayers, Kit, *North-East Passage to Muscovy: Stephen Borough and the First Tudor Explorations,* Sutton Publishing, 2005.

Mills, William James, ''Borough, Stephen,'' *Exploring Polar Frontiers: A Historical Encyclopedia,* ABC-CLIO, 2003, pp. 95–96. □

Carl Bosch

German chemist Carl Bosch (1874–1940) shared the 1931 Nobel Prize in Chemistry for his efforts to synthesize chemicals using high-pressure methods. As a developer of the Haber-Bosch method, Bosch overcame great challenges to produce large quantities of ammonia from atmospheric nitrogen; later, and with less commercial success, he worked to synthesize gasoline on a grand scale. Also trained in metallurgy, Bosch was equally comfortable with machinery and rose to the top levels of corporate scientific management.

The eldest of the six children of Carl and Paula Bosch, Carl (sometimes written Karl) Bosch was born on August 27, 1874, in Cologne, Germany. Bosch showed an early affinity for the sciences and mechanical items; as a boy, he enjoyed disassembling household objects to learn about their workings. His father, who had a successful business selling gas and plumbing supplies, encouraged him to study metallurgy, and in his late teenage years Bosch undertook an apprenticeship at a metallurgical plant. Upon enrollment at the Technische Hochschule in Charlottenburg in 1894, Bosch began studies in that field, as well as in engineering; he changed tacks two years later, however, and took up studies in chemistry at Leipzig University. Bosch completed his degree in organic chemistry under noted scientist Johannes Wislicenus, graduating from Leipzig in 1898.

The following spring, he took a position as a chemist with Germany's largest chemical company, Badische Anilin und Soda Fabrik (BASF), in Ludwigshafe, Rhine. Unlike most of the scientists as BASF, Bosch was willing and able to work with machinery; writing in *The Alchemy of Air,* Thomas Hager observed that while most of BASF's scientific staff enjoyed cultural pursuits and networking, Bosch ''liked to drink beer and go bowling.'' At BASF, Bosch joined a team of researchers under Dr. Rudolf Knietsch who were working on the recently-mastered production of synthetic indigo. This feat had been accomplished in 1897, and Tony Travis noted in *Chemistry and Industry* that it ''had brought great prestige to BASF, and encouraged its search for new challenges in chemical technology, especially those that might lead to diversification away from dyes.''

As a result of this search, BASF began conducting research into the potential artificial creation of nitrogen-based chemical compounds, such as ammonia and nitrates, through the process of fixating nitrogen present in atmospheric gases. These compounds had commercial application in industries ranging from food production to weapon-making, providing solid financial reasons for the research. At the time, Germany relied heavily on sodium nitrate imported from Chile; efforts to synthesize the chemical domestically had resulted in the Schönherr furnace, a device too expensive and inefficient to be a realistic replacement for imported chemicals. Bosch's background in metallurgy and skill with machinery made him a natural choice to join the efforts to devise a better way. One of his first chores was to duplicate and run tests on a machine designed by highly respected scientist Wilhelm Ostwald that reputedly generated ammonia using a process involving hot gases and an iron catalyst. Bosch soon found that, as Thomas Hager explained, "Ostwald's apparent success was only that—apparent. The ammonia he thought he was producing from the atmosphere was actually the result of contaminants in his machine." Ostwald was first bewildered and then angered by the unexpected information that a novice scientist had discovered a serious flaw in his mechanism, but Bosch refused to back down. Further experimentation supported Bosch's findings, and as a result of his competence on the project, he was soon promoted to a position heading up all of BASF's nitrogen research.

Developed Haber-Bosch Process

In 1902—shortly after his advancement at BASF—Bosch married Else Schilbach, and soon after, the couple had a son and then a daughter. Now supporting a family, Bosch was particularly driven to cement his position at BASF. Efforts to fixate nitrogen at BASF had stalled by 1908, when Fritz Haber approached BASF with a discovery he had made four years previously: the combination of hydrogen and nitrogen could—under high pressure conditions and with the presence of osmium or uranium as catalyst—synthesize significant amounts of ammonia. The following year, Bosch took on the task of devising machinery that could use Haber's method to produce ammonia on a much larger, industrial scale. The challenges seemed practically insurmountable; cheap catalysts had to be found to replace the expensive osmium and uranium, sophisticated machinery capable of withstanding the extreme heat and pressure had to be constructed, and huge quantities of pure nitrogen and hydrogen had to be generated. The costs—and the risks—of such a project were enormous.

Bosch quickly enlisted the services of other talented scientists and engineers, including Alwin Mittasch and Franz Lappe. Haber also joined the process. Much of the work done by the team covered new ground, and Bosch applied for dozens of new patents over the course of the project. Mittasch soon found that iron spiked with aluminum oxide and calcium could serve as an effective catalyst, and despite running 20,000 experiments over the course of a decade, a better replacement than this was never found. Bosch relied on existing techniques to refine pure nitrogen from liquid air, but some time was required before a method was determined of extracting pure hydrogen without producing dangerous amounts of carbon monoxide.

With these problems conquered, the development of a suitable machine began. Haber's small model had been constructed of steel, a material that became very brittle when placed in contact with hydrogen. Bosch solved this problem by using a pressurized two-chamber system: the inner chamber, made of steel, released the hydrogen safely into a reinforced outer chamber. In order to produce the high level of pressure necessary to process the chemicals on a large scale, Bosch needed a compressor that was more powerful, stronger, and less likely to leak than any that existed at the time. Hager noted that "[Bosch] wanted a machine that combined the strength of a sumo wrestler, the speed of a sprinter, and the grace of a ballerina." Challenges to the patents filed regarding the nitrogen fixation appeared in court, and were defeated in 1912. Slowly, Bosch built larger and larger machines, until in September 1913 a full-size commercial plant began operations at a site near Oppau. This plant was soon producing vast amounts of ammonia-based fertilizer. The Haber-Bosch method, as it came to be called, was a success.

Rose to Corporate Leadership

The advent of World War I in 1914 brought about increased demand for nitrogen-derived products, both as fertilizers and as components in the making of explosives. Bosch oversaw the expansion of the program as BASF established a research laboratory at Oppau and, in 1917, a new plant was opened at Leuna, far enough from the border to avoid the air harassment that the Oppau factory had endured since 1915. The plant at Leuna produced methanol and hydrogenated oil in addition to ammonia. Travis commented that "it was later claimed, probably with considerable exaggeration, that the ammonia synthesis had enabled the Germans to conduct an extended war." Regardless of whether it was the defining factor in Germany's ability to fight, unquestionably ammonia production ramped up considerably during the war, with over 200,000 tons coming out of BASF's two plants by the end of hostilities in 1918.

After the German defeat, Bosch and BASF made all possible effort to remove inventory and shut down equipment—particularly the ammonia factory at Oppau—to prevent the hitherto secret process of synthesizing ammonia from falling into foreign hands, thus eliminating BASF's commercial advantage. Although the British eventually discovered some of Bosch's techniques from two of his former employees, they were unable to produce the chemical nearly as successfully as did the BASF plants.

In 1919, Bosch became the managing director of BASF and waded into a period of crisis for the company; the labor movement was attracting workers throughout Germany, including those at BASF, and in 1921 an explosion destroyed part of the Oppau factory and the surrounding area, killing over 500 employees and injuring over three times that number. This explosion made the already somewhat withdrawn Bosch even more distant and businesslike. The following year, Bosch—along with other directors of

BASF—was found guilty of refusing to cooperate with French officials who had come to seize assets after Germany, in the midst of an inflationary crisis, stopped paying war reparations. Although Bosch was sentenced to eight years in prison, he remained in Heidelberg, from which the French could not legally extradite him. By the end of 1923, the situation had cooled, and Bosch's conviction and unserved sentence were forgotten.

In 1925, BASF combined with some of Germany's other major chemical companies to form IG Farben, and Bosch was named head of this corporate behemoth, the third-largest company in the world. He turned his attention to a new process devised by Friedrich Bergius that synthesized gasoline from coal and hydrogen. Although the process became technologically feasible, the discovery of vast oil reserves in the United States crushed any potential market for an expensive synthesized product; Bosch's synthesized gasoline was twice the price of traditionally produced fuel. Even so, Bosch shared the Nobel Prize in Chemistry in 1931 with Bergius in recognition of their work with high-pressure processes.

Resisted Nazi Ideals

The economic crisis that battered nations on both sides of the Atlantic caused a significant decline in Farben's revenue, and Bosch did not wear the damage well. The rise of the Nazi Party did little to improve his spirits, particularly after a heated meeting with Adolf Hitler in which Bosch defended the abilities of Jewish scientists and researchers. Bosch dedicated himself to securing the safety of his own Jewish employees while trying to secure a lucrative contract to sell the Nazis synthetic gasoline. He pushed back against Nazi goals, and in 1935 was moved to a position on Farben's board which effectively removed him from day-to-day leadership of the company.

In 1937, he became head of the Kaiser Wilhelm Institutes, a role that *World of Invention* characterized as "the highest position in executive management in German industry." Despite this prestigious job, Bosch was unhappy. He strongly disliked the Nazis, and in some ways felt that his discoveries were fueling an ideology that he found highly distasteful. By the time that Hitler invaded Poland in 1939, Bosch was experiencing both physical and mental declines. He died at Heidelberg on April 26, 1940, depressed and certain that Germany would suffer greatly as a result of the Nazi regime.

Throughout his lengthy career, Bosch received a great many honors, including honorary doctorates from the Technische Hochschules of Karlsruhe, Munich, and Darmstadt; the Agriculture College in Berlin; and Halle University. He also received the post of Honorary Senator from the University of Heidelberg in 1922, and from the University of Leipzig in 1939. That same year, Bosch became an Honorary Citizen of Frankfurt. Long after his death, Bosch continued to receive recognition for his work. In 2006, he and Fritz Haber were inducted in the National Inventors Hall of Fame in Akron, Ohio, in honor of their development of synthesized ammonia.

Books

Hager, Thomas, *The Alchemy of Air,* Harmony, 2008.
Notable Scientists: From 1900 to the Present, Thomson Gale, 2006.
World of Invention, Thomson Gale, 2006.

Periodicals

Chemistry and Industry, August 2, 1993.

Online

"Carl Bosch," *Nobel Lectures,* http://www.nobelprize.org/ (December 18, 2008).□

S. N. Bose

Indian mathematician, Satyendra Nath Bose, more commonly known as S.N. Bose (1894–1874) was known for his brilliant work in mathematics and physics. Bose also worked with many well-known scientists. While he accomplished many great things during his life, Bose's work with Albert Einstein developing the phenomenon known as the Bose-Einstein condensate (BEC) was an exceedingly important scientific discovery.

S.N. Bose was born on January 1, 1894 in Calcutta, India (now Kolkata). Bose's mother, Amodini Devi, received very little formal education, but still competently helped raise her seven children. Bose was the eldest of the seven children and the only boy. His father, Surendranath Bose worked as an accountant before becoming employed by the engineering department of the East India Railway. Later his father would open his own chemical and pharmaceutical company. Bose's father would also be tasked with the job of finishing raising his seven children as he lost his wife at a young age.

Education played an important role throughout Bose's life. As a boy he began his elementary education in a Calcutta school. Then in 1907, after his family had moved, he entered a Hindu school. At this school his mathematics teacher, Upendra Bakshi, was considered a legendary figure. There, fostered by his mathematics instructor and encouragement from the school's headmaster, Bose's interest in mathematics and science began to flourish. Bose's aptitude for mathematics stood out in high school when he scored 110 marks out of 100 on a mathematics exam. After the headmaster questioned his score, the teacher explained that he had given Bose extra marks, more than the allotted 100 because Bose solved the problems using more than one mathematical method.

After high school, Bose enrolled at the Presidency College of Calcutta. Bose chose to study the sciences although he did also have exceptional talents for languages and the humanities. He was a skilled reader of Bengali, Sanskrit, and English literature, and was also very familiar with poetry. He was also a great lover of music and the fine arts and played the flute and the Esraj, an instrument similar to the violin. During his college years Bose was fortunate to study with classmates such as Girijapathi Bhattacharya, Meghnad Saha, J.C. Ghosh, Nikhilranjan Bose, and J.N. Mukherjee, who would all go on to become well-known scientists. Bose was also acquainted with the freedom fighter Netaji Subashchandra.

Upon the beginning of World War I, members of independence-minded groups based in Bengal risked their careers to organize an armed rebellion against British colonial India. Some of Bose's friends joined these organizations, and left the country for Germany to gather arms. Bose, however, was under firm instruction from his father not to become caught up in any actions that may end his career. Being the eldest and only son of his family, Bose followed his father's orders; however, he remained a supporter of those fighting for the independence movement, also called the swadeshi movement, and aided them when he could. Sometimes Bose provided shelter, acted as a messenger, or helped the cause out with monetary contributions.

Life After College

Bose completed his Bachelor of Science degree in 1913. Before he finished his Masters of Science degree in 1915, he married Ushabati Gosh. His wife was the only daughter of an extremely wealthy doctor. Bose was only 20 years old when he was married, and although he was not eager to marry at such a young age while he was still in college, he could not go against his mother's wishes for him to marry. While it was common for the husband to accept a dowry for his wife, Bose, however, refused to accept one and also refused to accept monetary aid from his wife's family during difficult financial situations. Soon after Bose finished his Masters degree, he and his wife had their fist child. They would eventually have five children altogether, two sons and three daughters.

After completing his Masters, Bose could not find regular employment so he worked as a private tutor. He tried to work toward a doctorate in mathematics under Ganesh Prasad at the University of Calcutta, but never finished. In an article in *Physics Today* by Kameshwar Wali, Bose recalled his experience as a doctoral student. "After my MSc I too presented myself before Ganesh Prasad who was also my examiner though I had not fared as badly as the others [on Prasad's exam questions]. Dr. Prasad was kind to me at first but I was notorious for plain speaking. I found it difficult to bear his tirade against my teachers. I had dared to counter his adverse criticisms. This infuriated him. He said 'You may have done well in examination but that does not mean you are cut for research.' Disappointed, I came away. I decided to work on my own."

In 1916, Bose started a career at Calcutta University as a Lecturer in Physics. In 1921, Bose accepted a position at Dacca University as a reader in Physics. It was during this time that he wrote an important article pertaining to physics. Bose was dissatisfied with the current derivations of Planck's radiation law and so he developed an acceptable derivation based on Einstein's photon concept. The article was written in English and was only six pages long and it related to "Max Planck's Law" and "Light Quantum Hypothesis." He sent the article to *Philosophical Magazine* in late 1923 or early 1924, but the paper was rejected.

Bose then sent the article to Albert Einstein. In his letter to Einstein accompanying the article Bose asked for Einstein's opinion, as well as if he thought the paper was worthy enough to be translated into German and submitted for publication to the magazine *Zeitschrift für Physik*. Part of Bose's letter to Einstein was quoted on the Vigyan Prasar Science Portal website in the article *Satyendra Nath Bose The Creator of Quantum Statistics.* In his letter Bose noted, "Though a complete stranger to you, I do not feel any hesitation in making such a request. [W]e are all your pupils though profiting only of your teachings through your writings."

Einstein responded to Bose's letter noting the importance of Bose's subject matter, and he himself translated the article which was later published in the August 1924 issue of *Zeitschrift für Physik* under the title "Plancksgesetz Lichtquantenhypothese" ("Planck's Law and Light Quantum Hypothesis"). Einstein also included his own note with the article as is also shown on the Vigyan Prasar Science Portal website. He stated, "Bose's derivative of Planck's formula appears to me to be an important step forward. The method used here gives also the quantum theory of an ideal gas, as I shall show elsewhere." From Bose's work, the field of Quantum Statistics came into being.

Took a Two Year Sabbatical

Due to the success Bose found with his article about Planck's Law, he decided to apply for two years of research leave from Dacca University. Einstein wrote a postcard on Bose's behalf, and the Vice Chancellor of Dacca University granted Bose his leave after seeing the postcard from Einstein. Bose's two year sabbatical was used to enable Bose to travel to Europe and become more acquainted with the newest developments in his field.

Bose first arrived in Europe in October 1924. He first went to Paris intending only to spend a few weeks there before going to Berlin to work with Einstein. Bose ended up staying in Paris for a year, however, and while there, one of Bose's friends, Prabodh Chandra Bagchi introduced him to Sylvian Levi, the renowned French Indologist. Levi in turn gave Bose a letter of introduction to Paul Langevin. Bose's mission was to familiarize himself as much as possible with the most recent developments and theoretical and experimental physics as he could. Bose wanted to learn about radioactivity techniques from Marie Curie. It was Langevin who suggested Bose should work with Curie in her laboratory and gave him a letter of introduction.

Bose could speak French proficiently, but Curie was unaware of this so she was hesitant to let him work in her laboratory. Bose was the type of man not to draw attention to himself or his accomplishments, so instead of admitting to Curie that he had a good working knowledge of the French language, he waited a few months and studied the language further before returning to her laboratory to work. Although Bose accurately made difficult measurements of the piezoelectric effect (which is the generation of an electric charge in certain nonconducting materials, such as quartz crystals and ceramics, when they are subjected to mechanical stress) in Curie's laboratory, his desires to learn techniques in radioactivity went largely unfulfilled.

Also due to a letter from Langevin, Bose met Maurice de Broglie, known for his work with X-ray spectroscopy. Broglie allowed Bose to work side by side with Alexander Dauvillier, his chief assistant. In Broglie's laboratory, Bose learned the diverse techniques of crystallography as well as piqued an interest in the theoretical aspects of crystal behavior. After Bose spent about a year working with famous scientists in laboratories in Paris, he made his journey to Berlin to meet with Einstein.

Bose had to wait several weeks before he could take a meeting with Einstein who was traveling when Bose arrived in Germany in 1925. Bose did not work with Einstein, but with his help Bose met many influential German scientists such as Michael Polanyi and Walter Gordon, along with many others. With Polanyi, Bose was able to work with X-ray crystallography. He also became engaged in theoretical studies with Gordon. With Einstein's aid Bose was able to borrow books form the University Library and attend the physic's colloquium. After nearly two years in Europe, Bose returned to India. Although he learned a great deal, Bose did not publish any papers during his research expedition to Europe.

Later Years

After Bose returned from his stay in Europe his friends suggested he apply for the post of Professor in the Physics Department at Dacca University. Bose asked for a letter of recommendation from Einstein, who was a bit surprised by this request, as he felt Bose was the sure candidate; yet still he complied. Einstein's letter did not help Bose initially as the job was offered to someone else, but when the job was declined by the first prospect, it was then offered to Bose who accepted. He later became Head of the Department of Physics in 1927. While fulfilling his professorship at Dacca, Bose also became interested in experimental physics. He studied crystal structures, designed his own experimental equipment, and designed and constructed X-ray diffraction cameras. His research was not limited to physics though. Bose also was extremely interested in chemistry. He also started conducting research in organic chemistry.

After serving Dacca University for almost twenty-five years, Bose was appointed the Khaira Professor of Physics at Calcutta University in 1945. During 1953-54, Bose published five papers on the Unified Field Theory. Again, he consulted with Einstein on these papers. Einstein was unsure how these papers related to physics and told Bose so through detailed notes. Bose in turn wrote responses to Einstein's comments but hoped to reply to them personally at the celebration of the 50th anniversary of the theory of relativity. Unfortunately, Bose was not able to have that conversation as Einstein died in 1955. Bose was overcome with such emotion and grief over the death of his master (the term he used to address Einstein in all of his

letters) that he threw away the only copy of his important paper. Bose ultimately stopped work on the Unified Field Theory.

In 1956 Bose was appointed the Vice Chancellor of the Visva Bharati University at Shantiniketan founded by Rabindranath Tagore. Bose's methods and presence at the university, however, went against the established tradition of Visva Bharati. Unhappy with his position there, Bose left and returned to Calcutta in 1958. In that same year he was also elected Fellow of the Royal Society of London. In 1959, Bose was appointed national Professor, and he held that post until his death on February 4, 1974.

Legacy Continued

Bose may be best known for his work in the sciences, especially his work now known as the Bose-Einstein condensate (BEC). While neither man lived to see if their idea that if atoms were cooled to within a few billionths of a degree of absolute zero, the atoms would lose their identities and become a single coherent whole, the outcome did in fact happen. In 2001, the Nobel Prize for Physics was shared by three scientists, two Americans and one German, the men who created the BEC's first predicted by Bose and Einstein. Eric Cornell and Carl Wieman, professors at the University of Colorado, and Wolfgang Ketterle, a professor at the Massachusetts Institute of Technology, were awarded the prize for chilling atoms to a fraction over absolute zero.

Even after the two Americans and the German scientists won the Nobel Prize for Physics, Bose's legacy continues to live on as continued research takes place in the fields of science and mathematics. Today, an institute at Kolkata (formerly Calcutta) is named after Bose. It is called the S.N. Bose National Centre for Basic Sciences.

Periodicals

Economist, (US), July 7, 2001; February 1, 1997.
London Times, September 10, 2001.
Physics Today, October 2006.

Online

O'Connor, J.J., and E.F. Robertson, "Satyendranath Bose," http://www-gropus.dcs.st-and.ac.uk/ histroy/Printonly/Bose.html (December 18, 2008).
"Satyendra Nath Bose" http://www.vigyanprasar.gov.in/scientists/snbose/bosenew.htm (December 18, 2008).
Shanbhag, M.R., "Satyendra Nath Bose,"http://www.calcuttaweb.com/people/snbose.shtml (December 18, 2008). □

Antoinette Bourignon

The French-born religious leader and mystic Antoinette Bourignon (1616–1680) founded a Protestant sect that gained adherents in several European countries and anticipated the ideals of both the Enlightenment and, more distantly, the feminist movement.

ourignonianism, as her movement was known in English-speaking countries, was one of a number of offshoots of a broader movement known as Pietism—a strain of Protestantism that placed emphasis on personal faith as opposed to institutional religious structures or theological discussion. Indeed, Bourignon took it as a point of pride that she did not know the Bible in detail. Salvation, in her view, came purely from love of God, and even such central tenets of the Christian faith as Jesus Christ's crucifixion and resurrection were important to her only insofar as they contributed to this goal. Bourignon led a colorful life, much of which was spent on the road, and in her later years she founded a utopian religious community on an island in the North Sea. She believed herself to be divinely inspired and thought of herself as the bride of the Holy Ghost.

Born with Facial Deformity

Antoinette Bourignon de la Porte was born in Ryssel, in the Spanish-controlled Netherlands, on January 13, 1616. Ryssel is now the city of Lille, France. Brought up in the Roman Catholic faith, Bourignon used the French language in her 19 volumes of religious writings. Her father was a merchant. Bourignon's interactions with humans were largely negative from the beginning: she was born with a harelip, and her mother expressed disgust at her appearance. The defect was surgically repaired, but Bourignon grew up feeling inferior to her siblings in her parents' affections. Bourignon believed that their marriage was unhappy, and when

her mother tried to steer her toward the idea of marriage that was conventional for young women of the time, she pointed out that marriage had brought her mother little happiness.

Indeed, according to a nineteenth-century biography of Bourignon appearing on the Christian Classics Ethereal Library Web site, Bourignon once heard the voice of God saying, "Canst thou find a lover more perfect than I?" Another voice told her to forsake all earthly things. Bourignon wanted to spend her life in a convent as a Carmelite nun, but her parents forbade it. In 1636 they arranged a marriage between her and a local businessman. Bourignon repeatedly tried to push the date of the wedding back, and finally she sewed herself a monk's robe and used it one morning to make her escape by blending into the populace on the streets. She had one coin in her pocket. According to a story reproduced on the Distinguished Women Web site, she heard another voice, this one saying, "Where is thy faith—in a penny?" So she threw the coin away.

Bourignon would spend much of the next several decades on the road, living as a religious mendicant and preaching a personal brand of Christianity that increasingly diverged both from her inherited Catholic faith and from the new Protestant ideas that were making headway all over northern Europe. At one point she was captured and returned to her family, but she escaped again and sought refuge in the compound of the Catholic archbishop in the city of Mons. Several times she tried to form communities of like-minded individuals, with the idea that they would live together in poverty, but these failed. Her options widened after her father's death, for she filed a successful lawsuit against his second wife and gained control of his estate. In 1653 she took charge of an orphanage in Ryssel, trying to turn it into a cloistered community. In 1662 she was accused of cruelty to the children under her charge and fled the city once again.

Outlasted Companions

Bourignon later attracted adherents in the British Isles, especially in Scotland, and her memoir in dialogue form, known in English as *The Light of the World,* contained reflections on her wanderings. Asked whether they were not "dangerous for a Maid alone," she answered that she "was obliged to travel alone, for she had found no Body that would accompany her; and that many had indeed gone along with her for some Time, but upon the first Temptation, Hunger, or Incommodity, they had staid behind, not knowing how to endure Penitence because they had too much Love for themselves, and too little Affection to seek God; esteeming their Ease more than the Contentment there is in the loving and following of him: For this Cause they had left her."

She preferred to be on the move, and wrote: "Though I am a Stranger, yet I may be taken Notice of by staying long in one Place, which I do not desire; for Men are full of vain Curiosity, they would hinder my inward Repose and Quiet without any Profit; therefore I love rather to travel and continue unknown: For men cannot give me any Thing, nor I them. . . . I never learned any Thing from any Man; and as to the teaching of them, they have too much Presumption of their own Knowledge, to hearken to a Child as I am.''

Bourignon eventually began to distribute her talks in written form, as letters and essays, and her following grew. Unlike many other writers, whether on religious subjects or otherwise, she only began to write seriously after she had passed the age of 50. Bourignon's travels took her to Ghent and then to Mechlin (both now in Belgium). There she gained a supporter in Christian de Cort, the superior of a monastic Catholic community known as the Oratorians, who favored worship dominated by intense expressions of faith. Bourignon was also interested in the ideas of the radical Dutch Catholic theologian Cornelius Jansen who emphasized the doctrine of justification by faith and was thus close to the Protestant focus on the religious experiences of the individual believer.

Hoping to find a publisher who could give her writings wider dissemination, Bourignon settled in Amsterdam in 1667. The city was a hotbed of dissenting ideas, both Catholic and Protestant, and Bourignon plunged into the fray. She shared aspects of belief with various other religious leaders, including the controversial Dutch Reformed minister Jean de Labadie, and with another woman who espoused radical Pietist ideas, Anna Maria van Schurman. However, because of a combination of theological disagreements and the sort of personality conflict endemic among reformers with strong personalities, she ended up at odds with these reformers. Bourignon wrote sharp polemics attacking the Catholic church, and her own ideas were far enough out on the edges of established thinking that she stimulated plenty of attacks herself from detractors.

Emphasized Devotional Attitude

Essentially, Bourignon placed tremendous emphasis on personal faith, which she defined as love for God. She shared this emphasis with other Pietist figures, and she also joined with other Pietists in her strong distrust for institutional religious structures. But in other respects her beliefs diverged widely from existing Protestant and Catholic outlooks. The life and death of Jesus Christ, while important in her teaching, was not central to it; Christ's crucifixion, for Bourignon, was not sufficent to atone for human sinfulness. Rather, wrote Joyce Irwin in *Church History,* Bourignon believed that ''his saving role consists primarily of pointing the way to salvation rather than accomplishing it on behalf of humans.'' Humans had become distanced from a loving relationship with God, and, in Bourignon's view, Christ's trials had the function of helping them find their way back.

Bourignon placed little stock in the traditional Trinity of Father, Son, and Holy Spirit. Instead, she subdivided the Deity into another threefold concept: truth, mercy, and justice. Although she allowed that truth could be found in the Bible, she proclaimed herself proud that she did not know Scripture well and believed that a spirit of devotion was much more important. She did not believe in the baptism of babies. Nor did she accept the doctrine of predestination—the belief that human salvation is determined by God alone,

independent of human actions—a concept that was common to most of the radical Protestant sects of northern Europe. Because of her disregard for the authority of Scripture and for the influence of established churches, Bourignon is sometimes considered a forerunner of the freethinking spirit of the eighteenth-century Enlightenment.

Indeed, Bourignon had little use for existing churches at all. Her main quarrel with Labadie, one of her closest spiritual relatives, was that he was attempting to form a church of individuals who were regenerate, or religiously renewed. ''If you are true disciples of Jesus Christ,'' she wrote to him (as quoted by Irwin), ''it is a pity that you are attached to a particular church, since there is now no assembly in the world where the Holy Spirit presides.'' Bourignon has sometimes been called a quietist, a thinker who believes that his or her job is to clear away errors that keep the human mind from a state of quietude. Increasingly, as she grew older, she viewed herself as a source of direct revelation from God, even as a bride of God.

Tried to Secure Island Inheritance

Despite this focus on life beyond the material world, Bourignon's secular affairs were complicated in the last decade of her life. After de Cort's death in 1669, she stood to inherit his property. His holdings included a North Sea island, Nordstrand (now linked by an artificial peninsula to the German coast), where Bourignon planned to create a utopian community of worship without priests or ministers. The estate became embroiled in legal disputes, and Bourignon moved from Amsterdam to Haarlem, to the German-Danish Schleswig region, and finally to the German city of Husum, near Nordstrand, as she pursued the case's resolution.

At some point Bourignon obtained a small printing press, and she carried it with her on her travels. She issued tracts, polemics, and letters by the dozen, arousing spirited opposition and eventually the confiscation of her press by a local government. Nonetheless, word of her ideas began to spread, partly because of her sheer tirelessness as a writer. Her complete works, issued in Amsterdam beginning in 1680, ran to 19 volumes. In the German city-state of Hamburg in 1679, Bourignon was accused of sorcery by an army colonel who had been one of her followers, and took to the road once again. She died in Franeker, in what is now the Dutch province of Friesland, on October 30, 1680.

Despite the controversial nature of her ideas, Bourignon attracted a strong following that continued to grow even after her death. Bourignonianism was especially popular in Scotland, where among its adherents was the Rev. James Garden, professor of divinity at King's College in Aberdeen. His younger brother, the Rev. George Garden, was removed from the ministry after writing a book supporting Bourignon's ideas. Even in the late nineteenth-century United States, pragmatist philosopher William James wrote that he considered Bourignon a saint because of her uncompromisingly self-sacrificing ways. Although she was a clear forerunner of modern feminism, many of her writings still await rediscovery by scholars writing in English.

Periodicals

Irwin, Joyce, "Anna Maria van Schurman and Antoinette Bourignon: Contrasting Examples of Seventeenth-Century Pietism," *Church History,* September 1991, p. 301.

Online

"Antoinette Bourignon," Distinguished Women, http://www.distinguishedwomen.com/biographies/bourigno.html (November 15, 2008).

Bourignon, Antoinette, "An Abridgement of the Light of the World," *Eighteenth Century Collections Online,* Gale Group, http://www.galenet.galegroup.com (November 15, 2008).

"Bourignon de la Porte, Antoinette," *New Schaff-Herzog Encyclopedia of Religious Knowledge,* Christian Classics Ethereal Library, Calvin College, http://www.ccel.org/s/schaff/encyc/encyc02/htm/iv.v.ccl.htm (November 15, 2008).□

Émile Boutmy

Émile Boutmy (1835–1906) was deeply involved in reforming nineteenth-century France's political system. A political scientist and sociologist, Boutmy was the founder and longtime director of the École Libre des Sciences Politiques, which later became the required provider of a degree for any French youth planning on a career in politics or the uppermost ranks of the nation's civil service. H.S. Jones, writing in the *Oxford Dictionary of National Biography,* called the school "an immensely important influence on French public life. Its success testified both to the power of its founder's vision, and to his practical genius in translating that vision into reality."

B outmy was born on April 13, 1835, in Paris, where he would spend all of his life. In 1848, the year he turned 13, his family encountered some unexpected hardship following the death of Boutmy's father Laurent-Joseph, a journalist who also had business ventures. Fortunately Boutmy had a generous patron in the form of his godfather, Émile de Girardin, a leading journalist and politician. After attending two of the most rigorous college-preparatory schools in all of France—the Lycée Louis-le-Grand and the Lycée Henri IV, both located in Paris—Boutmy studied law before becoming a journalist himself.

Ideas Shaped by Political Turmoil

There was another significant event that occurred when Boutmy was entering his teen years: the French Revolution of 1848. This ousted the last monarch ever to rule France, King Louis-Philippe, and established the Second Republic, a four-year-long period of social upheaval marked by

historic reforms that touched every aspect of life in France. Boutmy's godfather, Girardin, was instrumental in aiding the rise of Louis-Napoléon Bonaparte, of the famed Bonaparte dynasty, to become president of the short-lived republic, which ended in 1852.

As a young man Boutmy came to befriend several influential figures who would play a role in the founding of the École Libre des Sciences Politiques. One was Hippolyte Taine, a philosopher and literary critic. Another was François Guizot, who served as prime minister of France from September of 1847 to February of 1848 and was responsible for mandating that every *commune,* or government-administrative unit in the country, offer primary-school education to its youngest citizens. In the 1860s, Boutmy began teaching courses in the history of civilizations at the newly founded École Spéciale d'Architecture in Paris. His first book, *Philosophie de l'architecture en Grèce* (Philosophy of Architecture in Greece), was published in 1870.

That same year, in July, France entered into a disastrous war against Prussia, its powerful German neighbor. Economics and territory were, as always, the main impetus behind the conflict, but the actual declaration of war came after a series of telegrams exchanged over an incident between Kaiser Wilhelm I of Prussia and the French ambassador to Prussia. The subsequent diplomatic correspondence, known as the Ems Dispatch because they originated in the German spa town of Bad Ems, were poorly translated and misinterpreted, and the perceived insults led France to declare war on Prussia. The conflict lasted ten months and led to a quarter of a million casualties and an ignoble defeat for France in which it was forced to give up the region of Alsace-Lorraine. With the defeat also came the collapse of the Second Empire of Louis-Napoléon, who had ruled as the Emperor Napoleon III since 1852.

Founded Elite National Academy

France became a parliamentary democracy once again, and this would be known as the Third Republic and endure until the onset of World War II. Less than a year after the end of the Franco-Prussian conflict, in February of 1872, Boutmy founded the École Libre des Sciences Politiques (Private School of Political Studies) and became its first director. Its goal was to educate and train an elite group of government professionals who could conduct affairs of state no matter what regime was in place—either a monarchy, republican parliamentary democracy, or some other form. The civil service had actually been created during the First French Empire under Napoléon Bonaparte, who ruled as Napoléon I. It was still deeply politicized, however, and had not yet achieved a necessary level of professionalism for its vital duties.

Boutmy's academy was founded on the principle that only qualified and rigorously educated professionals should conduct the most important matters of state. A degree from his school had become necessary for anyone wishing to enter the upper echelons of the vast French civil service. With the creation of the French civil service, a job inside certain government ministries required achievement, or a passing score on a rigorous examination, and the aim of Boutmy's École was to prepare students for these exams. The top four were the *Conseil d'Etat* (Council of State), which serves as the legal advisory body to the French president; the *Cour des Comptes,* or Court of Accounts, which audits government agencies and other semi-official bodies; the *Inspection Générale des Finances,* a particularly powerful auditor post; and the French Ministry of Foreign Affairs.

Boutmy hired high-ranking officials from each of the ministries to teach at the school. Moreover, it was a private school, with high tuition fees and no scholarships. "Boutmy aimed to provide France with a new elite, drawn from the traditional ruling classes, but justifying its pre-eminence through competence in the skills needed to lead society in an era of democratization," noted an essay on him in the *Biographical Dictionary of French Political Leaders since 1870.* Others involved in the founding of the school besides Boutmy and Taine were Ernest Renan, a noted philosopher and author of the bestselling *Vie de Jésus* (Life of Jesus); the historian Albert Sorel; and Pierre Paul Leroy-Beaulieu, an economist.

Authored Several Books

Boutmy himself taught constitutional history classes at his school for 17 years, and authored several books on that subject and other topics in political science. His published works include *Quelques Observations sur la réforme de l'enseignement supérieur* (Some Observations on the Reform of Higher Education), which appeared in 1876; *Études de droit constitutionnel* (Studies of Constitutional Law) from 1888; *Le recrutement des administrateurs coloniaux* (The Recruitment of Colonial Administrators), issued in 1895; and *Essai d'une psychologie politique du peuple anglais au XIXe siècle* (Essay on the Political Psychology of the People in 19th Century England).

This last book, which appeared in 1901, was widely read in Britain. In it, Boutmy wrote that the English were "peculiarly qualified for collective operations; they have a superior power of coalition and ability to work collectively which is unknown among races who are less active and more absurdly vain." A critique by A. L. Lowell that appeared in the *American Historical Review* remarked that Boutmy's "estimate of Englishmen does not differ essentially from that commonly accepted in France. He finds them highly individualistic, somewhat brutal, unsociable, lacking in sympathy, and among the uneducated masses stupid; but, on the other hand, from their very lack of sympathy, frank to the degree that reaches nobility of character, energetic from the need of activity, and conservative from their dislike of abstract ideas."

Though Boutmy was keenly interested in English political culture, he visited the British Isles only a few times, and never for any lengthy period. He once famously described the United Kingdom—the conjoined England, Scotland, Ireland, and Wales—as "four nations in a condition of permanent irritation with each other" according to Bill Jamieson's *Scotland's Ten Tomorrows: The Devolution Crisis—And How to Fix It.* In the early 1890s, the founders of the London School of Economics modeled their institution on Boutmy's Paris academy.

Boutmy also wrote about the United States in *Eléments d'une psychologie politique du peuple américain* (Elements of the Political Psychology of the American People), which appeared in 1902. Its chapters examined the role of the original colonies, westward expansion, immigration issues, and the role government should play in its citizens' lives. Lowell assessed the merits of this work, too, in the *American Historical Review,* and wrote that Boutmy "points out how much more ancient the conception of the nation is in Europe than in America . . . he says that the Americans have not the same feeling of patriotism as Europeans. That sentiment, he says, does not appeal to their imagination, their public spirit being based rather upon a super-abundance of individual energy and an enlightened conviction of self-interest."

Boutmy died on January 25, 1906, in Paris, and was survived by his wife Eugène Bersier, the daughter of a Protestant minister of some renown in France. Nearly four decades later, his school was one of the academies nationalized, or taken over by the French government, after the end of World War II. It was split into two entities: the Fondation Nationale des Sciences Politiques (National Foundation of Political Studies) and the Institut d'Études Politiques de Paris (Institute of Political Studies of Paris). The latter is known as *Sciences Po,* and it offers a multilingual undergraduate and graduate program. The highest positions in government are reserved for graduates of the École Nationale d'Administration, which was created in 1945. Its students must be graduates of Sciences Po. At the onset of the twenty-first century, France's entire civil service, which included teachers, police officers, transport workers, and government-office workers as well as the highest-ranking members of the courts, diplomatic corps, and finance ministries, numbered 1.9 million and was Europe's largest employer.

Books

Bell, David S., Douglas Johnson, and Peter Morris, editors, *Biographical Dictionary of French Political Leaders since 1870,* Association for the Study of Modern and Contemporary France/Simon & Schuster, 1990, pp. 31–32.

Boutmy, Émile, *Essay on the Political Psychology of the People in 19th Century England,* Armand, Colin, 1901.

Jamieson, Bill, *Scotland's Ten Tomorrows: The Devolution Crisis—And How to Fix It,* Continuum International, 2006, p. 28.

Matthew, H.C.G., and Brian Harrison, editors, *Oxford Dictionary of National Biography,* Volume 6: *Blackmore–Bowyer,* Oxford University Press, 2004, pp. 868–869.

Periodicals

American Historical Review, January 1902; October 1902.

Annals of the American Academy of Political and Social Science, November 1891.

New York Times Book Review, December 12, 1903. □

Edward George Bowen

British physicist Edward Bowen (1911–1991) was a key researcher and the prime mover behind the British military's development of military applications for radar in the years before the outbreak of World

War II. His discoveries contributed significantly to Britain's success in repelling German air attacks during the Battle of Britain in the early stages of the war.

Bowen had an unusual combination of visionary imagination and an ability to improvise in difficult circumstances. Spending much of his career in Australia after the war, he became an important figure in the early history of radio astronomy and also tried to devise methods of seeding clouds with dry ice or silver iodide in order to increase Australia's sparse rainfall totals. But it was Bowen's work in radar research that was most important. Lord Douglas, the commander-in-chief of Britain's Fighter Command, wrote (as Bowen himself reported in his memoir, *Radar Days,*) "I think we can say that the Battle of Britain might never have been won...if it were not for the radar chain" Bowen had helped to develop and shepherd through Britain's military bureaucracy.

Loved Radio as Youth

Born on January 14, 1911, in a village called Cockett near the Welsh city of Swansea, Edward George Bowen was the youngest of four children of a skilled steel mill worker and amateur church organist, George Bowen, and his wife, Ellen. Bowen remained proud of his Welsh origins and confidently adopted and continued to use the slightly derogatory Welsh nickname of Taffy. When he was about 11, shortly after commercial radio broadcasting began in Great Britain, Bowen became fascinated by the new medium. Scientifically gifted, he impressed his teachers and won a series of scholarships that enabled him to extend his education far beyond the norm for far-flung Wales: he attended Swansea's Municipal Secondary School, Swansea University College (where he switched from chemistry to physics, earning an honors degree in 1930 and a master's degree in 1931), and finally King's College at the University of London, where he earned a doctorate.

Bowen was admitted to King's College after one of his professors in Swansea noticed his interest in radio and thought it should be nurtured. Research for his degree took him in 1933 and 1934 to the British government's Radio Research Station in Slough, west of London, where he became familiar with the facility's cathode-ray direction-finder—a device used to determine the directional origin of a radio signal. At this time some in the British government worried that Germany's rising military might develop a radio-beam weapon, popularly known as a death ray, and some also wondered whether Britain might develop such a weapon for itself. The station superintendent, R.A. Watson-Watt, succeeded in convincing his superiors that the idea was impractical for both sides, but that radio energy might instead be used to detect planes in the air, well in advance of their entering visual range. The basic idea of radar went back to the early years of the twentieth century, but no one had previously advanced detailed ideas for its use in military combat.

Watson-Watt, a Scotsman, hired Bowen as a junior researcher, subjecting him only to a friendly interview in which he and a Scots deputy asked whether the Welsh Bowen could work effectively under two Scottish superiors. They challenged Bowen to sing the Welsh national anthem, a difficulty the flummoxed Bowen dodged by posing his interviewers the equally difficult challenge of singing Scotland's anthem. In June of 1935 Bowen joined the Radio Research Station as Junior Scientific Officer. Only at that point was the secret radar project revealed to the new employee, who hid the papers describing it between the sheets of his hotel bed and later returned from the hotel bar to find a hot water bottle on top of them. "That night," he wrote in *Radar Days,* "I had nightmares about swinging on the end of a gibbet on some lonely heath outside London. Next morning I made a point of chatting with the chambermaid and was relieved to find that she bore no resemblance to a Mata Hari but was a buxom country girl with an unmistakable Buckinghamshire accent."

Bowen moved with a group of researchers to the coastal Orfordness facility, now home to a major British Broadcasting System transmitter array. Assembling a rudimentary radar transmitter from a set of miscellaneous parts, he successfully demonstrated, on June 17, 1935, a visible radar reflection from a flying boat (an aircraft similar to a floatplane) at a range of 17 miles. By the beginning of the following year his radar unit could spot an approaching aircraft 100 miles away. At the time, the word "radar," an acronym for radio detection and ranging, was unknown (it was coined in 1941); Bowen's device was called an RDF, or radio direction finder. With these successes in place, Watson-Watt convinced the British military to authorize a more extensive radar program. The program split into two parts, one of them aimed at constructing a chain of radar stations to protect Britain's east coast. The other, highly speculative at the time, involved the idea of outfitting fighter planes with radar. Bowen was put in charge of the latter division and moved with other scientists into a large British country house, Bawdsey Manor.

Took Charge of Airborne Radar Project

"It was a delightful existence," Bowen recalled in *Radar Days.* "We worked hard and could often be found at work well after midnight. At the same time we were not averse to having a swim before lunch or a game of cricket on the magnficent lawn in front of the Manor before dinner." The Bawdsey team's first attempt at demonstrating its new radar station, in September of 1936, was a total failure: the planes were not detected until they were within audible range. But Bowen, working all night, set up the Orfordness transmitter and managed to make it work well enough for the second day's exercise to keep the Commander-in-Chief of Fighter Command Sir Hugh Dowding placated. Over the next two years, the team perfected a chain of radar stations covering England's eastern coast. When British prime minister Neville Chamberlain went to meet Adolf Hitler in Munich in 1938 on a doomed mission to try to placate the German dictator and stave off war, his plane was tracked by the Bawdsey group's radar stations, although Chamberlain was unaware of the tracking.

Bowen's specific task, that of fitting his new radar apparatus onto planes so that it could be used in combat, is difficult to imagine from the perspective of an era when transistors and other miniaturized electronic components are as common as nuts and bolts. Existing ground radars, noted the Australian Academy of Sciences Bowen biography, "would fill a small house, weighed several tons and took many kilowatts of power. Bowen decided that a viable airborne radar should not exceed 200 lbs. in weight, eight cubic feet in volume and 500 watts in power consumption and that, to reduce the aerodynamic drag of the antenna, the operating wavelength would have to be about one metre—a very short wavelength in those days." Bowen faced other problems, too, including the fact that fighter planes were not equipped with the alternating current required to power radar transmitters.

Between 1936 and 1939, with a combination of forward scientific thinking, engineering ingenuity, and an ability to lean on the Royal Air Force's suppliers and inspire them to new technological heights, Bowen solved these problems one by one. Numerous experiments with radio wavelengths pushed the entire science of radio forward. The system's sheer bulk was minimized by separating the radar's transmitter and receiver; transmitters were located on the ground, and planes were outfitted with receivers and indicators. Along the way were several more milestones in the history of radar. An unannounced test took place in September of 1937, when Bowen switched on his radar during a North Sea fleet exercise and, from the air with Navy and Coastal Command officers aboard, detected radar echoes of planes taking off from the battleship *Courageous.* This was, in the words of the Australian Academy of Sciences biography, "the first detection of an aircraft by a complete airborne radar," and Bowen himself called the event a landmark in the history of radar. In the midst of this critical activity, Bowen married Enid Vesta Williams, a science teacher; the couple raised three sons, Edward, David, and John.

Bowen spearheaded other technical breakthroughs, many connected with the radar detection of ships, and several major tests and demonstrations were carried out in the summer of 1939. But when war broke out in September of 1939 his focus partially changed from technical innovation to implementation. The scientists at the Bawdsey Research Station, by then known as the Air Ministry Research Establishment, was moved several times, with the personnel ending up at a maintenance facility in the Welsh town of St. Athan. Within a few months of the team's arrival, British aircraft were being equipped with AI (aircraft interceptor) or ASV (Air to Surface Vessels) radar at the rate of one per day. "It is very much to Bowen's credit that this was achieved in such difficult circumstances," noted the Australian Academy of Sciences.

Moved to U.S.

At this point Bowen began to experience personality conflicts with his superiors. The fruits of his innovations were reaped during the Battle of Britain; in addition to the key role played by Britain's chain of radar stations in neutralizing the effects of German air attacks, his AI radar took a deadly toll on German bombers. In May of 1941 more than 100 German aircraft were shot down during night raids by British planes, as compared with about 30 by ground-based antiaircraft guns. Bowen himself moved to the United States, where his job was to brief American scientists on the advances in radar technology that he and other British

researchers had achieved. His work led directly to the establishment of the Radiation Laboratory at the Massachusetts Institute of Technology (MIT) in late 1940; by the war's end the lab employed a staff of 4,000.

In 1943, with the tide of the war turning in the Allies' favor and his work in the United States approaching completion, Bowen accepted an offer from a group of Australian scientists to join the Radiophysics Laboratory in Sydney. Bowen would remain in Australia for the rest of his life, working on projects from the far-fetched (an attempt to correlate meteor showers to rainfall) to the potentially useful (stimulated by Australia's dry climate he became an early pioneer of cloud seeding), to the visionary. He was viewed as something of a boffin, an Anglo-Australian term denoting a brilliant but somewhat eccentric scientist. Many of his efforts from 1955 onward were applied to the development of the Parkes Telescope radioastronomy observatory, located in the desert several hundred kilometers west of Sydney, a project that he spearheaded.

Opened in 1961, the Parkes Telescope was one of the most advanced astronomy facilities in the world at the time, and it continues to operate today. As chairman of the Anglo-Australian Telescope commission, Bowen later supervised the development of an important optical telescope operated jointly by Australia and Great Britain; the Anglo-Australian Telescope was inaugurated in 1974. With a long list of honors beginning with the conferring of the Order of the British Empire in 1941, Bowen could have been honored even more frequently if he had agreed to take Australian citizenship, but he remained a Welshman to the end. He died in Sydney on August 12, 1991, after suffering for several years from the effects of a stroke.

Books

Bowen, Edward G., *Radar Days,* Adam Hilger, 1987.

Hanbury Brown, Robert, *Boffin,* 1991.

National Academy of Engineering (U.S. National Academy of Sciences), *Memorial Tributes: National Academy of Engineering, Volume 8 (1996),* p. 21.

Online

"Edward George Bowen: 1911–1991," Australian Academy of Science, http://www.science.org.au/academy/memoirs/bowen.htm (November 25, 2008).□

Abraham-Louis Breguet

French watchmaker and inventor Abraham-Louis Breguet (1747–1823) created timepieces that were in high demand among the European aristocracy of his day, both before and after the dramatic changes that the Revolution brought to France. He also devised several new mechanisms for the keeping and telling of accurate time. Sympathetic to republican politics, Breguet was a close friend of notable leftist figure Jean Paul Marat, but was nevertheless forced to flee the

country due to royalist connections. The Breguet watch company—founded by Breguet in 1775—has operated continuously since its inception and today produces luxury timepieces in Switzerland.

Abraham-Louis Breguet was born one of the seven children of a middle-class family in Neuchâtel, Switzerland, on January 10, 1747. His father, Jonas-Louis Breguet, died in 1758, leaving Breguet and two sisters partially orphaned; Jonas-Louis Breguet's cousin, Joseph Tattet, then married his widow, Marguerite (Bolle) Breguet, the mother of Abraham-Louis Breguet. The Tattet family hailed from nearby Les Verrieres and made a living both making and selling watches, the occupation in which the young Abraham-Louis Breguet would later make his mark.

Pursued Apprenticeship

Facts about Breguet's early life are scant. When he was fifteen, Breguet traveled to Versailles, home of the French royal court, to pursue an apprenticeship as a watchmaker presumably arranged by Tattet. He learned his art under respected craftsmen including Ferdinand Berthoud, who produced timepieces for the French monarch and the Navy, and Jean-Antoine Lépine, who made clocks for three different French kings. Within a few years, Breguet had also begun studies at the Collège Mazarin in Paris. There, the Abbé Joseph-François Marie instructed the young

apprentice in mathematics and culture, as well as reportedly introducing him to France's reigning monarch, Louis XVI. *Europa Star Online* said of the Abbé that "[t]his generous man would later take the young apprentice under his wing and provide protection and support for him and his younger sisters." During this time, Breguet also studied physics, astronomy, and the mechanical sciences. At some point prior to 1775, Breguet spent time in London, although precise details regarding his work there are slim. Writing in *It's About Time,* Paul Chamberlain argued that "[Breguet] acquired there the necessary skill to make jewels and may have been there for that purpose."

In about 1775, Breguet married Cécile-Marie-Louise L'huillier; the exact date of the marriage is unknown, but based on L'huillier's known birthyear—1752—it seems quite unlikely the marriage occurred before the early 1770s. The couple received assistance with the purchase of an apartment at 39 Quai de l'Horloge in Paris' Ile de la Cité as a wedding gift from L'huillier's father; the apartment was well-located in an area known for its prominent watchmakers, and Breguet would remain there throughout his life. (In fact, this apartment remained in the hands of Breguet's family for at least a century after the watchmaker's death.) In 1776, the couple had a son, Louis-Antoine. Although the couple had two other children, only this son survived childhood. Breguet's wife herself died after only a few years of marriage in 1780. The watchmaker never remarried, but instead relied on one of his younger sisters to assist with the management of his household throughout the remainder of his life.

In 1775, Breguet established his own watchmaking business at his apartment in the Ile de la Cité. He found success relatively quickly, assisted by his familial and social connections, and began providing watches to members of the aristocracy. The Duke d'Orléans became his first significant aristocratic client, and in 1782, the famed French queen Marie-Antoinette joined Breguet's client list. *Europa Star Online* noted that "with the queen's support, [Breguet's] reputation grew not only in France but all over the Continent." In 1784—less than ten years after opening his own company—Breguet received the designation of Master Watchmaker. He continued to attract clients from all facets of Europe's elite, which in turn helped him draw some of the finest craftsmen available to his business. Breguet was by all reports a beneficent employer and a skilled businessman, capable of putting his social skills to use to attract the kind of elite client to whom his company catered.

Associated with French Revolutionaries

Like many Frenchmen of his day, Breguet was interested in the growing republican movement taking place in Paris, a position that was not affected by his long-standing ties to the French aristocracy. Sometime in the late 1880s, Breguet met the radical political figure Jean Paul Marat—a fellow native of the Neuchâtel area of Switzerland—probably through Marat's sister, who produced watch parts for Breguet. Breguet became a member of the leftist Jacobin Club and eventually developed a close friendship with Marat. Despite Marat's increasing shift to the radical left, which Breguet did not share, the pair remained personal friends if not complete political allies.

Breguet remained in Paris during the early days of the French Revolution. In 1793, he assisted Marat with a dramatic escape from a royalist mob to a safehouse during one of the latter's visits to the city. When the mob appeared outside of a mutual friend's home where Breguet and Marat were dining, Breguet disguised Marat as a woman and then boldly strolled out of the house with the revolutionary through the crowd.

Breguet's own safety soon became endangered when the Revolutionary Committee ordered his death due to the watchmaker's longstanding royalist associations and in spite of Breguet's own revolutionary sympathies. In June 1793, Marat helped Breguet acquire a pass to travel safely to Switzerland; accompanied by his son and his sister, he soon escaped to that country. Although Breguet's son traveled to London to wait out the political turmoil in France, Breguet himself remained in Switzerland for the duration. Records of his stay there exist in the form of letters back to friends and relations in France; writing in *Smithsonian,* Allen Kurzwell noted that the letters "vividly describe a once-wealthy watchmaker reduced to concern about the shortage of lemons, eggs and lard, and the price of turkey and chicken."

Flourished in Later Years

In 1796, Breguet created a new payment system he dubbed "souscription," which allowed a purchaser to make a 25 per cent down payment on a particular watch and pay the remaining monies owed upon completion of the timepiece. A publicity brochure promoting this system was published the following year, and orders began rolling in. Kurzwell characterized the ensuing years as "the most comfortable period of his career," and by 1811, Breguet had achieved such success that his business brought in over 400,000 francs each year and employed dozens of watchmakers through the continent.

Breguet is associated with many improvements or inventions in the field of mechanical watchmaking, to the extent that Chamberlain commented that "[t]he ingenuity of Breguet has never been equaled and one never examines one of his productions without finding new evidences of it." The first invention with which Breguet is often credited is the "perpetuelle" watch in 1780; a device that relied on a system of pedometer winding, meaning that the natural movements of the wearer caused the watch to be self-winding. Modern scholarship, however, argues that watchmaker Abraham Louis Perrelet had designed the perpetuelle by 1777, and historical records document that watchmaker Hubert Sarton filed papers regarding such a watch in 1778.

Other inventions attributed to Breguet include a number of improved escapements—the "échappement naturel" in 1789; the constant force escapement in 1795; and the "tourbillon," or whirlwind, in 1801. In 1789, Breguet created a specialized ratchet key now known as the Breguet ratchet. He also designed a unique form of the ruby cylinder in the early 1790s and a "pendule sympathique," a contraption that wound and set watches overnight, in 1795. Well into his seventies, Breguet continued to innovate, working with Frédérick Louis Fatton to design the "encreur" timepiece in 1821.

Died at his Workshop

Experiencing practically no health problems other than failing hearing, Breguet continued to work in his later years. In 1814, he received an appointment to the Bureau of Longitude; the following year, he became the official Watchmaker to the Royal Navy. The year 1819 brought Breguet two major honors: first, King Louis XVIII nominated Breguet to the Académie of Sciences—recently reconfigured as the Institute of France—and soon after, Breguet was made a Chevalier of the prestigious Legion of Honor. He died at his workshop in Paris on September 17, 1823, at the age of 76, and was interred at Père Lachaise cemetery in Paris, where a statue of Breguet can still be seen today. The Breguet watchmaking firm—now owned by Swatch—has operated continuously since 1775 and still manufactures luxury mechanical timepieces in Switzerland.

The legacy of Breguet can be found not only in his own works and in the resilience of the Breguet watch company, but also in the works of his descendents. Breguet's son, Antoine-Louis, ran the family watchmaking business until 1833, when it was taken over by his own son and other relatives. This son, called Louis-Francois-Clément, was an inventor and scientist of some repute, accomplishing such diverse tasks as overseeing the building of telegraph lines, developing an electric clock and thermometer, and, according to tradition, building an early telephone for Alexander Graham Bell. Another descendent of Breguet—also named Louis—was active in aviation in the early 20th century, building an airplane in 1909, a hydroplane in 1912, and a precursor to the modern helicopter in 1917; this same descendent also founded the Compagnie des Messageries Aeriennes, which would later become Air France.

The many accomplished members of the Breguet family trace their lineage back to a man whom Chamberlain summed up by saying "[h]uman and brave, ingenious and resourceful, artist and artisan to whom mediocrity was unknown, Breguet shines as a star of the first magnitude, an inspiration to all lovers of the beautiful and good." Unquestionably, Breguet's contributions to the art of watchmaking remain relevant and important to contemporary life.

Books

Chamberlain, Paul M., *It's About Time,* Richard R. Smith, 1941.

Merriam-Webster's Biographical Dictionary, Merriam-Webster, 1995.

Periodicals

Smithsonian, May 1985.

Online

"Abraham-Louis Breguet," *Famous Watchmakers,* www.hautehorlogerie.org (January 7, 2009).

"Abraham-Louis Breguet, Keeper of Time" *Europa Star Online,* http://europastar.com/europastar/watch_tech/breghist.jsp (January 7, 2009).

"Abraham Louis Perrelet," *Famous Watchmakers,* www.hautehorlogerie.org (January 7, 2009). □

Laura Bridgman

Laura Bridgman (1829–1889) was the first deaf-blind individual ever to be taught the English language and educated beyond the level of simple manual tasks.

Bridgman lived half a century before Helen Keller, the deaf-blind author and lecturer whose story is taught to children around the world. As a result, her pioneering story has long been largely forgotten. Yet Keller herself cited Bridgman as a forerunner who made her own accomplishments possible, and she was taught by a woman who had worked with Bridgman and asked her for advice. Beyond its undoubtedly inspirational qualities, Bridgman's story is interesting because of its links to progressive intellectual and religious currents in the mid-nineteenth-century United States.

Laura Dewey Bridgman was born on December 21, 1829, in Etna, New Hampshire, near Hanover, into the farming family of Daniel and Harmony Bridgman. She was the third of three daughters; several younger brothers and sisters were born later. Bridgman suffered episodes of poor health as a baby but was quick with language, learning to speak in complete sentences and starting to try to read by the time she reached the age of two. But a month after her second birthday she and her two older sisters contracted scarlet fever. Her sisters died, and Laura was at death's door for a week. She began to recover, but her parents quickly realized that she was both blind and deaf, and she had also lost most of her sense of smell. Bedridden for two years, she finally grew stronger. She could still see light dimly in one eye, but that ability was lost after she walked into a spinning wheel spindle.

Bridgman remembered how to speak a few words after her illness, but, completely deaf, could not hear her own words or the answers of others. Gradually she forgot all traces of English and began to communicate in pantomime. She retained a basic curiosity about the world, helped with household work such as sewing and churning butter, and enjoyed country walks with a neighbor named Asa Tenny. But her parents found discipline a difficult job without the aid of language. Educational reformer Samuel Gridley Howe read about Bridgman in a newspaper and visited Hanover, offering to house and educate the young girl at his new Perkins Institute for the Blind in Boston (now the Perkins School for the Blind, in Watertown, Massachusetts), and Daniel and Harmony Bridgman readily agreed to the arrangement. Laura entered the school in 1837, when she was eight.

Howe's personality included a classically American mixture of humanitarian generosity, ambition, and fascination with new theories about human nature and psychology. He had recently returned from Europe, where he fought in the Greek war of independence against the Ottoman Empire and became acquainted with a range of new ideas. Like some Romantic-era poets and philosophers, he was fascinated by the idea of a pure human soul, untouched by the realm of experience. Howe believed that the human mind was not a blank slate shaped purely by experience, but that language,

thought, and even morality and conscience were distinct mental faculties that every human being possessed. In Bridgman, he saw an ideal vehicle for the testing of these ideas—if he could find a way to communicate with her. Howe also became a member of the Unitarian church, which rejected the biblical concepts of original sin as well as the divinity of Christ.

At first Bridgman was upset at being moved to the Perkins Institute, but she quickly adapted to her new surroundings. Soon Howe began his teaching program. He and his assistants attached labels with raised lettering to a variety of objects in a room. Bridgman was given a copy of the label and asked to feel it. Then she was led to the object itself, feeling its label until she could determine that it was the same as the detached one bearing the object's name. Within a few days she had realized that objects had names, and was attaching labels of her own to pieces of furniture. Next, Howe broke the labels into individual letters. Bridgman knew that they could be joined together to form the names she had learned, but it took her time to grasp the idea that she could make words of her own and express her ideas in language. Howe described a scene similar to one found in Helen Keller's writings, in which this knowledge came to Bridgman in a flash of inspiration, but it seems likelier that she acquired it gradually.

Howe's next step, now that Bridgman understood words and letters, was to teach her a manual alphabet, also known as fingerspelling—an alphabet of letters that can be formed by the hands (usually with one hand) and thus perceived visually or by touching the "speaker." After three months, Bridgman had learned about a hundred nouns. Then she began to learn about verbs, which enabled her to hold actual conversations with her teachers and with other blind students at the Institute. She also learned to write in a distinctive blocky script, using paper with small grooves to keep her writing neatly aligned, and within a year she could tell a short story. A year after that, she could write letters home.

By that time, Bridgman's mother had already come to visit her in Boston. A heartrending scene unfolded as Bridgman at first failed to recognized her mother's hands and clothes but then was overcome with emotion as her tactile memories reawakened. Such events, retold in Howe's annual reports on Bridgman's progress, began to publicize Howe's accomplishment, and visitors began to come to the Institute to see the deaf-blind girl who had learned to read and write. Bridgman, who always wore a ribbon across her damaged eyes, was soon famous across the city of Boston and then beyond, and young girls sometimes even gouged out the eyes of their dolls and named them Laura. Pretty and polite, Bridgman drew a steady stream of visitors. With the example of Helen Keller in mind, public excitement over Howe's accomplishment is difficult to appreciate, but it should be borne in mind that prior to Howe's efforts the deaf-blind were considered completely unable to learn.

Bridgman's fame became international when English novelist Charles Dickens came to visit and penned a glowing description of her in his *American Notes* (1842), writing in a letter to Howe that the visit to Bridgman and seeing Niagara Falls were the two highlights of his trip to the United States. Howe visited England in 1843 and was hailed as a deep thinker and teacher. His new bride, future "Battle Hymn of the Republic" text composer Julia Ward Howe, wrote (as quoted by Bridgman biographer Ernest Freeberg) that "London has rung with my husband's praises.... Everybody comes to see him, and to talk about Laura Bridgman."

Howe's marriage and increasingly frequent departures from the Perkins Institute caused changes in Bridgman's personality. Naturally enough on both counts, she had become deeply attached to Howe as a father figure and began to experience emotional swings as she entered adolescence. She had a tendency toward violent temper tantrums, and at one point a teacher who had ordered Bridgman to put a handkerchief in her desk noticed that she was becoming angrier and angrier. The teacher recounted (according to an early biography quoted on the Female Ancestors Web site) that Bridgman "uttered the most frightful yell I ever heard." She later learned to control these reactions to a degree. But something new came between teacher and student: Bridgman began to have religious ideas of her own.

Howe had envisioned a grand finale to his education of Bridgman in which he inculcated in her a Unitarian vision of a loving God who could be experienced by enlightened humans through an inborn organ of veneration in the brain. He tried to isolate her from the more conservative brands of Christianity that were contending for supremacy with reformers of like mind with Howe, but visitors exposed her to conventional ideas about the path toward salvation and everlasting life. To Howe's chagrin, Bridgman began to gravitate

back toward the Baptist faith of her parents. She moved back to New Hampshire for a time, returning to Boston after she became homesick for the Institute where she had spent most of her life. But she continued to spend summer vacations at her parents' farm. In the early 1860s, on one of those visits, she began attending a New Hampshire church after the death of her sister Mary. She taught the minister the manual alphabet so that she could converse with him. She was baptized in Thetford, Vermont. In her later years Bridgman wrote simple but original religious poetry.

Howe was absent from Bridgman's life for long periods as he became more deeply involved in the struggle to abolish slavery in the United States. But he continued to provide for his charge, working with early feminist Dorothea Dix to raise a fund to be used to support her. Bridgman lived out the rest of her life at the Perkins Institute, living in a small cottage on the grounds in her later years. Visitors gradually lost interest in her. "It's an old, bitter story in the disabled community," Bridgman biographer Elisabeth Gitter told Jennifer K. Ruark of the *Chronicle of Higher Education*. "Everybody loves a disabled child, but the adults suddenly aren't so cute." But Bridgman lived quietly, making money from small knitted or sewn items she would sell to visitors and sometimes giving the proceeds to the homeless when she was taken for walks around Boston. She had a keen sense of humor that she was even able to express in writing. Satirizing the Institute's strict program of moral teaching, she wrote in her journal after a rat invaded her room that "he ought to have a conscience on purpose to reprove himself very much. I must ask W. to please teach him about doing right & wrong."

As Perkins instructor Annie Sullivan prepared to go south to Alabama to try to teach Helen Keller to read and write, she familiarized herself closely with Bridgman's story and directly asked Bridgman for advice. Bridgman and Keller even met briefly a few years before Bridgman's death on May 24, 1889 (after which a plaster cast of her brain was made and placed in the Perkins School archives, where it still resides). Keller eventually outstripped Bridgman's accomplishments, writing essays and becoming known worldwide as a lecturer. But until that time Bridgman's story was told to nineteenth-century children, much as Keller's is a staple of school curricula today. Decades after Bridgman's death, no less a figure than the American philosopher and psychologist William James recalled (according to Freeberg) that "there could never have been a Helen Keller if there had not been a Laura Bridgman."

Books

Freeberg, Ernest, *The Education of Laura Bridgman: First Deaf and Blind Person to Learn Lanuage,* Harvard, 2001.

Gitter, Elisabeth, *The Imprisoned Guest: Samuel Howe and Laura Bridgman, the Original Deaf-Blind Girl,* Farrar, Straus & Giroux, 2001.

Lamson, Mary Swift, *The Life and Education of Laura Dewey Bridgman,* Houghton, Mifflin, 1881.

Periodicals

Chronicle of Higher Education, April 6, 2001.

Online

"Laura Bridgman," Female Ancestors, http://www.female-ancestors. com/daughters/bridgman.htm (December 5 2008). □

Charles Tilston Bright

English telegraph engineer Charles Tilston Bright (1832–1888) contributed to the growing 19th century communications field of telegraphy. He supervised the establishment of the first transatlantic telegraph cable and later oversaw the laying of underwater cables connecting distant points around the globe. Bright's efforts garnered him a knighthood, and he went on to serve as a member of the British Parliament.

The descendent of two eminent Yorkshire families, Charles Tilston Bright was born the youngest son of Brailsford Bright on June 8, 1832, near Wanstead, Essex, England. (Bright's grandmother, the goddaughter of famed Admiral Horatio Nelson, was the source of the family name Tilston.) Bright attended the Merchant Taylors School along with brothers William and Edward, where he showed greater talents in sporting than in academic pursuits. He particularly enjoyed boating, and showed an early interest in electricity and chemistry. A financial downturn in the Bright family prevented Bright and his brothers from pursing planned further studies at Oxford University.

Achieved Professional Success as a Youth

In about 1847, Bright took a position as a telegraph clerk with the nascent Electric Telegraph Company, working at Harrow railway station. Soon, his elder brothers joined him at the Electric Telegraph Company; William Bright quickly left for other pursuits, but Edward Bright, as Charles Bright noted in *The Life Story of Sir Charles Tilston Bright*, "was more or less in double harness with Charles throughout their lives." The two brothers began devising improvements for existing telegraphy equipment, noting their ideas in a log. These early ideas, including a design for a system to locate faults in telegraph wires, formed the basis of an 1852 patent.

In 1851, Bright left the Electric Telegraphy Company for a position as assistant engineer with the British Telegraph Company; however, he left that firm the following year to join the growing Magnetic Telegraph Company, where his brother was the manager, as its chief engineer. At this firm, Bright's initial duties lie primarily in the refining of the devices patented by the two brothers as well as the oversight of a growing telegraphic system throughout the British isles. These lines—over 7,000 miles in total—stretched as far as Scotland and Ireland and marked, in 1853, the first successful establishment of an undersea telegraph cable, for which Bright received general public accolades. In May 11 of that same year, Bright married Hannah

Taylor in Hull, England; the couple would later have two daughters, Agnes and Mary Angela, and one son, Charles.

Laid First Transatlantic Cable

By 1855, Bright and his brother had begun considering the technology required to successfully lay telegraphic cables in deep waters with the intention of creating a transatlantic telegraph line. Meanwhile, an American businessman, Cyrus Field, had independently become interested in a similar venture on the opposite side of the Atlantic. Bright met with Field in 1855 to discuss the possibility of such a project. The following year, Bright, Field, and John Watkins Brett established the Atlantic Telegraph Company to further the construction of a transatlantic line; a fourth business partner, Edward Orange Wildman Whitehouse, soon joined the enterprise. Armed with financial subsidies from both the American and British governments for the completion of a functional transatlantic line, the company began operation in October 1856. It took only a few short weeks to raise the necessary funds, primarily from backers of the Magnetic Telegraph Company, some of whom also took leadership roles in the Atlantic Telegraph Company. Bright served as engineer-in-chief of the new endeavor.

Soon, the route that the cable would take—reaching from Valentia Island, Ireland, to the town of Heart's Content in Trinity Bay, Newfoundland, Canada—was determined and plans were begun. The backers of the Atlantic Telegraph Company urged the rapid execution of the project, and Bright quickly began supervising the construction of the materials and hiring the necessary employees for the task. As the biographer Bright noted, the engineer's responsibilities were great: "He had to select ships suitable to carry two thousand five hundred miles of cable, and to prepare them to receive it, together with the machinery ... [and] there was the necessity for more or less constant attendance on the directors—meeting as they did almost daily—and the preparation of frequent reports." Bright also devised a somewhat more durable and sophisticated mechanism for feeding cable from ship to water.

On August 4, 1857, preparations were complete and Bright set out from Valentia Bay on one of the ships that would lay the transatlantic cable. The cable snapped only days later, however, and the attempt to cross the Atlantic was temporarily halted. Bright began preparations for a second attempt in earnest, seeking to repair the mechanical errors that had caused the breakage of the first cable. The following summer, the ships again set out, and again faced failure. Several directors of the Atlantic Telegraph Company resigned, but Bright refused to give up hope of success. A third attempt would bring that success, as the cable laying was at last completed on August 5, 1858. A few days later, Bright became the youngest person to receive a knighthood in recognition of his work on the project. Unfortunately, Bright faced disappointment three months later when the cable failed and telegraphic communications ceased. He began investigating the cause of the failure, and it was eventually determined that the cables had carried too much electrical power.

Formed Partnership and Served in Parliament

Despite the ultimate disappointment of the transatlantic cable, Bright continued to work with submerged cables. In 1860, he oversaw the completion of a series of cable for Spain. The following year, Bright decided to retire from his position as chief engineer and assume a consulting role with Magnetic, which he would hold until the nationalization of the telegraph in 1870. After retiring from his full-time post at the Magnetic Telegraph Company, Bright formed a partnership with Latimer Clark, who had worked for many years as an engineer with the Electric and International Telegraph Company. The pair soon presented a seminal report on the standardization of electrical units and measurements to the British Association for the Advancement of Science. In this paper, Bright and Clark suggested the use of the ohm, volt, ampere (amp), farad, and coulomb; twenty years later, these units were officially adopted by an international group and they remain in use today. Additionally, Bright and Clark investigated and developed an improved form of insulation for underwater telegraph cables.

In 1862, the British government approached Bright regarding the establishment of a submerged telegraph cable to India, enabling faster communication between England and its then-imperial holding. A line had been laid in the 1850s, but had broken down within days of completion; Bright became the technical adviser to the new Telegraph to India company, which was charged with the task of making these faulty lines functional. After inspection, Bright's partner Clark discovered that parts of the lines were unsalvageable

and plans were made to lay some new cable in the Persian Gulf area. Bright devised several improvements to existing telegraph cables for this project, including an insulation that deterred destruction of the cable by shipworms, a common problem in the region.

By November 1863, nearly 1,500 miles of cable had been made and the laying of the Indian line commenced. Bright traveled to Mumbai to await the completion of the project, which was being constructed in four parts stretching between the mouth of the Persian Gulf and the city of Karachi, on the northwestern tip of the Indian peninsula in what is now Pakistan. Bright then personally oversaw the laying of the cable between Gwadar—also located in present-day Pakistan—and the Persian Gulf during the winter and spring of 1864. The line was fully completed in May and Bright returned to England soon after.

In 1865, Bright decided to seek election as a Member of Parliament from Greenwich, choosing that location due to his long-standing ties with a number of its constituents who had worked for him during the construction of the transatlantic cable. He ran on a moderate platform and, attracting the support of both moderate liberal and conservative groups in the district, was elected as a Liberal to one of Greenwich's two Parliamentary seats alongside the sitting representative, Alderman Salomans. Bright was by all accounts a conscientious public servant; he held the seat until 1868, when he chose not to seek reelection due to his concurrent professional obligations. During his tenure, Bright worked to arrange for favorable terms for the telegraphic companies in the national government's buyout of the telegraph wires and to support issues related to impoverished Londoners.

Later Years and Legacy

In 1873, Bright settled with his family in the then relatively new neighborhood of South Kensington, London. He began work on a book about electricity and telegraphy, but as "a man of action rather than of words," as the biographer Bright accurately characterized him, he never completed this endeavor. Instead, Bright turned his attention to the problem of laying a telegraph line between Spain and the Canary Islands and visited Spain and Portugal to further these efforts; ultimately, his work contributed to the formation of the Spanish National Telegraph Company.

At about this time, Bright, along with his brother, became involved in the establishment of a mining operation in Serbia. The mines performed well, and the brothers acquired more land over the next few years; however, when Serbia and neighboring Montenegro declared war on the Ottoman Empire in 1876, both supplies and workers for the mines fell into short supply and the mines' profits dwindled. Despite efforts to return the operation to prosperity, the brothers eventually closed down the mines.

In the late 1870s, Bright experimented with a new fire alarm system capable of remotely alerting fire houses of blazes through telegraphic technology; this device was exhibited in Paris in 1881 and London in 1882 to great acclaim and was subsequently installed in London and other cities. He also became interested in the growing field of telephony and served as a consulting engineer to the new British Electric Light Company. Until the time of his death, Bright remained active in matters relating to the development and practical application of electrical light technology. In 1887, Bright served as president of the Society of Electrical Engineers and Electricians.

Bright had experienced ongoing health problems throughout the years and suffered from what his biographer Bright described as "various worries and the need of an entire rest from work." This declining health led to Bright's death from heart failure on May 3, 1888, in Abbey Wood, outside of London, England, at the age of 55. Following a funeral service, Bright was interred among his family members at Chiswick, London.

The contemporary press gave much notice to Bright's death, celebrating his contributions to the telegraphic field; an obituary in the *Electrical Review*, quoted by the biographer Bright, proclaimed: "We may, indeed, safely assume that so long as the broad Atlantic, separated by its broad expanse of water from this country, carries at its utmost depths the electric connecting chain of communication, so long will the name of the Atlantic and its first cable be connected with that of Charles Tilston Bright." Although time and the decline of the telegraph in the face of improved 20th century technology has diminished the fame of Bright, his contributions to the growth of intercontinental communications unquestionably helped shape the modern world.

Books

Bright, Charles, *The Life Story of Sir Charles Tilston Bright, Civil Engineer,* Archibald Constable & Co., 1908.

Online

"Sir Charles Tilston Bright," *Encyclopedia Brittanica Online,* http://search.eb.com/eb/article-9016452 (November 20, 2008).

"Timeline: The Great Transatlantic Cable," *American Experience: The Great Transatlantic Cable: Timeline PBS:* http://www.pbs.org/wgbh/amex/cable/timeline/index.html (December 21, 2008). □

Arthur Brisbane

The American journalist Arthur Brisbane (1864–1936) was among the most widely read newspaper writers of the early twentieth century, as well as one of the most powerful executives in the American newspaper world.

Brisbane did much to give the mass-market American newspaper its modern form. As an editor he had an almost unerring instinct for how to build circulation, relying on the sensational headlines and feature stories associated with so-called yellow journalism. He was quick to champion such innovations as color comics. But most of all, Brisbane was known for his own columns, which were read by millions of people every week. Literati might debate whether or not Brisbane was a talented writer, but he had a distinctive style that would be imitated for decades to come. American journalism was fundamentally shaped by his one-sentence paragraphs, loaded with high drama, filled with deep if sometimes crudely oversimplifying historical references, and effective in breaking down complex issues to a set of formulas to which readers could easily relate.

Arthur Brisbane was born on December 12, 1864, in Buffalo, New York. Brisbane's family, earlier members of whom had been among the earliest European settlers of western New York State, was both well-off and politically radical; his father, Albert Brisbane, was a follower of the utopian French socialist Charles Fourier. After his mother died when he was two, young Arthur Brisbane was raised in various households in the New York City area. He was sent to Europe to study when he was 13 and remained there for more than five years, soaking up contemporary trends in social thought from tutors. But he showed little interest in his father's socialist ideas.

Back in New York in 1883, Brisbane found himself at a loss regarding the direction of his career. His father pulled strings to get him installed as a reporter for the New York *Sun,* a newspaper that at the time had literary pretensions. The paper's rather dissolute veteran staff thought little of Brisbane's early writing efforts, but he got the chance to break into print when the regular sportswriter, assigned to cover a boxing match involving champion John L. Sullivan, was too drunk to file his story. Brisbane impressed *Sun* editor Charles Dana with a story in which he described in detail the dynamiting of a ledge over the East River as part of a public works project. When Albert Brisbane, after 18 months, pulled his son off the staff so that he could go on a family trip to Europe, Arthur wrote letters to Dana describing the goings-on in European capitals. After buttering up the editor in this way, Brisbane suggested that he return to the *Sun* payroll as its London correspondent, and Dana agreed.

Brisbane filed dispatches about the Jack the Ripper murders in London, and about the great political figures serving during the height of the British Empire. Through a friendship with the son of former British prime minister William Ewart Gladstone, he got to know the aging politician himself. He later recalled, as quoted in Oliver Carlson's *Brisbane: A Candid Biography,* that he "sat at the feet of the old religionist, learning from him all the tricks of moral and political hypocrisy." But the story that made Brisbane a marketable journalistic property was a vivid, tear-jerking account he wrote about Sullivan's defense of his heavyweight boxing title against Charley Mitchell in Paris, France, on March 10, 1888. He had become the *Sun*'s night editor during a stint in New York the previous year.

Among those paying attention to the rising young editor was the legendary newspaper magnate Joseph Pulitzer, who hired Brisbane away from the *Sun* in 1890. Pulitzer took Brisbane back to Europe once again as a traveling companion, turning him into a protégé and instructing him in the ways of the newspaper trade. Back in New York, Brisbane wrote feature articles and edited various editions of Pulitzer's *New York World.* In 1896 he became the editor of the *World*'s new Sunday edition. Brisbane brought the latest experiments in the newspaper industry, such as color comics, garish illustrations, and banner headlines, to bear on the new project. Among the journalistic institutions that got its start during Brisbane's tenure at the *World* was a comic strip called "The Kid of Hogan's Alley," by R.F. Outcault. Dubbed "The Yellow Kid" because of the bright yellow clothing of one of its characters, the strip in turn lent that name to the populist-oriented newspaper style, heavily influenced by Brisbane, that came to be called yellow journalism.

In 1896 and 1897, the circulation of the *Sunday World* was increasing at a rate of 11,000 subscriptions per week, and Brisbane was gaining a reputation as a journalist with a magic touch. But he wanted more—specifically, he wanted to see his own words in an editorial column on the front page. Taking matters into his own hands, he ran one of his own columns in a prominent spot. Pulitzer, who wanted the *World*'s editorials to reflect his own voice exclusively, sent him a telegram ordering that he stop. The result of the dispute was that, later in 1897, Brisbane accepted an offer from Pulitzer's rival, William Randolph Hearst, to become editor of the New York *Evening Journal.* It was the beginning of a relationship that would last for the rest of Brisbane's life: he would become Hearst's top lieutenant, and he was in large part the figure who shaped the products of Hearst's journalistic empire.

Spurred by circulation-based bonuses, Brisbane repeated and then exceeded his successes at the *World.* The *Evening Journal*'s circulation, which had stood at about 40,000 copies when Brisbane arrived, surpassed the daily *World*'s figure of 325,000 in just seven weeks. Brisbane did not let up, running garish headlines and often misleading stories, some of which have been blamed for fanning the war fever that led to the involvement of the United States in the Spanish-American War of 1898. As the *Journal*'s circulation soared toward the million-copy mark, Hearst rewarded Brisbane with salary increases, first to $50,000 and then to $70,000 a year. In 1900 Hearst sent Brisbane to Chicago to establish a new Hearst paper in that city, called the *American.* Brisbane remained the paper's official editor until his death, but he soon left subordinates in charge and returned to his office in New York.

In the late 1890s Brisbane became a fierce opponent of President William McKinley, even writing one editorial that contained veiled references to assassination, but after McKinley's assassination in 1901 he heaped praise on the slain leader. Such reversals were characteristic of Brisbane's political stances, which had a general populist flavor but tended to shift with the prevailing winds rather than being strongly fixed. Heavily pro-war in 1898, he opposed U.S. entry into World War I so vociferously that he was accused of sympathizing with Germany. He supported the succession of Republican presidents that ruled the United States in the 1920s but backed Franklin Delano Roosevelt in 1932, only to turn once again and become a foe of Roosevelt's New Deal economic stimulus measures.

Brisbane went on to start or acquire papers for Hearst in Washington, D.C., San Francisco, California, and Milwaukee, Wisconsin, where, as quoted in the *Dictionary of Literary Biography,* he complained to the local editor he had retained on staff that "the editorials you write make people think. Editorials should make people think they think." Brisbane's own editorials were accompanied by large, cartoon-like illustrations. During the roaring 1920s, his partnership with Hearst broadened beyond journalism into real estate; the two built New York's Ziegfeld Theatre and co-owned a group of hotels. Brisbane himself moved into a 3,000-acre estate in suburban Allaire, New Jersey, often sleeping in an open-air penthouse because he thought the fresh air was healthful. He married for the first time in 1912, at age 47. He and his wife, Phoebe Cary Brisbane, had six children: Seward, Sarah, Emily, Hugo, Alice, and Elinor.

Despite his business associations with Hearst and his many daily duties as editor, Brisbane found time to do plenty of writing of his own, and indeed it was as a writer that most Americans of his time would have recognized him. His daily editorials, which he composed aloud using a Dictaphone recording machine that he often carried with him as he was chauffeured around Manhattan, took him only 15 minutes to write. That left him time to write for magazines such as *Cosmopolitan,* which at the time was a general-interest news publication. Brisbane also wrote several books; some were compilations of his newspaper columns, but several, including *How to Be a Better Reporter* (1933) were written from scratch. From 1917 until the end of his life, Brisbane wrote a syndicated column called

Today, which at its peak appeared in more than 200 daily newspapers, often on the front page. Repackaged as *This Week,* Brisbane's columns appeared in about a thousand weeklies.

Evaluations of Brisbane as a writer varied. *Time,* in its Brisbane obituary, referred to what it and many other print outlets called "Brisbanalities"—trite observations such as "There is more in any woman than any man can learn in 50 lifetimes." But Brisbane's columns were highly readable, peppered with a seemingly effortless range of historical allusions, for which he could thank his European education. "Marie Antoinette staked thousands of louis at a time at Versailles," he wrote in an editorial on gambling that was reproduced in a collection appearing on the Project Gutenberg Web site. And "She was so wrapped up in gambling she could not see that her neck was in danger." Among Brisbane's most widely acclaimed journalistic accomplishments was a sympathetic interview he did with Christian Science founder Mary Baker Eddy, originally appearing in *Cosmopolitan* in 1907 and later expanded into a book. Brisbane's admirers were legion, and after his death, writer Damon Runyon told *Time* that "journalism has lost its all-time No. 1 genius." The magazine estimated that he had reached 30 million readers a day.

Brisbane took over the editorship of Hearst's tabloid *New York Daily Mirror* in 1934, but was unable to repeat his former turnaround magic. He left the paper's staff after two years. Brisbane suffered from cardiac problems in his last years but continued to write prolifically. He dictated part of a Christmas Day column on the evening of December 24, 1936, but was forced to stop and turn the remainder over to his son Seward. The conclusion was said to contain the only words ever to appear under Brisbane's name that he did not write himself. He died on Christmas morning in 1936.

Books

Carlson, Oliver, *Brisbane: A Candid Biography,* Stackpole, 1937.

Contemporary Authors Online, Gale, 2008.

Dictionary of Literary Biography, Vol. 25: American Newspaper Journalists, 1901–1925, edited by Perry J. Ashley, Gale, 1984.

Online

"Death of Brisbane," *Time,* January 4, 1937, http://www.time.com/time/magazine/article/0,9171,762350,00. html (December 19, 2008).

"The Historic Village at Allaire," http://www.allairevillage.org/Bios/ArthurBrisbane.htm (December 19, 2008).

"The Project Gutenberg Etext of Editorials from the Hearst Newspapers by Arthur Brisbane," Gutenberg.org, http://www.gutenberg.org/dirs/etext96/ehnab10.txt (December 19, 2008). □

Max Brod

The Czech Jewish writer Max Brod (1884–1968) produced a large body of fiction treating many aspects of European and later Israeli life, as well as nonfiction of various kinds. He remains best known, however, for preserving the writings of Franz Kafka, one of the greatest German-language writers of the twentieth century.

Brod came into possession of Kafka's writings because the two were friends—in Kafka's case among the few friends he had. With death from tuberculosis approaching, Kafka asked that his unpublished manuscripts be destroyed, but Brod decided that they should be available for future generations of readers. He took on the difficult task of editing writings in various stages of completion and organization, and readying them for publication. Later he wrote the first major biography of Kafka. Kafka's writings were sparse, consisting of three novels and a group of short stories. Brod, by contrast, was extremely prolific, publishing new writing during almost every year of his long life. Brod's own writings, strongly Central European in flavor, have attracted only a limited readership in the English-speaking world, but he remains well known in German-speaking countries and in Israel, where he settled after fleeing the Nazi seizure of Czechoslovakia in the months before World War II.

Suffered from Spine Ailment

Max Brod was born in Prague, then under the rule of the Austro-Hungarian monarchy, on May 27, 1884. Kafka was less than a year older, and both writers grew up in German-speaking Jewish families. Unlike Kafka (at least overtly), Brod would go on to focus on his Jewish identity in many of his writings. Brod's father, Adolf, worked at a bank, and the family had money to travel to Germany in search of treatment, ultimately unsuccessful, for Brod's curved spine. Brod was a talented student and overcame obstacles facing most Jews in Central European universities to obtain a law degree from the University of Prague in 1907. It was there that he befriended Kafka, who was also a law student, and both worked quietly for many years in the Austro-Hungarian government bureaucracy while pursuing their writing on the side. Kafka was an insurance lawyer, while Brod worked for 17 years for the empire's postal service. The two enjoyed going on hiking trips in the hills outside Prague. In 1913 Brod married Eva Taussig, the daughter of a Prague wholesaler. He was a press officer for the Republic of Czechoslovakia in the 1920s, and in 1929 he became an arts editor at the *Prager Tageblatt* newspaper.

At the university in Prague, Brod and Kafka were part of a group of several young intellectuals who helped shape Austrian culture between the two world wars. One was the poet and novelist Franz Werfel, later the author of *The Song of Bernadette.* Younger than Brod, he, like Kafka, benefited from Brod's encouragement. Although he wrote exclusively in German, his native language, Brod did not identify himself as a German writer. He greeted with enthusiasm the establishment of the independent nation of Czechoslovakia in the aftermath of World War I, spoke Czech, and worked closely with Czech-language writers. Among them was Jaroslav Hasek, whose novel *The Good Soldier Schwejk* Brod

adapted as a stage play. He also knew the composer Leos Janacek, translated the texts of some of Janacek's vocal music into German, and wrote his biography.

Brod's own writing career began in 1906 with the publication of a book of short stories called *Tod den Toten!* (Death to the Dead). His first novel, *Schloss Nornepygge* (Nornepygge Castle), was written in 1908 but not published until 1919; it did not attract attention in the Austrian capital of Vienna, but in Germany, the homeland of the expressionist movement, it won praise as an early example of that movement's techniques. Brod's early writings showed him experimenting with the various styles of the day, expressionism among them. Some of his books had the nihilistic turn-of-the-century mood associated with the bitter comedies of playwright Arthur Schnitzler, and Brod even coined a word, "Indifferentismus," to describe his one-man literary movement. *Schloss Nornepygge* was subtitled "Der Roman des Indifferenten," or The Novel of the Indifferent Man.

After this downbeat early phase, Brod became more interested in his Jewish identity. He wrote novels on several different kinds of Jewish themes. Some, such as *Arnold Beer: Das Schicksal eines Juden* (Arnold Beer: The Fate of a Jew, 1912), dealt with Jewish society in Prague and with the relationships between Jews and non-Jews. Brod also became interested in Zionism—the movement to establish a Jewish homeland in British-controlled Palestine—and the growing Jewish settlements in what became the nation of Israel played a part in several of Brod's novels of the 1920s

and 1930s. *Abenteuer in Japan* (1938), which dealt with a businessman who sees through a plan to resettle European Jews in Japan, was co-written with Brod's brother Otto, who later died in a Nazi concentration camp. Several of Brod's Zionist-oriented novels reflect tensions between Europe and Palestine in characters' lives. *Der H'gel ruft: ein kleiner Roman* (The Hill Calls, 1942), for example, features a woman named Ruth who lives on a kibbutz in Palestine but is also romantically involved with a Czech composer.

Heard Early Drafts of Kafka Novel

Brod's friendship with Kafka continued as his own career developed. As Kafka worked on *The Trial,* considered one of his greatest novels, he read his longhand manuscript aloud to Brod. In gratitude for Brod's having served as a sounding board, Kafka gave the manuscript to Brod as a gift in 1920. Brod's connection to Kafka's legacy deepened after Kafka's death from tuberculosis in 1924. Kafka had designated Brod as the executor of his literary estate, which at the time consisted of just a few published short stories. Kafka had asked that the manuscripts of his novels and his many unpublished short stores be burned, Weighing his promise to his friend against the value he saw in Kafka's works, he began working to make sense of Kafka's heavily revised manuscripts, several of which were uncertain in their chapter ordering. Later scholars have questioned some of Brod's editorial decisions, but his closeness to Kafka's creative process has counted in Brod's favor. *The Trial* was published (in German, as Der Prozess) in 1925. *Das Scholoss* (The Castle) followed in 1926, and the unfinished novel *Amerika* appeared in 1927.

Brod's connection with Kafka's manuscripts continued beyond that initial decision. As Kafka's literary executor, he retained a large collection of Kafka's personal materials. On the night before German troops rolled into Prague in March of 1939, Brod and his wife escaped into Romania, soon making their way to Tel Aviv in what was then British-ruled Palestine. He continued to administer Kafka's literary estate, shipping the materials to neutral Switzerland in 1956 when the Egyptian-Israeli conflict over the Suez Canal threatened to erupt into full-scale war. Finally, in 1961, he donated most of the Kafka material to the Bodleian Library at Oxford University in England; he had been requested to do so by the children of Kafka's sisters, who were killed during the Holocaust. He kept the manuscript of *The Trial* for himself, finally giving it to an acquaintance. It was sold at auction in 1988. Brod edited Kafka's diaries and wrote several nonfiction books about his friend.

Meanwhile, Brod's writings themselves commanded a wide readership. He was perhaps best known for a trio of historical novels: *Tycho Brahes Weg zu Gott* (1916, translated as *The Redemption of Tycho Brahe* in 1928), about the Danish astronomer named in the title; *Rëubeni, Fürst der Juden* (1925, translated as *Reubeni, Prince of the Jews* in 1928), which dealt with Judaism and the Spanish Inquisition; and *Galilei in Gefangenschaft* (Galileo in Prison, 1948), a treatment of the famed Italian astronomer's persecution at the hands of religious authorities. Brod considered the three novels a trilogy, titling it *Ein Kampf um*

Wahrheit, (or A Fight for Truth). *Rëubeni, Fürst der Juden* won the Czechoslovak State Prize for literature, and *Galilei in Gefangenschaft* was awarded Israel's Bialik Prize despite objections that the award should have gone to a Hebrew-language writer. Brod continued to write historical novels, a decision that probably dented his popularity after World War II as the historical novel fell out of fashion.

Depicted Prague in Fiction

However, Brod had many other interests as well. He wrote about contemporary events, touching on the establishment of the nation of Israel in *Unambo: Roman aus dem jüdisch-arabischen Krieg* (1949, translated in 1952 as *Unambo: A Novel of the War in Israel*). Several of his books dealt with love, either sentimental or erotic, and like his contemporary Thomas Mann he often focused in his writing on creative artists and their philosophical growth. One of his most important achievements lay in his depictions of the culturally rich city of Prague, the setting for novels as early as *Ein tschechisches Dienstmädchen* (A Czech Servant Girl, 1909), and *Stefan Rott oder Das Jahr der Entscheidung* (Stefan Rott, or, The Year of Decision, 1931), and continuing even after Brod settled in Israel.

In addition to novels, Brod wrote a large body of short stories, several plays and dramatic adaptations (of works by Kafka among others), poetry, criticism, and philosophical essays. A tireless writer, he issued some 95 books in all. Yet as of 1987, only seven of them had been translated into English. Despite the celebrity generated by his connection with Kafka, Brod suffered from a marked lack of popularity in the United States, where his works failed to hit the mark. Margarita Pazi contended in a *Modern Austrian Literature* essay reprinted in *Twentieth-Century Literary Criticism,* that this was primarily for two reasons: "The development and the changes in the author's spiritual and ethnic conceptions which motivated him to write these books were unfamiliar to the American public; also the readers were not prepared for his pronounced Jewish Central-European way of thinking and arguing or for the emotional intensity typical for the intellectuals of the 'Prague Circle.'" Brod remains an example of a writer well known in much of the literary world but comparatively neglected in Anglophone countries.

Brod worked beginning in 1939 as an advisor to the Hebrew Theatre in Tel Aviv, where he lived for the rest of his life. He was an enthusiastic supporter of the state of Israel, but he maintained close ties to European culture. Nearly every year he returned to Europe to give speeches and readings, and he did not avoid difficult visits; beginning in 1954 he traveled to West Germany, and in 1964 he returned to Communist-controlled Prague for a Kafka festival. In 1960 he wrote his autobiography, *Streitbares Leben* (Life of Struggle), and his 1966 book *Der Prager Kreis* (The Prague Circle) was a reminiscence of the cultural life of his native city. In 1968 Brod went on tour in West Germany. He died soon after returning home to Tel Aviv, on December 20, 1968.

Books

Dictionary of Literary Biography, Vol. 81: Austrian Fiction Writers: 1875–1913, Gale, 1989.

Pavlovski, Linda, and Scott T. Darga, eds., *Twentieth-Century Literary Criticism,* Vol. 115, Gale, 2002.

Weltsch, Robert, *Max Brod and His Age,* Leo Baeck Institute, 1970.

Periodicals

New York Times, September 20, 1988.

Online

Contemporary Authors Online, Gale, 2008. http://www.galenet.galegroup.com/servlet/BioRC (December 3, 2008).□

Heinrich Georg Bronn

German geologist and paleontologist Heinrich Georg Bronn (1800–1862) was a contemporary of British scientist Charles Darwin and translated Darwin's famous work, *On the Origin of Species,* into German in 1860. It was the first foreign translation of Darwin's landmark work that laid the foundation for modern biology, but the publication was nevertheless marked by some disagreements characteristic among scientific professionals. "Bronn did not translate everything to Darwin's liking," wrote Sander Gliboff in the *Journal of the History of Biology.* "He inserted a chapter-length critique of Darwin's argument, and he has often been criticized by Darwinian purists for his supposed mistakes, liberties, and obtuseness."

Bronn was born on March 3, 1800, in Ziegelhausen, a part of the larger German city of Heidelberg. Just a few years following his birth, the newly created Grand Duchy of Baden was created from the remnants of the Holy Roman Empire, and in 1815 the Duchy became part of the larger German Confederation. Baden's Heidelberg was an important cultural and administrative center of imperial Germany, as it had been for some centuries. The scenic, hilly city on the Neckar River was home to the University of Heidelberg, founded in 1386 as Germany's first university.

Studied Earth's Rock Strata

Bronn's father was a civil servant and held a post with the local forestry authority. One of seven children in a Roman Catholic family, Bronn gravitated toward the sciences at an early age, and chose a dual course in both natural history and cameral studies when he entered the famed university of his hometown. The cameral studies program was for students seeking a career in the civil service. He earned his doctoral degree in 1821, which came with a designation called a *habilitation* that permitted him to teach at the university level and conduct research.

The University of Heidelberg offered Bronn a teaching post in the department of natural history, where he taught courses in forestry, agriculture, mining and soils, and mineralogy; after 1833 he also took over duties as a professor of zoology and curator of the school's Zoological Cabinet. In the 1820s, however, he was still a specialist in the field of geology, and became particularly renowned for his work in what was then called stratigraphical geology, or the science of rock strata. This was a relatively new field at the time, with the pioneering work having been largely done by two British geologists of the previous century, William Smith and James Hutton. Working independently, they put forth theories about the age of the earth based on the fossils discovered in the various layers of rock known as strata.

Bronn conducted field work in Germany, the south of France, and northern Italy while teaching at Heidelberg, and for more than three decades he served as editor of *Jahrbuch für Mineralogie, Geognosie, Geologie, und Petrefackten-kunde* (Yearbook for Mineralogy, Geognosie, Geology, and Fossil Studies). He published scores of scientific papers and books, including an important study of the geology of the Heidelberg area in 1830, *Gaea Heidelbergensis, oder Mineralogische Beschreibung der Gegend von Heidelberg.* A year later, he published a work on the tertiary strata of Italy. At the time, "tertiary" was the more commonly used term for what scientists now refer to as the Cenozoic period.

In *Italiens Tertiär-Gebilde und deren organischen Einschlüsse,* which was published in Heidelberg in 1831, Bronn advanced the idea that "in successively more recent strata the number of extinct species diminishes while the number of modern species increases," according to Bert Hansen in the *Dictionary of Scientific Biography.* This and other theories helped Bronn earn a reputation as one of the leading experts in fossil geology in Europe at the time. He also espoused a new idea that fit in with other discoveries about the age of the earth itself, which was a question of immense scientific debate at the time. Gliboff, writing in the *Journal of the History of Biology,* encapsulated some of Bronn's ideas in a 2007 article. "Ever since its formation as a uniform, molten sphere, Bronn argues, the earth has been cooling. It has crusted over, contracted, cracked, and developed increasingly diverse and hospitable environments on its surface. Life has had to change constantly in order to keep up with a dynamic earth."

Published Exhaustive Index of Life Forms

One of Bronn's most important published tomes was *Handbuch einer Geschichte der Natur* (Handbook of a History of Nature), the first volume of which appeared in 1841. This first part was a physical history of the earth, while its second volume detailed the history of living organisms on earth. Though Bronn's theories about the interrelatedness of species shared some parallels with Darwin's groundbreaking 1859 work, *Origin of Species,* there were a few key differences. "In contrast to Darwin, who has natural

selection impose order and apparent purpose on nature's random variations, Bronn explains how nature can be orderly and law-governed, yet still produce a wild variety of landforms, mineral forms, plants, and animals," Gliboff explained in the *Journal of the History of Biology.* "He sees variation as the product of nature's laws, not as raw material to be further sorted and shaped." More importantly, at this stage of his career Bronn considered the multifarious array of life forms so great that he theorized they could only have been divinely wrought—in other words, the work of a higher power.

The third section of Bronn's *Handbuch* included the *Index Palaeontologicus,* a comprehensive record of all known fossils, and this remained a standard reference work for geologists and paleontologists for decades. Out of this same project came another significant work, *Die Klassen und Ordnungen des Thierreichs, wissenschaftlich dargestellt in Wort und Bild* (Classes and Orders of the Animal Kingdom). He wrote the volumes *Amorphozoa* (the term for organisms without a mouth, like sponges), *Actinozoa* (an obsolete term for animals like sea anemones), and *Malacozoa* (mollusks and other invertebrates), before he died in 1862, and others continued it.

Bronn's research work was prodigious, but his beliefs about the origins of life put him in conflict with some other renowned thinkers who were either his contemporaries or had preceded him. One of the earlier theorists was French naturalist Jean-Baptiste Lamarck, who believed that evolution was the result of natural laws—in other words, changes in species occurred entirely because of natural causes—rather than by supernatural forces or the work of a supreme being. Some of Lamarck's more complex ideas behind evolution were debated by both Bronn and Darwin, and Bronn is the link between the two naturalists, each of whom attained much more enduring fame than he would.

Argued for Divine Power

Bronn believed in what the German language calls *Urkraft,* or a primeval force, and initially disagreed with the theory that species evolved into new, more complex ones on their own. Lamarck's landmark work, published around the time of Bronn's birth, had argued that life forms change because they are adapting to their environment—mammals, for example, have teeth, which they need to eat. Bronn considered the vast complexity of life forms on earth as preordained. "Bronn is not out to prove the existence of God or infer His attributes," Gliboff noted in the *Journal of the History of Biology.* "Rather, Bronn's investigations begin from the assumption that God has already organized nature, endowed it with laws and forces, and that these need to be discovered and described."

Bronn's body of work had some esteemed supporters. In 1857, his essay on the *Laws of Evolution of the Organic World* won the French Academy of Sciences prize for its discussion of fossils and species extinction. In the years before his death in 1862, however, he appeared to be shifting away from his theories about Urkraft or any divine power. Scholars of evolutionary science date this to his 1858 work *Morphologische Studien über die Gestaltungs-Gesetze der Naturkörper überhaupt und der organischen insbesondere* (Morphological Studies of the Formative Laws of Natural Bodies in General and Organic Bodies in Particular).

Questioned Part of Darwin's Theory

Charles Darwin was a young English naturalist in the 1830s when he undertook a round-the-world voyage on the *HMS Beagle.* He published a journal of the voyage in 1839, which gained him immense fame, but it took him another two decades and considerable research into the field of geology before Darwin fully formulated his ideas in *On the Origin of Species,* which caused a sensation when it was published by the London house of John Murray in 1859. The work promoted Darwin's theory of natural selection, or the idea that nature "selects" for more favorable genetic traits, which became the foundation of modern biology.

Darwin's theory was immediately discussed, debated, and mostly heralded across the Western scientific community. Bronn had received one of ten copies that Darwin had sent out to German scientists whom he thought would be receptive to his ideas. Bronn reviewed it in the *Jahrbuch* for which he served as editor, and sent an inquiry to Darwin about translating it. He was offered the job, and carried out the first German translation, which appeared in early 1860. Despite the criticism Bronn would later be subject to for his disagreements with some of Darwin's ideas, the English scientist seemed pleased with the work. In a letter to Bronn, Darwin wrote, "On my return home, after an absence of some time, I found the Translation of the third part of the 'Origin,' and I have been delighted to see a final chapter of criticisms by yourself," the letter read, according to Gliboff's 2008 book *H.G. Bronn, Ernst Haeckel, and the Origins of German Darwinism: A Study in Translation and Transformation.* "I have read the first few paragraphs and final paragraph, and am perfectly contented, indeed more than contented, with the generous and candid spirit with which you have considered my view . . . I shall consider myself deeply indebted to you for the immense service and honour which you have conferred on me in making the excellent translation of my book."

Bronn won the Wollaston Medal from the Geological Society of London in 1861 for his work. He died a year later, on July 5, 1862, in Heidelberg. One of his students had been Louis Agassiz, from Switzerland. Years later, after Agassiz achieved prominence for his theories on comparative zoology, he went back to Germany and acquired Bronn's fossil collection for the Museum of Comparative Zoology at Harvard University.

Books

Gillispie, Charles Coulston, editor, *Dictionary of Scientific Biography,* Volume II: *Hans Berger–Christoph Buys Ballot,* American Council of Learned Societies/Charles Scribner's Sons, 1980.

Gliboff, Sander, *H.G. Bronn, Ernst Haeckel, and the Origins of German Darwinism: A Study in Translation and Transformation,* MIT Press, 2008.

Periodicals

Journal of the History of Biology, October 2007. ☐

Anne Brontë

Often overlooked by the greater achievements of her older sisters, English author Anne Brontë (1820–1849) was a talented novelist in her own right, though she remains the least celebrated of the three writing Brontë sisters. Before her death at 29, Anne Brontë published two books, *Agnes Grey* in 1847 and *The Tenant of Wildfell Hall* in 1848, both under the gender-concealing pseudonym Acton Bell.

Raised in Church Parsonage

The youngest of six children, Anne Brontë was born January 17, 1820, to Patrick and Maria Branwell Brontë. Anne Brontë's mother came from a family of wealthy merchants. Her father, a Cambridge University graduate, hailed from Northern Ireland and worked as a clergyman with the Anglican Church. Patrick Brontë was also an author. He published several books of prose and verse, often with a moral bent. The Brontës married in 1812. Between 1814 and 1820, Maria Brontë gave birth to six children—five girls and one boy.

In 1820, the family settled at a parsonage in Haworth, an industrial village in central England. Anne Brontë was born here. The Haworth parsonage was not a cheery place—the stone home was cold and bleak. Patrick Brontë feared fire and therefore allowed no curtains to be hung in the windows. In their front yard sat a cemetery, and the rear of the house backed up to moorland—a habitat of gently flowing hills covered with coarse grasses. The Brontë children enjoyed exploring the moorland; the landscape appeared in many of their novels.

In 1821, Maria Brontë died, leaving Patrick Brontë alone with six children. Anne Brontë was not even two years old at the time. Soon, Patrick Brontë's unmarried sister-in-law, Elizabeth Branwell, came to help out. Growing up, the children developed close ties to one another. They entertained each other and played together all day long, often exploring the moors.

Studied Literature, Religion

Patrick Brontë was highly educated and believed his daughters deserved to be schooled as well. In 19th century England, however, this idea was a bit radical, and the notion of the day was to educate a girl just enough to please her future husband. Girls typically learned such things as singing and needlework and possibly a bit of French. Patrick Brontë, however, believed all of his children had intellectual capabilities that should be fostered. He provided the children with adult books and subscribed to literary magazines. He encouraged their interest in the English romantic poet William Wordsworth and Lord Byron. To

save money, Patrick Brontë arranged to receive day-old copies of *The Times* from a friend because he wanted his children to keep informed of current events.

Family discussions centered on poetry and art and cultural and political affairs. In addition, the children received a rigorous religious education. They read the *Bible, Methodist Magazine* and the *Book of Common Prayer.* Patrick Brontë's Sunday sermons tended to focus more on damnation than salvation. In his sermons and writing, he cautioned his congregants to be wary of sin. Of the children, Anne Brontë was the one who took his message most to heart, and was the most devout. Morality and religion come up in *Agnes Grey,* a novel about a governess written by her later on. The protagonist, Agnes, is firm in her desire to teach her charges about Christianity and proper pious behavior. When Anne Brontë worked as a governess, she struggled in this area herself as well.

While the Brontë girls received a more expansive education than their female peers, Patrick Brontë still had some old-fashioned ideas about women's roles in society. His son, Branwell Brontë, received a more rigorous education than his sisters. Patrick Brontë worked with Branwell Brontë incessantly, hoping to prepare him for admission to Oxford or Cambridge. In *Agnes Grey,* Anne Brontë addressed the issue of educational inequity.

Patrick Brontë understood the need to raise his children so they would be able to earn a living. During this time, teacher and governess were about the only jobs available to middle-class working women. In 1824, a

wealthy clergyman named Rev. Carus Wilson opened a school for girls in Lancashire, a town about 50 miles to the northwest. The goal of the school was to turn out future governesses. He enrolled the oldest girls—Maria, Elizabeth, Charlotte and Emily Brontë. The place was horrid. The wash water froze in their frigid dormitory and they were fed a poor diet, causing their physical health to decline. In 1825, the eldest two Brontës—Maria and Elizabeth—died of tuberculosis they contracted while at the school. Patrick Brontë quickly withdrew the other two girls.

Escaped into Imaginary Worlds

The four remaining siblings, devastated by another loss, became closer than ever, creating their own little close-knit society. They spent their time reading, writing and drawing and escaped the harsh realities of their lives by creating imaginary worlds and writing tales of their inhabitants. Later on, these worlds and characters formed the foundations for their literary work.

The children were particularly inspired by a set of wooden soldiers Branwell Brontë received in 1826. Each of the children took a soldier and gave it a name and personality. Soon, they began writing tales of the soldiers' adventures and created a make-believe place called Glass Town. Charlotte and Branwell Brontë wrote volumes about the place. Inspired by their siblings, Emily and Anne Brontë created their own imaginary land, Gondal, which was ruled by a female leader. The children spent hours writing about these worlds.

At 15, Anne Brontë went off to boarding school, attending Miss Margaret Wooler's Roe Head School near Dewsbury. Her older sister, Charlotte Brontë, had gone there earlier and was currently teaching at the school. Emily Brontë attended for a time but was too homesick to continue. Anne Brontë stayed for about two years before she fell ill with gastritis and returned to Haworth in 1837.

In 1839, Anne Brontë left home to work as a governess, determined to make her own way in the world. A year later she went to Thorp Green Hall near York to serve as a governess for Edmund and Lydia Robinson. In time, she secured a position for her brother, Branwell, as a tutor for the Robinson's son. Branwell Brontë did not last long, however, and was dismissed for allegedly having an affair with Lydia Robinson. Anne Brontë quit in 1845.

Began Publishing Career

The year 1845 found the three Brontë sisters living back at home. None of them had any job prospects. Charlotte Brontë suggested they combine their best work into a poetry collection and seek publication. Each chose a gender-neutral pen name, fearing their work might be dismissed if publishers knew their true identities. In 1846 *Poems,* by Currer, Ellis and Acton Bell, was published. Charlotte Brontë chose the name Currer, Emily Brontë chose Ellis and Anne Brontë settled on Acton. In this manner they each kept their initials. The surname Bell was adopted from one of their father's assistants, a curate named Arthur Bell Nicholls, whom Charlotte Brontë later married.

The slim green volume failed to generate many sales; however, the Brontë sisters decided to push on and try their hand at fiction. Anne Brontë delved into *Agnes Grey*, which she had begun at Thorp Green. Charlotte Brontë worked on *The Professor* and Emily Brontë worked on *Wuthering Heights.* The young women fussed with their novels late into the night, sitting at the writing table in the parlor. They read passages to each other, paced the room and offered critiques of each other's work.

In 1847, a publisher offered to print *Agnes Grey* and *Wuthering Heights,* but rejected *The Professor.* The sisters had to help with the cost. Written as a first-person narrative, *Agnes Grey* tells the woeful tale of a put-upon governess named Agnes. Much of it was based on Anne Brontë's experiences as a governess. Throughout the book, Agnes is disgusted by the children's unruly behavior and their parents' failure to rein them in. In *The Brontës,* author Christopher Martin noted that in *Agnes Grey,* Anne Brontë said governesses lived a life of "minute torments and incessant tediums."

Wrote Controversial Novel

In 1848, Anne Brontë published *The Tenant of Wildfell Hall* under her pseudonym. *Wildfell Hall* explored the breakdown of a drunken adulterer named Arthur Huntingdon and the turmoil he causes his wife, Helen, who finds the courage to leave him and escapes to Wildfell Hall with their son. The character of Arthur was based somewhat on Anne Brontë's brother, who struggled to find his place in the world and turned to alcohol and opium after losing his tutoring job. After watching her brother slip away, Anne Brontë wanted to warn against the dangers of alcohol.

In the book, Helen escapes from her husband and befriends a farmer named Gilbert Markham. The book's narrative structure is sophisticated—part of the story is told through Helen's diary and part through the letters Markham writes his brother-in-law. Because it was pretty much forbidden for a woman to leave her husband during this time period, Anne Brontë made Helen nearly perfect, hoping readers would understand her plight and forgive her actions.

The book received mixed reviews, mostly because the subject matter was considered too lurid. Anne Brontë's frank portrayal of drunken degeneracy offended many critics who condemned the author for seeking self-gratification through debauchery. According to *The Brontës* by Rebecca Fraser, a review in the *Athenaeum* called *Wildfell Hall* "the most interesting novel which we have read for a month past."

Other reviewers denounced it as a women's fantasy tale and questions concerning the author's gender began to circulate. According to the *New York Times'* Michael Frank, in a second edition, Anne Brontë declared in the preface: "I am satisfied that if a book is a good one, it is so whatever the sex of the author may be. All novels are or should be written for both men and women to read." Anne Brontë defended the novel, saying it was not about amusing readers or even creating a piece of art. According to Fraser, Anne Brontë said she wrote the book with God's help to warn against vice. She acknowledged that the book might be offensive to some but believed that was necessary to make her point and save people from a similar fate.

By now, Charlotte Brontë had published *Jane Eyre* under her pseudonym, Currer Bell. The book was creating a stir both in England and the United States and critics began to wonder about the Bell brothers. At this time, Anne and Charlotte Brontë decided to tell their publisher the truth.

Work Censored After Death

In September 1848, Branwell Brontë died. A few months later, Emily Brontë died of tuberculosis. In January 1849, Anne Brontë began to show signs of deep decline due to tuberculosis. Anne Brontë had always enjoyed the seaside town of Scarborough and in May 1849 Charlotte Brontë took her sister there. By now, Anne Brontë was so weakened by the disease she had to be lifted in and out of the carriages and trains. They found lodging in a room that overlooked the bay. In this way, Anne Brontë spent her last days, gazing out the window at the sea. She died May 28, 1849, and was buried at St. Mary's Church in Scarborough because Charlotte Brontë could not bear to bring another body home for her father to bury.

During her life, Anne Brontë remained in the shadow of her sisters, whose Romantic novels were better-accepted. In addition, Charlotte Brontë disliked *Wildfell Hall* and refused to let the book be reprinted after Anne Brontë died. In this manner, Anne Brontë faded away from literary consciousness. "Charlotte didn't like *Wuthering Heights* or *The Tenant of Wildfell Hall,*" Brontë Parsonage Museum director Jane Sellars told the *South China Morning Post.* "She really does manipulate what happens to [Anne and Emily's] work and their reputations. She said she didn't know what they were doing when they were writing these books."

In the 20th century as critics reviewed the sisters and their work, Anne Brontë received acclaim for her strong feminist texts. Both of her books contain resilient female protagonists struggling for autonomy during a time when society was dominated by men. More than 150 years after Anne Brontë's death, fans were still paying homage to the writer who died so young. "People have planted flowers over the years and still leave flowers," Brontë Society director Alan Bentley told the *Daily Telegraph,* noting that flowers still arrive at the society's headquarters on the anniversary of her death.

Books

Fraser, Rebecca, *The Brontës: Charlotte Brontë and Her Family,* Crown Publishers, Inc., 1988.

Martin, Christopher, *The Brontës,* Rourke Enterprises, Inc., 1989.

Miller, Lucasta, *The Brontë Myth,* Alfred A. Knopf, 2003.

Periodicals

Daily Telegraph (London), December 29, 2004.

Irish Times, November 18, 2000.

New York Times, March 8, 1996.

South China Morning Post (Hong Kong), April 1, 1995 (Diversions).□

Heywood Campbell Broun

American journalist Heywood Broun (1888–1939) was among the most familiar voices of newspaper opinion during the period between World Wars I and II.

A committed liberal, Broun sometimes clashed with his employers and their editorial stances, but the results of those clashes were productive: Broun's daily column, "It Seems to Me," at first appearing in the *New York World* and later syndicated, became recognized as the first newspaper opinion column that was editorially independent of the paper or papers in which it appeared. Broun expressed opinions on many of the major issues of the day. Indeed, according to a friend quoted by Broun biographer Richard O'Connor, he had the tendency to "launch a crusade every hour," and his readership grew into the millions. His influence on American journalism was wide, for he was among the first newspaper writers to let his own personality shape his writing rather than aim for a neutral voice.

Angered German Teacher

Heywood Campbell Broun (the name was pronounced "Broon") was born on December 7, 1888, in Brooklyn, New York. He grew up solidly middle-class: his father, Heywood Cox Broun, came from England and had built a successful printing business. The three Broun children were taken to vacation in Europe by their mother, the former Henrietta Brose, and Heywood attended the Horace Mann School, a top-ranked private institution. Teachers noted his obvious writing skills, but his gift did not extend to foreign languages; on one occasion his German teacher, in frustration, threw an inkpot at him. In spite of that debacle, Broun was admitted to Harvard University and matriculated in 1906.

That made him part of Harvard's class of 1910, a group that produced an above-average crop of writers. Among Broun's classmates were John Reed, who chronicled the birth of the Soviet Union, and Alan Seeger, the doomed poet of World War I. Broun did well in his English classes but lacked the focus expected of a Harvard man, often spending time watching the Boston Red Sox play in the afternoons. With a dress style somewhere between rumpled and disheveled, he felt more comfortable among the hard-drinking journalists at the New York *Morning Telegraph,* where he interned during the summer, than in the halls of academe. Broun finished school at Harvard with the rest of his class, but because he failed a French course in his last semester he never officially received his diploma.

That did not stop the *Morning Telegraph* from hiring Broun as a sports reporter, at a salary of $20 a week. When he asked for a raise to $30 he was instead fired, but in 1912 he signed on with the New York *Tribune* as a copyeditor. Restless, he left after a few months in order to travel to China as a researcher for the Liebling and Company theatrical firm, with expenses covered but otherwise unpaid. The *Tribune* hired him back as a sportswriter when he

returned, and he happily spent his afternoons at the Polo Grounds, describing the exploits of the New York Giants in a rather literary style. The *Tribune* moved him to the position of drama critic in 1915. In this capacity he met, fell in love with, and briefly became engaged to the Russian dancer Lydia Lopokova, who later married economist John Maynard Keynes.

Married Pioneering Feminist

When the engagement ran aground, Broun began seriously dating his friend Ruth Hale, a feminist and member of the Lucy Stone League, which advanced the idea that women should keep their own names after marriage. On their first date, when they went for a walk in Central Park, Broun showed up in one brown and one black shoe. She and Broun married on June 7, 1917, after which they went to France so that Broun could take up a post as the *Tribune*'s World War I correspondent. He ruffled feathers with direct criticism of commanding General John J. Pershing, eventually resulting in the censorship of several of his articles by military police, but his dispatches also led to congressionally mandated reforms in the military supply chain. The *Tribune,* a Republican-leaning paper, was well disposed toward reports that reflected badly on Democratic president Woodrow Wilson, and did nothing to rein Broun in. Back in New York in 1918, Ruth Hale gave birth to the couple's only child, future sportscaster and author Heywood Hale Broun.

The easygoing Broun began to challenge himself more and more as his journalistic career progressed. When he became the *Tribune*'s literary editor in 1919, he used the post as a forum to express his own outlook and personality. His book reviews themselves had an unusual tone. "In his discussions of the new postwar school of novelists," noted O'Connor, "Heywood also attracted attention to himself by forcefully expressing his opinions at a time when book reviewing was still a rather genteel occupation and harsh criticism was regarded as unmannerly." In addition, Broun had his own column, "Books and Things," in which he adopted a voice approaching that of the modern newspaper columnist: he not only discussed books but also favored readers with discussions of the raising of his son, whom he called H. the 3rd in print. He argued against the use of baby talk with children.

The rival *New York World* was observing these developments with interest, and in 1921 Broun accepted an offer to join the staff of that paper. He was given his own daily column, "It Seems to Me," with more or less free rein to write about whatever he wanted. Broun quickly weighed in with support for Eugene V. Debs, the leader of the Socialist Party, who had been imprisoned during government anti-Communist actions in the aftermath of the war. Broun's liberal voice developed as he wrote columns attacking the Ku Klux Klan, condemning censorship (despite his own rather straitlaced views), and generally promoting the idea of a fair shake for ordinary Americans.

Broun's columns often had a humorous or satirical thrust, not always with deep political import. A whimsical reflection on "The Fall of Humpty-Dumpty," reproduced in the collection *Sitting on the World*, featured a psychiatrist who warned that "I could put him together again, but I give it as my professional opinion that he'd never be quite normal. I mean, I doubt very much whether you could ever get him to go up on the wall again." Broun's columns were compiled into several book-length collections. Always taking a relaxed attitude toward work, and often writing his columns at the last minute, Broun was actually industrious without seeming to be: he wrote 12 books, including two novels (1922's *The Boy Grew Older* and 1923's *The Sun Field*), as well as an examination of anti-Semitism called *Christians Only: A Study in Prejudice* (1931, with George Britt).

Fired After Attacking Employer

Broun's liberal politics often brought him into conflict with the official editorial views of the *World* and its publisher, Joseph Pulitzer. His sharply worded columns in support of accused anarchists Nicola Sacco and Bartolomeo Vanzetti did not accord with the *World*'s outlook, and he drew a brief suspension. Broun was a supporter of the controversial contraception advocate Margaret Sanger, and conflict flared again when he penned an article in the *Nation* that attacked the *World* for refusing to support a birth control exhibit. In place of his March 3, 1928 column, Broun found a notice saying that he had been released from the newspaper's staff due to disloyalty.

With his popularity still growing, Broun had little trouble finding a new forum. He moved to the *New York Telegram* and had the satisfaction of seeing it absorb the *World* and become the *World-Telegram* a few years later. Broun's new employer promised him a free editorial voice and paid him a $30,000 salary, exceeded at that time in the world of journalism only by political pundit Walter Winchell and gossip columnist Dorothy Thompson. Best of all, Broun's column was syndicated to other papers around the country. He was not the first syndicated columnist, but he was among the first of a type that became very common as the century went on: an editorial columnist providing a distinctive political voice and writing style, independent of the paper in which it appeared.

Broun was a well-known figure in New York in the late 1920s and early 1930s, spending much of his leisure time in famed literary haunts such as the Algonquin Hotel. In 1930 he ran unsuccessfully for the United States Congress as a Socialist. His marriage to Hale declined under the pressure of the individualism of both; Hale traveled to Mexico and obtained a divorce in November of 1933. The two remained friends, however, and during the illness that led to Hale's death in 1934, Broun was often at her bedside. In 1933 Broun named and co-founded the Newspaper Guild union, and he served as the union's first president. From then until the end of his life, he was reelected at the union's annual convention.

Broun married dancer Constantina Maria Incoronata Fruscella, also known as Connie Madison, in 1935. Although he had been indifferent to religion for much of his life, he converted to Roman Catholicism, and in 1939 he was baptized by priest and future religious broadcaster Fulton J. Sheen. By that time, Broun's daily readership was estimated to be at least one million. He wrote columns for the *New Republic* magazine and launched a small humorous publication of his own, *Connecticut Nutmeg* (soon renamed *Broun's Nutmeg*). Angered by cuts in some of his *World-Telegram* columns, Broun placed situation-wanted ads in rival papers and was hired by the *New York Post*. He was able to write only one column before he contracted pneumonia and died quite suddenly on December 18, 1939. President Franklin Roosevelt, quoted in the *Dictionary of American Biography*, eulogized him as "a hard fighter...undeterred by slander, calumny or thought of personal consequences."

Books

American Decades, Gale, 1998.

Broun, Heywood, *Sitting on the World,* Putnam, 1924.

Dictionary of American Biography, Supplements 1–2: To 1940, American Council of Learned Societies, 1944–1958.

O'Connor, Richard, *Heywood Broun: A Biography,* Putnam, 1975.

Riley, Sam G., *Biographical Dictionary of American Newspaper Columnists,* Greenwood, 1995.

Online

"Heywood Broun (1888–1939)," National Park Service, http://www.nps.gov/archive/elro/glossary/broun-heywood.htm (December 29, 2008).

"Heywood Broun," Spartacus Educational (UK), http://www.web311.pavilion.net/USAbrounH.htm (December 29, 2008).□

C

Cachao

The Cuban musician Israel López, known as Cachao, is credited as the inventor of the internationally popular mambo style, and he was musically influential far beyond his native country and the sphere of its popular dance music.

Music historian Ned Sublette told Enrique Fernandez of the *Miami Herald* that Cachao was "arguably the most important bassist in 20th-century popular music." The *descarga* jam sessions Cachao pioneered in the nightclubs of Havana in the 1950s were important incubators of Latin jazz and salsa. He did much to emancipate the bass from its accompanying role in dance and jazz ensembles, a development that presaged the instrument's ongoing importance in the American R&B genre. Sublette noted that R&B bass lines "have become such a part of the environment that we don't even think where they came from." Partially forgotten after coming to the United States after the Cuban Revolution, Cachao enjoyed a remarkable surge of late-life creativity in the 1990s and 2000s, as older forms of Cuban music began to receive their proper appreciation.

Grew Up in Martí House

Israel López was born on September 14, 1918, in Havana, Cuba. The house in which he grew up, on Calle Paula (Paula Street), was the birthplace of Cuban independence activist José Martí, and the family had to move out temporarily each year on Martí's birthday, January 28, as schoolchildren were brought to the house to commemorate the occasion. He grew up in a family that was devoted not only to music but specifically to the string bass. The number of bassists in his extended family has been estimated at anywhere from 40 to a perhaps exaggerated 100. Our house was a wreck," Cachao recalled in an interview quoted in England's *Daily Telegraph.* "There were instruments everywhere and people playing all the time." Israel López received the nickname Cachao because that was the last name of one of his older relatives, and in most of his professional activities he was known by that single name.

Cachao took lessons from his parents, who both played the bass, and he also played bongo drums as a child. At age eight he joined a kids' septet (on bongos) that also included future bandleader Roberto Faz. A year later, playing bass, he began his professional career as a bassist in an orchestra that accompanied silent films, a band that included another future Cuban music great, singer-pianist Bola de Nieve (Snowball, whose full name was Ignacio Villa). Cachao's parents emphasized training in classical music, and he took further lessons at a local conservatory. When he was 12 or 13 he was ready for a spot in the Havana Philharmonic Orchestra as a double bassist, even though at first he had to stand on a box to reach the strings of the instrument. Remaining a member of the orchestra until 1960, Cachao played under the batons of some of the greatest names in twentieth-century classical music, including German conductor Herbert von Karajan and Russo-French composer Igor Stravinsky.

The final applause of the orchestra's audience did not, however, signal the end of his evening's work. Cachao played in Havana dance ensembles, and in 1937 he and his cellist brother Orestes joined a small orchestra called Arcaño y sus Maravillas. The group's sheet music was stolen soon after their arrival, but the theft had the positive effect of stimulating the creativity of the López brothers, who were ordered to come up with new material, sometimes at the blistering pace of 28 new dances per week.

104

They eventually composed more than 3,000 pieces. At first they were mostly connected with the danzón, a formation dance with roots in the court dances of Europe. New influences from Afro-Cuban music were beginning to make their way into the genre, and sometimes one of the brothers would begin to repeat a section of a danzón, using the African word "mambo" (meaning singing or storytelling in Bantu) as a rhythmic text. Soon the word was attached to a repeated vamp-like pattern that might be attached to the end of a danzón.

The mambo was officially born when Cachao and Orestes composed a piece called "Danzón Mambo" in 1938. As with any other musical development, the mambo had various contributors to its early development. With its heavily rhythmic style, however, it quickly became identified with Cachao, the group's bassist. Cachao dubbed the new style "El Nuevo Rítmico," or the New Rhythm, but the term mambo was soon attached to it. He had various recollections about the initial reactions of Havana nightclub dancers. "This was the era of the syncopated beat," he was quoted as saying by Rebecca Mauleón in *Bass Player*. "We musicians began experimenting with that, and the dancers reacted instantly!" But in a *Miami Herald* article quoted by Fernandez, Cachao recalled the mambo's actual debut negatively: "Nothing happened! Here was this 180-degree turn. The whole orchestra was out of work for six months after that because people didn't understand that type of music."

Creation Popularized by Pérez Prado

Whatever the case, the mambo caught on quickly among Cubans and among the numerous American patrons of Havana's clubs, some of whom had connections to organized crime. The dance skyrocketed to international popularity around 1950 in the hands of Cuban-Mexican bandleader Dámaso Pérez Prado, often called "the King of the Mambo." Cachao did not begrudge Pérez Prado his success. "People think there could've been some antagonism," Cachao told Fernandez. But "if it weren't for him, the mambo wouldn't be known around the world." Pérez Prado in turn acknowledged the inspiration of Arcaño y sus Maravillas and other bands.

Cachao married his wife, Ester Buenaventura, in 1946, and the marriage lasted until her death in 2005. "A love like that never leaves you," he told Mauleón. "Everyone around was womanizing, but not me. There was only one woman for me my entire life." They had one daughter, María Elena. Finally leaving Arcaño y sus Maravillas in 1949, Cachao performed in a variety of bands and theatrical ensembles. As part of the José Fajardo Orchestra in the mid-1950s, he played the new cha-cha style. His second major innovation came at the end of that decade, when he organized various Cuban musicians into after-hours "descargas" (the word means "discharges"), relaxed sessions in which they could interact and play mambo, jazz, and other kinds of music. Beginning with 1957's *Descargas en Miniature,* Cachao released some of the descargas as albums. These were his first recordings under his own name, and they helped spread his name beyond Cuba.

That proved important after Fidel Castro's guerrillas overthrew the government of Fulgencio Batista in 1959. Under the Communist system Havana's nightlife largely came to a halt, although roots Cuban forms continued to flourish. Cachao was ambivalent about the question of leaving Cuba. His brother Orestes remained in Cuba. But the departure of Cachao's wife to join relatives in New Jersey tipped the scales. In 1962 Cachao left Cuba for a tour of Spain with the Ernesto Duarte Orchestra and stayed away for some months. He never returned to Cuba, and the island's government expunged his contributions to the many compositions that had shaped Cuban music, crediting them exclusively to Orestes. Rejoining his wife in New York, Cachao quickly found work with the relocated Fajardo orchestra and other musicians, including Eddie Palmieri and Chico O'Farrill. He was a fixture of New York's Cuban-American music scene through much of the 1960s. He recorded several more albums of descargas, including *Descargas at the Village Gate* (1966).

Struggled with Gambling Addiction

In the 1970s Cachao worked mostly in Las Vegas, often featured as a headliner at top hotels on the city's gambling "Strip." The real reason for his relocation to Las Vegas, however, was that he was a compulsive gambler, a trait to which he freely admitted. He remained in Las Vegas, losing almost all his assets at the casinos, but his wife remained faithful to him and finally persuaded him to leave the city. In 1978 Cachao moved to Miami, Florida. Largely forgotten as younger Latin musicians moved on to more contemporary styles, he made a living playing at weddings, quinceaños parties, and dance nights in clubs with various bands.

Cachao's rediscovery was brought about by Cuban-American actor Andy Garcia, who encountered *Descargas en Miniature* in a used record store in Miami's Little Havana neighborhood. Returning to the store the next day, he bought out the shop's entire stock of Cachao recordings and carried them around on cassette tape copies for several years. While making the film *The Godfather III* in San Francisco in 1989, Garcia had the chance to hear his idol in concert at a San Francisco Jazz Festival event. Introduced to the musician, Garcia offered to produce a major Cachao concert in Florida. The two discovered that Garcia's father had booked Cachao to play at all-ages dances in Garcia's Cuban hometown of Bejucal.

In 1994 Garcia made a documentary about Cachao, *Como su Ritmo No Hay Dos* (Like His Rhythm There Is No Other), and produced and released in conjunction with the film a new Cachao album, *Master Sessions, Volume One.* The album earned Cachao a Grammy Award for Best Tropical Latin Performance in 1995. This new exposure put the septuagenarian Cachao ahead of the curve in the world music scene, for the *Buena Vista Social Club* album released by a group of older Cuban musicians, working with U.S. guitarist Ry Cooder, touched off a surge of interest in classic Cuban popular forms. The instrumental tune that bore the "Buena Vista Social Club" title was one of the mambos composed by Cachao and his brother back in 1938. Orestes López's son and Cachao's nephew, Orlando López, nicknamed Cachaito, played bass in some of the Buena Vista Social Club ensembles and became a significant figure in Cuban music in his own right.

Cachao continued to release new music at a vigorous clip, telling his manager (according to Jon Pareles of the *New York Times*), "You've got years. I've got minutes." Cachao joined pianist Bebo Valdés on a trio album, *El Arte del Sabor,* that won a Grammy in 2003, and he took home a third Grammy for his 2004 release *Ahora Sí.* His tremendous contribution to the popular music of the Americas began to be recognized at the end of his life as he won a National Heritage Fellowship award from the National Endowment for the Arts and was given a star—number 2,219—on the Hollywood Walk of Fame. A series of 2005 concerts at San Francisco State University was filmed for a second documentary, *Cachao: Una Más* (Cachao: One More). The biggest blow to Cachao in his later years was the death of his wife in 2005, but he continued to perform, making his first appearance in Britain in 2007. He was in the planning stages of a new album, at age 89, when he died of kidney failure, in Coral Gables, Florida, on March 22, 2008.

Books

Broughton, Simon, ed., *World Music: The Rough Guide,* volume 2, The Rough Guides, 1999.

Contemporary Musicians, volume 34, Gale, 2002.

Periodicals

Daily Telegraph (London, England), March 24, 2008.
Entertainment Weekly, August 12, 1994.
Guardian (London, England), March 24, 2008.
Independent (London, England), March 24, 2008.
Latin Beat, September 2002.
Miami Herald, March 22, 2008; March 23, 2008.
New York Times, March 24, 2008.
Palm Beach Post, March 26, 2008.
San Francisco Chronicle, April 12, 2008.

Online

"Cachao," *All Music Guide,* http://www.allmusic.com (December 2, 2008).
"Cuban Music Icon 'Cachao' Dies at 89," MSNBC, http://www.msnbc.msn.com/id/23759333 (December 2, 2008).
Mauleón, Rebecca, "Cachao!," *Bass Player,* http://www.bassplayer.com/article/cachao/mar-08/33745 (December 2, 2008). □

Lott Cary

The African-American missionary Lott Cary (c. 1780–1828), a pioneer in developing the colony that became the independent nation of Liberia, was among the first blacks to serve as a missionary anywhere on the African continent.

Cary moved to Africa from his home in Richmond, Virginia, forsaking a relatively prosperous existence, with the aim of preaching the Christian gospel among Africa's peoples. His natural leadership skills, however, soon became essential to the life of the young colony. Cary was a self-taught physician who attended to African Americans plagued by unfamiliar diseases in their new land. He was a military leader who organized defenses against the attacks of native Africans intent on eradicating the colonial presence they saw as an invasion. Cary served as the vice-agent of the Liberian colony and for several years was its acting governor of Liberia. His detailed correspondence with his American sponsors has been preserved and offers valuable firsthand evidence regarding the life of the freed slaves who tried to make a new life on the continent from which their ancestors had been taken.

Little is known of Lott Cary's early life beyond the fact that he grew up as a slave. He was born into slavery around 1780, on a plantation in Charles City County, in Virginia's tobacco farming belt. Few slaves could read and write at the time, and Cary, like his parents, was illiterate as a young man. (There was no conclusive spelling of his last name, and the forms Cary and Carey have both been used.) The sole known hint of his future career was the prophecy of his grandmother, who had been brought from Africa and converted to Christianity, that he would one day return to Africa and preach the Christian gospel. The possibility was hard to imagine during Cary's early adulthood: rented out by his owner to work in a Richmond, Virginia, tobacco warehouse,

Cary was said by early biographer J.B. Taylor (writing in *Biography of Elder Lott Cary, Late Missionary to Africa*) to have "become rather dissipated in his habits, being frequently intoxicated, and allowing himself to indulge in profane swearing. He became increasingly vicious for two or three years after his settlement in Richmond."

What turned Cary's life around was a sermon given by a local Baptist elder on the biblical figure of Nicodemus, the Pharisee who helped to bury the body of Christ. Fascinated by the story, Cary acquired a copy of the New Testament and began trying to learn to read it, word by word and letter by letter. Tobacco workers who could read helped him at the beginning. When he could read the third chapter of the Book of John aloud, he applied himself to the task of learning to write. From that point onward, his sparse free time was spent in the pursuit of knowledge. Someone described by Taylor as a "gentleman," perhaps one of the warehouse's owners or overseers, once picked up a book he had seen Cary reading and discovered that it was *The Wealth of Nations,* the classic work by British economist Adam Smith.

Cary's conversion and subsequent education had two immediate effects. For one, he began to preach among African Americans living in Richmond. Showing an obvious aptitude for religious leadership, he was encouraged by local African-American churches, and was soon preaching over a wide area of the surrounding countryside. He became the pastor of Richmond's African Baptist Church. Second, Cary's leadership skills started to show themselves in the workplace as well. An observer quoted by Taylor felt "that his services at the warehouse were highly estimated, but of their real value no one except a dealer in tobacco can form an idea. Notwithstanding the hundreds of hogsheads that were committed to his charge, he could produce any one the instant it was called for; and the shipments were made with a promptness and correctness, such as no person, white or black, has equalled in the same situation."

Frequently given small bonuses by his employer, and also allowed to sell bits of leftover tobacco for his own profit, Cary began to save money. In 1813 he was able (for $850) to purchase his freedom and that of his two children by a first wife who by that time was deceased. He continued to work at the warehouse, and in 1815 he married for a second time. Given periodic raises, he was making the then-substantial salary of $800 a year by the late 1810s, and had purchased a small farm.

Cary's material success, however, collided with both his growing spiritual fervor and his awareness of the realities of being black in America. A new idea began to form in his mind after he and another young African-American convert, Colin Teague (or Collin Teage), began to attend night classes offered by a pair of white Baptist church members. There they began to hear about Africa, about how the continent was as yet mostly untouched by Christianity, and about the growing desire among Southern white leaders to resettle large numbers of American blacks in West Africa. Cary, Teague, and a group of similarly minded others formed the Richmond African Baptist Missionary Society in 1815. Required by law to have a white sponsor, they turned to one William Crane. He put Cary and Teague in touch with the growing American Colonization Society (ACS), a group dedicated to promoting the resettlement idea.

By about 1819, Cary had decided to move to Africa and to spend the rest of his life there doing missionary work. The offer of a raise in salary to $1,000 did not dissuade him from his aims, and in fact he liquidated most of his assets in preparing for the move. Racial discrimination played a major role in his desire to leave the United States. "I am an African, and in this country, however meritorious my conduct, and respectable my character, I cannot receive the credit due to either," he was quoted as saying by Taylor. "I wish to go to a country where I shall be estimated by my merits, not by my complexion; and I feel bound to labor for my suffering race." Newly ordained as a Baptist minister, and having delivered a stirring farewell sermon to his Richmond congregation, Cary set sail with Teague and a small group of other emigrants for the city of Freetown, part of a British colony in what is now Sierra Leone, in January of 1821. The trip took 44 days.

The enterprise started slowly, for neither Cary's group nor the larger ACS had any fixed plans as to how to go about acquiring land for the new colony. Cary and his fellow emigrants stayed for several months in Freetown, where Cary became a self-taught cooper (a maker of barrels and other wooden containers) to help make money for the group. Finally, in December of 1821, land was purchased from an African king at Cape Montserado, near the present-day city of Monrovia (which the settlers named for U.S. President James Monroe). Early in 1822, Cary led his group of missionaries to their new home, where they planted an American flag. Teague remained in Freetown.

The new settlement had a white governor, Jehudi Ashmun, but Cary quickly emerged as its day-to-day leader in many respects. Cary was the group's only Baptist missionary, and within the first year he established a church congregation, Sunday school, and missionary school that attracted several native African converts. By 1825 the church had some 60 members and its own sizable meeting house, and the school was serving 21 African children. Cary supervised construction of the new buildings, reported on their progress in letters to the ACS whenever a ship docked on the Liberian coast, and exhorted his sponors to send needed supplies.

Perhaps the most remarkable of Cary's resourceful efforts was his period of service as the colony's sole physician. Taylor commented that Cary's medical skills "resulted entirely from his good sense, observation, and experience," although he had occasional help from visitors whose knowledge exceeded his own. As new emigrants arrived from the United States, most of them lacked resistance to African diseases and fell ill within weeks, and one report estimated that more than half of Cary's time was spent in tending to the sick. One of the victims was Cary's second wife, who died soon after arriving in Liberia; he later married for a third time. In 1826 he hoped to return temporarily to the United States to report on the colony's activities, but it was decided that the need for his medical services in Liberia was too great to permit him to make the trip. He never saw his native country again.

Cary and Ashmun generally worked together well and regarded each other as friends, but one episode foreshadowed the tensions that led to the establishment of Liberia as an independent nation in 1847 and the decline of the colonization movement generally. Early accounts of Cary's life, written by colonization-oriented white Baptists, refer obliquely to the events involved, but what apparently occurred was that a dispute broke out between Ashmun and a group of the first Liberian settlers over whether newcomers would be allowed to till already cleared farmland or be given the task of establishing new farms on their own. Ashmun wanted those already settled in the colony to clear new land or work on other public projects, but that group, led by Cary, refused. As the dispute escalated, Ashmun tried to cut off food rations to Cary's group, whereupon Cary led a detachment that seized the colony's food warehouse. The disagreement eventually simmered down, and Cary was named vice-agent of the colony. In 1828, when health problems forced Ashmun to return to the United States, Cary was in line to become the colony's first black governor. But he never had the chance to assume the post.

Despite Cary's successes as a missionary, relations between the African-American colony and its surrounding African kingdoms were far from peaceful. Cary, who could also count good military instincts among his leadership skills, often was involved in raising men and materials to defend against hostile actions. This responsibility cost him his life in 1828, when conflict broke out between the colonists and an African group whom Cary accused of robbing one of the colony's workshops and of intercepting and destroying a letter he had sent to warn a slave trader who had encroached on one of the colony's facilities. Cary called out the colony's militia and, on November 8, gathered a group to make cartridges in one of the government buildings. A candle tipped over and ignited some loose gunpowder, causing a large explosion that killed eight people. One of those was Cary, who survived for two days and died on November 10, 1828. He was in every sense one of the founding fathers of the modern nation of Liberia, and his work continued with support from African Americans. The Lott Carey Baptist Foreign Mission Convention, established in 1897, continues to foster missionary and educational initiatives in Liberia such as the Lott Carey Mission School, a direct descendant of the one Cary himself established in the African jungles nearly two centuries ago.

Books

Brockman, Norbert, ed., *An African Biographical Dictionary,* ABC-CLIO, 1994.

Fitts, Leroy, *Lott Carey: The First Black Missionary in Africa,* 1978.

Smith, Jessie Carney, ed., *Notable Black American Men,* Gale, 1998.

Taylor, J.B., *Biography of Elder Lott Carey, Late Missionary to Africa,* Armstrong & Berry, 1837 (reproduced at Documenting the American South, http://www.docsouth.unc.edu/neh/gurley/gurley.html, accessed December 22, 2008).

Periodicals

Winston-Salem Journal (North Carolina), September 4, 1999, p. B9.

Online

Hammond, Leslie, "Lott Carey: Pioneer African American Missionary," http://www.urbana.org/wtoday. witnesses.cfm? article=26 (December 22, 2008).

"Sketch of the Life of the Rev. Lott Cary," Documenting the American South, http://www.docsouth.unc.edu/neh/gurley/gurley.html (December 22, 2008).□

Carlota, Empress of Mexico

Princess Charlotte of Belgium, later known as Empress Carlota of Mexico (1840–1927), came from a long line of royalty—she was the daughter, sister, wife and aunt of kings. She married the Austrian Archduke Maximilian, who became the emperor of Mexico through an ill-fated plot by Napoleon III to establish a monarchy in the Americas. After being tossed from the Mexican throne, Carlota went insane and spent the last 60 years of her life living in near seclusion in Belgium, becoming known as the "mad empress."

Born into Royal Family

One of three children, Carlota was born June 7, 1840, at the family's castle in Laeken, located on the outskirts of Brussels, Belgium. Her father was Leopold I, the king of Belgium. Her mother, Marie-Louise of Orleans, was the daughter of King Louis Philippe, the last king to rule France. At the time of Carlota's birth, her grandfather still occupied the throne in France. At her baptism, she was christened Marie Charlotte Amélie Augustine Victoire Clémentine Léopoldine.

When Carlota was 10 her mother died, leaving Leopold I in charge of her future. He made sure the young princess received an extensive education aimed at preparing her for a life in the royal court. Carlota studied math, history, drawing and piano. She could name each king of England and the dates they served. Growing up, Carlota enjoyed reading Plutarch—the famed priest and biographer who chronicled the lives of legendary Roman and Greek heroes. She also liked the music of Bach.

King Leopold I allowed his daughter to attend meetings of the councils of state, during which time official government matters were discussed. Early on, he recognized her abilities and lamented that she would not be able to follow in his footsteps toward the throne. According to *The Crown of Mexico* by Joan Haslip, the king wrote to a friend in 1851: "Charlotte is so much more attentive than her brothers. It is a tragedy she is not a little boy." Her brothers were Prince Philippe, who later became the Count of Flanders, and Prince Leopold II, who became king of Belgium in 1865.

By many accounts, Carlota took herself seriously, much like her father, inheriting little of her mother's humor. The young princess was known to keep a journal chronicling her physical and moral development. As Carlota hit adolescence, King Leopold I kept a tight reign on her existence. At social gatherings, she was only allowed to dance with

those of royal blood. If she wanted to waltz, she had to take one of her brothers as a partner. Since the waltz required a closer embrace than other dances, the king wanted to ensure no inappropriate touching would occur, which could possibly tarnish her name.

Married Austria's Archduke Maximilian

By the time Carlota was 16, her father was looking into matrimonial arrangements. She was presented to Prince George of Saxony; King Pedro V, who had just taken the throne in Portugal; and the Archduke Ferdinand Maximilian of Austria. Initially, Carlota's family favored Pedro V, who was the only ruling monarch to approach her. Carlota, however, did not care for him and voiced concern about moving to Portugal. According to *The Cactus Throne* by Richard O'Connor, Carlota's former governess, Countess Hulst, supported her views, telling her, "The Portuguese are only orang-utangs. They have no resources, not even a priest capable of understanding you."

Meanwhile, Maximilian continued visiting royal palaces in search of a bride. In the end, his mother decided he should marry the Princess. Maximilian spent time with King Leopold I's family at their chateau in Laeken so the young couple could get acquainted. They took heavily chaperoned walks through the gardens and rides through the woods. While the couple courted, representatives from each family negotiated the arrangements for the marriage. According to Haslip, in *The Crown of Mexico*, Maximilian

wrote his brother, describing Carlota this way, "She is small, I am tall, which is as it should be. She is a brunette and I am fair, which is also good. She is very clever, which is a bit worrying, but no doubt I will get over that."

The Archduke Maximilian and Carlota married on July 27, 1857, in Brussels. The bride was 17, the groom, 25. The newlyweds traveled to Italy for their honeymoon and the former princess was so inspired she changed her name to Carlota. Around this time Maximilian was appointed viceroy of the Kingdom of Lombardy-Venetia. Though located in northern Italy, the kingdom was part of the Austrian Empire. Around 1859, the Italians began to revolt against their Austrian rulers. As tensions mounted, Maximilian sent Carlota back to her father to live peacefully in Belgium. Eventually, he was removed from office and the couple retreated to Miramar, their stately castle on the Adriatic Sea near the Italian port city of Trieste. The white limestone and marble castle was built specifically for the couple.

Established Monarchy in Mexico

Meanwhile, trouble was brewing in Mexico and the French emperor, Napoleon III, was involved. Following the Mexican civil war, Benito Juárez came to power in the early 1860s. Juárez was a full-blooded Indian and leader of the Liberal Party, which was mainly composed of ranchers, lesser merchants and intellectuals who wanted to modernize Mexico. His party was fighting the Conservatives for control. The Conservative Party consisted of church officials, the army and large landowners. After Juárez came to power, he decided that his new government was not liable for the debts incurred by the previous government.

France was among Mexico's major creditors and this move by Juárez angered Napoleon III. He sent his troops to Mexico and in 1863 they ousted Juárez. At this time, Napoleon III called upon Maximilian and offered him the throne of Mexico. Napoleon III was not really interested in recouping his money—he wanted to set up a new colony in the Americas and envisioned sending hordes of French settlers. Maximilian was unsure but Carlota, lured by the opportunity to become an empress, pressed on, encouraging her husband to accept the offer. Likewise, pro-French Mexican conservatives who had been ousted from power urged Maximilian to go to Mexico. They suggested the Conservative Party would back his monarchy when in essence, all they desired was to oust Juárez.

To some extent, Emperor Maximilian and Empress Carlota were duped by Napoleon III, who made them believe the Mexican people wanted them there. In *Maximilian and Carlota,* author Gene Smith reprinted the telegram Emperor Maximilian received from his parents at their departure, suggesting that perhaps they knew the situation was tenuous. "Farewell. Our blessings—Papa's and mine—our prayers accompany you.... Farewell for the last time on your native soil, where alas! we may see you no more. We bless you again and again from our deeply sorrowing hearts." In perhaps what should have been seen as another premonition, Maximilian's majordomo from Miramar committed suicide before their departure because he did not want to go to Mexico.

Escorted by French troops, the royal couple took a boat to South America and landed at Veracruz, Mexico, in May 1864. The royal couple brought along some 85 attendants and 500 pieces of luggage. It did not take them long to realize the Mexican people did not want them ruling over their country. Nonetheless, Emperor Maximilian and Empress Carlota worked hard to secure the support of the people. In Mexico, she was known as Empress Carlota.

Empress Carlota gave her own money to charity causes. She and Maximilian restored Chapultepec, the ancient palace in Mexico City where they resided. In an effort to appease the people, the royal couple adopted the grandsons of the former Mexican Emperor Agustín de Iturbide, proclaiming them crown princes and heirs to the throne. They also toured the country, hoping to befriend its citizens. Empress Carlota traveled to Yucatán to visit the ruins of Uxmal, which had been a part of the Mayan civilization. They invited officials to banquets at the palace. It was impossible, however, to gain the trust of the Mexican people as Juárez kept up his opposition to the regime. In addition, Emperor Maximilian's liberal leanings caused him to lose the support of the Conservatives who initially supported him.

Ousted from Throne

Napoleon III eventually realized his plan to establish a satellite nation was going to fail and he began pulling French troops from Mexico. At this point, Emperor Maximilian knew he was in trouble. He considered withdrawing from the throne, but Empress Carlota was adamant they stay. In a letter to her husband, Empress Carlota spelled out several reasons for staying. According to O'Connor, in his book *The Cactus Throne*, she wrote: "Abdication amounts to pronouncing sentence on oneself, and writing oneself down as incompetent, and this is admissible only in old men and idiots, and is not a thing for a prince thirty-four years of age, full of life and hope in the future." She continued, "The moment one assumes responsibility for the destiny of a nation, one does it at one's own risk, at one's own danger, and one is never free to give it up."

The situation in Mexico continued to deteriorate and in 1866, Empress Carlota snuck back to Europe, hoping to secure help. She spoke to Napoleon III, but he refused to return his troops. A 1927 obituary published in the *New York Times* recounted Empress Carlota's exchange with Napoleon III. According to the article, she screamed at him: "I have got what I deserved! A granddaughter of Louis Philippe should never have trusted her future to a Bonaparte!"

At this point, Empress Carlota realized her husband was in real danger. She appealed to Francis Joseph, Maximilian's brother and the emperor of Austria. He refused to help. Next, she called upon Pope Pius IX and created such a scene in her hysteria that she was removed from the Vatican. Later, she was found walking the streets, jabbering incoherently. She never went back to Mexico.

Meanwhile, Juárez's backers captured Maximilian, tried him and sentenced him to death. He was executed by a firing squad on June 19, 1867. At this time, Empress Carlota was living at Miramar. In early 1868, family members visited her and transported her back to Laeken, her childhood home near Brussels. Eventually, she was told of her husband's execution and allegedly went mad. Empress Carlota lived her last 60 years in seclusion, cared for by her family. She passed her time playing cards, taking walks and reading books. Historians have long debated her state, wondering if she really went insane or pretended to have dementia to save her pride. She died on January 19, 1927, at the Castle of Bouchout, a 12th-century family estate near Laeken.

Books

Haslip, Joan, *The Crown of Mexico: Maximilian and His Empress Carlota,* Holt, Rinehart and Winston, 1971.

O'Connor, Richard, *The Cactus Throne: The Tragedy of Maximilian and Carlota,* G.P. Putnam's Sons, 1971.

Smith, Gene, *Maximilian and Carlota: A Tale of Romance and Tragedy,* William Morrow & Co. Inc., 1973.

Periodicals

New York Times, October 4, 1885; June 11, 1894; July 24, 1923; August 5, 1923; January 23, 1927.□

Juan José Carrera

The military leader Juan José Carrera (1782–1818) was one of Chile's founding fathers.

Juan José was the commander who provided the military muscle behind the political career of his brother José Miguel Carrera. He played a key role in establishing Chile's first semi-independent government, the Patria Vieja (Old Nation), served briefly as a member of its ruling junta, and fought in the battle that led to its demise, the so-called Disaster of Rancagua. In that battle, Carrera fought at the side of Chile's independence hero Bernardo O'Higgins, but as the pro-independence leadership splintered into factions, the Carrera brothers and O'Higgins ended up on opposite sides. As a result of that split, Carrera died in exile, executed by firing squad.

Descended from Spanish Aristocrats

Juan José Carrera was born on June 26, 1782, in Santiago, in what was the province of Chile in Spanish-controlled South America. He was the son of Ignacio de la Carrera, a colonel in the Spanish crown militia, and Paula Verdugo y Valdivieso. His full name in the Spanish system combined names from both his paternal and maternal families, becoming Juan José Carrera Verdugo. Descended from a long line of Spanish landowners and military officials, he had three younger siblings: a sister, Javiera, and two brothers, Juan Miguel and Luís. All would play parts in Chile's long and complex struggle for independence from Spain.

Carrera attended a school called the Carolino Convictori and soon began a military career. Both brothers rose through the militia ranks, and by 1811 Juan José had achieved the rank of sergeant major in the Grenadiers (grenade-throwers).

He was said to be a physically powerful man who could stop a wagon by grabbing the wheels, or pull a horse out of a well by the head. It was in that year that his brother Juan Miguel returned from Spain; he had been educated there and had participated in Spain's unsuccessful attempt to defend itself from invasion by Napoleon Bonaparte's expansionist French regime. The war in Spain started the chain of events that led to Chile's independence, and that of other South American countries: it left a power vacuum in Chile, with some groups swearing allegiance to the deposed Spanish King Ferdinand VII while others advocated more or less rapid moves toward freedom from Spain.

In this confused situation, the Carrera brothers moved quickly. In September of 1811 Juan José moved to declare himself commander of the Grenadiers. From this position he launched a series of quick coups d'état that, by November 15, had installed Juan Miguel and Bernardo O'Higgins as leaders of a new independent Government Junta of 1811. This event inaugurated the Patria Vieja. The new government began to promote liberal institutions modeled on those put in place by other revolutionary movements around the world; a new constitution was written, slavery was abolished, diplomatic relations with the United States were established, and a comprehensive education system, capped by a national library, was planned and begun.

Accused of Conspiracy

The position of Juan José in the new regime, however, was ambiguous. Considered a more volatile personality than Juan Miguel, he was suspected of conspiring with groups outside the new government, including the rival Larraín family and, even worse, the Royalist forces of the Viceroy of Peru, in order to further his own ambitions. By September of 1812 the situation had deteriorated to a point where Juan José and his Grenadiers were in open insubordination toward the government. For several weeks an outbreak of armed hostilities seemed to be a possibility, but the two brothers, despite ongoing tensions, worked out a temporary reconciliation. In the words of historian Stephen Clissold, quoted on the *Gendering Latin American Independence* Web site, Juan José was "conscious of his seniority [and] sometimes sullenly resentful of his more brilliant brother's pretensions, but his own manifest inferiority of gifts and personality always compelled his eventual submission." In 1813 Juan José temporarily joined the ruling junta itself.

These internecine rivalries were typical of the hastily organized Patria Vieja, a situation that became all the more serious inasmuch as many Chileans still favored Spanish control and welcomed the advance of a force of 2,000 men headed by the Peruvian viceroy, Ferndando de Ascabal. The Carrera brothers led Chilean troops in two clashes with the royalist forces, at Chillán and San Carlos, in 1813. Those battles ended badly for the Chileans, weakening the positions of both Carreras. Juan José participated in a coup in July of 1814 that reinstalled Juan Miguel as supreme director of the junta in place of Francisco de la Lastra. But a more serious rival was O'Higgins, who had been placed in command of the Chilean army following heavy losses at Chillán and San Carlos. The carreristas, as the Carrera faction was known, briefly came into armed conflict with

O'Higgins, but the two groups set aside their differences as Peruvian forces, under the leadership of Mariano Osorio, advanced toward Santiago in 1814. At this unlikely juncture, Carrera married Ana María Cotapos.

The Disaster of Rancagua, in which the Chilean patriots were routed by Osorio's forces, marked the end of the Patria Vieja and a temporary reimposition of royalist control. Juan José and Juan Miguel Carrera, as well as Bernardo O'Higgins, went into exile in Mendoza, a city in northwestern Argentina near the Chilean border. The city was then part of a short-lived U.S.–style United Provinces of South America, including the present countries of Argentina, Bolivia, and Uruguay. Its regional governor was General José de San Martín, who later forged an alliance with O'Higgins that eventually succeeded in driving the Spanish from all of southern South America. Rivalries among the exiled Chileans continued to fester, and Juan José Carrera incurred San Martín's enmity when he killed O'Higgins backer (and fellow Irish-Chilean) Juan MacKenna O'Reilly in a duel. He spent time in an Argentine prison, rejoining Juan Miguel and his younger brother Luís in Buenos Aires upon his release.

Planned Infiltration in Disguise

The bad blood between the Carrera and O'Higgins–San Martín factions continued to simmer, and the situation deteriorated further after Juan Miguel Carrera traveled to the United States in 1817. When he returned to the port of Buenos Aires with two purchased warships, O'Higgins received him coldly and refused to accept his help. Soon after this setback, Juan José and Luís Carrera began to plot ways to seize the mantle of Chilean independence for themselves. According to one later commentator it was their sister, Javiera, who hatched the plan that even Juan Miguel Carrera soon recognized as doomed: Juan José, disguised as a printer's apprentice, and the younger Luís, dressed as a teenage boy, would sneak into Chile and try to rejoin supporters there. Other conspirators would organize a military force that would place O'Higgins and San Martín under arrest and then try to cross the border.

The plan did not lack for grandiose detail. The conspirators agreed on the roles they would assume in the new Chilean government; Juan José was to be one of two top military commanders, and it was to be his responsibility to capture and try San Martín. The enterprise unraveled, however, even before Juan José's advance group crossed the Cordillera, the Andean mountain range separating the settled areas of Argentina and Chile. Luís Carrera, for reasons unknown, assaulted a postal carrier and stole the contents of his mail sack. He and his companions were arrested, and their confessions led to the arrest of Juan José at Barranquita, in Cuyo province, on August 20, 1817.

Imprisoned once again in Mendoza, Juan José had some months in which he hoped for rescue—which Javiera, by means of letters addressed to anyone she could think of, attempted to provide. The other conspirators evaded arrest until February of 1818, by which time O'Higgins and San Martín had invaded Chile themselves and were on the verge of final victory over the Spanish at Maipú. Since they now constituted a functioning Chilean government, the documents for the trial of Juan José and Luís in Mendoza had to be copied, taken across the Andes, and filed in Santiago, where O'Higgins and San Martín were otherwise occupied.

After its victory over the royalists seemed assured, however, the chief problem of the new Chilean government became the imprisoned Carrera brothers, who were charged not only with insurrection within the Chilean camp but also with attempting to overthrow local officials. After a brief trial, they were sentenced to death by firing squad on April 8, 1818. Luís, according to one chronicle, made confession to a priest, but Juan José stepped directly to the gallows. It took many shots to bring him down.

Books

Bizzarro, Salvatore, *Historical Dictionary of Chile,* Scarecrow, 1987.

Clissold, Stephen, *Bernardo O'Higgins, and the Independence of Chile,* Hart-Davis, 1968.

Collier, Simon, *A History of Chile, 1808–2002,* Cambridge University Press, 2004.

Kinsbruner, Jay, *Bernardo O'Higgins,* Twayne, 1968.

Online

"Juan José Carrera Verdugo," Gendering Latin American Independence: Women's Political Culture and the Textual Construction of Gender, 1790-1850, http://www.genderlatam.org.uk/PersonDetails.php?PeopleID=432 (January 26, 2009).

"Juan José Carrera," Icarito, http://www.icarito.cl/medio/articulo/0,0,38035857_0_351878266_1,00.html (January 26, 2009). □

Braulio Carrillo

Braulio Carrillo (1800–1845) was the third president of Costa Rica, ruling from 1837 to 1842 in two separate administrations. He proclaimed himself "dictator for life," but was exiled to El Salvador and later assassinated. Carrillo, however, was credited for enhancing the growth of agriculture and the coffee business in his country. He also ordered the construction of a road from San José, in the central part of the country, to the Caribbean coast. More than a century later, the route became a highway with an adjacent national park. The country named both in honor of Carrillo.

Carrillo was born in Cartago, Costa Rica, in 1800. He attended schools in Leon, Nicaragua, before traveling to Honduras, El Salvador, and Guatemala. He returned to Costa Rica in 1830.

Encouraged Growth of Coffee

After working in the financial department of the Supreme Court, Carrillo became Costa Rica's provincial governor, then its president, after the country, once a province of Guatemala, seceded from the five-member Federal Republic of Central America after it broke from Spain's rule in 1821. Carrillo filled out the term of José Rafael de Gallegos, who resigned amid reports of electoral taint, and served from 1835 to 1837. After Manuel Aguilar succeeded him, with Juan Mora as vice president, in 1837, he reclaimed the presidency one year later, taking advantage of disaffection with Aguilar.

Costa Rica, "although widely removed from the center of political intrigue and commotion in Guatemala . . . did not wholly escape the dissentions which disturbed the peace and retarded the prosperity of the other states," Ephraim George Squier wrote in *The States of Central America.* Costa Rican revolutions, though, were usually "less bloody" than those in such neighboring states as Guatemala and Nicaragua, Squier added, "owing, probably, rather to the circumstance of the concentration and homogeneousness of its population than to a higher morality or a more tolerant spirit."

John A. Booth and Thomas W. Walker, in *Understanding Central America,* called Carrillo the country's "first dictator-president." They wrote: "In the nineteenth century, the roots were planted for Costa Rican democracy, despite a conspicuous absence of democratic rule for much of the era. From 1824 to 1899, one Costa Rican government in five ended by coup d'ètat and the country was under military rule 44 percent of the time. During most of that epoch, the country was governed by moneyed rural families."

In his second administration, Carrillo eliminated foreign debt, which Costa Rica had accumulated since 1826, enacted penal and civil laws, and organized the court system. Carrillo also redesigned the Costa Rican flag in 1840.

Notably, he encouraged agriculture. In 1840 Carrillo authorized the sale of municipal lots, called *las paras,* provided that the buyers agreed to plant coffee on them. "This contributed to the emergence of a class of smallholding yeoman farmers that kept renewing itself by expanding the agricultural frontiers," Booth and Walker noted. Land grants for growers facilitated the cultivation of coffee, a practice that dated to the administration of Juan Mora Fernandez, Costa Rica's first ruler. "This quickly led to the establishment of a new Costa Rican elite, the coffee barons, who quickly put their power to use," the Web site *CentralAmerica.com* wrote.

Frustrated by restrictions placed upon his presidency, Carrillo imposed a coup and called himself "president for life" in 1838, effectively making himself a dictator. By then, Costa Rica had permanently withdrawn from the Central American federation. After Costa Rica learned of the independence, bitter disputes followed over whether it should join the federation or align with independent Mexico.

Carrillo decreed a new constitution, calling it the *ley de bases y garantia,* or law of rights and guarantees. Carrillo declaring himself a dictator "struck a major blow against democratic rule," Myron Weiner and Ergun Özbudun wrote in *Competitive Elections in Developing Countries,* adding that the decree eliminated "popular sovereignty and local government. The powerful office of *jefe politico* was created, combining the functions of mayor and justice of the peace." Squier called Carrillo "a man of energetic character, who exercised power without the intervention of legislature or ministers." He added: "For five years, from the period of the dissolution of the federation in 1839, to the first formal assumption of independent sovereignty in 1844, the state held an anomalous position, being, for the greater part of the time, under [Carrillo's] dictatorship.''

General Francisco Morazán, a Honduran who had been elected president of the federation in 1830, took advantage of unhappiness with Carrillo. Forces loyal to Rafael Carrera had routed Morazán at Gutemala City in 1840 and driven him into exile—Carrera represented conservatives who favored autonomy while Morazán sided with the pro-federalist liberals. ''Thus, conservatism became closely related to local autonomy and the breakup of the Central American federation,'' Leslie Bethell wrote in *Central America since Independence*. In 1842, Bethell added, ''Morazán returned, reorganized his army in El Savador with less support than he anticipated and then invaded Costa Rica, where he toppled Braulio Carrillo.'' Morazán pulled off the coup by winning the support of Costa Rican army leaders after he landed on the Pacific Coast.

''Unfortunately for Carrillo, the country disagreed with his [dictatorial] decision,'' Joseph Fullman and Nicola Mainwood wrote in their book *Costa Rica*. His lifetime presidency lasted just a few months before he was overthrown and sent to live in exile in El Salvador.'' Carrillo lived in El Salvador and was working in a mine in 1845 when a personal enemy killed him, taking advantage ''of the revolutionary condition of the country to perpetrate his vengeance,'' Joaquin Bernardo Calvo wrote in *Republic of Costa Rico*.

Morazán's rule was also short-lived. He declared Costa Rica a part of the federation, but was in charge for only six months. An insurgency overtook Morazán, who was convicted in a brief trial and shot to death by a firing squad on September 15, 1842.

Carrillo's rule, wrote Squier, ''gradually prepared the people for the proclamation of the state as a sovereign and independent republic, which took place on the event of his death in 1845.'' Since then, Costa Rica's government has largely consisted of a president and a 12-deputy Congress, with a vice president governing meetings.

Road, National Park Bear His Name

As the coffee industry expanded, Carrillo saw the need to construct a roadway to the Caribbean Sea from the Central Valley, to enhance deliveries to Europe. Without such access, ships had to circle around the southern tip of South America. ''Although this president was a merciless dictator, he is credited with conceiving the idea of building [such] a road,'' Stéphane G. Marceau, Francis Giguere, and Yves Seguin wrote in another book titled *Costa Rica*. A small road was finished in 1882, and nine years later a railway was constructed along the route, connecting San José and Limón. After several bridges were destroyed along the route, government officials abandoned the railway.

In 1977 the government resurrected the project of constructing a highway from San José, the national capital, through the mountains to the flatlands near the Caribbean coast. When nature advocates feared that highway construction would lead to overdevelopment and deforestation, the government conceived of a national park. Costa Rica has lost two-thirds of its forest land since the 1950s. ''Environmentalists,'' wrote the Web site Costa-Rica-Guide.com,

''used the value of the region as a watershed to leverage the establishing [of] the national park.'' The government opened Parque Nacional Braulio Carrillo (Braulio Carrillo National Park) on April 15, 1978. The road, named Autopista Braulio Carrillo, opened in 1987. Locals sometimes call it the Guápiles highway or the Siquirres highway. ''It is certainly one of the most spectacular in the country . . . and provides easy access to protected virgin tropical rainforest just a few kilometers from San José,'' Marceau, Giguere, and Seguin wrote. The road, however, is also vulnerable to landslides.

Braulio Carrillo National Park covers 113,400 acres, and is the largest park in the Central Valley, featuring hiking trails, overlooks, waterfalls, and an aerial tram. It includes about 500 species of birds and more than 150 species of mammals, and the heavy rainfall for the region benefits the plant life. Climate zones range from tropical to high-altitude rainforest.

Carrillo was a self-proclaimed dictator who was driven into exile and assassinated, yet a superhighway and a major national park bear his name. Fullman and Mainwood wrote that Carrillo's ordering of the roadway was ''one of the few success stories of his time in office.'' They added: ''the building of the motorway . . . was seen as the completion of Carrillo's vision, and so his name lives on.''

Carrillo also earned credit for laying the groundwork for the country's penal system. ''Costa Rica was the first of the Central American republics to effect complete emancipation from the Spanish and colonial laws, and one of the first countries of Spanish America to provide herself with laws in harmony with a new mode of political being and with the progress of civilization,'' Calvo wrote.''

Books

Bethel, Leslie, *Central America Since Independence,* Cambridge University Press Archive, 1991.

Booth, John A., and Thomas W. Walker, *Understanding Central America: Global Forces, Rebellion, and Change,* Westview Press, 2006.

Calvo, Joaquin Bernardo, *Republic of Costa Rica,* Rand McNally & Co., 1890.

Fullman, Joseph, and Nicola Mainwood, *Costa Rica,* New Holland Publishers, 2006.

Marceau, Stephane G., Francis Giguere, and Yves Seguin, *Costa Rica,* Ulysses Travel Guides, 2001.

Squier, Ephraim George, *The States of Central America,* Harper & brothers, 1858.

Weiner, Myron, and Ergun Ozbudan, *Competitive Elections in Developing Countries,* Duke University Press, 1987.

Online

''Braulio Carrillo National Park, Costa Rica,'' Costa-Rica-Guide.com, http://www.costa-rica-guide.com/Natural/Braulio.html, December 19, 2008.

''A Brief History of Costa Rica,'' CentralAmerica.com, http://www.centralamerica.com/cr/info/history.htm, December 19, 2008.

''Elections and Events 1812-1900,'' University of California, San Diego, http://www.ucsd.edu/portal/site/Libraries/menuitem.346352c02aac0c82b9ba4310d34b01ca/?vgnextoid=3eeee22617e14110VgnVCM10000045b410acRCRD, December 18, 2008.☐

Claire Lee Chennault

American airman Claire Lee Chennault (1893–1958), a hero of World War II, helped revolutionize the way air forces fight. During his years as an Army pilot and flight instructor, Chennault promoted the use of fighter planes in formations, instead of the solo dogfighting of World War I. He proved the effectiveness of his tactics in World War II, when his corps of American volunteer fighters, the Flying Tigers, played a key role in defending China and Southeast Asia from imperial Japan.

Chennault (pronounced shuh-NAWLT) was born on September 6, 1893, in Commerce, Texas, to Louisiana cotton planter John Stonewall Jackson Chennault and his wife Jessie Lee. Chennault grew up in northeast Louisiana. He enrolled at Louisiana State University in Baton Rouge in January of 1909, when he was 14 (a relatively common age to attend college in the early 1900s), then transferred to a state teacher's college in Natchitoches. He worked as a teacher in several states during the 1910s. He married Nell Thompson in 1911 and eventually had six sons and two daughters with her.

When the United States joined World War I in April of 1917, Chennault enlisted in the Army. Ever since seeing an airplane for the first time, at the Louisiana State Fair in Shreveport in 1910, he had wanted to be a pilot. Turned down when he applied for flight training, he managed to get transferred to the Army's only base for training pilots, Kelly Field in San Antonio, Texas. He convinced flight instructors there to give him informal training. He was transferred to Langley Field, Virginia, where he fought off a severe bout of influenza (an epidemic in 1918) and nearly died. After he recovered and the war ended, the Army at last approved him for formal flight training, and he returned to Kelly Field. He displayed a talent for flying fighter planes and soon became a flight instructor.

Chennault was discharged in April of 1920, but refused to give up on his dream of flying. "I have tasted of the air," he wrote in a letter to his father (quoted in *Claire Chennault: Flying Tiger* by Earle Rice Jr.), "and I cannot get it out of my craw." After a brief return to his family's cotton plantation, Chennault applied to the Army's new Air Service and was accepted. Chennault was one of the first students in the Army's new aerial fighting tactics course, which taught World War I's dogfighting tactics of one-on-one air combat. He became convinced that fighter planes would be more effective in war if they flew together in formations instead of alone. In 1923, he was named commander of a fighter squadron at Pearl Harbor, Hawaii. His fighters proved themselves in mock battles, sometimes overwhelming and embarrassing the Army's artillery forces and Navy's dive bombers.

Introduced Innovative Tactics

While instructing Army pilots in the late 1920s and early 1930s, Chennault promoted his tactic of flying fighter planes in two-man formations, a leader and wingman, and concentrating their firepower on a single target. The Army Air Corps in the 1930s disdained that idea, however, and was instead building a strategy around a large bomber plane, the "Flying Fortress," which it thought would be invulnerable to attack because of its speed and size. Chennault argued incessantly against this strategy, making several enemies in the Air Corps. He was not allowed to join the Army's Command and General Staff School, a sign that he was out of favor.

Chennault had one prominent supporter, however, in General John Curry, who assigned him to develop a three-man stunt flying team. Chennault spent three years flying Boeing P-12E fighters in air shows, executing complex acrobatic maneuvers in perfect formation. Playing off a popular song about a circus performer, the team called themselves "Three Men on a Flying Trapeze." For Chennault, the team held a greater purpose than stunt or spectacle. It demonstrated his theories about how to use fighter planes. A general in the Chinese Air Force saw their last performance, at an air show in Miami, Florida in January of 1936, and invited Chennault's two partners, John Williamson and Billy McDonald, to come to China as flight instructors.

Fought The War In China

Health problems, including chronic bronchitis and impaired hearing from years of flying in loud planes, forced Chennault to retire from the Army Air Corps in April of 1937. It appeared his military career was over. But that spring, the Chinese government hired Chennault as an adviser to its air force. Tensions between China and Japan were increasing, and Chiang Kai-shek, the president of China, and his wife, head of the country's aviation commission, realized that their air force needed reorganizing and better training.

Chennault and McDonald, his former stunt-flying partner, spent several days in Japan photographing shipping routes and industrial facilities, intelligence that would later prove extremely valuable. Next, Chennault inspected the Chinese Air Force and found that its pilots were poorly trained and that most of its planes were not ready for combat. On July 7, 1937, a month after Chennault arrived in China, a gunfight broke out between Chinese and Japanese forces at the Marco Polo Bridge near Beijing. It set off a war that eventually became part of World War II. A few days into the conflict, the Chinese air force proved its incompetence when it attempted to attack a Japanese warship that was bombarding the Chinese city of Shanghai. Instead, the pilots, flying in a fog, bombed part of Shanghai and could not hit the ship.

Though Chennault worked to improve the air force, the first few years of the war did not go well for China. Mercenaries hired to fly its planes performed poorly. By late 1940, Japan controlled most of China's main ports, and its air force dominated the country's skies. Chennault returned to the United States to seek help. The U.S. government quietly allowed China to buy 100 P-40 fighter planes from an American entrepreneur, and let Chennault recruit a volunteer force of 240 American military airmen.

Trained the Flying Tigers

The American Volunteer Group played a celebrated role in the air battles in Asia during World War II. They arrived in Burma in the summer and fall of 1941 and underwent training directed by Chennault. After hearing that the Japanese considered tiger sharks a sign of bad luck, they painted tiger shark faces on their planes' noses. Chinese soon nicknamed the pilots and their planes the "Flying Tigers."

"Fight in pairs," Chennault told his airmen (as quoted by Rice in *Claire Chennault: Flying Tiger*). "Make every bullet count. Never try to get every Japanese in one pass. Hit hard, break clean, and get in position for another pass. Never worry about what's going to happen next, or it will happen to you. Keep looking around. You can lick the Japanese without getting hurt if you use your head and are careful."

The Flying Tigers flew their first mission on December 20, 1941, less than two weeks after Japan attacked the United States naval base at Pearl Harbor, Hawaii, and the United States declared war. In the next seven months, the Flying Tigers shot down 300 enemy planes over China and Southeast Asia, while suffering only 26 casualties. The Flying Tigers inspired Americans in the early months of U.S. involvement in the war, when most news from elsewhere in the world was grim. "They had been transformed from ragtag, roisterous mercenaries, many of whom had never flown a fighter, into cool, highly skilled combat pilots," wrote James W. Canan in the *Washington Post*. "They beat the odds at nearly every turn by virtue of their superior airmanship, gunnery and tactics, which put a premium on fighters attacking in pairs."

Viewed as a Maverick

On April 15, 1942, Chennault was reinstated as a U.S. Army officer and given the rank of Brigadier General. On July 4, the Flying Tigers were admitted into the U.S. Army Air Forces. Chennault was named head of U.S. air forces in China. His new stint in the Army proved to be stormy, though. Other generals saw him as a renegade and disliked his outspokenness. They often disagreed with his strategies and demands for more planes and supplies. They also felt Chennault was too close to Chiang Kai-shek, whom they distrusted.

Some of the friction was personal. Chennault was a famously tough man, and even his craggy face was intimidating. American friends of his said (according to the *New York Times*) that he "looks as if he has been holding his face out of the cockpit and into a storm for years." He was difficult to work with, feuding during the war with other American generals, the British military, and sometimes even the Chinese. He wrote an insubordinate letter to President Franklin D. Roosevelt in 1943, asking to be named commander of all U.S. forces in China, a position held by his superior officer, Gen. Joseph Stilwell. *New York Times* writer Annalee Jacoby, reviewing Chennault's 1949 memoir, *Way of A Fighter,* joked that the book could also be called "'I Was Always Right,' or 'They Wouldn't Let Me Win the War,' or 'The Varmints and the Villians That Opposed Me.' Or, perhaps, simply 'Grrrr-r-r-r.'"

Roosevelt, however, agreed with many of Chennault's strategies. The president reacted to his letter by promoting Chennault to major general; creating the Fourteenth Air Force, with him in command; and permitting him to proceed with an air offensive against Japan. Starting in June of 1943, Chennault's Fourteenth Air Force destroyed at least 2,600 Japanese planes, sank 44 ships, and destroyed 600 bridges. It also carried out bombing raids on Japan itself.

While defending China, Chennault developed a deep affection for its people. The feeling was mutual. Americans called him the ultimate "China hand," a phrase meaning an American expert on China. Chennault argued that the United States should provide strong support to China's Nationalist government, and he felt American companies could benefit greatly from investment there. His advice, however, often went unheeded. In the summer of 1945, after Roosevelt's death, Chennault resigned from the military. He quietly made it clear that he felt that other United States officials had become too critical of Chiang's government and was not supporting it in its renewed fight against the Chinese Communists.

Returned to China

After resigning, Chennault returned to the United States, but only for five months. He divorced his wife, returned to China at the start of 1946, and in December of 1947 married Anna Chan, a young Chinese newspaper reporter and former nurse for the Flying Tigers. Chennault organized the Civil Air Transport, a major Chinese flight service that flew missions in support of Nationalist forces fighting the Communist uprising. When the Communists took over mainland China in October of 1949, Chennault followed the Nationalist government to the Chinese island of Taiwan. He and his partners sold the air service to the United States'

Central Intelligence Agency in 1950. Later known as Air America, it supported American forces during the Korean War and later, both French and American forces in Vietnam.

In December of 1957, Chennault announced to reporters in Taipei, Taiwan, that he had developed incurable lung cancer. He returned to the United States in January of 1958 for treatment at hospitals in Washington, D.C., and New Orleans. He underwent surgery that May at Ochsner Foundation Hospital in New Orleans and was readmitted there in early June of 1958. That summer, President Dwight D. Eisenhower and Congress enacted a bill promoting him from major general to lieutenant general on the military retirement list. On July 27, with his wife at his side, Chennault died from an arterial hemorrhage. He was 67. He is buried in Arlington National Cemetery.

Books

Rice, Earle, Jr. *Claire Chennault: Flying Tiger,* Chelsea House Publishers, 2003.

Periodicals

New York Times, January 30, 1949; July 28, 1958.
Washington Post, December 20, 1987; August 31, 1990.

Online

"Chennault, Claire Lee," *World Book Advanced 2008,* http://www.worldbookonline.com/advanced/article?id=ar108860 (December 14, 2008). □

Roy Cohn

American attorney Roy Cohn (1927–1986) was centrally involved in some of the most famous episodes of American political life in the 1950s. Widely reviled but also vigorously defended, he served as chief counsel for the U.S. Senate Permanent Subcommittee on Investigations, headed by the senator and anti-Communist crusader Joseph McCarthy.

U nusually public in that role, Cohn failed miserably, and indeed his failures contributed to McCarthy's precipitous downfall. For much of his life, however, Cohn was a behind-the-scenes figure—and he went to great lengths to remain that way. Later in life he made various claims about the significance of his contributions to, for instance, the espionage trials of American Communists Julius and Ethel Rosenberg. Because of the furtive nature of his work, however, such claims have been difficult for biographers to prove or disprove. Cohn's private style extended to his personal life; widely believed to have been homosexual, and eventually a victim of AIDS when it was a disease contracted primarily by homosexuals, Cohn nevertheless publicly disparaged gays and opposed any expansion of homosexual rights.

Lived with Mother into Adulthood

Roy Marcus Cohn was born on February 20, 1927, in Bronx, New York. From the start, his life was dominated by political influence, and by its relentless pursuit. His father, Albert Cohn, was a New York State Supreme Court justice who had risen through the ranks of New York's Democratic Party politics under the tutelage of political machine boss Ed Flynn. Equally influential was Cohn's mother, Dora Marcus Cohn, a millionaire's daughter who hoped to replicate her own father's success in the life of her son. Cohn remained close to his mother in adulthood, living with her in her Manhattan apartment until her death in 1967.

Cohn attended top private schools: the Community School for gifted students, Fieldston School in the Bronx, and Horace Mann preparatory school. While his classmates followed the fortunes of the New York Yankees baseball dynasty, Cohn observed the ways of the political animals who populated the Grand Concourse avenue that ran among the civic buildings of the Bronx. He enjoyed discussing law cases with his father, and in general he preferred the company of older people. By the time he was 15, Cohn had executed his first back room transaction: thanks to connections he made through an uncle, Bernie Marcus, he facilitated the purchase of a radio station by Generoso Pope, the father of a classmate. Pope rewarded Cohn with a $10,000 payment, part of which the teenaged Cohn kicked back to a Federal Communications Commission member.

Soon Cohn was fixing traffic tickets for friends and doing himself even bigger favors. Finishing high school a year early, he faced the prospect of being drafted during the final stages of World War II. Cohn escaped the draft by calling in a family favor from a congressional representative who nominated him for officer training at the U.S. Military Academy at West Point, New York. Then he stalled for time by failing the academy's physical academy three times in a row. With the war safely over, Cohn enrolled at Columbia University, and he was not above using a program for veterans to reduce his graduation requirements. He once again finished in three years, receiving a B.A. degree in 1945. Admitted to Columbia's law school, he blazed through his coursework and was awarded the LL.B. law degree in 1947.

Not yet 20 years old, he was not even eligible to take the New York State bar exam for another year. When he did take the exam he passed on the first attempt, a notable accomplishment. There was a job waiting for him as an assistant U.S. attorney in the Justice Department's appeals division. For several months he worked on routine cases involving narcotics and even stamp fraud, but he was hungry to see his name in newspaper headlines. He accomplished that goal by manufacturing publicity out of thin air: when a small-time gangster was arrested with a stash of counterfeit bills, Cohn called a journalist and claimed to have cracked a major counterfeiting ring. He manipulated Treasury Department office politics to produce comments from investigators that seemed to back up his claims. But even Cohn, who remained reticent about most of his subterfuges, later admitted that he had greatly exaggerated the arrest's significance.

Prosecuted Rosenbergs

In 1950 Cohn took a job as confidential assistant to U.S. Attorney Irving Saypol. Just 23 years old, he was tracked closely by journalists as he spent his evenings circulating around posh New York nightclubs cultivating old contacts and new ones. Cohn was at the center of the prosecution team during the 1951 trial of scientists Julius and Ethel Rosenberg, helping to bring about their conviction with his relentless questioning. He claimed to have discussed the sentencing with Judge Irving Kaufman, a breach of the law, and he may have persuaded the judge to sentence the possibly innocent Ethel Rosenberg to death.

Cohn moved to Washington, D.C., in 1952 to take a job as special assistant to U.S. Attorney General James McGranery. He did not fit in well at the Attorney General's office, clashing with his superiors after he charged that they were impeding his investigation into the presence of Communists on the American staff at United Nations headquarters in New York City. But his unsuccessful effort to obtain a perjury indictment against Johns Hopkins University professor Owen Lattimore, whom Cohn suspected of Communist sympathies, got the attention of McCarthy, whose charges of widespread Communist infiltration of American politics and culture had gained wide publicity. McCarthy, impressed by Cohn's anti-Communist zeal, hired him as the subcommittee's chief counsel. The other candidate for the job, ultimately unsuccessful, had been Robert F. Kennedy.

Cohn's first months on the job were not auspicious. He brought a friend, G. David Schine, on board as a consultant, although Schine's only apparent qualification for the job was an amateurish, self-published pamphlet called "Definition of Communism." The two embarked on an 18-day tour of European offices of the U.S. Information Agency (USIA), with the stated aim of purging USIA libraries of books sympathetic to Communism. The trip generated ridicule not only in European newspapers but in the United States, after the pair accused an American official in Germany, Peter Kaghan, of having signed a Communist petition. Kaghan dubbed Cohn and Schine "junketeering gumshoes," and the term stuck in the press. Kaghan, however, was fired from his job, and the hardworking Cohn made himself indispensable to McCarthy and his committee.

The mutual benefits of Cohn's relationship with McCarthy ran out, however, after Schine was drafted into the U.S. Army in late 1953. Cohn began making calls to have Schine assigned to a desk job, but this time, perhaps because of growing tensions between McCarthy and President Dwight D. Eisenhower, his dealmaking went nowhere. Cohn asked McCarthy for help, and McCarthy announced that he was launching an investigation of Communist influence in the army itself. The military hit back with a 34-page report documenting Cohn's calls, which included a threat to "wreck the army." As a result, the so-called Army-McCarthy hearings in April of 1954 turned from an extension of McCarthy's crusade into a debacle in which McCarthy himself came under close questioning from army lawyers, increasingly losing his composure, while Cohn wrote notes and shook his head, trying to rein him in. McCarthy and Cohn were actually cleared of the army's allegations of improper conduct, but McCarthy's influence was finished. Cohn resigned his position as counsel a few weeks after the hearings.

Built Successful Law Practice

Cohn still had many friends in high places, however, and the guest list at a banquet thrown in his honor in New York a few months later, including William F. Buckley and Westbrook Pegler, read like a roster of American conservative thought. Cohn moved back to New York, joining the law firm of Saxe, Bacon, and Bolan. He attracted high-profile clients, including future president Ronald Reagan, jet set rock-and-roll wife Bianca Jagger, mob boss Carmine Galante, and real estate magnate Donald Trump. Three times Cohn was a defendant instead of an attorney; he was tried three times on charges of bribery, fraud, and income tax evasion. Cohn maintained that he was the victim of a vendetta initiated by Robert F. Kennedy, who was U.S. Attorney General when the series of prosecutions began, and at the end of his second trial, in 1969, he defended himself in a dramatic seven-hour summation, delivered without notes. He was acquitted all three times.

The prosecutions intensified Cohn's reputation as a hard-to-beat courtroom scrapper, although his actual legal skills were said to have declined as time passed. He wrote several books, including *How to Stand Up for Your Rights* (1981). Cohn led a high-flying bachelor lifestyle, hosting lavish parties at his Manhattan apartment or at the Studio

54 nightclub with guests like novelist Norman Mailer and television personality Barbara Walters. Cohn's homosexuality, long rumored, became an open secret. In public, however, Cohn denounced homosexuals and strove to limit their rights. "He is so complex and contradictory," actor James Woods, who played Cohn in the cable television film *Citizen Cohn,* commented to Bernard Weinraub of the *New York Times.* "He once addressed a fund-raiser and delivered a diatribe about gays, and then promptly jumped into a limousine for Studio 54 and was flamboyant on the dance floor with his gay friends. This guy was so self-loathing."

At some point during the 1980s, Roy Cohn contracted the AIDS virus. Diagnosed in 1984, he maintained that he was suffering from liver cancer, but among his last string-pulling deals was one that allowed him to participate in trials of the early AIDS drug AZT, and he lobbied the Reagan administration for increases in AIDS research funding. In 1985 Cohn began an autobiography, eventually completed by his friend Sidney Zion, in which he disputed many of the charges that had been leveled against him during his lifetime. In 1986 Cohn faced disbarment proceedings in New York State, based on various charges, including one that he had failed to repay a $100,000 loan from a client. Cohn's legal counsel in the disbarment proceedings was future U.S. Attorney General Michael Mukasey. On June 23, 1986, he lost his license to practice law. Cohn died at a National Institutes of Health hospital in Bethesda, Maryland, on August 2, 1986, of AIDS-related complications. He is reputed to have owed the Internal Revenue Service an estimated seven million dollars. Cohn was a major character in the seven-hour play *Angels in America* (1991), by dramatist Tony Kushner.

Books

Gay & Lesbian Biography, St. James Press, 1997.

Von Hoffman, Nicholas, *Citizen Cohn: The Life and Times of Roy Cohn,* Doubleday, 1988.

Zion, Sidney, and Roy Cohn, *The Autobiography of Roy Cohn,* Lyle Stuart, 1988.

Periodicals

Globe & Mail (Toronto, Ontario, Canada), August 6, 1988.

Herald (Glasgow, Scotland), May 1, 2007.

New York Times, April 3, 1988; August 19, 1992.

U.S. News & World Report, January 27, 1986.

Online

Ward, Geoffrey C., "The Life and Times: Roy Cohn," *American Heritage,* http://www.americanheritage.com/articles/magazine/ah/1988/5/1988_5_12.shtml (January 16, 2009). □

Jane Colden

The early American botanist Jane Colden (1724–1766) was the first woman in the New World to become accomplished in the science of botany.

Homeschooled and partially self-taught, Colden corresponded with the great European botanists of the day. They in turn recommended her to Carl Linnaeus, the greatest botanist of them all. She was the first woman who had mastered the classification system that bore his name, a system that is still used as a taxonomy of all living things. Colden discovered the flower known today as the gardenia, and named it for the Scots botanist Alexander Garden. She catalogued more than 300 plants that she found near her family's home north of New York City, and her observations circulated among scientists in the Old World.

Jane Colden was born on March 27, 1724, in New York City. She was the fifth of ten children of Cadwallader Colden, a Scottish physician who had emigrated to Philadelphia in 1710, and his wife, Alice Christy (or Christie) Colden. The elder Colden was something of a Renaissance man and a jack-of-all-trades. He was widely read in physics, astronomy, and botany, and he maintained a substantial library of volumes in those fields. Cadwallader Colden was also quick to identify the financial advantages of holding political office in the New World; he moved to New York to take a position as Surveyor General, and he later served for several years as lieutenant governor of what was then the province of New York in British America. He accumulated the resources to build a handsome house in the hills outside Newburgh, New York, and he named it Coldengham.

Homeschooled by Mother

Jane Colden spent most of her childhood on this estate, surrounded by flora with folk names that might vary from one county to the next. The family home was too far from any town school for any of the Colden children to attend, so Jane and all of her eight living siblings were educated at home. Inasmuch as Cadwallader Colden's responsibilities frequently took him away from home, a key participant in this process was Jane's mother, Alice, and fortunately she was well equipped for the task. She had received a good education in Scotland, and she was a full partner in the intellectual discussions that occurred whenever the family could attract learned visitors to its remote homestead. Letters written by Jane's brother, the younger Cadwallader Colden, described their mother's gift for thorough and systematic teaching.

It was Jane's father, however, who noticed her special gift for botany. A strong believer in the education of women who argued their cause, he brought her books on plants and gardens, and shared with her the knowledge of the local ecosystem he had gained from visitors to Coldengham, such as Peter Kalm, Linnaeus's best student. He also translated Linnaeus's writings from Latin into English (although solidly educated, Jane Colden never learned the former language) and trained his daughter in the use of the Swedish scientist's exhaustive method, a novelty at the time. From her father, Colden also learned to use printer's ink to capture images of the leaves of plants, and she seems also to have become a competent artist.

Between the early 1740s and the time of her marriage in 1759, Colden preserved and classified some 400 varieties of plants, many of them native to the region north of New York City. She described them in great detail and made somewhat less detailed drawings. She apparently published several articles in European journals. She came to be regarded as an expert on American plant life, and she also wrote a book about cheesemaking, one of the first such manuals written in America. She also had a lively interest in insects and shells.

Sent Plants to Europe

Word got back to Linnaeus by way of scientists who visited Coldengham that Colden was the first woman to have mastered his system. She became part of the network of correspondents who sent him plant specimens from around the world, and she was probably the only woman among them. At least one of her plant descriptions found its way into Linnaeus's catalogue, for he mentioned the plant in one of his letters and used Colden's names for it— *Fibraurea,* or, as it was called in New York, gold thread. Colden's own writings noted the local names of plants and the uses folk medicine attached to them.

Leading European botanists thought well of Colden's work. Indeed, several suggested to Linnaeus that he name the *Fibraurea* plant after Colden—a rare honor among botanists. "This young lady merits your esteem, and does honour to your system," John Ellis wrote in a letter to the Swede, quoted in *Women in the Biological Sciences.* "She has drawn and described 400 plants in your method only; she uses English terms. Her father has a plant named called after him Coldenia, suppose you should call this [Gold thread] Coldenella or any other name that might distinguish her among your Genera." She was also well enough regarded by Linnaeus and other writers that she felt confident in correcting their mistakes from time to time.

Linnaeus apparently expressed appreciation for Colden's efforts, but he had already given the plant a different name (which was also dropped in favor of yet a third name, *Coptis groenlandica,* given by another botanist, Richard Salisbury, who found the plant independently). Colden herself was more assiduous about promoting the work of her colleagues: after describing a small shrub with white flowers, a Chinese native transplanted to Africa, England, and finally America, she named it the gardenia in Alexander Garden's honor.

Gave Up Botany After Marriage

For much of her life, Colden was occupied with her scientific work. She did not marry until age 35, late in life for a woman in the eighteenth century. Her husband, William Farquhar, was another Scottish immigrant who had come to New York to practice medicine. They married on March 12, 1759. Cadwallader Colden moved from his country estate to Flushing, on Long Island, in 1762, and Coldengham was demolished in 1845. Records suggest that Jane abandoned her botanical work after her marriage. Few records survive from the last part of her life. Colden died on March 10, 1766. This was shortly after the death of her only child, suggesting that both may have died from complications during childbirth.

Unfortunately, many of Colden's scientific manuscripts, including a "botanic dissertation" referred to by several other botanists, have been lost. However, her large catalogue of New York plants, housed in the British Museum, was edited by Harold Ricket and Elizabeth C. Hall and published in 1963 as *Botanical Manuscript of Jane Colden, 1724–1766* by the Garden Club of Orange and Dutchess Counties. Some of her correspondence is housed by the New York Historical Society, which has published selections from it.

Books

Grinstein, Louise S., Carol A. Biermann, and Rose K. Rose, *Women in the Biological Sciences,* Greenwood, 2000.

Notable Women Scientists, Gale, 2000.

Ogilvie, Marilyn Bailey, and Joy Dorothy Harvey, *The Biographical Dictionary of Women in Science,* Taylor & Francis, 2000.

Rossiter, Margaret W., *Women Scientists in America: Struggles and Strategies to 1940,* Johns Hopkins, 1982.

Online

"Jane Colden." *Dictionary of American Biography Base Set,* American Council of Learned Societies, 1928–1936. http://www.galenet.galegroup.com/servlet/BioRC (January 15, 2009). □

Louise Colet

During the 1840s and 1850s, French author Louise Colet (1810–1876) was a renowned figure in Paris's social and literary circles. A prolific writer, Colet churned out fiction, newspaper articles, poetry, and biography, as well as history and travel books. She is best known, however, for her fiery affair with French novelist Gustave Flaubert and is widely thought to have been the model for the protagonist and adulteress of his fictional masterpiece, *Madame Bovary.*

Colet was born into an upstanding French family. Her mother, Henriette Le Blanc Révoil, came from a long line of wealthy aristocrats. Her father, Henri-Antoine Révoil, grew up in a family of well-established merchants. Colet's father served as director of the Aix-en-Provence Postal Service. As a government employee, Révoil received a number of advantages, including free housing in one of the stately mansions owned by the town. It was here, on August 15, 1810, that Louise Révoil, later known as Louise Colet, was born.

Spent Childhood Devouring Books

Growing up, Colet spent her time reading, studying foreign languages, memorizing poetry and writing in her diary. Her five older brothers and sisters teased her for being an unsocial bookworm. As a child, Colet earned a reputation for her hot-headedness, a trait that would follow her into adulthood. Once, when her governess insisted she put down her books in favor of knitting, Colet slapped her face. Colet learned Italian from her father, for whom it was a second language. He told her stories of his childhood in Naples and sang her arias he learned at the opera. During the early 1800s, the French retained sovereignty over Naples, which later became part of Italy.

Colet's family lived in Aix-en-Provence throughout the winter but spent each summer at a country estate in Servanes. Colet's family had acquired the estate in the seventeenth century. Colet enjoyed her time there, as the chateau housed an extensive library of poetry and history. To escape the taunts of her siblings, Colet took long walks in the countryside with a book in hand. She began writing poems at age 12, and at 16 published them anonymously in the provincial newspapers.

According to *Rage & Fire,* a biography on Colet written by Francine du Plessix Gray, one of Colet's contemporaries described her childhood this way: "Louise lived quite apart, composing, in verse or prose, the most romantic little stories, repeating for herself, by the hour, the dramas swarming in her head. And when her brothers and sisters surprised her thus, conversing with her Muse, they oppressed her with their sarcasm and mockery."

As a well-educated woman, Colet was somewhat of an anomaly for her time. Many leading philosophers of the day, including the French thinker Joseph de Maistre, spoke out against the intellectual cultivation of girls, believing females had weaker minds. In addition, they worried that education would undercut women's devotion to domestic duties and upset the gender balance. Given the prevailing opinions of the day, it is understandable that Colet's siblings considered her quest for knowledge abnormal.

Married to Escape Family

In 1826 Colet's father died, and the family retreated to Servanes. As Colet grew older and money scarcer, her siblings worried that she would become a financial burden if they did not find a suitable husband for her. They tried to marry her off to a career army man, but she refused. In 1832 Colet met Julie Candeille, an accomplished former Paris musician, composer and actress. Candeille oversaw a salon in Nîmes and invited Colet to attend. A salon was a periodic gathering of distinguished guests who came together to study and discuss literature or art. At Candeille's salon, Colet shared her poetry and met other aspiring writers who convinced her she would be happier in Paris and be able to pursue her writing there.

In 1834 Colet's mother died, as did Candeille, leaving Colet in despair. She no longer had a reason to stay in Servanes, and her desire to move to Paris intensified. She had become acquainted with a flautist and violin player named Hippolyte Colet, who made his living playing in chamber music ensembles. He asked Colet to marry him, promising she could join him in Paris. They married in December of 1834.

Colet spent her first year in Paris trying to sell her writing, and finally had a poem accepted for publication in *L'Artiste.* Through her acquaintances from Nîmes, Colet slowly made her way into the Paris literary world. She was a stunning beauty, and her husband grew jealous of her associations,

forbidding her to wear anything but high-necked dresses. Colet wore her blond hair in ringlets and preferred azure-colored dresses that accentuated her blue eyes.

Launched Publishing Career

Colet published a book of poetry, *Fleurs du Midi* (Flowers of the South), in 1836. The book attracted the attention of the king's daughter, Marie d'Orléans, who enjoyed the poems so much she secured a small pension for Colet from the Ministry of Instruction, which funded artists and writers. Next, Colet concentrated on selling short pieces of prose, book reviews, and social commentaries to different periodicals. Hippolyte Colet's music career had failed to ignite, and he became resentful of his wife's growing achievements. He opened her mail and forged correspondence in her name, undermining her success. To make ends meet, he offered private music lessons to society ladies and took a mistress.

In 1839 Colet published another poetry collection, *Penserosa.* She also entered the prestigious Académie Française poetry competition and took first prize. After learning that the famed French philosopher and university lecturer Victor Cousin had voted for her in the contest, Colet sought to meet him, and soon he became her mentor and lover. By 1841 Colet was hosting her own salon, inviting Cousin's colleagues.

Colet and Cousin's affair became public, and a few months later Colet was pregnant. Most people in Paris's literary circles assumed Cousin to be the father of her child, since Colet's five-year marriage had yet to produce any offspring. Journalist Alphonse Karr picked up on the story. Karr edited a gossipy satirical monthly called *Les Guêpes* (The Wasps), in which he frequently attacked Cousin. In 1840 Karr wrote a piece suggesting that Cousin was the father of Colet's unborn child. Colet urged her husband to defend her by challenging Karr to a duel. Hippolyte Colet was a wiry musician who knew he was outmatched. He refused to challenge Karr, so Colet decided to defend her own name. Nearly nine months pregnant, she took a kitchen knife to Karr's home and stabbed him in the back, though the wound drew little blood.

According to *Rage & Fire,* Karr ridiculed Colet in his next issue. He wrote an account of the incident, suggesting that Colet staged the attack in an act of self-promotion. Karr wrote, "I certainly would have been gravely harmed if my attacker had struck me with a direct horizontal blow instead of lifting her arm high over her head in a tragedian's gesture, surely in anticipation of some forthcoming lithograph of the incident." Afterward, Karr proudly displayed the knife in a glass case with the inscription "Offered by Madame Colet...In the back."

Colet gave birth to Henriette Colet in August of 1840. For many years, Cousin provided Colet with a stipend for the child's expenses. In 1841 Colet published *La Jeunesse de Mirabeau,* a biography on the life of Comte Honoré-Gabriel de Mirabeau, a French writer and politician who was a leader in the French parliament during the early days of the French Revolution. The book gained some popularity and was serialized in at least one newspaper. Colet's next publications included a travel book on Provence, a region of Southern France, and *Les Coeurs Brisés* (Broken Hearts, 1843), a collection of romantic novelettes.

Met Gustave Flaubert

In July of 1846 Colet was posing for famed sculptor James Pradier when Gustave Flaubert paid a visit to Pradier's home. Flaubert had traveled to Paris to commission Pradier to create a sculpture of his sister, who had recently died. Colet and Flaubert met in Pradier's studio. She was 36; he was 24. The following evening Flaubert showed up on Colet's doorstep, and the two spent the evening discussing literature. Within days, an affair had begun.

Less than a week later, Flaubert returned to his country home in Croisset, France, a few miles from Rouen. He lived with his mother and spent his days writing, though he had yet to publish any work. Within hours of his return, Flaubert wrote the first of some 200 letters to Colet. In the first year-and-a-half of their relationship, Flaubert wrote about 100 letters, though they met in person only six times. Flaubert forbid Colet to visit him at his home. Sometimes they met in Mantes, a town on the rail line between Rouen and Paris. Flaubert's letters to Colet at times included grand passages where he professed his love and recalled their lovemaking; at other times, he wrote that he wished he had never met her. He blamed her for disturbing the progress of his work.

In many letters, Flaubert wrote about his work, sharing his ideas with Colet. He was busy writing *Madame Bovary*. At times, Flaubert took other lovers and made no point of hiding this information from Colet. Colet's letters to Flaubert did not survive; historians believe his family burned them so they could not be published.

Meanwhile, Colet stayed busy writing in order to support herself and her daughter. Hippolyte Colet died around 1848. During the 1850s, Colet wrote fashion copy and continued selling stories. Over the course of her career, she wrote for most of France's leading journals. Colet also took other lovers, including poets Alfred de Musset and Alfred de Vigny. These further strained her stormy relationship with Flaubert, who was spending longer periods of time living in Paris.

In 1855 Flaubert ended their relationship for good. He sent one final tart letter to Colet, suggesting that she leave him alone. Du Plessix Gray quoted from Flaubert's letter: "Madame: I was told that you took the trouble to come here to see me three times last evening. I was not in. And, fearing that your persistence might provoke me to humiliate you, wisdom leads me to warn you that I shall never be in."

Mocked in *Madame Bovary*

Flaubert's highly acclaimed novel *Madame Bovary* was serialized in 1856 and appeared in book form in 1857. Public outrage erupted over the book's content—thought obscene by many, it subsequently became a bestseller. The book focused on Emma Bovary, a doctor's wife who has an affair. Emma Bovary shared a lot in common with Colet. Like Colet, Emma grew up in the country reading romantic novels and yearning for a more fulfilling life in the city.

Emma has an affair with a man named Léon Dupuis. The book contains the famous description of an amorous ride taken by the couple in a horse-drawn cab, reminiscent

of one Flaubert and Colet took days after their initial meeting. Flaubert wrote about the ride in his letters. According to Julian Barnes's book *Something to Declare*, Colet derided *Madame Bovary* in an 1859 poem, calling it "a travelling-salesman's novel whose foul stench makes the heart retch."

In 1859 Colet published *Lui: A View of Him*. This biting novel was based on several real-life romances, including her affairs with Musset and Flaubert and Musset's romance with novelist George Sand. The book's raw depictions of Paris celebrities amused readers. During the 1860s Colet traveled extensively, working as a foreign correspondent for various French newspapers. She covered the Italian struggle for reunification, and in 1869 traveled to Egypt to report on the opening of the Suez Canal. In 1865 she published *Enfances Célèbres*, a book for young readers that explored the childhoods of famous people.

Colet died on March 8, 1876, at her daughter's home in Paris. She was 65. She was buried in Verneuil, France, alongside her husband's family. As for Colet's creative legacy, her image suffered from the disdain Flaubert and his peers heaped upon her in her later years. While her writing has not endured the test of time, Colet was popular and moderately successful during her lifetime because she wrote about the people and places that most interested her contemporaries.

Books

Barnes, Julian, *Something to Declare: Essays on France,* Alfred A. Knopf, 2002.

Fraser, Kennedy, *Ornament and Silence: Essays on Women's Lives,* Alfred A. Knopf, 1996.

Gray, Francine du Plessix, *Rage & Fire: A Life of Louise Colet,* Simon & Schuster, 1994.

Periodicals

Globe and Mail (Toronto, Ontario, Canada), April 30, 1994.

Independent (London, England), August 6, 1994.

New York Times, March 26, 1876, p. 6; April 15, 1923.□

James Bertram Collip

Canadian scientist James Bertram Collip (1892–1965) was a member of the University of Toronto team of researchers who discovered insulin, the hormone that regulates blood sugar, in the early 1920s. Insulin production was absent in those who suffered from diabetes, a chronic condition whose diagnosis was a virtual death sentence at the time. Regular doses of insulin meant that diabetics now had a safe, effective, and vastly life-prolonging treatment. When Collip and his colleagues developed a type of insulin in early 1922 that diabetics could inject daily, it "was one of the most dramatic events in the history of the treatment of disease," wrote Michael Bliss in *The*

Discovery of Insulin. "Those who watched the first starved, sometimes comatose, diabetics receive insulin and return to life saw one of the genuine miracles of modern medicine."

James Collip was born in Belleville, Ontario, on November 20, 1892, the son of a florist. Belleville was a modest-sized town on the Bay of Quinte on Lake Ontario's northern shore, where Collip attended a one-room high school and graduated at the age of 15. He entered college that same year, enrolling at Trinity College, which was part of the University of Toronto system. He earned an honors degree in physiology and biochemistry in 1912 after finishing first in his class, and was granted his master's degree in 1913. Remaining at the University of Toronto for the next three years to pursue a doctorate in biochemistry, he studied under Dr. Archibald B. Macallum, who was the first-ever head of the biochemistry department at the University of Toronto and helped turn its medical school into an esteemed research center.

Named Department Chair

After earning his Ph.D. in 1916, Collip joined the Faculty of Medicine at the University of Alberta in Edmonton. Despite a full teaching load and a young family at home, he spent long hours in his laboratory working on various experiments, and began to publish scores of scientific papers detailing his results. In 1920, he became professor and chair of the department of biochemistry—an extraordinary honor for a professional who had not yet reached his 30th birthday. His research specialty was blood chemistry. This was linked to a new field in medicine called endocrinology, or the study of disorders of the endocrine glands. Endocrine glands produced various hormones that regulated an array of physiological functions. One of his studies, for example, concerned the effect of adrenalin, the hormone from the pair of adrenal glands located near each kidney, on blood pressure.

In the spring of 1921, Collip took a sabbatical leave from the University of Alberta when he won a traveling scholarship from the Rockefeller Foundation. He returned to Toronto to conduct research at the pathology laboratory at Toronto General Hospital, which was the University of Toronto Medical School's teaching facility, and was also teaching courses at his alma mater. This brought him into contact with the team that was already working on a treatment for diabetes. Their supervisor was John J. R. MacLeod, a Scottish-born professor of physiology and pioneer in the field of carbohydrate metabolism. MacLeod was not actively involved in the lab work, but contributed suggestions and directed the team. The primary researcher was Frederick Banting, a Canadian and orthopedic surgeon by training who had turned to medical research after World War I. Banting believed that a viable treatment for diabetes was imminent, and was determined to bring that honor to the University of Toronto. Charles Best was the graduate student who was assigned as Banting's assistant.

Terrible Scourge Swiftly Took Victims

At the time, diabetes had long been known to humankind, but there was no effective treatment. Diabetes refers to a metabolic disorder characterized by inordinately high levels of glucose, or sugar, in the blood. Normally, blood glucose is converted by insulin into energy in the form of glycogen, which is stored in the liver and in muscle tissue. Diabetics suffer from a deficiency of insulin, which is produced in a part of the pancreas called the islets of Langerhans. The pancreas is located behind the stomach, and supplies various digestive enzymes to the small intestine. The lack of insulin means that in diabetics, their body begins to use fat as a source of energy, which results in rapid weight loss. This brings a host of other complications as the liver and cardiovascular systems are thrown into disarray, with the final and most fatal ones being coma and kidney failure. Diabetics often went blind, too, or suffered from gangrene infections in their extremities, which required amputation.

The term diabetes comes from an ancient Greek word meaning "to pass through," which may have been a reference to the excessive urination that is one of the major indicators of the disease. It was discussed by Greek physicians as early as the first century CE, but seven centuries prior to that an Indian physician named Sushruta wrote about it, calling it *madhumeha* or sweet urine disease; early on, it was noticed that ants seemed to like the urine of diabetics, which was found to contain an excessive amount of sugar. The word "diabetes" first appeared in English in the early fifteenth century, and *mellitus*—Latin for "honey"—was added in 1675. The root cause of diabetes seemed to be a genetic predisposition, and was also lifestyle- and diet-related. Until 1922, those who were diagnosed with the condition were generally given a prognosis of 18 months or less to live.

The link between the pancreas and diabetes was uncovered in 1889 by two German scientists, Josef von Mering and Oskar Minkowski, who removed the pancreatic organs of dogs, which then developed diabetes and died. In 1910, the English physiologist Edward Albert Sharpey-Schafer named the missing hormone in diabetics as insulin, from the Latin word for island, referring to the islets of Langerhans.

Experimented with Animals

In Toronto, Banting and Best also worked with dogs. In one group of animals, they tied off the pancreatic ducts, which caused them to atrophy. The ducts were then removed and found to contain higher levels of insulin. In another group, they purposefully caused diabetes in dogs, then injected them with the secretion from the first group, and the dogs did not die from diabetes. The next step would be creating a stable form of insulin for human injection. Banting and Best began experimenting with various mammals, asking slaughterhouses to supply sweetbreads, as animal pancreases were known. The insulin they made produced bad side effects in animals, but a University of Chicago researcher had experimented with mixing the secretion in alcohol, filtering it to remove impurities and then injecting it with some success in animals. MacLeod learned of these experiments when he was a professor at Western Reserve University in Cleveland, Ohio.

In December of 1921, Banting reported to MacLeod that he and Best had some success but needed help in finding a better form of the pancreatic extract. Some of the early batches that used toluene, saline, or alcohol in various combinations had no effect at all, while others produced immediately noticeable results when injected in the lab animals. Collip was sent by MacLeod to help in coming up with a formulation that worked—and worked consistently—in the research trials. He was known to be working on this by the second week in December in a lab at the Pathology Building.

After Christmas, Collip, Banting, and Best traveled to a meeting of the American Physiological Society held in New Haven, Connecticut, to report on their research. Banting made the presentation, but was unnerved by the crowd of esteemed researchers, and faced a barrage of questions. The far more experienced MacLeod stepped in to aid him, and the experience later rankled Banting and he began to feel that his supervisor was about to take full credit for the discovery, which was just around the corner. When Banting and Best, working separately and now in a sort of competition with Collip—who was considered MacLeod's ally—thought they came up with a stable compound, it was tested on January 11, 1922, at Toronto General Hospital on a 14-year-old boy named Leonard Thompson, who weighed just 65 pounds and was being given a 450-calorie, strictly controlled diet that was the only known way to help diabetics. The first injection was not a success, and Collip appeared to have been kept out of the controversial decision to try the insulin out on the first human subject.

Breach Never Healed

Collip tried grinding up the pancreatic organs of cattle and came up with a stable form sometime within the next ten days that January. Both Banting and Best claimed he came to tell them of his achievement, but then announced that he would not be sharing the method with them yet because he planned to apply for the patent on his own. He also said that MacLeod had approved of this plan. Reportedly Banting physically attacked Collip, and the professional discord between all parties intensified. "Collip's success fed the dissension among team members concerning who would be credited with the discovery," explained *Diabetes Forecast* writer Marcia Mazur. "They settled the argument on January 25, with Banting, Best, and Collip agreeing no one would patent the discovery independently."

Two days before that, Leonard Thompson had been given another injection, this one made from Collip's formulation, which were repeated almost daily. Within a week, the teen's condition had vastly improved. In February, efforts were underway to establish a full-time production facility at a laboratory owned by the University of Toronto on the outskirts of the city. According to Bliss's book, Collip was unable to replicate his work in the equipment at that lab. In the diabetic ward at the Toronto General Hospital, supplies had to be rationed out carefully. By late spring, however, a method had been devised, and Collip and Best presented two separate papers to the Royal Society of Canada meeting.

They then traveled to Indianapolis to share the discovery with chemists at Eli Lilly & Company, the pharmaceutical giant whose director of research had shown an interest in producing insulin in large quantities when he attended the American Physiological Society gathering in New Haven.

Contributed to War Effort

Collip then returned to his teaching post in Edmonton, though there had been talk of him remaining at the University of Toronto. In 1923, Banting and MacLeod were awarded the Nobel Prize for Medicine for the discovery of insulin, though Banting was adamant that Best should have been one of the recipients and shared his prize money with him; MacLeod did the same with Collip. Collip remained at the University of Alberta until 1928, when his mentor Macallum recommended him for the chair of the department of biochemistry at McGill University in Montreal, from which Macallum was retiring. He accepted and spent the next 13 years there. During World War II, he was given the rank of colonel by the Canadian armed forces and sent to the United States as a medical services liaison officer, though he commuted to a facility in Washington that was possibly conducting experiments to solve motion sickness in military personnel.

In addition to his contribution to the discovery of insulin, Collip also made significant scientific advances in a hormone secreted by the pituitary gland, adrenocorticotropic hormone, or ACTH. After 1947, he became dean of medicine at the University of Western Ontario in London, Ontario, and retired in 1961. He died in the city on June 19, 1965, following a stroke at the age of 72. With his wife Ray he had three children, two of whom became doctors. He often took his entire family with him in the early years of his career, when he crisscrossed parts of North America delivering research papers at professional meetings. According to reminiscences collected by R. L. Noble for an article that appeared later in 1965 in the *Canadian Medical Association Journal,* "Collip had early perfected an autoclaved baby formula which would keep for over a week on long trips to meetings."

Books

Bliss, Michael, *The Discovery of Insulin,* University of Chicago Press, 1982.

Periodicals

Canadian Medical Association Journal, December 25, 1965.
Diabetes Forecast, May 1991.
New York Times, December 6, 1922.□

Charlotte Corday

French assassin Charlotte Corday (1768–1793) is known in history for a single act that catapulted her from obscurity to infamy during the most heated period of the French Revolution. On July 13, 1793, she gained

entry to the home of a noted leader in the political uprising, Jean-Paul Marat, and stabbed him to death. Quickly taken into custody and brought to trial, Corday died by the guillotine four days later.

Corday was born Marie-Anne-Charlotte de Corday d'Armont on July 27, 1768, in St.-Saturnin-des-Ligneries, a town in the Orne region of Normandy. She came from an old aristocratic family and was descended from seventeenth-century French dramatist Pierre Corneille. Her father, Jacques François de Corday, bore the title *seigneur d' Armont,* and sent the 13-year-old Corday and her younger sister to a convent in Caen called Abbaye-aux-Dames after the death of their mother, Charlotte Marie Jacqueline Gaultier de Mesnival, in 1782.

Drawn into Revolutionary Fever

Abbaye-aux-Dames boasted an excellent library, where Corday was exposed to the writings of leading figures of the Enlightenment in France, a movement whose ideas about the rights of individuals would lead to the French Revolution later that decade. The key date in that event came July 14, 1789, when a Paris mob stormed the Bastille, a formidable prison-fortress in the city that had long been a symbol of the tyranny of the French monarchy over the people, who had no political power. In the decade leading up to this event, moreover, the lavish spending and privileges accorded the royal family and aristocratic classes had incited widespread rancor, and Louis XVI's financial support for American Revolutionary forces in their battle against France's longtime enemy, England, had brought the nation to the edge of bankruptcy. In Paris and other cities, unemployment was high, the price of bread and firewood rose exorbitantly, and starvation and sickness rose precipitously.

Corday had been born into an aristocratic family generally of the type to side with the monarchist cause, and it is known that her two brothers joined an army commanded by exiled princes engaged in suppressing the Revolution. Yet Corday's extensive reading had transformed her into a republican, or one who believed that France should enact a constitution and have some form of representative democracy. After 1791, she lived in the Norman city of Caen with a relative. The most significant events of the Revolution were taking place mainly in Paris, but after 1793 Caen emerged as a center for the Girondists, a faction of revolutionary political activists who had lost a crucial battle for control of the movement to their ideological foes, the Jacobins.

Jean-Paul Marat emerged as a respected political leader in the aftermath of the Bastille-storming. The Swiss-born physician published his own newspaper, which he named *L'ami du peuple* (Friend of the People), in which he displayed a gift for vivid prose in denouncing injustices and championing the poor. He was arrested several times for his strong views on the abolition of the monarchy, and went into hiding on occasion with fellow revolutionaries. Yet he also began to criticize some within the movement itself, which was dividing inside the National Convention, the legislative assembly,

along physical lines which gave rise to the terms "left" and "right" wings to denote political beliefs. The more conservative, right-wing side of the legislative body believed that France should adopt England's model of government, with a monarch but strong parliament and prime minister. The left-seated factions, led by a lawyer from the city of Arras named Maximilien Robespierre, had a far different vision for France's future.

The Onset of "The Terror"

Marat was allied with Robespierre and Georges Danton, another figure on the extreme left, and all emerged as leaders of the faction known as the Jacobins. By the summer of 1792, France was mired in both a civil war and a battle against its powerful enemy, Austria, and popular sentiment turned against King Louis XVI and his widely loathed Austrian-born wife, Marie Antoinette, both of whom had been under house arrest at the Palais des Tuileries Palace in Paris. The king's authority had been drastically curtailed by a constitution of 1791, but in August of 1792 more trouble broke out in Paris followed by what was known as the September Massacres of 1792.

The National Convention became a focal point over the fate of Louis XVI. Moderates believed his life should be spared, but Marat and others argued that the king had worked to undermine the Republic and thus was guilty of treasonous acts. The king's trial descended into a battle between Gironde and Jacobin sides, and Marat's anti-monarchist arguments stirred his fellow delegates. Louis XVI was beheaded in January of 1793, but Marat's invective had so alarmed the Girondists that a faction voted to indict him. A special Revolutionary Tribunal acquitted him in April of 1793, which was viewed as a significant victory for the left in France's revolutionary struggle. Shortly afterward, on the last day of May of 1793, an uprising occurred and the Girondists were forced to flee to Caen.

Thus the city where Corday lived became the center of opposition to Marat and the Jacobins. The unrest in Paris had continued, with mobs breaking into prisons and summarily executing scores of inmates, many of them aristocrats, high-ranking members of the Catholic church, or political prisoners. Marat, Robespierre, and Danton were blamed for failing to halt the violence.

Surprised Him in Bath

Marat was legendarily productive, but suffered from a mysterious skin condition that later scientists have described as eczema, psoriasis, or scrofula, which is a tuberculosis of the neck. A particularly virulent outbreak plagued him in July of 1793, and he became too ill to attend the sessions of the National Convention. Instead he spent the majority of his time in a special boot-shaped bathtub, fashioned from copper, known as a *sabot*. He wrote on an upturned wooden box while soaking in kaolin, a mineral compound, to soothe his skin. A turban soaked with vinegar wrapped around his head was another medicinal measure he undertook in an attempt to find relief.

In Caen Corday was drawn into Girondist circles, and was moved to act by their descriptions of the Jacobin terror in Paris, which Marat had urged in his writings and speeches. House-to-house searches had become commonplace, and in an effort to root out "counterrevolutionary" elements hundreds were taken into custody and summarily sentenced to death by guillotine. These actions began to reach a fever pitch as spring turned into summer in June of 1793.

Corday left Caen by stagecoach on July 9, arrived in Paris two days later, and took a room at the Hôtel de Providence on the rue des Victoires. On the morning of July 13, she purchased a new hat with green ribbons to replace the more commonplace bonnet-style one that marked her as a woman from Caen. She also bought an ebony-handled kitchen knife with a five-inch blade. She wrote *Adresse aux Français amis des lois et de la paix* (Speech to the French Who Are Friends of Law and Peace), and showed up at the National Convention to kill Marat, which she had hoped to do in full sight of the delegates for maximum effect. She learned he was at his home, located at 18 rue des Cordeliers, but it was widely known he had an "open-door" policy and regularly allowed ordinary citizens to present their case to him.

Corday went by hired carriage to the rue des Cordeliers and attempted to gain entry, but was turned away by the sister of Marat's fiancée shortly before noon. She wrote a letter, stating she had valuable information about the anti-Jacobin movement in Caen, but forgot to include an address. Around seven p.m. the same evening, she went back to Marat's door and gained entry with the day's bread-delivery person. Again, she was halted, this time by Simonne Evrard,

the fiancée, but claimed in a loud voice to have information that Marat would appreciate. He overheard the exchange and called out to Evrard to let the woman in.

Severed Vital Artery

Once there, Corday related information about anti-Jacobin activists in Caen, but Evrard was also present. Marat requested some more kaolin solution, which Evrard went to get, while Corday gave him several names, which he wrote down on a piece of paper on his desk. "Good," he said, according to Simon Schama's *Citizens: A Chronicle of the French Revolution*. "In a few days I will have them all guillotined." At that, Corday drew closer, pulled out the knife out from the folds of her dress, and plunged it into his chest. He cried out "À moi, ma chère amie!" ("Help me, my dear friend!"). A friend of Marat's who was in the house, Laurent Bas, rushed in, threw a chair at Corday, and then physically restrained her. The commotion that began with Marat's first scream could be heard in the street below, and soon medical professionals were attempting to staunch the bleeding—but beginner's luck was with Corday and she had severed the vital carotid artery. Marat died within minutes.

Corday was incarcerated at the Prison de l'Abbaye, and Schama's book noted that a black cat kept her company in her cell. Revolutionary justice was swift, and she was brought to trial immediately. During the proceedings she said that she was driven to kill Marat because "he was perverting France," according to *Citizens.*. "I have killed one man to save a hundred thousand. Besides he was a hoarder: at Caen they have arrested a man who bought goods for him."

Corday was executed by guillotine on July 17, 1793, in Paris. Legend holds that the assistant to the executioner, so outraged by her act, picked up her newly severed head and slapped it across the cheek, and bystanders near the scaffolding reported that the face visibly changed expression for a moment and her cheeks flushed. The Jacobins ordered an autopsy to determine whether she was a still a virgin because of the strong belief that she had been driven to commit such a shocking act of violence because of love for a man. The results showed that she was, disproving the rather counter-revolutionary sentiment that a woman was incapable of political violence by the sole virtue of her gender.

Both Attained Infamy

Corday's body was reportedly buried in a trench, though rumors persisted the skull was passed on through the Bonaparte family for several generations. The late Marat, meanwhile, became a national hero and the French Revolution's most famous martyr. Paris hosted his immense funeral, and for a time busts of him even replaced the crucifix in Roman Catholic churches during a brief period of anti-religious sentiment. Corday had believed that only a figure as influential as Marat could halt the violence, but her act instead triggered another wave of bloodshed, and the Revolution descended into its most appalling period.

Corday's act was immortalized in one of the best-known paintings of the nineteenth century, Jacques-Louis David's *Death of Marat*. The painter knew Marat personally and had been in the room just a few days before. In the painting, the slain Jacobin leader is posed similar to the angle of the famed *pietàs* of Italian Renaissance art, in which the suffering of Christ is portrayed in stark terms in order to convey suffering and stir the emotions of the viewer. "In the annals of criminality," wrote John Russell in the *New York Times,* this particular painting "will always rank high. It is plain, concise, unsparing. It could be a news photograph, or even a police photograph.... Like a veteran detective, David was a master of fact. He got the wound right. He got the long blade of the knife right, as well as the blood. He got the letter, word perfect, with which the assassin... had bluffed her way into the room. He got the quill pens right and the dark blue ink pot. He persuades us that this was where someone lived and worked—right up until he was killed."

Books

Schama, Simon, *Citizens: A Chronicle of the French Revolution,* Alfred A. Knopf, 1989.

Van Alstine, Jeannette, *Charlotte Corday,* W. H. Allen & Co., 1890.

Periodicals

New York Times, September 19, 1999. □

Francisco Hernández de Córdoba

Spanish explorer Francisco Hernández de Córdoba (died 1517) was the first European to explore Mexico's Yucatan peninsula. Although his expedition suffered significant defeats and Hernández de Córdoba himself died shortly after its conclusion, his reports helped persuade Spanish authorities to thoroughly investigate Mexico, thus paving the way for the later missions of conquerors such as Hernán Cortés and contributing to the lasting effects of Spanish colonization of the Americas.

Assembled Expedition to Mexico

Practically no details of Francisco Hernández de Córdoba's life prior to his exploration of the Mexican Yucatan peninsula survive. Originally from Spain, Hernández de Córdoba was a wealthy merchant living in Cuba by about 1510. Writing in *The Aztecs, the Conquistadors, and the Making of Mexican Culture,* Peter O. Koch noted that "[de] Córdoba, like so many other Spanish immigrants, had been lured to the island of Cuba by the guarantees of generous land grants, liberal rights to a native workforce, and rumors of untold wealth just waiting to be uncovered." Hernández de Córdoba became a well-known and respected Cuban landowner, and his business was sufficiently successful that he owned a number of

sailing vessels working throughout the area that would become the Spanish Main—the coastline of Central and parts of North and South America as well as portions of the Caribbean.

Probably in 1516, a small group of men headed by Antonio Alaminos hatched a plan to investigate the western lands with which Alaminos had had brief contact during previous expeditions. The costs of such a voyage were far beyond what Alaminos and his partners could themselves provide, so they approached Hernández de Córdoba as a potential backer and participant. Intrigued by the Alaminos' descriptions of his journeys, Hernández de Córdoba signed on and preparations for a significant expedition began.

These preparations quickly attracted the attention of Cuba's governor, Diego Velázquez, who demanded to become a partner in the expedition. With the governor's additional funding, the expedition added both a third ship to the two already commissioned by Hernández de Córdoba and an additional purpose: the taking of slaves. Although contemporary Spanish law prohibited enslaving native peoples unless those people fought against Spaniards, kidnappings of this type were quite lucrative and fairly common practice. Scholars disagree on Hernández de Córdoba's opinions on this task; contemporary sources state that members of the expedition were against the idea, while some have more recently argued that enslaving natives may have been among Hernández de Córdoba's goals all along.

With the attractions of Cuba not living up to the expectations of many of its immigrants—as Bernal Díaz del Castillo, a sailor who participated in Hernández de Córdoba's expedition, bluntly stated in *The Discovery and Conquest of Mexico,* "it [had become] evident that we were merely wasting our time"—Hernández de Córdoba, who was named captain of the expedition, easily recruited about 110 adventurers. Alaminos was named the fleet's chief pilot, with Pedro Camacho and Juan Alvarez serving as pilots of the other two ships. The two ships initially procured by Hernández de Córdoba offered ample space for crew and provisions, which included colored beads and other inexpensive items that the Spanish had successfully traded for valuable native goods in the past.

Ambushed at Great Cairo

With ships, crew, and supplies accounted for, the expedition sailed from the port of Ajaruco on February 8, 1517. Within two weeks, the ship had entered unknown waters; Díaz del Castillo noted that "we were in the open sea, and trusting to luck we steered toward the setting sea, knowing nothing of the depth of water, nor of the currents, nor of the winds which usually prevail in that latitude"—essentially, none of the pieces of information so vital to sixteenth century navigation and safety. The expedition survived a strong storm before sighting land: first what was probably the Isle de Mujeres, and, soon after, the Yucatan. Although the Yucatan lies on a peninsula, this fact was to remain unknown to the Spanish explorers. In *The Discovery of the Yucatan by Francisco Hernández de Córdoba,* Henry R. Wagner noted that "Alaminos... insisted that Yucatan was an island. Since, while with the Hernández expedition he did not see any of the peninsula south of Champóton, he must have reasoned from analogy, Cuba, Santo Domingo, and Jamaica were all islands and it was then believed that Florida was one also—ergo, land to the west which did not appear to be attached to a continental mass must also be an island." Indeed, this belief persisted for at least twenty years after the Hernández de Córdoba expedition.

A large town containing what appeared to be a pyramid was visible even before the ships reached shore; this structure inspired the Spanish to name this city, occupied by descendents of the Mesoamerican Mayan empire, Great Cairo. Soon, a group of Mayans paddled out in large wooden canoes to greet the Spaniards. The two parties, hampered by a lack of interpreters, made friendly gestures before about 30 Mayans boarded the Spanish ships. The Spanish gave the Mayans strings of glass beads in an effort to win their friendship. After the Mayans departed, Hernández de Córdoba and the expedition's other leaders spent some time considering whether to go ashore. The arrival of another Mayan deputation complete with sufficient canoes for the transport of the Spanish crew the following morning made their decision for them; after being hailed by the leader of the town with cries of "cones catoche," the Mayan phrase for "come to my houses," the entire Spanish party disembarked. Koch observed that "the massing of Mayans along the shore was somewhat disconcerting to [de] Córdoba, so the captain decided to play it safe by making sure that his men arrived in full battle gear."

Hernández de Córdoba's precautions proved to be justified. As the chief led the expedition toward the town, he called out to a waiting mass of Mayan warriors who attacked the Spanish, killing fifteen of them almost immediately. The Spanish fought back, eventually killing an equal number of Mayans and capturing two with the intention of training them as interpreters. Despite having numbers on their side, the Mayans retreated before the Spaniards' superior weaponry, and the expedition continued to Great Cairo. There, they discovered a square surrounded by what Díaz del Castillo described as "houses contain[ing] many pottery idols, some with the faces of demons and others with women's faces." They also found a great deal of gold and precious jewelry, which the party collected and took back to the ships.

Misadventures at Campeche and Champotón

Shaken by this experience, Hernández de Córdoba directed the expedition to travel cautiously, passing by other Mayan settlements visible from the coast. After two weeks, however, a lack of available fresh water forced the Spaniards to go ashore to replenish their supply. A smaller, well-armed group carted the water casks to a cache of fresh water and were in the midst of refilling those casks when a large group of Mayans unexpectedly appeared. After using sign language to explain that they came from the east and wished only to replenish their water supplies and return to their ships, the Spanish were invited to visit the Mayan's city, Campeche. There, the Spaniards visited a number of Mayan temples, where they were shocked by the signs of recent human sacrifice. The townspeople appeared friendly, that is, until a group of ten priests began piling flammable materials around the Spaniards, lit a fire, and made it known that

when that fire went out, the suddenly massed Mayan warriors would attack the Spanish party. Quickly, the Spanish party fled to their ships and sailed along the coast to the southwest.

After spending four days battling a strong storm, the expedition again went ashore seeking water, this time some distance from the town of Champotón. While filling their water casks, Hernández de Córdoba and his party again unexpectedly encountered a group of Mayan warriors, made even more intimidating this time by the addition of black and white face paint. As they had done previously, the Spanish indicated that they came from the east and wished only to fill their water casks; the Mayans retreated, leaving the encamped Spanish to debate whether to attack and plunder the town or to leave as quickly as possible. Díaz del Castillo reported what happened next: "while we were still taking counsel and the dawn broke, and we could see that there were about two hundred Indians to every one of us, and we said one to the other 'let us strengthen our hearts for the fight, and after commending ourselves to God let us do our best to save our lives.'"

The vastly superior Mayan force trounced the Spaniards, and Hernández de Córdoba soon realized that his party had no choice but to fight their way through the Mayan ranks and make for the beach. This they accomplished, although every solider except one suffered injuries, with Hernández de Córdoba taking at least ten arrows. By the time the Spanish managed to sail away—with the Mayans continuing to hurl missiles and arrows after them—nearly 50 of their number had perished, with more to follow in the days to come.

The End of the Expedition and Its Legacy

Alaminos, who had previously visited Florida as a member of Juan Ponce de León's exploration party, suggested that Hernández de Córdoba's expedition travel to that site rather than Cuba due to its proximity and plentiful fresh water supply. The much-reduced expedition party reached that site, delighting in its fresh waters for a brief time before a group of Floridians appeared and launched an attack. The Spanish fled to their ships and decided to return to Cuba.

After reaching Havana, Hernández de Córdoba met with the island's governor, Diego Velázquez, to report on the misadventures of his expedition. Some time after his meeting with Velázquez, Hernández de Córdoba died as a result of the injuries he had received during the battle at Champotón. The exact date of his death is unknown, although it certainly occurred in 1517. Contemporary sources place the event ten days after Hernández de Córdoba's return to Cuba—as early as May—but later evidence suggests that he may have survived for several months, perhaps until October or November.

Regardless of its precise timing, Hernández de Córdoba's death did not halt further Spanish exploration. Koch argued that Hernández de Córdoba's "stories of Indian towns built of carved stones instead of simple reeds and the description of natives who covered their nakedness in elegant attire was more than enough evidence that the Yucatan was home to an advanced civilization that...warranted further investigation." In 1518, four ships under the command of Juan de Grijalva—including two vessels that had taken part in Hernández de Córdoba's expedition—set out to further probe Mexican territory. The findings of both Hernández de Córdoba's and Grijalva's voyages encouraged Velásquez to put together a larger Mexican expedition. This party, led by famed conquistador Hernán Cortés, defeated the native Aztec empire and brought Mexico into the Spanish fold, giving Spain a significant foothold in the Americas and setting the stage for events to come. Although Hernández de Córdoba's name and accomplishments have been overshadowed by the explorers who followed in his wake, his actions as the first Spaniard in the Yucatan had a great and lasting effect on history.

Books

Díaz del Castillo, Bernal, *The Discovery and Conquest of Mexico,* Farrar, Straus and Cudahy, 1956.
Koch, Peter O., *The Aztecs, the Conquistadors, and the Making of Mexican Culture,* Macfarland and Co., 2006.
Wagner, Henry R., *The Discovery of the Yucatan by Francisco Hernández de Córdoba,* The Cortes Society, 1942.□

Mairead Corrigan Maguire

The Irish peace activist Mairead Corrigan Maguire (born 1944) helped to organize the first major demonstrations against violence between Protestants and Catholics in Northern Ireland. For her work, she was awarded the 1976 Nobel Peace Prize.

The organization Maguire founded during those initial protests, the Community of Peace People, continued to exist after the initial fervor of the peace movement in Northern Ireland had died down. Maguire herself withdrew from peace activism for a time in the 1980s, but then returned to her organizing activities with a renewed sense of ambition that broadened the scope of her activities to a global scale. Although the 1976 demonstrations failed initially to achieve their goals, Maguire had the satisfaction of seeing Northern Ireland take major steps toward peace in the late 1990s and early 2000s. Later in that decade she devoted much of her energy to the Israeli-Palestinian conflict in the Middle East.

Worked as Secretary to Beer Executive

Mairead (pronounced muh-RAID) Corrigan was born on January 27, 1944, in Belfast, Northern Ireland. Her father, Andrew Corrigan, was a window cleaning contractor. Maguire was the second of seven children, and the large Catholic family sometimes had trouble paying its bills. She attended Catholic schools but had to drop out at age 14 when her parents could no longer afford the tuition. At age 16 Corrigan took a job as a secretary, a profession at which she worked for most of the next two decades. For a year she attended a business school, Miss Gordon's Commercial College. Corrigan worked her way up in the secretarial field, and by the mid-1970s she had obtained a good position as confidential secretary to a managing director at the Guinness brewery.

The first hint of commitment to social activism in Corrigan's career was her involvement with a Catholic lay organization called the Legion of Mary, which combined Christian teachings with social services. Corrigan's contributions of time to the group continued into her adult years. Though Corrigan was Catholic, she felt little identification with the Provisional Irish Republican Army (IRA) and other militant Catholic groups that were agitating for the unification of Northern Ireland, which was under British control, with the Republic of Ireland to the south. She was not overly interested in politics, and insofar as her Catholic beliefs influenced her political feelings, they led her to reject the Provisional IRA and its violent tactics.

On August 10, 1976, the conflict in Northern Ireland, referred to by residents as "the Troubles," came to Corrigan's doorstep and took a brutal toll on her family. In the Catholic Andersontown neighborhood, a British patrol pursued a car driven by an IRA gunman, Danny Lennon, and one soldier fired a shot that killed him. Lennon's car jumped the curb onto the sidewalk and hit Corrigan's sister-in-law Anne Maguire and three of her children, pinning them against a railing. The children were killed, and Anne Maguire, shattered by grief, later committed suicide. Interviewed on television after the event, Corrigan and her brother-in-law Jackie Maguire decried the violence. Another woman, Betty Williams (who was of Catholic, Protestant, and Jewish background), witnessed the tragedy and spontaneously began going door to door collecting signatures on a petition calling for an end to the violence. Other women joined her, and the petition grew to include six thousand signers who took to the streets in peace marches.

Joined Marchers

The following day, Corrigan was looking out her parents' Andersontown window and saw Williams's marchers passing by. She joined them. The day after that, at the funeral of Anne Maguire's children, Corrigan and Williams called for a demonstration the following Saturday at the spot where the children had been killed. A journalist, Ciaran McKeown, joined the cause and helped publicize it. Ten thousand people, mostly women, turned out, and some of them brought babies in strollers. The following weekend's march doubled that turnout, and soon the peace marches were drawing 30,000 demonstrators.

The marches took place in both Catholic and Protestant neighborhoods, including those most strongly associated with the IRA and the Protestant Ulster Defence Association and Loyalist Volunteer Force paramilitary groups. Both Corrigan and Williams received hate mail and death threats, and became targets for denunciation from both Catholic and Protestant militant leaders. But Corrigan was evenhanded in her rejection of the violence coming from all sides— Catholic militants, loyalist Protestant groups, and the British military, which was accused of various human rights abuses. Her position was close to the classic nonviolent stance of Mohandas K. Gandhi and other modern peace campaigners. Corrigan believed, as quoted by Jesuit writer John Dear in an essay appearing on the Peace Heroes Web site, "that a peaceful and just society can be achieved only through nonviolent means and that the path to peace lies in each of our hearts."

Part of the peace movement's growth in the last months of 1976 was attributable to Corrigan's personal charisma and the impression of deep spirituality she gave when addressing even a sizable crowd. Among those who fell under her spell was the American folk singer and activist Joan Baez, who described Corrigan this way, as quoted on the Peace Heroes site: "The breath of God ran through her like a fair summer breeze. She was a smile. She was a prayer. She was endlessly brave, going into the streets and homes of 'the enemy' unarmed and with cheerful countenance. No evil could envelop her or even touch her. I'm sure she is all those things still. She will hate to read this, because she is also self-effacing, like some other saints."

Corrigan and Williams co-founded the Community of Peace People as an institutional extension of their activities in the streets of Belfast. The group's First Declaration read, as quoted on its Web site: "We have a simple message to the world from this movement for Peace. We want to live and love and build a just and peaceful society.... We reject the use of the bomb and the bullet and all the techniques of violence. We dedicate ourselves to working with our neighbours, near and far, day in and day out, to build that peaceful society in which the tragedies we have known are a bad memory and a continuing warning."

Awarded Nobel Prize

The pair won several awards for their work in 1976 and 1977. They were jointly awarded the Carl von Ossietzky Medal from the International League of Human Rights office in Berlin, West Germany, and they received several honorary doctorates from colleges and universities in the United States, including the Yale University Law School. They were granted an audience with Britain's Queen Elizabeth II in 1977. What cemented their international fame was the 1976 Nobel Peace Prize, again awarded to both women. The prize was actually given retroactively, in December of 1977. No award had been given in 1976; the prize committee's deliberations would already have been underway when Corrigan and Williams began to organize their marches.

By that time, however, Northern Ireland's peace movement had diminished in intensity. Sectarian violence continued, and marchers retreated to their religiously segregated neighborhoods. Mistakes by Corrigan and Williams also contributed to the movement's decline. Their initial decision to keep their Nobel Prize money (then $60,000 each) generated bad publicity, although Corrigan later gave away most of her share. Williams moved to the United States, and Corrigan to a small seaside town. In 1981 Corrigan married auto mechanic Jackie Maguire, the widower of her sister Anne. After that time she used the name Mairead Corrigan Maguire. The pair had two children of their own, and she raised her sister's three surviving children.

The Community of Peace People never entirely disappeared, however, even though it shrank to a core of about 50 members in the late 1980s. One of its grassroots activities was to bring Catholic and Protestant children together for two-week vacations. Corrigan carried her Nobel Prize medal in her pocket for several years, but in 1987 she gave it to a museum. Gradually she resumed her activities, focusing at first on emergency legal measures imposed by British forces that she believed were applied unfairly. She co-founded the Committee on the Administration of Justice, which argued for the repeal of British emergency security laws. In February of 1993 Corrigan and six other Nobel Prize laureates tried to visit Burmese Nobel Prize winner Aung San Suu Kyi, who had been placed under house arrest by her country's military rulers as a result of her efforts to promote human rights. The Burmese government refused to admit Corrigan's group into the country, so they visited refugee camps on the Thai-Burmese border instead, and publicized the plight of Burma's Karen ethnic group, members of which had been forced to flee persecution.

Visiting some 25 countries and meeting with Pope John Paul II, Corrigan evolved into an articulate and persistent international peace campaigner. Her opposition to violence at the state level was seemingly absolute. She condemned European and American bombing campaigns in the Balkan region of Kosovo, designed to stop ethnically based attacks by Serbs against Albanians, telling *Catholic New Times* that "you have to give peace processes time, and you don't do that by bombing." More generally, she rejected the idea of a just war laid out by various Catholic thinkers, under which the church might under certain conditions consider military action valid. "When the church speaks about the conditions for a 'just war,' the impression is given that in some situations the church 'blesses' war," she said, according to the *Catholic New Times.* In Japan, she argued against changes to that country's constitution that would loosen restrictions on military action.

Corrigan remained a consistent presence in international affairs in the 2000s. She opposed the American- and British-led wars in both Afghanistan and Iraq, believing that those who planned and executed the terrorist attacks of September 11, 2001, should be brought to justice by legal rather than military means. "Don't get stuck in the suffering of Sept. 11," Corrigan told an audience of American young people from an educational group called PeaceJam, as reported in the *National Catholic Reporter.* "If you get stuck in the suffering, you lose your creativity." In the first decade of the 2000s, Corrigan became involved in ongoing protests against Israel's military actions against Palestinian forces in the West Bank and Gaza regions. During one protest that brought attention to a wall under construction by the Israelis in the West Bank, she was hit in the leg by a rubber bullet. "This wall, contrary to what the Israelis say, will not prevent attacks and violence," she told the *Christian Century.* "What will prevent attacks and violence is a peace agreement between the two peoples."

Books

Brown, Ray B., *Contemporary Heroes and Heroines, Book I,* Gale, 1990.

Deutsch, Richard, *Mairead Corrigan/Betty Williams,* Woodbury, 1977.

Periodicals

America, May 7, 2007.

Catholic New Times, July 4, 1999.

Christian Century, April 20, 1994, p. 414; May 15, 2007.

Globe and Mail (Toronto, Canada), July 15, 1988.

International Herald Tribune, October 30, 2008.

Japan Times, May 5, 2008.

National Catholic Reporter, November 16, 2001; May 11, 2007; October 19, 2007.

News Letter (Belfast, Northern Ireland), August 9, 2001; January 27, 2003.

Post-Standard (Syracuse, NY), March 20, 2003.

Online

"First Declaration of the Peace People," Community of Peace People, http://www.peacepeople.com/PPDeclaration.htm (December 28, 2008).

"Mairead Corrigan," Nobel Foundation, http://www.nobelprize.org/nobel_prizes/peace/laureates/1976/ (December 19, 2008).

"Mairead Corrigan Maguire," Peace Heroes, http://www.peaceheroes.com/PeaceHeroes/maireadcorrigan.htm (December 19, 2008).

"Pied Pipers of Peace," *Time,* September 6, 1976, http://www.time.com/time/magazine/article/0,9171,918304,00.html (December 19, 2008).□

Michael Curtiz

Hungarian-born American film director Michael Curtiz (1888–1962) was responsible for several of the greatest hits of American cinema, most notably the World War II classic *Casablanca.*

Curtiz exemplified the role of the director within the studio system of American film in its first decades. He worked fast and effectively, turning out several films a year and tailoring his style to the requirements of the story being told. Histories of film rarely rank Curtiz with the great directors who had instantly identifiable styles. But the Hollywood film would not have been the same without him, and a resurgent interest and close study of his films among cineastes suggests that his work was shaped by the same forces of German expressionism and Scandinavian naturalism that influenced many of the other European-born directors active in early Hollywood. As biographer James C. Robertson pointed out in his book *The Casablanca Man: The Cinema of Michael Curtiz,* the director's "overall output from 1912 to 1961 remains one of the highest in cinema history. More than two-thirds of his approximately 160 films were made outside his own country, while about half of them were sound movies not in his native tongue."

Sold Theater Programs

One of five children, Michael Curtiz was born Mihaly Kaminar Kertesz (or, in the Hungarian naming system Kertesz Kaminar Mihaly) on December 24, 1888, in Budapest, then part of the Austro-Hungarian Empire. He was of Jewish descent, and he often joked that the stacks of wrapped presents he saw during Christmas season were intended for his own birthday. Curtiz's father, Ignatz, was a carpenter. The family was poor, and accounts of Curtiz's early life are fragmentary and sometimes contradictory. His mother, Aranka, apparently was active as an opera singer, and Curtiz appeared on stage with her in an 1899 production. He and his brothers sometimes sold programs in Budapest's theaters to earn extra money.

After graduating from Budapest's Markoczy School in 1906, Curtiz ran away from home and joined a traveling circus. He mastered the arts of juggling, mime, and even acrobatics before returning to Budapest in 1910 and enrolling at the Royal Academy of Theater and Art. There he studied not only acting and theatrical production but also languages—a boon during the international career he pursued. Curtiz directed and acted in student theatrical productions, and after graduating he became interested in the young art of cinema. Finding that there was no Hungarian film industry, Curtiz essentially created one from scratch. He directed *Today and Tomorrow* (1912), generally regarded as the first Hungarian film, and in 1913 he went to Denmark to study the new medium at the Nordisk Studios there.

Returning to Hungary, Curtiz directed about 40 silent films between 1912 and 1919. His career was interrupted by a term of service in the Austrian army during World War I that ended when he was transferred to a Red Cross

film unit after either being wounded in action or pulling strings to avoid that eventuality. The films Curtiz made in Hungary have been lost; anyone who rediscovered them would unlock a significant chapter in the history of early European cinema. Curtiz married actress Lucy Duraine (also known as Ilona Kovács Perényi) in 1915, and the couple had one daughter. In 1919 Hungary briefly came under the control of a Communist-oriented government, backed by the Soviet Union, that nationalized Hungary's film industry. Accounts differ as to whether Curtiz left Hungary at this point, or whether he worked for the new government film office and then departed after the leftist government collapsed as fighting dragged on in Eastern Europe.

Curtiz settled in Vienna and made the first of several modifications to his name, using the German form Michael Kertes. From 1919 to 1926 he worked for Sascha Studios, one of Austria's leading production houses. His films grew in scope. Two of them, *Sodom and Gomorrah* (1922) and a film called *Die Sklavenkönigin* (1924, later released in the United States as *Moon of Israel*), were blockbuster spectacles with biblical settings. *Moon of Israel* attracted the attention of American film executive Jack Warner, who invited Curtiz to come to Hollywood. He was accompanied on the journey by his second wife, actress Lili Damita, who later went on to marry the star of several Curtiz films, Errol Flynn. That marriage, like his first, ended in divorce, and Curtiz married screenwriter Bess Meredyth in 1929.

Experimented with Sound

Arriving in America at the age of 38, he began using the "Curtiz" spelling of his last name, pronouncing it "Kurt-ez," although most people gravitated naturally toward the Spanish-sounding "Kurt-eez." He made four silent films, the first of which was the gangster film *The Third Degree* (1926). That film featured experimental techniques drawn from the Central European cinema Curtiz knew well; at one point, the viewer's perspective shifts to follow a moving bullet. Soon Curtiz was entrusted with the Warner Brothers studio's attempts to develop full-fledged sound films. Several of the part-silent, part-sound films he made in the late 1920s, such as *Tenderloin* (1928) (initially billed as "a film with dialogue," according to its *New York Times* review), featured the Vitaphone technique, in which sound came from records synchronized with the film rather than being recorded onto the film itself.

In 1929 Curtiz released another biblical blockbuster, *Noah's Ark*. The film was only moderately successful at the box office, but it established Curtiz's reputation as a director who could bring a complex project to completion, and from then on he made films in a steady stream of perhaps three to six each year. The film, as noted by Hal Erickson of the *All Movie Guide*, also "set the standard for an utter lack of concern for the well-being of actors; several extras died during the climactic flood sequence, reportedly because Curtiz, hoping to [cause] genuine panic in his performers, had failed to inform them that they'd be deluged with tons of water."

Warner Brothers grew steadily in the 1930s, and Curtiz's career bloomed. His work in the 1930s is notable for its variety. Curtiz made two significant early horror films in color, *Dr. X* (1932) and *The Mystery of the Wax Museum* (1933), each drawing on the German expressionist horror films of the 1920s. He made gangster films, domestic dramas, and Westerns such as the acclaimed *Virginia City* (1940). The director sparked the careers of several major female stars over the course of his career; one was Bette Davis, who appeared in *The Cabin in the Cotton* and the crime drama *20,000 Years in Sing Sing*. In 1935 Curtiz introduced the then-unknown Australian swordsman Errol Flynn in the pirate swashbuckler *Captain Blood,* and that durably successful piece of entertainment inaugurated a series of 12 Curtiz-Flynn collaborations, ending only when Flynn tired of Curtiz's autocratic directing style.

Other actors associated with Curtiz included Edward G. Robinson, who starred in the director's adaptation of Jack London's novel *The Sea Wolf* (1941), and James Cagney. Cagney held lead roles in the gangster film *Angels with Dirty Faces* (1938) and *Yankee Doodle Dandy,* a biography of songwriter George M. Cohan. The latter film showed Curtiz's flair for brisk narrative pacing and his grasp of the details of American life, also strikingly on display in *Life with Father* (1947). The director immersed himself in American history prior to his successful U.S. citizenship application in 1937, and was disappointed when the examining officer only wanted to talk about his films. Curtiz never mastered the grammatical intricacies of English, and his malapropisms ("By the time I was your age, I was 15") were legendary among film crews.

Directed *Casablanca*

In terms of posthumous reputation, the high point of Curtiz's career was *Casablanca* (1942). With an all-star cast headed by Humphrey Bogart and Ingrid Bergman and its perfectly timed patriotic story line, the film was seen by some later historians as an accidental success for its director and studio. But neither critics nor audiences have seen it that way. Curtiz's direction was critically acclaimed, and the film brought him an Academy Award, his only one, for Best Director. Curtiz made the film's emotional scenes seem natural, something for which he showed a knack at several points in his career. Indeed, in the words of Curtiz's *Turner Classic Movies* (TCM) biography, the director's "highly developed visual approach combined with his technical mastery could elevate the most mundane material, and three of his finest films, *Yankee Doodle Dandy* (1942), *Casablanca* (1943) and *Mildred Pierce* (1945), make a virtue of melodrama and sentimentality."

Curtiz steered Joan Crawford to a Best Actress Oscar for *Mildred Pierce,* and he repeated his talent-spotting success with Doris Day, whom he directed in four films, including her debut, *Romance on the High Seas* (1948), and *I'll See You in My Dreams* (1952). In 1954 Curtiz left Warner Brothers for the Paramount studio and enjoyed the peak of his commercial success with *White Christmas,* starring Bing Crosby. The films from the later part of Curtiz's career are generally regarded as inferior to his earlier hits, but he entered the era of rock and roll in 1958 with the Elvis Presley film *King Creole.*

After closing out his career with *The Comancheros,* a Western starring John Wayne, Curtiz died in Los Angeles on April 11, 1962. "Curtiz left behind an impressive body of work possessing an incredibly consistent narrative energy," noted *Turner Classic Movies.* In the filmmaker's own words (quoted by TCM), "I put all the art into my pictures I think the audience can stand. I don't see black-and-white words in a script when I read it. I see action."

Books

International Dictionary of Films and Filmmakers, Volume 2: Directors, 4th ed., St. James, 2000.

Robertson, James C., *The Casablanca Man: The Cinema of Michael Curtiz,* Routledge, 1993.

Periodicals

Films of the Golden Age, Summer 1999.

New York Times, March 15, 1928.

Online

"Michael Curtiz," *All Movie Guide,* http://www.allmovie.com (January 17, 2009).

"Michael Curtiz," *Eighty-Odd Years,* http://www.eightyoddyears. com/bio-michael-curtiz.html (January 17, 2009).

"Michael Curtiz," *Turner Classic Movies,* http://www.tcm.com/ tcmdb/participant.jsp?spid=42547 (January 29, 2009).

"Michael Curtiz: Biography," *Lenin Imports,* http://www.leninimports. com/curtiz.html (January 17, 2009). □

Francesca Cuzzoni

The Italian singer Francesca Cuzzoni (1696–1778) was among the most renowned female opera stars of the eighteenth century.

The most notorious episode involving Cuzzoni was an onstage brawl between her and a rival Italian diva, Faustina Bordoni, in London in 1727. That conflict remains significant, for it shows the depth of the feelings that underlay operatic disputes of Cuzzoni's day. Recent scholarship, however, has tended to downplay the sensational aspects of the fight, and instead emphasize Cuzzoni's importance in shaping the style of the leading English operatic composer of the time, George Frideric Handel (1685–1759). Cuzzoni had a long and colorful career that took her across the European continent, but she ended her life alone, abandoned by those who had profited from her talent.

Studied with Organist

The daughter of violinist Angelo Cuzzoni and his wife, Marina Castelli Cuzzoni, Francesca Cuzzoni (coot-SOH-nee) was born on April 2, 1696, in the Italian city of Parma. Not much information has surfaced from the first part of her life. Cuzzoni studied music with a local organ builder, Francesco Lanzi, and by the age of 18 she was appearing on stage. Her first documented appearance was in a Parma staging of an opera called *La virtù coronata, o Il Fernando* (Fernando, or Virtue Crowned), in 1714. From there she moved on to the larger city of Bologna, where she appeared in four operas during the 1716–17 season.

For the following season, Cuzzoni landed a post as *virtuosa da camera* (chamber virtuosa) with a Tuscan noblewoman, the Grand Princess Violante. The position left her plenty of time to appear in opera houses around northern Italy: in Florence, Siena, Mantua, Genoa, and Reggio nell'Emilia. But the prize was the glittering city-state of Venice, where she appeared in 1718 in an opera called *Ariodante* by Carlo Francesco Pollarolo. Her future rival, Faustina Bordoni, appeared in the same production, and they shared the stage three more times in Venice over the next several years. Cuzzoni's reputation grew, and during the 1721–22 season she appeared in five separate Venetian productions.

That was enough to get the attention of Handel, who had been trained in Italy and was on the lookout for promising new operatic talent, having recently become the director of the Royal Academy of Music. Handel himself had moved from Italy to England a decade earlier, and a parade of Italian singers, composers, and instrumentalists had followed him. Imported Italian music aroused strong passions among England's growing theatre-going middle class, with singers gaining legions of fervent partisans. Handel dispatched composer and keyboardist Pietro Giuseppe Sandoni to bring Cuzzoni to England. On the return trip to London, Sandoni married the singer. Perhaps he sensed a source of ready wealth, for Cuzzoni was reported to be physically unattractive; the indefatigable English letter-writer Horace Walpole, as quoted by Isabelle Emerson in *Five Centuries of Women Singers,* wrote that "she was short and squat, with a doughy cross face."

At the time, female opera stars were not especially common. The fiery soprano roles of the Baroque era were generally sung by performers known as castrati—males castrated at the onset of adolescence in order to produce a high yet powerful male voice. The most popular singer in London at the time was an Italian castrato named Senesino. Change, however, was in the air.

Inspired Voluntary Surcharge

At the beginning of her London career, Cuzzoni resisted some of the musical directions Handel gave her. During rehearsals for her London debut in Handel's opera *Ottone,* she refused to sing the opera's key aria, "Falsa imagine." The young diva had met her match in the strong-willed composer, however. "I know quite well that you are a veritable devil," Handel said, according to Emerson, but I will let you discover that I, I am Beelzebub, the chief of devils." Handel then picked up Cuzzoni by the waist and told her that if she raised any more objections, he would throw her from the window. Cuzzoni sang the disputed aria during her debut at the King's Theatre on January 12, 1723. The audience response was rapturous, and Senesino found himself replaced by a new queen of London opera—much to the dismay of fans of the aging countertenor. Winton Dean and Carlo Vitali, writing in the *New Grove Dictionary of Music,* asserted that "Cuzzoni was the first female high soprano to distinguish herself in prime roles." Cuzzoni was already getting a salary of 2,000 pounds per season, and in March of 1723 a group of noblemen added a surcharge of 60 guineas per ticket to make sure the star soprano was satisfied.

Although the artistic relationship between Cuzzoni and Handel got off to a rocky start, it proved fruitful for both. Handel began to write arias that fit the dramatic and affecting quality of Cuzzoni's voice, which often reduced audiences to weeping, and the result was a series of hits, including *Giulio Cesare* (in which Cuzzoni sang the role of Cleopatra), *Rodelinda,* and *Flavio.* The typical Cuzzoni role was that of a heroine trapped by fate, pouring out her despairing feelings in a set of operatic laments (often in the 12/8 siciano rhythm) that became increasingly numerous as Handel refined the Cuzzoni formula. She might be a woman suffering from unrequited love, or separated from her beloved. The leading chroniclers of eighteenth-century music, Britain's Charles Burney and Germany's J.J. Quantz, both remarked on the beauty and appeal of Cuzzoni's voice, and the Italian vocal authorities Tosi and Mancini penned detailed appreciations of her technique. According to Emerson, Tosi described "the Sweetness of a fine Voice, a perfect Intonation, [and] Strictness of Time." Her range was said to extend from middle C to the C two octaves higher.

Cuzzoni, then, ruled the operatic roost in London until the arrival of Bordoni in 1726. The newcomer was a very different artist from Cuzzoni, with an athletic voice that emphasized sheer power and a flair for dramatic acting, which Cuzzoni lacked. At first, Handel exploited this natural contrast between his two star sopranos, writing operas that emphasized their vocal dissimilarity and using it to dramatic ends. But the sheer passion of Cuzzoni's admirers soon led to clashes with fans of the rising Bordoni, and the two singers, even though they had apparently gotten along well personally, found themselves cast as rivals. Gossipy newspaper articles fanned the flames, and passions intensified as partisans of the two singers exchanged catcalls in the theater during their performances.

Got Into Fight Onstage

Early in June of 1727, during a performance of the opera *Astianatte* by the Italian composer Giovanni Battista Bononcini, the tensions came to a head as Cuzzoni and Bordoni engaged in a hair-pulling fight on stage. The battle provoked waves of merriment among London's legion of press satirists, who produced various humorous drawings of the event. Cuzzoni was fired, but King George II, who was her partisan, ordered her reinstated. Cuzzoni and Bordoni suffered the indignity of having themselves parodied in the comic show *The Beggar's Opera,* but the conflict between them, and between their fans, cooled off later in the year. Cuzzoni was nevertheless out of a job when the Royal Academy met its demise in 1728, and both she and Bordoni left London temporarily.

Count Kinsky, the Austrian empire's ambassador in London, invited Cuzzoni to come to Vienna, but operatic producers there refused to meet her salary demand of 24,000 florins. She returned to Italy and sang in most of her homeland's major cities over the next decade, performing works by composers including the German-born Johann Adolf Hasse, who was Bordoni's husband. At one point Handel and a group of entrepreneurs launched a new Royal Academy, but Handel wanted no more of his quarrelling pair of sopranos and opted instead for new artists. Cuzzoni returned to London in the mid-1730s under the auspices of a new company, the Opera of the Nobility, but her spell over British audiences was broken.

Cuzzoni remained a major star, however, and the new, more natural operatic style of the mid-eighteenth century would have fit her voice well. During the Carnival season in 1739, she performed a pair of operas in the city of Turin and was paid the sizable fee of 8,000 lire. She traveled from there to Vienna and then, for the fall season of 1740, to Hamburg in northern Germany. She seems to have separated from Sandoni around this time, and the separation, combined with the age-related decline of her voice, wreaked havoc in her life. She continued to find operatic engagements, but the small fortunes she had received in fees during her youth evaporated. In the late 1740s she was imprisoned in the Netherlands due to her mounting debts.

Temporarily released on condition that she give concerts to pay off her creditors, Cuzzoni performed for the queen of France in 1750 and returned to London for the 1750–51 season, finding that audiences there had forgotten her. According to Emerson, Burney attended one of her concerts and reported that he "found her voice reduced to a mere thread." Cuzzoni returned to Italy after that, and apparently descended to severe poverty. Living in Bologna in her last years, she eked out a living by making buttons. Burney, who traveled to Bologna in 1770, did not see fit to visit her. Cuzzoni died in Bologna on June 19, 1778.

Books

Dean, Winton, and J. Merrill Knapp, *Handel's Operas: 1704–26,* Oxford, 1987.

Emerson, Isabelle, *Five Centuries of Women Singers,* Greenwood, 2005.

International Dictionary of Opera, 2 vols., St. James, 1993.

The New Grove Dictionary of Music and Musicians, 2nd ed., Macmillan, 2001.□

D

Marion Davies

Film star Marion Davies (1897–1961) emerged during Hollywood's silent era and made a largely successful transition to talkies during the late 1920s and early 1930s. Although her efforts were well-publicized and she worked with some of the biggest names in the film industry, the former show-girl-turned-screen actress is best remembered for her decades long affair with publishing tycoon William Randolph Hearst, which was the basis for the classic 1941 film *Citizen Kane.* Davies's love affair with a powerful man, however, is the only thing she had in common with Kane's fictional Susan Alexander. A vivacious on-screen comic with solid singing and dancing skills, Davies displayed effortless charm and youthful energy throughout her 20-year motion picture career.

Born Marion Cecilia Douras in Brooklyn, New York on January 3, 1897, she was the youngest of five children of Bernard Douras, an attorney and one-time city magistrate, and his wife Rose. Bored with public school, where she was constantly forced to wear a dunce cap in class, young Marion and sister Rose Marie followed in the footsteps of older sisters Ethel and Irene—already professional show girls—and attended Kosloff's Ballet School at age 13. During that same era, her older sister Irene—nicknamed Reine—saw a sign for Davies Real Estate and adopted Davies as her stage name. The other Douras sisters quickly followed suit, although Marion was the only sibling to make the name famous.

Part of a junior company called the pony ballet, she and other girls her age polished shoes and ran errands for the more experienced dancers in between lessons and recitals. She made her on-stage debut in a Washington, DC production of *The Bluebird* that same year. After a short trial in the pony ballet unit, the poised, yet high-spirited Davies began appearing in such Broadway musicals as *Chin Chin, Miss Information* and Jerome Kern's *Nobody's Home.* Later she augmented her show-business education with a stint at the Empire School of Acting, although she later confessed that her sights were never set on anything more than being a show girl.

Started as a Show Girl

Working as a fill-in dancer and extra at first, Davies realized her early ambition when she was hired to appear in the 1916 edition of the *Ziegfeld Follies.* Before her arrival, producer/showman extraordinaire Flo Ziegfeld had perfected the art of musical comedy on Broadway. Adding to the visual appeal of a revue featuring the top comedy and musical talents in the country were lines of gorgeous, scantily clad show girls. Less dancers than attractive window-dressing for the various productions, show girls were mainly required to be graceful and attractive in their skimpy—sometimes outlandish—costumes. Although a childhood stammer kept her from taking on meatier speaking roles, Davies proved a more than capable addition to Ziegfeld's shows which led to work in such musical revues as *Betty, Oh Boy, Miss 1917,* and *Words and Music.*

Davies, along with many of her contemporaries, enjoyed the attentions of college aged admirers who waited at the stage door, gifts in hand, hoping to lure an attractive show girl as their date for the evening. Dubbed "stage door Johnnys," their wealthier counterparts were often played as marks by the show

girls, who would encourage gift-giving, imply an impending romance, and then ditch the poor sucker when a better offer came along. Girls who did this were often referred to as gold diggers. It was under these circumstances that Davies met the single most important person of her adult life, William Randolph Hearst.

Hearst Made Her a Star

According to her autobiography, *The Times We Had,* Davies's relationship with publishing tycoon William Randolph Hearst was inevitable. As a child, she played games near his New York home. Later, after her stint in the 1916 *Ziegfeld Follies*—where she initially caught his eye—they began traveling in all the same social circles, and when she would take a wrong step, he would surreptitiously put things right. Initially, when the lonely publisher began to openly court Davies, she played him like any other married chump looking to cheat on his wife—she took his lavish gifts and gave him nothing in exchange. Early in their relationship, the millionaire gifted her with a diamond bracelet, which she promptly lost. She asked the 52-year-old spendthrift to get her another, and he did. Yet, she could tell that Hearst had deep feelings for her. It took a while, but she eventually returned those feelings. "I started out a gold digger," she was quoted as saying in the 2001 documentary *The Battle Over Citizen Kane,* "but I fell in love with him." All during their relationship, Hearst was married to another former show girl, Millicent Wilson, with

whom he had five sons. A strict Catholic, she refused to give Hearst the divorce he desperately wanted.

During this era, the motion picture business was split between New York City and Hollywood. As a result, Davies seized the opportunity—through her brother-in-law/producer Charles Lederer—to appear in the 1917 film *Runaway, Romany.* By her own admission, neither the film nor the story she reportedly wrote were very good. Hearst, whose company had been producing movie shorts and cartoons since 1915, however, was intrigued by Davies's beauty and artistic ambition and signed her to a long-term contract with his new Cosmopolitan Productions movie unit. In 1918, the pair moved out to Hollywood, where Hearst made a production and distribution deal with Paramount, and set out to make her a star.

Working as her producer and mentor, Hearst cast Davies in stiff period dramas such as *Cecelia of the Pink Roses,* turgid melodramas like *The Bell of New York,* and soppy romances such as *Enchantment.* Indeed, Davies made ten pictures with Hearst before they fashioned a hit, 1922's *When Knighthood Was in Flower.* The film's popularity could not ensure profits, however. Hearst spent fifteen times the normal film budget on the project and paid out a fortune redecorating the theater for the premiere showings. As part of a continuing publicity campaign, Hearst eventually spent over $7,000,000 publicizing her career. Further, he directed all his newspapers and magazines to run a favorable item on Davies in every issue—which they did until the very day he died. According to David Shipman's book *The Great Movie Stars,* MGM—starting in 1924—picked up the cost for Hearst's Cosmopolitan productions and paid the actress a whopping $10,000 per week in exchange for his newspaper chain supplying the studio as much positive publicity as was being drummed up for Davies. The ploy initially worked, but Hearst's outlandish methods created some serious drawbacks. Writing the introduction to Davies autobiography, director Orson Welles said of the non-stop publicity, "...that was less of a favor than might appear. That vast publicity machine was all too visible; and finally, instead of helping it cast a shadow—a shadow of doubt. Could the star have existed without the machine? The question darkened an otherwise brilliant career."

On several of her films, Davies is listed as a producer, but Hearst was clearly in charge. He sent volumes of telegrams to the directors, production managers, and technicians on Davies's films—something he seldom did for the other movies his company produced for both Paramount and MGM. Hearst's ham-handed directives inflated the budgets of Davies's films terribly, making many of them unprofitable. Moreover, he continually chose heavy dramatic parts for Davies when her gifts for mimicry and mugging suggested that she was a natural comedienne.

Occasionally, public demand caused Hearst to relent and let Davies just be funny. She is considered genuinely amusing in such films as *The Fair Co-Ed, The Patsy,* and her biggest hit *Show People.* The latter co-starred William Haines—a major star of the silent era—and featured a comic cameo appearance by Charlie Chaplin. It was her last full-length silent picture.

Starred in Early Talkies

During the early talking picture era, many of the great silent film stars fell by the wayside. Davies made her singing and talking debut in *The Hollywood Revue of 1929,* but made a far bigger splash the following year in *Marianne.* Originally filmed as a silent picture, it was redone as a musical comedy with Davies speaking with an appealing French accent. Such light-hearted family fare as *Peg O' My Heart* and *Polly of the Circus,* proved profitable, but other films tanked at the box office. Subsequently, MGM found it necessary to pair her with such top male stars as Leslie Howard, Robert Montgomery, Gary Cooper, and singing sensation Bing Crosby. In his autobiography *Call Me Lucky,* Crosby recalled that Davies had seemingly learned some extravagant habits from Hearst. The actress didn't show up on set until 11 o'clock and then brought with her an entourage containing hairdressers, make-up ladies, a secretary, and a five-piece orchestra that played solely for her amusement. The partying in Davies' full-sized bungalow slowed the production's pace to a crawl, but Crosby, who was being paid two thousand dollars a week, didn't care, "[f]or it was the most leisurely motion picture I ever had anything to do with. It took six months."

Davies's stint at MGM ended in 1934 after the studio refused to give her the lead roles in *The Barretts of Wimpole Street* and *Marie Antoinette.* Both went to Norma Shearer. Angered, Hearst moved her contract to Warner Brothers where she played alongside the likes of Dick Powell in *Page Miss Glory,* Clark Gable in the musical *Cain and Mabel,* and *Ever Since Eve* with Robert Montgomery. Despite her rocky box office track record at MGM, Warner's honcho Jack L. Warner is quoted in *The Great Movie Stars* as saying, "It may surprise the dour prophets to know that they all brought in a solid profit."

Despite her prolific work before then, after 1937 Davies never stepped in front of a motion picture camera again. Over forty and with steady drinking taking a toll on her looks, she could no longer play the dumb blonde or virginal heroine convincingly. More importantly, her chief benefactor, W.R. Hearst, was undergoing severe financial reverses and suffering poor health. Showing surprising loyalty, the actress sold all her jewels and real estate holdings and gave Hearst the proceeds. Then, she retired from the screen in order to take care of him.

Citizen Kane

Stories about Hearst and Davies are legend throughout Hollywood. Indeed, Hearst turned his San Simeon, California home into a castle so Davies could host lavish parties for all the Hollywood elite. More controversially, during a star-studded yacht party in 1924, film maker Thomas Ince died, reportedly of heart failure due to acute indigestion. The 2001 film *The Cat's Meow,* dramatizes the popular theory that a jealous Hearst shot Ince believing he was Charlie Chaplin, with whom he suspected Davies of having an affair. In the modern era, there exists open speculation that Hearst and Davies had a child out of wedlock that lived as Davies's niece and married Arthur Lake, the star of the Dagwood and Blondie movies. Yet none of the Hollywood legends and rumors have impacted public perception of the couple as thoroughly as Orson Welles's film debut *Citizen Kane.*

Welles's film, considered one of the greatest ever to be produced in Hollywood, is a fictional story that mirrors some of Hearst's rise as a publishing giant. He also based Kane's no-talent opera singer Susan Alexander on the story of a Chicago politician who built an opera house for his girlfriend. References to the drinking and picture puzzles supplied by screenwriter Herman Mankiewicz, a former San Simeon party goer, however, convinced Hollywood columnists that Welles and company were depicting the life of Marion Davies. "I thought we were very unfair to Marion Davies," Welles said in a 1982 interview shown in *The Battle Over Citizen Kane.* "Because we had somebody very different in the place of Marion Davies and it seemed to me to be something of a dirty trick and it does still strike me as something of a dirty trick—what we did to her. And I anticipated the trouble from Hearst for that reason."

Upon reading the script and hearing reports from his chief gossip columnist Louella Parsons, Hearst was enraged at the perceived slight to Davies. He encouraged the main Hollywood studios to buy the film from RKO and burn it and refused to allow his papers to carry ads for *Citizen Kane.* A fictionalized account of Hearst and Davies's reaction to Welles's masterwork is dramatized in the 1999 HBO film *RKO 281.* Ironically, Davies claims that neither she nor Hearst ever saw the film.

Davies stayed with Hearst until his death in 1951. Although never his legal wife, she was given 30,000 shares in the Hearst Corporation and control of his publishing empire in his will. Yet, in the end, all she wanted was recognition. She negotiated away her voting rights for a position as a Hearst Corporation consultant at a fee of $1 a year. Four months after Hearst's death, she married Capt. Horace Brown, a merchant mariner. Rumored to resemble a young Hearst, Davies and her new husband neared the brink of divorce twice but stayed together.

A shrewd investor in her own right, Davies made money buying and selling commercial real estate, including the Desert Inn in Palm Springs. In 1952, her gift of $1.9 million dollars helped establish a children's clinic at UCLA and she continued to champion the fight against childhood diseases with the Marion Davies Foundation. After a lengthy bout with cancer, Davies died on September 23, 1961.

Books

Crosby, Bing, as told to Martin, Pete, *Call Me Lucky: Bing Crosby's Own Story,* Da Capo, 1993, pg. 118–122.

Davies, Marion, edited by Pfau, Pamela and Marx, Kenneth S., *The Times We Had: Life with William Randolph Hearst,* Ballantine Books, 1975.

Shipman, David, *The Great Movie Stars: The Golden Years,* Hill and Wang, 1979; revised edition.

Online

"Marion Davies," *All Movie Guide,* http://www.allmovie.com/cg/avg.dll?p=avg&sql-2:1, (December 29, 2008).

"Marion Davies," *biographybase,* http://www.biographybase.com/biography/Davies_Marion.html (December 29, 2008).

"Marion Davies," *Britannica Online,* http://www.britannica.com/EBchecked/topic?152704/Marion-Davies/Britannica Online (December 29, 2008).

"Marion Davies," *Film Reference.Com,* http://www.filmreference.com/Actors-and-Actresses-Co-Da/Davies-Marion.html (December 29, 2008).

"Marion Davies," *Internet Broadway Database,* http://www.ibdb.com/person.php?id=37425 (December 29, 2008).

"Marion Davies," *Internet Movie Database,* http://www.imdb.com (September 8, 1999).

"Marion Davies, Consultant," *Time,* http://www.time.com/time/magazine/article/0,9171,856971,00.html (December 29, 2008).

"New Horizons," *Time,* http://www.time.com/time/magazine/article/0,9171,816622,00..html (December 29, 2008).

"William Randolph Hearst," *Internet Movie Database,* http://www.imdb.com (January 3, 2008).

Other

The Battle Over Citizen Kane, Warner Bros., 2001http://www.biography.com. □

Vittorio De Sica

The Italian filmmaker Vittorio De Sica (c. 1901–1974) invented the neorealist style in cinema in the years after World War II. Among these films depicting lower-class Italian life amid the difficult conditions prevailing in Italy after the war was *The Bicycle Thief* (*Ladri di Biciclette,* 1948), widely regarded as one of the greatest films ever made.

De Sica's neorealist style, with its low-budget, natural look and quasi-improvisational acting, was immensely influential and continues to shape many independent films. His career beyond neorealism, which occupied only a short stretch of a long period of filmmaking activity, is also noteworthy: he used his status as a star actor to finance his more adventurous directorial activities. Another De Sica film regarded as a classic came from the end of his life: *The Garden of the Finzi-Continis* (*Il Giardino dei Finzi-Contini,* 1971) examined the situation of Italian Jews under the rule of Italian Fascist leader Benito Mussolini.

Acting Ambitions Encouraged

Sources differ on whether De Sica was born in 1901 or 1902; his birthday was July 7. A native of Sora, in central Italy, he was raised in Naples. His bank clerk father, Umberto De Sica, was perhaps a frustrated performer and encouraged his son to try to become a star. Starting out in amateur theatrical productions as a child, De Sica was already comfortable under the footlights when he made his film debut in 1918 in a supporting role in *The Clemenceau Affair* (*Il Processo Clemenceau*). Although he studied accounting for a time, De Sica decided on acting as a career when he landed

a small part in 1922 in a theatrical company headed by actress Tatiana Pavlova.

Throughout the 1920s and 1930s, De Sica balanced theater and film with unusual success. He formed a theatrical company of his own, often using productions as starring-role vehicles for himself and his first wife, Giuditta Rissone. He appeared in several silent films, including *The Beauty of the World* (*La bellezza del mondo,* 1926). Later he made a successful transition to sound film with such films as *The Secretary for Everybody* (*La segretaria per tutti,* 1932). The handsome De Sica, whether on stage or screen, was one of Italy's matinee idols as a young actor.

During World War II De Sica began to try his hand at directing. His first film as a director was *Scarlet Roses* (*Rose scarlatte,* 1939). Although he never joined Mussolini's Fascist Party, he did work within the government-controlled film industry, and it was for that reason that he later turned to the subject matter of *The Garden of the Finzi-Continis.* "I wasn't a Fascist," he was quoted as saying by Geoff Pevere of Canada's *Globe & Mail,* "but I belong to a country that collaborated with Hitler. I wanted, out of conscience, to make the film." De Sica made several light comedies, but the film that pointed to his groundbreaking postwar work was *The Children Are Watching Us* (*I Bambini ci guardano,* 1942). The perspectives of children would likewise figure in plots or subplots of several of De Sica's neorealist classics. The film was scripted by Cesare Zavattini, who became De Sica's regular collaborator.

Pioneered Neorealist Style

The neorealist style was partly a virtue made of necessity; working in economically shattered postwar Italy, De Sica had little money available for production costs. He began to work on location, using natural light and mostly non-professional actors, whom he encouraged to perform in a spontaneous, realistic way. The first film to fully reflect his new approach was *Shoeshine* (*Sciuscià*, 1946), an examination of the lives of street orphans who, separated from their parents in the aftermath of the war, made a living by shining the boots of American soldiers. The film flopped in Italy itself but was released in the United States in 1947 and was given a Special Academy Award the following year.

At the time, there was no Best Foreign Language Film Oscar, but *Shoeshine* and De Sica's next film, *The Bicycle Thief* (*Ladri di Biciclette,* 1948), which received another special award, led Academy Awards presenters to establish the category several years later. *The Bicycle Thief,* with its simple story of a desperate father and son trying to recover a stolen bicycle, gained an international audience, but De Sica's position in Italy was precarious; his films enjoyed only spotty success, and his realistic stories were attacked by right-wing critics. His 1951 film *Umberto D,* which dealt with a retired government employee living in poverty alone with his dog, was denounced by Christian Democratic Party culture minister (and future Italian prime minister) Giulio Andreotti, according to London's *Guardian* newspaper, as "a wretched service to the fatherland."

After the total box office failure of *Umberto D,* De Sica began to agree to offers he had received from hit-oriented producers in the United States (David O. Selznick) and Italy (Carlo Ponti). During the filming of *Indiscretion of an American Wife* (originally titled *Stazione termini,* 1952), lead actress Jennifer Jones tried to flush a hat she disliked down a toilet. De Sica remarked that for the cost of the hat, he could have made *The Bicycle Thief.* A return to neorealist themes in *The Roof* (*Il Tetto,* 1956) was again financially unsuccessful, and for the next decade or so, De Sica would mostly align his filmmaking with studio demands.

Directed Award-Winning Sophia Loren Performance

For several years he was mostly visible as an actor, earning a Best Supporting Actor Academy Award nomination for an appearance in *A Farewell to Arms* (1957). Among his best regarded performances was one in the 1959 Roberto Rossellini film *General della Rovere*. He stepped behind the cameras again in 1960 with *Two Women* (*La ciocara*), the story of a widow and her daughter struggling to survive in postwar Italy. Lead actress Sophia Loren won an Academy Award for her performance in the film. De Sica won his first actual Best Foreign Film Oscar for *Yesterday, Today, and Tomorrow* (*Ieri, oggi, domani,* 1967), and he enjoyed an international hit in 1967 with the frothy comedy *Marriage, Italian Style* (*Matrimonio all'Italiana*). Many of his 1960s films, however, led reviewers to conclude that he was in decline as a serious creative force.

That formed another part of the motivation for De Sica's decision to film *The Garden of the Finzi-Continis,* which was based on an autobiographical novel by Giorgio Bassani. According to Pevere, De Sica called the film a work of "artistic vengeance." Indeed, the film was among De Sica's first to combine critical and popular success, winning a Golden Bear award at the Berlin Film Festival and an Academy Award for Best Foreign Language Film. It was turned down by nine international distributors and producers but was eventually financed by Swiss producer Arthur Cohn.

The story of *The Garden of the Finzi-Continis* is told through the eyes of Giorgio, a middle-class Italian student who becomes romantically involved with Micol, the daughter of a fabulously wealthy Italian Jewish aristocrat. Spanning the years from 1938 to 1943, the film juxtaposes images of their romance with the doomed world of idle luxury the Finzi-Continis inhabit, and with the gathering winds of political destruction outside the walls of their estate, as the rights of Italian Jews under the Mussolini regime are systematically stripped away. In making the film, De Sica cast stars in the lead roles, including French actress Dominique Sanda as Micol. But he returned to his practice of using nonprofessional actors in many of the subsidiary roles, casting locals from the city of Ferrara, where he filmed on location. The film was reissued in a restored version in 1997.

The final De Sica film to gain international release was *A Brief Vacation* (Una breve vacanza, 1973), produced once again by Cohn. The film reunited De Sica and Zavattini for the story of a woman who has a spiritual reawakening while on vacation at a health spa. After making one more film, *The Voyage* (Il viaggio, 1974), and appearing as an actor in the Andy Warhol–produced *Blood for Dracula* and several other films, De Sica was hospitalized in Paris, France. He died there after complications from lung surgery on November 13, 1974.

Books

International Dictionary of Films and Filmmakers, Volume 2: Directors, 4th ed., St. James, 2000.

Periodicals

Globe & Mail (Toronto, Ontario, Canada), January 24, 1997, p. C2.

Guardian (London, England), November 24, 1994, p. 12.

Online

"The Garden of the Finzi-Continis," *Bright Lights Film Journal,* http://www.brightlightsfilm.com/18/18_garden.html (January 25, 2009).

"A Noble Ruin: Remembering De Sica," *Senses of Cinema,* http://www.archive.sensesofcinema.com/contents/00/11/desica.html (January 25, 2009).

"Vittorio De Sica," *All Movie Guide,* http://www.allmovie.com (January 25, 2009).

"Vittorio De Sica," Sony Pictures Classics, http://www.sonypictures.com/classics/garden/crew/sica.html (January 25, 2009). □

Fèlix Hubert d'Hèrelle

French-Canadian bacteriologist Fèlix d'Hèrelle (1873–1949) is credited with the co-discovery of bacteriophage, a microscopic virus that attacks and kills bacteria. His research led to the development of phage therapy and helped advance the science of microbiology.

Essentially a self-taught microbiologist, d'Hèrelle became a leading pioneer in the field of molecular biology. His major contribution to science and medicine, the discovery of bacteriophage, found practical application outside of the laboratory and in the arena of public health. He spent much of his career investigating the impact of his discovery. While the established scientific community viewed him as an outsider, d'Hèrelle received international renown and important awards for his work. He not only helped advance microbiological research but he was also the first to use bacteria as a method of biological control of insect pests such as locusts.

Birth of an Adventurous Spirit

Fèlix d'Hèrelle was born on April 25, 1873, in Montreal, Quebec, Canada, to French immigrant Felix d'Hèrelle Sr., a member of a well-known French Canadian family, and Augustine Meert d'Hèrelle, a woman of Dutch descent. His father was 30 years older than his mother, and died when d'Hèrelle was only six years old.

After his father's death, d'Hèrelle moved with his mother and younger brother, Daniel, to Paris, France, where he received secondary education at the Lycée Condorcet and Lycée Louis-le-Grand schools. Possessing an adventurous disposition, d'Hèrelle traveled a great deal while growing up (as he would also do as an adult). During his teen years, he toured Western Europe on bicycle. After finishing his high school education, he traveled through South America. Afterward, he began studying medicine and completed his medical education at the University of Leiden in the Netherlands. In 1893 he married Mary Caire, a Frenchwoman he had met during his travels in Turkey. The couple eventually had two daughters.

Subsequently, d'Hèrelle moved with his wife and first daughter back to Canada, where he studied microbiology in his own home laboratory. He learned the science through book reading and by conducting his own experiments.

When he was 24, d'Hèrelle secured employment with the Canadian government, working on the fermentation and distillation of maple syrup. He also served as a medic for a geological expedition and, with his brother, he invested a great deal of money into an unsuccessful chocolate factory.

Moved to Latin American

In 1901, due to his bleak financial situation, d'Hèrelle was compelled to take a job in Guatemala City, Guatemala, where he became director of a bacteriology laboratory in a general hospital. He also taught microbiology at a Guatemalan medical school. In addition, he took a side job that involved developing a method of making whiskey from bananas. In all, d'Hèrelle enjoyed living in the rural country, but the rough environment and frequent illness made life hard for his family.

In 1907 d'Hèrelle accepted an offer from the Mexican government to continue his fermentation work, and he moved his family to a sisal plantation near Mérida, Yucatán, where he developed a successful method of producing schnapps from sisal hemp. The following year the Mexican government sent him back to Paris, where he supervised the construction of machines for mass production and continued his microbiological research. At the same time, d'Hèrelle spent his spare time working in a laboratory at the Pasteur Institute. At first he worked for free, but in 1909 he became a lab assistant, and in 1914 he became laboratory chief. He remained at the institute until 1921.

Discovered Bacteriophage

During this period, d'Hèrelle studied a bacterium (*Coccobacillus acridiorum*) that caused enteritis, or inflammation of the intestines, in locusts and grasshoppers. He surmised that he could apply this microbe to killing locusts. In a 1949 article in *Science News* titled "The Bacteriophage," portions of which appeared on the Memorial University (Canada) Web site, he wrote that in 1910, while in the Yucatan, he witnessed an invasion of locusts. After collecting and studying many of the sick insects, he found that he could "start epidemics in columns of healthy insects by dusting cultures of the [locusts' bacteria] coccobacillus on plants in front of the advancing columns: the insects infected themselves as they devoured the soiled plants."

In his research, d'Hèrelle grew bacteria on culture plates and saw empty spots on these plates. He theorized that the spots resulted from a virus that grew with and eventually killed the bacteria. As such, he felt that his observation could have significant implications for fighting diseases of the digestive tract. Appropriately, in 1916 he expanded his research to cultures of the bacillus that caused dysentery. Again, he observed the empty spots on the culture surfaces. Subsequently, he managed to filter out a substance from the feces of dysentery patients that consumed a culture broth of the bacillus in only a few hours.

Treated Soldiers During World War I

d'Hèrelle applied this knowledge to an investigation of dysentery afflicting World War I soldiers. He began by closely monitoring an individual patient, each day taking a feces sample that he filtered through porcelain to remove bacteria. He mixed samples of this filtrate with bacterial cells and spread them on agar plates. By the fourth day of observation, he began seeing plaques. In direct testing, he recovered material from a plaque and mixed it with a growing bacteria culture. According to the article posted on the Memorial University Web site, the following day he discovered that the culture was now clear, and that "all the bacteria had vanished, they had dissolved away like sugar in water." He immediately understood that "what caused

[the] clear spots was in fact an invisible microbe, a filtrable virus, but a virus which is parasitic on bacteria.''

On September 10, 1917, he produced a paper that announced his discovery. In the paper, which he titled "Sur un microbe invisible, antagoniste du bacille dysentérique" and presented to the French Academy of Sciences, he termed the bacteria-destroying substance "bacteriophage." Literally translated, the term means "eater of bacteria." During World War I, working with assistants that included his wife and daughters, d'Hèrelle would produce more than twelve million doses of medication for the allied military forces.

While d'Hèrelle was given joint credit with English scientist Frederick Twort for the discovery of bacteriophage, the name that he applied to the virus would endure. Further, his work would stimulate other research into bacteriophages. But he remained most interested in applying the knowledge to therapeutic agents. Throughout the rest of his life, he devoted most of his research to various types of bacteriophage that appeared concurrently with specific types of bacteria. After publishing his first paper on the bacteriophage phenomenon, he wrote more than one hundred articles and six books. These publications helped provide the foundation for the later work of molecular biologists.

Traveled around the World

Because of his adventurous spirit, combined with his research activities, d'Hèrelle lived and worked throughout the world during the 1920s and 1930s. In 1920 he traveled to French Indochina, where he investigated human dysentery as well as septic pleuropneumonia in buffaloes. Working under the auspices of the Pasteur Institute, he perfected his techniques for isolating bacteriophage. From 1922 to 1923, he served as an assistant professor at the University of Leiden. In 1924 he and his family moved to Alexandria, Egypt, where he served as director of the Bacteriological Service of the Egyptian Council on Health and Quarantine.

In 1927, responding to an invitation from the Indian Medical Service, he relocated to India, where he attempted to develop a cure for cholera by using the specific bacteriophage associated with the disease. The following year he accepted a position as a tenured professor of bacteriology at Yale Medical School, where he received a generous salary as well as guaranteed laboratory support. This was his first permanent position at a major research institution. His positions at the Pasteur Institute were untenured, and he never rose above the level of a laboratory employee. But d'Hèrelle only remained at Yale until 1933, when he resigned.

Worked in Russia

In 1934, d'Hèrelle went to Russia at the request of the government of the Soviet Socialist Republic of Georgia, to establish institutes focused specifically on the study of bacteriophage. These would be located in Tiflis, Kiev and Kharkov.

The Soviet Union welcomed d'Hèrelle as a scientific hero, as he possessed medical knowledge that could potentially treat diseases that were afflicting the region. He worked at the Tbilisi Institute in Georgia for about a year. During this period he wrote *The Bacteriophage and the Phenomenon of Recovery,* a book that he dedicated to Russian leader Joseph Stalin. d'Hèrelle, who was said to support communist ideals, intended to settle in Russia permanently, and started building a cottage on the Tbilisi Institute property. However, because of unstable political and civil conditions, he was forced to flee in 1937. He never returned and his book was banned.

d'Hèrelle returned to Paris, where he remained for the rest of his life, continuing his bacteriophage-related research. He worked to apply bacteriophage to treating various human and animal diseases such as dysentery, cholera, plague, and staphylococcus and streptococcus infections. Treatments he helped develop were widely used, particularly in the Soviet Union. However, chemical drugs and antibiotics later replaced the applications. Today, bacteriophage is used primarily as a diagnostic ultravirus.

Died in Paris

d'Hèrelle died on February 22, 1949, in Paris, following surgery related to pancreatic cancer. He was 75 years old. He was buried in Saint-Mards-en-Othe in the department of the Aube in France. By this time, he was essentially a forgotten man in the scientific community, despite his valuable work and adventurous spirit.

Even though d'Hèrelle was viewed as an outsider in the science community, he received numerous awards and honors during his life. In 1924 he was awarded an honorary medical degree from the University of Leiden. He also garnered honorary degrees from Yale, Montreal, and Laval universities. In 1925 the Amsterdam Academy of Sciences awarded him its prestigious Leeuwenhoek Medal. Before d'Hèrelle, Louis Pasteur had been the only other French scientist to receive the award. In 1947 he received the Medal of the Pasteur Institute. A year later the French Academy of Sciences presented d'Hèrelle with its Prix Petit d'Ormoy.

In the 1960s the Nobel Foundation placed d'Hèrelle's name on its list of notable scientists who had been worthy of receiving a Nobel Prize but did not. During his lifetime, d'Hèrelle was nominated for a Nobel Prize numerous times.

d'Hèrelle received recognition in other ways. In France, a street in Paris was named after him. Also, Sinclair Lewis's famous novel *Arrowsmith* (1925), which relates the story of a small-town physician who rises to the highest levels in the medical community, was partly based on d'Hèrelle's life.

Books

"Fèlix d'Hèrelle," *World of Microbiology and Immunology,* Thomson Gale, 2006.

Periodicals

Canadian Journal of Infectious Diseases and Medical Microbiology, January 2007.

New England Journal of Medicine, February 24, 2000.

Time, April 16, 1928.

Online

"Biochemistry 3107: Felix d'Herelle and the Discovery of Bacteriophage," *Memorial University,* http://www.mun.ca/biochem/courses/3107/Lectures/Topics/dHerelle.html (December 26, 2008).

"Phage History: The Discovery of Bacteriophage," *Intralytix.com,* http://www.intralytix.com/history.htm (December 26, 2008). □

R. R.R. Dhlomo

R.R.R. Dhlomo (1901–1971) was a South African writer of Zulu heritage whose 1928 novella *An African Tragedy* was the first work of fiction written by a black South African to appear in print in English. In it, wrote Lokangaka Losambe in *An Introduction to the African Prose Narrative,* Dhlomo "expresses his abhorrence of the sordid moral behaviour that a young individual who goes to the city is exposed to, and condemns the revolting living conditions of the slum areas of industrialized cities" like Johannesburg. Dhlomo's later output included several historical novels in the Zulu language, but to most black South Africans of his generation he was known as a prolific journalist for *Bantu World* and other publications.

O f Zulu ethnicity, Dhlomo was born Rolfus Reginald Raymond Dhlomo in 1901 in Siyamu, South Africa, near Pietermaritzburg in Natal Province, and attended the Ohlange Native Industrial Institute and later the Amanzimtoti Training Institute, which was renamed the Adams Teacher's Institute during his teen years. Both were schools founded for black South Africans and funded by foreign missionary-aid societies, but Ohlange was the result of a black scholar and activist, John Langalibalele Dube, who became the founding president of the African National Congress, or ANC, when it was created in 1912.

Worked at Johannesburg Mine

The Dhlomo family moved to Johannesburg that same year that the ANC was founded in response to new restrictions placed on blacks in the region, which was called the Union of South Africa at the time. After a bitter war for control between British settlers and their Dutch counterparts—known as Afrikaners—the two European groups settled into this uneasy alliance, with both unwilling to abandon control of the vast mines of gold and diamonds that had been uncovered late in the nineteenth century. The land grab effectively forced black South Africans into smaller and smaller parcels, and scores of families like Dhlomo's moved to the cities to find work.

Dhlomo's father, Ezra, worked as a medic in a mine, and their mother, named Sardinia Mbune Caluza Dhlomo, took in laundry. The family was among many who readily adopted European—and especially British—customs and morals in addition to Christianity. As a young man, Dhlomo worked as a clerk at the Johannesburg mine before turning to journalism; his brother Herbert, two years his junior, also studied at Adams College and worked as a librarian for a time before becoming a writer. Both were drastically affected by two important pieces of legislation in the history of segregated South Africa: the first was the Native Urban Areas Act of 1923, which delineated all urban centers as whites-only areas. Blacks were permitted to live in what became known as the townships, which were undeveloped areas that quickly became home to thousands of shanties; as late as the mid-1970s less than ten percent of the homes in Soweto, the largest Johannesburg township, had running water or electricity. The 1926 Colour Bar Act was also significant, for it prevented blacks from holding skilled-trades jobs in almost all sectors, including the mining industry.

Dhlomo's first published work was his novella, *An African Tragedy: A Novel in English by a Zulu Writer,* which was published by the Lovedale Institution Press in 1928. Lovedale was a settlement and school founded by Scottish missionaries a century before in Eastern Cape Province. "Dhlomo's novel chronicles the destruction of a male labor migrant in Johannesburg at the hands of a prostitute, contrasting this domineering urban female figure with the migrant's obedient and Christian wife in rural Zululand," noted Lynn M. Thomas, writing in the *Journal of African History* several decades later, for there seems to be no contemporary notice of *An African Tragedy*'s publication in either England or the United States despite the fact it was the first work of fiction by a black South African writer to appear in print. (Another work, Sol T. Plaatje's *Mhudi: An Epic of South African Native Life a Hundred Years Ago,* was published in 1930 but was thought to have been written around 1913.)

Tale May Have Been Autobiographical

A Web site entitled *KZN Literary Tourism* devoted to the literary history of KwaZulu-Natal, as Dhlomo's birthplace later became known, provides a brief excerpt from *An African Tragedy.* Its protagonist, Robert Zulu, has left behind a teaching position at a mission school in order to find better-paying work in Johannesburg. He did this because he needed money for a dowry for the woman he intended to marry, plus, "he thought, as most foolish young people think now-a-days, that town life is better in every way than country life; and that for a young, educated man to die having not seen and enjoyed town life was a deplorable tragedy."

A year after his short novel was published, Dhlomo went to work for a satirical publication called *The Sjambok,* a dreadful title that had multilayered implications in an increasingly racist South Africa. The term was an Afrikaans-language corruption of a Malay word for a type of whip used to drive cattle that was also used on slaves in the medieval history of the Indian Ocean Rim populations. *The Sjambok* was founded by a white journalist named Stephen Black with the intention of skewering South Africa's political elite, but lasted only two years before folding in 1931 after Black's death. One of Dhlomo's articles for it was titled "The Black Bolshevik Factory."

Dhlomo also wrote several short stories. One of them was "Juwawa," which dates back to 1930, and is a brief but compelling tale of a white mine boss who has died in an accident. The title character is his black employee, who has apparently consulted a witch doctor to find a solution to the ill treatment he receives by Garwin, the boss. Even Garwin's colleagues warned him about mistreating workers. "The white miners are presented as fearful, almost superstitious," wrote Christine Loflin in the 2003 volume *The Postmodern Short Story: Forms and Issues.* "They are concerned about Garwin, not because he has been beating black workers—this is apparently acceptable—but because he has been 'knocking *his* boys about.'" Loflin pointed out the white workers were well aware that suspicious accidents sometimes befell such workplace tyrants. Through one character, Dhlomo "implies that the mine tunnels are in fact an underworld, where different rules apply... Already, Dhlomo is setting up a dichotomy between the world aboveground, where whites are in control and can hit blacks with impunity, and the world belowground, where, alone with their own crew 'queer things' happen."

After the accident that is the focal point of "Juwawa," a standard commission of inquiry reviews the matter and decides that there is not enough evidence to cast the blame on Juwawa. His name, however, is put on the official blacklist and he can never work in a mine again—despite the fact that he was essentially exonerated. As Loflin noted, "here, Dhlomo reveals the double standard of the white community. They ignore their own system of justice and apply a different rule to black workers: even the appearance of wrongdoing must be punished."

Exhibited Misogynist Tendencies as Journalist

Dhlomo went on to work for two publications that catered to the large number of literate blacks in South Africa who, like himself, had received a solid education in missionary schools, and aspired to a certain middle-class respectability. One was *Bantu World,* a Johannesburg daily newspaper with about half of its 20 pages in English and the rest in various black languages such as Tswana, Sotho, Zulu, and Xhosa. Borrowed from the Zulu language was the word *AmaRespectable,* which was a somewhat derogatory term for blacks who fully embraced the comportment and moral lessons of the Christian missionaries. As Thomas wrote in the *Journal of African History,* the term and the concept presented a conundrum, for "what counted as respectable behavior for black South Africans living amid the harsh political realities and shifting cultural terrain of the 1930s was the subject of significant debate."

Thomas's essay examined a period of black feminist history in South Africa through the pages of *Bantu World.* Dhlomo became editor of its women's pages after the section debuted in October of 1932. This was an obviously irony-laden situation, for, as Thomas noted, that while there were a few "female writers featured on the women's pages, Dhlomo and a handful of male contributors framed most of the discussion. Together, they promoted an AmaRespectable urban femininity that would distinguish their daughters and wives from the disreputable female figures of the prostitute and skokian [a homemade alcoholic beverage] queen that black leaders had long associated with South Africa's towns."

Copying American and even some African-American publications, Dhlomo and his colleagues at *Bantu World* initiated a newspaper beauty contest for "Miss Africa." They were searching for the ideal representative of a new, modern version of African womanhood that would be judged by "The Son of Africa," probably the white-owner paper's black editor Victor Selope-Thema, and the two winners showed, not surprisingly, a penchant for modest dress with a European flair.

Vented Against Use of Cosmetics

One new trend that was coming into South Africa from abroad earned the scorn of Dhlomo and other editors at *Bantu World,* however, and this was the use of artificial cosmetics such as skin-lightening powder and red lipstick. In early 1933 the paper began an editorial campaign against these new imported products, claiming "that powders and lipsticks did 'not suit dark skins,'" Thomas reported from her research. "Black women," Dhlomo wrote, "should abandon their desire 'to turn themselves white', recognize 'the beauty of their natural coloring', and limit their use of cosmetics to moisturizing creams and hair lotions." Thomas also noted that the paper seemed to have received scores of letters in favor of their effort. She conceded that "in many regards, Dhlomo was a strong proponent of women's 'advancement'. He celebrated black women's educational and professional achievements, and advocated companionate marriages. When it came to black women wearing make-up, however, Dhlomo saw nothing redeemable." It is possible that poor and working-class women were the first black women to wear make-up, thereby contributing to Dhlomo's unease about AmaRespectable cosmetics use."

In 1935, *Bantu World* merged with another publication, *Ilanga lase Natal* (Natal Sun), which had been a pioneering Zulu-language newspaper founded in the city of Durban in 1903 by Dube, the first ANC president. Dhlomo continued to write for the paper, and also began writing a trio of historical novels about the famous Zulu leader Shaka Zulu and his half-brothers, Mpande and Dingane. These were all in the Zulu language, and include *Udigane kaSenzangakhona* from 1938 and *UShaka: Ukuxoxa kuka* from 1939. His 1946 novel, *Indlela Yababi* (The Evil Way) returned him to modern South African concerns in "a novel that deals with the decline of morals among the blacks in the slums of Johannesburg as reflected in the illicit love affair between the main characters and their involvement in delinquent practices," wrote Losambe in *An Introduction to the African Prose Narrative.*

Another scholar of South African history, Rebecca Hourwich Reyher, cited Dhlomo as having been involved in the official Zulu Succession hearings in the early 1940s. This turns up in the biography of one of several dozen wives of an uncrowned Zulu king, *Zulu Woman: The Life Story of Christina Sibiya,* with Reyher noting that Dhlomo had some involvement in the Enquiry Concerning the Zulu Succession. His last work was *UNomalanga kaNdengezi,* published in 1947. A year later, the long and divisive struggle between British colonialism and the more drastic

Afrikaner version ended with the election of the National Party in the 1948 general elections.

Little else was heard from Dhlomo after this point. He died in 1971, when South Africa was still two decades away from the end of apartheid. His brother was H.I.E. (Herbert Izaac Ezra) Dhlomo, who enjoyed some success as an English language playwright and poet during the 1930s and '40s.

Books

Haresnape, Geoffrey, "H. I. E. Dhlomo," in *Dictionary of Literary Biography*, Volume 225: *South African Writers*, edited by Paul A. Scanlon, Gale, 2000, pp. 150–156.

Loflin, Christine, "Multiple Narrative Frames in R.R.R. Dhlomo's 'Juwawa,'" in *The Postmodern Short Story: Forms and Issues*, edited by Farhat Iftekharuddin et al., Greenwood Publishing, 2003, pp. 223–232.

Losambe, Lokangaka, *An Introduction to the African Prose Narrative*, Africa World Press, 2004, pp. 108–109.

Reyher, Rebecca Hourwich, and Christina Sibiya, *Zulu Woman: The Life Story of Christina Sibiya*, Feminist Press, 1999, p. 210.

Periodicals

Journal of African History, November 2006.

Online

"Reginald Dhlomo," KZN Literary Tourism, http://www.literarytourism.co.za/index.php/Authors/Reginald-Dhlomo.html (accessed January 29, 2009). □

Bo Diddley

The 1950s recordings of American singer, songwriter, and guitarist Bo Diddley (1928—2008) were milestones in the evolution of rock and roll music from its rhythm and blues ancestors.

Diddley called himself the Originator, and indeed his influence on early rock and roll was matched by just a few other musicians. A characteristic rhythm heard in several of his most famous songs, given the name of the Bo Diddley beat, became widely familiar among rock percussionists and was copied, to Diddley's chagrin, in many dozens of later song. Even as he made records and played solos that pioneered the use of unusual effects on a guitar (often one he had made himself), Diddley drew on musical ideas, including the Bo Diddley beat, that came from the deepest wellsprings of the African-American tradition. Earlier musicians had built on the blues and other African-American forms to create new popular styles, but Diddley's innovations were profound.

Studied Violin

Bo Diddley, born on December 30, 1928, was a native of McComb, Mississippi. His birth name was Otha Ellas Bates.

He never knew his father, and his teenage mother, Esther Wilson, turned him over to her first cousin, Gussie McDaniel. McDaniel moved with Diddley and her own three sons to Chicago when Diddley was six years old, giving Diddley the name of Ellas B. McDaniel. Growing up on Chicago's South Side, Diddley was steered toward music by O.W. Frederick, a music teacher at Ebenezer Baptist Church. His first instrument was the violin, which he studied for eight years and sometimes played during concerts as an adult; he also played the banjo occasionally. Later he said that his guitar technique, which relied on a variety of slides around the fretboard rather than rapid fingering, was based on his early experiences as a violinist.

For several years Diddley attended Foster Vocational School, where he learned to build musical instruments, a talent that would serve him well in later years when he began to play his own distinctive box-shaped guitars (he built a guitar, a violin, and a bass at age 15). It was early in his career that he acquired the name Bo Diddley. The origin of the name is unclear. A diddley bow is a homemade one-stringed guitar (probably derived from an African instrument) that was still in use among African Americans when Diddley was young. Diddley himself later said that he had never played or heard of one at the time he was given the name, but the same may not have been true among his circle of Southern migrant friends that included many musicians. Diddley band member Billy Boy Arnold also claimed to have bestowed the name on the musician, saying that it meant a comical-looking man.

In any event, Bo Diddley made an ideal stage name when he began performing on street corners and in Chicago's blues-rich Maxwell Street Market during his teenage years. At first he performed with a washtub-playing friend, Roosevelt Jackson. The band expanded to include another guitarist and a harmonica player, and landed occasional gigs at the 708 Club and other South Side venues, and the group began calling themselves the Hipsters and later the Langley Avenue Jive Cats. In the late 1940s and early 1950s, Diddley also worked outside music as an elevator operator, meatpacker, paving crew member, and picture-frame factory worker, among other jobs. He also took up boxing for a time.

Featured Maraca Player in Band

By 1954 Diddley had refined his band into a form closer to the one that made him famous. He added a maraca player, Jerome Green, and perfected guitar tremolos that he could set against his unusual percussion section, which usually lacked the cymbals and bass that were the staples of many blues bands. That year the band sent a demo recording to the Chicago blues label Chess, getting word back that brothers Phil and Leonard Chess liked what they heard. In 1955 Bo Diddley's first 45 rpm record was released (on Chess's Checker imprint), with a song called "Bo Diddley" on the A side and "I'm a Man" on the reverse. Diddley would go on to make other successful recordings, but for sheer influence and historical importance, he never topped that initial pair of songs.

The songs were innovative even in the rapidly developing genres of rhythm and blues and rock and roll. For one thing, they were harmonically static, with no chord changes, relying entirely on rhythm, texture, and lyrics for musical effect. The rhythm underlying "Bo Diddley" was distinctive enough that it became known as the Bo Diddley beat. Difficult to represent in print, it might be described as a cycle of eight beats (or two bars) with accents on the first, the offbeat of the second, the fourth, the sixth, and the seventh beats. In Afro-Caribbean music it is known as the clave rhythm.

Diddley treated the Bo Diddley beat in fresh ways in each song, accenting it with his guitar or inflecting it according to whether the lyrics of the song were playful, boasting, or romantic. But just as the familiar "shave and a haircut, two bits" refrain had simplified the clave rhythm, rock and roll musicians found the Bo Diddley beat easy to imitate in its essentials. One of the first major hits based on it was Buddy Holly's "Not Fade Away" (1957). Diddley's focus on the various noises a guitar could make, as opposed to sheer playing speed, also influenced later musicians, including Jimi Hendrix. As Ned Sublette described it in *Smithsonian*, Diddley "was a key figure in the invention of psychedelic guitar. He found new ways to mess with the sound, making rhythm out of everything the pickups could detect." In 1957 he hired a female guitarist, Peggy Jones, thought to be the first woman to play the guitar in a rock and roll band; on stage she was called Lady Bo.

Diddley, meanwhile, found himself banned from television after appearing on the *Ed Sullivan Show* and performing "Bo Diddley" instead of the agreed-upon "Sixteen Tons." He experienced limited commercial success; recordings such as "Who Do You Love?" reached the top levels of rhythm-and-blues sales charts, but his only pop hit was the top 20 "Say Man" (1959), which featured comic spoken dialogue between Diddley and Green over a rhythmic background. He also at least co-wrote the 1957 Mickey & Sylvia hit "Love Is Strange," whose authorship remains in dispute. Diddley believed that he had never received proper payment for the music he composed. "I am owed," he was quoted as saying in London's *Guardian* newspaper. "I've never got paid. A dude with a pencil is worse than a cat with a machine gun."

Toured in Britain

After a moderate hit with 1962's "You Can't Judge a Book by Its Cover," Diddley left for Britain the following year to perform as part of package tour that included the youthful Rolling Stones. Most of the bands from the blues-oriented side of what became the British Invasion of American popular music admired Diddley's music and imitated it. Diddley himself had more commercial success in Britain than in the United States, placing several songs in the top 20 there, and he returned to Britain in 1973 to record *The London Bo Diddley Sessions*. In 1979 he was picked by the internationally popular British punk band the Clash as an opening act for their tour of the United States that year.

In the United States Diddley continued to perform and record for Chess and then for a succession of small labels, trying to adapt his style to new musical developments, though with little success. He hit a low point after his contract with Chess expired in 1974, by which time the label itself was on its last legs. Living in Los Lunas, New Mexico, he worked for a time as a deputy with the Valencia County sheriff's department. Diddley was married four times: to Louise Woolingham (around 1947), to Ethel Smith (from 1949 until the late 1950s), to a teenaged Southern white magazine saleswoman, Kay Reynolds, and to Sylvia Paiz (in 1992, ending before his death). He had four children, and at his death his descendants included 15 grandchildren, 15 great-grandchildren, and three great-great-grandchildren.

Diddley's touring career was unusually long, something he attributed to the fact that he avoided alcohol and drugs. In 1996 he issued the album *A Man Among Men*, featuring Keith Richards and Ron Wood of the Rolling Stones. He received various honors toward the end of his life, including invitations to perform at two presidential inaugural balls (for George H.W. Bush and Bill Clinton). In 1987 he was inducted into the Rock and Roll Hall of Fame. But he felt that he had never received proper remuneration or appreciation for his contributions. "I opened the door for a lot of people, and they just ran through and left me holding the knob," he told the *New York Times*. In the early 1980s Diddley moved to Archer, Florida, where he set up the last in a long series of home recording studios; his first, in Chicago, was among the first in existence. He amassed a collection of old cars, including a purple Cadillac hearse. Suffering from diabetes and cardiovascular problems, he died at his home on June 2, 2008.

Books

White, George R., *Bo Diddley: Living Legend,* Sanctuary, 1998.

Periodicals

Guardian (London, England), June 3, 2008.
New York Times, June 3, 2008.
Smithsonian, August 2008.
Variety, June 9, 2008.

Online

''Bo Diddley,'' *All Music Guide,* http://www.allmusic.com (January 24, 2009).
''Bo Diddley: Biography,'' *Rolling Stone,* http://www.rollingstone.com/artists/bodiddley/biography (January 24, 2009).
''Bo Diddley,'' Rock and Roll Hall of Fame, http://www.rockhall.com/inductee/bo-diddley (January 24, 2009). □

Frank Nelson Doubleday

American publisher Frank Nelson Doubleday (1862–1934) became one of the most famous, respected and influential leaders in the United States book publishing industry. Thanks to his business acumen and his great appreciation for literature, his firms not only provided fertile ground for famous authors but also advanced the industry through marketing innovations.

Frank Nelson Doubleday was born on January 8, 1862, in the Brooklyn section of New York City, New York, to William Edwards and Ellen M. (Dickinson) Doubleday. He was the sixth of seven sons in a family that included eight children. His father, a New York City clothing merchant, was the great-great-grandson of Jonathan Edwards (1703–1758), the Early American theologian, while his mother was the daughter of Horace Dickinson, who owned the first steamboat that ran the Saint Lawrence River rapids.

Education Interrupted

Growing up, Doubleday developed a fascination for the printing business and its technology. He even saved up his own money to purchase a small printing press, which he turned into a profitable tool by producing advertising handouts for local businesses.

Meanwhile, he attended a public school in Brooklyn and later enrolled in the Brooklyn Polytechnic Institute. His education was cut short, however, when his father's hat making business collapsed, a situation that compelled the fifteen-year-old Doubleday to seek full-time employment. Appropriate to his youthful interests, he landed his first job at Charles Scribner's Sons, a Manhattan-based publishing company. Starting at Scribner's in 1877, Doubleday spent the next twenty years at the firm, where he rose through the organizational ranks and took the lead on many substantial projects. In 1884, he helped revive Scribner's *The Book Buyer* magazine and served as its editor. In addition, he managed *Scribner's Magazine* when it was established in 1887. He also headed the company's subscription book department.

Started His Own Publishing Company

When Doubleday left Scribner's in 1897, he formed a partnership with Samuel Sidney McClure, who published *McClure's Magazine*). Together, they founded the publishing firm of Doubleday & McClure Company.

Established in March of that year, the new company quickly established its credentials. In its first year of existence, Doubleday & McClure published works by Frank Norris (the novelist best-known for the American classic, *The Octopus*), as well as Mary E. Wilkins Freeman and Hamlin Garland and Rudyard Kipling, the author and poet who became one of the best-loved writers in the English language. Doubleday published Kipling's *The Day's Work*.

From their working relationship, Doubleday and Kipling formed a long-standing friendship. In 1899, when Kipling became gravely ill while in New York, Doubleday was constantly by his side, providing support that contributed to the writer's recovery. Based on Doubleday's initials (F.N.D.), Kipling affectionately nicknamed Doubleday ''Effendi,'' an Arabic term that means Chief. The nickname, which was used by friends and family, became one of the most famous in the publishing industry. Later, Doubleday would even call his Locust Valley, New York home the ''Effendi Farm.'' However, Doubleday would reveal, according to a *New York Times* article, that ''Kipling himself never called me anything but Frank all his life.''

Severed Ties With McClure

As a successful publisher, Doubleday effectively coupled his deep appreciation of literature with an instinctive business savvy, a combination that guided his decisions. For instance, in 1898, Doubleday & McClure was contracted to manage the Harper & Brothers publishing company, a move encouraged by the partners' banker, J. Pierpont Morgan. Doubleday felt it best to back out of the agreement, however, after examining Harper's books and determining that the company's financial situation was desperate. This decision only contributed to a growing tension already existing between Doubleday and McClure, though. Finally, on December 31, 1899, the two men ended their partnership.

The following year, Doubleday attracted several new partners—including Walter Hines Page (former editor of *The Atlantic Monthly*), William H. Lanier (son of famed American poet Sidney Lanier), John Leslie Thompson and Samuel A. Everitt—and started a new publishing house: Doubleday, Page & Company.

More than just a book publisher, the new firm produced periodicals. In November 1900, Doubleday and Walter Page founded *World's Work*, a monthly magazine devoted to politics and national affairs (but particularly focusing on educational, agricultural and industrial conditions existing in the southern region of the United States). Page served as editor until 1913. The firm developed other magazine titles including *Garden and Home Builder* (which later became *American Home*), *Country Life in America*, *Short Stories*, *West*, and *Frontier*.

Established New Publishing Facilities

In 1910, Doubleday, Page & Company had become so successful that it outgrew its existing facilities, which included two buildings. As a result, Doubleday decided to relocate from Manhattan to Garden City, Long Island, transplanting the firm from the city to the country. The company also built and operated its own printing and production plant at the new location.

At the time, industry observers questioned the wisdom of these developments. For one thing, the relocation removed Doubleday, Page & Company from a major metropolitan publishing center. Secondly, few publishing companies owned and operated their own production facilities. But Doubleday scoffed at the expressed misgivings. "Many people prophesied its failure, but the idea of a failure never crossed my mind," wrote Doubleday in *The Memoirs of a Publisher*, an autobiography originally written for his family and eventually published in 1972, to help commemorate the company's 75th anniversary. "When we moved to Garden City, we took a great risk. But we all had in mind that if we could make the success that we thought we could, we might be of benefit to the whole publishing trade and induce others to follow our example. I was never able to figure out why an attractive factory would not make more money than an unattractive one."

And, indeed, Doubleday's new setting was quite attractive. The new facility's structure was designed along the lines of a Tudor mansion, in particular King Henry VIII's Hampton Court palace. Further, the company's new offices and production facilities were situated on landscaped grounds, and the surrounding gardens became almost as famous as the authors the company worked with and the volumes it published.

As the company continued growing, Doubleday acquired many other publishing firms and subsidiaries in the United States and in England, where he traveled each summer to find new authors. In 1920, on one of these trips, he bought the controlling interest of the William Heinemann of London publishing company when founder and senior partner William Heinemann died.

In February 1923, Doubleday formed a subsidiary called Garden City Publishing Company, Inc. Later subsidiaries would include Doran Book Shops, Inc., the Crime Club, Inc. and The Sun Dial Press, Inc.

Became an Industry Leader

In 1927, Doubleday bought the George H. Doran Company, a publishing firm that had been established in 1908. Following that acquisition, Doubleday's company eventually became known as Doubleday, Doran & Company, Inc. In that incarnation, the firm became one of the leading publishing houses in the United States. Writers who worked for the company included Kipling, T.E. Lawrence (better known as "Lawrence of Arabia") and Jack London.

One of the most famous writers in the stable was Joseph Conrad, whose contributions to world literature included *Lord Jim* and *Nostromo*. "I liked the things he wrote, so I thought he was worth a gamble," Doubleday once said of Conrad, according to the *Dictionary of American Biography*. "I financed him, and he was worth it."

Other famous writers that Doubleday would work with included O. Henry (pen name of the renowned short story writer William Sydney Porter), Gene Stratton Porter, Booth Tarkington, Ellen Glasgow, Edna Ferber and Kathleen Norris. Doubleday also published *The Jungle*, Upton Sinclair's famous work that exposed conditions in the food industry. It was a risky venture, as other publishing companies refused to touch Sinclair's manuscript. One of the problems was that Armour & Company, a leading meat product supplier, threatened to sue for libel over the work's depiction of the Chicago stockyards. But Doubleday was adamant and even advocated for an investigation into the conditions, and he even presented evidence to President Roosevelt. Partly as a result of Doubleday's efforts, new food and drug laws were subsequently passed.

Doubleday's company also provided training ground for people who eventually became leading figures in the publishing world, including Alfred A. Knopf, who would establish Alfred A. Knopf, Inc. as another leading New York publishing house. In addition, Robert F. DeGraff, founder of Pocket Books, began his career in the Doubleday organization. Henry Luce, who later started *Life* magazine, also worked at Doubleday early in his own career. Novelist Frank Norris worked at Doubleday, Page & Company as an editor and accepted Theodore Dreiser's first novel *Sister Carrie* for publication, a circumstance that led to one of Frank Doubleday's few misjudgments.

Sister Carrie, in part based on the experiences of one of Drieser's sisters, related the story of Carrie Meeber, who ventured from Indiana to Chicago to gain success in the big city. Circumstances forced her to compromise her values and become a mistress, however. In Dreiser's narrative, Carrie was rewarded, rather than punished, for her apparent sins. In his depiction, Dreiser placed blame on society rather than on his heroine. It was a groundbreaking theme, and Norris enthusiastically accepted the manuscript. Doubleday's partner, Walter Page, shared the editor's passion. However, Doubleday's wife Neltje (nee Neltje De Graff), who he had married in June 1886, was appalled by what she felt was the narrative's amorality. Doubleday shared her misgivings and, as he felt it was a commercially unviable book, tried to cancel the publishing contract. But Dreiser demanded that the publisher honor the agreement. Doubleday printed the work in 1900 but he still refused to advertise or widely distribute the book. Subsequently, another book publisher reissued it twelve years later, and *Sister Carrie* gained general release and garnered much acclaim.

Developed Important Social Connections

Doubleday remained president and chairman of the board of his company until 1927. During his tenure, he gained wide respect as an important publisher, and also endeared himself to many famous people. Besides Kipling and

Lawrence, his friends included Theodore Roosevelt, Christopher Morley, Mark Twain, British politician Ramsay MacDonald and James Barrie, author of *Peter Pan.*

Doubleday also played golf with U.S. industrial titans Andrew Carnegie and John D. Rockefeller. On the links, he asked for their business advice. In turn, they sought his counsel on literary matters. In fact, Doubleday helped Rockefeller put together his autobiography.

Doubleday also became a prominent figure in American society. He and his second wife, Florence Van Wyck, involved themselves in philanthropic activities and became well respected in New York Society. (Doubleday's first wife died on February 21, 1918. He married Van Wyck on November 27, 1918.)

Doubleday died on January 30, 1934, at his winter home in Coconut Grove in Florida, of a heart attack. He was 73 years old. Surviving him were his second wife, his daughter Dorothy, and son Nelson (by his first wife). Nelson succeeded his father as the Chairman of the Board of Directors of Doubleday, Doran & Company.

Influenced Industry Direction

Today, Frank Nelson Doubleday is recognized for revolutionizing the publishing industry by considering the enterprise as much a business as a literary pursuit. His innovations include publishing collected volumes of authors' works, book subscriptions and developing advertising and publicity campaigns. Moreover, at his Garden City publishing plant, he established a modern model for employee benefits and health care, as he felt that employee satisfaction provided a key to increased productivity and overall quality. In essence, it was not only the right thing to do but also made good business sense. Company facilities housed a hospital and dentist office, and company benefits included health and life insurance.

Nelson Doubleday (born June 16, 1889) carried on his father's tradition of innovation. He became president and resigned the position in 1946, the same year the firm changed its name to Double & Company. He retained his chairmanship post until his death in 1949.

Books

"Frank Nelson Doubleday," *Dictionary of American Biography, Supplements 1-2: To 1940,* American Council of Learned Societies, 1944-1958.

Frank Nelson Doubleday, *The Memoirs of a Publisher,* Doubleday & Co., 1972.

Periodicals

New York Times, October 6, 1996.

Chicago Tribune, November 8, 1900.

Online

"Frank N. Doubleday and Nelson Doubleday Collection, 1734-1966 (bulk 1890s-1940s): Finding Aid," *Princeton University Library-Manuscripts Division,* http://diglib.princeton.edu/ead/getEad?id=ark:/88435/tb09j566w (December 20, 2008).

"Theodore Dreiser," *American Masters: The American Novel,* http://www.pbs.org/wnet/americannovel/timeline/dreiser. html(December 20, 2008). □

John Sholto Douglas

Sir John Sholto Douglas (1844–1900) was one of the most intriguing figures in nineteenth-century Britain. The immensely wealthy Scottish noble inherited the family's Marquessate of Queensberry, and spent his lifetime indulging in various athletic pursuits typical of his class. Douglas was also a boxing enthusiast, and the guidelines that govern the sport are known as the Marquess of Queensberry Rules, though he did not actually author them but merely sponsored their publication. Later in life, he became embroiled in a rancorous legal dispute with the writer Oscar Wilde.

Born on July 20, 1844, in Florence, Italy, Douglas was the son of Archibald William Douglas, who inherited the Marquessate of Queensberry upon the death of his father in 1853. With that, the young Douglas became known as Viscount Drumlanrig, another title the family's first-born also carried. He is variously referred to as either the eighth or ninth Marquess of Queensberry, and the confusion stems from the fact that one notorious ancestor was formally removed from the official line, which had been created in 1682. That was the third Marquis, James Douglas, who was born in 1697 and died in 1715. He was known to be unstable since childhood, and was kept locked inside Queensberry House in Edinburgh. When the city erupted in unrest over the official Act of Union between England and Scotland in 1707, the boy escaped and killed another youngster, a boy who worked in the kitchen at nearby Holyrood Palace. The ten-year-old Douglas was discovered while eating his victim after having roasted him on the kitchen's spit, allegedly while still alive.

Inherited Title and Lands at 14

There were other tragic episodes in the history of the Douglas family as well. In 1858, Douglas's father accidentally shot himself while out hunting, and the wound was fatal. Published reports claimed he had been rabbit-hunting on his estate, Kinmount, in Dumfriesshire, Scotland, and was likely loading his double-barreled shotgun when it went off. "The national press speculated about the incident," noted Douglas Murray in his 2000 biography of Douglas's son, *Bosie: A Biography of Lord Alfred Douglas.* "The *Evening Herald* reported that 'in sporting circles a belief is expressed that the death was not accidental; he had recently sustained severe losses.'" A few years later, Douglas's younger brother, Lord Francis Douglas, plummeted four thousand feet to his death while climbing the Matterhorn at the age of 18. Francis was one of four Alpine climbers who fell, but only three bodies—all unrecognizable—were found, and Douglas embarked upon his own search mission, during which he nearly froze to death. He later wrote a poem about that night, "The Spirit of the Matterhorn," which expressed some of the atheistic views for which he would become known later in his life.

When Douglas inherited the family title upon the death of his father, he was just 14 years old and already serving in the Royal Navy. He had entered the Royal Naval College as a child, and became a midshipman by the age of twelve; at 15, he was promoted to naval lieutenant. In 1864, at the age of twenty, he entered Magdalene College of Cambridge University, and spent two years there but did not earn a degree. In 1866 he married Sibyl Montgomery, daughter of Alfred Montgomery, whom Murray described as "a magnificent wit and entertainer. Lisping, stuttering and effete, he was considered a fine conversationalist and companion. It seemed unlikely that he would marry." Montgomery did marry and produce a family, however, but that earlier reputation would later become an issue for his son-in-law.

In the same year of his marriage, Douglas became a co-founder of the Amateur Athletic Club (AAC), which was composed of students from the various colleges of Oxford and Cambridge universities. A year later, the AAC published a list of rules for boxing matches held under its sanction. They were probably the work of fellow AAC member John Graham Chambers, but Douglas sponsored their publication, and they became forever known as the Marquess of Queensberry rules. The code prohibited wrestling maneuvers, called for boxing gloves to be worn, limited rounds to three minutes, and specified that if a boxer went down, the referee would count aloud to ten before declaring the other boxer the winner.

Sent to the House of Lords

Douglas and Sibyl had four sons and one daughter in their 21-year marriage: Francis, Percy, Alfred—nicknamed "Boysie" or Bosie" by his mother—Sholto, and finally Edith in 1874. They raised their family at Kinmount, where Douglas engaged in his various sporting pursuits, including serving as Master of the Dumfriesshire Foxhounds hunt; he was also a skilled racer in equestrian events. The marriage faltered, however, because Douglas was often away from home for months at a time tending to his various hobbies, which included politics and adultery in addition to his sporting pursuits. The boys were educated at prestigious boarding schools and rarely saw their father.

Douglas eventually moved to London by himself. Sibyl filed for divorce in 1887 after he turned up at their house in Berkshire, accompanied by his mistress, in time for the festivities of Royal Ascot week, the annual horseracing event. Relations with his five children—aged 13 to 20 by then—became increasingly strained. According to Murray's biography, his son Bosie "recorded that from the age of twelve his father talked to him as though he was an adult, repeatedly expressing concern at his brother Jim's drinking—reportedly as many as four bottles of brandy a day on top of the claret, port and champagne he consumed at meals. Conversation initiated by his son, or anyone else, was generally received with a 'stony silence.'"

With his vast riches and sporting accomplishments, Douglas was a popular figure among other titled landowning peers in Scotland, who selected him to serve as their delegate to the British House of Lords in 1872. He was nominated again in 1880, but this time refused to take the Oath of Allegiance to the sovereign, in this case Queen Victoria, as required of all peers in the chamber. He claimed this was in conflict with his atheist views, for it required him to state, on a copy of the New Testament, "I . . . swear by Almighty God that I will be faithful and bear true allegiance to Her Majesty Queen Victoria, her heirs and successors, according to law. So help me God." He was refused his seat, though in 1888 the Oaths Act permitted members of both houses of parliament to deliver a Solemn Affirmation instead, which omitted the references to God.

Sold Family Estate

Another noted atheist who also refused his seat was Charles Bradlaugh, founder of the National Secular Society, who had been elected to the House of Commons and mounted the campaign that eventually resulted in passage of the Oaths Act of 1888. Douglas, in the interim, became president of the British Secular Union in 1881, which was a splinter group that broke from Bradlaugh's organization. In 1882, Douglas caused a disturbance during a theater performance of *The Promise of May*, a new work by England's poet-laureate Lord Tennyson. "Audiences generally had not reacted well to Tennyson's play and on the first night there had been booing and hissing from a group of atheists objecting to one of the characters, the evil Philip Edgar, an atheist, radical and hedonist," noted Murray in *Bosie*. "On the night Queensberry took his seat in the front row of the stalls he objected forcefully to the depiction of the atheist and was shouted down. When the scene drew to a close he attempted to explain his feelings to the audience but was promptly ejected from the theatre."

In the 1880s, Douglas sold Kinmount, which had been in the family since 1733, and the decision angered his sons and added to the already poor relations between the two generations. Despite his progressive views on religious beliefs, he was a noted homophobe, and as his sons grew into adulthood became convinced that they had been tainted by the genetic legacy of their maternal grandfather, Alfred Montgomery. Trevor Fisher, writing in the *New Statesman* more than a century later, noted that Douglas "became obsessed with the idea that the Montgomery family possessed a homosexual trait threatening his own sons, all the more so when his eldest son, Lord Drumlanrig, became private secretary to the Liberal politician, Lord Rosebery. Queensberry thought Rosebery to be the most prominent member of a homosexual clique operating incognito in the highest political circles. This fear turned him manic."

Lord Rosebery, born Archibald Primrose, helped secure for Francis, the eldest Douglas son, a baronetage from Queen Victoria. The current Viscount Drumlanrig and future Marquis of Queensberry thus became Baron Kelhead, which gave him a seat in the House of Lords. This further exacerbated the rift between father and son, and when Rosebery was serving as British foreign secretary, Douglas traveled to Bad Homburg, Germany, to threaten him if he did not release his son from employment. Rosebery had already received threatening letters from Douglas, and enlisted the help of the Prince of Wales, who strongly advised Douglas to leave the country, which he did. Two months later, in October of 1894, Francis died in yet another hunting accident, this one occurring during an outing at Quantock Lodge in Somerset. Again, it was ruled an accidental shooting, "but informed opinion suspected suicide, hinting at blackmail and the effect of his father's extraordinary behaviour," wrote Fisher in the *New Statesman* article.

Sued by Oscar Wilde

Even before the death of Francis, Douglas was already equally disturbed by his third son's friendship with the writer Oscar Wilde. Bosie was a poet of some renown by then, while Wilde was a successful playwright. As he had with Rosebery, Douglas appealed to Wilde to sever ties with his son, but Bosie harbored no love for his father and the tension seemed to bring him and Wilde closer. Douglas again tried to disrupt a theater performance, this time of Wilde's play *The Importance of Being Earnest* when it opened at St. James's Theater in London in February of 1895. A few days later, Douglas showed up at Wilde's club in London, the Albemarle, but Wilde was not there. The marquis scribbled a note on a calling card and handed it to the porter to give to Wilde. It read, "For Oscar Wilde ponce and somdomite," according to the *New Statesman*. Douglas had misspelled "sodomite," but later claimed that

he had meant to write "posing as a sodomite," a term that referred to a sexual act. At the time, in Britain and elsewhere, homosexuality was essentially a crime, because such acts were subject to criminal prosecution.

Urged on by Bosie, Wilde initiated a defamatory libel lawsuit against Douglas, who was arrested at a London hotel. In British libel law, the burden of proof is on the defendant, not the plaintiff—meaning that Douglas would have to show proof that Wilde had engaged in acts that could be classified as sodomy. His defense attorneys deposed a young man who earned a living from male prostitution and had kept a list of his clients on which Wilde's name was found. When it appeared that this young man and possibly others would be compelled to testify in what was already becoming Britain's most scandalous court case of the decade, the prosecution dropped the case, and the judge instructed the jury to enter a verdict of not guilty against Douglas, which they did. Wilde was arrested later that day for gross indecency, jailed, and convicted.

Despite the vicious tone of Douglas's accusations—he called Lord Rosebery, who was Jewish, exceedingly derogatory names, for example—Douglas became a hero to many in Britain for his personal crusade against homosexuality. He died in London on January 31, 1900. Wilde died later that year, his health having never recovered from his two-year prison term. Douglas's second son, Percy, inherited the Marquess of Queensberry title. Bosie died in 1945. The Wilde-Douglas trial was the centerpiece of the 1997 film *Wilde*, with Stephen Fry in the title role, Jude Law as Bosie, and Tom Wilkinson as Douglas.

Books

Murray, Douglas, *Bosie: A Biography of Lord Alfred Douglas*, Talk Miramax Books/Hyperion, 2000.

Periodicals

New Statesman, April 7, 1995.

Times (London, England), August 10, 1858. □

Le Duan

Le Duan (1908–1986) generated few headlines at the time, but for three decades, he was one of the most powerful leaders in North Vietnam. Le Duan, who survived ten years of imprisonment, was general secretary of the Vietnamese Communist Party and the driving force behind the communist victory in that country. His profile, however, was much lower than that of longtime party leader Ho Chi Minh. Le Duan oversaw a unified Vietnam from 1975 to 1986, when he struggled with domestic crises and international isolation.

were reluctant—to accelerate the fight in the south because the United States was providing help there. Between the 90,000 Communists in North Vietnam and a rising insurgency in South Vietnam, the Viet Cong, a total victory was plausible, Le Duan told Ho. Finally, Hanoi approved the aggressive stance, sending troops and supplies south. "It was Le Duan's first major victory within the party, and it would not be his last," Quynh wrote.

Emerged as Potent Hanoi Figure

In 1960, one year after he convinced Ho to accelerate in the south, Le Duan was elected general secretary of the Communist Party. He would keep that position until his death. Le Duan solidified his power, building the support of North Vietnam allies. "Ho Chi Minh, his health deteriorating, was becoming less and less involved in governmental decisions," Mark Moyar wrote in *Triumph Forsaken: The Vietnam War, 1954-1965.* "Responsibility for the country's detailed business no longer belonged to Ho at all but to Le Duan, and on large strategic issues Le Duan was becoming the dominant figure." Ho's role became essentially ceremonial. "I am better than Uncle Ho," Le Duan, as quoted by Moyar, told an associate. Also marginalized were such revolutionary veterans as 30-year Prime Minister Pham Van Dong and General Vo Nguyen Giap, the mastermind of the Viet Minh victory in the Battle of Dien Bien Phu that forced the 1954 accord. "Although Ho's international prestige and experience meant that he became Hanoi's chief diplomat, real power at home rested with Le Duan and his trusted deputies," Quynh wrote.

By 1961, assassinations of government officials and village chiefs escalated to 4,000 annually, forcing South Vietnam to ask the United States for help. The conflict escalated and in 1965, U.S. President Lyndon B. Johnson deployed more troops. Le Duan, meanwhile, remained in a tug-of-war in his own party over whether to push for all-out military victory—which he had favored—or continue to escalate the guerilla insurgency. When Ho died in 1969, Le Duan officially became North Vietnam's leader. In 1971, according to *Time* magazine, Le Duan implored North Vietnam's army to "shatter the U.S. imperialist plan of Vietnamizing the war." One year later, *Time,* acknowledging Le Duan's crafty and shadowy ways, called him "the most powerful figure in the North Vietnamese hierarchy."

"In some ways, Le Duan's career has been advanced as much by luck as by leadership," *Time* wrote, comparing him to Soviet leader Nikita Khrushchev. The magazine cited Le Duan's activities in the south that kept him away from the land-reform crisis in the north during the 1950s. The latter event led to the ouster of secretary-general Truong Chinh. Ho succeeded Truong, but delegated operations to Le Duan. Though Khrushchev, as quoted by *Time,* once said Le Duan "talks, thinks, and acts like a Chinese," Le Duan survived politically by conducting a difficult balancing act among his country, the Soviet Union, and China in his early years in charge, "threading his way between Moscow and Peking."

With Le Duan leading a new direction, the relationship between China and North Vietnam warmed in the mid-1960s. Hanoi lambasted the Soviet Union for signing a nuclear test-

L e Duan, whose name is revolutionary, not given, and is pronounced "LAY-zwan," was born to a peasant family on April 7, 1908 (some sources say 1907) in Quang Tri province, in what was French Indochina—later South Vietnam. He received a French colonial education before working as a clerk for the Vietnam Railway Company. He became a union activist and a founding member of the Indochinese Communist Party (ICP) in 1930.

Jailed over Union Activities

The French rulers sentenced him to the notorious "tiger cages" at the prison on Con Son Island in 1931, alleging subversive activities in connection with anti-French riots in the country. "His formative years were spent in colonial jails, which served to shape him into a determined and implacable revolutionary," Quynh Le wrote for British Broadcasting Corporation's Vietnamese service. Le Duan, however, was released only five years into a 20-year sentence and rejoined the ICP in 1936. Le Duan was rearrested in 1940 when the party was outlawed, and released when the Communist Viet Minh temporarily took power in 1945, upon the end of World War II.

Le Duan rose through the party ranks, at first coordinating guerilla activities. After the French left the country under the 1954 Geneva Accord, Vietnam was bifurcated into the Communist north and anti-Communist south. Le Duan ordered guerillas in the south to intensify their battle. He urged Ho and other Communist leaders—who at first

ban treaty with the United States, while a Le Duan-led group of militants discredited revisionists within the Vietnamese Communist Party. The victory by anti-revisionist factions and move toward China, meanwhile, created a chill in relations with the Soviets. Khrushchev early in 1964 implored Le Duan not to undermine the communist effort worldwide, and when he resisted, Moscow reduced its aid to Hanoi. Chinese leader Mao Zedong, meanwhile, encouraged the North Vietnamese to send more troops into South Vietnam and neighboring Laos.

Struggled as Leader of Unified Country

After North Vietnam captured Saigon in 1975 and evacuated the United States, Le Duan, the Associated Press wrote, was reported to have returned to Con Son and stood rigidly in front of his former cell for more than one hour. Le Duan coordinated the rebuilding of the south and its integration into a unified, communist Vietnam. He sought to emulate Ho in his detachment from political frays. Personally, he had the reputation of being secretive and rigid, a man not friendly with many. The Associated Press called Le Duan "one of the communist world's most durable liberals."

The war had left Vietnam isolated politically from the West. In addition, its relationship with neighboring China deteriorated. "Military adventurism, including a border war with China, has put Vietnam on bad terms with his neighbors," Charles Mohr of the *New York Times* wrote, as quoted in the *Encyclopedia of World Biography*. Le Duan charted his country on a warmer rapport with the Soviet Union. Christopher Lehmann-Haupt, also in the *New York Times,* called Le Duan "Brezhnev-like," comparing him to former Soviet leader Leonoid Brezhnev.

Poverty, however, was Vietnam's biggest challenge in the Le Duan years. "Despite the return of peace, for over a decade the country experienced little economic growth because of conservative leadership policies," the Central Intelligence Agency wrote on its CIA World Factbook Web site. The mass exodus of hundreds of thousands of so-called "boat people," many of whom died at sea, brought worldwide attention to the plight of many Vietnamese. "The people who suffered the most, many of them expelled from the country and perishing at sea as boat people, were the Chinese minority in Vietnam, who were feared as a potential fifth column in Beijing," Lehmann-Haupt wrote.

Le Duan, meanwhile, found leadership around him divided. He perceived enemies, even among some of his closest confidants. "In 1982, General Giap was forced out of the Politburo, the executive body of the Vietnamese Communist Party, after clashing with Le Duan," Lehmann-Haupt wrote. Le Duan's critics asserted political power should have been more spread out.

On July 10, 1986, Le Duan died in Hanoi of a kidney and heart ailment. Five days of national mourning followed the announcement. The Associated Press (AP), quoting Western diplomats in Hanoi, reported at the time that the Politburo had already removed Le Duan from elite leadership because of his health and age. "They said he probably would have been retired officially at the sixth Communist Party congress later this year," the AP wrote. Leaders named a street in Hanoi after Le Duan.

Diplomats envisioned a more moderate Vietnam, including rapprochement with the West and entrepreneurial incentives, after Le Duan's death. Later in 1986, the country enacted "doi moi," a series of economic incentives. "Vietnamese authorities have committed to increased economic liberalization and enacted structural reforms needed to modernize the economy and to produce more competitive, export-driven industries," the CIA World Factbook wrote on its Web site.

Le Duan's Legacy

Communists in North Vietnam, 30 years after unification, were divided over how to view Le Duan in retrospect. Since his death, however, the country has divided its three top positions among its northern, southern, and central regions, implying that leadership in the Le Duan years was too centralized. In 2006, two southerners were chosen to lead the country for the first time since unification.

Reflecting the changes since unification, the street in Hanoi that bears Le Duan's name featured Diamond Plaza, which the Associated Press called "a glittering, upscale department store where French perfumes and Italian shoes are sold to an urban, middle class. In the same area, a five-star hotel owned by a French conglomerate was across the street from the U.S. consulate.

"Though the North and South reunified three decades ago, the task of reconciliation still looms large," Tini Tran wrote for the Associated Press in 2005. In the same article, Prime Minister Phan Van Khai implored former enemies to "close the past, [and] look to the future." But, Tran added, "despite the government's message of reconciliation, lingering mistrust continues." For example, the government that year banned a book from pre-1975 that contained love songs.

"Economic stagnation marked the period after unification from 1975 to 1985," the CIA World Factbook wrote. "Vietnam is a densely populated developing country that in the last 30 years has had to recover from the ravages of war, the loss of financial support from the old Soviet Bloc, and the rigidity of a centrally planned economy." The book cited progress the country made in the immediate decade after Le Duan, and its rebound from the Asian financial crisis of the late 1990s.

The BBC's Quynh wrote that there is no compelling sentiment to revive discussions of leaders such as Le Duan. "At school, students are not taught about some uncomfortable episodes in the country's recent history," Quynh wrote. "But sooner or later, Vietnam will have to come to terms with the past by re-examining the enduring effects of Le Duan's regime."

Books

Moray, Mark, *Triumph Forsaken: The Vietnam War, 1954-1965,* Cambridge University Press, 2006.

Periodicals

New York Times, July 27, 1992.

Time, May 15, 1972.

Online

''Central Intelligence Agency: The World Factbook: Vietnam,'' https://www.cia.gov/library/publications/the-world-factbook/geos/vm.html, November 18, 2008.

''Duan Le,'' *Contemporary Newsmakers Online,* 2002, http://galenet.galegroup.com/servlet/BioRC?vrsn=149&OP=contains&locID=k12_biorc7&srchtp=name&ca=1&c=3&AI=U13013466&NA=Le+Duan&ste=12&tbst=prp&tab=1&docNum=H1000058317&bConts=35, November 13, 2008.

''Le Duan, 79; Headed Vietnam Communists,'' Associated Press, http://www.highbeam.com/doc/1P2-3775024.html, July 11, 1986.

''Vietnam Ambivalent on Le Duan's Legacy,'' BBC News, http://www.bbc.co.uk/2/hi/asia-pacific/5180354.stm, July 14, 2006.

''Vietnam Marks 30 Years since War's End,'' AP Online, http://www. highbeam.com/doc/1P1-108344268.html, May 1, 2005. □

E

Adolf Erman

German Egyptologist and lexicographer Adolf Erman (1854–1937), called "one of the revered patriarchs of Egyptology" by Jon Manchip White in his introduction to Erman's book *Life in Ancient Egypt,* contributed greatly to the study of Egyptian language and culture. His *Neuaegyptische Grammatik* (New Egyptian Grammar) has remained the standard work in its field for over a century, and Erman's efforts to implement academic rigor to the study of ancient Egypt laid the groundwork for essentially all later scholarship on the topic. Erman wrote extensively not only on the ancient Egyptian language, but also on its history and culture. His work in the organization and administration of the Egyptian Museum helped to solidify its collection of antiquities and develop its status as a premier museum of ancient Egyptian art.

The son of scientist and mathematician Georg Adolf Erman, Johann Peter Adolf Erman—commonly known as Adolf—was born in Berlin on October 31, 1854. His ancestors had originally come to Berlin to join a community of expatriated French Protestants from Geneva, Switzerland, around the turn of the 18th century, shortening their family name of Ermatinger to Erman. Despite several generations of residence in Berlin, the family retained ties to their French heritage; for example, Erman spoke French as his native tongue, and like the other males of his family attended school at the French Gymnasium in Berlin. He then pursued studies at the University of Berlin.

The field of Egyptology had exploded in the early part of the 1800s, drawing renewed attention from scholars. In 1842, King Frederich Wilhelm IV of Prussia tapped Richard Lepsius to investigate ancient Egyptian ruins; Lepsius' successes led to the formation of the Egyptian Section of the Royal Museums, and would in many ways serve as inspiration to Erman, a generation younger than Lepsius. In the early heyday of Egyptology, the field routinely offered exciting discoveries leading to great leaps of knowledge and was generally considered to be quite glamorous—particularly for a scholarly field. The European exploration of ancient Egyptian sites also caused many artifacts and even entire tombs to be removed from their rightful locations, a practice that L. Bull and W. F. Edgerton characterized in the *Journal of the American Oriental Society* as "reckless destruction."

It was against this somewhat romantic backdrop that Erman entered the Egyptological field. Writing in the introduction to Erman's *Life in Ancient Egypt,* Jon Manchip White noted that "[Erman] was fortunate in finding his vocation early." Indeed, Erman's first published article—describing but one of what would be many findings regarding Egyptian grammar—appeared in the *Zeitschrift für Agyptischen Sprache* (Journal for the Egyptian Language) in 1875. His first major scholarly work on ancient Egypt appeared in 1877 when he was but 23 years old; that same year, Erman completed his doctoral degree at the University of Berlin. He also began working that year as an assistant in the numismatic (coinage) department at the Royal Prussian Museum in Berlin, and many of his early works related to that field.

Achieved Lifelong Professional Success

In 1881, the Egyptian Section of the Royal Museums passed from one generation to the next when Erman inherited the position of Director from the retiring Lepsius. That same year, Erman became an assistant editor of the *Zeitschrift für Agyptischen Sprache,* a position he held until 1884; he later served as editor of that publication from 1899 to 1906, first alongside Heinrich Brugsch and later with Georg Steindorff. Erman achieved personal success as well in 1881 with his marriage to another German with French heritage, Käthe d'Heureuse. The couple, who later had five children—including a son, Peter, whose death at the Battle of the Somme during World War I was a source of lifelong anguish to Erman—remained married until Erman's death in 1937.

In 1881, Erman began teaching courses in Egyptology at the University of Berlin; three years later, he ascended to a professorship in that department, a position that he would hold until 1923. Writing in the *Journal of Egyptian Archeology,* W.E. Crum noted that Erman was "an inspiring teacher: enthusiastic, full of ideas and eagerly adopting promising suggestions from his hearers." He not only encouraged his pupils in their studies, but also developed lasting friendships with most of them; the wide majority of those who studied under Erman went on to find success in their own right. Among Erman's students was the American scholar James Henry Breasted, who is credited with establishing the study of Egyptology in the United States.

Prior to Erman's time, the study of Egyptian grammar had been undertaken as haphazardly as had the excavation of Egyptian archeological sites. Erman argued for the application of method and order to the interpretation of ancient texts as well as against the sometimes destructive archeological techniques of his day. Not all of his contemporaries agreed with these methods and the Egyptologist and his students received the somewhat derisive designation of the Berlin School. In noting the later decline in usage of this term coincident with the later acceptance of Erman's methodology as standard, Bull and Edgerton commented that "this history of a phrase may serve in some slight degree as a measure of the difficulties which Erman once encountered, and of the overwhelming success with which he patiently and laboriously faced them."

Influenced the Study of Egyptian Grammar

Crum observed that "though in time Erman was to set his mark upon every branch of [Egyptology], it was always by the problems of language that he was most attracted and it is as a philologist no doubt that he will be remembered." Erman began his grammatical studies early in his career and they defined much of the scope of his work throughout his life. One of Erman's earliest contributions to the study of the ancient Egyptian language was his realization that the language contained two distinct periods: Old Egyptian, encompassing those writings preceding about 1600 BC, and Late Egyptian, covering the era from 1600 to about 700 BC. (Modern scholarship includes a third grouping, Middle Egyptian.) The first edition of Erman's seminal work on Egyptian grammar, *Neuaegyptische Grammatik,* dating

from 1880, focused on the latter division; in his later years, Erman, despite failing vision, dictated a revised version of the text. This latter edition has served as a standard work in the study of Egyptian grammar since the time of its publication in 1933.

Erman published in 1889 a grammatical work, *Die Sprache des Papyrus* (The Language of the Papyrus), based on a recently discovered Middle Egyptian text. Five years later, he completed the *Aegyptische Grammatik* (Egyptian Grammar), a primer on the Egyptian language which Erman stated in its introduction was "designed to facilitate as far as possible, for the beginner, the acquisition of the Egyptian language and writing[.]" The scholar significantly revised this text as well in later life, producing the fourth edition of the book in 1928. One of Erman's crowning achievements was his *Wörterbuch der Aegyptischen* (Dictionary of the Egyptian Language), a massive undertaking with which Erman was assisted by many of his students; five volumes of this work appeared between 1926 and 1935.

Another of Erman's contributions to Egyptian philology lie in his work connecting the Coptic language—which flourished in Egypt from about the 100s AD and was written using Greek characters—with Egypt's earlier languages. Erman believed that an understanding of Coptic was crucial to the comprehension of texts written in hieroglyphic form. He also discerned the relationship between earlier Egyptian and the Semitic language family, which today includes Arabic and Hebrew.

Studied Egyptian Culture and Life

In addition to his extensive philological research, Erman researched and wrote on practically all aspects of ancient Egyptian life. Referring to these wide-ranging studies, Bull and Edgerton claimed that "it would be hard to overestimate the importance of Erman's work" for both its breadth and influence of generations of later scholars.

Erman's *Aegypten und aegyptisches Leben* (Life in Ancient Egypt) was first published in 1885, with a revision by Hermann Ranke following in 1923. This work extensively detailed facets of ancient Egypt life ranging from broad treatments of politics and religion to such minutiae as clothing and hairstyles in what White called "a rigorous and somewhat clinical spirit." Although previous treatments of Egyptian life existed—most notably Sir John Gardner Wilkinson's *Manners and Customs of the Ancient Egyptians,* dating from the 1840s—Erman's work presented the latest in Egyptological scholarship and did so in a way that was accessible to a popular audience.

In the years that followed, Erman turned his attentions more specifically to the nature and practice of ancient Egyptian religion. These effort led to the 1905 publication of *Aegyptische Religion* (Egyptian Religion), which Willeke Wendrich deemed a century later in the *Encyclopedia of Religion* "the oldest general overview of Egyptian religion that is still worth reading today," a testament to the lasting value of Erman's scholarship. This work, which presented the first book-length treatment of the topic, argued that Egyptian religion had been a natural response to unexplainable natural phenomena and an attempt to exert control over these at times dangerous events. The publication of the book did not end Erman's interest in the area, however, and he gathered his later findings into the expanded *Die Religion der Aegypter* (The Religion of the Egyptians), published in 1934.

Erman wrote and published extensively throughout his life. Other notable works include *Die Literatur der Aegypter* (The Literature of the Ancient Egyptians), a collection of ancient texts edited by Erman and published in 1923; and an autobiography, *Mein Werden und mein Wirken* (My Values and My Works), in 1929.

Death and Legacy

Erman's grandmother had been born a Jew; despite her later conversion to Christianity, Erman was harassed—although not directly persecuted—by the German Nazi regime in his later years. He experienced prolonged failing health toward the end of his life, suffering from near-total blindness by the time of his death. Despite this physical failing, he remained mentally sound and continued to work nearly until his last day. He passed away in Berlin on June 26, 1937, at the age of 82. During his long career, the Egyptologist had produced well over 275 written works, excluding his reviews and lectures. Bull and Edgerton claimed that "notwithstanding their great number, his publications were never hasty and never ill-considered . . . many of them have been superseded, but only after the labor of years and only by scholars who incorporated Erman's results in the foundations of their own work." As one of the first scholars to firmly apply a principled, scientific approach to the study of ancient Egypt and its language, Erman's contributions laid the foundations for contemporary knowledge of that long-ago era and have certainly assured his position in history.

Books

Encyclopedia Judaica, Vol. 6, 2nd ed. Eds. Michael Berenbaum and Fred Skolnik, Keter Publishing House Ltd., 2007.
Encyclopedia of Religion, Gale, 2005.
Erman, Adolf, *Egyptian Grammar,* Williams and Norgate, 1894.
Erman, Adolf, *Life in Ancient Egypt,* Dover, 1971.
"James Henry Breasted," *Encyclopedia of World Biography,* Gale Research, 1998.

Periodicals

Journal of the American Oriental Society, September 1938.
The Journal of Egyptian Archaeology, June 1937.□

F

Gabriele Falloppio

Italian anatomist Gabriele Falloppio (1523–1562) is credited with making several significant discoveries about human anatomy, particularly discoveries about the inner ear and the female reproductive system. In 1561 he identified the pathway from the ovaries, which in women of childbearing age carries an ovum, or egg, during the monthly reproductive cycle, to the uterus for the possibility of fertilization through sexual intercourse. Though Falloppio did not actually recognize its function, the pair of canals in which the ova travel are named the Fallopian tubes in his honor.

Falloppio was born in 1523 in Modena, Italy, to parents Geronimo and Caterina Falloppio. The Falloppios were an impoverished noble family, and the family's financial woes worsened when Geronimo died. Falloppio entered the Roman Catholic priesthood, and in 1542, the year he turned 19, he became a canon of the cathedral in Modena, a magnificent example of medieval European Romanesque architecture that was built in 1184. Canons were members of the clergy living together in a religious community that was attached to the local cathedral. His family's financial circumstances eventually improved, and he was able to enter the Medical College of Modena, where the historical record lists him as performing his first dissection of a human cadaver in December of 1544 under his teacher Niccolo Machella.

Earned Medical Degree at Ferrara

The practice of dissecting human corpses had long been subject to official and quasi-official bans, due to deep-seated cultural taboos. Ancient Greek physicians carried out legitimate scientific investigations on the dead, but subsequent Roman law—which was applied throughout much of Europe as the Roman Empire expanded in the first century C.E.—specifically prohibited the dissection of human cadavers. This was followed a century or so later by a decree from Pope Boniface VIII prohibiting a practice that had begun during the Crusades, when the bodies of dead Crusaders were boiled so that their bones could be returned to their birthplace in Christian lands for burial.

In the early 1300s, however, some northern Italian states began permitting the dissection of the corpses of executed criminals for scientific purposes. This reflected a flourishing of scientific inquiry in places like Bologna, Padua, Modena, and Ferrara, all of which were home to some of the first universities in Europe. Falloppio went on to earn his medical degree from the University of Ferrara in 1548.

The first public dissection on record took place in the early 1300s and was conducted by the anatomist Mondino de Liuzzi, whose published textbook *Anatomia mundini* (Mondino's Anatomy) became a standard reference work for the next three centuries. Liuzzi did not actually cut open the body, but instead supervised the work done by barber-surgeons, who in medieval times were permitted the practice of bloodletting for medical purposes. Liuzzi then pointed out the various parts of the body, many of whose actual functions remained shrouded in mystery. Such dissections also became a type of professional examination for prospective physicians. The custom was, however, to use only the bodies of executed criminals, and dissections were carried out in the colder months because of the risk of putrefaction.

Became Professor at Padua

Mondino's Anatomy was a significant improvement over the first and only comprehensive book of anatomy used in

157

Western Europe for more than a millennium. This was *Methodus medendi,* written by a Roman physician named Galen in 180 C.E. Galen treated gladiators, and his findings were gleaned from his observations of their gruesome injuries. He also dissected monkeys and tried to provide analogies between primate and human anatomy. Evelyn B. Kelly noted in *Science and Its Times* that "this often led to erroneous conclusions. Galen, for example, thought the uterus had two horn-like projections. He believed that male and female children developed in the right and left horn, respectively."

Falloppio joined the faculty at Ferrara in 1548, and was subsequently made the chair of its pharmacy faculty. In 1549 he moved to Pisa to take a post as professor of anatomy at its university, which was then the leading university in all of Italy. In addition to his teaching and research duties, he was a highly regarded physician with well-known patients, one of whom was Baldovino del Monte, the brother of Pope Julius III. Two years later Falloppio moved on to the University of Padua at the invitation of Cosimo I de Medici, who was the Grand Duke of Tuscany and one of the most influential figures in Europe at the time. This particular Medici was a major patron of the arts and played a key role in the Italian Renaissance.

Falloppio accepted the position at Padua in 1551 and held it for the next eleven years. He was chair of the school's anatomy and surgery departments, a professor of botany, and superintendent of the *Orto Botanico di Padova,* the

school's botanical garden and the world's oldest existing academic *horto medicinale,* or medicinal garden.

At Padua, Falloppio made his most important breakthroughs. He was a specialist in cranial anatomy, or the structure and systems of the skull, and is known for discovering and naming several of its parts. He wrote about the tympanum, or eardrum, the membrane that separates the outer ear from the middle ear, and explained for the first time how it works with the chain of ossicles, or tiny bones. He also identified the circular and oval windows known as *fenestrae* leading from the middle ear to the inner ear, and wrote about that relationship to the vestibula of the inner ear where the cochlea is located, which contains the actual sensory cells that permit hearing. Falloppio's investigations into other parts of the head yielded the discovery of the nasolacrimal ducts, or tear ducts, and the ethmoid bone, which serves as the barrier between the nasal cavity and the brain.

Discovered Fallopian Tubes

Falloppio's name is forever associated with the part of the female reproductive system that bears his name. For reasons that are lost to the historical record, he was able to dissect the corpses of women, children, infants, and even a fetus. His major study *Observationes anatomicae* (Anatomical Observations) was published in Venice in 1561, and it featured the first scientific description of the Fallopian tubes. Falloppio likened the pair to trumpets, or *tuba* because of their shape. Each linked one of two ovaries—the repositories for the female reproductive gametes known as ova, or eggs—to the uterus, where an egg arrives once a month to await possible fertilization by a male reproductive gamete known as a spermatozoon or sperm cell.

Falloppio did not recognize the function of the tubes in carrying the ova during a woman's monthly menstrual cycle, but he did describe finding bodies that had a watery fluid and others that had a yellowish fluid. Later scientists believe he may have been writing about ova and the nearby follicular cells. It would take another 200 years for anatomists to fully identify the parts of the female reproductive system and their functions. Falloppio's discoveries were significant, in part because of the gender bias among scientific professionals of the era. The generally accepted wisdom was that the male and female reproductive systems were essentially the same, with the male version the more perfect form and the female the inferior version. According to Kelly, the belief was that "because the female did not have adequate 'vital heat,' women could not make semen like the men, but produced milk instead. Women, in short, were leaky vessels full of holes, as evidenced by crying, milk production, and menstruation."

Falloppio's breakthrough 1561 tome also described and named the parts of the female genitalia, including the vagina, and advanced the correct theory that it was separate from the uterus. *Anatomical Observations* also contained a description of the clitoris, referencing the work of the esteemed Persian physician Avicenna, also known as Abu Ali Sina Balkhi, who died in 1037. "Avicenna makes mention of a certain member situated in the female genitalia which he calls *virga* or *albathara,*" Falloppio wrote, according to the scholarly work *Re-reading Sappho: Reception and Transmission.* He added, "Our anatomical writers have completely neglected this and do not even have a word for it."

Conducted Clinical Trial of Condoms

Falloppio also wrote about sexually transmitted diseases, and recommended the prevention of syphilis by the use of condoms. H. Youssef, in an article in the *Journal of the Royal Society of Medicine,* investigated reports on the history of condom use and debunked claims that the ancient Egyptians and Romans may have used the contraceptive and disease-preventive device. Youssef cited a work by Falloppio as "the earliest description of the condom," noting that this was published in 1564, two years after Falloppio's death. "He claimed to have invented a linen sheath and it was worn for protection against syphilis. He tried it on 1100 men, no more, no less—not one became infected."

Falloppio's published works included commentaries on the works of others, including a review of one by Hippocrates, the pioneering Greek physician who died around 370 BCE. He also wrote *Observations Anatomicae,* a commentary on *De Humani Corporis Fabrica* (On the Fabric of the Human Body), an important work by one of his contemporaries, a Belgian named Andreas van Wesel, known by the Latinized form of his name, Andreas Vesalius. Vesalius also taught at the University of Padua. Vesalius, Falloppio, and the Italians Realdo Colombo and Bartolemeo Eustachi were considered the four leading human anatomists of the Renaissance. Eustachi described the tube that links the inner ear to the pharynx and made many other important discoveries. Colombo was the first to correctly identify some functions of the pulmonary arteries, but had an intense professional rivalry with Vesalius, whose work was the most important and widely read book on anatomy for several generations because of its detailed illustrations.

Died Near Age 40

There were other publications attributed to Falloppio, but only a collected volume titled *Opera omnia,* published in Venice in 1584, is known for certain to have been from his hand. This was published posthumously, however, for Falloppio died of pulmonary tuberculosis on October 9, 1562, a year after he had accepted an offer from the University of Bologna to become its professor of practical medicine. He fell ill before beginning the job, and remained at Padua, where he died. At the University of Padua his teaching chair was filled by his former student, Girolamo Fabrici, also called Fabricius ab Aquapendente. Fabrici, in turn, taught the pioneering English physician and anatomist William Harvey, widely considered the founder of modern medicine for his research into the human circulatory system.

Falloppio also lent his name to the aquaeductus Fallopii, part of a cranial canal that carries the facial nerve some of the way from the brain to the middle ear. But the other part of the anatomy bearing his name is the much more commonly known one, and Falloppio's scientific legacy remains his research into female reproductive anatomy.

Before him, "the womb was a baffling space which gave birth to monstrous myths about womanhood," wrote Felipe Fernandez-Armesto in the *Times* of London, in a review of two books on feminist history. "With other 16th-century anatomists, he helped to start the Western world's biggest-ever revolution in perceptions of women. Before his time, it was possible to define woman as "Nature's bodged attempt to create an example of a better sex. Now her apparent deficiencies seemed moulded with the obvious perfection of divine design."

Books

Dictionary of Scientific Biography, Volume IV: *Richard Dedekind—Firmicus Maternus,* edited by Charles Coulston Gillispie, American Council of Learned Societies/Charles Scribner's Sons, 1980.

Porter, Roy, *Blood and Guts: A Short History of Medicine,* W. W. Norton & Company, 2004.

Re-reading Sappho: Reception and Transmission, edited by Ellen Greene, University of California Press, 1999.

Science and Its Times, Volume 3: *1450–1699,* Gale, 2001.

Periodicals

Journal of the Royal Society of Medicine, April 1993.

Times (London, England), November 16, 1995.

Online

"Gabriele Falloppio," *World of Health Online,* Thomson Gale, 2006. □

Enrico Ferri

Enrico Ferri (1856–1929), a prolific Italian professor, lecturer, and politician, was a pioneer in criminology, or the study of crime, as well as a longtime member of the Italian parliament and leader of Italy's Socialist Party. Though his theory that some people are born with a tendency to commit crimes is an outdated notion, and his support of Italian fascism near the end of his life hurt his reputation as a socialist, his ideas that crime can be measured and analyzed and that social conditions can affect crime rates are very familiar to modern criminologists.

The Academic Rebel

Ferri was born on February 25, 1856, in San Benedetto Po in Mantua, Italy. He entered high school at Mantua's Liceo Virgilio at the age of 15, and studied under the accomplished psychologist Roberto Ardigo, author of the book *Psychology as a Positive Science.* Ardigo's influence convinced Ferri to pursue a career in the social sciences. Ferri continued his studies at the University of Bologna in 1874, where he attended lectures given by prominent criminal law scholar Pietro Ellero.

In his final year at the university, Ferri wrote a groundbreaking thesis arguing against the concept of free will in criminal law. Back then, criminal law assumed that criminals bore a moral responsibility for their actions because they had free will, the capacity to choose to commit crimes. Instead, Ferri argued that laws should be based on social accountability—that, even if criminals were predisposed to commit crimes because of genetics or their social situation, they could still be punished, because they are members of society and because other people need protection from them.

After defending his thesis successfully in 1877, Ferri went on to study at the University of Pisa, where he established a reputation as an intellectual rebel. He studied the art of public speaking and debate, figuring it would help him in his intellectual arguments. "I forced myself daily— at spots removed from the traffic on the beaches, along the Arno [River] outside the city—to talk aloud for an hour at a stretch, improvising on some topic which I picked at random from a number of cards that I had prepared and put into my pocket," he once recalled, as quoted by Thorsten Sellin in a biographical essay accompanying the 1968 edition of Ferri's book *The Positive School of Criminology.*

In 1878 Ferri published his dissertation, announcing his intention to "apply the positive method to the science of criminal law," as quoted by Sellin. Positivism was the idea that the scientific method could be used to explain the social life of human beings. It included an emphasis on what is observable and measurable, and distanced itself from making moral judgments in order to look at what is, not at what ought to be.

Ferri sent a copy of his book to Cesare Lombroso, a natural intellectual ally who had recently published *The Criminal Man,* which applied Charles Darwin's theory of evolution to the study of crime. Lombroso argued that biology made some people more likely to commit crimes, and that criminals were throwbacks to a more primitive stage of human evolution. Lombroso even believed that likely criminals had different facial characteristics than other humans, such as differently shaped skulls with prominent jawbones and cheekbones. Such arguments are widely rejected in the twenty-first century, but they fit the intellectual trends of that era, which included social Darwinism—the idea that society, like biology, was guided by the survival of the fittest.

Ferri agreed with Lombroso, even coining the term "born criminal." He thought criminals had low intelligence and moral insensitivity and did not think ahead about the consequences of their actions. The criminal has "defective resistance to criminal tendencies and temptations, due to that ill-balanced impulsiveness which characterizes children and savages," Ferri wrote, according to Anthony Walsh and Lee Ellis in *Criminology: An Interdisciplinary Approach.* Since Ferri felt criminals were not rational, he did not believe in two of the common rationales for criminal punishment: rehabilitating criminals and deterring future crime. Instead, he believed in imprisoning criminals for as long as possible in order to protect others. He felt courts could actually calculate the danger a criminal posed to society,

and how blameworthy or understandable his or her motivations were.

Social Causes of Crime

In 1878 Ferri moved to Paris to study. He analyzed 50 years of statistics from French courts and discovered multiple factors that he thought led to crime or encouraged it. Some were physical, including climate and geography. Some were human, from age to gender to psychology. Others were social, from religion to economic conditions to population density. This view was much different than Lombroso's biological ideas, but it had one thing in common with them: it was based on observation, evidence, and facts. Ferri would later propose that governments try to reduce crime by enacting "penal substitutes," meaning laws designed to improve social conditions.

The next year, Ferri applied to join the faculty at the University of Turin. To win acceptance, he had to deliver a lecture to an examining committee. In it, he argued that jury trials for ordinary crimes should be replaced by trials before judges trained in social science and psychology. The lecture won him admission, and he published his lecture in 1880 to acclaim.

In 1884 Ferri published the first edition of his most influential book, *Criminal Sociology,* which summarized his theories about crime. That same year, he married Camilla Guarnieri, a woman from Florence. The couple had two sons and a daughter.

Socialist Leader

In 1886 Ferri took a bold step out of academia that led him into his other occupation, politics. He was hired as a lawyer for a group of peasants in his home province of Mantua. After disputes with their landlords, they had been charged with attempting to incite civil war. In court, Ferri offered a persuasive argument about the social and economic conditions that had led to the peasants' conflict. His clients were found not guilty. Two months later, apparently on the strength of his successful arguments in court, Ferri was elected to represent Mantua in the Italian parliament. He was re-elected eleven times, serving until 1924.

Elected without party affiliation, Ferri allied himself with the radical liberals in Parliament. He and his wife moved to Rome, where he continued to teach, write, and work as a defense lawyer. He also helped organize labor cooperatives for farm workers in Mantua. In 1890 Ferri was appointed to the faculty at the University of Pisa. Two years later he founded an academic journal, *La Scuola Positiva* (The Positive School), dedicated to his and Lombroso's approach to criminology. Ferri joined the new Italian Socialist Labor Party in 1893, and the university responded by firing him.

Ferri's belief that economic conditions determine people's behavior made him a natural fit in the Socialist Party. In hopes of spreading socialist ideas and improving the party's strength in Parliament, he became a lecturer, traveling across Italy to give lectures on economic, sociological, historic, and scientific topics. In 1896, when the Socialist Party decided to start a newspaper, *Avanti,* Ferri went on a three-week lecture tour to earn the money to found it. Ferri was a popular and extremely charismatic speaker. "The extreme beauty of the man, the magnificent head of curly hair, the penetrating gaze, the aquiline nose, the portentous voice with its warm and insinuating timbre, [all lead] directly to spectacular success in the law, in the university, and with the people," remarked Roberto Michels, a fellow socialist and scholar, as quoted in Richard Drake's *Apostles and Agitators: Italy's Marxist Revolutionary Tradition.*

Historians tend to consider Ferri less successful as a political leader than as a scholar. W. Hilton-Young, author of *The Italian Left: A Short History of Political Socialism in Italy,* called him a "turbulent and unstable figure" and complained, "His personal vanity and rather portentous style of speech and writing concealed the outlines, or perhaps the absence, of his ideas." Others have suggested that Ferri's ambition to become head of the party led him to change his mind too often, until no one was sure of his principles.

During the 1890s Ferri was one of the leaders of the radical wing of the Socialist Party, which did not want to compromise with other parties, and favored waiting to take power until capitalism failed. However, by 1900 Ferri was attempting to bridge the gap between radicals and the moderate socialists, who wanted to pursue specific reforms, such as improved labor conditions and compulsory education. That middle ground became attractive to many socialists. Ferri became director of *Avanti* in 1903, and he was elected leader of the Socialist Party at its congress in Bologna in 1904.

However, Ferri's time as party leader was not a huge success. He backed a general nationwide strike in 1904 to protest harsh police treatment of peasant organizations in Sardinia and Sicily. Voters did not approve, and the Socialists fared poorly in the next elections. In Parliament, Ferri's greatest accomplishment was in advocating an investigation of theft in the government's Navy Department. At one point, the minister of the navy sued him for criminal libel, but the case was dropped when the parliament named a commission to investigate the theft charges, and they were proven accurate.

By 1908 political trends were turning against Ferri. Economic conditions had improved in Italy, and the moderates in the Socialist Party came into favor. Ferri shifted his attention away from politics. "Ferri, acting in accordance with his fickle and unpredictable character, threw up parliament, party, press, and everything, and went on a lecture tour to America, from which it was understood he would not return for some time," wrote Hilton-Young. Ferri resigned as editor of *Avanti,* and a moderate reformist succeeded him as party leader.

Later Years

Ferri toured South America, delivering 80 lectures meant for the general public. He returned in 1910 to lecture to professional audiences. He continued to work as a scholar of crime, attending nearly every international congress of criminal anthropology and making Italian positivist ideas well-known in other nations. In 1912 he founded the School for Applied Criminal Law and Procedure in Rome to train judges and others who dealt with crime and criminals.

After World War I, Ferri came close to enacting his ideas about criminal punishment into law. A former classmate, Ludovico Mortara, became the Italian minister of justice in 1919 and named Ferri president of a commission to write a new criminal code. Positive criminologists dominated the commission, which presented its proposal in 1921. But Parliament, caught up in deep political turmoil, did not enact it.

Fateful Alliance With Fascism

By then, Benito Mussolini's Fascist Party was gaining strength, rearranging Italy's politics. In a move that greatly harmed his reputation, Ferri tried to form a bloc of socialists willing to support fascism. In 1924 Ferri decided not to run for re-election and left Parliament. The Fascist Party won the elections, the first major victory for a far-flung movement that would later overturn democracy and conquer most of Europe during World War II.

In 1927 Ferri was named to another commission to rewrite the criminal code. Its ideas were eventually adopted. In 1929, just before he died, Ferri wrote that the Socialist Party had failed "because it neither knew how to make a revolution nor wanted to assume the responsibility of power," according to Sellin. He praised the Fascist government for "putting into effect some of the principles and the most characteristic practical proposals of the positive school." In Ferri's last years, he wrote a book that summarized the positive school of criminology, *Principles of Criminal Law,* and completed a final edition of his classic book *Criminal Sociology.* He was nominated to the Italian Senate, but did not live to be confirmed to the seat. He died on April 12, 1929.

Ferri estimated that he had delivered 2,300 academic lectures and 600 public lectures on 40 topics, plus thousands more political speeches. In 1925, when he presented a lecture at the University of Rome, Thorsten Sellin was in the audience. In his essay accompanying *The Positive School of Criminology,* Sellin described the experience: "Slender of build, a head taller than most Italians, and with a shock of white curly hair and a white beard," he wrote, "[Ferri] was an imposing figure and still possessed, at seventy, the clarity of exposition and the manner of the great orator."

Books

De Grand, Alexander, *The Italian Left in the Twentieth Century: A History of the Socialist and Communist Parties,* Indiana University Press, 1989.

Di Scala, Spencer M., *Italian Socialism: Between Politics and History,* University of Massachusetts Press, 1996.

Drake, Richard, *Apostles and Agitators: Italy's Marxist Revolutionary Tradition,* Harvard University Press, 2003.

Ferri, Enrico, *The Positive School of Criminology: Three Lectures by Enrico Ferri,* University of Pittsburgh Press, 1968.

Hagan, Frank E., *Introduction to Criminology: Theories, Methods, and Criminal Behavior,* Wadsworth, 2002.

Hilton-Young, W., *The Italian Left: A Short History of Political Socialism in Italy,* Greenwood Press, 1975.

Knepper, Paul, *Explaining Criminal Conduct: Theories and Systems in Criminology*, Carolina Academic Press, 2001.

Miller, James Edward, *From Elite to Mass Politics: Italian Socialism in the Giolittian Era, 1900-1914*, Kent State University Press, 1990.

Walsh, Anthony, and Lee Ellis, *Criminology: An Interdisciplinary Approach*, Sage Publications, 2007. □

Archduke Franz Ferdinand of Austria

Archduke Franz Ferdinand of Austria (1863–1914) is best known for the way his life ended: he was assassinated in the Bosnian city of Sarajevo on June 28, 1914. The cascade of events that followed plunged Europe and the world into the Great War, later known as World War I.

At the time, Franz Ferdinand was the heir to the throne of the Austro-Hungarian Empire, not its ruler. He is not reckoned among Europe's great leaders, and, although he played a significant part, others' decisions were more responsible than his own for the war his death set in motion. Yet he was more than simply an individual whose course intersected with momentous historical events. Many of Franz Ferdinand's concerns as an adult were personal, not political—but rarely has the maxim that the personal is political been better exemplified than by his life and marriage.

Third in Line to Become Emperor

Franz Ferdinand was born on December 18, 1863, in Graz, Austria. His father was Archduke Karl Ludwig, brother of the Austrian Emperor Franz Joseph, and his mother, Maria Annunziata, was a Sicilian princess linked to the Austrian throne by central Europe's then vital web of royal marriages. He had two younger brothers, Otto Franz and Ferdinand Karl, as well as a younger sister. His full name, Franz Ferdinand Karl Ludwig Joseph Maria, reflected various facets of his ancestry. As Franz Ferdinand grew toward adulthood, he was only third in line for the throne of what, due to an 1868 agreement between Austria and Hungary, became the Austro-Hungarian Empire. Ahead of him were his father, Karl Ludwig, and the emperor's own son, Rudolf.

Franz Ferdinand was by many accounts an unremarkable child, and the most significant event of his early years was a large inheritance that came from a distant Italian cousin, Duke Francis V of Modena. The aging Italian nobleman had no direct heir, and he offered his vast riches to one of his young Austrian relatives on two conditions: that the young man take the noble title Duke of Este as part of his own name, and that he learn Italian. Franz Ferdinand managed, at age 12, to obtain a shaky grasp of Italian from his coterie of private tutors, with two results: he was henceforth financially set for a life of leisure, and as an adult he would be officially known as the Archduke of Austria-Este.

With what seemed to be only a slight chance of becoming emperor, Franz Ferdinand as a young man lived a carefree life as a lieutenant in the Fourth Dragoons company of the monarchy's army (a dragoon was skilled as both a foot soldier and a cavalry fighter). He began seeing Mizzi Caspar, a well-known Austrian stage actress of the 1880s, and wrote letters describing her as *wunderschön,* (wondrously beautiful) with the word underlined three times. Even as a teen he had had a passion for hunting, and in his twenties he had the time and money to indulge it in full. In the late 1880s he spent two years with a Hungarian regiment and got his first taste of the nationalistic passions that threatened the Austrian empire's unity. "The officers spoke in Hungarian even in front of me," he wrote home to Vienna, as quoted by biographer Gordon Brook-Shepherd in *Archduke of Sarajevo: The Romance and Tragedy of Franz Ferdinand of Austria,* "and the simplest German question produced the answer '*nem tudom*' ('I don't understand'). Military terms were translated into long-winded Hungarian phrases. In short, throughout the regiment, not a word of that German language so detested by the Hussars."

Shot Tiger in India

In 1889 the mentally unstable Prince Rudolf shot his 16-year-old mistress and then himself, bringing Franz Ferdinand a step closer to the throne. After his father renounced his own right of succession, Franz was regarded as the heir apparent. Perhaps with the intention of giving him some social and political seasoning, he was sent on a round-the-world military inspection tour, beginning on the Austrian battleship *Empress Elizabeth*. Setting off from Trieste in December of 1892, he made stops in Egypt and what is now Sri Lanka before undertaking an extended sojourn in India. There, despite a limited command of English, he hobnobbed with British nobility and made a point of combining business with pleasure. During a seven-day tiger hunt (involving 1,793 men, 25 elephants, 148 horses, and 39 dogs), he shot his first tiger. "I cannot describe my joy," he wrote, according to Brook-Shepherd. The trip finally took Franz Ferdinand across the Pacific to Canada and the United States, a country he found drab and dispiriting.

In 1895 Franz Ferdinand's smooth path through the corridors of power was interrupted by love. At a dance in Prague he met Countess Sophie Chotek, a 27-year-old Czech woman from a family of long, noble background in Bohemia, but not, as custom required of a marriage within the Austro-Hungarian monarchy, descended from royalty. Fully aware of this, the pair saw each other on the sly while maintaining a public image of innocent friendship as they played on the same side of the net in doubles tennis matches. Sophie was a lady-in-waiting (a sort of aristocratic assistant to a noblewoman) in the retinue of the Archduchess Isabella in Teschen, now in the Polish province of Silesia, and Isabella hoped that Franz Ferdinand would become enamored of one of her own unmarried daughters. Indeed, he often visited and seemed to be friendly with them.

The secret affair was exposed in spectacular fashion in 1898 when Franz Ferdinand left his pocket watch, an elaborate model that opened to reveal a photograph, on a tennis court at Isabella's residence. Isabella opened it, hoping to find a picture of one on her daughters, but instead she found Sophie's picture inside. The resulting scandal erupted 40 years before the affair between British King Edward VIII and American divorcee Wallis Simpson made headlines, but it was in some ways more serious, with ramifications that went to the top of the Austro-Hungarian government. A group of ministers, with the approval of Emperor Franz Joseph himself, tried to talk Franz Ferdinand out of marrying Sophie, whereupon he dug in his heels and announced that he was not only going to marry her but would also make her his Empress when the time came. Among his few backers was the emperor's wife, Maria Theresia.

Because it involved the fragile legitimacy of Austro-Hungarian rule, the issue was loaded with political significance beyond pure custom: the empire was a patchwork of small fiefdoms, all with restive populations speaking more than a dozen different languages, and all with a greater or lesser degree of nationalistic sentiment. The compromise eventually reached, with the assistance of top leaders from within the empire as well the Vatican, the Russian Tsar, and the German Emperor, was that the marriage could go ahead but would be "morganatic," meaning that Sophie and her children would have no claim upon the Austro-Hungarian throne or any of its royal privileges. Franz Ferdinand and his beloved were married in 1900, but this did not put an end to the controversy.

Became Enthusiastic Hunter, Gardener

"The sumptuous setting of the couple's Vienna residence also needs to be borne in mind," noted Brook-Shepherd, "to appreciate to the full the pain inflicted by the famous protocol pin-pricks the couple had to suffer whenever they visited the capital." Sophie was not supposed to appear in public with her husband or to ride in a carriage or car with him. Franz Ferdinand's personality, which tended toward the sarcastic and the standoffish, also worked against him, and the Emperor himself continued to give his nephew the cold shoulder. The Viennese began to refer to Franz Ferdinand as the loneliest man in the city, and he took refuge in hunting (his lifetime total was counted at an awe-inspiring 272,511 head of game) and in another passion, gardening. Yet the love story of Franz Ferdinand and his "Sopherl" had its admirers. Some newspapers in the empire's more remote corners hailed the Archduke as an independent man who could stand up to the stodgy old monarchy, and as the couple's three children grew, so did Sophie's reputation. She was given the rank of Duchess and began to appear more often at Franz Ferdinand's side—with ultimately fatal results.

As he neared the seat of power, Franz Ferdinand began to plunge into the Austro-Hungarian Empire's complex and perpetually crisis-ridden relationships with its satellite provinces. The government's Austrian and Hungarian halves experienced conflict, sometimes centered on Hungary's increasing repression of the ethnic minorities, including various South Slav groups, within its borders. Franz Ferdinand espoused a concept known as Trialism (as opposed to dualism), under which a confederation of groups in the Balkan region would form a third major power center in the empire, as a counterweight to Austria and Hungary. In general he favored stronger safeguards for the rights of the empire's many minorities, ultimately aiming toward a federal-style government that would replace the moribund central monarchy. These positions aroused the ire of hardliners in Vienna who argued for a tougher military stance against restive regions.

Franz Ferdinand's efforts to promote South Slavic influence cut two ways, however. The independent Balkan nation of Serbia also hoped to take its place at the head of a South Slavic confederation, and many nationalists in the Austro-Hungarian provinces of Bosnia and Herzegovina (just as in modern Bosnia) were sympathetic to the Serbs. When Franz Ferdinand visited the Bosnian capital of Sarajevo in June of 1914 for a military inspection, the ingredients for a tragedy were coming together. Top personnel in Serbia's intelligence agency dispatched members of a terrorist group, the Black Hand, to assassinate Franz Ferdinand in Sarajevo. The Serbian prime minister tried unsuccessfully to thwart the plot.

By the time Franz Ferdinand and Sophie arrived by train in Sarajevo on Sunday morning, June 28, 1914, six Serb assassins lined the route of their motorcade from the train station to Sarajevo's city hall. The first two were unable to get a clear shot at Franz Ferdinand's open car through the crowds, but a third, Nedjelko Cabrinović, hit the car with a hand grenade. Two people riding in the car were wounded, and after the official reception for Franz

Ferdinand had ended he asked to visit them in the hospital. The Austrian governor, Oskar Potiorek, advised Sophie to remain behind at the city hall, but she insisted on remaining at his side. Plans were hastily laid for a safer route, but Franz Ferdinand's driver became confused and lost his way. As he began to turn around, the car rolled slowly past one of the original group of six assassins, Gavrilo Princip.

He fired his gun several times, nearly at point-blank range, and a single bullet hit Franz Ferdinand in the neck and Sophie in the abdomen. Franz Ferdinand, hit in the jugular vein, knew he was dying. According to many accounts (one is quoted on the Web site austria-hungary.piczo.com), his last words were "Sopherl! Sopherl! Sterbe nicht! Bleibe am Leben f'r unsere Kinder!" (Little Sophie! Little Sophie! Don't die! Stay alive for our children!). But both were dead within minutes. War flared between Serbia and Austria-Hungary in the aftermath of the shooting, and other countries that had been allied with one or the other, all armed and on hair-trigger status, were drawn into the conflict before diplomacy had a chance to work. The result was four years of total warfare over much of the world.

Books

Brook-Shepherd, Gordon, *Archduke of Sarajevo: The Romance and Tragedy of Franz Ferdinand of Austria,* Little, Brown, 1984.

Online

"Archduke Franz Ferdinand," Trenches on the Web, http://www.worldwar1.com/biohff.htm (December 19, 2008).

"Franz Ferdinand," Spartacus Educational, http://www.spartacus.schoolnet.co.uk/FWWarchduke.htm (December 19, 2008).

"The Making of an Archduke," http://www.austria-hungary.piczo.com/?cr=7 (December 19, 2008).

"Who's Who: Archduke Franz Ferdinand," http://www.firstworldwar.com/bio/ferdinand.htm (December 19, 2008). □

G

Franz Joseph Gall

The German physiologist Franz Joseph Gall (1758–1828) is remembered mostly for his association with the now-discredited science of phrenology, or the study of brain function through examination of the shape of the head.

Although phrenology has not been taken seriously by scientists since the late nineteenth century, Gall's accomplishments remain worthy of note. He is viewed as the first investigator to realize that brain functions were localized—that different parts of the brain were connected with specific aspects of human thought. Gall made important discoveries in the anatomy of the brain, and he was among the first observers to connect aphasia (the loss of language ability) to an injury in a particular brain area. In addition to his occasional correct hypotheses, Gall set the stage for brain research in a broader sense. An indefatigable popularizer of his own ideas, he faced considerable resistance from religious authorities threatened by his purely physical explanations of thinking. Gall got the science wrong, but he was in some respects the founder of modern research into brain anatomy.

Noted Link Between Talents, Skull Shape

Born on March 9, 1758, Gall grew up in the village of Tiefenbronn, on the edge of the Black Forest in what is now the German state of Baden-Württemberg. His father was a devout Catholic of Italian background who had Germanized his name from Gallo to Gall. He was a merchant and at times the little town's mayor. Gall received the beginnings of a formal education from an uncle who was a priest. Showing promise, he was sent to several schools around Baden, which was an independent principality at the time. When he was 19 he went to nearby Strasbourg, France, to study medicine, and he became interested in comparative anatomy. He supplemented his coursework with his own observations: boys who were good with words, he thought, had skulls that were spacious in the front, and those with good memories had large, flared eye sockets.

In Strasbourg, Gall contracted typhus and was nursed back to health by a young woman whose last name was Lieser. The two soon married, but the marriage was honored more in the breach than in the observance; the couple had no children, but Gall had a son, Hammann, by one of several mistresses. Unapologetic about his dalliances, Gall quipped, according to the Who Named It? Web site, "Neither sin nor friends will ever leave me." In 1781 Gall left Strasbourg to study in Vienna with the reform-minded Dutch-Austrian physician Gerard van Swieten. He received a university degree there in 1785 and opened a medical practice of his own, picking up patients from among the ranks of the influential van Swieten's acquaintances.

Gall also began giving medical lectures, eventually publishing his ideas in a pair of books: *Philosophisch-Medicinische Untersuchungen über Natur und Kunst im kranken und gesunden Zustande des Menschen* (Philosophical-Medical Investigations of Nature and Art in Humans in Sick and Healthy Conditions) in 1791, and *Des Herren Dr. F. J. Gall Schreiben ü ber seinen bereits geendigten Prodromus über die Verrichtungen des Gehirns der Menschen und der Thiere* (Dr. F. J. Gall's Writings on His Already Concluded Studies of the Functions of the Brain in Humans and Animals) in 1798. He attracted various students, and one of them, Johann Christoph Spurzheim, became his collaborator for many

years, beginning in 1800. It was around this time that Gall's characteristic ideas about the brain and head shape were developed; the date of phrenology's founding is often given as 1796.

Founded Science of Brain Organs

Gall called his new science organology, meaning the study of the individual organs that he believed made up the brain. Spurzheim and other followers applied the name phrenology (*phrenologie* in German), derived from the Greek terms for "mind" and "study" (or "word"). Phrenology evolved in various directions over the course of the nineteenth century, but in the beginning it relied on a set of simple concepts. First, Gall argued, human thinking, both intellectual and moral, was innate. Specifically, mental faculties resulted from the structure of the brain rather than from religious inspiration. Second, Gall believed that each mental faculty came from a particular organ that was part of the brain. And finally, he believed that the degree to which each faculty might be developed in the case of an individual human could be determined by feeling an individual's skull, noting its protuberances and its overall shape.

In the end, Gall named 27 of these organs, 19 possessed by both humans and animals, the other eight uniquely human. In abbreviated form, they were responsible for the following traits of mind: reproductive instinct, love of offspring, affection and friendship, instinct of self-defense, carnivorous instinct (which Gall saw as the tendency toward

murder), guile and cleverness, feeling of ownership, pride, ambition, forethought, memory of things and facts, sense of place and space, memory of people and words, sense of language, colors, sounds and music, connectedness between numbers, mechanics and construction (with this began his list of uniquely human organs), comparative wisdom, sense of metaphysics, sense of satire and witticism, poetic talent, faculty of imitation, religious feeling, and firmness of purpose or perseverance. Gall and others published detailed diagrams correlating specific areas of the skull with individual organs.

"Today," noted John Oxlee of London's *Guardian* newspaper, in a summary of phrenology, "reading head bumps is viewed with some suspicion." In hindsight it may seem hard to understand phrenology's appeal, but the key to its popularity was that it was perhaps the first systematic attempt to explain brain function rationally. Until Gall began to disseminate his ideas, human mental faculties were generally thought to be connected with the spirit or the soul. Those concepts had centuries-old religious underpinnings, and indeed the Catholic Church reacted to Gall's ideas with an attempt at suppression: Holy Roman Emperor Francis II banned Gall's lectures by handwritten order in 1801.

The order was later relaxed somewhat, but Gall, with Spurzheim in tow, left Vienna in 1805. The pair toured Europe in order to expound upon their ideas, visiting Germany, the Netherlands, Switzerland, and Denmark. Gall's presentations were set up along the lines of lecture-demonstrations; he and Spurzheim would often visit institutions such as prisons, schools, or insane asylums, and would discuss their methods while gathering evidence on the spot. They gained admirers such as the German poet Johann Wolfgang von Goethe, who was an enthusiastic amateur scientist and had written his own pioneering description of aphasia. Gall, a showman like many other nineteenth-century medical figures, charged admission to his lectures, a practice for which he was sometimes criticized. But he plowed some of his profits back into the promotion of phrenology, publishing new books and pamphlets as often as he could.

Opened Medical Practice in Paris

In 1807 Gall and Spurzheim arrived in Paris. Gall opened a new medical practice, treating high-profile patients such as the novelist Stendhal (Henri-Marie Beyle), and he gave lectures at a hall called the Athenée while trying to earn the respect of France's large scientific establishment. A key part of this project was Gall's 1810 magnum opus, the multi-volume *Anatomie et physiologie du système nerveux en general, et du cerveau en particulier, avec des observations sur la possibilité de reconnaître plusieurs dispositions intellectuelles et morales de l'homme et des animaux, par la configuration de leur têtes* (Anatomy and Physiology of the Nervous System in General, and of the Brain in Particular, with Observations on the Possibility of Recognizing Various Intellectual and Moral Dispositions of Humans and Animals by the Configuration of Their Heads). Gall was eventually turned down for membership in the French Academy of Sciences, partly because emperor Napoleon Bonaparte was disappointed by Gall's analysis of his own skull, feeling that it pointed insufficiently to presumed noble qualities.

Members of the Academy raised grave doubts about phrenology from the start, but Gall's ideas gained wide currency in both Europe and the United States over much of the nineteenth century. Believers in phrenology included figures as diverse as the philosophers Georg Wilhelm Friedrich Hegel and Karl Marx, novelists Honoré de Balzac and Charlotte and Emily Brontë, poet Walt Whitman, U.S. President James Garfield, and Britain's Queen Victoria. Spurzheim moved to Britain and attracted new supporters for Gall's ideas there; one of them was George Combe (1788–1858). Ordinary people were fascinated by Gall's ideas, in much the same way as readers flock to astrological predictions today. It was once said that if a British household owned only three books, they would likely be the Bible, Bunyan's *Pilgrim's Progress,* and Combe's *System of Phrenology.*

What undermined phrenology's influence, even during Gall's own lifetime, was simple scientific experimentation; French scientists tried to replicate his results and reported that head shapes and mental traits showed few correlations. Phrenology's general appeal continued to grow, but scientists soon began to take it less seriously. Gall himself married one of his longtime mistresses, Marie Anne Barbe, after his first wife's death in 1825. Soon after that, he began to suffer from strokes and symptoms of heart disease. He died on his estate outside Paris on August 22, 1828, after a massive stroke. At his death he had a collection of more than 300 human skulls and brain casts.

By the end of the nineteenth century phrenology was in general decline. But it never died out completely; phrenology was still common enough to be among a group of services proposed for new taxation in a measure passed by the Michigan state legislature in 2007. And Gall's reputation was rescued from the realm of quackery by the growing scientific realization that specific parts of the brain were indeed responsible for specific mental functions, even if Gall's own diagrams of local brain functions were erroneous. Indeed, it emerged that two of Gall's brain organs, those for memory of words and the sense of language, were close to the actual parts of the brain responsible for those functions. Gall proposed in 1825 that loss of word memory was connected to specific brain injuries, and he was cited as influential by later aphasia researchers.

Gall's detailed dissections of brains led to several valid scientific insights: he was the first researcher to distinguish between so-called gray matter (made up of neural components) and white matter (which conducts impulses) in the composition of the brain, and he had several important insights into the configuration of nerves leading into the brain. Franz Joseph Gall was a pioneer in his field. The great French anatomist Paul Broca, quoted in a biography of Gall appearing on the Geocities Web site, wrote: "He had the undisputable merit of proclaiming the great principle of cerebral localization, which . . . it may be said . . . was the starting point of the discoveries of our century concerning the physiology of the encephalon."

Periodicals

Guardian (London, England), June 29, 1993.
Independent (London, England), October 31, 1998.

Online

"Extended list of services affected by new tax," Michigan Live, http://www.blog.mlive.com/michigan/2007/10/extended_list_of_services_affe.html (December 24, 2008).
"Franz Josef Gall," Geocities, http://www.geocities.com/SoHo/Workshop/4220/gall.html (December 24, 2008).
"Franz Joseph Gall," Phrenology, http://www.phrenology.com/franzjosephgall.html (December 24, 2008).
"Franz Joseph Gall," Who Named It?, http://www.whonamedit.com/doctor.cfm/1018.html (December 24, 2008).
"Phrenology: The History of Brain Localization," Brain & Mind, http://www.cerebromente.org.br/n01/frenolog/frenologia.htm (December 24, 2008). □

Mary Ellen Garber

American journalist Mary Garber (1916–2008) was one of the first female sports writers in the United States, and her success opened doors for future aspiring female sports journalists. She was more than just a pioneer, however, and throughout her long career, Garber exhibited levels of talent and professionalism that garnered her numerous awards.

By transgressing gender lines in the male-dominated field of sports journalism, Mary Garber paved the way for future female journalists in both the print and broadcast mediums. Talented and persistent, Garber became the only woman to receive what is considered sports journalism's highest honor: the Red Smith Award, an annual tribute bestowed by the Associated Press Sports Editors. She also became the first woman inducted into the U.S. Basketball Writers Hall of Fame. Her career spanned more than a half-century, and her courage, talent and professionalism still provide inspiration for aspiring sports reporters no matter their gender or race.

Early Life

The future sports writing legend was born as Mary Ellen Garber on April 19, 1916, at home on Riverside Drive in Manhattan, New York City. The Garbers later moved to New Jersey, living in Ridgewood until Mary, the middle child in a family of three girls, was eight years old. In 1924, her father, Mason Garber, who was a civil engineer, moved the family to Winston-Salem, North Carolina, where he started a construction business and built many of the city's architectural landmarks, including the Winston-Salem train station.

At a very early age, Garber developed a passion for both sports and journalism by perusing the lively prose and picture-rich game coverage offered by *The New York Daily News.* While growing up in Winston-Salem, Garber vividly displayed her tomboy tendencies by playing tackle football with neighborhood boys. She was also a big fan of Notre Dame gridiron coach Knute Rockne.

Mail correspondences with her grandmother allowed Garber to indulge her own journalistic impulses. Rather than writing conventional letters, which she considered boring, Garber composed letters that displayed a rudimentary front-page mockup, complete with headlines and stories, an activity that she called the "Garber News."

Pursuing her youthful interests, Garber later wrote sports stories for her high school and college alma mater Hollins College, an all-women's institution located in Roanoke, Virginia.

Became a Professional Journalist

Garber graduated from Hollins College (now Hollins University) in 1938 with a degree in philosophy. Two years later, she was hired to be the society editor of the *The Twin City Sentinel*, the Winston-Salem afternoon newspaper. She also covered general news. At the time, sports writing remained the province of male reporters. In 1944 (during World War II), however, she switched to sports coverage when the male teenager who put together the paper's sport page enlisted in the U.S. Navy. His departure essentially emptied the paper's sports department and Garber, who was still a passionate sports fan, eagerly volunteered to take his place.

When the sports editor resumed his job at the war's end, Garber was once again relegated to the news and society beats. In 1946, however, the editors of the *Sentinel* and its sister paper *The Winston-Salem Journal* realized that Garber understood sports better than fashion, so they moved her back to the sports department. As it turned out, she would continue writing about athletics on a full- or part-time basis until 2002. In the process, she would open doors for hundreds of future aspiring female sportswriters.

Encountered Male Chauvinism

Still, while she was in the right place at the right time to combine her journalistic and sports interests, her subsequent career course would not be easy. She met with resistance from athletic and journalism organizations, and she suffered indignities arising from gender discrimination and chauvinistic attitudes. For instance, in 1946, while covering a Duke University football game (which was part of her Atlantic Coast Conference [ACC] sports beat) she was not allowed in the press box, even though she came to the event with the proper press credentials. Instead, she was forced to work from the coaches' wives' box. The experience was almost unendurable from a professional standpoint. "All through the game the wives blabbed and the kids screamed, and I thought I would lose my mind," Garber recalled in 2000, in a *Sports Illustrated* interview.

Fortunately, her managing editor stood up for her. Indignant over Garber's treatment, he told the ACC athletic directors he would not send any reporters to cover their games. Faced with this threatened news blackout, ACC officials relented and allowed Garber access to the previously all-male press box. Still, when coaches and sportswriters were not ignoring her, they stereotyped her in gender terms. Once, during a high school basketball game, a player ripped his shorts, and the team's coach asked Garber if she could sew the damaged clothing.

For a long time, she was also excluded from important journalism and athletic organizations. Both the ACC Sportswriters Association and the Football Writers Association (FWA) denied her membership for many years. Ironically, after she was finally accepted as an ACC member, she would later serve as the organization's president. "More than anything else [the honor] tells me that I am accepted," she said when she accepted the position, according to an interview in *Sports Illustrated*.

In addition, she served on the board of directors of both the ACC and FWA. The ACC even named its annual award to the conference's best female athlete after Garber, an honor that implicitly recognized her perseverance as well as her journalistic skills. In the December 29, 2008 issue of *Time* magazine, which came out a little more than three months after Garber's death, Hall of Fame tennis player Billie Jean King, who advocated for gender equality throughout her career, wrote: "For most of her amazing career... [Garber] navigated uncharted waters. While Mary went quietly about her job, she understood that she was a pioneer for women, for sports and for all us. She understood the importance of breaking barriers but was still focused on getting a balanced story."

Covered Many Sports Beats

During the early part of her sports writing career, Garber covered high school and collegiate football and basketball games, but she would eventually cover many sports including baseball, softball, swimming, tennis, track and field, volleyball and wrestling in both recreational and academic arenas. Working in North Carolina, she had few opportunities to cover professional sports, but her scope of coverage expanded to include minor league baseball, international track and field events and the Davis Cup international tennis tournament.

Eventually, the local community came to appreciate the efforts of "Miss Mary," as Garber was affectionately known by friends, colleagues and fans, and people often helped her any way they could. Writing about Garber in 2008 in his *New York Times* column, renowned sports writer George Vecsey recalled that when she started covering college games in Raleigh, a security guard named John Baker regularly pulled athletes out of the locker rooms to provide her with quotes for her newspaper stories.

Athletes also came to recognize and appreciate her reportorial skills, and they demonstrated the respect that any insightful, talented and hard-working journalist—whether male or female—deserved. For an interview with the Women's Sports Foundation in the *Los Angeles Times*, Garber recalled an incident from the late 1940s, when she was covering a Winston-Salem Red Sox minor league baseball game: "I asked the Carolina League manager for a copy of [his team's] lineup, and he sneered and kind of laughed, 'You're a sportswriter?' About the same time, Bill Haywood, one of the best players in the league, walked by and said, 'Yes she is, and she's a darn good one.' That manager never gave me a hard time again."

Provided Coverage for Black Athletes

Garber not only breached gender-related barriers; she is now also remembered for providing extensive coverage for African-American high school and college athletes before they achieved widespread acceptance in the south, a region that remained segregated throughout the 1940s and 1950s, when Garber covered sports in the Winston-Salem area.

Clarence "Big House" Gaines, a black coach who headed the Winston Salem State University basketball for forty-seven years, recalled that Garber covered black players long before it became accepted or even popular. Interviewed by *Sports Illustrated* in 2000 (five years before he died), Gaines, a member of the Naismith Memorial Basketball Hall of Fame, said, "Nobody cared much about black players 40 years ago, but Miss Mary covered a lot of things that weren't too popular."

Earlier, in a 1990 interview for the Washington Press Club and printed in a *New York Times* article, Gaines noted, "There were two different worlds, black and white, and most news about black people ended up on the Sunday newspaper's 'colored page.' We had outstanding athletes here, and Mary came to write about them when no one else cared. Mary was always trying to help the underdog."

Indeed, Garber's coverage and consideration extended beyond established team stars—black or white, male or female—to include unsung players, second-string players who came off the bench and even team equipment managers. "She went out of her way to see that everybody got a fair shake," commented Gaines in the *Los Angeles Times,* who first met Garber in 1946 and became a close friend.

Inspired by Jackie Robinson

Appropriately, Garber garnered much of her own inspiration from Brooklyn Dodger shortstop and Major League Baseball Hall of Fame member Jackie Robinson, the man who stoically endured repeated—and often vicious—race-related humiliations when he broke professional baseball's "color barrier" during his 1947 rookie season. Garber observed Robinson up close when she traveled to Ebbets Field (the Dodgers' home stadium) to watch the team practice. "Jackie became the most important influence in my life," recalled Garber, during a *Sports Illustrated* interview in 2000. "When people would step on me and hurt my feelings, I would look at how he kept his mouth shut and did his job as best he could with the belief that someday he would be accepted."

In 1977, Garber voiced her appreciation in a *Sports Illustrated* column that honored Robinson's legacy. "Jackie is given credit for breaking the color line and giving thousands of black athletes a chance to play. But he did more. He made it possible for thousands of black athletes to fail or succeed on their own merits."

In her own way, Mary Garber accomplished the same thing for aspiring female sportswriters

Continued Working after Retirement

"Miss Mary" officially retired in 1986, when she was seventy years old. Her age required her retirement. She remained a

Journal sportswriter for sixteen years, however, covering sports on a part-time basis. A small woman (she was only five feet tall and weighed about ninety-five pounds) Garber was often described as a little old lady in sneakers. Her career finally ended in 2002, when age-related physical impairments forced her from the sidelines.

During her final years, she required daily medical care and lived in a nursing home. She died in Winston-Salem on September 21, 2008. Garber, who never married, was survived by a niece and three nephews. She was ninety-two years old.

Garber received numerous awards throughout her career. The most important came in 2005, when she received the Associated Press Sports Editors' Red Smith Award, named after the Pulitzer Prize-winning sports journalist and columnist. The annual honor, established in 1981, recognizes major contributions to sports journalism. Garber became the first and only woman to receive the award.

In 2006, the Association for Women in Sports Media renamed its pioneer award after Garber. Today, the Mary Garber Pioneer Award annually recognizes a role model for women in sports media. Recipients have included Julie Ward, former deputy managing editor of *USA Today*; Kristin Huckshorn, senior news editor for ESPN, and Lesley Visser, reporter for "CBS Sports."

In 1996, Garber was elected to the North Carolina Sports Hall of Fame and, in 2008, she became a member of the National Sportscasters and Sportswriters Association and Hall of Fame. In 2002, she became the first woman inducted into the United States Basketball Writers Hall of Fame.

Books

"Mary Ellen Garber," *Marquis Who's Who,* 2009.

Periodicals

Los Angeles Times, September 22, 2008.
Sports Illustrated, March 20, 2000.
The New York Times, May 3, 2008; September 22, 2008; September 23, 2008.
Time, December 29, 2008.
Winston-Salem Journal, September 22, 2008.□

Horatio Gates

American general Horatio Gates (c. 1727–1806) is best remembered for his leadership at the Battles of Saratoga, often considered the turning point in the American battle for independence. He served first in the British military, primarily in North America, before taking up the Patriot cause and becoming a commander in the Continental Army. Although much of his career was marked by disappointment, Gates's leadership contributed significantly to the American victory and hence the formation of the United States.

Early Years in England

According to tradition, Horatio Gates was born on July 26 of either 1727 or 1728 at Maldon, Essex, England. His father, Robert Gates, was perhaps a distant descendent of English nobility who has been identified as working at jobs as diverse as army officer, clergyman, and butler. His mother, Dorothea (Parker) Gates—who worked as a housekeeper for the second Duke of Leeds—took great interest in him as the only child from her second marriage. (Gates had an elder half-brother, Peregrine, from his mother's first marriage.) Gates's parents named him for his godfather, Horace Walpole, a well-known eighteenth-century statesman and writer.

The exact form of Gates's childhood schooling remains unknown, but his adult writing proficiency as well as his conversance with French and Latin suggests that he received a respectable education. As a result of this, Gates developed an interest in reading and acquired what Paul David Nelson, in his book *General Horatio Gates: A Biography,* called "habits of thinking and learning that helped him succeed in his career as a soldier."

After the death of the Duke of Leeds, Gates's parents began working for Charles Powlett, third Duke of Bolton, and relocated the family to Greenwich. Robert Gates was shortly afterwards appointed to the position of customs collector at Greenwich due to the Gates's connection with Powlett. Powlett also acquired a military post for Horatio Gates as an ensign with the Twentieth Regiment; Gates

briefly served as a lieutenant in Powlett's own regiment in 1745–1746 and as a regimental adjutant in Germany during the War of Austrian Succession.

Military Career Began in America

In 1749 Gates traveled to North America to serve as an aide to the governor of Nova Scotia, Colonel Edward Cornwallis, who would support Gates throughout his early career. Gates helped found the town of Halifax and was soon made a captain lieutenant under Colonel Hugh Warburton. By 1753, however, Gates hoped for greater advancement and returned to London in the hopes of obtaining a better commission. The outbreak of the French and Indian War a few months later led to an opportunity for Gates; he was offered the captaincy of the Fourth Independent Company of Foot, stationed in New York. Gates returned first to Halifax, where he married his longtime sweetheart, Elizabeth Phillips, on October 20, 1754, before continuing on to New York.

In the spring of 1755, Gates and his company joined Major General Edward Braddock's troops in Maryland. Seeking to join the conflict in the Ohio Valley, the army soon moved on to Pennsylvania, where they fell victim to a French-led ambush near Fort Duquesne in July of 1755. Gates suffered an injury during this battle that temporarily paralyzed his left arm and caused him to return to safer territory to recover. After Gates regained the use of his arm, he spent the next few years on patrol duty along the New York frontier. His son, Robert, was born during this period, in October of 1758.

Gates's stagnation in New York came to an end in 1759, when Cornwallis succeeded in securing him an appointment as brigade major under Brigadier General John Stanwix at Fort Pitt. The following spring, Brigadier General Robert Monckton took over the fort. Monckton and Gates organized a large peace conference attended by over 1,000 Native American representatives; this conference contributed to the British victory in the American theater of the French and Indian War in the fall of 1760.

The following year, Monckton led an attack in the French West Indies, taking Gates along as an aide. After the swift British victory, Gates took the news to London. Soon, Gates was rewarded with an appointment as major in Nova Scotia's Forty-Fifth Foot—to which Gates had been posted during his time in Halifax—and a sum of money with which to buy a lieutenant colonelcy. Writing in *The Generals of Saratoga: John Burgoyne and Horatio Gates,* Max M. Mintz noted that "it looked as though [Gates] had arrived."

Unfortunately for Gates, the lieutenant colonelcy never materialized and his career stagnated. His majority with the Forty-Fifth unavailable, a frustrated Gates served for a time as a political aide before returning to England. He became major of the Sixtieth Regiment in Quebec the following November, but continued to live in England on a leave of absence. In May of 1765, Gates took a post with the Seventy-Fourth Regiment—accepting a pay cut to do so—but remained in England until leaving the army altogether on March 10, 1769.

His military disappointments had made Gates somewhat disillusioned with the status quo. He became interested in the growing republican movement and considered turning his newfound political activism into a bid for Parliament. However, his failures continued and Gates decided to return with his family to America in August of 1772. He soon purchased a large tract of land near present-day Shepherdstown, West Virginia, and founded a plantation called "Traveller's Rest." In Virginia, Gates served as a lieutenant colonel in the colony's militia and as a justice of the peace, mostly foregoing public life. However, his radical political leanings crystallized into firm American patriotism.

Led Patriots to Victory at Saratoga

Up until the opening shots of the American Revolution, Gates remained on the sidelines at Traveller's Rest. On hearing the news of the conflict at Lexington, he promptly called on George Washington to volunteer for military service. Soon, Washington summoned Gates to Boston to help manage the administration of the ragtag Continental Army, a task that took advantage of his previous experience organizing large campaigns such as that of the French West Indies.

In May of 1776, Gates was promoted to major general and appointed to lead the campaign in Canada. However, American forces retreated from Canada, leaving Gates without a post. Instead, Gates joined the Northern Department, where he clashed with Major General John Schuyler over command. Schuyler prevailed, and Gates took control of Fort Ticonderoga. From that location he helped stop a British invasion from Canada before going south in December of 1776 to join up with General George Washington in New Jersey shortly before the latter famously crossed the Delaware River to attack forces at Trenton. Although Gates's troops participated in the action, Gates himself had pled illness and left for Philadelphia, where he spent the winter of 1777.

Gates used his position in Philadelphia to campaign for control of the Northern Department and eventually succeeded in wresting authority from Schuyler, who promptly traveled to Philadelphia to protest the decision. The *Encyclopedia of the American Revolution: Library of Military History* acknowledged that the "continual bickering between Gates, Schuyler, and congressional proponents of the two generals profited no one except Major General John Burgoyne, who threatened to invade New York from Canada in the spring of 1777." Burgoyne succeeded in capturing Fort Ticonderoga on Schuyler's watch in July of 1777 and pressed further inland towards the Hudson River. The Continental Congress returned command of the Northern Department to Gates the following month.

His command assured, Gates began the task of expelling Burgoyne from New York. He fortified Bemis Heights, located about ten miles from Saratoga, to block further advances into American territory. The first Battle of Saratoga also known as the Battle of Freeman's Farm took place at this location on September 19, 1777. Burgoyne's forces won the day, but did not manage to break Gates's line. The British again tested Gates's troops on October 7, 1777, in the Battle of Bemis Heights (the Second Battle of Saratoga). American troops led by Benedict Arnold repelled the attack, and Burgoyne faced an increasingly difficult situation as both his numbers and his supplies dwindled. Two days later, Gates led his army to surround the army of a retreating Burgoyne at Saratoga; there, Burgoyne surrendered to Gates on October 17, securing passage for his troops back to Britain with the promise that they would not again battle in America.

This agreement, as well as a perceived delay in the dispatch of Gates's notification of the victory to the Continental Congress, drew intense criticism. However, this criticism seems unwarranted; Randolph Greenfield Adams argued in the *Dictionary of American Biography* that, in the case of the notification, it was "certainly not fair as he wrote to President Hancock the day after the surrender, and sent the messages by his adjutant, Wilkinson." As the messenger traveled slowly, making many stops, Adams concluded that "Gates can hardly be blamed, save perhaps for choosing Wilkinson in the first place." Congress soon recognized Gates's accomplishments, awarding him a vote of thanks and a commemorative medal of the battle on November 4. Later that month, Congress elected Gates head of the Board of War.

The following year, Gates became embroiled in controversy as speculation arose that a number of military and political figures were planning to remove Washington from power and install Gates as commander of the Continental Army. It seems unlikely that Gates himself was a major participant of what came to be known as the Conway Cabal, and any rearrangement of senior command never came to be, as Washington publicly scorned the cabal. Gates developed what the *Encyclopedia of the American Revolution: Library of Military History* called "a profound and lasting dislike of Washington," and found his efforts to enact reform as head of the Board of War stymied. The scandal also led to a fruitless duel between Gates and Wilkinson in September of 1778.

In April of 1778, Gates returned to New York as commander of the Northern Department and established his base at Fishkill. That fall, he took over troops at Boston, and remained in New England throughout most of 1779. He returned to his home in Virginia for the winter of 1780, but was ordered to take over the command of the troubled Southern Department that June. He led troops at the disastrous Battle of Camden on August 16, where he was routed by the British army under Cornwallis. This defeat led to his removal from command, although a proposed inquiry into his actions was canceled in light of his previous accomplishments and the difficulty of the war. Seeking to clear his name, Gates fought for an inquiry, and in August 1782, Congress reversed the order removing Gates from command. He then traveled to the Continental Army's headquarters at Newburgh, Virginia, where he spent the remainder of the war assisting Washington.

Later Days and Legacy

The years 1783 through 1785 were difficult ones for Gates. He left the army to attend to his ailing wife, who died on June 1, and faced financial problems due to the continuing lack of pay from his service in the Continental Army. He became increasingly withdrawn from public life until after his 1786 marriage to Mary Vallance. In 1790, Gates decided to free his slaves and return to New York, where he would remain for the rest of his life. His last significant public service comprised one term in the New York legislature from 1800–1801.

Gates died in New York City at his home, Rose Hill Farm, on April 10, 1806, as the result of a lengthy illness. He was buried at Trinity Church in New York City. Nelson summed up Gates's legacy by saying, "Few of his supporters would have denied that he was not one of the greatest leaders in the struggle for American independence and that his life had produced a record of contradictions. But few of them would have agreed that he deserved bitter and general reproaches for his career." Although Gates may not have been lionized in American memory as were many of his contemporaries, his contributions to the founding of the United States are undeniable.

Books

Adams, Randolph Greenfield *Dictionary of American Biography,* American Council of Learned Societies, 1928–1936.

Mintz, Max M., *The Generals of Saratoga: John Burgoyne and Horatio Gates* Yale University Press, 1990.

Nelson, Paul David, *General Horatio Gates: A Biography,* Louisiana State University Press, 1976.

Encyclopedia of the American Revolution: Library of Military History, □

Charles Sidney Gilpin

American actor Charles Gilpin (1878–1930) became the first African American to play a starring role in a serious drama on Broadway when he appeared as Brutus Jones in Eugene O'Neill's *The Emperor Jones* in 1920.

Gilpin was a key figure in the nexus of African-American talent that generated the 1920s artistic movement known as the Harlem Renaissance. After his triumph in *The Emperor Jones,* which led to controversy when a formerly all-white awards banquet suddenly became a racially integrated event, Gilpin did much to encourage the development of serious African-American theater in the United States. His career up to that point had traversed many of the genres of African-American entertainment in the early twentieth century, both serious and comic, and his varied appearances showed him to be a performer of versatility and skill.

Became Apprentice in Newspaper Print Shop

The youngest of 14 children, Charles Sidney (or Sydney) Gilpin was born on November 20, 1878, in Richmond, Virginia. Gilpin's parents both had good jobs for African

Americans in that time and place. His father, Peter, was a steel mill worker, and his mother, Caroline, was a trained hospital nurse. He grew up in the Jackson Ward area, for decades the center of African-American business and entertainment in Richmond. Gilpin attended the St. Francis School, a segregated Catholic institution. At 12 he dropped out of school to become a "printer's devil," or apprentice, at the city's black-oriented newspaper, the *Richmond Planet.*

It was around that time that Gilpin made his first appearances as a singer. His fine baritone voice was apparent as soon as his voice changed, but opportunities in rigidly segregated Richmond were scarce. When Gilpin and his mother moved to Philadelphia in the early 1890s he sometimes got the chance to put on a song-and-dance routine in a saloon or at the variety shows that circulated through the area in the summer. In the 1890s, the chief source of employment for African-American performers beyond their purely local circles was the traveling minstrel show, a black counterpart to the blackface caricatures of white minstrelsy, which softened the racist edges of the form and developed indigenous forms of black entertainment such as the cakewalk. Gilpin was hired in 1896 by a minstrel show, Brown's Big Spectacular Log Cabin Company.

That venture lasted only two stops before it went bankrupt, but Gilpin quickly signed on with a second group, Perkus and Davis's Great Southern Minstrel Barnstormers. That ensemble too ran aground after several months, and Gilpin returned to Philadelphia. He held several jobs, including printer, barber, and boxing trainer, but the theatrical bug had infected him. In 1903 he jumped at the chance to join a group in Hamilton, Ontario, Canada, called the Carey and Carter Canadian Jubilee Singers. That engagement lasted two years and gave Gilpin valuable chances to connect with the growing network of black performers who were scratching out a living on North American stages.

Featured in Williams and Walker Show

At around this time (sources disagree as to whether the year was 1904 or 1906), Gilpin landed a role with the Smart Set, a touring African-American troupe organized by white producer Gus Hill. Gilpin played a politician named Remus Boreland. A major break came in 1905, when he joined a revue titled *The Two Real Coons* (the term, though derogatory, was in wide use among African-American performers at the time), starring the two leading black vaudevillians of the time, Bert Williams and George Walker. Gilpin was advertised as the show's baritone soloist. In 1907 he starred in a three-act musical called *The Husbands* with the Pekin Stock Company at Chicago's Pekin Theatre.

Over the next several years he appeared in shows such as *Captain Rufus* (1907), *The Mayor of Dixie* (1907, later adapted into the pioneering all-black Broadway musical *Shuffle Along*), *The Merry Widower* (1908), *The Chambermaid* (1908), and *The Man Upstairs* (1909), working in the Pekin Stock Company and its successor, Jesse A. Shipp's Stock Company. Like Williams and other black performers of the time, he appeared in the burnt-cork blackface makeup that African-American minstrelsy borrowed from the white minstrel show. Sometimes, however, Gilpin turned the tables and played white characters, using whiteface makeup.

Gilpin returned to vocal music between 1911 and 1913, touring the United States with the Pan American Octette. When he returned to New York, he began to move in the direction of an African-American theatrical art that extended beyond comedy revues. He appeared in the musical *The Old Man's Boy* in 1913 and 1914, also serving as the show's vocal director. In 1915 he joined the Anita Bush Players, the resident theatrical stock company at the Lincoln Theatre in Harlem. Initially known as the Anita Bush All-Colored Dramatic Stock Company, the group changed its name and began to mount more elaborate productions. When the company merged with the Lafayette Theatre Players (at Harlem's Lafayette Theatre), Gilpin emerged as its star. Such shows as *Across the Footlights, Within the Law, For His Daughter's Honor,* and *The Octoroon* attracted the attention of white newspaper critics. In the last-named play, Gilpin appeared in whiteface as a villainous plantation overseer, and earned acclaim from Harlem audiences.

By 1916 the Lafayette Theatre show *Southern Life* was being billed as a Charles Gilpin vehicle, with the Lafayette Stock Company advertised only for its supporting role. But in April of that year Gilpin quit the company during rehearsals for a show called *Paid in Full,* because of a salary dispute. His movements over the next two years have not yet been documented, but in 1919 he re-emerged in a starring role in a Broadway play, *Abraham Lincoln,* by British dramatist John Drinkwater. Gilpin played an African-American preacher named William Custis, who was modeled on abolitionist lecturer Frederick Douglass. Despite several handicaps in the conception of the role—Drinkwater's rendition of African-American dialect was stilted in the extreme, and his idea that Douglas was a minister was mistaken—Gilpin received positive attention for his performance.

Starred in O'Neill Drama

Around that time, the white playwright Eugene O'Neill was working on several experimental dramas involving black characters. One, *The Moon of the Caribees,* was produced with a white cast in blackface. Another short play with just four characters, *The Dreamy Kid,* was staged with black performers. But O'Neill's most extensive effort up to that time was *The Emperor Jones,* virtually a full-length monologue in which a Pullman porter becomes the dictator of a fictitious Caribbean island and gradually descends into madness. Gilpin auditioned for the role, difficult by any standard, and won it despite the presence of several white actors among the contenders. The show opened on November 1, 1920, at O'Neill's Provincetown Playhouse, recently moved to New York from Massachusetts, and that event marked the first star appearance on Broadway of an African-American actor in a serious full-length American drama.

Critical praise for Gilpin's virtuoso feat flowed from both black and white writers. The famed critic and essayist Alexander Woollcott wrote in the *New York Times,* as quoted in the *Dictionary of American Negro Biography*: "They have acquired an actor, one who has it in him to invoke the pity and terror and the indescribable foreboding

which are a part of the secret of *The Emperor Jones*." The show moved to the larger Princess Theatre and ran for 204 performances before being sent out on a national road tour. The National Association for the Advancement of Colored People (NAACP) awarded Gilpin its Spingarn Medal in 1921, and the Drama League selected Gilpin as one of ten individuals who had made the biggest contributions to American theater over the previous year. That award involved a banquet invitation, stirring controversy among white theater professionals who resisted the integration of the event. Gilpin's attendance at the dinner went off without incident, however, and by 1930 black historian James Weldon Johnson could write in his book *Black Manhattan,* "It is doubtful if a similar incident today could provoke such a degree of asininity."

Gilpin left the cast after disagreements with O'Neill. Of the reasons for the split, accounts differ as to the relative importance of Gilpin's alcohol abuse and/or his tendency to revise lines in the play that he considered offensive. Whatever the cause, O'Neill chose actor Paul Robeson for the London run of *The Emperor Jones,* and for its 1924 revival in New York. Despite the fact that Gilpin had originated the role and helped to bring O'Neill his 1921 Pulitzer Prize, Robeson became identified in the public mind with the role. Gilpin appeared in another 1924 play, *Roseanne,* winning less critical approval. O'Neill, however, later reflected that in his entire career he had encountered only one actor who fully embodied everything he had in mind for a character, and that that actor was Gilpin.

In addition to the example he had already set, Gilpin encouraged younger actors to pursue serious African-American drama. On a visit to Cleveland in the mid-1920s he was responsible for the creation of a new theatrical troupe, exhorting a group of young theater enthusiasts to focus on the details of African-American life around them. He made a $50 donation that helped launch the Karamu House theatre, which still exists, and the new Gilpin Players.

In his last years, Gilpin suffered from an unidentified ailment that caused him to lose his ability to speak. Working as an elevator operator, he was still able to appear in the all-black pro-temperance silent film *Ten Nights in a Barroom,* a milestone in early African-American cinema. After that his condition worsened, and he was cared for by his wife, Alma Benjamin, in the Trenton, New Jersey, suburb of Eldridge Park. She was either his second or third wife; his first marriage, to Florence Howard, produced a son, Paul Wilson, who was born in 1903. Gilpin died in Eldridge Park on May 6, 1930. He was buried in nearby Lambertville, but his body was then exhumed and taken to New York's Woodlawn Cemetery for reburial after an elaborate funeral.

Books

Dictionary of American Negro Biography, edited by Rayford W. Logan and Michael R. Winston, Norton, 1982.

Encyclopedia of the Harlem Renaissance, edited by Cary D. Wintz and Paul Finkelman, Routledge, 2004.

Haskins, James, *Black Theater in America,* HarperCollins, 1982.

Johnson, James Weldon, *Black Manhattan,* 1930 (rev. ed., Atheneum, 1968).

Notable Black American Men, Gale, 1998.

Online

"Charles Gilpin," Kennedy Center, http://www.artsedge.kennedy-center.org/exploring/harlem/faces/gilpin_text.html (December 19, 2008).

"Charles S. Gilpin," School of Information, Harlem Renaissance Exhibit, University of Michigan, http://www.si.umich.edu/CHICO/Harlem/text/gilpin.html (December 19, 2008).

"Gilpin, Charles Sidney (1878-1930)," The Black Past, http://www.blackpast.org/?q=aah/gilpin-charles-sidney-1878-1930 (December 19, 2008). □

Sheilah Graham

Raised in a London orphanage, Sheilah Graham (1904–1988) rose above her humble beginnings to become one of the best-read celebrity gossip columnists of all time. Savvy yet sarcastic, Graham dished out brutal judgments of the Hollywood elite for some 20 million readers in 175 newspapers during the mid-1950s. Graham is famously known for her relationship with U.S. novelist F. Scott Fitzgerald, which she detailed in a 1958 best-selling memoir *Beloved Infidel*.

Raised in Orphanage

The youngest of six children, Sheilah Graham was born Lily Shiel on September 15, 1904, in Leeds, England. Her parents, Louis and Rebecca Shiel, were of Russian-Jewish descent and arrived in England having fled the Ukraine to avoid the increasing persecution faced by Jewish citizens. Her father, an educated tailor who owned his own business, died of tuberculosis when Graham was an infant. In order to make ends meet, Graham's mother found work as a washerwoman in a local London bathhouse. They lived a poor, hungry existence, boarding in a basement slum where they slept on a sofa.

When Graham was six years old, her mother sent her to live at the Norwood Jewish Orphanage. Once inside the walls, her ash-blond hair was clipped to the scalp to help prevent the spread of lice and discourage runaways. It was a regular routine for the orphans and one that Graham despised. At the orphanage, hunger continued to be an issue for Graham. She often snuck into the kitchen to steal food, hiding scraps in her uniform, which consisted of knickers that tied at the knee. She cleverly discovered that she could carry food tucked down the legs of her knickers.

While at the orphanage, Graham took an interest in poetry. The headmaster would sometimes offer a small cash prize for the first child to memorize a particular poem. Graham won these contests frequently and soon turned to writing her own passages. She excelled in her schoolwork at the orphanage and even skipped a grade. Often, her essays were read aloud to the entire school. Graham showed so much promise that one of her teachers arranged for her to get a scholarship so she could attend high school and college. Graham was elated, figuring she would be able to rise above her bleak beginnings. Her mother, ill

with cancer, foiled those plans when she called Graham home to care for her, however.

Struggled to Support Self

At 14, Graham returned to the squalor of her early childhood and began caring for her mother. She found work at a factory, but after a heated fight with her mother over a housekeeping issue, she ran away. Graham secured work as a maid in the seaside resort town of Hove; the job lasted only a few months before Graham was notified that her mother was near death and all alone. Graham returned home again to look after her mother in her final days.

Seeking to support herself, Graham found a job selling a special U-shaped toothbrush at a cosmetics counter at Gamages, a popular London department store. There, she befriended a cosmetics worker who gave her the pet name "Sheilsy." The job ended when the toothbrush company went bankrupt. While on the job, she met a businessman named Maj. John Graham Gillam. He owned his own manufacturing company and agreed to hire her to sell his products.

They married in 1923. Graham was 19, while Gillam was in his mid-40s. Gillam lovingly chided Graham about her Cockney accent, acquired while living on London's working-class East Side, but he went on to help her refine her speech and learn proper manners. In time, she enrolled at the Royal Academy of Dramatic Art, where she took speech courses. At the academy, Graham also learned the art of entering a room—these skills served her later when she landed in Hollywood.

Became Chorus Girl

When Gillam's company suffered from financial difficulties, Graham decided to find work to help out. She decided to try for a job on stage, possibly in a musical-comedy. Before she went to her first audition, however, Gillam told her not to apply as "Mrs. Gillam" because no one would want to hire a housewife. He suggested she use the name Sheila Graham, taking the Sheila from her nickname Sheilsy, and adding Graham, his middle name. She liked the sound of it and added an "h" to Sheila, rendering it Sheilah, because she thought that was more distinguished.

Graham earned a role as a chorus girl in *Punchbowl,* and then joined the chorus line, in 1927, for *One Dam Thing After Another,* a Rodgers and Hart show starring Mimi Crawford. At the time, Crawford was one of the reigning stars of the musical stage. One night, Crawford was sick so Graham went on in her place to positive reviews. When that show ended, Graham earned a speaking part in British playwright Noel Coward's *This Year of Grace.*

Graham's stage life filled her with countless story ideas so she began putting them down on paper. She first wrote an article called "The Stage-Door Johnny, by A Chorus Girl." She sent it off to the *Daily Express,* which bought the piece. By 1929, Gillam was bankrupt, prompting Graham to write articles in earnest to pay the bills. She started hanging out with other writers and soon learned about syndication, which was popular in the United States. Intrigued, Graham decided to move to the United States. Gillam offered his blessing and promised to follow.

Moved to United States

In June 1933, Graham arrived in the United States with $100. She took her clippings to the *New York Mirror* and was hired but soon moved to the *Evening Journal,* where she wrote a provocative column called "Sheilah Graham Says." Her stories tended toward the sensational, with headlines such as, "Who Cheats the Most?"—a treatise on men most likely to be unfaithful.

In 1934, King Features dispatched her to London to write about the Duke of Kent's marriage to Princess Marina of Greece. Back in England, she visited Gillam and they decided to divorce. In 1935, she took a job as a Hollywood reporter for the North American Newspaper Alliance, spending the next three decades as a syndicated columnist.

Once in Hollywood, Graham distinguished herself by writing candidly about the stars. While Graham's work interested readers, it alienated her from the Hollywood elite. In her book *Beloved Infidel,* Graham reprinted a portion of an early article she wrote about Clark Gable, famous for his role in *Gone With the Wind.* "Clark Gable threw back his handsome head and exposed a chin line upon which a thin ridge of fat is beginning to collect." She also wrote that Joan Crawford was becoming a "tired, sallow-faced woman." At first, Hollywood studios were furious but in a short amount of time, the protests died down. Graham's column, "Hollywood Today," was well-read, which brought publicity, even if the celebrities or studios did not always like what she was saying.

Fell For Fitzgerald

Graham eventually fell in with the Hollywood elite and attended their parties, and in 1937 met F. Scott Fitzgerald at a social gathering. She was 26; he was 40. Best known as the author of *The Great Gatsby,* Fitzgerald was in Hollywood writing a screenplay. During one early rendezvous they went dancing and in *Beloved Infidel,* Graham recalled her emotions from that evening: "I thought, *this man is not forty, he is a young man, he is a college boy, he is utterly delightful.*" At the time, Fitzgerald was married, but his wife, Zelda, was locked in a sanitarium in Asheville, North Carolina.

Nonetheless, Graham and Fitzgerald started spending time together and began a relationship. Fitzgerald was struggling with his writing career and having trouble selling his work. He drank heavily at times. In 1938, they moved in together, living at a beach house in Malibu, California. Graham's steady work helped Fitzgerald financially, and he helped Graham with her writing, making her his protégé. Fitzgerald introduced Graham to the poetry of Keats and she was moved. With her spotty schooling at the orphanage and failure to attend past eighth grade, she realized her education was lacking, particularly in literature and history. To fill in her gaps of knowledge, Fitzgerald created the "F. Scott Fitzgerald College of One." Each day for two years he wrote out assignments for her to read and each evening they discussed them. She read Plutarch's *Lives,* as well as the work of Proust and Lord Byron. She studied Adolf Hitler's *Mein Kampf* and Karl Marx's *Das Kapital.*

The three and a half years Graham and Fitzgerald spent together were highly volatile, filled with ups and downs. At times Fitzgerald drank so heavily he could hardly function and was prone to depression. He even pulled a gun on her once. Other times, he sent her flowers or wrote her romantic poems. In 1940, Fitzgerald died—of an apparent heart attack—in her living room. She chronicled their affair in the 1958 best-seller *Beloved Infidel,* a title she borrowed from a love poem Fitzgerald wrote for her. The book was made into a movie in 1959 featuring Gregory Peck and Deborah Kerr in the starring roles.

Wrote Several Autobiographical Books

After World War II heated up, Graham returned to England to work as a war correspondent. There, she met Trevor Westbrook, an Englishman who oversaw the company that manufactured the Spitfire—a fighter plane used by the British during the war. They married in 1941 and divorced in 1946. During their marriage, Graham gave birth to two children—Wendy and Robert Westbrook.

After the war, Graham continued her work in Hollywood. Besides her newspaper column, she wrote regularly for *Photoplay,* a film magazine, and also had her own radio show. She raised her children in Beverly Hills. In 1953, Graham married Stanley Wojtkiewicz, but the marriage lasted only a few years. Graham's older child, Wendy, was raised to believe that Westbrook was her father. Later in life—after her mother's death—she discovered her father was actually the British philosopher A. J. Ayer, whom she knew as a family friend.

Throughout her life, Graham kept a lot of secrets, often lying about her age and her background. Her children, who have each written books about Graham, lamented that their mother was not forthcoming with the facts surrounding their lives. Graham revealed more in her books than she did to her children. Growing up, the children did not even know they were half-Jewish.

Graham continued writing right up until the end of her life. She wrote several autobiographical books, including *The Rest of the Story,* 1964; *College of One,* 1967; *Confessions of a Hollywood Columnist,* 1969; *The Real F. Scott Fitzgerald,* 1976; and *Hollywood Revisited: A Fiftieth Anniversary Celebration,* 1985.

Graham died November 17, 1988, at a hospital in West Palm Beach, Florida. A note of her passing in *Time* magazine quoted Graham from a previous interview, bemoaning that fact that, "I won't be remembered for my writing. I'll be remembered as Scott's mistress."

Books

Graham, Sheilah and Gerold Frank, *Beloved Infidel,* Henry Holt and Co., 1958.

Westbrook, Robert, *Intimate Lies: F. Scott Fitzgerald and Sheilah Graham Her Son's Story,* HarperCollins Publishers, 1995.

Periodicals

All Things Considered (NPR), July 2, 1992.
Los Angeles Times, November 19, 1988.
New York Times, November 19, 1988.
Time, November 28, 1988.
Washington Post, November 19, 1988.

Online

"We Remember: Sheilah Graham," Jewish Women's Archive, http://jwa.org/weremember/graham (December 16, 2008). □

Elisha Gray

American inventor Elisha Gray (1835–1901) sparked a lasting historical and scientific debate as to the true inventor of the telephone when he filed a patent notification for that device on the same day as Alexander Graham Bell. Although he is primarily remembered today for what the *World of Invention* called "one of the most remarkable coincidences in the history of invention," Gray was a prominent scientist in his day. He received over 70 patents in his lifetime for communications and electronic devices, including telegraphic equipment and a distant precursor of the fax machine.

The son of Quakers David and Christina Gray, Elisha Gray was born on August 2, 1835, near Barnesville, Ohio. Even as a child, he turned his energies to building and invention. In *The Telephone Patent Conspiracy of 1876: The Elisha Gray-Alexander Graham Bell Controversy and Its Many Players,* A. Edward Evenson described Gray's success, at the age of ten, in building a working telegraph station: "Mostly through ingenuity and improvisation, [Gray] had created a fully functional telegraph—and an engineer was born." Gray attended school in Barnesville until the age of 12, when the death of his father forced him to go to work. He first served as a blacksmith's apprentice, but soon turned to shipbuilding. He spent the next three-and-a-half years in a shipbuilding apprenticeship, finally qualifying to become a ship joiner, a person who worked with the wooden parts of ships.

Despite obtaining these skills, Gray hoped to return to formal schooling. An acquaintance who attended nearby Oberlin College suggested that institution, and Gray, by then 22 years old, soon began to study there. He attended Oberlin for five years, focusing on the physical sciences—particularly electricity—and supporting himself by doing carpentry work and building laboratory equipment for the college's science departments. While at Oberlin, Gray met Delia Shepherd, and the couple married in 1862 after Gray completed his studies.

First Inventions

Gray initially considered a career as a minister before he turned his attention to mechanical inventions at the suggestion of his mother-in-law. By 1867 Gray had begun working in the field of telegraphy—the use of the wireless telegraph for communication—and his first patent was for an improved, self-adjusting telegraph relay. Despite continuing to farm, he soon patented other telegraphic devices, including a telegraph switch, receiver, and printer, as well as an annunciator, or signal board, for use in hotels. Evenson commented that "not all of these devices brought in rich rewards, but they did bring him recognition in the telegraphic field as a serious inventor."

His success allowed Gray to give up farming and start a company in about 1870, called Barton and Gray, along with former telegraph operator Enid Barton. The business manufactured telegraphic and electrical supplies, with Gray acting as designer and Barton as production manager. Success came quickly, attracting the attention of Anton Stager, head of the Western Union Telegraph Company. By 1872 Stager had bought a one-third share of Barton and Gray. That year, the company relocated from Cleveland to Chicago and changed its name to the Western Electric Manufacturing Company. Soon, Western Electric became the primary supplier of electric goods to Western Union, which held a virtual monopoly on the telegraph system of the time.

By this time, Gray had stopped working as the company's head designer and secured the necessary financial support from fellow inventor Dr. Samuel S. White to dedicate all of his efforts to invention. Evenson noted that "this was the best of both worlds for Gray, an engineer's dream." Gray continued his professional affiliation with Western Electric, often using the company's laboratories.

Race for the Harmonic Telegraph

During the early- and mid-1870s, many inventors were investigating the possibility of a harmonic telegraph system. The original telegraph system had been capable of sending or receiving one message at a time along a given telegraph line. Although fast, this system was somewhat inefficient. In 1872 J.B. Sterns developed an improved system that allowed a single telegraph wire to both send and receive a message at the same time. Shortly after that, Thomas Edison introduced a quadruplex system that allowed for two incoming and two outgoing messages. Each of these developments had been quite lucrative, so it is unsurprising that several inventors—including Gray, Edison, and Alexander Graham Bell—sought an effective method to transmit 30 or 40 simultaneous messages, with Gray seemingly having the most success.

By this time, Bell had identified Gray as his principle rival in the race for the harmonic telegraph, although it seems unlikely that Gray had any particular knowledge of Bell. Bell's rivalry was reinforced in the spring of 1875 when, after showing interest in Bell's demonstration of his harmonic telegraphic system, a representative of Western Electric told Bell that Gray had developed a superior device. Gray had filed a patent application for this system on February 23, 1875; shortly thereafter, Bell filed an application that caused an "interference" with Gray's, meaning that the two applications were enough alike to require further examination. While Gray's harmonic telegraph patent application was tied up in the interference resolution process, another patent of Bell's that relied on similar technology was approved. Gray, upon seeing the publication of Bell's patent, became quite angry and presumably complained to the U.S. Patent Office. Eventually, Gray developed a harmonic telegraphic system capable of transmitting eight simultaneous messages, but this system proved to be ultimately unworkable and may simply have been too advanced for the technology of the time.

A Controversial Caveat

Gray had become interested in the idea of transmitting human speech over telegraph wires, but his financial backer, Dr. Samuel S. White, discouraged him from that line of inquiry in favor of the harmonic telegraph. Despite this, Gray had been quietly working on an idea involving liquid transmission and variable resistance. On February 11, 1876, he gave his assistant a packet containing a drawing and handwritten notes and asked him to have a caveat—a formal notice of intent to produce an invention then used by the U.S. Patent Office—produced from it. The following Monday morning, February 14, 1876, Gray dropped off his caveat at the Patent Office. That same day, Gardiner Hubbard, Bell's financial backer, decided to file a patent application for a voice-transmitting device that Bell had designed.

Recent scholarship has argued that this decision was not a coincidence. Records show that Bell had previously decided to wait to file the application pending the possibility of instead patenting the device in Great Britain; he had arranged with an acquaintance, George Brown, to file a patent on his behalf in Britain, and was awaiting a cable from Brown confirming that he had done so before filing for a U.S. patent. However, Hubbard filed the U.S. patent application, without consulting Bell, before the cable had arrived. Writing in *The Telephone Gambit*, Seth Shulman argued that "it strains credulity to imagine that Hubbard's hurried, unilateral action came only coincidentally on the exact date that Gray's caveat was filed." Although no proof exists that Hubbard had learned of Gray's intent to file the caveat, the rush with which Bell's application was handled makes it seem likely that he somehow had.

Conventional wisdom states that Bell's patent application arrived at the office two hours before Gray's caveat. This assumption has long been based on entries in the cash blotter maintained by the chief clerk, placing Bell's name higher on the list than Gray's. However, Evenson stated that contrary to typical patent office procedures, "the person who brought in Bell's application demanded that it be taken immediately to [a patent clerk]. . . . The clerk had no choice but to stop at the chief clerk's office, and request that Bell's application be entered immediately into the daily blotter." Even had Gray's application been delivered earlier in the day, it would not have been processed until later than Bell's due to this unusual event. As this blotter entry became the basis for the granting of the patent to Bell, it again seems likely that conscious steps were taken to ensure the placement of Bell's name toward the head of the list. Further investigation into the possibility of an interference, common practice when two notifications were filed so close together, was halted due to the decision that Bell's application had preceded Gray's caveat.

Gray, aware that Bell was working on a telephone but believing it to be based on electromagnetic properties rather than ones using his own liquid transmission system, completed his model and sold the rights to Western Union. Around the end of 1877, Western Union formed a company to compete with the recently launched Bell Telephone Company. Bell Telephone soon filed a lawsuit, and years of legal wrangling over the true inventor of the telephone began. An 1888 U.S. Supreme Court decision declared Bell to be the "first discoverer" of the process of electrically transmitting human speech, based on his 1876 patent.

Later Career and Death

In 1880 Gray returned to his alma mater, Oberlin College, as an instructor. He taught courses in electricity at the college for the remainder of his life. During his tenure at Oberlin, Gray continued his work developing electronic devices. Perhaps his most notable invention at this stage of his career was the TelAutograph, a forerunner of the modern fax machine. This instrument was capable of exactly reproducing words or images sent over telephone lines through the use of a special pen which accurately mimicked the motions performed by the sender in creating the content of the message. Gray debuted the TelAutograph at the 1893 Columbian Exposition (Chicago World's Fair), also serving as the chairman of the exposition's International Congress of Electricians. The TelAutograph became a popular piece of equipment for such businesses as banks and factories and remained in continuous production until it was superseded by the fax machine in the 1990s.

Gray was an active writer, publishing the technical works *Experimental Researches in Electro-Harmonic Telegraphy* in 1878, *Telegraphy and Telephony* in 1878, *Electricity and Magnetism* in 1900, as well as a popular scientific book, *Nature's Miracles,* explaining natural and scientific phenomena such as weather and electricity, also in 1900. He was also the recipient of a number of honorary degrees and the prestigious medal of the French Legion of Honor.

In the winter of 1901 Gray was in Newton, Massachusetts, hard at work on a new undersea signaling system to help protect ships in navigating shallow waters. He unexpectedly took ill on the afternoon of January 20 and collapsed later that evening, most likely as the result of a heart attack. Gray died in the early morning hours of the following morning, January 21. He was later interred at Rosehill Cemetery in Chicago, Illinois. Although Gray's fame has dwindled over the years, his many contributions to the field of electronics—and possible status as the true inventor of the telephone—have surely earned him a place in history as more than merely someone who reached the patent office a few hours too late.

Books

Evenson, A. Edward, *The Telephone Patent Conspiracy of 1876: The Elisha Gray-Alexander Bell Controversy and Its Many Players,* McFarland and Company, 2000.

Shulman, Seth, *The Telephone Gambit,* Norton, 2008.

Online

"Elisha Gray," *World of Invention,* reproduced in *Biography Resource Center,* http://www.galenet.galegroup.com/servlet/ BioRC (October 19, 2008).

"The Telephone Cases, 126 U.S. 1 (1888)," U.S. Supreme Court Center, http://www.supreme.justia.com/us/126/1/case.html (November 15, 2008). □

Janet Guthrie

Janet Guthrie (born 1938) blazed a trail when she became the first female race car driver to compete and finish in the world-famous Indianapolis 500 in 1977.

Like many women who have emerged as feminist icons, Guthrie did not set out to champion any particular cause, she just wanted to drive race cars on the same major circuits ruled by such down-home southern legends as Richard Petty and Cale Yarborough. When she could not find a sponsor for the big races, she assembled her own team and tackled the big-time circuit. She enjoyed few supporters and endured a lot of resistance from the sport's well-entrenched good-old-boy network, but by the time she got to the Indianapolis 500, she had not only proven herself as a driver, but had opened the doors for other women, Danica Patrick among them, to compete in America's fastest moving sport.

Raised in Rural Florida

Guthrie was born on March 7, 1938, in Iowa City, Iowa, to William Lain Guthrie, an Eastern Airlines pilot who later became an airport manager, and his wife, the former Jean Ruth Midkif, who was born in Brazil. One of five children, she moved with her family to the backwoods of Dade County in Miami when she was three years old. In her autobiography, Guthrie described their lifestyle as secluded, and her mother, though loving to her children, as emotionally distant from even her own closest friends. By contrast, her father proved outgoing, and displayed curiosity and imagination all his adult life. Indeed, Guthrie recalled that the elder Guthrie would amuse his children with his flight experiments, which included tossing chickens from the top of their windmill, or giving the surprisingly calm family cat a kite ride.

Janet Guthrie began her formal education at Miss Harris's Florida School for Girls in Biscayne, but her spirit was stoked by her family's weekly trips to the library in nearby Coral Gables. Most of the adventure stories that she read featured male heroes, but young Guthrie had no problem imagining herself as the focal point of the stories. Later, she cherished Tennyson's *Idylls of the King,* Scott's *Ivanhoe,* and all the books in the *Three Musketeers* series. Although well-read and very bright, she experienced the downside of living in such a rural area and missed having a normal social life with others her own age. She asked to attend

public school, but felt so out of place that she returned to the Harris school until graduation.

Living in a rural area where the now-endangered Florida panther howled through the nights and coral snakes and rattlers lived in abundance, Guthrie developed a fearless and adventurous spirit. When her father brought home a bicycle for her fourth birthday, she insisted on learning to ride without the aid of training wheels. She made her first parachute jump at age 16, practicing her landings by jumping off the roof of the family home. Following in her parents' footsteps, she worked at a nearby flying strip to pay for flying lessons, earning her pilot's license when she was only 17. Later, Guthrie met her first boyfriend by betting she could fly a Piper J-3 Cub higher than he could. Although their relationship only lasted a year, the young daredevil learned that she could break through societal barriers and still win. However, in the 1950s there was no such thing as a female commercial airline pilot. So Guthrie had to find another way to compete in a man's world.

Began Racing as a Hobby

Initially, Guthrie's quest for higher education at the University of Michigan did not go well. Picked for its excellence as an aeronautical engineering school, she was discouraged by the school's attitude toward the role of women. After a year she dropped out of the engineering program and went into physics, which seemed a better fit. At the end of her sophomore year, Guthrie took a year off from school to earn her

commercial pilot's license and flight instructor rating before hitchhiking around Europe for a couple of months. Upon returning, she resumed her studies, graduating in 1960 with a bachelor of science degree in physics.

Sorting through post-college job offers, Guthrie chose Republic Aviation, where she worked in research and development. Still passionate about flying, her job held her earthbound. Earning $125 a week working in Farmingdale, Long Island, New York, she considered buying a half-share in an airplane, but an ad for a 1953 Jaguar XK 120 M coupe caught her eye, and it was love at first sight. Taking out loans from a bank and a local finance company, she purchased the sports car. The following spring she discovered the world of gymkhanas. As applied to automobiles, gymkhanas are competitions of speed and accuracy. In large parking or asphalt areas, pylons mark out an intricate course that drivers try to drive through with speed and precision. The fastest time wins, but points are subtracted if the pylons are moved. Intrigued, Guthrie viewed several competitions before becoming a full-fledged competitor in 1961.

The next step in her evolution as a driver came with speed-oriented hill climbs, sometimes putting both car and driver in great personal risk. Guthrie risked several close calls, cracking up her beloved Jaguar, which forced her to occasionally drive other competitors' cars. Often looked upon as the driver to beat, and with her confidence growing, she began investigating the possibility of road racing. The likes of Evelyn Mull and Denise McCluggage, among others, had preceded her in the 1950s, but Guthrie was an admitted novice. Finally, in February of 1963 she began attending Sports Car Club of America (SCCA) competition drivers' school in Marlboro, Maryland. With her new Jaguar, an XK 140 MC roadster, she learned to inspect the track, recognize flags, how to slide off the road, and do battle in bumper-to-bumper, door-to-door competition.

After certification, Guthrie's beleaguered finances kept her from racing as frequently as she wanted to. Strictly amateur, when she blew an engine, she paid for it out of her own pocket, and she often had to do the mechanical work herself. When she needed a pit-crew, fellow workers at Republic Aviation were recruited. Later, Guthrie admitted that her preoccupation with racing had kept her from pursuing a master's degree. Moreover, the all-consuming passion sabotaged several potential romantic relationships. However, the rush of adrenaline that came with racing was something she was loath to give up. She began racing whenever time and money would permit. She won her first SCCA race in October of 1963, and began competing regularly in May of 1964. Aided in no small part by garage owner/mechanic and pit crew boss Ralph Farnham Jr., she competed at the SCCA National Championship race at Watkins Glen, where she finished sixth, a strong showing from a relatively new driver.

Racing was not the only avenue Guthrie pursued during that pre-feminist era. In 1964 she applied to NASA's Scientist-Astronaut Program. Although her test results advanced her to the second round of evaluations, all the female applicants were dismissed in 1965. That same year, Republic Aviation was bought by Fairchild Hiller. As a result, the Advanced Orbiting Solar Observatory program, where she worked as one of two experiment coordinators, was shut down. She ended up back in Long Island working temporarily at an aerospace company started by a few of her Republic colleagues, but when the company lost an important contract, the company folded.

Driving in curtain-raisers for major events and SCCA competitions, Guthrie began racking up wins and strong finishes, but without a sponsor and a world-class car, she struggled. For a time she existed on unemployment checks, and after her beloved Jaguar faltered one final time, she took a job as a publications engineer at Sperry Systems Management Division. The job would keep her solvent for the next four years, but racing was seldom far from her mind.

First Woman at Indy

Driving for sponsor Ring-Free, Guthrie, along with fellow drivers Liane Engeman and Donna Mae Mimms, had a strong finish at the 12 Hours of Sebring race in 1969, and finished first in the Under 2-Liter class the following year. In 1971 Guthrie began refitting a Toyota Celica, eventually running the company's first sport vehicle in 52 SCCA races. Dropping her job at Sperry, she became a full-time pro in 1972, driving under the banner of A-1 Toyota in Connecticut. By 1975 she was five thousand dollars in debt, with no savings or financial assets and a car that was not justifying her time and ambitions. Just as she was ready to quit, Toyota offered her a one-year contract to promote safe driving and small cars on radio and television.

As early as 1972, independent car designer and builder Rolla Volstedt had inquired about bringing Guthrie to the Indianapolis 500. Three years later, with a spot open for a second driver, Volstedt asked his top driver, Dick Simon, to check her out. "Rolla asked me to watch her in a race at Ontario speedway in California," Simon told *Time*. When Simon returned, he informed Volstedt, "You'd be stupid if you didn't sign her up." From the start, male drivers questioned her experience, physical strength, and mental toughness. Yet Volstedt, Simon, and her sponsor, Bryant Heating & Cooling, stood behind her as waves of anti-feminism emanated from the press.

Saddled by a balky car, Guthrie did not qualify for Indianapolis the first time around. As a concession to the public interest, she drove a test car during the preliminary time trials. However, in 1976 she became the first woman to compete in the NASCAR Winston Cup superspeedway stock car race. Driving a Chevrolet Laguna for owner Lynda Ferreri, with Kelly Girl as the sponsor, she would eventually run 33 races against such elite NASCAR drivers as Bill Elliot, Richard Petty, Bobby Allison, Johnny Rutherford, and David Pearson. She also became the holder of the women's world closed course speed record. At a time when women were not allowed in the pit areas and sidelines, many anti-feminist catcalls still rang from the sidelines, but Guthrie gradually earned respect from the other drivers.

The year 1977 was Guthrie's breakthrough year as a driver. In addition to being named Top Rookie at the Daytona 500, she returned to the Indianapolis 500, setting the fastest time on the first day of practice and the fastest time of any driver during the second weekend of qualifications. The

result of all that hard driving was historic: Guthrie became the first woman to qualify and compete in the famed Indianapolis 500. Unfortunately, 27 laps into the big race her car suffered mechanical problems, and she could not finish the race. However, Guthrie learned from her mistakes, and the following year she formed her own team and surprised many onlookers by finishing ninth, despite incurring a potentially debilitating injury for a driver. "She done a helluva job," driver Gordon Johncock told *Philadelphia Inquirer Magazine,* as posted on Guthrie's official Web site. "The woman drove 500 miles with a broken wrist. I don't know if I could have done it."

Guthrie competed at the Indy 500 again in 1979, finishing thirty-fourth, and continued to race on the NASCAR Winston Cup stock car circuit. After competing at every major venue the circuit had to offer, from Bristol and the Daytona 500 to the Pocono 500 and Talledega, Guthrie, frustrated by the lack of sponsorship, drove her last big NASCAR event in 1980. "I didn't decide to quit racing, believe me, I was forced out by lack of sponsorship," she told *Auto Week*. "There was nothing but turndowns." After driving in two endurance races for the Peugot factory team in 1985 and 1986, she retired from racing for good.

In 1989 Guthrie married American Airlines captain Warren Levine, and after a stint as a highway safety consultant, she became a spokesperson, appearing on such nationally televised programs as *Good Morning, America* and *James Michener's Sports in America*. She was inducted into the Women's Sports Hall of Fame in 1980, and her helmet and driving suit were given a place of honor in the Smithsonian Institute. The former driver re-entered the national consciousness in 2005 with the release of her autobiography, and again when Danica Patrick became the first female driver to best Guthrie's 1978 Indy 500 finish. To Guthrie it was no surprise that Patrick, who finished fourth in 2005 and became the first woman to win an Indy Car event in 2008, could compete at such a high level. Speaking with the *Sporting News,* Guthrie proudly observed, "The candidates are out there. It's just whether a top-notch team will give a woman an opportunity."

Books

Guthrie, Janet, *Janet Guthrie---A Life at Full Throttle,* Sports Classics Books, 2005.

Online

Autoweek, http://www.autoweek,com/apps/pbcs.dll/article?AID=/200505300430/FREE.505300705, (January 8, 2009).

"Janet Guthrie, The First Female Indianapolis 500 Driver, to be Honored on Capitol Hill May 7 at the 'SEMA Salute to Women in Motor Sports,'" *The Auto Channel,* http://www.theautochannel.com/news/press/date/19970506/press002203.html, (January 8, 2009).

"Janet Guthrie," *International Motor Sports Hall of Fame,* http://www.motorsportshalloffame.cpm/main/03_halloffame.htm, (January 8, 2009).

"Janet Guthrie," *International Women's Sports Hall of Fame,* http://www.womenssportsfoundation.org/News-and-Events.Awards/International-Womens-Sports-Hall-Of-Fame, (January 8, 2009).

''Janet Guthrie,'' *Internet Movie Database,,* http://www.imdb.com/name/nm0349273/, (January 8, 2009).

Janet Guthrie Official Web site, http://www.janetguthrie.com, (January 8, 2009).

''On the Right Track,'' *Time,* http://www.time.com/time/printout/0.8816,947686,00.html, (January 8, 2009).

''Patrick beats men and her doubters,'' *International Herald Tribune,* http://www.iht.com/bin/printfriendly. php?id=12178926, (January 8, 2009).

''Who is NASCAR's Danica?,'' *Sporting News,* http://www.sporting news.com/experts/lee-spencer/20050621-p.html, (January 8, 2009).□

Jean Harlow

Film actress Jean Harlow (1911–1937) exemplified the blonde bombshell persona long before the advent of Betty Grable, Marilyn Monroe, or Madonna. She made her first big splash in Howard Hughes's 1930 epic *Hell's Angels*, and became a major star at MGM, churning out a string of classic hit pictures until her shockingly abrupt death at the age of 26.

Born Harlean Harlow Carpenter on June 7, 1937, in Kansas City, Missouri, she was the daughter of Mont Clair Carpenter, a dentist, and Jean Poe Harlow. With her wealthy maternal grandparents living nearby, young Harlean—a combination of her mother's first and last names—lived in relative affluence. Raised with a nurse, nanny, chauffeur, and a menagerie of pets, she was the apple of her grandfather's eye as well as the repository for many of her mother's unrealized ambitions. Doted on by her mother, the youngster didn't realize that her name wasn't "the Baby" until she was sent to Miss Barstow's School, a private academy in Kansas City.

Mont Claire Carpenter ran a successful dentistry practice that afforded his family an 18-room mansion, but his marriage was in shambles. Dr. Carpenter came from humble Iowa working stock that valued hard work and education. By contrast, his wife was always looking for ways to break into high society or, later, ways to exploit their daughter's beauty and talent to her own benefit. Two days before their fourteenth anniversary, the Carpenters divorced. Dr. Carpenter allowed his wife sole custody of the 12-year-old Harlean and paid $200 a month in child support.

According to David Stenn's book *Bombshell—The Life and Death of Jean Harlow,* the former Mrs. Carpenter took the child support money with the sole purpose of moving to Hollywood in 1923. While the 34-year-old buxom blonde divorcee belatedly took a stab at an acting career—with no luck—she ensconced her daughter in the Hollywood School for Girls. Among Harlean's classmates were the daughters of MGM honcho Louis B. Mayer, famed director Cecil B. De Mille, and silent screen superstar Francis X. Bushman, along with two boys, future stars Joel McCrea and Douglas Fairbanks Jr. At the school, the blonde-haired, green-eyed child made quite an impression on the other girls, who were in awe of her adultlike sophistication and bravado.

Harlean Carpenter's Hollywood education was financed by her grandfather Skip Harlow. When he learned that his daughter had moved to a cheaper apartment to make the child support allotments stretch further, he threatened to disinherit his daughter if she didn't bring his granddaughter home. Back in Missouri, grandfather Harlow sent Harlean to Notre Dame de Scion, a strict Catholic school, in order to separate the mother and daughter. But he had underestimated their bond. After one month she begged to come home, and was enrolled in Miss Bigelow's School in Kansas City. Eventually, the youngster ended up at an all-girls boarding school in Lake Forest, Illinois, which mother Jean chose because her lover, a small-time grifter named Marino Bello, who had rumored mob connections, lived in nearby Highland Park.

While at school, 16-year-old Harlean was introduced to fellow student Charles McGrew II, the only child of a wealthy couple who had died in a tragic boating accident. He and Harlean fell in love, and the couple eloped and were married in Waukegan, Wisconsin, on September 21, 1927. A few months later, hoping to distance his bride from her controlling mother, McGrew moved to Beverly Hills, where his wife stumbled into a movie career.

Howard Hughes Made Her Famous

In Beverly Hills, Harlean McGrew befriended Rosalie Roy, an aspiring actress. One day she drove Roy to an audition at Fox Studios and waited for her inside the studio grounds, where company executives were stunned by her beauty. Initially, the future star took their letters of introduction to Central Casting and stuffed them in her purse as if they were a joke. However, friends dared her to take the letters around to various casting directors to see if she could actually get extra work. When she was accepted, she registered her professional name as Jean Harlow. Delighted, Harlow's mother and new husband Bello moved to Los Angeles to advise her career.

Fox paid Harlow $7 a day to work as an extra in such films as *Honor Bound, Moran of the Marines,* and *Fugitives.* At the Hal Roach Studios, she made $10 a day working on a two-reel comedy with comedian Charley Chase. Roach, second only to Mack Sennett in the pantheon of great slapstick comedy directors, admired Harlow's combination of beauty and nerve, and began casting her in bit parts as Harlean Carpenter before he signed her to a $100-a-week contract. Eventually she appeared in three silent Laurel and Hardy short comedies: *Liberty, Double Whoopee,* and *Bacon Grabbers.* However, before Roach could help her develop into one of his comedy stock players, Harlow begged out of her contract, citing the movie business's negative effect on her marriage. Harlow's husband became disgusted by his mother-in-law's influence on Harlean, and the young couple soon divorced.

Initially, leaving the Roach Studios seemed a mistake. As the sole support of her mother and stepfather, Harlow took on all the extra work she could, ranging from Al Christie two-reel comedies to uncredited parts in Charlie Chaplin's *City Lights* and the hit gangster film *Scarface.* Her luck began to change with a stunning bit part in fading sex symbol Clara Bow's 1929 film *The Saturday Night Kid.* Afterwards, the male lead in that picture, James Hall, recommended her for a film that millionaire aviator Howard Hughes was producing, *Hell's Angels.* Originally a silent picture, Hughes took so long to complete the film that it became outdated when Hollywood entered the new era of talking pictures. The first actress filmed, Greta Nissen, possessed a thick Norwegian accent that didn't match her character as the film changed to a talkie. After a screen test, Hughes signed Harlow to a five-year, $100-a-week contract, and cast her as the film's femme fatale.

The filming of *Hell's Angels* proved a trial for Harlow. Not only was she unprepared to act in a major bad girl role, but Hughes insisted on filming segments in a new Technicolor process. The end result was a performance that critics loathed but that caused a sensation with audiences. Dressed in form fitting gowns with no underwear underneath—she seldom wore it—and sporting white-blonde hair, the actress stunned audiences with her flashy looks and earthy sex appeal. Overnight, women hoping to emulate her impact on men were bleaching their hair and wearing the silken bell-bottom pajamas she wore in the film.

Harlow's impact on audiences did not mean that Hughes hastened to cast her in another film. He kept her busy with promotional tours and loaned her out to other studios, which didn't help enrich the actress. Warner Bros. paid Hughes $100 a week to have Harlow appear with James Cagney in the classic racketeer drama *Public Enemy,* but Harlow only received a total of $200. Hughes loaned her out for several more pictures, including *The Secret Six, Goldie,* and *Platinum Blonde,* the latter being the first of a two-picture deal with Columbia, arranged and financed by reputed gangster Abner "Longy" Zwillman. Finally the eccentric Hughes sold her contract to MGM for a reported $60,000.

Became a Major Star at MGM

By the time Harlow joined the MGM roster, she was an established sex symbol, one that critics decried but couldn't stop watching. During the making of *Platinum Blonde,* director Frank Capra was shocked at her lack of acting ability but awed by her vibrant screen presence. At MGM, however, her constant film work helped her build up skills as a comedienne, romantic lead, and heroine. After playing more bad girls in *Beast of the City* and *Red Headed Woman,* she and Clark Gable delighted audiences with the torrid romance enacted in John Ford's *Red Dust.* She proved surprisingly funny playing off such old pros as Wallace Beery, Lionel Barrymore, and Marie Dressler in *Dinner at Eight.* Moreover, she satirized her own image and behind-the-scenes circumstances with wicked zeal in the back-to-back smashes *Hold Your Man* and *Bombshell.*

Although she was one of the top box office stars of the 1930s, Harlow struggled with her personal life and finances.

Her mother and stepfather spent her money as fast as she could make it, and embarrassed and manipulated her constantly. Even worse was her luck with romantic relationships. In contrast to her public image, she was shy and intelligent in private, and desired a more mature man. She found one in Paul Bern. Twenty-one years her senior, Bern was an MGM production chief under wunderkind Irving Thalberg, and was known as "Father Confessor" to many of the actors. The two married on July 2, 1932, but any happiness they experienced did not last. A day after Harlow was confronted by her husband's former common law wife, Bern was found shot to death on September 5, 1932. Although foul play was rumored, the official cause of death was suicide.

Emotionally shattered, Harlow returned to work amid a great deal of public sympathy. While filming, she grew close to veteran cameraman Harold Rosson, 16 years older than Harlow, who had made her look appealing in many of her best films. Their 1933 marriage was a mistake made on the rebound, and the couple divorced eight months later. Biographer David Stenn claimed that she found the love of her life in actor and co-star William Powell. Recently divorced from Carole Lombard, Powell took it slow and found ways to tolerate Harlow's demanding family, although the couple never married.

Harlow demanded that her pay be augmented, and was put on suspension by MGM in 1934. During her time off, she co-wrote a novel with her friend Carey Wilson, titled *Today is Tonight*. In the story of a courageous young wife who hides financial ruin from her recently blinded husband, the heroine tells him that day is night so she can secretly earn a living in a nightclub. Eventually the book was sold to MGM, but a film was never produced. The book was released by Dell in 1965 during the height of the Harlow revival.

Died Young

By the mid-1930s, Harlow began paying a serious price for her blonde bombshell image. In addition to her hair being permanently damaged from too many bleachings—she wore wigs in her last films—the Catholic League of Decency began targeting her films and image as unwholesome. Smartly, she changed her hair color to light brown for 1935's *Riffraff*, co-starring Spencer Tracy. She demonstrated great chemistry with Tracy—they made three films together—and the film and the new look proved a smash. A greater sensation was caused by *Wife Versus Secretary*, in which Harlow played off Clark Gable and Myrna Loy. *Variety*, as quoted by Stenn, noted that "it is Harlow who profits most. She clicks in every scene without going spectacular. She shows she really can act something besides the vamp roles with which she has been chiefly identified." Now playing characters who displayed more heart than open sexuality, she scored big hits in *China Seas, Suzy* (co-starring Cary Grant), and one of the best screwball comedies of the era, *Libeled Lady*. The latter featured Tracy, Loy, and Powell, but Harlow provided most of the film's comic spark and romantic poignance.

Working one picture after another, Harlow's health began to turn sour during the filming of *Personal Property,* which co-starred Robert Taylor. She was slow to recover from a bout with influenza, and nearly died during a simple tooth extraction. Things got worse on the set of *Saratoga.* Experiencing severe abdominal pains and bloating, she was sent home, hospitalized with uremic poisoning, and on June 7, 1937, died of a cerebral edema. At the time, there was much speculation that mother Harlow's Christian Science beliefs had prevented early medical care that might have saved her daughter's life. In fact, however, doctors had been called in from the very start. Later it was determined that her kidneys had been deteriorating for quite some time, possibly the result of a childhood bout with scarlet fever.

Although Harlow never finished the principal filming on *Saratoga,* MGM completed the film, with Mary Dees doubling her body in long shots and Paula Winslowe imitating her voice. The final product was not her best film, but her legions of fans made it the highest grossing film of her career.

Harlow's star rose again when her films were broadcast on television during the 1950s and 1960s. At the peak of this newfound fame, two movies were released about her life, both titled *Harlow,* one starring Carroll Baker and the other Carol Lynley. Neither was successful. Perhaps national audiences were thinking of what Marilyn Monroe (whose look and career were inspired by Harlow's) once said, according to Stenn, when she turned down the lead in a proposed Harlow biopic: "I hope they don't do that to me after I'm gone."

Books

Shipman, David, *The Great Movie Stars—The Golden Years,* Hill and Wang, rev. ed., 1979.

Stenn, David, *Bombshell—The Life and Death of Jean Harlow,* Doubleday, 1993; pp. 195, 245.

Wallace, Irving, et al, *The People's Almanac Presents The Book of Lists 2,* Morrow, 1980; pp. 215-216.

Online

"Harold Rossen," *Internet Movie Database,* http://www.imdb.com/name/nm0005849/bio, (January 3, 2009).

"Jean Harlow," *All Movie Guide,* http://www.allmovie.com/cg/avg.dll?p=avg&sql-2:30456-T1, (January 3, 2009).

"Jean Harlow," *Internet Movie Database,* http://www.imdb.com/name/nm0001318/bio, (January 3, 2009).

"Jean Harlow," *NationMaster.com,* http://www.nationmaster.com/encyclopdeia/JeanHarlow, (January 3, 2009).

The Official Site of Jean Harlow, http://www.jeanharlow.com, (January 3, 2009).

"Paul Bern," *Internet Movie Database,* http://www.imdb.com/name/nm0075960/bio, (January 3, 2009).

"Portrait of Harlow: The Original Blonde Bombshell," *Classic Hollywood Bios,* http://www.classichollywoodbios.com/jeanharlow.htm, (January 3, 2009). □

Lorenz Hart

The American lyricist Lorenz Hart (1895–1943), known for his collaborations with composer Richard Rodgers, was one of musical theater's great creative figures.

In his early twenties, Hart made a living translating German musicals into English. He enjoyed spending time with musical theater people, and in 1918 one of them, small-time producer Philip Leavitt, introduced him to Rodgers, a Columbia student who enjoyed writing songs for collegiate shows. The two quickly landed a song, "Any Old Place with You," in a Broadway show called *A Lonely Romeo* (1919). Hart's rhymes (such as "go to hell for ya"/"Philadelphia") were distant from the romantic formulas that ruled the popular songs of the day. In 1920 the pair contributed songs to the musical *Poor Little Ritz Girl.*

For several years after that, Rodgers and Hart searched for their next hit. They wrote songs for amateur productions and charity events, spreading their names around New York's musical community. By 1925 they were thinking of calling it quits, but they received an offer to write songs for a two-night revue called *The Garrick Gaieties.* Hart responded with "Manhattan," an affectionate chronicle of New York romance ("The great big city's a wondrous toy / Just made for a girl and boy") that remains among his most beloved lyrics. The show was held over into a regular Broadway run, and the careers of Rodgers and Hart were launched in earnest.

Unlike many other composers and lyricists in the 1920s, Hart and Rodgers worked exclusively as a team; until the end of Hart's life, neither collaborated with anyone else. Between 1925 and 1931 they turned out songs prolifically for Broadway shows that were often defined more by the presence of a star vocalist than by a strong narrative. Even very early in his career, however, Hart was breaking new ground as a lyricist. For the 1927 musical *A Connecticut Yankee,* based on Mark Twain's novel *A Connecticut Yankee in King Arthur's Court,* he concocted the unique "Thou Swell," a mixture of contemporary and antiquated language that baffled producers at the time but has fascinated performers of Broadway song ever since. Other Rodgers and Hart standards of the late 1920s included "You Took Advantage of Me," from the show *Present Arms* (1928), and "*With a Song in My Heart,*" from *Spring Is Here* (1929).

Hart was both a witty wordsmith and a key innovator in the history of the American musical. His outlandish rhymes were rivaled for sophistication only by those of Ira Gershwin, and it was said that he could rhyme anything—and would. Hart and Rodgers expanded the creative boundaries of the musical genre. Yet Hart also had a way with simpler melancholy lyrics of loneliness that were, perhaps, close to his own experiences. The list of Rodgers and Hart standards for which Hart provided the lyrics is a long one, including such widely familiar titles as "Manhattan," "With a Song in My Heart," "The Lady Is a Tramp," "My Funny Valentine," "Thou Swell," and "Bewitched, Bothered and Bewildered."

Wrote Songs at Camp

Lorenz Hart, known to his friends as Larry and to his family as Lorry, was born on May 2, 1895, in New York City. Of Jewish background, he was a descendant on his mother's side of the German poet Heinrich Heine. Hart's father, Max, was an immigrant (his German surname was Hertz) who prospered by keeping his hand in a variety of enterprises, some of them of dubious legality. Growing up in Manhattan's Harlem neighborhood, Hart swung from luxury to straitened circumstances and then back again, with plenty of alcohol always on hand in the family home. He showed poetic talent early on, and at summer camp in upstate New York he wrote songs and skits for his fellow campers. Hart took classes at Columbia University in the mid-1910s but never graduated.

Moved to Hollywood

Rodgers and Hart continued to turn out hits in the early 1930s, including "Dancing on the Ceiling," from the musical *Ever Green* (1930). But the Depression slowed their activities as well as the stream of income that had primed Hart's late-night lifestyle. Living with his mother in a Manhattan apartment after his father's death, Hart would wait until his mother had gone to bed and then begin a round of partying that might last all night. Later he had a soundproof door installed in his own area of their apartment so that he could hold parties at home without disturbing her. Rodgers and Hart headed for Hollywood and wrote several film musicals. Some were successful, such as *Love Me Tonight* (1932), which spawned the hit "Isn't It Romantic?," but Hollywood did not suit Hart as well as his native city did.

While they were in Hollywood, Rodgers composed a tune with a gracefully descending pentatonic refrain, and Hart set several sets of lyrics to it. Metro-Goldwyn-Mayer producer Jack Robbins suggested that a simple commercial lyric would turn the song into a hit. "You mean something corny like 'Blue Moon?,'" Hart asked scornfully (the remark was quoted in a *Dictionary of Literary Biography* essay), but he complied with one of his simplest and most affecting lyrics. Despite Hart's low opinion of the song, "Blue Moon" became one of Rodgers and Hart's biggest hits, and the only one not directly connected with the larger entity of a film or stage show.

As Broadway recovered from its economic doldrums, Rodgers and Hart returned with new shows. Many of them were more ambitious in scope than their frothy 1920s musicals, and their production slowed to one or two new shows per year. *Jumbo* (1935) was a spectacular circus-musical hybrid that bombed at the box office but generated the ever-popular "The Most Beautiful Girl in the World" and "My Romance," the latter a song that showed the songwriting chemistry between Rodgers and Hart in its combination of Hart's text mentioning a "constantly surprising refrain" with Rodgers's ingenious harmonic twists.

Babes in Arms (1937), featuring choreography by George Balanchine, was something of an apotheosis of Rodgers and Hart's early shows, and it was densely packed with songs that became classics: another simple romantic sentiment in "Where or When," a bit of blues-diva attitude in "The Lady Is a Tramp," and a counter-to-type love song in "My Funny Valentine," another of Hart's most beloved lyrics. Hart's love songs were not matched by real-life romances; he never married, and some historians have concluded that he lived the concealed life of a homosexual in a time that was unsympathetic to that orientation.

Expanded Scope of Musical

With their last few shows, Rodgers and Hart took the musical in new directions. *The Boys from Syracuse* (1938) was the first of several musicals drawn on plays by Shakespeare (in this case *A Comedy of Errors*), and *Pal Joey* (1940), based on a set of downbeat short stories by John O'Hara, was among the first serious musicals with a naturalistic setting. It featured another Rodgers and Hart standard, "Bewitched, Bothered and Bewildered," as well as the intricately topical "Zip!" The show received mixed though generally positive reviews. After this time, Hart began to act in an alcohol-fueled and increasingly erratic manner.

He never lost his touch as a songwriter, and the Rodgers and Hart show *By Jupiter* (1942) was one of their biggest successes of all. Some have taken its signature song, "Nobody's Heart" ("Nobody's heart belongs to me / Heigh-ho, who cares?"), as an expression of Hart's own feelings. The following year, however, Rodgers had the idea for a new musical, based on the play *Green Grow the Lilacs,* a bright romance with a bucolic small-town setting. The hard-bitten Hart balked at the show that became *Oklahoma!,* and, with Hart now disappearing for days at a time on alcoholic binges, Rodgers was in no mood to push him. He took as a partner the lyricist with whom he would work for the rest of his life, Oscar Hammerstein II.

Rogers and Hart reunited later that year to write new songs for a revival of *A Connecticut Yankee,* but at the show's premiere Hart was ejected for causing a disturbance by singing loudly while pacing the aisles. His movements over the next few days are uncertain, but finally he was found half-conscious in his apartment, suffering from pneumonia. Penicillin, not yet officially approved, was flown in and administered at the order of First Lady Eleanor Roosevelt, but Hart died on the evening of December 22, 1943. The sheer intelligence of Hart's lyrics affected numerous songwriters who followed—even those, such as Stephen Sondheim, who affected a dislike for his work. "Which lyricist does Sondheim echo in his own labyrinthine rhyming and too-hip-for-the-room allusions?," asked Richard Corliss of *Time.* "In style and tone he is an avatar of Hart, and should be proud of it."

Books

American Song Lyricists, 1920–1960: Dictionary of Literary Biography, vol. 265, edited by Philip Furia, Gale, 2002.
Furia, Philip, *The Poets of Tin Pan Alley,* Oxford, 1992.
Nolan, Frederick, *Lorenz Hart on Broadway,* Oxford, 1994.
Thou Swell, Thou Witty: The Life and Lyrics of Lorenz Hart, edited by Dorothy Hart, Harper & Row, 1976.

Periodicals

Opera News, May 1995, p. 58.
Time, July 8, 2002.

Online

"Lorenz Hart: Biography," Songwriters' Hall of Fame, http://www.songwritershalloffame.org/index.php/exhibits/bio/C66 (January 18, 2009). □

Anna Held

The Polish-born French-American actress Anna Held (c. 1870–1918) was among the biggest theatrical stars in the United States during the first decade of the twentieth century.

Held was partly responsible for the annual variety-show extravaganza known as the Ziegfeld Follies, having suggested the idea to her professional and romantic partner, promoter Florenz Ziegfeld. For many years she was recognizable to theatergoers all over the United States, and to many in France as well, for her seductive stage presence and sexual humor, much of it worked into hit songs like "I Just Can't Make My Eyes Behave." Held helped Ziegfeld build his show business empire, but that was just one chapter in a colorful life that took her from rags to riches and finally to the battlefields of World War I.

Concealed Polish Birth

Helene Anna Held was the sole surviving child of a Jewish glove maker, Shimmle Held, who used the name Maurice, and his wife, Yvonne. She spent the first part of her life in Warsaw but later concealed this fact, insisting that she was

company of impresario Jacob Adler, and it was as a chorus girl that her career was launched. Soon she was playing lead roles. Her fellow chorus girls were jealous of her success, and she was attacked and beaten on one occasion. But from then on, there was no stopping her.

Held returned to Paris after Smith's Theater, where she had been appearing in *Gypsy Girl,* burned to the ground, killing 17 patrons. She had no trouble finding employment in the city's music halls, even though she refused to join the ranks of the *grandes horizontales* (literally, great horizontal ones, meaning courtesans) like some of her rivals. She became one of the top attractions in Paris, sometimes appearing at the finest music hall venue of all, the Folies-Bergère, and also making tours of western Europe's major capital cities. She cultivated a daring new feminine image, appearing in public riding the newly invented bicycle. In 1893 she met the aging Uruguayan playboy and gambler, Maximo Carrera, marrying him and converting officially to Catholicism (although she was never very religious). The marriage produced a daughter, Liane, who was probably conceived before the wedding. The youngster was raised in a convent, and Held was mostly absent from her life.

Arrival Advertised on Trash Receptacles

In 1896 Held was appearing at the Palace Theater in London when she began receiving flowers, then flowers draped with a diamond bracelet, from an American named Florenz Ziegfeld Jr. Soon he bribed his way into her dressing room. The two, Golden observed (all quotations, unless otherwise noted, come from her biography, *Anna Held and the Birth of Ziegfeld's Broadway*), "had a lot in common. Both were young, attractive, and ambitious. Both were risk-takers and rule-breakers. And both loved show business with every ounce of their beings." Ziegfeld resolved to bring Held to Broadway, paying off debts she had incurred during her marriage to Carrera and trying unsuccessfully to break her contract with the Folies-Bergère. Held eventually walked out on that contract, while Ziegfeld festooned trash cans on the streets of New York with posters reading "GO TO HELD!"

In her New York debut, *A Parlor Match,* Held played a spurious "ghost" who was made to emerge from a cabinet in the home of a dimwitted millionaire. The part was constructed to allow her to perform her first signature song, "Won't You Come and Play with Me?," which was actually written in German and then translated into English. Through its lyrics ("Won't you come and play with me? / For I have such a way with me."), the song exploited Held's mix of coquettishness and confidence. For her first few years in America, Held delivered songs like these in a Parisian accent, which added to her image of sophistication and pleasantly naughty sexuality.

Held was a uniquely talented performer, but Ziegfeld's promotional genius contributed mightily to her success. Both believed there was no such thing as bad publicity, and they claimed to be disappointed if a day passed when Held's name did not appear at least once in the pages of New York's sensational newspapers. Ziegfeld's first publicity stunt was his best: he told reporters that Held bathed in fresh milk, adding what he thought was the realistic detail that he had had to return one shipment to a dairy because

French by birth. As a result, her date of birth remains uncertain. The date of March 18, 1873, was given in many early accounts of her life, but her gravestone gave the year as 1872. Held's biographer, Eve Golden, whose examination of the roles Held played as a teen is extensive, contended that she was probably born around 1870.

It was not only the common deceptive tendencies of major stars in this respect that might have made Held lie about her age. Her life in Warsaw likely involved major trauma, for her family was forced to flee Poland for Paris during a serious outbreak of anti-Jewish violence in 1881. She would also hide her ancestral affiliation with Judaism for much of her life, even though being Jewish was not a serious impediment to success in American show business. At first Held experienced Paris as a wonderland, but soon she was forced to go to work as a factory seamstress. There were no child labor laws in France at the time, and working conditions were horrific. But Held sometimes entertained her coworkers with songs she had learned, and they told her she could earn extra money by singing for tips on the street.

After Held's father died in 1884, she and her mother moved to London. They were unable to locate the relative they thought was living there, and with Yvonne Held now also in poor health they soon found themselves in dire straits. When her mother died, Anna Held was on her own—at age 12, as she told the story, but actually in her mid-teens. A neighbor who knew that Anna spoke Yiddish and could sing offered to help her join the Jewish theater

the milk had gone sour. The ploy touched off a milk-bathing fad, and the revelation that the whole story was a hoax (when the outraged dairy owner sued for libel) did nothing to diminish Held's burgeoning name recognition. In 1897 Held divorced Carrera and moved into Ziegfeld's 13-room suite at the Ansonia Hotel; the two were never formally wed, but their relationship was recognized in 1904 as a common-law marriage.

Although her first few shows were only moderately successful, Held had a major hit with *Papa's Wife* in 1899. For that show Ziegfeld outfitted Held in the latest Parisian fashions and exploited news stories that she was one of the first women to drive a car of her own: she drove off the stage at the end of the first act. Ziegfeld never quite matched the milk bath story for publicity, but continued to feed the press colorful Held stories. A fall from her bicycle became the occasion for a claim that she had jumped off in order to stop a runaway carriage that was headed in the direction of a retired jurist. At one point, Ziegfeld probably staged the theft of Held's jewels from a train headed for Cleveland; they were returned to her under murky circumstances. Held, who was not let in on the details of the plan, was not amused.

Held spent a lot of time on the road, for in pre-cinema days touring shows were crucial to the theatrical economy. In New York itself, her biggest shows were 1905's *The Parisian Model* (in which she introduced another hit song, "I Just Can't Make My Eyes Behave") and 1908's *Miss Innocence.* The humor in Held's shows, often based on mild double entendres, seems tame today but was sometimes attacked as indecent. Such attacks only increased the take at the box office. According to Golden, the *Boston Telegraph,* in its review of *The Parisian Model,* pointed out that "Bostonians are stumbling over one another in the clamor to have their moral sense shocked."

Suggested Idea for Ziegfeld Follies

Held occasionally wrote song lyrics herself, but her major offstage contribution was the formation of her backup singers and dancers into an ongoing group called the Anna Held Girls. They were part of the inspiration for the Ziegfeld Follies, an annual spectacular staged on Broadway between 1907 and 1931. The Follies were originally Held's idea, based on her experiences at the Folies-Bergère, and on whose elaborate stage shows the Ziegfeld Follies were modeled. Held herself appeared in the Ziegfeld Follies only once, in a short film included in the 1910 show. That was the year Halley's Comet dazzled Americans with its appearance on its once-in-76-years-cycle, and the film showed an animated comet with Held's face replacing its nucleus.

By that time, the personal relationship between Held and the womanizing Ziegfeld had deteriorated, owing to his very public appearances with showgirl Lillian Lorraine, whose real name was Mary Ann Brennan. Held had looked the other way when Ziegfeld strayed briefly in the past, but when he installed Lorraine in a room one floor above his and Held's suite at the Ansonia, she packed her bags and moved out. They were divorced, without the benefit of ever marrying, in 1912, but their professional relationship was too important to both to give it up completely, and Ziegfeld continued to manage the performer's career. The break became permanent, however, at a New Year's Eve party at the Astor Hotel in 1913 where Ziegfeld ignored both women and took up with Billie Burke, who had come to the party as the date of writer W. Somerset Maugham; Ziegfeld and Burke later married.

Held's durable popularity remained undamaged on both sides of the Atlantic, and there were few other actresses who were able to command top dollar for the better part of two decades. Held had always proclaimed her love of France and espoused her French identity, even when confronted with evidence to the contrary, such as a 1908 Detroit newspaper interview with a neighbor who had known her in Poland. World War I, however, changed her life. As the conflict deepened into the grind of trench warfare, Held made physically hazardous journeys to the battlefront to entertain French troops, and she raised funds for relief operations. In 1916 she found time to star in the Broadway musical *Follow Me,* produced by Ziegfeld's arch-rivals, Lee and Jacob Shubert. She also appeared that year in the Hollywood silent *Madame la Presidente,* which was her only feature film role.

Follow Me received good reviews and went on a successful road tour, but Held complained of unusual aches and pains during its run. Early in 1918, in Milwaukee, she collapsed on stage. Diagnosed with multiple myeloma, she was confined to a room at New York's Savoy Hotel as press gossips speculated as to whether Ziegfeld would visit. He did not, and she died on August 12, 1918. Memories of Held were stirred by actress Luise Rainer's portrayal of her in the 1936 film *The Great Ziegfeld,* for which Rainer won an Academy Award. Interest in her remarkable career flowered anew as historians began to investigate the roots of Broadway and modern American theater.

Books

Golden, Eve, *Anna Held and the Birth of Ziegfeld's Broadway,* University Press of Kentucky, 2000.

Slide, Anthony, *Encyclopedia of Vaudeville,* Greenwood, 1994.

Periodicals

Palm Beach Post, July 23, 2000, p. J6.

Online

"Ziegfeld 101: Anna Held," Musicals 101, http://www.musicals101.com/ziegheld.htm (December 28, 2008).□

Zelma Cleota Henderson

American civil rights figure Zelma Henderson (1920–2008) served as a plaintiff in the 1954 school desegregation case *Brown v. Board of Education of Topeka, Kansas* described by the National Park Service on their website as "one of the most pivotal opinions ever rendered by [the Supreme Court]." Herself a

victim of discrimination, Henderson participated in the case in the hopes of encouraging better understanding between black and white schoolchildren. The effects of the legal victory—and Henderson's legacy—can be seen in the integrated schools present today throughout the United States.

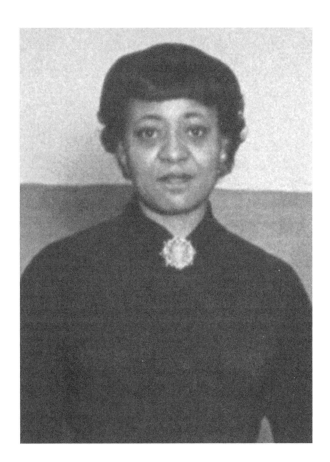

The daughter of farmers, Zelma Henderson was born Zelma Cleota Hurst on February 29, 1920, in Colby, Kansas. Colby, a small town located in western Kansas, was home to only two African American families at the time of Henderson's birth. While Henderson was still a child, her family relocated to nearby Oakley, Kansas. Because contemporary Kansas law allowed only for the segregation of elementary schools in communities with populations exceeding 15,000—a figure neither Colby nor Oakley contained—Henderson attended integrated schools. Henderson's son Donald commented in his mother's *New York Times* obituary that Henderson "never had a problem out there" despite being one of few African Americans in her community.

After completing schooling in Oakley, Henderson moved to Kansas's capital, Topeka, where she enrolled at the Kansas Vocational School to study cosmetology. In Topeka, Henderson had her first widespread experiences with segregation and discrimination. Unlike the previous schools she had attended, the Kansas Vocational School was segregated. Topeka also was home to segregated movie theaters and other public facilities—the municipal swimming pool banned African Americans except for one day per year—although the level of segregation was not as high as in the southern United States. Henderson found when she applied for the clerical jobs for which her typing skills qualified her, she was instead offered domestic work; in fact, African Americans in Topeka at the time were actively discouraged from taking secretarial courses due to a supposed lack of jobs. In 1943, Henderson began a home-based beauty salon; that same year, she married Andrew Henderson, an employee of the Goodyear Tire and Rubber Company. The couple had a daughter, Vicki, two years later, soon followed by a son, Donald.

Beginnings of *Brown v. Board of Education*

During the years leading up to the filing of *Brown v. Board of Education*, the National Association for the Advancement of Colored People (NAACP) and others had challenged the legality of segregation. In fact, the first legal challenge to school segregation by African Americans had preceded the American Civil War with the case of *Roberts v. City of Boston*, and Kansans had initiated 11 cases challenging school segregation in the state between 1881 and 1949. Perhaps the best known and unquestionably the most influential decision regarding segregation prior to *Brown v. Board of Education* was the 1892 case *Plessy v. Ferguson*. This decision established the "separate-but-equal" doctrine that characterized segregated public institutions ranging from restaurants to railway cars throughout parts of the United States during the first half of the 20th century.

By the 1940s, NAACP leaders such as Thurgood Marshall had decided to push for a legal end to segregation, despite concerns by many African Americans, including teachers, regarding the practical effects of desegregation. James T. Patterson noted in *Brown v. Board of Education: A Civil Rights Milestone and Its Troubled Legacy* that many African American believed that "the NAACP...should contest inequality, not segregation. It should push to ensure the "equal" part of "separate-but-equal."

Zelma Henderson, however, disagreed with the wisdom of the separate-but-equal doctrine. Because the population of Topeka well exceeded the requisite 15,000, Henderson's children were required to attend a segregated elementary school. (Kansas law did not require the segregation of junior or high schools, although many school activities such as dances and sports remained segregated.) The forced bussing to a distant school frustrated Henderson, who remembered her own positive experiences as a student at integrated schools. Writing in *The Topeka Capital-Journal*, Barbara Hollingsworth noted that "it wasn't the quality of the education that bothered Henderson...but black and white children needed to have the opportunity to play together and understand each other."

By 1950, Henderson had become a member of the NAACP. That year, the Topeka chapter of the NAACP under the direction of McKinley Burnett began organizing a class-action lawsuit challenging the state's school segregation laws. When Henderson was asked to become one of the plaintiffs in the case, she soon agreed; ultimately, the suit—deliberately named for its sole male plaintiff, the Reverend Oliver Brown—would represent thirteen total Topeka parents. In a 2004 *Associated Press* news story marking the fiftieth anniversary of the decision in *Brown v. Board of Education,* Henderson explained her reasons for signing onto the case this way: "I wanted my children to know all races like I did. It means a lot to a person's outlook on life. No inferiority complex at all, that's what I wanted for my children as far as race was concerned." The case was officially filed in February 1951. The U.S. District Court that initially tried the case found against the parents represented by *Brown v. Board of Education* based on the precedent set by *Plessy v. Ferguson,* and NAACP lawyers quickly moved to file an appeal. The case moved on to the United States Supreme Court.

A Hard Won Victory

At about the time of the filing of *Brown v. Board of Education,* the NAACP had filed similar challenges to school segregation around the country. The first of these had begun in Clarendon County, South Carolina, in 1948 and addressed the woefully inadequate conditions present in segregated African American schools in the county. The case was initially thrown out, but was reorganized as the class-action suit *Briggs v. Elliot* in 1951. That same year, three other lawsuits in addition to *Brown v. Board of Education* challenged school segregation: *Belton v. Gebhart* in Wilmington, Delaware; *Davis v. County School Board of Prince Edward County* in Prince Edward County, Maryland; and *Bolling v. C. Melvin Sharpe* in Washington, D.C. Because all five suits sought similar legal outcomes, they were bundled with *Brown v. Board of Education* for the purposes of the Supreme Court trial, first held in December 1952.

NAACP civil rights lawyer Thurgood Marshall—who would later go on to become the first African American justice of the Supreme Court—argued the case for the prosecution, and prominent lawyer John W. Davis led the defensive team. The prosecution's arguments lie in the rights granted by the Fourteenth Amendment to the U.S. Constitution, which granted all native-born residents of the United States full citizenship rights and was intended to grant citizenship to former slaves after the Civil War. Specifically, Marshall claimed that segregation encroached on the right to equal protection under the law granted by the amendment, arguing that African American children suffered from a sense of inferiority brought about by segregation.

As with many controversial cases, however, political and social issues seemed certain to inform the court's decision as much as pure interpretation of the law. The court's overall reluctance to rule on the hot button issue led to a delay; eventually, the court ordered that the case be argued anew in December 1953. During the interlude, Chief Justice Fred Vinson—who had opposed forcing the legal desegregation of schools—had died and was replaced by Earl Warren, a California governor with a history of supporting civil rights legislation. Despite the support of a narrow majority of the nine justices in December 1953, the court again delayed a decision, as Warren hoped to gain the support of the dissenting justices in order to deter protest from southern states. By May, Warren had his wish,

and the court issued a unanimous decision striking down school segregation on May 17, 1954. In his decision, as referenced from the *Find Law* website, Warren wrote, "We conclude that in the field of public education the doctrine of 'separate but equal' has no place. Separate educational facilities are inherently unequal." Zelma Henderson and her fellow plaintiffs had won.

A Legacy of Equality

Schools in Topeka had began taking steps to integrate even before the Supreme Court handed down its decision in *Brown v. Board of Education.* The integration was, in Henderson's opinion, completed quickly and smoothly; her own two children finished out their elementary school educations not in the segregated schools in which they had begun, but in fully integrated schools. African American teachers and administrators in Topeka began rising to prominence, with the first African American principal of a formerly segregated white school taking office with great success in 1962. Henderson returned to her regular life, remaining active in her church and community. Henderson's husband passed away in 1971, followed in 1984 by her daughter, Vicki.

Henderson rarely discussed her involvement in the case until the later years of her life when, as the last surviving plaintiff of *Brown v. Board of Education,* Henderson and her views on the case and on the state of civil rights in the United States were often sought. In 2005, the United States Postal Service honored civil rights landmarks, including the decision of *Brown v. Board of Education,* with a series of commemorative postage stamps entitled "To Form a More Perfect Union." In an *Associated Press* news story about the event, Henderson expressed her approval of the set by commenting, "I think we all need reminders of what some of our people went through."

Henderson was diagnosed with pancreatic cancer around the beginning of April 2008, and passed away as a result of the illness about six weeks later, on May 20, in Topeka. Her funeral took place a few days later at St. John's African Methodist Episcopal Church in Topeka, and she was interred at Mount Hope Cemetery. Henderson's death was much noted by the public due to the accomplishments that Henderson and her fellow plaintiffs had made over fifty years before. In an article which appeared in the *States News Service,* speaking at Henderson's funeral, Kansas Governor Kathleen Sebelius stated, "Mrs. Henderson reminds us that ordinary people can do extraordinary things; that change comes with acts of courage and moral stamina in the face of daunting odds.... Henderson and her 12 fellow plaintiffs changed the face of America." Unquestionably, Henderson's legacy lies in her contributions to the radical changes made during the civil rights era and the lasting impact of the case with which she will long be associated on the students of schools throughout the United States.

Books

Patterson, James T., *Brown v. Board of Education: A Civil Rights Milestone and Its Troubled Legacy,* Oxford University Press, 2001.

Periodicals

Associated Press, April 30, 2004.
Associated Press, August 30, 2005.
The New York Times, May 22, 2008.
States News Service, May 28, 2008.
The Topeka Capital-Journal, May 21, 2008.

Online

"Brown v. Board of Education Court Cases in Prelude to Brown, 1849–1949" *Brown Foundation for Educational Equity,* http://brownvboard.org/research/handbook/prelude/prelude.htm (January 5, 2009).
"Brown v. Board Finding Aid Part 8.1" *Kansas State Historical Society,* http://www.kshs.org/research/collections/documents/personalpapers/findingaids/brownvboard/BrownPart81Bios.htm#HendersonZ (January 5, 2009).
"U.S. Supreme Court: Brown v. Board of Education, 347 U.S. 483 (1954)" *FindLaw: Cases and Codes,* http://caselaw.lp.findlaw.com/scripts/getcase.pl?court=US&vol=347&invol=483 (January 5, 2009).
"Zelma Cleota Hurst Henderson," *Find a Grave Memorial,* http://www.findagrave.com (January 4, 2009).☐

Robert William Holley

American scientist Robert Holley (1922–1993) shared the 1968 Nobel Prize in physiology of medicine for his efforts in determining the structure and sequence of ribonucleic acid, or RNA. The biochemist led a team of researchers who painstakingly isolated, sequenced, and determined the structure of the alanine transfer RNA molecule, contributing greatly to the then-nascent field of genetics. Later in his career, Holley conducted research into cell growth and division that supported the growing scientific understanding of cancer and aided in efforts to develop more effective treatments for that disease.

One of four brothers, Robert William Holley was born on January 28, 1922, in Urbana, Illinois. Both his father, Charles Elmer Holley, and his mother, Viola Esther (Wolfe) Holley were teachers. Growing up in Illinois, California, and Idaho, Holley developed an early interest in nature and life. By his teenage years, Holley had returned to Illinois. He attended Urbana High School—where he was the school's yearbook photographer—and graduated in 1938. He subsequently enrolled at the University of Illinois to study chemistry and received a bachelor's degree in the subject in 1942.

Holley then enrolled at Cornell University in Ithaca, New York, to pursue graduate work in organic chemistry. The advent of World War II temporarily halted Holley's graduate work. From 1944 to 1946, the scientist served as a civilian researcher at the United States Office of Research and Development at Cornell University Medical College; in this role, he was part of the five-member team that was responsible for the first successful chemical synthesis of penicillin. After the close of international hostilities, Holley returned to his regular graduate studies. He completed his doctorate in organic chemistry under Professor Alfred T. Blomquist at Cornell in 1947, and then traveled to Washington State College in Pullman, Washington, to pursue studies as an American Chemistry Society Postdoctoral Fellow.

During this era, Holley also met chemist and math teacher Ann Lenore Dworkin. The couple married on March 3, 1945, and later had one son, Frederick. Holley's biography in *Les Prix Nobel en 1968* noted that the family "especially enjoy[ed] the ocean and the mountains," a reflection of Holley's lifelong interest in the natural world.

Began Research into RNA

After completing his fellowship in Washington in 1948, Holley returned to New York State, where he took up an assistant professorship at the Geneva Experiment Station, a division of Cornell University. Holley advanced to an associate professorship in 1950; on sabbatical for the 1955–1956 academic years, Holley held the post of Guggenheim Memorial Fellow at the California Institute of Technology's Biology Division in Pasadena, California.

Modern genetic research had its genesis in 1941 with the discovery that genes housed the information needed to make proteins; later, it was determined that proteins controlled various chemical reactions within the body that established individual variation among people. In 1953, James D. Watson, Francis Crick, and Maurice Wilkins identified the double-helix structure of DNA, which was hypothesized to be made up of chemical chains called nucleotides. These nucleotide sequences were thought to hold the information for the sequencing of specific amino acids, and thus be the building blocks of proteins. From the mid-1950s, a flurry of scientific activity into the structure and sequencing of different genetic material took place, and it was in this rapidly-changing scientific world that Holley would make his mark.

At the California Institute of Technology, Holley began researching protein synthesis, with a focus on the composition of nucleic acids, which house genetic information within cells. These experiments marked Holley's first explorations into the specific field of molecular chemistry that would later define his career. The *World of Chemistry* proposed that "his course that may have been inspired, at least in part, by Crick's suggestion that adaptor molecules of some sort must be involved in the transition of genetic information into proteins."

As a result, Holley became interested in the structure of transfer RNA (tRNA), the substance responsible for the transfer of specific amino acids into ribosomes, which then use that genetic information to create protein molecules. Speaking in his 1968 Nobel lecture as recorded on the Nobel Prize website, Holley stated that "for a chemist, the existence of amino acid-specific, low molecular weight RNAs was very intriguing. It seemed possible that these RNAs might be small enough to permit detailed structural studies. This would be of great interest because it is the nucleotide sequences of nucleic acids that provide specificity and enable nucleic acids to carry out their many vital functions."

Back in Cornell, Holley became a Research Chemist at the Plant, Soil, and Nutrition Laboratory of the United States Department of Agriculture, and was later promoted to a Professor of Biochemistry and Molecular Biology in 1964. In this role, Holley led a team of researchers in efforts to isolate a small quantity of tRNA from a given substance; because tRNA varies relative to each of the twenty amino acids, one form of RNA had to be chosen for study. Holley selected yeast due to its ready availability in large quantities. Indeed, those large quantities were needed: Holley successfully isolated a tiny quantity of tRNA from 300 pounds of yeast, a feat requiring three years of work. Of the three types of tRNA isolated by the researchers—alanine, tyrosine, and valine—alanine was selected for further study due to its higher level of purity. Writing in *The Scribner Encyclopedia of American Lives Thematic Series: the 1960s,* Adi R. Ferrara noted that "since both molecular biology and genetics were in their infancy in the early 1960s, Holley's task was momentous."

With alanine tRNA successfully isolated, Holley and his team turned their attention to determining the sequence of each of the substances contained within the molecule's 77 subunits. This task required another four years of intensive work, in the course of which Holley was also able to determine how alanine was fixed to its tRNA molecule. Holley's *New York Times* obituary noted that these years

of work were summed up "in a two-sentence abstract in a scientific journal in 1965: "The complete nucleotide sequence of an alanine transfer RNA, isolated from yeast, has been determined. This is the first nucleic acid for which the structure is known."" (It would later be learned that all tRNA have structures similar to one another.) This discovery contributed greatly to the understanding of the role of protein synthesis in genetics; within five years of Holley's findings, scientists had fully explained the process of genetic coding through further research, with Holley's work playing a significant role in that explanation.

In 1968, Holley shared the Nobel Prize in Physiology of Medicine with scientists Marshall W. Nirenberg and Har Gobind Khorana. Each man had independently conducted research into related topics in the field of genetics—Nirenberg into the nature and function of messenger RNA, and Khorana into the synthesis of nucleic acid as it related to the genetic code. Holley, receiving the award in recognition of his work with tRNA, shared the accompanying prize money with fellow researcher Elizabeth Keller, who had determined the structure of tRNA based on the completed alanine sequencing, and reputedly shared that discovery with Holley in a Christmas card.

Later Research into Cell Growth and Division

Holley remained at Cornell until 1966, serving as head of the Biochemistry Department during the 1965–1966 academic year. In 1966, he took a sabbatical to travel to the Salk Institute for Biological Studies and the Scripps Clinic and Research Foundation in La Jolla, California. He would remain at the Salk Institute as a fellow and professor until the time of his death over 25 years later, as well as serving as an adjunct professor at the University of California at San Diego from 1969.

At the Salk Institute during the 1970s, Holley began conducting research into the nature of cell growth in humans and other mammals. This research held important ramifications for the understanding of the nature of cancerous cell growth, as well as the way that the body heals large and small injuries. Although cell growth is a natural function of the body, cancerous cells grow rapidly and are uncontrolled; Holley's studies sought to determine both the factors that contributed to this rapid growth and those that could inhibit cell growth and division.

This research first led to the conclusion that peptide and steroid hormones—proteins derived from amino acids that serve a variety of functions within the body—were, along with nutrients, responsible for the growth and division of cells. The *World of Chemistry* observed that "he found that types of cells prone to develop into tumors responded dramatically to these growth factors, dividing rapidly in response to very low hormone levels." Further experimentation showed that hormones caused different reactions in different types of cells and that cell density played a key role in cell growth, as well as that certain growth factors supported the creation of proteins. Holley also considered non-hormonal factors in cell growth, including the role of sugars and amino acids, finding that only certain amino acids such as glutamine exerted a noticeable influence on the process.

Holley worked to find the molecular sequence of some of the cell growth and inhibiting factors that he studied, much as he had done with tRNA years previously. Improved technology eased the process, and Holley successfully sequenced molecules including a growth inhibitor in monkey cells that was later shown to be identical to a human growth factor, TGF-beta 2.

In addition to determining factors in cell growth, Holley considered those that inhibited the development of cells. He found that these inhibitors prevented DNA from replicating and hence providing the needed information for cell growth; the inhibitors also led to increased production of certain proteins. Holley determined that despite the equalizing effects of cell growth and inhibiting factors on DNA, the production of hormones as a result of these factors was unaffected. Extant cells continued to grow in the presence of a growth inhibitor, but cell division came to a halt. Dr. Brian Henderson of the Salk Institute described the important of the research in Holley's *New York Times* obituary by saying that the "discoveries deepened our understanding of cell growth and opened new possibilities for the diagnosis and treatment of cancer and other diseases."

Holley died at the age of 71 on February 11, 1993, at home in Los Gatos, California as the result of lung cancer. During his career, his research into RNA earned Holley a great deal of recognition in addition to the prestigious Nobel Prize. In 1965, Holley won the Albert Lasker Award in Basic Medical Research and the Distinguished Service Award of the U.S. Department of Agriculture, and in 1967 he received the U.S. Steel Foundation Award in Molecular Biology of the National Academy of Sciences. The scientist held membership in numerous professional organizations, including the National Academy of Sciences, the American Chemical Society, the American Society of Biological Chemists, the American Association for the Advancement of Science, and the American Academy of Art and Sciences.

Books

Ferrara, Adi R., "Holley, Robert William," *The Scribner Encyclopedia of American Lives Thematic Series: The 1960s,* Charles Scribner's Sons, 2003.

Fisher, John E., "Robert William Holley," *The Scribner Encyclopedia of American Lives, Volume 3: 1991–1993,* Charles Scribner's Sons, 2001.

"Robert William Holley," *Science and Its Times, Vol. 7: 1950–Present,* Gale Group, 2000.

"Robert William Holley," *World of Chemistry*, Thomson Gale, 2006.

Periodicals

The New York Times, February 14, 1993.

Online

"Genetics," *Encyclopedia Brittanica,* http://search.eb.com/ (January 16, 2009).

Holley, Robert W., "Alanine transfer RNA," *Nobel Lecture, December 12, 1968,* http://nobelprize.org/nobel_prizes/medicine/laureates/1968/khorana-lecture.html (January 16, 2009).

"Robert W. Holley," *Les Prix Nobel/Nobel Lectures,* http://nobelprize.org (January 16, 2009).□

Henry Clay Hooker

American rancher Henry Clay Hooker (1828–1907) was a leading citizen of Arizona in the decades before it became a state. A livestock herder who earned a small fortune supplying beef to the U.S. Army in the 1860s, Hooker founded the Sierra Bonita Ranch near Tucson in 1872, which became the first cattle ranch in Arizona.

Henry Clay Hooker was born on January 10, 1828, in Hinsdale, a town in the southwestern corner of New Hampshire on the Connecticut River. His family was descended from one Reverend Thomas Hooker, a Puritan who emigrated from England in 1633 to Massachusetts Bay Colony, but left with a hundred or so followers in 1636 to found the Colony of Connecticut.

Owned California Store

Little is known about Hooker's early life. He apparently moved West at the onset of the California Gold Rush of 1848, and was a store proprietor in Placerville by 1853. Known back then as Hangtown, Placerville is in the Sacramento metropolitan area and earned its original name for its strict application of frontier justice to captured miscreants. During the Gold Rush years, it was one of the largest cities in California.

During his later years Hooker was often referred to in the press as "Colonel," which probably stemmed from his service in the Union Army during the U.S. Civil War. Back in Placerville, he suffered heavy financial losses when a fire swept through the town and destroyed his store. He knew that the new center of mining activity was Carson City, Nevada, and that miners there were undersupplied. Using his savings, he bought 500 turkeys and drove them across the Sierra Nevada Mountains and over the state line, and was able to sell them at a handsome profit to miners subsisting mainly on bacon and beans.

From there, Hooker headed south and east to what was then called Arizona Territory. It was sparsely populated by Native Americans and a few Spanish ranching and mining settlements, but had come under U.S. federal jurisdiction and was also the site of a few scattered military outposts. Its most inhabitable region ran along what is today the U.S. southern border with Mexico. Arizona was first explored by Spanish conquistador Francisco Vàsquez de Coronado in the 1540s, and then settled by missionaries who worked to convert the indigenous Apache to Roman Catholicism. Spanish colonists moved into the area in late 1600s to exploit Arizona's veins of silver ore, and after Mexico declared itself independent from Spain in 1821 the area was part of the Mexican state of Sonora. It came under American control after the conclusion of the Mexican-American War in 1848. Five years later, in 1853, the area south of Gila River—which would include the lands Hooker later owned—was acquired from Mexico by the U.S. government in a transaction known as the Gadsden Purchase.

Founded Arizona's First Cattle Ranch

Hooker is known to have had contracts with the U.S. Army from 1867 to 1870 to supply beef to its posts in eastern Arizona as well as to mining camps and Indian agencies. He owned roughly 15,000 head of cattle at the time of his 1871 marriage to a woman named Susan, and a year after that was taking some of his herd through the Galiuro Mountains when the cows stampeded. "By the time Hooker and his cowboys caught up with them, they were grazing on lush grass near a broad valley with an abundant supply of water," wrote W. Lane Rogers in the *Willcox Range News.* Hooker was elated by the view and its fertile possibilities, and struck a claim for some land.

Hooker and his cows had discovered Sulphur Springs Valley, which runs a hundred miles between mountain ranges and two deserts, the Sonoran and Chihuahuan, and is situated about 80 miles east of Tucson. Hooker found an old Spanish *hacienda,* or ranch, that had been deserted since the early 1800s during a period of conflict between the Spanish settlers and the Apache. The area he originally fenced off was some 800 acres, which made it the largest permanent settlement in Arizona Territory at the time. It also boasted *cienegas,* or springs, as well as plentiful grasslands for his cattle to graze. He called the place Sierra Bonita Ranch, after the Spanish term for 'beautiful mountain."

Within a few short years Hooker became one of the most prosperous citizens in the Territory. He worked to forge positive relations with the Apache, whose raids on his cattle cost him profits. His ranch was also the first to bring superior cattle stock to the American West. At the time, the cattle used to supply meat was generally of an inferior but hardy breed, but Hooker shipped in Durham and Hereford cows from back East and began breeding them with great success. His business prospered further after 1880 when the tracks of the Southern Pacific Railroad reached Tucson on their path eastward. Near to Sierra Bonita a small construction camp was set up that would eventually become the town of Willcox, Arizona. Once the Southern Pacific Railroad stretched into Texas, Willcox served as a major shipping point for Hooker's cattle. He also bred prized stallions, and an article from the *Rocky Mountain News* in 1885 reported that he sold the entire herd for a sum of $37,000.

Friendly with Earp Brothers

Around this same time Hooker acquired a nearby property in Muleshoe, which boasted hot springs favored by nineteenth-century Americans as a restorative good-health measure. He opened a resort called Hooker's Hot Springs, which in addition to its 115-degree pools featured "a croquet lawn, tennis courts and billiard tables," wrote *New York Times* travel writer Rob Nixon. Its proprietor "buttonholed travelers alighting from the Willcox train and promised them quick cures for their pimples and dyspepsia. In the closing years of the 19th century, Hooker's Hot Springs buzzed with 400 visitors each summer. But Western spoilers—stagecoach robbers, rustlers, droughts and flash floods—

ruined Mr. Hooker's dream of turning Muleshoe into a badlands rendition of Baden-Baden in Germany."

Another nearby town was Tombstone, Arizona, a mining community which took its name from the warning given to the discoverer of its vein of silver ore located in the middle of Apache-controlled lands. Founded in 1879, the town's population exploded with new miners, but it was also isolated and the target of armed opportunists—mostly cattle rustlers and horse thieves referred to as "Cow Boys" in the press of the day—from nearby areas. In 1881, Tombstone became the site of the legendary Shootout at the O.K. Corral, a brief gunfight that actually took place at a local lumber yard and remains one of the emblematic examples of the lawlessness and violence of the Old West.

In his lifetime, Hooker knew several prominent men involved in that shootout or other episodes that became part of the lore of the Old West. A young ranch hand he hired later became famous as the outlaw Billy the Kid, a horse thief probably named William Henry McCarty who claimed to have killed 21 men by the time he was 21. McCarty was a figure in the Lincoln County War, a conflict between local business owners and a group of outlaws known for horse thievery and other crimes that were common in the free-for-all atmosphere of the Arizona and New Mexico Territories. Hooker was also friendly with Wyatt Earp, the local sheriff and another well-known name from the era. Earp's brother Morgan was a U.S. marshal in Tombstone who was shot dead in a pool hall in the town in March of 1882. Wyatt and his brother Warren sought to avenge the killing on what became known as the Earp Vendetta Ride. Earp's posse, which had federal support, pursued another group of local law-enforcement personnel who had engaged in election fraud in Cochise County. The two well-armed groups never met, but Earp's posse hid out for a time on Hooker's Sierra Bonita Ranch during the three-week episode.

Died in Los Angeles

In the quarter-century since Hooker had established his ranch, it grew to immense proportions through his various acquisitions and enterprises. At its peak, its acreage was 250,000 and Hooker owned 20,000 head of cattle. In 1898, he built a home for his family in Los Angeles, where his wife and daughter preferred to be. He was also said to have prospered from real estate investments in Southern California he shared with Wyatt Earp and Tombstone mayor John Clum. Hooker died in Los Angeles on December 5, 1907, at the age of 79.

Hooker's son Edward inherited the Sierra Bonita property. Edward married a woman named Forrestine Cooper, who later penned a novel about life in Arizona Territory titled *When Geronimo Rode.* Published in 1924, her story recounted the final years of the Apaches, who had fought bitterly to keep their lands as far back as the Spanish era of the region. Hooker has occasionally been portrayed in other novels and in film. In the 1993 movie *Tombstone,* he was played by Charlton Heston. The Sierra Bonita Ranch is still owned by Hooker's descendants and is a National Historic Landmark. The original corral and bunkhouse, both made from durable adobe brick, still stand, as does the fort that Hooker had built to ward off Apache raids.

Periodicals

Daily Evening Bulletin (San Francisco, CA), March 4, 1882, p. 4.

Los Angeles Daily Times, October 13, 1882; July 10, 1883.

New York Times, November 1, 1998.

New York Times Book Review, January 1, 1933, p. BR8.

Rocky Mountain News (Denver, CO), August 29, 1885, p. 2; September 09, 1885, p. 6.

Willcox Range News, November 11, 2008.

Online

"Colorful Characters," MyCochise.com, http://www.mycochise.com/characters.php (January 7, 2009).

"Henry Clay Hooker," Plunge Creek Cowboys, http://www.plungecreekcowboys.com/Plunge%20Story/henry_clay_hooker___one_of_the_f.htm (January 3, 2009).

"Hooker Family Genealogy Forum," Genealogy.com, http://www.genforum.genealogy.com/hooker/messages/1597.html (January 7, 2009)

"The Nature Conservancy Preserves Boast Colorful Past," Nature Conservancy, http://www.nature.org/wherewework/northamerica/states/arizona/preserves/art22002.html (January 7, 2009).

"Sierra Bonita Ranch," U.S. National Historic Landmarks Program, http://tps.cr.nps.gov/nhl/detail.cfm?ResourceId=94&ResourceType=Building (January 3, 2009). □

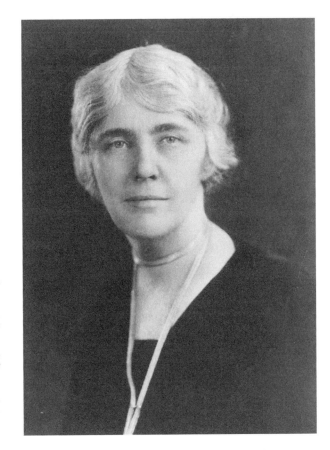

Lou Henry Hoover

During her time in the White House, Lou Henry Hoover (1874–1944) helped usher in a new era of modern first ladies who were notable public figures in their own right. An energetic activist and frequent speechgiver, Hoover was a visible first lady who championed her own causes in such a way that they supported her husband's policies. She was the first president's wife to give a radio address and used her notoriety to promote both her and her husband's agendas.

The older of two daughters, Lou Henry Hoover was born March 29, 1874, in Waterloo, Iowa, to Florence Weed and Charles Delano Henry. Records indicate she was not given a middle name and was simply called Lou Henry. Her parents hailed from the railroad town of Wooster, Ohio, and had settled in Waterloo in 1872. Charles Henry ran the local bank. He was an avid outdoorsman and naturalist who enjoyed teaching Hoover to fish, ride horses, camp, trap rabbits, shoot a rifle and identify area wildflowers and grasses. Charles Henry also took his daughter on trips down the nearby Cedar River. During the summers, Hoover canoed down the river; during the winters, she ice-skated across its frozen surface. She also liked to play baseball.

Enjoyed Unconventional Upbringing

As a country banker, Charles Henry moved frequently. In 1879 the family lived briefly in Corsica, Texas. They also spent time in Kansas. Around 1885 they headed west, taking the Santa Fe and Southern Pacific railroads to California. The family settled in Whittier, a newly founded Quaker settlement just south of Los Angeles with about 1,000 people. Charles Henry opened a bank and the family lived in an apartment above the business. They worshiped with the Quakers and later, when an Episcopalian Church was built, they attended services there.

Once in California, Hoover continued to take trips with her father. Sometimes, the father-daughter duo wandered off into the wilderness for weeks at a time, living off the land. These trips sparked Hoover's later interest in geology and also helped her develop an independent spirit and thirst for adventure. This upbringing, unconventional for a girl during the late 19th century, instilled in Hoover an enormous sense of confidence in herself and in females in general. In high school she wrote essays calling for women's suffrage and equality.

When she was 16, Hoover entered the State Normal School at Los Angeles, intending to become a teacher. In 1892 she transferred to the San Jose State Normal School to be closer to family members, who had moved to Monterey. Hoover graduated in 1893 and returned home to work as a cashier in her father's bank. In time, she received an appointment to teach third-graders but found she disliked the vocation.

Bucked Female Conformity

In the summer of 1894, Hoover attended a geology lecture titled "Bones of the Earth" given by John Casper Branner, a Stanford University professor. The lecture rekindled Hoover's interest in the natural sciences, prompting her to enroll at Stanford for the fall term. Living in Palo Alto and attending Stanford, Hoover was finally out from under her parents' wings. She matured into an independent spirit and upset her parents when she bought a "wheel"—as the first bicycles were called. These early bikes, with a four-foot-tall front wheel, were awkward to ride. Since the rider sat so high above the center of gravity, falls were frequent. For a culture just moving away from Victorian values, riding a "wheel" was unladylike.

Free-spirited and frugal, Hoover preferred sleeping in a hammock instead of buying a bed, which also upset her parents. Hoover had grown up a tomboy and continued to buck female conformity through her young adulthood. At Stanford, she lived a carefree life. She joined the Kappa Kappa Gamma sorority and took part in political discussions and debates.

During her studies at Stanford, Hoover studied Latin and majored in geology, where she was the only female in the department. While there, Hoover befriended one of Branner's lab assistants, a senior named Herbert Hoover, though she called him Bert. The two spent a lot of time studying together and when he graduated and went to work for the U.S. Geological Survey, he asked if he could write.

Hoover finished up her studies and graduated in 1898, becoming the first female to earn a geology degree from Stanford. No job offers came her way. During this time period, men did not think women were capable of doing jobs in the scientific fields. In *Lou Henry Hoover,* author Nancy Beck Young reprinted part of a letter Hoover wrote to a friend shortly after graduation. In the letter, Hoover lamented that her degree was an A.B., which "unfortunately does not stand...for 'A Boy'—ah, what wouldn't I give just about now to be one! They would not want me to stay meekly at home."

Became World Traveler

Hoover returned home and turned her attention to social activism, which would become a lifelong passion. In 1898, the United States was involved with the Spanish-American War. Hoover spent her time rolling bandages for the Red Cross to support the troops. Her future took a turn in 1899 when she received a marriage proposal telegram from Herbert Hoover. Herbert Hoover had been working for a British mining company in Australia. He wrote that he would be traveling to China and departing from San Francisco, and he asked her to accompany him. Herbert Hoover arrived in Monterey a few days before their February 10, 1899, wedding, which took place at her parents' home.

Within 24 hours, the newlyweds boarded the *SS Coptic* bound for China. Once settled in Tientsin, a coastal city south of Beijing, Hoover studied Chinese and often accompanied her husband on trips to various mines, collecting samples to send back home to Branner at Stanford. Their stay in China was not entirely peaceful. By 1900, the Boxer Rebellion was

in full swing. The Boxers began a revolt against foreigners and Christians, fearing their attempts to exert influence over their country. It was called the Ei Ho Chiang—or "Closed Fist" movement, and for a period Tientsin was under siege with frequent attacks. Shells dropped around the Hoovers' home. Tientsin was home to many foreigners, including Americans, the British, French and Russians, making it a prime target for the Boxers. The residents were asked to patrol the community's perimeter at night and Hoover took her turn.

By 1902, the Hoovers were living in London but took frequent trips. As a mining engineer, Herbert Hoover traveled extensively to inspect mines, and Hoover often accompanied her husband on these missions. She went to Egypt, India, Australia, New Zealand, Burma, Japan and Russia. On August 4, 1903, Hoover gave birth to Herbert Charles Hoover Jr. A second son, Allan Henry Hoover, followed on July 17, 1907. The children began traveling within weeks of their births.

Hoover liked to write and was especially fond of penning biographical essays. She persuaded her husband to help her translate *De Re Metallica,* a Latin tome on mining and metallurgy published in 1556. It was an important work in the fields of mining, refining and smelting. The Hoovers spent about five years completing the translation, which was published in 1912 and earned them a Gold Medal award from the Mining and Metallurgical Society of America in 1914.

Began Career in Social Activism

By 1910, Herbert Hoover was working as an independent mining consultant based in London. The Hoovers were independently wealthy and able to live off investments. In 1914, World War I erupted in Europe, leaving thousands of U.S. citizens stranded. They poured into London seeking help. Hoover leapt into action and worked with the Society of American Women in London to provide clothing, food and shelter for stranded U.S. women and children.

Herbert Hoover was appointed chairman of the Commission for the Relief of Belgium. Belgians were struggling because Germany had invaded their country and thousands were suffering from starvation. Hoover helped secure money to finance a food ship for Belgium while her husband worked through diplomacy, speaking with enemy forces and asking that the food be allowed to pass through to those in need. When the United States entered the war in 1917, President Woodrow Wilson appointed Herbert Hoover director of the U.S. Food Administration and the Hoovers relocated to Washington, D.C.

Because the United States had to provide food for its own troops and for the Allies, Herbert Hoover was concerned about a food shortage at home. He trumpeted a food conservation program, challenging the nation to change its eating habits and not be wasteful. He instituted programs called Meatless Mondays and Wheatless Wednesdays. Hoover did her part, offering food-saving tips to the nation in a feature for *Ladies' Home Journal.*

Around this time Hoover began working with the Girl Scouts, becoming a troop leader in Washington, D.C., and helping the girls grow vegetables in a "war garden." She also enjoyed the opportunity to take the girls exploring outdoors. Hoover believed in the organization's mission of helping girls learn self-sufficiency while contributing to their communities and gaining a respect for the natural world through outdoor adventures. In the 1920s, Hoover joined the National Amateur Athletic Federation (NAAF), serving as vice president and overseeing the women's division. The NAAF's mission was to promote physical fitness among Americans.

Moved to White House

After the war, Herbert Hoover was appointed Secretary of Commerce under President Warren G. Harding. In 1928, he received the Republican Party's nomination for president and went on to win the election. As first lady, Hoover envisioned herself as a communicator and spokeswoman for the White House. In 1929 she gave a radio address, becoming the first president's wife to utilize this medium to reach the public. During her four years on Pennsylvania Avenue, Hoover gave several talks. She spoke about her work with the Girl Scouts and the athletic association, and urged girls to go into fields dominated by men. She also discussed the Depression, which struck the United States just as her husband took office.

President Hoover tried to combat the nation's downward economic spiral by promoting volunteer efforts. He was leery of calling for a legislative bailout because he thought it would make citizens dependent on the federal government. In radio addresses and in countless speeches, First Lady Hoover promoted volunteerism. She mobilized 250,000 Girl Scouts to provide volunteer relief work, thus melding her causes with her husband's policies. In addition, Hoover donated family money to many relief causes and sent money, anonymously, to those in need. Hoover's philanthropic efforts were not reported until after her death. While Hoover was public and vocal with her social activism, she kept a low profile regarding her family and private matters.

Hoover caused an uproar in 1929 when she invited Jessie DePriest—an African American—to a White House tea. DePriest was married to U.S. Rep. Oscar DePriest, the first African American elected to Congress in the 20th century. Newspapers and state legislatures across the country lambasted her for inviting a black person into the White House. Hoover abolished other outdated social customs as well, such as allowing pregnant women to visit reception lines from which they had previously been banned.

Suffered From Husband's Unpopularity

In 1932, Herbert Hoover lost the election to Franklin D. Roosevelt. Herbert Hoover was an extremely unpopular president because of his stiff demeanor and inability to solve the nation's financial crisis. After leaving Washington, the Hoovers split their time between their Palo Alto home and an apartment at the Waldorf-Astoria in New York City. Hoover continued her work with the Girl Scouts and promoted relief efforts for people in Nazi-occupied countries. She also volunteered for the California League of Women Voters and the Salvation Army.

Despite Hoover's achievements and the precedents she set as first lady, she never received much credit or praise for her accomplishments during her lifetime. In the end, her husband's unpopularity tarnished her name and image. Hoover died of a heart attack on January 7, 1944, at their New York City apartment. She was 68. Hoover was initially buried in Palo Alto, but after Herbert Hoover died in 1964, she was moved to West Branch, Iowa, to be buried next to him in his hometown.

Books

Colbert, Nancy A., *Lou Henry Hoover: The Duty to Serve,* Morgan Reynolds Inc., 1998.

Gould, Lewis L., ed., *American First Ladies: Their Lives and Their Legacy,* Garland Publishing Inc., 1996.

Young, Nancy Beck, *Lou Henry Hoover: Activist First Lady,* University Press of Kansas, 2004.

Periodicals

New York Times, January 8, 1944, p. 13.

Online

"Lou Henry Hoover: A Biographical Sketch," Herbert Hoover Presidential Library and Museum, http://hoover.archives.gov/education/louhenrybio.htm (December 23, 2008).□

Alan Hovhaness

American composer Alan Hovhaness (1911–2000) fused Eastern and Western influences into a highly personal yet accessible synthesis that continued to gain new adherents over the composer's remarkably long life and creative career.

For much of that career, Hovhaness's style was regarded as conservative. He rejected the atonality (the absence of a fixed note or chord to which the music tends to return) of much 20th-century classical music, likening the idea of a tonal center to natural phenomena. "To me, atonality is against nature," Hovhaness was quoted as saying in the *Daily Herald* of Arlington Heights, Illinois. "It is the center of everything that exists. The planets have the sun, the moon and the earth. The reason I like oriental music is that everything has a firm center. All music that has a center is tonal." Yet by the end of the century, Hovhaness looked more like an innovator than like a conservative. His incorporation of non-Western influences, including those from India, Korea, and Japan, into his music prefigured that of many other composers. Hovhaness was one of the first composers to use aleatoric or chance techniques in his music, where performers played within certain parameters rather than reproducing notes on the page. And his music often had a mystical attitude, expressed by means of extreme technical simplicity, that anticipated the hugely popular minimalist style.

Devised Notation System as Child

Hovhaness was born Alan Vaness Chakmakjian in Somerville, Massachusetts, near Boston, on March 8, 1911. His father, Haroutioun Hovanes Chakmakjian, was a chemistry professor, an Armenian who came from a town in what is now Turkey. His mother, Madeleine, was of Scottish background and tried to get her son to minimize his Armenian roots. He grew up as Alan Vaness, but after her death he changed the surname to Hovaness (based on his father's father's last name), Armenianizing it further to Hovhaness in 1940. Many observers commented on how spontaneously Hovhaness made music, jotting down melodies on music paper while pushing a grocery cart or waiting while his wife shopped. He started composing at the age of four, at first using a notation system he made up himself, and once said that he never specifically decided that he wanted to be a composer; it simply came naturally to him.

Hovhaness's parents did not approve of his musical orientation and forbade him to play the small organ they had in the house. He showed interest in astronomy (and would for the rest of his life), but composing had the strongest hold on him. His parents would confiscate his music manuscripts when they found them, so he would sometimes write music in the bathroom and hide it under the tub. Hovhaness also developed another way of evading his parents' restrictions: he would compose late at night, after they had gone to bed. That turned into a lifelong habit; Hovhaness generally slept until early afternoon and worked

late into the evening. Another pattern that was set early in his life was close communion with nature; he loved to go for long hikes among New England's hills and mountains.

After writing several full-length operas in collaboration with a high school classmate, Hovhaness enrolled at Tufts University, where his father taught. He studied with composer Frederick Converse and was also inspired by the monumental music of Finnish composer Jean Sibelius. Hovhaness and his first wife (of an eventual six) Martha traveled to Finland to meet Sibelius, who became godfather to their daughter. Hovhaness wrote dozens of pieces, many for small ensembles, and some of them began to gain attention in Boston's vigorous concert scene. One of his orchestral pieces won the Samuel Endicott Prize in 1933, and in 1937 his Exile Symphony (which later became designated as the Symphony No. 1 in an eventual series of 67 symphonies) was performed in Britain by the BBC Midland Orchestra. The work's title referred to Turkish human rights abuses of Armenians.

In the early 1940s Hovhaness became more and more interested in Armenian music, closely studying the works of the little-known Armenian composer and priest Komitas Vartabed, sometimes known by the single name of Komitas. "To me, he's the original minimalist, and it was through Komitas that I got the idea of saying as much as possible with the fewest possible notes," Hovhaness said in an interview quoted on his website. In 1942 Hovhaness won a scholarship to study composition at the prestigious Tanglewood Music Center in western Massachusetts, but he found that other composers at the center, including Leonard Bernstein and Aaron Copland, received his music negatively and even ridiculed it.

Destroyed Manuscripts

This episode seems to have produced a temporary crisis for Hovhaness, who destroyed many of his youthful works—perhaps up to the often-cited figure of a thousand compositions, although the actual number was probably lower. Hovhaness claimed that he had discarded his music merely because he was moving to a smaller apartment that had no room for them, but later interviews revealed the degree to which the Tanglewood rejection had made clear to him how far he stood from the modern American compositional mainstream. Hovhaness's creativity quickly reasserted itself, however. In 1944 he formed an orchestra devoted to the performance of music written in pure intervals (i.e., in scales where the tuning of notes is not slightly distorted to permit the performance of music in any key), and later that year he emerged with one of his major works, *Lousadzak*, a concerto for piano and orchestra.

The work was unlike any other piano concerto composed up to that time. The piano part was entirely monophonic (in a single line), using techniques borrowed from Armenian and Turkish music. At certain junctures the orchestral strings were given a short figure to repeat, but were allowed to determine the speed themselves, with no requirement to align themselves with the other players. Hovhaness called this technique the "spirit murmur," and he hit on it at least 15 years in advance of European avant-garde compositions that featured something similar. The work won Hovhaness the respect of the American experimentalists John Cage and Lou Harrison, both of whom were interested in non-Western traditions.

For the first part of his life, Hovhaness made a living independently of the university teaching posts and foundation grants that have sustained most contemporary classical composers. In the late 1940s and early 1950s, his financial situation was dire, but he cobbled together a living from various sources, including help from a group called the Friends of Armenian Music, support at times from several of his wives, playing the organ at an Armenian church, and a three-year stint teaching at the Boston Music Conservatory. Hovhaness enjoyed little prestige among the American compositional establishment, which by the 1950s leaned toward the rigid Austrian-originated system known as 12-tone music or serialism, which disregarded and even disdained popular appeal.

Hovhaness's music held plenty of appeal for American symphony orchestra audiences, however; its tranquil, almost hypnotic qualities sold tickets and recordings in much the same way as would the music of minimalists like Steve Reich and Philip Glass several decades later. The British-American orchestral conductor Leopold Stokowski became a key Hovhaness backer, leading the premiere of the composer's Symphony No. 2 ('Mysterious Mountain'') in Houston in 1955. That became one of Hovhaness's most durably popular pieces, and commissions for new music began to flow in from orchestras, radio and television programs, and theatrical producers (Hovhaness wrote a score for the Clifford Odet's play *The Flowering Peach*).

Studied Eastern Traditions

Once again broadening his horizons, Hovhaness became something of an ethnomusicologist. He traveled to Greece in the mid-1950s and followed up that journey with another to India in 1959 and 1960. There, in Madras (now Chennai), he studied south Indian classical music and wrote works for an all-Hovhaness concert that included the piano concerto *Arjuna* and the Symphony No. 7 (''Nanga Parvat''), presented at the Madras Music Festival to acclaim from Indian journalists. Hovhaness made similar trips, each musically successful, to Japan in 1960 and to Korea in 1962. By that time, with about a dozen new compositions a year to his credit, Hovhaness's list of published compositions was well over 200 items long. With his Symphony No. 19 (''Vishnu''), which depicted in musical form the creative forces of the universe, Hovhaness synthesized Indian ideas with extensive use of chance techniques.

Hovhaness's round-the-world travels concluded in 1962 with a residence at the University of Hawaii, and the following year he moved to Seattle, Washington. He served during the 1966–67 season as composer-in-residence for the Seattle Symphony Orchestra, and the musical atmosphere of the West Coast, oriented toward the musical cultures of the Pacific Rim, suited him more than that of the Northeast, although the commission for one of Hovhaness's most successful works, 1969's *And God Created Great Whales* (which included tapes of humpback whale sounds), came from the New York Philharmonic Orchestra. He settled permanently in Seattle in 1971, and a few years after that he met Japanese

soprano and actress Hinako Fujihara at a concert devoted to his music. In 1977 she became Hovhaness's sixth wife, and the two remained married for the rest of his life.

Fujihara formed a record label, Fujihara Records, to distribute Hovhaness's music, and she took over some of his business affairs, which had reached considerable dimensions by the time they married. A 1975 Hovhaness royalty statement showed that nearly all of Hovhaness's compositions had sold at least one copy, and the choral piece *From the Ends of the Earth* had sold 5,640. Hovhaness was able to live comfortably off his music during his later years, partly because he continued to compose prolifically and even speeded up rather than slowing down. Commissions flowed in from major symphony orchestras, university groups, and smaller ensembles around the Northwest, with Seattle Symphony Orchestra conductor Gerard Schwarz emerging as another major Hovhaness champion. Between 1980 and 1989 Hovhaness wrote about 80 works, including 20 full-length symphonies.

When illness finally forced him to stop composing in 1996, Hovhaness's list of publications ran to some 434 opus (work) numbers—a remarkable achievement in a world in which the popularity of classical music was declining. Hovhaness died in Seattle on June 21, 2000, of stomach problems. He also left many unpublished works, and Hinako Fujihara Hovhaness reported finding numerous others among the stacks of papers in his studio. ''He deserves major status, because he wrote some of the best music around,'' Lou Harrison was quoted as saying in the *New York Times*. ''When he first came along, there were the 12-toners, and there were the Americanists, and neither camp knew what to make of him. But now there's a resurgence of interest in the kind of qualities that characterize his music: melody, clarity, discipline, beauty. We'll be hearing more of Alan, I'm sure.''

Books

Contemporary Musicians, volume 34, Gale, 2002.

Periodicals

Daily Herald (Arlington Heights, IL), June 30, 2000, p. 7.

Guardian (London, England), June 28, 2000, p. 24.

Independent (London, England), June 26, 2000, p. 6.

New York Times, May 20, 2001, p. AR33.

Scotsman (Edinburgh, Scotland, United Kingdom), July 27, 2000, p. 16.

Seattle Times, April 22, 2001, p. F5.

Online

''Alan Hovhaness: The Composer in Conversation with Bruce Duffie,'' http://www.bruceduffie.com/hovx.html (January 6, 2009).

''Hovhaness, Alan Biography,'' Naxos Records, http://www.naxos.com/composerinfo/Alan_Hovhaness_20949/20949.htm (January 6, 2009).

Shirodkar, Marco, ''Alan Hovhaness Biographical Summary,'' http://www.hovhaness.com (January 6, 2009). □

Elizabeth Jane Howard

In a publishing career spanning more than five decades, British author Elizabeth Jane Howard (born 1923) produced more than 15 books and an introspective autobiography. She is best known as the author of the much-loved Cazalet Chronicles, a four-book series offering an account of British domestic life in the years surrounding World War II. Since her first book appeared in 1950, Howard has been praised by critics for her tightly drawn scenes, keen-witted dialogue and astute ability to reveal the real-life, day-to-day intricacies of human nature.

Struggled Through Childhood

Elizabeth Jane Howard—known as Jane—was born into an affluent London family on March 26, 1923. Her mother, Katharine Margaret [Somervell] Howard, was an accomplished dancer who had performed with the Ballets Russes, an itinerant ballet company. Howard's mother, who went by Kit, gave up her career to marry. Howard's father, David Liddon Howard, worked in the family's timber business. The Howards were well-off—there were cooks, gardeners, chauffeurs and nannies.

When Howard was a youngster, the family lived in West London. Howard spent her days in the company of her rage-filled nanny, often relegated to the home's nursery. The nanny took her for walks in Kensington Park and Howard looked on with envy at the children who were allowed to splash in the pond and get dirty. One time, Howard's nanny locked her in the linen closet after her little brother cut himself on a tin car in the nursery while he was alone with Howard. The lesson solidified for Howard the notion that boys mattered more than girls, which was true in her family. Her two brothers received a proper education, while Howard was casually taught the basics at home.

In a podcast interview with CBC radio host Eleanor Wachtel, Howard recalled that early on, she dreamed of escaping. As a child, Howard said, she used to look out the window of her home and gaze upon the sea of chimney pots. She would pretend these funnels were the smokestacks of large ships that were coming to take her away. One thing Howard wanted to escape was her mother's indifference—the two never bonded. Kit Howard had given birth to a girl a year before Howard was born and that baby had died. That child had also been named Jane. In the CBC interview, Howard recalled overhearing her mother tell another relative that she did not like little girls. Her mother's constant attack on her self-image left Howard feeling like she was never good enough.

Howard's father was fun-loving but immature and unable to handle the demands of a family. Howard's relationship with her father took an abrupt turn once she reached adolescence and he began making advances at her. Howard believed her father's problems stemmed from the battlefield and the fact that people from his generation did not talk about their experiences during World War I or receive counseling to help them readjust to civilian life.

"He was 17 when he joined up and suffered four years of atrocious sights and sounds. As a consequence of the shock he had suffered when he was young, he had never grown up," Howard told Clare Colvin of the *Independent*. "I didn't blame him, and he would have been horrified if he had known of the damage he had done."

Sought Escape Through Marriage

In 1940, Howard joined a student repertory company in Devon, England. Around this time she met a young naval officer named Peter Scott, son of the famed Arctic explorer Robert Scott. Scott was home on sick leave when the two met. He was a naturalist and painter and enjoyed creating artwork in Howard's likeness. "I was bowled over at the attention he gave me," Howard told the *Daily Mail*'s Anne De Courcy. "He drew me a lot and that was very flattering."

They married in 1942. Howard was 19; Scott was in his thirties. With World War II in full swing and so many men off fighting and dying, there was a lot of pressure for couples to marry and procreate. "Wartime marriages were murder," Howard told the *Daily Mail*'s Lynda Lee-Potter. "You can't have a relationship with somebody you hardly ever see—and when you do, you think it may be for the last time." Their daughter, Nicola, was born in 1943. Within a few years, they separated.

After leaving her husband, Howard figured it would be nearly impossible for her to support herself and her daughter. She ended up leaving Nicola in the care of her own mother and in the care of her ex-husband, who could afford a nanny. Howard did not spend much time with her daughter, repeating the cycle of neglect she had suffered through.

Published First Novel

During the war, Howard worked as a broadcaster for the BBC (British Broadcasting Corporation). She also began to write, creating the plot and characters that would become her first novel, *The Beautiful Visit*. Published in 1950, the book was about a girl trying to escape her family. *The Beautiful Visit* won the John Llewellyn Rhys Prize, a British literary award given for the best piece of fiction by an author under 35.

Howard wrote the book while working part-time and living on coffee, toast and smoked herring. Though one reviewer called *The Beautiful Visit* "delicately introspective," Howard was not fond of the finished piece. Howard told the CBC that she knew nothing of plot structure or literary devices when she wrote the book. Howard called it "a good try."

During the 1950s, Howard supported herself by working as an editor at Chatto publishers. In 1956, she published *The Long View*, a book that explored a failed marriage in reverse-chronological order. In a 1956 review in the *New York Times*, one critic called Howard's style "a rare combination of wit and wisdom, humor and intensity." *The Sea Change* followed in 1959. This book was borne out of an exploration of personality traits. Howard began by pondering the question of which traits a person could change and which traits were fixed.

During the 1950s, Howard had affairs with writers Cyril Connolly and Kenneth Tynan. Howard, a stunning ingénue, had men chasing her all the time and she was never quite sure what to do about it. She was completely oblivious to her beauty. No longer wanting the role of mistress, she decided to settle down and in 1959 married an Australian broadcaster named James Douglas-Henry. The marriage proved uneventful and they divorced in 1964.

Met, Married Famed British Author

In 1962, Howard helped organize the Cheltenham Literature Festival and met British novelist Kingsley Amis, who was married. After the festival, Amis called her in London and asked to meet for a drink. They soon became lovers and Amis' wife left him. In 1965, Howard and Amis married. Their first years were filled with bliss. In 1969, they settled into a stately home in Hertfordshire, England. The two burgeoning writers worked together, facing each other across a double desk. Howard wrote a few books during her 15-year marriage to Amis, but her output was slow because of domestic duties. Howard spent a lot of time forging relationships with Amis' children. Martin Amis became a novelist and credited Howard with introducing him to Jane Austen and inspiring him to buckle down in his studies so he could succeed.

Kingsley Amis encouraged his wife to write but she failed to get much down on paper. "I just didn't have the energy," Howard told the *Daily Mail*'s De Courcy. "I spent much of the time cooking. My mother lived there for the last six years of her life, my brother lived there, a painter friend lived there and there were Kingsley's children in the holidays and all their friends. Sometimes I was cooking for 25."

As the years went by, their relationship deteriorated and Howard found herself crying more and more. Her doctor prescribed valium. Amis developed a drinking problem. They became resentful of each other. In 1980, she left. Amis never forgave her, never spoke to her again and refused to see her before his death. He made it a point during interviews to tell journalists that the worst thing that ever happened to him was his marriage to Howard. Speaking to the CBC, Howard noted that his remarks stung. "I think I found it difficult when Kingsley went about saying what a bad thing it was he'd ever met me."

Kingsley drank heavily, but it was not the drinking that ultimately drove Howard away—it was his loathing. Speaking to the *Independent*, Howard put it this way: "I don't think it's easy to live with someone who drinks too much, but in the end I couldn't live with someone who disliked me so much, as well. You can go on living with someone who doesn't love you, but what is really killing is someone who dislikes you." Howard was terrified to leave, though, because she did not know if she could earn a living and she did not like being alone.

Came Into Her Own

In 1990, Howard published *The Light Years,* which introduced readers to the affluent Cazalet family. She continued their saga in *Marking Time* (1991), *Confusion* (1993) and *Casting Off* (1995). This quartet of books, known as the Cazalet Chronicles, covers the Cazalet family from 1937 to 1947. Howard set out to write a book that captured life in Britain both before and after the Great War. She reasoned that many books chronicled battles and life on the front lines, but none discussed family life on the home front. She had to look no farther than her own family to get ideas for the epic drama.

The Cazalet Chronicles caught the nerve of the British people and went on to sell more than a million copies. The Cazalet Chronicles have a semi-autobiographical flare, evident in the characters of the young girls living through the war. The chronicles cover a vast cast of characters, and Howard was praised for depicting each one superbly, showing their quirks and shortcomings. In 2001, the BBC adapted the books into a television mini-series.

After leaving Amis, Howard gave up on love and settled into life on her own. Then, in her 70s, she fell for another suitor, a man who wooed her through letters. She discovered he was a con artist after catching him in a lie. Out of the pain and revelation of this experience came *Falling* (1999), which Howard considered her best book. In 2002, she followed with *Slipstream,* a candid and self-critical autobiography in which she focused a microscope on her own life and mistakes. She discussed her childhood, her mother, her quest for love and her romantic entanglements with poet laureate Cecil Day-Lewis and authors Laurie Lee, Arthur Koestler and Romain Gary. Howard chose the title *Slipstream* because she felt she had lived her life in the "slipstream" of events.

Howard continued to write into her eighties, enjoying a solitary life in an 18th century farmhouse in Suffolk, England. She moved there in 1990. Her daily routine included gardening and writing. "Regularity is very important," she told the *Scotsman*'s Gillian Glover. "I do believe that now. People expect dancers and musicians to practice every day, and I think it's the same for writers. That way, the muscles stay in trim." In 2008, Howard published *Love All.* Set in the 1960s, the book was a domestic drama depicting middle-class rural life.

Speaking to the CBC, Howard acknowledged that it took her a long time to grow up and figure out how to live her life—how to not make the same mistakes over and over. She said she had gotten smarter with age and was not as irritable or impatient as in her younger days. "So by the time I'm 100, I'll be truly marvelous," she quipped.

Periodicals

Daily Mail (London), November 3, 1993, p. 15; December 15, 1994, p. 9.

Guardian (London), November 2, 2002, p. 9.

Independent (London), November 9, 2002, p. 28.

New York Times, April 29, 1956, p. 326.

Scotsman, April 13, 2003, p. 14.

Sunday Times (London), October 12, 2008, p. 7; November 16, 2008, p. 28 (Home).

Other

"Eleanor Wachtel Speaks with British Novelist Elizabeth Jane Howard, Author of the Famous Cazalet Chronicles," *Words At Large* podcast, CBC Radio, http://www.cbc.ca/wordsatlarge/blog/2008/10/eleanor_wachtel_speaks_with_br.html (February 12, 2009). □

John Hunter

British surgeon John Hunter (1728–1793), considered the forefather of modern surgery and pathological anatomy, was one of the most influential surgeons of his day. Despite having little formal training in his field, Hunter became a respected authority on anatomy and dissection. His investigations into animal and human anatomy greatly increased scientific knowledge of the subject and laid the groundwork for modern medical practices in fields as diverse as dentistry and artificial resuscitation.

The child of farmer John Hunter, Sr., and Agnes Hunter, John Hunter was born at Long Calderwood, Lanarkshire, Scotland on February 13, 1728. Hunter was the tenth child born and seventh surviving, with three older siblings having died before his birth. The elder Hunter was considerably older than his wife and uninterested in his youngest son, leaving the boy to be spoiled by his mother and four older sisters. Hunter had little interest in book learning, often shirking class in favor of independent observations of nature. Writing in *The Knife Man: The Extraordinary Life and Times of John Hunter, Father of Modern Surgery*, Wendy Moore noted that Hunter "always preferred to believe the evidence of his own eyes rather than the recorded views of others." At the age of thirteen, Hunter quit formal schooling; that same year, his father died, leaving Hunter—whose two elder brothers had already left the family fold to pursue medical careers—to help out on the farm.

With the exception of a brief stint as a trainee carpenter in Glasgow, Hunter remained on the farm until the age of 20, when he moved to London to assist his elder brother, William, at his recently founded anatomy school. Hunter enjoyed his work, despite being charged with the illegal and somewhat gruesome task of sourcing the corpses used in the school's anatomy lectures, and showed an early talent for the dissection and preparation of anatomical specimens, if not for the social graces of London. As John Kobler noted in *The Reluctant Surgeon*, "[Hunter] was as prickly a Scot as ever crossed the Tweed, and his fine-feathered brother would find it easier to make an anatomist out of him than a gentleman."

Soon, Hunter's skills as a dissector and anatomist were such that he began instructing some of his brother's students in that field. During the warmer months of 1749 and 1750, when the heat made dissection particularly repugnant, Hunter studied practical surgery at Chelsea Hospital

with William Cheselden. Following Cheselden's death in 1752, Hunter worked with Percivall Potts at St. Bartholomew's Hospital, and, later, as a surgical student at St. George's Hospital. These studies were the extent of his formal medical training; Hunter's general distaste for academics prematurely terminated his brief enrollment at Oxford University and ultimately meant that, as noted in *Science and Its Times, Volume 4: 1700–1799,* "he never completed a course of studies in any university and never really attempted to become a doctor." The lack of qualified surgeons and inadequate medical training of the day, however, allowed talented individuals such as Hunter to excel in the surgical field despite having no official diploma.

In the mid-1750s, Hunter began treating patients, first in 1753 as a Master of Anatomy of the Surgeon's Corporation and, from 1756, as a hospital surgeon at St. George's; he would become a governor of that institution in 1760, a post he retained throughout his life. At about this time, Hunter began conducting experiments on both live and dead animals such as dogs and sheep that allowed him to better understand the biological processes of the body. (These activities, although considered unconscionable today, were generally accepted by Hunter and his contemporaries.)

Private Practice and Experimentation

By 1760, Hunter had served as his brother's assistant for 12 years and was ready to strike out on his own. He joined the British army—then embroiled in the Seven Years War—as a surgeon, traveling to France and Portugal in the course of his duties. While treating soldiers injured by gunshots, Hunter determined that the best cure for such injuries was, as Moore put it, "leaving the injury alone... [and] letting nature take its course, even to the extent of leaving bullets embedded permanently in their wounds." These observations served as the basis for Hunter's later treatise *Inflammation and Gun-Shot Wounds,* published in 1794 shortly after the surgeon's death.

Following the conclusion of the war in 1763, Hunter returned to London and began a dentistry practice with James Spence. Dentistry, although a dire necessity for contemporary Londoners, was practiced in a rather slipshod manner, with barbers and blacksmiths sometimes performing tooth extractions. Hunter's qualifications as a surgeon lent the practice an unusual level of quality; writing shortly after Hunter's death, Jessé Foot commented in his *Life of John Hunter* that "Spence soon found his house crowded by all the fashion of the age." This association continued until at least the latter part of the decade. Hunter's work led to the publication of *The Natural History of the Human Teeth* in 1771 and *A Practical Treatise on the Diseases on the Teeth,* which combined provided a sourcebook for the development of modern dentistry in following years.

Hunter's practice did not prevent him from continuing his medical experimentation. He became intrigued by the possibility of grafting body parts from one animal to another; the results ranged from moderate success to, in the case of a human tooth stuck into a cock's comb, a bizarre failure. His findings, however, helped support later research into the field of human organ donation. In 1765, Hunter purchased a large property near London's western edge, where he built a home and established a menagerie suitable for his experiments. Over the next several years, Hunter investigated such diverse topics as the effects of freezing temperatures on bodies, the best way of healing injured Achilles tendons—a condition from which Hunter himself suffered—and the bodily structures of exotic animals such as whales and crocodiles. Hunter would continue these sorts of experiments throughout his career, eventually collecting a lifetime of findings in the 1786 treatise *Observations of Certain Parts of the Animal Oeconomy.* In 1767, Hunter was elected to a fellowship in the Royal Society; that same year, he officially received a surgical diploma and was made a surgeon at St. George's Hospital.

Hunter undertook a life-altering experiment in 1767: infecting himself with venereal diseases. Syphilis and gonorrhea were both highly common and practically impossible to cure during the eighteenth century, with the most common treatment being the application or ingestion of mercury, which caused side effects nearly as bad as the disease itself. Popular medical theory of the day held that the two diseases were different facets of the same infection, and Hunter set out to prove this theory. He first undertook the injection of gonorrhea and began monitoring his symptoms to determine if the former disease exhibited the symptoms of the latter, thus proving that they were one and the same infection. When he discovered that all expected symptoms did appear, he erroneously concluded that his theory was correct. As Moore pointed out, however, "the

experiment had been doomed from the outset, since Hunter had plainly used infected matter containing both syphilis and gonorrhea bacteria." Hunter published his conclusions in the 1786 *Treatise on the Venereal Disease and Treatise on the Blood,* and suffered ill health probably resulting from this experiment throughout the remainder of his life.

Lectures and Museum Specimens

Despite Hunter's unusual interests and rough manners, he attracted the romantic interest of the much-younger polished society girl Anne Home. Confident that the prescribed dosage of mercury had rid him of his self-inflicted venereal diseases, he married Home at St. James's Church on July 22, 1771. The couple soon had four children; of these, two died in childhood, one suffered from a mental illness, and the fourth remained in good health throughout most of her life. Hunter's wife—a poet who composed the lyrics to one of Haydn's canzonets—maintained a social presence, giving parties and holding salons, even amidst the visual and olfactory reminders of Hunter's experimental work.

In the early 1770s, Hunter embarked on a course of lecturing, hoping to bring surgical knowledge to those pupils who showed an interest in the subject. Kobler noted that Hunter's "maiden efforts, halting, cumbrous, often couched in the idiom of the streets, produced more laughter than enlightenment." Indeed, popular medical opinion on Hunter's lectures was split; his goal—to provide students with the anatomical theory necessary for them to understand the workings of the human body—was a departure from commonly accepted surgical teaching methods, and thus not entirely accepted by the medical establishment. Over time, the number of attendees at these lectures grew somewhat to include both surgical students and interested members of the lay public. Eventually, Hunter's pupils carried his ideas throughout the British Isles and even to Europe and the nascent United States, giving them an impact reaching far beyond the walls of Hunter's home.

Hunter faced an unusual challenge in 1775 when he was approached with the task of embalming a deceased woman such that her body could remain above ground, a requirement of her will for her husband to inherit. Hunter successfully tackled the challenge, producing a corpse of such quality that the husband in question dressed and displayed the body of his wife in a glass case six days a week. Toward the end of the 1770s, Hunter became interested in the possibilities of reviving the dead, particularly those who had drowned. In pursuit of this goal, he recommended fast action to restart breathing through the use of artificial resuscitation and tested the application of electricity to restart the heart, a distant precursor to the modern practice of defibrillation. Around this time, Hunter also gained the title of Surgeon Extraordinary to King George III.

Later Years and Death

By the early 1780s, Hunter and his brother William had experienced increasingly cool relations; a rift between the two had not been resolved by the time of the latter's death in 1783 and Hunter found himself absent from his brother's will. Nevertheless, Hunter soon moved his household to new quarters in the fashionable Leicester Square area of London. This home included a lecture space and museum area for Hunter's prized specimens, including preserved animal and human body parts, skeletons of all types—including one of an eight-foot-tall Irishman—and other teaching aids. These specimens would be purchased by the British government in 1799; some can still be seen today at the Royal College of Surgeons' Hunterian Museum in London. Hunter continued lecturing and experimenting through the 1780s, becoming interested in animal inter-breeding and ancestry, challenging the traditional religion-based views of the subject accepted at the time.

During this era, Hunter won a number of professional honors. In 1781, he was elected to the Royal Society of Gothenberg. Two years later, he gained membership in the Royal Society of Medicine and Royal Academy of Surgery of Paris. Hunter—who had retained his army post—became the deputy surgeon general of the army, its second-highest medical position, in 1786. He also became the surgeon general and inspector general of hospitals in 1790.

Hunter suffered an unexpected collapse and died on October 16, 1793, while arguing on behalf of two Scottish pupils who, like Hunter himself, wished to study surgery but had not completed formal apprenticeships at a Board of Governors meeting at St. George's Hospital. Hunter's body underwent an autopsy following his death, and the cause of death was determined to be heart failure related to an attack of angina, a condition from which Hunter had suffered since the early 1770s. He was buried on October 22, 1793, at St. Martins-in-the-Fields, where he remained until 1859, when he was re-interred at Westminster Abbey in London.

Books

Foot, Jessé, *The Life of John Hunter*, Becket, 1794.

Kobler, John, *The Reluctant Surgeon: The Life of John Hunter*, Heinemann, 1960.

Moore, Wendy, *The Knife Man: The Extraordinary Life and Times of John Hunter, Father of Modern Surgery*, Broadway Books, 2005.

Science and Its Times: Volume 4: 1700–1799, Gale Group, 2001.

World of Biology, Thomson Gale, 2006.

*World of Invention,*Thomson Gale, 2006.□

Zakir Hussain

The Indian percussionist Zakir Hussain (born 1951) has bridged Indian and Western musical styles, becoming one of the creators of cross-cultural genre referred to as world music.

Hussain has operated from within a secure position in his own North Indian classical tradition: play-ing the tabla, a pair of contrasting hand drums that form the rhythmic foundation of many Indian classical performances, he gained a reputation as one of the instrument's

greatest living exponents. Since moving to the United States in 1970, however, Hussain has been open to a great variety of the musical influences that have come his way. He was part of the 1970s group Shakti, which pioneered the fusion of jazz and Indian music, and his collaborators since then have come from fields as diverse as jazz, rock, country, and classical music. Hussain never curtailed his musical experiments, telling Law-rence B. Johnson of the *Miami Herald* that "[i]f I think I play well enough now, I might as well hang up my boots. It's not about the goal; it's about the journey. This is a learning expe-rience all through your life."

Taught Percussion Rhythms as Baby

Born Zakir Hussain Allarakha Qureshi on March 9, 1951, in Bombay (now Mumbai), India, Hussain had a famous father; tabla player Ustad Alla Rakha Qureshi often per-formed with star sitar player Ravi Shankar (who later became the father of vocalist Norah Jones). As the elder musician held his infant son in his arms, he would often be singing tabla rhythms to him, using a uniquely Indian method, known as solkattu, of producing percussion rhythms with the voice. The training caught on: Hussain easily mastered various styles of tabla playing, and he was performing in concert by the time he was seven.

As a teenager, Hussain was a regular concert attraction and was considered something of a prodigy, performing with top North Indian instrumental and vocal musicians. He was acclaimed as the next phenomenon of Indian classical music, but as he entered his late teens he began to suffer the burnout that has plagued many youthful prodigies: audiences demanded ever more spectacular feats of virtuosity that would have been at odds with his development as a well-rounded musician. Looking for a way out, Hussain volunteered to replace his father as Ravi Shankar's tabla player on a 1970 tour of the U.S. Initially, Ustad Alla Rahka opposed the idea, believing that his son should concentrate on continuing to make a name for himself in Indian music. But the father had shown a tendency toward experimentation himself, recording an album with jazz drummer Buddy Rich in 1965, and he eventually gave the go-ahead for his son's departure.

The tour went well, and Shankar recommended Hussain for a teaching position at the University of Washington. The three years Hussain spent in Seattle were important in his musical development, for in India he had been immersed in a tradition that had a profound history but was in many ways contained within itself. Suddenly he heard other Asian classical traditions, from China, Japan, and Korea that were as old as India's. He met African musicians, and he soaked up the American jazz and rock that were all around him. In the early 1970s Hussain moved to northern California to join a music program founded by Indian sarod player Ali Akbar Khan. He met his wife, Toni, an Indian dancer, and settled in San Anselmo in the northern San Francisco Bay Area.

Lived at Hart Ranch

Another Bay Area artist who had an impact on Hussain's career was Mickey Hart, the drummer for the improvisationally oriented rock group the Grateful Dead and a musician with a strong interest in world traditions. The meeting was originally brought about by Hussain's father, who had been approached by Hart for lessons and guessed that the rock musician and his son might enjoy a fruitful collaboration. At first Hussain was put off by the rampant drug use in Hart's circle, and later he talked about it with Brad Kava from the *San Jose Mercury News*. "My father said he was too old and set in his ways, but here is my son.... And here was this young Indian kid who didn't drink or smoke, and he was throwing me right into that den!" Living at Hart's Marin County ranch for six months, Hussain succeeded in avoiding the drug scene and formed a group called the Tal Vadya Rhythm Band, later renamed the Diga Rhythm Band. The group's self-titled 1976 album with Hart, according to Derek Beres of *Sing Out!* magazine, is "sometimes considered the first true 'world music' project, in terms of how broadly the foundation of cultures involved reached."

Better known, however, was another group in which Hussain had become involved: he formed Shakti with British-born jazz guitarist John McLaughlin and South Indian violinist Lakshminarayanan Shankar, known as L. Shankar and unrelated to Ravi Shankar. The group released its debut album, *Shakti*, in 1975. It met with only moderate success, for Shakti's record label, Columbia, was unsure of how to market the album's unusual stylistic mix featuring fiery guitar solos by McLaughlin answered by long passages of solkattu from Hussain. Shakti released two more albums: *A Handful of Beauty* (1976) and *Natural Elements* (1977). The

group dissolved in 1978, but the reputation of its music grew consistently as listeners became more familiar with cross-cultural fusions. All three Shakti albums remained in print more than 30 years after their initial release.

Shakti was influential not only in the West but also in India itself, where its joining of North and South Indian styles counted as a major innovation. The two styles were not just different dialects of a single musical language but drew on different procedures and methods of study although they ultimately shared a common source. "Indian musicians became much more open after Shakti towards the idea of trying things not only within the realms of Indian music but by stepping out of Indian music and into any traditions they felt comfortable with," Hussain explained to Anil Prasad of *Innerviews*. "Shakti was one of the first combinations of musicians trying to do something that crossed all musical boundaries. We didn't approach each other thinking 'Okay, you play South Indian, I play North Indian and he'll play jazz, then see what happens.' We just jumped into the wagon and took a ride together."

Hussain's career as a film composer began in 1979 with *Apocalypse Now*, which used about 14 minutes (mostly at the film's end) of the 90 minutes of music the musician submitted to director Francis Ford Coppola. In the 1980s he devoted much of his energy to film scores and worked several times with the British production team of Ismail Merchant and James Ivory, several of whose films were set in India. His score for *Heat and Dust* earned an award nomination at the Cannes Film Festival in 1983. Hussain continued to write film scores, and in 1996 he composed the opening music for the Summer Olympics in Atlanta, Georgia.

Won Indian Government Honor

Beginning in 1986 with *Making Music*, Hussain released a series of more than 20 albums under his own name. That album was on the avant-garde-jazz-oriented ECM label, but he soon formed his own label, Moment, not only to distribute his own music but also to give other Indian musicians a space in which they could maintain control over the recording process. Some of Hussain's own albums were in Western fusion idioms, but many captured performances in the pure North Indian classical tradition. The 1988 album *Tabla Duet* was recorded with his father. Hussain's long career in the West did not dent his standing among traditionalist devotees in India; he continued to perform there, at times accompanying Ravi Shankar, and he won several of India's major cultural awards, including the Padma Shri title denoting civilians of merit. In the U.S., he received a National Heritage Fellowship in 1999. As of 2005 he was performing more than 150 concerts a year.

In the West, the range of Hussain's collaborations continued to broaden in the 1990s and 2000s. Perhaps the most critically successful was the 1992 album *Planet Drum*, which reunited Hussain with Hart and earned the first Grammy ever awarded for Best World Music Album as well as several other awards. That album, perhaps more than any other, made Hussain a familiar name among general North American audiences (he was featured on many of its tracks, not only those in Indian idioms) and catapulted world music to the status of a viable and ongoing commercial category. Hussain also appeared as a guest on albums by an impressive variety of other artists, including rock musicians Van Morrison and George Harrison, jazz players Billy Cobham and Pharoah Sanders, the Kodo drummers of Japan, and the symphony orchestras of New Orleans and Hong Kong. He composed music for dance, providing the score *Lines* (which won an Izzie, or Isadora Duncan Award) to choreographer Alonzo King in 1998 and later worked with the Alvin Ailey Dance Theater and choreographer Mark Morris. The latter collaboration was part of cellist Yo-Yo Ma's Silk Road Project, a multimedia set of concerts and recordings exploring connections between East and West. Hussain toured with a reconstituted Shakti (without L. Shankar) under the name Remember Shakti in the late 1990s.

In 2006 Hussain extended his range still farther, joining progressive bluegrass banjoist Bela Fleck and bassist Edgar Meyer to compose a Triple Concerto for Banjo, Bass, and Tabla; the three performed the work together with the Nashville Symphony Orchestra at the reopening of that city's Schermerhorn Hall. The work received performances by other major orchestras over the next several years. Returning to India in 2007, Hussain was asked by the Indian government to compose a song marking the 60th anniversary of the country's independence. That song, "Jai Hind," was recorded by both popular and classical Indian singers. By that time, with Indian music heard as a component of popular songs and even television commercials all over the world, Hussain could look back on a considerable even if still unfinished legacy. In the words of France's

Mondomix website, "If the Indian Tabla is as well known today as the Cuban conga, it is above all thanks to one quite extraordinary musician, Zakir Hussain."

Books

Contemporary Musicians, volume 22, Gale, 2001.

Periodicals

Globe & Mail (Toronto, Canada), November 8, 2000.
Guitar Player, November 2006, p. 56.
Houston Chronicle, May 5, 2005, p. 6.
Miami Herald, May 2, 2008; May 6, 2008.
San Francisco Chronicle, April 14, 2002, p. 49.
San Jose Mercury News, September 21, 2006.
Sing Out!, Winter 2008, p. 150.
Times of India, February 14, 2006; December 16, 2007.

Online

Prasad, Anil, "Remember Shakti: Four People as One," "Zakir Hussain: Crossing Musical Boundaries," *Innerviews,* http://www.innerviews.org/inner/shakti.html (January 3, 2009).
"Zakir Hussain," All Music Guide, http://www.allmusic.com (January 3, 2009).
"Zakir Hussain," Mondomix, http://zakir_hussain.mondomix.com/en/artiste.htm (January 3, 2009).
"Zakir Hussain," Moment! Records, http://momentrecords.com/zakir.html (January 3, 2009).
"Zakir Hussain Profile," I Love India, http://www.iloveindia.com/indian-heroes/zakir-hussain.html (January 3, 2009).☐

Ibn Bajja

The medieval Spanish writer and philosopher Abu Bakr Muhammad ibn Bajja (c. 1085–1139) was among the most influential thinkers to emerge from the Iberian peninsula during the period of Islamic control. Ibn Bajja is also known as Avempace, a Latin adaptation of his name. His works were widely read in medieval Europe within the Islamic tradition, and his influence was strong among Christian and Jewish writers as well.

During the Islamic period, extending from roughly the eighth century C.E. until 1492, the Muslim-ruled areas of what is now Spain and Portugal were called Al-Andalus or Andalusia. In many respects, Al-Andalus represented a golden age of philosophy, music, and mathematics. The region was plagued by religious warfare, but many rulers pursued enlightened policies of tolerance and encouragement of knowledge. Islamic philosophers, writing in Arabic, took the lead in rediscovering and extending the heritage of Greek philosophy and science, particularly as exemplified in the writings of Aristotle. Ibn Bajja preceded most of these philosophers and was one of the first to grasp the impact of Greek thought in its totality. Like Aristotle, Ibn Bajja was a polymath—a thinker whose knowledge extended across many disciplines. His writings, some of them cut short and left incomplete, extended beyond philosophy as the term is generally understood into mathematics, astronomy, music, physics, biology, and medicine. He was also noted as a poet who served some of the regional Islamic rulers of Iberia.

Grew Up in Highly Cultured Principality

Accounts of Ibn Bajja's life are sketchy, with much of what is known about him dependent on the recollections of later philosophers and large parts of his career missing from the record altogether. He was born in Zaragoza (also known as Saragossa), Spain, probably around 1085. Zaragoza at the time was the seat of a small Islamic emirate called the Banu Hud after its dynastic rulers, who were among the most educated and cultured of the entire region. Al-Mutaman ibn Hud, who was probably king when Ibn Bajja was born, was himself the author of a key mathematical treatise, *The Book of Perfection*. It is likely that Ibn Bajja's education took place in this milieu, which may have inspired his own philosophical efforts. He traveled to the city of Seville, some 800 kilometers distant, so that he could acquire instruction in astronomy there.

In the early twelfth century, an ethnically Berber dynasty called the Almoravids conquered much of southern and eastern Iberia. They came to Zaragoza in 1110. Ibn Bajja became closely connected to these rulers for most of his career, serving the Almoravid governor of the region, Ibn Tifalwit, as vizier or high-ranking minister in the mid-1110s. He was attractive to the Almoravids at first because of his skill as a rhetorician, and he was pressed into service as a speechwriter. Later he seems to have been accepted into the inner circles of the Almoravid rulers, sharing music and wine with them and writing court poetry of various kinds. When Ibn Bajja went on a diplomatic mission to meet with the deposed Hud king, he was imprisoned for several months for unknown reasons.

Nor did he find political stability when he returned to Zaragoza. The city was conquered by mixed Aragonese and French forces under Aragon's King Alfonso I (known as Alfonso the Warrior) and came under Christian control. Ibn

Bajja left the area, and hard information on his movements over the next decade and a half has been difficult to establish. Ibn Bajja is thought to have lived in various cities around Spain and North Africa, including Granada, Almería, and Oran. He may have served Yahya ibn Yusuf ibn TashufŽn, another scion of a North African dynasty, as vizier, and for part of his life he made a living as a physician. Other physicians are known to have been jealous of his skills and knowledge. Ibn Bajja was apparently something of a controversial figure in other fields as well; his poetry came under criticism from rivals, and his unique mixtures of religious and political philosophies did not always sit well in Almoravid circles. Nevertheless, he enjoyed a long career as a writer and was sought after as a teacher and adviser, although some of his writings, perhaps due to the rapidly changing political circumstances in which he found himself, were left unfinished.

Expounded Aristotelian Ideas

Although their chronology has not been fully established, Ibn Bajja's mature writings seem to fall into two groups. He seems to have begun by writing commentaries on Aristotle's ideas, expounding, critiquing, and refining them. In these treatises, which included *The Book of Animals,* Ibn Bajja sometimes combined Greek ideas with more advanced observations made by scientists in the Middle East. His *Discourse on Astronomy* was less concerned with the ideas of Aristotle than with those of another major Greek thinker, the astronomer Ptolemy. After writing his commentaries on Greek thought, Ibn Bajja went on to develop his own theory of knowledge, as well as a related set of ideas concerning how the philosophically minded might live in an imperfect world. While these works were also influenced by Greek ideas, they were of a more personal nature.

The Aristotelian system of knowledge encompassed many fields of inquiry, with overarching principles, such as deductive reasoning and the scientific method, covering them all. In his *Book of Demonstration,* Ibn Bajja expanded on the critique of Aristotle undertaken by an earlier Islamic philosopher, al-Farabi. Ibn Bajja outlined the issues that the scientific method raised in various fields, such as mathematics and biology. His ideas on physics mostly mirrored those of Aristotle, but he introduced new concepts (such as that of "fatigue" or resistance in the motion of bodies) that would prove fertile when they reached the mainstream of European science and philosophy: writers such as Thomas Aquinas and John Duns Scotus did not read Ibn Bajja's writings directly, but they were influenced by him through the works of Ibn Bajja's followers. The greatest late medieval physicist of them all, Galileo Galilei, was once thought to have been inspired by Ibn Bajja in the famous demonstration in which he dropped two balls of different weights off the Leaning Tower of Pisa to show that they would hit the ground at the same time. It is now doubted, however, that Galileo had direct contact with Ibn Bajja's ideas (and the Leaning Tower of Pisa story itself is thought to be fictional).

Ibn Bajja wrote widely on biology and medicine in such works as *The Book of Animals, The Discourse on Plants,* and the *Book on the Two Experiments Concerning Ibn Wafid's Drugs.* His approach throughout is systematic in the Aristotelian fashion. For example, he divides the subject of medicine into three subfields: the knowledge of objects (such as the body), the knowledge of medical aims, and the knowledge of technology and techniques. His discussions of biology are detailed and intriguing, even if mostly untenable from the point of view of modern science. Ibn Bajja broke with Aristotle but supported the work of Arab scientists in affirming the existence of male and female plants. In the realm of human sexuality, Ibn Bajja agreed with Aristotle (and disputed the great Roman physician Galen) in his observation that women may produce a semen-like fluid during sex, but that this fluid is not directly involved in reproduction.

Addressed Treatise to Student

It was probably later in his life that Ibn Bajja developed his theory of knowledge—his epistemology—and set it forth in a series of writings. One of those writings, the so-called *Epistle of Farewell,* was addressed to Ibn al-Imam, one of Ibn Bajja's students (who is known to have been with Ibn Bajja in Seville in 1136), on the occasion of the student's embarkation on a long journey. In it, Ibn Bajja expanded on the idea of spiritual health he had developed in other writings. He told the student that intellectual pleasure resulted from the discovery of traces of larger truths, and that pleasure itself existed in various degrees, the highest of which was scientific pleasure. In general, combining Greek and Islamic strains of thought, Ibn Bajja contended that knowledge and the soul develop by stages from purely physical phenomena to the levels of rationality and philosophy. Following a line of thought descending from Plato, he distinguished among various types of intelligible forms, proceeding from concrete to abstract, and he was especially reminiscent of Plato when he used the metaphor of dwelling in a cave to explain the ways ordinary people perceive the realm of forms.

Ibn Bajja generally viewed life as developing in stages; life, he believed, developed from plants to animals to reasoning beings, which he considered the highest. At the top of the pyramid was the philosopher, who inquires into universal truths. From this idea, Ibn Bajja developed the concepts (in treatises called *Management of the Solitary* and *Essay on the Conjunction of the Intellect with Human Beings*) of *al-ittisal,* or conjunction, and *al-tawwahud,* meaning solitude or union. In the words of Shams C. Inati, writing on the Web site muslimphilosophy.com, these are "the two most essential pillars on which Ibn Bajja's philosophy rests." They refer to states of mind of the philosopher. Al-ittisal occurs when the philosopher encounters universal truths, while al-tawwahud describes the position of the philosopher in society. Ibn Bajja, again following Plato and his intellectual descendants, went on to apply his ideas to the descriptions of an ideal city, the virtuous city, where inhabitants are happy because they have achieved perfection through holding true opinions. In an imperfect city, the inhabitants hold false opinions. Those, however, who live in imperfect cities but find the truth exist in a solitary state; Ibn Bajja (here borrowing from earlier Islamic writers but refining their ideas) calls them "weeds" or "weed-men."

During the last years of his life, Ibn Bajja seems to have worked mostly in North Africa. He died in the city of Fez, in present-day Morocco, in May of 1139—because, according to later stories, rival physicians resented his success and poisoned him, perhaps with an eggplant. He was said to have an arrogant personality that alienated those around him. However, his ideas were transmitted by his student Ibn al-Imam and by later writers in medieval Iberia, forming part of the great corpus of Islamic works that did much to reawaken Western interest in the accomplishments of the ancient Greeks and to reinvigorate the spirit of inquiry in Western philosophy and science.

Books

Complete Dictionary of Scientific Biography. Vol. 1, Scribner's, 2008.

Glick, Thomas F., Steven John Livesey, and Faith Wallis, eds., *Medieval Science, Technology, and Medicine: An Encyclopedia,* Routledge, 2005.

Online

"Ibn Bajja," Stanford Encyclopedia of Philosophy, http://www.plato.stanford.edu/entries/ibn-bajja (October 22, 2008).

"Ibn Bajja, Abu Bakr Muhammad ibn Yahya ibn as-Say'igh (d. 1138)," Islamic Philosophy Online, http://www.muslimphilosophy.com/ip/rep/H023.htm (October 22, 2008). □

Kon Ichikawa

Japanese filmmaker Kon Ichikawa (1915–2008) was among the great figures of 20th-century cinema, producing several works regarded as classics over a career lasting more than 70 years. His works ranged from comedies and mysteries to adaptations of classic literature to innovative documentary and semi-fictional films.

As a result of this diversity, Ichikawa was sometimes undervalued in comparison with the other directors who put Japan on the global cinematic map from the late 1940s to the early 1960s—instantly identifiable directors such as Akira Kurosawa and Yasujiro Ozu. Ichikawa often said that he simply made films he liked; he was not motivated by any underlying theme. Yet critics detected orientations that linked together his various films: he often focused on individuals in extreme situations, and he was interested in the stresses inherent in contemporary Japanese society, particularly those related to the family. Ichikawa was more comfortable with purely commercial filmmaking than were his contemporaries, who often struggled to get their films made. "He made not just art films, but also melodramas, documentaries, mysteries and others . . . and he brought to all of them a technique and craft that showed he took the works seriously no matter the subject," critic Tadao Sato told the *Japan Times.* "Even his light entertainments had class."

Injured in Baseball Accident

Kon Ichikawa was born in Uji-Yamada (now Ise), in Mie Prefecture, Japan, on November 20, 1915. His father died a short time later, and his mother supported the family by opening a kimono shop. Although he lived to be 92, he was in poor health for much of his childhood. From the start, drawing and painting were his best subjects in school, and he began to take art classes whenever he could. Ichikawa tried out for his high school baseball team, but an accident on the field in which he was hit by a ball injured his spine so severely that he was forced to drop out of school. Sent to live with relatives in the country, he soaked up the samurai action films that were among the few available forms of local entertainment.

By 18, Ichikawa had decided he wanted to pursue a career in the film industry himself. Thanks to his art skills, he landed a job in the animation department of the J.O. Studio in Kyoto. The Japanese animation scene was growing rapidly, and Ichikawa, who nurtured a lifelong admiration for the films of Walt Disney, quickly took on varied responsibilities at the studio. He devised new characters, wrote scripts for them, worked on continuity, and was taught how to direct animated films. The J.O. Studio, after several mergers, evolved into Toho, one of the major companies that made up the tightly knit Japanese studio system. Working full-time for Toho, Ichikawa learned about other aspects of the film industry. He always stressed the importance to his artistic development of his career as an animator, however, and critics detected compositions in scenes in his films that seemed to be derived from animation techniques. In fact, some of his films, such as *Mr. Pu* (1953) were adapted from printed comics.

Twice during World War II, Ichikawa received the red card that summoned him to report for military duty, but both times he was rejected for service due to health problems. As Japan recovered from the devastation of the war, Ichikawa was ready to begin his career as a feature director. In 1945 he made a puppet film called *A Girl at Dojo Temple,* but it was improperly submitted to American censors for approval and was later lost. Moving to the rival Shintoho studio, he made the melodrama often regarded as his debut, *A Flower Blooms,* in 1948. The film dealt with the weakness of Japan's middle class before the war. Ichikawa made *365 Nights* for the same studio later that year and enjoyed his first commercial success.

Wife Worked on Screenplays

Ichikawa's first marriage ended in divorce, but in 1948 he married screenwriter Natto Wada. The couple had two sons, and Wada became Ichikawa's professional partner as well. She wrote the scripts for many of his films from the late 1940s until the mid-1960s, and during the period regarded as the peak of Ichikawa's career—from about 1954 to 1965—they worked closely together. During that period, Ichikawa's films reveal a sharply satirical attitude toward Japanese society. In the 1954 film *A Billionaire,* a hapless tax collector with a fear of nuclear attack visits a comic variety of delinquent taxpayers and finally moves into a ramshackle house that he thinks will be safe, only to discover that his next-door neighbors, a family of 18, are trying to manufacture a bomb of their own. In the dark comedy *The Key* (1959), Ichikawa depicted a wealthy but aging man who bribes his son-in-law to have an affair with his young wife, hoping that his own jealousy will stave off his own impotence. The film was adapted from a novel by Tanizaki Junichiro, and many other Ichikawa films drew on classic or contemporary Japanese literature for source material.

Very different in tone was Ichikawa's widely acclaimed *The Burmese Harp* (1956), the story of a former Japanese soldier in Burma after Japan's surrender at the end of World War II. The soldier has become a Buddhist monk and attempts as far as possible to bury the bodies of his fallen comrades. The film, on which Ichikawa was called in to replace the ailing director Tomotaka Tasaka, earned an Academy Award nomination for Best Foreign Language Film. It was followed by another antiwar film, *Fires on the Plain* (1959), which depicted cannibalism among Japanese soldiers stranded in the Philippines.

One sign of the close connection between Ichikawa's cinematic images and the currents of Japanese society was that he was able to make convincing films about actual events; several of these were among his most convincing and characteristic works. *Conflagration* (1958) was based on a novel by Yukio Mishima (*The Burning of the Golden Pavilion*), which in turn was based on the 1950 destruction of a centuries-old Buddhist temple by a disturbed young worshipper. Ichikawa's *Tokyo Olympiad* (1965), the last film on which he worked with Wada, was a documentary of an entirely innovative type, anticipating the unusual perspectives of later documentarians. Its subject was the 1964 Olympic Games in Tokyo, but, especially in its uncut 165-minute version, the film focused closely on the spectators at the Games.

Made Genre Films

Many of Ichikawa's films were both serious and innovative, but he also worked comfortably within the boundaries of Japanese genre cinema and still won critical acclaim. He made edgy mysteries (*Ten Dark Women,* 1961), family dramas (*Her Brother,* 1960), and a curious film about childhood (*I Am Two,* also known as *Being Two Isn't Easy,* 1962). *The Actor's Revenge* (1963), is an over-the-top camp drama about a female impersonator in the kabuki theater form who sets out to avenge the deaths of his parents. Olaf Moller, writing in *Film Comment,* called *The Actor's Revenge* "total cinema at its most outrageous." *The Wanderers* (1973) was a satire on the yakuza (Japanese organized crime) films of that time.

Ichikawa remained prolific over his entire career, with more than 70 features to his credit by the time of his death plus numerous earlier films to which he contributed in some capacity. He continued to direct new films at a consistent clip during the 1970s and 1980s. Some of these equaled the innovative energy of his earlier films; *I Am a Cat* (1975) was told from the point of view of a suicidal feline. But Ichikawa's prolific output somewhat diluted his critical reputation. "Today," Moller wrote in 2001, "he's regarded as a master who's lost his touch, a relic from another era stubbornly refusing to retire, and, worst of all, a sellout." During his later years he often made new versions of his earlier films such as a second *The Burmese Harp* (1985).

Critical hesitation did not diminish Ichikawa's commercial success in Japan, however, as films such as the mystery thriller *The Inugami Family* (1976) became major hits. Many of Ichikawa's later films were mysteries, a form for which he had a particular affection. He enjoyed the novels of British mystery author Agatha Christie and often used the name Shitei Kuri (a Japanese rendering of the name Agatha Christie) as a pseudonym. He also made a 26-part television serial of the classic Japanese novel *The Tale of Genji.* In 2001 Ichikawa was given a lifetime achievement award at the Montreal Film Festival. Ichikawa's last film was *Clan of the Inugami,* a remake of *The Inugami Family,* which appeared in 2006 when the director was 91. He died in Tokyo on February 13, 2008.

Books

Allyn, Jon, *Kon Ichikawa—A Guide to References and Resources,* Hall, 1985.

International Dictionary of Films and Filmmakers, Volume 2, 4th ed., St. James, 2000.

Quandt, James, ed. *Kon Ichikawa,* Cinematheque Ontario, 2001.

Periodicals

Film Comment, July-August 2001, p. 30.
Guardian (London, England), February 14, 2008, p. 38.
Independent (London, England), February 15, 2008, p. 40.
Japan Times, February 14, 2008.
New York Times, February 14, 2008, p. C12.
Sight and Sound, Spring 1966, p. 85.
Times (London, England), March 11, 2008, p. 72.
Variety, February 18, 2008, p. 49.

Online

"Kon Ichikawa," *Senses of Cinema,* http://archive.sensesofcinema.
com/contents/directors/04/ichikawa.html (January 10, 2009).

"Kon Ichikawa: Profile," BBC Four, http://www.bbc.co.uk/bbcfour/
cinema/features/kon-ichikawa.shtml (January 10, 2009). ☐

Hayato Ikeda

**Hayato Ikeda (1899–1965) began his career as a
bureaucrat in Japan during World War II. Following
the war, Ikeda played a critical role in rebuilding his
nation. First as finance minister, then as trade minister, and finally as prime minister, Ikeda helped
propel Japan to the forefront of the world economy.**

Hayato Ikeda was born on December 3, 1899, in
Takehara in southern Japan. Born to a successful
sake brewer's family, Ikeda lived a privileged
childhood. Sake is an alcoholic beverage made from rice.
Though little information is available, it is known that Ikeda
received a good early education.

Later he studied law and economics at Kyota Imperial
University, and graduated with a law degree in 1925. After
graduating, Ikeda went immediately into public service,
beginning his career as an official in the tax office of the
Prefectures for the Ministry of Finance.

Ikeda remained at the Ministry of Finance for several
years. Then in the 1930s, a rare skin disease called pemphi-
gus left Ikeda bedridden. Unable to work, Ikeda dropped
out of politics for several years. He sought medical care
and religious relief, visiting both hospitals and Buddhist
shrines and temples. During the course of his recovery,
Ikeda became a vegetarian.

War and Postwar

Ikeda recovered from his illness just at the outset of World
War II. He served in a largely bureaucratic capacity during
the war, and had little to do with foreign affairs or external
matters that affected the nation's conduct abroad. In 1945
Ikeda became the chief of the tax bureau in the Ministry of
Finance. Two years later, Prime Minister Shigeru Yoshida
appointed Ikeda as the deputy, or vice minister, of finance.
Ikeda served in that position until 1948, and had great
esteem for Yoshida.

In January of 1949, Ikeda won his first seat in the
national legislature, known as the Diet. As a member of the
House of Representatives, the lower house of the Diet, Ikeda
soon became the minister of finance. Yoshida was still prime
minister, and Ikeda continued to support his policies. World
War II had ended, leaving Japan devastated by the conflict
and its aftermath. The United States and the Allied Powers,
who won the war, stripped Japan of its military power. Yoshida, Ikeda, and others in Japan's new government set about
rebuilding Japan into a world economic power.

As finance minister, Ikeda focused on reducing inflation. Inflation is the rate at which prices in an economy
increase. High inflation means that prices increase by large
amounts, making it more difficult for people and businesses
to buy goods. Inflation in Japan was very high following
World War II.

Ikeda worked with U.S. banker Joseph Dodge to find
solutions to Japan's high inflation. Dodge, the chairman of
the Detroit Bank, had come to Japan in 1948 to evaluate the
nation's struggling postwar economy. He also assisted in
rebuilding Germany's economy. Dodge's recommendations became known as the Dodge Line, and Ikeda supported most of its measures. In particular, Ikeda agreed that
Japan had to balance its national budget in order to reduce
inflation. A nation's budget is its plan for earning and
spending money. A balanced budget means that a nation
does not spend more money than it takes in.

Ikeda served as finance minister until 1952. During
that time, he also accepted an appointment as Minister of

International Trade and Industry. As trade minister, Ikeda worked to pass policies that favored large industry in order to strengthen Japan's position in world trade. Unfortunately, policies that favored big industry often harmed smaller businesses. The unpopularity of such policies forced Ikeda to resign his ministerial post in response.

Ikeda stayed on as finance minister. He served the remainder of the 1950s as either Minister of Finance or Minister without Portfolio. A minister without portfolio retains his or her office and has certain ministerial powers but does not head a particular department of government. Even without portfolio, Ikeda remained a strong voice in Yoshida's administration.

In 1950 the United States went to war again, this time in Korea. Japan was able to win U.S. military contracts during this war. Producing goods for the U.S. military helped jump-start the Japanese economy. Japan—and Ikeda—also played a key role in the Korean peace negotiations that began in 1951 and dragged on for two years.

That same year, Ikeda and other Japanese officials decided to address Japan's military position. Ikeda joined a delegation that went to San Francisco, California, to negotiate a final peace between Japan and the Allied Powers of World War II. As part of the settlement of World War II, Japan had passed a new constitution in 1947, under which it could neither make war on another nation nor maintain a standing army. To ensure that Japan abided by the terms of the peace treaty and its new constitution, the Allied powers had stationed occupying forces in the country.

The 1952 Treaty of San Francisco provided for the end of the Allied occupation of Japan. It also allowed Japan to maintain a national self defense force. The purpose of this defensive military force was to maintain peace, order, security, and independence in the nation. The national constitution still prohibited Japan from using its military in an aggressive capacity. Ikeda played a crucial role in finalizing this agreement, not only through his participation in the San Francisco talks but also in follow-up negotiations with U.S. Assistant Secretary of State Walter S. Robertson in 1953.

Final talks between Japan and the United States in 1954 resulted in the U.S.-Japan Mutual Defense Assistance Agreement. This agreement not only allowed Japan to increase its defense forces but also provided for splitting the cost of rebuilding Japan's military between the United States and Japan. It also encouraged U.S. investment in Japan. The U.S. stance on Japan and Japan's rearmament caused a great deal of outcry, both outside and within Japan.

Political Unrest and a New Prime Minister

In 1956, after the completion of talks and signing of agreements, Japan was admitted to the United Nations, an international body set up to maintain peace, protect human rights, and mediate among nations. In 1960 Japan and the United States also negotiated a new mutual defense treaty, called the Treaty of Mutual Cooperation and Security. This new agreement prompted further protest. Thousands of people gathered outside the Japanese Diet in Tokyo to demand the dissolution of the government. Although this unrest destabilized Japan's government, it led to Ikeda's rise in rank.

Japan had gained a new prime minister, Nobusuke Kishi, in 1957. Against outstanding opposition and criticism, Kishi signed the mutual defense agreement with the United States in June of 1960. He then resigned, leaving a vacuum of power in the Liberal Democratic Party and in the prime minister's office.

Ikeda moved to gain support for the agreements, and quickly won the backing of Yoshida. Kishi also threw his support behind Ikeda, and on July 14, 1960, Ikeda became the president of the Liberal Democratic Party. A few days later he was elected the nation's 58th prime minister in a special session of the Diet. Ikeda took office on July 19.

Ikeda's Leadership

As Prime Minister, Ikeda continued to focus most of his efforts on building Japan's economy. Although he maintained a pro-Western stance and worked to maintain good relations with the United States, Ikeda largely kept Japan out of international conflict. Under Ikeda's foreign policy, Japan maintained open contact with many nations, including China and the Soviet Union, both of whom the United States viewed as key opponents in the Cold War.

The first action of Ikeda's administration was to resolve a long-running labor dispute at the Miike Mine of Mitsui Mining Company. Ikeda intervened in 1960 and called for mediation between the company and the workers. Although the resolution was viewed as largely pro-company and anti-labor, it did prevent further violence and provide for the return of many workers to the mine.

Ikeda and his administration intervened in several labor disputes, but the major platform of Ikeda's government program was the Income Doubling Plan. Ikeda promised to double the national income in ten years, to achieve complete employment, and to increase the standard of living in the country. Under Ikeda, the government expanded public works, increased employment, reduced taxes and inflation, removed trade barriers, and increased exports. Ikeda also promoted a social security program.

Investment in Japan's public sector led to increasing private investment, and the economy took off. Ikeda's economic policies proved largely successful. The national income doubled not in ten years but in just over four. Ikeda's successes secured him and his party re-election twice.

Although Ikeda wanted to keep Japan out of the Cold War and international conflict, he did work to normalize relations—or open and maintain peace talks—with other nations. He pursued trade not only with western nations but also with the Soviet Union and China. In 1961 Ikeda met with Korean leader Park Chunghee to improve relations with the nation that Japan had once invaded. Between 1961 and 1964, Ikeda visited with many foreign leaders in North America, Europe, and Asia, including U.S. President John F. Kennedy.

In April of 1964, Ikeda led Japan to join the Organization for Economic Cooperation and Development. Formed in 1948, this international body brought more than two dozen countries together to support free markets and economic cooperation. That same year, Japan also hosted the 18th Olympic Games, an important event in securing Japan a prominent place on the world stage and reinvigorating its national economy.

Hosting the Olympics spurred a rampant period of economic development and internal improvements. New roads, highways, and subways were built, and Japan's first high-speed bullet train launched, connecting Tokyo and Osaka. Public facilities and utilities also received huge amounts of investment. New buildings and other structures went up. Employment boomed, and the games themselves led to large increases in tourism and other spending.

Unfortunately, by the time of the Olympics, Ikeda had also been diagnosed with throat cancer and his health was rapidly declining. Ikeda made it through the Olympics, announcing his resignation from the ministry and from public life on October 25, 1964, the day after the closing ceremony. Ikeda left office on November 9. His friend and former colleague, Sato Eisako, succeeded him as prime minister.

Ikeda's Legacy

Ikeda died less than a year after leaving office, on August 18, 1965. He had devoted most of his life to public service. Little information is available about Ikeda's private life, though it is known that he was married twice. His first wife died early in his career, in the 1930s, and he remarried not long after. He had children with his second wife.

Ikeda presided over the largest period of economic growth in Japan's history. By the mid-1960s, at the end of his term, Japan's average economic growth was above 10 percent. On its Web site, the Liberal Democratic Party of Japan noted that "the Ikeda administration was able to accomplish great things both at home and abroad." The Web site went on to explain that the "bold economic policies" of Ikeda's administration helped lead to "Japan's even more active participation in international trade that further fueled the economy's expansion."

Ikeda's policies enabled Japan not only to recover from the devastation of World War II and the country's subsequent Occupation, but to actually surpass most other nations in the world economy. Today, Japan remains an economic superpower, thanks largely to policies and programs initiated in Ikeda's time.

Books

Encyclopedia of Modern Asia, Vol. 3, Charles Scribner's Sons, Gale, 2006.

LaFeber, Walter, *The Clash,* W. W. Norton & Company, 1997.

Matray, James I., *Japan's Emergence as a Global Power Explained,* Greenwood Press, 2001.

Scalapino, Robert A., and Junnosuke Masumi, *Parties and Politics in Contemporary Japan,* University of California Press, 1964.

Periodicals

Bulletin of Concerned Asian Scholars, Vol. 23, 1991, pp. 30–43.
Time, November 29, 1963.

Online

"Chapter Four: Period of President Ikeda's Leadership," *Liberal Democratic Party of Japan,* http://www.jimin.jp/jimin/english/history/chap4.html (October 16, 2008).

"Hayato Ikeda," *Biografias y Vidas,* http://www.biografiasyvidas.com/biografia/i/ikeda.htm (October 16, 2008).

"Hayato Ikeda," *NationMaster,* http://www.nationmaster.com/encyclopedia/Hayata-Ikeda (October 16, 2008).

"Hayato Ikeda, History of Japan," *World History Database,* http://www.badley.info/history/Ikeda-Hayato-Japan.biog.html (October 16, 2008).

"Ikeda, Hayato," *Columbia Encyclopedia,* http://www.bartleby.com/65/ik/Ikeda-Ha.html (October 16, 2008).

"Ikeda, Hayato," *Encyclopedia Britannica,* http://www.search.eb.com/eb/article-9042091 (October 16, 2008).

"Postwar (since 1945)," *japan-guide.com,* http://www.japan-guide.com/e/e2124.html (January 10, 2009).

"The Rise of the Japanese Miracle," *All Empires,* http://www.allempires.com/article/index.php?q=The_Rise_of_the_Japanese_Miracle (October 16, 2008).

"Self Defense Force," *japan-guide.com,* http://www.japan-guide.com/e/e2138.html (January 10, 2009). ☐

J

Joseph Joachim

Austrian violinist and composer Joseph Joachim (1831–1907) was one of the greatest European performers of the nineteenth century, and also, through his teaching as well as his example, one of the most influential.

Even in an age of violin "titans," noted David Schoenbaum of the *New York Times,* "there was general agreement that two were more titanic than the others: the eminently Italian Niccolo Paganini... and the definitively Central European Joseph Joachim." The two violinists were quite different in the way they presented themselves: Paganini was a model for all the showman virtuosi who came after him, but Joachim was a serious musician devoted to the ideas of beauty and perfection. Several of the major composers of the late 19th century wrote new violin concertos (pieces for violin and orchestra) for Joachim, and he did much to incorporate the violin works and the difficult string quartets of Beethoven into the standard classical repertory. His friends included Brahms and Schumann, whom he also introduced to each other. In short, Joachim stood at the center of the German-Austrian musical tradition that continues to fundamentally shape classical music today.

Made Recital Debut at Seven

Joseph Joachim was born June 28, 1831 in the small town of Kittsee in the Austrian Empire; the town is now in Austria, near Bratislava, Slovakia. Like many other musicians around the cultural crossroads of central Europe, he had a multicultural upbringing. When he was two, his family moved to Pest, now part of the city of Budapest, Hungary,

and he has sometimes been described as Hungarian. Raised in the Jewish faith, he later adopted Lutheranism and regarded himself as culturally German, however. Joachim took violin lessons from a local teacher named Szervaczinski or Serwaczynski, who presented him in recital at the tender age of seven.

Soon it was clear that there was no more for the teachers in Pest to give the young prodigy, and he was sent to the imperial capital of Vienna. His first teacher there was Joseph Hellmesberger, but, according to Joachim's 1907 interview in the *Times* of London, "this master feared that nothing could overcome the boy's deficiencies" acquired during years of substandard instruction in Hungary. Joachim ended up a student of Vienna Conservatory professor Joseph Böhm, a direct associate of Beethoven, who rebuilt the young violinist's technique. In 1843 the preteen Joachim moved on to Leipzig, Germany, where a major new conservatory had been established. Composer Felix Mendelssohn, the conductor of the city's famed Gewandhaus Orchestra, proclaimed that Joachim's conservatory education was over.

Joachim gave a concert with Mendelssohn, singer Pauline Viardot, and pianist Clara Schumann shortly after arriving in Leipzig. For several months he studied privately with violinist Ferdinand David and composer Moritz Hauptmann, and then the 12-year-old was ready for stardom. Mendelssohn took him to England, where he performed for Queen Victoria. Joachim played a series of concerts in England, where he remained popular for the rest of his life; a performance of Beethoven's violin concerto with Mendelssohn conducting took place at the Philharmonic Society on May 27, 1844, and was famous for years afterward. The Beethoven concerto—not especially flashy but musically profound—became one of the pillars of Joachim's repertoire, and he did much to cement the work's ongoing place on concert programs.

Became Royal Music Director

Returning to the Continent, Joachim settled in Leipzig. He rose to the rank of associate concertmaster in the Gewandhaus Orchestra. For some time, Joachim worked within the musical patronage system of what remained of the small monarchies and noble realms that coalesced into the modern nation of Germany. In 1850, he left to become the concertmaster of the court orchestra of the Duchy of Saxe-Weimar in the city of Weimar. He remained there for three years but clashed with the mercurial Franz Liszt, who at the time dominated the court's musical life. In 1853 Joachim became royal music director for the Kingdom of Hannover, becoming active as a composer and conductor during this time. Some of Joachim's theatrical overtures date from this period of his career.

During this period of residence in central Germany, Joachim became friendly with both Clara Schumann and her ailing husband Robert, originally gaining their attention with an 1853 performance in Düsseldorf. He gave the 20-year-old Viennese composer Johannes Brahms a letter of introduction to the Schumanns, resulting in a long creative relationship (and a serious flirtation) between Brahms and Clara Schumann. Joachim continued to compose, and with Robert Schumann and Albert Dietrich he wrote an extremely unusual collaborative sonata for violin and piano (each composer wrote one of the three movements) based on the notes F-A-E—based on Joachim's personal motto, "Frei aber Einsam" (free but lonely). Before succumbing to syphilis-induced insanity, Schumann wrote a violin concerto for Joachim.

Although he had converted to Lutheranism by that time (and enthusiastically backed the Prussian side in the Franco-Prussian War in 1870), Joachim attempted to stand up for the rights of Jewish musicians, whose situation in German lands was always tenuous. In 1865 he resigned his post in Hannover in protest over discrimination against a Jewish composer. By that time, Joachim's reputation as a violinist had risen to its height. Joachim was famous not only as a soloist but also for his participation in string quartet performances of music by Mozart and Beethoven. The modern image of the string quartet as an intellectual dialogue among equals owes much to Joachim; his contemporary Ole Bull, when he played string quartets, would seat himself alone on stage as first violinist, relegating the other players to a spot behind the curtain. In 1869 he formed his own Joachim Quartet.

In 1868 Joachim became director and professor of violin at Berlin's Hochschule für Ausübende Tonkunst (College for Applied Musical Arts). The school was largely Joachim's own creation, and this was an important post that gave him the opportunity to shape the talents of the next generation of central European violinists. Among the many young violinists who traveled to Berlin to study with him were several who, like Joachim, were either Jewish, came from the distant lands of Eastern Europe, or both. They included Leopold Auer, Hungary's Jenö Hubay, and Poland's Bronislaw Huberman. Joachim remained close to Brahms and gave the composer technical pointers as he shaped his violin concerto, one of the greatest works in the genre. Joachim, with Brahms conducting the orchestra, gave the work's premiere in 1879. Auer trained many of the Eastern European violinists who settled in the United States in the 20th century, and much violin teaching in the U.S. even today remains only a few steps removed from Joachim's direct influence.

Suffered Through Messy Divorce

In 1863, Joachim married the vocalist Amalie Weiss, and the couple had six children. The marriage dissolved in spectacular fashion when Joachim accused his wife of cheating on him with the music publisher Fritz Simrock. Joachim's German-language biographer Beatrix Borchard attributed strains in the marriage to Joachim's attempts to control his wife's activities—she had resumed her operatic career after raising their six children. Friends of the couple split into two camps, and the relationship between Joachim and Brahms was temporarily ruptured. That friendship was not patched up until Brahms wrote a concerto for violin, cello, and orchestra in 1887, and Joachim performed the solo violin part at the premiere.

Even the bad publicity resulting from the divorce could not do much to dent Joachim's popularity, and by the 1880s he was considered perhaps the greatest violinist in the world. In European capitals from London to St. Petersburg, a concert by Joachim was a hot ticket. He played concertos by Beethoven, Brahms, Mendelssohn, or one of his own, often a "Hungarian" concerto in which he drew on the music he had heard as a youth. The Czech composer Antonín Dvorák and the Dane Niels Gade both wrote new concertos for Joachim. He also carried forward Mendelssohn's rediscovery of the music of Johann Sebastian Bach, performing the composer's fiendishly difficult sonatas and partitas for unaccompanied violin.

Despite his fame and his exalted attitude toward the art of music, Joachim was a generous figure who retained traces of his gregarious Eastern European youth. He enjoyed telling jokes in German dialect, and he was always ready to sit down in a string quartet with a group of amateurs or to help a colleague find a rare violin. Despite the conflict with his wife, he did not try to put obstacles in the way of the careers of the late 19th century's few female composers, and he was a lifelong friend to Jewish musicians.

Joachim was richly honored later in life, with several honorary degrees, a Stradivarius violin presented by the British prime minister, and a portrait by painter John Singer Sargent among his tributes. One of his last works was an Overture in C major, a birthday gift for Germany's Kaiser Wilhelm II. Joachim's death in Berlin on August 15, 1907, was followed by an elaborate funeral encompassing five wagons filled with flowers. A Norwegian-American violin maker, Knute Reindahl, devised a tribute of his own: a violin topped by a small Joachim head instead of the usual wooden scroll. "In Joseph Joachim," wrote in the *Times,* "the world has lost not merely the greatest violinist of our time, but a man of exceptional beauty of nature and character."

Books

Fuller-Maitland, J.A., *Joseph Joachim,* John Lane, 1905.

Slonimsky, Nicolas, ed. emeritus, *Baker's Biographical Dictionary of Music and Musicians,* centennial ed, Schirmer, 2001.

Periodicals

American Record Guide, September 1999, p. 176.

New York Times, September 15, 1985; August 12, 2007, p. AR19.

Times (London, England), August 16, 1989.

Online

"Joseph Joachim: Life," http://www.karadar.it/Dictionary/joachim.html (January 15, 2009).□

Ollie Johnston

American film animator Ollie Johnston (1912–2008), as part of his work in the animation studio of producer and director Walt Disney, created some of the most familiar images in the history of animated film, and significantly advanced the emotional impact of the genre.

Johnston's career began with *Snow White and the Seven Dwarfs,* Disney's first feature film, and continued through the heyday of Disney Productions. His contributions were important to such Disney classics as *Pinocchio* and *Fantasia,* and the groundbreaking *Bambi*

(1942) was fundamentally shaped by his work. Johnston, whom Disney referred to as one of the elite "Nine Old Men" who defined the style of his animated films, continued his affiliation with Disney for his entire working life, contributing to Disney films through the 1960s and 1970s. In the words of Walt Disney's nephew Roy E. Disney, as quoted by Pat Saperstein of *Variety,* "Ollie was part of an amazing generation of artists, one of the real pioneers of our art, one of the major participants in the blossoming of animation into the art form we know today.... He brought warmth and wit and sly humor and a wonderful gentleness to every character he animated."

Attended Grade School on Stanford Campus

Oliver Martin Johnston was born in Palo Alto, California on October 31, 1912. In view of his long life (he died at 96), Johnston surprisingly suffered from serious health problems as a child. He lived through major childhood diseases (whooping cough, measles, and chicken pox), contracted pleurisy, and broke several bones. Athletics helped to restore his health; he was an enthusiastic football player, hiker, swimmer, and track and field participant who could often been seen working out in a field near Stanford University. Johnston's father was a professor of Romance Languages there, and Johnston himself enrolled at Stanford in 1931, after graduating from Palo Alto High School. His grade school classes were even held in a school on the Stanford campus. Johnston's future animation colleague

Frank Thomas, according to John Canemaker of the *Wall Street Journal,* made the accurate guess that "Ollie is stuck together with spit and string but will outlast everyone."

Johnston attended Stanford for three years, majoring in art and considering a career as a magazine illustrator. For his last year he moved to Chouinard Art Institute in Los Angeles (now part of the California Institute for the Arts), graduating from there in 1935 and getting the chance to mix with creative people in the burgeoning Hollywood film industry. Johnston moved to Southern California with Thomas, who had already landed a job with Disney, and in 1935 he himself was hired at a salary of $17 a week as an assistant to animator Fred Moore. At first he was an "in-betweener," producing drawings that linked together the main scenes created by more senior animators. The first films he worked on were Mickey Mouse shorts: *Mickey's Garden* (1935), *Pluto's Judgment Day* (1935), and *Mickey's Rival* (1936).

Still an assistant as *Snow White and the Seven Dwarfs* went into production for its 1937 release, Johnston worked on the animation of the impressively individualized dwarfs in that film. After another Mickey Mouse short, *The Brave Little Tailor* (1938) was particularly successful, Disney elevated Johnston to principal animator, along with Moore, for *Pinocchio* in 1940. The image of Pinocchio's nose growing as his lies are discovered was Johnston's creation, although the bird's nest that appears at the end of the scene was suggested by another animator. Johnston also animated the scene in which the puppet Pinocchio comes alive. His work on that scene inspired one of Disney's rare compliments. "I sure like those Pinocchios you're doing," Disney barked as he walked by Johnston's workspace, according to a *Wall Street Journal* article. Johnston demurred, saying that he was just following the example of the other animators. "I don't give a damn where you get it. Just keep doing it!" Disney ordered.

Studied Animal Anatomy

Johnston worked on *Fantasia* in 1940 before being promoted, with Thomas, to the position of supervising animator for 1942's *Bambi,* the story of the life of a young deer. The pair sweated over the details of their new assignment, going to the zoo and watching films of animals. "We had a guy who was a real authority on animal anatomy," Johnston recalled (as quoted in the *Times* of London). "Walt hired him to come teach us all about the anatomy of deer muscles." Sometimes Johnston used his own anatomy as a model. "If you shrug your shoulders, you feel how they work," Johnston said, according to the *Times* of London. "If you squint your eyes and open them wide you can feel how it stretches your face," Among the film's crucial moments, Johnston soon realized, would be the one in which hunters shoot Bambi's mother. Johnston was developing a style in which motion and drawn facial expressions were more important than dialogue in involving the audience, and this moment was tailor-made for his growing abilities.

The scene became a classic tear-jerker that affected several generations of audience. "It showed how convincing we could be at presenting really strong emotion," Johnston was quoted as saying in the *Albany Times Union.*

Some thought of Johnston's techniques, and Disney's style in general, as sentimental, but as the *Independent* noted, when *Bambi* appeared in 1942, "the very achievement of bringing animal drawings to life and triggering an emotional response in a mass audience was little short of groundbreaking." With his career in full flower, Johnston married his wife, Marie, in 1943. The marriage lasted until 2005 and produced two sons.

Now often outsourced to lower-wage markets, animation is difficult, time-consuming work. In his early years with Disney, Johnston and Thomas spent long hours at the studio—"eating, sleeping and drinking animation," in the words of Thomas's son Theodore in a 1995 documentary about the pair, according to the article from *Insight on the News.* After World War II their hours became more regular, although they never gave up their rigorous preparation for each film. As they devised the elderly Good Fairies in *Sleeping Beauty* (1959), they closely observed the gaits and hairstyles of elderly women in a local supermarket. Johnston worked on all the Disney classics of the 1950s, including *Cinderella* (1950), *Alice in Wonderland* (1951), *Peter Pan* (1953), and *Lady and the Tramp* (1955).

Modeled Cat on Self

Two more of Johnston's most touching inventions came in films made in the 1960s. In 1961's *101 Dalmatians,* he was responsible for many of the scenes involving the parents of the 101 Dalmatians, Pongo and Perdita, and in particular for one scene in which Pongo gives Perdita a consoling lick after she is frightened by the hated Cruella De Vil. The magical friendship between wild child Mowgli and the bear Baloo in *The Jungle Book* (1967), including their song-and-dance routine "The Bear Necessities," was also Johnston's work. Disney died before the completion of that film, but Johnston's career continued to flourish with such films as *The Aristocats* (1970) and *Robin Hood* (1973). In his last film, 1977's *The Rescuers,* Johnston created a cat named Rufus that he admitted was modeled on himself with its mustache and warm personality.

Johnston retired in 1978 due to hand tremors, an inherited condition, that finally worsened to a point where it was difficult for him to draw. That gave him more time to pursue a passion for model trains—which Disney also enjoyed. His enthusiasm manifested itself in 1946 in a set of railroad tracks and small-gauge locomotive he constructed on his property in La Cañada Flintridge, California, and finally in the refurbishing of a full-size 1901 steam engine that he installed on half a mile of track near his vacation home in suburban San Diego.

Several animators in the generation after Johnston benefited from his training, including Andreas Deja, John Lasseter, and Brad Bird (who observed to Canemaker that drawings "flowed out of him [Johnston] like water"). Johnston and Thomas passed on their knowledge and experiences in a series of four books, beginning with *The Illusion of Life: Disney Animation* in 1981. That book remains a standard text for aspiring animators, and it was followed by books on sight gags (1987), on *Bambi* specifically (1990), and on Disney's villains (1993). The documentary *Frank and Ollie,* about Thomas and Johnston, appeared in 1995.

Vitally interested in developments in animation, Johnston tried out a new computer paint system at the Lucasfilm studios in Northern California near the end of his life. In 2005 he was awarded the National Medal of the Arts by President George W. Bush in a White House ceremony. Moving in his old age to Sequim, Washington to be closer to his son Ken, Johnston died there on April 14, 2008.

Periodicals

Albany Times Union, April 17, 2008, p. P25.
Economist, April 26, 2008, p. 109.
Guardian (London, England), April 17, 2008, p. 34.
Independent (London, England), April 17, 2008, p. 24, 34.
Insight on the News, July 15, 1996, p. 34.
New York Sun, April 16, 2008, p. 12.
Times (London, England), April 17, 2008, p. 67.
Variety, April 16, 2008, p. 2.
Wall Street Journal, April 22, 2008, p. D9.

Online

Official Frank Thomas and Ollie Johnston website, http://www. frankandollie.com (January 17, 2009).
"Ollie Johnston (Animation)," Disney Legends, http://legends. disney.go.com/legends/detail?key=Ollie+Johnston (January 17, 2009). □

Chuck Jones

American animator and filmmaker Chuck Jones (1912–2002) became famous for the comic characters he created for the animated films of the Warner Brothers studio, including the Roadrunner and his hapless nemesis, Wile E. Coyote.

J ones also expanded the visual vocabulary of many of the other Warner Brothers animated characters he inherited, such as Bugs Bunny, Daffy Duck, and Porky Pig. More generally, he set Warner Brothers on a different path from its chief rival in the American animation field, Walt Disney Studios. Thanks in large part to Jones's work, Warner Brothers cartoons became humorous, satirical, and anarchic whereas Disney's were sentimental and idealistic. In the words of *Senses of Cinema,* "Chuck Jones can be plausibly described as the most influential individual in the history of animated film."

Watched Chaplin Filming

A native of Spokane, Washington, Charles Martin Jones was born September 21, 1912. His parents were fruit farmers, and when he was six months old they moved to Los Angeles, growing oranges and then avocados on a farm on still semi-rural Sunset Boulevard. The Charles Chaplin Film Studio was a few blocks away, and the young Jones liked to watch through the gates as the famous film comedian honed scenes to the perfect timing that made them classics. He also landed occasional roles as an extra in the slapstick

comedies of director Mack Sennett. Jones was the youngest of four children, all of whom were encouraged to develop their artistic abilities. His two older brothers became artists, and his sister a fashion designer.

At Franklin High School in Los Angeles, Jones drew cartoons for the school newspaper and yearbook. He finished high school at the age of 15 and enrolled at Chouinard Art Institute, which was later to become the destination of other animators including Disney's Ollie Johnston. Graduating in 1930 when the film industry was plunging into the Great Depression, Jones took whatever work he could get, which included puppeteer and dollar-an-image sidewalk sketch artist. In 1931 he entered the animation industry as a cel washer—an assistant who rinsed off animators' celluloid sheets so that they could be reused—at Celebrity Productions, run by animation pioneer and early Disney associate Ub Iwerks (Ubbe Ert Iwwerks). At one point he was fired temporarily; the secretary who delivered the bad news, Dorothy Webster, became Jones's first wife.

Jones was soon promoted to a job with animator Grim Natwick as an "in-betweener," an assistant who performed the tedious work of making the transitional drawings that connected the main poses sketched by a head animator. That lasted until 1933, when Celebrity Productions closed. Jones landed with Leon Schlesinger Productions, a fertile animation studio that provided short films under contract to Warner Brothers and was eventually absorbed into the larger company. Jones was given a job in the company's new cartoon production unit, a hotbed of creativity where both Daffy Duck and Porky Pig were first devised. The company's animators benefited from Schlesinger's hands-off attitude toward the creative team's activities, and Jones worked his way up from in-betweener to story writer, gag-smith, animator, and finally assistant director. His first credit came in 1935 as an animator on the short subject *Buddy of the Legion.*

The film, a military parody about an attack by a group of Amazons or warrior women, contained comic elements that would not have been apparent to children. "We never made cartoons for children in those years," Jones was quoted as saying in the *Independent.* "Our shorts were made to support Warner's features, like *I Was a Fugitive From a Chain* and *Dr. Ehrlich's Magic Bullet.*" Other early Jones films lacked the element of madcap comedy or visual ingenuity for which he later became known, focusing more on sheer elegance of animation instead.

Worked Under Tex Avery

In 1935 Jones got a new boss who was also a key shaper of the Warner Brothers style. Fred Avery, known as Tex, presided as director over a team of Warner animators in an old silent film studio not-so-affectionately dubbed Termite Terrace. Jones worked on seven Avery features between 1936 and 1938. Another member of Jones's team was animator Ben Hardaway, nicknamed Bugs, who sketched out a rabbit that gained the in-house nickname of Bugs's Bunny, later slightly shortened. Jones was soon to develop the rabbit's look and urbane personality. In 1938, Jones was elevated to director (often termed "supervisor" on animated films of those days) when Friz Freleng, another future animation giant (who had originally hired Jones at Schlesinger Productions), moved to the MGM studio. His first film, depicting a cat on guard against some pretzel-stealing mice, was called *The Night Watchman.*

Jones directed other films with unique characters, such as *Dog Gone Modern* and *Little Lion Hunter* (both 1939), the latter featuring a mynah bird whose odd gait is accompanied by an excerpt from Felix Mendelssohn's *Fingal's Cave.* The young African lion hunter himself, Inki, became the subject of a Jones series in the 1940s. Jones sometimes worked on Warner's Merrie Melodies and Looney Tunes series of animated visual accompaniments to classical music compositions, introduced to compete with Disney's Silly Symphonies. Soon he also took over running the Warner Brothers series involving Daffy Duck (with *Daffy Duck and the Dinosaur,* 1939) and Porky Pig. In 1941 he introduced a character of his own, Conrad Cat, first featured in *The Bird Came C.O.D.* and later incorporated into Daffy Duck and Porky Pig storylines. Jones took over the Bugs Bunny franchise with 1940's *A Wild Hare* and for many years afterward was responsible for his appearance and development.

The next several years proved busy and lucrative for the animator. Jones won an award for the non-humorous patriotic short *Old Glory* in 1940. He showed his originality with the 1942 film *The Dover Boys,* a satire on 1890s melodrama that expanded the expressive content of the animation genre. During World War II he directed several episodes of the Private Snafu series, developing a character created by director Frank Capra. Jones also collaborated with Dr. Seuss

creator Theodor Geisel on the Private Snafu films, which were distributed to American military servicemen.

The period after the war marked Jones's personal golden age, in which he put the formal elegance of some of his early films together with original characters that had endless potential for comic development. The first of these was the debonair, seemingly French skunk Pepe le Pew, whom Jones modeled partly on his own personality. "Pepe was very much like me," Jones was quoted as saying in the *Independent.* "Irresistible. He doesn't know he's a stinker!" Pepe was introduced in 1945 in *Odor-able Kitty* and brought Jones's producers an Academy Award with *For Scent-imental Reasons.* Three Jones films won Oscars, although the only award given to him specifically was for *The Dot and the Line* (1965). Despite the time-consuming nature of animation in the precomputer era, Jones was extremely prolific in the postwar years, directing between seven and ten films in most years between 1949 and 1958.

Introduced Roadrunner

Many of these films featured the duo of the Roadrunner and Wile E. Coyote, perhaps Jones's most characteristic creations. The Roadrunner films, the first of which was *Fast and Furry-ous* (1949), were "displays of perfect animation," noted the *Independent,* "totally visual without the need of any verbal expressions or explanations." Each film featured an increasingly outlandish series of attempts by the coyote to catch the roadrunner, ending more often than not in the coyote's plunge off a cliff, preceded by a helpless look toward the audience. Jones also turned out numerous films featuring Bugs Bunny and Elmer Fudd, the most famous of which was the operatic parody *What's Opera, Doc?* (1957).

After the Warner Brothers animation studio closed in 1962, Jones worked briefly for Disney and MGM, directing *Tom and Jerry* cartoons for the latter. He soon established his own company, Chuck Jones Enterprises, which created nine half-hour animated films for television. These included *Rikki Tikki Tavi* and *The White Seal.* In 1970, he became Vice-President of Children's Programming for the ABC television network. Jones and his daughter, Linda, created a business selling limited-edition drawings based on Jones's animated films. Dorothy Jones died in 1978, and Jones married his second wife, Marian Dern, soon after that. In the late 1970s he drew a syndicated comic strip, *Crawford.*

Various honors came Jones's way late in life, including a one-man retrospective at New York's Museum of Modern Art. In 1995 he received a special Lifetime Achievement Academy Award. He wrote an autobiography, *Chuck Amuck,* in 1989. He never rested on his laurels, however. He signed a contract at age 82 to make five new films based on the old Warner Brothers characters; the last, *Chariots of Fur,* appeared in 1996. Jones was making new drawings until a month before his death, which came in Corona del Mar, California, on February 22, 2002.

Books

International Dictionary of Films and Filmmakers, Volume 4: Writers and Production Artists, 4th ed., St. James, 2000.

Jones, Chuck, *Chuck Amuck,* Farrar, Straus & Giroux, 1989.

Kenner, Hugh, *Chuck Jones: A Flurry of Drawings,* University of California Press, 1994.

Periodicals

Chicago Sun-Times, January 15, 2006.
Entertainment Weekly, March 8, 2002, p. 22.
Independent (London, England), February 25, 2002, p. 6.
New York Times, February 24, 2002, p. 26.
Time, March 4, 2002, p. 80.

Online

"Chuck Jones, 1912–2002," Chuck Jones official website, http://www.chuckjones.com/bio.php (January 15, 2009).
"Chuck Jones, Master of Character Animation," *Senses of Cinema,* http://archive.sensesofcinema.com/contents/directors/02/jones.html (January 15, 2009). □

Hamilton Jordan

Hamilton Jordan (1944-2008) was the driving force behind Democrat Jimmy Carter's ascension to the U.S. presidency in 1976. At 34, Jordan became the youngest ever White House chief of staff. The bright but often swashbuckling Jordan "was portrayed in the press as either a political wunderkind or a hell-raising pariah," Drew Jubera and Tom Bennett wrote in the *Atlanta Journal-Constitution.* Jordan had numerous battles with cancer before his death in 2008 of mesothelioma, and wrote a best-selling book about his experience with the illness.

Jordan, who pronounced his name "JER-din," was born William Hamilton McWhorter Jordan on September 21, 1944, in Charlotte, North Carolina. His father was stationed there during World War II. After the war his family returned to Albany, Georgia, where he grew up. According to Jubera and Bennett, Jordan called Albany "a place where I didn't meet a Catholic or a Republican until I was 18." Jordan's Albany High School classmates voted him mostly likely to become governor.

Jordan earned a political science degree from the University of Georgia. There, he worked on the campaign for Carl E. Sanders's successful run for governor, and in the Washington, D.C., office of Senator Richard B. Russell. The *Journal-Constitution* related that Jordan once stuffed envelopes with a newsletter in which Russell promised to win the fight against school integration.

Racial Incident Changed His Views

Jordan's perspective began to change in December of 1961, when his father took him to a downtown Albany protest march led by civil rights worker Martin Luther King Jr. The family's housekeeper participated. Jordan's father, a segregationist who worked in the insurance industry, urged the protesters to leave when police arrived, and chased them into an alley. "For the first time, I felt real shame in my life, watching quietly while decent people and children . . . were herded into the alley just like animals. Later I would mark that day as a moment of moral failure in my life," Jordan said, according to the Atlanta newspaper.

Charted Course to White House

Jordan took to Carter and his more centrist racial views after hearing him at an Albany Elks Club luncheon in 1966, when Carter ran unsuccessfully for governor. Jordan wrote the candidate, and to his surprise, Carter called in response and offered him a job. According to the *Journal-Constitution,* when Jordan told Carter he was working full-time spraying mosquitoes, Carter said, laughing, "I'm going to have a hard time getting elected if people like you can't choose between mosquitoes and me."

Jordan, however, took up Carter's offer and helped the upstart campaigner finish third. After serving in Vietnam for the refugee relocation group International Voluntary Services, Jordan returned to Georgia and became Carter's campaign manager for his follow-up run for governor in 1970. Carter won this time, beating Sanders in a runoff and Republican Hal Suit in the general election.

In 1972, shortly before Republican Richard M. Nixon's landslide presidential victory over George S. McGovern, Jordan showed Carter an 80-page white paper that plotted Carter's path to the White House in 1976. It urged Carter to enhance his national profile by writing a book, meeting with foreign officials on trade matters, and furthering his position with the Democratic National Committee. Carter embraced the proposal and Jordan established a Washington office, working solo.

Two years after Nixon resigned in mid-term amid the Watergate scandal, Carter defeated Nixon's replacement, Gerald R. Ford, in the 1976 national election. "I played some hunches," Jordan told *Atlanta Magazine,* as quoted in the *Journal-Constitution.* "I look smart only in retrospect because we won."

'Georgia Mafia' Runs Washington

Jordan, by then Carter's top confidant, became chief of staff at age 34. Jordan, whom Rick Lyman of the *New York Times* called "a thick-set and rough-hewn man with piercing dark eyes and a rapier wit that knew how to draw blood," was part of a group known as the Georgia Mafia. It included press secretary Jody Powell and budget director Bert Lance. "Together, they became a large part of the public face of the administration, distrustful of Washington traditions and disdainful of pomp," Lyman added.

Carter gave Jordan wide latitude in the White House. Jordan was a point man in the drive to enact the Panama Canal treaty that passed stewardship of the canal linking the Atlantic and Pacific oceans to host country Panama, as well as the attempts, albeit unsuccessful, to free hostages held at the U.S. Embassy in Teheran, Iran. The Carter administration was also marked by a panic involving gasoline prices and long lines at the pump in the summer of 1979.

"Mr. Jordan developed something of a difficult reputation during his White House years," Lyman wrote. Among its other pressing issues, the White House had to release a 33-page statement denying that Jordan had spat at a woman in a nightclub, and defuse rumors that he had made distasteful remarks to the wife of Egypt's ambassador at a party. Jordan denied the accusations, as did the ambassador's wife and others in attendance at the event.

A special counsel was appointed to investigate accusations in 1979 that Jordan had used cocaine at the Studio 54 nightclub in New York City. Officials from the U.S. Department of Justice questioned Jordan for more than ten months. Club owners were under federal indictment for tax evasion and were attempting to plea bargain for lighter sentences, and a federal grand jury in February of 1980 decided it would not indict Jordan. Still, he repeatedly had to beat back a reputation he held in some circles as "an ill-mannered, wisecracking social boor," according to the *Journal-Constitution* article.

Jordan got closely involved with the hostage crisis, which began on November 4, 1979, when militants stormed the American Embassy in Teheran and took about 70 hostages. The crisis lasted 444 days, ending on January 20, 1981, the day Carter's successor, Ronald Reagan, took office. Jordan later wrote that the desire to redeem himself with Carter had strongly motivated his involvement. Carter, however, lost his re-election bid to Reagan in November of 1980, with political pundits citing Carter's plummeting approval rating during the hostage situation.

Fragmentation Helped, Hurt Carter

The Carter administration, anchored by its Georgians, was often at odds with the Washington establishment and its own party in Congress. One year after Carter's re-election defeat, Jordan gave a lengthy interview with scholars at the Miller Center of Public Affairs at the University of Virginia. According to David S. Broder in the *Washington Post,* Jordan said that Carter had secured the Democratic nomination and subsequent election in 1976 "because of the fragmentation that had taken place" within the Democratic Party. Discord within the party in the 1968 and 1972 campaigns, and the influx of reform-minded candidates, Carter included, after Nixon's 1974 resignation, enabled Carter to split the seams and occupy the White House. The same dynamic, however, worked against Carter at re-election time. "Because Carter ran against the Washington establishment, he had no claim on their loyalty—and they easily spurned him," Jordan told his interviewers, according to Broder. Selecting party insider Senator Walter Mondale from Minnesota didn't appease Carter's opponents, and discord within the White House was common.

Jordan, who taught at Emory University in Atlanta from 1981 to 1982 and published *Crisis: The Last Year of the Carter Presidency* in 1982, ran for the U.S. Senate in 1986, narrowly losing the Democratic primary to Wyche Fowler. Though a runoff loomed, Jordan stepped aside at Fowler's request, and Fowler won the general election. "I called Hamilton and basically asked him to get out of the race so that we could beat the Republicans in the fall. A couple of days later—I'll never forget—he graciously threw his support to me. I've admired his courage and loyalty all these years," Fowler remarked, according to Drew Jubera and Jim Auchmutey in another article in the *Journal-Constitution.*

Increasingly unhappy with the two-party system, Jordan advocated a third major party, and in 1992 became co-chairman of Texas businessman H. Ross Perot's independent presidential campaign. Perot finished a distant third that year behind Democratic winner Bill Clinton and Republican incumbent George H.W. Bush. In addition, Jordan served as the executive director of the Association for Tennis Professionals (ATP) from 1987 to 1990. Through politicking and shrewd negotiation, Jordan was instrumental in reinventing the organization as the ATP Tour, and cutting lucrative marketing deals. "We were easy for him," Raymond Moore, head of the Men's Tennis Council, said of Jordan in the *Los Angeles Times.* "If he could take a peanut farmer and make him president of the United States, tennis was putty in his hands."

Took Up Fight against Cancer

Jordan was a longtime and highly visible advocate for cancer research. The disease struck Jordan himself in 1985. He fought a long battle against the disease, which he chronicled in his 2001 book *No Such Thing as a Bad Day: A Memoir.* He implored cancer patients to take control of their own treatment and offered a list of suggestions for those suffering from the disease.

He married pediatric nurse Dorothy Henry in 1981; together they founded Camp Sunshine, in Morgan County,

Georgia, for cancer-stricken children. After the Jordans's daughter, Kathleen, contracted juvenile diabetes, they founded Camp Kudzu, also in Georgia, for similarly affected children. Jordan also founded the Georgia Cancer Coalition.

Jordan died on April 20, 2008, of cancer at his Atlanta home. He was 63. Former Cable News Network president and chief executive Tom Johnson, as quoted by Jubera and Auchmutey, called Jordan "the bravest fighter I have ever met. He fought and he fought and he fought." Jordan left his wife and three children, Hamilton Jr., Kathleen, and Alexander.

The Jordan Legacy

An overflow crowd paid tribute at a memorial service for Jordan at the Carter Center in Atlanta. President Carter said of Jordan, according to the Jubera and Auchmutey, "No other human being affected my life and career more beneficially than Hamilton Jordan." The Atlanta newspaper went on to say that Jordan "was remembered as a political genius, a loving husband and father, an unrepentant jokester, an enjoyer of cocktails and especially as a cancer survivor and warrior advocate for others afflicted with the disease."

Former budget director Lance said of Jordan, as quoted in the same article, "It took a lot of courage to face what we faced in Washington. He went through what I went through. I called it 'the Lance toe-test'—that's where you go out on the front stoop and turn the *Washington Post* over with your toe. If your name is above the fold, you know it's going to be a bad day. Hamilton and I had to face all of that."

Former Carter pollster Patrick Caddell, in the same article, praised Jordan for his doggedness. "Hamilton was always at his best when our backs were to the wall," he said. "He never faltered."

Online

"Hamilton Jordan, Carter's Right-Hand, Dies at 63," *New York Times,* http://www.nytimes.com/2008/05/21/us/21jordan.html?hp, May 21, 2008.

"Hamilton Jordan, President Carter's Chief of Staff, Dies," *Atlanta Journal-Constitution,* http://www.ajc.com/metro/content/metro/stories/2008/05/20/hamilton_jordan_obituary_carter.html, May 20, 2008.

"Hamilton Jordan Remembered at Memorial Service," *Atlanta Journal-Constitution,* http://www.ajc.com/northfulton/content/metro/stories/2008/05/23/jordan_0523.html, May 23, 2008.

"Hamilton Jordan's Message to Obama," *Washington Post,* http://www.washingtonpost.com/wp-dyn/content/article/2008/05/28/AR2008052802918.html, May 29, 2008.

"Jordan Used Political Skills to Help Tennis," *Los Angeles Times,* http://www.articles.latimes.com/2008/may/27/sports/sp-dwyre27, May 27, 2008. □

K

Brian Keenan

Born in Northern Ireland, Brian Keenan (1940–2008) began life in a country divided by religious differences and a long history of conflict. At the age of 28, dismayed by the problems he saw in Belfast, Keenan joined the newly formed Provisional Irish Republican Army (IRA). Rising quickly through the ranks of the IRA, Keenan became known as the mastermind behind many of the organization's deadliest bombing campaigns in the United Kingdom. In 1980 Keenan was convicted for his involvement in numerous terrorist attacks in Britain, and was sentenced to 18 years in prison. After his release 13 years later, however, Keenan played a pivotal role in negotiating peace in Northern Ireland, and was heralded as a major force behind the disarmament of the IRA.

Keenan was born in the early 1940s to Harry and Jean Keenan in Northern Ireland, either in Belfast or in Swatragh. At that time, World War II raged in Europe, and another conflict was brewing inside the small country of Northern Ireland.

The English and the Irish had been fighting for control of the island since the twelfth century. In 1919 the Irish Republican Army (IRA) formed to fight for Irish independence from Britain. After two years of fierce fighting, the British and the Irish agreed to divide Ireland. The six northeastern counties, where a majority of the population were Protestants and wanted to remain part of Britain, became Northern Ireland. The remaining 26 counties became the Irish Free State. However, many Irish Catholics throughout the island still wanted one united, independent Ireland.

Keenan was born to an Irish Catholic family in the predominantly Protestant Northern Ireland. Keenan's father, Harry, was a serviceman in the British Royal Air Force. During World War II, Harry Keenan served in England at Packlington RAF Bomber Command Base. Ironically, 40 years later his son would walk the same grounds—as an inmate at the recently built Full Sutton Prison.

From City to Country and Back Again

While Keenan's father was serving in England, his mother remained in Northern Ireland, looking after Keenan and his four siblings. In 1941 their home in Belfast was destroyed during a bombing attack called the Belfast Blitz. Jean Keenan moved the children to the countryside, where they lived in Swatragh for the remainder of the war.

Harry Keenan returned to his family at the end of the war in 1945. Together, they moved back to Belfast to rebuild their lives. Even though they were not involved directly in sectarian disputes, Keenan and his family could not escape the effects of the conflict. Like other Irish Catholic families in Northern Ireland at the time, the Keenans suffered discrimination that kept them mired in poverty.

Union Worker

At age 16, Keenan went to work as an apprentice electronics engineer, and joined the Electrical Trade Union (ETU). During his time as a union worker, Keenan began to recognize the class disparity that had resulted from the split between Irish Catholics and Protestants, and he became more interested in politics and economics.

Two years after beginning his apprenticeship, Keenan moved to England to find more work. There he became a

television repairman, and for a time he partnered with his brother in Corby, Northamptonshire. While in Corby, he met Chrissie, the woman he would marry. Also during his time in Corby, Keenan damaged a cigarette machine while he was drunk and angry, and was arrested. The incident would have dramatic consequences years later.

From Corby, Keenan went to Luton, where he continued his apprenticeship and ETU membership by working at a factory that made guided missiles. Keenan soon attended his first trade union convention as a delegate, and met union members who were involved in the Campaign for Nuclear Disarmament (CND). The CND workers refused to make missiles designed for offensive purposes and only built missiles designed for defense.

By the mid-1960s, Keenan had returned to Belfast and was working as a foreman at Grundig, a German electronics plant. Now in management, Keenan witnessed for himself the discriminatory hiring practices that had become commonplace in Northern Ireland. When Keenan refused to hire an under-qualified Protestant applicant, another foreman informed him that the hire had been prearranged. After that, Keenan became a union shop steward and began organizing workers' strikes to demand equitable working conditions and hiring practices.

The IRA

As Keenan became more involved in union activism, Northern Ireland was disintegrating into sectarian violence between Catholics and Protestants. More and more Catholics were beginning to protest voter discrimination and unfair living and working conditions. As they did so, British officials began to crack down, restricting civil rights, banning marches, and attacking protestors. This period of escalating tensions and violence became known as "the Troubles."

By 1969 Keenan had six children to provide for, but had earned a reputation as a radical activist and been blacklisted by the unions. As violence in Belfast mounted, he joined the IRA Volunteers. That year, a mob of Protestants loyal to Britain swarmed a Catholic neighborhood, and Keenan's parents were forced to flee their home. Keenan and other IRA volunteers swept in to help their families escape.

The back-and-forth attacks threatened to throw Northern Ireland into another civil war. Northern Ireland officials finally asked the British army to intervene and restore order. The IRA split, as some members supported the intervention in favor of peace and others opposed it. The Official IRA renounced violence and pledged to continue supporting peaceful forms of protest against the British government. The Provisional IRA, also known as the Provos, vowed to continue fighting for complete independence.

Became a Weapons Master

In 1970 Keenan pledged himself to the Provos. For the next ten years, he would be a significant force behind the Irish part of the bloody campaign that became known as "the Long War." Between 1969 and 2000, more than 3,000 people would be killed in this conflict between British and Irish forces.

Skilled in both weaponry and strategy, Keenan rose through the ranks of the Provos quickly. By August of 1971, Keenan had become the quartermaster for the Belfast Brigade of the Provos. He recruited fighters, obtained weapons, and planned numerous bombings in Belfast.

As quartermaster, Keenan reached beyond Irish organizations for support. In 1972 he traveled to Tripoli, Libya, to negotiate with Libyan President Muammar al-Gaddafi for arms and financial support. He also met with leaders in East Germany, Lebanon, and Syria. Keenan was no longer just a weapons master; he was an arms smuggler, and he was a good one.

In 1973 Keenan was promoted to the post of quartermaster general for the Provos. Although he continued recruiting arms and members for the organization, he also took control of the Provos' offshore bombing campaign in England. Two years later, Keenan traveled to Britain to lead the terror unit in London. In the subsequent four years, Keenan and his group were responsible for dozens of bombings in and around London. Their activities resulted in at least 16 civilian deaths.

While planning with the Provos in London, Keenan made a mistake. He left traces of himself at an apartment in Crouch Hill—his handwriting on crossword puzzles and his fingerprints on bomb-making plans. When the British police raided the apartment in December of 1975, they seized these items and subsequently found a match with fingerprints on file for the arrest in Corby a decade earlier. British officials issued a warrant for Keenan's arrest.

Arrest and Conviction

By the time Keenan was identified as a terrorist, he had disappeared again. He soon resurfaced in Ireland and Northern Ireland. In 1977 he became the Provos' director of operations.

In the spring of 1979, Keenan's activities caught up with him. While traveling from Dublin, Ireland, to Belfast, Keenan's car was stopped by the Royal Ulster Constabulary. They arrested Keenan on the 1975 warrant. A year later, he was tried in London and found guilty on 18 charges of planning terrorist acts. The judge sentenced Keenan to 18 years in prison.

From Prisoner to Peacemaker

Keenan served 13 years of his sentence in the prison at Leicester, England. During that time, his perspective began to change. He still believed that Ireland should be one united nation, but he began to work toward those goals in a different way.

Keenan had long been a supporter of IRA leader Gerry Adams. In the early 1980s, when Adams moved away from the militant activities of the Provos and began building up the political wing of the IRA, known as Sinn Fein, Keenan gave his continued support. In 1982 Keenan wrote a strong letter endorsing Adams's efforts to win office in the Northern Ireland Assembly. In the letter, quoted in the U.K.'s *Independent,* Keenan wrote: "To those of us who have struggled for years in a purely military capacity, it must be obvious that if we do not provide honest, recognizable political leadership on the ground, we will lose that war for peace."

In 1993 Keenan was released on parole. At the time, the IRA and Sinn Fein had begun holding peace talks with British officials. To the surprise of many, Keenan joined that effort. In August of 1994, Keenan stood by as the IRA declared a ceasefire.

The peace talks did not go far. Officials demanded that the IRA disarm before any peace could be concluded. Many IRA leaders, including Keenan, rejected disarmament. In early 1996 the ceasefire ended, and the IRA bombed the Dockland area of London, causing the deaths of two people.

Public pressure against the continued violence increased, and in 1997 the IRA reinstated its ceasefire and Sinn Fein officials re-joined the peace talks. Those talks led to the signing of the Good Friday Agreement in 1998. Under the Good Friday Agreement, all nonviolent parties in Northern Ireland would share political power, and Northern Ireland would remain a part of the United Kingdom as long as a majority of the population supported it.

The success of the Good Friday Agreement hinged on the disarmament of the IRA, and in 1999 Keenan engaged in secret disarmament talks.

Peaceful Death, Mixed Legacy

Despite the provisions of the Good Friday Agreement, the IRA was not eager to disarm. Their mass store of weapons gave them negotiating power. However, global public opinion worked against them. The demands for peace in Northern Ireland had mounted throughout the 1990s, and resistance to violence was strong.

Then, on September 11, 2001, Islamic terrorists hijacked four planes and attacked buildings in the United States, causing the deaths of more than 3,000 people, mostly civilians. Public sentiment against all forms of terrorism grew, and the IRA lost any platform to pursue change through violence. On October 23, the Provisional IRA, with Keenan's support, announced the end of its armed struggle and began disarming. Four years later, the IRA officially announced its complete disarmament.

Earlier in 2005, Keenan had left the IRA after being diagnosed with cancer. Though removed from official negotiations, he remained a public figure, making periodic appearances at rallies and ceremonies in Ireland.

Keenan died on May 21, 2008. He was cremated at Roselawn Cemetery in Belfast, and former IRA leaders carried an honorary coffin through the city's streets. Thousands of mourners gathered to witness the procession.

As a unionist and labor activist, Keenan pursued many positive changes on behalf of the Catholic population in Northern Ireland. As an IRA weapons master, strategist, and terrorist, he planned and helped perpetrate many devastating attacks on Irish and British soil. As a participant in the peace talks among Irish and British groups, he helped bring an end to more than 800 years of violence.

Jonathan Powell, an aide to former Prime Minister Tony Blair, had once called Keenan "the biggest single threat to the British state," as noted in Dublin's *Irish Independent.* But in the end, Keenan was praised for his efforts to restore peace to the nation he loved so dearly. At his death, Keenan left Northern Ireland a mixed legacy of unrepentant violence and devoted idealism.

Books

Lucent Terrorism Library: Terrorists and Terrorist Groups, edited by Stephen Currie, Lucent Books, 2002 (November 12, 2008).

Moloney, Ed, *A Secret History of the IRA,* W.W. Norton & Company, 2002.

Periodicals

Daily Telegraph (London, England), May 22, 2008.

Guardian (London, England), May 22, 2008, p. 42.

Independent (London, England), February 19, 2000; May 22, 2008.

Irish Independent, May 26, 2008, p. 11.

New York Times, May 23, 2008.

Observer (London, England), May 25, 2008, p. 5.

Online

"The Brian Keenan Interview," SAOIRSE32, March 27, 2008, http://www.saoirse32.blogsome.com/2008/03/28/the-brian-keenan-interview/trackback (October 16, 2008).

"Brian Keenan (Ireland, Provisional IRA)," About.com, http://www.terrorism.about.com/od/groupsleader1/p/BrianKeenan.htm (October 16, 2008).

"Former IRA guerilla leader Brian Keenan dies," May 21, 2008, Reuters online, http://www.reuters.com/articleID=USL21858666 20080521 (October 16, 2008).

"Irish Republican Army," *Encyclopedia Britannica,* http://www.search.eb.com/eb/article-9042782 (October 16, 2008).

"Keenan, Brian," *Britannica Book of the Year 2009,* http://www.search.eb.com/eb/article-9443600 (October 16, 2008). □

Ned Kelly

Ned Kelly (1854–1880), Australia's most famous outlaw, stole horses and robbed banks, spent almost two years on the run, and was hanged for shooting a policeman. Because he defied colonial-era Australian authority and cast his crime spree as a reaction to injustice, Kelly has come to embody parts of his nation's unruly, rebellious spirit. Even today, Australians argue over whether he was a hero or an irredeemable criminal.

Ned Kelly was born in 1854 in Beveridge, near Melbourne, Australia. His father, John "Red" Kelly, was one of the 50,000 Irish convicts relocated to Australia by the British government as punishment. He had been convicted of stealing two pigs in 1841. His mother, Ellen, had come to Australia with her parents to flee the Irish famine of 1840, but found more poverty and discrimination there. Kelly's father, convicted of stealing horses, died in prison in 1866, when Kelly was 12. The oldest of eight children, Kelly was left the responsibility of providing for his family.

Aspired to be a Bushranger

The Kellys lived in Victoria, then a British colony, now an Australian state. In the 1860s, Victoria's society was divided into small farmers, known as selectors, and farmers who owned large ranches, known as squatters. The selectors often owned small plots of land with poor soil, while squatters were wealthy and held most of the power in the colony. Selectors often struggled to make a living, and some stole cows and horses from the squatters. The police generally defended squatters and dealt harshly with selectors.

Wild and defiant, the Kelly family often clashed with police and came to see them as enemies. At age 14, Kelly was arrested for stealing ten shillings from a man. After his release, eager to become an outlaw, he spent time as a sort of apprentice to legendary bushranger Harry Power. (Bushrangers were Australian country bandits; their place in their nation's imagination is similar to that of the American cowboy.) In 1870 Kelly was sentenced to a six-month prison term for assault. Soon after his release, at age 20, he was arrested again for receiving a stolen horse. The policeman who arrested him beat him savagely with his pistol. Kelly received a three-year prison sentence. Released in 1874, he went for the next three years without any known confrontations with law enforcement.

After prison, Kelly cut timber and worked as a sawmill foreman. He also prospected for gold. Meanwhile, he developed many skills valuable to an Australian frontiersman. He was an expert rider and rifleman and an intimidating bare-knuckled boxer.

The Kelly Gang

The legend of Ned Kelly began in April of 1878, when police officer Alexander Fitzpatrick went to the Kelly home to arrest Kelly's brother Daniel, age 16 or 17, on a horse-stealing charge. By some accounts, Fitzpatrick, assigned to command the local police station for a few days, chose to confront the Kellys despite warnings not to do so. A confrontation followed, its details disputed at the time and mythologized afterward. According to Fitzpatrick, Ned Kelly shot him in the wrist. The Kellys said Ned had not been home, that Fitzpatrick had merely cut himself on a door lock, and that family members attacked Fitzpatrick only after he made an advance on Ned and Dan Kelly's 15-year-old sister, Kate.

Dan Kelly escaped with Ned to Victoria's forested mountains, known as the Wombat Ranges. Authorities issued warrants for their arrest on charges of wounding with attempt to murder. Their mother, Ellen, and her son-in-law and a family friend were arrested on charges of aiding and abetting and sentenced to long jail terms. Ned and Dan Kelly's friends Steve Hart and Joe Byrne joined the brothers in their hideout. Four constables tried to find them. The Kellys, who knew the area better, found the constables first. In an ambush on October 28, 1878, near the colorfully named Stringybark Creek, they killed three of the four constables. It was the first murder of a police officer in Victoria in ten years, and the first killing of multiple officers in the history of British rule in Victoria.

The Kelly brothers and their friends, who became known as the Kelly Gang, set out on a crime spree. They carried out daring bank robberies in the towns of Euroa in December of 1878 and Jerilderie in February of 1879. Kelly left a long written statement behind at Jerilderie, justifying his actions by pointing to Irish colonists' grievances against the British authorities. (The letter bore Kelly's name, but Byrne, the most literate member of the gang, may well have written it.) "It will pay Government to give those people who are suffering innocence, justice and liberty," read the letter left in Jerilderie, as quoted by Andrew Sayers in the book *Sidney Nolan: The Ned Kelly Story.* Otherwise, the letter said, "Fitzpatrick will be the cause of greater slaughter to the Union Jack"—the flag of Great Britain— "than Saint Patrick was to the snakes and toads in Ireland."

The Parliament of Victoria declared the Kelly Gang outlaws, authorized citizens to shoot them on sight, and offered a two thousand-pound reward for their capture. Authorities searched for the gang throughout northeast Victoria with the help of Aboriginal trackers—native Australians skilled at tracing people's paths—but failed to find them. For more than a year, the gang remained at large, and the incompetence of the police search was widely mocked.

Finally, in June of 1880, a friend of Joe Byrne's, Aaron Sherritt, tipped off police to the gang's location. Byrne responded by finding Sherritt and killing him. This gave authorities the necessary clue to Kelly's location, and a train full of police traveled to the town of Glenrowan, in northern Victoria, to confront him.

Last Stand

The Kelly Gang, ready for a fight, devised a plan to derail the train and kill the police. (Some have said the gang wanted to start a rebellion and make northern Victoria an independent country, but many historians disagree.) To prepare for the confrontation, the gang stole plow blades from local farmers and built homemade suits of armor and helmets by bolting the blades together.

Before the police train arrived, the gang occupied the Glenrowan Inn, also known as Mrs. Jones's Hotel, and took 60 prisoners. They spent a weekend celebrating with athletic contests and drinking games, even competing with their prisoners. However, the police, tipped off to the plot, got off the train before the spot where the gang had pulled up the tracks. They surrounded the hotel. Kelly's gang donned their armor and faced off against about 50 police.

A bloody 12-hour gun battle broke out. Several hostages were struck by bullets and killed. In the middle of the battle, Ned Kelly emerged from the hotel, wearing his helmet and armor, and was shot in the leg and captured. During a brief lull in the fighting, the surviving hostages were released. Police set fire to the hotel to end the battle. Dan Kelly, Byrne, and Hart were found dead inside. They appeared to have committed suicide to avoid surrender.

News of the battle spread across Australia, attracting intense public attention. Kelly was held in the Melbourne Jail and charged with murdering one of the constables at Stringybark Creek. Kelly's lawyer, David Gaunson, interviewed his client at length and then gave an account of the conversation to the newspaper *Age.* (Critics suggested the article's elevated language could not have been Kelly's, but Alex C. Castles, author of *Ned Kelly's Last Days: Setting the Record Straight on the Death of an Outlaw,* considered the article an authentic expression of Kelly's thoughts, rephrased by Gaunson.)

"Let the law of the land strike me down if it will, but I ask that my story might be heard and considered," Gaunson quoted Kelly as saying, according to Castle. "If my life teaches the public that men are made mad by bad treatment, and if the police are taught that they may not exasperate to madness men they persecute and ill treat, my life will not be entirely thrown away."

Kelly stood trial in October of 1880 and was found guilty. "It is not that I fear death; I fear it as little as to drink a cup of tea," he said in court, according to Castles. "On the evidence that has been given, no juryman could have given any other verdict." Kelly's final replies to the prosecutor and judge are among the most famous in Australian courtroom history. "The day will come when we shall have to go to a bigger court than this," he said to the prosecutor after he argued for execution. "There we shall see who is right and who is wrong." When the judge sentenced him to die, Kelly replied either, "Yes, I will meet you there," or "I will see you there where I go."

Some citizens started a campaign to spare Kelly's life, but to no avail. He was hanged on November 11, 1880, at the age of 26.

The Legend Grows

Ever since that time, Kelly has been a controversial figure in Australia, a vicious outlaw to some and a rebellious hero to others. Many settlers of Australia were ex-convicts, and many were Irish immigrants in a land ruled, like their homeland, by the British. Kelly embodied Australians' defiance of authority they saw as oppressive. "So greatly warped were the minds of a small section of the colonists that these criminals had many sympathizers," reported an article in the 1889 book *Cassell's Picturesque Australia* (quoted by Mark Juddery in *History Today*), "and among young Australians there was a tendency to rank them with Robin Hood . . . and other partly mythical outlaws."

Soon after Australia became an independent country in 1901, Kelly's legend was revived, thanks to the 1906 feature-length film *The Story of the Kelly Gang.* The film was ambitious, impressive for its day and extremely popular. It spawned a popular genre of bushranger movies, films about outlaws in the Australian bush country that were similar to American cowboy movies. Audiences cheered when the Kellys won battles against the film's bad guys (the police). "It is the sort of bellow-drama that the lower orders crave for, and two-thirds of Australia will want to see it— the two thirds that believe Ned Kelly was a greater man than George Washington," complained a reviewer for the conservative publication *Bulletin,* as quoted by Juddery.

Later generations also retold the Kelly legend. In the 1940s alone, Douglas Stewart, a poet born in New Zealand, wrote a play in verse about him; writer Max Brown wrote *Australian Son,* a biography of him; and Sidney Nolan began painting a series of modernist artworks depicting Kelly in the Australian landscape that have been exhibited worldwide. Several more films have been made about him, including the 1970 movie *Ned Kelly,* in which British rock star Mick Jagger played the outlaw, and a 2003 movie of the same name, starring Heath Ledger.

Kelly has remained a folk hero to many Australians, who pride themselves on their toughness, courage, and disrespect for authority. The Australian phrase "game as Ned Kelly" is a compliment recognizing deep courage. Australia issued a postage stamp in 1980 to mark the one hundredth anniversary of his death. One of Nolan's Kelly paintings hangs outside the office of the country's prime minister. The spot where the Glenrowan Hotel stood is now a national heritage site, and in 2008 scientists announced that they believed they had located the mass grave where Kelly and 31 other executed criminals were buried.

Books

Castles, Alex C., *Ned Kelly's Last Days: Setting the Record Straight on the Death of an Outlaw,* Allen & Unwin, 2005.

Sayers, Andrew, *Sidney Nolan: The Ned Kelly Story,* Metropolitan Museum of Art, 1994, pp. 9-14.

Periodicals

History Today, January 2008.

Observer (London, England), November 30, 2003.

Washington Post, January 28, 2001, p. T8.

Online

"Kelly, Ned," *World Book Advanced,* http://www.worldbookonline. com/advanced/article?id=ar724738 (December 14, 2008).

"Ned Kelly," *Australian Government Culture and Recreation Portal,* http://www.cultureandrecreation.gov.au/articles/nedkelly (December 14, 2008).

"'Ned Kelly's burial site' found," *BBC News,* http://www.news.bbc. co.uk/go/pr/fr/-/2/hi/asia-pacific/7285907.stm (December 14, 2008). □

Margery Kempe

The English mystic Margery Kempe (c. 1373–after 1438), late in her life, dictated an account of her life and spiritual development called *The Book of Margery Kempe*. Despite questions about exactly what its contents represent, it is generally regarded as the first autobiography in the English language.

Kempe, who was illiterate, had her words taken down by scribes. *The Book of Margery Kempe* existed for centuries in just a single copy, buried in the library of an old English mansion. It was rediscovered in 1934, and since then has been translated several times into Modern English from the Middle English original. Several generations of scholars have had the opportunity to examine Kempe's book, and have reached sharply differing conclusions about its aims, its veracity, and its relationship to other forms of religious literature in Kempe's time. What is not in dispute, however, is that Kempe had an extraordinary life, and that the story she told is a compelling one for any reader.

Daughter of Town's Mayor

Essentially, what is known about Kempe comes from *The Book of Margery Kempe*. Histories of the English seacoast town where she lived, however, have confirmed many of its external details. Kempe was born around 1373 in King's Lynn, referred to by Kempe and many other residents simply as Lynn. The town was on England's east coast, in the county of Norfolk. A member of the Hanseatic League of mercantile cities, it enjoyed unusual prosperity, thanks to a location that was ideal for trade with the Low Countries. Kempe was the daughter of John Burnham (also referred to as John de Burnham or John Brunham), who served five terms as Lynn's mayor and for a time was a member of England's parliament. Atypically for medieval England in the wake of the great plague of the middle fourteenth century, she had a background that might be described as solidly middle class.

With this background, it would have been normal for Kempe to learn to read, but for whatever reason, she did not. She referred in her book to some kind of sin that she committed as a young woman, refusing to elaborate on what it was. Given the importance of sexuality in the later development of Kempe's life, it is possible that the sin was of a sexual nature. She married John Kempe, the son of a tanner or fur seller, in 1393, and the marriage was apparently happy enough for a time.

Kempe's spiritual journey began after the birth of her first child, which was unusually difficult. At the time, noted Lynn H. Nelson in a lecture on Kempe appearing on the Virtual Library Web site, "Gynecology and obstetrics were not only ignored, but the suggestion that there should be some concern in these fields was regarded as evidence of a sick mind." After the biblical Eve brought about humanity's fall from a state of grace, women were apparently thought to deserve whatever pain they had to endure. Kempe survived, but she and her child were both sick for some time after the birth. Kempe reacted by assuming that her trials were due to a spiritual deficiency, and she asked for a priest to whom she could confess the sin she had committed before her marriage.

The priest was unsympathetic and berated Kempe, not even permitting her to receive absolution for the sin. Kempe, perhaps suffering from what would now be called postpartum depression, lost control of her emotions and began to scream and utter blasphemies. She tried to throw herself from the window of her room, and, after she was locked in a room, to bite through the veins of her own wrists. She was then chained to her bed, where she raved incoherently. After she had been locked up for eight months, Kempe experienced a vision in which she saw Jesus sitting at the foot of her bed. "Daughter," he said (according to Nelson), "why have you forsaken me when I never forsook you?"

Operated Brewery

The vision had the effect of restoring Kempe's mental equilibrium. Although the townsmen who had been watching her advised against it, John Kempe set his wife free and gave her the keys to the storeroom where she had been kept. She plunged back into the life of the world, buying herself new clothing and opening a brewery. She later organized a milling operation. The brewery was apparently quite successful for several years, but both these businesses eventually failed. Meanwhile, Kempe continued to have more children—14 of them by the time she was 40.

During this period, Kempe reportedly began to have more religious visions—of Christ, the Virgin Mary, various saints and, increasingly, God himself. She began to believe that she should take a vow of chastity. John Kempe at first took a dim view of the plan, and several more children were born. However, according to Nelson, after Margery called out the words "Oh Dear Jesu Christ, Save me, Jesus!" as John approached her, John lost his desire for her. Kempe, however, seemed not quite ready for chastity herself, and made sexual advances to a young man she met outside a church. "He ran away," Nelson recounted, "yelling that he would rather be cut up for the stewpot than sleep with her." Kempe's religious visions deepened, and she began to exhibit what those around her often considered eccentric behaviors, such as refusing to eat herring.

Around 1413, two developments presaged a new phase in Kempe's spiritual life. First, she succeeded in severing herself permanently from a normal relationship with her husband. She had recently inherited a substantial sum of money from her father, enough to make her financially independent, while John Kempe's business had gone sour, leaving him deeply in debt. Margery, informing John that she would prefer seeing him killed to having sex with him again, proposed that she pay off his debts in return for his signing a contract of chastity, and he had little choice but to agree. Second, at about this time Kempe began to manifest outward signs of religious ecstasy, in the form of sounds whose exact nature is difficult to ascertain. She used the word "cry," but it is not clear whether she was weeping, or shouting, or something else. The Book of Margery Kempe used the Latin phrase "nota de clamore" to describe her utterances, a term that was used for the expressions of penitential wailing by monks in monasteries. Modern writers have suggested that she might have suffered from epileptic seizures; from a medieval point of view, as Kempe realized, such behavior might be regarded as a sign of either great devotion or demonic possession.

After long vigils and several fasts in Lynn's St. Margaret's church, Kempe set off in 1414 on a pilgrimage to Jerusalem. Her first stop was at the Shrine of St. Thomas a Becket in Canterbury, where she correctly identified the secret sin of a monk as lechery toward married women. The monk proclaimed her a holy woman, but local townspeople, afraid of her strange behavior, formed a mob and chased her away. Accompanied by her husband, Kempe sought out various ecclesiastical authorities and asked for permission to clothe herself entirely in white. During one of these visits, the Archbishop of Canterbury gave her enough money to begin her journey to Jerusalem.

Made Multiple Pilgrimages

Passing through Konstanz in present-day Germany, she arrived in Rome and made great observances of piety at each of the city's large collection of religious shrines, weeping and moaning. In 1415 she finally arrived in Jerusalem, where her religious utterances began to include full-throated screams. "She could not keep herself from crying and roaring though she should have died for it," read a modern translation of The Book of Margery Kempe, as quoted in the Southern Review. Kempe's Jerusalem pilgrimage was followed by another to Compostela, in Spain, and then by a series of voyages across England.

After that, Kempe's life seems to have quieted down. Her husband was injured in an accident and became an invalid, and Kempe cared for him until his death. One of Kempe's sons was apparently as oriented toward travel as his mother, and he made his way to what is now Gdansk, Poland, returning with his wife to England for a visit in 1431. He died at around the time of John Kempe's death, and Margery may have dictated the beginnings of The Book of Margery Kempe to her son's wife at this time. She accompanied the widow back to Poland, traveling mostly by land and making stops at shrines along the way. By the end of her return journey to England, Kempe was destitute, but she managed with the help of friends to return to Lynn. A priest took over as her scribe, and The Book of Margery Kempe as it is known today was set down between 1436 and 1438. The book was known to later theologians, but its circulation was apparently limited. The date of Kempe's death is unknown; she is mentioned in the logbooks of Lynn's Trinity Guild in 1439, but there is no further record of her after that.

Modern knowledge of The Book of Margery Kempe seems to have been limited to a pamphlet issued by Dutch publisher Wynken de Worde nearly a century after Kempe's activities, until a copy of the book itself surfaced in 1934 in the library of an English mansion called Pleasington Old Hall. Since then, the book has generated a substantial body of literature. The remarkable events it describes can be interpreted in many ways. For a generation of male scholars raised on psychoanalytic theory, Kempe was, to use the terminology of the time, hysterical, and the contents of the book were regarded with skepticism. The sexual imagery in the book also lent itself to other psychological interpretations. According to the Southern Review, Kempe wrote many descriptions (in modern translation) of Jesus seeking an intimate connection with her: "I want you to love me, daughter, as a good wife ought to love her husband. Therefore you can boldly take me in the arms of your soul and kiss my mouth, my head, and my feet as sweetly as you want." Later investigators also questioned the truth of the events in the book, but for a different reason: Kempe's accounts ran parallel to medieval tales of saints' lives, and it is an open question whether The Book of Margery Kempe should be regarded as autobiography, fiction, or a unique mixture of both. Recent research has focused on the ways in which Kempe's highly personal relationship with the divinity was related to the religious trends that were developing around her. Kempe was not the only worshipper of her time to prefer direct communication with God and Jesus to the structures of institutional religion: groups such as the Lollard movement prefigured the attitudes that were ultimately to lead to the Protestant Reformation in Europe. Kempe has remained a unique figure whose testimonies are distinctive even among the prolific literature of religious writings by women of the medieval era.

Books

Atkinson, Clarissa, *Margery Kempe: Genius and Mystic,* Cornell University Press, 1983.

Gallyon, Margaret, *Margery Kempe of Lynn and Medieval England,* Lutterworth, 2004.

World Eras, Vol. 1, Gale, 2001.

Periodicals

Southern Review, Summer 2002, p. 625.

Online

"The Book of Margery Kempe: Introduction," University of Rochester, http://www.lib.rochester.edu/camelot/teams/kempint. htm (January 15, 2009).

"Margery Kempe (b. 1373–d. 1438)," King's College, Cambridge, http://www.departments.kings.edu/womens_history/margery kempe. htm (January 15, 2009).

"Margery Kempe," St. Margaret's Church, King's Lynn, http://www. stmargaretskingslynn.org.uk/margery_kempe.htm (January 15, 2009).

"Margery Kempe (1373–post 1438)," WWW Virtual Library, http://www.vlib.us/medieval/lectures/margery.html (January 15, 2009).□

Shibasaburo Kitasato

Japanese physician and bacteriologist Shibasaburo Kitasato (1852–1931) is noted for his important contributions to the world's understanding of disease and how the human body combats infection. He also is credited with discovering the bacterium that causes bubonic plague.

Early in his career as a physician and bacteriologist, Shibasaburo Kitasato became interested in studying microbes and their link to certain diseases. His subsequent research and discoveries placed him in a small, elite group of distinguished researchers, including Louis Pasteur, Robert Koch, Emile Roux and Emil von Behring, who formed the foundations for the fields of bacteriology and immunology. Kitasato's interests and research led to significant contributions to bacteriology, particularly tetanus and diphtheria. He was among the first scientists to discover tetanus bacillus (Clostridium tetani), the bacteria that causes tetanus, as well as the bacteria responsible for the bubonic plague.

The future world-renowned scientist was born on December 20, 1852, in Oguni, on Japan's southern island of Kyushu. He was the eldest son in a family that lived in an isolated mountain village. His father was the village's mayor.

Kitasato began his medical studies at Igakusho Hospital, which later became the Kumamoto Medical School. He studied under Dutch physician C.G. van Mansvelt. When his mentor left the facility, Kitasato enrolled at the University of Tokyo Medical School, where he completed his studies and earned his medical degree in 1883. Following graduation, he conducted bacteriological research at the Central Sanitary Bureau of the Ministry of Home Affairs. He worked in the field of public health, focusing on cholera epidemics and preventing outbreaks of infectious diseases.

Studied with Robert Koch in Germany

In 1885 the Japanese government sent Kitasato to the Hiygienisches Institute in Berlin, Germany, to study bacteriology and infectious diseases in the laboratory of the world-famous scientist Robert Koch (1843-1910). His laboratory attracted students from all over the world. Koch had recently gained international attention for his pioneering work in the emerging field of bacteriology, after spending years isolating and culturing certain germs. He also tracked down the microbes responsible for various diseases. In 1877 he established the sources of anthrax. In 1882 and 1883 he established the sources of tuberculosis and cholera.

Under Japanese government sponsorship, Kitasato remained in Berlin until 1891. During that six-year period he was taught Koch's painstaking methods for the culturing and experimentation related to various microbes. Under Koch, he also studied the organisms of cholera, typhoid fever, and anthrax, and also published a number of important papers about his research.

Helped Develop Antitoxins

While in Berlin, Kitasato garnered substantial notoriety for his work on tetanus and diphtheria. In 1889 he accomplished what many then considered to be impossible: He developed a procedure that enabled the growth of a pure culture of the tetanus bacillus bacteria Clostridium tetani, the bacteria that causes what is commonly called lock-jaw. It proved to be one of his greatest achievements. One of the elements that made it so remarkable was that Kitasato was the first to employ anaerobic methodology; that is, growing germs without contact with air.

As a result of his work, Kitasato became the first to understand that tetanus is a disease of intoxication. He discovered that the tetanus bacillus secreted a toxin that, in a dilute form, could be employed as an agent to produce immunity to tetanus. The discovery of a tetanotoxin by Danish internist Knud Faber (1862-1956) in 1890 confirmed his views.

Also in 1889, Kitasato demonstrated the power of blood serum for treating tetanus, working with fellow researcher Emil von Behring, the German microbiologist who later received the Nobel Prize in Physiology or Medicine in 1901 for developing a serum therapy for diphtheria. Their partnership provided the world with valuable information that helped explain the workings of the immune system. Specifically, the collaborating scientists found that animals injected with tetanus-causing microbes produced antitoxins in their blood. These antitoxins neutralized the toxins produced by the microbes. In addition, such antitoxins could be injected into healthy animals to make them immune to the microbes.

On December 4, 1890, Kitasato and Behring made history when they published the results of their research in the German medical journal *Deutsche Medizinische Wochenschrift.* In their paper, they clearly delineated three important facts: the bacillus produced a soluble toxin; animals injected with this substance developed the neutralizing antitoxin; and the antitoxin was specific.

The importance of their work was boldly underscored during World War I, when antitoxins were administered in precautionary fashion to wounded soldiers. Previously, soldiers had contracted tetanus infections when their open wounds came into contact with soil, which resulted in many fatalities. During World War I, deaths from tetanus were dramatically reduced.

Essentially, Kitasato and Behring's work helped give birth to the science of immunology, and their ongoing research helped advance the field. Shortly after their tetanus collaboration, Behring demonstrated that the same conclusions applied to diphtheria. Later, Kitasato would discover an anthrax antitoxin.

Returned to Japan

In 1891 Kitasato left Germany. He had received many offers to work abroad, but he decided to return to Japan. He brought back with him his vast learning and important discoveries, which he subsequently passed on to students and scientists in his homeland, in turn significantly advancing research in Japan.

Upon his return, Kitasato established his own laboratory, funding its creation with his own money. There, he continued his studies and research related to microbes and infectious diseases. At first this was a private bacteriological enterprise. However, the Japanese government eventually subsidized Kitasato's ongoing work. Funding covered Kitasato's research as well as the training of other scientists, and the institute became a center for the development of talented bacteriologists. Some of Kitasato's notable students included Togo Aoyama, Kigoshi Shiga and Toju Hata. The Japanese government later took over the facility.

Discovered Cause of Bubonic Plague

Today, many consider the discovery of the cause of bubonic plague to be Kitasato's most notable achievement.

Around the time that Kitasato left Berlin and returned to Japan, a devastating outbreak of the bubonic plague was spreading in the Eastern portion of the world, leaving a high death toll in its wake. It had spread through the trade routes in southern China, and in 1894 it hit Canton with violent force. The Japanese government became understandably alarmed, as the outbreak appeared headed toward Hong Kong, which was downriver from Canton.

The first case in Hong Kong was identified on May 8, 1894. Less than a week later, 20 more advanced cases were reported. Most of these occurred in Tai Ping Shan, a densely populated Chinese neighborhood adjacent to the Tung Wah Hospital, where hospital admissions rapidly increased. At the epidemic's height, nearly 100 new cases were reported each day, and temporary hospitals were established. Further, plague riots erupted in the epidemic's wake, and violent and fearful mobs reportedly hindered removal of plague patients from the hospital. Physicians needed to arm themselves with guns, and gunboats were called in to restore order.

When the plague struck Hong Kong, the Japanese government sent for Kitasato to study the disease. By this time, Kitasato was regarded as a national hero and one of the greatest bacteriologists in the world. He arrived from Tokyo on June 12, and by June 14 he had set up a temporary laboratory. He worked with Aoyama, and the two began tracking down the disease's cause. Ultimately, Kitasato managed to isolate and identify the bacillus that led to bubonic plague.

Soon after he started his work, Kitasato saw a bacillus in a post-mortem patient specimen. At first he questioned the significance, because the post-mortem examination occurred eleven hours after patient death. But he went ahead and inoculated a mouse, and then saw a similar bacillus in another patient's blood sample. It was then reported that Kitasato had been able to isolate the bacillus of the plague.

However, when the outbreak hit Hong Kong, the French government also sent a delegation of scientists to investigate the plague's cause. One of these was Swiss researcher Alexandre Yersin (1863-1943), who had studied in the French laboratory of Louis Pasteur. Yersin, who arrived in Hong Kong on June 15, was living in Indochina (which later became Viet Nam) when the plague struck. He was a young and distinguished scientist who had previously isolated the diphtheria exotoxin with Emile Roux. He, too, managed to isolate the bubonic plague bacillus, and at almost the same time as Kitasato.

Kitasato was the first to publish, and his work appeared in the British medical journal *The Lancet* in 1894. For many years, he was credited with the discovery. Eventually, however, it became known as the Kitasato-Yersin bacillus. Initially, Yersin named the bacillus Pasteurella pestis, after his famous mentor. More recently, it became officially known as Yersinia pestis, but Kitasato is still given credit for his simultaneous discovery.

Later Career

Other important discoveries would follow. Four years later, Kitasato and his student Kigoshi Shiga were able to isolate and identify the organism that caused dysentery. In his later career, Kitasato also studied the mode of infection in tuberculosis.

In 1899, after the Japanese government took over his laboratory and renamed it the Imperial Japanese Institute for Infectious Diseases, Kitasato was appointed as the institute's director. However, when the government consolidated the institute with the Ministry of Education in 1914, Kitasato resigned his position. He disagreed with the government's move, as he felt that his research and discoveries had practical applications for public health and thus should be included in the hygiene department within the country's Ministry of the Interior. Kitasato's staff also turned in their resignations.

Subsequently, Kitasato founded the Kitasato Institute at Shirokane, a non-profit organization situated across the bay from Tokyo. At the same time that he was establishing his new institute, Kitasato accepted a position with the University of Keio. His primary responsibilities included recruiting and organizing the educational institution's new medical faculty. Eventually, he became the first dean of the University's medical faculty. In 1923, in recognition of his remarkable contributions to medicine, Kitasato was named the first chairman of the Japanese Medical Association.

Kitasato died on June 13, 1931, in his home in Nakanojo, Konshu. He was 75 years old. During his long and distinguished career, Kitasato received numerous honors and awards from several countries. When he left Germany, he was awarded the title of "Professor," becoming the first non-German to receive the distinction. In 1917 Japanese Emperor Taisho appointed Kitasato to the House of Peers. In 1924, for his services to science and humanity—and specifically for his contributions to the control of infectious diseases—Taisho bestowed on Kitasato the title of Baron of the Japanese Empire.

The institute that he founded still exists today as Kitasato University, which was established in 1962. Because of his work with the bubonic plague and other infectious diseases, Kitasato is regarded as a leading pioneer in the field of bacteriology.

Books

"Kitasato Shibasaburo," *Science and Its Times, Vol. 5: 1800-1899*. Gale Group, 2000.

Periodicals

Canadian Medical Journal, August 1931.
The Lancet, July 5, 1997.

Online

"Kitasato, Shibasaburo," *UPEI.ca,* http://www.upei.ca/ xliu/multiculture/kitasato.htm (December 21, 2008).
"Shibasaburo Kitasato," *World of Biology Online,* http://www. galenet.galegroup.com/servlet/BioRC (December 21, 2008).□

Wellington Koo

V.K. Wellington Koo (1888–1985), China's greatest diplomat of the twentieth century, represented his nation during both world wars and played a role in forming the United Nations and its predecessor, the League of Nations. Flawlessly polite and dazzlingly eloquent, he famously defended his nation's interests at the Paris Peace Conference in 1919 and before the League of Nations in the 1930s. To other world leaders, he represented a modern face of China as it strove to rise from colonized subjugation to worldwide power and influence.

Learning Western ways

Born Vi Kyuin Koo on January 29, 1888, in Shanghai, China, Koo was the third son of a successful merchant. He became known as Wellington because the English name was considered similar to his given name, but he was often referred to as V.K. Wellington Koo, combining

the Chinese and English names. During Koo's childhood, Shanghai was dominated by foreign nations, a result of unequal treaties forced upon a weak China. Koo, like many Shanghai residents of his generation, grew up familiar with people from other countries and wanted to learn about foreign culture and languages, instead of being hostile to them like many rural Chinese of the time. But he was also patriotic, eager to help China shake off its subjugation and become an equal among nations.

After studying at St. John's College, an American missionary school in Shanghai, Koo came to the United States as a student in 1904 and enrolled at Columbia University in New York. He was his class's best debater and public speaker, and spoke fluent English and French. He earned three degrees from Columbia: a bachelor's degree in 1908, a master's degree in 1909, and a doctorate in 1912. Before he left for Columbia, Koo's father had arranged his son's marriage to a woman in Shanghai, but Koo divorced his first wife in 1908, feeling that arranged marriages were not modern and that his wife, who lacked an education and knew little of the wider world, was not a good match for him.

In 1912 Koo returned to China and became English secretary to Yuan Shih-kai, president of the newly unified Republic of China. Next, he went to work at the country's foreign ministry. When World War I began in 1914, Koo wrote the document that announced China would be neutral in the conflict. After Japan took over German possessions in China's Shantung Province, a peninsula near Beijing, Koo took part in tense diplomatic discussions between Japan and China over the territory. In 1915, while still in his twenties, Koo was sent to Washington as the Chinese minister to the United States. He married his second wife, May Tong Koo, in 1913, and had two children with her. She died in the 1918 influenza epidemic.

A Hero in Paris

In January of 1919, Koo traveled to France as part of the delegation representing China at the Paris Peace Conference, which officially ended World War I. Koo helped create the charter of the League of Nations. He supported U.S. President Woodrow Wilson's proposed structure for the league, which included an executive council made up of five large powers and four smaller nations. Koo also argued that China should be given direct control of the territory Japan still held in Shantung Province. At age 32, Koo was already carrying himself with distinguished authority, impressing other nations' diplomats and leaders, even though his nation's bargaining position was not strong. Georges Clemenceau, prime minister of France, described Koo as "a young Chinese cat, Parisian of speech and dress, absorbed in the pleasure of patting and pawing the mouse, even if it was reserved for the Japanese," as quoted by Margaret MacMillan in *Paris 1919: Six Months That Changed the World.*

When the conference took up the Shantung Province question, Koo gave a powerful speech full of references to international law. Koo, as quoted by MacMillan, called Shantung "the cradle of Chinese civilization" and argued that foreign control of the strategic peninsula would make it a "dagger pointed at the heart of China." That April, however, the leaders of the United States, Great Britain, and France concluded that they had to agree to give Shantung to Japan to secure Japanese approval of the peace treaty. Koo refused to sign the Treaty of Versailles because of the Shantung issue. (China did sign it later that year.) On a personal level, Koo's time in Paris was more rewarding: he fell in love with a young, wealthy Indonesian woman, Hui-lan Oei, who became his third wife.

Conflict at Home

China made Koo its minister to Great Britain in 1920. A year later, Koo was one of China's representatives at the Washington Conference, obtaining promises from Japan and the Western nations that they would gradually reduce their influence and territorial claims in China. In late 1921, Koo returned home and reluctantly devoted his attention to China's tumultuous domestic politics. "It had always been my desire to bring about a revision of China's unequal treaties," he later said, according to Stephen G. Craft's *V.K. Wellington Koo and the Emergence of Modern China,* "and I had no taste for politics or political rivalry." However, Koo had become a respected leader. One poll of Chinese teachers and students named him the third greatest living person in China.

During the 1920s, governments in China were frequently replaced, while opposing forces controlled different regions of the nation. Koo briefly served as foreign minister, finance minister, and acting prime minister of the government based in Beijing. While foreign minister, he reestablished diplomatic relations with Russia, which had been cut off in 1917 after the Russian Revolution. Koo pursed a diplomatic, gradual strategy for asserting Chinese rights in international affairs. But the Nationalist and Communist forces vying for control of China saw Koo and the Beijing governments as too soft, too accommodating to other nations. After the Nationalists, led by Chiang Kai-Shek, took control of most of the country in 1928, a warrant was issued for Koo's arrest. He fled to Europe and lived there for about a year.

Debating at the League of Nations

In 1930 Koo returned to China to serve as an adviser to Zhang Xueliang, an ally of Chiang's who controlled the province of Manchuria. "I wanted to leave the political sphere, and had the intention of giving up my diplomatic and political life altogether," Koo later recalled, according to Craft. But a crisis soon broke out in Manchuria that brought Koo back to diplomatic service. The Japanese army, which did not want Chiang's Nationalists to control Manchuria, invaded the province in 1931. Chiang formed a commission to decide how to react, and Koo was named Zhang's representative on it. In 1932 Koo was also named the Chinese representative on the League of Nations' commission on the Manchurian issue. Koo returned to Manchuria, at great personal risk, to observe conditions there.

Later that year, the Chinese government appointed Koo minister to France and a delegate to the League of Nations. In a speech to the league's executive council, Koo eloquently denounced Japan's determination to expand onto the Asian continent. "The double-armed Continental policy of expansion, which is the crystallization of several centuries of teaching by Japanese warriors, is aimed at China as the first stage of the conquest of Asia, and to be carried out from the north and from the south, just as a virulent scorpion attacking its victims by its foreclaws and its tail," Koo said, according to *The Rise and Fall of the League of Nations* by George Scott.

The League failed to effectively address the Manchuria crisis. However, Koo again impressed observers from other nations. "Few people are more typical of the new China than Dr. Wellington Koo," wrote a British newspaper columnist, as quoted in Koo's wife's memoir, *No Feast Lasts Forever.* "American by training, smooth, polished, infinitely patient and gentle, there is no diplomat of the Western world who can surpass him in poise and suavity."

After returning to China in 1934, Koo was reappointed ambassador to France in 1936. War broke out the following year between China and Japan, which invaded the Chinese mainland and bombed Chinese towns, causing mass casualties. The long, brutal war eventually became part of World War II. Koo argued China's case at the League of Nations and the Nine-Power Conference in Brussels, Belgium, but the League, whose influence was rapidly weakening, took no effective action. In the years leading up to World War II, Koo continued to argue that the League should take a stand against Japan's aggression in Asia and against Germany's military offensives in Europe. Craft agrued in *Diplomacy & Statecraft* that Koo was not merely representing China's national interest. "From 1913 to 1939, Koo wanted the

League to take action against Japan because inaction meant the ultimate death of the international organization," Craft wrote. "The League's credibility would be lost by a failure to deal with Japan."

Koo was right. The League of Nations dissolved soon after World War II began, in September of 1939. The war left Koo deeply disappointed in the Western democracies. "In meeting crises, democracies are clumsy and slow to act, whereas dictators count upon surprise attack and rapid crushing of victims," he lamented in his diary, according to Craft in *V.K. Wellington Koo and the Emergence of Modern China.*

Wartime ambassador

Koo was still ambassador to France when German troops took over Paris in 1940. He followed the French government to its temporary capitals in Tours, then Vichy. In 1941 he was named ambassador to Great Britain and moved to London. He pressed the British government to aid China in its fight with Japan. But Britain, focused on its fight against Germany, provided less help than Koo had hoped. He served in London through the end of World War II, managing the tense military alliance and different war aims among China, Great Britain, and the United States. He negotiated a 1943 treaty with Britain that abolished the last remnants of its unequal treaties with China. As the war neared its end, Koo advocated the formation of the United Nations, arguing that a stronger international organization with more police powers was needed to replace the ineffective League of Nations.

In 1946 Koo was transferred to Washington to become China's ambassador to the United States. He tried to convince the U.S. government to take the side of Chiang's Nationalist government in its civil war against Communist forces, but with only partial success. After the Communists took over China in 1949, Koo continued to serve as ambassador for the Nationalist government, which relocated to the Chinese island of Taiwan. During seven more years as ambassador, Koo criticized China's Communist regime, accusing it of extracting diplomatic concessions from the United States by holding on to U.S. prisoners from the Korean War. The Communists' "feverish military aggression," he claimed, according to Bart Barnes of the *Washington Post,)* was "destroying the basic virtues of the Chinese people."

Retirement

In March of 1956 Koo resigned as ambassador, weary of the anxiety of international crises and his diminished standing as a representative of Taiwan instead of mainland China. In 1957 the United Nations General Assembly elected Koo a judge on the International Court of Justice. He served ten years there, becoming vice-president of the court. In 1967 he left the court and moved to New York City. In 1976 Koo donated 500 hours of spoken memoirs, recorded over 17 years, to Columbia University. The next year, Columbia held celebrations of Koo's ninetieth birthday. Koo died of a heart ailment on November 13, 1985, at age 97, at his home in Manhattan.

Books

Craft, Stephen G., *V.K. Wellington Koo and the Emergence of Modern China,* University Press of Kentucky, 2004.

Koo, Madame Wellington, *No Feast Lasts Forever,* Quadrangle, 1975.

MacMillan, Margaret, *Paris 1919: Six Months That Changed the World,* Random House, 2003.

Scott, George, *The Rise and Fall of the League of Nations,* Macmillan, 1973.

Periodicals

Diplomacy & Statecraft, November 2000.

New York Times, November 16, 1985.

Washington Post, November 16, 1985.□

Fred Korematsu

Asian-American Fred Korematsu (1919–2005) is most remembered for challenging the legality of Japanese internment during World War II. His case, *Korematsu v. The United States,* is still considered a blemish on the record of the Supreme Court and has received heightened scrutiny given the indefinite confinement of many prisoners after the terrorist attacks on September 11, 2001. Awarded the Presidential Medal of Honor, he is considered a leader of the civil rights movement in the United States.

Fred Korematsu was a 22-year-old welder when the Japanese bombed Pearl Harbor on December 7, 1941. A Nisei—which means an American citizen born to Japanese parents—he was one of four brothers and grew up working in his parents' plant nursery in Oakland, California. Prior to the bombing he had tried to enlist in the military but was turned down due to poor health. Before Pearl Harbor, he was employed by a defense contractor in California. At the time of the attack he was having a picnic with his Italian-American girlfriend. Years later he told the *San Francisco Chronicle,* "I was just living my life, and that's what I wanted to do." It was for this simple reason that he eventually became known as a civil rights leader.

American reaction to an attack on United States' soil was both swift and harsh. Asian-Americans soon found themselves the targets of ridicule and attacks. On February 19, 1942, President Franklin D. Roosevelt issued Executive Order 9066, which granted the leaders of the armed forces permission to create Military Areas and authorizing the removal of any and all persons from those areas. Roosevelt justified these actions in the opening paragraph of the order by declaring, "the successful prosecution of the war requires every possible protection against espionage, and against sabotage to national-defense material, national-defense premises and national-defense utilities." This statement effectively pronounced Japanese-Americans on the West Coast as traitors because even though Executive Order 9066 allowed the military to remove any person from designated areas, only those of Japanese descent were ordered to leave.

Ignored Internment Order

The California, Washington, and Oregon coasts as well as the sections of California and Arizona along the Mexican border were declared Military Area 1. All Japanese aliens and Americans of Japanese descent living in those areas were ordered to report to staging areas in order to be taken to internment camps. It is estimated that over 100,000 people, of which over 70% were American citizens, were affected. Korematsu and his family were told to register at a former racetrack south of San Francisco where detainees would eventually be transferred to a more permanent camp in Utah. He did not comply with the military order and instead fled to Nevada with his girlfriend, whom he intended to marry. At her suggestion he assumed the alias Clyde Sarah and went so far as to have plastic surgery on his eyes in attempt to disguise his Japanese features. The surgery was not a success but he continued to claim he was of Hawaiian or Spanish descent whenever he was asked. The couple returned to the Bay area, and on May 30, 1942 he was arrested for failing to report to an internment camp. Korematsu recalls in a *San Francisco Chronicle* article that the next day a local newspaper ran the headline, "Jap Spy Arrested in San Leandro."

Matt Bai recounted in the *New York Times* that soon after his arrest, Korematsu received a visit from Ernest Besig, executive director of the American Civil Liberties Union of Northern California. Besig was looking for an appropriate case to challenge the constitutionality of the internment. Korematsu agreed to go to court. Besig posted $5000 bail for Korematsu's release; however, the military took him back into custody before he even left the jail. He was held in Tanforan, the same racetrack his parents had been sent to. While there, he slept in a horse stall and was eventually transferred to a camp in Topaz, Utah where he remained until the end of the war. During this incarceration, Besig continued to advance *Korematsu v. The United States* in court.

Supreme Court Upheld Conviction

The case eventually came before the Supreme Court in 1944. In a 6–3 decision the high court ruled that Korematsu's arrest was not unconstitutional. Writing for the majority, Justice Hugo L. Black stated that, "It should be noted, to begin with, that all legal restrictions which curtail the civil rights of a single racial group are immediately suspect. That is not to say that all such restrictions are unconstitutional. It is to say that courts must subject them to the most rigid scrutiny. Pressing public necessity may sometimes justify the existence of such restrictions; racial antagonism never can." Black went on to claim, "Korematsu was not excluded from the Military Area because of hostility to him or his race. He was excluded because we are at war with the Japanese Empire, because the properly constituted military authorities feared an invasion of our West Coast and felt constrained to take proper security measures, because they decided that the military urgency of the situation demanded that all citizens of Japanese ancestry be segregated from the West Coast temporarily." In short, the court determined that the need to protect the nation from

attack outweighed Korematsu's rights as an individual. In a scathing dissent, Justice Robert Jackson argued, "Korematsu has been convicted of an act not commonly a crime. It consists merely of being present in the state whereof he is a citizen, near the place where he was born, and where all his life he has lived." Jackson further notes that, "A military order, however unconstitutional, is not apt to last longer than the military emergency. Even during that period a succeeding commander may revoke it all. But once a judicial opinion rationalizes such an order to show that it conforms to the Constitution, or rather rationalizes the Constitution to show that the Constitution sanctions such an order, the Court for all time has validated the principle of racial discrimination in criminal procedure and of transplanting American citizens."

For decades after the event, the internment of Japanese-Americans on the West Coast during World War II received little attention. The military determined the extreme measure was a necessary war time endeavor. The American citizens forced into relocation camps considered the topic taboo and rarely, if ever, discussed their experiences. The public in general focused on the defeat of the Nazis and the resulting post-war economic boom. Even Korematsu tried to forget what had happened. In a 2001 documentary on the case recorded in an article in *The Seattle Times,* attorney Peter H. Irons told filmmaker Eric Paul Fournier, "He felt responsible for the internment in a backhanded way, because his case had been lost in the Supreme Court." Indeed, throughout his imprisonment and after his release Korematsu was often shunned by fellow Asian-Americans who viewed him as unpatriotic and a trouble-maker.

Challenged The Ruling

After WWII, Korematsu once again returned to the San Francisco area. He married and had two children, a son and a daughter. He also became a draftsman. In a 2004 *San Francisco Chronicle* article, he revealed how difficult life was because of his arrest. He stated, "After I was released in 1945, my criminal record continued to affect my life. It was hard to find work. I was considered to be a criminal." It was not until the 1980s that Korematsu would revisit his past, and, in the process, change the future. In fact, it was the attorney Peter H. Irons who first approached Korematsu about reopening his case. According to a 2005 *Los Angeles Times* article, the University of California San Diego professor was planning to write a book about the internment. While researching the topic he stumbled across memos written by Justice Department officials challenging the legitimacy of military claims that Japanese-Americans were a threat during WWII. One memo went so far as to accuse Solicitor General Charles Fahy of lying before the Supreme Court in order to obtain Korematsu's conviction. Irons took this evidence to Korematsu and convinced him to reopen the case. Together they assembled a team of lawyers, many of Japanese descent whose own parents had been forced into internment camps.

The new case was significant in that it tested whether the entire internment policy was constitutional, whereas the previous case had only challenged the constitutionality of

Korematsu's conviction. U.S. District Judge Marilyn Hall Patel presided over the court proceedings. Korematsu's lawyers introduced a petition for a writ of coram nobis—a scarcely used legal tactic to reverse a decision based on error of fact. In an effort to quash the matter quickly, the US Justice Department offered Korematsu a pardon—a release from the penalty of an offense. His obituary in the March 31, 2005 *Los Angeles Times* indicates he refused the offer by saying "As long as my record stands in open court, any American citizen can be held in prison or concentration camps without a trial or hearing." According to an Annie Nakao article in the *San Francisco Chronicle*, Patel vacated Korematsu's conviction stating, "Korematsu stands as a caution that in times of distress the shield of military necessity and national security must not be used to protect governmental actions from close scrutiny and accountability."

Brought About Policy Changes

Since the end of WWII, the US government has been forced to address the decision to imprison thousands of loyal citizens. In 1976, President Gerald Ford issued Proclamation 4417 which revoked all authority conferred by Executive Order 9066, declaring the original Order a mistake. In 1988, President Ronald Regan considered the internment was an injustice and signed the Reparations Bill for Japanese-Americans which authorized $20,000 to each surviving detainee. In 1998, President Bill Clinton awarded Korematsu the Presidential Medal of Freedom, the highest honor given a civilian in the United States. Recorded on the *Presidential Medal of Freedom* website, during the ceremony Clinton said, "In the long history of our country's constant search for justice, some names of ordinary citizens stand for millions of souls—Plessy, Brown, Parks. To that distinguished list today we add the name of Fred Korematsu." Despite these advances, the nation continues to face challenges in balancing national security and individual freedom.

In the wake of the terrorist attacks on 9-11, the United States government claimed authority to indefinitely detain citizens and non-citizens alike as "enemy combatants" without charging them with any crime. The Center for American Progress reports that as recently as January 14, 2004,

Korematsu filed an Amicus Curiae brief with the Supreme Court in the case of *Rumsfeld v. Padilla*. In that brief he states, "by allowing the Executive Branch to decide unilaterally who to detain, and for how long, our country will repeat the same mistakes of the past." The Supreme Court agreed with him and ruled that enemy combatants are entitled the opportunity to contest the claims made against them by the government. Korematsu died March 30, 2005. Dale Minami, Korematsu's long time attorney noted in the *Seattle Times* "He had a very strong will. He was like our Rosa Parks. He took an unpopular stand at a critical point in our history." Sadly, Korematsu did not live to see the government comply with the court's decision in the Padilla case.

Periodicals

New York Times, December 25, 2005.
San Francisco Chronicle, December 12, 2004; April 10, 2005.
Seattle Times, March 31, 2005.

Online

Agrast, Mark, "Remembering Fred Korematsu (1919-2005)," http://www.americanprogress.org/issues/2005/04/b489061.html/print.html (December 16, 2008).
Black, Hugo L., "Korematsu v. United States Majority Opinion," http://www.law.umkc.edu/faculty/projects/ftrials/conlaw/korematsu.html (December 16, 2008).
"Children of the Camps: Internment History," http://www.pbs.org/childofcamp/history/eo9066.html (December 5, 2008).
"Evacuation To Be Carried Out Gradually," http://www.sfmuseum.org/hist8/evac.html (December 16, 2008).
"Fred Korematsu Speaks Out on Racial Profiling and Scapegoating," http://www.reclaimdemocracy.org/articles_2004/fred_korematsu_racial_profiling.html (December 14, 2008).
Jackson, Robert, "Mr. Justice Jackson, dissenting," http://tourolaw.edu/patach/Korematsu/JACKSON.asp (December 16, 2008).
Korematsu, Fred, "Brief of Amicus Curiae" http://supreme.lp.findlaw.com/supreme_court/briefs/03-1027/03-1027.mer.ami.korematsu.pdf (December 10, 2008).
"Medal of Freedom," http://www.medaloffreedom.com/FredKorematsu.htm (December 9, 2008).
"Of Civil Rights and Wrongs: The Fred Korematsu Story." Dir. Eric Paul Fournier. PBS, 2001. □

L

Mary Ann Lamb

British writer Mary Ann Lamb (1764–1847) remains known as the author of a classic of children's literature, *Tales from Shakespeare*, which was published under the name of her brother, Charles Lamb, although it was primarily her work.

Lamb's name is also attached to a notorious incident: while suffering from severe mental illness, she murdered her mother in 1796. As a result of the tragedy and of Lamb's unusual status as a female writer in the early nineteenth century, her life, personality, and writings have remained partially obscure. Even the basic events of her life are difficult to reconstruct, for they were originally recounted only in correspondence among the participants in those events—participants who assumed background knowledge and referred elliptically to what was happening. Mary Lamb's writings were long regarded as secondary to those of her better-known brother Charles, but recent scholarship has begun to flesh her out as an individual.

Had Access to Lawyer's Library

Mary Ann (or Anne) Lamb was born on December 3, 1764, in London; Charles was more than a decade younger. Unlike many of their literary contemporaries, they were of lower middle class origins; their mother, Elizabeth Field Lamb, came from Hertfordshire farm stock, while their father, John Lamb, was a scrivener or scribe—a copyist—in the offices of a London lawyer named Samuel Salt. John Lamb had minor literary ambitions, and at one point published a collection of poetry and prose. The central fact of the childhood of Mary and Charles (and one older brother,

John) was that Salt took an interest in the family's well-being and emerged as their benefactor. The Lambs lived in an apartment just below Salt's in a big law office building called the London Temple, and both Charles and Mary received top-notch educations. Mary attended Mr. William Bird's School, and she was permitted to browse among the books in Salt's library and to attend theatrical performances.

Neither sibling could go on to pursue higher education, however; Mary as a woman was barred, and Charles suffered from a stutter that ruled out the likely course of studying for the priesthood. Their free education ended with Salt's death in 1792, and Charles went to work for the British East India Company. They had to move out of the London Temple, and began a series of often debilitating moves among various houses and apartments. Charles's job was unpaid at first, and Mary was forced to take up dressmaking in order to support the entire family, as both of their elderly parents were in poor health. Their care fell mostly to the overworked Mary, and that care became more time-consuming after her mother lost the ability to walk. The brief periods of respite the siblings enjoyed came primarily from their friendships with literary figures they had met at school, including the poet Samuel Taylor Coleridge.

As of the mid-1790s, there were few signs of the catastrophe that was approaching Mary. Indeed, it was Charles Lamb who showed signs of mental instability, and he was hospitalized briefly at a private asylum called Hoxton (or Hogesdon) House during the winter of 1795–1796. But on September 22, 1796, after several days of behavior that had unsettled her family, it was Mary, somehow irritated by a young female apprentice, who began swinging a table knife and chasing the girl around the family's dining room. Mary's mother called on her to stop, whereupon Mary, screaming, turned on her mother with the knife and stabbed her in the

237

mother's murder." He added, "I had confidence enough in her strength of mind, and religious principle, to look forward to a time when even she might recover tranquillity."

Never charged with murder, Mary was moved to housing that Charles was able to arrange for her, that he described as being in the London borough of Hackney. It is not clear whether this was another asylum, an independent apartment, or a kind of halfway house. In 1799, after her father's death, Mary returned to live with Charles at an apartment in Pentonville in north-central London.

Soon after her return they had to move, for word of the murder had spread among the local population. This became a recurring pattern, for Mary's illness was episodic. Periodically she would be hospitalized in various places, for periods lasting from a few weeks to several months. Charles learned to recognize the symptoms of an oncoming attack, however, and she never again did violence to herself or anyone else. A story widely told in the years after Mary's story became common knowledge recounted how the brother and sister would walk arm in arm, weeping, toward a sanatorium. The relationship between Charles and Mary was one of mutual dependence. In fact, he sometimes regarded her as his protector. "I know I have been wasting and teazing her life for five years past incessantly with my cursed drinking and ways of going on," Charles wrote to Dorothy Wordsworth in 1805, as quoted on the Middlesex University site. "But even in this up-braiding of myself I am offending against her; for I know that she has cleaved to me for better, for worse; and if the balance has been against her hitherto, it was a noble trade."

Published *Tales from Shakespeare*

During the first decade of the nineteenth century, the Lambs enjoyed relative stability. Living in an apartment near their childhood home in the Temple, they cultivated friendships among British writers and thinkers. One of them was the proto-socialist philosopher William Godwin (the father of Mary Shelley), whose wife had suggested that he launch a publishing enterprise devoted to books for children. Godwin asked the Lambs to provide a child's introduction to Shakespeare's plays, to be published in individual pamphlets and eventually in a two-volume set, and by 1806 Charles Lamb could report that the work was well underway, and that (according to a letter posted on the Middlesex University site) "Mary has done them capitally." Of the 20 tales, published in 1807, Mary, by Charles's own account, wrote 14; Charles did the other six, mostly tragedies. However, Godwin insisted that Charles be listed as the sole author.

The *Tales from Shakespeare* were in prose form. They put the motivations of Shakespeare's characters into terms children could understand, but they were notable for the way they avoided oversimplifying Shakespeare's complex situations. Mary Lamb did an admirable job of transferring the madcap spirit of the playwright's comedies into prose. The *Tales from Shakespeare* have never gone out of print, and the Lambs followed them up with another volume, *The Adventures of Ulysses*, that retold the events of Homer's *Odyssey* in chronological sequence. Mary Lamb on her own wrote *Mrs. Leicester's School: Or, the History of Several Young Ladies Related by Themselves*, featuring common stories of childhood

heart. She began throwing other knives and forks around the room, wounding her father in the forehead. The apprentice summoned Charles and the family landlord to the terrible scene, but they were too late to save the life of Elizabeth Lamb.

Confined in Asylum

Up until she began to show signs of illness, Mary was described as calm and reasonable. The Lambs managed to keep most accounts of the tragedy out of the public records, so it is not wholly clear what happened to Mary next. A jury was convened by the local coroner and returned a verdict of lunacy, or temporary insanity. Mary was apparently confined for a year in an asylum in Islington, a somewhat more humane place than the notorious Bedlam hospital for the criminally insane (still in existence as Bethlem Royal Hospital). It is thought that she may have suffered from what would now be called manic depression, and that she gradually returned to a more lucid state.

On October 3, Charles Lamb wrote a letter to Coleridge, quoted in an extensive chronology of the Lambs' lives posted on England's Middlesex University Web site, describing his visit to the asylum: "My poor dear dearest sister, the unhappy and unconscious instrument of the Almighty's judgments to our house, is restored to her senses; to a dreadful sense and recollection of what has past . . . but tempered with religious resignation, and the reasonings of a sound judgment, which in this early stage knows how to distinguish between a deed committed in a transient fit of frenzy, and the terrible guilt of a

experiences. That book was published in 1809 with "Anonymous" substituted for the author's name, but another book, *Poetry for Children, Entirely Original* (1809), bore Mary Lamb's name. *Mrs. Leicester's School* was successful for several decades but eventually fell out of publishers' catalogues. In 1815 Lamb wrote an essay, "On Needlework," that described the lives of constant hard work that many women knew.

Charles Lamb went on to write other books and to become well known as an essayist in the 1820s. Mary, on the other hand, was a woman virtually without a public face—even more so because, due to the treatment protocols of the time, disturbing the patient was thought to worsen the symptoms of her illness, so she was mostly forbidden to have visitors while she was institutionalized. Charles fell in love with an actress, Fanny Kelly, in the late 1810s and proposed marriage. Unwilling to face the consequences of Mary's deteriorating health, she declined his proposal. After that, the Lambs adopted a young Italian girl, Emma Isola.

Mary's attacks became more frequent as she grew older, and she was eventually unable to care for herself. After Charles Lamb's death in 1834 she was cared for by a nurse, and then in a home belonging to her nurse's sister. She died on May 20, 1847, at the age of 82. For many years, biographical material mentioned her mostly in connection with her brother, but a biography of Mary alone by Anne Gilchrist appeared in Boston in 1883, and her life and writing have furnished rich sources of material for feminist scholars and those interested in the relationship between creativity and madness.

Books

Aaron, Jane, *A Double Singleness: Gender and the Writings of Charles and Mary Lamb,* Clarendon Press, 1991.

Anthony, Katharine, *The Lambs: A Study of Pre-Victorian England,* Hammond, 1948.

Dictionary of Literary Biography, Vol. 163: British Children's Writers, 1800–1880, Gale, 1996.

Online

"Charles and Mary Lamb: Their Web Biographies," Middlesex University, London, http://www.mdx.ac.uk/WWW/STUDY/ylamb.htm (January 15, 2009).

"Reflections of Love: Mary Lamb, Percy Shelley, and The Keepsake Literary Annual," University of Florida, http://www.nwe.ufl.edu/los/kberes.html (January 15, 2009). □

David Lean

The films of British director David Lean (1908–1991) were emblematic of high quality British cinema from the years after World War II until the 1980s.

Whether working within the dimensions of a small, intimate story as in his early film *Brief Encounter,* or in the epic settings of cinematic classics like *The Bridge on the River Kwai* or *Lawrence of Arabia,* Lean was a director consumed by his craft. With an early background as

an editor, he was one of the few directors who edited his own films, and no detail was too small to escape his personal attention. Crews working on his epic *Ryan's Daughter* reported waiting for hours until the cloud formation Lean wanted for a scene came into view. Actress Katharine Hepburn, as quoted by Peter B. Flint of the *New York Times,* wrote that to make a film with Lean was "to work with someone who really knows what he is doing—who has an enthusiasm for working in film beyond one's imagination—whose capacity for work has no end—whose determination is to produce the best possible result—to whom nothing matters—discomfort, exhaustion—so long as it contributes to a perfect result. My admiration for David is infinite."

Forbidden to Watch Movies

David Lean was born on March 25, 1908, in the south London suburb of Croydon. His father, Francis, was an accountant. The family adhered to the Quaker faith, and the boy who would become one of Britain's greatest directors was not allowed to watch movies at all when he was young; they were considered sinful. Sent to the Quaker Leighton Park School in Reading, England, Lean sneaked out to see the silent film of the Sherlock Holmes novel *The Hound of the Baskervilles* and was fascinated. At his parents' urging, he signed on as an apprentice in his father's office. In 1927, however, he got a job as a tea boy at the French-owned Gaumont studio. His responsibilities were expanded to include messenger services, holding the clapper number board that marked the beginning of each filmed scene, and finally assisting the camera operator.

By 1930 Lean was editing the newsreels that were shown with most feature films in those days. His skills as an editor developed in tandem with the new vocabulary of sound film. In 1933 he edited his first feature, the low-budget *Money for Speed,* and his reputation grew. By the late 1930s he was serving as editor on the top productions of the British film industry, including two adaptations of plays by George Bernard Shaw: *Pygmalion* (1938) and *Major Barbara* (1940). His first directing credit came with the wartime drama *In Which We Serve.* Officially listed as co-director with screenwriter Noël Coward, he actually controlled most of the filming, inasmuch as Coward was playing a leading role. The film juxtaposed action sequences with soldiers' recollections of their domestic lives.

Lean also worked with Coward on his next three films, *This Happy Breed* (1944), *Blithe Spirit* (a 1945 adaptation of Coward's durably popular comic play), and *Brief Encounter* (1945), the concise story of a man and woman tempted by the prospect of adultery. Although its length was just 86 minutes, the film's romantic themes, amplified by careful use of lighting and a score of traditional classical music, foreshadowed the sweeping, formal, yet emotional style of Lean's later films. *Brief Encounter,* in the words of the British Film Institute, "announced Lean as a true poet of the cinema," and it is widely regarded as the first film classic in his oeuvre. Lean's next three films were literary adaptations: *Great Expectations* (1946) and *Oliver Twist* (1948) drew on novels of Charles Dickens, and *Passionate Friends* (1949) was based on a novel by H.G. Wells. In these works, hints of the style of Lean's later films were apparent in his use of long, atmospheric passages that emphasized a detail of the plot.

Filmed Story of Supersonic Flight

Passionate Friends (1949) and 1950's *Madeleine* featured Lean's third wife (of six), Ann Todd. Except for the dramatic adaptation *Hobson's Choice* (1954), Lean's films of the mid-1950s were on a larger scale that suggested his epic masterpieces to come. *The Sound Barrier* (1952), about the first pilot to fly faster than the speed of sound, and *Summer Madness* (1955, also known as *Summertime* and *Midsummer Madness*), starring Hepburn and set in the lush environment of the city of Venice, Italy, both featured Lean's characteristically close connection between setting and story, drawn on increasingly larger canvases.

After that, for the rest of his life, Lean made only five films. His films, in a word, were blockbusters. They were expensive to make, and he outgrew the dimensions of Britain's film industry and wrangled with foreign producers such as the American Sam Spiegel and Italy's Carlo Ponti. Actors had to be ready for filming schedules lasting months or even years, involving extensive location shooting. But what made film industry figures ready to make these sacrifices was that Lean's final films were, with the exception of 1970's *Ryan's Daughter,* all major critical and box office successes. Several were acclaimed as classics.

None received more acclaim than the 161-minute *The Bridge on the River Kwai* (1957), which earned seven Academy Awards, including Lean's first Best Director award. Filmed in the jungles on the island of Sri Lanka, standing in for Burma during World War II, the film traced the relationship under pressure of the commander of an imprisoned British unit, Colonel Nicholson, and his Japanese counterpart, Colonel Saito. With room in his cinematic structure to depict conflicting motivations and personality flaws within his individual characters, Lean forged a gripping wartime drama that has rarely been matched. The film's memorable "Colonel Bogey Theme" was played at Lean's funeral.

Filmed *Zhivago* Outside Russia

Equally famous were *Lawrence of Arabia* (1962), featuring breathtaking on-location desert scenes in its story of British military officer and author T.E. Lawrence, and *Doctor Zhivago* (1965), based on the novel of the same name by Boris Pasternak and packed with evocative Russian scenery filmed in various locations around the world, although not in Soviet Russia. Running for 197 minutes in its final release (and later restored to the 220-minute length Lean preferred, *Doctor Zhivago* drew some criticism for its gargantuan scale, but it was a major success at the box office. Both films drew on the talents of screenwriter Robert Bolt and cinematographer Freddie Young, Lean's regular collaborators during the final stage of his career.

The criticism intensified with Lean's *Ryan's Daughter* (1970), an adaptation of the Gustave Flaubert novel *Madame Bovary* that was set in Ireland after the Easter Rising of 1916. While Vincent Canby of the *New York Times* conceded that "this kind of extravagant film making is often lovely to look at," he suggested that "it becomes, toward the third hour, as boring as cloud-watching." The film's epic quality was out of step with the politically turbulent times in which it was made, and it dented Lean's reputation for box office magic. Partly as a result of that, and partly because he was personally discouraged by the film's negative reception, Lean did not make another film for 13 years, although he did make a documentary for New Zealand television, *Lost and Found: The Story of An Anchor,* in 1978. That film came about while Lean was planning a never-realized film about the mutiny on the ship Bounty in 1789.

Lean's final film, *A Passage to India* (1984), restored his reputation. Adapted from a novel by E.M. Forster, the film featured a script by Lean himself depicting the aftermath of a rape accusation in British colonial India. Despite the director's advancing age, on-location shooting in India's Marabar Caves brought to life the story's central episode. *A Passage to India* received two Academy Awards, and Lean was knighted by Britain's Queen Elizabeth II in the year of its release.

Lean planned yet another film, an adaptation of Joseph Conrad's novel *Nostromo,* to be set in South America. But he was slowed by throat cancer, and died in London of pneumonia on April 16, 1991, shortly before shooting was to begin. Often honored in his later years, he received a Lifetime Achievement Award in 1990 from the American Film Institute. The British Film Institute listed three of his films—*Brief Encounter* (number two), *Lawrence of Arabia* (number three), and *Great Expectations* (number five)—in the top five of its list of the 100 greatest British films ever made.

Books

International Dictionary of Films and Filmmakers, Volume 2: Directors, 4th ed., St. James, 2000.

Silverman, Stephen, *David Lean,* Abrams, 1989.

Periodicals

Atlantic, February 1994, p. 104.

Globe & Mail (Toronto, Ontario, Canada), May 3, 1991, p. D1.

New York Times, April 17, 1991; September 14, 2008, p. 22.

Times (London, England), April 17, 1991.

Online

"David Lean," *Senses of Cinema,* http://www.archive. sensesof cinema.com/contents/directors/04/lean.html (January 14, 2009).

"David Lean: Biography," British Film Institute, http://www.bfi.org. uk/lean/intro.php?isec=biography (January 14, 2009).

"David Lean (1908–1991)," Britmovie.co.uk, http://www.britmovie. co.uk/directors/d_lean (January 14, 2009). □

Lotte Lenya

The Austrian-born actress and singer Lotte Lenya (1898–1981) embodied the worldwide image of German culture between the two world wars: satirical, sexy, and hard-bitten.

That image took shape during the various stages of Lenya's career. Married to the composer Kurt Weill, she interpreted songs and theatrical creations of his that became hits in both Europe and the United States, to which she fled after the Nazi takeover of Germany in 1933. Lenya solidified her image with roles in various hit films, and for many years she served as a caretaker of Weill's legacy. In the words of Bruce Eder of the *All Movie Guide,* Lenya "was arguably, along with Marlene Dietrich, the most enduringly popular performing star to come out of pre-war/pre-Nazi Germany."

Performed in Circus as Child

Lenya was born Karoline Wilhelmine Charlotte Blamauer on October 18, 1898, in Vienna, Austria. Her father was a hansom cab driver, her mother a laundress. Her performing career began early at a neighborhood circus, where, at age four, she danced, walked a tightrope, and did acrobatics. Lenya's father was abusive, and according to her biographer Donald Spoto, she was forced into prostitution when she was about 11. Lenya's mother and an aunt who worked as a housekeeper in Zurich, Switzerland, conspired to help her escape her life on the streets, and finally they succeeded. Lenya got a job as an au pair in Zurich and became an apprentice actress at the Stadttheater. By 16 she was appearing as a dancer or in small parts in major theater or in operetta productions such as Franz Lehar's *The Merry Widow.*

Neutral Switzerland was a good place for an aspiring actress during World War I, when many creative artists fled the war-depleted cities of their own countries. Lenya found a mentor, Zurich theatrical director Richard Revy, who encouraged her to choose a stage name. They settled on Lotte Lenja, Lotte being an abbreviation of her middle name Charlotte, and Lenja an adaptation of the name of a character in the Anton Chekhov play *Uncle Vanya.* When she moved to the United States, she changed Lenja to Lenya, which reproduced the name's German pronunciation in an English spelling. After the war's end, Lenya moved to Berlin, where experimental drama took root in the early 1920s. She landed a role in a German translation of Shakespeare's *Twelfth Night* and auditioned for a role in a children's dance production with music by a then-unknown composer, Kurt Weill.

Lenya and Weill were both present at that audition, but their relationship did not develop at that time. She appeared in contemporary plays by the likes of Georg Büchner and Franz Wedekind, and in 1924 she and Weill met again. By the following year they were living together, and in 1926 they married. The marriage was not always a stable one, for Weill was devoted to composing above all, and Lenya had other men in her life. Their artistic partnership, however, was consistently fruitful. Lenya appeared as Bessie in the *Mahagonny Songspiel,* a 1927 concert piece that served as a sketch for Weill's later three-act opera *Aufstieg und Fall der Stadt Mahagonny* (The Rise and Fall of the City of Mahagonny). Both versions included the hit "Alabama Song," sung by Lenya. The real breakthrough for both Lenya and Weill came the following year with *Die Dreigroschen Oper* (The Threepenny Opera), an acidly satirical adaptation by Weill and Bertolt Brecht of a semi-popular English opera of the eighteenth century.

Appeared in *Threepenny Opera* Film

Playing Jenny, the prostitute who turns the criminal Macheath ("Mack the Knife") over to the police, Lenya had another hit with her first-act song "Seeräuber Jenny," also becoming well known for her performance of its English version, "Pirate Jenny." Lenya never learned to read music, and her voice was not conventionally beautiful; one German critic compared it to shattered glass. But in its tense alternation between gravelly stretches and a tight vibrato, it was instantly identifiable. Lenya was a major star in Berlin during the years immediately preceding the Nazis' ascent to power, and in 1931 she appeared in the film version of *Die Dreigroschen Oper* directed by G.W. Pabst.

Lenya sometimes said that she and Weill fled German fascism together, but in fact their marriage was in a difficult phase in 1933, and she took the opportunity to walk away from her adopted country while at a casino in Monaco with a lover. She and Weill were actually divorced in 1933, but that did not stop her from appearing in Weill's new music-dance film *The Seven Deadly Sins,* which had its premiere in Paris. The couple reunited when both landed in New York, and they remarried in 1937.

Both threw themselves into American life, speaking English to the exclusion of German. In the 1940s they settled in New City, New York, located in Rockland County. Weill composed a series of successful musicals, but things were harder for Lenya with her marked German accent. In 1937 she appeared in the biblical stage pageant *The Eternal Road,* with music by Weill, and in a 1945 operetta by Weill and Ira Gershwin, *The Firebrand of Florence.* She made occasional nightclub appearances before the war at Le Ruban Bleu in New York. Mostly, however, her career was on hiatus during the World War II years. She was hit hard by Weill's death in 1950 but married editor George Davis the following year. Lenya got a taste of the continuing appeal of Weill's music when she performed at a Weill memorial concert at New York's Town Hall; the event was so successful that it was repeated every year until 1965.

What sparked the revival of Lenya's career in the United States was the appearance in 1952 of an English adaptation of *Die Dreigroschen Oper* as *The Threepenny Opera,* by composer Marc Blitzstein. The show was mounted in 1954 at the Theater de Lys in New York's Greenwich Village, with Lenya, at Davis's encouragement, reprising her original role of Pirate Jenny. *The Threepenny Opera* ran until 1961, earned Lenya a Tony Award in 1956, spawned the first cast recording of an off-Broadway show, and added Weill's stylized German cabaret jazz to the American popular vocabulary once and for all. The hit song "Mack the Knife" was recorded by jazz artist Louis Armstrong (with Lenya in the studio at the time) and by pop singer Bobby Darin.

Recorded LP Albums

Between 1955 and 1960 Lenya recorded six LP albums for the Columbia label, including *Lotte Lenya Sings Berlin Theatre Songs of Kurt Weill* and an English-language companion, *September Song and Other American Theatre Songs of Kurt Weill.* Though Lenya was in her late fifties, her voice retained its characteristic timbre. She made other recordings during this period, including the spoken-word release *Invitation to German Poetry. The Seven Deadly Sins* was revived by the New York City Ballet, again with Lenya, in 1958. George Davis died in 1957, after which Lenya married artist Russell Detwiler. He, too, died young (at age 44, in 1962), after a history of alcohol abuse.

Despite these personal setbacks, Lenya's star kept rising with the American public as she enjoyed several prominent film roles during the 1960s. Lenya's new film career began with *the Roman Spring of Mrs. Stone,* an adaptation of a play by Tennessee Williams. In 1963 she played the film part with which she remains most often identified: that of the Soviet spymaster Rosa Klebb in the James Bond film *From Russia with Love.* She also appeared in *Ten Blocks on the Camino Real* (1966), *The Appointment* (1968), and *North Dallas Forty* (1976), and made a cameo appearance as a masseuse in *Semi-Tough* the following year, in which she remarked onscreen to male lead Burt Reynolds that all American men had sexual problems. In 1966 she returned to the stage as Fräulein Schneider in the original Broadway production of *Cabaret*—a musical strongly influenced by Weill's idiom. She also appeared on stage at the University of California at Irvine in the Brecht play *Mother Courage* in 1971.

Lenya was a familiar figure on television talk shows during her later years, suffering from health problems but never losing her characteristic verve. She was increasingly active with the Kurt Weill Foundation, which was established in 1962 in order to promote Weill's music. After a long illness, Lenya died of cancer in New York on November 27, 1981. Various successors, including opera star Teresa Stratas and German cabaret singer Ute Lemper, showed strong traces of her influence.

Books

Spoto, Donald, *Lenya: A Life,* Little, Brown, 1989.

Periodicals

Globe & Mail (Toronto, Ontario, Canada), September 7, 1996, p. C19.
Independent (London, England), October 13, 1998, p. 9.
New Leader, May 15, 1989, p. 12.
New Yorker, May 14, 2007, p. 150.
Opera News, November 1998, p. 38.

Online

"Lotte Lenya," *All Movie Guide,* http://www.allmovie.com (January 15, 2009).
"Lotte Lenya Biography," Kurt Weill Foundation, http://www.kwf.org/kwf/lotte-lenya (January 15, 2009). □

Wilhelm von Lenz

Although Wilhelm von Lenz (1809–1883) made his way into Russian politics, he is best known for his contributions in the field of musicology. His studies of the 18th century composer Ludwig van Beethoven earned international acclaim. As Beethoven's renowned biographer, Lenz produced multiple volumes of work examining the composer's life and music. Lenz also reviewed—and befriended—many other renowned composers, including Franz Liszt and Frédéric Chopin.

nformation about Wilhelm von Lenz's early years is limited. Lenz was most likely born on May 20 or June 1, 1809, though some sources have also placed his birth on June 13, 1808. He was born in what was then Riga, Russia, though the city is today located in the modern nation of Latvia along the Baltic Sea. Half-German and half-Russian, Lenz would remain in Riga through early adulthood. There, he attended school and began his musical education.

Studied with the Great Pianists

In 1828, Lenz traveled to Paris, France, one of the great centers of European music. He went to France in order to study under the pianist Friedrich Kalkbrenner of Berlin. Lenz later wrote that he was walking to one of his regular lessons with Kalkbrenner when he saw a poster advertising a concert by Hungarian composer and pianist Franz Liszt. Printed on bright yellow paper with giant black letters, the poster instantly caught Lenz's attention. The concert was later that night, and Liszt would be playing the E Flat Major Piano Concerto of Ludwig von Beethoven, the pianist that Lenz most admired.

Lenz immediately resolved not only to attend the concert that evening but also to appeal to Liszt to accept him as his student. Though Lenz was unable to speak with Liszt at the concert, he was greatly impressed by him. More than 40 years later, Lenz would write of Liszt in *The Great Piano Virtuosos of Our Times,* "Liszt does not just play at the piano; he tells at the piano, the story of his own destiny, which is linked to, and reflects, the progress of our time."

Still determined to study with Liszt, Lenz obtained the pianist's address from the clerks at Schlesingers, a music store in Paris. The clerks told Lenz that Liszt was not a teacher, but Lenz drove to Liszt's home to try to convince Liszt to take him as a student. Liszt came down to speak with Lenz, and asked the young musician to play for him. Lenz played Carl Maria von Weber's "Invitation to a Dance." Lenz later claimed that Liszt was so grateful to Lenz for introducing him to Weber's music that he agreed to mentor him.

Lenz spent the rest of 1828 studying with Liszt in Paris. Primarily, they worked on Beethoven's pieces together. Lenz then returned to St. Petersburg, Russia, to live and work. He stayed in St. Petersburg for nearly 14 years, but it is unclear what he did during that time. In 1842, Lenz decided to return to Paris and continue his studies.

On his return to Paris, Lenz took up again with Liszt. He lived near the music store, and spent his afternoons studying with Liszt. They branched beyond Beethoven to study Weber, Frédéric Chopin, and other great musicians of the century. In the evenings, Lenz joined Liszt in his social outings and met other musicians and composers. He soon found himself able to expand his studies.

Through Liszt, Lenz met Johann Baptist Cramer, the founder of Lancaster Pianoforte School, and began studying with him when Liszt left Paris. Liszt had also left a calling card for Lenz to use in order to meet Chopin. Lenz wrote that he made use of the card and called on Chopin at his home one afternoon. Like Liszt, Chopin agreed to meet with Lenz and asked him to play. He then accepted Lenz as his student. According to Lenz, he spent a great deal of time with Chopin, and Lenz seems to have made many contacts as a result of his friendship with the French pianist.

As with Liszt, Lenz would later praise Chopin as a great man and a great musician. In *The Great Piano Virtuosos of Our Time,* Lenz writes, "Chopin's tone-colour is like that of Raphael [*sic.* a respected Renaissance artist]. He is the Raphael of the piano, though one must not seek his Madonnas [*sic.* a famous work of Raphael's] in the churches—but in Life."

Russian Politician and Writer

Some time between the mid-1840s and 1852, Lenz returned to St. Petersburg. His friend Chopin would die in 1849, and Lenz reportedly stated that Chopin died not of consumption, the official cause, but of a broken heart. Consumption was a term used at the time to describe a disease called tuberculosis, which mainly affects the lungs.

On returning to Russia, Lenz moved into a new field when he was appointed Imperial Councilor of State. Despite the distraction of politics and governing, Lenz remained devoted to his musical interests. He took fair advantage of the time away from his teachers and friends in France to work on his own private studies.

From 1852 through 1855, Lenz worked on what would become his most famous written work, *Beethoven and His Three Styles.* Published in three volumes, this study not only provided a close analysis of Beethoven's style and works but also examined the composer's life.

Lenz followed these first volumes by immediately launching into another study. From 1855 through 1860, Lenz wrote and published five volumes entitled *Beethoven, an Art Study.* In the first of these volumes, known as *Beethoven, a Biography,* Lenz adopted an idea from an earlier music writer and divided Beethoven's large body of work into three periods— early (1794-1800), middle (1801-1814), and late (1814-1827). Critics accused Lenz of choosing arbitrary time periods, but his framework eventually became the accepted structure for examining Beethoven's music.

Beethoven

Together, *Beethoven and His Three Styles* and *Beethoven, an Art Study* firmly established Lenz as a musicologist, or one who scientifically studies music.

Lenz's friend Liszt wrote to him in a letter dated December 2, 1852 and found on the website entitled *Letters of Franz Liszt:* "[Y]ou have really understood Beethoven, and have succeeded in making your imagination adequate to his by your intuitive penetration into the secrets of his genius."

Beethoven (1770–1827) was one of the most notable musicians and composers of the 19th century. Today, his music remains well-loved and respected. Born to a musical family, Beethoven's father began training him early, and the talented boy went on to study with some of the greatest musicians in Europe. In 1801, however, Beethoven began to lose his hearing, and it continued to decline in subsequent years until he was diagnosed as completely deaf in 1817. Lenz judged Beethoven's deafness as contributing to the unique compositions and performances that set him apart. Though Lenz never met Beethoven, he remained one of the musician's most committed fans and reviewers.

Further Studies

In 1868, Lenz met the French composer Louis Hector Berlioz in St. Petersburg. Soon after, Lenz decided to take up his musical studies again. That autumn, he traveled to Berlin, Germany, to hear the pianist Carl Tausig perform. Tausig and Lenz shared a mutual friend, Liszt, and Lenz was eager to meet and hear him.

Unfortunately, Lenz fell ill and was unable to attend Tausig's Berlin performance. He sent the composer a kind note expressing his apologies, and Tausig responded by coming to visit Lenz. Lenz reported that Tausig promised to visit him every day, because they were both friends of Liszt.

Tausig largely kept his promise, and visited Lenz regularly. Lenz returned the courtesy by visiting Tausig at his home as well. The two talked about not only music but also philosophy. Lenz stayed in Berlin for six weeks, playing and studying music with Tausig before returning to St. Petersburg again.

In 1870, Tausig came to St. Petersburg. Lenz met with his friend before he played for a packed audience at the Hall of Nobles. Lenz also attended the performance, and praised Tausig's heartfelt performance of the composers Bach, Beethoven, Liszt, Weber, Mozart, Chopin, and others. Lenz would later say of Tausig in *The Great Piano Virtuosos of Our Time,* "In Tausig's nature, humanism was predominant, like the artistic height on which he stood. Dark clouds gathered early over his life. The artist took refuge from them in his Art." For Lenz, Tausig's music was as much about his emotion as about his ability.

The Piano Masters

Soon after Tausig's visit, Lenz began work on his next book, *The Great Piano Virtuosos of Our Time.* Although the book was presented as a critical analysis of four composers—Liszt, Chopin, Tausig, and Adolf Henselt—the book was as much narrative of Lenz's personal experiences with these composers. Lenz had met, studied with, and befriended all four composers, including Henselt, whom Lenz first encountered in St. Petersburg in 1838 when the composer began teaching at the royal education institutions.

Henselt trained many Russian music teachers, and spent most of his life in St. Petersburg. Lenz noted that Henselt rarely gave public performances but generally played only for himself and his close circle of friends and students. Still, Lenz spoke highly of Henselt as a musician, as a composer, and as a friend in his book: "Henselt is . . . a distinct personality. To imitate Henselt's performance is impossible, because it is specifically individual."

In *The Great Piano Virtuosos of Our Time,* Lenz honored Liszt, Chopin, and Henselt as piano masters in their own right, and praised Tausig for his genuine spirit and wonderful performances. He also drew comparisons among the four musicians and their contemporaries. The anecdotes of the pianists revealed as much about Lenz's life and the experience of musicians at the time as it did about the science of their trade.

End of a Musical Life

The Great Piano Virtuosos of Our Time was Lenz's last major work. He may have written other smaller pieces but they have not survived. Like many educated people of the 19th century, Lenz wrote letters with this friends and acquaintances. Letters exchanged with Liszt and Chopin reveal his ongoing interest in music.

Little is known about how Lenz spent his final decade. Having given much of his life to the world of music and some measure of time to Russian politics, Lenz seems to have spent his final ten years in a quieter fashion.

The precise date of Lenz's death is debated. Sources cite January 19 and January 31, 1883. After his death, Lenz was remembered not for his contribution to government but for his interest in and study of the great pianists and composers of his time. Today, he is most well-known for his detailed analysis of Beethoven's work and style.

In a letter dated December 2, 1852 and found on the website entitled *Letters of Franz Liszt,* Liszt wrote Lenz: "You assume alternately the gait of the mole and of the eagle—and everything you do succeeds wonderfully, because amid your subterranean maneuvers and your airy flights you constantly preserve, as your own inalienable property, so much wit and knowledge, good sense and free fancy. If you had asked me to find a motto for your book I should have proposed this, 'Inciter et initier,' as best summing up, according to my ideas, the aim that you fulfill by you twofold talent of distinguished writer and musician ex professo."

For Liszt and others, Lenz was a man who had much to offer in his life and who left behind several great works that have helped contribute to the modern understanding of 19th century European music and society.

Books

"Lenz, Wilhelm von," ed. Stanley Sadie and John Tyrrell, *New Grove Dictionary of Music and Musicians,* Macmillan Publishers Limited, 2001.

von Lenz, Wilhelm, *The Great Piano Virtuosos of Our Time,* ed. Philip Reder, Kahn & Averill, 1983.

Periodicals

The Boston Globe, December 16, 2008,.

Online

"91. To Wilhelm von Lenz in St. Petersburg," *Letters of Franz Liszt,* http://www.globusz.com/ebooks/Liszt/00000103.htm (October 16, 2008).

"Beethoven, Ludwig van," *Encyclopedia Britannica,* http://search.eb.com/eb/article-21592 (October 16, 2008).

"Beethoven, Ludwig van," *The Columbia Encyclopedia, Sixth Edition,* http://www.bartleby.com/65/be/Beethove.html (December 3, 2008).

"Chopin 150: Memories," *Pianos and Pianists,* http://www.mvdaily.com/articles/1999/10/ppvonlnz.htm (October 16, 2008).

"musicology," *Encyclopedia Britannica,* http://search.eb.com/eb/article-9054439 (October 16, 2008).

"Wilhelm Lenz," *Music Encyclopedia,* http://www.answers.com/topic/wilhelm-lenz (December 22, 2008).□

Francisco León de la Barra

A lawyer and a diplomat, Francisco León de la Barra (1863–1939) earned international recognition for serving a term as interim president of Mexico in 1911. For nearly six months, León de la Barra helped maintain an imperfect peace in a country that had been rocked by revolution. Following public elections, León de la Barra stepped down and returned to the field of international law, where he was most comfortable. As a diplomat, León de la Barra served as an envoy and ambassador to nations on three continents.

Francisco León de la Barra was born on June 16, 1863, in Querétaro in central Mexico, the son of Bernabé León de la Barra and María Luisa. His father had come to Mexico from Chile and risen successfully through the ranks of the military. He was a general when León de la Barra, the first of seven sons, was born.

Shortly after León de la Barra's birth, France invaded Mexico and tried to install Emperor Maximillian as its ruler. Bernabé León de la Barra fled with his wife and his 15-day-old son to the United States to escape French forces. They remained in the United States for two years. In 1865 León de la Barra's father returned to Mexico and fought in the battle at Querétaro, which resulted in the capture of Emperor Maximillian. Following a revolt and seizure of power by Porfirio Díaz, the León de la Barra family settled in Mexico City.

Early Career

After León de la Barra completed his primary studies, he enrolled at the National Preparatory School in Mexico City, graduating at the top of his class in 1884. Subsequently, Joaquín Baranda, who was the minister of education and foreign relations, appointed León de la Barra to serve as a mathematics instructor at the school. Years later, in 1897, León de la Barra was appointed to chair the department of logic.

During his time as a teacher, León de la Barra also worked to finish his law degree at Escuela Libra de Derecho.

At the law school, he specialized in international law and became a respected lecturer. He also produced several treatises on international law. When he completed his degree, he opened a private law practice.

For León de la Barra, being a lawyer, teacher, and writer was not enough. During the 1890s he also delved into politics. His family had contacts with the ruling Díaz regime, and León de la Barra benefited from that connection. Díaz arranged for him to be appointed as a council member in Mexico City, and beginning in 1891, León de la Barra served three terms in the federal legislature, the National Chamber of Deputies.

In 1892 León de la Barra represented Mexico at the Ibero-American Judicial Conference in Madrid, Spain, celebrating the 400th anniversary of Christopher Columbus's voyage to the Americas. During that visit he met Queen Isabella II, and received the Order of Carlos III, the first of many medals conferred on him by foreign leaders.

The Diplomat

León de la Barra's poise, legal expertise, and scholarly approach were highly praised, and he began receiving more diplomatic appointments. In 1896 he officially joined the diplomatic corps and served as an envoy to various nations in South America, North America, and Europe. In 1898 Díaz's Foreign Minister, Ignacio Mariscal, hired León de la Barra as a consultant on international law, to assist in settling numerous international disputes, especially those involving conflicting territorial claims.

In 1902 León de la Barra accepted an appointment as a Mexican delegate to the Conference of American States. More commonly known as the Pan-American Conference, this meeting of nations in the Americas was meant to foster trade and other open relations among the governments of North and South America. Two years later, León de la Barra was sent as a diplomatic envoy to Brazil, Uruguay, Argentina, and Paraguay, and Díaz then appointed him as the envoy to Belgium and Holland.

For the next four years, from 1905 to 1909, León de la Barra and his first wife, María Elena Barneque, lived in Belgium and traveled throughout Europe. León de la Barra developed a love for the French people, culture, and landscape that would lead him back to the country many years later.

In 1906 León de la Barra represented Mexico at another Pan-American Conference. The member nations each agreed to send a delegate to The Hague peace conference in the Netherlands the following year. The meeting was intended to bring together representatives from various nations in an effort to establish peaceful international relations.

In 1909 León de la Barra suffered personal tragedy with the death of his wife. He was left with two young sons, Francisco and Julio. At the same time, he accepted a mission as ambassador to Washington, D.C., to work on improving relations between Mexico and the United States. With his sons, León de la Barra relocated to the American capital for the next two years.

In the United States, León de la Barra impressed U.S. officials with his diplomacy, and regularly dealt with President William Howard Taft. In 1911, León de la Barra married his widowed sister-in-law, Refugio Borneque, and she joined him in Washington.

León de la Barra focused largely on territorial issues while in the United States, and succeeded in staving off conflict over the shifting course of the Rio Grande, which formed much of the U.S.-Mexican border, and over rights to the Colorado River. The negotiations helped lay the groundwork for settlement of these issues over the next decade.

León de la Barra's most critical task as ambassador came when the Mexican Revolution erupted in 1910, and Díaz gave him the task of preventing U.S. intervention in Mexican affairs. Díaz feared that the United States would side with the leader of the revolt, Francisco I. Madero, who sought to overthrow him.

Presided Over Interim Regime

In May of 1911, León de la Barra reluctantly returned to his country to take up a new post—that of president. The Mexican Revolution had succeeded in unseating Díaz, and the dictator had relinquished power in the Treaty of Ciudad Juárez. As part of the treaty, Díaz had agreed to hand over power to León de la Barra as interim president until free and open elections could be held. Parties on both sides of the revolution had agreed to León de la Barra's appointment because they felt he was an honest official who was not strongly aligned with any political party.

León de la Barra took office on May 25, 1911, and served as interim president until November of that year. In his inaugural address, as recorded in Peter V.N. Henderson's *In the Absence of Don Porfirio,* León de la Barra assured the Mexican people: "The happiest day of my public life will be that on which, within the shortest time compatible with the electoral law and the welfare of the country, I can deliver up the power that today I receive to the citizen elected by the republic."

Many issues faced León de la Barra as president, but he lacked the power to effectively address many of them. As a temporary ruler, he was largely concerned with keeping the peace and securing free and fair elections. Until that time, León de la Barra tried to maintain a balance between the old order of Porfirians and the new movement of maderistas under Madero; between urban interests and rural; between landowners and peasants who worked the land. However, many historians as well as his contemporaries criticized León de la Barra for letting various conflicts spiral into violence.

During León de la Barra's short rule, the agrarian Zapata Rebellion in southern Mexico got underway. Following the Mexican Revolution, many rural groups anticipated sweeping land reforms that would redistribute parcels of land from wealthy plantation holders to the masses of people who worked the land for subsistence. León de la Barra was committed to land reform, but he would not open talks until rural forces, in particular the Zapatistas, had disarmed. When León de la Barra ordered government forces to disarm the rebels, violence flared.

According to *Don Porfirio,* for most of his months in office, León de la Barra also worked to secure what he called "effective suffrage," and protect every eligible voter's right to vote. He refused to run for office himself, and refused any attempts to delay the elections. On October 1, popular elections were held, and although León de la Barra did not respond to efforts to enact woman suffrage, the elections themselves were widely regarded as the first truly democratic elections in Mexico up to that time.

As expected, Madero won in a landslide, with nearly 95 percent of the vote, and León de la Barra officially—and with great relief—stepped down as president.

Life After the Presidency

At Madero's request, León de la Barra stayed on in government. He was elected governor of the State of Mexico and then a senator in the federal legislature. In 1913, when the military leader Victoriano Huerta instituted a coup leading to the assassination of Madero, León de la Barra was implicated in the plot, but his part, if any, was never clear and never proven. Huerta appointed León de la Barra as his foreign secretary, but León de la Barra was already setting his sights outside Mexico.

When revolution broke out again in 1914, León de la Barra, his wife, and their children left Mexico for the last time, and moved to Paris, where they had relatives. Officially, León de la Barra had accepted a post as the Mexican minister in France, but he never returned to his homeland and largely pursued his own career and interests.

Once settled in Paris, León de la Barra began teaching international law at the University of Paris at the Sorbonne. To supplement that work, he opened a private law practice, and also undertook scholarly pursuits, reviewing the work of other legal minds and producing his own treatises on international law.

Following World War I, León de la Barra assisted the French government during peace negotiations at Versailles, and began working with the International Court of Justice and the various tribunals established under the Treaty of Versailles. For much of the 1920s, he served as a judge and arbitrator at The Hague, eventually becoming president of the Permanent Court of Arbitration there.

As World War II approached, León de la Barra's health began to fail. In 1939, when León de la Barra's health had further declined, his wife took him to Biarritz in Southern France, where he died on September 23, 1939. He was buried there at the Sabou Cemetery. He had outlived all of his children and left behind his second wife and the couple's grandchildren.

León de la Barra rose to politics at a time of great change in Mexico, and he served as his nation's president during a period of volatile transition. He dedicated his life to public service and to the advancement of international law, and his actions as president, as a legal scholar, and as a diplomat helped shape not only the Republic of Mexico but also the conduct of international bodies today.

Books

Coerver, Don M., Suzanne B. Pasztor, and Robert M. Buffington, *Mexico*, Abc-Clio Inc., 2004, (January 12, 2009).

Henderson, Peter V.N., *In the Absence of Don Porfirio: Francisco León de la Barra and the Mexican Revolution*, Scholarly Resources Inc., 2000.

Periodicals

Journal of Latin American Studies, August 2001, p. 623.
New York Times, September 18, 1911.

Online

"Francisco León de la Barra," Transl., *Instituto de Educacion de Aguascalientes,* www.iea.gob.mx/efemerides/efemerides/biogra/flbarra.html (October 16, 2008).

"Francisco León de la Barra," *NationMaster Encyclopedia,* http://www.nationmaster.com/encyclopedia/Francisco-León-de-la-Barra (October 16, 2008).

"Francisco Madero," *Encyclopedia Britannica,* http://search.eb.com/eb/article-9049888 (October 16, 2008).

"León de la Barra, Francisco," *Historical Text Archive,* 2003, http://www.historicaltextarchive.com/sections.php?op=viewarticle&artid;=586 (October 16, 2008).□

Mary Livermore

Mary Livermore (1820–1905) was one of the most successful of the lecturers and writers who toured the country in the late 19th century, preparing the way for the eventual institution of woman suffrage and for the prohibition of liquor.

L ivermore came to these causes later in her career, having already amassed a striking variety of life experiences. As a young woman, she underwent a profound spiritual conversion, rejecting the Baptist faith of her parents. That conversion led Livermore into an intellectually fruitful marriage and a long career as an editor, devoting her energies to her adopted Universalist church and to the cause of the abolition of slavery. During the Civil War, she lent her considerable organizational abilities to the medical arm of the Union cause, serving as director of a branch office of the U.S. Army's medical and sanitation service. In this way Livermore experienced the devastation of the war firsthand, and she later wrote about it in great detail. With a remarkable career that intersected many of the major social movements of the time, Mary Livermore remains an underappreciated figure in American history.

Memorized Catechism

The fourth child of Timothy and Zebiah Vose Rice, Livermore was born Mary Ashton Rice in Boston, Massachusetts, on December 19, 1820. Her parents were devout Baptists who held to the hard-core Calvinist belief in predestination of salvation, and Livermore received an extremely strict religious upbringing. She had to repeat endlessly a catechism, or a set of questions and answers illustrating religious doctrine, that was administered by her father. "If that catechism is lost, hopelessly, I can at any time reproduce it, question and answer, verbatim et literatim, for it is burned into my memory forever," Livermore wrote in her auto-biography, *The Story of My Life: The Sunshine and Shadow of Seventy Years.* She recalled long Sundays in unheated churches, with a strict prohibition against reading any book but the Bible or even eating.

Many aspects of Livermore's religious instruction took root in her mind. She read the Bible in its entirety every year from the time she was old enough to do so until she was 23. As a child, she liked to pretend that she was a preacher, using the kitchen table as a pulpit, or even preaching in the family's woodshed to a congregation of pieces of wood, "sitting" in long pews of unsplit logs. She had doubts from the start, however, about Calvinist doctrine. When she was seven or eight years old, her younger sister was born. Livermore asked her parents to send the girl back to God rather than take the chance that she might grow to be one of the souls condemned to hell with no recourse for avoiding it. When Livermore was a young woman, her doubts deepened: her younger sister Rachel, suffering badly because she had been born with a curved spine, died a painful death in Livermore's presence. Livermore had no way of knowing whether the innocent girl was among the elect who would be saved.

Educated at the Hancock Grammar School and the Female Seminary of Charlestown (although her schooling was interrupted by a two-year interval the family spent as pioneer farmers in western New York state), Livermore set about trying to answer the questions in her mind. Already employed by the seminary to teach French and Latin, she learned ancient Greek so that she could read parts of the Bible in the original language. Increasingly troubled, she took a job in 1839 as a tutor on a plantation in Virginia. Over her three years there, she observed the injustices and the growing strains in the system of slavery. She was sickened for days after witnessing the brutal whipping of a slave. By the time she returned to Massachusetts in 1842 to take a position as a schoolmistress in Duxbury, she was committed to the abolitionist cause.

Religious Counseling Bloomed into Romance

On Christmas Eve of 1843, she stopped into a Universalist church in Duxbury because she was attracted by the hymn singing she heard. Although the Baptists did not consider the Universalists to be Christians, she introduced herself to the pastor, Daniel Livermore, and asked him questions about the church. He gave her a pamphlet called "Moral Argument Against Calvinism" by the liberal New England theologian William Ellery Channing, among other readings, and the two began to meet frequently for religious discussions that turned into a courtship. Despite resistance from within Mary's family, the couple married in 1845 and had three daughters, one of whom died young. They moved from Duxbury to Fall River, Massachusetts, Stafford Center, Connecticut, Weymouth, Massachusetts, Malden, Massachusetts, and Auburn, New York between 1845 and 1857 as Daniel Livermore took up new ministerial posts.

Unsatisfied in her church wife role, Mary began to write. She published two books, a set of temperance stories called *Thirty Years too Late* (many had been originally written for a children's temperance group she organized called

the Cold Water Army) and *A Mental Transformation,* a reflection on her own spiritual evolution. The family settled in Chicago after the illness of their daughter Marcia put a stop to their plans to move to Kansas to found an anti-slavery settlement in the territory that was contested by pro- and anti-abolition forces. They acquired a Universalist newspaper, *The New Covenant,* which Mary helped to edit, and she founded a home for elderly women and a hospital for women and children.

The skills she acquired in these enterprises served her well after the outbreak of the Civil War, which inspired the formation of numerous relief organizations. In the Northern states, the United States Sanitary Commission was formed to coordinate their activities. Livermore quickly divested herself of her editorial responsibilities and became involved in the Northwest Sanitary Commission, working directly as part of soldier relief groups, and she was appointed co-director of the U.S. Sanitary Commission's Chicago office in December of 1862. This was not a desk job. Livermore traveled extensively near the front lines, working with groups that tended directly to the wounded. She recalled offering to take dictation of a letter to the mother of a dying soldier who insisted instead that she should help his comrade first.

Wartime experiences convinced Livermore that women's contributions to American society were being suppressed because women did not have the right to vote. Not particularly attracted by the suffrage movement before the war, she organized Chicago's first woman suffrage convention in 1868 and became editor of the pro-suffrage newspaper *The Agitator* the following year. When that paper merged with Boston's *Woman's Journal,* the Livermores moved back to the Boston area. They settled in suburban Melrose, where Mary Livermore lived for the rest of her life. She became co-editor of the *Journal* with early feminists Lucy Stone and Julia Ward Howe, the author of the text of "The Battle Hymn of the Republic."

Began Lecturing

Soon a speakers' bureau asked Livermore to take to the lecture circuit full-time. Daniel, who had become the minister at a Universalist church in the town of Hingham, did not object to the plan—quite the opposite, in fact. "It is preposterous," he said (as quoted in the website of the Unitarian Universalist Association), "for you to continue baking and brewing, making and mending, sweeping, dusting, and laundering, when work of a better and higher order seeks you.... You need not forsake your home, nor your family; only take occasional absences from them, returning fresher and more interesting because of your varied experiences." "There was force in his manner of stating it," Mary recalled later in her autobiography, "and the matter was settled."

She was an effective lecturer, traveling all over the U.S. and visiting Europe several times to talk on women's rights, religion, history, and temperance, which inspired the members of the Massachusetts Woman's Christian Temperance Union to elect her as president for a 20-year period. She estimated that she gave one lecture, entitled "What Shall We Do with Our Daughters?," more than 800 times. Lists of her speaking engagements do not include the numerous addresses she gave in Universalist churches. Livermore also became president of the Massachusetts Woman's Suffrage Association and was connected with various other progressive organizations.

Along with several magazine articles, Livermore wrote two compelling books about her experiences: *My Story of the War: A Woman's Narrative of Four Years Personal Experience* (1888) and *The Story of My Life, or, The Sunshine and Shadow of Seventy Years* (1897). After Daniel Livermore's death in 1895, she became interested in Spiritualism and sometimes claimed to be communicating with him from beyond the grave. Although her schedule slowed in her last years, she continued to give lectures well into her ninth decade of life. Livermore died at her home in Melrose on May 23, 1905.

Books

Livermore, Mary, *The Story of My Life: The Sunshine and Shadow of Seventy Years,* Worthington, 1897.

Venet, Wendy Hamand, *A Strong-Minded Woman: The Life of Mary Livermore,* University of Massachusetts Press, 2005.

Online

"Major Figures in Civil War Medicine: Livermore, Mary Ashton Rice (1820–1905)," Reynolds Historical Library, University of Alabama at Birmingham, http://www.uab.edu/reynolds/CivilWarMedFigs/Livermore.htm (January 14, 2009).

"Mary and Daniel Livermore," Unitarian Universalist Association, http://www25.uua.org/uuhs/duub/articles/livermorefamily.html (January 14, 2009).

"Mary Livermore," http://www.marylivermore.com (January 14, 2009).

"Mary Livermore," Spartacus Schoolnet, http://www.spartacus.schoolnet.co.uk/USAWlivermore.htm (January 14, 2009).□

Carole Lombard

Attractive and versatile, with a strong sense of comic timing, American actress Carole Lombard (1908–1942) defined the feminine on-screen style of the so-called screwball comedies emerging from Hollywood in the 1930s.

Lombard's films were anything but one-note affairs. She played socialites, small-town girls, criminals, and even a Polish actress in her classic final film, *To Be or Not to Be.* In each role she played she seemed natural and likable, and she could elevate even mediocre material. Lombard's love life also blazed trails; her marriage to her sometime co-star Clark Gable was one of the great Hollywood romances during the period before World War II. Lombard's death in a 1942 plane crash came as a shock to a nation that had just plunged into the war, and it cut short a career that had already placed her among Hollywood's legends.

Reputedly Discovered Playing Baseball

Born Jane Alice Peters on October 6, 1908, Lombard was a native of Fort Wayne, Indiana. She spent her early years there in a sizable home on Rockhill Street, but when she was six years old her parents separated. Lombard, her mother, Elizabeth, and her two brothers moved to Los Angeles, where Lombard attended Fairfax High School. She also took dancing and acting classes. Lombard won her high school's title of May Queen in 1924, but by that time her film career was already underway. An often-told story held that director Allan Dwan noticed Lombard playing baseball with some boys on a Los Angeles street and thought she would be a natural for a part as a tomboy in his film *A Perfect Crime* (1921).

In 1924 Lombard dropped out of high school to join a theater company, and the following year she was signed to a contract by the 20th Century Fox studio. From then until the end of her life, she would make three or more films almost every year, but she took time off in 1927 to finish her high school courses and earn a diploma. In *A Perfect Crime* she was billed as Jane Peters, but when she joined Fox she was made Carol Lombard; the final "e" was added to her first name in 1930. Lombard's first film for Fox was a Western, *Hearts and Spurs.* She made three more films for the studio in 1925, and teamed with director Howard Hawks for *The Road to Glory* the following year. In an auto accident later in 1926 she suffered facial scarring and was dropped by Fox as a result.

Lombard bounced back, making a series of short subjects for the studio of silent film pioneer Mack Sennett in the late 1920s. Sennett specialized in slapstick comedies. Although films such as *The Swim Princess* (1928) were artistically slight, working in a fast-paced environment opposite such veteran stars of the silent screen as Billy Bevan, Mack Swain, Chester Conklin, and Billy Gilbert honed the young actress's sense of comic timing. Lombard began to land small roles in such feature-length films as 1928's *Me, Gangster,* directed by Raoul Walsh. In 1929 she made her first sound film, *High Voltage,* for the Pathé studio, and the following year she was signed to a seven-year contract by Paramount.

At first, Lombard made more headlines off the screen than on. It took several years for her restless, madcap personality to emerge. In her earlier films, such as 1931's *Man of the World,* in which she played a delicate high-class young woman deceived by an extortionist, "she could," in the words of Gary Arnold of the *Washington Times,* "be mistaken for other aspiring starlets of the period." That same year, after an intense courtship, Lombard married her *Man of the World* costar, William Powell. The marriage ended in divorce in 1933, but Powell and Lombard remained friends. He became a key backer of her career, recommending her for the starring role in one of her greatest comedies, *My Man Godfrey* (1936). Lombard costarred with Clark Gable in 1932's *No Man of Her Own.* Although their romance was still several years in the future, the film marked the only time they appeared together on screen as costars.

Starred Opposite Barrymore

Lombard's real breakthrough came in 1934, when she reunited with Hawks for *Twentieth Century,* prompting the director (according to Terrence Rafferty of the *New York Times*) to describe her as a "marvelous girl—crazy as a bedbug." In the film Lombard played an actress, Lily Garland, who is trying to break free of her mentor and former lover, a director played by legendary actor John Barrymore. Lombard found her cinematic style opposite the powerful Barrymore, and her high-energy performance won the admiration not only of Hawks but also of Barrymore, who sent her an autographed photo with an inscription calling her the finest actress he had ever worked with.

Twentieth Century touched off a series of Lombard successes that, although she appeared in dramas occasionally, mostly fell into the screwball category. They included *My Man Godfrey* (1936), in which Lombard played a socialite who falls in love with the family butler, and 1937's *Nothing Sacred,* where she had the role of a Vermont woman who feigns a fatal illness so that a New York tabloid newspaper can tell the story of her last days and boost its circulation—while she sees the Big Apple at the paper's expense. That film had a screenplay by top Hollywood writer Ben Hecht, and most of Lombard's films attracted Hollywood's A-list writing and directing talent.

When Lombard crossed paths with Clark Gable again at a party in Hollywood in 1936, her career was in full swing. Making three films and three radio programs that year, she earned a near-industry-high of $465,000. Her romantic life was less successful, as she suffered through unrequited attractions to actor Gary Cooper and vocalist Russ Columbo. Despite the fact that Gable was married to socialite Ria Langham, however, sparks flew between Lombard and Gable. Lombard indulged Gable's passion for duck hunting and, after the two had a lovers' quarrel, sent him a pair of live doves as a peace offering. Lombard's jealousy toward Gable's female leads only intrigued the womanizing actor. In 1937 *Photoplay* magazine would include the pair in a snarky list of "Hollywood's Unmarried Husbands and Wives."

Lived in Valley Farmhouse

After Gable paid out a large settlement and won a divorce from Langham, he and Lombard were married on March 29, 1939, during a short break in Gable's work on *Gone with the Wind.* The couple moved into a farmhouse in the then-rural San Fernando Valley, constructing for themselves an idyllic rural scene in which they called each other Ma and Pa, and raised horses, dogs, and chickens. In 1940 Lombard began to lay the groundwork for a long-haul career, temporarily forsaking comedy for two serious films, *Vigil in the Night* and *They Knew What they Wanted.*

After the entry of the United States into World War II in December of 1941, Lombard volunteered to appear at a January rally in her home state of Indiana in order to sell war bonds. The rally was a success, with $2.1 million in bonds sold. Lombard, along with her mother and 15 servicemen, boarded a Trans World Airlines flight to Los Angeles. The plane stopped in Las Vegas to refuel, taking off again at 4 a.m. on January 16, 1942. Just over 20 minutes later the plane slammed into Mount Potosi, southwest of Las Vegas. Lombard was the first military-related American female fatality of World War II. A frantic Gable came to join the search and ended up taking the bodies of the 33-year-old Lombard and her mother back to Los Angeles to be buried at Forest Lawn cemetery. He refused offers from the U.S. Army to give Lombard a military funeral and from the Hollywood Victory Committee to erect a Lombard monument, instead carrying out Lombard's written wishes for a simple family funeral in which she would be clothed in white.

President Franklin Roosevelt sent a telegram of condolence that was widely publicized, and Gable enlisted in the Air Force and served as a gunner on bombing missions in Europe. At the time of her death, Lombard had already completed *To Be or Not to Be,* a comedy about a troupe of actors in Nazi-occupied Poland. The film was poorly timed in several respects, one being a scene in which Lombard asked what could go wrong on a plane, but it is now recognized as one of her finest films, and one that would have pointed the way to a rich future for its still-youthful star.

Books

International Dictionary of Films and Filmmakers, Volume 3: Actors and Actresses, 4th ed., St. James Press, 2000.

Maltin, Leonard, *A Pyramid Illustrated History of the Movies,* Pyramid, 1976.

Matzen, Robert D., *Carole Lombard: A Bio-Bibliography,* Greenwood, 1988.

Swindell, Harry Win, *Screwball: The Life of Carole Lombard,* Morrow, 1975.

Periodicals

New York Times, November 23, 2008.

People, February 12, 1996.

Washington Times, October 5, 2008.

Online

"Carole Lombard Bio," http://www.carolelombard.org (January 16, 2009).

"Carole Lombard," The Biography Channel (UK), http://www.thebiographychannel.co.uk/biography_story/300:136/1/Carole_Lombard.htm (January 16, 2009).

"The Queen of Hollywood," Mount Potosi Canyon Ranch, http://www.mountpotosi.com/history.htm (January 16, 2009). □

Lon Nol

Lon Nol (1913–1985) rose through the ranks of power in Cambodia in the 1950s and 1960s. In 1970, with American support, he orchestrated a military coup to overthrow Cambodia's ruling Prince Norodom Sihanouk. As war waged in neighboring South Vietnam, Nol opened Cambodian territory to the U.S. military and seized control of the government. His policies helped mobilize the communist guerilla forces known as the Khmer Rouge, and ultimately led to a bloody civil war.

Born on November 13, 1913, Lon Nol grew up in Prey Vêng Province in eastern Cambodia along the border with Vietnam. He was born into a middle class, landholding family in a country fraught with disparities between urban and rural and landowners and landless.

At the time, France maintained colonial power over Cambodia as well as over other territories in southeastern Asia, then called Indochina. Nol's father, Lon Hin, served as a minor official in the colonial government, and his grandfather had once been the provincial governor. Nol was raised to follow in their footsteps.

When Nol was old enough, he was sent to a French colonial school, the Lycée Sisowath in the capital city Phnom Penh. He received an elementary education there, and then attended the Lycée Chasseloup-Laubat in Saigon, now known as Ho Chi Minh City, in Vietnam. When he finished school, Nol followed his father and grandfather into civil service.

Rising Through the Ranks of Government

In 1934, Nol joined the French colonial administration as a member of the Judicial Service. Within a few years, he rose to become a magistrate in the Siem Reap Province in northwestern Cambodia. A decade later, in 1946, he was appointed as the provincial governor of Kratie Province along the Vietnam border. He remained there for several years before becoming the head of the national police in 1951.

In the 1950s, France began losing its hold on its colonies in Indochina. Weakened by World War II, French resources were stressed and local movements in the colonies were challenging French rule. Strong opposition in Vietnam grew around rural-based communist guerillas. Other interests supported independence but opposed communist rule and wanted to maintain a governing style similar to that of the colonial powers.

Nol joined with the nationalist push to secure independence but set himself against the communist movement. In 1952, he joined the Cambodian army as a lieutenant and quickly rose to a position of leadership as an area commander. He battled Vietnamese communist forces in eastern Cambodia, determined to push them back.

Meanwhile, his former schoolmate King Norodom Sihanouk also joined the regional push for independence from France. When Cambodia won its independence on November 9, 1953, Sihanouk took power, largely with western approval. He set about stabilizing the existing government structure as conflict increased in neighboring Vietnam.

In 1954, the Geneva Agreements officially recognized the independence that had already been won by Vietnam, Laos, and Cambodia, but competing interests in Vietnam plunged the region into war. Even as France pulled out of the area, the United States began sending money, weapons, advisors and eventually troops to support western-approved regimes, including Cambodia's Sihanouk, and stamp out what was considered a growing communist threat.

Nol supported Sihanouk and continued opposing any communist forces. In 1954, he was appointed as provincial governor, this time of Battambang Province. The following year, Sihanouk abdicated, or gave up, the throne to his father, Norodom Suramarit, but stayed on as Prime Minister. Sihanouk then called on Nol to serve as Defense Minister and Army Chief of Staff.

In 1960, Suramarit died and Sihanouk again became head of the government, though he took the lesser title "Prince" in place of "King." Nol rose to become the commander of the armed forces even as Sihanouk declared a policy of neutrality in the Cold War and in Vietnam. Sihanouk maintained that Cambodia favored neither the North nor the South, and allowed both access to Cambodian territory.

Nol continued to support Sihanouk but he was never entirely happy with the neutrality policy. Throughout the escalation of the conflict in Vietnam, which led to strained ties between Sihanouk and the United States, Nol remained a critical and seemingly loyal player in Sihanouk's government. In 1963, Nol became Sihanouk's Deputy Prime Minister. Then, from 1966 to 1967, he served as Prime Minister. In 1968, Nol slid over to serve as Defense Minister, but he returned to the position of Prime Minister in 1969.

By the end of the 1960s, not only had U.S. officials grown frustrated with Sihanouk's neutrality but so, too, had officials in Cambodia, including Nol and Sihanouk's cousin Sirik Matak, who was serving as Deputy Prime Minister. Nol wanted to take a more aggressively pro-Western and anti-communist stance, and he would soon seize his chance to do so.

Change in Power

Early in 1970, Nol went to France to receive medical care. At the same time, Sihanouk was touring countries in Europe and Asia on official visits. When Sihanouk reached France, Nol returned to Cambodia, where Matak, as Prime Minister, was overseeing government operations.

At the time, North Vietnamese communist forces were arrayed in eastern Cambodia, using the borderlands as a base of operations. Nol, Matak, and others found this unacceptable, but Sihanouk allowed it under the neutrality policy. On returning to Cambodia, Nol decided to move against this policy.

In March, Nol organized a series of demonstrations against the North Vietnamese and issued an ultimatum demanding that the communist forces withdraw from Cambodia or suffer attack. Thousands of people turned out in Phnom Penh in support of the demonstrations, but North Vietnam ignored the ultimatum. In response, on March 15, Nol requested that the South Vietnamese forces, supported by the United States, shell North Vietnamese targets inside Cambodia, and they did.

Sihanouk, though furious about the demonstrations, the ultimatum, and the shelling, did not return. He went from France to the Soviet Union, and was in Moscow when his cousin Matak and Nol decided to initiate a coup and seize power. The morning of March 18, Nol and Matak convinced the Cambodian National Assembly to unanimously vote to depose Sihanouk, and the leader was removed from power.

Nol, as Prime Minister, was granted emergency powers over the nation, and Matak stayed on as Deputy Prime Minister. People in the cities largely supported the change in power, but Sihanouk was popular among rural communities. The move not only upset the political balance within Cambodia but also invited the Vietnam War into the country.

Nol abandoned Sihanouk's neutrality policy and immediately established close ties with the United States and South Vietnam. He allowed U.S. and South Vietnamese forces to use Cambodia as an operations base and organized the national army against not only the North Vietnamese but also against a growing Cambodian communist movement, called the Khmer Rouge.

At the same time, Sihanouk set up a government in exile in China and moved to align with the Khmer Rouge in hopes of regaining power. Sihanouk became a rallying point for the Khmer Rouge to recruit support across rural Cambodia. Accusations of corruption and heavy-handed policies also hurt Nol and encouraged the growth of the communist guerilla force. Soon, Cambodia plunged into a civil war.

The United States and South Vietnam supported Nol's government and military with funds and supplies but their own forces were mired in Vietnam. Nol found his government largely on its own to defend against the incursion of the Khmer Rouge, and most historians agree that Nol was not prepared to do so.

In August and September 1970, Nol launched the first of two large-scale attacks against the Khmer Rouge. The offensive failed horribly. A few months later, Nol suffered a stroke and temporarily gave up power in order to recover. He spent two months in Hawaii receiving treatment, but he never entirely recovered. With U.S. help, he returned to Cambodia to reclaim power, but both he and the nation were in a worse state than before.

In August 1971, Nol launched the second large-scale attack intended to rout the Khmer Rouge. Again, it failed. Nol was forced to call on the United States for assistance, and U.S. bombing became a regular occurrence in the Cambodian countryside. The destruction caused by the bombing campaign only increased the ire against Nol and helped the Khmer Rouge gain ground.

In October, as the situation worsened, Nol declared a state of emergency and enacted repressive measures against the media and citizens. Several months later, on March 10, 1972, he suspended the nation's constitution and seized total control of the nation. Nol declared himself President, Prime Minister, and commander of the armed forces. He was inaugurated four days later.

Nol's apparent hold on power was weakening fast, however. War raged around and within Cambodia, and Nol's national army had been forced into a largely defensive posture, dependent on U.S. supplies, weaponry, and bombing. By August 1973, the United States had dropped more than 2 million tons of bombs on the Cambodian countryside. This air campaign and Nol's own repressive stance cost him rural Cambodia and positioned the Khmer Rouge to seize the rest of the country.

By 1975, Nol and his national forces held just the capital Phnom Penh and a few isolated areas in northwestern

Cambodia. The Khmer Rouge held the rest of the nation and was advancing on the capital. As the guerillas neared Phnom Penh, Nol, who was a great believer in magic and sorcery, reportedly sprinkled a circular line of magic sand around the city to protect it. The magic did not work.

Apparently not willing to trust his own fate to spells, Nol fled Cambodia on April 1, 1975, taking his wife and ten children with him. Most of the rest of his government, including Matak and Nol's brother Lon Non, remained. Two weeks later, the Khmer Rouge seized the capital.

Exile

Nol lived the rest of his days in exile. He fled first to Indonesia, and from there, he went to Hawaii. With him, he took $1 million in U.S. currency. He was in Hawaii when the Khmer Rouge executed the remaining members of Nol's government and forcibly emptied the cities of their inhabitants.

The leader of the Khmer Rouge, Pol Pot, wanted to establish an agrarian communist nation. He forced all of the nation's urban residents to move to the countryside. Thousands died on the forced marches, and many others were killed. Cambodia soon fell into the bloodiest period of its long history.

Meanwhile, Nol and his family remained safe in Hawaii until 1979, when they moved to Fullerton, California. There, Nol lived with his wife, Sovanna Nol, until his death. On November 17, 1985, Nol succumbed to heart disease in St. Jude's Hospital. He left behind his wife, nine of their ten children, six grandchildren, and a distant country that was still trying to recover from decades of violence.

In 2008, more than 30 years after Nol had fled Cambodia, his eldest son, Lon Rith, returned to the struggling nation. The Khmer Rouge had long since collapsed. Rith, then an economist in California, had decided to run for Prime Minister as a member of the Khmer Republic Party. He did not win.

Like other politicians and soldiers, Nol gave a large part of his life to civil service. He left behind, however, a legacy of corruption and bloodshed. Flanked by a brutal war, it was Nol's political maneuvers that led Cambodia into the conflict in Vietnam and enabled an even more brutal regime to seize power in Cambodia. Today, nonprofit organizations and international aid groups are still working to clear the landmines and cluster bombs from Cambodian lands while the Cambodian people struggle to rebuild their nation.

Books

Ayres, David M., "Lon Nol," *Encyclopedia of Modern Asia,* Eds. David Levinson and Karen Christensen, Vol. 3, Charles Scribner's Sons, 2002.

"Lon Nol," *Vietnam War Reference Library,* Vol. 2, Eds. Kevin Hillstrom, Laurie Collie Hillstrom, and Diane Sawinski, U*X*L, 2001.

The Columbia Encyclopedia, Sixth Edition, Columbia University Press, 2007.

Periodicals

Globe & Mail, (Toronto, Canada), November 18, 1985.
People's Daily, (Beijing, China), April 21, 2008.
The New York Times, April 4, 1981; November 18, 1985.
The Sunday Times, (London, England), October 24, 2004.
The Times, (London, England), November 19, 1985.
Time, September 28, 1970; December 2, 1985.

Online

"Banyon Tree, The: Untangling Cambodian History," *Cambodia,* http://www.mekong.net/cambodia/banyan2.htm (October 16, 2008).

"Cambodia," *Encyclopedia Britannica,* http://search.eb.com/eb/article-52488 (October 16, 2008).

Carvin, Andy, "The Coup: Opportunities for Nixon and the Khmer Rouge," *Before the Holocaust,* http://www.edwebproject.org/sideshow/history/coup.html (October 16, 2008).

"General Lon Nol," http://www.khmerkampongspeu.org/lonnol.htm (October 16, 2008).

"Lon Nol," *Chronology of Cambodian History,* http://angkor1431.tripod.com/index/id26.html (October 16, 2008).

"Lon Nol," *Encyclopedia Britannica,* http://search.eb.com/eb/article-9048822 (October 16, 2008).

"Lon Nol," *Online Encyclopedia of Mass Violence,* February 2008, http://www.massviolence.org/Lon-Nol (October 16, 2008). □

Annie Londonderry

In 1895, Annie Londonderry (1870–1947) astounded the world by pedaling thousands of miles around the globe on a bicycle. Her journey began in Boston and took her through nearly a dozen countries. Supposedly begun as a challenge to win $10,000, Londonderry's travels became an international sensation, not the least because she was a Victorian woman embarking alone on a bicycle and telling fantastic stories along the way.

From Childhood to Motherhood

I n 1870, Annie "Londonderry" Kopchovsky was born to a Jewish family in what was then Riga, Russia. Today, her birth city is part of Latvia. Londonderry was one of five children born to Levi (Leib) and Beatrice (Basha) Cohen. At the age of four or five, her family emigrated to the United States and settled in Boston.

Little is known about Londonderry's early childhood. Unfortunately, Londonderry's parents both died in 1887, leaving Londonderry and her brother to raise their younger siblings. The following year, Londonderry married Simon "Max" Kopchovsky, an Orthodox Jewish man who worked as a peddler.

Within the first four years of their marriage, Kopchovsky and Londonderry had three children—Mollie, Libbie, and Simon. Both parents worked, and by 1894, Londonderry was working at Pope Manufacturing Company, which made bicycles. She may also have been working in advertising for several Boston newspapers.

A Wager

Londonderry's infamous journey began in 1894. On June 25, a crowd of nearly 500 onlookers gathered outside the Boston State House to see off Londonderry and her 42-pound women's Columbia bicycle.

A few weeks earlier, Londonderry had reportedly accepted the wager of two Boston businessmen. The challenge was this: Londonderry had to ride her bicycle around the world, covering at least 9,000 miles by wheel, and earn $5,000 over the course of her travels. She would collect signatures from American consuls along the way to prove that she had spanned the globe. If she succeeded, she would win $10,000.

Reporters and others have since debated the existence of the two businessmen or their wager. Londonderry's great-grandnephew, Peter Zheutlin, who documented much of her life and travels in his 2007 book *Around the World on Two Wheels,* speculated that Londonderry herself had come up with the idea of riding around the world and had invented the wager to gain attention.

Whether the wager existed or not, Londonderry headed out on a bicycle supplied by the Pope Manufacturing Company. As she prepared to leave, Mrs. J.O. Tubbs of the Women's Christian Temperance Union (WCTU) paid her a penny to wear the white ribbon of the WCTU and a representative from the Londonderry Lithia Spring Water Company paid her $100 to carry an advertising sign for the company on her bicycle and to use the name "Londonderry" during her travels. Having earned her first $100, Londonderry mounted her bicycle and sped away.

A Change in Course

Clad in a long skirt, Londonderry headed west. She averaged 8 to 10 miles per hour through Rhode Island and New York, where she redesigned her clothing. When she left again, she wore bloomers, or loose-fitting pants, beneath a shorter skirt, giving her more freedom to ride.

Londonderry was an unusual sight. Although the bicycle itself had gained popularity and many women rode, a woman riding alone through the countryside, bearing advertising signs and ribbons, and wearing pants beneath a short skirt was definitely an unusual thing. After all, Londonderry had set out at a time when women had not yet gained the right to vote.

Londonderry followed bike routes mapped in tour books, railroad tracks, and the Erie Canal. She slept where she could, sometimes finding lodging in hotels or rooming houses, other times sleeping under bridges and in barns.

Nearly two months after leaving New York City, Londonderry reached Chicago, Illinois. She had traveled hundreds of miles and lost 20 pounds in the process, but she was three months into her 15-month journey and she still had most of the United States—and the world—to go.

While in Chicago, Londonderry realized that she could not keep going the way that she had planned. Winter was coming, and she would not clear the Great Plains and the Rocky Mountains before the season made them impassable. She decided to turn around, restart the clock from Chicago, and head east around the globe. She negotiated a new arrangement with the Sterling bicycle company, and traded her Columbia bike for a 21-pound men's Sterling roadster. She also traded her improvised skirt and bloomers for a standard pair of bloomers.

On October 14, 1894, Londonderry set out again, tracing her trail back east. She had an easier time on that journey, riding in pants on a lighter bike and having gained strength and experience from the first leg of her venture.

Two weeks later, in Buffalo, Londonderry again traded in her clothing, this time adopting a small men's riding suit. She rode for New York City, part of the way by bicycle and part of the way by train. In New York City, on November 24, she boarded an ocean liner bound for France.

From Europe to Asia

Londonderry reached Le Havre, France, in early December. Throughout December and January, Londonderry would travel, mostly by bike, across the French countryside. Along the way, she earned money by advertising goods for businesses and giving lectures about her trip.

As she reported her experiences, Londonderry changed and embellished her story. Over the course of her journey, Londonderry became known for spinning fantastic tales. She not only invented stories about highway robberies but also made up details about her own past, including that she was a doctor, a law student, and a wealthy heiress. Zheutlin would later claim that Londonderry did this not so much out of deliberate dishonesty but out of a great sense of mischief. Londonderry knew what type of story would grab the public's attention, and that is what she tried to give them.

Londonderry rode into Marseilles at the southern tip of France in mid-January 1895. From there, she sailed across the Mediterranean Sea aboard the steamship *Sydney.* Londonderry would cover thousands of miles aboard this ship, leading one reporter to claim that she spent more time traveling "with her bike" than "on her bike."

The *Sydney* stopped first in Alexandria, Egypt. Londonderry reportedly did short tours in Egypt, riding her bicycle in bursts and visiting Port Said. From Egypt, she rode or sailed to Jerusalem, Israel, and on to Yemen, Colombo (now Sri Lanka) off the southern tip of India, and then to mainland India. She then claimed to ride overland from India to China, but travel logs show that she actually took the *Sydney* from India to Singapore, and then to Vietnam, Japan, and China.

In late February, Londonderry claimed to travel with two war reporters from Japan when they went to China to cover the closing days of the Sino-Japanese War. Londonderry reported that she landed in Port Arthur in the thick of battle, and was injured when she and a British missionary, F.A. Moffatt, fell through an icy river. She claimed that they were captured and imprisoned by the Japanese. Londonderry maintained that the Japanese held her prisoner for three days, and that after she was released, she biked across the Korean peninsula and through Siberia before returning to Japan.

While all these adventures were supposedly happening, historical evidence suggests that Londonderry was actually hopping from spot to spot on the *Sydney.* The ship's travel logs show that she sailed from Singapore to Vietnam in mid-February and from there to Hong Kong, where she did a short two-day tour. She apparently left Hong Kong on February 21 and reached Shanghai, China, the next day.

Though Londonderry appears to have stayed in China a few days, she did not have time to travel to Nagasaki and back with war reporters, foray into battle, and become imprisoned. Instead, she seems to have sailed directly to Nagasaki and then to Kobi and Yokohama. It is unclear whether she traveled by ship or ventured overland on her bicycle.

On March 9, 1895, the global part of her adventure ended. Londonderry boarded another ship in Yokohama to cross the Pacific Ocean. Though she had traveled thousands of miles by ship in a matter of weeks, Londonderry later said that she often left the ship and rode her bicycle during her stops. To earn money, Londonderry had continued advertising for businesses on her bicycle, giving lectures, and working odd jobs, often selling things. She also sold pictures of herself. She spent some of her earnings on specially prepared photographs called lantern slides, which she used in her lectures.

The Home Stretch

Nearly six months after leaving New York, Londonderry arrived back in the United States. She reached San Francisco, California, on March 23, 1895, having covered about 20,000 miles, though her cyclometer showed that she had ridden her bike only 7,280 of those miles.

Londonderry spent two weeks in San Francisco, where she met with reporters, gave lectures, had her portrait done, organized her slides, and answered her mail, which consisted of more than 4,000 letters. True to form, her stories were exciting, detailed, and more than a little outlandish.

From San Francisco, Londonderry rode down the California coast, often disappearing from the public eye along the way. She reached Los Angeles, then a small city of 40,000 people, in about five weeks. Beyond Los Angeles stretched the vast southwestern United States, a dry and sparsely settled region. Londonderry aimed her bike for Phoenix in what was then the Arizona Territory and followed the Southern Pacific Railroad tracks. The days were hot, and the nights were bitterly cold. Along the way, she may have caught a ride on the railroad, but it seems clear that she did bike a great deal of the distance.

Londonderry continued to make many short stops, giving lectures and interviews and earning money. After Phoenix, she headed for El Paso, Texas, riding the rail part of the way. At El Paso, Londonderry turned north, reaching Denver, Colorado, a month later, and then riding east toward Wyoming. Londonderry admitted to riding the Santa Fe Railroad part of the way north, but because much of the land through which Londonderry rode was still the "wild west," she may have ridden the rails as much for safety as for time.

In Cheyenne, Wyoming, Londonderry again hefted her bicycle onto a train for the passage across much of what is now Nebraska. In Columbus, she got back on her bike and rode to Iowa, breaking her wrist during a collision outside of Gladbrook. She rode the rest of her journey in a cast and sling.

On September 12, 1895, Londonderry finished her incredible journey. Flanked by two Iowa cyclists, she rode through Chicago, and laid her bicycle down on the steps of the Wellington Hotel at 1 in the afternoon. Londonderry

reclaimed her married name, Kopchovsky, and her trip ended on a surprisingly quiet note, without the parades and crowds of its beginning.

In 15 months, Londonderry had traveled around the world, with her bike when not on it. She had cycled between 9,000 and 10,000 miles altogether, and had earned just over the required $5,000.

Back to Normal

After her ride, Londonderry returned quickly to Boston, where she collected her $10,000 prize and reunited with her husband and children. Within a month, the family moved to New York.

For a time, Londonderry worked as a reporter for the *New York World* under the byline Nellie Bly, Jr. She first wrote an extraordinary account of her adventure, which was printed in the *World* on October 20. Subsequently, she wrote several features, including one about a women-only stock exchange near Wall Street and one about a charitable home for wayward girls. She also went on a short adventure to cover a story about a "wild man" who had reportedly frightened an entire town in Massachusetts.

Londonderry's journalism career did not last, however. In 1897, she gave birth to her fourth child, Frieda. She had already sent her other children to live in boarding schools, and Frieda was soon sent to a foster family in Maine. For unknown reasons, Londonderry lived a brief spell in Ukiah, California, where she worked as a saleslady.

After the turn of the century, Londonderry returned to her husband in New York. Together, they opened their first garment business, Kay & Company. In the 1920s, their first shop was destroyed in a fire, but they used the insurance money to start a new business, Grace Strap & Novelty in Manhattan.

The Fading of Fame

Londonderry stayed with her husband and their business the rest of their lives. Her infamous story had long since lost its luster, and she lived—and died—in obscurity.

In 1946, Londonderry's husband, Max, died. The following year, on November 11, Londonderry passed away as well. She worked up until a few days before, and finally succumbed to a stroke. She left behind her four children and one granddaughter, Mary, who would help her great-grandnephew Zheutlin piece together her story half a century later.

Though Londonderry undertook to ride the globe for her own reasons, her globetrotting highlighted the skills and strength of women. Her public presence, her words, and her personality helped win recognition for all women. As Zheutlin wrote, "Though not an active feminist or a suffragist, [Londonderry] was willing to act on her dreams in the face of what would have been, for most women, overwhelming social forces. . . . In this regard she was a true feminist, willing to ride past the limitations [put on] women to seek fulfillment of her unconventional dreams. She was, in this sense, heroic, though she didn't always act heroically." Perhaps most importantly, though, her adventure made for a fantastic story.

Books

Zheutlin, Peter, *Around the World on Two Wheels: Annie Londonderry's Extraordinary Ride,* Citadel Press Books, 2007.

Periodicals

AZ Daily Star, March 27, 2008.
Bicycling, May 2007, p. 56.
Booklist September 1, 2007, p. 44.
Kirkus Reviews September 15, 2007.
New England Quarterly, vol. LXXVIII, no. 4, December 2005, pp. 617Û630.
Winston-Salem Journal January 13, 2008, p. A22.

Online

"Annie Londonderry," *Annie Londonderry,* http://www.annie londonderry.com (October 16, 2008).
"Annie Londonderry: A Global Sensation," *Spokeswoman Productions,* http://www.spokeswomanproductions.com/aboutannie.html (October 16, 2008).□

Katherine von Bora Luther

German nun Katharina von Bora (1499–1552) became the wife of Martin Luther after leaving her religious community in the midst of the social upheaval brought on by Luther's Protestant Reformation. Though she was the closest confidant of the man whose actions would forever alter the course of world history, von Bora remains a shadowy figure in the historical record. Her husband, however, left behind writings in which he praised her devotion and work ethic.

V on Bora was born on January 29, 1499, at her family estate called Lippendorf in Kobenhagen, a city near Leipzig. At the time, Leipzig was the capital of Electoral Saxony, a medieval kingdom in what is the present-day east German state of Saxony. Electoral Saxony took its name from the fact that its hereditary ruling family was among a select group given the power to elect the Holy Roman Emperor. During von Bora's lifetime that leader was Frederick III, also known as Frederick the Wise, a progressive reformer and founder of the university in Wittenberg, a city on the Elbe River that would become the center of the Reformation.

Ensconced in Convent

Von Bora came from a noble family, but they were not wealthy and the family's situation seemed to have worsened after her mother, Katharina Anna von Haugwitz or Haubitz, died when von Bora was five. Hans der Jüngere von Bora, her father, was left a widower with five children, but soon remarried and sent von Bora and her sister to a convent. This was a commonplace practice among young women of von Bora's station in life, where money was exchanged between noble families in arranged marriages. For families with no assets, like the von Boras, committing daughters to the safety of a religious community was the best alternative if the young women were deemed financially ineligible for marriage.

Two aunts of von Bora's, in fact, were nuns. Her first years were spent at the cloistered community of Benedictine nuns in Brehna, in the vicinity of Halle, but her father later transferred her to Marienthron in Nimbschen, a Cistercian-order convent near Grimma. Magadalene von Bora, her father's sister, was also there, while her mother's sister, Margarete von Haugwitz, was the Mother Superior. On October 8, 1515, von Bora took her formal religious vows, which committed her to a life of chastity, poverty, and prayer.

Von Bora was just 16 years old when she took her vows, which were irrevocable according to church law at the time, it was impossible for a woman to undergo a change of mind about her vows and leave the community. Yet some women chose to make their religious vows because they had—like von Bora—been living there since early childhood and had no experience with the outside world.

In some cases, convents and abbeys were not the oasis of tranquility and religious devotion they seemed to be to the outside world. Abuse in all forms occurred, and some members felt no genuine religious calling and realized they were trapped there for the remainder of their lives. There were many other unsavory aspects of Christianity in Europe during von Bora's early years. The Church in Rome, founded by St. Peter in the first century, by then had become the dominating figure in religious as well as social, economic, and political life for centuries by then, and yet there was a growing dissatisfaction over what was viewed as its rampant abuses of power.

Martin Luther's Reformation

A German born 15 years before von Bora named Martin Luther became the leader of a reform movement, which was known as the Protestant Reformation. A native of Eisleben, Luther grew up in the mining town of Mansfield and studied law at the University of Erfurt. In 1505, a year after the five-year-old von Bora was given over to the convent, he experienced a religious awakening and entered an order of Augustinian monks in Erfurt.

Luther was aware that the Church—which was headed by the Pope in Rome and administered by various bishops, archbishops, and other powerful appointed clergy at the ground level—had some corrupt practices, but when he began to study theology and made a visit to Rome in 1510, he was reportedly appalled at the luxurious lifestyle of Church officials there. He earned his doctorate in 1512 and joined the faculty of the University of Wittenberg. He also began to preach at the Wittenberg Castle Church.

One church practice that irked both Luther and Frederick III was the selling of indulgences. In the religious parlance of the day, an indulgence was a grant given by the Pope for a partial remission of time to be spent in purgatory, a waiting room of sorts in the afterlife before admittance into heaven. Indulgences could be purchased for a price, which meant that even the worst sinners could be forgiven in the eyes of God merely through monetary payment. Frederick had prohibited their sale, but the faithful could travel to a nearby state where a priest named Johannes Tetzel was selling them. Tetzel had been sent from Rome by Pope Leo X to raise money for the rebuilding of St. Peter's Basilica.

Tetzel's actions prompted Luther to write his famous *95 Theses*, which he nailed to the door of the Wittenberg Castle Church—a public bulletin board of the era—in an act that sparked the Protestant Reformation. Luther asserted that the Bible should be the spiritual guide for all believers, and that any baptized Christian was actually a member of the clergy in God's eyes.

Inspired to Break Free

Luther's act was a daring one, for previous clerics who had questioned Church practices and gained a following were condemned as heretics, defrocked, and in some cases burned at the stake. Frederick was Luther's powerful protector in his battle with Pope Leo X, but even he could not prevent the proclamation of the dire Edict of Worms by the pope's ally, Holy Roman Emperor Charles V. The edict banned Luther's writings and ordered his arrest. Frederick arranged for him to be kidnapped and hid in a royal castle at Wartburg. Luther remained there for nearly a year, during which time he worked on his translation of the New Testament into German—his most important contribution to the spread of the Protestant Reformation.

Word of the renegade priest had spread throughout Germany and much of Europe by the early 1520s and prompted scores of similar rebellions. Von Bora was apparently one of the many priests and nuns who had come across Luther's secret pamphlets and were inspired to leave their religious communities. She made contact with Luther, who arranged for Leonhard Köppe, a herring merchant and city official in Torgau, to rescue her and eleven other women who wished to leave Marienthron. Köppe's daughter was among the dozen, and while legend asserts that the nuns were smuggled out in herring barrels on Köppe's wagon on Easter Eve of 1523, they actually just hid among the barrels. At the time, smuggling nuns was a capital offense, punishable by death in the lands of the Holy Roman Empire.

Von Bora and her sister-nuns' plight had so moved Luther that shortly after the event, which took place on April 4, 1523, he wrote a pamphlet titled "Why Nuns May, with God's Blessing, Leave the Cloisters." He commended Köppe's actions, which prompted scores of similar abductions. What to do with the twelve women, however, was a more immediate question; Köppe had brought them to Wittenberg, and Luther agreed to help them find husbands, because living on their own was not possible.

Married Luther in 1525

Von Bora and the others were initially taken in by various supporters. She herself first stayed at the home of Philipp Reichenbach, the Wittenberg city clerk, and later moved to the household of the painter Lucas Cranach the Elder and his wife Barbara. Two years after the Marienthron escape, von Bora remained the sole unmarried nun, and she reportedly said to a close associate of Luther's, Nikolaus von Amsdorf, that either he or Luther would suit her as a spouse. Luther was not married, having originally followed Rome's teachings on the subject of priests and celibacy, but during the Reformation had come to see that the required vow of celibacy was widely ignored. He believed it was right for a man to have a wife, even a priest, but was reluctant to marry himself because he still feared death as a heretic.

Von Bora and Luther were married in private on June 13, 1525, and a public ceremony was held on June 27. She was 26 years old at the time, and he was 42. Frederick had died several weeks earlier and was succeeded by John Frederick, the new Elector of Saxony, who gave the newlyweds a former Augustinian monastery called the Black Cloister as a wedding gift. A few years later Luther purchased some farmland outside Leipzig from von Bora's brother, a property known as Zulsdorf. Extant documents about the family's financial matters show that von Bora was a skilled manager of both properties. The Black Cloister contained brewing works, and beer was made and sold there. Its rooms were rented out to university students, but became a hospital during outbreaks of epidemic diseases. The farm at Zulsdorf became a profitable cattle-breeding site. In letters her husband refers to her as "the boss of Zulsdorf" and notes that she rose every morning at 4 a.m. to accomplish the long list of tasks in her busy day.

The Luthers had six children together, one of whom died in infancy and another at the age of 13. They also took in four foster children, one of them a nephew of von Bora's named Fabian. The family lived in turbulent times, however. The Reformation led to a Peasants' Revolt in Germany and several other sites across Europe, and in Germany the new religion's more fanatical adherents murdered those still loyal to Rome while plundering churches, monasteries, and the palatial estates of the nobles. Even within the Protestant movement itself various factions arose, and Luther became embroiled in a long and bitter dispute with French theologian John Calvin.

Poverty Marred Final Years

In 1545 and 1546, Luther made three visits to his family in Mansfield in order to settle a dispute over the control of his family's mining interests that involved a local noble. On the third and final visit, he took ill and died at Eisleben, leaving von Bora a widow with four biological children, several foster wards, and an uncertain future. Local authorities requested that the family move out of the Black Cloister into smaller quarters, but she refused. Later in 1546, however, war broke out between an alliance of northern German princes loyal to Protestantism and the Holy Roman Empire. The conflict was known as the Schmalkaldic War and took its name from the Schmalkaldic League of Protestant-allied princes. When the armies of Charles V neared, von Bora and her family were forced to flee to the cathedral city of Magdeburg. They returned when the hostilities subsided but were forced out once more as the battlefield neared Wittenberg. This time, they settled in Braunschweig. In July of 1547, they returned to find both the Zulsdorf farm and the Black Cloister sacked and in ruins.

Von Bora was given some financial support from John Frederick, and the princes of the Anhalt dynasty also are on record as helping the family. Despite this, von Bora's final years were marked by poverty and hardship. In 1552, another outbreak of the Black Plague swept through the region, and that year's harvest failed, too. Von Bora took her children to Torgau, a city on the Elbe River, but on the way there her wagon was involved in an accident and she was badly injured. She died three months later on December 20, 1552, at the age of 53. She was buried in St. Mary's Church in Torgau. Her only daughter to live to adulthood, Margarete, married into an old Prussian noble family called von Kunheim. Their descendants include Paul von Hindenburg, a German military hero during World War I who was elected president of Germany in 1932.

Von Bora is considered the exemplar for the spouses of Protestant clergy, for she was among the first wives in modern Christianity to live and pray on equal footing with her husband. In the Lutheran Church Calendar of Saints, her feast day is celebrated on December 20.

Online

"My Lord Katie: Katharina von Bora Luther," Concordia Historical Institute, http://chi.lcms.org/katie/ (December 19, 2008).□

Enid Lyons

Born in a logging village on the Australian island of Tasmania, Dame Enid Muriel Lyons (1897–1981) rose to become one of the best known women in

Australia. First as the wife of Prime Minister Joseph Lyons and then as the first woman elected to the Australian House of Representatives, Dame Lyons traveled throughout the country, making speeches and working tirelessly on the issues that concerned her. As the mother of 12 children and as a politician often concerned with caring for the Australian people, Dame Lyons became known as "Australia's Greatest Mother."

Enid Burnell was born to William and Eliza Burnell on July 9, 1897. The second of four children, Lyons had a modest beginning. Her father was a sawyer, or a logging worker responsible for sawing wood. Lyons was born and raised in a small logging village in western Tasmania, an island off the southern tip of Australia. She and her siblings were raised among the sawmills. Later in life, Lyons recalled, as reported on the *Australians* website, "I was born in what would be called I suppose very poor circumstances. My father was a working man, worked at a sawmill, and always my memories of my early childhood revolve around little bush sawmills."

Raised to Value Education

Both of Lyons' parents were hard workers, and her mother was as active as she was determined to see her children do well. A member of the Women's Christian Temperance Union and a supporter of the Labor Party, Eliza Burnell also picked up odd jobs washing and sewing to make extra money. She wanted her four children to have an education, and the money that she earned went to pay for their schooling.

Lyons started off at Stowport and Burnie State Schools. She received a basic education that prepared her to pursue training as a teacher. Around 1912, at the age of 14, Lyons enrolled in Hobart Teachers' College. A few years later, while working as a trainee teacher at Burnie State School, Lyons met a former schoolteacher turned politician. Though he was 18 years older than her, they embarked on a short courtship and married within two years.

Became a Prime Minister's Wife

On April 28, 1915, at the age of 17, Lyons married Joseph Aloysius Lyons. At the time, her new husband was Treasurer of Tasmania and Minister for Education and Railways, but he had greater ambitions. He would rise through the political ranks of Australia quickly, and Lyons would rise with him.

Lyons was eager to marry Joseph and begin a family. She not only converted to Catholicism to wed but also left her position as a teacher in training. The year after their marriage, Lyons gave birth to the first of 12 children, a son that they named Desmond. That same year, the Lyonses had a house called Home Hill built at Devonport in Tasmania. Within two years, they had their first daughter, Sheila, with Enid following in 1919 and Kathleen in 1920.

That same year, Lyons gave her first political speech. She had always been interested in politics and her marriage to Joseph Lyons afforded her a new way to become involved. Though she spent a great deal of time with her children, she also traveled with her husband, and campaigned on his behalf and on behalf of her own political interests. Her first foray into public speech was intended to gain the support of women for her husband and for the Labor Party. Lyons also addressed issues of public responsibility and the need for equality for women. The public soon came to recognize that Lyons was a gifted speaker in her own right.

By 1925, Lyons had given birth to three more children—Moira, Kevin, and Garnet, who died in infancy. Lyons felt the call to politics herself at this point and decided to run for a seat in the legislature. In 1925, Lyons and her mother both ran for the seat representing Denison. Lyons ran as a Labor candidate and nearly won, losing the election by only 60 votes.

Meanwhile, Lyons' husband was still pursuing his political aims. In 1929, Joseph Lyons won a seat in the federal Parliament. This victory was wonderful and celebrated, but it led to a great change in the family's life. As a member of Parliament, Joseph Lyons had to move to Canberra on the Australian mainland.

Lyons, now the mother of nine children—Barry, Brendan and Rosemary having been born in the ensuing years—remained in Tasmania at the family home. Though she was pleased for and proud of her husband, she had to manage the household and care for her children largely on her own. To make matters more difficult, Lyons had been suffering bouts of ill health that led her in and out of the hospital. It would take doctors another 40 years to figure out that much of her repeated illnesses were the result of a broken pelvic bone.

Being a tough woman, however, she worked through it and the family persevered. Lyons and the children traveled to Canberra at times, and Joseph Lyons returned home when he could. The family remained close despite their periods of separation, and in 1931, Lyons gave birth to another son, Peter. That same year, when Joseph Lyons decided to shift from the Labor Party to the new United Australia Party and run for Prime Minister, his wife supported him wholeheartedly.

In 1932, Joseph Lyons was elected Prime Minister of Australia. For the next seven years, the family would move back and forth between the official residence of prime ministers, known as the Lodge, in Canberra and their family home in Devonport. In 1933, Lyons gave birth to her last child, Janice.

Throughout the 1930s, because of the demands of politics, the family was separated a great deal. Both Lyons and her husband were often traveling, making speeches, addressing important issues of the day, and visiting with other officials. In 1935, Lyons accompanied her husband to England. Together, they attended the Royal Jubilee Celebration for King George V and Queen Mary. Two years later, they returned to England for the coronation of King George VI.

As the Prime Minister's wife, Lyons traveled a great deal on her own. She constantly worked to raise more support for her husband and the United Australia Party, but she also focused a great deal on issues of importance to her. Lyons was very concerned about women's issues. She addressed many women's associations and conferences, and worked with organizations such as the Victorian Women Citizens' Movement and the Sydney Feminist Club. Throughout this time, Lyons continued to struggle with her health, and in the mid-1930s, her husband's health began to decline as well.

Then, in 1939, Lyons' husband died, leaving the nation without its prime minister, his 11 surviving children without their father, and Lyons without her dearest friend and partner.

Forged Ahead

Following her husband's death, Lyons retired from public life. Later, she would say that she had a breakdown, and that her health suffered terribly. She withdrew to Tasmania to grieve and to determine how to move forward on her own. At the time, many of her children were enrolled in boarding school.

In 1943, Lyons reappeared on the public scene to pursue politics in her own right. That year, the federal representative of Darwin retired, opening the seat to election. Lyons decided to run as a member of the United Australia Party. A strong, experienced speaker, she focused on issues of interest to families and women, and she won by 160 votes.

Lyons became the first woman member of the Australian House of Representatives and one of the two first women members of the federal Parliament. In 1943, and recorded in an online interview from the *Australian Broadcast Corporation,* she addressed the House for the first time: "[T]his is the first occasion on which a woman has addressed this house. For that reason, it's an occasion which for every woman in the Commonwealth marks in some degree a turning point in history."

Lyons worked devotedly and earned a great amount of respect in Parliament and in the nation. She was re-elected twice, in 1946 and in 1949. The Prime Minister also appointed her Vice President of the Executive Council, a largely honorary role that made her the first woman to hold a ministerial office. Though she was socially conservative, opposing abortion and divorce and encouraging the growth of families, Lyons focused mostly on issues of equality and support for women and families. She opposed socialism and believed in free markets, but she strongly supported programs providing for the public welfare.

In 1948, Lyons lobbied for and helped pass a bill supporting a woman's right to maintain her citizenship when she married a non-citizen. In 1950, she successfully worked to extend the child endowment to include a first child and helped raise the allowances paid to servicewomen returning from duty. The child endowment was a certain amount of money paid to families for each child that they had to help with the expenses of child rearing.

During that time, Lyons also worked to extend maternity health care, to reduce discrimination in employment, to increase women's representation in Parliament, and to raise the widow's pension, or support received by widows following a husband's death. Her efforts earned her references as "the mother figure in Parliament" and "an ideal national housekeeper." Lyons seemed to embrace these roles. Lyons once said as found on the *Australians* website, "The foundation of a nation's greatness is in the homes of its people," and she focused much of her effort on providing for the homes of Australia.

Lyons had struggled much of her life with poor health. She had undergone numerous hospitalizations and surgeries over the years, and as she aged and picked up work, her health continued to cause her problems. In 1951, she retired from politics for good.

Lyons did not retire from public life, however. Her health recovered enough to enable her to remain active in non-governing ways. She traveled throughout Tasmania, speaking to people and organizations about issues that continued to concern her. She also began writing. From 1951–1952, Lyons worked as a newspaper columnist for *Woman's Day,* and from 1951–1954, she wrote as a columnist for the *Sun.* She also served as a member of the Australian Broadcasting Commission for a little more than a decade, from 1951–1962.

On May 11, 1957, Lyons was awarded the Dame Grand Cross of the Order of the British Empire for her life of public service to Australia. Two decades later, she was awarded the Dame of the Order of Australia. Both honors carried a great deal of esteem, and Lyons was the second of only two women to receive the Order of Australia. Thereafter, she became commonly known as Dame Lyons.

Lyons also wrote three books in the final decades of her life. In 1965, she published her autobiography, *So We Take Comfort,* and in 1969, she followed that with a collection of essays and anecdotes, *The Old Haggis.* Three years later, she completed a book entitled *Among the Carrion Crows,* which reflected on her experiences in politics.

The late years of her life were largely spent in the private world of her home and family. She stayed at Home Hill, the first house of her marriage and her residence for the better part of 60 years, until her death. On September 2, 1981, she died there at the age of 84. The Australian government afforded Lyons a state funeral, and she was buried next to her husband at Mersey Vale Lawn Cemetery.

Lyons was survived by 11 of her 12 children. She left their family home to the Australian people. Today, it is a house museum managed by the National Trust of Tasmania. She also left a great legacy, exemplifying the strength, skill, and determination of women and demonstrating to all Australians the need for compassion toward their fellow citizens and for public accountability and responsibility at all levels of government, business, and family life.

In her 1943 speech, the first speech ever given by a woman to the House of Representatives and documented on the *ABC Rural* website, Lyons had said: "I believe, very sincerely, that any woman entering the public arena must be prepared to work as men work; she must justify herself not as a woman, but as a citizen; she must attack the same problems, and be prepared to shoulder the same burdens." As a wife, mother, politician, and citizens, Lyons did her best to live up to this statement.

Books

"Lyons, Enid (1897–1981)," *Dictionary of Women Worldwide: 25,000 Women Through the Ages,* Eds. Anne Commire and Deborah Klezmer, Vol. 1, Yorkin Publications, 2007.

Online

"4 Dame Enid Lyons," http://www.naa.gov.au/naaresources/ publications/research_guides/pdf/joseph_lyons/chapter_four. pdf (January 8, 2009).

"Dame Enid Lyons," *ABC Online,* http://www.abc.net.au/gnt/ history/Transcripts/s951058.htm (October 16, 2008).

"Dame Enid Lyons," *Australians,* http://www.abc.net.au/ schoolstv/australians/elyons.htm (October 16, 2008).

"Joseph Aloysius Lyons," *Encyclopedia Britannica,* http://search.eb. com/eb/article-9049541 (October 16, 2008).

"Lyons, Enid Muriel (1897–1981)," *Australian Women,* http://www. womenaustralia.info/biogs/AWE0105b.htm (October 16, 2008).

"Lyons, Joseph Aloysius (Joe) (1879–1939)," *Australian Dictionary of Biography—Online Edition,* http://ww.adb.online.anu.edu. au/biogs/A10018b.htm (October 16, 2008).

Mackenzie, Michael, "Great Speeches of Rural Australia—Enid Lyons," *ABC Rural,* http://www.abc.net.au/rural/telegraph/ speeches/lyons.htm (October 16, 2008).

Sells, Anne, "Enid Lyons 1897–1981," *200 Australian Women,* http://www.200australianwomen.com/names/172.html (October 16, 2008). □

M

Joseph Leo Mankiewicz

American film director and producer Joseph L. Mankiewicz (1909–1993) was among the most critically acclaimed filmmakers of the post–World War II period, combining sharp dialogue with complex narrative techniques.

Mankiewicz won two Academy Awards for *All About Eve* (1950), one of the most celebrated films of its time. As significant as that or any of Mankiewicz's other individual awards, however, was the fact that the films he directed won an impressive overall total of 48 Academy Awards. Mankiewicz was a superb screenwriter, a sensitive handler of actors, and a skillful producer with a fine instinct for promising material, especially when it came to adaptations from other media. He did make one major mistake in judgment, and as a result he is partly remembered for his participation in *Cleopatra* (1963), one of Hollywood's epic flops.

Graduated from College at 19

Joseph Leo Mankiewicz was born on February 11, 1909, in Wilkes-Barre, Pennsylvania,. He was one of two sons born to Franz and Johanna (Blumenau) Mankiewicz. At the time, Franz Mankiewicz was a schoolteacher, but because he hoped for a better job as a college professor, the family moved to New York in 1913. Joseph graduated from the competitive Stuyvesant High School at 15 and enrolled at Columbia University, completing a degree in English in 1928, at age 19. His older brother was Herman Mankiewicz, who later wrote the screenplay for the Orson Welles–directed classic *Citizen Kane.*

Mankiewicz, who thanks to his family background spoke German fluently, took off to see Europe after graduation, landing in Berlin. Herman Mankiewicz, who was an executive with the Paramount studio at the time, installed his brother in a position translating the intertitles—the intermittent screens containing dialogue or verbal narration in silent films—from German to English in German films destined for export. Mankiewicz moved back to the United States in 1929, and soon got a similar job writing intertitle screens at Paramount. The advent of sound films soon put an end to that position, but by then Mankiewicz had his foot in the door and quickly took advantage of chances to show he could write original dialogue. Herman Mankiewicz served as a mentor to his younger brother for a time, and later the two brothers became intensely competitive. After *Citizen Kane,* however, Herman's star faded.

By 1934 Mankiewicz had written or worked on 16 screenplays at Paramount, many of them comedies. Among his most durable products from this time was the screenplay for comedian W.C. Fields's *If I Had a Million,* which introduced the familiar Fields catchphrase "my little chickadee." The full line, "My little magpie . . . my little chickadee . . . my little tomtit," delighted Fields, who gave the young screenwriter a $50 tip, just ten dollars less than Mankiewicz's weekly salary at the time. In 1933 or 1934 Mankiewicz, receiving a substantial raise to $1,250 a week, moved to the MGM studio.

He had hoped to direct films there, but the studio's co-founder Louis B. Mayer made him a producer instead, telling him, according to Steve Daly of *Entertainment Weekly,* "You have to learn to crawl before you can walk"—a description that Mankiewicz later called "as good a definition of a producer as any." Mankiewicz's eye for actors, and combinations of actors, began to develop during this period. He cast Joan Crawford in several well-regarded films and later was

responsible for the first teaming of Spencer Tracy and Katharine Hepburn. To Hepburn's objection that Tracy was too short for her, Mankiewicz (according to Daly) rejoined, "Don't worry. He'll cut you down to size."

Garland Affair Sparked Move to MGM

Mankiewicz's personal life was often turbulent. He married three times. By his first wife, Elizabeth Young, he had a son, Eric, although the marriage lasted only from 1934 to 1937. Mankiewicz married his second wife, Rosa Stradner, in 1938, and had two more sons by her. That marriage lasted until 1958, although it was threatened by a long affair Mankiewicz had with the much younger and increasingly unstable actress Judy Garland in the 1940s. The affair also incurred the displeasure of MGM executives, causing Mankiewicz to sign a new contract with 20th Century Fox. The contract gave Mankiewicz considerable creative freedom, allowing him to choose from among directing, writing, and production.

Mankiewicz quickly repaid Fox's investment. Reporting to the legendary executive Darryl F. Zanuck, he made eight films between 1943 and 1952, nearly all critically acclaimed and commercially successful. Most of them were based on preexisting novels or plays, although the pioneering anti-racism film *No Way Out* (1950), which launched the careers of actors Sidney Poitier and Ossie Davis, was based on an original screenplay by Mankiewicz and Lesser Samuels. Mankiewicz hits from this period included *The Ghost and*

Mrs. Muir (1947), one of several Mankiewicz films featuring unusually strong female characters, and *House of Strangers* (1949), starring Edward G. Robinson as an immigrant bank executive who loses control of his business to his sons. The film made use of Mankiewicz's favored flashback technique, which often resulted in complex but always clear narrative structures.

In 1949 Mankiewicz took home Academy Awards for Best Director and Best Screenplay for *A Letter to Three Wives,* a comedy-drama about three women who each receive a letter from a fourth woman who informs them that she is going to run off with one of their husbands. That film also made use of the flashback technique. Mankiewicz's double Academy Award repeat in 1950 with *All About Eve* established him as a member of Hollywood's directorial A-list, and the film remains perhaps the high point of Mankiewicz's career. The screenplay bristled with pungent Mankiewicz one-liners, as when aging and contentious Broadway star Margo Channing (Bette Davis) warns a party crowd, "Fasten your seat belts. It's going to be a bumpy night." A measure of Mankiewicz's mastery came with the film's 14 Academy Award nominations, a record that was equaled by *Titanic* in 1998 but not yet exceeded. In 1951 Mankiewicz, who disliked Los Angeles, moved his family back to New York and installed his Oscars on a mantelpiece beneath a picture of his father.

After the 1952 spy film *Five Fingers,* whose postproduction changes by Zanuck met with bitter resistance from Mankiewicz, the director left MGM and embarked on a career as a freelance producer-director. In 1954 he formed his own production company, Figaro, Inc. Mankiewicz's films of the 1950s maintained his reputation for high quality. Two adaptations of major dramas, *Julius Caesar* (1954, from Shakespeare) and the grim *Suddenly Last Summer* (1959, from Tennessee Williams), earned Academy Award nominations for their respective stars, Marlon Brando and Elizabeth Taylor.

During the three-year production of *Cleopatra,* Mankiewicz was brought in as a replacement for initial director Rouben Mamoulian. The gigantic film bogged down in problems, including an emergency surgery episode involving star Elizabeth Taylor, numerous script rewrites, expensive shooting in Italy, and skyrocketing costs across the board. Mankiewicz, in a press conference quoted by Peter B. Flint of the *New York Times,* complained that the film was "shot in a state of emergency" and "wound up in blind panic." The director eventually screened a seven-and-a-half hour version of the film for producers, but it was cut down to four hours for its final release. *Cleopatra* cost an unheard-of $44 million in the end and was widely considered an epic failure, although television showings eventually resulted in a small profit. The film essentially put an end to Mankiewicz's career, and he made only one more film, the mystery *Sleuth* in 1972.

Film fashions were changing by the 1960s, and Mankiewicz's dialogue-rich but static style had become slightly old-fashioned. His films nevertheless had many admirers, not only in America but also in France, where they received close attention in such periodicals as *Cahiers du Cinema* (Film Notebooks). Mankiewicz was regarded as one of the most cultured figures in the film industry. "It was...a rare experience to work with a 'Hollywood' director who was not only widely read but in some areas deeply read," Daly quoted *Cleopatra* costar Richard Burton as saying. Mankiewicz married Rosemary Matthews in 1962, and this third marriage lasted until the end of his life. He died on February 5, 1993, in his adopted hometown of Bedford in Westchester County, New York.

Books

Dick, Bernard, *Joseph L. Mankiewicz*, Twayne, 1983.

International Dictionary of Films and Filmmakers, Volume 2: Directors, 4th ed., St. James, 2000.

Periodicals

Entertainment Weekly, March 1, 20002, p. 118.

Guardian (London, England), February 8, 1993, p. 13.

New York Times, November 24, 1992; February 6, 1993.

Online

"Joseph L. Mankiewicz," *Senses of Cinema*, http://www.archive.sensesofcinema.com/contents/directors/05/mankiewicz.html (January 13, 2009).

"Joseph L. Mankiewicz," Turner Classic Movies, http://www.tcmdb.com/participant.jsp?participantId=121045 (January 13, 2009). □

Marie, Marquise de Sévigné

A member of the French aristocracy during the reign of King Louis XIV, Marie de Sévigné (1626–1696) was a devout and meticulous letter-writer. In countless notes to friends and family, she offered eyewitness accounts of public and political events and described the riches of the royal court and the misery of the common peasant, painting a clear picture of life during 17th century France. More than 1,000 of her letters survive, praised for both their historical and literary value.

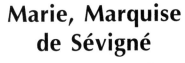arie de Sévigné was born Marie de Rabutin-Chantal on February 5, 1626, in Paris. She was the third child born to Celse-Bénigne de Rabutin and Marie de Coulanges, though she was the only child to make it past the first year of life. Sévigné's father came from a long line of nobility that hailed from Burgundy and had served the monarchy for decades. Her mother grew up in a wealthy family of financiers—part of the nouveau riche bourgeois.

Sévigné's father, the Baron de Chantal, had a reputation as a bit of a hothead who loved to duel and gamble. Shortly after Sévigné's birth, he got into trouble with the king of France for his rabble-rousing and decided to leave Paris for awhile until things settled down. He volunteered for service, hoping to regain the favor of the king. The Baron de Chantal traveled to Île de Ré, an island off the west coast of France. At the time, the inhabitants were engaged in a dispute with England's King Charles I over the treatment of the Huguenots, which escalated into a battle that erupted on July 22, 1627. The Baron de Chantal lasted through several hours of fighting against the English, eventually dying of 27 spear wounds.

Sévigné remained in Paris with her mother, living at her maternal grandparents' home in Place Royale, one of the most desirable areas of Paris. The Place Royale, developed by Henry IV, consisted of a number of elaborate, four-story-tall row houses of white stone and rose-colored brick surrounding a large square. The stately homes were sold to noblemen and the wealthy bourgeois. The Coulanges family home at Place Royale housed some 40 people. Sévigné's aunts and uncles and cousins lived there, as well as a number of servants.

In 1633, Sévigné's mother died. Within a few years, her grandparents died, too, leaving her orphaned at the age of 10. At this time, her father's family got involved and demanded custody of the orphan—and future heiress. Everyone wanted a piece of her wealth, and family members from both her maternal and paternal sides fought for custody. Eventually, an archbishop awarded guardianship to an uncle, Philippe II de Coulanges.

Sévigné continued to live at the Place Royale with the Coulanges family and received an outstanding education. She learned Latin, Spanish, and Italian. She read Latin classics, some in their original language, others translated into Italian. As was the tradition of the day, her education focused on literature over science. She was well-read, even among her peers, and enjoyed history, philosophy and theology. Like other wealthy girls from high-society families, she also received training to help her become a proper "lady." This included singing, dancing and riding lessons, as well as elocution training. Famed French writer and poet Jean Chapelain, a friend of the family, was among her mentors.

Married and Widowed

In 1644 Sévigné became engaged to a Breton nobleman named Henri de Sévigné. Also known as the Marquis de Sévigné, he came from an upstanding family with a good name but little wealth. Their wedding was set for May 1644 but had to be postponed because the Marquis de Sévigné was injured in a duel. After his recovery, they married on August 3, 1644, in a church ceremony that took place two hours after midnight, as was customary during that time. The bride was 18; the groom, 21. For their honeymoon, the couple retreated to the groom's turreted family chateau in Brittany—to an estate called Les Rochers, which means The Rocks (The home was built of gray rock). After her marriage, she was known as the Marquise de Sévigné.

Their first child, Françoise-Marguerite de Sévigné, was born in 1646. Charles de Sévigné followed in 1648. The Marquis de Sévigné was not very good at managing money, however, and the Marquise de Sévigné's family intervened on her behalf, separating their estates before he could empty her of her wealth. Besides being wasteful with money, the Marquis de Sévigné was a womanizer. He frequently left the Marquise de Sévigné and the children in Brittany, then went to Paris for what he called business.

In February 1651 the Marquis de Sévigné got involved in a duel over his mistress. He was pierced in the heart and died, leaving the Marquise de Sévigné widowed on her 25th birthday. In the end, his death afforded the Marquise de Sévigné a rare opportunity for a woman of the 17th century—absolute autonomy over her own life. In the 17th century, women lived according to the directives of their husbands, but the Marquise de Sévigné was able to live the rest of her life as she pleased, free from her husband's demands.

In the years after her husband's death, the Marquise de Sévigné devoted herself to raising her children. Her son, Charles de Sévigné, eventually joined the military. In 1669, the Marquise de Sévigné's daughter, Françoise-Marguerite, married Francois-Adhémar de Monteil de Grignan, who hailed from an illustrious noble family. At first, the Marquise de Sévigné's daughter remained in Paris with her. A grandchild was born in 1670.

Began Letter-Writing

In early 1671, the Marquise de Sévigné's daughter had gone to Provence to live with her husband, and her son-in-law had been appointed lieutenant-governor of Provence. It was at this time that de Sévigné began her intense correspondence. She often wrote 20 to 30 pages a day. Most of de Sévigné's letters were written to her daughter, whom she missed terribly. For 25 years, the Marquise de Sévigné kept up a nearly nonstop dialogue with her daughter through weekly letters.

De Sévigné spent the remainder of her life moving about from place to place. She lived in Paris off and on, staying connected to the Parisian social scene. In Paris, she resided at the Hôtel Carnavalet. She spent time in Brittany, at her husband's ancestral home. During part of the time, she traveled to Vichy to soak in the local spas as a treatment for her rheumatism. The thermal springs at Vichy had been used for therapeutic treatments since Julius Caesar's time. She also took extended visits to Provence to stay with her daughter and grandchildren.

While de Sévigné's letters to her daughter often touched on the personal, her letters to friends and other relatives read more like newspaper dispatches. The Marquise de Sévigné worked much like a reporter, telling people what was happening in the world around her. During this period in history, before newspapers were prevalent, people got their news from letters, and it was a common understanding that letters would be copied and passed around a community. The Marquise de Sévigné wrote her letters knowing they would be circulated. Her letters were well-written and tinged with humor and sorrow at the same time. Through her accounts, historians have learned a considerable amount about France during the 17th century.

In 1664 Nicolas Fouquet, France's Superintendent of Finance, went on trial for mismanaging funds. It was a huge ordeal, as Fouquet was well-liked and many noblemen spoke out on his behalf. The Marquise de Sévigné was friends with the Marquis de Pomponne, who was also friends with Fouquet. By the time Fouquet went on trial, Pomponne had been banished from Paris. The Marquise de Sévigné reported the proceedings to Pomponne in some 40 letters, offering a detailed account of the legal process during King Louis XIV's regime. The Marquise de Sévigné was able to obtain a close account of the proceedings because one of her friends served as a court reporter.

Enjoyed Collecting, Disseminating News

The Marquise de Sévigné relished in her ability to send her daughter news from Paris. In *Madame de Sévigné: A Life and Letters,* Frances Mossiker included translations of many of the Marquise de Sévigné's letters. In one letter to her daughter, the Marquise de Sévigné wrote, "I am going, now, to make the rounds to see if I can hear something amusing to tell you." She went on to say, "You know how I love to pick up gossip for your diversion." When big events happened in Paris, the Marquise de Sévigné was sure to be there so she could report the news to others. One such event included the execution of the Marquise de Brinvilliers, a serial killer, in 1676. She murdered her husband, brother and sisters in an effort to inherit their property. Prior to killing them, she had tested her poison on patients at various charity hospitals around Paris.

In recounting the execution, the Marquise de Sévigné wrote her daughter a letter that appears in *Madame Sevigne: A Life and Letters:* "Now, at last, it is over and done with. La Brinvilliers has gone up in smoke...Her poor little body was tossed, after the execution, into a raging fire, and her ashes scattered to the winds! So that, now, we shall all be inhaling her! And with such evil little spirits in the air, who knows what poisonous humor may overcome us?" In the letter, the Marquise de Sévigné also discussed the crowd. "Never has the city been so aroused, so intent on a spectacle." The Marquise de Sévigné's nonchalance concerning the event may come across as cold, but read within the context of her lifetime, it serves to illustrate the notion that life during the 17th century was cruel and people simply accepted that fact. If someone did something wrong, it was expected that they would suffer the consequences.

In other letters the Marquise de Sévigné reported on her visits to the Palace of Versailles to see the king. In this correspondence, she discussed what the members of the royal court wore—from their clothes to their hairstyles to their jewelry. She also reported on the games they played and the conversations that occurred. In one letter from *Madame Sévigné: A Life and Letters,* de Sévigné noted how the king and his noblemen spent the afternoon gambling for gold coins—with the king's mistress holding his cards for him. Afterward, the visitors took carriage rides. "Later, everyone amuses himself according to his fancy...Some go out on the Canal in gondolas, again to the sound of music...At ten o'clock, they all come in for the performance of a comedy...At the stroke of midnight, supper is served...And that is how Saturday is spent at Versailles."

Letters Published

On April 17, 1696, the Marquise de Sévigné died at the family chateau in Grignan. Within a few months, her letters began appearing in print. Several of her letters were included in a memoir of her cousin, the Count de Bussy-Rabutin. Several years later the Marquise de Sévigné's granddaughter decided to publish a proper edition and began compiling letters.

In 1725, 28 of the Marquise de Sévigné's letters appeared in *A Selection of Letters from the Marquise de Sévigné to Mme de Grignan Her Daughter, Containing Many Events of Interest in the History of the Reign of Louis XIV.* The book was so popular that a two-volume edition of 138 letters was published the next year. For the next several decades, various editions of her letters were published for public consumption.

In 1891, publishers released yet another edition, titled *The Best Letters of Mme de Sévigné.* A review in the *New York Times* quoted a French critic, who praised the volume. The critic summed up the lure of the Marquise de Sévigné's letters, noting, "Philosophy, politics, art, anecdotes, bright sayings, all are embodied in her letters, but told with ease and without constraint."

Books

Mossiker, Frances, *Madame de Sévigné: A Life and Letters,* Columbia University Press, 1985.

Ojala, Jeanne A. and William T. Ojala, *Madame de Sévigné: A Seventeenth-Century Life,* Berg, 1990.

Tancock, Leonard, *Madame de Sévigné: Selected Letters,* Penguin Books, 1982.

Periodicals

New York Times, May 10, 1891, p. 19; September 28, 1902, p. 4; March 7, 1926, p. BR11; January 8, 1984, p. G24.□

Glenn Luther Martin

In 1912, U.S. aviation pioneer Glenn Martin (1886–1955) founded his own aircraft company, becoming one of the first manufacturers to provide planes for the U.S. military. During the 1930s and '40s, the Glenn L. Martin Co. gained notoriety for its development of bombers and seaplanes, including the torpedo-carrying B-26 Marauder, utilized during World War II, and the China Clipper, a flying boat used by Pan American Airlines as it introduced trans-Pacific flights in the mid-1930s.

Glenn Luther Martin was born January 17, 1886, in Macksburg, Iowa, to Araminta and Clarence Martin. His mother was orphaned as a child after her father, a Union soldier, died during the Civil War. Clarence Martin hailed from Pennsylvania but made his way west as a young man, tagging along behind the farmers and railroads in their push toward the Pacific Ocean. By the time Martin was a toddler, the family had moved to Liberal, Kansas, where Clarence Martin opened a hardware store, selling farm implements and home-building materials to area homesteaders. Martin had an older sister named Della, but she was institutionalized in 1911 and rarely spoken of again. It is thought she was schizophrenic.

Developed Interest in Kites, Cars

Like many children living on the Kansas Plains, Martin took to kite-flying. He developed his own design for a box kite, which outperformed the simple geometric kites the other children constructed. Martin entered his kites in contests and after winning he offered to make kites for the other kids—for a quarter apiece. He even sold kites on payment plans.

By the time Martin entered high school, the family had relocated to Salina, Kansas, where Martin secured a job in a bicycle shop. He dropped out of high school after two years and attended Kansas Wesleyan Business College, which was located in Salina. Around this time, automobiles were just taking off and Salina soon had its first auto shop. Fascinated with mechanics, Martin went to work in a garage and learned to make automobile repairs. Mechanics were in high demand because these early models constantly broke down.

In 1905 the family moved to an apricot ranch in Santa Ana, California, where the mechanically-minded Martin opened his own garage. He hired a mechanic to do much of the work so he could concentrate on becoming a car distributor for both Ford and Maxwell. In Santa Ana, Martin was known for his eccentricities. One time, he drove a Ford up the courthouse steps to demonstrate the vehicle's horsepower. He was meticulous with his appearance and

painfully introverted, arousing talk around town. In *Barons of the Sky,* author Wayne Biddle wrote that most accounts of Martin described him as "girlish and annoyingly prim" yet possessing "a steely sense of commerce."

Obsessed With Notion of Flight

Somewhere along the way, Martin turned his attention from the road to the sky. The Wright brothers made their famed flight in 1903 and by 1906, do-it-yourself glider kits had become fairly popular. Martin experimented with gliders in the Santa Ana hills and eventually got the idea to attach a Ford motor to one in hopes of making an airplane. This first attempt failed, and the simple flying machine whipped Martin around and around in circles as he clutched the framework in distress.

Unwilling to give up, Martin decided to try again. He rented an abandoned church and began constructing a biplane with the help of several local mechanics. He read newspaper accounts of the Wright brothers, hoping to learn something about their design. While some biographers take a romantic view of Martin's plane-designing, describing the way he studied bridge-building books to gain an understanding of structural stresses and strains, Biddle contended that Martin, with his farm-boy schooling, was not smart enough to understand the mathematics and could have done little more than look at the pictures.

Sometime in 1909, Martin and his mechanics completed the machine, which looked much like the biplane

formulated by U.S. aviator Glenn Curtiss. In order to get the machine outdoors, Martin had to tear down the front of the church. He moved the aircraft to a nearby ranch for further testing. Martin claimed to have made his first successful flight in August 1909, going about 100 feet. Some historians, such as Biddle, suggest this plane was underpowered and may not have actually flown but served as a successful prototype in helping Martin learn the principles of flight. By mid-1910, Martin had constructed another aircraft, this one lighter and with more horsepower. In August 1910, the *Los Angeles Times* carried the first documented story of Martin making a successful flight.

Gained Notoriety as Exhibition Pilot

Because airplanes were so new and few, many folks did not believe they actually worked—or would work. Even after flights had been documented, many people believed these accounts to be a hoax. Those dabbling with planes were often considered lunatics—Martin included. A 1942 *New Yorker* profile on Martin included a letter from the family's doctor, who wrote Martin's parents, urging them to persuade Martin to stop wasting his time on planes. "For Heaven's sake," the doctor wrote, "if you have any influence with that Wild-eyed, Hallucinated, Visionary young man, call him off before he is killed. Have him devote his energies to substantial, feasible and profitable pursuits, leaving Dreams to Professional Dreamers."

By November 1910, Martin was holding exhibitions to demonstrate his crude, cockpitless flying machine. In no time, he made a name for himself by performing at county fairs. By 1911, Martin had become a highly celebrated barnstormer, though he lacked the glitz and charisma of his fellow flamboyant fliers. In comparison, Martin looked like a preacher in his flying outfit, which consisted of a black suit, a white-collared shirt and sensible helmet. He was nicknamed "the Flying Dude." Over the next several years, Martin appeared in countless aircraft exhibitions and took part in races, mostly because the business was lucrative. Martin set a number of aviation firsts. He was the first to deliver mail by plane, the first to deliver newspapers by plane, the first to aid police by chasing bandits in a plane, and the first to drop a bouquet into a beauty queen's lap during a county fair coronation.

Founded Own Company

In 1912 he officially founded the Glenn L. Martin Co. with an infusion of cash earned from his flying feats. He had been building planes in Santa Ana but around this time moved operations to Los Angeles. Martin understood airplanes had a bright future for both passenger service and military operations. Martin's company developed a seaplane, which was basically a biplane mounted on a kayak-shaped pontoon. In 1912, Martin strapped a compass to his leg, placed an inner tube around his neck and flew the seaplane from Newport Bay, California, to Santa Catalina Island and back. Flying more than 20 miles there and 20 miles back, Martin broke the record for ocean flight. Not only had he flown longer over water than anyone else, he also completed the first round-trip, overwater flight. In 1909, French pilot Louis

Blériot had flown across the 26-mile English Channel but only went one way. Martin's flight generated excitement in Southern California as investors began to see how planes might revolutionize transportation.

To generate further interest in his business, Martin began conducting mock aerial battles at exhibitions. He also dropped bombs—flour sacks filled with blasting powder that detonated on impact. Martin used these "bombs" to destroy mock cardboard forts, hoping to entice the military. He dropped parachutists and predicted that parachuting soldiers would one day be important to the military. As his fame grew, orders rolled in. Martin built two planes for noted U.S. stuntman Lincoln Beachey. Hollywood, enticed by the idea of using planes in motion pictures, called on Martin, who charged up to $700 a day for himself and a plane. His most noteworthy appearance was in *The Girl of Yesterday,* a 1915 flick about a society girl who goes for a plane ride.

As World War I erupted in Europe in 1914, Martin turned his attention to bombers, anticipating that it was only a matter of time before U.S. troops would be involved in a similar conflict. His company developed the Martin MB-1, a large biplane bomber that was delivered just after the war ended. Over the next decade demand for bombers and airliners increased dramatically. In 1929, Martin moved his manufacturing facility to Middle River, Maryland. Located on water, and near Washington, it was a great place to test and manufacture airplanes.

Pioneered Bombers, Seaplanes

In the 1930s, Martin's company created the twin-motored Martin B10, which had a range of 1,800 miles and could carry 2,400 pounds of bombs in its deep belly. Hitting speeds of up to 250 miles per hour, the B10 was fast enough to evade enemy planes. The U.S. Army ordered about 150. Argentina ordered 35 and The Netherlands asked for more than 100. This monoplane earned Martin a 1932 Robert J. Collier Trophy for achievement in aeronautics. Incidentally, the plane was a hard sell at first with some Congressmen calling Martin a "merchant of death," insinuating he wanted nothing more than to profit from war.

In 1935 Martin's company rolled out the China Clipper flying boat for Pan American Airlines. In the early 1940s, the Martin Co. introduced the B-26 Marauder, which became important during World War II. By 1943, with planes in full production to support the war, Martin employed some 70,000 workers. During this period, Martin's company also pioneered a giant seaplane known as the Mars. With a wingspan of 200 feet, the Mars—wider than a Boeing 747—was the largest seaplane ever built. The Navy received seven of these four-engine planes and used them to transport supplies and wounded soldiers across the ocean during World War II and the Korean War.

Through the 1940s, military orders kept the company in the black and Martin himself adopted an opulent lifestyle. He owned a 106-foot yacht, a 16-cylinder Cadillac and had a palatial estate on the Eastern shoreline. He was known for his stiff, double-breasted, high-collared suits. Martin was a lifelong bachelor; his mother lived with him until she died in 1953. There are no accounts of Martin being romantically involved with anyone. Biddle has suggested he was gay.

Ran Into Financial Trouble

Martin received a major setback in the late 1940s when his company fumbled the development of the Model 2-0-2, meant for the airline industry. In a rush to beat the competition, Martin invested heavily in the plane's development and rushed its production. Its service record was poor, however. One 2-0-2 crashed due to metal fatigue, and as a result, orders were canceled. The company lost $20.9 million in 1947, forcing Martin to take a $25 million loan from the Reconstruction Finance Corporation.

In 1948, the company lost another $15.5 million. With the United States no longer at war, military orders dwindled, exacerbating the company's cash-flow problem. In 1949, Martin gave up his management position, realizing the company would no longer be able to secure loans with his name on the books. In 1961, Marietta purchased the company, forming Martin Marietta. As for Martin, after being locked out of the company, he spent his remaining years giving speeches at aviation ceremonies. He died of a cerebral hemorrhage on December 5, 1955, at his farmhouse in Chestertown, Maryland. He was interred at the Fairhaven Mausoleum in Santa Ana, placed next to his mother.

Martin's life and aeronautical achievements are commemorated at the Glenn L. Martin Maryland Aviation Museum in Baltimore, a place aviation buffs visit to learn more about this man who took an early interest in flight and went on to found one of the leading aircraft manufacturers of the 20th century. From 1909 to 1960, the Glenn L. Martin Co. produced some 80 types of aircraft, impacting everything from commercial air travel to military operations. Martin's name and company live on, now part of Lockheed Martin, the largest defense contractor in the United States.

Books

Biddle, Wayne, *Barons of the Sky,* Simon & Schuster, 1991.

Harley, Ruth W., *Glenn L. Martin: Boy Conqueror of the Air,* Bobbs-Merrill Co., 1967.

Pattillo, Donald M., *Pushing the Envelope: The American Aircraft Industry,* University of Michigan Press, 1998.

Periodicals

Los Angeles Times, September 28, 2003.

New York Times, March 15, 1929; May 9, 1937; January 21, 2007.

New Yorker, November 28, 1942; December 5, 1942.

Time, May 29, 1939.

Washington Post, November 12, 1993.

Online

"Glenn Luther Martin," Glenn L. Martin Maryland Aviation Museum, http://www.marylandaviationmuseum.org/history/glenn_martin/index.html (December 16, 2008). □

Giulietta Masina

Giulietta Masina (1921–1994) was a veteran Italian performer best known for her roles in films made by her husband, the legendary director Federico Fellini. She starred in 1954's *La strada* (The Road) and *Le notti di Cabiria* (Nights of Cabiria) three years later, both of which won Academy Awards for best foreign film of the year. Critics often described Masina's characters in these two films as the female version of Charlie Chaplin for her waiflike innocence and unassailable optimism. "She is not just the main actress in a number of my films," her husband once said, according to *Guardian* writer Ronald Bergan, "but their inspiration as well."

The future film star was born Giulia Anna Masina on February 22, 1921, in San Giorgio di Piano, a city in northern Italy's Bologna region. Her father Gaetano was a music teacher and violinist, while her mother, Anna Flavia Pasqualin Masina, taught school. She was the last of their four children, and in her teens went to live with an aunt in Rome, where she attended a school run by nuns of the Ursuline order. She then went on to Rome's Sapienza University, where she earned a degree in literature.

Married Fellini in 1943

Masina's first acting experiences came in college productions, and after graduating she joined a musical-comedy group in Rome. She came to the attention of Fellini, who was writing radio scripts at the time, and he cast her in his 1943 serial radio play, *Terziglio.* The pair also fell in love and were wed on October 30 of that same year.

During this period of Masina's life, Italy experienced terrible hardships resulting from the Fascist dictatorship of Benito Mussolini and his alliance with Nazi Germany; in 1943, Allied forces invaded the Italian peninsula and the war turned against Germany, but there was a period of extreme adversity for most Italians. The end of the war in 1945 ushered in a period of exuberance and experimentation in the arts, especially in the cinema. One of the leading directors was an already-established filmmaker, Roberto Rossellini, who cast Masina in her film debut in an uncredited role in 1946. That movie was *Paisà,* a story set during the German occupation. Both Rossellini and Fellini became the leading figures in a new movement dubbed neorealism for their films' frank, unsentimental portrayals of modern life.

Masina's first credited role came in 1948 in an adaptation written by Fellini and filmed by Alberto Lattuada, *Senza pietà* (Without Pity), another World War II-set tale. Next, she won a supporting role in the gritty *Persiane chiuse* (Behind Closed Shutters), a 1950 drama about a woman searching for her missing sister in the rough areas of Genoa. That same year, her husband cast her in his first film, *Luci del varietà,* (Variety Lights), which Fellini co-directed with Lattuada. The story centered on a performing troupe and featured Masina as a member having an affair with the manager until the arrival of an attractive new performer. "Already her round animated baby-face and bright eyes proved her a singular personality and talented performer," wrote Bergan in the *Guardian* about Masina's effort.

Starred in *La strada*

Masina's next role came in *Cameriera bella presenza offresi...* with a script written by Fellini, and in 1952 she had a supporting role in *Wanda la peccatrice* (The Shameless Sex). She also appeared in *Lo sceicco bianco* (The White Sheik), her husband's debut as a solo director in 1952. Another role that year came as the factory worker in Rossellini's *Europa '51,* which starred Ingrid Bergman as a wealthy woman who suffers a family tragedy and then attempts to lead a more charity-focused life, but her family institutionalizes her for her good works.

Masina became an international star with *La strada,* which had its premiere at the 1954 Venice Film Festival among a stellar number of other classics, including Marlon Brando's starmaking turn in *On the Waterfront,* Alfred Hitchcock's *Rear Window,* and *The Seven Samurai* from Japanese filmmaker Akira Kurosawa. *La strada* centered on the relationship between a brutal, selfish circus strongman played by Anthony Quinn and his pitiful companion, Gelsomina. Quinn's character, named Zampano, has actually purchased Gelsomina from her impoverished family because he needs a cook, sexual partner, and assistant for his performances. The pair eventually joins a circus near Rome, where Zampano's temper lands him in jail temporarily. Offered the chance to flee the abusive relationship with a kindly acrobat-clown, Gelsomina chooses to wait for Zampano, but tragedy follows.

The film, with its bleak portrayal of those on the outskirts of Italian society, did not initially win the hearts of Italian critics, which caused Masina no small amount of grief. "Can you imagine my crisis?" she recalled in an interview with *New York Times* journalist E. J. Dionne Jr. years later. "Because I thought I had ruined Federico." The film soon found its audience, however, and went on to win the 1956 Academy Award for best foreign language film. Writing in the *New York Times* about of Masina's starring role, the critic A. H. Weiler called her "an extremely versatile performer who mirrors the simple passions and anxieties of the child-like girl with rare and acute perception," Weiler wrote. "She is expert at pantomime, funny as the tow-headed, doe-eyed and trusting foil and sentient enough to portray in wordless tension her fear of the man she basically loves."

Unforgettable as *Cabiria*

Masina appeared next in *Il bidone* (The Swindlers), a 1955 project by her husband that reunited her with the American actor who played her potential savior in *La strada*, Richard Basehart. Her next film cemented her reputation in Italian cinema as one of the country's most appealing—and heartrending—tragic heroines. *Le notti di Cabiria* (Nights of Cabiria) premiered at the Cannes Film Festival in May of 1957, and went on to win Fellini his second Academy Award for best foreign language film. Masina played Cabiria, a prostitute in Rome who suffers a series of degrading experiences but remains optimistic about the possibility of true love in her future. She is unexpectedly hired by a movie star, who then unceremoniously casts her out, goes on a religious pilgrimage, elicits laughs and jeers from an audience when a hypnotist extracts her secret wishes for a less degrading life, and falls in love with a shy, seemingly caring man, who swindles her out of her life's savings.

The film earned Masina several awards, including best actress honors at Cannes. A restored version was released in 1998, which features a scene cut from the original version because it displeased Italy's Roman Catholic-dominated film censorship board. In the missing footage, Cabiria accompanies a man who distributes food to the homeless who live in Rome's underground caves, where she will likely have to spend her final years, too. Despite the wrenching subject matter, *Nights of Cabiria* is consistently hailed as a classic, and one of Fellini's best works out a career full of cinematic triumphs. "There is more grace and courage in the famous image of Giulietta Masina smiling through her tears," wrote Janet Maslin in the *New York Times* at the time of the rerelease, "than there is in all the fire-breathing blockbusters Hollywood has to offer."

Despite the acclaim she won in what was just her first decade as a film star, Masina was actually more wary about her career because of those accomplishments. "Success," she told Dionne, "means being careful not to make mistakes because you develop a certain kind of fear. You are scared to accept roles which are different. You are scared

that you will cancel the success you had. You are scared to disappoint the critics and the public."

Hosted Radio Show

After *Nights of Cabiria*, Masina appeared in the women's prison movie, *Nella città, L'inferno* (Hell in the City) alongside another top Italian star of the era, Anna Magnani. Her next project, 1960's *La Grande Vie* (The High Life), earned critical barbs for its attempt to portray a seemingly amoral young woman—Masina's Doris—who filches her friends' boyfriends in carefree, comic light. That was a critical and commercial failure, and Masina went into semi-retirement following it. She returned to the screen in 1965 with *Giulietta degli spiriti* (Juliet of the Spirits), which her husband wrote and directed. Some of her fans were perplexed by the apparently semi-autobiographical tale of an affluent housewife in Rome in an unhappy marriage to an adulterous man—even more so because prior to its release, Masina's comeback was hyped as Fellini's tribute to his wife. "In a way, I'm ashamed of it," Fellini would only say about the story to *New York Times* writer Robert F. Hawkins, who visited the set when the film's actual plot was still a topic of intense speculation.

Juliet of the Spirits would be the last major starring role for Masina for two decades. She appeared in a 1967 flop, *Non stuzzicate la zanzara* (Don't Tease the Mosquito), an early work by Swiss filmmaker Lina Wertmüller, and in her first English-language role two years later in *The Madwoman of Chaillot*, which starred Katherine Hepburn. Though Hawkins, visiting the set of *Juliet of the Spirits* a few years earlier, had observed as Fellini "fed her lines, hints, suggestions of moods to which she was to react," he wrote in the *New York Times*, and "Masina overcame the difficult test, responding mimically, superbly, vividly, bringing to life the nuanced reactions he desired," Masina later said that working with her husband was stressful for her. With directors other than her husband, she told Dionne in the *New York Times* in 1986, "I feel freer, as strange as it may seem. I would like to understand him immediately, without his explaining, and he wants me to understand, and so I become defensive because I'm scared of making mistakes."

From 1966 to 1969 Masina hosted a popular radio show in Italy, *Lettere aperte* (Open Letters), which had been based on her popular newspaper column of the same name. She answered reader mail on the air, largely from advice-seekers. She did some television work and was active in the United Nations Children's Fund (UNICEF). She and Fellini made one final film together, *Ginger e Fred* (Ginger and Fred), in 1986. The movie co-starred her with Marcello Mastroianni, the handsome star who had been in many Fellini films, but this was the first time they worked together. "Just as Miss Masina's roles in earlier Fellini films called upon her to be sold into the circus and forced into prostitution, she now finds herself conned into coming back, against her better judgment, by her broken-down former dancing partner," Dionne wrote. They once had a hit nightclub act long ago, and reunite for a vacuous television show. "These are lovely performances, observant, original and infinitely appealing," noted Richard Schickel in *Time.* "When we, and Fellini, are lucky, his taste for flash and trash does not overwhelm what he really has to say; instead, it makes a useful contrast to simpler truths, and makes us grateful for them, as we are in *Ginger & Fred.*"

Masina's final film was *Aujourd'Hui Peut-Être* (A Day to Remember), released in 1991, in which she played an aging French matriarch determined to sell her house and land rather than let her ungrateful children inherit the valuable property. It was a bittersweet cinematic finale for Masina, who had no children. Early in her marriage, she fell down a flight of stairs and suffered a miscarriage; another pregnancy resulted in the birth of Pierfederico in March of 1945, but the infant died a month later from respiratory problems. She died of cancer in Rome on March 23, 1994, five months after the loss of her husband, who died a day after their fiftieth wedding anniversary. Masina's career was an extraordinary one, but she reflected in the 1986 *New York Times* interview that it had all been pre-ordained. "I didn't decide anything," she told Dionne. "It was destiny which decided for me."

Books

International Dictionary of Films and Filmmakers, Volume 3: *Actors and Actresses,* fourth edition, St. James Press, 2000.

Periodicals

Guardian (London, England), March 24, 1994, p. 16.

Interview, January 1994, p. 76.

New York Times, July 17, 1956, p. 19; October 29, 1957, p. 34; October 4, 1964, p. X7; March 23, 1986; July 3, 1998.

Time, March 31, 1986, p. 74.

Times (London, England), April 7, 1958, p. 10.□

Hans J. Massaquoi

German-born American journalist Hans J. Massaquoi (born 1926) had a unique story to tell in his 1999 memoir *Destined to Witness.* Massaquoi's unusual circumstances were indicated by the book's subtitle: "Growing Up Black in Nazi Germany."

Massaquoi faced constant danger living as a teenager in and near the city of Hamburg during the horrors of World War II. Yet for the most part he did not witness the worst of those horrors: he was never sent to a concentration camp himself. He became a unique observer of the lives of ordinary Germans during the war and the Holocaust. He was most certainly an outcast in German society at the time, but was still living and working among them in a way that Jews and other minorities marked for death could not. Indeed, as a child, Massaquoi was as fascinated by Nazi pageantry and as susceptible to Adolf Hitler's spell as were his white classmates.

Descended from Liberian Diplomat

Hans-Jürgen Massaquoi, born on January 19, 1926, in Hamburg, was the grandson of Momolu Massaquoi, Liberia's consul general in that city and the hereditary king of the Vai people of West Africa. Momolu Massaquoi's son Al-Haj grew up in an atmosphere of privilege befitting a high-ranking diplomat, studied at Trinity College in Dublin, Ireland, and, while on vacation, began a relationship with a German nurse, Bertha Baetz, whom he met at a party at Momolu Massaquoi's Hamburg villa. After Hans-Jürgen's birth, Al-Haj returned to his studies, and his son spent the first few years of his life in his grandfather's household. Whenever he would recite racist German nursery rhymes he had learned, Momolu would laugh and tell him stories from African tribal lore.

The Massaquoi family broke up in December of 1929, when both Momolu and Al-Haj were forced to return to Liberia during the unfolding of a major political scandal there: the president of the small nation, founded as a refuge from slavery in the United States, stood accused of selling Liberians into forced labor on a Spanish-controlled island off the Nigerian coast. Hans-Jürgen Massaquoi was in poor health, having suffered through a bout with diphtheria and several other serious childhood diseases, and his mother decided it would be safer to raise him in Germany. Massaquoi suffered the stares and remarks of passers-by and the humiliation of seeing Africans caged like animals at a display at Hamburg's Hagenbecks Zoo, but he made friends with other children in the working class Hamburg neighborhood where he and his mother lived in a cold water flat.

On Massaquoi's first day of school in 1932, other children taunted him with chants of "Neger, Neger, Schornsteinfeger" ("Negro, Negro, chimneysweep," as quoted in *Destined to Witness*). But Massaquoi was as enthusiastic as his classmates when Adolf Hitler rode through Hamburg at the head of a parade—even though his mother had no love for the Nazi Party and removed a swastika Massaquoi had asked a babysitter to sew onto his sweater. "The Nazis put on the best show of all the political parties," Massaquoi told Audrey Fischer in an article in the *Library of Congress Information Bulletin*. "There were parades, fireworks and uniforms—these were the devices by which Hitler won over young people to his ideas. Hitler always boasted that despite parents' political persuasion, Germany's youth belonged to him."

Attempted to Join Hitler Youth

Massaquoi's life during much of the 1930s was marked by an extreme kind of double consciousness. A sequence of disturbing incidents made clear the danger he was in as a result of the Nazi doctrine of racial purity. In 1934, shortly after the beginning of formal National Socialist rule, he was pulled into a beer hall by a group of drunken Nazi storm troopers and held up on stage as an example of the effects of racial mixing; he was fortunate to be rescued by his very angry mother. He found his neighborhood playground closed to non-Aryans (Aryans are Germanic peoples). Yet he idolized Adolf Hitler, even after his attempt to join the Hitler Youth organization was rebuffed with contempt. The principal of Massaquoi's school, a well-known philologist named Wriede, lost no opportunity to humiliate him, but other teachers tried to soften the blow and encouraged him to develop his musical and athletic gifts.

Athletics provided a refuge for Massaquoi, who was inspired by the exploits of African-American boxer Joe Louis and Olympic track-and-field star Jesse Owens. "Both men had a profound and lasting effect on my life, since they instilled me with genuine pride in my African heritage at a time when such pride was extremely difficult to come by," he wrote in *Destined to Witness*. Despite restrictions against non-Aryans in the sport, he became a talented amateur boxer and a competent soccer player. Among his friends were a group of Hamburg's so-called swing kids, young people who enjoyed American jazz and wore their hair long despite frequent harassment from Hitler Youth gangs. Massaquoi's mother lost her hospital job because she had a mixed-race son, and Massaquoi faced the wrath of a Nazi teacher who told him that when the Nazis were finished with the Jews, people like him would be next. Nevertheless, they lived a more normal life than did their few Jewish acquaintances, even after the outbreak of war in September of 1939. Massaquoi knew no other black people in Germany at all.

With university studies and professional preparation barred to him, Massaquoi had few choices as to an adult career. A hiring officer who believed that Germany would soon recapture its African colonies agreed to let him become an apprentice in a machine shop on the grounds that engineers familiar with African cultures would soon be needed there. Beginning in 1940, Massaquoi spent several years at the Lindner A.G. machine firm, mastering various skills there although he had had little exposure to mechanical training during his schooling. Among his co-workers he found some who were devoted to the German war effort, but others who ridiculed it; he was aware that concentration camps existed but was unsure what happened there. He even had a German girlfriend named Gretchen Jahn for a time, and the two sometimes used air-raid blackouts as a cover for clandestine meetings. Massaquoi still retained a degree of loyalty to the German state, until he tried to enlist in the German army during the war and was asked how he dared to show his face at the recruiting office.

Fled Hamburg

British and American bombing of Hamburg in 1943, codenamed Operation Gomorrah, reduced much of that city to rubble, including Massaquoi's place of employment. He and his mother fled Hamburg for the nearby small town of Harburg, where Massaquoi had spent time when he was young. Retracing the steps of some of his childhood walks, he came to the fence of what he came to learn much later was the Dora-Mittelbau concentration camp, and saw smoke rising from what he later realized was a crematorium. He narrowly evaded arrest by local police who thought he was a spy. Soon he and his mother returned to Hamburg, and he was still there when British troops entered the city in the summer of 1945, near the war's end.

In *Destined to Witness*, Massaquoi speculated on why he was not sent to the camps himself. He attributed his survival, he wrote, to "two fortunate coincidences. Unlike Jews, blacks were so few in numbers that they were relegated to low-priority status in the Nazis' lineup for extermination. Also, the unexpectedly rapid advance of the Allied military juggernaut kept the Nazis preoccupied with their own survival and in many cases crushed the Gestapo executioners before they could put the finishing touches on their racial cleansing. Thus I fell through the cracks of modern history's most extensive, most systematic mass-murder scheme."

With only a rudimentary grasp of English at first, Massaquoi managed to sign on as an interpreter with a company of British soldiers. He soon forsook British English for American as he tried to put together a living in the difficult conditions of postwar Hamburg, and his skills on trumpet and clarinet were good enough to earn him occasional gigs as a jazz musician. In 1948 Massaquoi was reunited with his father in Liberia, and two years later he moved to the United States, where some of his mother's relatives already lived. She settled in suburban Chicago and lived until 1986. Massaquoi was drafted into the U.S. military because of a clerical error, but did not contest the order to report for duty because he felt that military service would aid his eventual (and indeed successful) effort to become a citizen.

Serving during the Korean war as a paratrooper at the still-segregated 82nd Airborne Division based at Fort Bragg, North Carolina, Massaquoi experienced American-style racial discrimination as he traveled around the South. After his term of service was over, the Servicemen's Readjustment

Act, popularly known as the G.I. Bill, made it possible for him to earn a journalism degree from the University of Illinois in 1957. Before graduating, he joined the staff of the black-oriented Johnson Publishing Company in Chicago as an associate editor at *Jet* magazine. He soon joined Johnson's flagship publication, *Ebony*, and in 1967 he began a long tenure as *Ebony*'s managing editor. In 1984 Massaquoi was interviewed by oral historian Studs Terkel for his 1984 book *The Good War*. *Ebony* publisher John H. Johnson and author Alex Haley helped convince Massaquoi to write *Destined to Witness*, which appeared in 1999 and became a bestseller in Germany—a country Massaquoi still considered home. In 2001 actress Whoopi Goldberg acquired the cinematic rights to his story.

Books

Contemporary Black Biography, vol. 30, Gale, 2001.
Massaquoi, Hans J., *Destined to Witness: Growing Up Black in Nazi Germany*, Morrow, 1999.

Periodicals

Independent on Sunday (London, England), July 8, 2001.
Jet, December 6, 1999, p. 23; April 23, 2001.

Online

"Growing Up Black in Nazi Germany: The Remarkable Life of Hans Massaquoi," *Library of Congress Information Bulletin*, http://www.loc.gov/loc/lcib/0003/black_nazi.html (January 27, 2009). □

Bat Masterson

American lawman Bat Masterson (1853–1921) helped tame the wild west during the 1870s before embarking on a career as a gambler, boxing corner man and sportswriter.

S porting a bowler hat and a well-groomed moustache, he was an expert marksman who practiced both his fast draw technique and accuracy constantly—in short, Masterson earned his reputation as an Indian scout, buffalo hunter, sheriff, gambler, and gunman. History has no accurate number of how many men he gunned down in the line of duty, but in violent situations he was certainly fearless and deadly, with many well-documented killings to substantiate his legend.

During the 1950s, when television and motion pictures picked up on his legend—eschewing many of the actual facts—they transformed the inveterate gambler and gunfighter into a continental style bon vivant. A man of the people, the real Masterson was badly flawed, but far more colorful.

Born in Canada, Raised in the American West

Many sources state that Masterson was born and raised on a farm in either Fairview or Iroquois, Illinois. However, both

The Lawmen and *Bat Masterson—The Man and the Legend* offer proof that he was born in St. Georges of Henryville Parish in the Canadian province of Quebec on November 26, 1853. Further, his parents—Thomas Masterson Sr. And Catherine McGurk Masterson—had him baptized under the French name Bartholomew, which became the basis for his famous nickname, Bat. The family, which included siblings Edward, James, Nellie, Thomas Jr., George and Emma, moved across the border seeking virgin farmland sometime in 1861. The Mastersons tried their collective hands at making homes in New York state, Iroquois County and Fairfield, Illinois, and Missouri before settling in Grant Township, Kansas, 14 miles northeast of Wichita. The elder Masterson took his sons Ed and Bartholomew with him to construct a sod house in which the family would live. Indifferent to schooling, the youngsters honed their skills as marksmen by hunting for fresh meat to put on the family dinner table. When they became accomplished enough, they left home to make a living. It was during this time that he began to sign his name as William Barclay Masterson.

Initially, the Masterson brothers worked for a subcontractor grading a five-mile section of road for the Atchison, Topeka, and Santa Fe railroad. When they were tricked out of most of their pay and left stranded in Dodge City, Edward returned home, but young Bat latched on with a group of buffalo hunters. Seen today as wasteful slaughter of a species, during its time buffalo hunting supplied meat and hides for railroad workers, the military, and local construction crews. Further, it cleared the land of cumbersome wild life where railroad lines and new townships were springing up. Eventually, Ed joined his brother and both worked as skinners and stock tenders, which meant in addition to shooting buffalos, they would cut the hides of the animal's carcass and prepare them for shipment back east. During this era, the Mastersons met several men who would serve alongside them as lawmen including Charlie Trask, Tom Nixon, Dave Morrow, Neal Brown, Fred Singer, and the legendary Wyatt Earp. In addition to perfecting his marksmanship, Masterson—just a few months past the age of eighteen—developed his love of gambling and drinking in the buffalo hunting camps.

In 1874, Masterson's brothers Ed and Jim had returned to Kansas when Bat and fellow buffalo hunter Billy Dixon were caught in the middle of an attack by Comanche Indians at the small town of Adobe Walls. Led by chief Quona Parker, the Comanches were angered by the U.S. Government's broken promises to clear the buffalo hunters from the plains and mustered two hundred warriors to stage a violent uprising. Masterson, Dixon and the townspeople valiantly defended their turf, but fighting lasted on and off for six days and four settlers were killed along with two dozen attacking Native Americans. The attack was one of many that would sweep the Great Plains over the next two years. When General Nelson A. Miles received word of the incident, he deployed troops and hired Masterson and Dixon—revered as heroes in nearby Dodge City—as Indian scouts, positions both would hold intermittently over the next few years.

Became a Legendary Lawman

Although Masterson was a fine rifle shot, he did not make his reputation with a pistol until January 24, 1876 in Sweetwater, Texas, when he was provoked into a gun battle with Sgt. Melvin A. King at the Lady Gay Saloon. Upon entering the barroom, King was enraged at Masterson's attentions to saloon girl Molly Brennan and began to shoot. Reportedly, Brennan jumped in front of Masterson to protect him and both were wounded; Brennan was killed. Shot in the hip, Masterson fell to the floor where he drew his gun and shot King dead. The incident proved to be the legendary gunfighter's only face-to-face gun battle. His wounds necessitated the use of a cane, which along with his derby hat and dandified style of dress, became a sartorial trademark. Some accounts claim the cane—which he often used as a bat to subdue criminals, was the origin of his famous nickname "Bat." Masterson had been known as "Bat" for years prior to the incident, however.

The following year Masterson returned to Dodge City as a partner in the Lone Star Dance Hall, a place that allowed him to indulge his twin passions of carousing and cards. A dispute with local sheriff Larry Degen resulted in Masterson taking employment as a Ford County sheriff's deputy alongside old friend Wyatt Earp. Later that fall, Masterson was elected county sheriff, and his brother Ed became marshal for the city of Dodge. Immediately, the younger Masterson proved his mettle, leading a successful posse in the capture of six train robbers including Dave Rudabaugh, who would one day ride with the infamous Billy the Kid.

The Masterson brothers were complete opposites as law enforcement agents. Older brother Ed was friendly and easy going, preferring to talk drunks and rowdies out of troubling situations. By contrast, younger brother Bat had no qualms about reaching for his weapon when trouble arose. Rapidly growing, Dodge City attracted a fair number of undesirables. On April 9, 1878, the elder Masterson was fatally wounded as he tried to wrestle a gun away from a couple of drunken cowboys. Some biographies claim that Bat Masterson avenged his brother's shooting, but newspaper accounts of the day have Ed Masterson shooting his attackers before succumbing to the wounds he incurred. After escorting his late brother to a full military style funeral, Bat Masterson returned to Dodge with his brother Jim, who was made deputy marshal and later city marshal.

Once hunters had rendered buffalos nearly extinct as a species, Dodge City was transformed into a wide open cattle town filled with hard core drinking, gambling and random gunfire. Masterson's reputation as a crack shot and relentless pursuer did much to keep the often volatile town from exploding into violence. Ironically, the notorious gunman seldom fired his weapon at lawbreakers, choosing to use the barrel of his Colt .45 as a blackjack or his fists to settle one-on-one skirmishes. In 1879, his appointment as a United States Deputy Marshal enhanced his authority statewide. That same year, he and thirty men were called upon to keep the peace on behalf of the Atchison, Topeka, and Santa Fe railroad in the so-called railroad wars with the Denver and Rio Grande line.

Falsely charged with fraud by a local newspaper, Masterson lost the next election to George Hinkle in 1880, although his younger brother Jim remained city marshal. Rather than seek another law enforcement post, the elder Masterson began a career as an itinerant gambler and part-time faro dealer in various western locations. Drinking and gambling as he pleased, he ended up in Tombstone, Arizona with Wyatt Earp, but left before the famed showdown at the O.K. Corral between the Earps, Doc Holliday and the Clanton gang. After a period of speculative gold mining and extensive travel, Masterson was appointed sheriff of Trinidad, Colorado in 1882, but after a controversial year that ended the town's outlaw era, he returned to Dodge City.

As the decade wore on, participation in gambling, music halls and sports dominated Masterson's life more than law. His last known gunfight in 1881 had him swapping bullets with two men bothering his brother. His last job as a peace officer came in 1892 in Denver while he was running the Denver Exchange Club. A renowned womanizer, Masterson had met pretty blonde showgirl Emma Walters and married her in 1891, but often left her alone for months at a time while he traveled. Not surprisingly, the couple had no children.

Wrote Boxing Column

In addition to casino gaming, Masterson enjoyed wagering on horse races and professional boxing. An inveterate fan of the Sweet Science, Masterson began to offer his views in a sports column for *George's Weekly*, a Denver newspaper. Further, during the boomtown years when prize fights drew huge crowds, the former sheriff acted as cornerman, referee, manager, and promoter. Masterson also worked the corner of Jake Kilrain when he lost the title to John L. Sullivan in the last bare knuckle heavyweight championship bout in 1889. He also lost a great deal of money backing prize-fighter Charlie Mitchell in his losing effort against "Gentleman Jim" Corbett, and even more betting on Corbett's loss to "Battling Bob" Fitzsimmons. Still a feared gunman, he guarded the $10,000 prize money for the Peter Maher—Bob Fitzsimmons 1896 heavyweight title fight held outside of El Paso, Texas at the behest of Judge Roy Bean himself. That year, he opened the Olympic Athletic Club in an old Denver Salvation Army barracks, where he sponsored and refereed regular bouts. In time, he earned a reputation as a shrewd judge of boxing talent.

Constantly in dispute with local figures and drinking heavily, Masterson was formally asked to leave Denver in 1902. Offered a position on the *Morning Telegraph* in New York City, Masterson—who was arrested for illegal gambling his first day there—was later delighted to find that he was something of a pre-sold celebrity. During an 1881 interview in Gunnison, Colorado, a Dr. W.S. Cockrell pointed Masterson out as a man-killer to a gullible newspaper reporter and proceeded to spin a yarn in which the sheriff killed 26 men and lopped off the heads of bandits as proof of capture. It was all blarney. Newspapers such as the *New York Sun* nonetheless picked up the reporter's story and a nation dissatisfied about the rapidly diminishing old west accepted the tall tales as fact. Subsequently, the faded gunfighter enjoyed a measure of fame and credibility in the Big Apple.

In New York, novelist and editor Alfred Henry Lewis befriended Masterson and wrote the highly fictionalized biography of the former gunslinger's life and times on which most movies and television shows eventually based their portrayals. Aside from mounting a slander suit against a former enemy who claimed he shot Mexicans in the back while they were drunk—Masterson was awarded $3,500 in damages—the former lawman did very little to curtail the inaccuracies in his biography. He was busy penning his popular thrice weekly column *Masterson's Views on Timely Topics* for the *Morning Telegraph,* wherein he primarily covered boxing, but dabbled in politics, theater, and events of the day. When not working as a reporter, he also penned a series of stories about his old gunfighter friends and cultivated a very important new friend, President Theodore Roosevelt.

Roosevelt was so enamored with Masterson's wild west reputation that he would often delay important matters of state to hear the tales of Adobe Walls and Dodge City from the man who lived it. Moreover, the President offered Masterson the post of U.S. Marshal of the Oklahoma Territory, but the aging sportswriter wisely turned it down. In 1904, Roosevelt appointed Masterson a United States Federal Marshal for the Southern District of New York State. The job, which paid a solid $2000 a year for keeping the peace in the grand jury room, did not interfere with his newspaper work. When Roosevelt was voted out of office in 1912, President Taft purged the government of all of the former president's appointments, including Masterson's. The two remained in close touch, however, until Roosevelt's death in 1919.

Masterson continued writing for the *Morning Telegraph* until October 21, 1921, when, suffering from the ravages of diabetes, the 67-year-old columnist died of a heart attack. He was found slumped over the typewriter that contained his philosophical observations about the $12,000 purse paid to prizefighter Rocky Kansas while farmers toiled a lifetime to earn as much. "Yet there are those who argue that everything breaks even in this old dump of a world of ours," he wrote in his last column that appeared in the *Morning Telegraph* after his death, as recorded by Robert K. DeArment in *Bat Masterson: The Man and the Legend.* "I suppose these ginks who argue that would hold that because the rich man gets ice in the summer and the poor man gets it in the winter things are breaking even for both. Maybe so, but I swear I can't see it that way..." One of the true icons of the wild west, Bat Masterson was buried at the Woodlawn Cemetery in the Bronx section of New York City.

Books

DeArment, Robert K., *Bat Masterson—The Man and the Legend,* University of Oklahoma Press, 1979.

Horan, James D., *The Lawmen,* Grammercy Books, 1980; pg. 21-74.

"William Barclay Masterson," *Dictionary of American Biography Base Set,* American Council of Learned Studies, 1928–1936.

Online

"Bat Masterson," *Answers.Com,* http://www.answers.com/topic/bat-masterson (January 21, 2009).

"Bartholomew 'Bat' Masterson," *Sangres.Com,* http://www.sangres.com/history/batmasterson.htm (January 21, 2009).

"Bat Masterson," *HistoryNet,* http://www.historynet.com/bat-masterson.htm/print (January 21, 2009).

"Bat Masterson (1854–1921)," *Find a Grave Memorial,* http://www.findagrave.com/cgi-bin/fg/cgi?page=gr&GRid=683 (January 21, 2009).

"Biography for William Barclay 'Bat' Masterson," *Internet Movie Database,* http://www.imdb.com/name/nm1330875/bio (January 21, 2009). □

Wilhelm Maybach

Wilhelm Maybach (1846–1929) was a German inventor whose pioneering technical innovations helped to launch the automotive industry. Maybach was a longtime associate of Gottlieb Daimler, and in 1890 the pair founded the Daimler Motoren Gesellschaft, or Daimler Motor Company. A decade later, Maybach's newly designed Phoenix automobile caused a sensation when it was introduced in Europe. The 1901 models were renamed Mercedes, but Maybach's involvement with the firm he founded dissolved in acrimony a few years later. That company would eventually become Mercedes-Benz.

Wilhelm Maybach was born on February 9, 1846, in Heilbronn, a city in the southern German state of Württemberg. He was the only son of six children, and his father was a carpenter who moved

the household to Stuttgart around 1854. Two years later, Maybach's mother died, and he was 13 when his father died in 1859. Relatives found a school for him in Reutlingen, where his talent for industrial design and engineering was recognized and encouraged by his teachers. Later in his teens he was hired at a workshop that made engines used to power heavy machinery.

Teamed with Gottlieb Daimler

Maybach's boss was Gottlieb Daimler, who was twelve years his senior. Daimler also realized that Maybach possessed a strong talent for industrial design and engineering, and in 1869 when Daimler was hired by the Maschinen-Gesellschaft Karlsruhe AG—a locomotive manufacturer located in another city in Württemberg—he signed the contract only with the stipulation that Maybach be hired as his assistant. Three years later, in 1872, Daimler was once again recruited by a major player in Germany's industrial revolution, Deutz-AG-Gasmotorenfabrik in Köln in the northern German state of North Rhein-Westphalia. Daimler was hired to serve as Deutz's technical director. Maybach, meanwhile, was its chief designer.

Deutz was founded by Nikolaus Otto, and in 1876 Otto won a patent for the four-stroke engine, which would prove an ideal formulation for the internal-combustion device. Maybach reportedly took the "Atmospheric Gas Engine" to the 1876 Philadelphia Exposition and demonstrated its workings for the thousands who came through Machinery Hall. After this point, however, nearly everything in the history of the development of the automobile industry becomes complicated and rife with lawsuits and rival claims. Otto's patent was the subject of a court case, and his claim was eventually overturned.

In 1878 Maybach married Bertha Habermaas, and their first son was born a year later. Two more boys followed, and one of them would carry on his father's legacy in the automotive industry. All grew up near the separate home workshop—actually a converted greenhouse—in which their father spent many hours behind their house on Taubenheimstrasse in Bad Cannstatt, a leafy part of Stuttgart. In fact, once Maybach and Daimler quit Deutz, so much activity was happening in the greenhouse that the neighbors feared they were counterfeiting money and notified the police.

Success with First Marine Engine

Maybach and Daimler had left Deutz to form their own joint venture to develop a better internal combustion engine. Maybach applied for and was granted a patent on a novel type of four-stroke engine in 1885, which operated at 600 rotations per minute, more than three times as fast as Otto's model. Maybach's engine was also much lighter, weighing in at a hundred pounds. It was this new, lightweight engine that made the first artificially-powered vehicles possible. Another crucial invention of this era was the carburetor, which was patented by Karl Benz in 1885. The carburetor was the method by which the fuel was delivered to the engine. A few years later, Maybach would perfect another type of carburetor that proved to be even more efficient.

Maybach and Daimler mounted their engine on a wooden bicycle and called it a *Reitwagen,* or riding car. They received a patent for that on August 29, 1885. In 1886, they twinned it with a small boat and successfully tested it out on the nearby Neckar River. The marine engine proved to be a top seller for their fledgling venture, and they began licensing the rights to produce it in other countries. Their first American partner was New York piano manufacturer William Steinway.

By 1887 Maybach and Daimler's newly built factory in Seelberg Hills had nearly two dozen employees. Maybach handled all the design aspects, while Daimler ran the financial end of the business. They were convinced that their engines were ideal for road transport, and began coming up with different versions. There was what is recorded as the first gas-powered motorized public transit system, which was essentially a two-sided bench covered by a canopy and mounted on a platform; with the help of a modified rail track it moved passengers from one part of Bad Cannstatt to another. There was even a taxi fleet run by Daimler's son Adolf, in the late 1880s in downtown Stuttgart.

Renamed Model the "Mercedes"

Maybach and Daimler exhibited the first automobile that was not a modified horse carriage or other type of existing vehicle at the 1889 Paris World's Fair, and its enthusiastic reception helped them land some wealthy backers for the next stage of their venture. In November of 1890, they founded the Daimler Motoren Gesellschaft (Daimler Motor Company, or DMG). A series of squabbles with two of the main investors, however—munitions manufacturers and financiers Max von Duttenhofer and Wilhelm Lorenz—meant that they soon lost control of their own company. Von Duttenhofer and Lorenz apparently wanted to merge with Otto's Deutz, to which Maybach and Daimler strenuously objected. Maybach left in February of 1891 when he was not given a seat on the management board, but Daimler financed Maybach's workshop though he remained with DMG for the next two years.

Maybach teamed with another son of Daimler's, Paul, to build a new engine and an entirely new vehicle. They dubbed the car the "Phoenix," from the mythical tale of a bird that dies in a fire but rises again out of the ashes. This featured the first true gasoline-powered engine, which had four cylinders and a spray-nozzle carburetor. This type of carburetor allowed it to be powered by liquid gasoline, not the "town gas" previously used to power engines. Town gas was a vapor that was the byproduct of burning coal, wood, or other materials; it was used to illuminate the gaslights in major cities around the world by then. Maybach used gasoline, which was a highly flammable byproduct of crude oil, which worked well with his carburetor design.

Maybach was rehired by DMG in 1895, after a new investor came on board and demanded that both company founders be rehired. He held the title of chief engineer, and worked to produce impressively fast race cars that were soon being tested in exciting new automobile races in the most scenic parts of Western Europe. On March 6, 1900, Maybach lost his longtime ally and collaborator when Daimler died of a heart condition. A new investor turned up in the form of a semi-retired Austrian merchant named Emil Jellinek, who had bought one of the first Phoenix motorcars and loved it. Jellinek lived in the South of France by then, and daily competed with his far wealthier neighbor and fellow auto enthusiast, a Rothschild from the European banking dynasty, to determine which of the two owned the faster car.

Jellinek asked Maybach to produce an even faster model, one that could reach the dizzying speech of 25 miles per hour, and Maybach agreed, though he had reservations. The first try was a failure, for the car had too high a center of gravity to be safe, and in a race in the South of France the car lost control, crashed into a boulder, and killed its driver. Maybach returned to the drawing board and came up with a new design with a longer wheelbase and lower center of gravity. Jellinek agreed to buy the first 36 of them at a total cost of $130,000, with two provisions: that he would have exclusive rights to sell DMG cars in Austria-Hungary, France, and Belgium, and that the Phoenix would be renamed in honor of his ten-year-old daughter, Mercedes, whose name was Spanish for "mercy."

Forced Out Once Again

Maybach's newest vehicle caused a sensation and irrevocably altered human history. "The Mercedes was hailed in the motor press as the first modern automobile, the foundation upon which almost every design since the turn of the last century has been based," wrote Dennis Adler in

Daimler & Benz: The Complete History. "The 1901 Mercedes introduced steel, instead of wood, for the chassis, a honeycomb radiator in front of the engine, a gated gear change lever, driven rear wheels, and four-passenger seating, a simple formula which has prevailed, with few changes to the basic concept, for over 100 years."

With the success of the new Mercedes, Maybach was finally able to convince the DMG board to devote the company's resources to manufacturing automobiles, not just engines. He continued to produce innovations, including the six-cylinder engine in 1903 and a 120-horsepower engine designed specially for flight. There were still problems, however—now with Daimler's two sons, who each wanted control of the company for themselves. In 1907 Maybach left DMG once again to form his own company with his son Karl. He turned to producing engines that powered the massive airships invented by Count Ferdinand von Zeppelin that were being tested in southern Germany at the time. Maybach's new venture was called Luftfahrzeug-Motoreinbau GmbH (Airship Engine Company), and eventually relocated to Friedrichshafen on Lake Constance in southwestern Germany, where Zeppelin built his hydrogen-fueled behemoths. He still hoped to return to automobile manufacturing, however, and registered the name "Maybach-Motorenbau GmbH."

During World War I, Maybach's company produced more than 2,000 plane engines for the German war effort. After the war, the Zeppelin works were closed, and Maybach and his son were able to try automobile production once again. At the 1921 Berlin Automobile Exposition, they introduced the Maybach W3 limousine, a six-cylinder luxury car that reached a top speed of 65 miles per hour. The vehicles competed with another high-priced line still produced under the Mercedes nameplate by DMG, but in 1926 DMG merged with its longtime competitor, Benz & Cie, founded by Karl Benz in Mannheim in 1883. The company became Daimler-Benz, but would used Mercedes-Benz as their brand name.

World's First V12 Car

Maybach's company never equaled the success of the one he had founded that had ousted him not once but twice, but he and his son Karl did produce some legendary automobiles on their own that became extremely rare collectors' items later in the century. In 1929, their firm introduced the world's first car with a mighty V12 engine, known simply as the Maybach 12. This and several other models produced before World War II were both immense and expensive, on par with British automaker Rolls-Royce and Hispano-Suiza, a joint Spanish-Swiss venture. All of these companies produced both chauffeur-driven and smaller cars that were the favorite of kings, film stars, and various political despots and industrial tycoons.

Maybach died in Stuttgart on December 29, 1929, at the age of 83. His son Karl continued the company, and during World War II it switched to diesel engine production. The company survived as an engine manufacturer for several years after the war until Karl Maybach struck a deal with Mercedes-Benz to make diesel engines. This apparently gave the age-old rival the right to the Maybach marque, and in 2002 the newest iteration of the original DMG, DaimlerChrysler, introduced the Maybach 62, an ultra-luxury car and one of the largest passenger cars on the market. There is also a shorter Maybach, the 57, priced around $450,000, which bears some resemblance to Mercedes S-Class vehicles but is largely built by hand and extravagantly customized for the individual buyer.

Books

Adler, Dennis, *Daimler & Benz: The Complete History,* Collins, 2006.
"Wilhelm Maybach," *World of Invention,* Thomson Gale, 2006.

Periodicals

Automotive Design & Production, August 2002, p. 44.
Independent on Sunday (London, England), November 21, 2004, p. 73.□

Earle Willard McHenry

Canadian biochemist Earle Willard McHenry (1899–1961) was a nutritional pioneer. McHenry headed the nutrition department at the University of Toronto upon its founding in 1946 and also wrote two important books: *Basic Nutrition* and *Foods without Fads: A Basic Guide to Nutrition.*

McHenry was born on January 25, 1899. He initially studied chemistry, but while lecturing in the physiological hygiene department at the University of Toronto, he took a particular interest in nutrition. McHenry earned his bachelor's, master's, and doctorate degrees from that university.

Studied Chemistry at First

He joined its staff in 1927, working in the School of Hygiene and Connaught Laboratories. Early in his career, he wrote several scientific papers, often about ascorbic acids and their relation to vitamin deficiency. In one such writing, McHenry and university colleague Murray Graham summarized in the *Biochemical Journal:* "Vegetable tissues do not appear to contain a mechanism to prevent the aerobic oxidation of ascorbic acid. Hence they generally contain appreciable quantities of reversibly oxidized ascorbic acid. . . . Several vegetables show an increased titration value after heating for a short period, or after acid hydrolysis. The increase is believed to be due to the liberation of ascorbic acid from a compound which is soluble in water but insoluble in trichloroacetic acid."

In another paper, written with Eric James Reedman and Margaret Sheppard and titled *The Physiological Properties of Ascorbic Acid: An Effect upon the Weights of Guinea-Pigs*—also published in the *Biochemical Journal*—McHenry discussed the use of paired feeding in nutritional investigations of amino acids and vitamin B-1. Conducting a test with guinea pigs, he said the control animals lose appetite and weight, and then die, after ten to twelve days. "Ascorbic acid prevents a loss in [weight] in animals paired with the control group," wrote McHenry, who added that the eating disorder anorexia reflects a deficiency of amino acids as much as one of vitamin B-1. "The difference in weight . . . is believed to be due to alterations in metabolism, waterbalance, and food absorption caused by a lack of ascorbic acid," he summarized.

In 1946, the school established a separate nutrition department, with McHenry in charge. He expanded his study from basic research to public health. McHenry was the first president of the Nutrition Society of Canada upon its founding in 1957, and also chaired the Canadian National Nutrition Committee. In addition, he was president of the Canadian Physiological Society and the Canadian Federation of Biological Societies. He also participated on several government committees on North American policy, including the American Institute of Nutrition, for which he served both on the editorial board and as a council member.

Needs Vary by Region

In writing *Basic Nutrition* for college students, McHenry "presented the more fundamental considerations of the science of nutrition in order that the student might better understand the reasoning of the recommended intakes of the various nutrients," George H. Beaton, an associate professor of nutrition at the University of Toronto, wrote in its foreword. McHenry himself contended that while nutritional requirements do not vary by race, "the practical application of such information should be regional," and added that a "program for improving nutrition in Pennsylvania might not be suitable in Louisiana and would be quite unsuitable in Angola or India."

McHenry acknowledged that scientific research about the subject was nascent at the time. He hoped, however, that the book would lessen the stigma of nutritionists as disreputable. Citing papers by his research colleagues, he said commercial exploitation of vitamins, a fairly new topic at the time was still uncontrolled.

He broke down what affects the food habits of people, including availability. While people in the United States and Canada eat wheat because it is easily available, people in southern China will similarly consume rice. "Thus, climate and soil conditions determine the choice of food in many parts of the world," wrote McHenry in *Basic Nutrition,* who added that economics were closely related. "In prosperous countries the availability of food has been altered markedly by modern transportation, methods of storage and preservation and by modern processing."

He keenly observed that many people associated race with food choice, while admitting that it was difficult to gauge. Still, "religious ordinances may have a pronounced effect on food use." As an example, he cited the forbidding of meat on certain days—Roman Catholics at the time could not do so on Fridays—or at all.

McHenry realized that while milk and cheddar cheese are good providers of calcium, nutritional recommendations to the public are based at least partly on "the modern status of the dairy industry. There is no doubt that dependence must be placed on milk and cheese to furnish the generous intakes of calcium commonly recommended. However, it is debatable whether large intakes of milk always are advisable or necessary." In *Basic Nutrition* he contended that "so much emphasis has been placed on the use of milk in the United States and Canada that it is difficult to realize that these countries are unusually favored with large supplies of milk. Many other countries are much less fortunate.... [But] food practices in other countries may enable people to obtain calcium from sources not familiar in the United States or Canada."

McHenry's work offered a straightforward view of reasons behind excessive weight. "The only successful treatment of obesity or its prevention is the continuous consumption of less food (in energy value) than has been the custom. The reverse is true of underweight.... Lack of determination is the main reason for the failure of reducing regimens. No magical pill, however, expensive, or freak or faddish treatment can replace the will to eat less."

Vitamin needs to offset disease risk, he added, are small enough to readily obtain from foods. "Excess amounts of water-soluble vitamins are removed rapidly from the body by excretion in the urine. Meals, composed of foods selected to meet requirements, are the best means of obtaining vitamins," McHenry argued.

The Journal of the American Dietetic Association praised the book. "Dr. McHenry brings to the task of writing a text on nutrition a wide experience in research and in teaching graduate and undergraduate students," the association wrote in a passage that publisher J.B. Lippincott Company included in the book. "The book is perhaps unique among elementary texts for conveying the questioning spirit characteristic of research."

'Appalled at Misinformation'

McHenry's second book, *Foods Without Fads,* evolved from his public speeches, newspaper and magazine articles, and from answering many questions from the public. "It pays to eat wisely and not spend money on pills," he instructed in the book. "Like other workers in nutrition, I have been appalled at the quantity of misinformation passed out.... In the past 50 years a large amount of scientific information has become available. Much of this has been validated by repeated research. Some more recent reports concern research in progress and cannot yet be accepted as valid.... While misinformation is available in various fields, nutrition is particularly confused by pseudo experts and by some popular writers."

He said parents should be especially vigilant about food use during a child's second year, and around age ten or eleven. "Youngsters feel that they are growing up and becoming adult," McHenry observed in *Foods Without Fads.* "At this time, we see all too frequently the giving up of foods like milk, which are thought to be childish. If we want children to grow normally and to become healthy adults, we should be concerned about the development and preservation of good food habits as part of the general health picture."

McHenry also advised against using food as a reward or punishment, particularly regarding sweet foods. Youngsters, he wrote, may develop a sweet tooth for them. Conversely, nagging children about food may result in children using food as a leveraging chip. "Whether a child develops good habits depends upon the attitude of the parents," he noted. "To start with, we provide for children foods which are selected on a health basis. We set an example by eating those foods ourselves.... It is never wise to make an issue of a child's refusal to eat. Good food habits should be a matter of course."

Additionally, McHenry argued against what he called rationalizations by overweight people who blame thyroid glands, digestive processes, and family history. "People store fat and become overweight because they eat more than they need," he wrote in his commonsense approach. "We have all heard it said that stout people enjoy food. The impression is given that it is impossible to be a connoisseur of food without eating a lot. This is not true. Food can be enjoyed and savored without gluttony.... The pleasure of smoking a good cigar is not increased by smoking five cigars in rapid succession. Half a pound of tender, nicely cooked steak is just as appealing as two pounds."

While advising that weight maintenance helps minimize risk of such illnesses as diabetes, heart ailments, and gallbladder ailments, McHenry urged realistic expectations about the limitations of nutrition in fighting disease. "While the wise selection of food will help to maintain health, it cannot be assumed that an unusually high level of health can be produced by nutrition. A claim to this effect is unjustified."

Among the benefits of nutritional meals, he wrote, are healthy childbirths and adolescent growth, money savings, heightened interest, and maintaining health regardless of age. "Food intake is not the only factor involved in the maintenance of health; it is one factor which we don't need to neglect," he wrote. "Good food selection means good meals. Good meals are worth eating."

McHenry was at the forefront of nutritional awareness. He wrote two books on the subject, and was working on a third, *Nutrition: a Comprehensive Treatise,* when he died on December 20, 1961, in Toronto. Beaton finished the third book, which was published in 1966. In an update of *Basic Nutrition,* published after McHenry's death, Beaton wrote, "It was the sincere hope of the author that this book might help the student to appreciate the need for caution in interpreting dietary recommendations and the need to adapt these recommendations to the situation—environmental or physiologic—as it might exist."

The Canadian Council of Food and Nutrition sponsors an award in McHenry's name annually, and the Canadian Society for Nutritional Sciences presents it. The Earle Willard McHenry Award recognizes nutrition-related service by a Canadian or Canadian-based person. Teaching, leadership through professional associations, administrative or material support, research breakthroughs and "creating an atmosphere of public acceptance" all qualify a person for consideration, the society said on its website. The award consists of a monetary prize and a scroll.

Books

McHenry, Earle, *Basic Nutrition,* J.B. Lippincott, 1957.
McHenry, Earle, *Foods without Fads,* J.B. Lippincott, 1960.

Periodicals

Biochemical Journal, June 28, 1935; June 25, 1938.

Online

"About CSNS: Earle Willard McHenry Award," Canadian Society for Nutritional Sciences Website, http://www.nutritionalsciences.ca/content/awards.asp (December 21, 2008).

"McHenry, Earle Willard," *Canadian Encyclopedia,* http://www.thecanadianencyclopedia.com/index.cfm?PgNm=TCE&Params=A1ARTA0004912 (November 23, 2008).☐

George Wilhelm Merck II

Chemical industry executive, George Wilhelm Merck (1894–1957) was an informal man, but also a person who had a strong energy for work and research. His enthusiasm for his work and continuing research in the drug industry influenced many, especially his co-workers. He led his company on a continual search for new products and increased sales while maintaining a high ethical standard.

George Wilhelm Merck was born in New York City to George Merck and Friedrike Schenck. His mother was a native of Antwerp, Belgium. His grandfather was the senior partner of Merck Chemical Works in Darmstadt, Germany. Merck's father, also a native German, was sent to New York in 1890 to manage the sales office and warehouse in the United States.

Merck's father wanted to expand the manufacturing of the company's pharmaceuticals; however, the New York offices in which he worked did not afford him the space required for this endeavor. In 1900, the company was moved to a 150-acre tract of land in Rahway, New Jersey. New York City offered a good place for the company to start import offices, but New Jersey offered more space, lower taxes, and easy access to ports and to New York City for Merck's manufacturing plant. By 1908 Merck and Company was incorporated and the senior George Merck became its president.

While his father grew the family's business, Merck's youth was spent in West Orange, New Jersey. He went to Newark Academy and Morristown School, then attended Harvard and majored in chemistry, receiving his Bachelor of Arts degree in 1915. Originally, Merck planned to go to Germany after he graduated from Harvard for graduate school, but World War I prevented him from doing so. Instead, he stayed in New York and New Jersey and worked in a variety of positions at the Merck and Company laboratories, before becoming a plant manager after the United States entered the war. The war brought great wealth to American chemical manufacturers. Merck's father, who became an American citizen in 1902, voluntarily gave up 80 percent of the company stock representing the company's claims by German relatives. By 1918,

Merck and Company was reorganized with the elder Merck as president and Merck II as vice-president. Then in 1919, the shares which Merck senior had given up were bought back by him and American financial interests in which he did business.

In 1917, Merck married his first wife, Josephine Carey Wall. Together they had two sons, but the marriage ended in divorce. Then, in 1926, he married Serena Stevens and together they had three more children, two girls and a boy.

Built Business

In 1925, George Wilhelm Merck was appointed president of Merck and Company. In 1927, he merged the firm with Powers-Weightman-Rosengarten Company, which was a Philadelphia company that produced fine chemicals. With Merck as president, he worked to bring new products and increased sales to his company. He also broke new ground in the realm of scientific research for the pharmaceutical industry. During that time, most chemical research was done on academic campuses. In order to lure academic scientists who scoffed at industrial research to his company, he vastly expanded his laboratories in Rahway. By 1933, he created a campus atmosphere and introduced an interdisciplinary approach to research. Merck encouraged his company's scientists to deeply explore their experiments and investigations, and also allowed them to publish their findings.

Several years after Merck took over as president, the company began research with vitamins. In 1934, Dr. Randolph

Major, Merck's head of research received a call from Biochemist Robert Runnells Williams. In his call Williams told Major that he had isolated a small quantity of B and wondered if the Merck laboratories would be interested in working with him to help supply him with a more natural substance, establish its molecular structure, and possibly try to synthesize it. Major, acting as Merck's representative was interested. For over a year the Merck laboratories at Rahway worked on producing B. In 1936, with the help of Merck, Williams succeeded in synthesizing the vitamin. B was now able to be made cheaply and easily and Merck moved into large scale production. B was not the only vitamin tackled; soon the company was making a variety of vitamins such as riboflavin or B, niacin, vitamin C, and many more. Vitamins were being sold nationwide at drugstores, and the United States government was encouraging producers of processed foods to add vitamins to enrich the foods.

Merck and Company did not only produce vitamins, however. Shortly after vitamins found themselves widely accepted and used across the nation, Merck began working with sulfas and antibiotics. Although countries like France and Germany first brought the idea of sulfa drugs out into the open with the drug Prontosil, a drug that would kill the streptococcus germ that often caused deadly infections, other companies would look to patent sulfa variants. Merck chemists worked with a sulfa called sul-faquinoxalne. The researchers at Merck and Company thought they could not produce anything useful with the drug because it was not safe for human use; however, they did find the drug was excellent in protecting chickens against a deadly parasitic disease.

Antibiotics soon replaced sulfas and Merck and Company narrowly missed out on producing penicillin. In the pharmaceutical world, the story is told that Merck and Company missed out on the early stages of penicillin because the company was determined to find a way to synthesize the drug. Merck explains the situation differently, however. In the article "What the Doctor Ordered" featured in the August 1952 edition of *Time* magazine, Merck stated, "The government asked us to put up a plant, but insisted Merck apply for Government money to finance it. I said 'No, that would make it look as if we were lobbying. We won't do it.'" This statement helped demonstrate the ethical standards Merck and Company held in high esteem. Although Merck missed out on penicillin, the company moved ahead with the next major antibiotic, streptomycin. Dr. Selman Waksman from Rutgers found that a soil bacteria made something that killed many germs which penicillin did not kill. He brought his findings to the laboratories at Rahway, which contributed greatly with its output.

Merck and Company would then go on to aid Edward Calvin Kendall, a biochemist from the Mayo Clinic in discovering cortisone. Kendall began the synthesis process and Merck completed it. In the 1952 *Time* article, Kendall called Merck's work on the project "the most complicated chemical processes ever carried out in a commercial laboratory on a production scale." Although the production of cortisone was originally touted as the cure for arthritis, doctors found that the drug could not be given over long periods of time without causing other risks. In spite of this, Kendall and the Mayo Clinic's Dr. Philip Hench shared a Nobel prize for their part of the work on the drug. Merck and Company helped them achieve this honor, and according to *Time*, they believed "cortisone, like its predecessors, is not a goal but a direction marker; they know the road is long, but they believe they are on the right road." Merck continued to push his company to find, research, and process new pharmaceutical advances.

Balanced Many Obligations

While Merck worked tirelessly to grow his family's business, he was also involved in many other endeavors. In 1933 Merck aided in writing the National Recovery Administration code. From 1942–1945 he also was a member of the National Research Council Committee on Drugs and Medical Supplies. In 1951 he was appointed by President Harry S. Truman to the board of the National Science Foundation, and then reappointed to the board in 1954 by President Dwight D. Eisenhower. From 1949–1952 Merck was president of the Manufacturing Chemists' Association. Merck also served as director for many other organizations, including the American Foundation for Tropical Medicine, the American Cancer Society, the National Conference of Christians and Jews, the National Industrial Conference Board, and the Save-the-Redwood League.

In addition to these responsibilities, Merck was presented with a job in 1942 during World War II. President Franklin D. Roosevelt appointed Merck as the director of the War Research Service. This service was a civilian agency that was responsible for the research and development of all biological warfare. By 1944, this work became a part of the Chemical Warfare Service of the War Department. Merck was named the chairman of the Biological Warfare committee in addition to acting as a consultant to the secretary of war. After the war Merck was awarded the Medal of Merit. From his work during this time, Merck predicted and advised that biological warfare would pose a greater threat to humanity than that of the atomic bomb.

Merck was also actively known for his involvement in environmental conservation. A 1952 *Time* magazine article, in which Merck was featured on the magazine's front cover, discussed Merck's devotion to nature. The article stated, "Merck climbs his jeep and sets out for a jolting ride over the 2,000 rugged Vermont acres which he is trying to bring back, after a century of neglect, into efficient use as a useful farm and forest land. He has supervised the planning of 90,000 evergreens, and would rather swing a brush hook to clear the undergrowth than play golf—or even tennis." Merck's passion for conservation would continue with the help of his family even after his death.

After the war, Merck saw a change in competition in the pharmaceutical industry. Merck and Company had previously acted as an ingredient supplier, but when the war ended, however, Merck and Company sought to merge into a phase where drugs could be produced and ready to be sold in finished form without further processing. To help Merck gain an advantage in these new markets, the company merged with Sharp and Dohme in 1953. Sharp and

Dohme was a company with an excellent reputation and an experienced sales force, and they were well regarded among doctors and druggists.

Merck became chairman of the board of Merck and Company in 1949. The next year, he resigned as the company's president. He held his position as chairman of the board until his death in 1957 in West Orange, New Jersey.

Founded the Merck Family Fund

George Wilhelm Merck established the Merck Family Fund in 1954. As stated by his granddaughter, Patience Merck Chamberlin, on the Merck Family Fund website, "He created the fund for two principal reasons: to do good with the resources acquired through the company's success, and to create an opportunity to regularly bring family members together." His philanthropic vision still lives on. Although the Fund has a strong staff, The Merck Family Fund is still a family run foundation. As Merck desired, the trustees of the Fund are his lineal descendants.

The Merck Family Fund focuses its grants on two areas. The first encompasses protecting the natural environment, an issue which Merck personally held near and dear to his heart. The Fund has two priorities under this area. The article "Profile: Merck Family Fund" which appeared in *Nonprofit World Funding Alert* stated the first priority of the fund was "the protection of vital ecosystems in the eastern United States and supporting the shift toward environmentally sustainable economic systems, incentives, and behaviors." According to the same article, the second area the Merck Family Fund supports is "strengthening the social fabric and physical landscape of the urban community." This area encompasses communities that have little resources to make changes, but are experiencing hardships either socially, economically, or environmentally. The article "Profile: Merck Family Fund" maintained that "the Fund focuses its grantmaking on two areas: creating green and open spaces and supporting youth as agents of social change."

Although George Wilhelm Merck passed away at the age of 62, and few of his grandchildren knew him, his legacy remains in The Merck Family Fund. His ethics, character, and expectations for a better world are carried out through The Fund. His willingness to find new advances in the pharmaceutical world will live on in and will have far-reaching effects on the work that is done in the future.

Books

Young, James Harvey, *Dictionary of American Biography, Supplement 6: 1956-1960,* American Council of Learned Societies, 1980.

Periodicals

Financial World, May 30, 1989.

Nonprofit World Funding Alert, July 2008.

Time, August 18, 1952.

Online

Chamberlin, Patience Merck, "Letter from Trustee," http://www.merck.ff.org/letter_trustee.html (December 28, 2008).

"Executive Speeches," http://www.merck.com/newsroom/executive_speeches/120150.html (December 28, 2008). □

Vincente Minnelli

American filmmaker Vincente Minnelli (1903–1986) brought the American movie musical to a peak of imaginative fantasy in the post–World War II period with such films as *An American in Paris* (1951).

Even when he was working outside the musical genre, Minnelli's films were lush productions, suffused with color and dreamlike atmospheres. Minnelli, wrote Bosley Crowther in the *New York Times,* "'wisely relied on color and the richness and character it gives to images." In *Meet Me in St. Louis* (1944), Minnelli launched the adult career of actress Judy Garland, who would become his first wife, and he made several well-regarded serious films. But it was the rich images of his musicals, as carefully staged as the photographs in a fashion magazine, for which he is best remembered. Indeed, Minnelli was sometimes regarded during his own lifetime as a director who prized style over substance. But his reputation was international, and he is now regarded as a true auteur—a director with a personal cinematic vision—of a sort that American cinema has only rarely produced.

Grew Up Around Tent Shows

Even the first name by which Vincente Minnelli was known was a piece of artifice. He was born Lester Anthony Minnelli on February 28, 1903, in Chicago, Illinois. Other birth years appear in various sources, but Minnelli's gravestone carries the 1903 date. He was the son of Vincent Charles Minnelli, a musician and the operator of a traveling tent repertory show called the Minnelli Brothers' Tent Theater. His mother, the former Mina Le Beau, sometimes appeared as a singer in her husband's productions. Young Lester grew up partly on the road, surrounded by the low-budget illusions of a mobile theater. To make it possible for him to attend school, he was sometimes lodged with relatives, principally in Delaware, Ohio. As silent films began to squeeze out the tent shows, Minnelli's father began working as a musician in central Ohio. Lester's formal education ended when he graduated from high school in Delaware.

As a high school student, Minnelli enjoyed literature and art above everything else. He moved back to Chicago after finishing school, and his skill with a sketch pad quickly landed him a job setting up window displays at the Marshall Field's department store. It was around this time that he began to use the name Vincente. Minnelli's job at Marshall Field's placed him in close proximity to the movie palaces of the city's center, which at the time still mounted elaborate stage revues. He landed a job as a

costume designer with the Balaban and Katz chain of movie theaters, and later added the position of set designer to his resume.

After Balaban and Katz merged with the New York Paramount-Publix chain, Minnelli moved to New York and continued doing design work for the new company. He got a break when actress Grace Moore asked him to design sets and costumes for the 1932 operetta *DuBarry*, in which she was to star. By the mid-1930s Minnelli was directing Broadway revues such as *At Home Abroad* (1935) and the *Ziegfeld Follies of 1936*—elaborate productions with little or no plot but plenty of elaborate song-and-dance numbers. In 1937 Minnelli took a stab at cinema, directing a segment of the film *Artists and Models* for the Paramount studio, but he later returned to New York.

Directed All-Black Musical

Minnelli's definitive move to Hollywood came in 1940, when MGM executive Arthur Freed courted and finally signed him to the studio. MGM would remain Minnelli's home for most of his career. For several years he was an assistant, designing scenes in films such as *Babes on Broadway* (1941). His first film as director was *Cabin in the Sky* (1943), a musical with an all-black cast featuring singer and dancer Lena Horne. That commercially successful film earned Minnelli another turn behind the camera the following year for *Meet Me in St. Louis*. Minnelli's characteristic style, formed during his period of stage work, was

already in evidence in those two films, which featured such elements as fantasy and the vivid use of color.

In 1945 Minnelli married Judy Garland, the youthful female lead of *Meet Me in St. Louis,* who used the film as a springboard to adult stardom after becoming famous as a child actress in *The Wizard of Oz.* In the late 1940s Garland began a long struggle with substance abuse, and the marriage ended in 1951. The couple had one daughter, Liza Minnelli, who went on to become a star on Broadway and in film, including an Academy Award-winning turn in the film *Cabaret.* Minnelli married three more times and had another daughter, Christiane Nina Miro, by his second wife, Georgette Magnani. Biographical writings and dramatic treatments of the lives of Minnelli and Garland have suggested that Minnelli may have been a homosexual, although Minnelli specialist Joe McElhaney, writing on the Web site *Senses of Cinema,* contended that "a person who married four times and had two children was one whose sexuality was, at the very least, complicated."

Minnelli directed Garland in the romance *The Clock* (1945) and the musical *The Pirate* (1948), and his next films showed his talent for working established stars into his personal style. *Father of the Bride* (1950) featured Spencer Tracy and Elizabeth Taylor in a comedy that became a major hit, and Minnelli's next major musical, *An American in Paris* (1951), paired dancer Gene Kelly with the then-unknown young French actress Leslie Caron, in a film based not on a play or novel but on songs and classical compositions by George Gershwin. The film ended with an 18-minute dance sequence, using the Gershwin composition that gave them film its name. The French film historian Jean-Pierre Coursodon, quoted by Crowther, called the passage "unquestionably the greatest set piece in the entire history of the film musical."

Made van Gogh Film Biography

Minnelli's films of the mid-1950s were infused with a similarly experimental spirit. *The Band Wagon* (1953) was a musical about musicals themselves, and was mirrored by *The Bad and the Beautiful,* a serious, non-musical treatment of Hollywood culture, shot in black and white. After a pair of high budget adaptations of stage musicals, *Brigadoon* (1954) and *Kismet* (1955), Minnelli made the critically acclaimed *Lust for Life* (1956), a biography of Dutch-French artist Vincent van Gogh that seemed to be drenched in the explosive colors of van Gogh's canvases themselves. Minnelli also directed a string of successful comedies, including *Designing Woman* (1957).

With *Gigi* (1958), based on a short novel by the French writer Colette, Minnelli hit another career peak, fusing songs by Alan Jay Lerner and Frederick Loewe with ornate scenes of French life in the story of a young woman who finds her way from courtesan-in-training to marriage. The French settings of Minnelli's two most famous films (*Gigi* was filmed on location, while *An American in Paris* mostly used Hollywood studio sets) fit well with the director's natural orientation toward elegance. "I don't think Vincente ever understood middle class," said Minnelli set decorator Keogh Gleason, as quoted by McElhaney. "He . . . thought everybody dined with candles and a crystal chandelier." *Gigi* brought Minnelli an Academy Award for Best Director.

Minnelli had further hits with the downbeat drama *Some Came Running* (1958) and the musical *Bells Are Ringing* (1960), featuring Judy Holliday. But the more naturalistic film environment of the 1960s was inhospitable to the big budget musical, and Minnelli's output decreased. After several flops and unambitious films, he turned to the rising singer and actress Barbra Streisand for the musical *On a Clear Day You Can See Forever* (1970). Minnelli's career ended on an unhappy note with the musical *A Matter of Time,* starring his daughter Liza Minnelli. Minnelli disowned the final version of the film after it was heavily cut by studio executives.

Minnelli's third marriage, to Denise Gigante, was celebrated in 1960 but ended in divorce in 1971. He married Lee Anderson in 1971. Minnelli wrote an autobiography, *I Remember It Well,* in 1974, and at the end of his life he received several honors from the French government, including the Legion of Honor in 1986. He died on July 25 of that year in Beverly Hills, California, after a long battle with emphysema and pneumonia. A galaxy of stars attended his funeral, where Minnelli's wife, Lee, and daughter Liza were escorted by the then-chart-topping vocalist Michael Jackson.

Books

International Dictionary of Films and Filmmakers, Volume 2: Directors, 4th ed., St. James Press, 2000.

Minnelli, Vincente, with Hector Arce, *I Remember It Well,* Doubleday, 1974.

Naremore, James, *The Films of Vincente Minnelli,* Cambridge, 1993.

Vincente Minnelli: The Art of Entertainment, edited by Joe McElhaney, Wayne State University Press, 2008.

Periodicals

Globe & Mail (Toronto, Ontario, Canada), July 31, 1986, p. D4.

New York Times, July 26, 1986.

Online

"Minnelli, Vincente (1913–1986)," *glbtq: an encyclopedia of gay, lesbian, bisexual, transgender & queer culture,* http://www.glbtq.com/arts/minnelli_v.html (January 19, 2009).

"Vincente Minnelli," *All Movie Guide,* http://www.allmovie.com (January 18, 2009).

"Vincente Minnelli," *Senses of Cinema,* http://www.archive.sensesofcinema.com/contents/directors/04/minnelli.html (January 18, 2009).

"Vincente Minnelli," Turner Classic Movies, http://www.tcm.com/tcmdb/participant.jsp?spid=132580&apid=151450 (January 19, 2009).□

Paul Moody

The American inventor Paul Moody (1779–1831) provided much of the engineering ingenuity that made the Massachusetts textile industry the equal of any in the world in the early nineteenth century.

It was Francis Lowell and other entrepreneurs who conceived and built the massive brick mills that still dominate the landscape of northeastern Massachusetts today. Moody was not a businessperson or an executive. But it was he who designed some of the key machines that filled Lowell's mills, and he supervised the machine shops where the looms for the weaving rooms were built. In the words of John N. Ingham, writing in the *Biographical Dictionary of American Business Leaders*: "Although Moody was not an entrepreneur, it was his mechanical genius that was to a large degree responsible for the development of the cotton textile industry in the United States."

Took Weaving Job at 12

Paul Moody was born on May 21, 1779, in Byfield, in the town of Newbury in the northeastern corner of Massachusetts. The Moody family's roots in Massachusetts dated back to the early seventeenth century. Paul's father, Captain Paul Moody, had fought in the battle of Lexington in the Revolutionary War and rose to become a commander of a Newbury regiment. The younger Paul Moody had five (or six) older brothers who were all educated at the local Governor Dummer Academy. From the beginning, however, Paul preferred to make a living with this hands. At age 12 he got a job as a hand weaver at a woolen mill in the nearby town of Waltham.

For several years, Moody bounced from job to job—not because he had trouble holding down a position, but because he was hungry with curiosity about the various machines used in the factories where he worked, and was intent on understanding them for himself. He worked at the nail-making plant of one Jacob Perkins, and by 1800 he felt secure enough in his prospects to marry Susannah Morrill of Amesbury, Massachusetts; the couple had three sons. The Perkins nail plant moved to Amesbury the following year, and Moody followed, but then he moved to the firm of Kendrick and Worthen, which manufactured carding machines—machines that brush out raw fiber. Joining this company early in the new century, he remained there until 1812, accumulating more and more general knowledge of textile manufacturing operations.

That year, Moody and one Ezra Worthen went into business together manufacturing satinets—satins with an admixture of cotton—naming their new firm the Amesbury Wool and Cotton Manufacturing Company. In 1813, however, Moody was lured away after a visit by Francis Cabot Lowell, one of the great early visionaries of American industry. Lowell had visited cotton mills in England in 1810 and was determined not just to replicate them in America but to exceed their accomplishments. He hired the best equipment designers he could find (individuals who would now be called engineers), and chief among these was Moody. In 1814 Lowell formed the Boston Manufacturing Company, with headquarters in Waltham, Massachusetts. Moody's first task was to construct a machine shop where the new factory's equipment would be built.

Developed Power Loom

Moody remained at the Waltham plant for the next 11 years, and those years saw a revolution in the way cloth was manufactured, as well as deep changes in the social structure of New England, as young women began streaming from the region's small towns to work on what were essentially America's first assembly lines. Working from Lowell's ideas, Moody first developed a power loom that harnessed the water power of the region's streams, rivers, and later canals. Completed in the autumn of 1814 in Moody's machine shop in Waltham, the loom, in Ingham's words, "was to be the generating spark that brought the great Waltham textile industry to life."

The patent for the power loom went to Lowell and his partner, Patrick Tracy Jackson. Soon Moody's name began to be recorded as the inventor of devices that improved the efficiency of the Waltham plant and helped it compete with and often surpass its English counterparts. In 1816 he and Lowell visited a machinist in the town of Taunton, planning to purchase a device that would wind yarn on bobbins, or large spools. Just as Lowell was about to conclude the purchase, Moody took him aside and suggested that he could invent a machine that would spin yarn directly onto the bobbins, making the machine unnecessary. The so-called filling frame, which Moody perfected in 1819, was an entirely novel invention that drove down the cost of making cotton fabric.

Another Moody patent, granted in 1818, was for soap-stone rollers on a dressing machine. His most important innovations were the "double speeder," a moving or roving frame credited to Moody and Lowell, and the dead-spindle system of spinning, an improvement on the live-spindle devices in use in England and in Rhode Island. The double speeder was the subject of a lawsuit by another Waltham mechanic who felt his rights as inventor had been infringed upon, but a court found in Moody's favor. In his book, *Lowell as It Was, and as It Is,* the Rev. Adolphus Henry Miles noted that an expert witness named Bowditch "was afterward heard to say that seldom had his mind been more severely taxed, for the 'double speeder' required for its construction the greatest mathematical power of any piece of mechanism with which he had become acquainted."

Designed Device After Hearing Description

Another piece of equipment Moody contributed to the Waltham mill was a governor that regulated the speed at which the mill wheels turned, so that the entire mill apparatus would be powered consistently. The story of how that contribution came about, recounted by Miles, is indicative of Moody's personality. Lowell recalled having seen one in England, with "two iron balls, suspended on two rods, connected at one end like a pair of tongs." The balls, Lowell remembered, might be driven apart if the mill wheels turned too quickly, and would set in motion machinery that would close the mill's water gate (or open the gate if the flow was too slow).

Lowell suggested that the device be ordered from England, but, wrote Miles, "Mr. Moody, on his ride to Waltham, could not get those balls out of his mind. They were flying round in his brain the whole of that day and night. The next morning he went to the shop and chalked out the plan of some wheels, which he ordered to be made." Asking Lowell whether the order had been sent to England and learning

that it had not, he produced his model, which served as the basis for governors in use in Lowell into the 1830s.

In 1821 Moody was granted other patents connected with devices for spinning cotton and making cotton rope. In 1823 Lowell began building new mills in the city that now bears his name (it was then East Chelmsford), and Moody and other mechanics from his shop were transferred there to set up the new operation. The Waltham mill was compensated to the tune of $100,000 for the loss of their services. Moody built a new machine shop, the Lowell Machine Works, to supply the new mills, and he put in place the fundamentals for their revolutionary success. According to the National Park Service's online archive, "The shop underlay Lowell's textile industries: fabricating machines that turned cotton into cloth, building water-wheels, turbines, and steam engines that provided the power, and making shafts, gears, and pulleys that transferred power within the mill." It also supplied mills outside Massachusetts and produced early railroad locomotives.

Not much is known about Moody's life outside of the workplace. He was said to be a supporter of the temperance movement, and he was active in promoting public education. Moody did not live to share in the wealth that the Lowell mills created. Just as they were reaching full speed, he died in Lowell after a three-day illness, on July 8, 1831; he was 52 years old. "When the history of the progress of mechanical invention in this country shall be written," wrote Miles, "the name of Paul Moody will be honored as one of the chief men in this line of distinction."

Books

Dictionary of American Biography Base Set, American Council of Learned Societies, 1928–1936.

Ingham, John N., *Biographical Dictionary of American Business Leaders,* Greenwood, 1983.

Miles, Rev. Henry Adolphus, *Lowell as It Was, and as It Is,* Powers and Bagley, 1845.

Online

"The Lowell Machine Shop," National Park Service, http://www. nps.gov/archive/lowe/loweweb/Lowell_History/lowe_machine_ shop.htm (January 14, 2009). □

Henry Morgan

Welsh buccaneer Sir Henry Morgan (1635–1688) roamed the Caribbean Sea as a privateer of much ill fame before becoming the royally-sanctioned deputy governor of Jamaica. A controversial figure in his own day, Morgan gained and lost royal favor for his raids on Spanish-held cities throughout the Caribbean and Americas. One of the most successful and well-known buccaneers of the 17th century, Morgan remains an inspiration for contemporary films and literature.

Water: Captain Morgan's Great Pirate Army, the Epic Battle for the Americas, and the Catastrophe That Ended the Outlaws' Bloody Reign, learned several important lessons that would aid his later career: "how not to lead troops in the New World, how not to attack a fortified Spanish position, how not to enlist the local Indians to your cause, and how not to share power between commanders."

In Jamaica, Morgan joined the ranks of the privateers—royally-sanctioned pirates authorized to raid the ships of nations hostile to England—headquartered at the new English city of Port Royal. Morgan had already achieved the position of captain by the time of his first excursion as a privateer in 1661, a probable indication of his success in earlier conflicts. Under the command of Christopher Mings, Morgan participated in a successful raid on the Spanish-held city of Santiago, Cuba. This excursion was followed by another to San Francisco de Campeche. Soon, his success under Mings would encourage Morgan to strike out on his own.

By November 1663, Morgan was ready to lead his own expeditions. Still using Port Royal as a base of operations, the young privateer led four ships across the sea and attacked Villahermosa, Mexico. The successful raid turned sour when Morgan discovered that Spanish soldiers had captured his ships, effectively cutting off his means of return to Port Royal. Soon, however, the force managed to coerce a number of rude sailing vessels, and began pillaging along the coast, including a particularly profitable attack on the city of Gran Granada. Talty noted that this technique "would became an emblem of [Morgan's] expeditions: Always act as if you have the upper hand, even if you don't." By the time Morgan returned to Jamaica, his privateering skills were sharply honed and his reputation was growing on both sides of the Atlantic.

Shunned a Comfortable Retirement

During Morgan's absence, his uncle Edward Morgan had been appointed the Lieutenant Governor of Jamaica; Sir Thomas Modyford had become the island's new royal governor. Upon his return to the island in 1665, Morgan became enamored with Edward Morton's daughter, Mary Elizabeth, and the couple married probably sometime in the first half of the following year.

Morgan had become extremely wealthy as a result of his raids; Pope commented that "he could have left the sea after his brief encounter with it and . . . settled into the comfortable life of a prosperous Jamaica planter . . . [but] it was a way of life that did not seem to appeal to him." Indeed, Morgan soon held dual admiralties in both the Port Royal Militia—the body responsible for protecting the island of Jamaica from attack—and the Brethren of the Coast, the unofficial governing organization of the pirates working throughout the Spanish Main.

In late 1667, the privateer sent out a call for men to join a new expedition; by spring 1668, about 700 pirates had assembled near Cuba under Morgan's command. The buccaneers decided to attack the inland Cuban city of Puerto del Príncipe, previously untouched by buccaneers. Morgan and his men captured and looted the city, but discovered that their haul was less fruitful than anticipated. Grumblings appeared among the men, and the French members of the party withdrew from the expedition. Morgan, determined to

Although Henry Morgan's exact birth date and location remains unknown, baptismal records suggest that he was born in 1635. His birthplace is given alternately as Penkarne or Llanrhymney—both in Wales—and his father was probably Robert Morgan, a lesser relation of the influential Morgan family residing at Tredegar. Morgan grew up in what were likely modest surroundings in Wales, presumably hearing war stories about his mercenary uncles, Thomas and Edward; the latter was stationed near Morgan's family home and may have provided the young buccaneer with basic military training. Of formal schooling, Morgan completed little. Dudley Pope argued in *The Buccaneer King: The Biography of the Notorious Sir Henry Morgan, 1635–1688* that "from what we know of his personality in adulthood, Henry Morgan spent [his youth] thinking of very little else except war and soldiering."

In late 1654, Morgan joined an expedition of conquest to the West Indies as an ensign under the command of General Robert Venables and Vice-Admiral William Penn. The ship arrived at the British island of Barbados on January 29, 1655, and in April of that year continued on to attack the Spanish city of Santo Domingo on the island of Hispaniola. The invasion was a disaster, and a force much reduced by disease abandoned the attack, moving on to Jamaica. Even in its weakened state, the English army easily captured the poorly populated, mostly agricultural island in May 1655. Disease and a general lack of food and hygiene continued to wreak havoc on the men. Morgan survived this difficult period, and as Talty noted in *Empire of Blue*

raid another city and increase the profitability of the voyage—and, thus, protect his admiralty of the Brethren—roused his supporters and set off for a new target, this one larger and better protected than any that they had previously attacked: Portobelo, Panama.

What Morgan knew that the others did not was that the famed defenses of the city had been weakening for months. The Spanish soldiers protecting the city had not been paid and often left the city's defenses understaffed. Morgan and his men invaded the city, taking prisoners that became a human shield behind which the buccaneers crouched as they approached the nearer of Portobelo's two forts. Within 24 hours, Morgan controlled the city; in negotiations with the Spanish, he demanded a hefty ransom in exchange for leaving the city relatively unmolested. The pirate force left Portobelo encumbered by vast amounts of gold, silver, and slaves, and Morgan had effectively regained the trust and respect of his men.

Morgan's next major raid, on the city of Maracaibo, Venezuela came swiftly on the heels of the force's return to Port Royal. The residents of the city fled, leaving it open to the buccaneers. Morgan then moved on the city of Gibraltar, on the opposite side of Lake Maracaibo. There, the force found more treasure, but soon faced a serious problem: the Spanish, led by Don Alonzo, had learned of their presence and blocked the only route back to the open seas and Jamaica.

Quickly, Morgan devised a plan. Working at night, the buccaneers fitted up one of their ships with flammable materials, creating a fireship, and sent it hammering into Don Alonzo's man-of-war. Talty argued that "after this stunning reversal of fortune, [Morgan] became *the* buccaneer commander." Morgan and his men were still trapped, however—now back at Maracaibo—for Don Alonso had taken up a position in a castle from which he could fire on the buccaneer's ship if they attempted to sail away. The townspeople—more than ready to be rid of Mogran and his men—ransomed their city to the buccaneers and negotiated with the Spanish for their safe passage. After negotiations fell through, Morgan tricked Don Alonzo and managed to sail back to Port Royal, arriving in May 1669.

Destroyed Panama City

Political changes had altered the atmosphere of Port Royal during the buccaneers' absence. Morgan soon learned that the royal sanction that had legalized his attacks against Spanish settlements was gone. The following year, the tentative peace between the English and Spanish began to break down as the Spanish retaliated against the island of Jamaica for the attacks on their settlements. Morgan—in his role as leader of the Port Royal Militia—was empowered to protect the island against the Spanish by whatever means he deemed necessary. He gathered a massive force and set out in December 1670 to recapture Providence—an English settlement previously taken by the Spanish—and launch an attack on Panama City.

Days later, the buccaneers arrived at Providence, and after a bit of military theatrics, took the island. Morgan decided that the next stop was San Lorenzo, a fort at the mouth of the Chagres River. A buccaneer force overcame the Spanish resistance, and Morgan led the remainder of the fleet toward the site. Morgan and his forces, 1,500 strong, disembarked to travel along the Chagres River to Panama City.

The buccaneers met little resistance from the terrified Spaniards. The residents of the city, greatly intimidated by the numbers and ruthless reputation of the buccaneers, prepared for the onslaught. Before long, Morgan and his men had taken the city—but the city had been filled with powder kegs, and began burning down around the looting buccaneers. Despite this devastation, they remained at the ruined city for nearly a month, leaving on February 24, 1670. By that time, Morgan faced internal problems; the pirates had begun to believe that the treasure was not as rich as they had expected and agitate against Morgan's leadership.

The buccaneers returned to the mouth of the Chagres and there divided the spoils, learning that their fears of a relatively low take were accurate. The rank and file complained that Morgan had reserved the best treasure for himself, but this seems unlikely; the sheer number of men involved simply depressed the amount of treasure per person. Morgan had also begun to hear rumors of a peace treaty between England and Spain, leaving his recent actions against Panama City on doubtful legal ground. He sailed for Port Royal with no warning and only a fraction of his force.

Became Deputy Governor of Jamaica

By June 1670, news of the events at Panama City had reached Europe. The Spanish were shocked and angered; Talty commented "to the Spanish there was no possibility that the invasion could have gone ahead without approval at the very highest levels of English government." The English made diplomatic efforts, including issuing an order of arrest for Jamaican governor Modyford. Morgan became increasingly concerned as events unfolded; his concerns proved to be justified when an order for his own arrest arrived in Port Royal. He landed in London in August 1672 and found that the political winds had already begun turning in his favor. Rising tensions between England and the Netherlands gave Jamaica a new enemy, and the king eventually turned to Morgan for advice on how to protect the island. The king was so taken with the buccaneer that he named him deputy governor of Jamaica and even knighted him.

In 1676, Morgan returned to Jamaica as its second-in-command. He began strengthening Port Royal's defenses and, ironically, worked to eliminate piracy in Jamaica's waters. The feared and revered buccaneer transformed into an English bureaucrat. This shift is not as dramatic as it appears; throughout his career, Morgan saw himself as a loyal Englishman dedicated to the cause of king and country. He served as deputy governor until 1683.

Morgan became increasingly ill in later life, suffering from the effects of extended heavy drinking. After the best efforts of Jamaica's imported doctors, including forced vomiting, failed to improve Morgan's condition, he turned to native folk doctors with a similar lack of luck. Talty argued that "Morgan really needed . . . rest and a different lifestyle, but he refused to change." This refusal led to his death in Port Royal on August 25, 1688, at the age of 53.

So that all of Morgan's associates could pay their respects, Jamaica's governor offered a 24-hour amnesty to anyone attending the deceased buccaneer's funeral. Soon, a motley collection ranging from pirates to government officials began visiting the King's House, where Morgan's body lay in state. The funeral ceremony was held at St. Peter's Church, and Morgan received a 22-gun salute after he was interred at the Palisadoes cemetery, which—perhaps suitably—sank into the Caribbean Sea less than five years later as the result of an earthquake that devastated Port Royal.

Morgan's name and reputation have long survived the man himself. In fictionalized form, the buccaneer has appeared in numerous films, novels, and television programs, and his life has served as material for documentaries examining piracy. As long as people remain fascinated by tales of swashbucklers on the high seas, it seems certain that the legendary pirate will live on.

Books

Esquemeling, John, *The Buccaneers of America*, Dorset Press, 1987.

Pope, Dudley, *The Buccaneer King: The Biography of the Notorious Sir Henry Morgan, 1635–1688*, Dodd, Mead, & Company, 1977.

Talty, Stephen, *Empire of Blue Water: Captain Morgan's Great Pirate Army, the Epic Battle for the Americas, and the Catastrophe That Ended the Outlaws' Bloody Reign*, Crown, 2007. □

Moritake Arakida

Moritake Arakida (1473–1549) was the Japanese Shinto priest and poet credited with originating the *haikai* or 'comic linked-verse' style of Japanese poetry that eventually produced the loftier *haiku* style many readers are familiar with today.

M oritake Arakida was born in 1473, possibly in the city of Ise in the Mie prefecture, Japan, although there is no record in English as to the exact location of his birth. It is difficult to determine whether the drought of biographical information on Arakida is the result of a scarcity of sources, or simply a scarcity of sources in English. The late translator Kenneth Yasuda was an expert on Arakida, and his colleague, Professor Emerita Sumie Jones of Indiana University's East Asian Language and Culture and Comparative Literature departments, confirmed that there is likely no current text in English that offers comprehensive biographical details for this seasoned poet. An entry on Arakida in the *Encyclopedia of Shinto*—one of the few resources in English that has mentioned Arakida's heritage and non-poetic duties—related that he was a "member of the priesthood (*shinshoku*) of the Inner Shrine (Naiku) at the Grand Shrines of Ise (Ise Jingu) in the period of Warring Provinces (*sengoku*, ca. 1457–1568) . . . [and] the ninth son of Suppliant Priest (*negi*) Sonoda Morihide and

grandchild of famed author Fujinami Ujitsune (1402–1487)." Beyond these few facts, however, little information is readily available to scholars and other interested parties.

Poetic Metamorphosis

In order to understand Arakida's significance, one must first take a crash course in Japanese poetry—specifically the journey from *renga* to *haiku*. A forward to *The Classic Tradition of Haiku* explained the evolution of these Japanese poetic forms, beginning with "twelfth-century *renga* (literally 'linked songs' or 'linked verses'—the word for poem and song in Japanese is the same), an elegant literary pastime in which poets, singly or in groups, improvised connecting stanzas to create long poems of up to 10,000 verses." *Renga* was displaced in the sixteenth century, when "*haikai-no-renga* raged as a national fad. *Haikai,* from two words meaning 'sportive' and 'pleasantry,' meant unusual or offbeat and is translated (somewhat deceptively) as 'comic linked verse.'" It was this humorous and surprising poetic form that Arakida mastered and popularized, eventually prompting the *hokku*—*renga's* starting or opening verse—to become independent and be renamed *haiku* (*hai* unusual and *ku* verse) in the twentieth century.

As both a poet and a priest, Arakida split his time and energies between spiritual and literary pursuits. He studied *renga* with Iio Sogi (1421–1502), among others, and while he never became a prominent poet in that medium, an entry in *The Princeton Companion to Classical Japanese Literature* verified that his *haikai* sequence *Haikai no Renga Dokugin Senku* (*A Thousand-Stanza Solo Haikai Sequence*), better known today as *Moritake (Dokugin) Senku* (Moritake's Thousand-Stanza [Solo] Sequence), contributed immensely to the evolution of *haikai*.

An entry on *haikai* in the *Dictionary of Oriental Literature* defined it as a "Japanese poetic form . . . [with] unconventional diction or exaggerated, humorous treatment of conventional themes . . . [that] retained greater freedom, tolerating and even encouraging . . . an earthiness that might on occasion make even Chaucer blush." Its lack of literary posturing made it very popular with the masses, and the same entry reported how Arakida found himself pushing for "the acceptance of *haikai* as a genre independent from *renga*." Sharing this goal was poet Yamazaki Sokan (1465–c.1553), who believed that any insolence was permitted as long as it got a laugh, while Arakida held that the emphasis should remain on true wit and respectability. Sokan and Arakida have often shared the credit for popularizing and developing the *haikai* form, but the style, content, and tone of their work was drastically different, and for many years Sokan's more vulgar style remained more popular that Arakida's more refined works.

Final Days

Arakida, whose personal style was known as *Ise haikai*, was given the position of head priest of the Inner Ise Shrine when he was 69. He is noted for using his art to urge readers to preserve traditional morals, through works that were published in *Yo no naka hyakushu* (One Hundred Poems of the World), also known as *Ise rongo* (the Ise

Analects). He died in August of 1549 in Uji, Japan, at the age of 77, although sources have disagreed as to the exact day of his death.

Living Through Legacy

Over time, Arakida's importance has trickled through the ages to assert itself in multiple cultures. Teimon haikai, a school established by poet Matsunaga Teitoku (1571–1653), brought attention back to Arakida and his work. Arakida also inspired and influenced much later Japanese poets, such as *haiku* master Matsuo Basho (1644–1694), celebrated as a poetic innovator who helped revive the great traditions of poets like Arakida. The *haiku* is a stylistic descendant of the clever and comical linked verse established by Arakida, and Basho—a member of Nishiyama Soin's (1605–1682) Danrin school—pursued Arakida's ideals initially, but quickly focused on elevating the 17-syllable *haiku* to the serious art form it is today.

Arakida's influence even managed to cross oceans as well as cultures. His poem *Rakka eda ni* (A fallen petal), which features the image of a butterfly being mistaken for a fallen petal returning to its branch, inspired and informed American Modernist expatriate poet Ezra Pound's (1885–1972) essay *Vorticism* (1914), and made Arakida briefly famous in both Europe and America. Pound believed that Japanese literature could significantly stimulate English verse.

While there are scholarly arguments regarding exactly where and how Pound in particular was exposed to the Japanese mediums, other poets have borrowed Arakida's *Rakka eda ni* conceit time and again. American poet Amy Lowell's (1874–1925) two-line verse *Autumn Haze,* with a speaker who mistakes a maple leaf for a dragonfly, was a perfect example.

The Jingu History Museum of Ise's Outer Shrine houses a statue of Arakida, and a memorial to his spirit was preserved on his property sometime in the 1640s and later relocated at the Uji Jinja shrine. Hundreds of thousands of people still make a pilgrimage to *Ise Jingu* (the Grand Shrine of Ise) every new year, and Arakida's grave draws poets and readers alike, all wishing to pay homage to Arakida as the founder of *haiku.*

Books

Cassell's Encyclopaedia of World Literature, edited by S.H. Steinberg, Cassell and Company, 1953.

The Classic Tradition of Haiku, edited by Faubion Bowers, Dover Publications, 1996.

Dictionary of Oriental Literatures, edited by Jaroslav Prusek, Basic Books, 1974.

Encyclopedia of World Biography, Gale, 2004.

Keene, Donald, *World Within Walls,* Columbia University Press, 1999.

Miner, Earl, *Japanese Linked Poetry,* Princeton University Press, 1979.

Miner, Earl, Hiroko Odagiri, and Robert E. Morrell, *The Princeton Companion to Classical Japanese Literature,* Princeton University Press, 1985.

Periodicals

Harvard Journal of Asiatic Studies, June 1992.

The Mie Times, February/March 2007.

Monumenta Nipponica, Spring 1976.

Online

"Arakida Moritake," *Encyclopedia of Shinto,* http://www.themargins.net/bibliography.html (October 23, 2008).

"Arakida Moritake," *The Margins,* http://www.eos.kokugakuin.ac.jp/modules/xwords/entry.php?entryID=413 (October 23, 2008).

"Arakida Moritake," *The Samurai Archives,* http://www.wiki.samurai-archives.com/index.php?title=Arakida_Moritake (October 23, 2008).

"Kenneth Yasuda and Moritake Arakida," (e-mail from Indiana University professor Sumie Jones [joness@indiana.edu]) (November 4, 2008).□

Giorgio Moroder

The Italian producer and songwriter Giorgio Moroder (born 1940) has exerted a fundamental influence on the development of contemporary popular dance music.

The string of hits with which Moroder was associated in the late 1970s, many of them recordings he produced for vocalist Donna Summer, virtually defined the disco genre and pioneered a key role for digital electronics in popular music. Moroder has also been successful as a composer, notably of music for films, whose soundtracks have brought him three Academy Awards. Moroder was one of the first pop producers to create an extended remix of a song, and his influence has continued to resonate in trance music and other electronic genres.

Attended Art School

Giovanni Giorgio Moroder was born on April 26, 1940, in Ortisei, in northern Italy's Tyrol mountains. Moroder, who lived in Germany for many years, sometimes used a German variant of his name, Hansjörg Moroder; the area in which he grew up is marked by both Italian and German cultural influences. There were several creative artists in Moroder's family background, and he began his education at an art school in Ortisei. He moved on to attend high school in the regional capital of Bolzano. But his real interest lay with the guitar, which he first began to play at age 16 or 17. After graduating from school at 19, Moroder joined a dance band and began to travel around Europe as a musician.

Moroder played with a variety of bands in the 1960s, few of which lasted long. He has mentioned a performance at the luxurious Savoy Hotel in London, with a group called the Happy Trio, as a highlight of his early years in the music business. In 1967 he settled in Berlin, Germany, and began to work on songwriting seriously. Moroder took naturally to

the growing complexity of the recording studio of those days, and made a few demo recordings of his own. In 1969 he released a single called "Looky, Looky," and he produced a German-language hit by vocalist Ricky Shayne called "Ich springe alle Ketten" (I Break All the Chains).

In the early 1970s Moroder moved his base of operations to Munich, Germany, although he continued to divide his time between Munich, Berlin, and his home country. In Munich he established the Musicland studio, whose clients included the Rolling Stones and Led Zeppelin. In 1972, as Giorgio (or Giorgio & Friends in the United States), Moroder recorded an album of his own called *Son of My Father*. The album's title track was a minor hit and was covered by the British band Chicory Tip. It was around this time that Moroder met British songwriter Pete Bellotte, and the two began to work as a songwriting team.

The pair hired American vocalist Donna Summer as a singer for the demos they pitched to various groups, and creative musical chemistry began to develop between Moroder and Summer, who had also lived for several years in Germany and spoke the language well. For a Dutch label they recorded the 1974 album *Lady in the Night* (which Bellotte produced, but for which Moroder was the lead songwriter on most of the tracks), which reached high chart levels in several European countries. In early 1975, Moroder and Summer together devised the composition that would make them both famous. Moroder had been listening to the breathy 1969 French duet "Je t'aime . . . moi non plus" by Serge Gainsbourg and Jane Birkin, and had

the idea of trying to write a song in the same vein. He asked Summer to think of a hook, and she suggested "I love to love you," which Moroder and Bellotte extended into a standard three-and-a-half-minute single, "Love to Love You Baby." According to Summer, and quoted by Ben Sisario on the *Blender* Web site, Casablanca Records president Neil Bogart listened to the song as if it were in the context of a sexual encounter and reported back: "You know what? I wish I could have a good 20 minutes of this song."

Pioneered Extended Remix

Bringing the session musicians back into the studio—for digital sequencing was not yet in common use—Moroder reworked the original material and added new variations to create a 17-minute version of the song. In so doing, Sisario noted, Moroder "virtually invented the extended remix," which became a staple of popular dance music. The remix actually had various antecedents, including the dub genre of Jamaican music, but Moroder's production was pioneering in other respects as well: the song's percussive use of wah-wah guitar and heavy bass line marked a milestone in the development of what would soon be called disco music. Moroder also set the mood for Summer to produce the 23 simulated orgasms that became the song's most notorious feature: he had her lie down alone in a darkened studio, whereupon he recalled to Sisario, she nailed the 17-minute track "in one take."

The sexual nature of "Love to Love You Baby" resulted in a ban by the British Broadcasting Corporation, condemnation in the United States from the Rev. Jesse Jackson, and in general a level of controversy that boosted sales and made the song a standard in clubs where disco was growing, such as New York's Studio 54. Moroder continued to experiment, producing further important innovations and another major hit in 1977 with Summer's "I Feel Love" (from the album *I Remember Yesterday*), which the *New Musical Express* Web site called "an electronic production masterpiece, especially considering the technology available at the time." In the words of James Rotondi, writing in *Remix*, the song's "almost purely electronic soundscapes and motorlike beats make 'Love to Love You Baby' sound downright organic by comparison. If trance and house have a proper antecedent on the continent that loves them most—besides Kraftwerk—it's clearly Moroder."

Under Moroder's guidance, Summer became the reigning queen of disco in the late 1970s, issuing albums at a rate of up to two per year. Among her other hits was the Bellotte–penned "Hot Stuff," from the 1979 double album *Bad Girls*. That year marked disco's high-water mark, but Moroder made an effective turn back to rock styles on his final album with Summer, *The Wanderer* (1980). He produced several of the rock-oriented numbers that became ubiquitous in dance clubs in the early 1980s, including Blondie's "Call Me" (1982, which he also co-wrote).

Penned Film Scores

Meanwhile, Moroder continued to pursue his own songwriting and recording projects. His 1979 album *E=MC2*, according to *New Musical Express*, was the first in history to be recorded live to a digital medium. The soundtrack medium, with its mix of song and musical atmospherics, was ideally suited to Moroder's talents as a composer, and during his heyday he received the most recognition from his industry peers for his film scores rather than for his production work. Moroder earned three Academy Awards for his film scores, beginning with *Midnight Express* in 1978. He also scored or contributed songs to *The Never Ending Story, American Gigolo, Scarface,* and several other songs. He scored three more major hits in the mid-1980s with songs that appeared in films, receiving Academy Awards in 1983 for *Flashdance* and in 1986 for *Top Gun.*

By that time, Moroder's decade of contributions to the pop mainstream was drawing to a close, and he was devoting himself more often to a remarkable variety of personal interests. In 1984 he composed a controversial new score to the German silent film *Metropolis* that, in contrast to earlier silent film scores, featured pop and electronic elements. He ventured into automotive design, working with Claudio Zampolli and Marcello Gandini on a 16-cylinder, $600,000 Italian sports car called the Cizeta Moroder Super Sport, which won first prize at the Philadelphia Design Contest. In the 1990s Moroder worked as a visual artist, experimenting with digital media in paintings and videos that were exhibited in Germany, England, and the United States. One of his short films took a pair of first prizes at the Palm Springs Film Festival in 1993.

Moroder continued to keep a hand in music, issuing albums of his own while reuniting with Summer as producer and earning a Grammy Award for the 1997 track "Carry On." His influence resonated in the trance and Hi-NRG genres, and, in Rotondi's words, "anywhere a quarter-note disco pulse meets a snippet of Rhodes piano, a swirling synth-string section and a big Jupiter-esque sequenced bass throb." Various remixes of his own recordings have appeared, and he has produced a stage version of *Flashdance.*

Books

Contemporary Musicians, volume 63, Gale, 2008.

Periodicals

Billboard, February 19, 2000, p. 31.

Remix, September 1, 2002.

Online

"Giorgio Moroder Biography," *All Music Guide,* http://www.allmusic.com (January 23, 2009).

"Giorgio Moroder Biography," *New Musical Express,* http://www.nme.com/artists/giorgio-moroder (January 23, 2009).

Giorgio Moroder Official Web site, http://www.giorgiomoroder.com/bio/m_bio.html (January 23, 2009).

"Giorgio Moroder: Short Biography," Discog.Info, http://www.discog.info/moroder-bio.html (January 23, 2009).

Sisario, Ben, "The Greatest Songs Ever!: Love to Love You Baby," *Blender,* December 2006, http://www.blender.com/guide/articles.aspx?id=2209 (January 23, 2009). □

N

Antonín Novotný

Czechoslovakian politician Antonín Novotný (1904–1975) ruled his nation ruthlessly during some of the most perilous years of the Cold War. As head of Czechoslovakia's Communist Party from 1953 to 1968, he kept the organization and the country firmly allied with the Soviet Union—to the dismay of many Czechs and Slovaks who considered their lands to be part of the Western European family of nations. So firm was Novotný's grip that it actually sparked a movement within the party itself to oust him from power, and the success of that launched a brief, but brutally suppressed period of democratic reform in 1968 known as the Prague Spring.

Novotný was born on December 10, 1904, in Letňany, which later became part of the city of Prague. At the time of his birth, Prague was one of the regional capitals of the Austro-Hungarian Empire, which held control over a wide swath of Central Europe. Novotný's mother died when he was four years old. His father was a bricklayer and belonged to the Czech Social Democratic Party, which Novotný also joined as a young man. When World War I ended in 1918, the losing Austro-Hungarian Empire was dissolved and its constituent republics were granted full independence. The Czechs shared a similar language to their neighbors to the east, the Slovaks, and so both were united into the new nation of Czechoslovakia. Tomáš G. Masaryk, the leader of the Czech independence movement, became the nation's first president.

Co-Founded Czechoslovakian Communist Party

As a young man, Novotný trained as a machinist and worked as a locksmith and metalworker. He became one of the founding members of Czechoslovakia's Communist Party, the Komunistická strana Československa, or KSČ, in 1921 when an ideological split occurred within the Social Democratic Party. Rising through the KSČ ranks, he eventually became a full-time party functionary and is known to have served as a delegate to the Seventh Congress of the Communist International, or Comintern, held in Moscow in 1935. The Comintern was the Soviet Union's international-outreach effort that urged other native Communist parties to foment revolution on their own soil.

By 1937, Novotný had risen to become head of the Prague branch of the KSČ, and was soon deployed in the Czech province of Moravia to run the party organization there. In September of 1938, a historically German area of western Czechoslovakia was invaded by Nazi Germany, and six months later the entire country capitulated to Nazi forces. With that event, the KSČ and other political opposition parties of the left were outlawed.

Novotný and others were forced to go underground, where they worked to undermine Nazi rule. Within six months, German troops had invaded neighboring Poland, an act that formally began World War II. Novotný's activities came to the attention of the Gestapo, or secret police unit of the Nazi occupation government, and he was arrested in September of 1941 and sent to the Mauthausen-Gusen concentration camp in Austria.

Survived Nazi Labor Camp

Mauthausen was actually a series of several linked camps established by Nazi Germany for slave labor purposes, and its principal detainees were those whom the Nazis classified

several non-KSČ members of the cabinet resigned as a protest move, hoping to force new elections. The KSČ, meanwhile, had installed a few of its members in key police and security posts. The country's internationally respected foreign minister was Jan Masaryk, son of Czechoslovakia's founder, who sought to position the new Czechoslovakia as a bridge between the Soviets and the West. On March 10, 1948, Masaryk's body was found in the courtyard of Czernin Palace, part of the Hradčany Castle, which housed government offices and official residences. His death was ruled a suicide.

Became Party Chief

KSČ leaders consolidated power over the next five years, and Novotný played a crucial role in the tightening of the Czechoslovak-Soviet alliance. He became a member of the Politburo after the ouster of two KSČ members who voiced objections to KSČ policy; Novotný replaced Rudolf Slánský, who was accused of spying for the United States and executed in 1952. When Klement Gottwald, the longtime KSČ leader, died of heart disease in 1953, Novotný became First Secretary of the party. The country's nominal president was another Communist, Antonín Zápotocky, but when he died of a heart attack in office in 1957, Novotný succeeded him in that post, too. He was "re-elected" by the vote of KSČ-filled National Assembly in November of 1964.

Novotný ruled both the party and the nation with a ruthlessness that characterized—and in few instances even exceeded—his fellow pro-Soviet native Communist leaders in neighboring Eastern Bloc countries during this era. He even followed the lead of Moscow when, in 1956, Soviet premier Nikita Khrushchev denounced the excesses of the Stalin era. Novotný was present at that Twentieth Party Congress when Khrushchev made his famous announcement deriding the cult of personality that Stalin had fostered.

Back in Prague, Novotný dutifully made a similar denunciation of the late Gottwald, claiming that the KSČ had wrongfully given his former mentor credit for "merits that belonged to the Party and to the masses," according to a *New York Times* article from 1961. He accrued new foes within his party for this transgression, but also had a powerful protector. "Novotny's relationship with Khrushchev was particularly close," noted the *Times* of London, "and this helped him to survive the various attacks on 'Stalinism' which in Czechoslovakia were frequently veiled attempts to undermine the position of Novotny and the system of arbitrary power which he personified."

Ruled by Fear

The Eastern Bloc was a secretive place during the Cold War era, but foreign-policy experts in the West believed there was strong opposition within the KSČ to Novotný. One enemy was believed to be Rudolf Barak, a Politburo member who may have tried to stage an internal coup within the KSČ in the early 1960s as the country's economic troubles worsened. Barak was ousted from his post, and then tried and convicted on charges of embezzlement of public funds. Even small steps hinting at potential reform in the state-controlled media in Czechoslovakia were ruthlessly suppressed. "We have always denied the independence of

as enemies of the Reich. Among them were known Communists and members of socialist organizations as well as homosexuals and Romany, or gypsies. Novotný survived his four years in Mauthausen by becoming a *kapo,* or a prisoner given special privileges by camp guards for maintaining control of their barrack or work unit. The camp was liberated by U.S. troops on May 5, 1945, in the final days of World War II. Novotný returned to Czechoslovakia, which was now occupied by Soviet troops, and rejoined the newly reestablished KSČ.

Even before the defeat of Nazi Germany by combined Allied forces of the United States, Britain, and the Soviet Union, Soviet leader Josef Stalin and his U.S. and British counterparts had formulated a plan for temporarily dividing up the map of Europe. This was agreed upon to help restore all Nazi-occupied countries to their former sovereign states, but after 1945 the Soviets and the West worked to install regimes friendly to each of their respective political ideologies. Thus places like France, Denmark, and the Netherlands saw a rather speedy return to parliamentary democracies, but the Soviet-occupied lands of Eastern Europe fell into the hands of Communist organizations.

In 1946, Novotný returned to his former post as head of the Prague region of the KSČ, and was also given a post on its Central Committee. In the first years following the war, a coalition government called the National Front ruled the newly liberated Czechoslovakia, and the KSČ was one of the six member parties. Disagreements arose within the National Front over foreign policy, and in February of 1948

the press from the party and its ideas and we definitely deny it still,'' Novotný once bluntly stated, according to the *New York Times*. ''Although we are concerned with the liveliness and the fascination of the contents of our papers, we are still more concerned with their party position, with their Communist firmness and clarity.''

A postwar baby boom occurred in the Eastern European nations, much like in the United States, and *New York Times Magazine* writer Richard Eder visited Prague in the fall of 1967 and reported that throngs of teenagers crowded the streets each evening sporting jeans, mini-skirts, and other styles habitually derided by the KSČ as evidence of Western decadence. Eder cited some economic reforms over the past few years to which Novotný had apparently conceded, and found an increasing liberalization in the press, which was tentatively expressing dissenting opinions to KSČ dogma. Weeks later, Eder's newspaper reported that Novotný appeared to be in the midst of a genuine power struggle within the party. In early December, Soviet leader Leonid Brezhnev made an unexpected visit to Prague to meet with high-ranking KSČ officials in closed-door sessions.

Brezhnev's efforts backfired. In January of 1968, Novotný submitted his resignation as head of the KSČ. His successor was a known reformer named Alexander Dubček, who had until then headed the Slovak branch of the party. Under Dubček, the Slovak half of the nation began to move toward a less-censored press, and the movement quickly spiraled out of control. In early March, several regional party congresses were convened, and opposition to Novotný remaining in the president's office became evident. ''In a major departure from tradition, most of the party meetings held secret ballots and elected new slates of officers for the party units involved,'' noted Harry Schwartz, a *New York Times* correspondent. ''Actual secret elections have been a rare occurrence in Czechoslovak political life during the last two decades.''

Ousted from Posts, Party

That same weekend, a celebration at a cemetery near Prague marking the 20th anniversary of the death of the younger Masaryk turned into a major protest event. Within days, both the Czechoslovak National Assembly as well as the KSČ-controlled Central Council on Trade Unions signed off on a letter urging Novotný to step down as president, too, which he did on March 22, 1968. In June, he was expelled from the party he had helped found nearly 50 years earlier.

Dubček's reforms lasted just five months. On the night of August 20, 1968, Soviet troops and tanks invaded Czechoslovakia from the east, along with significant numbers of military personnel from Poland, East Germany, and other Eastern Bloc countries. Moscow sent advisors to return the KSČ to the correct Marxist-Leninist path, and no other major opposition effort ever occurred in Eastern Europe until August of 1989. The loss of those satellite nations over that summer and fall of 1989, along with the breaching of the Berlin Wall, finally brought down the Soviet Union exactly two years later in August of 1991.

Novotný never lived to see Czechoslovakia rejoin the West. Though he was reinstated to the KSČ in 1971, his health had declined, and he played no further role in the Communist regime of the man who succeeded Dubček, the hardliner Gustáve Husák. Novotný died in Prague on January 28, 1975, at the age 70, probably from a blocked artery caused by an earlier heart attack. He was married and had one son, Antonin Jr., who headed a major book-exporting firm during his father's peak years of power. During the Prague Spring of 1968, the younger Novotný was pilloried as a symbol of the excesses of the party elite because of his wealthy lifestyle.

Periodicals

New York Times, November 20, 1957, p. 1; November 22, 1961, p. 3; November 13, 1964, p. 8; December 20, 1967, p. 1; March 11, 1968, p. 2; March 13, 1968, p. 2; March 23, 1968, p. 1; January 29, 1975, p. 29.

New York Times Magazine, November 12, 1967, p. 265.

Times (London, England), January 29, 1975, p. 19.□

O

Nuala O'Faolain

Irish journalist and author Nuala O'Faolain (1940–2008) rose to literary prominence after the publication of the acclaimed *Are You Somebody? The Accidental Memoir of a Dublin Woman* in 1996. This memoir, with its unflinching description of a troubled childhood and lifelong struggles with loneliness, struck a chord on both sides of the Atlantic. In both her writing and her lifestyle—the bisexual O'Faolain never married or had children—the writer challenged the traditional Irish society of her youth. O'Faolain's shift to full-time authorship in the later years of her life also produced a second memoir, a successful first novel, and a respected biography.

Grew Up Among Books and Bitterness

The second of nine children, Nuala O'Faolain was born on March 1, 1940, in Dublin, Ireland. Her father, author and journalist Tomas O'Faolain, wrote a gossip column for the *Dublin Evening Press* using the pseudonym Terry O'Sullivan and was frequently absent from the family home; her mother, Catherine O'Faolain, was desperately unhappy in her marriage and spent much of her time pregnant, reading, and growing increasingly dependent on alcohol. Most of O'Faolain's childhood was spent in the countryside around Dublin, where according to *The Guardian* she "followed a familiar path of waywardness, academic brilliance and books." From a young age, O'Faolain honed her observation skills by people watching in the streets of Dublin on family trips to visit her grandmother in the city

and developed a love of reading inspired by her mother's near-dependence on the written word as a form of protection from the outside world.

At the age of fourteen, O'Faolain enrolled at St. Louis's Convent boarding school in County Monaghan, a drastic departure from her Dublin-area explorations with dancing, smoking, and boys. After completing her education three years later, O'Faolain returned to Dublin, where she won a scholarship to University College Dublin. There, she studied English but soon dropped out and moved to London, taking a job as a menial hospital worker. She later returned both to Dublin and to University College. At loose ends upon completing her English degree, O'Faolain pursued a scholarship program in Medieval Literature at the University of Hull in Yorkshire, England. By the winter of 1961, O'Faolain had entered Hull, although she found herself ill-suited to scholarly life; writing in *Are You Somebody?*, she commented that "I was no scholar. I began to wither....I had wanted to try to be independent. But I couldn't stand the loneliness." She remained at Hull for only a year before returning to Dublin hoping to win a major Irish scholarship that would afford her the opportunity to study elsewhere, and perhaps, to marry a man with whom she had a long-standing relationship. Although the marriage was not to be, the scholarship was, and O'Faolain entered Oxford University to pursue post-graduate studies at the age of 23.

Had Early Career in Academia

Her studies at Oxford completed, O'Faolain took a job in Dublin with the English department of University College. She became acquainted with writers and artists of the day—including fiction writer Mary Lavin and film producer Jon Huston—but found that Dublin's literary circles of the

1960s, then closely tied to Dublin's pubs, had little respect for women as writers or intellectuals. For a time, O'Faolain was engaged, but at the last minute called off the wedding in the face of her family's disapproval.

In Dublin, O'Faolain taught both regular courses at University College and night courses at the People's College; this latter role provided a natural segue to a position she took in 1970 with the BBC producing television content to support Great Britain's new distance learning-based Open University. In this role, she relocated to London and traveled extensively, including a visit to Iran to help with the establishment of a similarly open university in that country. At the BBC, O'Faolain was also active in a special production unit allowing average Britons the opportunity to make television programs. Throughout this period of her life, O'Faolain was romantically attached to English writer and art critic Tim Hilton; O'Faolain had always felt a certain ambivalence toward England due to what she believed to be an abundance of classism and snobbery in English society, and her relationship with Hilton held no exception to this internal struggle.

Found Success as Producer and Columnist

In 1977, O'Faolain returned to Dublin and began working for Radio Telefis Eireann (RTE), Ireland's public broadcaster. Her work at RTE reflected a growing national interest in programming dedicated to the dual causes of feminism and women's issues, often described from the perspective of ordinary Irish women. Writing in *Are You Somebody?*, O'Faolain declared that she "did pioneering pieces on incest, prostitution, abortion, women's pay and employment, contemplative nuns, health issues, Unionist women and their views on Southern women, the fall-out within their families of the activities of "supergrasses" both loyalist and republican... world issues for women, the Hormone Replacement Therapy debate, how to run a 10k race, where in Ireland there are the most unmarried men... and so on. It was serious, and it was fun."

In some ways, O'Faolain found her return to Ireland to be a relief. The rising violence linked to the Irish republican movement of the 1970s had caused her to feel somewhat ill at ease in England, as tensions between Irish and English grew across the board. Despite this relief and her success at RTE, O'Faolain continued to face personal problems. In *Publisher's Weekly*, Yvonne Nolan commented that by the late 1970s, O'Faolain "was a broken woman, drinking too heavily and finally seeking treatment for alcoholism." In 1979, O'Faolain became pregnant and had a miscarriage; ultimately, she remained childless throughout her life, a state which she both embraced and regretted.

Soon, O'Faolain began a life-defining relationship with civil rights activist and journalist Nell McCafferty. This relationship lasted for nearly 15 years, and helped O'Faolain regain control of herself both physically and emotionally. The 1980s proved to be a pivotal decade for O'Faolain; her work as a producer and, after 1986, a weekly columnist at the *Irish Times* propelled her to fame throughout Ireland. O'Faolain's television series *Plain Tales*, a collection of interviews of everyday Irish women, garnered her a Jacob's

Award, Ireland's highest television honor, in 1985. The following year, she joined the staff of the *Irish Times,* and it was in this role that O'Faolain began to develop her voice as a writer. As with her television work, O'Faolain's newspaper columns often addressed issues rarely spoken of in contemporary Irish society, bringing such diverse topics as divorce—legalized in Ireland only in the 1990s—and Dublin's first gay bed and breakfast to a widespread audience.

Experienced Later Literary Fame

A planned collection of some of these columns led to the writing of the work that defined the remainder of O'Faolain's career: the autobiographical *Are You Somebody? The Accidental Memoir of a Dublin Woman.* Initially conceived as an introduction to a collection of previously published pieces, the memoir grew quickly into a full-length work and was published with only a short print run in 1996. The memoir caught the attention of the Irish public and was printed on a wider scale before becoming a bestseller in both England and the United States. A brutally honest retelling of her life, *Are You Somebody?* laid bare O'Faolain's difficult childhood, complicated personal relationships, and reliance on alcohol as well as the writer's internal struggles with herself as a middle-aged Irish woman. O'Faolain later commented in *The Writer* that "I was only able to be so candid because I thought nobody would ever read it." The success of this memoir catapulted O'Faolain to literary stardom.

In 1999, O'Faolain received a residency at the Yaddo artists' colony in Saratoga Springs, New York. Although she had not originally intended to remain in New York after completing her stay at Yaddo, the fruits of her residency—the beginnings of a novel—led to a contract with Riverhead Books and an extended stay in New York City. Three months later, O'Faolain had written her first novel, *My Dream of You,* published to great critical and popular success in 2001. Writing in the *New York Times,* Catherine Lockerbie argued that "the real virtues of *My Dream of You* are... entirely traditional: they lie in involving storytelling and in the depiction of a vivid and warm cast of characters, people about whom it is possible to care."

O'Faolain soon returned to the familiar territory of autobiography, documenting the unexpected success of *Are You Somebody?* and her familial and personal relationships in *Almost There: The Onward Journey of a Dublin Woman,* published in 2003. Like its predecessor, *Almost There* became an international bestseller and earned O'Faolain critical acclaim. *Contemporary Authors Online* quoted a *Women's Review of Books* article on this second memoir as claiming that "O'Faolain's delineation of loneliness, wrenching in *Are You Somebody?*, reappears here, raw as a wound, in words as starkly beautiful as a stripped bone."

O'Faolain's final published book, *The Story of Chicago May,* appeared in 2005. This non-fiction piece gave the biography of a late 1800s Irish-American prostitute and became O'Faolain's most decorated literary work, earning the author the French literary Prix Femina Etranger in 2006. That same year, the writer received an honorary doctorate from Great Britain's Open University, with which she had herself worked three decades previously.

A Public Death

Around the beginning of April 2008, O'Faolain was diagnosed with metastatic cancer: the disease had begun in her lungs and spread to her brain and liver. She chose to forego chemotherapy, a treatment which would not have cured the disease but could have prolonged her lifespan. Regretfully, O'Faolain left New York City for Ireland, where she lived out her few remaining days.

Having bared her life to the public eye through her two memoirs, O'Faolain—perhaps unsurprisingly—gave a tear-filled interview about her battle with the illness and her approaching death in April 2008 with Irish radio station RTE and printed in *The Independent,* commenting that "even if I gained time through the chemotherapy it isn't time I want. Because as soon as I knew I was going to die soon, the goodness went out of life." *The Guardian* later described the impact of this interview by noting that "even in Ireland, where death is readily acknowledged, the interview sparked a remarkable public reaction because of the searing honesty and total lack of sentimentality."

Just a few weeks after her RTE interview, O'Faolain died in Dublin during the night of May 9, 2008, as a result of her illness. She was 68 years old. Writing in the *New York Times* shortly after O'Faolain's death, Maura J. Casey stated that "although [O'Faolain's] mortal life has ended, her words, her sympathy and insights, are here. Even if, at the end, she could find little to believe in, her writing helped her legions of readers believe in her and in the validity of their own experiences." O'Faolain herself passed judgment on her life in *Almost There,* commenting that "the truth is that my life has always been a mixture—I have sunk low, but I hung on; I do get lost, but I find my way back. I plainly do know things even though I think I don't." Despite this somewhat optimistic summation, O'Faolain struggled throughout her life with feelings of loneliness and failure, two emotions which informed her writing and in some ways defined her actions. Regardless of her own beliefs, O'Faolain's forthright literary self-examination and strong voice seem likely to guarantee her legacy as a memoirist and storyteller for years to come.

Books

Contemporary Authors, Gale, 2008.

O'Faolain, Nuala, *Almost There: The Onward Journey of a Dublin Woman,* Holt, 1998.

O'Faolain, Nuala, *Are You Somebody? The Accidental Memoir of a Dublin Woman,* Holt, 1998.

Periodicals

The Guardian, May 12, 2008.

New York Times, March 4, 2001; May 11, 2008; May 13, 2008.

Publishers Weekly, March 12, 2001.

The Writer, February 2002. □

Hermann Oberth

In 1923, Romanian-born rocket scientist Hermann Oberth (1894–1989) published his groundbreaking work *By Rocket to Interplanetary Space.* The book helped popularize the idea of building rockets for space exploration. Oberth is also credited with coining the term "space station."

Hermann Julius Oberth was born June 25, 1894, in Transylvania, which at the time was part of the Austro-Hungarian empire. Following World War I, the area was ceded to Romania. Oberth's parents were Julius and Valerie Krasser Oberth. His father was a doctor. As a child, Oberth lived in Schässburg, a small village in Transylvania that lacked modern conveniences. Growing up, Oberth lived without electricity and telephones yet was able to envision a truly modern future where people would orbit the earth and live on space stations.

Dreamed of Space Travel

At the age of 11, Oberth read *From the Earth to the Moon,* a science-fantasy novel by French author Jules Verne. The book tells the tale of a group of U.S. Civil War veterans who become obsessed with the idea of creating a large cannon for the purpose of launching themselves to the moon. The idea captivated Oberth. He re-read the book so many times he nearly had it memorized. In the book, Verne described Sir Isaac Newton's laws of motion, prompting the young Oberth to conduct experiments examining those laws. With the help of his physics teacher, Oberth began to explore the mathematics of putting a person in space. He also built a model of the rocket-blaster Verne described in the book.

Throughout his teen years, Oberth continued to ponder the idea of spaceflight. He wondered how weightlessness might affect humans. To answer this question, he conducted experiments at the swimming pool. Despite his interest in mathematics and physics, Oberth entered Germany's University of Munich in the fall of 1913 to study medicine. Oberth's father insisted that his oldest son follow in his footsteps.

Ideas Rejected

In 1914, with the eruption of World War I, Oberth left school to serve with the Austro-Hungarian army. Injured in the line of duty, Oberth ended up in a field ambulance unit. In the book *To A Distant Day,* author Chris Gainor references a conversation of Oberth's in which he declared how fortunate he was to have landed in the medical unit. "This was a piece of good luck, for it was here that I found that I should probably not have made a good doctor."

Serving in the ambulance unit afforded Oberth some free time to develop more theories on spaceflight and rockets. He drew up plans for an 82-foot-long explosives-carrying rocket. Oberth believed such a weapon might

could carry people to distant worlds. He visualized a space station that could be supplied by smaller rockets and suggested it be made to rotate slowly so as to mimic gravity for the crew. He discussed the shape a rocket should be to limit drag and theorized about the optimal angle of trajectory.

In the book, Oberth hypothesized that space travelers would need to lie down during a launch because the force of gravity would be too great to withstand otherwise—NASA later adapted this strategy. Oberth told about special ''diving suits'' people might wear so they could take a spacewalk. He envisioned that some day in the future, there might even be a flying ship that could lift off like a rocket, dock with a space station and come back to earth. He suggested that telescopes could be placed into orbit to provide data about the solar system.

The book's first printing quickly sold out. Almost immediately, scientific journals began carrying articles refuting Oberth's ideas. Oberth's proposed rocket was a recoil rocket, meaning it was propelled through space by spewing out liquid-fuel exhaust gases from its base. Several scientists dismissed this idea, believing that a rocket would not work in the vacuum of space with no air to push against. According to an article by Marsha Freeman in *World & I,* one mathematician printed a response to Oberth that read, ''It will not be possible to travel around in space because of the enormous wear on material. We think that the time has not yet come to deal with this problem, and probably it will never arrive.''

Inspired Space Enthusiasts

Just as Verne's science-fiction book inspired Oberth to look toward the skies, Oberth's scientific book inspired a new generation to fantasize about spaceflight. Impressed with Oberth's vision, Austrian writer Max Valier published *Der Vorstoss in der Weltenraum* (*A Dash Into Space*). This nontechnical book, written for the lay reader, successfully spread Oberth's ideas to the masses.

Small clubs for space enthusiasts popped up across Europe, including the German-based Verein für Raumschiffahrt, or VfR, which stood for the Society for Space Travel. Founded in 1927, the group's mission was to entice the public's interest in spaceflight and raise money to fund experiments based on Oberth's ideas. The group published a journal, *Die Rakete,* to disburse information among all of the amateur rocket and space societies in Europe. By 1929, the VfR had 1,000 members.

Valier joined the group, as did Oberth. One of the society's first projects included experimenting with rockets to propel vehicles on the ground. Working with Fritz von Opel—of the German automobile manufacturer Opel—they built a rocket-powered car. Meanwhile, Oberth had earned his teaching certificate and was working as a teacher to support his family.

Worked on Rockets

In 1928, German film director Fritz Lang lured Oberth to Berlin to help produce a movie on space travel for the Ufa Film Co. Called *Frau im Mond,* or *Woman in the Moon,* the

help end the war. He showed the designs to German officials who dismissed him as a dreamer.

The war ended in 1918 and Oberth married Mathilde Hummel, who was also from Schässburg. They had four children. Oberth returned to the University of Munich to finish his degree, having persuaded his father to let him study aerodynamics and physics. He transferred to Göttingen University and later, the University of Heidelberg.

In 1922, Oberth presented his thesis on astronautical engineering to the faculty at the University of Heidelberg. They refused, however, to award Oberth his doctorate because they thought the thesis was more visionary than scientific. To the professors, his ideas seemed sketchy, though they were backed by mathematical theorems. Part of the problem was that no one knew anything about his science.

Published Diatribe on Rockets, Spaceflight

Knowing his work was sound, Oberth decided to publish his ideas about spaceflight. For the scientific community, he wanted to include the mathematics he had worked out concerning rocketry. Oberth knew this would limit readership so he included sections describing the fantastic possibilities of space exploration, hoping to reach a broader audience. Published in 1923, *Die Rakete zu den Planetenräumen* (*By Rocket to Interplanetary Space*) created a buzz in Europe.

While the book contained sophisticated mathematical proofs and a discussion of two-stage liquid-fuel rockets, it was also visionary in nature. He proposed spacecrafts that

movie was about four men, a woman and a boy who rocket to the moon. Oberth was asked to serve as a technical consultant. In addition, the film company asked Oberth to build a liquid-fueled rocket from scratch—a rocket that could be launched at the film's debut. Oberth agreed to the project because he thought it might help him secure future funding for his rocket research.

The project afforded Oberth the opportunity to work with bringing liquid oxygen and fuel together for combustion. The work was dangerous, however, and Oberth, working alongside a number of amateurs, was injured during an explosion. There were other setbacks as well and Oberth failed to deliver a working rocket by the movie's 1929 premiere. *Frau im Monde* failed to generate much interest but the movie did conceive of the notion of a pre-flight countdown. The words "10 seconds to go" appeared on the screen, followed by "6-5-4-3-2-1-FIRE."

Oberth, somewhat disgraced by his failure, returned to teaching and conducting experiments with the VfR. He published *Wege zur Raumschiffahrt* (*The Way to Spaceship Travel*) in 1929. This was a much-longer revised edition of his original work. That same year, the VfR launched its first liquid-fuel rocket, the Kegeldüse, which was derived from the German word for cone. A university student named Wernher von Braun helped Oberth on this project. For the next several years, the VfR built and exploded rockets, tweaking the design each time. Oberth's rocket design at this time consisted of an outer shell made of copper lined with baked sandstone. In the early 1930s, as the Great Depression set in, however, the VfR ran into trouble. With funds dwindling, the VfR could no longer afford its experiments. Oberth moved back to Romania to teach.

Von Braun wanted to continue the rocket experiments so he persuaded the German army to fund his work. In time, he created the V2 based on many of Oberth's innovations. Von Braun worked out of the German army's research center in Peenemünde. In 1941, Nazi officials sent Oberth to join von Braun in Peenemünde. Oberth was given the title of consulting engineer, though officials did not expect him to do much. Mostly, Oberth was placed there so he would not be able to share his rocket research with Germany's enemies. As he investigated the research, Oberth became impressed with von Braun's progress.

Von Braun developed the V2 for space travel but Adolf Hitler, who came to power in 1933, had other ideas. He launched the long-range, liquid-fuel V2 at England during World War II. At the end of the war, von Braun surrendered to U.S. troops, figuring he would be spared because of his rocket knowledge. The United States, eager to stay ahead of the Russians with regards to missiles, appointed von Braun to head up the development of U.S. military rockets.

Lived to See Visions Realized

In 1955, von Braun invited Oberth to the United States to serve as a scientific advisor at the Marshall Space Flight Center in Huntsville, Alabama. Von Braun was working on the Redstone Rocket, which launched the first U.S. satellite into orbit. He was also working on development of the Saturn V, which eventually sent astronauts to the moon. Oberth stayed for a couple of years, returning to Germany to retire in 1958.

Oberth continued to write about his ideas and published *The Moon Car* in 1959. This book included detailed descriptions and illustrations of a lunar surface vehicle. Oberth spent the remainder of his life in Nuremberg and was often visited by space enthusiasts who wanted Oberth to critique their ideas. He died at a Nuremberg hospital on December 28, 1989, after witnessing many of his visions come true. His life is commemorated at the Hermann Oberth Space Travel Museum in Feucht, Germany.

While Oberth's work in rocketry helped bring missiles into existence, his vision was for them to bring people together in space. Writing in *Aviation Week* in 1986, he said, "Surely we must learn that by making war we cannot solve any problems . . . We should, therefore, enter the door to space by utilizing the strength of our youth to realize a world that is better and more just. In my 91st year, I know such a world can happen if we all join together to explore space in cooperation rather than separately in jealously and greed. Our world is much larger than just the Earth and our minds must look outward to the heavens, knowing now that orbital travel can challenge us with new frontiers."

Books

Gainor, Chris, *To A Distant Day: The Rocket Pioneers,* University of Nebraska Press, 2008.

Oberth, Hermann, *Man into Space,* Harper & Brothers, 1957.

Wulforst, Harry, *The Rocketmakers,* Orion Books, 1990.

Periodicals

Astronomy, January 2004, pp. 48-52.

Aviation Week, January 6, 1986, p. 96.

New York Times, January 30, 1931, p. 3; January 31, 1931, p. 8; December 31, 1989, p. 32.

Washington Post, November 7, 1985, p. C1.

World & I, December 1994, p. 206.□

Chukwuemeka Odumegwu Ojukwu

Nigerian political and military leader C. Odumegwu Ojukwu (born 1933) led the Ibo people of Eastern Nigeria in their attempt to secede and establish the independent Republic of Biafra in 1967. After a three-year war in which a million people died, many of starvation, Ojukwu went into exile. He moved back to Nigeria in 1982, but his attempts to return to political prominence have been mostly unsuccessful.

The Path to Leadership

Ojukwu was born on November 4, 1933, in Zungeru, a small town in northern Nigeria. He was the son of Sir Louis Ojukwu, a millionaire businessman from Eastern Nigeria who had made his fortune in trucking and real estate and been knighted by the queen of

a Nigerian battalion, and served in a United Nations peace-keeping force in the Congo. In 1963 he was promoted to lieutenant colonel, and at the end of 1964 he was named commander of Nigeria's Fifth Battalion.

The Coup

Nigeria became independent of Great Britain in 1960, but its democratic government was torn by competition among ethnic groups and regions, assassinations and jailings of major political figures, and corruption. The upheaval Ojukwu had foreseen came in January of 1966, when several military officers, all Ibo, attempted to overthrow the republic. They assassinated Nigeria's prime minister and the premiers of the country's northern and western regions. However, army chief J.T.U. Aguiyi-Ironsi, also an Ibo, did not join the coup. Nor did Ojukwu, who remained loyal to Ironsi and helped keep his battalion's region free from riots. When Ironsi put down the coup and assumed power as head of state, he rewarded Ojukwu by appointing him the military governor of the Eastern Region of Nigeria.

Ironsi quickly alienated northern Nigerians by promoting mostly Ibo military officers and by attempting to make Nigeria a unified republic instead of a federation of regions. In July, Ironsi was assassinated in a counter-coup in which northern Nigerians attacked and killed about 200 Ibo soldiers. A lieutenant colonel from the north, Yakubu Gowon, became head of state.

Ojukwu refused to recognize Gowon as Nigeria's leader and began asserting his own authority in eastern Nigeria. In August of 1966 he told an assembly of representatives from the east that the region should create its own army and conduct its own foreign policy. This alienation from the central government increased in September, after mob violence broke out against the Ibo in northern Nigeria, and federal authorities and the northern regional government did not protect them. Between 5,000 and 50,000 Ibo were murdered. More than a million fearful Ibo fled from the north and west to their homeland in eastern Nigeria.

As refugees crowded into the eastern region, creating an economic crisis, Ojukwu ordered non-easterners out, saying he could not guarantee their safety. Many Ibo argued for secession from the rest of Nigeria or the breakup of the country into several smaller nations. A meeting between Ojukwu and Gowon in Aburi, Ghana, in January of 1967 failed to solve their disputes. Their disagreements escalated.

Rallied People of Biafra

"We were now thoroughly convinced that only our separate political existence could guarantee our basic needs of survival and security of life and property," Ojukwu recalled later, according to Dan Jacobs in *The Brutality of Nations.* On May 30, 1967, Ojukwu announced that the eastern region would break away and become a separate nation, the Republic of Biafra. Gowon responded by sending federal troops to the area Ojukwu controlled. A civil war began.

"Fellow countrymen, proud and courageous Biafrans, this is your moment," Ojukwu said in a radio broadcast on June 30, 1967, according to *The History of Nigeria* by Toyin Falola. "When we go to war, it will be a war against Nigeria,

England. Ojukwu grew up in his family's mansion in Lagos. He went to secondary school at Kings College in Lagos, and at age 13 attended Epsom College in Surrey, England. He majored in modern history at Oxford College in England, where he played on a rubgy team. He received his bachelor's degree in 1955. After college, Ojukwu, defying his father, joined the Nigerian civil service instead of going into business. He spent two years as an administrative officer in eastern Nigeria, working on roads and culverts and getting to know ordinary people in his father's native region.

Ojukwu was an Ibo, one of Nigeria's three largest ethnic groups, a fact that explains much about his rise to power. The Ibo, concentrated in Eastern Nigeria, prospered under British colonial rule, learning English and embracing British culture more often than other Nigerians. Many Ibo became doctors, lawyers, successful traders, government officials, and military officers. However, as they migrated across Nigeria, their wealth stoked resentment in Nigerians of other ethnicities.

In 1957 Ojukwu joined the army, becoming the first Nigerian soldier with an Oxford degree. The decision horrified his father. But Ojukwu did not really foresee a career as a soldier. He was positioning himself for political power. He later explained, according to John J. Stremlau in *The International Politics of the Nigerian Civil War, 1967-1970)*, that he realized Nigeria was "headed for an upheaval and that the army was the place to be when the time came." Ojukwu spent two years in officer training in Britain, was assigned to

for it is Nigeria that has vowed that we shall not exist. With God on our side, we shall vanquish."

The force of Ojukwu's personality helped unify Biafra. "Ojukwu . . . is a charismatic figure who possesses a towering ego, a quick mind, and a keen appreciation of political intrigue," Stermlau wrote. "His full beard and piercing stare became a symbol of Biafran resistance that was recognized around the world."

The Biafran forces fought intensely, while the poorly organized Nigerian federal military struggled to defeat them. Ojukwu and other Biafran leaders warned the Ibo that the Nigerian forces would completely exterminate them if they lost the war. Biafran's radio station also used religious differences in its propaganda, depicting the federal forces as Muslim hordes out to destroy the Christian Ibo.

In May of 1968, federal forces took over the eastern city of Port Harcourt, cutting Biafrans off from the ocean. That effectively blockaded Biafra and caused massive starvation. Ojukwu argued that the federal government was committing genocide against the Ibo. Many Westerners agreed. The war was one of the first to be widely televised, and many people worldwide, moved by images of starving Ibo children, donated to relief efforts. Charity agencies sent food and other materials, and a few Western nations, such as France and Portugal, supported the Biafran military effort.

The war, which lasted two and a half years, cost one million lives. Many of its victims starved to death. The outnumbered Biafran military was defeated in January of 1970. Ojukwu fled into exile in the Ivory Coast. His warnings that the Ibo would be massacred after defeat proved untrue. Gowon immediately declared an amnesty for all rebels.

Many Nigerians blamed Ojukwu for the civil war, arguing that he had declared independence because of his ambition. However, the idea was not just his. Most Ibo shared his desire to secede. The deeper causes of the war were shared by all of Nigeria: ethnic rivalries, a failed central government, and military officers more concerned with themselves and their region than the nation. Other critics, including some Ibo, argued that Ojukwu had waited too long to accept defeat, prolonging the starvation the war caused.

Returned from Exile

Ojukwu spent 12 years in exile in the Ivory Coast. He went into business, starting transportation, construction, and quarrying companies. In 1982 he received a pardon from Nigerian President Shehu Shagari, erasing criminal charges of rebellion. He returned to Nigeria that June. Thousands of supporters greeted him at the airport. Nigeria had returned to a civilian government in 1979, so hopes were high among some Ibo that Ojukwu would return to politics and again become a powerful figure.

Ojukwu renewed a bitter rivalry with another Ibo politician, Nnamdi Azikiwe, who had renounced Biafra's independence effort during the civil war and had later become head of the Nigerian People's Party, popular among the Ibo. In January of 1983, Ojukwu gave a dramatic speech in Aba, a prominent Ibo city, announcing he was joining Shagari's National Party of Nigeria and arguing that other Ibo should do the same. "Separatism, founded on a siege mentality that erupts in confrontation with

everything non-Ibo, is no road," Ojukwu told the crowd, according to Leon Dash of the *Washington Post.* "It will lead to isolation, political arthritis and hence defeat."

Ojukwu was named one of the National Party's vice chairmen. He ran for the country's Senate in the 1983 elections and also campaigned for Shagari's re-election, but his Senate race dissolved into controversy. Official election results showed him losing to his opponent, but a judge ruled that fraud had taken place and that Ojukwu was the rightful winner. However, the dispute became moot when another military coup overthrew the civilian government.

Ojukwu was among hundreds of people detained by the military government in 1984. He spent several months in the Kiri Kiri jail in the Nigerian capital of Lagos. Once released, Ojukwu became a businessman in Lagos. In 1987 a court ordered the government to return his family's mansion to him, two decades after the army had seized it during the civil war.

Looking back at the war 20 years later, Ojukwu acknowledged that his ideal of an independent Biafra had proven unrealistic. "I believe that Nigeria as a result of the war has learned that an ethnocentric political movement, no matter where, would not be viable," he told Blaine Harden of the *Washington Post.* "I believe that any leader of any group in Nigeria today should be seeking greater integration. I believe the name of the game is nation-building." However, he contended that the Nigerian government still discriminated against the Ibo in awarding federal projects and using quotas to limit how many Ibo could be admitted to the country's best universities. "We are constantly asking ourselves, are we being treated as the underdog?" he said.

Returned to Politics

In the 1990s, after another military coup, Ojukwu became an ally of Nigerian military ruler Gen. Sani Abacha. He participated in a 1994 constitutional conference that Abacha's critics called a sham. They demanded instead that the results of the annulled 1993 elections be respected. "We are here on a mandate—the mandate that the people of Nigeria have given to Nigeria," Ojukwu argued, according to Cindy Shiner of the *New York Times.* "If there is any person who thinks another mandate is more important, that person should just resign from this house and get out."

When democracy returned to Nigeria in 1999, Ojukwu swung back toward ethnic politics, joining other Ibo leaders who insisted on setting aside powerful positions for people from their region. "It is already 28 years since we were said to have been defeated in a war as a result of which they continuously rubbed our nose in the dust," Ojukwu protested, according to Falola. "We no longer will ask for pardon or acceptance. We have already suffered for too long." Ojukwu ran for president of Nigeria in 2003 as head of the new All Progressives Grand Alliance. However, he came in a distant third, with only 3 percent of the vote. In the next presidential election, in 2007, he fared even more poorly.

In 2008 Ojukwu was granted a Nigerian army pension, a gesture of reconciliation toward the military leaders of the Biafra revolt. At the pension ceremony, he complained that the government referred to him as a lieutenant colonel, though Biafra had named him a general. But he was mostly conciliatory. "This is one of the rare occasions," he said, as quoted by Kingsley Omonobi on AllAfrica.com, "that makes one really feel proud to be part of this country."

Books

Falola, Toyin, *The History of Nigeria,* Greenwood Press, 1999.

Forsyth, Frederick, *The Biafra Story: The Making of An African Legend,* Pen & Sword, 2007.

Jacobs, Dan, *The Brutality of Nations,* Alfred A. Knopf, 1987.

Mwakikagile, Godfrey, *Ethnic Politics in Kenya and Nigeria,* Nova Science Publishers Inc., 2001.

Stremlau, John J., *The International Politics of the Nigerian Civil War, 1967-1970,* Princeton University Press, 1977.

Periodicals

New York Times, June 19, 1982; September 21, 1983; July 14, 1987; April 17, 2003.

Washington Post, March 4, 1983; April 9, 1983; August 7, 1983; October 4, 1984; June 27, 1988; August 4, 1994.

Online

"Nigeria: Ojukwu Gets Pension, 38 Yrs After Civil War," *AllAfrica. com,* http://www.allafrica.com/stories/200801150101.html (January 4, 2009).

"Odumegwu Ojukwu," *Encyclopedia Britannica Online,* http://www.britannica.com/EBchecked/topic/426372/Odumegwu-Ojukwu (December 28, 2008). □

Keisuke Okada

Keisuke Okada (1868-1952) served as an admiral in the Imperial Japanese Navy and was Japan's prime minister in the mid-1930s. Okada was also instrumental in the initiative for peace with the United States and in the removal of Hideki Tojo as prime minister at the end of World War II. Okada survived an assassination attempt by rebel troops in 1936 by hiding in a maid's closet for a few days, then escaping in disguise.

Okada was born on January 21, 1868, in Fukui Prefecture. He graduated in 1889, ranked seventh among eighty, from the fifteenth class of the Imperial Japanese Naval Academy. He graduated from the Naval War College. Okada's early assignments included midshipman on the Kongo, an ironclad ship, and the Naniwa, a protected cruiser. He was promoted to sublieutenant in 1890 and lieutenant in 1894. After his promotion to lieutenant commander, Okada served on such battleships as the Fuji and the Shikishima.

Working up the ranks, Okada became commander, captain, rear admiral, and vice-admiral. He assumed the admiral's title in 1924. Twice Okada served as a Navy minister—in 1927 and 1932, under prime ministers Tanaka Giichi and Makoto Saito, respectively.

Revolt, Assassination Try Undermined Him

In 1934 Okada became Japan's prime minister. Insurrection among increasingly militaristic factions was among his biggest challenges. It was the focal point of the 1932 assassination of Tsuyoshi Inukai. "The assassination marked the end of parliamentary democracy sought by Inukai and the beginning of the nation's slide into militarism," the *Japan Times* wrote. Okada exiled Sadao Araki, a hard-liner in a military-political group calling itself the Imperial Way, and brought in Nagata Tetsuzan, a moderate whom Araki himself had exiled under the Saito administration. Okada promoted Tetsuzan to general and made him director of military affairs in the Army ministry.

Two years after taking office, Okada faced a revolt that undermined him politically, though he did survive an attempt on his life. Marius B. Jansen, in his book *The Making of Modern Japan,* called the revolt "the largest [in Japan], perhaps, since the Satsuma Rebellion of 1877." In 1935 Saburo Aizawa was convicted and executed for the stabbing death of General Nagata Tetsuzan, who had stifled plots against the government. The public trial of Aizawa "became a circus for ultranationalist emotionalism," Jansen wrote.

The hysteria fueled what became the young officers' revolt, on February 26, 1936. It featured a series of moves that involved about 1,400 officers. Civilian extremists and young officers collaborated on an overthrow attempt. "In a late winter snowfall assassination squads moved out to remove the principal conservative members of the authority structure," Jansen wrote. The rebels awakened former prime minister Saito, who had become lord privy seal admiral, and shot him to death in his bedroom; they did likewise to Jotaro Watanabe, the inspector general of military education, and to Takahashi Korekiyo, the finance minister. Other top officials were wounded or escaped. "Between 1921 and 1936, three Japanese prime ministers had fallen victim to assassins, and a fourth, Admiral Okada, had barely escaped death," Ben-Ami Shillony wrote in *Politics and Culture in Wartime Japan.* "The wartime government of Japan had clamped down on the extreme rightists, but there were always hot-headed young officers and right-wing civilians who might be ready to 'destroy the traitors around the throne.'"

"The most important squad was assigned to eliminate the prime minister," Jansen wrote, of Okada. The insurgents moved on the prime minister's residence, the *Kantei,* in Tokyo, at which Inukai had been assassinated. "The soldiers quickly took possession of the official residence, only to err by shooting Admiral Okada's brother-in-law, who resembled him somewhat, instead of the prime minister, who escaped by hiding in a closet. Okada was declared and assumed to be dead, but he managed to slip out of the residence in disguise a few days later."

"The uprising was soon suppressed and key rebels were executed. But it led to increased military influence on the government and drove Japan into waging war in China from 1937 to 1945," the *Japan Times* wrote. As for Okada, shortly after the assassination attempt, he resigned as prime minister.

Continued to Wield Influence

Okada officially retired in 1938, but would play a major role in the downfall of Tojo and the acceleration of the peace talks with the United States during World War II. Former prime ministers, called *jushin,* often advised emperors on political appointments, which "provided them with a high status and instilled in them a sense of responsibility," Shillony wrote. Tojo, while maintaining outwardly courteous relations with the *jushin,* kept the group at arm's length. Tojo's friend, General Sato Kenryo, referred to the likes of Okada as "a bunch of old gentlemen," according to Shillony.

As World War II continued from 1941 through 1945, the *jushin,* of which there were seven in 1944, considered the war a lost cause and became disillusioned with Tojo. They also worried that a major defeat would trigger an insurrection within the military that could topple the imperial structure. Okada "became convinced that Tojo should go," Shillony wrote. Relatives who were military insiders updated Okada on war details, including his oldest son, Commander Sadatomu Okada, who was the chief of the operation section of the naval headquarters.

On August 8, 1943, Okada dispatched a relative to try and convince Tojo's lord keeper of the privy seal that the prime minister should step down. The exchange led to a meeting with the prime minister that Okada had hoped would lead to a rebuke by the *jushin.* "The veiled purpose of this move was to discredit the Tojo regime with the ultimate objective of forcing its retirement. Admiral Okada, the prime instigator, believed that a general peace would be impossible as long as Tojo remained in office," said a passage from *Reports of General MacArthur: Japanese Operations in the Southwest Pacific Area, compiled from Japanese demobilization bureau records and posted on the U.S. Army Center of Military History Web site.*

Tojo, accompanied by other top officials, controlled the meeting. "Far from rebuking the prime minister, senior statesmen found themselves being lectured by him. The desired confrontation did not materialize," Shillony wrote. The *jushin,* however, were undaunted. Military defeat and domestic economic problems had effectively shaken Tojo's regime.

After Tojo reshuffled his cabinet in a move to further consolidate his power, Navy minister Shigetaro Shimada had even more clout, doubling up as chief of staff. Okada sought to use his navy contacts to try to bring down Shimada, create a rift between the army and navy, and force Tojo to resign. After Okada met with Shimada, saying the latter's dual titles were improper, Tojo summoned Okada, criticizing him "for trying to weaken the cabinet at such a grave moment in history," according to Shillony. The meeting ended with the sides still at an impasse.

On June 15, 1944, nine days after American and British forces landed in Normandy, France, to open a long-awaited second front in Europe, U.S. troops descended on Saipan in the Mariana Islands. Vice-Admiral Chuichi Nagumo, who had overseen efforts at the December 7, 1941, bombing of Pearl Harbor in Hawaii and the Battle of Midway six months later, coordinated the Japanese efforts. The Americans, however, outnumbered the Japanese by roughly 70,000 to 30,000, and held a superior balance of air and sea power. A blame game ensued in Japan after that country's withdrawal. "After three weeks of desperate resistance, the last defenders of the island made a suicidal charge against the Americans and were annihilated," Shillony wrote. "Vice-Admiral Nagumo committed suicide. The doorway to Tokyo was open."

"By late spring of 1944, they had gained sufficient strength and confidence to urge their views more strongly," the MacArthur report said, of the senior statesmen. "In mid-July the disastrous loss of Saipan gave them an opportunity to press for the resignation of the Tojo government. Tojo, realizing the graveness of the situation, tried to settle it by reorganizing his Cabinet but this attempt failed." As Japan's position in the war weakened, internal calls for Tojo's resignation intensified. An assassination plot failed to materialize; so, too, did another Tojo cabinet reorganization, this time intended to placate opponents. The Okada faction, in pushing for Cabinet replacements, had an agenda of ending the war as soon as possible. The MacArthur report related that "Admiral Okada and his associates felt that now, at last, they had reasonable hopes of attaining this difficult objective."

After a series of costly military defeats, punctuated by Saipan, Tojo resigned on July 18, 1944. He was found guilty two years later of war crimes, and was hanged on December 23, 1948.

Okada himself died on October 10, 1952, at age 84.

Books

The Making of Modern Japan, Belknap Press of Harvard University Press, 2000.

Politics and Culture and Wartime Japan, Oxford University Press, 1981.

Online

"Doors Close after 73 Years, 42 Leaders," *Japan Times Online,* http://www.search.japantimes.co.jp/cgi-bin/np20020423b5. html, April 23, 2002.(November 30, 2008).

"Graduates of Naval Academy Class 15th," Materials of IJN, http:// homepage2.nifty.com/nishidah/e/px15.htm#a001, (November 30, 2008).

"Reports of General MacArthur," *U.S. Army Center of Military History,* http://www.history.army.mil/books/wwii/MacArthur% 20Reports/MacArthur%20V2%20, August 6, 2005 (November 30, 2008).

"Rundown of Japan's 14 Class-A War Criminals," *China Daily,* http://www.chinadaily.com.cn/english/doc/2005-06/08/content_ 449596.htm, August 6, 2005 (November 30, 2008).

"Scar of the *Kantei,*" Prime Minister of Japan and His Cabinet, http://www.202.232.190.90/foreign/vt2/main/01/photo-kizuato 01.html, (November 22, 2008).□

King Oliver

American cornetist and bandleader Joseph "King" Oliver (c. 1884 –1938) was among the most successful and influential musicians during the first years of jazz.

Oliver's influence is difficult to pin down precisely, for he had already been performing for some years by the time the first jazz recordings were made. Nevertheless, the music by Oliver that has survived provides a perfect example of the collective improvisation on existing music that is thought to have given birth to jazz itself. Oliver was the immediate mentor of one of the greatest jazz musicians of them all, trumpeter Louis Armstrong. He was one of the first jazz musicians to bring the new music from New Orleans to Chicago, and the one who brought Armstrong north to play in his Creole Jazz Band. Several of Oliver's own compositions, including some generally associated with Armstrong, remain jazz standards.

Birth Date Unknown

Joseph Nathan Oliver was, depending on which historian's conclusions are accepted, born either in New Orleans or on Salsburg Plantation, near the hamlet of Aben, Louisiana, on the Mississippi River west of New Orleans. No firm evidence of his date of birth has surfaced, and Oliver, who may not have known exactly how old he was, gave conflicting answers when he had to provide ages or birth years for official documents (census counts, a marriage certificate, a World War I draft card) later in life. Researcher Peter Hanley has concluded that December 19, 1884, was his probable date of birth. Oliver's father was named Nathan Oliver, but there are several individuals, including a traveling preacher, who could have been the one involved. His mother, Virginia Jones, known as Jinnie, apparently moved to New Orleans and worked there as a domestic servant.

The family, including a half-sister, Victoria, settled in the poverty-ridden but musically rich Uptown section of New Orleans. After Oliver's mother died in 1900, Victoria took charge of his welfare. Oliver himself went to work shortly after that, spending several years as a butler for a white New Orleans family. He lost his left eye as a teenager, perhaps in a fight. His first musical activities came early in the new century, with the New Orleans outdoor marching bands that helped to spawn jazz. Performing at first on the trombone and soon on his chosen instrument, the cornet, he is thought to have played with the Olympia, Onward, Original Superior, and Eagle brass bands. New Orleans jazz observer Edmond Souchon, quoted by Gary Giddins in the book *Visions of Jazz*, wrote of hearing Oliver "blasting the heavens and shaking the blackberry leaves in funeral parades through the fringes of his neighborhood." By 1910 he was playing in the booming taverns of the Storyville red-light district as well. In 1911 he married Stella Dominick (or Dominique); they later separated but apparently did not divorce.

Oliver's own mentor was trombonist and bandleader Edward "Kid" Ory, with whom he worked through much of the 1910s decade. It was Ory who bestowed upon Oliver the nickname "King." In 1917 the federal government mandated the shutdown of Storyville's nightlife establishments because of the prostitution associated with them. Historians disagree over whether the closure caused jazz musicians to begin seeking work in other cities; the reason could as easily have been that the music was new, exciting, and ready to spread. In any event, Ory moved to Los Angeles in 1919, and Oliver followed a large migration of African Americans up the Mississippi River in the same year, where he landed in Chicago and joined bandleader and bassist Bill Johnson (who had invited him north) at the Dreamland Ballroom on the Near West Side.

In 1920 Oliver formed a band of his own, performing at Dreamland and another key early Chicago jazz site, the Pekin Inn on South State Street. Sometimes he played sets at both clubs on the same night, ending the first at about 1 a.m. and then continuing until dawn at the other establishment. Oliver rejoined Ory in California in 1921 but was back in Chicago by mid-1922, ready to introduce King Oliver's Creole Jazz Band at Lincoln Gardens, an elegant establishment on East 31st Street on the South Side, on June 17. The new band was to become a seminal force in jazz.

Attracted Top Musicians, Including Armstrong

Oliver's stature was reflected in the stellar lineup of musicians he attracted. Brothers Johnny and Baby Dodds, on clarinet and drums respectively, maintained the traditional New Orleans group improvisation sound along with bassist Johnson and trombonist Honore Dutrey. But Oliver also identified two striking new talents of immense importance who would, as it happened, go on to marry each other: pianist Lillian Hardin and cornetist Louis Armstrong, who had not yet switched to the trumpet.

The cornet duos of Oliver and Armstrong were captured on a set of 1923 recordings by the Creole Jazz Band, which became the first African-American New Orleans–style band captured on records. But they were even more compelling when heard live, not restricted to the confines of a three-minute 78 rpm record, and the music was inspirational for the group of young white Chicago jazz musicians who were coming of age on the city's far West Side. Guitarist Eddie Condon, quoted by Giddins, wrote that "the music poured into us like daylight running down a dark hole. The choruses rolled on like high tide, getting wilder and more wonderful. Armstrong seemed able to hear what Oliver was improvising and reproduce it himself at the same time. It seemed impossible, so I dismissed it; but it was true."

Those 1923 recordings included "Dippermouth Blues," which included an Oliver solo that stretched over three blues choruses. The solo has been an essential part of the education of jazz cornetists and trumpeters ever since. Other Oliver compositions, including "West End Blues" (which inspired one of Armstrong's greatest solos), were taken up by Armstrong and other jazz players even as the solo aspect displaced Oliver's New Orleans ensemble conception. When Armstrong left the group in 1924, the Creole Jazz Band gradually drifted apart. Oliver recorded several duets with pianist Ferdinand "Jelly Roll" Morton in 1925, taking over an existing band that year and renaming it the Dixie Syncopators. Oliver's largest group, including three saxophones and a tuba, the Dixie Syncopators settled in for a recurring dance gig at the Plantation Cafe on 35th Street.

Declined Cotton Club Engagement

That group continued to bring Oliver respectable business, but the stylistic cutting edge of jazz was shifting elsewhere. In 1927 Oliver followed Armstrong and other musicians eastward to New York, attempting to reestablish the Dixie Syncopators there. He was dogged by a mixture of ill health, questionable judgment, and bad luck. Oliver turned down a regular engagement at Harlem's Cotton Club, which soon launched the spectacularly successful career of bandleader Edward Kennedy "Duke" Ellington—a mistake that must have been hard for Oliver to live down, inasmuch as Ellington's trumpeter and cornetist James "Bubber" Miley played in a style heavily influenced by Oliver. Another player whose style showed marks of contact with Oliver was the Chicago cornetist Francis "Muggsy" Spanier.

Oliver continued to perform with a variety of bands around New York, making several elegant recordings as King Oliver & His Orchestra. Sometimes he backed vocal soloists such as blues diva Sippie Wallace. But work dried up for many musicians as the Depression deepened in the early 1930s, and Oliver was troubled in addition by severe periodontal disease that may have been caused by his fondness for eating sugar sandwiches when he was younger. By 1935 he could play a cornet only with difficulty and pain. Taking increasingly more ragged bands on tours of the Midwest and South, he eventually ran completely out of money. He made his way to Savannah, Georgia, where he found a job as a janitor in a poolroom. Oliver died in Savannah on April 8, 1938.

The fact that recordings captured only the end of Oliver's peak years as a performer may have distorted evaluations of his importance in histories of early jazz, which tend to focus on Armstrong, Morton, and others. Souchon believed that his best performances came in New Orleans, where he was never recorded. And the musical relationship between Oliver and Armstrong deserves close investigation. Armstrong quickly developed a style of his own, but in interviews and his own writings he was expansive in acknowledging Oliver's influence, and in 1923 they joined together into a musical unit.

Books

Giddins, Gary, *Visions of Jazz,* Oxford, 1998.
Williams, Martin, *King Oliver,* Barnes, 1960.

Online

"Joe 'King' Oliver (1885–1938)," Red Hot Jazz Archive, http://www.redhotjazz.com/kingo.html (January 30, 2009).
"Joe 'King' Oliver," *Jazz: A Film by Ken Burns,* Public Broadcasting System, http://www.pbs.org/jazz/biography/artist_id_oliver_joe_king.htm (January 30, 2009).
"King Oliver," *All Music Guide,* http://www.allmusic.com (January 30, 2009).
"King Oliver," Doctor Jazz, http://www.doctorjazz.co.uk/portnewor.html#koliver (January 30, 2009).
"King Oliver," *Jazz Review,* http://www.jazzreview.com/article details.cfm?ID=168 (January 30, 2009). □

Ahmed Orabi

Ahmed Orabi (1841–1911) was an Egyptian military leader. In 1881 and 1882 he led the so-called Orabi Revolt against Egypt's hereditary ruler, or khedive, and his British supporters.

That revolt, noted Robert Tignor in *Modernization and British Colonial Rule in Egypt, 1882–1914,* "has been viewed by many observers as one of the earliest nationalistic uprisings in the Middle East." It shared features with many of the conflicts that have plagued the region in the years since: a rise in Islamic consciousness and a desire to resist Western cultural encroachment played a role, as did class and regional conflicts within the area. Such tensions have in turn been reflected in Egyptian evaluations of Orabi himself in the years since his death.

Attended Islamic Institute

Ahmed (or Ahmad) Orabi has also been known as Arabi or Urabi in different systems of transliterating Arabic, and during his rise to power he was given the title of Pasha, indicating a high-ranking official in the Ottoman Empire with which Egypt was associated. Born in 1841 (or 1840), he was the son of a small landowner in Horiyeh, near Zagazig in the lower Nile River delta. In Egyptian terms Orabi was a peasant, or *fellah.* In his book *Secret History of the English Occupation of Egypt,* Wilfrid Scawen Blunt, a British supporter of Orabi's rise to power, described him as a "typical fellah, tall, heavy-limbed, and somewhat slow in his movements, [seeming] to symbolize that massive body strength which is so characteristic of the laborious peasant of the Lower Nile." But Orabi's father was something of a local leader, and the family saw to it that their son was educated. He attended village schools and, contrary to charges later leveled against him by his opponents, was not illiterate. As an adolescent he was sent to study for several years at the Islamic Al-Azhar University in Cairo.

The system that gave Orabi his basic education was a product of the reforms instituted in Egypt by Muhammad Ali, the founder of the modern Egyptian state, and his descendants over the course of the nineteenth century. Another institution shaped by these rulers was the Egyptian military, which grew into a powerful force rivaling that of the Ottoman Empire, headquartered in Istanbul and officially the entity that ruled Egypt. Orabi was drafted into the Egyptian army when he was 13. Despite his young age, he rose rapidly into the army's officer corps, achieved a promotion every year, and reached the rank of colonel by the time he was 20. Blunt remarked that although Orabi got on well with the Europeans he encountered, "he knew no language . . . but his own, and maintained his integrity free from the European vices that are so easily acquired." Orabi served in the war waged by Egypt against Ethiopia in the early 1870s, and his suspicion of Egypt's elites grew when he was briefly arrested at one point in a botched illegal attack hatched by higher-ups in the government.

By the 1870s, Egypt's program of modernization had begun to run into financial trouble. One factor was the building of the Suez Canal, connecting the Mediterranean and Red Seas, between 1859 and 1869. Although the canal was financed primarily by French and Ottoman investors, Egypt bore heavy construction and labor costs. Said Pasha, Muhammad Ali's son, who ruled Egypt from 1854 to 1863, was an ineffective financial manager who drove Egypt deeper into dept with profligate spending, and matters grew worse under the next khedive, Said Pasha's nephew Ismail. Resentment grew among members of the Egyptian army, limited in size by an earlier agreement with the British government. All these events made an impression on Orabi, but it was not only the Europeans who aroused his anger and that of other officers his age. He and other descendants of Egyptian villagers occupied reserved low-level posts, but the ranks of top-level officers were filled by Turks and Circassians—an ethnic group of highly trained fighters from what is now southern Russia. When Orabi reached the rank of colonel, that marked, for the time being, the ceiling on his military career.

Joined Secret Society

As Egypt's financial situation worsened, key institutions such as railroads fell partly under the control of European creditors. By 1877 payments on Egypt's national debt consumed more than 60 percent of the country's gross revenues. Egyptian intellectuals began to talk openly of creating a modern constitutional democracy, free of foreign control, and a secret society in the army, of which Orabi was one of the first members, formed in 1876 and planned ways of ridding the military of Turkish and Circassian control. The conflicts in Egyptian society deepened after khedive Ismail was forced out in 1879 by the Ottoman Sultan Abdul Hamid II, under pressure from European powers. Ismail was replaced by his son, Tawfiq. By that time, European finance ministers partially controlled the government's purse strings, and in 1880 an international committee implemented measures further restricting Egypt's use of its own revenues.

Such measures provoked anger across a wide swath of Egyptian society, but khedive Tawfiq was seen as more obedient than Ismail to orders from London, Paris, and Istanbul, and there was as yet no popular figure around whom the dissenters might coalesce. Orabi set about making sure that he would become that figure. He formed contacts and friendships with leading constitutionalists in Egypt, such as the legislator Muhammad Sharif Pasha, and with sympathetic Europeans such as Blunt. Within the repressed ranks of native Egyptians in the army, he had already emerged as a leader, and in 1880 his secret group of army officers informally joined forces with an existing secret organization called the National Society, made up of democratic activists and intellectuals. The coalition, with Orabi as its head and spokesman, began to press Tawfiq for reforms. As their influence grew, so did their motto: "Egypt for the Egyptians!."

The conflict grew when Tawfiq installed a reactionary Circassian, Osman Rifky, as Minister of War—in Blunt's words, "an extreme representative of the class which for centuries had looked upon Egypt as their property and the fellahin as their slaves and servants." Orabi and a group of other officers made several peaceful attempts to present their grievances against Rifky to the government. Then, in February of 1881, Orabi and his group were invited to an army barracks at Kasr el Nil, ostensibly to discuss the role to be played by Orabi's Fourth Regiment in the wedding of Princess Jamila, the khedive's sister. Rifky placed the Egyptian officers under arrest. But Orabi had foreseen this turn of events. He believed that Rifky's plan was to put his group on a nearby Nile River steamer, take them upriver, and drown them. Therefore, a large company of friendly soldiers appeared on the scene, unwilling to carry out Rifky's orders and ready with a list of demands of their own. These included the resignations of Rifky and other ministers, some of them Europeans, and an increase in the size of the army.

Tawfiq, unsure of his level of support from the sultan (who was waiting to determine the direction of the evolving power struggle), backed down and agreed to install the nationalist Mustafa Sami as Minister of War. An emboldened Orabi, in the words of Peter Mansfield writing in *The British in Egypt,* "became a national hero." His following among the heavily taxed Egyptian masses burgeoned, while the various foreign forces with their fingers in the Egyptian treasury looked on with increasing concern. In September of 1881 a force of 4,000 Egyptian soldiers with Orabi at their head marched on the khedive's Abdeen Palace, demanding the institution of a constitutional government. Orabi again believed he was threatened by subterfuge and again had taken the advance precaution of gathering a large force. The weakened khedive, according to a British officer quoted by Mansfield, asked rhetorically, "What can I do? We are between four fires. We shall be killed." He largely agreed to Orabi's demands, installing the constitutionalist Muhammad Sharif Pasha at the head of a new cabinet.

Named Minister of War

At that point, it looked as though Orabi had achieved a peaceful transfer of power. His primary quarrel was not with Europe, or with Christianity (he was a follower of what today would be called moderate Islam), but with the ongoing domination of Egypt, and Egypt's army specifically, by Ottoman Turks and Circassians. The underlying dynamics of European imperialism, however, soon reasserted themselves. Then, as now, the Middle East was an important crossroads for the transfer of raw materials; the Suez Canal connected England with the Indian plantations that supplied its growing industrial machine, and other European countries had similar interests in ensuring a compliant Egypt. Two critical events occurred in January of 1882: Orabi himself became Egypt's Minister of War, and Britain and France delivered a hostile diplomatic communiqué known as the Joint Note, affirming their support for the embattled khedive, who by then was reduced to heading what increasingly looked like a shadow government.

From that point on, even as various parties (including Blunt, religious leaders of several faiths, the Ottoman sultan Abdul Hamid, and moderates on both the British and Egyptian sides) pleaded for calm, the political situation quickly deteriorated. Europeans began to flee the Egyptian capital, and the trickle turned into a flood after riots broke out in June of 1882 in the city of Alexandria, with considerable loss of life among both Arabs and Europeans. The British and French responded with a massive show of naval force in the Mediterranean Sea off the Egyptian coast, which only had the effect of inflaming the passions of the Egyptian public even further. With the situation spiraling out of control, British warships shelled Alexandria in July of 1882.

British marines landed in Alexandria in August and quickly overran the city, the Suez area, and the towns of Port Said and Ismaila. They installed Tawfiq at a palace in Alexandria, while Orabi continued as de facto leader in Cairo, bolstered by a fatwa, or religious edict, from three Islamic leaders at his alma mater, Al-Azhar, that declared Tawfiq a traitor. Egyptian solidarity, however, yielded before superior British power. In September Orabi led an Egyptian contingent to block the British forces under Gen. Sir Garret Wolseley at Tel El-Kabir, but was quickly defeated and fled the battlefield. Thus began a British occupation of Egypt that lasted until 1956 and continues to shape the politics of the turbulent region today.

The British did not want to make Orabi into a martyr, so they allowed him to go into exile in British-controlled Sri Lanka. He arrived there in 1883, leaving his pregnant first wife (he later married three more times) behind and in charge of some of his property. Sri Lanka's small Muslim minority treated him as a hero, but he faced harassment from British soldiers and was forced to live on a small fixed allowance granted by British authorities in Egypt. In 1901, nearly blind, he was allowed to return to his homeland. He received a chilly welcome there, for rumors had spread that he had accepted a bribe to capitulate to British forces at Tel El-Kabir, and a younger generation of nationalists accepted the story. Orabi died in poverty in Helwan, Egypt, on September 21, 1911. His reputation was not rehabilitated until the establishment of the Egyptian Republic under president Gamal Abdel Nasser in the 1950s. At that time he once again became known as an Egyptian national hero.

Books

Berdine, Michael D., *The Accidental Tourist: Wilfrid Scawen Blunt, and the British Invasion of Egypt in 1882,* Routledge, 2005.

Blunt, Wilfrid Scawen, *Secret History of the English Occupation of Egypt,* Knopf, 1922.

Cole, Juan, *Colonialism and Revolution in the Middle East,* Princeton, 1993.

Mansfield, Peter, *The British in Egypt,* Weidenfeld and Nicolson, 1971.

Mayer, Thomas, *The Changing Past: Egyptian Historiography of the Orabi Revolt, 1882–1983,* University of California Press, 1988.

Tignor, Robert L., *Modernization and British Colonial Rule in Egypt, 1882–1914,* Princeton, 1966.

Vatikiotis, P.J., *The History of Modern Egypt: From Muhammad Ali to Mubarak,* 4th ed., Johns Hopkins University, 1991.

Online

"Far and Away," *Egypt Today,* October 2004, http://www.egypttoday.com/article.aspx?ArticleID=2483 (October 15, 2008).

"From Intervention to Occupation, 1876–82," *Egypt: A Country Study* (Library of Congress, 1990), http://www.countrystudies.us/egypt/25.htm (October 15, 2008). □

Henry Fairfield Osborn

American paleontologist and geologist Henry Fairfield Osborn Sr. (1857–1935) served as president of the American Museum of Natural History for a quarter-century and was one of the leading names in his field in the early twentieth century. Though some of his scientific claims and beliefs were later discredited,

Osborn did much to excite interest in paleontology with new fossil discoveries that were being uncovered around the world and carefully studied by scientists. He also turned the Museum of Natural History into a New York City cultural landmark through an ambitious expansion program during his tenure. In the *New Yorker,* Claudia Roth Pierpont described him as "a brilliant curatorial impresario," who was responsible for exhibiting dinosaur skeletons "with murals of living dinosaurs lumbering about the earth—images that were so widely reproduced that by the turn of the century the fantastical dragons had become as much a part of American childhood as baseball or cowboys and Indians."

O sborn was born on August 8, 1857, in Fairfield, Connecticut, the son of William Henry Osborn and Virginia Reed (Sturges) Osborn. Both sides of his family were among New England's wealthy, old-money elite: his middle name was taken from his birthplace, which his mother's ancestors had founded in the seventeenth century. One of his mother's sisters, Amelia, was the first wife of legendary financier J. P. Morgan. Osborn's father was one of the early investors in the Illinois Central Railroad.

Veered from Theology to Geology

Osborn grew up with an older sister and two younger brothers, one of whom drowned in the Hudson River in his teens. The family lived in New York City and at Castle Rock, an estate on the Hudson River near the U.S. Military Academy at West Point. Deeply religious in his teens, Osborn entered Princeton College in 1873 and discovered his love of geology and scientific inquiry during these years. He graduated in 1877 and that same year made his first fossil-collecting trip to Wyoming and Colorado with three other students. His career as an expert in vertebrate paleontology was launched by a number of articles he wrote about the findings on this and subsequent trips, which appeared in scientific journals.

Osborn's postgraduate schooling included the study of human anatomy at Bellevue Medical College in New York City and courses at Cambridge University in England. In 1881 he became an assistant professor of natural science at Princeton, and also wed Lucretia Perry, who hailed from the famed Rhode Island clan that also produced U.S. naval commanders Oliver Hazard Perry and Matthew Perry.

Osborn and his wife lived in Princeton until 1891, when he accepted a post at Columbia University to establish its department of biology. Five years later, he was also made professor of zoology. As an academic he rose to prominence as an expert on fossil proboscideans, the mammals whose distinguishing characteristics include a trunk and tusks; the prehistoric mammoths and mastodons he studied are the genetic predecessors of modern-day elephants. The word "dinosaur" first came into use in the 1840s to describe fossil remains of vertebrates that seemed

helped popularize dinosaurs in the public imagination and instilled an enduring interest in the creatures that seems to seize all children at a certain early-elementary age.

The Museum of Natural History's fossil collection grew to epic proportions during Osborn's 25-year tenure as president. A number of renowned fossil hunters were hired or mentored by Osborn during this era, including Barnum Brown, who brought back several important finds in the earliest years of the twentieth century from the Hell Creek Formation area of southeastern Montana and later the Red Deer River in Alberta, Canada. Another was Roy Chapman Andrews, the explorer on whom the fictional Indiana Jones of movie fame was based and whose expeditions in China and Mongolia in the 1920s unearthed the first dinosaur eggs. Osborn also promoted the work of Charles R. Knight, who became the preeminent artist of the era with his immense dinosaur murals as well as the sculptures he created for the Museum and its rivals, including the Field Museum of Natural History in Chicago.

Named the T. Rex

One of the key events in the history of the Museum during Osborn's era was the February of 1905 unveiling of a massive dinosaur skeleton called the brontosaurus, or "thunder lizard." It was 67 feet in length and became the showpiece of the Museum's newly opened Dinosaur Hall. Osborn did not name that beast, but did provide scientific nomenclature for many others, including tyrannosaurus rex, or "tyrant lizard." The first "T. Rex" remains found by modern paleontologists were uncovered by Brown at the Montana quarry site in 1902, and a partially reassembled skeleton went on display at the Museum in December of 1906. The immense size of one of the last of the non-avian dinosaurs that roamed the prehistoric West fascinated scientists and the public alike, aided by Osborn's expert marketing of the new display promoting what was called the largest animal ever to walk the earth. A more complete skeleton was found a few years later, and after cleaning and restoration it made its debut at the Museum in 1915.

Osborn was also responsible for naming the pentaceratops ("five-horned face" in Greek) in 1923, a smaller dinosaur with huge spiked protuberances underneath its eyes, and the velociraptor, or "swift thief," in 1924. The latter beast was featured in computer-generated form in the 1993 Hollywood film *Jurassic Park*. As a scientist, Osborn made a few errors in describing or characterizing some of these extinct animals. The velociraptor was actually much smaller than Osborn claimed, and was later discovered to have had feathers. He also misrepresented the eohippus, an ancestor of the horse, whose name is Greek for "dawn horse," as being "the size of a small fox terrier," a quote that was repeated consistently in elementary school textbooks for generations. In reality, the eohippus was actually about two feet long and nine inches in height, much smaller than an actual fox terrier. The comparison was made so often that anthropologist Stephen Jay Gould actually tracked it in an essay, "The Case of the Creeping Fox Terrier Clone," in his 1992 book *Bully for Brontosaurus: Reflections in Natural History.*

to be a cross between birds and lizards. The word is a combination of two Greek words—*deinos,* or "terrible," and *sauros,* or lizard.

Expanded Dinosaur Collection

Concurrent with the position at Columbia was one with the American Museum of Natural History in New York City, which had been founded in 1869. Osborn was invited to organize its new department of mammalian paleontology. He became president of the Museum in 1908, and continued his already-considerable efforts in fundraising, expansion, and public relations, which launched a new mania for dinosaurs. By this point he had given up his regular course load at Columbia University, but was still listed on the faculty as a research associate. He became a member of the U.S. Geological Survey in 1900 and held the title of senior vertebrate paleontologist with the Service in 1924; he also worked for its Canadian counterpart.

As a preeminent expert in vertebrate paleontology, Osborn did much to advance scientific inquiry in the field, authoring scores of professional papers and a number of textbooks. He also turned the Museum into the leading force in finding new fossil specimens, with its staff of scientists and curators working to classify the immense new dinosaur skeletons being found in the American West. Curators assembled the skeletons for displays that gave visitors a sense of wonder and awe at the fierce creatures that ruled the earth for 80 million years. Such attractions

Promoted Pair of Spurious Finds

In the early 1920s, Osborn engaged in a public battle with William Jennings Bryan, a well-known American politician who ran for president several times. Bryan bolstered his political ambitions by attacking the science of Darwinism, or the theory that humans are descended from apes. The controversy played out on the pages of the *New York Times*, and Osborn's arguments were laid out in a book called *Evolution and Religion*. Some of Osborn's beliefs rested in part on the theory of orthogenesis, which is sometimes called autogenesis. Popularized by German zoologist Theodor Eimer in the 1890s, orthogenesis held that evolutionary changes are predetermined—in other words, evolution is driven by a mysterious force, either internal or external.

A few months after the newspaper debate with Bryan began, Osborn published a scientific paper on Hesperopithecus, which the media dubbed "Nebraska Man"—coincidentally, Bryan's home state. In the scientific journals of the day, Hesperopithecus was described as a type of higher ape and heralded as the first higher primate in North America—thus a possible human ancestor. The publication was based on the discovery of a single tooth in Nebraska, which was later discovered to have come from a peccary, a type of pig. Another notable controversy was that of the Piltdown Man, named after skeletal remains found at a site in England in 1912. Part of a skull and jaw were heralded as belonging to an early form of human being, but were revealed four decades later as merely a human skull paired with the jawbone of an orangutan. Yet Osborn, like many others, was misled by the discovery, which he wrote about in his 1927 book *Man Rises to Parnassus: Critical Epochs in the Prehistory of Man*.

Embroiled in Immigration Debate

Osborn was also a proponent of eugenics, or the belief that humankind could be improved through selective breeding, where reproduction would be carefully monitored for so-called "favorable traits" such as height and skin color. He allied with a lawyer, conservationist, and fellow eugenics supporter, Madison Grant, to found the Galton Society in 1918. Its meetings took place in Osborn's office in the Museum, and in 1921 the Museum even hosted the Second International Congress of Eugenics. Osborn gave the opening address, in which he said, according to Pierpont, that "we are engaged in a serious struggle to maintain our historic republican institutions through barring the entrance of those who are unfit to share the duties and responsibilities of our well-founded government." Osborn further maintained that the "unfit" would remain permanently so, since "education and environment do not fundamentally alter racial values."

The Galton Society supported a new and much more restrictive immigration bill, and on April 3, 1924, the *New York Times* published an editorial written by Osborn that bore the title "Lo, the Poor Nordic!" In it, he asserted that "there is incontestable evidence that other countries, aided by foreign steamship companies, are endeavoring to "send us the people they believe they can spare and retain the people they believe they need." He also claimed that the Nordic race, to which he belonged, originated in the western part of Asia and came to Northern Europe in 12,000 B.C.E., a theory that has since been debunked. The myth of Nordic superiority, however, would be used a decade later by Adolf Hitler, the leader of Nazi Germany, who began a program to exterminate Jews, Romany, the developmentally disabled, and other peoples the Nazis deemed undesirable based on the principals of eugenics.

Osborn retired from the Museum of Natural History in 1933, and died two years later at Castle Rock on November 6, 1935. He and his wife had five children, although one died in infancy. One son, Henry Fairfield Osborn Jr., became the longtime president of the New York Zoological Society, and also authored the influential 1948 book *Our Plundered Planet*, which warned of a coming global catastrophe because of the modern era's careless management of natural resources.

Books

Biographical Dictionary of American and Canadian Naturalists and Environmentalists, edited by Keir B. Sterling et al., Greenwood Press, 1997, pp. 592–596.

Dictionary of American Biography, Supplements 1-2, American Council of Learned Societies, 1944-1958.

Dictionary of Scientific Biography, Volume X, edited by Charles Coulston Gillispie, American Council of Learned Societies/ Charles Scribner's Sons, 1980, p. 241.

Periodicals

Natural History, May 2005, p. 34.

New Scientist, October 1, 2005, p. 31.

New Yorker, March 8, 2004, p. 48.

New York Times, February 15, 1905, p. 9; December 30, 1906, p. 21; April 8, 1924, p. 18.

Obituary Notices of Fellows of the Royal Society, December 1936, pp. 67-71. □

P

E. Sylvia Pankhurst

English reformer and voting rights advocate E. Sylvia Pankhurst (1882–1960) dedicated her life to radical politics, working first alongside her mother and sister as a suffragist in Great Britain, and later independently of her family as an agitator for increasingly leftist causes both at home and abroad.

A complex figure with ties to a diverse array of radical political movements during the first half of the twentieth century, Pankhurst is remembered today—like the other Pankhurst women—primarily for her association with the women's suffrage movement. Her efforts certainly contributed to the granting of the vote to women over the age of 30 in 1918, which led to full, equal suffrage for men and women in Great Britain in 1928. Unlike her mother and sister, however, Pankhurst took her fight for equality into other realms, making her mark on radical movements from communism to anti-fascism, from pacifism to pan-Africanism.

An Unusual Upbringing

Estelle Sylvia Pankhurst, who was usually called Sylvia, was born the second daughter of Richard and Emmeline Pankhurst on May 5, 1882, in Old Trafford, near Manchester, England. Richard Pankhurst, a lawyer with strong radical political leanings, was 20 years older than his wife, Emmeline, a well-educated political activist who became a renowned suffragist in her own right. The first Pankhurst daughter, Christabel, had been born in 1880 and was her mother's favorite child throughout her life; June Purvis commented in *Europe 1789–1914: Encyclopedia of the Age of Industry and Empire* that Christabel "was the brightest and prettiest of the three daughters, which caused considerable rivalry with her two younger sisters...Sylvia and Adela." Both Pankhurst sons, Frank and Harry, died before reaching adulthood.

The Pankhurst family moved several times during Sylvia Pankhurst's childhood before settling in the London area. There, Pankhurst met many of her parents' acquaintances active in the growing radical movements. She also became exposed to politics, attending speeches and meetings. In the early 1890s the family again moved, first to Southport and then back to the Manchester area. Pankhurst's formal education was somewhat haphazard, although she did attend school both in Southport and later in Manchester. Writing in *E. Sylvia Pankhurst: Portrait of a Radical,* Patricia W. Romero noted that "already the victim of so many moves and of such eccentric parents, [Pankhurst] made few, if any friends in these crucial teenage years...and became involved—perhaps excessively so—with the causes and concerns of her parents."

In 1895 Richard Pankhurst stood for Parliament as a member of the Independent Labor Party. Sylvia Pankhurst, along with the rest of the family, assisted in his campaign and was quite crushed when he lost the election. However, Pankhurst's mother successfully won a seat on the Chorlton Board of Poor Law Guardians, inaugurating a period of much political activity among the Pankhurst women. After her father's death two years later, Pankhurst enrolled on a scholarship at the Manchester School of Art to study design. She was an accomplished student, winning a national silver medal for mosaic design, a Primrose Medal, and a school scholarship that enabled her to study mosaic art in Venice, Italy. She later continued her artistic studies on a scholarship at the Royal College of Art in London.

Fought for Women's Rights

Upon her return to England, Pankhurst designed the interior for the new Pankhurst Hall, built in Manchester in honor of her father, despite the hall's refusal to allow women as members. This policy angered Pankhurst and her family, and the women soon formed an independent group dedicated to the promotion of women's rights. This group—known as the Women's Social and Political Union, or WSPU—saw its membership grow steadily after its first meeting in 1903. Pankhurst returned to London to continue her artistic studies, sending money to her mother to support the WSPU whenever possible. Her direct involvement remained slight, however, until after the WSPU's relocation to London from Manchester a few years after its formation. In 1906 Pankhurst was arrested while protesting on behalf of some WSPU members on trial in London; she was sentenced to 14 days in prison. Writing in the autobiographical *The Suffragette Movement: An Intimate Account of Persons and Ideals,* Pankhurst noted that "the protest resulted in securing for us the consideration accorded to other people, and perhaps even a little more." This event marked the beginning of Pankhurst's involvement in what was termed "militant," as opposed to peaceful, protest activities.

Pankhurst continued her suffragist activities following her release from prison, at times breaking with the policies set forth by her mother and sister Christabel; one of Christabel's first actions on relocating to London in 1906 had been to end the involvement of women from the working class East End, who had been recruited by her sister. Sylvia Pankhurst also maintained ties with the Independent Labor Party after the other Pankhursts broke away from that organization in 1907. Demonstrations in support of women's suffrage continued apace, with more than 4,000 occurring between May and November of 1910 alone. Suffragists suffered an unexpected disappointment when a bill allowing severely restricted voting rights for women failed to pass Parliament in 1911. Pankhurst remained committed to the cause despite undergoing forced feeding during a hunger strike and several prison sentences. Iris Noble noted in *Emmeline and her Daughters: The Pankhurst Suffragettes* that "Sylvia had found in herself a capacity to *be* a crusading leader, and she enjoyed it."

In 1911 Pankhurst's first book, a non-fiction account of the women's movement up to 1909 called *The Suffragette,* was published to popular success. Pankhurst traveled to the United States on two speaking tours and spent several months out of 1911 and 1912 traveling throughout that country. Upon her return to England, Pankhurst found the leadership of the WSPU at odds over the use of increasingly militant actions, and her split from her sister and mother soon widened. Christabel Pankhurst had fled Britain for Paris, but refused Sylvia's request to lead the WSPU in her absence. Instead, Sylvia Pankhurst established the East London Federation of Suffragettes in 1912, and in 1914 was expelled from the WSPU altogether. That same year, she founded a radical newspaper, *The Women's Dreadnought,* to spread news and information regarding the suffrage movement.

A Shift to Socialism

Soon after her split from the WSPU, Pankhurst became active in the World War I opposition movement. A pacifist, she gradually shifted the focus of her activities from women's suffrage to socialism. *The Women's Dreadnought* featured editorials and stories regarding food shortages, wages,

relief efforts, and pacifism, while the East London Federation of Suffragettes became the Workers Suffrage Federation in 1916, showing the recent encompassment of socialist ideology. Emmeline and Christabel Pankhurst's support for the war further increased the rift within the family. Sylvia Pankhurst supported the revolution in Russia, hoping it would lead to Russian withdrawal from the war and perhaps inspire Britain to do the same.

Although that withdrawal did not occur, Pankhurst continued to support Bolshevik politics. She helped form the first Communist Party in Britain and called for revolution within the country. Pankhurst traveled to Petrograd (St. Petersburg) where she met with Soviet leader Vladimir Lenin. In 1920 she was arrested for sedition in Britain and began supporting radical views that did not follow Lenin's stated policies. She was sentenced to prison in 1921, and shortly after her release was expelled from the Communist Party she had worked to organize.

By about 1925 or 1926, Pankhurst had become romantically involved with Italian anarchist Silvio Corio, whom she had probably met in the late 1910s. The two developed what Romero called "a working partnership that lasted until the end of Corio's life." Pankhurst, who had wished to have a child for several years, was delighted to welcome a son, Richard, in December of 1927 as a result of her union with Corio. Despite her mother's disapproval, Pankhurst refused to marry Corio, and publicly announced the birth of Richard without revealing the identity of the father. Pankhurst had become further estranged from her mother after the latter announced a bid for Parliament as a Conservative in 1927, and some believe that Pankhurst's open acknowledgement of the baby was a stab at her mother; the shock of the announcement may have contributed to Emmeline Pankhurst's death in June of 1928. In the years that followed, Pankhurst became a vocal advocate for unmarried mothers, publishing a book titled *Save the Mothers: A Plea for a National Maternity Service* in 1930.

Indeed, the 1930s became a fruitful literary period for Pankhurst. She published three of her best-known works during this time: the autobiographical work *The Suffragette Movement: An Intimate Account of Persons and Ideals* in 1931, *The Home Front: A Mirror to Life in England during the World War* in 1932, and *The Life of Emmeline Pankhurst: The Suffragette Struggle for Women's Citizenship* in 1935.

Years of Ethiopian Support

From the mid-1930s until her death, Pankhurst was heavily involved in the pro-Ethiopia movement. After Italian fascist forces occupied that nation in 1935, Pankhurst began publicly agitating to draw attention to and raise funds for the Ethiopian plight. She began a paper, the *New Times and Ethiopia News,* to promote Ethiopian independence and the actions of Emperor Haile Sellassie, although she did not visit the country in person until 1944, well after the end of fascist control. On this trip, she was awarded the Order of Sheba and a Patriot's Medal with Five Palms in recognition of her work on behalf of the nation. Her dedication to this movement caused Pankhurst to become increasingly anti-British and anti-Italian, and at times irrationally pro-Ethiopian, supporting such ideas as the Ethiopian annexation of Somalia. The events of World War II passed Pankhurst by practically unnoticed in the face of her crusade on behalf of Ethiopia.

Pankhurst's efforts exhausted her, leading to nervous strain and even a heart attack in April of 1953. Her son, Richard, now fully grown, increased his presence at the *New Times and Ethiopia News*, although Pankhurst continued her role as editor. In 1954 longtime partner Corio passed away, and Pankhurst accepted Selassie's invitation to move to Ethiopia permanently. Preparations for the move took some time, and Pankhurst—along with her son, who joined the faculty of the university at Addis Ababa—finally moved to Africa in 1956, the same year as the *New Times and Ethiopia News* ceased publication. In Ethiopia, Pankhurst founded a new publication, the *Ethiopian Observer*, which she edited until the time of her death.

On September 27, 1960, at the age of 78, Pankhurst died in her sleep at her home in Addis Ababa. Romero noted that both "friends and former opponents joined in paying final respects" to the well-known figure. Ethiopian emperor Haile Sellassie granted Pankhurst a state funeral, which he and the royal family attended, and he permitted her burial in a location honoring Ethiopia's heroes. Her eulogy offered what Pankhurst, with her longstanding devotion to her adopted home, would likely have considered high praise: "Since by His Imperial Majesty's wish you rest in peace in the earth of Ethiopia, we consider you an Ethiopian."

Books

Noble, Iris, *Emmeline and Her Daughters: The Pankhurst Suffragettes,* Julian Messner, 1971.

Pankhurst, E. Sylvia, *The Suffragette Movement: An Intimate Account of Persons and Ideals,* Longmans, Green and Co., 1931.

Romero, Patricia W., *E. Sylvia Pankhurst: Portrait of a Radical,* Yale University Press, 1987.

Online

"E. Sylvia Pankhurst," *Contemporary Authors Online,*

"Europe 1789–1914: Encyclopedia of the Age of Industry and Empire,* .

"Sylvia Pankhurst," *Historic World Leaders,* reproduced in *Biography Resource Center,* http://galenet.galegroup.com/servlet/BioRC (October 19, 2008).□

William Edward Parry

The British explorer William Edward Parry (1790–1855) was the commander of three key expeditions that searched for the elusive Northwest Passage through the Arctic Ocean, north of what is now the Canadian mainland.

Parry served on the English side during the War of 1812, had a long career as a government official, and went into private enterprise as the administrator of a company working to open up the Australian frontier. But he remains most famous for his Arctic explorations, whose value was in no way diminished by the fact that they were unsuccessful in finding a way by sea from Greenland to Alaska. Parry spent four winters in the Arctic, making huge strides in procedures for equipping explorers for travel in that frozen region. A faithful journal keeper, he was an important early ethnographer of the Inuit whom he met, and who did much to keep him and his men alive on one of his voyages. Parry mapped much of the Arctic, was the first European to sail west of 100 degrees longitude in the Arctic Ocean, and on another expedition came closer to the North Pole than anyone else until nearly 50 years later.

Served in War of 1812

The fourth son of physician Caleb Hillier Parry and his wife, Sarah, William Edward Parry was born in Bath, England, on December 19, 1790. He was an adventurer from the beginning, joining England's Royal Navy before he turned 13. During the Napoleonic Wars of the nineteenth century's first decade, he served on ships in the English Channel and the Baltic Sea. Promoted to lieutenant in 1810, he got his first experience of far northern waters aboard the *Alexandria,* a ship assigned to protect the whaling station at Spitsbergen, Norway, from attack. When the War of 1812 broke out, Parry was transferred to North America and saw action in 1814 during a British attack that destroyed 27 American ships in the Connecticut River.

After he returned to England in 1817, Parry's career of Arctic exploration began when he was assigned to the crew of an expedition led by commander John Ross. Parry became commander of the *Alexander,* one of two ships that set off from London in April of 1818. The ships traveled all the way up the west coast of Greenland and arrived at the mouth of Lancaster Sound, at the northern end of what is now Baffin Bay. Ross, for reasons that remain unclear, became convinced that the way through Lancaster Sound was blocked by a mountain range, which he duly named Croker's Mountains after a British official. Parry remained unconvinced, and indeed Ross took considerable criticism from his superiors after he turned the ships around and returned home via the east coast of Baffin Island. With the Russian and American governments also keen on opening up a way through the Northwest Passage, British administrators faced pressure to find a route first.

Parry, therefore, was firmly in line as commander of a second voyage, which had specific orders to investigate the Lancaster Sound passage. Parry led two vessels, the *Hecla* and the *Griper,* west into the sound as the Arctic winter approached in 1819. Navigating among treacherous icebergs, he got as far as the southern shore of what he named Melville Island, at about 110 degrees longitude west. That made him the winner of a 5,000-pound prize offered by the British Parliament to the first explorer to pass the 100-degree mark. As the days grew shorter, Parry's ships were soon almost enclosed in sea ice. Crews had to saw for three days before they reached a small harbor on Melville Island.

It was as much in shepherding his crew through the sunless winter as in navigating at sea that Parry showed his skills as a commander. He insulated his ships with snow and outfitted them with piping that was used to transmit heat throughout the crew's quarters in temperatures that dipped as low as 55 degrees below zero. Parry understood the importance of foods containing what would later be called vitamin C in combating scurvy, and he brought large stores of lemon juice and some vegetable soup to supplement the ship's stores of salted meat and the game they could occasionally shoot on the Arctic tundra.

Mounted Plays on Board

He also understood that psychological factors might be as important as physical ones. Parry assigned the crewmen of the *Hecla* and *Griper* regular tasks such as scouring the decks with stones. For amusement they might be treated to a tune Parry himself played on a fiddle, or they might attend productions of the Royal Arctic Theatre, whose all-male casts mounted their first production on November 5, 1819, the first day with no sunrise. Later a weekly crew newspaper, the *North Georgia Gazette and Winter Chronicle,* provided additional diversion.

In the spring of 1820 Parry had high hopes of continuing on to the west and finding the way to Alaska. But while the fall of 1819 had been mild, the next spring was cold, and the ships were unable to leave Melville Island until August. By the end of that month, Parry realized that he had to give up. Returning to England with only one sailor's life lost, he was greeted as a hero. Anxious to try again, Parry left London in May of 1821 with the *Hecla* and a

replica called the *Fury.* This trip did not penetrate as far to the west as had the 1819 voyage, but it likewise yielded an abundance of information.

This time Parry sailed to the south and west of Baffin Island, aiming to enter an inlet called Repulse Bay that had been discovered by earlier explorers. He proved conclusively that it offered no access to points west, so he worked his way up the eastern shore of the peninsula that the bay interrupted. Forced to stop for the winter on an island, Parry and his crew struck up an acquaintance with a group of Inuit who gave them pointers on winter survival and drew them maps of points north and west. These maps turned out to be quite accurate, but Parry was once again frustrated by the weather. The ships could not leave the island until July, and they made it only as far as a channel Parry named the Fury and Hecla Straight before being forced to set up camp on the Inuit-inhabited Igloolik Island.

Forced to Abandon Ship

Parry filled his notebooks with information on the Inuit during the 11 months he spent on Igloolik, but he was low on provisions, and with the crew in poor health he decided to return to England in August of 1823. He made one more voyage, in 1824 and 1825, taking the route that was finally used by Norwegian explorer Roald Amundsen when he sailed through the Northwest Passage between 1903 and 1905. This attempt was the least successful; after overwintering on Baffin Island, the *Fury* was damaged in a storm on July 30, 1825. The ship was finally abandoned, and Parry returned with the whole crew on the *Hecla.* On this trip Parry again interacted with the Inuit, and he brought back a pair of goggles they used to avoid snow blindness.

Between the second and third voyages, Parry had been given the title of hydrographer in the Royal Navy, and in 1826 he married a wealthy woman named Isabella Stanley. They had eight children, and after her death Parry had three more by his second wife, Catherine Hankinson. He might have appeared ready to settle down in London, but instead continued with his adventurous ways. In 1827 he took a crew of 13 on the *Hecla* north from Spitsbergen to try to reach the North Pole. Finally caught in ice heading southward he abandoned the effort, but he passed the 82 degrees north latitude line; no European went farther north until 1876.

Parry worked at the Royal Navy's Hydrographic Office for two more years, and in 1829 he was knighted. After that, wanderlust took hold once again and he took a four-year leave from the Navy in order to travel to Australia and serve as the Australian Agricultural Company's commissioner, managing its vast landholdings in what was then British colonial Australia. Back in Britain by 1834, he held several government positions in the later part of his life: assistant poor-law commissioner for the county of Norfolk (1835–1836), administrator for the reorganization of the Home Packet Service parcel post office (1836–1837), controller of steam machinery in the Royal Navy (1837–1846), and captain and superintendent of the Royal Clarence Victualling Yard and Haslar Hospital (1846–1852), after which he retired. This talented leader, however, was drawn out of retirement to take a post as lieutenant governor of the Greenwich Hospital in 1854. Contracting cholera during an epidemic that year, he went to a spa at Bad Ems, near Koblenz in what is now Germany, to try to recover, but he died there on July 8 or 9, 1855. Participants in several later, although unsuccessful, Northwest Passage expeditions, had consulted him for advice.

Books

Berton, Pierre, *The Arctic Grail: The Quest for the Northwest Passage and the North Pole,* Viking, 1988.
Explorers and Discoverers of the World, Gale, 1993.
Fleming, Fergus, *Barrow's Boys: The Original Extreme Adventurers,* Atlantic Monthly Press, 1998.

Periodicals

Geographical, August 1999, p. 91; September 2000, p. 84.

Online

"Parry, Sir William Edward," Dictionary of Canadian Biography Online, http://www.biographi.ca/009004-119.01-e.php?&id_nbr=4123(January 18, 2009).
"Parry, Sir William Edward (1790–1855)," *Australian Dictionary of Biography,* http://www.adb.online.anu.edu.au/biogs/A020282b.htm (January 18, 2009). □

Thomas Joseph Pendergast

American political leader Thomas J. "Tom" Pendergast (1872–1945) served for only two terms on the city council of Kansas City, Missouri. Yet, in the words of an essay appearing on the Web site of the Missouri Secretary of State (State Archives), he was "the politician with the greatest effect on Missourians during the twentieth century."

After he left the city council in 1914, Pendergast's only formal title within the political establishment was chairman of the Jackson County Democratic Club, the Democratic Party organization in and around Kansas City. Yet for much of the period between the two world wars, he was more powerful than most of Missouri's elected officials, many of whom owed their positions to him. Pendergast was the boss of a political machine—a network linking voter turnout operations with political patronage. Such machines existed in several American cities between about 1875 and 1975, but Boss Pendergast's operation was for many years unique in its scope and effectiveness, electing numerous Democrats to political office in a predominantly Republican state. Pendergast's ability to turn out the vote was phenomenal," noted the Secretary of State's office. "Not only did many of the poorest people in Kansas City vote regularly, but did so frequently at each election. Indeed, in some wards voter turnout often approached one hundred percent, when it did not exceed it. Even more miraculously, the dead would rise at each election in numbers that would astonish an expectant Christian."

Worked for Brother as Bookkeeper

Thomas Joseph Pendergast was born on July 22, 1872, in St. Joseph, Missouri. His large Irish immigrant family had come to Missouri by way of Gallipolis, Ohio. Pendergast's father was a manual laborer, but Thomas's older brother James took the first step toward family wealth when he moved to Kansas City, Missouri, and racked up large winnings at the racetrack, thanks to the efforts of a horse named Climax. He invested the money in a tavern and brothel, which he named Climax as well, and then opened a second establishment. In 1890 he invited his brothers to move to Kansas City to work in his growing operation, and young Tom Pendergast, who had been educated in public and Catholic schools in St. Joseph, signed on as saloon bookkeeper.

Kansas City was growing rapidly in the last decades of the nineteenth century, and James Pendergast quickly saw that the city government could become a rich source of money and influence. He established a local Democratic Party club, Kansas City's first, and won a seat on the city council in 1892. James Pendergast's political organization, centered in the West Bottoms and North End neighborhoods that were home to his businesses, formed the nucleus of the future Pendergast machine. Tom and his brother Michael started out as low-level workers in the organization, and Tom was appointed deputy marshal for Jackson County in 1896. The Pendergast brothers soon became the people to see if one wanted a job as a Kansas

City police officer, and Tom Pendergast's influence as a source of patronage grew further when James named him the city's superintendent of streets, just as the city's elaborate network of boulevards and fountains was being constructed. In the first decade of the new century he served for several years as a county marshal, and from 1910 until 1914 he was an elected alderman, representing Kansas City's First Ward.

The area was an ethnic stew of workers—Germans, Italians, Irish, African Americans, and many others, all drawn to Kansas City's growing industries. Some prospered, but many others needed help, and the Pendergast brothers often provided it. After 1910, as his health declined, James Pendergast took less of an interest in the family's political operations. Tom Pendergast set out to widen his sphere of influence, and the consistent flow of dollars he steered toward the city's downtrodden provided him with an unshakable base of support. Meanwhile he accumulated a considerable personal fortune, extending the family saloon business into liquor wholesale operations and later acquiring a concrete factory, the Ready Mix Concrete Company.

Distributed Food at Holidays

"What's government for if it isn't to help the people?," he observed, according to the Secretary of State Web site. "If anybody's in distress, we take care of them—especially in the poor wards.... We never ask about politics." Pendergast was a superior political organizer, and he knew it: "I know how to select ward captains and I know how to get to the poor. Every single one of my ward workers has a fund...and when a poor man comes to old Tom's boys for help we don't make one of those...investigations like these city charities." Thanksgiving and Christmas baskets went out under the Pendergast name at holiday time. In 1911 Pendergast married Carrie Snyder. The couple raised three adopted children, Marceline, Eileen, and Thomas.

By the early 1920s, Pendergast's influence extended beyond the first ward and across the city of Kansas City. True to his saloonkeeper roots, he discouraged enforcement of the prohibition against alcoholic beverages mandated by the 18th Amendment to the U.S. Constitution and ratified in 1919. Partially as a result, Kansas City became an important center for the new musical genre of jazz in the 1920s and 1930s. In spite of his growing power, Pendergast had to divide the flow of patronage jobs with a Democratic Party rival, Joseph Shannon. The rivalry had existed long enough that the two factions had acquired nicknames: Pendergast Democrats, who tended to be white ethnic voters and African Americans, were called "Goats," while Shannon's supporters, often native-born, middle class, and Protestant, were "Rabbits."

Despite pressure from state authorities due to alleged fraud in the 1920 elections, Pendergast set out to extend his realm over all of Jackson County, where Kansas City was located. To muscle out Shannon and gain control of Kansas City's growing suburbs, he took a three-pronged approach. He leaned on wealthy contractors who benefited from city work. In middle class neighborhoods he organized new political clubs with a more genteel atmosphere than that of the rough-and-tumble city ward offices, sponsoring such events as bridge parties and dances. And, most significantly in terms of American political history in general, he endorsed a squeaky-clean candidate with rural Missouri roots, Harry S. Truman, for county judge in the 1921 elections.

Truman, who had served with Pendergast's nephew in World War I, won the election, going on with Pendergast's help to win several other judicial and administrative posts. Shrewdly endorsing a series of political reforms that he quickly saw he could turn to his own benefit, Pendergast gained total control over Kansas City's government in 1926 as the city council's size was reduced from 32 to nine members. Shannon's supporters were edged out, and Pendergast's eight city department directors controlled a payroll of 37,000 workers. Pendergast's new suburban supporters were rewarded with big tax breaks on projects they undertook in the city.

Distributed New Deal Largesse

The Pendergast machine reached its peak between 1926 and 1935. His ability to contribute a margin of about 100,000 votes in Jackson County for Democrats running in statewide elections gave him influence all over Missouri as well, and by the time Truman won election to the U.S. Senate in 1934, both of Missouri's senators and its governor were Pendergast allies. Pendergast's base of operations was a nondescript building at 1908 Main Street in Kansas City. "To this Mecca," observed U.S. Federal Judge Merrill Otis and quoted on the aforementioned Web site, "came he who would be governor, he who would be senator, he who would be judge and he who was content to be only a keeper of the [dog] pound." Federal projects that came to Missouri thanks to President Franklin Roosevelt's New Deal stimulus projects in the 1930s were largely funneled through Pendergast's organization.

Finally, though, Pendergast and his supporters overreached. In the 1936 elections, which were again marked by widespread fraud allegations, Pendergast backed apple farmer Lloyd Stark for Missouri governor. Stark won the election, but after that he had a falling-out with Pendergast and successfully backed a rival candidate for a Missouri Supreme Court seat in 1938. More than 250 of Pendergast's party workers were convicted of vote fraud in 1937 and 1938. President Roosevelt, alarmed by Pendergast's reputation for corruption, increasingly began to work with Stark instead in disbursing funds to Missouri. When investigators examined various aspects of the Pendergast machine, it emerged that Pendergast had mediated between insurance companies and state regulators and had collected a large fee that he did not report on his federal income tax returns—perhaps because he was beset by mounting gambling debts.

In 1939 Pendergast was convicted of income tax evasion. While he was serving 15 months at the federal prison in Leavenworth, Kansas, his organization shrank but was still powerful enough to control several Kansas City wards, and to play a key role in promoting Truman's selection as Roosevelt's running mate at the 1944 Democratic Convention. Truman, however, is thought to have acted independently of Pendergast's influence in the Senate and to have been unaware of the excesses of the machine in its last years. Pendergast died of heart disease in Kansas City on January 26, 1945.

Books

Ferrell, Robert H., *Truman & Pendergast,* University of Missouri Press, 1999.

Larsen, Lawrence H, and Nancy J. Hulston, *Pendergast!,* University of Missouri Press, 1997.

Periodicals

Wisconsin State Journal, June 27, 1999, p. F3.

Online

"FAQ: How was Pendergast associated with the career of Truman?," Harry S. Truman Library & Museum, http://www.trumanlibrary.org/trivia/penderga.htm (January 20, 2009).

"Missouri's Most Important Politician," Missouri Secretary of State—State Archives Publications, http://www.sos.mo.gov/archives/pubs/article/article.asp (January 20, 2009).

"The Pendergast Machine," Kansas City, Missouri, Police Officers Memorial, http://www.kcpolicememorial.com/history/pendergast_3.html (January 20, 2009). □

Erwin Friedrich Maximilian Piscator

Born in Germany at a time of great political change, Erwin Piscator (1893–1966) used the theater to communicate his political and social views. Through his productions, Piscator demanded an end to war and militarism and sought to promote the needs of ordinary working people. He earned great renown not only for the message of his plays but also for the method itself. Piscator was an innovator who sought to connect every performance to the entire theater and its audience by mechanizing the stage and using whatever media form and technological device might best complement the production.

Childhood, Education, and War

Erwin Piscator was born to Carl Piscator and Antonia Laperose in Ulm, a village in central Germany, on December 17, 1893. His father was a merchant, and the family lived a largely middle-class lifestyle.

Early on, Piscator's family moved from Ulm to Marburg. There, he attended the Volkshochschule until 1913 when he went on to Munich University. At the university, Piscator initially studied philosophy, art history, and the German language. During his studies, he took classes under two theater historians, Arthur Kutscher and Max Hermann. After that experience, Piscator shifted his focus to the dramatic arts and the history of theater. He began volunteering at the Hof Theater and the Bavarian Court Theater in Munich.

Then war erupted, and from 1914 through 1918, World War I consumed most of Europe. Like most other German young men of his age, Piscator was conscripted, or forced to join the Germany army. From 1915 through 1917, he served in the infantry, operating radios as a signaller on the front lines of the battle. His experiences on the battlefield resulted in a life-long opposition to war and military aggression.

While he served, Piscator wrote poems and submitted them to the literary magazine *Die Aktion.* The magazine published several of Piscator's poems in 1915 and 1916. Then, in 1917, while fighting in the First Battle of Ypres, Piscator was wounded and hospitalized. Rather than send him back to battle on the front, his superiors reassigned Piscator to the army theater unit. Piscator spent the remainder of the war entertaining his fellow soldiers in Belgium.

Mixing Politics and Theater

World War I ended in 1918, and Piscator returned to Germany. There, he joined the newly formed German Communist Party. He was committed to working for better conditions for the working class of Germany. That same year, Piscator attended a meeting of the revolutionary Soldiers' Council in Hasselt and gave his first political speech.

In 1919, Piscator went to Berlin and began working in experimental theater. Like his colleagues, Piscator recognized the power of the theater to communicate ideas. Back in 1916, through the theater, Piscator had come into contact with a group of Dadaists, a movement of artists and reformers who challenged traditional forms of expression. Through the Dadaists, Piscator realized that the stage did not have to be just a stage. It could be anything, and he could do whatever he could figure out to do with it.

Piscator quickly became interested in using inventive staging techniques, such as mobile stages, as well as mechanical devices and multiple forms of media to create a "total theater" experience between the actors and the audience. For Piscator, the theater was not just a means of entertainment but a vehicle for information, organization, and reform. In *Documentary Theatre in the United States,* Hugh Rorrison is quoted as saying that Piscator's method aimed to "fuse audience and stage action and turn the performance into a public meeting."

In 1920, Piscator married Hilde Jurezyss, and helped found the Proletarian Theatre in Berlin. *Proletarian* refers to the working class, and the theater group was organized to perform in working class districts. At its height, it had about 5,000 members. The troupe performed in workers' clubs, admitted unemployed workers without charge, and recruited many of its performers and participants from the working class.

Documentary Theatre cited Piscator's own explanation of theater's suitability cooperative action: "Collective effort is rooted in the very nature of theater. No other art form, with the exception of architecture and orchestral music, relies so heavily on the existence of a community of like-minded people as does theater."

Piscator welcomed the input of the entire cast and crew in revising every production during rehearsal. He also continued experimenting with staging, media, and technological devices. When the group put on *Russia's Day,* written by Lajos Barta, the stage became a large world map. Unfortunately, the theater was short lived because of finances, and it closed in April 1921.

Over the next two years, Piscator worked with writer Hans Rehfisch to put together a proletarian Volksbühne (People's Theater) at the Central-Theater in Berlin. They staged several productions, including *The Power of Darkness* by Leo Tolstoy, whose works Piscator greatly revered. Though this undertaking did not last either, it did launch Piscator's reputation and commit him to the theater.

People's Theater

In 1924, Piscator went to work at the established Volksbühne of Berlin, and served as the director there until 1927. Piscator produced many plays at the Volksbühne and was able to experiment with various types of staging and mechanization. The May 1924 production of *Flags,* by Alfons Paquet, included the use of projections on either side of the stage flanking the live action. The 1926 performance of Paquet's *Tidal Wave* also involved projections as well as a moving stage. In later productions, Piscator would refer to the use of projections as "the theater's fourth dimension."

Piscator was quite busy during the 1920s. In addition to directing at the Volksbühne, he also produced two revues for the Communist Party during the German elections of 1924–1925. In the *Red Riot Review,* Piscator launched the action with an argument in the auditorium. The main actors of the play emerged from the audience and carried the action to the stage. He also incorporated dance, gymnastics, dozens of sketches, communist songs, and projections. The second revue, *In Spite of Everything,* also made use of projections. Piscator used a large amount of newsreel footage from World War I as well as recorded speeches and photographs. The stage itself was mechanized, revolving to show the action from multiple perspectives.

In 1927, Piscator worked with the architect Walter Gropius to design his own "total theater," which would immerse the audience in a complete theatrical experience. Gropius later explained, as quoted in *Documentary Theatre,* that the goal of total theater was "to force the audience into close contact with the scenic action, to make them participate in the playing and not to allow them to withdraw behind the curtains."

Piscator wanted the theater building to be fully mechanized and suitable to various forms of staging and the most modern technology. He envisioned projecting films and images not only on the stage but also on the surrounding walls and ceilings. He wanted the audience's seating to be able to move. The design was extraordinary, but it was not realized because of the expense; Piscator would soon succeed in getting his own theater, however.

In 1927, Piscator left the Volksbühne and started the Piscator Studio at the Theater on Nollendorfplatz. He produced numerous plays over the next several years, including Ernst Toller's *Hurrah! We're Alive!* in which he had a multi-room house structure built on a revolving stage so he could project images onto multiple screens as the action unfolded.

One of Piscator's most elaborate productions was *Rasputin, the Romanoffs, the War, and the People who Rose up against Them,* also staged at the Nollendorfplatz in 1927. For this play, Piscator used 12 acting spaces constructed inside a mechanized half-globe structure that could open and close and rotate. Piscator incorporated film footage of the Russian royal family and other relevant footage. He asked the former Kaiser Wilhelm of Germany to appear and deliver a historic quote, but instead the former Kaiser sued the company and the German government ordered the quote removed from the performance. In its place, Piscator had the actor deliver a presentation about the censorship.

In 1929, Piscator published his first and only book, *Das politische Theater,* a treatise on the use of theater for political purposes.

Emigration

In the early 1930s, Piscator's wife Hilde left him, and the onset of worldwide depression and the rise to power of the Nazis in Germany began to hurt his theater—as well as most other German theaters. In 1931, Piscator was jailed briefly for failing to pay taxes on his theater company. Although he managed to put on several more performances in the next few years, he ultimately decided to flee Germany and the increasing militarism of the Nazi regime.

For several years, Piscator had been traveling between Berlin and Moscow in Russia, working on various theatrical and dramatic productions. So in 1934, it seemed natural for Piscator to make his first move from Germany by going to Moscow to direct the film *The Revolt of the Fisherman.* After completing the film, Piscator traveled to other European cities, ending up in Paris, France, in 1936.

While in Paris, friends warned Piscator not to return to Russia either because the government there had begun imprisoning and executing artists, writers, and any others who were deemed a threat. Unsure what to do next, Piscator stayed in France for two years, but he did not produce much while there. He did, however, meet his second wife, the dancer and choreographer Maria Ley. They were married in April of 1937, and together, they decided to emigrate to the United States in 1939.

In the United States, the Piscators found great success. The newly wed couple settled in New York City and opened the Dramatic Workshop and Studio Theater at the New School for Social Research. They would stay in New York City, teaching and producing drama, for the next 12 years. During his tenure at the workshop, Piscator taught such renowned actors, playwrights, and directors as Marlon Brando, James Dean, Tennessee Williams, Harry Belafonte, and Walter Matthau. In 1941, Piscator's friend and collaborator Bertolt Brecht also joined him at the workshop. Brecht would adopt and popularize many of Piscator's most innovative methods.

But Piscator's politics would bring him trouble in the United States as well. When the Cold War set in following the end of World War II, Piscator and many of his colleagues found themselves subjected to increasing suspicion. Eager to avoid the investigations of U.S. Senator Joseph McCarthy, Piscator left the United States and returned to Germany in 1951. His wife, however, stayed in New York City to manage the Dramatic Workshop.

Back Home

As Germany, now divided into West and East Germany, struggled to recover from the destruction of the war, Piscator and others were determined to revive the theater. Piscator worked on a few productions in Hamburg, West Germany, before returning to the Volksbühne, in West Berlin, as a director. Among the plays he directed in the early 1950s were Rolf Hochhuth's *The Representative* and *The Soldiers* and Peter Weiss's *The Investigation,* which addressed economic conditions that made the concentration camp at Auschwitz possible.

In 1958, Piscator was appointed the manager of the Volksbühne, and in 1962, he became its artistic director. During that time, he continued to produce topical performances that brought the most critical issues of the time to the stage.

Piscator spent the remainder of his life as the artistic director of the Volksbühne. He continued to use innovative techniques in his set design and staging. Piscator considered one of his greatest accomplishments to be the dramatic production of Tolstoy's epic *War and Peace.* Piscator had reportedly spent much of his life devising mechanical stages and other devices for the sole purpose of producing Tolstoy's story on stage.

On March 30, 1966, Piscator died in Stanberg, West Germany. His wife, Maria, was still living and working in New York. Two decades later, she would appeal to the nonprofit group Elysium, which fostered artistic exchanges between Europe and the United States, to institute the Erwin Piscator Award in her husband's honor.

Piscator's legacy was one not only of theatrical creation but also of political and social activism. He strove to bring to the stage stories meant to inform, challenge, and motivate people to take action in their own lives. With his mechanized stages, use of projections, and other devices, Piscator blended the stories of the plays with historical background and contemporary context. *Documentary Theatre* recorded Piscator's explanation of his genre: "The most primitive explanation of [epic theater] would be that it is like a novel in that it presents not only dramatic action, but also describes the surrounding social and political circumstances." Piscator repeatedly drew connections between the past and the present—and above all, he pulled his audiences into the productions with the actors.

The website for the Erwin Piscator Award further elaborated, "Piscator believed in theat[er] as an instrument...to relate human beings to their societies, to their environment and to the world around them."

Piscator was considered the originator of epic theater, a dramatic style meant to convey social, economic and political messages rather than simply to entertain. His productions blurred the lines between the performers and the audience, making those who came to watch his productions more than mere observers. For Piscator, everyone in the theater was a participant. Piscator inspired generations of actors, directors, and producers to emulate his inventive methods to bring the audience into the performance, the story, and the significance of the moment.

Books

The Oxford Illustrated History of Theatre, Ed. John Russell Brown, Oxford University Press, 1995.

Dawson, Gary Fisher, *Documentary Theatre in the United States: An Historical Survey and Analysis of Its Content, Form, and Stagecraft,* Greenwood Press, 1999.

Grant, Neil, *History of Theatre,* Hamlyn, 2002.

Hartnoll, Phyllis, *The Theatre: A Concise History,* Revised Edition, Thames and Hudson, Inc., 1985.

Willett, John, *The Theatre of Erwin Piscator,* Eyre Methuen, 1978.

Online

"epic theatre," *Encyclopedia Britannica,* http://search.eb.com/eb/article-9032777 (October 16, 2008).

"Erwin Piscator," *Encyclopedia Britannica,* http://search.eb.com/eb/article-9060183 (October 16, 2008).

"Erwin Piscator (1893–1966)," *Tezzaland,* http://homepages.tesco.net/ theatre/tezzaland/webstuff/piscator.html (January 7, 2009).

"Erwin Piscator Award," *EBTC,* http://www.elysiumbtc.org/frame.html (October 16, 2008).

"Piscator, Erwin," *Columbia Encyclopedia,* http://www.bartleby.com/65/pi/Piscator.html (October 16, 2008).

"theatre," *Encyclopedia Britannica,* http://seach.eb.com/eb/article-39424 (October 16, 2008).

"Volksbühne am Rosa-Luxemburg-Platz," Transl., http://www.volksbuehne-berlin.de/volksbuehne/english_information/?PHPSESSID=c3c778b27510bc2e97abd66a35573534 (January 7, 2009). □

Juan Pizarro

Spanish conquistador Juan Pizarro (c.1495–1536) was one of four brothers who conquered the area in South America that is now Peru, on behalf of European interests. Although less well-known than his older brother Francisco, Pizarro contributed greatly to the rise of Spanish domination in the region; his leadership at the siege of Cuzco both aided the Spanish victory there and led to his relatively early death.

The four Pizarro brothers hailed from Trujillo, Estremadura, Spain, and shared one father but many mothers. Their father, Gonzalo Pizarro, was a Spanish infantry officer; his wife, Isabel de Vargas, was the mother of only the second Pizarro brother, Hernando, who was born sometime in the late 1470s. The eldest Pizarro brother, Francisco, had been born sometime in the early- to mid-1470s. His mother, called alternately Francisca González or Morales, has been sometimes identified as the mother of both third son Juan, born in the mid-1490s, and youngest brother Gonzalo, born in the early 1500s. However, the years separating the births of the younger three brothers make it unlikely that González was indeed the mother of Juan and Gonzalo; recent scholarship identifies Juan Pizarro's mother as María Alonso, who may or may not have also been Gonzalo Pizarro's mother.

Experienced Impoverished Youth

Juan Pizarro's early years remain as obscured as his maternal line. It is known that all the Pizarro brothers grew up in extreme poverty, and all but Francisco learned to read and write. Writing in *Brothers of Doom: The Story of the Pizarros of Peru,* Hoffman Birney noted that the Pizarros' father "bequeathed a tall, straight body, superb physical strength and powers of endurance, a natural skill with sword and lance, and lean, patrician features" to the four brothers. Juan Pizarro particularly was also reported to have thirsted for wealth—presumably as a result of his own poverty—from a young age. Philip Ainsworth Means noted some of Pizarro's less savory qualities in *Fall of the Inca Empire and the Spanish Rule in Peru: 1530–1780,* stating that Pizarro was "poor, proud, and avaricious, qualities which led [him] to do and dare anything for the sake of sudden wealth."

Participated in the Conquest of Peru

Francisco Pizarro had spent the first two decades of the sixteenth century exploring the Americas, eventually becoming lieutenant governor of Panama. During the 1520s, however, he joined forces with Diego de Almagro and Hernando de Luque and began exploring lands south of Panama in the hopes of discovering fabled riches. Francisco Pizarro's group eventually came into contact with the Inca Empire at the city of Tumbez in the northern Tawantinsuyu. Believing this city to be only the tip of what Means called "the long-dreamt-of golden empire," Pizarro returned to Spain to lobby King Charles I and Queen Isabella for approval to explore and conquer the lands of Peru. In July of 1529, Queen Isabella signed the Capitulación, or Agreement, of Toledo, granting Francisco Pizarro commanding authority, much to the disappointment of Almagro, who received only the command of Tumbez.

The Agreement placed various conditions on Pizarro's conquests and required him to recruit at least 150 Spaniards in only six months before returning to the Americas. Among these Spanish recruits was Juan Pizarro, along with brothers Hernando and Gonzalo and a few other relatives, presumably driven by desire for wealth. The Spanish party set out for Panama in two ships in late January of 1530, despite Francisco Pizarro's inability to recruit the full 150 men demanded by the Agreement. About a year later, the small army—some 200 altogether, including Juan Pizarro—began their journey of conquest. Almagro, although initially reluctant to participate in the expedition at all, agreed to remain in Panama to gather reinforcements before following Pizarro's party at a later date.

Landing first at a spot far distant from Tumbez, the force endured a long and difficult overland voyage, eventually reaching the island of Puña in the Gulf of Guayaquil. There, the Spanish fought a battle against the native inhabitants of the island and found themselves embroiled in local disputes. The conquering party left the island after Hernando de Soto arrived from Panama, accompanied by additional men and horses. The enlarged army crossed to the Peruvian mainland and traveled to Tumbez, only to find the city in ruins, reportedly destroyed as a result of an Incan civil war. Leaving the site of Tumbez in the spring of 1523, the party spent several months exploring northwestern Peru. Their numbers were again swollen by reinforcements brought by Sebastián de Banalcázar and Hernando de Soto, although about 60 members left the invading force to form the first Spanish settlement in Peru, San Miguel de Piura.

The reduced force left San Miguel and turned inland toward the Inca Empire in November of 1532. The Incas had been in the midst of a civil war between two factions headed by Huascar and Atahualpa; as the Spaniards began their journey, the civil war was coming to a close with Atahualpa as the victor. Francisco Pizarro, learning of the conflict, decided to try to use it for his own ends, and set on a course for Atahualpa's camp at Cajamarca. The Inca leader sent gifts to the Spaniards and decided not to attack them. John Hemming noted in *The Conquest of the Incas* that "the Spaniards were fortunate that Atahualpa had decided not to oppose their march into the mountains.... Less professional Inca armies destroyed a force as large as this in similar mountainous country four years later." Upon arriving at Cajamarca, the Spaniards were intimidated by the large and well-organized camp. However, they managed to overcome a guard of about 7,000 to capture the Inca leader, who had greatly underestimated the Spaniards' power. Atahulpa later paid a massive ransom of gold and silver to obtain his freedom, but was executed by Francisco Pizarro in July of 1533.

Juan Pizarro then accompanied the Spanish forces to the Inca capital of Cuzco. There, the Spanish first dedicated themselves to finding and distributing Inca wealth before turning to matters of government. The Incan Manco was established as a puppet ruler in early 1534, with the empire truly being controlled by Francicso Pizarro as governor. By the end of 1534, Francisco Pizarro had left Cuzco to deal with a fellow conquistador, Gonzalo Maldonado, who had violated Pizarro's recent order to halt all looting and treat the native Incans respectfully. Juan Pizarro, along with younger brother Gonzalo, was left in charge of a small garrison at Cuzco except for a brief period during which Francisco Pizarro's longtime partner in exploration, Almagro, took control.

Soon, Francisco Pizarro returned control of the city to Juan and Gonzalo, and Almagro departed shortly afterward to inspect his new lands in Chile. During the summer of 1535, the Incan Manco was becoming increasingly disenchanted with Spanish rule; the actions of Hernando Pizarro, back in Cuzco after a trip to Spain, only served to fuel his anger. By the fall of that year, Manco had determined to lead the Inca people against the Spanish. He escaped from Cuzco, but was soon discovered by Juan Pizarro and others; upon his return to the city, Manco was imprisoned. During his imprisonment, both Juan and Gonzalo Pizarro left Cuzco to deal with small uprisings. By the time Hernando Pizarro returned to Cuzco from Spain in January of 1536, Juan Pizarro had ordered that Manco be released from captivity. Soon, all of the Pizarro brothers except for Francisco, who was then in the new Spanish capital of Lima, were back in Cuzco. Manco asked for and received permission to leave the city, ostensibly to participate in ceremonies but in fact to stage a rebellion.

Died at the Siege of Cuzco

In the spring of 1536, Manco spearheaded what Means described as "a final and desperate attempt to capture the traditional capital of his empire," gathering a massive army of Incan warriors—estimates of the number of soldiers range from 100,000 to 200,000—and leading them to Cuzco. A lengthy siege ensued when as few as 200 Spanish fighters defended the city against the massive Inca onslaught. Manco had managed to trap Francisco Pizarro and his army at Lima, preventing them from coming to assist the forces of Juan, Hernando, and Gonzalo Pizarro at Cuzco. Birney offered a somewhat fantastic explanation of the Spaniards' defense, stating that "the direct intervention of Saint James and the Virgin saved Hernando Pizarro and his men... A miracle, of course, but one must be willing to accept the miraculous if there is to be any explanation of why the tiny force of battle-weary horsemen and foot soldiers was not overwhelmed by the sheer weight of numbers." Whatever the reason—and probably at least somewhat due to their superior armor and weaponry—the Spanish forces successfully held the city for several months in the face of seemingly impossible odds.

The Inca forces had made their base in the fortress of Sacsayhuamán near Cuzco. From this location, they could easily attack the city not only on foot, but also by throwing stones, burning objects, and other missiles towards the Spanish enclosure. The Spaniards determined that recapturing the fortress was vital to their continued survival, and assigned Juan Pizarro to lead the attack. He gathered about 50 Spanish horsemen and set out on the dangerous trek up to the fortress.

Days before the attack on Sacsayhuamán, Pizarro had been struck in the head by an arrow. The injury made wearing a helmet particularly painful and Pizarro thus chose to forego head protection. This decision turned out to be fatal one. Shortly after reaching the walls of the fort, Pizarro was struck on the head by a large rock. He lingered for about two weeks before dying at Cuzco as a result of his injuries on May 16, 1536. Pizarro left the bulk of his wealth to his brother Gonzalo—ignoring the Inca woman with whom he had been involved and the daughter she had borne him—and the remainder to religious and charitable causes in both Panama and Spain. The Spanish forces fought on, and, bolstered by troops brought by the returning Almagro in 1537, managed to defeat the Inca revolt.

Although the remaining Pizarro brothers themselves died or, in the case of Hernando, returned to Spain within about a decade of Juan Pizarro's death, they built an enduring Spanish empire in Peru. Of the four brothers, Birney judged Juan Pizarro to be "by all indication the best of the lot." Although he has been overshadowed throughout history by the successes of his siblings, particularly Francisco, Juan Pizarro played an important role in the conquest of the Inca empire and helped establish the groundwork for further European exploration and settlement.

Books

Birney, Hoffman, *Brothers of Doom: The Story of the Pizarros of Peru*, G.P. Putnam's Sons, 1942.

Hemming, John, *The Conquest of the Incas*, Harcorut Brace Jovanovich, 1970.

Means, Philip Ainsworth, *Fall of the Inca Empire and the Spanish Rule in Peru: 1530–1780,* Charles Scribner's Sons, 1932.

Europe, 1450 to 1789: An Encyclopedia of the Early Modern World,'' □

Jan Hird Pokorny

Jan Hird Pokorny (1914–2008) was a Czech-born architect who achieved prominence during his decades-long career in New York City. Pokorny fled the Nazi invasion of Czechoslovakia at the onset of World War II, but maintained ties to his homeland through various émigré-organizations in the New York area. In 2006, he was interviewed by *New York Times* journalist Joseph Berger for an article about lingering immigrant pockets on the Upper East Side. Berger described the architect as "a specialist in preservation," but also noted that "he himself is a preserved specimen of the gallant European, a breed that has almost vanished in the razzle-dazzle of modern life."

An only child, Pokorny was born on May 25, 1914, in Brno, a large city in Czechoslovakia, but his parents later moved to Prague. His father, Jaroslav, was a prominent electrical engineer who became an assistant general director of Škoda Works, an industrial powerhouse that was the largest company of its type in the country. The senior Pokorny also served as president of the Czechoslovak Electrotechnical Association and authored articles for professional journals and even books on subjects in his field.

Escaped to Sweden

Pokorny graduated from the engineering-architecture program at the Czech Technical University of Prague in 1937, and practiced architecture briefly in the city before Nazi Germany first annexed part of Czechoslovakia and then fully invaded the neighboring land by 1939. Pokorny fled first to Sweden, and then obtained a student visa to attend Columbia University in New York City in 1940. The Škoda Works factories, meanwhile, began churning out Panzer tanks and other heavy artillery for the German military effort. His father was briefly jailed by the Nazis, and eventually emigrated to the United States after the war.

Pokorny earned his master's degree from Columbia in 1941, and went to Detroit, where in a somewhat ironic twist he worked for two architectural firms in Detroit that were hired to convert Ford automotive factories over to tank production for the U.S. war effort to defeat Nazi Germany. Back in New York City in 1944, he was hired as an architect by Skidmore, Owings & Merrill in New York City, where he spent two years before establishing his own firm with his wife, Elizabeth Hird, who was also an architect. Pokorny took his wife's surname as his middle name.

When he first arrived in Manhattan, Pokorny settled in a neighborhood of Czech émigré families located around the East 70s-numbered streets near Second Avenue in a section of the Upper East Side that was known as Yorkville. The area was also home to many other European refugees, from the East 60s north to the East 90s. "It was very funny, the Czechs, next to the Hungarians, next to the Germans—just as it was in Europe," Pokorny told Berger, the *New York Times* writer. "When you walked the streets, you heard Czech spoken."

Designed College Facilities

Professionally, Pokorny built a reputation in the first half of his career as an talented architect of college-campus buildings. Some of the commissions he won include buildings for Centenary College in Hackettstown, New Jersey, and at the State University of New York at Stony Brook. For the Bronx-based Lehman College, he designed its Speech and Theater Building, the Performing Arts Center, and the Leonard Lief Library. For his alma mater, Columbia University, he supervised the renovation of Lewisohn Hall, formerly the School of Mines building and originally built by a top New York City architect of the early twentieth century, Arnold Brunner.

Pokorny began to win important restoration jobs in the second half of his long career. By then he was divorced from Hird and remarried, and had began and ended a six-year partnership with another architect as Pokorny & Pertz. In 1977, he reestablished his own eponymous firm, which for many years had offices in his home. "It was very similar to an atelier atmosphere, very unstructured and familial," recalled Michael Devonshire, a firm partner and director of conservation, in a tribute to Pokorny published in *The Architect's Newspaper.* "It was the norm that at everyone's birthday we would sit at his huge George Nakashima dining room table and have Slivovitz and cake. Often, if one arrived early, Jan would already be at his desk, but in his pajamas."

One of the significant commissions won by Pokorny's firm was the renovation of the historic Schermerhorn Row at the South Street Seaport, located near the East River between Front, John, South and Fulton Streets. Its buildings date back to 1812, making them one of the oldest commercial blocks in the United States, and Pokorny found an unusual construction method once his team began excavations: there was a layer of salt water beneath Schermerhorn Row, which kept the wooden footings supporting the heavy brick buildings from rotting in the water. "Nobody bothered to examine the foundations of buildings torn down in lower Manhattan to see how ingeniously they were done," Pokorny told George W. Goodman in the *New York Times.* "The old builders knew that salt water would preserve the condition of wood that is just as clean and strong as it was the day it went in. By maintaining the original foundations, the project saved $1 million for improvements we can see."

Appointed to Landmarks Preservation Commission

Pokorny's firm also won a commission to restore the Brooklyn Historical Society building located at 128 Pierrepont

Street in Brooklyn Heights. This was one of the first buildings in the United States to use a terra-cotta façade, and the renovation work had to be done with excessive care in order to preserve the original decorations dating back to 1881. Eventually, Pokorny's expertise led to a plum appointment on the New York City Landmarks Preservation Commission in 1996. The Commission—upon whose decisions sometimes millions of dollars in development money often hinge—is known for its capriciousness, and Pokorny was sometimes at odds with his commissioner-colleagues. In 2007, they reviewed a proposal for "a 30-story glass tower addition to a five-story building on the Upper East Side," explained *New York Times* writer Bruce Weber. "During a contentious hearing on the proposed project, he passed out copies of a print that showed the Leaning Tower of Pisa, which was begun in 1173, beside the Dome of Pisa, a century older. Adding a vertical tower to a horizontal base or placing it nearby, Mr. Pokorny said, 'has been done in history many times.'"

A fellow of the American Institute of Architects, Pokorny also taught at Columbia University School of Architecture from 1958 to 1974, and served as director of its evening program in architecture from 1957 to 1973. After 1974, he held the title of professor of architecture at Columbia's Graduate School of Architecture, Planning and Preservation, and professor emeritus after 1982. He was a trustee of the Grand Central Terminal Trust Fund and held the vice presidency of the Fine Arts Federation of New York City. From 1987 until his death he was president of the Bohemian Benevolent and Literary Association of New York City, which worked to preserve the landmark Bohemian National Hall on 73rd Street between First and Second Avenues. The building—once the center of social life for Czech émigrés like himself earlier in the century—still housed a ballroom, bowling alley, and even a shooting range.

When Pokorny's father Jaroslav came to America in 1948, he became treasurer of the American Fund for Czechoslovak Refugees, which aided fellow émigrés. The senior Pokorny died in 1958, and his son took his seat on the board a year later. From 1964 to 1971 Pokorny served as board secretary, and chaired the body from 1971 until his death. He had a son, Stefan Alexander, with his second wife Marise Angelucci, whom he wed in 1967.

Pokorny died after a long illness on May 20, 2008, in New York City, at the age of 93. In the tribute that appeared in *The Architect's Newspaper,* a colleague on the Landmarks Preservation Commission, Richard M. Olcott, commended Pokorny's ability "to serenely reside above the fray and get to the issues and the truth, and then find the way forward. I will miss that, and New Yorkers will too, whether they know it or not."

Periodicals

New York Times, September 2, 1958, p. 25; January 9, 1983; December 29, 1996; February 11, 2001; March 14, 2004; April 7, 2006; May 23, 2008.

The Architect's Newspaper, June 25, 2008. □

R

Manfred von Richthofen

German aviator Manfred von Richthofen (1892–1918) gained international repute as the World War I combat pilot whom the press dubbed "the Red Baron." Flying in lightweight armed aircraft that were an important technological advance in aerial warfare at the time, the handsome, aristocratic flyer took down 80 British planes in a relatively short career before he was himself felled in the final months of the war. Richthofen, noted Jonathan M. Young in *Air Power History*, "conquered the skies and the imagination at a time when war degraded from a noble endeavor to an industrial and impersonal slaughter."

Richthofen was born on May 2, 1892, in what was then known as Breslau, Germany, but later became Wrocław, Poland. He was the second of four children of Albrecht Richthofen, a cavalry officer with the Prussian army, and the family's aristocratic title dated back to 1661. The Richthofens were permitted to append the term *Freiherr*, or "free lord" to their name, whose nearest English equivalent is "baron."

Entered Military Academy

When Richthofen was nine year old, his father retired and the family moved to a smaller town called Schweidnitz (present-day Świdnica, Poland), where the surrounding countryside and nearby estates of his grandparents provided ample opportunity for hunting, his favorite sport. At the age of eleven, he entered a military academy in Wahlstatt (now Legnickie Pole, Poland), where he struggled academically, but excelled in all physical activities; by this point he had grown into a top-notch equestrian and famously accurate hunter. In 1909, at the age of 17, he enrolled in the Royal Prussian Military Academy near Berlin, and after graduating in 1911 began his career with a commission as *rittmeister*, or "riding master," with the Prussian cavalry. In military parlance, rittmeister was the cavalry equivalent of the rank of army captain.

Richthofen's duties centered primarily on patrolling the border with Poland, and in his off-duty hours he entered horse races. World War I broke out in August of 1914, and the complex tangle of alliances essentially pitted imperial Germany and the Austro-Hungarian Empire against Britain, France, Russia and, in the final months of the war, the United States. Richthofen's cavalry unit, known as the Uhlan (Lancer) Regiment, was first sent to participate in an attack on Belgium and Luxembourg. There, the man-to-man combat on horseback that Richthofen had dreamed of since boyhood—and which dated back to ancient times—had suddenly been supplanted by new and fearsome technology. Troops dug themselves into deep, muddy trenches and used mortar shells, artillery rockets, machine guns, and even new chemical agents to roust the enemy from their position and gain territory.

Richthofen found this new style of warfare gruesome, and after taking part in the first battle of Verdun requested a transfer to the fledgling German air force, called the *Fliegertruppe*, or air service. He trained not as a pilot but rather as the second person in a two-person bomber crew whose duties involved visual reconnaissance duties. He made his first flights over Russia, but then persuaded a friend to teach him how to fly—not in the heavy, noisy bombers, but rather in the new lightweight planes used in air-combat warfare. He crashed in his first solo fight, but walked away uninjured.

enamel—which was the Kingdom of Prussia's highest military order. He also became commander of his own fighter squadron, called the *Jagdstaffel* 11, or Fighter Squadron 11.

Richthofen earned the nickname the "Red Baron" because he ordered that his personal aircraft—later a series of planes made by the Albatros aircraft manufacturing facility near Berlin——be painted bright red in order to make it more visible to German ground troops; in this early era of air aviation, ground forces sometimes had a difficult time recognizing the type of their own and the enemy's aircraft and insignia, and being shot at by one's own side was not an uncommon occurrence. The other members of Richthofen's squadron followed suit, and their array of brightly hued planes was soon dubbed the Flying Circus. The French press began calling Richthofen *le diable rouge,* or "the Red Devil," and both this and "red baron" were soon picked by the British and U.S. newspapers.

Became Famous War Hero

In the summer of 1916 Richthofen joined the Royal Prussian Fighter Squadron, and recorded his first "kill" in the air on September 17, 1916. These pilots flew in formations looking for enemy aircraft, then began chasing individual planes in order to get close enough to fire. Aerial combat had made a significant technological advancement a year earlier with the introduction of a new type of plane by Dutch aviation pioneer Anthony Fokker, which allowed pilots to point their planes in the enemy's direction and fire its attached weaponry at the same direction. Richthofen soon began racking up a kill rate of nearly one a week. His second came on Sunday, September 24, and he wrote about it in a letter to his parents, noting "the heart beats a little faster when the opponent, whose face one has just seen, goes roaring down from 4,000 metres," he said, according to Peter Kilduff's *Richthofen: Beyond the Legend of the Red Baron.*

Most of the air combat that Richthofen engaged in with British, Canadian, or Australian pilots took place in the skies above the same northwestern corner of France anchored by the city of Lille, near both the border with Belgium and the English Channel. Back home in Germany, word of Richthofen's growing number of air victories against the enemy became an effective part of the war propaganda machine, and he was celebrated as the most daring of Germany's newly created and highly effective air corps. In January of 1917, Kaiser Wilhelm II awarded him the Order Pour le Mérite—also known as the "Blue Max" because of its blue

Survived Shot to Head

Encouraged to write his memoirs, the celebrated air ace complied, but felt uncomfortable with the fame and publicity his exploits had brought. *Der Rote Kampfflieger* (The Red Fighter Pilot) was published in August of 1917, and copies were given to every German soldier, sailor, or flyer. By then Richthofen had been given a new command post as head of the *Jagd Geschwader I,* or Hunting Wing I. On July 6, 1917, he was shot down by a British fighter for the first time, suffering a gunshot wound to his head while in flight. In 1999, a German physician named Henning Allmers authored an article that appeared in the British medical journal *The Lancet* after having been permitted by Richthofen's descendants to review the official medical records. Quoting from the official military debriefing after the accident, Allmers reported that Richthofen "had a feeling of total blindness and the engine sound was heard as if from a great distance. After regaining his senses and control over his limbs, he estimated that the time of paralysis lasted for only a minute. He descended to an altitude of 50 m[eters] to find an appropriate landing spot until he felt that he could no longer fly the aircraft."

Richthofen was taken to a field hospital in Kortrijk, Belgium, where he seemed to make a quick recovery. As he wrote on his autobiography, "I had quite a respectable hole in my head, a wound of about ten centimeters across which could be drawn together later; but in one place clear white bone as big as a *Taler* [large-sized coin] remained exposed," he wrote, according to Kilduff's biography. "My thick Richthofen head had once again proved itself." The bullet had not entered Richthofen's skull, and instead was thought to have glanced off his head, but the wound had not healed and a piece of the skull remained visible. Doctors ordered him not to return to flight yet, but after a visit to his family he returned to combat on August 16, 1917, where he shot down his 58th enemy plane that same day. He was ill afterward, however, and underwent surgery to remove a piece of bone that seemed to be causing trouble in the still-healing head wound. He went on to down another plane on the 26th of August, and two more in the first week of September.

Richthofen's record stalled for a time due to poor weather conditions for flying, so he instead used his presence in Berlin and other German cities to shore up public support for the war. At his family home in January of 1918, his mother noticed a marked change in his personality—her boisterous, energetic son now seemed distant and quiet. Medical historians later in the twentieth century wondered if Richthofen's accident had brought on classic symptoms of what is more commonly known as a traumatic brain injury, whereby the actual force of the injury to the skull and brain—whether penetrating or not—results in a range of symptoms, from blurred vision and headaches to memory loss and depression. Around this time Richthofen wrote another chapter in his autobiography which appeared in later editions. According to Kilduff, Richthofen noted that in rereading earlier chapters, "I smile at my own insolence. I am no longer so insolent in spirit." He went on to note that some of his superiors were suggesting that he should retire from the skies, and he seemed to sense that German military officials placed more value on his status on the ground as a celebrity. "I would be miserable with myself if now, burdened with glory and decorations, I were to become a pensioner of my own dignity in order to save my precious life for the nation, while every poor fellow in the trenches endures his duty as I do mine."

Legendary Appeal Endured

On March 3, 1918, Richthofen downed another British plane, which resulted in the capture of two prisoners of war and his sixty-fourth kill. His eightieth came on April 20, 1918, over Villers Brettoneux near Amiens, France. On the next day's flight, he suffered a gunshot wound to the chest over the Somme River in France and died in the crash. In a somewhat surprisingly twist, the British troops who recovered his body buried him with military honors in the cemetery of a church in nearby Bertangles. His body was later disinterred and reburied at a famous military cemetery in Berlin, the Invalidenfriedhof, with full military honors. Years later, the Berlin Wall was built to separate the West German enclave of West Berlin from the German Democratic Republic and its capital, East Berlin, where the Invalidenfriedhof now lay. Because the grave was so close to the Wall, Richthofen's surviving siblings petitioned the East German government for permission to remove his casket once again and rebury it in a family plot in Wiesbaden, Germany.

Richthofen was just 25 years old when he died on April 21, 1918, and he remains one of the most celebrated of war heroes in German history—though some military historians believe that his kill record of 80 planes may not be entirely accurate. Even the matter over whether or not he was physically fit to fly after his plane went down in July of 1917 remained the subject of debate among aviation buffs and medical experts decades later. In 1966, nearly five decades after the end of World War I, the term "Red Baron" was still a part of popular culture, especially when Charles Schulz's long-running cartoon strip *Peanuts* began featuring its clever beagle, Snoopy, atop his dog house wearing aviator goggles and imagining he is piloting one of the British air corps' famous "Sopwith Camel" aircraft in

pursuit of the Red Baron. That same year, a novelty song titled "Snoopy Versus the Red Baron" became a Top Ten hit on both the British and U.S. charts.

Richthofen has been portrayed in films and movies on several occasions, and in 2008 the English-language biopic *The Red Baron* debuted in German theaters as reportedly the most expensive German movie ever filmed. German screen idol Matthias Schweighöfer played Richthofen, and British actor Joseph Fiennes portrayed Roy Brown, the British pilot thought to have fired the fatal shot. More remarkable than its $28 million budget, however, was the fact that it was the first German film to celebrate a military hero made after the nation's ignominious 1945 defeat in World War II.

Books

Kilduff, Peter, *Richthofen: Beyond the Legend of the Red Baron,* John Wiley & Sons, 1993.

Periodicals

Air Power History, Winter 2006.
Lancet, August 7, 1999.
Maclean's, April 21, 2008.
New York Times, April 29, 1918.
Variety, April 14, 2008. □

César Ritz

The creator of the Ritz hotel chain, Swiss-born hotelier César Ritz (1850–1918), created new standards of luxury in the hospitality industry.

The man whose name became synonymous with high style was born on February 23, 1850, in the tiny Swiss village of Niederwald. The last of 13 children of Johann-Anton Ritz and his wife, Kreszentia, he grew up speaking the Valaisian dialect of German. Johann-Anton Ritz was angered that César showed no aptitude for dealing with the cows on the family's dairy farm, but Kreszentia persuaded her husband to send the youth to the larger town of Sion to go to school. Ritz arrived in Sion in 1863. He learned to speak French and standard German, but otherwise he was an indifferent student. In despair, Ritz's family paid a hard-earned 300 Swiss francs to the Hôtel des Trois Couronnes in the city of Brigue to land him a place as an apprentice wine steward.

Even this plan did not work well. According to Kenneth James in his book *Escoffier: The King of Chefs,* Ritz's boss, a Monsieur Escher, told him, "You'll never make anything of yourself in the hotel business. It takes a special knack, a special flair, and it's only right I should tell you the truth: you haven't got it." Ritz was fired after a year and moved to a job as a waiter at a Jesuit monastery, but could not hold even that job, because the monks said he was insufficiently religious. After a miserable few months of doing odd jobs at the monastery, Ritz was at the end of his rope. Rather than return home to the cow barns of Niederwald, he followed other European young people to Paris, hoping to get a job connected with the Paris Exhibition of 1867, an early world's fair.

Thrown completely on his own resources, and thrilled by the high life and bright lights of Paris, Ritz finally began to focus on getting ahead in the hospitality industry. Owning just one suit, he got a job at the Hôtel de la Fidélité. He was fired from that job after an incident involving a young Russian baroness, and he lost another job as a waiter at a quick-lunch establishment. But his reasons for getting fired were improving: he lost the waiter job because he broke too many dishes in an attempt to become the restaurant's fastest server, and according to Switzerland's César Ritz Web site, his co-workers called him "César le rapide." Landing another job as an assistant waiter at a full-service establishment on the Rue St.-Honoré, he advanced to the post of manager after two years. He was still only 19.

Fled Paris During Franco-Prussian War

Acting on a tip from a friend, Ritz got a job and a real taste of high-class service as a waiter at Voisin, one of Paris's best restaurants. Business dried up as troops moved through Paris during the Franco-Prussian War in 1871, and Ritz was forced to get work in a café catering to prostitutes in order to earn enough money for train fare back to Switzerland. Returning to Niederwald temporarily, he became the maître d' at the Hôtel Splendide. He returned to Paris after the war's end but then moved to Vienna, prompted by another major exhibition there, and for several years he followed the wealthy and the well-born around Europe to their haunts on the French Riviera, to Lucerne, and to the casino city of Monte Carlo, Monaco. At each stop, Ritz gained experience and landed positions with more and more responsibility.

In 1881 Ritz was made general manager of the Grand Hotel in Monte Carlo. He gained professional admiration and a lifelong customer after receiving a reservation telegram from Prince Albert Edward of Britain, the future King Edward VII. Finding that there were no rooms with a private bath available, Ritz marshaled a team of plumbers and carpenters, who installed a bathroom just ahead of the prince's arrival. When Ritz's head chef, Jean Giroix, was lured away by a competing hotel in Paris in 1884, Ritz trumped that move by hiring the chef who had trained Giroix: Auguste Escoffier, a master cook regarded as the father of modern French cuisine. The two remained business partners for many years. In 1887 Ritz married Marie-Louise Beck, a hotelkeeper's daughter from Strasbourg. The couple raised two sons, Charles and René, and Marie-Louise would take a strong interest in her husband's business affairs. The following year, Ritz purchased the Restaurant de la Conversation in the German spa town of Baden-Baden.

Ritz's breakthrough came in 1890, when he was hired to refurbish and reopen the Savoy Hotel in London, owned by theatrical impresario and longtime Gilbert & Sullivan operetta presenter Richard D'Oyly Carte. Ritz brought in Escoffier as head chef and mounted a full-scale effort to turn the hotel into an outpost of Continental elegance in a country that rarely ate out or treated itself to luxury. Chatting up the British press and even members of Parliament, Ritz promoted the idea that men and women could go out for dinner together (dining had previously been largely all-male). Sunday dinner at the Savoy became a meeting place for London's beautiful people, and in 1896 Elizabeth de Granmont reputedly became the first woman to smoke a cigarette in London, using the Savoy as her venue. Escoffier heightened the atmosphere of sophistication by refusing to answer if addressed in English.

Opened Hotel with 16-Course Meal

After a slow start, the new Savoy became hugely successful. Ritz capitalized on his momentum by opening other hotels. The Grand Hotel in Rome (1891), capitalized by the sale of Ritz's smaller properties in Baden-Baden and elsewhere, was said to be the world's first hotel with a private bath in each guest room. Ritz outdid himself in the Eternal City with the St. Regis Grand Hotel, opened in 1894 at a cost of three and half million lire. For the opening reception, Escoffier prepared a 16-course meal for each of the thousand guests on hand. In 1896 Ritz and Escoffier joined together in an official partnership called the Ritz Hotel Development Company.

These varied activities took Ritz's attention away from the Savoy, and by founding the new company he was effectively going into competition with the Savoy's owners. In addition, London's food industry swirled with rumors that vendors had to pay "commissions" to Escoffier in order to place their products in the Savoy's kitchens—in spite of his princely salary of 40,000 pounds annually. Further, one estimate held that in the first months of 1897, managers and staff had consumed over 3,000 pounds' worth of alcohol on the house, with another 3,400 pounds' worth unaccounted for. Both Ritz and Escoffier were fired later that year in a spectacular scene that saw 16 of Escoffier's French and Swiss cooks brandishing kitchen knives in a standoff with London police.

Prince Albert, among other London glitterati, backed Ritz in the ensuing controversy, and the firing did not slow down Ritz's career in the least. In 1898 he opened the small but exquisitely elegant Hôtel Ritz in Paris at 15 Place Vendôme, converting two older buildings. Later that year he oversaw the opening of London's Carlton Hotel, which became a formidable competitor to the Savoy. These and Ritz's other properties formed the nucleus of the future Ritz-Carlton hotel chain, which expanded to Madrid, Barcelona, and Budapest, and eventually around the world. In the first years of the twentieth century, Ritz supervised the construction of one of his greatest hotels, the Ritz Hotel in London. It was London's first large steel-frame building, and it featured a special bell-pull for the doormen to use when royalty rolled up to the entrance.

Ritz became known as the king of hoteliers and the hotelier to kings. Although his competitors could not divert the forward progress of his career, his hectic schedule began to take its toll. In 1902 he suffered a breakdown, whereupon Marie-Louise Ritz and Escoffier began to play a greater role in managing the Ritz empire. In 1906 his condition worsened, and he was hospitalized in Lausanne, Switzerland. Although he remained in a sanatorium for most of the rest of his life, he was able to make occasional visits to Niederwald.

César Ritz died in a hospital in Kssnacht, Switzerland, near Lucerne, on October 26, 1918. Marie-Louise Ritz continued to manage the Ritz hotels until 1953, when their son Charles took over. The direct involvement of the Ritz family in the hotels that bear their name (along with César Ritz's original logo, combining, perhaps in Albert's honor, a crown and a lion, a symbol for a financial backer) ended in 1976, but many of these establishments remain among the global hospitality industry's most luxurious properties. It was from the Hôtel Ritz in Paris that Princess Diana of England departed just before the auto accident that claimed her life.

Books

James, Kenneth, *Escoffier: The King of Chefs,* Continuum, 2002.

Periodicals

Evening Standard (London, England), May 24, 2006.
International Herald Tribune, January 16, 2004.
Observer (London, England), October 30, 1994.
Sunday Times (London, England), December 5, 2004.

Online

"César Ritz," Practically Edible, http://www.practicallyedible. com/edible.nsf/encyclopaedia!openframeset&frame=Right& Src=/edible.nsf/pages/cesarritz!opendocument (January 20, 2009).
"Learning & Traveling – Wanderlust," César Ritz, http://www. caesar-ritz.ch/en/lehrjahre.html (January 20, 2009).
"Our History," Ritz-Carlton Hotels, http://www.corporate. ritzcarlton.com/en/About/OurHistory.htm (January 20, 2009).
"Ritz, Cesar," The Most Famous Hotels in the World, http://www. famoushotels.org/article/480 (January 20, 2009).□

John Roebuck

English physician, chemist, inventor and entrepreneur John Roebuck (1718–1794) played an important role in advancing the Industrial Revolution in the British Isles, particularly Scotland. He is remembered today for introducing lead condensing chambers into the manufacture of sulfuric acid. He also patented a process for converting cast iron into malleable iron. He is probably best known, however, for his partnership with inventor James Watt, which led to the development of a highly efficient steam engine.

John Roebuck, who would grow up to become a scientist, inventor and entrepreneur, was born in Sheffield, England in 1718. His father, who was a master cutler, owned and operated a thriving manufacturing business. Roebuck came from a family of religious dissenters who disagreed with the views of England's established church. Because of his family's oppositional stance, Roebuck was denied the conventional avenues of education. Thus, he attended grammar school at the Northampton Academy of

Dr. Philip Dodridge, in Sheffield. There, Roebuck distinguished himself as a gifted student. Roebuck's father originally wanted to take his son into his business, but Roebuck was more attracted to science. Fortunately, his father encouraged his interests.

Became Interested in Chemistry

Roebuck studied medicine at the University of Edinburgh, the Scottish higher education institution established in 1582. At the University, in addition to his medical studies, Roebuck developed a strong interest in chemistry by attending the lectures of William Cullen, a renowned Scottish physician and educator, and Joseph Black, a Scottish chemist and physicist. At the university, Roebuck engaged in various chemical research activities that included advancement of the refining of precious metals and the production of chemicals.

In 1738, Roebuck enrolled at the University of Leyden in the Netherlands, where he continued his medical education, graduating with a medical degree in 1743. Following graduation, he returned to England, and set up a medical practice in Birmingham. He devoted a great deal of his time to chemical studies and experiments, however, and particularly those involving practical applications of chemistry.

During this period, he served as a chemical consultant to local industries. His activities and experiments led to an association with Samuel Garbett (1717–1803), a Birmingham industrialist and ironmaster who manufactured hardware. Eventually, Roebuck abandoned his medical practice to pursue his business relationship with Garbett. The two men established a company that applied acids to the recovery of precious metals, particularly gold and silver, from old plated products.

Mass-produced Sulfuric Acid

In 1746, applying his chemical education gained from Edinburgh and Leyden, Roebuck developed a way to mass-produce sulfuric acid, which was an integral component for several industrial processes. In ensuing years, sulfuric acid would become an important industrial chemical. Today, it is used in lead-acid storage batteries, papermaking, production of fertilizers, manufacture of chemicals and many other industrial processes.

Roebuck's mass-production method involved the use of large, lead condensing chambers which represented an advance over the conventional glass vessels, which were fragile. This early achievement would prove to be one of Roebuck's most important innovations to the chemistry field.

Moved to Scotland

The partners ran into a major problem, though: the man who owned the basic patent for the manufacture of sulfuric acid initiated legal action. As a result, presumably to avoid litigation in the English courts, Roebuck and Garbett relocated their operations to Prestonpans, a town located on the eastern coast of Scotland near Edinburgh. In 1749, they established Prestonpans Vitriol Manufacturing, a large factory that focused on production of sulfuric acid. Initially, Roebuck enjoyed a regional monopoly on such large-scale production. However, his methods became widely utilized by other companies because had not secured appropriate patents.

Still, the business proved very profitable, and earned Roebuck a great deal of money. Enthused by his success, and seeking to diversify, Roebuck sought to enter the iron-making field. Roebuck and Garbett came into contact with William Cadell, a businessman from Cockenzie, Scotland. Up to this point, Cadell had failed in attempts to establish an iron manufacturing plant, and he turned to Roebuck to help him succeed.

With this association, Roebuck began actively directing his efforts toward iron manufacturing. In 1760, Roebuck, Garbett and Cadell, along with Roebuck's three brothers (Benjamin, Ebenezer and Thomas), established the Carron Iron Works, on the banks of the Carron River in Stirlingshire County in Scotland, near Falkirk, which sits at the halfway point between Edinburgh and Glasgow. The site provided a water source and large supplies of iron, coal and limestone. For many years Carron was the largest foundry in the British Isles.

At this new facility, Roebuck introduced several improvements in production processes, including the conversions of cast iron into malleable iron by the action of a hollow pit-coal fire artificially blasted with a forceful draft of air. The method transformed breakable cast iron into a more resilient, compliant and, thus, more useful form. In addition, with this new method of iron production, Roebuck helped lay the foundation for development of later and more advanced blast furnaces. Further, presumably learning from his past mistake, he secured a patent for this method in 1762.

Entered Partnership with James Watt

Roebuck's next business venture, however, would turn out to be less successful and resulted in dire financial consequences. In the mid-1760s, he leased some coal mines at Bo'ness, a town located west of Edinburgh, which he hoped to use to supply coal to the Carron Iron Works plant. At these mines, he employed Newcomen engines—developed by English engineer Thomas Newcomen—to handle water, but the mines flooded much faster than the engines could handle. This problem led to another significant association.

Joseph Black, whose lectures influenced Roebuck at the University of Edinburgh, heard about Roebuck's problem. He introduced his former student to Scottish inventor and mechanical engineer James Watt (1736–1819). Starting at the age of nineteen, Watt worked as a mathematical instrument maker but later became interested in improving the steam engines invented by Newcomen and Thomas Savery, another English engineer, that were primarily used to pump water out of mines. Watt eventually developed a more efficient and powerful steam engine that could possibly solve Roebuck's problem.

Watt's technology was only in its early stages of development, however—up to this point, he had only been working with models—and it proved inadequate to the envisioned task. Roebuck installed Watt's prototypes into several of his mines, but a severe flood forced the mines to be shut down.

By this time, Roebuck had moved into the Kinneil House in Bo'ness, one of the family homes of the Duke of Hamilton, and he invited Watt to Kinneil to discuss further development of his steam engine. Watt visited Roebuck in May 1768 and they discussed a possible partnership. Nevertheless, one of Watt's main problems involved money. He had borrowed heavily from Black and had taken on a large debt. Despite his earlier problems with Watt's prototype, Roebuck still firmly believed in the strong potential for the steam engines. He provided Watt with financial support to perfect the technology in return for a two-thirds share of the invention. Also, Roebuck allowed Watt to live at Kinneil while building a new engine. Today, Roebuck is probably best remembered for the financing he provided Watt, as their partnership led to the development of the first commercially viable condensing steam engine, which was introduced and patented in 1769. In improving the Newcomen engine, Watt had determined the properties of steam—more specifically, the relation of steam density to temperature and pressure—and he designed a separate condensing chamber that prevented large steam loss in the cylinder and enhanced vacuum conditions. The patent covered these elements as well as other improvements such as steam jacketing, oil lubrication and a cylinder insulation that maintained high temperatures for maximum efficiency.

Suffered Financial Problems

But Roebuck's problems with his Bo'ness business, as well as his unsuccessful attempts to manufacture alkali, led to financial troubles that forced him to give up his share in Watt's engine to English engineer and manufacturer Matthew Boulton, who owned the Soho Engineering Works in Birmingham, England.

Boulten took over Roebuck's interest in 1775. Subsequently, he and Watt continued researching and patenting several other significant inventions, including a rotary engine that drove various types of machinery, a double-action engine that admits steam alternately into both cylinder ends, and a steam indicator that records an engine's steam pressure.

Meanwhile, Roebuck's surrender of his share in Watt's technology relieved him of some of his debt, but he eventually had to give up his interest in the Bo'ness plant. Ultimately, he suffered bankruptcy. He remained associated with the Bo'ness operation, but only as a wage-earning employee in a managerial position.

Because of his circumstances, Roebuck decided to take up farming on a large scale at Kinneil. He also founded the Bo'ness Pottery Company in 1784. In that way, Roebuck's name became strongly associated with the development of pottery in the region. He took over the South Pottery business and made coarse brownware from local clay. He also imported clays from Cornwall, Devon and Dorset to produce high-quality cream-colored and white stonewares. By 1789, he was supplying pottery to dealers in eastern and central Scotland and, by 1793, he had expanded the business and built extensions to the original premises. Earlier, in 1751, Roebuck, Garbett and Cadell, seeking to diversify their business activities, had established a pottery business in Prestonpans.

Died in 1794

Still, in the latter part of his life, agricultural activities took up most of Roebuck's time. Described as a man of "middle stature, square in frame without being stout, ruddy in complexion with finely modelled features," according to the *Bo'ness Pottery* website, Roebuck passed away when he was seventy-six years old. He died on July 15, 1794, surrounded by his wife and children.

He was buried in the Carridien parish churchyard, and his friends and family erected a tombstone the bears a long epitaph that serves as an appropriate testament to the man and his accomplishments. Translated from Latin, the epitaph reads: "Underneath this tombstone rests no ordinary man, John Roebuck, M.D., who, of gentle birth and of liberal education, applied his mind to almost all the liberal arts. Though he made the practice of medicine his chief work in his public capacity to the great advantage of his fellow citizens, yet he did not permit his inventive and tireless brain to rest satisfied with that, but cultivated a great number of recondite and abstruse sciences, among which were chemistry and metallurgy. These he expounded and adapted to human needs with a wonderful fertility of genius and a high degree of painstaking labour; whence not a few of all those delightful works and pleasing structures which decorate our world, and by their utility conduce to both public and private well-being he either devised or promoted.

"Of these the magnificent work at the mouth of the Carron is his own invention. In extent of friendship and of gentleness he was surpassing great, and, though harassed by adversity or deluded by hope and weighed down by so many of our griefs, he yet could assuage these by his skill in the arts of the muses or in the delights of the country.

"For most learned conversation and gracious familiarity no other was more welcome or more pleasant on account of varied and profound learning, his merry games and sparkling wit and humour. And, above all, on account of the uprightness, benevolence, and good fellowship in his character."

Online

"Dr. John Roebuck," *Falkirk Local History Society*, http://www.falkirklocalhistorysociety.co.uk/home/index.php?id=135&PHPSESSID=b6f47e1ca45ceb7fa539ab150997649f (December 20, 2008).

"Dr. John Roebuck," *Gazetteer for Scotland*, http://www.geo.ed.ac.uk/scotgaz/people/famousfirst244.html (December 20, 2008).

"James Watt," *IdeaFinder.com*, http://www.ideafinder.com/history/inventors/watt.htm (December 20, 2008).

"John Roebuck," *Bo'ness Pottery*, http://bonesspottery.co.uk/roebuck.aspx (December 20, 2008)

"John Roebuck (1718-1794)," *Online Encyclopedia*, http://encyclopedia.jrank.org/RHY_RON/ROEBUCK_JOHN_1718_1794_.html (December 20, 2008).

"Significant Scots: Dr. John Roebuck," *ElectricScotland.com*, www.electricscotland.com/history/other/roebuck_john.htm (December 20, 2008).

"The Industrial Revolution's Indispensable Entrepreneur," *Objectivist Center.org*, http://www.objectivistcenter.org/cth--723-The_Industrial_Revolutions_Indispensable_Entrepreneur.aspx (December 20, 2008).□

Nicholas Roerich

The Russian artist Nicholas Roerich (1874–1947) produced more than 7,000 paintings and sketches, many of them landscapes suffused with rich colors that reveal the artist's mystical attitude toward the natural world and the universe.

Roerich had a long, eventful, and unusual life. His paintings are of considerable importance, and he was a significant figure in a movement, spanning many decades and several countries, that aimed toward the unity of all the arts. The pioneering ballet *The Rite of Spring*, one of the central cultural events of the 20th century, was at least partly Roerich's idea. Later in life, Roerich began to try to generalize his artistic ideals outward into political activity. As much as anyone else, he is responsible for the now generally accepted idea that cultural artifacts should be protected in wartime. During a three-year sojourn in the United States, Roerich had an impact on the development of modern art and music in that country. Roerich's mystical attitudes eventually led him to settle in India, where he spent almost the last quarter century of his life.

Joined Archaeological Dig as Child

The son of a prominent lawyer, Nicholas Konstantinovich Roerich was born in St. Petersburg, Russia, on October 9, 1874. The family numbered many artists and scientists among their friends, and Nicholas's curiosity was stimulated and encouraged. When he was nine, an archaeologist took him along on an excavation being carried out at the site of some ancient mounds. Roerich collected coins, plants, and minerals, and above all he showed a talent for drawing the things he saw. He resolved to become an artist, but his father ordered that he study law instead. The two compromised: in 1893, Roerich enrolled at both St. Petersburg University and the Academy of Art.

In the fertile cultural atmosphere of the old imperial city, it did not take long for the arts to capture the better part of Roerich's energy. Through the writer Vladimir Stasov, Roerich met composers like Modest Mussorgsky and Nicolai Rimsky-Korsakov, as well as operatic vocalists. The operas of German composer Richard Wagner fascinated him; Wagner believed in the idea of a *Gesamtkunstwerk* or total art work, fusing music with text, dance, painting, and stage design. Roerich began to think along the same lines, and his thinking took a step forward when he met dance producer Serge Diaghilev. The two edited a short-lived but important magazine called *The World of Art*.

Roerich then spent a year touring Europe and acquainting himself with the latest artistic trends. On his return he married Helena Shaposhnikova, an architect's daughter and Mussorgsky's niece. The pair had two sons, Yuri (in 1902) and Sviatoslav (in 1904), and Helena fundamentally affected Roerich's thinking: feminine archetypes would play important roles in his art and philosophy. Roerich worked for several years as Secretary of the School of the Society for the Encouragement of Art, where he instituted a new interdisciplinary

began. Even at this point he and his family wanted to go to India; his fascination with Indian culture had begun when he met the poet Rabindranath Tagore. But he did not yet have the resources for the grand plans he had in mind. By way of Stockholm, where he mounted an art show, and England, where he designed sets for a production of a Russian opera, he made his way to the U.S. in 1920.

Roerich's stay in the U.S. was important both for him and for the American arts scene. He designed sets for a production of Wagner's *Tristan and Isolde* at the Chicago Lyric Opera and painted landscapes in New Mexico and Maine. He formed a new Master Institute of United Arts in New York, based on the curricula he had instituted in St. Petersburg, and he attracted major figures such as artist George Bellows and composer Deems Taylor to serve on the school's faculty. Most important for Roerich and his family was that he attracted friends in high places, putting an end to what had up until then been a financially precarious existence.

One was stockbroker Louis Horch, who financed a substantial new Roerich Museum on Riverside Drive (which still exists, now located on 107th Street) and subsidized Roerich's travels through India (which he first saw in 1923), Tibet, the Soviet Union, and later Japan. The paintings that he made during this trip, according to materials from an exhibition of Roerich paintings shown at Oglethorpe University, were the first Western artworks depicting Tibet and Central Asia. It was during this period that Roerich began to think on a world scale, and perhaps to show signs of eccentricity. He found a manuscript in a Tibetan monastery that he claimed showed Jesus Christ had visited India. Roerich produced a series of paintings depicting Christ and other religious leaders in the Himalaya mountains, with overtones suggesting the unity of all religions. His visits to his homeland were apparently aimed at gaining political influence, for he later abandoned his contacts with the Soviet government in favor of a plan to create a new country in Siberia, with himself as head of state.

Drafted Treaty

Roerich's other ideas, however, were more concrete. He believed in the power of the arts and culture to promote peace, a concept he summarized in the Latin phrase Pax Cultura. He drafted and promoted an international agreement, called the Roerich Pact, stating that cultural treasures should be protected in wartime. The campaign was symbolized by a so-called Banner of Peace bearing a red circle enclosing three spheres on a white field; the spheres had various interpretations but essentially symbolized common bonds of culture, spirit, and humanity. Roerich attracted the attention of President Franklin Roosevelt and U.S. Secretary of Agriculture Henry Wallace, and the U.S., along with a group of Latin American countries, signed the Roerich Pact in 1935. European countries, which would soon be drifting toward war, did not ratify the pact, but its general principles have gained currency.

Wallace, who had a personal orientation toward the occult and admired Roerich's ideas, was especially impressed by Roerich and sometimes called him "the guru." "Long have I been aware of the occasional fragrance from the other world which is the real world. But now I must live in the outer world

curriculum, and as a museum assistant. Then, in 1903, he and Helena embarked on a tour of 40 Russian cities, looking for archaeological and artistic traces of their distant pasts.

Roerich's exposure in the West began in 1906, when Diaghilev staged an exhibition of works by Russian painters in Paris, including 16 canvases by Roerich. Diaghilev spearheaded a vogue for Russian music in France, and in 1909, Roerich designed sets for a Diaghilev-produced production of Rimsky-Korsakov's *Ivan the Terrible,* starring the famed Russian bass Fyodor Chaliapin. That stimulated in Roerich's mind an idea for a more radical project: a ballet with original music and sets, set in pagan, prehistoric Russian and touching on sexuality and the shocking theme of human sacrifice. Stravinsky also claimed credit for the idea, but when the audience rioted and shouted insults at the 1913 premiere he was nonplussed. Roerich, however, merely observed that the audience was behaving like the primitive people being depicted in the ballet itself.

Moved to U.S.

In 1915 Roerich contracted pneumonia and was sent to a sanatorium in Finland to recuperate. He painted the bleak countryside of the Karelia region, and for much of his life he would paint landscapes, rooted in the places he visited but with vivid color schemes that indicated psychological states and spiritual ideas. Roerich was outside of Russia during the unstable year of 1917, when the Czarist monarchy was overthrown and the period of Communist rule

and at the same time make over my mind and body to serve as fit instruments for the Lord of Justice," wrote the Secretary of Agriculture to Roerich in a letter quoted in *American Heritage*. Believing that Roerich commanded admiration in the Soviet Union and various Asian countries, he agreed to send the artist on an expedition aimed at gathering drought-resistant seeds in Central Asia.

The expedition turned out to be something between a failure and a fiasco. Roerich's group, which included increasingly disillusioned Agriculture Department scientists, sent back few useful materials. Worse, during a sojourn in the northern Chinese city of Harbin, he began to gather a group of Russian exiles and, on the pretext that he was planning travel into dangerous areas, began to build a stock of small arms. He even received, thanks to Wallace's intervention, rifles and ammunition from a U.S. infantry unit stationed in China. His real plan, as the Soviets soon guessed, was to carry out his Siberian takeover scheme, and U.S. State Department officials worried that Roerich's activities had the potential to cause major diplomatic incidents or worse. By 1935 Wallace had withdrawn his support, but the episode occasionally resurfaced during his future political career as Roosevelt's vice president and as a presidential candidate in 1948.

Roerich was readmitted to India, thanks to the intervention of British diplomatic officials anxious to defuse tensions. He finally retired to a home and a small cultural center, the Urusvati Himalayan Research Institute, that he had established in the Kullu Valley, in the Himalayan foothills in northern India. The Institute fell into disuse but was reconstructed by a German admirer of Roerich's and now houses exhibits on the Roerich family and a collection of plant specimens. Roerich's family members accompanied him on all his adventures, and his son Sviatoslav married Indian actress Devika Rani after meeting her and proposing to her on the spot. He continued to paint prolifically, and the bulk of his roughly 7,000 surviving works depict the Himalayas in various ways. In his later years, he cultivated a friendship with Indian prime minister Jawaharlal Nehru. Roerich died in Kullu on December 13, 1947.

Books

Archer, Kenneth, *Nicholas Roerich,* Parkstone, 2000.

Decter, Jacqueline, *Nicholas Roerich: The Life and Art of a Russian Master,* Park Street Press, 1989.

Encyclopedia of Occultism and Parapsychology, 5th ed., Gale, 2001.

Periodicals

American Heritage, March 1989.

Globe & Mail (Toronto, Ontario, Canada), September 7, 1996, p. F1.

Guardian (London, England), February 1, 1994, p. 12.

Online

"Biography," Nicholas Roerich Museum, http://www.roerich.org/ (January 18, 2009).

"Nicholas Roerich: The Mystical Journey," Oglethorpe University, http://museum.oglethorpe.edu/Roerich2004/Roerich2004.htm (January 18, 2009).

"Roerich's Family," International Roerich Memorial Trust (India), http://www.roerichtrust.org/home.htm (January 18, 2009).

"The Roerichs' Family," International Center of the Roerichs (Russia), http://www.icr.su/eng/family/ (January 18, 2009). □

Ernst Röhm

During Adolf Hitler's rise to power, German military officer Ernst Röhm (1887–1934) commanded the Storm Troopers, a paramilitary wing of the Nazi Party. Over time, Hitler grew anxious of Röhm's influence. Fearing Röhm as a potential rival, Hitler had him executed in 1934.

Excelled at Warfare

R öhm was born November 28, 1887, in Munich, Germany. His father worked as a senior railway official in Bavaria, a region of southeast Germany. As a child, Röhm dreamed of joining the military. He attended a military academy and was commissioned as an officer in 1908. During World War I, which erupted in 1914, Röhm served as company commander of the 10th Bavarian Infantry, where he earned a reputation as a reckless and fearless soldier. Röhm was wounded three times and each time asked to be returned to the front lines. He emerged from the war with a number of scars on his face. Röhm lost part of his nose during the war and a bullet left a deep groove along his left cheek.

The war ended with Germany in defeat, leaving Röhm deeply infuriated. Germany lost a portion of its territory, and in addition, the Treaty of Versailles, signed at the end of the conflict, placed restrictions on Germany's military. Röhm was determined to restore the glory of the German army. He detested the authority of the Weimar Republic, which had come to power following the German Revolution at the end of the war.

The situation in Germany proved volatile. The country was suffering from losses in the war as well as an economic depression. A number of political parties began vying for power. These parties set up paramilitary groups to safeguard their interests. One such group was the Freikorps—or "Free Corps"—a private militia aimed at combating the left-wing Marxist party. The Freikorps claimed its mission was to restore Germany's prominence and power. Röhm liked this idea, so he joined the Freikorps von Epp, a Bavarian faction headed by Colonel Franz Ritter von Epp.

In addition to his involvement with the Freikorps, Röhm continued his association with the German military. After the war, the treaty called for weapons, including armored cars and machine guns, to be destroyed. Röhm persuaded his superiors to let him salvage the weapons. He maintained that the weapons could not be used for serious warfare and therefore posed no threat to Allied forces but could be used to fend off the spread of Communism within the country. In this manner, Röhm accumulated a secret stockpile of weapons. Whenever people threatened to report his secret arsenal, Röhm's henchmen went after them.

Joined Nazi Party

Along the way, Röhm befriended members of the radical right. With hyperinflation setting in and Germany suffering from reparations imposed at the end of the war, middle class citizens lost their savings and found themselves unemployed. The working class became increasingly despondent and began joining forces with the right wing, which championed a platform of Nationalism and said it would work to renegotiate the Treaty of Versailles to ease the economic situation. Röhm liked this idea.

In October 1919, Röhm heard Hitler speak at a National Socialist German Workers' Party rally in Munich. He was so impressed with Hitler's oratorical skills and charisma that he joined the group, later known as the Nazi Party. Röhm believed Hitler was the perfect frontman for the right wing and he began supporting the party with money funneled through his department. Röhm encouraged his peers to join the party as well.

Röhm's homosexuality was no secret at this point; it was something he flaunted. Röhm believed homosexual men were superior to all others. He pointed to Caesar, Alexander the Great, Charles XII of Sweden and Frederick the Great—all conquerors and all homosexuals, Röhm said, according to *Hitler's Elite,* a book by Louis L. Snyder. Röhm advocated that gay men have no sexual relations with women because it would tarnish their purity. He was distressed by the increasing rights women were gaining and thus disliked the idea of a democracy. Röhm

envisioned a future state in Germany where homosexuals were viewed with high regard.

While Röhm's sexuality distanced him from some up-and-coming leaders of the Nazi Party, Hitler took it in stride. He admired Röhm's gift for tactical planning and organizing and recognized his abilities to train militiamen. Hitler understood that he would need a ruthless paramilitary organization to back him up in his rise to power. He knew Röhm would be helpful in that respect.

In 1921, the Allies asked the German government to disband the Freikorps. The crafty Röhm kept his militia in place, however, by creating a new organization—a "Gymnastics and Sports Division"within the Nazi Party. By late 1921 this militia group was known as the Sturmabteilung—or Storm Section—abbreviated as SA. The SA was, in effect, a group of bully men who provided protection at meetings and intimidated political enemies. They were also known as the Storm Troopers or brown shirts, due to their uniforms.

Jailed for Treason

In 1923, Hitler attempted to seize power through a "putsch," or coup d'etat, backed by Röhm and the Storm Troopers. The putsch failed and both Hitler and Röhm were arrested and jailed for treason. Röhm, embarrassed by the failed overthrow and public trial that followed, left the Nazi Party. Röhm was also frustrated with Hitler. Hitler believed the SA should be no more than a political front for the Nazi Party, meaning the SA should take orders from the party, while Röhm thought of the Storm Troopers as a military movement in their own right.

After quitting his leadership position with the SA, Röhm threw himself into a number of homosexual relationships. He failed to find meaningful work. For a time, he peddled patriotic publications as a traveling salesman and also worked in a machine factory. Röhm struggled to fit into civil society, however. He missed the order of the military and accepted a position as a military instructor in South America training the Bolivian army.

In the September 1930 elections, the Nazi Party won a number of victories. Because the other ruling parties had failed to find a solution to the country's economic woes, more and more voters were placing their trust in the Nazi Party. Meanwhile, tensions mounted within the party itself. The Berlin SA destroyed party headquarters, claiming they were not receiving their fair pay, and other SA members were growing anxious at the slow pace of the party's takeover. They did not like that the Nazi Party was attempting to seize power through legitimate means. The SA members wanted a revolution and they wanted it without delay.

Hitler was in a tough position. He needed the SA to do his dirty work but could not afford to have them rising up. To fix internal problems within the SA, Hitler invited Röhm back to Germany and placed him in charge of the SA. Hitler knew Röhm could keep the SA under control.

Appointed Head of Storm Troopers

In 1931, Röhm was appointed Chief of Staff of the SA. Röhm was a brutal leader and under his command the SA won countless street battles against other parties. Under Röhm's guidance, the SA mastered the art of bullying and intimidation. Through their ruthless tactics, they quashed the electoral activity of other parties, thus helping the Nazis rise in power. Röhm also recruited a large number of men he had romantic relationships with in the Freikorps and made them senior SA commanders.

While tensions within the ranks of the SA subsided, Hitler and Röhm continued to disagree about the SA's future role. Röhm wanted the SA and the regular German army combined into one unit under his command. Röhm also envisioned a second revolution—a revolution of the working class. Hitler, however, shared no such vision. In 1933, Hitler was sworn in as chancellor of Germany. By the late 1930s, he had secured supreme political power.

Röhm believed Hitler would choose him for a high office within the German army. Once in power, though, Hitler had little use for the SA and grew leery of the group's loyalty. The SA predated Hitler and had its own agenda. Since the early 1930s, Hitler had been relying on the Schutzstaffel—or SS—for protection so he did not need SA members to work as bodyguards. In addition, Hitler knew his association with the SA—filled with homosexuals— hurt his chances of gaining the support of the more conservative factions.

The SA kept trumpeting its quasi-socialist, anti-capitalist, anti-tradition ideas, causing alarm among the big-business rank and file who supported Hitler's rise to power. More and more, Hitler grew nervous of the SA and Röhm, who now had some two million men under his command and access to stores of weapons. Hitler called on Röhm in early June 1934, urging him to reign in the SA and quit calling for a Second Revolution. Hitler told Röhm he would not disband the SA, despite pressure from Nazi Party brass, though he ordered the SA to take a leave from service while he sorted things out.

Executed by Order of Hitler

By mid-June 1934, rumors were spreading that the SA planned a putsch. Some historians believe these rumors were perpetuated by Nazi Party leaders who wanted Röhm and the SA out of the picture. They contend Röhm had no plans for a putsch. The SA, after all, complied with Hitler's orders to take a leave. Röhm went to vacation in Bad Wiessee, a spa town in Bavaria. Many SA members joined him.

On the morning of June 30, 1934, Hitler—backed by the SS and the police—arrived at the hotel where Röhm was staying. He burst into Röhm's room and announced his arrest, as Röhm scrambled from bed. Röhm and his SA colleagues were then taken to a Munich prison. Röhm was given a copy of a special edition of the *Völkischer Beobachter* (*People's Observer*), the paper of the Nazi Party. The special edition offered a story detailing how Röhm and the SA were planning a putsch to seize control of the party. Röhm was also given a pistol with one bullet and urged to take the honorable way out.

Röhm refused to use the pistol on himself and was summarily executed by SS guards. According to Anthony Read, author of *The Devil's Disciples: Hitler's Inner Circle,* Hitler made this brief announcement after the incident: "The former Chief of Staff Röhm was given the opportunity to draw the consequences of his treacherous behaviour. He did not do so and was thereupon shot." Hitler told the press that Röhm was planning a conspiracy alongside Nazi Party politician Gregor Strasser and Gen. Kurt von Schleicher, who served as German chancellor before Hitler took over. They were executed as well. Hitler claimed he was simply trying to stop a treasonous assault and the executions were done in the name of defending the nation.

A countless number of Hitler's rivals lost their lives during this purge, which came to be known as the "The Night of the Long Knives." Over a 48-hour period, many members of the SA were executed, as well as others on the party's "Reich List of Unwanted Persons." Under the cover of foiling a conspiracy, the Nazi Party eliminated its potential rivals. In *Devil's Disciples,* Read said records of the purge were destroyed, making it impossible to know how many were executed. Hitler said 58 traitors were executed and 19 were killed while trying to escape. Some historians, however, have placed the number of victims at close to 1,000. Besides those executed, hundreds were placed into concentration camps under protective custody, never to be heard from again.

"The Night of the Long Knives" marked Hitler's final push to power, cementing his position as the supreme ruler of Germany. Hitler had, in effect, declared himself the judge and juror of the land. Rivals began to fear for their lives, realizing that Hitler would not hesitate to execute anyone who stood in opposition to his ideas.

Books

Read, Anthony, *The Devil's Disciples: Hitler's Inner Circle,* W. W. Norton & Co., 2003.

Smelser, Ronald and Rainer Zitelmann, editors, *The Nazi Elite,* New York University Press, 1993.

Snyder, Louis L., *Hitler's Elite: Biographical Sketches of Nazis Who Shaped the Third Reich,* Hippocrene Books, 1989.

Periodicals

Daily Mail (London), July 2, 1994, p. 30.

History Today, November 2001, p. S5.

Independent (London), June 30, 1994, p. 22.

New York Times, July 1, 1934, p. 3.□

S

Antonio Salieri

The Italian composer Antonio Salieri (1750–1825) is familiar to classical music audiences primarily for a story that began during his lifetime and has come down, via the hit play and film *Amadeus,* to the present day: the story that Salieri poisoned Wolfgang Amadeus Mozart and killed him.

That tale, as told by those who have dramatized it, reflects badly on Salieri's abilities as a composer: he is presented as an ordinary man consumed by jealousy when faced with Mozart's seemingly divine talent. Yet no observer of Mozart's time would have recognized that picture—or taken the poisoning story seriously, and it is now regarded as almost certainly untrue. Salieri was almost on an equal footing with Mozart in late 18th-century Vienna. Even if close observers noticed a quality of genius in Mozart's music that Salieri lacked, Salieri was well entrenched in a better job than Mozart had, and there was no reason for him to feel jealous. Far from being immediately forgotten, Salieri's music was performed and admired well into the 19th century, and in recent years some of his works have been revived after decades of obscurity.

Antonio Salieri was born on August 18, 1750, in the small town of Legnago in northeastern Italy; his father was a merchant, and Salieri was his eighth child. The area at the time had political and cultural ties to the Austrian empire whose center was Vienna. One indicator of Salieri's enduring popularity is that as late as the middle 19th century he was the subject of a biography by the early American musicologist Alexander Wheelock Thayer (1817–1897), who also wrote a biography of Beethoven. Thayer told numerous stories about Salieri's childhood, such as one in which the youth cold-shouldered a local organist monk because, as he explained to his father later, he thought little of the monk's organ playing.

Educated in Venice after Father's Death

Whatever the accuracy of these stories, they suggest that Salieri gained attention early for his abilities. He studied the violin with his much older brother Francesco, who had himself studied with the great violin virtuoso Giuseppe Tartini, and he also took organ lessons at a church. When Salieri was 15, his father died. A family friend from Venice, the nobleman Giovanni Mocenigo, took him to that port city and made sure that he was able to continue studying singing and music theory. His teacher, Ferdinando Pacini, was set to appear in an opera composed by the visiting Austrian court composer Florian Gassmann, and Pacini introduced Salieri to Gassmann. Impressed by Salieri's talent, Gassmann invited him to come to Vienna for further study.

The invitation was a major stroke of good fortune, for it placed Salieri at the emerging center of European musical life. He studied opera with the aging Pietro Metastasio, the greatest librettist of the middle 18th century, and he gained a second major mentor in composer Christoph Willibald Gluck. Vienna's musical scene was flourishing under the patronage of the music-loving Emperor Joseph II. Salieri worked hard and sometimes picked up excess commissions when Gassmann became overscheduled. His first opera, now lost, was *La vestale,* staged in Vienna in 1768. He filled in for Gassmann as the composer of a comic work called *Le donne letterate,* which appeared in 1769 and gained its 19-year-old composer acclaim. Salieri soon turned to serious opera with *Armida* (1771), and he scored a hit with *La fiera di Venezia* the following year.

Salieri's style, influenced by the simplicity favored by Gluck, was already confident and assured by this time. The contemporary Italian soprano Cecilia Bartoli, who has championed Salieri's music, reflected to Roderic Dunnett of the *Independent* on the high quality of an excerpt from *Armida,* calling it "an immensely mature, four-section, double recitative and aria written for Rinaldo, who is overwhelmed by his love for Armida. The emotions are so real and so varied and he handles his material with such amazing clarity and simplicity." Also impressed was Joseph II, who praised Salieri's abilities to his sister, Marie Antoinette, and other European nobles. When Gassmann died in 1774, Salieri took over as *Kapellmeister,* or music director, of the imperial court's Italian opera theater. The following year he married Theresia Helferstorfer (or Helfersdorfer); the pair had eight children.

Initially Deprived of Credit for Opera

Just as he had with Gassmann, Salieri began to take over assignments he received at the recommendation of the aging Gluck. In 1778 he wrote the opera *Europa Riconosciuta* for the opening of the still-flourishing La Scala opera house in Milan, and he had perhaps his greatest international success with *Les Danaïdes,* which had its premiere in Paris in 1784. Gluck paid Salieri an indirect tribute when he at first tried to pass the work off as his own, and the work was still being performed in Paris decades later. French composer Hector Berlioz, born in 1803, wrote of seeing the opera as a young man (as quoted by John W.

Freeman in *Opera News*): "I was like a lad with the inborn instincts of a sailor who, never having seen anything but fishing boats on a lake, suddenly finds himself transported to a triple-decker in midocean. I hardly slept a wink the night after that performance."

Salieri worked for several years in Paris on the strength of his relationship with Gluck, and he scored a second success with *Tarare* (1787). That work featured a libretto by the French playwright Pierre Beaumarchais, the author of *The Barber of Seville* and of the play on which Mozart's *The Marriage of Figaro* was based. He returned to Vienna to take a position in 1788 as court composer, the highest position in the Viennese musical hierarchy. During these years, he became aware of the talents of Mozart, who (contrary to the portrayal in *Amadeus*) was just six years younger than himself.

Certainly the two were rivals, contending for space on opera stages at the imperial court and elsewhere in Vienna. And there is some evidence that Salieri was ahead of the curve in recognizing Mozart's as a talent greater than his own; he said to a colleague (according to Freeman) that "If this fellow keeps on like this, he'll put us all out of business." Yet there is scant evidence from the 1780s and 1790s that Mozart and Salieri were enemies. Mozart, during his final illness in 1791, did suspect that he had been poisoned, and speculated that rival Italian composers at the court were to blame. But he did not mention Salieri, whom he invited to the rather out-of-the-way premiere of his opera *Die Zauberflöte* (The Magic Flute). Salieri's enthusiasm for the music was appreciatively noted by Mozart in a letter to his wife, and the older composer served as a pallbearer at Mozart's funeral in 1791. The symptoms of Mozart's final illness were consistent not with poisoning but with the kind of lung infection that killed many people in the era before antibiotics.

Gave Lessons to Schubert

Salieri retired as court composer after the death of Joseph II in 1790. In the revolutionary years of the 1790s, musical styles began to show a shift from sheer melody toward a larger dramatic scope that pointed toward the music of Beethoven. Salieri's output slowed somewhat, although new Salieri operas appeared throughout the decade. Among his important later works was *Falstaff* (1799), one of the first operatic adaptations of a play by William Shakespeare. He also wrote symphonies, choral music, and some chamber music. He was valued as a teacher; among his students were Mozart's son Franz Xaver and the young genius of the next Viennese generation, Franz Schubert. The influence of Salieri can be seen in some of Schubert's early music. Salieri also gave some lessons to the young Beethoven. He disliked Beethoven's music but nevertheless helped mount a benefit performance of Beethoven's *Wellington's Victory* in 1813. Among Salieri's other students were pianist Carl Czerny and even the young Franz Liszt.

The story that Salieri had poisoned Mozart gained new life in Salieri's old age, when he confessed to Mozart's murder but later retracted the confession. Salieri was suffering from dementia, and the confession was not taken seriously, either at the time (the composer Gioacchino Rossini joked about it to Salieri), or by later historians. Yet the story continued to fascinate musical observers. The by-then-deaf Beethoven mentioned it in the written notebooks he used to carry on conversations, and Russian writer Alexander Pushkin devoted a short play, *Mozart and Salieri,* to the tale. Salieri died on May 7, 1825, in Vienna.

Pushkin's play served as the basis for an opera by Russian composer Nicolai Rimsky-Korsakov in 1898, and its general outline was followed in Peter Shaffer's 1979 play *Amadeus,* a hit that was filmed in 1984 by director Milos Forman. Shaffer depicted Salieri as a man angry at God that such talent should have been bestowed on the crass and brash Mozart, while his own diligent career somehow merited a lesser portion of divine favor. Shaffer's depiction of Mozart in the play drew on new evidence about his personality, but nothing has surfaced to suggest any culpability on Salieri's part in Mozart's death. In the years since the play and film appeared, performances of Salieri's music have become more common; Bartoli has sung arias from his operas in concert, and symphony orchestras have pitted his music against Mozart's in mock musical duels.

Books

Braunbehrens, Volkmar, *Maligned Master: The Real Story of Antonio Salieri,* Fromm, 1992.

International Dictionary of Opera, 2 vols., St. James, 1993.

Sadie, Stanley, ed., *The New Grove Dictionary of Music and Musicians,* 2nd ed., Macmillan, 2001.

Thayer, Alexander Wheelock, *Salieri: Rival of Mozart,* repr. ed., Philharmonia of Greater Kansas City, 1989.

Periodicals

Detroit Free Press, September 15, 2006.

Evening Standard (London, England), September 27, 2004, p. 87.

Guardian (London, England), December 19, 2003, p. 10.

Independent (London, England), December 22, 2003, p. 11.

International Herald Tribune, January 5, 2005, p. 10.

New Statesman, September 8, 2003, p. 40.

Opera News, March 28, 1998, p. 26; October 2003, p. 22.

Online

"Antonio Salieri," WBAI Radio: Here of a Sunday Morning, http://www.hoasm.org/XIIC/Salieri.html (January 19, 2009). □

Dorothy L. Sayers

The British writer Dorothy L. Sayers (1893–1957) was the creator of Lord Peter Wimsey, one of the most popular and enduring characters in mystery fiction.

S ayers herself valued her other writings above her 11 mystery novels and about two dozen short stories. She wrote religious essays and dramas, including one in a pioneering contemporary idiom, and later in life she did translations of classic literary works. But it was the mysteries, which have never gone out of print since they were first published, for which she is best remembered. The

Lord Peter Wimsey tales contain intriguing mixtures of elements—from up-to-the-moment criminological techniques to academic arcana, humor, vivid descriptions of English settings, and scenes and aspects of Sayers's own life—that continue to fascinate mystery readers.

Learned French and Latin

Dorothy Leigh Sayers was born in Oxford, England, on June 13, 1893. She was the daughter of an Anglican minister, the Rev. Henry Sayers, and Helen Leigh Sayers. Her father, who was also a teacher in a school that housed young choral singers at Oxford University, educated her strenuously from the start, and she learned both Latin and French as a child. The family moved out of Oxford into a large country house in a fen, or non-acidic wetland, landscape that provided the setting for Sayers's classic novel *The Nine Tailors* (1934). She was homeschooled, with the help of tutors and a governess, until she was 15, when she enrolled at the Godolphin School, a private institution in Salisbury. Sayers was withdrawn and somewhat unpopular, but she had some of her poems and fiction published in the school's magazine.

Sayers won a scholarship to Somerville College, an all-female division of Oxford University, in 1912. Somerville was depicted in thin disguise as Shrewsbury College in the novel *Gaudy Night* (1935). While at Oxford, Sayers published a book of poetry, *Op. 1.* She earned a B.A. degree in French, taught that language at Hull High School in Yorkshire for two years, became a secretary to a war veteran in France who was suffering from post-traumatic stress disorder, and worked as a manuscript reader for the Oxford publisher Blackwell. In 1920 Sayers received an M.A. degree with honors in medieval studies from Oxford, becoming one of the first women to earn an advanced degree there.

Sayers's personal life as a young woman was unhappy. She fell in love with novelist John Cournos and hoped to marry him, but the relationship came to nothing. Sayers also had a son by automobile salesman Bill White. She concealed the birth from biographers and even from her parents, sending the child to be raised by a cousin, Ivy Shrimpton. In 1926 Sayers married journalist Oswald Atherton Fleming, an alcohol abuser who was only intermittently employed. For much of her career, Sayers was the main breadwinner for the couple, and she sent money to help in the upbringing of her son as well.

Worked in Advertising Agency

Although she would eventually return to scholarly work, the young Sayers found the university atmosphere oppressive and took a job as an advertising copywriter with the Benson's agency in London, beginning in 1922. She remained there for seven years, and the world of advertising formed the setting for her novel *Murder Must Advertise* (1933). The work sustained Sayers as she established her career as a mystery writer. The question of whether she took up the mystery genre as a way of paying her bills is, like many other questions about Sayers's career, difficult to answer definitively, but she was, in any event, successful from the beginning.

Sayers's first mystery novel, *Whose Body?* (1923), introduced her sleuth Lord Peter Wimsey, who would become permanently identified with her work. Like Sayers herself, Wimsey was something of a mixture, and that was a major part of his appeal—he emerged as a multifaceted individual. He was well educated, with a wide range of knowledge that enabled him to step into undercover roles on occasion (as in *Murder Must Advertise*). Like Sayers's former employer, he had suffered from shell shock after service in World War I. He wore a top hat, dressed stylishly, and delivered witty lines worthy of Sayers's contemporary P.G. Wodehouse. He was an expert cricket player, and a lover of books. And he aged as Sayers did, developing in real time over the course of her oeuvre. Wimsey was, in short, a sleuth readers cared about.

The other Lord Peter Wimsey novels of the 1920s were, like *Whose Body?*, destined to become mystery classics. These included *Clouds of Witness* (1926), *Unnatural Death* (1927), and *The Unpleasantness at the Bellona Club* (1928). Sayers cofounded the Detection Club, a group of mystery writers (including Agatha Christie and G.K. Chesterton) who promoted the idea that mysteries ought to reach their resolutions through pure reasoning on the part of their detective heroes, not through the intervention of external events. With other Detection Club members, Sayers wrote collaborative novels (such as 1931's *The Floating Admiral*) that, alone among her full-length fiction, do not feature Lord Peter Wimsey as protagonist. She also wrote and published 11 short stories featuring a different detective, business traveler Montague Egg.

Sayers continued to produce future mystery classics in the 1930s. She introduced a second detective, Harriet Vane, who over the course of several novels (including 1932's *Have*

His Carcase) began to fall in love with Wimsey. The novel that introduced Vane, 1930's *Strong Poison*, is thought to contain elements of Sayers's relationship with Cournos, and Vane is sometimes seen as an alter ego of the novelist herself. Among Sayers's most famous books is *The Nine Tailors*, notable for rich background descriptions including a detailed explanation of change ringing, the quasi-mathematical system of bell-ringing employed in rural British churches.

Wrote Religious Radio Plays

Gaudy Night (1935) was among several Sayers novels that were made into films, and the success of the Peter Wimsey series seemed undiminished. After beginning a new novel in 1938, however, Sayers abruptly gave up fiction writing. She never renounced her mysteries, however, and she served as president of the Detection Club for the last eight years of her life. The final novel was completed in 1996 by writer Jill Paton Walsh and given the title *Thrones, Dominations*. A devout Anglican, Sayers for several years devoted herself to religious dramas broadcast on the BBC radio network. The most famous of these was *The Man Born to Be King* (1942), a serial radio play devoted to the life of Jesus Christ and written in straightforward modern English.

Had the play been presented on stage, Sayers would have been in violation of the law: stage impersonation of a divine figure was against the law in Britain until 1968. But radio drama was a loophole. Despite strong protests from fundamentalist Christians—"A sinful man presuming to impersonate the Sinless One! It detracts from the honour due to the Divine Majesty," ran a letter to the editor quoted by Mary Brian Durkin in an article appearing on the Religion Online website—the drama attained considerable popularity by the late 1940s and was rebroadcast many times.

During World War II Sayers lived in a cottage in the small town of Witham. She was well known for keeping a pet pig named Francis Bacon, but wartime food shortages eventually compelled her to cook and eat him. Beginning in the war years she increasingly turned to writing religious essays and tracts. She believed that theology should be communicated in language that average readers could understand, collecting a group of her essays into the volume *Creed or Chaos? and Other Essays in Popular Theology* in 1947. Her religious writings have never attained the celebrity of her novels, but she is recognized as part of a group of Christian-oriented writers, including C.S. Lewis, T.S. Eliot, and J.R.R. Tolkien, who influenced British culture in the middle 20th century, and close readers have found Christian themes even in her mysteries. Those books are marred, however, by the occasional expression of anti-Semitic sentiments.

In 1950 Sayers received an honorary Doctor of Letters degree from the University of Durham. In 1955 she produced a long poem, *The Story of Adam and Christ*. At the end of her life she returned to the medieval studies she had pursued at Oxford, and completed a translation of the French epic *The Song of Roland* that she had begun earlier. After teaching herself medieval Italian, she embarked on a new translation of Dante's *Divine Comedy*, finishing most of it before her death in Witham on December 17, 1957. Her Dante translation, which accomplished the difficult feat of replicating the metrical scheme of the original, remains in use.

Books

Concise Dictionary of British Literary Biography, Volume 6: Modern Writers, 1914–1945, Gale, 1991.

Hone, Ralph, *Dorothy L. Sayers: A Literary Biography,* Kent State University Press, 1979.

Reynolds, Barbara, *Dorothy L. Sayers: Her Life and Soul,* St. Martin's, 1993.

St. James Guide to Crime & Mystery Writers, 4th ed., St. James, 1996.

Online

"Biography," Dorothy L. Sayers Society, http://www.sayers.org.uk/ (January 20, 2009).

"Dorothy L. Sayers," MysteryNet, http://www.mysterynet.com/sayers/ (January 20, 2009).

"Dorothy L(eigh) Sayers (1893–1957)," Books and Writers, http://www.kirjasto.sci.fi/dlsayers.htm (January 20, 2009).

Durkin, Mary Brian, "Dorothy L. Sayers: A Christian Humanist for Today," http://www.religion-online.org/showarticle.asp?title=1267 (January 20, 2009).□

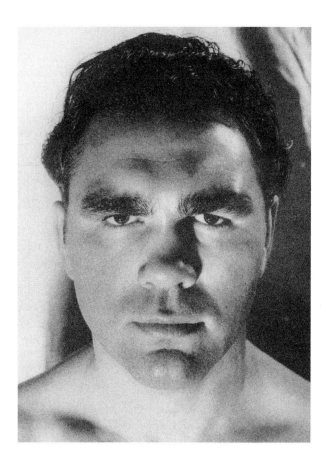

Max Schmeling

German boxer Max Schmeling (1905–2005) became a national hero in Fascist Germany when he twice fought the African-American Joe Louis in 1936 and 1938.

It was a role Schmeling accepted reluctantly, for he never subscribed to the National Socialist ideology and had tried to keep Adolf Hitler's regime at arm's length. Schmeling was a man caught between sport and ideology. In the United States Schmeling was vilified as a Nazi athlete, and, like those of many other Germans, his actions were morally ambiguous in the years just before and during World War II. Decades later, however, it also emerged that he had, at considerable risk to his own safety, protected German Jews and helped them to leave the country. Perhaps the truest measure of Schmeling's personality was the friendship that eventually developed between him and Louis, the boxer with whom he had shared the spotlight in the 1930s. Both boxers spoke of their fights as pure athletic contests, unencumbered by the ideas and world events that overshadowed them.

Inspired by Dempsey Films

Maximilian Adolph Otto Siegfried Schmeling was born in the village of Klein Lucknow in northeastern Germany, in the Berlin region. His father was a ship's navigator who had traveled around the world and encountered the sport of boxing, which was rarely seen in rural Germany at the time. Schmeling took up the sport when he was young, and his ambitions were strengthened when he saw a film of American heavyweight champion Jack Dempsey in action. As an adult, Schmeling bore more than an incidental resemblance to Dempsey in look and physique. With little athletic infrastructure to support him, he was largely self-taught as a boxer. In Arthur Bülow, the editor of a magazine called *Boxsport,* he found a patron and advisor.

Schmeling turned professional in August 1924 and won his first fight by knockout over Kurt Czapp in the sixth round. He fought nine more times in 1924 and won eight of those matches, losing only to Max Dieckmann by knockout. Moving to Berlin to seek out better management, he began to work with trainer Max Machon. Two years later he knocked Dieckmann out in the first round to become Germany's light heavyweight champion, and in 1927 he defeated Fernand Delarge to take the European light heavyweight title. He was the first German to hold that belt, which he successfully defended in December of 1927 and January of 1928.

His triumphs helped popularize boxing in Germany, and he found himself a celebrity. Coming into contact with the top cultural figures of Germany's Weimar Republic, Schmeling resolved to broaden the perspectives he had brought from his small-town origins. According to his biography from the Public Broadcasting System website, "I said to myself, 'You're a man from a humble background, what you didn't learn in school, you'll learn now. Catch up.'" Among his friends was the satirical artist George Grosz, who painted his portrait. Schmeling began to wear tuxedos purchased at an elegant Berlin shop owned by David Lewin. He moved up to the heavyweight class and became German champion at that weight level when he knocked out Franz Diener in a Berlin bout early in 1928.

With little left to accomplish in Europe, Schmeling wanted to take on new challenges in the U.S. Needing a manager familiar with the American boxing scene, he turned to a Jewish handler, Joe Jacobs, who often went by the Yiddish form of his name, Yussel. In the late 1920s this was not an issue, but after the Nazi takeover of the German government in 1933 it was frowned upon. Jacobs succeeded in getting Schmeling a place in the elimination series that followed the retirement of heavyweight champion Gene Tunney. Schmeling defeated Paolino Uzcudun and then faced off against Jack Sharkey for the title on June 12, 1930. He won the bout on a disqualification after being hit with a low blow.

Received Wedding Gift from Hitler

The decision was controversial, even for Schmeling himself, but after defending his title with a victory over Young Stribling in 1931 he was generally recognized as the world heavyweight champion. He was the first continental European to be so honored. Adolf Hitler took an interest in the new German champion, and when Schmeling married actress Anny Ondra, he sent the couple a Japanese maple tree. Schmeling and Ondra remained together through the tumultuous events of the next decade, and their marriage lasted until Ondra's death in the 1980s. Schmeling lost the title to Sharkey in 1932 in another controversial decision that saw Tunney and numerous other American observers claim that Schmeling had been robbed of a victory. For a short time, at least, Schmeling gained popularity in the U.S.

Hitler and his propaganda minister, Joseph Goebbels, wanted to exploit this popularity and began to shower Schmeling with attention. Although he was to some extent uneasy, visits with Germany's heads of government were impressive for the former small-town boy. In 1936, when there was talk that the United States might boycott the Olympic Games to be held in Berlin that year, Schmeling was dispatched to paint a rosy picture of life in Germany and to assure American officials that Jewish and black American athletes would not face mistreatment there. At the same time, he was allowed to use Jacobs as his manager only outside Germany, where Jewish participation in boxing was forbidden. After a mixed record in the mid-1930s, Schmeling scored several more victories in Germany and by 1936 was in line for another fight for the heavyweight crown, this one against 22-year-old Joe Louis.

By that time Schmeling was 31, an age at which most boxers' skills have begun to decline. Louis was undefeated, a phenomenon of the boxing world. Observers gave the German little chance, and he entered the ring in Yankee Stadium on June 19, 1936 as an 8-to-1 underdog. But Schmeling studied the young Louis's fight films closely, noticing a slight lowering of Louis's left hand at certain points that would allow Schmeling to come in with his right—his best punch. As Schmeling pummeled Louis with rights and took control of the fight, noted *Sports Illustrated,* "the crowd's latent racism began to surface. Before Schmeling finally knocked out Louis, he could hear ringside cries of 'Kill him! Kill him!'" After a 12th-round knockout, Schmeling returned to Germany a hero, flown home in the zeppelin *Hindenburg.*

The win put Schmeling in line to fight the other top heavyweight contender, James J. Braddock, but a threatened boycott scotched plans for the bout. Louis fought Braddock instead, and defeated him, setting up a rematch with Schmeling for June 22, 1938. By that time, tensions between Germany and much of the rest of the world had risen sharply, and Schmeling was received in the U.S. as a representative of Nazi ideology. He required a full cordon of police to protect him in New York, and he was showered with banana peels, cigarette packs, soda cups, and spit as he walked into the ring. Louis's son Joe Louis Barrow Jr. observed to *Sports Illustrated* that "[t]he parallels between my father and Max were quite considerable. Max had never really experienced prejudice till he came back over here in '38 and had pickets and felt hatred. Then he realized what so many whites never do—exactly what it is blacks have to go through."

Sheltered Jews on Kristallnacht

There was no hero's welcome for Schmeling this time after he was knocked out by a pumped-up Louis in the first round and hospitalized for two weeks with a pair of broken vertebrae. Privately, however, Schmeling felt relief on one level; if he had won, he later wrote (according to *Sports Illustrated*) that he would have been doomed to become "the 'Aryan Show Horse' of the Third Reich." Schmeling never joined Hitler's National Socialist Party, and the depth of his opposition to the Nazis manifested itself on Kristallnacht, the "night of broken glass" of November 9, 1938, when Nazi gangs rampaged through Germany in anti-Jewish riots at the instigation of Goebbels, and 30,000 Jews were arrested. Schmeling sheltered David Lewin's two teenage sons, Werner and Henri, in a Berlin hotel room for two days. Schmeling never discussed the incident; it was revealed only much later by Henri Lewin, who became a noted Las Vegas hotelier. "If they had caught him hiding us, they would have shot him," he told *Sports Illustrated,* Let me tell you: If I had been Max Schmeling in Germany in 1938, I wouldn't have done it."

His high status with the Nazi regime gone, Schmeling was drafted into the German army in 1940. He was 34; at the time it was mostly only young men of around 20 who were being drafted, but Schmeling's conscription occurred at the direct bidding of Germany's sports ministry. He served in a paratroop brigade and jumped into British fire on the Mediterranean island of Crete, but passed out during his descent because he was suffering from a stomach ailment. Hospitalized in Greece, he incurred further German enmity by refusing to denounce either the British who had captured him or the U.S., which he called his second home.

After the war, in desperate financial straits, Schmeling returned to the boxing ring several times to raise money. Thanks to the influence of a former New York State boxing commissioner who had become an executive at the Coca-Cola corporation, Schmeling was given a key franchise when Coca-Cola expanded into West Germany; settling in the Hamburg area, he reaped a generous share of Germany's postwar economic boom. In 1954 he returned to the U.S., invited to referee a boxing match in Milwaukee. He drove to Chicago to visit Louis, who agreed that the political meanings attached to their fights had been unimportant; they began a friendship that lasted until Louis's death in 1981. Schmeling helped Louis with mounting medical bills late in life and paid for his funeral. He published three autobiographies that left some questions about his experiences before the war unanswered, but he did assert in one of them that he and other Germans were well aware of the deportation of Jews to concentration camps. Schmeling died in Hollenstedt, near Hamburg, on February 2, 2005, just short of his 100th birthday.

Books

Margolick, David, *Joe Louis vs. Max Schmeling, and a World on the Brink,* Knopf, 2005.

Notable Sports Figures, 4 vols., Gale, 2004.

Schmeling, Max, *Max Schmeling: An Autobiography,* Bonus, 1998.

Periodicals

New York Times, February 5, 2005, p. A15; December 3, 2005, p. B13.

Sports Illustrated, December 3, 2001, p. 64; February 14, 2005, p. 19.

Times (London, England), September 2, 2006, p. 14.

Online

"Heavyweight Legend Schmeling Dies," BBC News, http://news.bbc.co.uk/sport2/hi/boxing/4235901.stm (January 24, 2009).

"Max Schmeling (1905–2005)," Public Broadcasting System, http://www.pbs.org/wgbh/amex/fight/peopleevents/p_schmeling.html (January 24, 2009). □

Peter Markham Scott

Sir Peter Markham Scott (1909–1989) was one of Britain's leading conservationists of the twentieth century. An ornithologist and artist as well, Scott was instrumental in the creation of the World Wild Fund for Nature (WWF), and designed its appealing panda bear logo. He served as WWF chair for more than 20 years, and played a vital role in several international conservation treaties. "A brilliant communicator, he awakened generations to the wonder of wildlife and then to the perils facing it," asserted his *Times* of London obituary, "with an increasing emphasis on conservation of habitat, long before being 'green' became fashionable."

Peter Markham Scott was named after the fictional *Peter Pan* character, the boy who never grew up. The author of *Peter Pan,* J.M. Barrie, was a friend of his parents and also became his godfather. Scott was born on September 14, 1909, in London, and never knew his father, the famed Antarctic explorer Robert F. Scott. He was still an infant when his father left on his ill-fated expedition to the South Pole in

the spring of 1911. The elder Scott was already famous for his 1901–04 Antarctic expedition, but became a martyr and legend after losing the unofficial race to the South Pole to Roald Amundsen of Norway, then perishing on the frozen turf with four other men on the 800-mile return trip to base camp. Their trip back had been derailed by terrible weather conditions and a lack of supplies, with the men falling ill to hunger and frostbite; a fifth companion had even walked away from the party, realizing that his failing state was imperiling the others.

Suffered from Dyslexia

A search party found the body of Scott's father and his fellow explorers in November of 1912, along with a diary that the elder Scott had kept of his journey—including a chronicle of the heartbreaking final days—and a letter he wrote to his wife, Kathleen Bruce Scott, with his hopes for their only child. "Make the boy interested in natural history, if you can," he urged her, according to *New York Times Magazine* writer Sophy Burnham. "It is better than games; they encourage it at some schools. . . . Above all, he must guard, and you must guard him, against indolence. Make him a strenuous man."

Scott's mother, a sculptor, heeded the advice, and encouraged an interest in birds at an early age. In 1922 she wed Edward Hilton Young, a British Treasury official who later became Lord Kennet of the Dene, and a year later gave birth to Scott's half-brother. Peter was 14 years old by then, and he began boarding at the Oundle School, near Peterborough, that same year. By then his passion for ornithology was so strong that he managed to keep various animals in his room and once even caught a bat during choir practice, which the boys then furtively passed around. In 1927 he entered Trinity College at Cambridge University with the goal of becoming a biologist, but his hopes of attaining a degree in natural sciences were hampered by dyslexia. By this point, however, he was already a talented artist with a specialty for drawing animals, and switched his degree course to art history in his third year. He graduated in 1931, then took further art courses in Germany. In 1933 he had his first exhibition of paintings in London.

Scott grew into an avid athlete with a particular talent for sailing and skating. At the 1936 Summer Olympics he won a bronze medal for Britain in the single-handed sailing event at the famous Berlin Games, though the actual sailing races took place in the port city of Kiel. Like other well-born English men and women, he participated in seasonal fox and grouse hunts, but later abandoned shooting as his interest in conservation grew. When World War II erupted, he enlisted in the Royal Navy and served on the fleet's destroyers that were deployed in the North Atlantic. He became commander of a squadron of gun boats in the English Channel, and also worked with Navy officials on effective new camouflage techniques for smaller destroyers, which involved painting ships in varying shades to confuse enemy ships and planes. Midway through his war service he married Elizabeth Jane Howard, who would later achieve prominence as a novelist, and earned the first of several official honors when he was named to the Order of the British Empire.

Founded Wetlands Trust

Scott ran in the 1945 general elections on the Conservative (Tory) Party ticket for the Wembley North district of London, but lost. He and his wife lived on Edwardes Square in the city, and their daughter Nicola was born in 1943, but the marriage was effectively over by 1947, when Howard left him. A few months later, Scott fulfilled one of the duties of his new job with the British Broadcasting Corporation (BBC), as a commentator at the royal wedding of the future Queen of England, Princess Elizabeth, to Prince Philip, the Duke of Edinburgh.

In addition to his BBC job, Scott continued to paint, and he wrote a number of articles on wildlife for various publications, including *Country Life*. He also traveled to the United States for a gallery exhibition of his work in New York City, and returned on board the *Queen Mary* with a collection of animals given to him by the curator of the Bronx Zoo. He acquired a country property near Bristol in the village of Slimbridge, and established the Severn Wildfowl Trust, which became the Wildfowl and Wetlands Trust in 1955. His house in Slimbridge was located near an area of mudflats adjacent to the Severn River, and the house itself overlooked a pond delightfully named Swan Lake.

The scenic setting provided ample artistic opportunities, but conservation efforts were Scott's paramount interest. His Trust's first significant success was a captive breeding program for the Nene, or Hawaiian goose. There were less than

four dozen left in Hawaii at the time, but a few were sent to Slimbridge by the Hawaiian Board of Agriculture and Forestry in 1950, and three years later nine new goslings had hatched. In 1951 Scott made a research trip to Iceland to search for the breeding grounds of the pink-footed goose. Along on the trip were his longtime friend James Fisher, whose father had been headmaster of Oundle School, and the Severn Trust secretary Philippa Talbot-Ponsonby. They traveled far inland and discovered a temporary settlement where some 1,700 pairs of the geese were breeding. They ringed the goslings at the age of two weeks, in order to identify their migratory patterns, and Scott chronicled the experience for the *Times* of London. "One might think that a 'grounded' wild goose would be easy to catch, but the Pinkfoot has evolved extremely efficient protective behaviour during this vulnerable flightless period," he wrote. "As soon as danger is detected, often at a range of a mile, the group of geese, perhaps 20 strong, perhaps 100, begins to run uphill. With a level start an adult goose runs uphill substantially faster than a man."

After tagging a thousand birds, Scott's expedition returned to Reykjavik, Iceland's capital, where he and Talbot-Ponsonby were wed on August 7, 1951. They had two children: a daughter, Dafila, born in 1952, and a son named Falcon, born in 1954. As British television expanded during that decade, so did Scott's presence in the medium. He served as host of the BBC's first regular program on natural history, *Look*, which ran from 1955 to 1981. The series made him a household name and a beloved weekly fixture in Britain, a nation with an unusually high proportion of bird watchers.

Took Up Gliding

Scott was also a published author. His account of the Iceland trip, *A Thousand Geese*, was written with Fisher and published in 1953. His autobiography, *The Eye of the Wind*, appeared in 1961, just as Scott's newest hobby, gliding, began to consume more of his time. His first airborne experience came in 1956 with a 19-minute flight at an altitude of 1,000 feet with the instructor of the local gliding club in Bristol. It was an ideal hobby for a bird lover such as Scott, for glider flight involved conquering the earth's gravitational pull with the help of wind currents. "By your own knowledge and cunning you are keeping yourself up, using natural power to do it," he wrote, according to Elspeth Huxley's 1993 biography, *Peter Scott: Painter and Naturalist*. "It is a gloriously uplifting feeling."

Scott won the British national gliding title in 1963, and later that decade served as president of the British Gliding Association. He remained involved in yachting, too, and skippered the *Sovereign* in the 1964 America's Cup race. He was knighted by Queen Elizabeth II in 1973, made a Companion of Honour in 1987, and also became a Fellow of the Royal Society that same year. By then he had accrued an impressive list of achievements, but it was his conservation work that garnered him the most accolades. In 1961 he and a trio of scientists and conservationists founded the World Wildlife Fund, which was later renamed the World Wide Fund for Nature (WWF). He designed its famously recognizable panda logo and served as its chair from 1961 to 1982.

At the helm of the WWF, Scott took an active role in arguing for international cooperation for the protection of flora and fauna. This included the 1971 Convention of Wetlands of International Importance, also known as the Ramsar Convention, and the 1973 Agreement on Conservation of Polar Bears, signed by the governments of the United States, the Soviet Union, Canada, Denmark, and Norway. He was also active in the United Nations World Heritage Convention of 1972, which created the UNESCO World Heritage sites, and the 1973 Convention on International Trade in Endangered Species of Wild Fauna and Flora, also known as CITES. This last international treaty was the work of the International Union for Conservation of Nature (IUCN), and from 1963 to 1980 Scott chaired its Survival Service Commission (which later became the Species Survival Commission), and launched the *Red Data* guides, an annual listing of the world's endangered species and plants. Scott's devotion to his cause was so ardent that he eventually returned the Order of the Falcon, which had been awarded to him by the government of Iceland for his conservation work, because of Iceland's continued involvement in the whaling trade.

Intrigued by Mythic Monster

Scott stepped down as chair of the WWF in 1982, but after 1985 became its honorary chair. Incidentally, he was nominally involved in the enduring controversy over the Loch Ness Monster, a supposed prehistoric beast that several people claimed to have sighted in a deep, 23-mile-long freshwater lake in the Scottish Highlands. Scores of well-funded expeditions have been devoted to proving or debunking the myth that a giant aquatic creature resembling a dinosaur lives in Loch Ness. Scott was one of the founders of the Loch Ness Phenomena Investigation Bureau in the 1960s, and is credited with giving the mythic beast its scientific name, *Nessiteras rhombopteryx*, in order to allow it to be registered as an endangered species. The ancient Greek moniker means "the wonder of Ness with the diamond shaped fin," but others have also pointed out that it is also an anagram of "Monster hoax by Sir Peter S."

Scott died of a heart attack on August 29, 1989, in a Bristol hospital. Eight years earlier, during his interview with Burnham, he recalled an encounter with U.S. astronaut Neil Armstrong, who had recounted just how majestic the earth looked from space, prompting in Armstrong a wave of homesickness. The planet, Scott told Burnham, is the "only one that is a home for man. We have to look up to it and look after it."

Books

Huxley, Elspeth, *Peter Scott: Painter and Naturalist,* Faber & Faber, 1993.

Periodicals

New York Times Magazine, April 27, 1980, p. SM23.

Times (London, England), July 11, 1951, p. 5; August 25, 1951, p. 5; August 31, 1989.□

Madeleine de Scudéry

French writer Madeleine de Scudéry (1607–1701) was one of the most prolific and well-known women authors of her day. "La Mademoiselle de Scudéry," as she was more commonly called, wrote lengthy novels, hosted a weekly literary salon in her Paris home in the 1650s, and was a longtime fixture at the court of Louis XIV. "The translations of her books formed part of a body of literature describing new, 'French' styles of living that were imitated by elite circles in England, Germany, Italy, and Spain," noted Elizabeth C. Goldsmith in Volume 268 of the *Dictionary of Literary Biography: Seventeenth-Century French Writers.*

Scudéry was born into a wealthy family in the port city of Le Havre, France, on November 15, 1607. She was named in honor of her mother, Madeleine de Martel de Goutimesnil, and was one of five children. Both parents died by the time she was seven years old, however, and Scudéry was sent to live with an uncle in Rouen, the main city in Normandy. It was not uncommon for young women from wealthy French families to receive a rather solid education—by contrast to their counterparts elsewhere on the Continent—but Scudéry appears to have been schooled further than most, as evidenced by her extensive knowledge of the literature of ancient Greece and Rome.

Scudéry seems to have followed her older brother, Georges, into a literary career. He had spent several years in the French military, and after his discharge moved to Paris. His first play, *Lygdamon et Lidias; ou, La Ressemblance,* was first staged in 1630, around the time he began his association with the Théâtre du Marais; after 1637, he wrote plays for the Hôtel de Bourgogne, a Parisian theater troupe with royal patronage. Scudéry joined her brother in Paris in 1637, where they shared a home in the city's Marais district for several years.

Wrote Under Brother's Name

Scudéry's first published work was *Ibrahim ou L'Illustre Bassa* (Ibrahim or the Illustrious Bassa), which appeared under her brother's name in 1641. The four-volume novel was based on a tale well known throughout medieval and Renaissance Europe, about a slave at the court of the sultan of the Ottoman Empire that had been passed down through the centuries. "Drawing liberally from published descriptions of Constantinople to evoke a plausible backdrop for her exotic story," noted Goldsmith, "Scudéry devised a series of romantic plots and subplots linking sentimental adventure with political tensions between different social groups—Christians, Muslims, Romans, Persians, and Turks. The narrative is punctuated with digressions in which the characters tell each other stories and converse on the moral and philosophical implications of their situation."

In 1642, Georges was appointed governor of the fort of Notre-Dame-de-la-Garde in Marseilles, the Mediterranean port city, and Scudéry seems to have lived in that city for a

time, too, though they both later returned to Paris around 1647. Her second work, which was also published under her brother's name and likely co-authored with him, too, was *Les Femmes illustres ou Les Harangues héroïques*– published several years later in English translation as *Les Femmes Illustres, or The Heroick Harrangues of the Illustrious Women,* which featured imaginary letters from well-known women throughout history.

Scudéry was reportedly one of the top contenders for a prestigious position as governess to the Mancini nieces of Cardinal (Jules) Mazarin, who served as France's prime minister under King Louis XIII and his successor Louis XIV. Though the powerful Mazarin chose someone else for the job, the fact that Scudéry was considered shows that she was a favorite at court and known for both her intelligence and moral character.

Contender for Longest Book Honor

In 1649, the first installment of Scudéry's longest work, *Artamène ou Le Grand Cyrus,* appeared in print. Again, the work was published under her brother's name, but Scudéry was widely known to be its author. The story unfolded through ten volumes between 1649 and 1653 and was translated into English as *Artamenes, or The Grand Cyrus, an Excellent New Romance* almost immediately; there were also German, Italian, and even Arabic versions. It remains one of the longest works of fiction ever published, with its 2.1 million words beating Marcel Proust's *À*

la recherche du temps perdu (Remembrance of Things Past), which contains 1.5 million words, and the 1.2 million words in *Mission Earth,* a science fiction tale from Church of Scientology founder L. Ron Hubbard.

Artamène is set in antiquity, but there are obvious parallels to current events and even life at the French royal court. Scudéry centers the tale at the court of Cyrus, the founder of the Persian Empire before his death around 530 BCE. The tenth volume is dominated by the recounting tale of Sapho, the ancient Greek lyric poet and the first woman writer ever to be known by her true name and gender. In Scudéry's final installment, "Sapho's retreat to the land of the Amazons occasions a description of a kind of female utopia, where women govern according to carefully elaborated codes of love and gallantry and where intellectual pursuits and writing are the highest vocations a woman can pursue," noted Goldsmith in the *Dictionary of Literary Biography* essay.

Some literary critics consider *Artamène* as a response to the Fronde, a civil war that raged in France from 1648 to 1653, which coincided almost exactly with the publication of its ten volumes. The actual conflict pitted the powerful Cardinal Mazarin, who was responsible for policies that were viewed as limiting to the French aristocratic classes, against Louis II de Bourbon, the powerful Prince of Condé who commanded a small army in his insurrection against the crown. In Scudéry's novel, a prince named Clèandre is accused of plotting against King Crésus and jailed, just as Condé had been imprisoned in the fort in Scudéry's hometown, Le Havre. Writing in the journal *L'Esprit Crèateur,* the scholar Joan DeJean called the novel "a unique example of *bel esprit* not only produced during civil war but as a commentary on the actions and the effects of such conflict.... Scudéry formulates an intricate questioning of the right to kingship in which controversial issues—Who deserves to be king? Should merit play a role in the designation of a monarch?—are discreetly woven in filigree throughout her tales of love unrequited and deferred."

Launched Literary Salon

Scudéry was a friend of Catherine de Vivonne, the Marquise de Rambouillet, a well-known Parisian hostess whose literary salon was an important center of French cultural life in the 1630s and '40s. In 1653, Scudéry launched her own salon, which she called the *Société du samedi* (Saturday Society). She co-hosted it with the writer Paul Pellisson, and its regular attendees included Madame de Sévigné, a renowned writer whose energies were devoted to voluminous correspondence, and Marie-Madeleine, the Comtesse de Lafayette, author of one of the first historical novels, *La Princesse de Clèves.*

Though Scudéry and her brother were both members of Louis XIV's court, there were tensions during the Fronde, and both appeared to support the Condé faction. For a time, her brother was forced to leave Paris to avoid arrest. In 1654, he married and set up his own household. Though neither achieved any significant remuneration from their writing, Scudéry did appear to be able to support herself, and her works were extremely popular with readers of the era. At one point, demand for new installments of her latest novel was so high that her Paris publisher, Augustin Courbé, was forced to reprint earlier volumes to satisfy demand.

That highly anticipated work was *Clélie: Histoire romaine,* which appeared in ten volumes beginning in 1654. Its final installment was published in 1660. In 1655, it was translated into English as *Clélia, An Excellent New Romance.* Like her previous opus, this work was based in part on ancient literature—in this case, the legacy of the Roman scholars, Livy and Plutarch—in imagining a romantic hero, Artaxander, and his love for Mellicinda. The work is notable for Scudéry's invention of the "Carte du pays de Tendre" (Map of the Land of Tenderness), a large map around which several characters gather and carry on a lengthy discussion typical of Scudéry's books. The map-as-allegory would be used many other times in literature, but in Scudéry's world the characters seek to reach love via stops in the villages of Generosity and Exactitude, while avoiding the community called Forgetfulness and the Lake of Indifference.

Expressed Independence of Mind

Scudéry's *Clélie* was also notable for its proto-feminist sentiments. While her characters discuss romantic attachments at length, their "speculations about marriage were perceived by some as subversive—a challenge to existing norms of behavior for women and a menace to conjugal harmony," noted Goldsmith in the *Dictionary of Literary Biography.* "Nicolas Boileau-Despréaux published a lengthy satire of novels in which he singled out *Clélie* and the 'Carte du pays de Tendre' as encouraging dangerous thinking that would ultimately lead to female adultery and the decline of marriage as a social institution." Scudéry had other detractors, too, including the playwright Molière, who poked fun at the in-jokes and word games of salon devotees in his 1659 satire *Les Précieuses ridicules* (The Pretentious Young Ladies). A later work by him, *Les Femmes Savantes* (The Learned Ladies) is also considered another jibe at Scudéry, Rambouillet, and their circle.

During the 1660s, Scudéry wrote a trio of novellas that were all published anonymously in Paris and never translated into English. They are *Célinte, Mathilde d'Aguilar,* and *La Promenade de Versailles.* She and Pellisson also involved themselves in a political intrigue involving Louis XIV's longtime minister of finance and wealthy arts patron, Nicolas Fouquet, whose power and influence bred rivalry at court and resulted in his arrest, three-year trial, and imprisonment. Pellisson even wrote a long treatise arguing on behalf of Fouquet's innocence, which resulted in his own five-year jail term.

Scudéry switched to nonfiction quite late in her writing career. Her *Discours sur la gloire* of 1671—translated several years later as *An Essay upon Glory*—won her the first-ever prize for authors from the esteemed Académie Française that same year. In 1680, she published the two-volume *Conversations sur divers sujets* (Conversations upon Several Subjects), followed by several similar works over the next dozen years that enjoyed a devoted readership for the instruction they provided on the art of learned discourse. Some of the titles were even used as textbooks at a renowned Saint-Cyr academy near Paris, founded and run by the

Marquise de Maintenon (Françoise d'Aubigné Scarron), the mistress of Louis XIV. The school was created with the goal of educating young women from aristocratic but impoverished families, and as Goldsmith noted in the *Dictionary of Literary Biography* essay, Madame de "Maintenon was not pleased with the effect they had on young readers, and she had them removed from St.-Cyr when she realized they were not serving the practical purpose she had intended—teaching young girls how to speak well—but rather were having the effect of encouraging daydreams and fantasy."

Despite her dalliances with movements that were somewhat seditious, Scudéry remained in the good graces at court, and was awarded a royal pension in 1683. She continued writing well into her ninetieth year, though her literary style had fallen out of fashion. She died in Paris on June 2, 1701, at the age of 93. So renowned a figure was she, however, that more than a century later the German Romantic writer E.T.A. Hoffmann made her the titular character in his novella *Das Fräulein von Scuderi: Erzählung aus dem Zeitalter Ludwig des Vierzehnten* (Mademoiselle de Scudéri: A Tale from the Times of Louis XIV), which is considered the first detective novel ever written in the German language.

Books

Goldsmith, Elizabeth C., "Madeleine de Scudéry," in *Dictionary of Literary Biography,* Volume 268: *Seventeenth-Century French Writers,* edited by Françoise Jaouën, Yale University, Gale, 2002, pp. 342–350.

Periodicals

L'Esprit Créateur, Fall 1989, pp. 43–51.□

Norma Shearer

Canadian-American actress Norma Shearer (1902–1982) was among the most bankable stars of the 1930s, with a versatile intelligence that allowed her to succeed in roles ranging from high drama to sexual adventuress.

S hearer today is not mentioned in the same breath as female contemporaries like Greta Garbo and Joan Crawford, but her career was notable in many respects. For one, she was among the few stars of the silent film era to make the transition to "talkies" successfully. For another, her life might be described as a rags-to-riches story, a triumph over a difficult childhood. And Shearer embodied the free spirit of American cinema for the few years before censorship codes came into full force in the 1930s. "Norma Shearer has killed our grandmothers," wrote a commentator in *Motion Picture Magazine* (as quoted by Mick LaSalle in *Complicated Women: Sex and Power in Pre-Code Hollywood*). "She has killed what they stood for. She has murdered the old-time Good Woman. She has cremated the myth that men will never marry 'that

kind of woman.' She has abolished 'that kind of woman.' There remain—free souls.''

Adopted Fashion-Forward Hair Style

Shearer and her publicists were unusually successful in obscuring her true date of birth, but it is now thought that she was born on August 10, 1902. She was born in the then English-speaking suburb of Westmount, near Montreal, Quebec, Canada. Her full name was Edith Norma Shearer; Edith was the name of her energetic and ambitious mother. Her father, Andrew, was a construction contractor of Scottish background. During the first part of Norma's life, the family was prosperous. She was educated partly at home, and Edith had the idea of making her into a piano prodigy. Shearer attended the Montreal School for Girls and Westmount High School, heightening her mother's ambitions for her when she won a beauty contest at age 15. She was the first girl at Westmount to bob her hair.

Shearer had no problem with sharing in those ambitions. She had wanted to be a performer ever since seeing the vaudeville act the Dolly Sisters when she was a child, and the *Perils of Pauline* series of silent film actress Pearl White transferred her dreams to the cinema. But the family's financial condition had worsened by the time Shearer was a teen. Andrew Shearer had lost most of the family's funds, and he and Edith separated. Edith Shearer and her three children moved into a tiny low-budget apartment. Edith Shearer made her move when she managed to

wangle a letter of introduction for Norma to New York theatrical producer Florenz Ziegfeld. But to finance the trip to New York, Norma had to sell her piano—and older sister Athole sold her beloved bulldog.

After arriving in 1920, Shearer got off to a very slow start in New York. She, along with Athole and Edith, landed parts as extras in short subjects, and Norma even landed a part in the feature *The Stealers.* But the three of them lived in a $7.50-a-week apartment that had only a double bed, a cot with no mattress, and no private bath. Both Ziegfeld and director D.W. Griffith, for whom Shearer worked as an extra in *Way Down East,* advised Shearer that she did not have what it would take to become a star actress, and indeed she seemed an unlikely candidate. She did not have the willowy look the silver screen favored; she needed dental work; and she had a slight cast in her right eye— an occasional inability to make it focus in tandem with the left. In early 1921, the family returned to Montreal.

Shearer did not give up, however. She found modeling jobs in Montreal and used them as a springboard to similar work in New York, soon landing on a billboard over Columbus Circle as ''Miss Lotta Miles,'' promoting a tire company. An agent got her more small film roles and even lead roles in *Channing of the Northwest* (1922) and *A Clouded Name* (1923). Muscle exercises helped reduce the cast in Shearer's eye, although close observers of her films can still spot it. Shearer's break came in 1923, reputedly after Mayer Company executive Irving Thalberg had spotted the Miss Lotta Miles billboards. She was signed to a six-month contract at a salary of $250 a week, with transportation for herself and her mother to California included. Later Athole and younger brother Douglas would join them; Douglas, as a sound engineer, won 12 Academy Awards, more than Norma Shearer ever even had in her sights.

Played Two Roles in Film

The Mayer Company merged with Metro Studios and the Goldwyn Company to become Metro-Goldwyn-Mayer, or MGM, and Shearer found herself a developing property of one of the Hollywood studio system's most successful manifestations. In 1924 she was featured in such films as *The Snob* and *Empty Hands*—not top-dollar MGM productions, but they did provide opportunities for her to gain fans and industry notice. Her personal life was less happy; she was romantically linked to *Empty Hands* director Victor Fleming but was dropped short of her goal of marriage. In *He Who Gets Slapped* (1924), Shearer worked with immigrant Swedish director Victor Seastrom. Perhaps the greatest critical success among her silent films was *Lady of the Night* (1925), in which she played two different roles, rich girl Florence, and streetwise Molly. That same year, Shearer came in fourth, behind only Marion Davies, Ramon Navarro, and John Gilbert, in a poll of movie theater owners who were asked to rank stars by popularity.

Shearer joined with Navarro for her first big-budget MGM spectacular, the Ernst Lubitsch–directed *The Student Prince,* in 1927. The film was a hit, and Shearer was a marquee attraction. A week after the film was released, Shearer and Thalberg married. They had two children, Irving Jr. (who became a professor of philosophy) and Katherine (later owner of the Explorers Bookshop in Aspen, Colorado). Shearer successfully juggled career and motherhood, taking time away from the screen when her children were young and to be with Thalberg as his health deteriorated, but each time engineering a triumphant return.

Part of the reason she was able to do so was that by the mid-1930s she had accumulated a longer record of success than most of her actress peers: her career, like those of few other performers, spanned the eras of silent and sound film. In making the switch she was aided by her brother, Douglas, who arranged for her an appointment with a University of Southern California professor who analyzed how she would sound in the new medium. Shearer's first sound film was *The Trial of Mary Dugan* (1929), in which she played a woman in her 30s with considerable experience with men. The film earned MGM a $400,000 profit, but another early Shearer 'talkie,' *The Hollywood Revue of 1929,* was a bomb.

Shearer realized that reinventing herself as a figure identified with a confident sexuality was important to her career, but Thalberg was skeptical. She won him over with a portfolio of seductive photos taken by Hollywood photographer George Hurrell (at Navarro's suggestion), and Thalberg cast her in the risqué *The Divorcee* in 1930. The move brought Shearer and MGM another hit, and Shearer won the 1930 Academy Award for Best Actress. For several years Shearer was in Hollywood's sexual vanguard. Silent-film buffs, noted LaSalle, may smile when they see Shearer "going on a self-described 'orgy' through Europe in *Strangers May Kiss*. What the modern audience is less likely to appreciate is that in 1931, this sort of story was both shocking and extremely new."

Appeared as Poet Elizabeth Barrett Browning

By the time *Smilin' Through* was released in 1932, Shearer was being billed as the First Lady of the Screen. With the edge taken off her image by the institution of the Production Code in the early 1930s (which detailed new industry standards of morally acceptable content), she balanced sexy roles with prestige films such as an adaptation of Eugene O'Neill's stage play *Strange Interlude* (1932) and the critically admired *The Barretts of Wimpole Street* (1934), a film biography of poet Elizabeth Barrett Browning. Shearer was hit hard by Thalberg's death from pneumonia in 1936, and she was absent from the screen for some time after contracting the disease herself. In the late 1930s, however, she was romantically linked with actors James Stewart, George Raft, and the teenaged Mickey Rooney, as well as tycoon Howard Hughes.

After conducting aggressive negotiations with MGM executives over her future and over the residual profits from Thalberg's estate, Shearer signed a new six-film contract with the studio in 1937. Director George Cukor's elaborate version of *Romeo and Juliet* bombed that year, perhaps because the 35-year-old Shearer made an unconvincing 14-year-old Juliet, but Shearer proved her continuing power as a screen draw with the 1938 hit *Marie Antoinette*. Shearer was originally slated to play Scarlett O'Hara in *Gone with the Wind,* but her still substantial legion of fans reacted negatively to the idea, and the role went to Vivien Leigh instead. Shearer's consolation prize was the

equally well regarded and only somewhat less successful *The Women,* a film with an all-female cast in which she received top billing over a host of other stars.

Shearer had one more hit with *Escape* in 1940, but her last few projects were less distinctive than many of her earlier releases. Her last film was *Her Cardboard Lover,* released in 1942. In that year she married ski instructor Martin Jacque Arrougé. The two signed a prenuptial agreement, which was rare at the time, protecting the rights of Shearer's children to Thalberg's fortune, and the marriage lasted until Shearer's death. On one ski trip, she met the then-unknown actress Janet Leigh and helped to further her early career. Shearer contemplated a return to the screen several times in the late 1940s and remained visible for a time in Hollywood, selecting the actor Robert Evans to play Thalberg in the Lon Chaney biography *Man of a Thousand Faces* in 1957. In her later years she would deny her identity to fans that recognized her in public, and she became increasingly wary of press photographers. Shearer suffered from deteriorating eyesight and poor health, and in 1980 she moved into a nursing home, the Motion Picture Country House and Lodge in Woodland Hills, California. She died there on June 12, 1982.

Books

Lambert, Gavin, *Norma Shearer: A Life,* Knopf, 1990.

LaSalle, Mick, *Complicated Women: Sex and Power in Pre-Code Hollywood,* St. Martin's, 2000.

Quirk, Lawrence J., *Norma: The Story of Norma Shearer,* St. Martin's, 1988.

Periodicals

People, June 25, 1990, p. 29.

Online

"Norma Shearer," All Movie Guide, http://www.allmovie.com (January 21, 2009).

"Norma Shearer," Turner Classic Movies, http://www.tcmdb.com/participant.jsp?participantId=175586 (January 21, 2009).

"The Story of Queen Norma Shearer: First Lady of the Films," Hollywood Legends, http://hollywood-legends.webs.com/ladyofthenight/bio.htm (January 21, 2009). □

Albert Spalding

The American sporting goods executive Albert G. Spalding (1850–1915) founded the company whose athletic gear still bears his name. On the field, he was one of the most accomplished stars of baseball in the 19th century.

Beyond these accomplishments, Spalding shaped the culture of baseball in fundamental ways that are still apparent today. It was Spalding who took baseball out of the realm of adult male gamblers and drinkers, redefining it as a clean family sport. Spalding was the first

took up the game out of sheer loneliness. Spalding himself told the story of how he was watching a game from beyond the centerfield fence, caught a ball coming toward him with his right hand, and threw it back to the catcher without a bounce. Impressed, the other boys recruited him as a pitcher. In 1863, a group of Rockford merchants formed a baseball team called the Forest City Club (or Forest Citys), and the teenaged Spalding joined the squad as a pitcher in 1865. In an early example of the power of sports to trump academics, the team's founders leaned on Spalding's high school principal to excuse his absences on game days.

The dimensions of Spalding's talent became clear in 1867 when the Washington Nationals, often considered the best team in the U.S., visited Illinois to play in a tournament (league play was still in the future). They drubbed the host Chicago Excelsiors 49–4, but the obscure Forest City Club, with Spalding on the mound, beat the Nationals 29–23. Spalding was recruited by the Chicago team and played there for a short time, but then returned to Rockford, took classes at Rockford Commercial College, worked as a grocery clerk, and continued to play for the local team. In 1870 he notched another major pitching victory, this one against the Cincinnati Red Stockings.

Won 54 Games in Season

The Red Stockings were managed by Harry Wright, who later moved to Boston and began to organize a new Boston Red Stockings team as well as baseball's first major league, the National Association of Professional Base Ball Players. Spalding and two other Rockford players were signed to the Red Stockings, and Spalding joined the team in 1871. From 1872 to 1875 his dominance of the National Association was impressive. Pitching every day, for baseball rules allowed only one pitcher per team at this point, he had more than 200 wins, topping every other pitcher up to that time for whom reliable statistics exist. In 1875 his record was 54 wins and 5 losses. That same year he married Sarah Josephine (Josie) Keith, and the couple had one son, Keith.

Spalding also got a chance to develop his organizational skills when Wright picked him to put together an American baseball exhibition tour in England. The Boston team showed its skills by winning not only most of the exhibition baseball games but also a series of cricket matches against English teams. Despite these successes, Spalding was frustrated by one aspect of professional baseball: like boxing, it flourished in a rough-and-rowdy atmosphere rife with alcohol and gambling. When Chicago entrepreneur William Hulbert began to organize the new National League, with stricter regulation of both, Spalding jumped at the chance to return to Illinois. In 1876 he became pitcher, captain, and manager of the Chicago White Stockings—the ancestor not of today's Chicago White Sox but of the Cubs.

Spalding notched 47 wins for the White Stockings in 1876, but because of the grueling conditions of early baseball his career as a player was almost over. He moved to first base in 1877, and in 1878 he played only one game. He moved to the position of secretary within the White Stockings organization, and after Hulbert's death in 1882 he took over as president. Under Spalding's leadership, the White Stockings evolved into one of baseball's first

to see the enormous possibilities for cross-merchandising the game of baseball offered. The idea of an official provider of equipment to a sports organization originated with Spalding, as did spring training. And he was among the first to promote baseball outside the United States. "The railroads had Commodore Vanderbilt. Big steel had Andrew Carnegie. Big oil, John D. Rockefeller. Baseball had Albert Goodwill Spalding," wrote documentarians Geoffrey Ward and Ken Burns (as quoted in *Investor's Business Daily*).

Raised on Farm

Albert Goodwill Spalding, known as "Big Al" during his days as a pitcher, was born in the farm town of Byron, Illinois, on September 2, 1850. His family was well off when he was young; his father, James Lawrence Spalding, was a prosperous farmer and property owner, and his mother, Harriet Irene Goodwill Wright Spalding, also brought financial resources to the marriage. Spalding had a younger sister, born in 1854, and a brother, James Walter Spalding, born in 1856. In 1858, however, the elder James Spalding died. Part of the family moved to the city of Rockford, Illinois—a completely unfamiliar environment for the farm-raised Albert Spalding, who later recalled that he was almost housebound by the fear of meeting strangers in the street.

Various stories have purported to recount how Spalding became acquainted with the game of baseball. One version held that a Civil War veteran taught Spalding and other Rockford boys how to play, another that Spalding

dynasties. They won the league pennant in 1880, 1881, 1882, 1885, and 1886. Among Spalding's innovations was spring training, which he instituted by sending the White Stockings players to Hot Springs, Arkansas in 1886. He also organized a six-month round-the-world baseball all-stars' world tour that made stops in Hawaii, New Zealand, Australia, Sri Lanka, Egypt, Italy, and the British Isles.

Opened Store with $800 Investment

All of these accomplishments came as Spalding was developing a second career. In 1876, with his younger brother, he opened the A.G. Spalding & Brother sporting goods shop at 118 West Randolph in Chicago's center. Two years later they were joined by Spalding's brother-in-law, and the name was changed slightly to A.G. Spalding & Brothers. In 1879 the firm began to manufacture baseballs, gloves, bats, baseball wear, and other items. Its growth was spectacular: launched with $800 of Spalding's own money, A.G. Spalding & Brothers had $4 million in capital by 1892.

The year before that, Spalding resigned as president of the White Stockings so that he could devote all his time to his burgeoning sporting-goods business. His promotional ideas and his instincts for new directions in which to take the firm were brilliant. The company's first product was the Spalding baseball, which he offered to National League teams for free, and even paid $1 per dozen balls for the privilege of being able to claim that the Spalding was the official ball of he National League. The lack of a formal agreement was no impediment to Spalding's plans; when the National League refused to sanction his *Spalding's Official Baseball Guide,* he marketed it successfully nevertheless. The Spalding firm designed the first basketball, and became the first American maker of golf clubs, and printed annual almanacs for other sports followed.

In the early 20th century, Spalding waded into an ongoing debate about baseball's origins. In his 1911 memoir, *America's National Game,* Spalding argued in favor of the now-familiar but then quite new idea that the game had been devised by Abner Doubleday in Cooperstown, New York in 1839. The preponderance of evidence, in the opinion of baseball historians, points instead to a slow evolution of baseball from the English game of rounders, from which the diamond-shaped field and some of baseball's terminology clearly developed. But the force of Spaulding's reputation was such that the Doubleday story became and remains a staple of American childhood.

After Josie Spalding's death in 1899, Spalding married a childhood friend, Elizabeth Churchill Mayer. Spalding and Mayer are thought to have carried on a relationship prior to that, resulting in the birth of an illegitimate son named Spalding Brown Spalding. Albert Spalding's nephew, also named Albert Spalding, became a famous concert violinist. Spalding and his new wife moved to the San Diego, California area so that the new Mrs. Spaulding could be close to a community practicing the ideas of the philsophico-religious system known as theosophy. Spaulding wanted to run for the U.S. Senate as a Republican in 1910, but he lost in the party's caucus to candidate John D. Works. Spaulding died in Point Loma, California on September 9, 1915. He was inducted into the Baseball Hall of Fame in 1939.

Books

Biographical Dictionary of American Sports: Baseball, rev.ed., Greenwood, 2000.

Levine, Peter, *A.G. Spalding and the Rise of Baseball,* Oxford, 1985.

Spalding, A.G., *America's National Game,* American Sports Publishing Company, 1911.

Periodicals

Investor's Business Daily, August 7, 2002, p. A3.
New York Times, September 12, 1915.
Sports Illustrated, April 15, 1985, p. 12.

Online

"Al Spalding," Baseball Biography Project, http://bioproj.sabr.org/bioproj.cfm?a=v&v=l&bid=1274&pid=13395 (January 17, 2009).□

J.G. Taylor Spink

J.G. Taylor Spink (1888–1962) inherited the *The Sporting News* from his father, Charles Spink. Through diligent promotion and canny marketing, he transformed the "Bible of Baseball" into one of the most influential sports publications of the twentieth century.

Spink oversaw publication of *The Sporting News* from 1914 until his death in 1962. During that time, he and his staff chronicled baseball's greatest era of change. The introduction of the American League, the switch from the dead-ball era to the rise of great home-run sluggers such as Babe Ruth, Lou Gehrig, and Jimmie Foxx, the breaking of the color barrier, night games, and expansion teams—all were covered during his watch. Further, the publication's own selections of All-Star and Most Valuable Players (MVPs) influenced Major League Baseball to stage a yearly All-Star game. The Baseball Writers of America also began giving out a regular MVP award for outstanding play. Further, in the years before pervasive television coverage, *The Sporting News* was considered the most reliable source for scrupulously researched statistics and up-to-date news on every major sporting event.

Started Young

Born John George Taylor Spink on November 6, 1888, he was the son of Charles Claude Spink, a publisher, and Marie Taylor Spink. The Spink family had emigrated from Canada during the Civil War, and Taylor Spink's uncles William and Al had become sportswriters, the latter founding *The Sporting News* in 1886. His father, the more business-minded Charles Spink, was homesteading in South Dakota when he was called back to St. Louis to help put the publication on a firm financial footing. "The paper was having a hard row to hoe and made little headway until he took hold of its business management," Al Spink was quoted as saying in an article posted on *The Sporting News*'s Web site, *SportingNews.com*. ''From that day it prospered.''

Al Spink, cash-strapped from his investment in an unsuccessful play, sold his stock to brother Charles a short time later, but running the magazine remained a family affair. Both of Taylor Spink's parents worked on the publication, and while he was still in grade school the youngster himself sold copies on the street like a regular newsboy. So ambitious was the lad that he added the *Saturday Evening Post* to the batch of periodicals he sold. After dropping out of school during the tenth grade, he worked as a stock boy with the Rawlings Sporting Goods Company and as a copy boy for the *St. Louis Post-Dispatch.*

After a year working outside the family business, Spink joined *The Sporting News* before he turned 18. Apprenticing as a copy boy, writer, and assistant editor, he learned his trade from the ground up. In time he began to branch out, writing entertainment reviews for the *New York Morning Telegraph* of stage productions passing through St. Louis, and in 1909 he put out the very first *Sporting News Record Book*. Further, his greatest coup came when he convinced American League president Ban Johnson to let him act as the official scorer for baseball's World Series, a position he held for ten years.

Reported to have a volatile temper, Spink was deeply passionate about baseball, and often argued with his father about the hot topic issues of the day. When the Federal League was formed as a competitor to the already established National and American Leagues, the elder Spink supported the upstart league, but Taylor Spink believed the new league could not last. Further, he argued that the *The Sporting News*'s support angered Major League Baseball owners and its fans, resulting in a dwindling readership. Before the Federal League collapsed in 1915, the younger Spink's view had prevailed and *The Sporting News* had withdrawn its support.

Took Over *The Sporting News* in 1914

At the age of 25, Spink married the former Blanche Keene, and the couple later had two children, son Charles Claude Johnson and daughter Marie Taylor. As the couple honeymooned, news came that the elder Spink had died. Suddenly in charge of the family business, the couple worked seven days a week redrafting the periodical to fit the times. Coverage was expanded, more correspondents were added—including such newsprint stars as Ring Lardner and Fred Lieb—and statistics were keenly emphasized.

At times, *The Sporting News* seemed less a product of adversarial journalism than the house organ for Major League Baseball, taking stands the paper deemed in the best interests of the game. In an unofficial quid pro quo, baseball owners and the baseball hierarchy helped the publication when it was in danger of folding. For example, during World War I, circulation per issue dropped from over 12,000 to an unprofitable 5,000. Reacting to the news that soldiers stationed overseas were eagerly passing around dog-eared copies of the publication, Spink prevailed upon American League president Ban Johnson to buy 150,000 copies of the publication for distribution to the Armed Services. Major League club owners and Spink himself upped that number

an additional 30,000 copies by 1917. Subsequently, despite a shortage of materials, Spink's was the only major baseball publication to survive the financial hardships of World War I. The windfall was repeated during World War II, when baseball bought and distributed 400,000 copies per week to American servicemen.

Spink helped investigate the 1919 ''Black Sox'' scandal—eight Chicago White Sox players who had agreed to throw the World Series—but earned the enmity of the game's first commissioner, Judge Kennesaw Mountain Landis, by supporting the White Sox in print. Landis, termed a ''show boat judge'' by John Sayles in Ken Burns's 1994 television documentary *Baseball*, enjoyed absolute power as commissioner and capriciously banned Spink from his beloved World Series official scorer post as a result of the publication's stand on the issue. Yet the post-''Black Sox'' era proved to be the most lucrative for *The Sporting News*, thanks in no small part to the clean sportsmanlike image both Landis and Spink encouraged, and the onset of the live-ball/home-run era. The live-ball era was the result of rule and equipment changes instituted in 1920 that brought a more tightly-wound, livelier ball that seemed to jump off the bat, as well as the outlawing of the use of foreign substances by pitchers.

In 1925 *The Sporting News* introduced its yearly picks for the best players at each position and for best right- and left-handed pitchers. This feature proved so popular that Major League Baseball adopted the idea for their annual All-Star game. Later in the decade, Spink and company began selecting the Most Valuable Player in each league, which led to an annual pick voted upon by the Baseball Writers of America. The publication also pre-figured the Fantasy Baseball concept by composing theoretical lineups of various players throughout history. Typical were proposed lineups of a team filled with players of Polish extraction versus a team solely made up of Italians.

During baseball's greatest early era, *The Sporting News* was an indispensable part of the game for fans, players, and even club owners. So important was the weekly 16-page publication that it was given the nickname the ''Bible of Baseball.'' According to *SportingNews.com*, the name first emanated from Jack Potter, son of a former Philadelphia Phillies co-owner, who pointed out the paper's publisher/editor and said, ''That's Taylor Spink, and he writes the Baseball Bible.''

Expanded Coverage During the 1940s

The key to the paper's success was its vast network of correspondents, who reported from wherever major and minor league baseball was played. This system allowed *The Sporting News* to keep staff budgets low while providing readers with fresh national coverage. Typical of these correspondents was the future radio voice of the Detroit Tigers, broadcaster Ernie Harwell. Just a teenager when he began sending in reports about the minor league Atlanta Crackers, Harwell continued contributing deep into his career as a broadcaster, sometimes penning Spink's column for him, ''because he was too busy to write his own column,'' Harwell told *The Sporting News*. ''I was one of [those correspondents]. Spink never left his office in St. Louis, but if you read his ghostwritten column, you'd think he was visiting all the major league parks." More of an idea man and editorial director than a writer in his later years, Spink's use of ghost writers extended to the 1947 biography of Judge Kennesaw Mountain Landis, titled *Judge Landis and Twenty-Five Years of Baseball.*

In 1941, after A.G. Spalding and Brothers stopped publishing their annual baseball guide, Spink received permission from baseball to take up the slack. Subsequently, baseball guides and reference books bearing *The Sporting News* logo—particularly *Sporting Goods Dealer* and *The Baseball Register*—became big moneymakers for the company, establishing Spink's personal fortune.

Another farsighted enterprise was the 1946 introduction of an eight-page tabloid called *The Quarterback.* The football-oriented publication ran both as a separate publication and as a pull-out section of *The Sporting News.* Baseball fans who were offended by the inclusion of football news were encouraged to simply extract the magazine from the publication. Not many did. By guessing that post-World War II audiences would be hungry for coverage of sports ranging from football and basketball to boxing, basketball, and golf, Spink stayed current with reader tastes.

Throughout the paper's early run, Spink often embraced opinions, only to later refute them. Night games were such an issue, and the breaking of baseball's color barrier was another. In a 1942 column, *The Sporting News* excused Major League Baseball's reluctance to allow black players on their teams, saying, according to an article on Baseball Library.com, that members of each race "prefer to draw their talents from their own ranks and both groups know their crowd psychology and do not care to run the risk of damaging their own game." However, after Jackie Robinson made his sensational 1947 debut with the Brooklyn Dodgers, the paper voted him Rookie of the Year. "Robinson was rated and examined solely as a freshman player in the big leagues—on the basis of his hitting, his running, his defensive play, his team value," Spink told *Time.* "The sociological experiment that Robinson represented, the trail-blazing he did, the barriers he broke down did not enter into the decision."

A Legendary Figure

As television coverage spread baseball's commercial viability to different parts of the country during the 1950s, Spink was the first to predict expanded leagues, interleague play, and possible sites for new teams. However, the canny publisher was afflicted with emphysema, and in late 1961 he became chairman of the board and allowed his son, C.C. Johnson Spink, to take over as the full-time publisher. As he was ineligible to be inducted into baseball's Hall of Fame in Cooperstown, the Baseball Writers' Association of America presented baseball's elder statesman with the Bill Slocum Award in January of 1962, and during the same year the association created the J.G. Taylor Spink Award for excellence in baseball writing.

Since the creation of the award, respected journalists ranging from Ring Lardner, Hugh Fullerton, and Jim Murray to Peter Gammons have been honored, but the very first award was given to Spink himself. *Sports Illustrated,* which would eventually overshadow *The Sporting News,* spoke of Spink's lasting contributions: "He had kept baseball's

books straight, he had been invaluable to writers, to scouts, to all the more dedicated fans whose appetite for baseball news and figures is never sated. He had stood for good things, he had spoken out against some bad things. He had maintained great faith in the national game, he had preserved a great personal integrity on the big issues."

J.G. Taylor Spink died of a heart attack on December 7, 1962. The weekly paper he gave his life to, *The Sporting News,* was published by his son until 1977, when C.C. Johnson Spink sold it to the *Times Mirror* publishing group.

Online

"Alfred Henry Spink," *Contemporary Authors Online,* http://www.galenet.galegroup.com/servlet/BioRC, (January 14, 2009).

"Ask the Sports Expert," *The Sporting News,* http://www.sportingnews.com/archives/sports2000/numbers/163466.html, (January 14, 2009).

"The Ballplayers - Sporting News, The," *Baseball Library.com,* http://www.baseballlibrary.com, (January 14, 2009).

"History of the Sporting News 1886-1900," *The Sporting News-The Vault,* http://www.sportingnews.com/archives/history/1886a.html, (January 15, 2009).

"History of the Sporting News 1920-1942," *The Sporting News - The Vault,* http://www.sportingnews.com/archives/history/1920a.html, (January 14, 2009).

"History of the Sporting News 1962-1977," *The Sporting News - The Vault,* http://www.sportingnews.com/archives/history/1962a.html, (January 14, 2009).

"J.G. Taylor Spink," *Baseball Library.com,* http://www.baseballlibrary.com/ballplayers/player.php?name=JG_Taylor_Spink, (January 14, 2009).

"J.G. Taylor Spink Award," *National Baseball Hall of Fame and Museum,* http://www.baseballhalloffame.org/hifers/spink.jsp, (January 14, 2009).

"John George Taylor Spink," *Contemporary Authors Online,* http://www.galenet.galegroup.com/servlet/BioRC, (January 14, 2009).

"My turn: A baseball life comes full circle," *The Sporting News,* http://www.sportingnews.com/basebvall/articles/20030409/467774.html, (January 14, 2009).

"Rookie of the Year," *Time,* http://www.time.com/time/printout/),8816,798173,00.html, (January 14, 2009).

"The Sporting News," *St. James Encyclopedia of Popular Culture,* http://www.findarticles.com/p/acticles/mi_glepc/ai_2419101147, (January 9, 2009).

"The Sporting News faces uncertain future," *The Free Library,* http://www.thefreelibrary.com/The_Sporting+News+faces+uncertain+future-a057487385, (January 9, 2009).

"Taylor Spink is First-class, *Sports Illustrated - SI Vault,* http://www.vault.sportsillustrated.cnn.com/vault/article/magazine/MAG1072319/index.htm, (January 14, 2009). □

Ernst Stuhlinger

German rocket scientist Ernst Stuhlinger (1913–2008), played an important role in helping to start America's space program. He worked for the United States government along with Wernher von Braun helping to launch the satellite Explorer 1. Stuhlinger was greatly involved with the Apollo Moon Program, and worked to design the guidance and navigation

systems for the Saturn V, which is still the world's largest launch vehicle.

E rnst Stuhlinger was born in Niederrimbach, Germany on December 19, 1913. His father was a schoolmaster. Stuhlinger was educated at the Oberrealschule and obtained a PhD in physics at the age of 23 from the University of Tübingen. Stuhlinger was described as a robust young man who rode his bike around the Alps. After graduating, he worked at the Berlin Institute of Technology as an assistant professor for five years. While there he performed research in cosmic rays and nuclear physics. He also took part in the German atomic energy program.

In 1941, Stuhlinger was sent to Russia as an infantry soldier and would later move up the ranks to corporal. He served on the Russian front, was wounded at the Battle of Moscow, and managed to survive the Battle of Stalingrad. Few in his unit survived that battle.

In 1943, Stuhlinger went to work with Wernher von Braun at Peenemunde. In an interview with the IEEE Spectrum Online in the article "Remembering Sputnik: Ernst Stuhlinger" he described von Braun as "the most impressive person I ever met in my life." Under von Braun, Stuhlinger worked on improving the guidance system of the V-2 rocket, one that was produced under the supervision of the SS using slave labor. The rocket was erratic, however, but nevertheless toward the end of World War II was used to attack London. In the obituary published in the *Washington Post*, Martin Weil

noted a 1995 article in the *Huntsville Times* where Stuhlinger spoke of his work regarding the V-2 rockets during the war. He called the Nazi era "extremely deplorable." Weil also quoted Stuhlinger from the *Huntsville Times* article as stating, "We were convinced that the war would be over before new systems could be used on military rockets...We were convinced that somehow our work would find application in future rockets that would not aim at London, but at the moon."

After Hitler's suicide and as the allies advanced, many in von Braun's team, however, were moved to southern Germany by force. Stuhlinger was not among those moved, so he and 20 other team members hid near Weimar, and they remained in that location until the war ended. It took several weeks for his group to hear that those with von Braun had surrendered to the Americans; in total, over 100 scientists surrendered to the Americans. The Americans were eager to learn of the knowledge of these German engineers and scientists, so the United States Government relocated leading members of the team, including Stuhlinger, to Texas under the secret Operation Paperclip plan.

Early Work in America

Stuhlinger remained in Texas at Fort Bliss from 1946 until around 1950. There, the German scientists and engineers worked for the Army Ordinance Corps. Working for the Army Ordinance Corps, the German scientists and engineers' advances allowed the Army to test approximately 70 V-2 rockets. In an obituary from the *New York Sun* documenting Stuhlinger's life, he was once quoted as saying the scientists and engineers at Fort Bliss were known as "PoPs—prisoners of peace." Around 1950, the group was moved from Fort Bliss to Huntsville, Alabama, and there the group worked for the Army Ballistic Missile Agency's Redstone Arsenal, continuing to develop more powerful and larger rockets.

Stuhlinger was a quiet man and a behind-the-scenes worker compared to the more outgoing von Braun. Although they both worked for NASA's Marshall Space Flight Center in the early period of the space age, the von Braun team built and improved several generations of rockets while Stuhlinger was the head of the Research Office at the Redstone Arsenal. He oversaw a project working to launch an Earth-orbiting satellite on one of von Braun's missiles. Even though the Navy's Vanguard rocket took priority in 1955, Stuhlinger continued to work in Huntsville to develop the Redstone, as the team hoped to use it as a space launcher. It was also in 1955 that Stuhlinger became a naturalized American citizen.

Sputnik

The Soviet Union launched Sputnik 1 on October 4, 1957, the first man-made object to orbit the Earth. America was shocked that the Soviet Union launched a satellite prior to it launching one of its two Navy Vanguard satellites. In an effort to rebound and compete with the Soviet Union, the space race was born.

Stuhlinger first heard about the launching of Sputnik in a New York taxi cab on the way to the airport where he was flying to a meeting of the International Astronautical Federation in Barcelona. Stuhlinger was not overly surprised by the Soviet Union's launch, as he had been following the remarks of many Russian dignitaries and felt they had something big coming. Stuhlinger had even gone to his superiors in the Army regarding his suspicions that the Russians were about to launch a satellite, but was told the Russians could not accomplish the launch. While rehashing these thoughts in the cab, Stuhlinger vowed to congratulate the Russians on their success while at the conference in Barcelona. He then hoped that the launch of Sputnik would be a wake-up call to the Americans, and that the realization would allow von Braun and his team to continue the satellite project, Explorer, which was on hold at that time. Stuhlinger's obituary in the *New York Times* quoted an interview given to the *New York Times* in 2007 for the 50th anniversary of Sputnik, where Stuhlinger said, "I immediately felt a kind of thankfulness to the Russian colleagues, because it was a wonderful wake-up call for us Americans."

Sputnik was indeed a wake-up call for the Americans. In an effort to catch up with the Russians quickly, the United States Army Ballistic Missile Agency, which included the von Braun team, along with the Jet Propulsion Laboratory in California were set to the task of getting the Explorer 1 satellite into orbit as quickly as possible.

Stuhlinger worked diligently to help launch the Explorer 1. In order for the satellite to achieve orbit, the timing of the second-stage firing had to be extremely precise. Unfortunately, there was no time for very detailed tests or designs. In order to aid in the execution of the second-stage firing, Stuhlinger went home and worked in his garage. There he came up with a timing device made of ordinary screws, nuts, and wires. In Cape Canaveral, Florida, on the night of January 31, 1958, just 84 days after the launching of Sputnik, Explorer 1 was launched. Stuhlinger pressed the button to signal the timing device that would trigger the second-stage firing. He had to press the button at exactly the precise time for it to work, which it did. He then became known as "the man with the golden finger," as was stated in the *New York Times* 2008 obituary recounting Stuhlinger's life. 1958 was a big year for Stuhlinger: just weeks before the Explorer 1 was launched Stuhlinger and his wife had their first child. Reporting on Stuhlinger's life, the *New York Sun* mentioned an article from the *Los Angeles Times*, where Stuhlinger's wife, Irmgard Lotze Stuhlinger, is quoted as saying, "Okay, I had my little satellite. Now you have yours."

The space race between the Soviet Union and the United States continued. Prior to the launch of the Explorer 1, the Soviet Union had launched a second satellite, Sputnik 2. After the launch of the Explorer 1, however, the United States successfully launched the Vanguard 1, which was the second artificial satellite launched into Earth orbit.

Continued Success

Stuhlinger also worked during the 1950s to develop designs for a solar-powered spacecraft after being inspired by the 1939 book *Possibilities of Space Flight* by Hermann Oberth. He began researching the replacement of chemical rocket engines with ion engines. According to the article in the *Independent,* the chemical engines were inefficient, but the ion engines "could accelerate electrically charged gases to very high velocities without the need for high temperatures." The *Independent* also claimed that he presented a paper at the 1955 International Astronautical Congress in Vienna called "Possibilities of Electrical Space Ship Propulsion." Stuhlinger's research in this type of new technology prompted its use in modern unmanned space missions.

In the 1960s, Stuhlinger acted as the director of the Marshall Space Flight Center Space Sciences Laboratory. He published the textbook *Ion Propulsion for Space Flight* in 1964. Then, in 1968, he was promoted to Associate Director for Science. He was also very involved with the Apollo Moon program and the early planning for exploration on the moon. He worked with the team that developed the guidance and navigation systems for the Saturn V. During 1973 and 1974, Stuhlinger supervised the creation of the solar X-ray telescope, which flew on the Skylab space station and generated a host of new data about the Sun.

Stuhlinger retired from the Marshall Space Flight Center in 1975. He moved on to work as an adjunct professor and senior research scientist at the University of Alabama Huntsville. In 1993, he co-authored the biography *Wernher von Braun: Crusader for Space.* Then, in 2005 he was awarded the medal for Outstanding Achievement in Electric Propulsion by the Electric Propulsion Society.

Stuhlinger died in his home in Huntsville, Alabama at the age of 94 on May 25, 2008. Stuhlinger was survived by his wife Irmgard, two sons Tillman and Christoph, and his daughter Susanne. His neighbor and Huntsville friend, Ralph Petroff commented in the May 25, 2008 issue of the *Washington Post* that Stuhlinger "was one of the chief figures of 'the golden age of space exploration.'" Furthermore, Petroff noted in the same article that Stuhlinger "'was enormously grateful to the United States' for his life here. Having seen firsthand the effects of the erosion of civil liberties in Nazi Germany, he was 'more than delighted to live in a free society' . . . [he] loved everything about America."

Periodicals

Daily Telegraph, (London, England), June 23, 2008.

Independent, (London, England), June 11, 2008.

London Times, May 30, 2008.

New York Sun, May 28, 2008.

New York Times, May 28, 2008.

Washington Post, May 27, 2008.

Online

"Remembering *Sputnik*: Ernst Stuhlinger," http://www.spectrum.ieee.org/sputnik (January 1, 2009).

"Stuhlinger, Ernst," http://www.britannica.com/EBchecked/topic/1443783/Ernst-Stuhlinger (January 2, 2009). □

Anne Mansfield Sullivan

American educator Anne Mansfield Sullivan Macy (1866–1936) has been called "the miracle worker" for her revolutionary instruction of blind and deaf student Helen Keller. Left with compromised eyesight herself after a childhood illness, Sullivan overcame her own challenges to become Keller's beloved lifelong teacher and companion. Her dedication to her pupil's success defined her life and made Keller's many achievements possible.

Faced Childhood Challenges

Like many others, Thomas and Alice (Cloesy) Sullivan left their home in Limerick, Ireland, for the United States as a result of Ireland's Great Famine in the late 1840s. They settled in Feeding Hills, Massachusetts, where Johanna Sullivan—called "Annie" throughout her life—was born on April 14, 1866. Two more girls and two boys followed, although only two Sullivan children besides Anne survived infancy.

Sullivan's childhood was marked by a seemingly endless series of tragedies. Writing in *Helen and Teacher: The Story of Helen Keller and Anne Sullivan Macy,* Joseph P. Lash noted that "the destitution of the Sullivans was starker and more desolate than even that of [other contemporary poverty-stricken Irish immigrants]." Alice Sullivan contracted tuberculosis while Anne Sullivan was an infant, and a few years later suffered a fall that left her unable to walk unaided. Thomas Sullivan had a sharp temper exacerbated by a drinking problem, and often beat his equally headstrong daughter Anne. Anne Sullivan's situation worsened when, at the age of five, she was afflicted with trachoma, an infectious eye disease that steadily caused her sight to deteriorate. After Alice Sullivan died in about 1875, Sullivan lived briefly with her father before he permanently deserted his family. Sullivan's healthy sister Mary went to live with relatives, while the partially blind Sullivan and her brother Jimmie, who suffered from a tubercular hip, went to live at the Tewksbury poorhouse.

Sullivan's biography in *Contemporary Heroes and Heroines, Book II* described Tewksbury as "notorious...a squalid facility that served as combination prison, asylum, and hospital." Although Jimmie Sullivan died shortly after arriving at Tewksbury, Anne Sullivan remained there for four years, living among the destitute, the deformed, and the dangerous. Her opportunity came in 1880 when the head of the State Board of Charities, Frank B. Sanborn, came to inspect Tewksbury. After fearfully following behind Sanborn's group, Sullivan approached the men as they were leaving and begged to be allowed to leave the poorhouse and attend school. This plea was granted and in October of 1880, Sullivan entered Boston's Perkins Institution for the Blind. While attending the school, Sullivan underwent two surgeries that enabled her to see well enough to read and thread a needle. Although she faced near-constant humiliation and struggle as a result of her early social and educational neglect, Sullivan graduated from the Perkins Institution with honors in 1886.

Became Helen Keller's Teacher

Her education complete, Sullivan faced a new dilemma: finding a job. The solution came in the form of a letter from Arthur Keller of Tuscumbia, Alabama, to Perkins Institution director Michael Anagnos, requesting a recommendation for a governess to his six-year-old daughter, who could not see, hear, or speak. Anagnos wrote to Sullivan about the position, and—despite her disinclination to work as either a governess or a teacher—Sullivan accepted. After spending some time studying the case of Laura Bridgman, a deaf and blind girl who had developed a remarkable command of language, Sullivan arrived in Tuscumbia on March 3, 1887, to meet her somewhat tempestuous new charge, Helen Keller. Keller later described this encounter in her book *The Story of My Life,* saying, "I went to the door and waited on the steps....I felt approaching footsteps. I stretched out my hand....Some one took it, and I was caught up and held close in her arms who had come to reveal all things to me, and, more than all things else, to love me."

Keller had had little discipline, and Sullivan's first efforts were divided between establishing rules and order and creating a system of communication between herself and the young girl. The ensuing battles of will soon ended in Sullivan's favor, and Keller's education commenced in earnest. Sullivan had noticed that although Keller knew some words, she did not understand the connection between words and physical objects. Using a system of hand signs to convey letters and, thus, words, Sullivan managed to help Keller make this connection several weeks after her arrival by spelling out the word "water" while holding Keller's hand under running water. This breakthrough—the oft-mentioned "miracle"—allowed Keller to experience the world as never before and strengthened the growing bond between teacher and pupil.

From that point on, Keller proved to be an enthusiastic student. She increasingly relied on Sullivan, and Sullivan in return devoted herself to helping the girl learn by experiencing the world firsthand. Sullivan reported on Keller's progress to Anagnos, who followed the case with much fascination. Soon Helen began to learn to write, and sent letters to the students of the Perkins Institution and to its director. These letters caused Anagnos to write glowingly of student and teacher, setting off a maelstrom of publicity. The pair traveled to Boston in the spring of 1888, stopping en route to meet with President Grover Cleveland in Washington, D.C.

Once in Boston, Keller appeared publicly at the Perkins Institution's graduation. Sullivan and Keller then stayed with Anagnos for a time, during which Keller impressed him with her knowledge and intellectual thirst. Sullivan took her charge to spend the summer on Cape Cod before returning to Perkins to study throughout the autumn. Even after returning to Tuscumbia in late 1888, both Sullivan and Keller's thoughts went often to Boston.

The following year, Sullivan was compelled to return to that city to have treatments done on her eyes, which had become strained from her exertions with Keller. This trip, over three months long, would prove to be the longest time that Sullivan spent away from Keller for the rest of her life. Later that year, both Sullivan and Keller settled in Boston so that Keller could attend Perkins. Keller performed well, and Sullivan even began working with an instructor at the school to teach Keller vocal speech, an ambitious but ultimately unsuccessful goal. During this time, Keller's renown earned her many social invitations, but Sullivan often found herself ignored. Sullivan's biography in *Contemporary Heroes and Heroines, Book II* noted that "many people outside of the academic community were unaware of her role in Helen's success and regarded her as little more than a servant. It was an image she was never able to shake completely, perhaps because she so willingly took a back seat to her pupil and downplayed her own accomplishments."

As the Kellers' ability to pay for their daughter's education faltered, several benefactors stepped in to support both Keller and Sullivan. The pair relocated for a time to New York City, where Keller attended the Wright-Humason School, before returning to Boston so that Keller could enroll at the Cambridge School for Young Ladies. Keller developed a dream of attending college, and Sullivan dedicated herself to helping Keller succeed in this goal.

Acted as a Constant Companion

In 1900 Keller entered Radcliffe College with Sullivan by her side, becoming the first blind or deaf person to pursue a university education. Sullivan's assistance was integral to Keller's academic success; she attended lectures alongside her student, translating the information using sign language, and helped Keller complete her reading and writing assignments. As a result of this, and much to Keller's dismay, Sullivan experienced great eye strain and was ordered to rest her vision. A replacement for this task, Lenore Kinney, was found, to Keller's obvious relief: "I have never ceased to bless her for my restored peace of mind," commented Keller in *Teacher: Anne Sullivan Macy*. Both Sullivan's and Keller's hard work paid off in 1904, when Keller graduated with honors from Radcliffe. Keller purchased a home in Wrentham, Massachusetts, and the pair went there to live.

Around 1902, Keller began work on an autobiography, *The Story of My Life*. This work was aided not only by Sullivan, but also by editor John Macy, a Harvard graduate. Macy remained in the pair's lives after the publication of the book, helping Keller with her schoolwork, and although Macy was ten years younger than Sullivan, the two developed a romantic relationship. Sullivan was to all appearances in love with Macy, but was reluctant to accept any of his repeated marriage proposals. Despite misgivings, Sullivan eventually relented and married Macy in 1905. Macy moved into the home that Sullivan and Keller already shared in Wrentham.

The three lived together for a time, but the difficulties Sullivan had feared soon came to fruition; her dedication to Keller prevented her from giving adequate attention to her husband, and the marriage soon became strained. Money was short, as all three relied on Keller's income, and Macy

drank heavily. Although the Macys never divorced, the marriage effectively ended with a permanent separation in 1914 after many failed attempts at reconciliation. After Macy's departure, the Scottish Polly Thomson came to live with the two women, and supported Sullivan in her work with Keller.

At the close of the 1910s Sullivan accompanied Keller to Hollywood, where the latter's life was made into a film called *Deliverance*. Although Keller appeared as herself in the later scenes of the picture—her inability to speak clearly not presenting a problem in this era of silent film—*Deliverance* was a commercial failure. Keller and Sullivan next toured the vaudeville circuit, where they enjoyed greater success. By the mid-1920s, the pair had become active in supporting the American Federation for the Blind and spent much of the remainder of the decade working on fundraising appeals for the organization.

Experienced Decline in Later Years

Sullivan's final years were marked by increasingly poor eyesight and failing health. She deteriorated throughout the 1920s, experiencing eye pain and cataracts; during this time, more and more of her work was taken over by Polly Thomson, although Sullivan did assist Keller in a revision of her autobiography. Despite traveling in the early 1930s to restful destinations such as Scotland, the Catskills, and Jamaica, Sullivan seemed increasingly tired and disinterested in life. Keller wrote in *Teacher* that "the fixed idea haunted her that old age was more difficult than to die, for it meant less to give at once life and all its blessings than to renounce it detail by detail." The loss of eyesight particularly seemed to prey on Sullivan.

On October 20, 1936, Sullivan died at her home in Forest Hills, New York, as a result of heart failure. Following a funeral at the Marble Collegiate Church in New York City on October 21, Sullivan was cremated; her ashes were interred at the National Cathedral in Washington, D.C., on November 2, making her the first woman to so receive this honor as a result of her work. People around the world paid tribute to Sullivan's memory, perhaps none so heartbrokenly as her longtime student and friend, Helen Keller, who wrote in *Teacher*: "She was lent to me from the Lord so that I might develop my own personality through darkness and silence, and I dared not ask for more, except that He render me worthier of His gift."

Books

Keller, Helen, *The Story of My Life,* Doubleday, 1902, 1903, 1905, 1954.

Keller, Helen, *Teacher: Anne Sullivan Macy,* Doubleday, 1957.

Lash, Joseph P., *Helen and Teacher: The Story of Helen Keller and Anne Sullivan Macy,* Delacorte Press/Seymour Lawrence, 1980.

Waite, Helen E., *Valiant Companions: Helen Keller and Anne Sullivan Macy,* Macrae Smith, 1959.

Contemporary Heroes and Heroines, Book II, reproduced.□

Gloria Swanson

American actress Gloria Swanson (c. 1897–1983) was among the most prominent performers of the silent film era and, perhaps more than any other, exemplified the glamorous lifestyles associated with early Hollywood cinema.

Swanson appeared bedecked with jewelry in such high-budget films as *Madame Sans Gene* (1925). She socialized with wealthy American entrepreneurs and with a European nobleman whom she married. "Through the 1920s," wrote Peter B. Flint in the *New York Times,* "Miss Swanson was Hollywood's top box-office magnet." After making a successful transition to sound films, Swanson entered a temporary retirement. She reemerged in one of cinematic history's legendary comebacks with *Sunset Boulevard* (1950), starring as an aging silent film actress. In fact, it is for her classic performance in *Sunset Boulevard* that Swanson remains best known among ordinary film viewers.

Traveled Because of Father's Army Job

Both the spelling of Swanson's real name, which has appeared as Gloria May Josephine Svensson and Gloria Josephine Mae Swenson, and her birth year, which has been given as March 27, 1897 or 1899, remain uncertain. Of partly Swedish background, she was born in Chicago. Her father, Joseph was a civilian employee of the United States Army, and the family moved first to Key West, Florida, and then to San Juan, Puerto Rico, during her childhood. They returned to Chicago around 1912 and settled on the city's North Side, which was one of the centers of the early film industry. As Swanson's father settled into a new career running a beer garden, Swanson took singing and art lessons on the side while attending Chicago public schools.

Swanson's film career began almost by chance in 1913, when an aunt was visiting the family in Chicago and took her to visit the Essanay Studio on Argyle Street. The two watched the filming of a short subject called *At the End of a Perfect Day,* and Swanson, on impulse, asked whether she could be an extra. A director who noticed the teenager's distinctively intense good looks altered the film in order to slightly expand Swanson's onscreen time. Over the next two years, she became a regular in small parts with Essanay (including one in comedian Charlie Chaplin's first feature, *His First Job*) and enjoyed having extra money to spend on high-fashion outfits. Looking toward life as a star, she began using the surname Swanson during this period.

While making the film *Sweedie Goes to College* in 1915, Swanson met actor Wallace Beery. He soon proposed marriage, and both Swanson and her mother, Adelaide, followed Beery to Hollywood. They married in 1916. Swanson, in her memoir, *Swanson on Swanson,* described a violent episode of marital rape on their wedding night. Beery is alleged to have given her poison to induce the abortion of her resulting pregnancy; they soon separated and were divorced in 1919. Swanson, as quoted in a biography on the Compass Rose website, later said, "I not

only believe in divorce, I sometimes think I don't believe in marriage at all." By the following day, she observed in *Swanson on Swanson,* "I was now a member of the great conspiracy of silence. I had joined it the moment I stifled my screams after Wally said to be quiet or I would wake up the whole hotel."

Performed in Sennett Comedies

Swanson's path to stardom, like that of many other silent stars, led through the comedies made by producer-director Mack Sennett. Those films made liberal use of shots of Swanson and other young actresses in bathing suits. But she made the best of them. "I did comedies as [Italian actress Eleanora] Duse might have done them—the more serious I became, the funnier the scene became," she was quoted as saying by Flint.

Hungering for more substantial roles, Swanson moved through several studio contracts in the late 1910s. In 1919 she married film executive Herbert Somborn. That marriage produced a daughter, Gloria, but it too quickly broke down, and Swanson began a relationship with director Marshall Neilan. What took the edge off these personal difficulties was Swanson's growing success on the screen. The director who made her a star was Cecil B. DeMille, who cast her in sharp marital farces like *Male and Female* and *Don't Change Your Husband.* Swanson gained a spot opposite a major star, Rudolph Valentino, in *Beyond the Rocks* (1922). That film helped give her a reputation for elegance, with ads promising the appearance of the star in 50 luxurious new gowns. Believing, correctly, that she had arrived as a star, she began to match her onscreen image with a lavish personal lifestyle.

In 1924, Swanson became perhaps the first Hollywood star to travel to Europe to make a film on location. During the filming of *Madame Sans Gene,* released in 1925, Swanson become romantically involved with her French translator, the Marquis Henri Le Bailly de la Falaise de la Coudray. In a development that warmed the hearts of Hollywood publicists, the two married in Paris. The Marquis was rich in heritage but cash-poor, and Swanson supported him when he returned with her to Hollywood. With him on her payroll along with 11 servants in her 24-room Beverly Hills mansion, Swanson faced major ongoing expenses. She could afford them; she was said to be only the second woman to have earned a million dollars (the first was financier Henrietta "Hetty" Green). Swanson's generosity did not stop the Marquis from having an affair with starlet Constance Bennett, however, and perhaps it was because Swanson herself had become involved with Massachusetts businessman Joseph P. Kennedy, the father of future U.S. president John F. Kennedy.

Kennedy lent money and expertise to Swanson's plan to take control of her own career. She produced several of her own films under the aegis of the United Artists studio. *The Loves of Sunja* was unsuccessful, but Swanson's next film, *Sadie Thompson,* (1928) was a hit that earned Swanson an Academy Award nomination for Best Actress. The film was based on a play (itself adapted from a W. Somerset Maugham story) about a conflict that develops between a prostitute working among U.S. troops in the Pacific and a minister who condemns her but is also attracted to her. Swanson's career in silent film ended with the lurid big-budget fiasco *Queen Kelly,* which was released only in Europe in a truncated form. In the U.S., the new "talkies" were already sweeping the old genre away. A segment of *Queen Kelly* eventually resurfaced in *Sunset Boulevard* as an example of the talents of Norma Desmond, the silent film star played by Swanson in the films.

Took Hiatus from Films

Swanson's career in sound films got off to a promising start with the 1929 drama *The Trespasser,* which brought her another Academy Award nomination. Swanson also had a pleasant singing voice that she deployed in *Tonight or Never* (1931) and *Music in the Air* (1934). But her career slowed somewhat in the 1930s, perhaps because her glamorous image fit poorly with the cultural environment of the Great Depression years. By 1934, Swanson had also been at the top of her profession for nearly 15 years. After *Music in the Air* she made no more films until the screwball comedy *Father Takes a Wife* in 1941. That film bombed, and she spent another nine years in retirement. Swanson kept busy with light theatrical appearances, and she also marketed lines of cosmetics and low-priced clothes. In 1948 she became one of television's first talk-show hosts with *The Gloria Swanson Hour.*

Swanson was not director Billy Wilder's first choice to play falling star Norma Desmond—Mae West, Pola Negri, and Mary Pickford were offered the role—but Swanson made lines like "I *am* big; it's the movies that got small" completely her own. The downbeat murder drama reunited Swanson with her silent film directorial collaborators Cecil B. DeMille and Erich von Stroheim, who appeared in the film as actors (DeMille as himself, Stroheim as Norma's chauffeur). Swanson was nominated for a third Academy Award but lost to *Born Yesterday* star Judy Holliday. *Sunset Boulevard,* however, has proven the more durable cultural icon, inspiring a long-running stage musical of the same name.

The film did not serve to revive Swanson's career; its follow-up, a comedy called *Three for Bedroom C,* was a flop. Swanson made a few more films, including the made-for-television *Killer Bees* (1974). She was seen on television making guest appearances on *The Beverly Hillbillies,* among other series. Swanson closed out her film career with the all-star vehicle *Airport 1975.* She also made successful stage appearances in her later years, including the 1971 hit comedy *Butterflies Are Free.*

In her later years Swanson remained visible to the press and energetically involved in new projects such as the promotion of vegetarian cuisine. Whenever possible, she took pains to point out that her own gregarious personality bore no resemblance to that of the reclusive and destructive Norma Desmond. Swanson's fourth (to sportsman Michael Farmer) and fifth (to stockbroker William Davey) marriages both ended in divorce, but in 1976 she married writer William Dufty, and the union lasted for the rest of her life. Swanson published an unusually successful memoir, *Swanson on Swanson,* in 1980; in her preface Swanson credited "my husband, William Dufty, who tirelessly helped me research and prepare all the early material," but the book named Swanson alone as author. She died after a brief struggle with heart disease in New York on April 4, 1983.

Books

International Dictionary of Films and Filmmakers, Volume 3: Actors and Actresses, 4th ed., St. James, 2000.

Swanson, Gloria, *Swanson on Swanson,* Random House, 1980.

Quirk, Lawrence J., *The Films of Gloria Swanson,* Citadel, 1988.

Periodicals

People, February 16, 1976.

Online

"Gloria Swanson," All Movie Guide, http://www.allmovie.com (January 18, 2009).

"Gloria Swanson," Turner Classic Movies, http://www.tcmdb.com/participant.jsp?participantId=187518 (January 18, 2009).

Starr, Steve, "Gloria Swanson," Compass Rose Cultural Crossroads, http://www.compassrose.org/uptown/GloriaSwanson.html (January 18, 2009). □

T

Edward Lawrie Tatum

Edward Lawrie Tatum (1909–1975) could be considered a geneticist, biochemist, or even biologist, as he mastered all of these fields. He is widely known for his work with genes and then later bacteria. In 1958, Tatum was awarded the Nobel Prize in physiology or medicine along with George Beadle and Joshua Lederberg.

Edward Lawrie Tatum was born in Boulder, Colorado, the first of three children to parents Arthur Lawrie Tatum and Mabel Webb Tatum. Tatum's father held two degrees, an M.D. and a PhD in pharmacology. His mother also excelled in academics as she was one of the first females to graduate from the University of Colorado. As a child, Tatum enjoyed swimming and ice-skating. He also especially enjoyed music and played the trumpet and French horn. His love of music would last his entire life. As is evidenced by their careers, medicine and science played an important role in the Tatum household. Edward would become a research scientist, his brother a doctor, and his sister a nurse.

Tatum began his post-secondary education at the University of Chicago in 1925. He studied at their Experimental School for two years before transferring to the University of Wisconsin at Madison in 1929. His father had moved the family there after accepting the position as chair of the physiology department. Tatum contemplated becoming a geologist, but declared his major instead in chemistry during his senior year. He graduated from the University of Wisconsin in 1931.

In 1932, Tatum received his master's degree in microbiology. Only two years later, he earned his PhD in biochemistry. Tatum researched cellular biochemistry and the nutritional needs of bacterium for his dissertation; this research and his work with microorganisms such as yeast, mold, and bacteria would be the foundation of his later work.

Tatum stayed at the University of Wisconsin as a research assistant in biochemistry for a year after receiving his doctorate. In the summer of 1934 Tatum also married the daughter of a lumber dealer, June Alton. Together they had two daughters, Margaret Carol and Barbara Ann.

Tatum earned a fellowship from the General Education Board from 1936–1937. This fellowship allowed him to study bacteriological chemistry at the University of Utrecht in the Netherlands under Fritz Kogl. While working in Kogl's laboratory, he researched the nutritional needs of fungi and bacteria.

Collaborated with George Beadle

While working in Holland, Tatum was contacted by George Beadle, a geneticist doing studies on *Drosophila melanogaster* (the fruit fly). Beadle, who had previously worked at the California Institute of Technology, was now employed by Stanford University and was in need of a biochemist to work with him as he continued his research with the fruit fly. Beadle was looking to discover the enzymes that were responsible for the inherited eye color in fruit flies.

After leaving his position in Holland in 1937, Tatum took a job as a research associate at Stanford University working in the department of biological sciences. He began work with Beadle. Over the course of four years, the two men were able to determine that kynurenine was the enzyme that determined the eye color of the fruit fly. Their success with fruit flies then led them to consider other theories regarding the relationship between biochemical reactions and genes; however, they realized the fruit fly was not the best living thing in which to test their theories.

Tatum and Beadle did a great deal of work together researching the best organism in which they could continue their experiments. After reviewing the literature, they agreed to use *Neurospora crassa,* or pink mold, which commonly grows on bread. There were many advantages in working with pink mold including that its nutritional needs had already been well studied and widely known, it reproduced at a fast rate, and it had the capability of reproducing both sexually and asexually.

The scientists began their work with pink mold in the spring of 1941. At that time scientists worked with genes without fully understanding what a gene could do. In the 1940s, geneticists used the work of Gregor Mendel as their foundation. Mendel's theory suggested that an inherited characteristic is caused by combining two hereditary genes, which are given by the parental cells. Mendel also theorized about dominant and recessive genes and how they are expressed by an organism. Tatum and Beadle used Mendel's theories as their basis as they caused deliberate mutations in the pink mold.

Tatum and Beadle first researched the nutritional needs of the pink mold because they already understood its biochemical processes well. They used X-rays to cause genetic mutations to some genes. They theorized that if genes controlled biochemical reactions, then the genes which had been damaged would show modifications in their ability to produce nutrients such as vitamins or amino acids. Their theory was correct. The first strain of mold that Tatum and Beadle identified was no longer able to make

vitamin B. They determined this after 299 tries. Then they crossed this mutated strain with a normal strain and found that the offspring inherited the genetic defect, based on what they learned about inheritance patterns from Mendel. *World Biology* noted that their research would be known as the "one gene, one enzyme" theory. In 1941, Tatum and Beadle's theory was published in the *Proceedings of the National Academy of Sciences.*

Tatum and Beadle's work with pink bread mold was used during World War II. The methods they used were applied to produce a large quantity of penicillin, another type of mold. In 1944, Tatum did work for the U.S. Office of Scientific Research and Development at Stanford; he served as a civilian staff member. Soon industries followed using the method of Tatum and Beadle to measure amino acids and vitamins in tissues and foods.

After the war ended, Tatum accepted a post at Yale University in 1945, the position of an associate professor of botany. He was promised that he would be allowed to create a program of biochemical microbiology within that department, and in 1946, Tatum did create that program and later became a professor of microbiology at Yale.

Worked with Bacteria

In March of 1946, Tatum met Joshua Lederberg, who was at Yale during a break from medical school at Columbia University. Together Tatum and Lederberg began researching the bacterium *Escherichia coli.* When they first started working together the scientific community believed that *E. coli* reproduced asexually, but the team proved that assumption wrong. The two scientists mixed cultures of two different mutant bacteria and from them a third strain, showing characteristics of each parent, was reproduced. Tatum called the result genetic recombination, which showed biparental inheritance could take place in bacteria. Their research provided geneticists with a new organism in which to experiment. Lederberg chose not to continue with his medical degree at Columbia and instead earned his PhD from Yale.

Tatum returned to Stanford in 1948 as a professor of biology. A new administration was now in place at Stanford and asked Tatum to return for a position that best suited his experience. During this period at Stanford, Tatum helped create the department of biochemistry. In 1956, Tatum became a professor of biochemistry as well as the head of the department, and also began working more diligently at promoting science at an administrative level. He was a key player in relocating the Stanford Medical School to the university campus in Palo Alto from its home in San Francisco.

Other key events took place for Tatum during 1956 as well. He and his first wife June divorced, and in December of that year he remarried Viola Kantor, the daughter of a Brooklyn dentist. She was a staff employee at the National Foundation (March of Dimes). The two were married in New York, and due in part to Tatum's personal life, he moved back to the East Coast. In 1957, he accepted a position at the Rockefeller Institute for Medical Research (now Rockefeller University). There he continued to influence young scientists as well as work on his own research in genetics.

Tatum also served on a variety of committees. He served as president and vice-president of the Scientists' Institute for Public Information, where his brother, Howard, also held a position. Additionally, he served on the board of directors of Mead Johnson, and acted as a consultant in microbiology for Merck and Company. Tatum worked in many groups associated with the National Research Council, and was the first chairman of the board of trustees of the Cold Spring Harbor Laboratory of Quantitative Biology in Long Island. Additionally, in 1959, he testified on behalf of the National Scientific Foundation before a congressional committee.

In 1958, Tatum's work with Beadle was recognized as they shared the award of the Nobel Prize in physiology or medicine. Tatum and Beadle shared one half of the prize for their work demonstrating the regulation of chemical processes in a cell by genes. Lederberg received the other half of the Nobel Prize for work done apart from Tatum. An excerpt of Tatum's Nobel lecture is quoted in *World of Genetics.* He contended that "with real understanding of the roles of heredity and environment, together with the consequent improvement of man's physical capacities and greater freedom from physical disease, will come an improvement in his approach to, and understanding of, sociological and economic problems."

During Tatum's later life, he demonstrated a great interest in social issues, and spoke about population control. During 1965 and 1966 he reached out to other Nobel laureates in science to promote birth control and family planning. Statements were made appealing to the Vatican and Pope Paul VI, who wrote a papal document against birth control for Catholics during this time.

During his final years, Tatum was marred by ill health, and he lost his second wife in 1974. Tatum was married again later that year to Elsie Bergland, who survived him when he died on November 5, 1975, at the age of 65. Tatum died in his home in New York City after a long-term illness.

During his time Edward Tatum was a noted and respected man in the science community. In addition to his Nobel Prize, he also was awarded the Remsen Award of the American Chemical Society. Furthermore, he was elected to the National Academy of Sciences, and was a founding member of the *Annual Review of Genetics* In 1957, Tatum also joined the editorial board of *Science.* Today Tatum's papers from the years 1930–1975 fill twenty-five feet of space in the Rockefeller University Archives.

Present day researchers and scientists have used Tatum's methods and research for continued study. In 2003, 77 researchers revealed the genome sequence of the bread mold *Neurospora crassa,* a feat that represents another stage in the history of research on this fungus begun by Tatum and Beadle. Professor Oded Yarden of the Hebrew University of Jerusalem Faculty of Agricultural, Food and Environmental Quality Sciences commented on the project in *Life Science Weekly* and said, "This first decoding of the *Neurospora* genome constitutes a breakthrough in the deeper understanding of the genetic base of this representative of the fungal kingdom. There are consequences as well for other life forms, including man." Furthermore, Professor Yarden remarked in the article, "The ease and speed with which we can conduct experimental work with this fungus will spur research on other genetic frameworks, leading to progress in developing future genetic-based medical treatment." This new research is based off the tenants of Tatum's work, and will continue to help aid in the progress and understanding of modern day genetics.

Books

Dictionary of American Biography, supplement 9: 1971–1975, Charles Scribner's Sons, 1994.

World of Biology, Thomson Gale, 2006.

World of Genetics, Thomson Gale, 2006.

Periodicals

Life Science Weekly , May 26, 2003. □

Germaine Tillion

Germaine Tillion (1907–2008) was one of France's leading intellectuals of the left. An anthropologist who conducted major studies of North African cultures when she began her career in the 1930s, Tillion was active in the French Resistance during World War II and spent three years in a Nazi concentration camp for it. She later became involved—as both an author and even an unofficial government emissary—in France's long and bitter war over independence for its colony of Algeria. "I am always on the side of those who are under attack," she told interviewer Alison Rice in *Research in African Literatures* a few years before her death. "I am on the side of those who receive the blows."

Tillion was born on May 30, 1907, in Allègre, a city in France's south-central Haute-Loire department, where her father was the local magistrate. He died when she was 17, which prompted her mother—an art historian and later writer and editor of the *Guides Blue* travel guides—to move the family to Paris. There, Tillion entered the recently established Institut d'Ethnologie, a leading college for students of anthropology. She earned her degree in 1932, and two years later embarked upon her first major research mission to Algeria, which at the time was a colony of France with a large population of native French. Tillion traveled to the isolated Aurès Mountains in eastern Algeria to study indigenous Berber culture, and was immediately struck by the similarities between the Berber community and that of the Auvergne region where she spent her childhood. "I was expecting to find savages, sublime people," the *Times* of London quoted her as saying, "and what I found was the French peasantry!"

Arrested by Nazis

Tillion was back in France by 1939, when World War II erupted in Europe, and was devastated when the French government surrendered to the invading troops of Nazi Germany in June of 1940. She took part in one of the first organized resistance groups working to sabotage or undermine the occupation forces and save French Jews from deportation to concentration camps. Her group was formed by colleagues she knew from the Museée de l'Homme (Museum of Man) in Paris. Her cell was discovered, and two members were executed; in August of 1942 she was arrested by the Gestapo, or German secret police, at Paris's Gare de Lyon train station.

Tillion was detained at both La Santé and Fresnes, two notorious Paris-area prisons, and at one point was told by a guard she would be shot momentarily by him. "I began to think about life, about the philosophy of life. And I shrugged my shoulders," she recalled in the interview with Rice, and the guard commented on the gesture. "And at that moment, I came to and realized that he was there and I told him, 'Oh, excuse me sir, I had forgotten you.' This staggered him so much that he began to gasp for air and then…he began yelling and he left. The fact that I had forgotten him, that sent him off in a rage."

In October of 1943, Tillion was deported to Ravensbrück, a concentration camp near Berlin, Germany, that housed mainly women prisoners. Approximately two out of every three of the 130,000 detainees there did not survive,

but Tillion was one of the fortunate ones. A few months later, her mother also turned up there after being caught working for the Resistance, but tragically died in Ravensbrück just a few months before the end of the war in 1945. Tillion penned an account of her time there, titled simply *Ravensbrück,* which was published in 1946; she also revised it for republication on two other occasions. "If I survived," she reflected in the book, according to the *Times* of London, "it was largely and mainly out of luck, and then from anger, the desire to reveal these crimes and, finally, because of a coalition of friendship—for I had lost the visceral desire to live."

Met with Rebel Leaders

Her health restored, Tillion pursued her doctorate in ethnology and resumed her research journeys to Algeria. In 1954, however, the National Liberation Front (FLN) began a campaign of covert action against the French colonial government which took the form of bombings and other terrorist acts. The French retaliated forcefully, and an eight-year-long war commenced that proved to be one of the most deadly and drawn-out battles for independence fought in the twentieth century. It was also a turning point for the rise of an allied Arab league of nations, and tore the social fabric of France apart as well, with young and old, leftist and conservative, bitterly divided over whether the colony—home to thousands of French-Algerians by then—should be granted sovereignty.

Tillion had much to say on the topic, having spent a great deal of time in Algeria. Her first book, *Algérie en 1957,* was published in 1958 and translated into English the same year as *Algeria: The Realities.* In it, she argued that the North African land would descend into utter turmoil should France remove itself entirely, and this view was roundly criticized by some leading French intellectuals who wholeheartedly supported the Algerian independence cause, including Simone de Beauvoir, who termed Tillion's stance as *saloperie,* or "filth," according to *Guardian* writer Julian Jackson. Yet Tillion had a strong supporter in Albert Camus, the well-known French-Algerian writer, who hailed her book for the insight it brought to the complexities of the matter. "No one, either in Algeria or throughout the world, can henceforth discuss the Algerian problem without having read what an understanding and cultivated woman has written about my misunderstood, desperate native land, now stirred by a heart-rending hope," Camus said, according to a 1958 review in the *New York Times.*

From friends in Algeria, Tillion learned that some of the key leaders of the FLN knew of her work and wanted to meet her. The FLN men were shadowy figures at the time, and Tillion later realized she had met with its chief, Yacef Saadi, who remarked, "You see that we are neither criminals nor murderers," to which Tillion replied, "you are murderers," according to her *New York Times* obituary. She did manage to secure a promise from Saadi to stop the bombing campaign, and in turn the French government agreed to halt the torture and execution of suspected FLN members.

Penned Groundbreaking Work on Endogamy

Tillion wrote a second tome, which was published in France in 1960 as *Ennemis-complémentaires* and in English translation a year later as *France and Algeria: Complementary Enemies.* At this point, the French-Algerian War was still ongoing, but was in its eighth and final year. "We are fighting for nothing," she wrote. In it she also revealed details about her meeting with Saadi, and those passages *New York Times Book Review* critic Henry Giniger found "especially moving for they show a great deal of the desperate rebel psychology, the strange atmosphere of Algeria and the author's humanitarian involvement (to the point where she risked her life)."

Additionally, Tillion was affiliated with France's National Centre for Scientific Research (CNRS), and from 1958 to 1980 taught at the School for Advanced Studies in the Social Sciences in Paris. Her career spanned more than six decades, and though she would be best remembered for her *Ravensbrück* memoir and her efforts to bring peace to Algeria, she was also the author of a notable study on patriarchy in the Mediterranean world, *Le harem et les cousins,* which appeared in 1966. It has been published twice in English translation—once under the title *The Republic of Cousins: Women's Oppression in the Mediterranean,* and years later as *My Husband, My Cousin: Clans and Kinships in Mediterranean Societies.* Writing in the *Weekly Standard* a few months after Tillion's death in 2008, the critic Ann Marlowe termed the book and its author "largely unknown in the United States outside academic circles. Yet 40 years after its publication, *The Republic of Cousins* offers fresh and even startling insights into the Muslim world."

Tillion explains in her 1966 study that even in Christian areas of the Mediterranean basin—such as parts of Lebanon and even the southern France of her childhood—marriage between close relatives remained common well into the early decades of the twentieth century. While the practice is more commonly associated with Muslim and Arab cultures, the custom reflected something Tillion termed "'saving all of the girls of the family for the boys of the family,'" Marlowe noted. "Her thesis is that in societies where women have inheritance rights (and giving daughters half the portion of sons was one of Mohammed's great breaks with Arab tribal codes), they are married off to paternal first cousins wherever possible. This keeps the family's land in the patrilineage."

This practice is called endogamous marriage, or marrying within a defined social group, and provides much of the impetus for women being kept in seclusion, or hidden by a veil when in public. The veiling of women decreed by law in some Islamic countries is one of the most controversial aspects of the religion for non-believers, but as Tillion explains in other parts of *Le harem et les cousins,* this particular geographical region of the world has a history of some shared customs that actually pre-date any codified religious law. Archeological digs of Neolithic sites, for example, show that neither of the two groups of Mediterranean peoples who became Muslims and Jews seemed to eat pork products, which their faith prohibits, because the sites do not contain any pig bones.

"Women...Are Crushed Intellectually"

In the interview with Rice, Tillion discussed Islamic fundamentalism of the modern age, and linked it to endogamy.

"I am convinced that in Algeria it is women who carry the Islamic movements," she said. "They do this because they are not as advanced as the men in their thinking—I say this even though you and I are feminists—because they travel less. There is nothing like travel (metaphorical as well as literal) to open up the mind, but women who must remain in place are crushed intellectually."

In 1999, Tillion was awarded the Grand Croix of the French Legion d'Honneur, the highest Legion of Honor category. She was only the fifth woman ever to attain the Grand Cross. A collection of her writings was published in 2000 as *Il était une fois l'ethnographie* (Once Upon a Time There Was Ethnography), though a precious store of her earliest research—which she was carrying with her in a suitcase on the day of her arrest at the Gare de Lyon station—vanished forever. In May of 2007, on the occasion of her hundredth birthday, she was grandly feted by various official bodies and cultural organizations. She died eleven months later on April 19, 2008, at her home in Saint-Mande near Paris.

In her final years, Tillion offered a balanced view on the growing problem of illegal immigration in Europe. "I have intervened on behalf of those without papers," she said in the interview with Rice. "All those who are here should be allowed to live in peace! If they are already managing to live here, why create constant obstacles by bothering them day in and day out with papers?" She also had strong opinions on the so-called global war on terror. "Effectively fighting against terrorists does not mean increasing the number of military operations," she asserted in *Research in African Literatures.* "It means fighting against what causes terrorism.... The greatest error the United States is currently making is to think that international military operations can stop a seventeen-year-old child from acting. The focus should be placed instead on alleviating the pain in the most sensitive regions of the world, beginning with Jerusalem."

Books

Tillion, Germaine, *Ravensbrück,* Anchor Press, 1975.
Tillion, Germaine, *The Republic of Cousins: Women's Oppression in the Mediterranean,* Interlink, 1990.

Periodicals

Guardian (London, England), April 24, 2008.
New York Times, July 7, 1958, p. 25; April 25, 2008.
New York Times Book Review, July 16, 1961.
Research in African Literatures, Spring 2004.
Times (London, England), April 24, 2008.
Times Literary Supplement, October 17, 1958.
Weekly Standard, June 30, 2008.□

Mabel Loomis Todd

American editor and author Mabel Loomis Todd (1856–1932) is best remembered as the earliest collector and editor of the works of Emily Dickinson. Her efforts produced the first three published volumes of Dickinson's poetry as well as a volume of

the poet's letters. In her time, Todd was also a well-known lecturer and writer on many topics, ranging from science to foreign travel, and she was an avid supporter of civic causes.

The only child of Mary Alden Wilder and Eben Jenks Loomis, Mabel Loomis Todd was born on November 10, 1856, in Cambridge, Massachusetts. Her father, to whom Todd was quite dedicated, worked as mathematician for a nautical almanac and had a deep love of nature and learning. His job took him to Washington, D.C., in 1867, where Todd and her mother joined him the following year. The family had little money and moved often from boardinghouse to boardinghouse, with Todd and her mother spending summers in New England. Although this unsettled existence did not seem to disconcert Todd, it did help shape her personality. Writing in *Austin and Mabel: The Amherst Affair and Love Letters of Austin Dickinson and Mabel Loomis Todd,* Polly Longsworth argued that "the lack of social privacy and emphasis on keeping up appearances inherent in boardinghouse life left clear marks on her behavior. For Mabel, a public parlor or dining room comprised a small stage which she learned to dominate with her conversational and artistic gifts." As a teenager, Todd spent much of her time writing, painting, and practicing voice and piano. She also enthusiastically attended the Georgetown Female Seminary in Washington, D.C., although an illness prevented her from completing her studies.

In late 1874, Todd moved to Boston to study at the New England Conservatory of Music. She returned to Washington, D.C., in 1876, where the following year she met David Peck Todd, an assistant at the U.S. Naval Observatory. The couple married on March 5, 1879, and Todd gave birth to the couple's only child, daughter Millicent, on February 5, 1880.

Arrived in Amherst

In 1881 David Todd received an appointment as professor of astronomy at Amherst College in Massachusetts. The Todds relocated to the small town of Amherst, where the beautiful and outgoing Mabel Todd soon became popular. Among Todd's first friends in Amherst were the socially prominent Dickinson family; the *Guide to the Mabel Loomis Todd Papers* noted that this "proved to be a fateful association." During the summer of 1882, Todd was a frequent guest at Evergreens, the home of Susan and Austin Dickinson. Her friendship with Sue Dickinson and her son, Ned, soon grew to include Sue Dickinson's husband, who was then the Treasurer of Amherst College. Todd and Austin Dickinson shared a mutual enjoyment of the natural world and displayed congenial temperaments; in September of that year, the pair confessed to their growing affection for each other and an intense and lengthy affair began. Over time, David Todd learned of his wife's relationship with Austin Dickinson, but does not seem to have strenuously objected; Sue Dickinson, who suspected the affair, was more noticeably incensed.

Todd's romantic connection with Austin Dickinson and her continued—if later unsurprisingly strained—friendship with Sue Dickinson led to her acquaintanceship with Austin Dickinson's spinster sisters, Lavinia and Emily, who lived next door to Evergreens at the Dickinson Homestead. Although Todd never met the reclusive Emily Dickinson in person, she began a correspondence with her in 1882 that lasted until the poet's death three-and-a-half years later. Through her many visits to the Homestead, Todd became a close friend of Lavinia Dickinson and was aware of the works of Emily Dickinson.

Worked with Emily Dickinson's Poems

Soon after Emily Dickinson's death in 1886, Lavinia Dickinson carried out the poet's wishes to burn many of her manuscripts and letters; however, she also discovered a box full of poems that Emily Dickinson had not left orders to destroy. Lavinia Dickinson approached Todd and asked her to send on these poems to a publisher. However, seeing the poet's scrawling penmanship and somewhat bewildering system of notation, Todd explained that she believed the work was considerably more complex than Lavinia Dickinson had anticipated. The poet's sister then sought assistance from Sue Dickinson, but finding her uninterested, returned to Todd.

Working with Colonel Thomas Wentworth Higginson, Todd then took on the chore of copying and interpreting the poems sometime in 1887. She continued work on the poems into 1889, urged on by the impatient Lavinia Dickinson. According to *Ancestors' Brocade: The Literary Debut of Emily Dickinson*, Millicent Todd Bingham, Todd's daughter, quoted her mother's description of the task thus: "Most of them I came to know lovingly by heart, and I was strengthened and uplifted. I felt their genius, and I knew the book would succeed." Despite this confidence, Todd faced many editorial challenges in addition to the difficulties of handwriting and notation. Emily Dickinson had, in writing her poems, often included several possible choices for a particular word, leaving Todd to discern which option best expressed the poet's voice. Also, in her later works, Dickinson had used little punctuation and only scattered capital letters, muddying the intended placement of the beginnings and ends of lines and stanzas; throughout her writing, the poet committed errors in spelling and grammar, forcing Todd to consider which mistakes warranted correction and which reflected the poet's style.

The first completed volume of Emily Dickinson's poetry appeared to great critical and public success in 1890. Within months of the initial publication, Todd and Lavinia Dickinson began planning for a follow-up volume. Todd threw more of her time and energy into the project, despite receiving little pay, and this second volume was completed in 1891. This work marked the end of Higginson's involvement with the poetry, leaving Todd to edit on her own a collection of Emily Dickinson's letters that was published in 1894.

Legal Battle with the Dickinsons

In 1895 Austin Dickinson died, reputedly as the result of overwork. Todd spent a long time in mourning after his death; according to Longsworth, "Her plight as Austin's unacknowledged widow was exquisitely bitter, solaced only by keeping a long-ago pledge to wear mourning publicly for him, an impropriety that shocked many townspeople and could not avoid enraging Sue Dickinson." Further strain erupted between Todd and the surviving Dickinsons after she approached Lavinia Dickinson regarding a promised inheritance from Austin, who had conferred a great deal of property to his sister with instructions for her to, in turn, pass that property on to Todd. However, Lavinia Dickinson felt a certain amount of reticence to surrender this bequest to Todd, presumably influenced by Sue Dickinson's anger and by a wish to keep the Dickinson land in the family proper. She was also motivated by a desire to avoid scandal, for no legitimate reason seemed to exist to justify such a large bequest to Todd—her work on Emily Dickinson's poems was not deemed significant enough—and to follow through with the bequest was guaranteed to bring about social scandal.

Eventually, Lavinia Dickinson deeded the Todds a long strip of land from the Dickinson plot abutting that of the Todds, which had been promised to that family for quite some time. Neither of the women reported this agreement to Sue Dickinson, and when the widow became aware of the agreement in 1896, she hotly protested Todd's right to any of the goods and property belonging to her late husband—even two pieces of art that had been openly left to Todd in Austin Dickinson's will. Probably urged on by Sue Dickinson, Lavinia Dickinson filed a lawsuit against Todd in May of 1896, accusing Todd of acquiring her signature on the deed through fraudulent measures. Todd, who had been away for several months, was both stunned and angered upon learning of the suit in August of that year.

Todd continued with her work, having readied a third volume of Dickinson's poems for publication in 1896, and busied herself with lecturing. However, the heretofore friendly relations between Lavinia Dickinson and Todd came to an end, and Todd endured the growing scandal surrounding the lawsuit and, by extension, her affair with Austin Dickinson, which had previously been something of an open secret. In February of 1898, the trial at last took place, with testimony focused primarily on Todd's claim to the land as recompense for her services as Emily Dickinson's editor. Longsworth wrote that "truth may have been on Mabel's side, but circumstances were running against her," and the court found in favor of Lavinia Dickinson in spring 1898. The rift between the two families was complete.

Later Years and Legacy

After the verdict, Todd wanted no continued affiliation with the Dickinson family, which led to a long delay in the publication of Emily Dickinson's remaining poems. Instead, Todd dedicated herself to the scholarly and philanthropic pursuits which had characterized much of her life outside of the Dickinsons; she was founder of the Amherst Historical Society, and was active in the Daughters of the American Revolution and the Massachusetts State Federation of Women's Clubs. She also continued lecturing throughout New England, helped raise money for a new observatory at Amherst, and accompanied her husband on research trips

to such far-flung locations as Chile, Tripoli, and the Andes Mountains. The first of two cerebral hemorrhages in 1913 left Todd's right hand and foot permanently impaired, but did not prevent her from visiting Russia the following year alongside her husband.

Todd wrote about her voyages for magazines including the *Nation* and the *Century,* and published two full-length travel books, *Corona and Coronet* (based on her visits to Japan) in 1898 and *Tripoli the Mysterious* in 1912. She also published two volumes of poetry. One, *A Cycle of Sonnets,* was the work of a cousin, which Todd edited and released in 1896, and the other, *A Cycle of Sunsets,* represented her own work, published in 1910. Additionally, Todd wrote a scientific work, *Total Eclipses of the Sun,* which was published in 1894.

Todd's schedule of writing and lecturing slowed significantly after her first cerebral hemorrhage. In 1917 David Todd's increasingly erratic mental stability led to his forced retirement from his position at Amherst, and the couple relocated to Coconut Grove, Florida. Five years later David Todd was placed in a mental institution. Despite her physical challenges, Mabel Todd continued to write, lecture, and participate in the community. At the urging of her daughter, Todd again returned to her work as an editor of Emily Dickinson's work in 1930, producing a new edition of Dickinson's letters that restored those previously omitted. Todd suffered another cerebral hemorrhage, which led to her death on October 14, 1932, at her summer residence on Hog Island, Maine. She was interred at Wildwood Cemetery in Amherst.

Even after her death, Todd continued to influence the literary legacy of Emily Dickinson; Millicent used manuscripts that she had inherited from her mother as the basis of a new 1945 volume of Dickinson's poetry. Certainly, Todd's own legacy remains inextricably linked with that of the poet, for her editorial judgment shaped the form of Dickinson's published poems and letters still read today.

Books

Bingham, Millicent Todd, *Ancestors' Brocade: The Literary Debut of Emily Dickinson,* Harper and Brothers, 1945.
Longsworth, Polly, *Austin and Mabel: The Amherst Affair and Love Letters of Austin Dickinson and Mabel Loomis Todd,* Farrar Straus Giroux, 1984.
Dictionary of American Biography,

Online

"Guide to the Mabel Loomis Todd Papers," *Guide to the Mabel Loomis Todd Papers: Finding Aid,* http://mssa.library.yale.edu/findaids/eadPDF/mssa.ms.0496c.pdf (January 1, 2009). □

Alice B. Toklas

American writer and editor Alice B. Toklas (1877–1967) was the life companion of the modernist poet and essayist Gertrude Stein. Their relationship remains one of the most famous gay female romantic partnerships of the 20th century.

Toklas devoted much of her life to managing and organizing Stein's writings, and her own career as a writer began only after Stein's death. Yet her position in relation to Stein was more than that of an assistant. The two women had a complex relationship that encompassed both romantic and literary aspects. One of Stein's most famous writings was a memoir written from Toklas's point of view. Toklas's own writings shed light on the Parisian literary milieu in which she and Stein played an important role—and no mention of her contributions would be complete without mention of her probably unwitting popularization of hashish brownies and fudge.

Planned Career as Pianist

Alice Babette Toklas was born in San Francisco, California on April 30, 1877. She shared with Stein an upper middle-class Jewish background. Her father, Ferdinand, was a businessman who had interests in Seattle, Washington as well as San Francisco, and the family moved there in 1890. Alice, after a good education in private schools, enrolled at the University of Washington in 1893. Her first ambition was to be a concert pianist, and she studied music both at the university and privately. Toklas was forced by the illness of her mother, Emma Levinsky Toklas, to cut short her studies in 1894 and to return to San Francisco. As a young woman she struggled with her lesbian sexual orientation in the absence of role models that would help her embrace it.

Emma Toklas died in 1897, and Alice lived an uneventful life for most of the next decade as a homemaker for several of her male relatives. It was the San Francisco earthquake of 1906 that shook her out of this existence. After the quake, she encountered Gertrude Stein's brother Michael, who she had met on a family trip to Europe and who owned a building in San Francisco and had come to check on its condition. Fascinated by his stories of Parisian life, Toklas borrowed money from a journalist friend, Harriet Levy, to finance the transatlantic trip and arrived with Levy in Paris in September of 1907. On her first night there, she met Gertrude Stein.

Their relationship was close and intense from the beginning, but initially it took a professional form. Toklas began typing manuscripts and doing other editorial work for Stein, and soon the friendship of the two women deepened into love. Stein was in the early stages of her career, and Toklas, who considered Stein a genius, served as a source of encouragement. They began to travel together in the company of Stein's brother Leo, and it was on one of those trips, in Fiesole, Italy, that Stein suggested a life partnership to Toklas. Back in Paris, Stein made a formal marriage proposal, and Toklas moved in with Stein at 27 Rue de Fleurus. Gertrude Stein's formerly close relationship with her brother Leo became more distant.

Established Salon

Toklas and Stein immersed themselves in Parisian culture. During World War I, under the auspices of the American Fund for the French Wounded, they distributed relief supplies, using a Ford car they had shipped from the United States. They bought paintings by Henri Matisse, Paul Cézanne, and Pablo Picasso when such works could be had for a paltry sum, and their home became what the French called a salon—an intellectual-social gathering place—that was popular with both French and expatriate American creative figures. Among their friends they numbered Picasso, novelists Ernest Hemingway and F. Scott Fitzgerald, and singer Paul Robeson. Even in hip Paris, homosexual relationships at the time had to be kept tightly under wraps, and the two generally did not discuss the romantic aspects of their relationship. Their letters, published after the deaths of both, made clear the depth and long duration of their mutual affection.

The couple privately assigned Stein the dominant or husband role in the partnership, but friends who knew them both well (among them was Hemingway, who recorded his observations in *A Movable Feast*) noticed that it was often Toklas who seemed to direct their activities. Toklas's activities as an editor were important to Stein's literary development, and it was Toklas who realized the catchy quality of Stein's trademark line, "A rose is a rose is a rose," and encouraged Stein to place emphasis on it. Toklas started and managed a small publishing company, Plain Edition, that was devoted exclusively to Stein's writings. An indicator of the complexity of their interpersonal roles was the publication in 1933 of *The Autobiography of Alice B. Toklas,* which, despite its name, was written by Stein. In that book Stein depicted herself from Toklas's point of view. *The Autobiography of Alice B. Toklas,* following on several books of highly experimental poetry by Stein, became one of her most widely read works. Toklas was also the unnamed object of much of Stein's love poetry.

One of the major puzzles in Toklas and Stein's story has been how the pair, as Jewish lesbians, managed to remain in Nazi-occupied eastern France and avoid deportation, probably to a concentration camp, during World War II. Literary researcher Janet Malcolm has suggested that they owed their safety to the intervention of right-wing French gay scholar Bernard Fay, who was close to the collaborationist French leader Marshal Philippe Pétain. Several times Toklas and Stein faced the danger of arrest, but through a combination of well-timed moves and advance warnings from Fay and his associates, they emerged unscathed and even entertained American soldiers at their home toward the war's end. After the war, Fay was arrested as a Nazi collaborator, and Toklas wrote letters on his behalf. One, quoted by Malcolm in *The New Yorker*, read, "He [Fay] has been in Fresnes prison since the liberation accused of hating communists (who doesnt) acting against the masons (who wouldnt in France) hating the English (the large majority of Frenchmen do) hating the Jews (is he alone?)."

Published Cookbook

Stein died in 1946, and for some years Toklas occupied herself with the management of Stein's literary estate. She had never thought of herself as a writer, and she may have turned to writing in her old age partly due to financial problems. This said, she produced several successful books that were unusual in form and cast light both on Stein's career and on the Parisian literary milieu of which they had both been part. The most famous was *The Alice B. Toklas Cook Book,* which appeared in 1954. The book did indeed contain recipes—part of the attraction of the Stein-Toklas salon was Toklas's cooking, which was reputedly superb. But it also included diverse reminiscences about Stein and other literary figures. Indeed, Toklas seemed to be trying to replicate Stein's spare, telegraphic prose in her own writing.

The British edition of that volume also included a recipe for "Haschich Fudge," which anyone could whip up on a rainy day. "This is the food of Paradise . . .," the recipe introduction went on (as quoted in the Straight Dope newspaper column). "It might provide an entertaining refreshment for a Ladies' Bridge Club or a chapter meeting of the DAR." The recipe, however, was not Toklas's but had been contributed by an artist friend, Brion Gysin. American editors spotted the marijuana ingredient and removed the recipe, but it nevertheless became famous with the rise of the 1960s counterculture. Toklas herself was said to be worried that readers would think that Stein's literary creativity had been drug-fueled.

Toklas published another cookbook, *Aromas and Flavors of Past and Present,* in 1958. She emerged less satisfied with this effort because editors altered her recipes to suit American tastes, and she said that she herself would not use the book. The volume contains Toklas's observations on the philosophy of cuisine, however, and it has been widely used and reprinted. In 1963, at the age of 86, Toklas issued her memoir, *What Is Remembered.* In that book she

recalled her last conversation with Stein as she lay dying in a Paris hospital: "What is the answer? I was silent. In that case, she said, what is the question?"

In 1957, Toklas converted to the Catholic faith. Part of the reason, she told friends, was the Christian concept of the afterlife; she believed that she would be reunited with Stein in heaven. Toklas lived in a monastery in Rome for almost a year in 1960 and 1961. Evicted from the Rue de Fleurus apartment, she was nearly destitute in her last years but was aided by friends. Toklas, a chain smoker, died in Paris on March 7, 1967, at age 89.

Books

Contemporary Authors Online, Gale, 2009.

Gay & Lesbian Biography, St. James, 1997.

Malcolm, Janet, *Two Lives: Gertrude and Alice,* Yale, 2007.

Simon, Linda, *The Biography of Alice B. Toklas,* Doubleday, 1977.

Souhami, Diana, *Gertrude and Alice,* Pandora, 1991.

Stein, Gertrude & Alice B. Toklas, *Baby Precious Always Shines: Selected Love Notes Between Gertrude Stein and Alice B. Toklas,* St. Martin's, 1999.

Periodicals

New Yorker, June 2, 2003, p. 59.

People, February 12, 1996, p. 127.

Online

"Alice B. Toklas brownies: the recipe!," The Straight Dope, http://www.straightdope.com/columns/read/880/alice-b-toklas-brownies-the-recipe (January 21, 2009).

"Alice B. Toklas (1877–1967)," Books and Writers, http://www.kirjasto.sci.fi/toklas.htm (January 21, 2009). □

Elsa Triolet

The Russian-born French writer Elsa Triolet (1896–1970) was a prolific creator whose novels touched on several of the great themes of 20th-century life, the fight against fascism during World War II chief among them.

C ritical opinions have differed as to the literary merit of much of Triolet's output, and for many years she was generally mentioned in connection with her husband, poet and novelist Louis Aragon. The reputations of both writers suffered because of their tolerant attitude toward the murderous regime of the Soviet Union and its leader, Joseph Stalin, in the 1930s. But Triolet, who avoided formal Communist affiliations and rejected Soviet policies later in life, has attracted attention independently of her association with Aragon. Her novels written during and after World War II offer some of the most penetrating accounts available of French life during that period.

Escaped Russian Revolution by Marrying

Of Jewish background, Elsa Triolet was born Ella Iurievana Kagana in Moscow, Russia, on September 25, 1896. She was also known as Elsa Kagan. Triolet's father, Yuri Kagan, was a prosperous attorney specializing in contract law; her mother, Helena, was a concert pianist. Both Elsa and her older sister, Lili, gravitated as teenagers toward Moscow's literary cutting edge, and both became romantically involved with the poet Vladimir Mayakovsky; Elsa, according to her biographer Lachlan Mackinnon, may have become pregnant by him and had an abortion. During the Russian revolution in 1917, she met a French military official, André Triolet, and left with him when he returned to Paris. The two married in 1918.

The couple moved to Tahiti, but a bored Elsa returned to Europe alone, staying first in London until she ran out of money, and then in Paris, where she had friends and lovers. Although her marriage to André Triolet ended in divorce, Elsa retained her first husband's surname for the rest of her life. The sojourn in Tahiti also provided the raw material for Triolet's first novel, *Na Taiti* (In Tahiti), which appeared in 1925 and, like its two successors within Triolet's output, was written in Russian. Other early Triolet novels were translated into French but enjoyed little success. Triolet's powers as a literary muse developed during this period as she rejected the Russian writer Viktor Shklovsky but agreed to keep corresponding with him as long as he agreed to avoid the subject of love in their exchanges; Shklovsky recycled these into a novel called *Zoo, or Letters Not About Love.*

Triolet had liaisons with several other top creative figures, and Russian novelist Maxim Gorky, among others, encouraged her to develop her literary gifts. Triolet met Louis Aragon, then mostly known as a surrealist poet, in 1928. They moved in together within a year and married in 1939. Each partner in the marriage stimulated the other to new literary production; Aragon wrote five volumes of love poetry, each with the name "Elsa" in the title, and Triolet published her first French-language novel, *Bonsoir Thérèse* (Good Evening, Therese) in 1938. She also wrote a book in French about Mayakovsky in 1939, and for much of her life she was active as a critic and translator in the field of Russian literature.

Wrote Novels Based on Resistance Movement

Triolet was active in the French Resistance during World War II. Her writings were eventually overshadowed by those of another famous literary wife, Simone de Beauvoir, but Triolet arguably took more risks in the fight against Nazism than did Beauvoir and her husband, Jean-Paul Sartre. Triolet wrote patriotic short stories and an allegorical epic novel, *Le Cheval blanc* (The White Horse, 1943), whose denouement was set on the battlefield during the war; the book was read avidly by prisoners the Germans had confined. During the later stages of the war Triolet was forced to publish her writings underground using the pen name Daniel Laurent. Her book *Les Amants d'Avignon* (The Lovers of Avignon, 1945) earned her the prestigious Prix Goncourt, and she was also awarded the Medal of the Resistance for her wartime activities.

Les Amants d'Avignon contained unusually detailed descriptions of Resistance activities. The story's heroine, Juliette, travels around France, trying to locate possible hideouts for Resistance fighters. At one point she is arrested by German authorities but escapes through a set of tunnels under the city of Lyon. Triolet's observations of the chaos of postwar Europe were equally accurate. In 1947's *Les Fantômes armés* (Armed Ghosts) she examined the corruption that took root in parts of defeated Germany after the war and eventually led to the triumph of Communism in the country's eastern half. *Personne ne m'aime* (No One Loves Me, 1946) and *Les Fantômes armés* were republished together as *Annie-Marie* in 1952.

During the postwar period, Triolet began to attract attention outside France; *L'inspecteur des ruines* (1948), the story of a concentration camp survivor, appeared in both Britain and the U.S. as *The Inspector of Ruins* in the early 1950s. She and Aragon became enmeshed in political controversy around this time, for both defended the policies of the Soviet government and hobnobbed with diplomats from the newly Communist governments of Eastern Europe. She and Aragon earned criticism in France at the time and also from later observers; Derwent May of the *Times* of London wrote in 1992 that "long after the war they were still traveling around on junkets in eastern Europe with Party bosses who were putting their own writers into jail." Triolet never actually joined the Communist Party of France, but she wrote drama reviews for the Communist-leaning *Les Lettres Françaises* between 1948 and 1951.

Translated Plays by Chekhov

Despite the criticism, Triolet continued to write prolifically. In the 1950s she completed new translations of the plays of Anton Chekhov into French, and her novels took up aspects of postwar French life. *Le Cheval roux; ou, Les Intentions humaines* (The Red Horse; or, Human Intentions, 1953) treated the subjects of nuclear war and nuclear energy, while *Roses à crédit* (Roses on the Installment Plan, 1959) was a satire on consumerism, depicting an activist young woman who becomes obsessed with electronic gadgets. One of the most acclaimed among Triolet's later books was *L'âme* (The Soul, 1963), another novel about a concentration camp survivor, this one female. Those two books, together with *Luna-Park* (1959) formed a loosely connected trilogy called *L'Age de Nylon* (The Age of Nylon).

First Triolet, and then, partly under her influence, Aragon, soured on Communism in the 1960s. Triolet spoke out in support of dissident Soviet writers Andrei Sakharov and Alexander Solzhenitsyn, encouraging Aragon to publish their works in *Les Lettres Françaises,* and both condemned the Soviet invasion of Czechoslovakia in 1968. As early as 1957, Triolet mocked the dullness of Socialist Realist art in her novel *Le monument* (The Monument), the story of an artist commissioned to produce a giant sculpture of Stalin. He realizes that the sculpture has spoiled the views of the old city in which he lives, and he eventually commits suicide.

Views of Triolet's life and legacy have diverged considerably. In the opinion of George Melly of England's *Guardian* newspaper, "She destroyed a considerable poet and turned him into a Soviet apologist," and Miranda Seymour of the *Sunday Times,* ascribing some of Triolet's fame to Aragon's influence, wonders "whether he was really doing his wife a favour in forcing such prominence on her lesser gifts.'' But Dominque Jullien, who organized one of the first U.S. conferences devoted to Triolet's work, argued that, even more so than that of Aragon, deserved to be better known.

Triolet was active until the end. In the 1960s she edited a collection of Russian poetry in French, and her last novels were among her most experimental. *Ecoutez-voir* (Look and Listen, 1968) included photographs in the text and at several points injected Triolet herself into the narrative. Triolet's last book, *Le Rossignol se tait à l'aube* (The Nightingale Falls Silent at Dawn, 1970), contained autobiographical elements. Triolet died in Moulin de Saint-Arnoult, France, on June 16, 1970, and various well-known writers, including Chilean poet Pablo Neruda, participated in her funeral.

Books

Contemporary Authors Online, Gale, 2009.

Dictionary of Literary Biography, Volume 72: French Novelists, 1930–1960, Gale, 1988.

Mackinnon, Lachlan, *The Lives of Elsa Triolet,* Chatto & Windus, 1992.

Periodicals

Economist, October 4, 1997, p. 90.

Romantic Review, January–March 2001, p. 3.

Sunday Times (London, England), January 19, 1992 p. 9.

Times (London, England), January 25, 1992, p. 42.□

V

Erich von Stroheim

Austrian-born American director and actor Erich von Stroheim (1885–1957) made some of the most ambitious films of the silent cinema era. Among general moviegoers he is equally familiar as an actor specializing in German military character roles, and for his memorable supporting part in *Sunset Boulevard* (1950).

Stroheim's work as a director might be characterized as extreme in scope and theme. His masterpiece was *Greed* (1924), which ran some nine hours in its now-lost original version. In an era when directors worked prolifically, he made only seven complete silent films. His autocratic behavior on the set, motivated by an obsessive attention to detail, was legendary in Hollywood. Stroheim's self-presentation was as inventive as his films. Even more so than other show-business figures, he embroidered the events of his life and claimed many experiences he had fabricated out of whole cloth. The facts of Stroheim's life began to emerge clearly only several decades after his death in 1957.

Claimed Noble Background

Stroheim's American inventions began with his name. When he arrived in the United States in 1909, he told an immigration officer at Ellis Island that his name was Erich Oswald Hans Carl Maria von Stroheim. Later he tacked a "von Nordenwald" (or "und Nordenwald") onto the end of that name. For some time, he claimed to be a count, the son of an officer in the army of the Austro-Hungarian Empire. The truth was more commonplace: born Erich Oswald Stroheim in Vienna,

in what was then the Austro-Hungarian Empire, on September 22, 1885. Both his parents were Jewish; his father, Benno Stroheim, operated a hat shop with a small manufacturing facility in the back. His mother, Johanna Bondy, came from what is now the Czech Republic.

The Vienna in which Stroheim grew up was, culturally, a strange mix of imperial tradition and avant-garde art that was often described as decadent. Much of Stroheim's life until his period of prominence in Hollywood, because of his inveterate tale-spinning, has been difficult to reconstruct with precision, but his biographer Arthur Lennig has suggested, based on evidence in Stroheim's writings, that he was familiar with the plays of Arthur Schnitzler and the modern music of Gustav Mahler and Richard Strauss. But what fascinated Stroheim the most was the pageantry of the Austro-Hungarian military, often on display in the streets of Vienna. From the time when he was young, Stroheim wanted to become a soldier.

An indifferent student, Stroheim was sent to a business school in the city of Graz; the plan was for him to take over his father's business. Having none of it, he tried to enlist in the Austrian army. On his first attempt, in Graz in 1906, he was turned down immediately. At the end of that year in Vienna, he received a rather dubious commission that required him to pay his own expenses, but even that lasted only five months before his discharge. Stroheim later made one more attempt to join the military before giving up. He departed for the U.S. in 1909, sailing from Bremen, Germany. Some versions of his life depict his decision as the result of an agreement to leave Vienna in exchange for having his debts paid off by a relative, but it seems equally likely that he simply wanted to reinvent himself.

Stroheim's first years in the U.S. are sparsely documented. In New York he apparently cobbled together a living writing for German-language newspapers. He claimed to

have served in the U.S. Army and to have been offered an officer's post in the army of Mexico as well, but these stories too are now regarded as fabrications; he apparently served for two months in the New York National Guard before being discharged from that force as well. Working as an agent for a hat firm, he made his way to the West Coast and settled in San Francisco. In 1912 he wrote a play in the Schnitzler mold called *In the Morning,* later retitled *Brothers.* Performed at Lake Tahoe resort where Stroheim was working, the play was ridiculed, but his efforts did not go for nothing: he met a group of actors who told him about Hollywood's growing film industry, and he moved on to Los Angeles.

Appeared in Griffith Films

Stroheim landed small parts in *The Birth of a Nation* (1915) and *Intolerance* (1916), two epics by director D.W. Griffith that exceeded all previous films in their length and scope. It seems to have been during this period that Stroheim began to flesh out his imagined noble past. He offered his services to filmmakers as a military advisor and began to affect a soldier's persona, walking the streets dressed as a German officer and wearing a monocle even at the height of World War I. He seemed to be building a personality that was suited to being filmed; when he met Universal Studios president Carl Laemmle, he pitched a story in which he would star as an Austrian lieutenant who becomes involved with the wife of a vacationing American physician. Further, Stroheim insisted that only he had the proper knowledge to

direct the film. When Laemmle agreed, Stroheim's directing career was underway. As his career was progressing during this period, Stroheim married and divorced three times, fathering two sons.

Stroheim's next film, *The Devil's Passkey* (1920), also dealt with the temptations of Americans in Europe, and his films rapidly expanded in scope. *Foolish Wives* (1922) was billed as Hollywood's first film with a million-dollar budget. Its sexual themes resulted in bans in several American cities. Stroheim was taken off his next production, *Merry-Go-Round,* by Universal executive Irving Thalberg, as its budget ballooned. But Stroheim's reputation as a cinematic genius was beginning to take shape.

Nothing could have prepared Thalberg or anyone else for the scope of Stroheim's next project. The director read the Frank Norris novel *McTeague,* about the life of a San Francisco dentist whose life spirals downward into violence and obsession because of money lust. Retitling the story *Greed,* Stroheim set out in 1924 to film it in every detail—and to add material on top of that. His obsessive pursuit of realism led him to demand that actors film the shocking denouement in the blazing heat of the Mojave Desert. Working from a staggering 446 reels of raw film, Stroheim produced a version between 42 and 47 reels long, lasting between eight and ten hours in screenings.

Stroheim whittled that version down to 28 reels, then to 22, resulting in a four-hour film. He argued that it could be shown over two evenings, but the studio rejected both that and a subsequent 15-to-18-reel version edited by Stroheim's assistant. Finally the film was taken out of Stroheim's hands, cut to ten reels (running under two hours), and released to audience bewilderment at the lack of continuity. Nevertheless, *Greed* became a cinematic classic that was cited in several critics' polls as one of the greatest films ever made. Thalberg ordered Stroheim's raw footage destroyed, according to different reports because he wanted to make sure it would never be released, or because he wanted to recover the silver from the film stock. The four-hour *Greed* was partially reassembled in 1999 by editor Rick Schmidlin, working from still photographs of scenes from the missing portions.

Film Financed by Kennedy Shelved

Toning down his grand visions somewhat, but inserting foot-fetish scenes unrelated to the original operetta, Stroheim scored a hit with *The Merry Widow* in 1925. The following year, having claimed to have done so already several times in the past, he became an American citizen. Back in the MGM studio's good graces, he spared no expense in filming *The Wedding March* (1927), drawing on his own experiences of Vienna's prewar luxury. That film was eventually divided into two parts, *The Wedding March* and *Honeymoon,* when it was released after seven months of filming. Stroheim's final silent film was a grand fiasco that remained unfinished. At the behest of star Gloria Swanson and her paramour and financier at the time, entrepreneur Joseph P. Kennedy, in 1928 Stroheim began filming *Queen Kelly,* a lurid story of a German girl forced into prostitution in Africa. Partly because production dragged on into the period when sound films had become fully established, the film was shelved, although a cut version was released in Europe. *Queen Kelly,* too, has been restored and has found admirers among film historians.

Stroheim made one sound film, *Walking Down Broadway* (1933), but it was never released, although a few scenes from it were incorporated into the film *Hello, Sister.* He returned to acting, taking an appropriate turn as a film director obsessed with realism in *The Lost Squadron* (1931) and co-starring with Greta Garbo in *Desire Me* the same year. By the mid-1930s Stroheim was out of money and would take whatever film work he could get, including at one point wardrobe consultant at the MGM studio. In his later years he worked mostly in Europe, where he was much admired. Of his various performances as German military officers, perhaps the greatest came in French director Jean Renoir's *Grand Illusion* (1938). In 1942 he appeared in the Broadway comedy *Arsenic and Old Lace,* replacing Boris Karloff, and the following year he played German general Erwin Rommel in *Five Graves to Cairo.*

Stroheim's most famous role as an actor, however, still lay in the future. In 1950 he was reunited with Swanson, playing the butler to Swanson's fallen star Norma Desmond in *Sunset Boulevard.* Footage from *Queen Kelly* was used to illustrate the silent-film stage of Desmond's career in the film. Stroheim wrote several novels, but never gave up on his ambition of returning to the director's chair. He also wrote several screenplays toward the end of his life. He had more success, however, with novels: *Paprika* (1935) sold well in the U.S., and he had other novels published in France, where he starred as composer Ludwig van Beethoven in the film *Napoléon* (1955). He was beginning to write what would have doubtless been an interesting memoir when he died in Maurepas, France, near Paris, on May 12, 1957, after suffering from spinal problems. His influence looms large in the work of American directors such as King Vidor and William Wyler, as well as Europeans such as Luis Buñuel. In Lennig's words, "The living, breathing Erich von Stroheim was so outrageous that only a gifted scenario writer could have invented him, as indeed was the case."

Books

Koszarski, Richard, *Von: The Life and Films of Erich von Stroheim,* Limelight Editions, 2001.

Lennig, Arthur, *Stroheim,* University of Kentucky Press, 2000.

Periodicals

Atlantic, September 1987, p. 73.

Guardian (London, England), August 31, 2002, p. 18; July 30, 2004, p. 10.

Star Ledger (Newark, NJ), December 4, 1999, p. 41.

Variety, September 13, 1999, p. 73.

Online

"Erich von Stroheim," All Movie Guide, http://www.allmovie. com (January 23, 2009).

"Erich von Stroheim: Biography," Lenin Imports, http://www. leninimports.com/erich_von_stroheim.html (January 23, 2009). □

Lurleen Wallace

Lurleen Burns Wallace (1926–1968) served as governor of Alabama for just 16 months between 1967 and 1968 at the tail end of the most troubled era in her state's history. Wallace was the wife of Alabama Democrat George Wallace, whose political career attained national prominence for his strident opposition to court-ordered desegregation of schools and other public institutions. One of the last of a handful of women to hold public office as a result of their husbands' ambitions, Wallace was often characterized by the press as a demure Southern homemaker. She died in office from cancer in May of 1968 at the age of 41.

Wallace was born Lurleen Brigham Burns on September 19, 1926, in Tuscaloosa, Alabama. Her father Henry worked as a laborer on river barges and later as a crane operator, and the family also owned a small farm. She grew up with a brother and graduated early from Tuscaloosa County High School in 1942 by taking summer school classes. She was just 15 and hoped to become a nurse, but nursing-school enrollees had to be at least 18, so she took courses at the Tuscaloosa Business College while working in a Kresge's five-and-dime store in her hometown.

Married Future Governor

At Kresge's Wallace met a young man who had graduated from the University of Alabama Law School in 1942 and was awaiting deployment in the U.S. Army Air Corps, the forerunner of the U.S. Air Force. She was captivated by the charming George Wallace, who came from a relatively modest semi-rural background like herself. When they wed on May 21, 1943, she was just 16 years old.

During the first years of their marriage, George Wallace's military duties in the midst of World War II uprooted them several times. At one point, they lived in a converted chicken coop when he was posted at a military base in New Mexico. She was 18 when her first child, a daughter they named Bobbi Jo, was born in 1944. A second daughter, Peggy Sue, arrived six years later, followed by their only son, George III, in 1951. After a ten-year hiatus which included a trial separation after Wallace became irate over her politician-husband's long absences and rumored infidelities, a fourth child was born in 1961 who they named Janie Lee.

Wallace was often described as a housewife whose only job had been at the five-and-dime, and during her husband's political rise she showed little interest in campaigning or becoming a public figure. Instead she preferred the duties involved in raising her children, and liked to fish at a lakefront cottage she and her husband bought. She also took flying lessons with the hopes of earning her pilot's license. At campaign rallies, she was present, but never gave stump speeches for her husband.

Became Popular First Lady

George Wallace became Alabama's assistant attorney general a year after they married, and in 1946 won a seat in the Alabama House. He became a state judge in 1953—where he gained a reputation as one of the more moderate jurists in a state where an African-American man had been sentenced to death for theft in 1958—but lost his first attempt to become governor when he was bested at the primary stage by an ardent segregationist. He stepped up his

anti-civil rights rhetoric, and won the 1962 governor's race by a landslide.

As governor, George Wallace consistently defied federal court orders and Department of Justice efforts to desegregate schools and public institutions in his state. School desegregation had actually been the letter of the land since the famous U.S. Supreme Court decision *Brown v. Board of Education* back in 1954, but many in the Southern states—descendants of slave-holders, or poor whites competing with blacks for scarce jobs in the era before the South's economic boom—were fiercely opposed to integration efforts, especially when they were imposed at the federal level.

As First Lady of Alabama, Wallace kept the governor's mansion in Montgomery, the state capital, which also served as the home for her four children, open to the public seven days a week. She was a lifelong teetotaler and refused to serve alcohol at official dinners and receptions. Her husband, meanwhile, took his political ambitions to the national stage: playing on the strong opposition in the South to passage of the U.S. Civil Rights Act of 1964, George Wallace entered the Democratic presidential race in 1964 and made a surprising showing in a few primaries, but failed to win the party's nomination. He hoped to run again in 1968, and returned to Alabama to finish out his term as governor.

Won Only Election by Landslide

Alabama's constitution permitted just one term as governor, and George Wallace tried but failed to have this reversed by

the state legislature. In February of 1966, Lurleen Wallace announced her candidacy for the governor's office in what was widely viewed as a ploy by her husband to retain control of the office. Though lawmakers occasionally permitted a widow to serve out the remainder of her late husband's term as a legislator, there was just one precedent for a state electing a woman governor to succeed her husband, and this had happened in Texas in 1924 when Miriam "Ma" Ferguson was elected to office after her husband was impeached. That same year, Nellie Tayloe Ross was permitted to run for governor in a special election after her husband died in office, and was sworn in to finish his term.

Alabama voters loved Wallace as a candidate, just as they had when she was the state's First Lady. She was petite, attractive, and demure—attributes that were considered emblematic of Southern femininity. She handily won the Democratic nomination for the gubernatorial ticket in 1966 and faced no genuine Republican challenger in the race. In the South at the time, the Republican Party was still viewed by many white voters as the pro-minority party because it had been founded by Abraham Lincoln, who proclaimed the end of slavery during the midst of a long and bloody Civil War over the matter during his term as president. While some questioned her level of experience to govern a state of 3 million where the chief executive had the power to grant last-minute acts of clemency in death-penalty cases, few expected that she would be carrying out any of the actual political duties herself. She claimed that her husband would be "her #1 assistant," according to the Web site for the Public Broadcasting Service (PBS) series *The American Experience.*

Wallace was elected on November 8, 1966, in a landslide victory, taking 100,285 votes over her Republican opponent's 39,072 votes. When she was sworn in on January 16, 1967, she was the only female governor in the nation. A few months later, she and her husband were the subjects of a lengthy profile in the *New York Times Magazine* titled "The Queen of Alabama and the Prince Consort." Journalist Ray Jenkins visited her in her office in the Montgomery State Capitol building, and recounted a legislative battle over a proposed pay raise for lawmakers twinned with a highway funding bill—securing passage of both required the usual behind-the-scenes deal-making. In the biased language of the day, Jenkins wrote that Alabama's new governor "didn't worry her pretty head over such distasteful matters. . . . Grimy politics was handled across the hall by a man who held no office but that of honorary general in the state militia," referring to George Wallace. Jenkins described the current situation as "a Queen-Prime Minister relationship: Mrs. Wallace handles the ceremonial and formal duties of state, Mr. Wallace draws the grand outlines of state policy and sees that it is carried out."

Resisted Desegregation Orders

There were two episodes in Wallace's career as governor where she was known to have exerted the power granted to her by the state constitution and by her mandate from voters: she refused to permit a holdover from her husband's administration to remain on the job, and secured additional funding for the developmentally disabled and the mentally ill after a traumatic visit to two institutions that housed both. In most matters, however, she simply carried out her husband's political agenda, such as her speech to a joint session of the state legislature in March of 1967. Responding to a federal court order on desegregation, she requested that legislators vote to place the entire Alabama public school system under the power of her office as a new strategy to fight the specter of African-American and white students attending the same schools. She claimed that parents would resist the order to desegregate, and that would open up the possibility of the state being forced to prosecute parents. "We in Alabama will not put parents in jail," a *New York Times* report from Homer Bigart quoted her as saying. The state eventually complied with the federal order, however.

Less than three months after that speech, Wallace announced that the cancer she had battled two years earlier had returned. She had been diagnosed with uterine cancer in 1965 and underwent radiation therapy and then a hysterectomy shortly before she had announced her candidacy for governor, but doctors discovered a growth in her abdomen that had spread to the colon. Following surgery in early July of 1967, she underwent another round of radiation therapy, but a few months later she informed her staff that there was now a tumor that was affecting her spinal nerves. She made her final public appearance as Alabama governor in late December during the Blue-Gray Football Classic, an all-star college match-up that revived the annual North-South tensions from the Civil War a century earlier. She also made a final appearance in early January on behalf of her husband's presidential campaign as he ran as the candidate of a newly created third party, the American Independent Party. She underwent three additional surgeries in the first months of 1968, and died in the early hours of May 7, 1968, at home in the governor's mansion.

Because Wallace died in office, she was accorded the full honors of a state funeral, and more than 20,000 mourners came to pay their respects—some waiting in line for four or five hours. On the day of her funeral on May 9, all government offices and schools in Alabama were closed, and most businesses followed suit. Her lieutenant governor, Albert Brewer, took over, and her husband resumed his campaign for the White House, which was not successful. He did manage to win election as governor in 1970, and the law barring consecutive terms was overturned. He was elected again in 1974 and 1982.

Husband Returned to Governor's Mansion

Nearly four years to the day of his wife's death, George Wallace was shot by an unstable, attention-seeking loner named Arthur Bremer during a rally for his 1972 presidential campaign. The shooting left him paralyzed and wheelchair-bound for the rest of his life, and Bremer's story later inspired the character of Travis Bickle in Martin Scorsese's 1976 film *Taxi Driver*. In one of the more intriguing turns of American political history, he later recanted much of his previous stance against civil rights in the years before his death in 1998.

More than four decades after her election, Wallace remains the only female governor in Alabama history. Until Kathleen Blanco was elected to lead Louisiana in 2003, Wallace was the only woman governor of a Deep South state. Jacksonville State University's School of Nursing is named in her honor, as are many other Alabama institutions and places, including Lake Lurleen and Lake Lurleen State Park in Tuscaloosa County. "Unfortunately, people will generally think of her only as someone who stood in for her husband," Jackson R. Stell, curator of the Lurleen B. Wallace Museum in Montgomery told *New York Times* journalist David Margolick. "But the programs she began in mental health, youth services and state parks have been a great help to the state of Alabama. No one was ashamed of Lurleen Wallace as Governor."

Books

Dictionary of American Biography, Supplement 8: *1966–1970*, American Council of Learned Societies, 1988.

Periodicals

New York Times, January 15, 1963, p. 9; February 25, 1966, p. 18; December 1, 1966, p. 46; March 31, 1967, p. 19; May 7, 1968, p. 1; June 19, 1991.
New York Times Magazine, May 21, 1967, p. SM27.

Online

"Lurleen Burns Wallace," Alabama Department of Archives & History, http://www.archives.state.al.us/govs_list/g_walllu.html (January 27, 2009).
"Lurleen Wallace," *American Experience* (*George Wallace: Settin' the Woods on Fire*), PBS.org, http://www.pbs.org/wgbh/amex/wallace/peopleevents/pande06.html (January 27, 2009).□

John Nelson Wanamaker

John Wanamaker (1838–1922) founded the American retailing empire that bore his family's name as a young man in nineteenth-century Philadelphia, and went on to become one of America's wealthiest citizens. For generations, his Philadelphia flagship store was one of the largest and most lavish department stores in the United States, and served as a model for the industry in the twentieth century. Wanamaker was also active in numerous political, charitable, and civil organizations, and served as U.S. Postmaster General in the 1890s.

Wanamaker was born on July 11, 1838, in Philadelphia, Pennsylvania, to Nelson Wanamaker and Elizabeth Deshong Kochersperger. His father was of mixed German and Scottish ancestry, while his mother was a descendant of French Huguenots who had

Presbyterian church, where he founded its Bethany Sunday School in 1858. Two years later, he married Mary Erringer Brown.

In April of 1861—the same month that the U.S. Civil War broke out—Wanamaker and his brother-in-law Nathan Brown opened the doors of Wanamaker & Brown's Oak Hall Men's and Boy's Clothing Store on Sixth and Market Streets in Philadelphia. In its first week, the store made $24.67, and Wanamaker reportedly took the $24 out of the till and went to the *Philadelphia Ledger* to buy more advertising space. A firm believer in marketing, Wanamaker once famously said, according to Thomas Forbes in *Adweek's Marketing Week*, "I am certain that half of the money I spend on advertising is wasted. The trouble is, I don't know which half." Forbes's article discussed the enduring status of Wanamaker's quote in the advertising business.

Oak Hall, as it was known, soon became the largest menswear retailer in the United States, with branches in Pittsburgh; New York City; Richmond, Virginia, and a few cities in the Midwest. Brown, his partner, died in 1868. A year later, Wanamaker opened his second business, which was called John Wanamaker & Company, which sold clothing as well as household goods at its 818 Chestnut Street address. Wanamaker's ads trumpeted his store's motto: "One price and goods returnable." The "one price" guarantee was a significant advance, because haggling over price was still commonplace between merchants and customers in this era. The return policy was also somewhat novel, and earned Wanamaker the enmity of other local merchants.

Involved in 1876 Centennial Celebrations

In 1875, Wanamaker—by then one of Philadelphia's leading business figures—acquired a former railroad depot at Broad and Market Streets. He was involved in the staging of a major religious-revival event in the city featuring the evangelist preachers Dwight Moody and Ira Sankey, and the site hosted that weeks-long event in late 1875. Afterward, it became the venue for Philadelphia's Centennial Exposition in 1876, for which Wanamaker chaired two board committees. He also traveled to Europe to visit the impressive retail establishments known as "department stores," such as Bon Marché in Paris. In March of 1877, John Wanamaker & Co.'s "Grand Depot" store opened for business in the renovated train station.

Wanamaker's Grand Depot was Philadelphia's first department store. It resembled retail establishments elsewhere that operated under some of the same principles, such as Alexander T. Stewart's Marble Dry Goods Palace and Rowland Macy's immense store, both in New York City. It sold men's and women's clothing, various household items, and fabrics, and within a decade would branch out into sporting goods, furniture, and even newfangled household appliances. Some 70,000 shoppers turned up on its first day of business, and a staff of 1,000 clerks was there to serve them. Wanamaker had designed the immense, lavish space as a destination—meaning anyone was welcome to visit without any pressure to buy something. There were rest rooms, a post office counter, and even a telegraph office. The Grand Depot was also the first major retail establishment to use new electric lighting, and a series of pneumatic tubes

immigrated to the United States to flee religious persecution. Wanamaker was the first of seven children in the family and spent his earliest years in a frame house near what were then the city limits of Philadelphia. He came from a moderately prosperous background, for his grandfather and father owned a local brickyard, which thrived until a larger competitor forced them out of business. In 1850, the entire family moved to Indiana to try their luck at farming, but soon returned to Philadelphia.

Headed Philadelphia YMCA Office

Around 1851, the 13-year-old Wanamaker went to work as an errand runner for a Philadelphia publishing house. He also became active in the local Presbyterian church—though he had attended both Methodist and Reformed churches with his family in his earliest years—and was a youthful temperance, or anti-alcohol, crusader and Sunday-school teacher. His parents thought he was destined for a career in the ministry, but instead Wanamaker became a salesperson at a men's clothing store in the city. Ill health forced him to quit around 1857, and he spent some time out West to recuperate from a bout with tuberculosis. Back in Philadelphia, he was hired as the secretary for the local branch of the Young Men's Christian Association (YMCA) at an annual salary of $1,000, which made him the first paid YMCA executive in the United States. A deeply religious young man, Wanamaker abstained from alcohol and tobacco and was active in his local

speeded up charge-account transactions, which Wanamaker was also among the first merchants to offer. The store quickly became a Philadelphia landmark and meeting place, as Wanamaker hoped it would be.

Wanamaker and his wife had six children, two of whom did not survive into adulthood. His sons Thomas and Rodman became executives with the company. There were also two daughters, Mary, known as Minnie, and Elizabeth, who was called Lillie. Wanamaker's staunch conservative views, on both politics and religion, put him at odds for a time with Thomas, the eldest, who struck out on his own in 1899 and bought the *North American* a Philadelphia newspaper, which published the columns of prominent leftist writers. Rodman stayed with the company and is credited with establishing a network of European wholesalers for the store, which offered an impressive range of imported luxury goods previously unavailable in the United States.

Became U.S. Postmaster

Some of those luxury goods were available only at Wanamaker's New York City branch, which opened in 1896 after Wanamaker bought Alexander T. Stewart's famous Cast Iron Palace at Astor Place. By then, Wanamaker's founder and chief executive officer was one of the most famous tycoons of America's Gilded Age, and appeared in newspaper reports in 1888 as the first person to have a life insurance policy valued at $1 million because of his various business holdings; the *New York Times* notice said that he had surpassed the $750,000 policy carried by John B. Stetson, manufacturer of the eponymous cowboy hat.

Wanamaker was an ardent Republican, and was a key fundraiser for Benjamin Harrison, the party's presidential candidate of 1888. Harrison won and appointed Wanamaker to serve as Postmaster General, which was a cabinet position at the time. Wanamaker is credited with establishing the practice of commemorative stamps, and supporting a new but controversial initiative at the time, Rural Free Delivery (RFD). It began in limited areas during his tenure as Postmaster, and went into full effect in 1896, three years after he stepped down when Harrison's term expired. His stint was also notable for his successful campaign against the sale of lottery tickets through the mail, which effectively banned all legitimate lottery games until official state-run lotteries came into being in the 1960s.

Like previous Postmasters General, Wanamaker took office and immediately fired some 30,000 Post Office employees who held their jobs thanks to the political patronage of the outgoing administration, and replaced them with Republican loyalists. A few years earlier, however, Congress had enacted the 1883 Pendleton Civil Service Act, which was supposed to prohibit this kind of wholesale job losses and cronyism, which was known as the "spoils system." Theodore Roosevelt, a young Republican reformer, had been appointed by Harrison to head the U.S. Civil Service Commission, and fought for stepped-up enforcement of the Pendleton Act because of Wanamaker's actions. Roosevelt was so successful in the job that the next president, Democrat Grover Cleveland, kept him on as head of the Commission.

Built Palatial New Store

In 1896, Wanamaker attempted to become one of Pennsylvania's two U.S. senators, but lost the contest, which at the time took place in sessions of state legislatures. He was also unsuccessful in his bid to become the Republican candidate for Pennsylvania governor in 1898. His business ventures, however, continued to prosper. Just before World War I, he commissioned Chicago architect Daniel H. Burnham to build a new flagship Wanamaker's store, and the twelve-story landmark took up an entire city block at Thirteenth and Market streets. Burnham also designed a new Wanamaker's for 770 Broadway in New York City, which boasted a million square feet of retail space.

Wanamaker's new flagship store in Philadelphia opened in 1910 with a rooftop athletic field for employee use. It was one of several novel benefits that Wanamaker offered his employees, including medical care, pensions, and profit-sharing. Continuing education was also a pet project—though he had left school by age 13, he was proud of his sons, both of whom were graduates of Princeton University—and the adult-education courses he offered his employees eventually became the John Wanamaker Commercial Institute. Not surprisingly, Wanamaker was also a staunch foe of unions, and forcefully fought any attempts by his workers to organize.

Wanamaker's stores sold the first generation of automobiles made by Detroit industrialist Henry Ford, and even some of the first airplanes available on the consumer market. He died on December 12, 1922, at the age of 84 in his manor home, Lindenhurst, in Cheltenham, Pennsylvania. He left a fortune estimated at $100 million, and was predeceased by his son Thomas. Rodman, who was ill with a kidney ailment at the time, inherited control of the stores. The younger Wanamaker died just a few years later, and is remembered as the founder of the Professional Golfers' Association of America, or PGA. His Palm Beach estate was later acquired by the Kennedy family, and used by U.S. President John F. Kennedy as the Winter White House. In the early 1990s, it became famous as the site of an alleged sexual assault by one of the late president's nephews, William Kennedy Smith.

Wanamaker's stores had suffered a similarly ignominious fate by then. After Rodman Wanamaker's death in 1928, the company was run by a family trust. In 1978, it was sold to Carter Hawley Hale, a department store company whose holdings included The Broadway stores in southern California and Neiman-Marcus. In 1986, the chain was acquired by Woodward & Lothrop, a Washington, D.C. retailer, which filed for bankruptcy in 1994. The remaining stores were sold off. Wanamaker's Philadelphia flagship store eventually became a Macy's. Wanamaker's city home at 2032 Walnut Street later became the site of a luxury condominium tower.

Books

Dictionary of American Biography, American Council of Learned Societies, 1928-1936.

Sobel, Robert, and David B. Sicilia, *The Entrepreneurs: An American Adventure,* Houghton Mifflin, 1986.

Periodicals

Adweek's Marketing Week, October 8, 1990.
New York Times, July 5, 1888; December 13, 1922. □

Jack Webb

American actor, producer, and screenwriter Jack Webb (1920–1982) is known internationally for his portrayal of Sergeant Joe Friday in the television police drama *Dragnet,* which began its run as a radio program in 1949.

Not so well known among the millions of viewers who have watched Friday's dour requests for "just the facts" is the degree to which Webb shaped *Dragnet* and by extension the entire history of the television police show. Well over a half century after *Dragnet* went on the air, the show's mannerisms and conventions were still easily visible in such programs as *Law & Order.* Webb created *Dragnet,* wrote many of the program's scripts, and was responsible as producer for several other successful series. "The story you are about to read is true. The names have not been changed to protect the innocent," wrote Bruce Fretts of *Entertainment Weekly,* recalling and parodying *Dragnet*'s unforgettable opening voice-over (which asserted that the names *were* changed). "The fact that the previous two sentences still resonate in the public memory," Fretts commented, "should be testament enough to the enduring legacy of Jack Webb."

Suffered from Asthma

John Randolph "Jack" Webb was born in Los Angeles on April 2, 1920. His father, Samuel Webb, left the family prior to his son's having registered any memory of him. Jack Webb was raised in poverty near downtown Los Angeles by his mother, Margaret Smith, and by a grandmother. To make things worse, Webb suffered from asthma. The disease was so severe during the first part of his childhood that he was unable to attend school, and he was taught to read by his grandmother, using food cartons in the household kitchen. By the time Webb was nine, his condition improved sufficiently that he was allowed to enroll in elementary school, and he went on to attend Los Angeles's Belmont High School. As an adult, despite his condition, he sometimes smoked three packs of cigarettes a day.

Webb's instincts as a producer showed themselves even before he graduated from high school in 1938; with funds for the school's athletic program running short, he mounted several variety shows as fundraisers. His grateful classmates elected him student body president. Also a talented cartoonist, Webb received an offer of admission, including an art scholarship, from the University of Southern California. He decided that he had to earn money to support his family, however, and worked in the early 1940s as a sales clerk in a men's clothing store. Then he got a job in a stamping plant that made tank parts for the United

States Defense Department. As his family's chief means of financial support, Webb was given a deferment enabling him to avoid the military draft. He nevertheless enlisted in the Army Air Force in 1943 and became a pilot trainer at Laughlin Field in Del Rio, Texas.

After leaving the Air Force, Webb landed a job as an interviewer and announcer at radio station KGO in San Francisco. For a time he hosted an early morning show devoted to jazz, which remained a lifetime passion; he eventually amassed a collection of more than 6,000 jazz recordings. In 1946 Webb played the title role in *Pat Novak for Hire,* a radio series about a private detective. The following year Webb married actress Julie London. The couple had two children, Stacey and Alisa, before divorcing in 1953; Webb later married three more times. A friendship with the writer of *Pat Novak for Hire,* Richard Breen, led Webb to move back to Los Angeles as both men decided to try to break into films. Webb landed more radio roles, and he was impressed by the quasi-documentary style of the 1948 film *He Walked by Night,* in which he had a bit part.

Consulted Police in Developing *Dragnet*

During a period of unemployment that year, Webb hit on the idea of developing projects himself rather than waiting for work to come to him. Combining the hard-bitten writing of *He Walked by Night* with the suggestion of a police officer acquaintance, he developed a series based on everyday police work. He rode around in squad cars and perused Los

Angeles Police Department case files as he developed scripts for the new series, again setting a precedent of consultation with actual officers for what would come to be called the police procedural drama. For the lead character, played by Webb himself, he chose the name Joe Friday because, he believed, it carried no special ethnic identification. Webb immersed himself in the details of police work in order to create a hyper-realistic atmosphere, and the Los Angeles police, for their part, gave the new show official approval.

Dragnet went on the air on the NBC radio network in June of 1949. Fatima cigarettes signed on as a sponsor that fall, and the show's popularity steadily increased as Webb worked out the various formulas, including a distinctive musical theme, that gave the show its flavor. In 1951 *Dragnet* moved to television, but there was an overlap of several years between the television and radio versions. The NBC television *Dragnet* ran until 1959, by which time Joe Friday's supposed admonition "Just the facts, ma'am" was part of the American lexicon. Curiously, the line never appeared in that exact form; "all we want [or need] are the facts, ma'am" were usually the actual words Friday spoke; the familiar version comes from later comic treatments of the easily lampooned program. Each episode of the show dealt with a single case, tracked through mundane details such as filling out forms as well as a dramatic denouement. At its peak, *Dragnet* was the second most popular show on U.S. television, behind only *I Love Lucy.*

Webb also had parts in several films, including *The Men* (1950), in which he played a paraplegic opposite the young Marlon Brando, and *Sunset Boulevard* (also 1950). *Dragnet* became a feature film in 1954, with Webb as both director and star. Webb also tried to extend the precise realism of *Dragnet* to several other films he directed, including *Pete Kelly's Blues* (1955), which had a 1920s jazz setting, and *The D.I.* (1957). *Pete Kelly's Blues* was also turned into a television series under the aegis of Webb's new production company, Mark VII. By the late 1950s the company was reaping profits from *Dragnet,* which became one of television's first syndicated rerun successes.

Revived *Dragnet* Series

In the early 1960s Webb produced and narrated for *General Electric True,* another real-life series, and he briefly served as head of television production for the studio that originated that show, Warner Brothers. Webb's judgment, however, was less accurate outside the crime and reality genres, and he soon returned to acting and directing under the Mark VII umbrella. One of his first new projects was a made-for-television *Dragnet* film (1966), which spawned a revival of the *Dragnet* television series that ran until 1970. Officially its initial name was *Dragnet '67,* with the year changed for each new season. Webb used Joe Friday's conservative image as a vehicle for negative treatments of the 1960s counterculture, whose members were sometimes depicted in drug-related storylines. These *Dragnet* episodes, too, were successful in syndication.

Webb parlayed the success of the new *Dragnet* into new production opportunities, and he was particularly successful as producer with *Adam-12,* a police show that ran from 1968 until 1975. Mark VII scored its first hit outside the police

genre with *Emergency!,* which ran from 1972 until 1977 and focused on a group of paramedics. Webb's ex-wife Julie London appeared as Nurse Dixie McCall in that show, which lasted five seasons in a time slot opposite the major situation comedy hit of the time, *All in the Family.*

The veteran-rookie squad-car pairing of *Adam-12* became a staple of police procedural shows, and *Emergency!* provided a foretaste of the medical jargon and realistic atmosphere of *ER* and other future shows with hospital settings. Webb, who (according to *Time*) described himself as a "demon at work," produced other shows during the 1970s, including *Hec Ramsey* and *Chase* (both 1973–1974) and *Project U.F.O.* (1978–1979). But none of his creations was as influential as *Dragnet,* whose elements, from its opening voice-over to its documentary-style camera work, have been perennially imitated—and parodied on television, in printed comics, and in music and literature. Indeed, the third appearance of *Dragnet* on film, in 1987, was a spoof treatment.

Webb was planning a third *Dragnet* television series, in which he was set to reprise his role as Joe Friday, when he died after a massive heart attack in Los Angeles on December 23, 1982. Outside of radio and television his accomplishments included a true-crime book, *The Badge: True and Terrifying Crime Stories That Could Not Be Presented on TV* (1958) and several recordings, including a version of the song "Try a Little Tenderness" that appeared on compilations of misfiring celebrity vocals in the 1990s. After his death, the Los Angeles Police Department, which had sometimes used *Dragnet* episodes as training films, flew its flags at half staff, retired Joe Friday's badge number, 714, and participated in his funeral with a full 17-gun salute.

Books

Contemporary Authors Online, Gale, 2009.

Moyer, Daniel, and Eugene Alvarez, *Just the Facts, Ma'am: the Authorized Biography of Jack Webb,* Seven Locks Press, 2001.

The Scribner Encyclopedia of American Lives, Volume 1: 1981–1985, Charles Scribner's Sons, 1998.

Periodicals

Entertainment Weekly, March 5, 1999, p. 50.

Time, January 3, 1983, p. 88.

Online

"Jack Webb," Filmbug, http://www.filmbug.com/db/34608 (January 17, 2009).

"Jack Webb," Internet Movie Database, http://www.imdb.com (January 17, 2009). □

Sunita Williams

Indian-American astronaut Sunita Williams (born 1965) spent 195 days in space during a mission to the International Space Station in 2006-07, setting a female endurance record for consecutive number of days

in space. During the trip, Williams also completed the first marathon by an orbiting astronaut. Anchored to a treadmill, she ran the Boston Marathon in tandem with those competing in the event on the earth below.

Raised on East Coast

Williams was born Sunita Pandya on September 19, 1965, in Euclid, Ohio. Friends call her Suni. Her father, Deepak Pandya, grew up in India and studied there before relocating to the United States in 1958. A noted neuroscientist, he taught at both Harvard and Boston universities. Her mother, Bonnie Pandya, was of Yugoslav descent and worked as an X-ray technician.

Williams spent her childhood in Needham, Massachusetts, an historic Colonial suburb southwest of Boston. She was nearly four years old when Neil Armstrong walked on the moon. Williams watched the historic landing on television, never dreaming that one day she would go to space. Growing up, Williams' parents encouraged her to pursue an active lifestyle, and she engaged in camping and swimming competitively. By the time she was an adult, Williams was hooked on triathlons, windsurfing, snowboarding, and running.

Initially, Williams thought she might study veterinary medicine. As a child, she was interested in science, having grown up in a household where it was common to find pictures of brains sitting on the kitchen table. Her father, a neuroscientist, was constantly studying brains. As Williams' 1983 graduation from Needham High School approached, she contemplated going to Columbia University but did not want to be saddled with student loans. Her brother attended the U.S. Naval Academy in Annapolis, Maryland, and encouraged her to apply, suggesting she would love the physical aspects of the program. Speaking to *Nirali Magazine,* Williams discussed her decision, saying she asked herself, "Ooh, do I want to live in New York City and have school bills or have this adventurous career?" In the end, she headed to the Naval Academy, graduating with a degree in physical science in 1987.

Worked as Naval Test Pilot

In July 1989, Williams became a Naval Aviator—or pilot. After training, she was assigned to the Helicopter Combat Support Squadron 8 based in Norfolk, Virginia. Williams was deployed to the Mediterranean, the Red Sea and the Persian Gulf to support 1990's Operation Desert Shield after Iraq invaded Kuwait. She remained overseas for 1991's Operation Provide Comfort, which was aimed at helping Kurds displaced by the war. Williams' job involved transporting goods between ships—she moved everything from bombs to eggs.

As Williams moved through the ranks she briefly contemplated becoming an astronaut but thought there was no way she would be accepted into the program. Williams was a Navy pilot, but she had learned to fly helicopters. She figured NASA preferred Navy pilots with jet-training because the space shuttle was more like a jet than a helicopter. During test-pilot school, her class visited the Lyndon B. Johnson Space Center in Houston and she met astronaut John Young, who went to the moon twice. Young mentioned how he had to master the art of flying a helicopter in order to land a module on the moon. With those words, Williams' whole outlook changed. She realized NASA had a place for helicopter pilots. She graduated from the U.S. Naval Test Pilot School in 1993 and became a test pilot, but in the back of her mind, she was dreaming of space. Over the course of her career, Williams has logged some 2,770 hours in flight, piloting more than 30 different aircraft.

In 1995, Williams earned her master's degree in engineering management from the Florida Institute of Technology. In time, she was assigned to the Norfolk, Virginia-based *USS Saipan,* an amphibious assault ship. She was deployed aboard the *USS Saipan* in 1998 when she found out she had been selected for NASA's astronaut training corps. Williams had unsuccessfully applied once before but that was prior to earning her master's degree.

Began Astronaut Training

Williams moved to Houston and began astronaut training in August 1998. She trained for some eight years before her first mission in 2006. Astronaut training proved thorough and intensive. Williams learned to fly a Northrop T-38 Talon, a supersonic trainer used by the U.S. Air Force. She took survival training. She learned Russian and spent a great deal of time in Moscow working with the Russian

Space Agency to learn about Russia's contributions to the space station.

Williams also spent time underwater living on the ocean floor in an aqua-laboratory called the NEEMO 2, which stands for NASA Extreme Environment Mission Operations. NEEMO is used to simulate an anti-gravity environment similar to the one astronauts endure in space. Williams also studied the space station itself, including its cooling and heating systems. She spent many days in virtual reality simulators learning to work a robotic arm. She received training to help her respond to emergencies and malfunctions that might occur aboard the space station.

Spent Six Months in Space

On December 9, 2006, Williams left the earth aboard the space shuttle *Discovery* and headed for the International Space Station. The mission was not without danger. This was the first shuttle to launch since the 2003 *Columbia* disaster when the *Columbia* disintegrated over Texas during re-entry. Williams' mother took the risk in stride. "It's no worse than when she was flying helicopters during the Gulf War or working as Navy test pilot," Bonnie Pandya told the *Cape Cod Times'* Aaron Gouveia.

During the six-month-long mission, Williams lived with two others in an area roughly the size of an airliner. Each morning, mission control sent them a schedule for the day. Work days on the space station last 12 hours and include two hours of exercise and a meal break. Williams and her Russian crewmates expanded the living quarters and upgraded the station's electrical system so it would pull power from solar panels that had been added during a previous mission.

In carrying out these tasks, Williams completed four spacewalks, spending a total of 29 hours and 17 minutes outside the space station. One task included adding a small structural truss to the orbiting laboratory. Williams had practiced her spacewalk tasks in a neutral buoyancy lab—or pool—before going into space, but the real walks still shook her nerves. Her four spacewalks set a new record for a woman and held until 2008 when U.S. astronaut Peggy Whitson completed five during her stay at the space station.

Ran Marathon Aboard Space Station

While aboard the space station, Williams completed another space first—running a marathon. Her sister, Dina Pandya, was going to run the Boston Marathon on April 16, 2007, and Williams wanted to join her. She taped a race number, 14,000, to a space station treadmill, tethered herself on with a bungee harness to simulate the pull of gravity and ran the race simultaneously with runners on the earth. Williams ran while watching a laptop of live feeds from the actual race. She wore Boston Red Sox socks and completed the 26.2-mile race in 4 hours, 24 minutes and 10 seconds while the space station floated more than 210 miles above the ground. Williams ran at speeds of up to eight miles per hour during the race while the space station flew through the air at more than five miles each second and completed more than two rotations around the earth.

Williams also participated in medical experiments aimed at helping scientists get future astronauts ready for deep space missions—possibly to the moon or Mars. These experiments consisted of sticking to a special diet regimen and fitness program aimed at limiting the bone and muscle mass loss that occurs while living in space.

On June 22, 2007, Williams came back to earth aboard the shuttle *Atlantis,* landing in California at Edwards Air Force Base. From there, she was ferried back to Ellington Field, in Houston, where her mother, sister and husband, Michael Williams (who had formerly flown helicopters), were waiting with her Jack Russell Terrier, Gorby. She had spent 195 days in space, setting a record for longest spaceflight by a woman, besting the record set by U.S. astronaut Shannon Lucid more than a decade before.

After such a long time in space living without the pull of gravity, Williams struggled to readjust. She felt nauseous the first few days as her inner organs readapted to life with gravity. After landing, Williams spent 45 days in a rehabilitation program to strengthen her bones and muscles. While Williams enjoyed her time in space, she was happy to be home. "It was nice to smell that sage air, feel the desert breeze, and it was really nice to put feet on the ground," she told the *Houston Chronicle's* Mark Carreau a few days after landing.

Hoped to Return to Space

Williams is only the second woman of Indian heritage to go into space. In 2003, Kalpana Chawla became the first. Chawla was born in India and immigrated to the United States. She died in the *Columbia* disaster in 2003. To honor her own heritage, Williams took a copy of the *Bhagavad Gita* into space, as well as a small statue of Lord Ganesh. The *Bhagavad Gita* is Hinduism's sacred scripture and Lord Ganesh is an elephant-like deity worshipped by many Hindus. Being a woman and being half-Indian makes Williams a rarity in the world of astronauts.

Williams prefers to keep a low profile and has said that her gender and ancestral background have not hampered her in any way. "It's been pretty transparent—maybe I've been lucky or avoided acknowledging that I'm different," Williams told *Nirali Magazine.* "If you don't acknowledge there's a difference the people around you won't acknowledge there's a difference, and I think that's beneficial. But I do think that there's a little determination and persistence that came from my dad. I'm not going to let anybody tell me I can't do anything, that's for sure." Williams is a member of the Society of Experimental Test Pilots, Society of Flight Test Engineers and the American Helicopter Association.

Like the many astronauts who have gone before her, Williams came home with a changed worldview. Speaking to *Reader's Digest,* Williams put it this way: "When you have that perspective of being far away and looking back at the planet, you don't see the hustle and bustle or the borders. You see a very peaceful place. Gandhi tried to instill the feeling of oneness in all of us. Seeing our planet from space, you understand that." As for the future, Williams has said she would love to go to the moon but would gladly return to the space station. If so, she is likely to set more firsts for female astronauts.

Periodicals

Boston Globe, January 18, 2007, p. Reg. 1.
Cape Cod Times (Hyannis, MA), June 18, 2007; July 4, 2007.
Christian Science Monitor, October 2, 2007, p. 19.
Houston Chronicle, June 29, 2007, p. B1.
Reader's Digest, November 2008.
Statesman (India), April 18, 2007.

Online

"Astronaut Bio: Sunita Williams," Lyndon B. Johnson Space Center, http://www.jsc.nasa.gov/Bios/htmlbios/williams-s.html (December 16, 2008).
"Working Woman: Sunita Williams," *Nirali Magazine,* http://niralimagazine.com/2004/10/working-woman-sunita-williams/ (December 16, 2008).□

Charlie Wilson

For most of his career in Congress, Charlie Wilson (born 1933) was known primarily as a handsome lawmaker from East Texas who was often seen in the company of attractive women and occasionally ran afoul of the House Ethics Committee. Over the years, however, Wilson's role in what was the largest and most expensive covert military operation in Central Intelligence Agency history became known, and in 2007 he was the focus of a major Hollywood film, *Charlie Wilson's War,* which depicted his influence in winning nearly $5 billion in secret aid for Afghanistan guerrillas battling the occupying forces of the Soviet Union. "It never leaked because nobody wanted it to," he told Sandra McElwaine in *Time.* "Everybody was pulling for [the mujahideen]. It was amazing and will never, never, ever happen again."

Born Charles Nesbitt Wilson on June 1, 1933, Wilson grew up in Trinity, Texas, where his father was an accountant for a timber company. The drama and excitement of World War II turned the young Wilson into a military history buff, but his political career was shaped by a terrible incident when he was 13 in which his beloved dog Teddy strayed one time too many into the neighbor's yard, and subsequently died a terrible, ten-minute-long death in front of him. Teddy had apparently been fed something that contained finely crushed glass, and Wilson blamed his neighbor, who was a city council member. Wilson first poured gasoline on the man's well-tended garden and set it on fire, then decided to make sure that the neighbor did not win the upcoming election by providing rides to African-American voters. The neighbor lost his council seat by 16 votes. Later that evening, Wilson went

to the man's house and told him he had lost the election, adding "You shouldn't poison any more dogs," according to *Charlie Wilson's War : The Extraordinary Story of the Largest Covert Operation in History,* a book by former CBS News producer George Crile that became the basis for the 2007 movie.

After high school, Wilson entered the elite U.S. Naval Academy at Annapolis, Maryland, but graduated in 1956 near the bottom of his class. He went on to serve four years in the Navy, returning home in 1960 to win a seat in the Texas House of Representatives on the Democratic Party ticket. In 1966, he made a successful run for the Texas senate, and six years later was elected to the U.S. House of Representatives from the Second Congressional District of Texas of Lufkin, Texas. At that point, he gave up his other job managing a lumber yard.

Elected to Congress

Arriving in Washington in 1973, Wilson soon gained a reputation as one of the more hard-partying of the 435 members of Congress. His marriage soon ended, and he enthusiastically indulged in all the social rituals of the era, even becoming part-owner of a K Street discotheque called Élan. The statuesque beauties who ran his Congressional office were dubbed "Charlie's Angels," after the popular television show of the era, and after a decade his lifestyle began to catch up with him. In early 1983, NBC News caught wind of a story that Wilson was the target of an ongoing federal drug investigation, and later that year he skillfully evaded arrest for a hit-and-run accident on a Potomac River bridge.

The "Cocaine Charlie" headlines were the result of Wilson's association with Paul Brown, who hosted a lavish weekend at Caesars Palace in Las Vegas in June of 1980 that included models and hot tubs in the high-roller suites. Wilson was there with his girlfriend at the time, and the group was supposed to meet with Hollywood producers to discuss a television drama series centered on behind-the-scenes political intrigue in Washington. Wilson gave Brown $29,000 to invest in the project, which never came to fruition. Brown appeared to have been operating a scam, and Wilson retaliated for his losses by having Brown prosecuted for interstate stock fraud. Brown was convicted and served four months, and then claimed to have evidence that Wilson had used cocaine that weekend, and on other occasions, too. Federal investigators launched a secret inquiry that also ensnared two other House members, but fizzled after Brown was deemed too unreliable a witness.

Other tales of Wilson's escapades regularly landed him in trouble of one form or another, but Lufkin voters regularly returned him to office. Years later, he reflected in an interview with Paul Burka in *Texas Monthly*, "If you live a clean life and have one bad escapade, it'll kill you politically. People think you're a phony. But when your whole life is escapades, they forgive you." The stories attached to Wilson's name were legendary: he took a former Miss World contestant on a weekend jaunt aboard the U.S.S. *Saratoga*, an aircraft carrier, at taxpayers' expense; he invited a belly dancer he knew to Egypt, where they hobnobbed with the country's defense minister; he treated his companion of four years, who had been Miss USA 1978, on a trip to Pakistan and used a military plane for part of the journey. A Defense Intelligence Agency officer barred them, citing proper procedure, from using it for the return flight, so Wilson contacted the president of Pakistan, General Muhammad Zia-ul-Haq, who sent a plane. The Defense Intelligence Agency later lost two planes and a crucial exemption from an important budget-trimming bill of the 1980s as retribution for the incident, for Wilson sat on the influential House Defense Appropriations committee.

Mixed with CIA Agents

One final, almost cinematic anecdote from Wilson's storied career involved the leader of Nicaragua, Anastasio Somoza, who had been a longtime ally of the United States in Central America until the Carter Administration began to distance itself because of human rights violations. Wilson and a Central Intelligence Agency agent who was already under suspicion for various abuses of office met Somoza in Miami. They were there to discuss the possibility of sending covert U.S. aid to rid Nicaragua of the left-wing Sandinista guerrillas that had been mounting a fairly successful offense to unseat Somoza. Wilson's cohort named an exorbitantly high sum that the dictator would need to pay, and the notoriously frugal Somoza declined. Wilson had brought with him to Miami a woman named Tina Simons, and Somoza was there with his longtime paramour, Dinorah Sampson. After many drinks,

Somoza danced with Simons and behaved inappropriately; Sampson attacked both of them and had to be pulled off.

Nicaragua's guerrilla war intensified in subsequent weeks, and Somoza was forced to flee the country. He went to Bolivia, where he was assassinated; newspaper photographs showed Sampson running from the car that had been hit by both gunfire and a small rocket. The CIA agent with Wilson on that Miami trip was later arrested in the Bahamas and sentenced to a lengthy prison term for other misdeeds. Wilson's date, Simons, testified at the agent's trial and subsequently disappeared into the federal witness protection program. Carter's successor, Ronald Reagan, would later carry out a covert operation against the Sandinista government by funding the right-wing Contra army.

Gust Avrakotos was another CIA figure whom Wilson befriended. He was a longtime CIA case officer and division chief and would play a key role in what became known as "Charlie Wilson's War." A third, almost improbable figure in the tale was Joanne Herring, a wealthy Houston socialite with connections to oil money and her state's Republican elite. An ardent anti-communist, Herring was made honorary consul to Pakistan, and befriended President Zia. She marshaled all of her resources to send humanitarian help when Pakistan's neighbor, Afghanistan, was invaded by the hard-line Communist regime of the Soviet Union in December of 1979. The Soviets had sensed strife in this part of southwestern Asia—a revolutionary student movement had recently ousted the Shah of Iran and taken dozens of U.S. Embassy officials hostage—and moved to occupy the mountainous, resource-poor, and predominantly Muslim nation. Afghanistan had scant military strength to mount any serious counteroffensive to the Red Army, but scores of men began fighting a guerrilla war, in some cases armed with only rocks and knives. Young Muslims from across the Middle East soon came to join the battle, which was deemed a *jihad*, or holy war, as fighters known as *mujahideen*.

Herring had dated Wilson and enlisted his support to fight the Communist occupation. She convinced him to visit a refugee camp in Pakistan to see the wounded and maimed guerrilla fighters and civilians who had fled Afghanistan, and Wilson was appalled. "I decided on the spot that if these people were brave enough to fight, then I was going to help them," he recalled in the interview with Burka for *Texas Monthly*.

Persuaded Colleagues to Fund Secret War

Wilson used his position on the House Defense Appropriations Subcommittee to win medical aid to help the mujahideen, and then billions in covert military aid. The arms were funneled into Afghanistan with the help of the Pakistani government after purchases were arranged with the help of two U.S. allies in the Middle East, Egypt and Israel. Avrakotos had long been known inside the Agency for his skills in carrying out successful clandestine operations, and was a significant figure in arranging the deals and shipments. Wilson was the point person in Washington for the funding, and traveled to the region several times a year often to supervise the results. By the summer of 1988, the Soviets were beginning to pull out, and the ultimately unsuccessful invasion of Afghanistan is commonly cited by historians as the beginning of the end of the Cold War.

Earlier that year, in the spring of 1988, Wilson had taken a crew from the CBS newsmagazine *60 Minutes* into Afghanistan. They also spent time in Pakistan, where correspondent Harry Reasoner interviewed President Zia. The president famously said on camera, "If there is a single man who has played a part that shall be recorded in history in golden letters, it is that right honorable congressman, Charles Wilson." When pressed further about Wilson's role, Zia was evasive. "I'm afraid, Mr. Reasoner, that it is too early to explain it all to you. All I can say is 'Charlie did it.'" The words "'Charlie Did It" actually became the title of the *60 Minutes* story, which also included an interview with Wilson filmed in Afghanistan in which he wore mujahideen-style dress on horseback and enthused about delivering a comeuppance to the Soviet Union for their covert role in the Vietnam War.

Zia died in a mysterious plane crash in August of 1988 along with the U.S. ambassador to Pakistan. Avrakotos had already fallen victim to internal CIA politics and been ousted from his post in the Agency's Near East division. Wilson retired from Congress in 1995 and became a political consultant. After 1988, both Afghanistan and Pakistan endured years of political instability that had not abated by the twentieth anniversary of the end of the war. In fact, the Soviet-Afghan war served as an extremely effective training ground for future Islamic fundamentalists. One was a wealthy Saudi Arabian and devout Muslim, Osama bin Laden, who ran training camps for the mujahideen. Bin Laden went on to found the rogue organization al-Qaeda, and one of al-Qaeda's allies has been a hard-line Islamic militant group in Afghanistan known as the Taliban, which has been accused of hiding bin Laden in the aftermath of the 9/11 terrorist attacks on the United States. "No one had heard of the Taliban," Wilson said in his own defense to *Dallas Morning News* journalist Michael Granberry. "They didn't exist until 11 years after the Russians were defeated." Wilson also asserted that the United States should have devoted funds to rebuilding the war-torn country. "We let chaos develop in Afghanistan. I tried hard to pull the other way, but my colleagues were tired of listening to me."

In the 2007 film version of Crile's book, Wilson was played by Tom Hanks; Philip Seymour Hoffman was cast as Avrakotos, and Julia Roberts played the role of Joanne Herring. The movie was released three months after Wilson survived heart transplant surgery. "I told them to keep me alive till the movie comes out," he told McElwaine in the *Time* interview. "I feel pretty good."

Books

Crile, George, *Charlie Wilson's War : The Extraordinary Story of the Largest Covert Operation in History,* Atlantic Monthly Press, 2002.

Periodicals

Dallas Morning News, December 22, 2007.

Texas Monthly, December 1995, p. 122.

Time, December 17, 2007, p. 79.

Online

"Charlie Did It," *60 Minutes,* http://www.cbsnews.com/video/ watch/?id=4556228n%3fsource=search_video(February 17, 2009). □

Tokugawa Yoshinobu

The brief reign of Japanese shogun Tokugawa Yoshinobu (1837–1913) ended the shogunate system of semi-feudal rule in Japan.

Yoshinobu (the family name, or in this case the clan name, is placed first in the Japanese naming system) was chosen as shogun in 1866 and by 1868 resigned his position, bringing to an end a system of government that had lasted for well over two centuries. His immediate reason was to spare Japan the trauma of all-out civil war, and indeed his departure precipitated several years of military conflict. The deeper levels of the backdrop against which Yoshinobu's life and career unfolded involved Japan's long isolation from Western influence and the internal conflicts that beset the country in the second half of the 19th century as it attempted to come to grips with the inevitability of that influence. His resignation was outwardly tendered in order to restore the most traditional of Japanese institutions, the imperial throne. But its ultimate effect was to put Japan on its unique path to modernity.

Yoshinobu was a ceremonial name, given when the young nobleman began to walk a path that led toward his becoming shogun one day. He was born on October 28, 1837, as Shichiroma, meaning "seventh son," indeed as the seventh son of Tokugawa Nariaki, the ruler of the Mito domain and a scion of the Mito clan, one of the three branches of the Tokugawa house that had produced the line of shoguns running back to the year 1600. He was also given the name of Keiki, and for much of his life he was known as Tokugawa Keiki. The shoguns were military rulers who had united at that time and had come to constitute the true system of government in Japan, centered in Edo, known today as Tokyo. The emperor's palace, at that time, was located in the ancient city of Kyoto.

Slept Between Swords

Keiki, accordingly, was given a traditional upbringing that included aspects of the traditional samurai warrior culture. Because a samurai was supposed to lie perfectly straight when asleep, it was said that Nariaki ordered that a pair of swords be place, blade inward, to either side of the youngster's pillow (which was made of wood), so that if he rolled around in his sleep he would cut himself. With his father's approval, he was adopted by a different and more prestigious branch of the Tokugawa house, the Hitotsubashi clan. Nariaki had spotted the potential for greatness in his son, and in the Hitotsubashi house, he believed, Keiki would have a better chance at eventually becoming shogun.

The curriculum for a young member of the bafuku, or shogunal system, was both traditional and rigorous, including studies in Japanese and Chinese, calligraphy, literature, horseback riding, javelin throwing, archery, fencing, and shooting on horseback. Yoshinobu had to spend long hours repeating, in Chinese, the classical writings of Confucius, a task he hated; when a tutor threatened to burn his finger if he did not apply himself more diligently, the boy silently extended an index finger and took the punishment, declaring that anything would be better than more Confucian recitation. He preferred physical tasks such as fishing. When told by a fisherman that he should learn to throw a particular kind of net properly, he took the net into his garden and began practicing obsessively, mastering the skill in a single month. The shogun himself, Ieyoshi, noted the self-directed quality of Keiki's learning, thought to be an essential leadership quality. When he was later introduced to the concubine who would meet his sexual needs,

he showed intense curiosity about her anatomy and made detailed sketches of it.

In 1847, Keiki became the official head of the Hitotsubashi household and was permitted to take the family name of the wider clan, Tokugawa. With the favor of Shogun Ieyoshi, his education proceeded rapidly; competent tutors were pleased to find their stipends increased, and the shogunate buzzed with rumors that Ieyoshi intended to make Keiki his heir. Ieyoshi, the 12th shogun since the institution of the nationwide shogunate, was Keiki's uncle by marriage; his wife, Sachi, was Keiki's mother's sister. Wider currents of history, however, were flowing through Japan and made Keiki's succession uncertain.

On July 8, 1853, Commodore Matthew Perry of the United States Navy sailed a flotilla of ships into Tokyo Bay and demanded that the shogunate open Japanese cities to international trade. For two centuries, as the European powers colonized the globe, the shoguns had kept Japan almost completely free of foreign influence. Perry's demand was backed by superior military force, and the shogunate had little choice but to agree to it in a deliberate way. Three days after Perry's arrival, Shogun Ieyoshi died. His successor, Iesada, was an ineffectual leader in poor health; he died in 1858. By that time, Keiki was ready to assume the position of shogun. The shogunate during those years was beginning to suffer from severe internal strains as well as external threats, however, with the traditional Choshu and Satsuma domains edging toward rebellion.

Placed Under House Arrest

Keiki was passed over in favor of Tokugawa Yoshitomi, who became Shogun Iemochi in 1858. It was Iemochi's adviser Ii Naosuke, however, who held the reins of power, and under his near-dictatorial rule Japan's internal situation worsened. Naosuke signed trade agreements with the West, which increased the strength of a nationalist, anti-Western faction that gathered under the slogan "revere the emperor, expel the barbarians!" Naosuke responded with a crackdown, known as the Ansei Purge, during which Keiki was placed under house arrest and made to give up his leadership of the house of Hitotsubashi.

After Naosuke's assassination in 1860, Keiki was rehabilitated. In 1862 he was nominated and confirmed as the shogunal regent, a traditional post as guardian that made him a key adviser to Iemochi. He placed relatives and other allies in key positions in the shogunate and attempted to counter the activities of Choshu forces, commanding fighters who repelled an attack by Choshu forces in 1864. Keiki still faced challenges from nationalist factions, but he realized that, in the words of Ryotaro Shiba's *The Last Shogun: The Life of Tokugawa Yoshinobu*, "inflamed antiforeign rhetoric was antishogunate radicalism in disguise."

In 1866, the 20-year-old Iemochi died of what is thought to have been beriberi. During his illness he designated an infant member of the Tokugawa family as his successor, but the shogunate, beset by renewed Choshu attacks and other crises on every side, turned to Keiki instead. Never a leader driven by strong personal ambition, he was reluctant to accept the post at first, but on January 10, 1867, he became Tokugawa Yoshinobu, the 15th and last shogun. Three weeks after that the Emperor Komei died, removing another pillar of the shogunate's support; he had worked within the traditional shogunal system, but his successor, Mutsuhito, later known as Emperor Meiji, was oriented toward reform.

Modernized Japanese Military

Yoshinobu moved quickly to neutralize the forces that were threatening shogunal rule. He introduced various reforms into the internal workings of the bafuku. Most important, he set out to modernize Japan's armed forces. He sought and received the aid of military advisers from France and, after negotiating new trade agreements with the U.S., purchased military equipment from that country as well. He seemed to be on the path to rejuvenating the moribund shogunate—but it was that very fact that proved his undoing. His successes stimulated a new alliance between the Choshu and Satsuma clans, which in 1867 began the campaigns of the Boshin War (1867–1869). Their aim was to formally restore power to the emperor; the more moderate factions among them would agree to the installation of Yoshinobu as head of a shogunal house of lords.

Hoping to bring about the end of the shogunate with as little violence as possible, Yoshinobu agreed to this arrangement and resigned as shogun on November 10, 1867, thus transferring his powers to the emperor. That event began an era in Japanese history known as the Meiji Restoration. Fighting flared among the rival clans in the first part of 1868, but Yoshinobu, who understood the forward-looking directions the Meiji regime would take, made another step in favor of peace by abandoning the Tokugawa forces at a point short of full-scale war. He pledged loyalty to the emperor and retired to the ancestral Tokugawa home at Shizuoka, living for the rest of his life mostly out of public view. He fathered 21 children who survived to adulthood. Disturbed by a burglary at his compound, he later moved to Tokyo, where he died on November 21, 1913. Various historical treatments of the late shogunate have recounted the events of Yoshinobu's life, but among the most readable is Ryotaro Shiba's *The Last Shogun.* Though published as a novel in Japan, the book might be called a nonfiction novel; the provider of its English introduction, Frank Gibney, wrote that the book "can safely be called history for all practical purposes."

Books

Beasley, William G., *The Modern History of Japan,* Praeger, 1962.

Totman, Conrad, *The Collapse of the Tokugawa Bakufu, 1862–1868,* University of Hawaii Press, 1980.

Shiba, Ryotaro, *The Last Shogun: The Life of Tokugawa Yoshinobu,* Kodansha, 1998.

Online

Huffman, James, "The Meiji Restoration Era, 1868–1889," Japan Society, http://aboutjapan.japansociety.org/content.cfm/the_meiji_restoration_era_1868-1889 (January 24, 2009).☐

Z

Vera Zasulich

Russian revolutionary Vera Ivanovna Zasulich (1849–1919) achieved international notoriety in 1878 for her unsuccessful attempt on the life of the governor of St. Petersburg, Fyodor Trepov. An intelligent, attractive political activist in her late twenties at the time of the incident, Zasulich belonged to a group of leftist radicals in St. Petersburg, the capital of imperial Russia at the time, who were determined to end the tyranny of autocratic rule under Tsar Alexander II.

Zasulich was born on August 8, 1849. One source claims she came from Mikhaylovka, in the *oblast,* or administrative district of Volgograd, but historian Ana Siljak, author of a definitive 2008 biography of Zasulich titled *Angel of Vengeance: The ''Girl Assassin,'' the Governor of St. Petersburg, and Russia's Revolutionary World,* cites her place of birth in Smolensk Oblast, near the city of Gagarin which was known as Gzhatsk at the time of Zasulich's birth. The sensational news reports surrounding Zasulich's case noted that she was the daughter of affluent landowners, but in reality her family was impoverished, and after her father died when she was three her mother was forced to send her to live with relatives, whom Zasulich resented for their wealth and Francophile airs.

Moved to St. Petersburg

Zasulich's relatives thought she might be best suited to a life as a governess, so she was sent to a finishing school near Moscow. After the end of her final term there, she took a job as a court clerk in Serpukhov, which was also near Moscow, around 1867. She ran into one of her long-lost sisters one day on a Moscow street, who reported that their eldest sibling, Ekaterina, was living independently in St. Petersburg and had become involved in socialist circles. In 1868, Zasulich moved to the capital and set up a small bookbinding enterprise with her sisters. She was already attracted to leftist political ideologies by this time, and began teaching literacy classes to factory workers.

Zasulich fell in with a group of radical St. Petersburg University students attracted to the anarchist philosophies of a young, charismatic man named Sergei Nechaev. As a political ideology, anarchism held that all systems of government are a form of tyranny and should be abolished. They became known as the Nihilists, from the Latin word for ''nothing'' *nihil,* and believed that the Russian peasants who were still eking out a living on the land would become the catalyst for an overthrow of the state. This idea differed from the teachings of German philosopher Karl Marx, whose landmark 1848 work, *The Communist Manifesto,* argued that the oppressed urban workers in industrialized cities would be the vanguard of the revolution.

Zasulich met Nechaev at a book-club discussion group in the fall of 1868, but he fled the country a few months later. Tsarist Russia's dreaded ''Third Department,'' more formally known as the Political Surveillance and Investigations arm of the police, began tracking down recipients of a flood of politically inflammatory materials being sent by mail to Moscow and St. Petersburg addresses from abroad, and Zasulich was soon identified as one of Nechaev's associates. Questioned by police, she denied knowing him, but covert police work implicated another woman along with Zasulich's sister Alexandra, and Zasulich was consequently arrested and taken to ''The Lithuanian Castle,'' a notorious St. Petersburg prison.

Harassed and Exiled

Zasulich spent 13 months in solitary confinement, and in May of 1870 was transferred to another prison, Peter and Paul Fortress, which had a reputation as a place of torture for political prisoners. By then, Nechaev had returned to Russia under an alias, and had grown increasingly fanatical. An associate of his who disagreed with his tactics was found murdered, and the tsar's secret police correctly pinned the crime on Nechaev; all of those already imprisoned were also implicated, including Zasulich. Then, in March of 1871, the charges against her were suddenly dropped, and she was released to the custody of her mother. Ten days later, she was rearrested, and was duly informed she was being sent to a small town in Novgorod Oblast. One of the guards who accompanied her gave her his coat, and she was left in the tiny town with a single ruble and orders to report to the local police chief once a week. A church caretaker and his family took her in, but she was summoned to return to St. Petersburg to testify at the Nechaev trial in June.

Following the trial, Zasulich was granted permission to live with her mother in Tver, a city near Moscow, but fell into revolutionary activities there, too, and was sent into exile once more in the summer of 1872. This time she was accompanied by her sister Ekaterina and brother-in-law, and the trio settled in Soligalich, another remote, impoverished village known for its bitterly cold winters. After a year of no suspicious activity, she was allowed to leave in January of 1874 and moved to the city of Kharkov in the south, ostensibly to train as a midwife. There she met a fellow revolutionary, Maria "Masha" Kolenkina, and the two moved to the main city of Ukrainian Russia, Kiev.

A new idea had taken hold among Russian radicals by then: to arm the peasants in the countryside. This final, inept attempt to incite a major peasant revolt against the tsar was also discovered, and led to scores of arrests. One of those arrested in St. Petersburg was a man named Aleksei Emelianov, who used the alias Arkhip Bogoliubov. During his time in St. Petersburg's much-vaunted House of Preliminary Detention—designed as a progressive, supposedly European model of incarceration—Bogoliubov came to the attention of General Fyodor Trepov, the governor of St. Petersburg. Trepov already had a reputation as a notorious brute as a military commander who dealt harshly with rebellions in Poland in 1830 and 1863, and Bogoliubov reportedly refused to remove his hat in Trepov's presence. Trepov ordered that Bogoliubov be flogged with birch rods, which incited prison riots and an official inquiry that found that far from being a model of a humane jail, the St. Petersburg House of Preliminary Detention contained areas with secret isolation cells where well-known dissidents lived in tiny rooms, the floors covered in human excrement and maggots crawling everywhere. The report unleashed a massive public outcry, and even more moderate Russians began to agree with the radicals, conceding that many of the supposed reforms of Tsar Alexander II were superficial at best.

Those arrested in the peasant-revolt conspiracy were brought to court in what was called the Trial of the 193, the number of those charged. The trial ended on January 23, 1878, with a surprising verdict: 90 were acquitted, while the others were sentenced to either time served or house arrest. The outcome is considered an important moment in Russian political history, demonstrating that the tsar's government—and judicial reforms that had been enacted—was in effect powerless to suppress legitimate opposition.

The Trepov Incident

By then Zasulich and Kolenkina had moved to St. Petersburg, and their shared three-room apartment on English Street welcomed many of the same political persuasion and became known as the English Commune. The plot against Trepov had been in place for several months by then, and was set to go into effect on January 24: Kolenkina was to appear at the office of Vladislav Zhelekhovski, the state prosecutor in the Trial of the 193, and shoot him; at nearly the same time, Zasulich would appear in Trepov's office, where the morning hours offered the chance for ordinary citizens to come in and ask for official favors. She planned to pose as a governess named Elizaveta Kozlova to ask for a document called a certificate of conduct, which was necessary to obtain a teaching job. She wore a suitably subdued dress and over it a shawl large enough to hide her weapon, an English Bulldog pistol.

According to Siljak's book, when Zasulich's turn came, she handed her petition to Trepov, and "without a word the governor took her formal request, marked it with a pencil, and turned to the next petitioner. When his back was turned, Vera pulled the revolver out of the folds of her thick cloak. She pulled the trigger twice, then dropped the gun to the floor." Trepov screamed, and blood began seeping through his uniform jacket. In the chaos that ensued, a guard struck Zasulich in the face with such force she was knocked to the floor, at which point he began kicking her.

Zasulich had expected to die on the spot, and her calm surprised her interrogators. The incident prompted headlines around the world, as much for the shock of an attempt on the life of such a high public official as for the fact that a woman was the perpetrator. Trepov survived his two shots, but retired from his post as governor. Around St. Petersburg, Zasulich had the sympathies of the poor but also that of some members of the nobility, who considered Trepov to be a thug. Students and leftists collected funds for Zasulich's legal defense, and an excellent lawyer named Peter Alexandrov defended her masterfully. Alexandrov used the flogging of Bogoliubov as a centerpiece of his arguments, and the first witnesses called were those who had been tortured or maltreated by Trepov. When she took the stand, she said simply that she had "decided, at the cost of my own life, to prove that no one should be sure they are beyond punishment when they violate human dignity," according to Siljak.

A jury found Zasulich not guilty, and massive crowds awaited the result outside the St. Petersburg courthouse. She was even grabbed and carried aloft by jubilant supporters, much to her consternation, but escaped into the safety of a carriage—which the crowds then followed. The losing side reacted predictably, and harassed the crowd; after the police fired shots, riots ensued. Furthermore, Zasulich's troubles were far from over: after hearing a rumor that an arrest warrant had been issued once again in her name, she was forced to move from one hiding place to another. When she heard word that the Russian Senate was about to overturn the jury verdict, she fled to Switzerland.

Rejected Acts of Terrorism

Zasulich's act spawned a wave of other assassination attempts, some of which were successful. Most notable was Nikolai Mezentsov, head of the dreaded Third Department. Even Alexander II was assassinated in 1881 after four failed attempts. Zasulich was reportedly horrified by the wave of copycat terrorist acts she had inspired, and distanced herself from the idea that it would take acts of violence to overturn a monolith as immense as Tsarist Russia.

In her later years, Zasulich lived in London and became a well-known writer on Marxist theory. She even translated some of Marx's writings into Russian, which became widely read among the Russian intelligentsia and helped to foment another political movement— leading to the founding of the forerunner of the Communist Party of Russia, the Russian Social Democratic Labor Party (RSDLP), in 1898. Two years later, she and that party's exiled leader, Vladimir I. Lenin, co-founded *Iskra* (Spark) a Marxist newspaper, with four other associates. In 1903, at the Second RSDLP Congress, the party split into two factions, the Bolsheviks and Mensheviks. Zasulich allied with the latter, more moderate group. She was finally able to return to Russia after the 1905 Revolution, but opposed the October Revolution of 1917 in which the Bolshevik faction triumphed over a Menshevik-allied provisional government and seized power. The Communist Party of the Soviet Union, as the Bolsheviks would eventually rename themselves, remained in power until 1991.

Zasulich died in St. Petersburg, which had been renamed Petrograd at the time, on May 8, 1919, just a few months shy of her seventieth birthday. For many years after her attempt on Trepov, she remained a famous but reclusive figure throughout much of Europe. The Russian novelist Fyodor Dostoevsky attended her trial and reportedly modeled some dialogue used by the lawyer in *The Brothers Karamazov* on Alexandrov's stirring arguments. Oscar Wilde's first play, the long-forgotten *Vera, or the Nihilists,* was based on her case, and female Nihilist assassins turned up in other pieces of literature, including sir Arthur Conan Doyle's "The Adventure of the Golden Pince-nez."

Books

Siljak, Ana, *Angel of Vengeance: The "Girl Assassin," the Governor of St. Petersburg, and Russia's Revolutionary World,* St. Martin's Press, 2008.

"Zasulich, Vera Ivanovna," *Encyclopedia of Russian History,* edited by James R. Millar, Macmillan Reference USA, 2004. □

Ferdinand von Zeppelin

German aviation pioneer Ferdinand von Zeppelin (1838–1917) is credited with inventing the dirigible airship that became synonymous with his name. Zeppelin was a retired military officer who spent the last

quarter century of his life designing and building the first prototypes before finally securing development funding from the imperial German government. In the years before World War I, Zeppelin's well-publicized saga aroused German patriotic fervor and became a symbol of the nation's technological progress.

Zeppelin's full name was Ferdinand Adolf August Heinrich Graf von Zeppelin, with *graf* being the German equivalent of "count." His family was part of the landed aristocracy and was said to have received its title from Theodoric, the king of the Visigoths in the fifth century. He was born on July 8, 1838, in Konstanz, a city on the shores of a large lake of the same name—but known as the *Bodensee* in German—located on the border between southwestern Germany and Switzerland. His father was Friedrich Jérôme Wilhelm Karl Graf von Zeppelin, a minister at the Württemberg royal court. His mother, Amélie Françoise Pauline Macaire d'Hogguer, was descended from a family of French Huguenots, or adherents of the Protestant faith. The family home was Schloss Girsberg, a castle in Emmishofen, Switzerland, on the shores of Lake Konstanz. Zeppelin had two siblings: a sister, Eugenia, and his brother Eberhard.

Saw Combat in U.S. Civil War

Zeppelin was educated at Stuttgart's Polytechnic School and earned a degree in civil engineering from the University of Tübingen. He also trained at the Ludwigsburg Military Academy near Stuttgart, and entered the Prussian cavalry around 1858 as a lieutenant. At the time, the loosely allied German states were dominated by the Kingdom of Prussia in the north, along the Baltic coastline, which boasted a superior military force. During Zeppelin's lifetime all the German properties would eventually unite into what was known as the German Empire.

In his youth, Zeppelin was intrigued by steamships and other new modes of transportation. His interest in aviation was sparked by a trip to the United States, where he was posted as Prussia's military attaché during the U.S. Civil War. He met with President Abraham Lincoln at the White House when he arrived, and was given a pass by Union Army General Ulysses S. Grant that allowed him to travel with the federal troops.

With the Union Army on its Peninsular Campaign in southeastern Virginia, Zeppelin was intrigued by the work of the Union Army Balloon Corps, which carried out aerial reconnaissance missions to ascertain Confederate troop strength and movements. Thanks to the work of a self-taught American inventor named Thaddeus S. C. Lowe, the Corps sent tethered, hydrogen-filled balloons aloft, and personnel aboard used telescopes to spy on the enemy. Lowe and Union Army officials would not permit Zeppelin to go up in one of the craft, so he traveled by steamboat to St. Paul, Minnesota, where a former Balloon Corps officer named John Steiner was giving demonstration rides. Zeppelin filed a formal report with his Prussian superiors on the usefulness of balloons in military reconnaissance.

Back in Germany, Zeppelin saw combat once again in the Austro-Prussian War of 1866, and was part of an ill-fated reconnaissance mission in the first hours of the Franco-Prussian War in 1870. He escaped then only by taking a French mount after his own horse was injured, and was promoted to colonel for his bravery. For the next 20 years, he held various positions in imperial Germany's tightly run, extremely advanced military apparatus, including commanding a fort. He retired in 1891 with the rank of brigadier general.

Built First Airship

Still fascinated by balloon aircraft, Zeppelin made another visit to the United States in 1869 for his own research purposes, and came up with his first design in 1874. Unlike other balloon-craft, his ship was a cylinder, not a sphere, and he came up with a novel way of preventing it from deflating upon descent—which happened because of the change in air pressure—by designing an aluminum frame that kept it rigid. It was covered on the outside by tightly stretched cotton over the frame. Inside that vast space were separate chambers for the hydrogen gas that provided the lift, and these chambers could be refilled individually if necessary. He set forth his intention in letters that were pleas to potential investors to fund his project. "I intend to build a vessel," he wrote, according to Frederic William Wile's *Men Around the Kaiser: The Makers of Modern Germany*, "which will be able to travel to places which cannot be approached—or only with great difficulty by other means of transport; to undiscovered coasts or interiors; in

a straight line across land and water where ships are to be sought for; from one fleet station or army to another, carrying persons or despatches; for observations of the movements of hostile fleets or armies, not for active participants in the operations of actual warfare."

Zeppelin obtained a patent for his dirigible, or steerable, airship design in 1895. A year later, he won a grant from the German Society of Engineers to help fund construction of a prototype at a property on the shores of Lake Konstanz. He also formed a company, contributing more than $100,000 of his own fortune, called Luftschiffbau-Zeppelin, or Zeppelin Airship Manufacturing. His first airship, named *LZ 1* or Luftschiff-Zeppelin 1, rose from a floating hangar on Lake Constance on July 2, 1900, carrying five people to a height of 1,300 feet for a nearly four-mile trip across the lake. Zeppelin's achievement attracted huge crowds, and there was tremendous interest in his subsequent demonstrations. This was more than three years before the Wright Brothers made the first powered airplane flight at Kitty Hawk, North Carolina.

Over the next few years Zeppelin made significant improvements in the design and engineering of his airships. There were two rudders that aided steering, and a pair of internal-combustion engines—also a relatively recent invention—provided by the Daimler firm in Stuttgart, the forerunner company of automaker Mercedes Benz. He secured additional funds through a state-run lottery in Württemberg, and finally German military officials began to show interest. In August of 1908, Zeppelin's *LZ4* attempted to fly for 24 hours straight without landing, which was a parameter set by German officials who were considering a major investment in his company. Engine trouble, however, forced Zeppelin and the airship to land near Echterdingen, near Stuttgart, and it broke free from its mooring during a thunderstorm with severe winds. The combustible hydrogen exploded, and the thousands of onlookers who had come out to see Zeppelin take off again saw instead German soldiers flying into the air as they tried to keep the craft tethered. "When the smoke had cleared away, it was found that the airship had been totally consumed," wrote the correspondent for the *Times* of London. "A more dramatic finish to these much-advertised experiments could scarcely be conceived."

Won Government Support

This setback did little to dampen enthusiasm for airships, however—either Zeppelin's or the public's. In sympathy, a National Zeppelin Fund was launched, and donations poured into its coffers. The German army bought his *LZ3*, renaming it the *Z1*, and the defense ministry commissioned a fleet and contributed $1.5 million for Zeppelin to construct a factory in Friedrichshafen on the shores of Lake Konstanz. Furthermore, Zeppelin was also awarded the Order of the Black Eagle from Kaiser Wilhelm, who hailed him as "the greatest German of the twentieth century," according to the book *Men Around the Kaiser*.

In the five years before World War I broke out, Zeppelin's airships carried adventure-seekers across Lake Konstanz and other sites on excursion rides. The Friedrichshafen works built about 130 of the craft, including the first one for the German Navy, which Zeppelin helmed in its maiden voyage over the North Sea. With the outbreak of war in 1914, the military-commissioned dirigibles were loaded with bombs and flown over Belgium and England in some of the first instances of aerial bombardment in the history of warfare; the bombs that dropped on the area of Great Yarmouth in Norfolk were the first to cause civilian casualties. These incidents caused a great deal of alarm among the public, and British authorities used the inimitable shape of the Zeppelin airship as a symbol of the enemy.

Despite the bombing incidents, Zeppelin's airships were ineffective for use in combat. Because they were slow-moving—reaching a top speed of about 80 miles per hour—they were easy targets for anti-aircraft weaponry. The fact that they were lumbering, easily seen orbs of a highly flammable gas was also a drawback, especially after British arms manufacturers developed a new type of exploding bullets to take them down. Zeppelin was reportedly not pleased with the German military's deployment of his aircraft, believing they were more ideally suited to reconnaissance missions. "I have one great ambition," he said in 1915, according to the *Times* of London, "and that is to connect Europe with America by an aerial route. I am an old man now, but I feel I must live for that....To go on a peaceful mission—to demonstrate that Zeppelins were made for other purposes besides warcraft."

Company Revived in the 1920s

The world was still at war on March 8, 1917, when Zeppelin died of pneumonia in Berlin at the age of 78. After the war's end, one of the terms of the 1919 Treaty of Versailles forbid the construction of any new aircraft—either the engine-powered type or the Zeppelin airships—in Germany. Zeppelin's successor at the company, Hugo Eckener, sought to keep the firm at the forefront of the technology despite that ban, and in 1924 piloted the first transatlantic voyage by an airship in order to deliver a new one to the U.S. military, which had commissioned it. Two immense civilian aircraft followed—the *Graf Zeppelin*, which made more than 600 transatlantic crossings after its launch in 1928, and the *Hindenburg*, which was the largest aircraft of any type when it went into service in 1936. Unfortunately the *Hindenburg* also became a byword for the dangers of dirigibles when it caught fire in Lakehurst, New Jersey, on May 6, 1937, killing 36 passengers and crew.

Zeppelin provided a generous endowment in his will for a foundation to be located in Friedrichshafen, which was charged with supporting research into dirigibles that would benefit humankind. The foundation played an instrumental role in the revival of the airship business in the 1980s, and a new company called ZLT, or Zeppelin Luftschifftechnik, launched a new fuel-efficient airship in 1997.

The British experiences with Zeppelin's airships gave rise to the phrase *like a lead Zeppelin,* meaning a balloon filled with the metal, not gas. In the late 1960s a new British rock band called Led Zeppelin emerged, and their name had been inspired by a quote from the drummer for The Who, Keith Moon, who reportedly remarked upon hearing that former Yardbirds guitarist Jimmy Page wanted to call the band The New Yardbirds that the name "would probably go over like a lead zeppelin," according to the online *Rolling Stone* interview. The way Zeppelin's name has become synonymous with the airships is only one indication of the way his legacy remains.

Books

"Count Zeppelin," in Frederic William Wile's *Men Around the Kaiser: The Makers of Modern Germany,* Bobbs Merrill, 1914, pp. 54–62.

Maslaniec, Kyla, "Ferdinand Adolf August Heinrich, Graf von Zeppelin," *Science and Its Times,* edited by Neil Schlager and Josh Lauer, Volume 6: *1900 to 1949,* Gale, 2000, pp. 602-603.

"Zeppelin, Count Ferdinand," in *Information Annual 1915: A Continuous Cyclopedia and Digest of Current Events,* R.R. Bowker, 1916, pp. 660–661.

Periodicals

International Herald Tribune, August 5, 2008, p. 3.

Times (London, England), August 6, 1908, p. 3; March 9, 1917, p. 7; July 8, 1938, p. 7.

Online

"The Long Shadow of Led Zeppelin," *Rolling Stone,* http://www.rollingstone.com/news/coverstory/long_shadow_of_led_zeppelin, (January 31, 2009). □

HOW TO USE THE *SUPPLEMENT* INDEX

The *Encyclopedia of World Biography Supplement (EWB)* Index is designed to serve several purposes. First, it is a cumulative listing of biographies included in the entire second edition of *EWB* and its supplements (volumes 1-29). Second, it locates information on specific topics mentioned in volume 29 of the encyclopedia—persons, places, events, organizations, institutions, ideas, titles of works, inventions, as well as artistic schools, styles, and movements. Third, it classifies the subjects of *Supplement* articles according to shared characteristics. Vocational categories are the most numerous—for example, artists, authors, military leaders, philosophers, scientists, statesmen. Other groupings bring together disparate people who share a common characteristic.

The structure of the *Supplement* Index is quite simple. The biographical entries are cumulative and often provide enough information to meet immediate reference needs. Thus, people mentioned in the *Supplement* Index are identified and their life dates, when known, are given. Because this is an index to a *biographical* encyclopedia, every reference includes the *name* of the article to which the reader is directed as well as the volume and page numbers. Below are a few points that will make the *Supplement* Index easy to use.

Typography. All main entries are set in boldface type. Entries that are also the titles of articles in *EWB* are set entirely in capitals; other main entries are set in initial capitals and lowercase letters. Where a main entry is followed by a great many references, these are organized by subentries in alphabetical sequence. In certain cases—for example, the names of countries for which there are many references—a special class of subentries, set in small capitals and preceded by boldface dots, is used to mark significant divisions.

Alphabetization. The Index is alphabetized word by word. For example, all entries beginning with *New* as a separate word *(New Jersey, New York)* come before

Newark. Commas in inverted entries are treated as full stops *(Berlin; Berlin, Congress of; Berlin, University of; Berlin Academy of Sciences).* Other commas are ignored in filing. When words are identical, persons come first and subsequent entries are alphabetized by their parenthetical qualifiers (such as *book, city, painting).*

Titled persons may be alphabetized by family name or by title. The more familiar form is used—for example, *Disraeli, Benjamin* rather than *Beaconsfield, Earl of.* Cross-references are provided from alternative forms and spellings of names. Identical names of the same nationality are filed chronologically.

Titles of books, plays, poems, paintings, and other works of art beginning with an article are filed on the following word *(Bard, The).* Titles beginning with a preposition are filed on the preposition *(In Autumn).* In subentries, however, prepositions are ignored; thus *influenced by* would precede the subentry *in* literature.

Literary characters are filed on the last name. Acronyms, such as UNESCO, are treated as single words. Abbreviations, such as *Mr., Mrs.,* and *St.,* are alphabetized as though they were spelled out.

Occupational categories are alphabetical by national qualifier. Thus, *Authors, Scottish* comes before *Authors, Spanish,* and the reader interested in Spanish poets will find the subentry *poets* under *Authors, Spanish.*

Cross-references. The term *see* is used in references throughout the *Supplement* Index. The *see* references appear both as main entries and as subentries. They most often direct the reader from an alternative name spelling or form to the main entry listing.

This introduction to the *Supplement* Index is necessarily brief. The reader will soon find, however, that the *Supplement* Index provides ready reference to both highly specific subjects and broad areas of information contained in volume 29 and a cumulative listing of those included in the entire set.

INDEX

A

"A"
see Arnold, Matthew

"A.B."
see Pinto, Isaac

AALTO, HUGO ALVAR HENRIK (born 1898), Finnish architect, designer, and town planner **1** 1-2

AARON, HENRY LOUIS (Hank; born 1934), American baseball player **1** 2-3

ABAKANOWICZ, MAGDALENA (Marta Abakanowicz-Kosmowski; born 1930), Polish sculptor **25** 1-3

Abarbanel
see Abravanel

ABBA ARIKA (c. 175-c. 247), Babylonian rabbi **1** 3-4

ABBAS I (1571-1629), Safavid shah of Persia 1588-1629 **1** 4-6

ABBAS, FERHAT (born 1899), Algerian statesman **1** 6-7

ABBAS, MAHMOUD (Abu Masen; born 1935), Palestinian statesman **27** 1-3

Abbas the Great
see Abbas I

Abbé Sieyès
see Sieyès, Comte Emmanuel Joseph

ABBEY, EDWARD (Edward Paul Abbey; 1927-1989), American author and environmental activist **27** 3-5

ABBOTT, BERENICE (1898-1991), American artist and photographer **1** 7-9

ABBOTT, DIANE JULIE (born 1953), British politician and journalist **26** 1-3

ABBOTT, EDITH (1876-1957), American social reformer, educator, and author **26** 3-5

ABBOTT, GRACE (1878-1939), American social worker and agency administrator **1** 9-10

ABBOTT, LYMAN (1835-1922), American Congregationalist clergyman, author, and editor **1** 10-11

ABBOUD, EL FERIK IBRAHIM (1900-1983), Sudanese general, prime minister, 1958-1964 **1** 11-12

ABC
see American Broadcasting Company (United States)

ABD AL-MALIK (646-705), Umayyad caliph 685-705 **1** 12-13

ABD AL-MUMIN (c. 1094-1163), Almohad caliph 1133-63 **1** 13

ABD AL-RAHMAN I (731-788), Umayyad emir in Spain 756-88 **1** 13-14

Abd al-Rahman ibn Khaldun
see Ibn Khaldun, Abd al-Rahman ibn Muhammad

ABD AL-RAHMAN III (891-961), Umayyad caliph of Spain **1** 14

ABD AL-WAHHAB, MUHAMMAD IBN (Muhammad Ibn Abd al-Wahab; 1702-1703-1791-1792), Saudi religious leader **27** 5-7

ABD EL-KADIR (1807-1883), Algerian political and religious leader **1** 15

ABD EL-KRIM EL-KHATABI, MOHAMED BEN (c. 1882-1963), Moroccan Berber leader **1** 15-16

Abdallah ben Yassin
see Abdullah ibn Yasin

ABDELLAH, FAYE GLENN (born 1919), American nurse **24** 1-3

ABDUH IBN HASAN KHAYR ALLAH, MUHAMMAD (1849-1905), Egyptian nationalist and theologian **1** 16-17

Abdu-l-Malik
see Abd al-Malik

ABDUL RAHMAN, TUNKU (1903-1990), Former prime minister of Malaysia **18** 340-341

ABDUL-BAHA (Abbas Effendi; 1844-1921), Persian leader of the Baha'i Muslim sect **22** 3-5

ABDUL-HAMID II (1842-1918), Ottoman sultan 1876-1909 **1** 17-18

ABDULLAH II (Abdullah bin al Hussein II; born 1962), king of Jordan **22** 5-7

'ABDULLAH AL-SALIM AL-SABAH, SHAYKH (1895-1965), Amir of Kuwait (1950-1965) **1** 18-19

ABDULLAH IBN HUSEIN (1882-1951), king of Jordan 1949-1951, of Transjordan 1946-49 **1** 19-20

ABDULLAH IBN YASIN (died 1059), North African founder of the Almoravid movement **1** 20

ABDULLAH, MOHAMMAD (Lion of Kashmir; 1905-1982), Indian political leader who worked for an independent Kashmir **22** 7-9

Abdul the Damned
see Abdul-Hamid II

ABE, KOBO (born Kimifusa Abe; also transliterated as Abe Kobo; 1924-1993), Japanese writer, theater director, photographer **1** 20-22

ABE, SHINZO (born 1954), Japanese prime minister **28** 1-3

ABEL, IORWITH WILBER (1908-1987), United States labor organizer **1** 22-23

ABEL, NIELS (1802-1829), Norwegian mathematician **20** 1-2

ABELARD, PETER (1079-1142), French philosopher and theologian **1** 23-25

ABERCROMBY, RALPH (1734-1801), British military leader **20** 2-4

ABERDEEN, 4TH EARL OF (George Hamilton Gordon; 1784-1860),

393

Air pioneers
see Aviators

Air pressure (physics)
Amontons, Guillaume **29** 3-5

Aircraft (aeronautics)
instrumentation
Bowen, Edward George **29** 84-86
manufacturers
Martin, Glenn L. **29** 265-267

Airplane-crash victims
Lombard, Carole **29** 249-251

AITKEN, WILLIAM MAXWELL (Lord
Beaverbrook; 1879-1964), Canadian
businessman and politician **1** 94-96

AKBAR, JALAL-UD-DIN MOHAMMED
(1542-1605), Mogul emperor of India
1556-1605 **1** 96

AKHENATEN (Amenhotep IV; c. 1385-c.
1350 B.C.), Egyptian pharaoh and
religious leader **25** 5-7

AKHMATOVA, ANNA (pseudonym of
Anna A. Gorenko, 1889-1966), Russian
poet **1** 96-97

AKIBA BEN JOSEPH (c. 50-c. 135),
Palestinian founder of rabbinic Judaism
1 97-98

AKIHITO (born 1933), 125th emperor of
Japan **1** 98-99

AKIYOSHI, TOSHIKO (born 1929),
Japanese musician **24** 10-12

AKUTAGAWA, RYUNOSUKE (Ryunosuke
Niihara; 1892-1927), Japanese author
22 13-14

Al Qaeda (Islamic terrorist group)
Wilson, Charlie **29** 379-381

Alabama (state, United States)
Wallace, Lurleen Burns **29**
370-372

AL-ABDULLAH, RANIA (Rania al-Yasin;
born 1970), Queen Rania of Jordan **25**
8-10

ALAMÁN, LUCAS (1792-1853), Mexican
statesman **1** 99-100

Alamein, 1st Viscount Montgomery of
see Montgomery, Bernard Law

Alaminos, Antonio (flourished 16th
century), Spanish explorer
Córdoba, Francisco Hernández de
29 126-128

Al-Andalus
see Andalusia (region, Spain)

Alanine (amino acid)
Holley, Robert W. **29** 191-193

ALARCÓN, PEDRO ANTONIO DE
(1833-1891), Spanish writer and
politician **1** 100-101

ALARCÓN Y MENDOZA, JUAN RUIZ DE
(c. 1581-1639), Spanish playwright **1** 101

ALARIC (c. 370-410), Visigothic leader **1**
101-102

Alau
see Hulagu Khan

ALA-UD-DIN (died 1316), Khalji sultan of
Delhi **1** 102-103

ALAUNGPAYA (1715-1760), king of
Burma 1752-1760 **1** 103

AL AQQAD, ABBAS MAHMOUD (Abbas
Mahmud al Aqqad; 1889-1964),
Egyptian author **24** 25-27

ALBA, DUKE OF (Fernando Álvarez de
Toledo; 1507-1582), Spanish general
and statesman **1** 103-104

AL-BANNA, HASSAN (1906-1949),
Egyptian religious leader and founder of
the Muslim Brotherhood **1** 104-106

Albategnius
see Battani, al-

AL-BATTANI (Abu abdallah Muhammad
ibn Jabir ibn Sinan al-Raqqi al Harrani
al-Sabi al-Battani; c. 858-929), Arab
astronomer and mathematician **25**
10-12

ALBEE, EDWARD FRANKLIN, III (born
1928), American playwright **1** 106-108

Albemarle, Dukes of
see Monck, George

ALBÉNIZ, ISAAC (1860-1909), Spanish
composer and pianist **1** 108-109

ALBERDI, JUAN BAUTISTA (1810-1884),
Argentine political theorist **1** 109-110

ALBERS, JOSEPH (1888-1976), American
artist and art and design teacher **1** 110

ALBERT (1819-1861), Prince Consort of
Great Britain **1** 110-112

ALBERT I (1875-1934), king of the Belgians
1909-1934 **1** 112

ALBERT II (born 1934), sixth king of the
Belgians **1** 112-113

Albert the Great
see Albertus Magnus, St.

Alberta, University of
Collip, James Bertram **29** 121-123

ALBERTI, LEON BATTISTA (1404-1472),
Italian writer, humanist, and architect **1**
113-115

ALBERTI, RAFAEL (born 1902), Spanish
poet and painter **18** 13-15

ALBERTUS MAGNUS, ST. (c. 1193-1280),
German philosopher and theologian **1**
115-116

ALBRIGHT, MADELEINE KORBEL (born
1937), United States secretary of state **1**
116-118

ALBRIGHT, TENLEY EMMA (born 1935),
American figure skater **23** 3-6

ALBRIGHT, WILLIAM (1891-1971),
American archaeologist **21** 1-3

ALBUQUERQUE, AFONSO DE (c.
1460-1515), Portuguese viceroy to India
1 118-119

Alcántara, Pedro de
see Pedro II

Alchemists
see Scientists, Arab

ALCIBIADES (c. 450-404 B.C.), Athenian
general and politician **1** 119-120

ALCORN, JAMES LUSK (1816-1894),
American lawyer and politician **1**
120-121

ALCOTT, AMOS BRONSON (1799-1888),
American educator **1** 121

ALCOTT, LOUISA MAY (1832-1888),
American author and reformer **1** 122

ALCUIN OF YORK (730?-804), English
educator, statesman, and liturgist **1**
122-123

ALDRICH, NELSON WILMARTH
(1841-1915), American statesman and
financier **1** 123-124

Aldrin, Buzz
see Aldrin, Edwin Eugene, Jr.

ALDRIN, EDWIN EUGENE, JR. (Buzz
Aldrin; born 1930), American astronaut
18 15-17

ALDUS MANUTIUS (Teobaldo Manuzio;
1450?-1515), Italian scholar and printer
21 3-5

ALEICHEM, SHOLOM (Sholom
Rabinowitz; 1859-1916), writer of
literature relating to Russian Jews **1**
124-125

ALEIJADINHO, O (Antônio Francisco
Lisbôa; 1738-1814), Brazilian architect
and sculptor **1** 125-126

ALEMÁN, MATEO (1547-after 1615),
Spanish novelist **1** 126

ALEMÁN VALDÉS, MIGUEL (1902-1983),
Mexican statesman, president
1946-1952 **1** 126-127

ALEMBERT, JEAN LE ROND D'
(1717-1783), French mathematician and
physicist **1** 127-128

ALESSANDRI PALMA, ARTURO
(1868-1950), Chilean statesman,
president 1920-1925 and 1932-1938 **1**
128-129

ALESSANDRI RODRIGUEZ, JORGE (born
1896), Chilean statesman, president
1958-1964 **1** 129-130

AMORY, CLEVELAND (1917-1998), American author and animal rights activist **26** 14-16

AMOS (flourished 8th century B.C.), Biblical prophet **1** 205

AMPÈRE, ANDRÉ MARIE (1775-1836), French physicist **1** 205-206
Ampère, Jean-Jacques **29** 5-7

AMPÈRE, JEAN-JACQUES (1800-1864), French essayist **29** 5-7

AMUNDSEN, ROALD (1872-1928), Norwegian explorer **1** 206-207
Parry, Sir William Edward **29** 311-313
Scott, Sir Peter Markham **29** 339-341

AN LU-SHAN (703-757), Chinese rebel leader **1** 239-240

ANACLETUS II (c. 1090-1138), antipope 1130-1138 **29** 7-9

ANACREON (c. 570-c. 490 B.C.E.), Greek lyric poet **29** 9-11

Anacreontea (poems)
Anacreon **29** 9-11

ANAN BEN DAVID (flourished 8th century), Jewish Karaite leader in Babylonia **1** 207-208

Anatomia mundini (Mondino's Anatomy; book)
Falloppio, Gabriele **29** 157-159

Anatomy (science)
cranial
Falloppio, Gabriele **29** 157-159
educators
Hunter, John **29** 202-204
reproductive
Falloppio, Gabriele **29** 157-159

ANAXAGORAS (c. 500-c. 428 B.C.), Greek philosopher **1** 208-209

ANAXIMANDER (c. 610-c. 546 B.C.), Greek philosopher and astronomer **1** 209-210

ANAXIMENES (flourished 546 B.C.), Greek philosopher **1** 210

ANAYA, RUDOLFO ALFONSO (born 1937), Chicano American author **27** 17-19

ANC
see African National Congress (ANC)

ANCHIETA, JOSÉ DE (1534-1597), Portuguese Jesuit missionary **1** 210-211

Andalusia (region, Spain)
ibn Bajja, Abu Bakr Muhhamad **29** 207-209

ANDERSEN, DOROTHY (1901-1963), American physician and pathologist **1** 212

ANDERSEN, HANS CHRISTIAN (1805-1875), Danish author **1** 212-214

ANDERSON, CARL DAVID (1905-1991), American physicist **1** 214-215

ANDERSON, IVIE MARIE (Ivy Marie Anderson; 1905-1949), African-American singer **28** 10-12

ANDERSON, JUDITH (1898-1992), American stage and film actress **1** 215-216

ANDERSON, JUNE (born 1953), American opera singer **1** 216-218

ANDERSON, MARIAN (1902-1993), African American singer **1** 218-219

ANDERSON, MAXWELL (1888-1959), American playwright **1** 219-220

ANDERSON, SHERWOOD (1876-1941), American writer **1** 220-221

ANDO, TADAO (born 1941), Japanese architect **18** 17-19

ANDRADA E SILVA, JOSÉ BONIFÁCIO DE (1763-1838), Brazilian-born statesman and scientist **1** 221-222

ANDRÁSSY, COUNT JULIUS (1823-1890), Hungarian statesman, prime minister 1867-1871 **1** 222-223

Andrea da Pontedera
see Andrea Pisano

ANDREA DEL CASTAGNO (1421-1457), Italian painter **1** 223-224

ANDREA DEL SARTO (1486-1530), Italian painter **1** 224-225

ANDREA PISANO (c. 1290/95-1348), Italian sculptor and architect **1** 225-226

ANDREAS-SALOMÉ, LOU (Louise Salomé; 1861-1937), Russian-born German author and feminist **28** 12-14

ANDRÉE, SALOMON AUGUST (1854-1897), Swedish engineer and Arctic balloonist **1** 226

ANDREESSEN, MARC (born 1972), American computer programmer who developed Netscape Navigator **19** 3-5

Andreino
see Andrea del Sarto

ANDREOTTI, GIULIO (born 1919), leader of Italy's Christian Democratic party **1** 226-228

ANDRETTI, MARIO (born 1940), Italian/American race car driver **1** 228-230

ANDREW, JOHN ALBION (1818-1867), American politician **1** 230-231

ANDREWS, BENNY (1930-2006), African American artists **25** 23-25

ANDREWS, CHARLES MCLEAN (1863-1943), American historian **1** 231

ANDREWS, FANNIE FERN PHILLIPS (1867-1950), American educator, reformer, pacifist **1** 231-232

ANDREWS, JULIE (Julie Edwards; born 1935), British singer, actress, and author **25** 25-28

ANDREWS, ROY CHAPMAN (1884-1960), American naturalist and explorer **1** 232-233

ANDREYEV, LEONID NIKOLAYEVICH (1871-1919), Russian author **29** 11-13

ANDRIĆ, IVO (1892-1975), Yugoslav author **24** 21-24

ANDROPOV, IURY VLADIMIROVICH (1914-1984), head of the Soviet secret police and ruler of the Soviet Union (1982-1984) **1** 233-234

ANDROS, SIR EDMUND (1637-1714), English colonial governor in America **1** 234-235

ANDRUS, ETHEL (1884-1976), American educator and founder of the American Association of Retired Persons **19** 5-7

Angel of the Crimea
see Nightingale, Florence

ANGELICO, FRA (c. 1400-1455), Italian painter **1** 235-236

ANGELL, JAMES ROWLAND (1869-1949), psychologist and leader in higher education **1** 236-237

Angelo de Cosimo
see Bronzino

ANGELOU, MAYA (Marguerite Johnson; born 1928), American author, poet, playwright, stage and screen performer, and director **1** 238-239

Anglican King's College
see Toronto, University of (Canada)

ANGUISSOLA, SOFONISBA (Sofonisba Anguisciola; c. 1535-1625), Italian artist **22** 22-24

Animal experimentation (medicine)
Hunter, John **29** 202-204

Anna Comnena
see Comnena, Anna

ANNA IVANOVNA (1693-1740), empress of Russia 1730-1740 **1** 240-241

ANNAN, KOFI (born 1938), Ghanaian secretary-general of the United Nations **18** 19-21

ANNE (1665-1714), queen of England 1702-1714 and of Great Britain 1707-1714 **1** 241-242

ANNE OF BRITTANY (1477-1514), queen of France 1491-1498 and 1499-1514 **29** 13-15

ANNE OF CLEVES (1515-1557), German princess and fourth wife of Henry VIII **27** 19-21

ANNENBERG, WALTER HUBERT (1908-2002), American publisher and philanthropist **26** 16-18

ANNING, MARY (1799-1847), British fossil collector **20** 14-16

Annunzio, Gabriele d'
see D'Annunzio, Gabriel

ANOKYE, OKOMFO (Kwame Frimpon Anokye; flourished late 17th century), Ashanti priest and statesman **1** 242-243

ANOUILH, JEAN (1910-1987), French playwright **1** 243-244

ANSELM OF CANTERBURY, ST. (1033-1109), Italian archbishop and theologian **1** 244-245

Anson, Charles Edward
see Markham, Edwin

Anthoniszoon, Jeroen
see Bosch, Hieronymus

Anthony, Mark
see Antony, Mark

Anthony, Peter
see Shaffer, Peter Levin

ANTHONY, ST. (c. 250-356), Egyptian hermit and monastic founder **1** 246-248

ANTHONY, SUSAN BROWNELL (1820-1906), American leader of suffrage movement **1** 246-248

Anthony Abbott, St.
see Anthony, St.

Anthony of Egypt, St.
see Anthony, St.

ANTHONY OF PADUA, SAINT (Fernando de Boullion; 1195-1231), Portuguese theologian and priest **21** 7-9

Anthrax bacillus (bacteriology)
Kitasato, Shibasabura **29** 230-232

Anthropology (social science)
North African societies
Tillion, Germaine **29** 358-360

Antibiotics (medicine)
Merck, George Wilhelm **29** 279-281

ANTIGONUS I (382-301 B.C.), king of Macedon 306-301 B.C. **1** 248-249

ANTIOCHUS III (241-187 B.C.), king of Syria 223-187 B.C. **1** 249-250

ANTIOCHUS IV (c. 215-163 B.C.), king of Syria 175-163 B.C. **1** 250

Antiochus the Great
see Antiochus III

Anti-Semitism
Italy
Anacletus II **29** 7-9

ANTISTHENES (c. 450-360 B.C.), Greek philosopher **1** 250-251

Antitoxins (medicine)
Kitasato, Shibasabura **29** 230-232

ANTONELLO DA MESSINA (c. 1430-1479), Italian painter **1** 251-252

Antoninus, Marcus Aurelius
see Caracalla

Antonio, Donato di Pascuccio d'
see Bramante, Donato

ANTONIONI, MICHELANGELO (1912-2007), Italian film director **1** 252-253

Antonius, Marcus
see Antony, Mark

ANTONY, MARK (c. 82-30 B.C.), Roman politician and general **1** 253-254

Anushervan the Just
see Khosrow I

Any Old Place with You (song)
Hart, Lorenz **29** 184-186

ANZA, JUAN BAUTISTA DE (1735-1788), Spanish explorer **1** 254-255

AOUN, MICHEL (born 1935), Christian Lebanese military leader and prime minister **1** 255-257

Apache Indians (North America)
Hooker, Henry Clay **29** 193-195

Apache Napoleon
see Cochise

APELLES (flourished after 350 B.C.), Greek painter **1** 257

APESS, WILLIAM (1798-1839), Native American religious leader, author, and activist **20** 16-18

APGAR, VIRGINIA (1909-1974), American medical educator, researcher **1** 257-259

APITHY, SOUROU MIGAN (1913-1989), Dahomean political leader **1** 259-260

APOLLINAIRE, GUILLAUME (1880-1918), French lyric poet **1** 260

Apollo program (United States)
Stuhlinger, Ernst **29** 349-351

APOLLODORUS (flourished c. 408 B.C.), Greek painter **1** 261

APOLLONIUS OF PERGA (flourished 210 B.C.), Greek mathematician **1** 261-262

Apostate, the
see Julian

APPELFELD, AHARON (born 1932), Israeli who wrote about anti-Semitism and the Holocaust **1** 262-263

APPERT, NICOLAS (1749-1941), French chef and inventor of canning of foods **20** 18-19

APPIA, ADOLPHE (1862-1928), Swiss stage director **1** 263-264

APPLEBEE, CONSTANCE (1873-1981), American field hockey coach **24** 24-25

APPLEGATE, JESSE (1811-1888), American surveyor, pioneer, and rancher **1** 264-265

APPLETON, SIR EDWARD VICTOR (1892-1965), British pioneer in radio physics **1** 265-266

APPLETON, NATHAN (1779-1861), American merchant and manufacturer **1** 266-267

APULEIUS, LUCIUS (c. 124-170), Roman author, philosopher, and orator **20** 19-21

Apulia, Robert Guiscard, Count and Duke of
see Guiscard, Robert

Aquinas, St. Thomas
see Thomas Aquinas, St.

AQUINO, BENIGNO ("Nino"; 1933-1983), Filipino activist murdered upon his return from exile **1** 267-268

AQUINO, CORAZON COJOANGCO (born 1933), first woman president of the Republic of the Philippines **1** 268-270

ARAFAT, YASSER (also spelled Yasir; 1929-2004), chairman of the Palestinian Liberation Organization **1** 270-271

ARAGON, LOUIS (1897-1982), French surrealist author **1** 271-272
Triolet, Elsa **29** 364-366

ARAKIDA MORITAKE (1473-1549), Japanese poet **29** 287-288

Arango, Doroteo
see Villa, Pancho

ARANHA, OSVALDO (1894-1960), Brazilian political leader **1** 272-273

ARATUS (271-213 B.C.), Greek statesman and general **1** 273-274

ARBENZ GUZMÁN, JACOBO (1913-1971), president of Guatemala (1951-1954) **1** 274-276

ARBER, AGNES ROBERTSON (nee Agnes Robertson; 1879-1960), English botanist **28** 14-16

Arblay, Madame d'
see Burney, Frances "Fanny"

ARBUS, DIANE NEMEROV (1923-1971), American photographer **1** 276-277

ARCARO, EDDIE (George Edward Arcaro; 1916-1997), American jockey **27** 21-23

football players
Berry, Raymond **29** 57-59
race car drivers
Guthrie, Janet **29** 178-181

ATKINS, CHET (Chester Burton Atkins; 1924-2000), American musician **22** 28-30

ATKINS, VERA (Vera Maria [May] Rosenberg; 1908-2000), English intelligence agent **28** 16-18

ATKINSON, LOUISA (Louisa Warning Atkinson; 1834-1872), Australian author **22** 30-33

Atlantic cable (communications)
Bright, Charles Tilston **29** 91-93

Atlantic Telegraph Company
Bright, Charles Tilston **29** 91-93

ATLAS, CHARLES (Angelo Siciliano; 1893-1972), American body builder **21** 14-15

Atom (physics)
radioactivity
Barkla, Charles Glover **29** 46-48

Atomic bomb (weapon)
espionage
Berg, Moe **29** 50-52

Atomic energy, peaceful use of
see United Nations–atomic energy

Atonality (music)
Hovhaness, Alan **29** 197-199

ATTAR, FARID ED-DIN (c. 1140-c. 1234), Persian poet **1** 359-360

ATTENBOROUGH, RICHARD SAMUEL (born 1923), English actor and filmmaker **18** 21-23

Attic Bee
see Sophocles

ATTILA (died 453), Hun chieftain **1** 360

ATTLEE, CLEMENT RICHARD (1st Earl Attlee; 1883-1967), English statesman, prime minister 1945-1951 **1** 361-362

Attorneys general
see statesmen, American

ATWOOD, MARGARET ELEANOR (born 1939), Canadian novelist, poet, critic, and politically committed cultural activist **1** 362-364

AUBERT DE GASPÉ, PHILIPPE (1786-1871), French-Canadian author **1** 364

AUDEN, WYSTAN HUGH (1907-1973), English-born American poet **1** 364-366

AUDUBON, JOHN JAMES (1785-1851), American artist and ornithologist **1** 366-367

AUER, LEOPOLD (1845-1930), Hungarian violinist and conductor **20** 22-24

AUERBACH, RED (Arnold Red Auerbach; Arnold Jacob Auerbach; 1917-2006), American Basketball coach **27** 25-28

AUGIER, ÉMILE (1820-1889), French dramatist and poet **29** 20-22

AUGUSTINE, ST. (354-430), Christian philosopher and theologian **1** 367-370
influence of
Baius, Michael **29** 31-33

AUGUSTINE OF CANTERBURY, ST. (died c. 606), Roman monk, archbishop of Canterbury **1** 370-371

Augustine of Hippo
see Augustine, St.

AUGUSTUS (Octavian; 63 B.C.-A.D. 14), Roman emperor 27 B.C.-A.D. 14 **1** 371-373

AUGUSTUS II (1670-1733), king of Poland and elector of Saxony **1** 373-374

Augustus the Strong
see Augustus II, (1696-1763)

AULARD, ALPHONSE FRANÇOIS VICTOR ALPHONSE (1849-1928), French historian **1** 374

Aulnay, Seigneur d'
see Charnisay

AUNG SAN (1915-1947), Burmese politician **1** 374-375

AUNG SAN SUU KYI (born 1945), leader of movement toward democracy in Burma (Myanmar) and Nobel Peace Prize winner **1** 375-376

Aung Zeya
see Alaungpaya

AURANGZEB (1618-1707), Mogul emperor of India 1658-1707 **1** 377

AUSTEN, JANE (1775-1817), English novelist **1** 377-379

AUSTIN, JOHN (1790-1859), English jurist and author **22** 33-35

AUSTIN, JOHN LANGSHAW (1911-1960), English philosopher **1** 379-380

AUSTIN, MARY HUNTER (1868-1934), American author **23** 23-25

AUSTIN, MOSES (1761-1821), American pioneer **29** 22-24

AUSTIN, STEPHEN FULLER (1793-1836), American pioneer **1** 380-381
Austin, Moses **29** 22-24

Australia, Commonwealth of (island continent)
British colonization of
Kelly, Ned **29** 226-228

Austria-Hungary (former kingdom, Central Europe)
nationality issue
Franz Ferdinand **29** 162-164

Austrian Succession, War of (1740-1748)
British forces
Gates, Horatio **29** 169-172

Authors, American
autobiographies
Massaquoi, Hans J. **29** 270-272
biographers (20th century)
Bernstein, Carl **29** 52-54
playwrights (20th century)
Baker, George Pierce **29** 33-35
poets (19th-20th century)
Todd, Mabel Loomis **29** 360-362

Authors, Czech
Brod, Max **29** 95-97

Authors, English
novelists (20th century)
Howard, Elizabeth Jane **29** 200-202
Sayers, Dorothy L. **29** 335-337
religious writers (19th-20th centuries)
Sayers, Dorothy L. **29** 335-337
translators
Sayers, Dorothy L. **29** 335-337

Authors, French
essayists (11th-15th century)
Bourignon, Antoinette **29** 80-83
letters (correspondence)
Sévigné, Marie de **29** 263-265
novelists (16th-17th century)
Scudéry, Madeleine de **29** 341-343
novelists (20th century)
Triolet, Elsa **29** 364-366
playwrights (19th century)
Augier, Émile **29** 20-22
poets (19th century)
Colet, Louise **29** 119-121
religious writings
Bourignon, Antoinette **29** 80-83

Authors, German
lexicographers
Erman, Adolf **29** 154-156

Authors, Greek (ancient)
poets
Anacreon **29** 9-11

Authors, Irish
nonfiction writers
O'Faolain, Nuala **29** 294-296
novelists
O'Faolain, Nuala **29** 294-296

Authors, Italian
poets (16th century)
Aretino, Pietro **29** 16-18
satirists
Aretino, Pietro **29** 16-18

Authors, Japanese
poets
Arakida Moritake **29** 287-288

Authors, Jewish
Brod, Max **29** 95-97

Authors, Russian
biographers
Lenz, Wilhelm von **29** 243-245
critics
Andreyev, Leonid Nikolayevich **29** 11-13

BACON, FRANCIS (1909-1992), English artist **1** 421-422

BACON, NATHANIEL (1647-1676), American colonial leader **1** 424-425

BACON, PEGGY (Margaret Francis Bacon; 1895-1987), American artist and author **25** 29-31

BACON, ROGER (c. 1214-1294), English philosopher **1** 425-427

Bacteria (microorganisms)
d'Hérelle, Félix Hubert **29** 140-142

Bacteriology (science)
foundations
d'Hérelle, Félix Hubert **29** 140-142
Kitasato, Shibasabura **29** 230-232
penicillin
Tatum, Edward Lawrie **29** 356-358

Bacteriophage (bacteriology)
d'Hérelle, Félix Hubert **29** 140-142

Bad Hand
see Fitzpatrick, Thomas

BAD HEART BULL, AMOS (1869-1913), Oglala Lakota Sioux tribal historian and artist **1** 427-428

Badajoz, battle of (1812)
Azara, José Nicolás de **29** 24-26

BADEN-POWELL, ROBERT (1857-1941), English military officer and founder of the Boy Scout Association **21** 16-18

BADINGS, HENK (Hendrik Herman Badings; 1907-1987), Dutch composer **23** 26-28

Badische Anilin und Soda Fabrik (BASF; German company)
Bosch, Carl **29** 76-78

BADOGLIO, PIETRO (1871-1956), Italian general and statesman **1** 428-429

BAECK, LEO (1873-1956), rabbi, teacher, hero of the concentration camps, and Jewish leader **1** 429-430

BAEKELAND, LEO HENDRIK (1863-1944), American chemist **1** 430-431

BAER, GEORGE FREDERICK (1842-1914), American businessman **22** 39-41

BAER, KARL ERNST VON (1792-1876), Estonian anatomist and embryologist **1** 431-432

BAEZ, BUENAVENTURA (1812-1884), Dominican statesman, five time president **1** 432-433

BAEZ, JOAN (born 1941), American folk singer and human rights activist **1** 433-435

Baffin Island (Baffin Land; Arctic Ocean)
Parry, Sir William Edward **29** 311-313

BAFFIN, WILLIAM (c. 1584-1622), English navigator and explorer **1** 435-436

BAGEHOT, WALTER (1826-1877), English economist **1** 436-437

BAGLEY, WILLIAM CHANDLER (1874-1946), educator and theorist of educational "essentialism" **1** 437-438

BAHÁ'U'LLÁH (Husayn-'Ali', Bahá'u'lláh Mírzá; 1817-1982), Iranian religious leader **28** 21-23

BAHR, EGON (born 1922), West German politician **1** 438-440

Baianism
Baius, Michael **29** 31-33

BAIKIE, WILLIAM BALFOUR (1825-1864), Scottish explorer and scientist **1** 440

BAILEY, F. LEE (born 1933), American defense attorney and author **1** 441-443

BAILEY, FLORENCE MERRIAM (1863-1948), American ornithologist and author **1** 443-444

BAILEY, GAMALIEL (1807-1859), American editor and politician **1** 444-445

BAILEY, MILDRED (Mildred Rinker, 1907-1951), American jazz singer **23** 28-30

BAILLIE, D(ONALD) M(ACPHERSON) (1887-1954), Scottish theologian **1** 445

BAILLIE, ISOBEL (Isabella Baillie; 1895-1983), British singer **26** 27-29

BAILLIE, JOANNA (1762-1851), Scottish playwright and poet **28** 23-25

BAILLIE, JOHN (1886-1960), Scottish theologian and ecumenical churchman **1** 445-447

BAIUS, MICHAEL (1513-1589), Belgian theologian **29** 31-33

BAKER, ELLA JOSEPHINE (1903-1986), African American human and civil rights activist **18** 26-28

BAKER, GEORGE PIERCE (1866-1935), American educator **29** 33-35

BAKER, HOWARD HENRY, JR. (born 1925), U.S. senator and White House chief of staff **18** 28-30

BAKER, JAMES ADDISON III (born 1930), Republican party campaign leader **1** 447-448

BAKER, JOSEPHINE (1906-1975), Parisian dancer and singer from America **1** 448-451

BAKER, NEWTON DIEHL (1871-1937), American statesman **1** 451

BAKER, RAY STANNARD (1870-1946), American author **1** 451-452

BAKER, RUSSELL (born 1925), American writer of personal-political essays **1** 452-454

BAKER, SIR SAMUEL WHITE (1821-1893), English explorer and administrator **1** 454-455

BAKER, SARA JOSEPHINE (1873-1945), American physician **1** 455-456

BAKHTIN, MIKHAIL MIKHAILOVICH (1895-1975), Russian philosopher and literary critic **1** 456-458

BAKST, LEON (1866-1924), Russian painter **29** 35-37

Bakufu (shogun military government)
see Japan–1185-1867

BAKUNIN, MIKHAIL ALEKSANDROVICH (1814-1876), Russian anarchist **1** 458-460

BALAGUER Y RICARDO, JOAQUÍN (1907-2002), Dominican statesman **1** 460-461

BALANCHINE, GEORGE (1904-1983), Russian-born American choreographer **1** 461-462

Balanchivadze, Georgi Melitonovitch
see Balanchine, George

BALBO, ITALO (1896-1940), Italian air marshal **29** 37-39

BALBOA, VASCO NÚÑEZ DE (c. 1475-1519), Spanish explorer **1** 462-463

BALBULUS, NOTKER (c. 840-912), Swiss poet-musician and monk **11** 434-435

BALCH, EMILY GREENE (1867-1961), American pacifist and social reformer **1** 463-464

BALDOMIR, ALFREDO (884-1948), Uruguayan president 1938-1943 **29** 39-41

BALDWIN I (1058-1118), Norman king of Jerusalem 1100-1118 **1** 464-465

BALDWIN, JAMES ARTHUR (1924-1987), African American author, poet, and dramatist **1** 465-466

BALDWIN, ROBERT (1804-1858), Canadian politician **1** 466-468

BALDWIN, ROGER NASH (1884-1981), American civil libertarian and social worker **25** 31-33

BALDWIN, STANLEY (1st Earl Baldwin of Bewdley; 1867-1947), English statesman, three times prime minister **1** 468-469

Baldwin of Bewdley, 1st Earl
see Baldwin, Stanley

Baldwin of Boulogne
see Baldwin I, king

Bassianus
see Caracalla

BATES, DAISY MAE (née O'Dwyer; 1861-1951), Irish-born Australian social worker **2** 52-53

BATES, HENRY WALTER (1825-1892), English explorer and naturalist **2** 53-54

BATES, KATHARINE LEE (1859-1929), American poet and educator **2** 54-55

BATESON, WILLIAM (1861-1926), English biologist concerned with evolution **2** 55-57

BATISTA Y ZALDÍVAR, FULGENCIO (1901-1973), Cuban political and military leader **2** 57-58

BATLLE Y ORDÓÑEZ, JOSÉ (1856-1929), Uruguayan statesman and journalist **2** 58-59

BATTEN, JEAN (1909-1982), New Zealander aviatrix **26** 33-35

BATTLE, KATHLEEN (born 1948), American opera and concert singer **2** 59-60

BATU KHAN (died 1255), Mongol leader **2** 60-61

BAUDELAIRE, CHARLES PIERRE (1821-1867), French poet and art critic **2** 61-63

BAUER, EDDIE (1899-1986), American businessman **19** 13-14

Bauer, Georg
see Agricola, Georgius

BAULIEU, ÉTIENNE-ÉMILE (Étienne Blum; born 1926), French physician and biochemist who developed RU 486 **2** 63-66

BAUM, HERBERT (1912-1942), German human/civil rights activist **2** 66-73

BAUM, L. FRANK (1856-1919), author of the Wizard of Oz books **2** 73-74

Baumfree, Isabella
see Truth, Sojourner

BAUR, FERDINAND CHRISTIAN (1792-1860), German theologian **2** 74-75

BAUSCH, PINA (born 1940), a controversial German dancer/choreographer **2** 75-76

Bavarian art
see German art

BAXTER, RICHARD (1615-1691), English theologian **2** 76-77

BAYLE, PIERRE (1647-1706), French philosopher **2** 77-78

Bayley, Elizabeth
see Seton, Elizabeth Ann Bayley

BAYNTON, BARBARA (1857-1929), Australian author **22** 46-48

BAZIN, ANDRÉ (1918-1958), French film critic **28** 32-33

BBC
see British Broadcasting Corporation

BEA, AUGUSTINUS (1881-1968), German cardinal **2** 79

BEACH, AMY (born Amy Marcy Cheney; 1867-1944), American musician **23** 30-32

BEACH, MOSES YALE (1800-1868), American inventor and newspaperman **2** 79-80

Beaconsfield, Earl of
see Disraeli, Benjamin

BEADLE, GEORGE WELLS (1903-1989), American scientist, educator, and administrator **2** 80-81
    Tatum, Edward Lawrie **29** 356-358

BEALE, DOROTHEA (1831-1906), British educator **2** 81-83

BEAN, ALAN (born 1932), American astronaut and artist **22** 48-50

BEAN, LEON LEONWOOD (L.L. Bean; 1872-1967), American businessman **19** 14-16

BEARD, CHARLES AUSTIN (1874-1948), American historian **2** 84

BEARD, MARY RITTER (1876-1958), American author and activist **2** 85-86

BEARDEN, ROMARE HOWARD (1914-1988), African American painter-collagist **2** 86-88

BEARDSLEY, AUBREY VINCENT (1872-1898), English illustrator **2** 88-89

BEATLES, THE (1957-1971), British rock and roll band **2** 89-92

BEATRIX, WILHELMINA VON AMSBERG, QUEEN (born 1938), queen of Netherlands (1980-) **2** 92-93

BEAUCHAMPS, PIERRE (1636-1705), French dancer and choreographer **21** 27-29

BEAUFORT, MARGARET (1443-1509), queen dowager of England **20** 29-31

BEAUJOYEULX, BALTHASAR DE (Balthasar de Beaujoyeux; Baldassare de Belgiojoso; 1535-1587), Italian choreographer and composer **21** 29-30

BEAUMARCHAIS, PIERRE AUGUST CARON DE (1732-1799), French playwright **2** 93-94

BEAUMONT, FRANCIS (1584/1585-1616), English playwright **2** 95

BEAUMONT, WILLIAM (1785-1853), American surgeon **2** 95-96

BEAUREGARD, PIERRE GUSTAVE TOUTANT (1818-1893), Confederate general **2** 96-97

Beautiful Visit, The (novel)
    Howard, Elizabeth Jane **29** 200-202

Beaverbrook, Lord
see Aitken, William Maxwell

BECARRIA, MARCHESE DI (1738-1794), Italian jurist and economist **2** 97-98

BECHET, SIDNEY (1897-1959), American jazz musician **22** 50-52

BECHTEL, STEPHEN DAVISON (1900-1989), American construction engineer and business executive **2** 98-99

BECK, JÓZEF (1894-1944), Polish statesman **29** 48-50

BECK, LUDWIG AUGUST THEODOR (1880-1944), German general **2** 99-100

BECKER, CARL LOTUS (1873-1945), American historian **2** 100-101

BECKET, ST. THOMAS (1128?-1170), English prelate **2** 101-102

BECKETT, SAMUEL (1906-1989), Irish novelist, playwright, and poet **2** 102-104

BECKHAM, DAVID (David Robert Joseph Beckham; born 1975), British soccer player **26** 36-38

BECKMANN, MAX (1884-1950), German painter **2** 104-105

BECKNELL, WILLIAM (c. 1797-1865), American soldier and politician **2** 105-106

BECKWOURTH, JIM (James P. Beckwourth; c. 1800-1866), African American fur trapper and explorer **2** 106-107

BÉCQUER, GUSTAVO ADOLFO DOMINGUEZ (1836-1870), Spanish lyric poet **2** 107-108

BECQUEREL, ANTOINE HENRI (1852-1908), French physicist **2** 108-109

BEDE, ST. (672/673-735), English theologian **2** 109-110

BEDELL SMITH, WALTER (1895-1961), U.S. Army general, ambassador, and CIA director **18** 30-33

BEEBE, WILLIAM (1877-1962), American naturalist, oceanographer, and ornithologist **22** 52-54

BEECHAM, THOMAS (1879-1961), English conductor **24** 46-48

BEECHER, CATHARINE (1800-1878), American author and educator **2** 110-112

BEN BELLA, AHMED (born 1918), first president of the Algerian Republic **2** 148-149

BENDIX, VINCENT (1881-1945), American inventor, engineer, and industrialist **19** 18-20

BEN-GURION, DAVID (born 1886), Russian-born Israeli statesman **2** 160-161

BEN-HAIM, PAUL (Frankenburger; 1897-1984), Israeli composer **2** 161-162

BEN YEHUDA, ELIEZER (1858-1922), Hebrew lexicographer and editor **2** 181-182

BENALCÁZAR, SEBASTIÁN DE (died 1551), Spanish conquistador **2** 145-146

BENAVENTE Y MARTINEZ, JACINTO (1866-1954), Spanish dramatist **2** 146-147

BENCHLEY, ROBERT (1889-1945), American humorist **2** 150-151

BENDA, JULIEN (1867-1956), French cultural critic and novelist **2** 151-152

BENEDICT XIV (Prospero Lorenzo Lambertini; 1675-1758), Italian pope **23** 32-35

BENEDICT XV (Giacomo della Chiesa; 1854-1922), pope, 1914-1922 **2** 153-154

BENEDICT XVI (Joseph Alois Ratzinger; born 1927), Roman Catholic pope (2005-) **26** 295-297

BENEDICT, RUTH FULTON (1887-1948), American cultural anthropologist **2** 154-155

BENEDICT, ST. (c. 480-547), Italian founder of the Benedictines **2** 154-155

Benedict of Nursia, St.
see Benedict, St.

BENEŠ, EDWARD (1884-1948), Czechoslovak president 1935-1938 and 1940-1948 **2** 155-157

BENÉT, STEPHEN VINCENT (1898-1943), American poet and novelist **2** 157-158

BENETTON, Italian family (Luciano, Giuliana, Gilberto, Carlo and Mauro) who organized a world-wide chain of colorful knitwear stores **2** 158-159

BENEZET, ANTHONY (1713-1784), American philanthropist and educator **2** 159-160

Bengan Korei
see Muhammad II, Askia

BENJAMIN, ASHER (1773-1845), American architect **2** 162-163

BENJAMIN, JUDAH PHILIP (1811-1884), American statesman **2** 163-164

BENJAMIN, WALTER (1892-1940), German philosopher and literary critic **20** 32-34

BENN, GOTTFRIED (1886-1956), German author **2** 164

BENN, TONY (Anthony Neil Wedgewood Benn; born 1925), British Labour party politician **2** 164-166

BENNETT, ALAN (born 1934), British playwright **2** 166-167

BENNETT, ENOCH ARNOLD (1867-1931), English novelist and dramatist **2** 167-168

BENNETT, JAMES GORDON (1795-1872), Scottish-born American journalist and publisher **2** 168-169

BENNETT, JAMES GORDON, JR. (1841-1918), American newspaper owner and editor **2** 169-170

BENNETT, JOHN COLEMAN (1902-1995), American theologian **2** 170-171

BENNETT, RICHARD BEDFORD (1870-1947), Canadian statesman, prime minister 1930-1935 **2** 171-172

BENNETT, RICHARD RODNEY (born 1936), English composer **2** 172

BENNETT, ROBERT RUSSELL (1894-1981), American arranger, composer, and conductor **21** 32-34

BENNETT, WILLIAM JOHN (born 1943), American teacher and scholar and secretary of the Department of Education (1985-1988) **2** 172-174

Bennett of Mickleham, Calgary, and Hopewell, Viscount
see Bennett, Richard Bedford

BENNY, JACK (Benjamin Kubelsky; 1894-1974), American comedian and a star of radio, television, and stage **2** 174-176

BENTHAM, JEREMY (1748-1832), English philosopher, political theorist, and jurist **2** 176-178

BENTLEY, ARTHUR F. (1870-1957), American philosopher and political scientist **2** 178

BENTON, SEN. THOMAS HART (1782-1858), American statesman **2** 178-179

BENTON, THOMAS HART (1889-1975), American regionalist painter **2** 178-179

BENTSEN, LLOYD MILLARD (1921-2006), senior United States senator from Texas and Democratic vice-presidential candidate in 1988 **2** 180-181

BENZ, CARL (1844-1929), German inventor **2** 182-183

Berbers (North African people)
Almoravids
ibn Bajja, Abu Bakr Muhhamad **29** 207-209

BERCHTOLD, COUNT LEOPOLD VON (1863-1942), Austro-Hungarian statesman **2** 183-184

BERDYAEV, NICHOLAS ALEXANDROVICH (1874-1948), Russian philosopher **2** 184-185

BERELSON, BERNARD (1912-1979), American behavioral scientist **2** 185-186

BERENSON, BERNARD (1865-1959), American art critic and historian **20** 34-35

BERG, ALBAN (1885-1935), Austrian composer **2** 186-187

BERG, MOE (1902-1972), American baseball player and spy **29** 50-52

BERG, PAUL (born 1926), American chemist **2** 187-189

BERGER, VICTOR LOUIS (1860-1929), American politician **2** 189-190

BERGMAN, (ERNST) INGMAR (1918-2007), Swedish film and stage director **2** 190-191

BERGMAN, INGRID (1917-1982), Swedish actress **20** 35-37

BERGSON, HENRI (1859-1941), French philosopher **2** 191-192

BERIA, LAVRENTY PAVLOVICH (1899-1953), Soviet secret-police chief and politician **2** 192-193

BERING, VITUS (1681-1741), Danish navigator in Russian employ **2** 193-194

BERIO, LUCIANO (1925-2003), Italian composer **2** 194-195

BERISHA, SALI (born 1944), president of the Republic of Albania (1992-) **2** 195-197

BERKELEY, BUSBY (William Berkeley Enos; 1895-1976), American filmmaker **20** 38-39

BERKELEY, GEORGE (1685-1753), Anglo-Irish philosopher and Anglican bishop **2** 197-198

BERKELEY, SIR WILLIAM (1606-1677), English royal governor of Virginia **2** 198-199

BERLE, ADOLF AUGUSTUS, JR. (1895-1971), American educator **2** 199-200

BERLE, MILTON (1908-2002), American entertainer and actor **18** 37-39

BERLIN, IRVING (1888-1989), American composer **2** 200-201

BERLIN, ISAIAH (1909-1997), British philosopher **2** 201-203

BERLINER, ÉMILE (1851-1929), American inventor **20** 39-41

BERLIOZ, LOUIS HECTOR (1803-1869), French composer, conductor, and critic **2** 203-205

BERLUSCONI, SILVIO (born 1936), Italian businessman and politician **25** 48-50

BERMEJO, BARTOLOMÉ (Bartolomé de Cárdenas; flourished 1474-1498), Spanish painter **2** 205

BERNADETTE OF LOURDES, SAINT (Marie Bernarde Soubirous; 1844-1879), French nun and Roman Catholic saint **21** 34-36

Bernadotte, Jean Baptiste
see Charles XIV John

BERNANOS, GEORGES (1888-1948), French novelist and essayist **2** 206-207

BERNARD, CLAUDE (1813-1878), French physiologist **2** 208-210

BERNARD OF CLAIRVAUX, ST. (1090-1153), French theologian, Doctor of the Church **2** 207-208
Anacletus II **29** 7-9

BERNARDIN, CARDINAL JOSEPH (1928-1996), Roman Catholic Cardinal and American activist **2** 210-211

Bernardone, Giovanni di
see Francis of Assisi, St.

BERNAYS, EDWARD L. (1891-1995), American public relations consultant **2** 211-212

BERNBACH, WILLIAM (1911-1982), American advertising executive **19** 20-22

BERNERS-LEE, TIM (born 1955), English computer scientist and creator of the World Wide Web **20** 41-43

BERNHARDT, SARAH (Henriette-Rosine Bernard; 1844-1923), French actress **2** 212-214

BERNIER, JOSEPH E. (Joseph-Elzéan Bernier; 1852-1934), Canadian explorer **23** 35-37

BERNINI, GIAN LORENZO (1598-1680), Italian artist **2** 214-216

BERNOULLI, DANIEL (1700-1782), Swiss mathematician and physicist **2** 216

BERNOULLI, JAKOB (Jacques or James Bernoulli; 1654-1705), Swiss mathematician **23** 37-39

BERNSTEIN, CARL (born 1944), investigative reporter **29** 52-54

BERNSTEIN, DOROTHY LEWIS (born 1914), American mathematician **2** 217

BERNSTEIN, EDUARD (1850-1932), German socialist **2** 218

BERNSTEIN, ELMER (1922-2004), American composer **27** 44-46

BERNSTEIN, LEONARD (1918-1990), American composer, conductor, and pianist **2** 218-219

Bernstein, Ludvik
see Namier, Sir Lewis Bernstein

BERRA, YOGI (born 1925), American baseball player, coach, and manager **29** 54-57

Berrettini, Pietro
see Cortona, Pietro da

BERRI, NABIH (born 1939), leader of the Shi'ite Muslims in Lebanon **2** 220-222

BERRIGAN, DANIEL J. (born 1921), activist American Catholic priest **2** 222-223

BERRUGUETE, ALONSO (1486/90-1561), Spanish sculptor **2** 223-224

BERRY, CHUCK (born 1926), African American performer **2** 224-226

BERRY, MARY FRANCES (born 1938), African American human/civil rights activist and official **2** 226-229

BERRY, RAYMOND (born 1933), American football player and coach **29** 57-59

BERRYMAN, JOHN (John Allyn Smith, Jr.; 1914-1972), American poet and biographer **19** 22-25

BERTHIER, LOUIS ALEXANDRE (1753-1815), French soldier and cartographer **20** 43-44

BERTHOLLET, CLAUDE LOUIS (1748-1822), French chemist **2** 229-230

BERTILLON, ALPHONSE (1853-1914), French criminologist **2** 230-231

BERTOLUCCI, BERNARDO (born 1940), Italian film director **18** 39-41

BERZELIUS, JÖNS JACOB (1779-1848), Swedish chemist **2** 231-233

BESANT, ANNIE WOOD (1847-1933), British social reformer and theosophist **2** 233-234

Besht
see Baal Shem Tov

Besig, Ernest, (1904-1998), ACLU director
Korematsu, Fred **29** 234-236

BESSEL, FRIEDRICH WILHELM (1784-1846), German astronomer **2** 234-235

BESSEMER, SIR HENRY (1813-1898), English inventor **2** 235-236

BEST, CHARLES HERBERT (1899-1978), Canadian physiologist **2** 236-237
Collip, James Bertram **29** 121-123

Beta
see Eratosthenes of Cyrene

BETANCOURT, RÓMULO (1908-1990), Venezuelan statesman **2** 237-238

BETHE, HANS ALBRECHT (1906-2005), Alsatian-American physicist **2** 238-239

BETHMANN HOLLWEG, THEOBALD VON (1856-1921), German statesman **2** 239-240

BETHUNE, HENRY NORMAN (1890-1939), Canadian humanitarian physician **2** 240-241

BETHUNE, MARY MCLEOD (1875-1955), African American educator **2** 241-242

BETI, MONGO (Alexandre Biyidi; born 1932), Cameroonian novelist **2** 242-243

BETJEMAN, JOHN (1906-1984), Poet Laureate of Britain 1972-1984 **2** 243-245

BETTELHEIM, BRUNO (1903-1990), Austrian-born American psychoanalyst and educational psychologist **2** 245-246

BETTI, UGO (1892-1953), Italian playwright **2** 246

BEUYS, JOSEPH (1921-1986), German artist and sculptor **2** 246-248

BEVAN, ANEURIN (1897-1960), Labour minister responsible for the creation of the British National Health Service **2** 248-249

BEVEL, JAMES LUTHER (born 1936), American civil rights activist of the 1960s **2** 250-251

BEVERIDGE, ALBERT JEREMIAH (1862-1927), American statesman **23** 39-41

BEVERIDGE, WILLIAM HENRY (1st Baron Beveridge of Tuccal; 1879-1963), English economist and social reformer **2** 251-252

BEVERLEY, ROBERT (c. 1673-1722), colonial American historian **2** 252

BEVIN, ERNEST (1881-1951), English trade union leader and politician **2** 252-253

Bewitched, Bothered and Bewildered (song)
Hart, Lorenz **29** 184-186

Beyle, Marie Henri
see Stendhal

BHABHA, HOMI JEHANGIR (1909-1966), Indian atomic physicist **2** 253-254

BHAKTIVEDANTA PRABHUPADA (Abhay Charan De; 1896-1977), Hindu religious teacher who founded the International Society for Krishna Consciousness **2** 254-255

BITRUJI, NUR AL-DIN ABU ISHAQ AL (c. 1150-1200), Spanish Moslem astronomer **2** 296

BITZER, BILLY (George William Bitzer; 1872-1944), American cinematographer **21** 36-38

BIYA, PAUL (born 1933), president of Cameroon **18** 41-43

Biyidi, Alexandre
see Beti, Mongo

BIZET, GEORGES (1838-1875), French composer **2** 296-297

BJELKE-PETERSEN, JOHANNES (''Joh;'' born 1911), Australian politician **2** 297-299

BJERKNES, VILHELM (1862-1951), Norwegian meteorologist **20** 48-50

BJØRNSON, BJØRNSTJERNE (1832-1910), Norwegian author **2** 299-300

BLACK, CONRAD MOFFAT (born 1944), Canadian-born international press baron **2** 300-301

BLACK, HUGO LAFAYETTE (1886-1971), American jurist **2** 301-303
Korematsu, Fred **29** 234-236

BLACK, JOSEPH (1728-1799), British chemist **2** 303
Roebuck, John **29** 326-328

BLACK, SHIRLEY TEMPLE (born 1928), American actress and public servant **2** 303-305

Black Death (1348)
see also Bubonic plague
Kitasato, Shibasabura **29** 230-232

BLACK ELK, NICHOLAS (1863-1950), Oglala Sioux medicine man **2** 305-306

Black Hand (terrorist group)
Franz Ferdinand **29** 162-164

BLACK HAWK (1767-1838), Native American war chief **2** 308

Black Hundred movement (Russia)
Andreyev, Leonid Nikolayevich **29** 11-13

Black is beautiful (philosophy)
Dhlomo, R.R.R. **29** 142-144

Black Jack
see Pershing, John Joseph

Black Prince
see Edward the Black Prince

''Black Sox'' scandal, 1919
Spink, J.G. Taylor **29** 347-349

Black Spartacus
see Turner, Nathaniel

Black Spurgeon
see Turner, Henry McNeal

BLACKBEARD (Edward Teach; 1680-1718), English pirate **21** 38-41

Blackbody radiation
see Radioactivity (physics)

BLACKBURN, ELIZABETH HELEN (born 1948), Australian biologist **18** 43-45

BLACKETT, PATRICK M.S. (1897-1974), British physicist **2** 306-307

BLACKMUN, HARRY (1908-1999), United States Supreme Court justice **2** 309-310

''Black-robe Voyageur''
see Lacombe, Albert

Blacks
see African American history (United States); Africa

Blackshirts (Italian politics)
Balbo, Italo **29** 37-39

BLACKSTONE, SIR WILLIAM (1723-1780), English jurist **2** 310-311

BLACKWELL, ALICE STONE (1857-1950), American editor **29** 61-63

BLACKWELL, ANTOINETTE BROWN (1825-1921), American minister and suffragette **21** 41-43

BLACKWELL, ELIZABETH (1821-1910), American physician **2** 311-312

BLACKWELL, EMILY (1826-1910), American physician and educator **19** 27-29

BLAGA, LUCIAN (1895-1961), Romanian poet and philosopher **24** 52-54

BLAINE, JAMES GILLESPIE (1830-1893), American statesman **2** 312-313

BLAIR, BONNIE (born 1964), American athlete **23** 42-44

Blair, Eric Arthur
see Orwell, George

BLAIR, FRANCIS PRESTON (1791-1876), American journalist and politician **2** 313-315

BLAIR, JAMES (1655-1743), British educator and Anglican missionary **2** 315-316

BLAIR, TONY (born 1953), British prime minister **18** 45-47

BLAKE, EUBIE (James Hubert Blake; 1883-1983), African American composer and pianist **25** 50-53

Blake, Nicholas
see Lewis, Cecil Day

BLAKE, WILLIAM (1757-1827), English poet, engraver, and painter **2** 316-318

BLAKELOCK, RALPH ALBERT (1847-1919), American painter **2** 318

BLAKEY, ART (Arthur Blakey; Abdullah Ibn Buhaina; 1919-1990), African American jazz musician **27** 46-48

BLANC, LOUIS (1811-1882), French journalist, historian, and politician **2** 318-319

BLANC, MEL (1908-1989), American creator of and voice of cartoon characters **2** 319-320

BLANCHARD, FELIX (''Doc'' Blanchard; born 1924), American football player and military pilot **21** 43-45

BLANCHARD, JEAN-PIERRE FRANÇOIS (1753-1809), French balloonist **28** 36-38

BLANCHE OF CASTILE (1188-1252), French queen **21** 45-47

BLANCO, ANTONIO GUZMÁN (1829-1899), Venezuelan politician, three-times president **2** 320-321

Blanco party (Uruguayan politics)
Baldomir, Alfredo **29** 39-41

BLANDIANA, ANA (born Otilia-Valeria Coman, 1942), Romanian poet **2** 321-322

BLANDING, SARAH GIBSON (1898-1985), American educator **2** 322-323

BLANKERS-KOEN, FANNY (Francina Elsja Blankers-Koen; born 1918), Dutch track and field athlete **20** 50-52

BLANQUI, LOUIS AUGUSTE (1805-1881), French revolutionary **2** 323-324

Blashki, Philip
see Evergood, Philip

BLAVATSKY, HELENA PETROVNA (Helena Hahn; 1831-1891), Russian theosophist **22** 67-69

BLEDSOE, ALBERT TAYLOR (1809-1877), American lawyer, educator, and Confederate apologist **2** 324-325

BLEULER, EUGEN (1857-1939), Swiss psychiatrist **2** 325

BLEY, CARLA (nee Carla Borg; born 1938), American composer and pianist **26** 40-42

BLIGH, WILLIAM (1754-1817), English naval officer and colonial governor **2** 325-326

Blind
education of
Bridgman, Laura Dewey **29** 88-91

Blixen-Finecke, Baroness
see Dinesen Blixen-Finecke, Karen

BLOCH, ERNEST (1880-1959), Swiss-born American composer and teacher **2** 326-327

BLOCH, ERNST (1885-1977), German humanistic interpreter of Marxist thought **2** 327-328

BLOCH, FELIX (1905-1983), Swiss/American physicist **2** 328-330

BLOCH, KONRAD (born 1912), American biochemist **2** 330-332

BLOCH, MARC (1886-1944), French historian **2** 332-333

BLOCK, HERBERT (Herblock; 1909-2001), American newspaper cartoonist **2** 333-334

BLODGETT, KATHARINE BURR (1898-1979), American physicist **24** 54-56

BLOK, ALEKSANDR ALEKSANDROVICH (1880-1921), Russian poet **2** 335

BLONDIN, JEAN FRANCOIS GRAVELET (Charles Blondin; 1824-1897), French tightrope walker and acrobat **27** 48-50

Bloody Mary
see Mary I

BLOOM, ALLAN DAVID (1930-1992), American political philosopher, professor, and author **2** 335-337

BLOOM, HAROLD (born 1930), American literary critic and educator **28** 38-40

BLOOMBERG, MICHAEL (Michael Rubens Bloomberg; born 1942), American businessman and politician **28** 40-42

BLOOMER, AMELIA JENKS (1818-1894), American reformer and suffrage advocate **2** 337

BLOOMFIELD, LEONARD (1887-1949), American linguist **2** 338

BLOOR, ELLA REEVE ("Mother Bloor"; 1862-1951), American labor organizer and social activist **2** 338-340

BLÜCHER, GEBHARD LEBERECHT VON (Prince of Wahlstatt; 1742-1819), Prussian field marshal **2** 340-341

Blue Moon (song)
Hart, Lorenz **29** 184-186

Blues (music)
Diddley, Bo **29** 144-146

BLUFORD, GUION STEWART, JR. (born 1942), African American aerospace engineer, pilot, and astronaut **2** 341-343

BLUM, LÉON (1872-1950), French statesman **2** 343-344

BLUME, JUDY (born Judy Sussman; b. 1938), American fiction author **2** 344-345

BLUMENTHAL, WERNER MICHAEL (born 1926), American businessman and treasury secretary **2** 345-346

BLY, NELLIE (born Elizabeth Cochrane Seaman; 1864-1922), American journalist and reformer **2** 346-348

BLYDEN, EDWARD WILMOT (1832-1912), Liberian statesman **2** 348-349

Blythe, Vernon William
see Castle, I. and V.

Bo Diddley (song)
Diddley, Bo **29** 144-146

Boadicia
see Boudicca

Boanerges
see John, St.

BOAS, FRANZ (1858-1942), German-born American anthropologist **2** 349-351

BOCCACCIO, GIOVANNI (1313-1375), Italian author **2** 351-353

BOCCIONI, UMBERTO (1882-1916), Italian artist **2** 353-354

BÖCKLIN, ARNOLD (1827-1901), Swiss painter **2** 354-355

BODE, BOYD HENRY (1873-1953), American philosopher and educator **2** 355-356

Bodenstein, Andreas
see Karlstadt

Bodhisattva Emperor
see Liang Wu-ti

BODIN, JEAN (1529/30-1596), French political philosopher **2** 356-357

BOEHME, JACOB (1575-1624), German mystic **2** 357

BOEING, WILLIAM EDWARD (1881-1956), American businessman **2** 357-358

BOERHAAVE, HERMANN (1668-1738), Dutch physician and chemist **2** 358-359

BOESAK, ALLAN AUBREY (born 1945), opponent of apartheid in South Africa and founder of the United Democratic Front **2** 359-360

BOETHIUS, ANICIUS MANLIUS SEVERINUS (480?-524/525), Roman logician and theologian **2** 360-361

BOFF, LEONARDO (Leonardo Genezio Darci Boff; born 1938), Brazilian priest **22** 69-71

BOFFRAND, GABRIEL GERMAIN (1667-1754), French architect and decorator **2** 361

BOFILL, RICARDO (born 1939), post-modern Spanish architect **2** 362-363

BOGART, HUMPHREY (1899-1957), American stage and screen actor **2** 363-364
Bacall, Lauren **29** 29-31

BOHEMUND I (of Tarantò; c. 1055-1111), Norman Crusader **2** 364

BOHLEN, CHARLES (CHIP) EUSTIS (1904-1973), United States ambassador to the Soviet Union, interpreter, and presidential adviser **2** 364-366

BÖHM-BAWERK, EUGEN VON (1851-1914), Austrian economist **2** 366

Böhme, Jakob
see Boehme, Jacob

BOHR, AAGE NIELS (born 1922), Danish physicist **25** 53-55

BOHR, NIELS HENRIK DAVID (1885-1962), Danish physicist **2** 366-368

BOIARDO, MATTEO MARIA (Conte di Scandiano; 1440/41-1494), Italian poet **2** 369

BOILEAU-DESPRÉAUX, NICHOLAS (1636?-1711), French critic and writer **2** 369-371

Boisy, Francis
see Francis of Sales, St.

BOIVIN, MARIE GILLAIN (née Marie Anne Victorine Gillain; 1773-1841), French midwife and author **25** 55-56

BOK, DEREK CURTIS (born 1930), dean of the Harvard Law School and president of Harvard University **2** 371-372

BOK, EDWARD WILLIAM (1863-1930), American editor and publisher **22** 71-73

BOK, SISSELA ANN (born 1934), American moral philosopher **2** 372-374

BOLAÑO, ROBERTO (1953-2003), Chilean author **28** 42-45

BOLEYN, ANNE (1504?-1536), second wife of Henry VIII **18** 47-49
Babington, Anthony **29** 27-29

Bolingbroke, Henry
see Henry IV (king of England)

BOLINGBROKE, VISCOUNT (Henry St. John; 1678-1751), English statesman **2** 374-375

BOLÍVAR, SIMÓN (1783-1830), South American general and statesman **2** 375-377

BOLKIAH, HASSANAL (Muda Hassanal Bolkiah Mu'izzaddin Waddaulah; born 1946), Sultan of Brunei **18** 49-51

BÖLL, HEINRICH (1917-1985), German writer and translator **2** 377-378

Bolshevik Revolution
see Russian Revolution (1917; October)

Bolsheviks (Russian politics)
supporters
Andreyev, Leonid Nikolayevich **29** 11-13
Borodin, Mikhail Markovich **29** 72-74

BOWIE, DAVID (David Robert Jones; born 1947), English singer, songwriter, and actor **18** 58-60

BOWLES, PAUL (1910-1999), American author, musical composer, and translator **19** 31-34

BOWLES, SAMUEL (1826-1878), American newspaper publisher **2** 464

BOWMAN, ISAIAH (1878-1950), American geographer **2** 464-465

BOXER, BARBARA (born 1940), U.S. Senator from California **2** 465-468

Boxers
see Athletes–boxers

Boy bachelor
see Wolsey, Thomas

BOYD, LOUISE ARNER (1887-1972), American explorer **22** 73-74

Boyd, Nancy
see Millay, Edna St. Vincent

Boyd Orr, John
see Orr, John Boyd

BOYER, JEAN PIERRE (1776-1850), Haitian president 1818-1845 **2** 468-469

BOYER, PAUL DELOS (born 1918), American biochemist **25** 62-65

BOYLE, ROBERT (1627-1691), British chemist and physicist **2** 469-471
Amontons, Guillaume **29** 3-5

Boyle's law (physics)
Amontons, Guillaume **29** 3-5

BOYLSTON, ZABDIEL (1679-1766), American physician **2** 471

Boys from Syracuse, The (musical)
Hart, Lorenz **29** 184-186

Boz
see Dickens, Charles

BOZEMAN, JOHN M. (1837-1867), American pioneer **2** 471-472

Bozzie
see Boswell, James

BRACKENRIDGE, HUGH HENRY (1749-1816), American lawyer and writer **2** 472-473

BRACTON, HENRY (Henry of Bratton; c. 1210-1268), English jurist **21** 54-55

BRADBURY, RAY (born 1920), American fantasy and science fiction writer **2** 473-474

Bradby, Lucy Barbara
see Hammond, John and Lucy

BRADDOCK, EDWARD (1695-1755), British commander in North America **2** 474-475

BRADFORD, WILLIAM (1590-1657), leader of Plymouth Colony **2** 475-476

BRADFORD, WILLIAM (1663-1752), American printer **2** 476-477

BRADFORD, WILLIAM (1722-1791), American journalist **2** 477

BRADLAUGH, CHARLES (1833-1891), English freethinker and political agitator **2** 478
Douglas, Sir John Sholto **29** 148-150

BRADLEY, ED (1941-2006), African American broadcast journalist **2** 478-481

BRADLEY, FRANCIS HERBERT (1846-1924), English philosopher **2** 481-482

BRADLEY, JAMES (1693-1762), English astronomer **2** 482-483

BRADLEY, JOSEPH P. (1813-1892), American Supreme Court justice **22** 74-77

BRADLEY, MARION ZIMMER (born 1930), American author **18** 60-62

BRADLEY, OMAR NELSON (1893-1981), American general **2** 483-484

BRADLEY, TOM (1917-1998), first African American mayor of Los Angeles **2** 484-485

BRADMAN, SIR DONALD GEORGE (born 1908), Australian cricketer **2** 485-486

BRADSTREET, ANNE DUDLEY (c. 1612-1672), English-born American poet **2** 486-487

BRADWELL, MYRA (Myra Colby; 1831-1894), American lawyer and publisher **24** 64-66

BRADY, MATHEW B. (c. 1823-1896), American photographer **2** 487-488

BRAGG, SIR WILLIAM HENRY (1862-1942), English physicist **2** 488-489

BRAHE, TYCHO (1546-1601), Danish astronomer **2** 489-490

BRAHMAGUPTA (c. 598-c. 670), Indian mathematician and astronomer **26** 44-46

BRAHMS, JOHANNES (1833-1897), German composer **2** 490-492
associates
Joachim, Joseph **29** 214-216

BRAILLE, LOUIS (1809-1852), French teacher and creator of braille system **2** 492-493

Brain (human)
Gall, Franz Joseph **29** 165-167

BRAINARD, BERTHA (Bertha Brainard Peterson; died 1946), American radio executive **28** 47-48

BRAMAH, JOSEPH (Joe Bremmer; 1749-1814), English engineer and inventor **20** 58-59

BRAMANTE, DONATO (1444-1514), Italian architect and painter **2** 493-494

BRANCUSI, CONSTANTIN (1876-1957), Romanian sculptor in France **2** 494-496

BRANDEIS, LOUIS DEMBITZ (1856-1941), American jurist **2** 496-497

BRANDES, GEORG (Georg Morris Cohen Brandes; 1842-1927), Danish literary critic **23** 45-47

BRANDO, MARLON (born 1924), American actor **2** 497-499

BRANDT, WILLY (Herbert Frahm Brandt; 1913-1992), German statesman, chancellor of West Germany **2** 499-500

BRANSON, RICHARD (born 1950), British entrepreneur **19** 34-36

BRANT, JOSEPH (1742-1807), Mohawk Indian chief **2** 500-501
portraits
Ames, Ezra **29** 1-3

BRANT, MARY (1736-1796), Native American who guided the Iroquois to a British alliance **2** 501-503

BRANT, SEBASTIAN (1457-1521), German author **2** 503-504

BRAQUE, GEORGES (1882-1967), French painter **2** 504-505

Braschi, Giangelo
see Pius VI

BRATTAIN, WALTER H. (1902-1987), American physicist and co-inventor of the transistor **2** 505-507

Bratton, Henry de
see Bracton, Henry de

BRAUDEL, FERNAND (1902-1985), leading exponent of the *Annales* school of history **2** 507-508

BRAUN, FERDINAND (1850-1918), German recipient of the Nobel Prize in Physics for work on wireless telegraphy **2** 508-509

BRAY, JOHN RANDOLPH (1879-1978), American animator and cartoonist **21** 55-57

BRAZZA, PIERRE PAUL FRANÇOIS CAMILLE SAVORGNAN DE (1852-1905), Italian-born French explorer **2** 509-510

BREASTED, JAMES HENRY (1865-1935), American Egyptologist and archeologist **2** 510-511
Erman, Adolf **29** 154-156

BROOKS, GWENDOLYN (born 1917), first African American author to receive the Pulitzer Prize for Literature **3** 24-26

BROOKS, MEL (Melvin Kaminsky; born 1926), American actor, playwright, and film and theatre producer/director **23** 48-50

BROOKS, PHILLIPS (1835-1893), American Episcopalian bishop **3** 26

BROTHERS, JOYCE (Joyce Diane Bauer; born 1927), American psychologist who pioneered radio phone-in questions for professional psychological advice **3** 26-28

BROUDY, HARRY SAMUEL (born 1905), American philosopher, teacher, and author **3** 28-29

BROUGHAM, HENRY PETER (Baron Brougham and Vaux; 1778-1868), Scottish jurist **22** 83-85

BROUN, HEYWOOD (1888-1939), American journalist **29** 97-99

BROUWER, ADRIAEN (1605/06-1638), Flemish painter **3** 29-30

BROWDER, EARL RUSSELL (1891-1973), American Communist leader **3** 30-31

BROWN, ALEXANDER (1764-1834), American merchant and banker **3** 31-32

BROWN, BENJAMIN GRATZ (1826-1885), American politician **3** 32-33

BROWN, CHARLES BROCKDEN (1771-1810), American novelist **3** 33

BROWN, CHARLOTTE EUGENIA HAWKINS (born Lottie Hawkins; 1882-1961), African American educator and humanitarian **3** 34

BROWN, GEORGE (1818-1880), Canadian politician **3** 35-36

BROWN, GORDON (James Gordon Brown; born 1951), British politician **28** 48-50

BROWN, HELEN GURLEY (born 1922), American author and editor **3** 36-37

BROWN, JAMES (1928-2006), African American singer **3** 37-39

BROWN, JOHN (1800-1859), American abolitionist **3** 39-41

BROWN, JOSEPH EMERSON (1821-1894), American lawyer and politician **3** 41-42

BROWN, LES (Leslie Calvin Brown; born 1945), American motivational speaker, author, and television host **19** 36-39

BROWN, MOSES (1738-1836), American manufacturer and merchant **3** 42-43

BROWN, RACHEL FULLER (1898-1980), American biochemist **3** 43-44

BROWN, ROBERT (1773-1858), Scottish botanist **20** 61-63

BROWN, RONALD H. (1941-1996), African American politician, cabinet official **3** 44-47

BROWN, STERLING (Sterling Allen Brown; 1901-1989), American literary critic **28** 51-54

BROWN, TINA (Christina Hambly Brown; born 1953), British editor who transformed the English magazine *Tatler*, then the United States magazines *Vanity Fair* and the *New Yorker* **3** 47-48

BROWN, TONY (William Anthony Brown; born 1933), African American radio personality **24** 68-70

BROWN, WILLIAM WELLS (1815/ 16-1884), African American author and abolitionist **3** 48-49

Brown v. Board of Education of Topeka (1954)
        Henderson, Zelma **29** 188-191

Browne, Charles Farrar
    see Ward, Artemus

BROWNE, SIR THOMAS (1605-1682), English author **3** 49-50

BROWNE, THOMAS ALEXANDER (Rolf Bolderwood; 1826-1915), Australian author **22** 85-87

BROWNER, CAROL M. (born 1955), U.S. Environmental Protection Agency administrator **3** 50-52

BROWNING, ELIZABETH BARRETT (1806-1861), English poet **3** 52-53

BROWNING, ROBERT (1812-1889), English poet **3** 53-55

BROWNLOW, WILLIAM GANNAWAY (1805-1877), American journalist and politician **3** 55-56

BROWNMILLER, SUSAN (born 1935), American activist, journalist, and novelist **3** 56-57

BROWNSON, ORESTES AUGUSTUS (1803-1876), American clergyman and transcendentalist **3** 57-58

Broz, Josip
    see Tito, Marshal

BRUBACHER, JOHN SEILER (1898-1988), American historian and educator **3** 58-59

BRUBECK, DAVE (born 1920), American pianist, composer, and bandleader **3** 59-61

BRUCE, BLANCHE KELSO (1841-1898), African American politician **3** 62-63

BRUCE, DAVID (1855-1931), Australian parasitologist **3** 63

BRUCE, JAMES (1730-1794), Scottish explorer **3** 63-64

Bruce, James (1811-1863)
    see Elgin, 8th Earl of

BRUCE, LENNY (Leonard Alfred Schneider; 1925-1966), American comedian **19** 39-41

Bruce, Robert
    see Robert I (king of Scotland)

BRUCE OF MELBOURNE, 1ST VISCOUNT (Stanley Melbourne Bruce; 1883-1967), Australian statesman **3** 61-62

BRUCKNER, JOSEPH ANTON (1824-1896), Austrian composer **3** 64-65

BRUEGEL, PIETER, THE ELDER (1525/ 30-1569), Netherlandish painter **3** 65-67

BRÛLÉ, ÉTIENNE (c. 1592-1633), French explorer in North America **3** 67-68

BRUNDTLAND, GRO HARLEM (1939-1989), Norwegian prime minister and chair of the United Nations World Commission for Environment and Development **3** 68-69

Brunei, Sultan of
    see Bolkiah, Hassanal

BRUNEL, ISAMBARD KINGDOM (1806-1859), English civil engineer **3** 69-70

BRUNELLESCHI, FILIPPO (1377-1446), Italian architect and sculptor **3** 70-72

BRUNER, JEROME SEYMOUR (born 1915), American psychologist **3** 72-73

BRUNHOFF, JEAN DE (1899-1937), French author and illustrator **19** 41-42

BRUNNER, ALOIS (born 1912), Nazi German officer who helped engineer the destruction of European Jews **3** 73-74

BRUNNER, EMIL (1889-1966), Swiss Reformed theologian **3** 74-75

BRUNO, GIORDANO (1548-1600), Italian philosopher and poet **3** 75-76

Bruno of Toul (Egisheim)
    see Leo IX, St.

BRUTON, JOHN GERARD (born 1947), prime minister of Ireland **3** 76-77

BRUTUS, DENNIS (born 1924), exiled South African poet and political activist opposed to apartheid **3** 77-78

BRUTUS, MARCUS JUNIUS (c. 85-42 B.C.), Roman statesman **3** 79-80

Brutus, Quintus Caepio
    see Brutus, Marcus Junius

BUTTERFIELD, JOHN (1801-1869), American financier and politician **3** 184-185

BUTTON, DICK (Richard Totten Button; born 1929), American figure skater and sports commentator **23** 55-57

BUXTEHUDE, DIETRICH (1637-1707), Danish composer and organist **3** 185-186

By Jupiter (musical)
Hart, Lorenz **29** 184-186

By Myself (autobiography)
Bacall, Lauren **29** 29-31

By Rocket to Interplanetary Space (book)
Oberth, Hermann Julius **29** 296-298

BYRD, RICHARD EVELYN (1888-1957), American admiral and polar explorer **3** 186-187

BYRD, WILLIAM (1543?-1623), English composer **3** 187-188

BYRD, WILLIAM (1652-1704), English colonial planter and merchant **3** 188-189

BYRD, WILLIAM II (1674-1744), American diarist and government official **3** 189-190

BYRNE, JANE (born 1934), first woman mayor of Chicago **3** 190-191

BYRNES, JAMES FRANCIS (1879-1972), American public official **3** 191-192

BYRON, GEORGE GORDON NOEL (6th Baron Byron; 1788-1824), English poet **3** 193-194

C

CABELL, JAMES BRANCH (1879-1958), American essayist and novelist **3** 195-196

CABET, ÉTIENNE (1788-1856), French political radical **3** 196

CABEZA DE VACA, ÁLVAR NÚÑEZ (c. 1490-c. 1557), Spanish explorer **3** 197

CABEZÓN, ANTONIO (1510-1566), Spanish composer **3** 197-198

CABLE, GEORGE WASHINGTON (1844-1925), American novelist **3** 198-199

CABOT, JOHN (flourished 1471-1498), Italian explorer in English service **3** 199-200

CABOT, RICHARD CLARKE (1868-1939), American physician **3** 200

CABOT, SEBASTIAN (c. 1482-1557), Italian-born explorer for England and Spain **3** 200-201
Borough, Stephen **29** 74-76

Caboto, Giovanni
see Cabot, John

CABRAL, AMÍLCAR LOPES (1924-1973), father of modern African nationalism in Guinea-Bissau and the Cape Verde Islands **3** 202-203

CABRAL, PEDRO ÁLVARES (1467/68-1520), Portuguese navigator **3** 203-204

Cabrera, Manuel Estrada
see Estrada Cabrera, Manuel

CABRILLO, JUAN RODRÍGUEZ (died 1543), Portuguese explorer for Spain **3** 204-205

CABRINI, ST. FRANCES XAVIER (1850-1917), Italian-born founder of the Missionary Sisters of the Sacred Heart **3** 205

CACCINI, GIULIO (c. 1545-1618), Italian singer and composer **3** 205-206

CACHAO (1918-2008), Cuban musician **29** 104-106

Cactus Throne, The (book)
Carlotta **29** 108-110

CADAMOSTO, ALVISE DA (c. 1428-1483), Italian explorer **3** 206-207

CAEDMON (650-c.680), English Christian poet **20** 66-67

CADILLAC, ANTOINE DE LAMOTHE (1658-1730), French explorer and colonial administrator **18** 69-71

CADMUS, PAUL (1904-1999), American painter **27** 64-66

CAESAR, (GAIUS) JULIUS (100-44 B.C.), Roman general and statesman **3** 207-210

CAESAR, SHIRLEY (born 1938), African American singer **3** 210-211

Caetani, Benedetto
see Boniface VIII

CAGE, JOHN (1912-1992), American composer **3** 211-214

CAGNEY, JAMES (1899-1986), American actor **21** 68-71

CAHAN, ABRAHAM (1860-1951), Lithuanian-American Jewish author **3** 214

CAILLIÉ, AUGUSTE RENÉ (1799-1838), French explorer **3** 214-215

CAIN, JAMES (1892-1977), American journalist and author **19** 50-52

CAJETAN, ST. (1480-1547), Italian reformer; cofounder of the Theatines **3** 215-216

Calabria, Duke of
see Guiscard, Robert

CALAMITY JANE (Martha Jane Cannary; 1852-1903), American frontier woman **3** 216

CALATRAVA, SANTIAGO (born 1951), Spanish/Swiss architect **27** 66-68

Calcutta, University of (India)
Bose, S.N. **29** 78-80

CALDECOTT, RANDOLPH (1846-1886), English artist and illustrator **19** 52-55

CALDER, ALEXANDER (1898-1976), American sculptor **3** 216-218

CALDERA RODRÍGUEZ, RAFAEL (born 1916), president of Venezuela (1969-1974) **3** 218-219

CALDERÓN, ALBERTO P. (1920-1998), Hispanic American mathematician **3** 219-220

CALDERÓN, FELIPE (Felipe de Jesús Calderon Hinojosa; born 1962), Mexican politician **27** 68-70

CALDERÓN, PEDRO (1600-1681), Spanish poet and playwright **3** 221-222

CALDERÓN FOURNIER, RAFAEL (born 1949), president of Costa Rica (1990-) **3** 222-223

CALDICOTT, HELEN BROINOWSKI (born 1938), Australian physician and activist **18** 71-73

CALDWELL, ERSKINE (1903-1987), American novelist **3** 223-224

CALDWELL, SARAH (1924-2006), long-time artistic director, conductor, and founder of the Opera Company of Boston **3** 224-226

Caletti-Bruni, Pietro Francesco
see Cavalli, Pietro Francesco

CALHOUN, JOHN CALDWELL (1782-1850), American statesman **3** 226-228

Caliari, Paolo
see Veronese, Paolo

CALIGULA (12-41), Roman emperor 37-41 **3** 228-229

Calixtus II, (Guido of Vienne; died 1124), pope 1119-1124
Anacletus II **29** 7-9

CALLAGHAN, EDWARD MORLEY (1903-1990), Canadian novelist **3** 229-230

CALLAGHAN, LEONARD JAMES (born 1912), Labor member of the British Parliament and prime minister, 1976-1979 **3** 230-231

CALLAHAN, DANIEL (born 1930), American philosopher who focused on biomedical ethics **3** 231-233

CALLAHAN, HARRY (1912-1999), American photographer **20** 67-69

CHAMPOLLION, JEAN FRANÇOIS (1790-1832), French Egyptologist **3** 421

CHAN, JACKIE (Chan King-Sang; Sing Lung; born 1954), Chinese actor **27** 81-83

Chanakya see Kautilya

CHANCELLOR, RICHARD (died 1556), English navigator **3** 422
    Borough, Stephen **29** 74-76

CHANDLER, ALFRED DU PONT, JR. (1918-2007), American historian of American business **3** 422-423

CHANDLER, RAYMOND, JR. (1888-1959), American author of crime fiction **3** 423-425

CHANDLER, ZACHARIAH (1813-1879), American politician **3** 425-426

CHANDRAGUPTA MAURYA (died c. 298 B.C.), emperor of India 322?-298 **3** 426

CHANDRASEKHAR, SUBRAHMANYAN (1910-1995), Indian-born American physicist **3** 426-429

CHANEL, COCO (born Gabrielle Chanel; 1882-1971), French fashion designer **3** 429

CHANEY, LON (Alonzo Chaney; 1883-1930), American actor **19** 68-70

Chang Chiao see Chang Chüeh

CHANG CHIEN (1853-1926), Chinese industrialist and social reformer **3** 429-430

CHANG CHIH-TUNG (1837-1909), Chinese official and reformer **3** 430-431

CHANG CHÜ-CHENG (1525-1582), Chinese statesman **3** 431-432

CHANG CHÜEH (died 184), Chinese religious and revolutionary leader **3** 432-433

CHANG HSÜEH-CH'ENG (1738-1801), Chinese scholar and historian **3** 433

Ch'ang-k'ang see Ku K'ai-chih

CHANG PO-GO (died 846), Korean adventurer and merchant prince **3** 433-434

CHANG TSO-LIN (1873-1928), Chinese warlord **3** 434-435

CHANNING, EDWARD (1856-1931), American historian **3** 435

CHANNING, WILLIAM ELLERY (1780-1842), Unitarian minister and theologian **3** 435-436

CHAO, ELAINE (Elaine Lan Chao; born 1953), Asian American government administrator **27** 84-86

Chao K'uang-yin see Zhao Kuang-yin

CHAO MENG-FU (1254-1322), Chinese painter **3** 436-437

CHAPIN, F(RANCIS) STUART (1888-1974), American sociologist **3** 437-438

CHAPLIN, CHARLES SPENCER (1889-1977), American film actor, director, and writer **3** 438-440

CHAPMAN, EDDIE (Arnold Edward Chapman; 1914-1997), British criminal and spy **28** 69-72

CHAPMAN, GEORGE (1559/60-1634), English poet, dramatist, and translator **3** 440-441

CHAPMAN, JOHN (Johnny Appleseed; c. 1775-1847), American horticulturist and missionary **21** 77-78

CHAPMAN, SYDNEY (1888-1970), English geophysicist **3** 441

CHAPONE, HESTER (Hester Mulso; 1727-1801), British author and critic **28** 72-74

CHARCOT, JEAN MARTIN (1825-1893), French psychiatrist **3** 442

CHARDIN, JEAN BAPTISTE SIMÉON (1699-1779), French painter **3** 442-443

CHARGAFF, ERWIN (1905-2002), American biochemist who worked with DNA **3** 444-445

CHARLEMAGNE (742-814), king of the Franks, 768-814, and emperor of the West, 800-814 **3** 445-447

CHARLES (born 1948), Prince of Wales and heir apparent to the British throne **3** 448-450

Charles I (king of Bohemia) see Charles IV (Holy Roman emperor)

Charles I (king of Spain) see Charles V (Holy Roman emperor)

CHARLES I (1600-1649), king of England 1625-1649 **3** 450-452

CHARLES II (1630-1685), king of England, Scotland, and Ireland 1660-1685 **3** 452-454

CHARLES II (1661-1700), king of Spain 1665-1700 **3** 454

CHARLES III (1716-1788), king of Spain 1759-1788 **3** 454-455

Charles IV (king of Two Sicilies) see Charles III (king of Spain)

CHARLES IV (1316-1378), Holy Roman emperor 1346-1378 **3** 455-456

CHARLES IV (1748-1819), king of Spain 1788-1808 **3** 456-457

CHARLES V (1337-1380), king of France 1364-1380 **3** 459-460

CHARLES V (1500-1558), Holy Roman emperor 1519-1556 **3** 457-459
    and Lutheranism
        Bora, Katharina von **29** 256-258

CHARLES VI (1368-1422), king of France 1380-1422 **3** 460-461

CHARLES VII (1403-1461), king of France 1422-1461 **3** 461-462

CHARLES VIII (1470-1498), king of France 1483-1498 **3** 462-463
    relatives
        Anne of Brittany **29** 13-15

CHARLES X (1757-1836), king of France 1824-1830 **3** 463-464

CHARLES XII (1682-1718), king of Sweden 1697-1718 **3** 464-466

CHARLES XIV JOHN (1763-1844), king of Sweden 1818-1844 **2** 205-206

CHARLES, RAY (Robinson; born 1932), American jazz musician–singer, pianist, and composer **3** 469-470

CHARLES ALBERT (1798-1849), king of Sardinia 1831-1849 **3** 466

CHARLES EDWARD LOUIS PHILIP CASIMIR STUART (1720-1788), Scottish claimant to English and Scottish thrones **3** 466-467

Charles Louis Napoleon see Napoleon III

Charles Martel see Martel, Charles

Charles Philippe (Count of Artois) see Charles X (king of France)

Charles of Luxemburg see Charles IV (Holy Roman emperor)

CHARLES THE BOLD (1433-1477), duke of Burgundy 1467-1477 **3** 467-469

Charles the Great see Charlemagne

Charles the Mad see Charles VI (king of France)

Charles Scribner's Sons (publishing house)
    Doubleday, Frank Nelson **29** 146-148

Charlie Wilson's War (film)
    Wilson, Charlie **29** 379-381

Charlier, Jean see Gerson, John

CHARNISAY, CHARLES DE MENOU (Seigneur d'Aulnay; c. 1604-1650), French governor of Acadia **3** 470-471

Charolais, Count of see Charles the Bold

Chrysostom
see John Chrysostom, St.

CHU YUAN-CHANG (Hongwu; T'ai Tsu; Kao-ti; 1328-1398), Chinese emperor (1368-1398) **21** 79-81

CHU, PAUL CHING-WU (born 1941), Chinese-American experimentalist in solid-state physics **4** 37-39

CHU HSI (Chu Fu-tzu; 1130-1200), Chinese scholar and philosopher **4** 40-43

CHU TEH (1886-1976), Chinese Communist military leader **4** 54-55

Chu Ti
see Yung-lo

Chu Yüan-chang
see Hung-wu

Chub
see Ward, Artemus

CHULALONGKORN (Rama V; 1853-1910), king of Thailand 1868-1910 **4** 43-45

CHUN DOO HWAN (born 1931), army general turned politician and president of the Republic of Korea (South Korea); 1981-1988 **4** 45-47

CHUNG, CONNIE (born 1946), American correspondent and resporter **4** 47-48

CHUNG, JU YUNG (1915-2001), Korean businessman **23** 72-74

CHUNG, KYUNG WHA (born 1948), Korean violinist **23** 74-76

Ch'ung Ch'eng
see Shih Ko-fa

Ch'ungnyong, Prince
see Sejong

Chung-shan
see Sun Yat-sen

CHUNG-SHU, TUNG (c. 179-104 B.C.), Chinese man of letters **4** 48-49

CHURCH, FRANK FORRESTER, III (1924-1984), American politician **28** 78-80

CHURCH, FREDERICK EDWIN (1826-1900), American painter **4** 49-50

Church of England
see England, Church of

Church of Rome
see Roman Catholic Church

Churchill, John
see Marlborough, 1st Duke of

CHURCHILL, WINSTON (1871-1947), American novelist **4** 50-51

CHURCHILL, SIR WINSTON LEONARD SPENCER (1874-1965), English statesman **4** 51-53

CHURRIGUERA, JOSÉ BENITO DE (1665-1725), Spanish architect and sculptor **4** 53-54

CHYTILOVÁ, VERA (born 1929), Czech filmmaker **24** 85-87

CICERO, MARCUS TULLIUS (106-43 B.C.), Roman orator and writer **4** 55-58

CID, THE (Cid Campeador; 1043-1099), Spanish medieval warrior **4** 58-59

Ciguë, La (Hemlock; play)
Augier, Émile **29** 20-22

CILLER, TANSU (born 1946), prime minister of Turkey (1993-) **4** 59-60

CIMABUE (flourished late 13th century), Italian painter **4** 60-61

CIMAROSA, DOMENICO (1749-1801), Italian opera composer **4** 61-62

CINQUE, JOSEPH (c. 1813-c. 1879), West African slave leader **4** 62

Cione, Andrea di
see Orcagna

Cisneros, Francisco Jiménez de
see Jiménez de Cisneros, Francisco

CISNEROS, HENRY G. (born 1947), first Hispanic mayor in Texas **4** 62-64

CISNEROS, SANDRA (born 1954), Hispanic American short story writer and poet **4** 64-65

CISSÉ, SOULEYMANE (born 1940), Malian filmmaker **4** 65-66

Cistercians (religious order)
Bora, Katharina von **29** 256-258

Citizen Kane (film)
Davies, Marion **29** 135-138

CITROËN, ANDRÉ-GUSTAVE (1878-1935), French automobile manufacturer **4** 66-68

City government
see Municipal government

Ciudad Juárez, Treaty of
de la Barra, Francisco León **29** 245-247

Civil War, Nigerian-Biafran (1967-1970)
Ojukwu, Chukwuemeka Odumegwu **29** 298-301

Civil War, Russian
see Russian Revolution (1918-1920)

Civil War, United States (1861-1865)
ACCOUNTS OF
foreign visitors
Zeppelin, Count Ferdinand von **29** 387-389

CLAIBORNE, LIZ (Elizabeth Claiborne Ortenberg;1929-2007), American businesswoman and clothing designer **4** 68-69

CLAIR, RENÉ (née René Lucien chomette; 1898-1981), French film director and screenwriter **25** 90-93

CLANCY, TOM (born 1947), American author **4** 70-71

CLAPHAM, SIR JOHN HAROLD (1873-1946), English economic historian **4** 71

CLAPP, MARGARET ANTOINETTE (1910-1974), American author, educator, and president of Wellesley College (1949-1966) **4** 71-72

CLAPPERTON, HUGH (1788-1827), Scottish explorer of Africa **4** 72-73

CLAPTON, ERIC (born 1945), English guitarist, singer, and songwriter **18** 90-92

CLARE, JOHN (1793-1864), British Poet **26** 69-71

CLARENDON, 1ST EARL OF (Edward Hyde; 1609-1674), English statesman and historian **4** 73-75

CLARE OF ASSISI, SAINT (Chiara Offreduccio di Favoronne; 1194-1253), Italian relisious leader **23** 76-78

CLARK, GEORGE ROGERS (1752-1818), American Revolutionary War soldier **4** 75-76

CLARK, HELEN ELIZABETH (born 1950), New Zealand prime minister **25** 93-95

CLARK, JOHN BATES (1847-1938), American economist **4** 76-77

CLARK, JOHN MAURICE (1884-1963), American economist **4** 77-78

CLARK, KENNETH B. (born 1914), American social psychologist **4** 78-79

CLARK, KENNETH M. (Lord; 1903-1983), English art historian **4** 79-80

Clark, Latimer (1822-1898), English engineer
Bright, Charles Tilston **29** 91-93

CLARK, MARK WAYNE (1896-1984), American general **4** 80-81

CLARK, TOM CAMPBELL (1899-1977), President Harry S. Truman's attorney general and Supreme Court justice **4** 81-82

CLARK, WILLIAM (1770-1838), American explorer and soldier **4** 82-83

CLARK, WILLIAM ANDREWS (1839-1925), American copper entrepreneur and politician **4** 83-85

CLARKE, ARTHUR CHARLES (1917-2008), English author **18** 92-94

CLARKE, KENNETH HARRY (born 1940), Conservative politician and Great Britain's chancellor of the exchequer (1993-) **4** 85-87

COEN, JAN PIETERSZOON (c. 1586-1629), Dutch governor general of Batavia **4** 133

COETZEE, J(OHN) M. (born 1940), white South African novelist **4** 133-135

COFFIN, LEVI (1789-1877), American antislavery reformer **4** 135

Coffin, Lucretia
see Mott, Lucretia Coffin

COFFIN, WILLIAM SLOANE, JR. (1924-2006), Yale University chaplain who spoke out against the Vietnam War **4** 135-137

COHAN, GEORGE MICHAEL (1878-1942), American actor and playwright **4** 137-138

Cohen, Bennett, (Ben Cohen; born 1951)
see Ben & Jerry

Cohen, George Morris
see Brandes, Georg Morris

COHEN, HERMANN (1842-1918), Jewish-German philosopher **4** 138-139

COHEN, MORRIS RAPHAEL (1880-1947), American philosopher and teacher **4** 139-140

COHEN, WILLIAM S. (born 1940), American secretary of defense **18** 96-98

Cohn, Arthur, (born 1927), Swiss movie producer
de Sica, Vittorio **29** 138-139

COHN, FERDINAND (1829-1898), German botanist **20** 95-97

COHN, ROY MARCUS (1927-1986), American lawyer and businessman **29** 116-118

COHN-BENDIT, DANIEL (born 1946), led "new left" student protests in France in 1968 **4** 140-141

COKE, SIR EDWARD (1552-1634), English jurist and parliamentarian **4** 141-142

Colba
see Cuba

Colbath, Jeremiah Jones
see Wilson, Henry

COLBERT, JEAN BAPTISTE (1619-1683), French statesman **4** 142-143

COLBY, WILLIAM E. (1920-1996), American director of the Central Intelligence Agency (CIA) **4** 143-145

Cold War (international politics)
European attitude
Novotný, Antonín **29** 291-293

COLDEN, CADWALLADER (1688-1776), American botanist and politician **4** 145-146
Colden, Jane **29** 118-119

COLDEN, JANE (1724-1766), American botanist **29** 118-119

COLE, GEORGE DOUGLAS HOWARD (1889-1959), English historian and economist **4** 146-147

COLE, JOHNNETTA (born 1936), African American scholar and educator **4** 147-149

COLE, NAT (a.k.a. Nat "King" Cole, born Nathaniel Adams Coles; 1919-1965), American jazz musician **4** 149-151

COLE, THOMAS (1801-1848), American painter **4** 151-152

COLEMAN, BESSIE (1892-1926), first African American to earn an international pilot's license **4** 152-154

COLERIDGE, SAMUEL TAYLOR (1772-1834), English poet and critic **4** 154-156
associates
Lamb, Mary **29** 237-239

COLERIDGE-TAYLOR, SAMUEL (1875-1912), English composer and conductor **28** 80-83

COLES, ROBERT MARTIN (born 1929), American social psychiatrist, social critic, and humanist **4** 156-157

Colet, Hippolyte, (1808-c. 1851), French musician
Colet, Louise **29** 119-121

COLET, JOHN (c. 1446-1519), English theologian **4** 157-158

COLET, LOUISE (1810-1870), French poet **29** 119-121

COLETTE, SIDONIE GABRIELLE (1873-1954), French author **4** 158-159

COLIGNY, GASPARD DE (1519-1572), French admiral and statesman **4** 159-160

COLLETT, CAMILLA (nee Camilla Wergeland; 1813-1895), Norwegian author **26** 73-75

COLLIER, JOHN (1884-1968), American proponent of Native American culture **4** 160-162

COLLINGWOOD, ROBIN GEORGE (1889-1943), English historian and philosopher **4** 162

COLLINS, BILLY (born 1941), American poet **28** 83-85

COLLINS, EDWARD KNIGHT (1802-1878), American businessman and shipowner **4** 162-163

COLLINS, EILEEN (born 1956), American astronaut **4** 163-165

COLLINS, MARVA (born Marva Deloise Nettles; b. 1936), African American educator **4** 165-167

COLLINS, MICHAEL (1890-1922), Irish revolutionary leader and soldier **4** 167-168

COLLINS, WILLIAM (1721-1759), English lyric poet **4** 168-169

COLLINS, WILLIAM WILKIE (1824-1889), English novelist **4** 169-170

COLLIP, JAMES BERTRAM (1892-1965), Canadian biochemist **29** 121-123

COLLOR DE MELLO, FERNANDO (born 1949), businessman who became president of Brazil in 1990 **4** 170-172

Colonna, Oddone
see Martin V

Colorado party (Uruguay)
Baldomir, Alfredo **29** 39-41

COLT, SAMUEL (1814-1862), American inventor and manufacturer **4** 172-173

COLTRANE, JOHN (1926-1967), African American jazz saxophonist **4** 173-174

COLUM, PADRAIC (1881-1972), Irish-American poet and playwright **4** 174-175

COLUMBA, ST. (c. 521-597), Irish monk and missionary **4** 175-176

COLUMBAN, ST. (c. 543-615), Irish missionary **4** 176

Columbia College (New York City)
see Columbia University (New York City)

Columbia University (New York City)
architecture
Pokorny, Jan Hird **29** 320-321

COLUMBUS, CHRISTOPHER (1451-1506), Italian navigator, discoverer of America **4** 176-179

COLWELL, RITA R. (born 1934), American marine microbiologist **4** 179-180

Comanche Indians (North America)
Masterson, Bat **29** 272-274

COMANECI, NADIA (Nadia Conner; born 1961), Romanian gymnast **18** 98-100

Comédie-Française (French state theater)
Augier, Émile **29** 20-22

COMENIUS, JOHN AMOS (1592-1670), Moravian theologian and educational reformer **4** 180-181

COMINES, PHILIPPE DE (c. 1445-1511), French chronicler **4** 181

Comintern
see International, Third (Comintern; 1919-43)

COMMAGER, HENRY STEELE (1902-1998), American historian, textbook author, and editor **4** 181-183

Commedia (Dante)
see Divine Comedy, The (poem; Dante)

DAVIS, ELMER HOLMES (1890-1958), American journalist and radio commentator **22** 133-136

DAVIS, GLENN (1925-2005), American football player **21** 101-103

DAVIS, HENRY WINTER (1817-1865), American lawyer and politician **4** 415-416

DAVIS, JEFFERSON (1808-1889), American statesman, president of the Confederacy 1862-1865 **4** 416-418

DAVIS, JOHN (c. 1550-1605), English navigator **4** 419

Davis, John W., (1873-1955), American lawyer and politician
Henderson, Zelma **29** 188-191

DAVIS, MILES (1926-1991), jazz trumpeter, composer, and small-band leader **4** 419-421

DAVIS, OSSIE (1917-2005), African American playwright, actor, and director **4** 421-422

DAVIS, RICHARD HARDING (1864-1916), American journalist, novelist, and dramatist **4** 422-423

DAVIS, SAMMY, JR. (1925-1990), African American singer, dancer, and actor **4** 423-424

DAVIS, STUART (1894-1964), American cubist painter **4** 424-425

DAVIS, WILLIAM MORRIS (1850-1934), American geographer and geologist **4** 425-426

DAVY, SIR HUMPHRY (1778-1829), English chemist and natural philosopher **4** 426-427

DAWES, HENRY LAURENS (1816-1903), American politician **4** 427

DAWSON, WILLIAM LEVI (1899-1990), African American composer, performer, and music educator **4** 427-428

DAY, DOROTHY (1897-1980), a founder of the Catholic Worker Movement **4** 428-429

DAYAN, MOSHE (1915-1981), Israeli general and statesman **4** 429-431

DAYANANDA SARASWATI (1824-1883), Indian religious leader **4** 431

DE ANDRADE, MARIO (Mario Coelho Pinto Andrade; born 1928), Angolan poet, critic, and political activist **4** 434-435

DE BEAUVOIR, SIMONE (1908-1986), French writer and leader of the modern feminist movement **4** 440-441

DE BOW, JAMES DUNWOODY BROWNSON (1820-1867), American editor and statistician **4** 441-442

DE BROGLIE, LOUIS VICTOR PIERRE RAYMOND (1892-1987), French physicist **4** 442-444

DE FOREST, LEE (1873-1961), American inventor **4** 459-460

DE GASPERI, ALCIDE (1881-1954), Italian statesman, premier 1945-1953 **4** 462-463

DE GAULLE, CHARLES ANDRÉ JOSEPH MARIE (1890-1970), French general, president 1958-1969 **4** 463-465

DE GOUGES, MARIE OLYMPE (born Marie Gouzes; 1748-1793), French author **23** 85-88

DE GOURNAY, MARIE LE JARS (1565-1645), French author **23** 88-90

DE HAVILLAND, SIR GEOFFREY (1882-1965), British aviator and aeronautical engineer **25** 101-103

DE HIRSCH, MAURICE (Baron de Hirsch; 1831-1896), Austro-Hungarian financier and philanthropist **24** 104-106

DE KLERK, FREDRIK WILLEM (born 1936), state president of South Africa (1989-) **4** 466-468

DE KOONING, WILLEM (1904-1997), Dutch-born American painter **4** 468-469

DE LA BARRA, FRANCISCO LEÓN (1863-1939), Mexican statesman **29** 245-247

DE LA MADRID HURTADO, MIGUEL (born 1934), president of Mexico (1982-1988) **4** 471-472

DE LA ROCHE, MAZO LOUISE (1879-1961), Canadian author **4** 474-475

De la Warr, Thomas West, English colonial governor of Virginia
Argall, Samuel **29** 18-20

DE LEMPICKA, TAMARA (Maria Gorska; Tamara Kuffner; 1898-1980), Polish American artist **24** 106-109

DE LEON, DANIEL (1852-1914), American Socialist theoretician and politician **4** 479-480

DE L'ORME, PHILIBERT (1510-1570), French architect **9** 519

DE MILLE, AGNES (1905-1993), American dancer, choreographer, and author **4** 486-488

De Motu Animalium (On the Movement of Animals; book)
Borelli, Giovanni Alfonso **29** 69-72

DE NIRO, ROBERT (born 1943), American actor and film producer **21** 103-106

DE PISAN, CHRISTINE (1363-1431), French poet and philosopher **24** 109-111

DE QUINCEY, THOMAS (Thomas Quincey; 1785-1859), British author **27** 98-100

De Revoire, Paul
see Revere, Paul

DE SANCTIS, FRANCESCO (1817-1883), Italian critic, educator, and legislator **4** 505

DE SAUSSURE, FERDINAND (1857-1913), Swiss linguist and author **24** 111-113

DE SICA, VITTORIO (1901?-1974), Italian filmmaker **29** 138-139

DE SMET, PIERRE JEAN (1801-1873), Belgian Jesuit missionary **4** 509-510

DE SOTO, HERNANDO (1500-1542), Spanish conqueror and explorer **4** 510-511
Pizarro, Juan **29** 318-320

DE VALERA, EAMON (1882-1975), American-born Irish revolutionary leader and statesman **4** 514-515

DE VALOIS, NINETTE (Edris Stannus; 1898-2001), English choreographer and ballet dancer **25** 103-105

DE VERE, EDWARD (Earl of Oxford; 1550-1604), English author **25** 105-107

DE VRIES, HUGO (1848-1935), Belgian botanist in the fields of heredity and the origin of species **4** 516-518

DE WOLFE, ELSIE (1865-1950), American interior decorator **20** 107-108

Deadwood Dick
see Love, Nat

Deaf, the
deafness victims
Amontons, Guillaume **29** 3-5
education of
Bridgman, Laura Dewey **29** 88-91

DEÁK, FRANCIS (1803-1876), Hungarian statesman **4** 431-432

DEAKIN, ALFRED (1856-1919), Australian statesman **4** 432-433

DEAN, JAMES (James Byron Dean; 1931-1955), American actor and cult figure **4** 433-434

DEANE, SILAS (1737-1789), American merchant lawyer and diplomat **4** 435-437

Death of Marat (painting)
Corday, Charlotte **29** 123-126

DEB, RADHAKANT (1783-1867), Bengali reformer and cultural nationalist **4** 437

DEBAKEY, MICHAEL ELLIS (born 1908), American surgeon **4** 437-438

DEBARTOLO, EDWARD JOHN, SR. AND JR., real estate developers who specialized in large regional malls **4** 438-440

DEBS, EUGENE VICTOR (1855-1926), American union organizer **4** 444-445

DEBUSSY, (ACHILLE) CLAUDE (1862-1918), French composer **4** 445-447

DEBYE, PETER JOSEPH WILLIAM (1884-1966), Dutch-born American physical chemist **4** 447-448

DECATUR, STEPHEN (1779-1820), American naval officer **4** 448-449

Decimus Junius Juvenalis
see Juvenal

DEE, JOHN (1527-1608), British mathematician and astronomer **25** 107-110

DEE, RUBY (born Ruby Ann Wallace; born 1924), African American actor **4** 449-452

DEER, ADA E. (born 1935), Native American social worker, activist, and director of Bureau of Indian Affairs **4** 452-454

DEERE, JOHN (1804-1886), American inventor and manufacturer **4** 455

DEERING, WILLIAM (1826-1913), American manufacturer **4** 455-456

DEES, MORRIS S., JR. (born 1936), American civil rights attorney **4** 456-457

DEFOE, DANIEL (1660-1731), English novelist, journalist, and poet **4** 457-459

DEGANAWIDA (also DeKanahwidah; c. 1550-c. 1600), Native American prophet, leader, and statesman **4** 460-461

DEGAS, (HILAIRE GERMAIN) EDGAR (1834-1917), French painter and sculptor **4** 461-462

DEHLAVI, SHAH WALIULLAH (Qutb-ud-Din; 1703-1762), Indian religious leader **28** 92-94

DEISENHOFER, JOHANN (born 1943), German biochemist and biophysicist **23** 90-93

DEKKER, THOMAS (c. 1572-c. 1632), English playwright and pamphleteer **4** 465-466

DELACROIX, (FERDINAND VICTOR) EUGÈNE (1798-1863), French painter **4** 469-471

DELANCEY, STEPHEN (1663-1741), American merchant and politician **4** 473

DELANY, MARTIN ROBINSON (1812-1885), African American army officer, politician, and judge **4** 473-474

Delattre, Roland
see Lassus, Roland de

DELAUNAY, ROBERT (1885-1941), French abstract painter **4** 475-476

DELBRÜCK, MAX (1906-1981), German-born American molecular biologist **4** 476-478

DELCASSÉ, THÉOPHILE (1852-1923), French statesman **4** 478-479

DELEDDA, GRAZIA (Grazia Maria Cosima Damiana Deledda; 1871-1936), Italian author **24** 113-115

DELEUZE, GILLES (1925-1995), French Philosopher **28** 94-96

DELGADO, JOSÉ MATIAS (1768-1832), Salvadoran political leader **24** 115-117

DELL, MICHAEL SAUL (born 1965), American businessman **23** 93-95

Della Robbia, Luca
see Robbia, Luca della

DELLINGER, DAVID (born 1915), American pacifist **4** 480-481

DELORIA, ELLA CLARA (1889-1971), Native American ethnologist, linguist, and author **22** 136-138

DELORIA, VINE, JR. (1933-2005), Native American author, poet, and activist **4** 481-484

DELORS, JACQUES (born 1925), French president of the European Commission and chief architect of Western Europe's drive toward market unity by 1992 **4** 484-486

DEL PILAR, MARCELO H. (1850-1896), Philippine revolutionary propagandist and satirist **4** 486

DELAY, TOM (Thomas Dale Delay; born 1947), American politician **26** 83-85

DEMILLE, CECIL BLOUNT (1881-1959), American film director and producer **4** 488-490
    Swanson, Gloria **29** 354-355

DEMIREL, SÜLEYMAN (born 1924), Turkish politician, prime minister, and leader of the Justice party **4** 490-493

Democratic party (United States)
    leaders (Missouri)
        Pendergast, Thomas J. **29** 313-315

Democratic Republic of Vietnam
see Vietnam, North (Democratic Republic of Vietnam)

DEMOCRITUS (c. 494-c. 404 B.C.), Greek natural philosopher **4** 493-494

DEMOIVRE, ABRAHAM (1667-1754), Franco-English mathematician **4** 494-495

DEMOSTHENES (384-322 B.C.), Greek orator **4** 495-496

DEMPSEY, JACK (William Harrison Dempsey; 1895-1983), American boxer **4** 496-497
    Schmeling, Max **29** 337-339

DEMUTH, CHARLES (1883-1935), American painter **4** 497-498

DENG XIAOPING (Teng Hsiao-p'ing; 1904-1997), leader in the People's Republic of China (PRC) in the 1970s **4** 498-500

DENIKIN, ANTON (1872-1947), Russian soldier **20** 108-111

DENKTASH, RAUF (born 1924), president of the Turkish Republic of Northern Cyprus (1985-) **4** 500-502

DENNING, ALFRED THOMPSON (Tom Denning' 1899-1999), British judge and author **22** 138-140

Dennis, Ruth
see St. Denis, Ruth

Dentistry (medical science)
    Hunter, John **29** 202-204

DENVER, JOHN (Henry John Deutschendorf, Jr.; 1943-1997), American singer and songwriter **27** 100-102

DEODORO DA FONSECA, MANOEL (1827-1892), Brazilian statesman, president 1890-1891 **4** 502

Deoxyribonucleic acid (DNA)
    Holley, Robert W. **29** 191-193

DEPARDIEU, GERARD (born 1948), French actor **27** 102-105

Department store (retail business)
    Wanamaker, John **29** 372-375

DERAIN, ANDRÉ (1880-1954), French painter **4** 503

DEREN, MAYA (Eleanora Solomonovna Derenkovskaya; 1917-1961), Ukrainian American author and filmaker **23** 95-97

DERRICOTTE, JULIETTE ALINE (1897-1931), African American educator **22** 140-141

DERRIDA, JACQUES (1930-2004), French philosopher **4** 503-505

DERSHOWITZ, ALAN MORTON (born 1938), American lawyer **26** 85-87

DESAI, ANITA (née Anita Mazumdar; born 1937), Indian author **25** 110-113

DESCARTES, RENÉ (1596-1650), French philosopher and mathematician **4** 505-508

Desert Fox
see Rommel, Erwin

Desiderio da Settignano
see Settignano, Desiderio da

Designers
    costumes
        Bakst, Leon **29** 35-37
    stage sets
        Bakst, Leon **29** 35-37

Despréaux, Nicholas Boileau
see Boileau-Despréaux, Nicholas

DESSALINES, JEAN JACQUES
(1758-1806), Haitian nationalist and politician **4** 511-512

Destined to Witness (autobiography)
Massaquoi, Hans J. **29** 270-272

Destouches, Louis Ferdinand
see Céline, Louis Ferdinand

Detective stories
see Mystery fiction (literary genre)

DETT, ROBERT NATHANIEL (1882-1943),
African American composer, conductor, and music educator **4** 512

Dettonville, Amos
see Pascal, Blaise

DEUTSCH, KARL WOLFGANG
(1912-1992), American political scientist **4** 512-514

DEVERS, GAIL (Yolanda Gail Devers; born 1966), American athlete **25** 113-115

DEVLIN, BERNADETTE (McAliskey; born 1947), youngest woman ever elected to the British Parliament **4** 515-516

DEVRIES, WILLIAM CASTLE (born 1943),
American heart surgeon **4** 518-519

DEW, THOMAS RODERICK (1802-1846),
American political economist **4** 519

DEWEY, GEORGE (1837-1917), American naval officer **4** 520

DEWEY, JOHN (1859-1952), American philosopher and educator **4** 520-523

DEWEY, MELVIL (1851-1931), American librarian and reformer **4** 523-524

DEWEY, THOMAS EDMUND
(1902-1971), American lawyer and politician **4** 524

DEWSON, MARY WILLIAMS (Molly; 1874-1962), American reformer, government official, and organizer of women for the Democratic party **4** 525

D'HÉRELLE, FÉLIX HUBERT (1873-1949),
Canadian bacteriologist **29** 140-142

DHLOMO, R.R.R. (1901-1971), Zulu writer **29** 142-144

Dhu'l-Aktaf
see Shahpur II

Diabetes (medicine)
Collip, James Bertram **29** 121-123

DIAGHILEV, SERGEI (1872-1929), Russian who inspired artists, musicians, and dancers to take ballet to new heights of public enjoyment **4** 525-527
sets commissioned
Bakst, Leon **29** 35-37
Roerich, Nicholas **29** 328-330

DIAGNE, BLAISE (1872-1934), Senegalese political leader **4** 527

DIAMOND, DAVID (1915-2005),
American composer and teacher **4** 527-529

DIANA, PRINCESS OF WALES (born Diana Frances Spencer; 1961-1997), member of British royal family **4** 529-533

DIAS DE NOVAIS, BARTOLOMEU (died 1500), Portuguese explorer **4** 533-534

DIAZ, ABBY MORTON (nee Abigail Morton; 1821-1904), American author and activist **26** 87-89

Díaz, Manuel Azaña
see Azaña Díaz, Manuel

DÍAZ, PORFIRIO (José de la Cruz Porfirio Díaz; 1830-1915), Mexican general and politician **4** 534-536
associates
de la Barra, Francisco León **29** 245-247

Diaz, Rodrigo
see Cid, The

DÍAZ DEL CASTILLO, BERNAL (c. 1496-c. 1584), Spanish soldier and historian **4** 536-537

DÍAZ ORDAZ, GUSTAVO (1911-1979),
president of Mexico (1964-1970) **4** 537-538

DICK, PHILIP K. (Philip Kindred Dick; 1928-1982), American science fiction writer **28** 96-98

DICKENS, CHARLES JOHN HUFFAM
(1812-1870), English author **4** 538-541
adaptations
Lean, David **29** 239-241

DICKEY, JAMES (1923-1997), American poet **19** 87-89

Dickinson, Austin, (1828-1895)
Todd, Mabel Loomis **29** 360-362

DICKINSON, EMILY (1830-1886),
American poet **4** 541-543
Todd, Mabel Loomis **29** 360-362

DICKINSON, JOHN (1732-1808),
American lawyer, pamphleteer, and politician **4** 543-544

Dickinson, Lavinia, (1833-1899)
Todd, Mabel Loomis **29** 360-362

DICKSON, LAURIE (William Kennedy Laurie Dickson; 1860-1935), British inventor and filmmaker **20** 112-113

Dictatorship (government)
Latin America
Carrillo, Braulio **29** 112-113

DIDDLEY, BO (1928-2008), American musician **29** 144-146

DIDEROT, DENIS (1713-1784), French philosopher, playwright, and encyclopedist **5** 1-2

DIDION, JOAN (born 1934), American author **20** 113-116

DIEBENKORN, RICHARD (born 1922),
American abstract expressionist painter **5** 2-4

DIEFENBAKER, JOHN GEORGE
(1895-1979), Canadian statesman **5** 4-5

DIELS, (OTTO PAUL) HERMANN
(1876-1954), German organic chemist **5** 5-6

DIEM, NGO DINH (1901-1963), South Vietnamese president 1955-1963 **5** 6-7

DIESEL, RUDOLF (1858-1913), German mechanical engineer **5** 7

DIETRICH, MARLENE (née Marie Magdalene Dietrich; 1901-1992),
German actor **25** 115-117

DIKE, KENNETH (Kenneth Onwuka Dike; 1917-1983), African historian who set up the Nigerian National Archives **5** 7-8

DILLINGER, JOHN (1903-1934),
American criminal **5** 9

DILTHEY, WILHELM CHRISTIAN LUDWIG (1833-1911), German historian and philosopher **5** 10

DIMAGGIO, JOE (born Giuseppe Paolo DiMaggio, Jr.; 1914-1999), American baseball player **5** 10-11

DIMITROV, GEORGI (1882-1949), head of the Communist International (1935-1943) and prime minister of Bulgaria (1944-1949) **5** 11-13

Din, Muslih-al-
see Sadi

DINESEN BLIXEN-FINECKE, KAREN
(a.k.a. Isak Dinesen; 1885-1962),
Danish author **5** 13-14

DINGANE (c. 1795-1840), Zulu king **5** 14-15

DINKINS, DAVID (born 1927), African American politician and mayor of New York City **5** 15-18

Dinosaur (extinct reptile)
Osborn, Henry Fairfield, Sr. **29** 306-308

DINWIDDIE, ROBERT (1693-1770),
Scottish merchant and colonial governor **5** 18-19

DIOCLETIAN (Gaius Aurelius Valerius Diocletianus; 245-c. 313), Roman emperor 284-305 **5** 19-20

DIOGENES (c. 400-325 B.C.), Greek philosopher **5** 20-21

DURAS, MARGUERITE (Marguerite Donnadieu; 1914-1996), French author and filmmaker **26** 92-95

DÜRER, ALBRECHT (1471-1528), German painter and graphic artist **5** 159-161

DURHAM, 1ST EARL OF (John George Lambton; 1792-1840), English statesman **5** 161-162

DURKHEIM, ÉMILE (1858-1917), French philosopher and sociologist **5** 162-163

DURRELL, GERALD MALCOLM (1925-1995), British naturalist and conservationist **24** 123-126

DURRELL, LAWRENCE (1912-1990), British author of novels, poetry, plays, short stories, and travel books **5** 163-164

DÜRRENMATT, FRIEDRICH (1921-1990), Swiss playwright **5** 164-165

DUVALIER, FRANÇOIS (Papa Doc; 1907-1971), Haitian president 1957-1971 **5** 165-166

DUVALIER, JEAN CLAUDE (Baby Doc; born 1949), president of Haiti (1971-1986) **5** 166-168

DVOŘÁK, ANTONIN (1841-1904), Czech composer **5** 168-169

DVR
see Vietnam, North (Democratic Republic of Vietnam)

DWIGHT, TIMOTHY (1752-1817), American educator and Congregational minister **5** 169

Dyck, Anthony van
see Van Dyck, Anthony

Dye (color matter)
Bosch, Carl **29** 76-78

DYLAN, BOB (born Robert Allen Zimmerman; b. 1941), American singer, songwriter, and guitarist **5** 170-171

DYSON, FREEMAN JOHN (born 1923), British-American physicist **5** 171-173

DZERZHINSKY, FELIX EDMUNDOVICH (1877-1926), Soviet politician and revolutionary **5** 173-174

E

E. coli (bacterium)
see Escherichia coli (bacterium)

Dzhugashvili, Iosif Vissarionovich
see Stalin, Joseph

EADS, JAMES BUCHANAN (1820-1887), American engineer and inventor **5** 175-176

EAKINS, THOMAS (1844-1916), American painter **5** 176-177

EARHART, AMELIA MARY (1897-1937), American aviator **5** 177-179

EARL, RALPH (1751-1801), American painter **5** 179

EARLE, SYLVIA A. (Born Sylvia Alice Reade; born 1935), American marine biologist and oceanographer **5** 180-181

EARNHARDT, DALE (1951-2001), American race car driver **22** 156-158

EARP, WYATT BARRY STEPP (1848-1929), gun-fighting marshal of the American West **5** 181-182
Hooker, Henry Clay **29** 193-195
Masterson, Bat **29** 272-274

Earthquake (seismology)
Amontons, Guillaume **29** 3-5

EAST, EDWARD MURRAY (1879-1938), American plant geneticist **5** 182-183

EASTMAN, CHARLES A. (1858-1939), Native American author **5** 183-185

EASTMAN, GEORGE (1854-1932), American inventor and industrialist **5** 186

EASTMAN, MAX (Max Forrester Eastman; 1883-1969), American poet, radical editor, translator, and author **5** 187-188

EASTWOOD, ALICE (1859-1953), American botanist **22** 158-160

EASTWOOD, CLINT (born 1930), American movie star and director **5** 188-190

EATON, DORMAN BRIDGMAN (1823-1899), American lawyer and author **5** 190-191

EBADI, SHIRIN (born 1947), Iranian author and human rights activist **25** 124-126

EBAN, ABBA (Abba Solomon Eban; 1915-2002), Israeli statesman, diplomat, and scholar **5** 191-192

EBB, FRED (1935-2004), American lyricist **21** 113-115

EBBERS, BERNIE (born 1941), American businessman **20** 122-124

EBBINGHAUS, HERMANN (1850-1909), German psychologist **5** 192-193

EBERT, FRIEDRICH (1871-1925), German president 1919-1925 **5** 193-194

Ebony (magazine)
Massaquoi, Hans J. **29** 270-272

EBOUÉ, ADOLPHE FELIX SYLVESTRE (1885-1944), African statesman, governor of French Equatorial Africa **5** 194

ECCLES, MARRINER STODDARD (1890-1977), American banker **22** 160-162

ECCLES, SIR JOHN CAREW (1903-1997), Australian neurophysiologist **5** 195-196

ECEVIT, BÜLENT (1925-2006), Turkish statesman and prime minister **5** 196-197

Echaurren, Roberto Matta
see Matta Echaurren, Roberto Sebastian Antonio

ECHEVERRÍA, JOSÉ ESTÉBAN (1805-1851), Argentine author and political theorist **5** 197-198

ECHEVERRIA ALVAREZ, LUIS (born 1922), president of Mexico (1970-1976) **5** 198-200

ECK, JOHANN MAIER VON (1486-1543), German theologian **5** 200

ECKERT, JOHN PRESPER (1919-1995), American computer engineer **20** 124-126

ECKHART, (JOHANN) MEISTER (c. 1260-c. 1327), German Dominican theologian **5** 200-201

ECO, UMBERTO (born 1932), Italian scholar and novelist **18** 128-130

École des Sciences Politiques (France)
Boutmy, Émile **29** 83-84

EDDINGTON, SIR ARTHUR STANLEY (1882-1944), English astronomer **5** 201-202

EDDY, MARY BAKER (1821-1910), American founder of the Christian Science Church **5** 202

EDELMAN, GERALD MAURICE (born 1929), American neuroscientist **27** 106-108

EDELMAN, MARIAN WRIGHT (born 1939), lobbyist, lawyer, civil rights activist, and founder of the Children's Defense Fund **5** 202-204

EDEN, ANTHONY (1897-1977), English statesman, prime minister 1955-1957 **5** 204-205

EDERLE, GERTRUDE (born 1906), American swimmer **19** 98-100

EDGERTON, HAROLD EUGENE (1903-1990), American inventor **28** 109-111

EDGEWORTH, MARIA (1767-1849), British author **5** 205-206

EDINGER, TILLY (Johanna Gabriella Ottelie Edinger; 1897-1967), American paleontologist **22** 163-164

EDISON, THOMAS ALVA (1847-1931), American inventor **5** 206-208

Editors, American
book editors
Todd, Mabel Loomis **29** 360-362
Toklas, Alice B. **29** 362-364
magazines and journals (19th-20th century)
Blackwell, Alice Stone **29** 61-63
newspapers (19th-20th century)
Brisbane, Arthur **29** 93-95

ELIZABETH II (born 1926), queen of Great Britain and Ireland **5** 266-269

ELIZABETH BAGAAYA NYABONGO OF TORO (born 1940), Ugandan ambassador **5** 269-271

ELIZABETH BOWES-LYON (Elizabeth Angela Marguerite Bowes-Lyon; 1900-2002), queen of Great Britain and Ireland (1936-1952) and Queen Mother after 1952 **5** 261-263

ELIZABETH OF HUNGARY (1207-1231), saint and humanitarian **5** 271-272

ELLINGTON, "DUKE" EDWARD KENNEDY (born 1899), American jazz composer **5** 273-274

ELLIS, HAVELOCK (Henry Havelock Ellis; 1959-1939), British psychologist and author **20** 126-128

ELLISON, RALPH WALDO (1914-1994), African American author and spokesperson for racial identity **5** 274-275

ELLSBERG, DANIEL (born 1931), U.S. government official and Vietnam peace activist **5** 275-277

ELLSWORTH, LINCOLN (1880-1951), American adventurer and polar explorer **5** 277

ELLSWORTH, OLIVER (1745-1807), American senator and Supreme Court Chief Justice **21** 115-117

ELSASSER, WALTER MAURICE (1904-1991), American physicist **5** 277-278

ELWAY, JOHN (born 1960), American football player **23** 98-100

ELY, RICHARD (1854-1943), American economist and social reformer **21** 117-120

EMERSON, RALPH WALDO (1803-1882), American poet, essayist, and philosopher **5** 278-280

EMINESCU, MIHAIL (1850-1889), Romanian poet **5** 280-281

EMMET, ROBERT (1778-1803), Irish nationalist and revolutionary **5** 281-282

EMPEDOCLES (c. 493-c. 444 B.C.), Greek philosopher, poet, and scientist **5** 282

Emperor Jones, The (play and film)
    Gilpin, Charles **29** 172-174

ENCHI, FUMIKO UEDA (1905-1986), Japanese author **23** 100-102

ENCINA, JUAN DEL (1468-1529?), Spanish author and composer **5** 283

ENDARA, GUILLERMO (born 1936), installed as president of Panama by the U.S. Government in 1989 **5** 283-284

ENDECOTT, JOHN (1588-1655), English colonial governor of Massachusetts **5** 284-285

ENDERS, JOHN FRANKLIN (1897-1985), American virologist **5** 285-286

Endocrinology (science)
    Collip, James Bertram **29** 121-123

Endogamy
    Tillion, Germaine **29** 358-360

Enemy combatants
    Korematsu, Fred **29** 234-236

ENGELS, FRIEDRICH (1820-1895), German revolutionist and social theorist **5** 286-288

Engine (machine)
    Maybach, Wilhelm **29** 274-277

England, Church of
    separation from Rome
        Babington, Anthony **29** 27-29

ENGLAND, JOHN (1786-1842), Irish Catholic bishop in America **5** 288

ENNIN (794-864), Japanese Buddhist monk **5** 288-289

ENNIUS, QUINTUS (239-169 B.C.), Roman poet **5** 289

ENRICO, ROGER (born 1944), American businessman **27** 111-112

ENSOR, JAMES (1860-1949), Belgian painter and graphic artist **5** 289-290

Environmental activists (European)
    Scott, Sir Peter Markham **29** 339-341

EPAMINONDAS (c. 425-362 B.C.), Theban general and statesman **5** 291-292

EPÉE, CHARLES-MICHEL DE L' (1712-1789), French sign language developer **21** 120-122

EPHRON, NORA (born 1941), American author, screenwriter and film director **18** 130-132
    Bernstein, Carl **29** 52-54

Epic theater
    Piscator, Erwin **29** 315-317

EPICTETUS (c. 50-c. 135), Greek philosopher **5** 292

EPICURUS (c. 342-270 B.C.), Greek philosopher, founder of Epicureanism **5** 292-294

Epimanes
    see Antiochus IV (king of Syria)

EPSTEIN, ABRAHAM (1892-1945), Russian-born American economist **5** 294-295

EPSTEIN, SIR JACOB (1880-1959), American-born English sculptor **5** 295-296

EQUIANO, OLAUDAH (1745-c. 1801), African author and former slave **5** 296-297

ERASISTRATUS (c. 304 B.C.- c. 250 B.C.), Greek physician and anantomist **5** 297-298

ERASMUS, DESIDERIUS (1466-1536), Dutch author, scholar, and humanist **5** 298-300

ERASMUS, GEORGES HENRY (born 1948), Canadian Indian leader **5** 300-301

ERATOSTHENES OF CYRENE (c. 284-c. 205 B.C.), Greek mathematician, geographer, and astronomer **5** 301-302

ERCILLA Y ZÚÑIGA, ALONSO DE (1533-1594), Spanish poet, soldier, and diplomat **5** 302

ERDOS, PAUL (1913-1996), Hungarian mathematician **22** 166-168

ERDRICH, LOUISE (Karen Louise Erdrich; born 1954), Native American author **23** 102-105

ERHARD, LUDWIG (1897-1977), German statesman, West German chancellor 1963-66 **5** 302-304

ERIC THE RED (Eric Thorvaldsson; flourished late 10th century), Norwegian explorer **5** 304

ERICKSON, ARTHUR CHARLES (born 1924), Canadian architect and landscape architect **5** 304-306

ERICSON, LEIF (971-c. 1015), Norse mariner and adventurer **5** 306-307

ERICSSON, JOHN (1803-1889), Swedish-born American engineer and inventor **5** 307-308

Erie Canal (New York State)
    Ames, Ezra **29** 1-3

ERIGENA, JOHN SCOTUS (c. 810-c. 877), Irish scholastic philosopher **5** 308-309

ERIKSON, ERIK HOMBURGER (1902-1994), German-born American psychoanalyst and educator **5** 309-310

ERLANGER, JOSEPH (1874-1965), American physiologist **5** 310-311

ERMAN, ADOLF (1854-1937), German Egyptologist and lexicographer **29** 154-156

ERNST, MAX (born 1891), German painter **5** 311-312

ERNST, RICHARD (Richard Robert Ernst; born 1933), Swiss Chemist **27** 112-114

Erotic art
    Aretino, Pietro **29** 16-18

ERSHAD, HUSSAIN MOHAMMAD (born 1930), Bengali military leader and president of Bangladesh (1982-1990) **5** 312-314

Fatih
see Mehmed the Conqueror

FAUCHARD, PIERRE (1678-1761), French dentist **26** 103-105

FAULKNER, BRIAN (1921-1977), prime minister of Northern Ireland (1971-1972) **5** 393-395

Faulkner, Thomas J.R., Liberian politician
Barclay, Edwin **29** 44-45

FAULKNER, WILLIAM (1897-1962), American novelist **5** 395-397

FAURÉ, GABRIEL URBAIN (1845-1924), French composer **5** 397-398

FAUSET, JESSIE REDMON (1882-1961), African American writer and editor **20** 135-138

FAUST, DREW GILPIN (Catherine Drew Gilpin; born 1947), American historian and university president **28** 116-118

FAVALORO, RENE GERONIMO (1923-2000), Argentine physician **24** 131-133

FAWCETT, MILLICENT GARRETT (1847-1929), British feminist **5** 398-400

FAWKES, GUY (Guido Fawkes; 1570-1606), English soldier and conspirator **27** 123-125

Faÿ, Bernard, (1893-1978), French historian
Toklas, Alice B. **29** 362-364

FAYE, SAFI (born 1943), Senegalese filmmaker and ethnologist **5** 400-401

FECHNER, GUSTAV THEODOR (1801-1887), German experimental psychologist **5** 401-402

Federal League (baseball)
Spink, J.G. Taylor **29** 347-349

FEE, JOHN GREGG (1816-1901), American abolitionist and clergyman **5** 402-403

FEIFFER, JULES RALPH (born 1929), American satirical cartoonist and playwright and novelist **5** 403-404

FEIGENBAUM, MITCHELL JAY (born 1944), American physicist **5** 404-405

FEIGL, HERBERT (born 1902), American philosopher **18** 135-137

FEIJÓ, DIOGO ANTÔNIO (1784-1843), Brazilian priest and statesman **5** 405-406

FEININGER, LYONEL (1871-1956), American painter **5** 406-407

FEINSTEIN, DIANNE (Goldman; born 1933), politician, public official, and San Francisco's first female mayor **5** 407-408

FELA (Fela Anikulapo Kuti; 1938-1997), Nigerian musician and activist **21** 127-129

FELICIANO, JOSÉ (born 1945), Hispanic American singer and guitarist **19** 109-110

Feliks
see Litvinov, Maxim Maximovich

FELLER, BOB (Robert William Andrew Feller; born 1918), American baseball player **21** 129-131

FELLINI, FEDERICO (1920-1993), Italian film director **5** 408-409
Masina, Giulietta **29** 268-270

Felt, Mark, FBI Associate Director and "Deep Throat"
Bernstein, Carl **29** 52-54

FELTRE, VITTORINO DA (1378-1446), Italian humanist and teacher **5** 409-410

Feminist movement
see Women's rights

Feminists
American
Blackwell, Alice Stone **29** 61-63
Livermore, Mary **29** 247-249

FÉNELON, FRANÇOIS DE SALIGNAC DE LA MOTHE (1651-1715), French archbishop and theologian **5** 410-411

FENG KUEI-FEN (1809-1874), Chinese scholar and official **5** 411-412

FENG YÜ-HSIANG (1882-1948), Chinese warlord **5** 412-413

Feodorovich, Pëtr
see Peter III, (Peter Feodorovich; 1728-62)

FERBER, EDNA (1887-1968), American author **5** 413

FERDINAND (1865-1927), king of Romania 1914-1927 **5** 413-414

FERDINAND I (1503-1564), Holy Roman emperor 1555-1564, king of Hungary and Bohemia 1526-64 and of Germany 1531-1564 **5** 414-415

Ferdinand II, grand duke of Tuscany
see Medici, Ferdinand II de', (1610-1670)

Ferdinand II (king of Aragon)
see Ferdinand V (king of Castile)

FERDINAND II (1578-1637), Holy Roman emperor 1619-1637, king of Bohemia 1617-1637 and of Hungary 1618-1637 **5** 415

FERDINAND II (1810-1859), king of the Two Sicilies 1830-1859 **5** 415-416

Ferdinand III (king of Naples)
see Ferdinand V (king of Castile)

FERDINAND III (1608-1657), Holy Roman emperor 1637-1657, king of Hungary 1626-1657 and of Bohemia 1627-1657 **5** 416-417

Ferdinand V (king of Spain)
see Ferdinand V (king of Castile)

FERDINAND V (1452-1516), king of Castile 1474-1504, of Sicily 1468-1516, and of Aragon 1479-1516 **5** 417-418

FERDINAND VII (1784-1833), king of Spain 1808 and 1814-1833 **5** 418-420
colonial revolts
Carrera, Juan José **29** 110-112

Ferdinand von Hohenzollern-Sigmaringen
see Ferdinand (king of Romania)

FERGUSON, ADAM (1723-1816), Scottish philosopher, moralist, and historian **5** 420-421

FERGUSON, HOWARD (1908-1999), Irish musician and composer **18** 137-138

FERLINGHETTI, LAWRENCE (Lawrence Monsato Ferling; born 1919), American poet, publisher and bookstore owner **27** 125-127

FERMAT, PIERRE DE (1601-1665), French mathematician **5** 421-422

FERMI, ENRICO (1901-1954), Italian-American physicist **5** 422-424

Fermoselle
see Encina, Juan del

FERNÁNDEZ DE LIZARDI, JOSÉ JOAQUIN (1776-1827), Mexican journalist and novelist **5** 424-425

Fernández, José Manuel Balmaceda
see Balmaceda Fernández, José Manuel

Fernando
see Ferdinand

FERNEL, JEAN FRANÇOIS (c. 1497-1558), French physician **5** 425-426

Ferrante
see Ferdinand

FERRARO, GERALDINE (born 1935), first woman candidate for the vice presidency of a major U.S. political party **5** 426-428

FERRER, GABRIEL MIRÓ (1879-1930), Spanish author **5** 428

FERRER, IBRAHIM (1927-2005), Cuban musician **26** 105-107

FERRER, JOSÉ FIGUÉRES (born 1906), Costa Rican politician **5** 428-429

FERRERO, GUGLIELMO (1871-1942), Italian journalist and historian **5** 429-430

FERRI, ENRICO (1856-1929), Italian criminologist **29** 159-162

FERRY, JULES FRANÇOIS CAMILLE (1832-1893), French statesman **5** 430

FEUCHTWANGER, LION (1884-1958), post-World War I German literary figure **5** 430-432

FEUERBACH, LUDWIG ANDREAS (1804-1872), German philosopher **5** 432

FEYNMAN, RICHARD PHILLIPS
(1918-1988), American physicist **5**
432-434

FIBIGER, JOHANNES (Johannes Andreas
Grib Fibiger; 1867-1928), Danish bacteriologist and pathologist **21** 131-133

FIBONACCI, LEONARDO (c. 1180-c.
1250), Italian mathematician **5** 434-435

FICHTE, JOHANN GOTTLIEB
(1762-1814), German philosopher **5**
435-436

FICINO, MARSILIO (1433-1499), Italian
philosopher and humanist **5** 436-437

FIEDLER, ARTHUR (1894-1979), American
conductor of the Boston Pops **5** 437-438

FIELD, CYRUS WEST (1819-1892),
American merchant **5** 438-439
Bright, Charles Tilston **29** 91-93

FIELD, DAVID DUDLEY (1805-1894),
American jurist **5** 439-440

FIELD, MARSHALL (1834-1906), American
merchant **5** 440-441

FIELD, SALLY (Field, Sally Margaret; born
1946), American actress and director **24**
133-135

FIELD, STEPHEN JOHNSON (1816-1899),
American jurist **5** 441-442

FIELDING, HENRY (1707-1754), English
novelist **5** 442-444

FIELDS, DOROTHY (1905-1974),
American lyricist **26** 107-109

FIELDS, W. C. (stage name of William
Claude Dukenfield; 1879-1946),
American comedian **5** 444

FIENNES, CELIA (Cecelia Fiennes;
1662-1741), British travel writer and
diarist **28** 118-121

Fieschi, Sinibaldo de'
see Innocent IV

**FIGUEIREDO, JOÃO BATISTA DE
OLIVEIRA** (born 1918), Brazilian army
general and president (1979-1985) **5**
445-446

Figuéres Ferrer, José
see Ferrer, José Figuéres

FILLMORE, MILLARD (1800-1874),
American statesman, president
1850-1853 **5** 447-448

FILMER, SIR ROBERT (died 1653), English
political theorist **5** 448

Fils de Giboyer, Le (play)
Augier, Émile **29** 20-22

The Final Days (book)
Bernstein, Carl **29** 52-54

FINCH, ANNE (Anne Kingsmill Finch;
1661-1720), English poet **27** 127-129

FINK, ALBERT (1827-1897), American
railroad engineer and economist **21**
133-135

FINKELSTEIN, RABBI LOUIS (born 1895),
American scholar and leader of
Conservative Judaism **5** 448-450

FINLAY, CARLOS JUAN (1833-1915),
Cuban biologist and physician **5** 450

FINNEY, CHARLES GRANDISON
(1792-1875), American theologian and
educator **5** 450-451

FIORINA, CARLY (Cara Carleton Sneed;
born 1954), American businesswoman
25 131-133

FIRDAUSI (934-1020), Persian poet **5**
451-452

Firestone Co. (tires; industry)
Barclay, Edwin **29** 44-45

FIRESTONE, HARVEY SAMUEL
(1868-1938), American industrialist **5**
452-453

FIRESTONE, SHULAMITH (born 1945),
Canadian feminist **27** 129-131

FIRST, RUTH (1925-1982), South African
socialist, anti-apartheid activist, and
scholar **5** 453-454

First Ladies
Hoover, Lou Henry **29** 195-197

FISCHER, BOBBY (1943-2008), American
chess player **5** 454-456

FISCHER, EMIL (1852-1919), German
organic chemist **5** 456-457

FISCHER, HANS (1881-1945), German
organic chemist **5** 457-459

**FISCHER VON ERLACH, JOHANN
BERNHARD** (1656-1723), Austrian
architect **5** 459-461

FISH, HAMILTON (1808-1893), American
statesman **5** 461-462

FISHER, ANDREW (1862-1928), Australian
statesman and labor leader **5** 462

FISHER, IRVING (1867-1947), American
economist **5** 462-463

FISHER, JOHN ARBUTHNOT (Baron
Fisher of Kilverstone; 1841-1920),
British admiral **22** 171-173

FISHER, SIR RONALD AYLMER
(1890-1962), English statistician **5**
463-464

FISHER, RUDOLPH (Rudolph John
Chauncey Fisher; 1897-1934), African
American author **28** 121-123

FISK, JAMES (1834-1872), American
financial speculator **5** 464-465

Fiske, Helen Marie
see Jackson, Helen Hunt

FISKE, JOHN (1842-1901), American
philosopher and historian **5** 465-466

FISKE, MINNIE MADDERN (Mary Augusta
Davey; 1865-1932), American
"realistic" actress who portrayed Ibsen
heroines **5** 466-467

FITCH, JOHN (1743-1798), American
mechanic and inventor **5** 467-468

FITCH, VAL LOGSDON (born 1923),
American physicist **24** 135-138

Fitz-Boodle, George Savage (pseudonym)
see Thackeray, William Makepeace

FITZGERALD, ELLA (1918-1996),
American jazz singer **5** 468-469

FITZGERALD, FRANCES (born 1940),
American author **5** 469-470

FITZGERALD, FRANCIS SCOTT KEY
(1896-1940), American author **5**
470-472
Graham, Sheilah **29** 174-176

FITZGERALD, GARRET (born 1926), Irish
prime minister (1981-1987) **5** 472-474

FITZHUGH, GEORGE (1806-1881),
American polemicist and sociologist **5** 474

FITZPATRICK, THOMAS (1799-1854),
American trapper, guide, and Indian
agent **5** 474-475

FIZEAU, HIPPOLYTE ARMAND LOUIS
(1819-1896), French physicist **5** 475

FLAGLER, HENRY (1830-1913), American
industrialist **21** 135-137

FLAGSTAD, KIRSTEN MALFRID
(1895-1962), Norwegian opera singer
25 133-135

FLAHERTY, ROBERT (1884-1951),
American documentary filmmaker **5**
476-477

FLAMININUS, TITUS QUINCTIUS (c.
228-174 B.C.), Roman general and
diplomat **5** 477

FLAMSTEED, JOHN (1646-1719), English
astronomer **5** 477-478

FLANAGAN, HALLIE (1890-1969),
American director, playwright, and
educator **5** 478-479

FLANNAGAN, JOHN BERNARD
(1895-1942), American sculptor **5** 480

FLAUBERT, GUSTAVE (1821-1880),
French novelist **5** 480-482
associates
Colet, Louise **29** 119-121

Flavio (opera)
Cuzzoni, Francesca **29** 132-134

Flavius Claudius Julianus
see Julian the Apostate

FRANKENHEIMER, JOHN (1930-2002), American filmmaker 22 182-185

FRANKENTHALER, HELEN (born 1928), American painter 6 56-57

FRANKFURTER, FELIX (1882-1965), American jurist 6 57

Frankish empire
see Holy Roman Empire

FRANKLIN, ARETHA (born 1942), African American singer and songwriter 6 58-60

FRANKLIN, BENJAMIN (1706-1790), American statesman, diplomat, and inventor 6 60-64

FRANKLIN, SIR JOHN (1786-1847), English explorer 6 68-69

FRANKLIN, JOHN HOPE (born 1915), pioneer African American historian 6 65-67

FRANKLIN, MILES (1879-1954), Australian novelist 6 68-69

FRANKLIN, ROSALIND ELSIE (1920-1958), British physical chemist and molecular biologist 6 67-68

FRANKLIN, WILLIAM (c. 1731-1813), American colonial administrator 6 69-70

FRANKS, TOMMY RAY (born 1945), American military leader 25 142-144

FRANZ FERDINAND (1863-1914), archduke of Austria 29 162-164

Franz Josef
see Francis Joseph

FRASER (PINTER), LADY ANTONIA (born 1932), popular British biographer, historian, and mystery novelist 6 70-71

FRASER, MALCOLM (born 1930), prime minister of Australia (1975-1983) 6 71-73

FRASER, PETER (1884-1950), New Zealand prime minister 1940-49 6 73-74

FRASER, SIMON (1776-1862), Canadian explorer and fur trader 6 74-75

FRASER-REID, BERT (born 1934), Jamaican chemist 20 145-146

Frau im Mond (Woman in the Moon; film)
Oberth, Hermann Julius 29 296-298

FRAUNHOFER, JOSEPH VON (1787-1826), German physicist 6 75-76

FRAZER, SIR JAMES GEORGE (1854-1941), Scottish classicist and anthropologist 6 76

FRAZIER, EDWARD FRANKLIN (1894-1962), African American sociologist 6 77

FREARS, STEPHEN ARTHUR (born 1941), British filmmaker 28 127-129

FRÉCHETTE, LOUIS-HONORÉ (1839-1908), French-Canadian poet 6 77-78

FREDEGUND (Fredegunda, Fredegond; c. 550-597), Frankish queen 20 146-149

FREDERICK I (1123-1190), Holy Roman emperor 1152-1190 6 78-79

FREDERICK II (1194-1250), Holy Roman emperor 1215-1250 6 79

FREDERICK II (1712-1786), king of Prussia 1740-1786 6 81-84

Frederick III (duke of Saxony)
see Frederick III (elector and duke of Saxony)

Frederick III (duke of Swabia)
see Frederick I (Holy Roman emperor)

FREDERICK III (1415-1493), Holy Roman emperor and German king 1440-1493 6 84-85

Frederick III, (1463-1525), elector and duke of Saxony 1486-1525
Bora, Katharina von 29 256-258

Frederick V (archduke of Austria)
see Frederick III (Holy Roman emperor)

Frederick Augustus I-II (elector of Saxony)
see Augustus II-III (king of Poland)

Frederick Barbarossa
see Frederick I (Holy Roman emperor)

Frederick of Hohenstaufen
see Frederick II (Holy Roman emperor)

Frederick the Great
see Frederick II (king of Prussia)

Frederick the Wise
see Frederick III (elector of Saxony)

FREDERICK WILLIAM (1620-1688), elector of Brandenburg 1640-1688 6 85-86

FREDERICK WILLIAM I (1688-1740), king of Prussia 1713-1740 6 86-87

FREDERICK WILLIAM III (1770-1840), king of Prussia 1797-1840 6 87

FREDERICK WILLIAM IV (1795-1861), king of Prussia 1840-1861 6 87-88

FREDHOLM, ERIK IVAR (1866-1927), Swedish mathematician 24 147-149

Free and Accepted Masons
see Freemasonry (Masonic Fraternity)

Free French (World War II)
see France–1940-46

FREED, JAMES INGO (1930-2005), American architect 6 88-90

FREEH, LOUIS J. (born 1950), director of the Federal Bureau of Investigation (FBI) 6 90-91

FREEMAN, DOUGLAS SOUTHALL (1886-1953), American journalist 6 91-92

FREEMAN, ROLAND L. (born 1936), American photographer of rural and urban African Americans 6 92-93

Freeman's Farm, battle of (1777)
see Saratoga, battles of (1777; Bemis Heights and Freeman's Farm)

Freemasonry (Masonic Fraternity)
Ames, Ezra 29 1-3

FREGE, GOTTLOB (1848-1925), German mathematician and philosopher 6 93-94

FREI MONTALVA, EDUARDO (born 1911), Chilean statesman 6 94-95

Freikorps (German paramilitary group)
Röhm, Ernst 29 330-332

FREIRE, PAULO (born 1921), Brazilian philosopher and educator 6 95-96

Freire, Rómulo Gallegos
see Gallegos Freire, Rómulo

FRELINGHUYSEN, THEODORUS JACOBUS (1691-c. 1748), Dutch Reformed clergyman and revivalist 6 96-97

FRÉMONT, JOHN CHARLES (1813-1890), American explorer and politician 6 97-98

FRENCH, DANIEL CHESTER (1850-1931), American sculptor 6 98-99

French Academy (established 1635)
Ampère, Jean-Jacques 29 5-7
Augier, Émile 29 20-22

French Academy of Sciences (established 1666)
Gall, Franz Joseph 29 165-167

French and Indian War (1754-1763)
British forces
Gates, Horatio 29 169-172

French Indochina
see Indochina, French (former nation, southeast Asia)

French literature
drama (19th-20th century)
Augier, Émile 29 20-22
poetry (19th-20th century)
Colet, Louise 29 119-121

French overseas empire
AFRICA
North Africa (Algeria)
Tillion, Germaine 29 358-360

French Resistance (World War II)
literary activity
Triolet, Elsa 29 364-366
political activity
Tillion, Germaine 29 358-360

French Revolution (1789-1799)
1792-1795 (1ST REPUBLIC)
Reign of Terror (1793-1794)
Corday, Charlotte 29 123-126

FRENEAU, PHILIP MORIN (1752-1832), American poet and journalist **6** 99-100

FRERE, SIR HENRY BARTLE EDWARD (1815-1884), English colonial administrator **6** 100-101

FRESCOBALDI, GIROLAMO (1583-1643), Italian composer and organist **6** 101-102

FRESNEL, AUGUSTIN JEAN (1788-1827), French physicist **6** 102-103

FREUD, ANNA (1895-1982), British psychoanalyst **18** 150-153

FREUD, LUCIAN (born 1922), British painter **20** 149-151

FREUD, SIGMUND (1856-1939), Viennese psychiatrist, founder of psychoanalysis **6** 103-106

FREYRE, GILBERTO (1900-1987), Brazilian sociologist and writer **6** 106-107

FREYTAG, GUSTAV (1816-1895), German novelist, dramatist, and critic **6** 107-108

FRICK, HENRY CLAY (1849-1919), American industrialist and financier **6** 108-109

Friday, Joe (television character) Webb, Jack **29** 375-376

FRIEDAN, BETTY (Betty Naomi Goldstein; 1921-2006), women's rights activist and author **6** 109-111

FRIEDMAN, MILTON (1912-2006), American economist **6** 111-112

FRIEDRICH, CARL JOACHIM (1901-1984), German-born educator who became a leading American political theorist **6** 113-114

FRIEDRICH, CASPAR DAVID (1774-1840), German romantic painter **6** 114-115

FRIEL, BERNARD PATRICK (born 1929), author, teacher, and playwright from Northern Ireland **6** 115-116

FRIEND, CHARLOTTE (1921-1987), American medical researcher **26** 115-117

FRIES, JAKOB FRIEDRICH (1773-1843), German philosopher **6** 116-117

FRINK, ELISABETH (1930-1993), British artist **26** 117-118

FRISCH, KARL VON (1886-1982), Austrian zoologist **6** 117-118

FRISCH, MAX (born 1911), Swiss novelist and dramatist **6** 118-119

FRISCH, OTTO ROBERT (1904-1979), Austrian-British nuclear physicist **6** 119-120

FROBERGER, JOHANN JAKOB (1616-1667), German composer and organist **6** 120-121

FROBISHER, SIR MARTIN (c. 1538-1594), English explorer **6** 121-122

FROEBEL, FRIEDRICH WILHELM AUGUST (1782-1852), German educator and psychologist **6** 122-123

FROHMAN, CHARLES (1860-1915), American theatrical producer **6** 123-124

FROISSART, JEAN (c. 1337-after 1404), French priest, poet, and chronicler **6** 124-125

From the Earth to the Moon (novel) Oberth, Hermann Julius **29** 296-298

FROMM, ERICH (1900-1980), German writer in the fields of psychoanalysis, psychology, and social philosophy **6** 125-127

Fronde, Wars of the (France; 1648-53) Scudéry, Madeleine de **29** 341-343

FRONDIZI, ARTURO (1908-1995), leader of the Argentine Radical Party and Argentine president (1958-1962) **6** 127-128

FRONTENAC ET PALLUAU, COMTE DE (Louis de Buade; 1622-1698), French colonial governor **6** 128-130

Frontiersmen, American
folk heroes
Masterson, Bat **29** 272-274
explorers, guides, and scouts
Austin, Moses **29** 22-24

FRONTINUS, SEXTUS JULIUS (c. 35-c. 104), Roman magistrate, soldier, and writer **6** 130

FROST, ROBERT LEE (1874-1963), American poet **6** 130-133

FROUDE, JAMES ANTHONY (1818-1894), English historian **6** 133-134

Fruit fly
see Drosophila

FRUNZE, MIKHAIL VASILIEVICH (1885-1925), Soviet military leader **6** 134

FRY, ELIZABETH (1780-1845), British reformer **6** 134-136

FRY, WILLIAM HENRY (1813-1864), American composer **6** 136-137

FRYE, NORTHROP (Herman Northrop Frye; born 1912), Canadian literary scholar **6** 137-139

FUAD I (1868-1936), king of Egypt 1922-1936 **6** 139

FUCHS, KLAUS (Klaus Emil Julius Fuchs; 1911-1988), German-born British physicist and espionage agent **28** 129-131

FUCHS, LEONHARD (1501-1566), German botanist **20** 152-152

FUCHS, SIR VIVIAN (1908-1999), English explorer and geologist **6** 140

FUENTES, CARLOS (born 1928), Mexican author and political activist **6** 141-142

FUERTES, LOUIS AGASSIZ (1874-1927), American naturalist and artist **24** 152-153

FUGARD, ATHOL (born 1932), South African playwright **6** 142-143

FUGGER, JAKOB (Jacob Fugger; 1459-1525), German banker **21** 147-149

Fugitive slaves
see African American history (United States)

FUJIMORI, ALBERTO KEINYA (born 1938), president of Peru **6** 143-145

FUJITA, TETSUYA (Theodore ''Ted'' Fujita; 1920-1998), Japanese American meteorologist **27** 135-137

FUJIWARA KAMATARI (614-669), Japanese imperial official **6** 145

FUJIWARA MICHINAGA (966-1027), Japanese statesman **6** 145-146

Fujiwara-no Daijin
see Fujiwara Kamatari

FUKUI, KENICHI (born 1918), Japanese chemist **23** 111-112

FUKUYAMA, FRANCIS (born 1952), American philosopher and foreign policy expert **6** 146-147

FULBRIGHT, JAMES WILLIAM (1905-1995), American statesman **6** 147-149

FULLER, ALFRED (1885-1973), American businessman and inventor **19** 117-118

FULLER, JOHN FREDERICK CHARLES (1878-1966), British soldier and author **22** 185-186

FULLER, META WARRICK (1877-1968), American sculpter **23** 112-114

FULLER, MILLARD (born 1935), American lawyer and social activist **18** 153-155

FULLER, RICHARD BUCKMINISTER (born 1895), American architect and engineer **6** 149-150

FULLER, SARAH MARGARET (1810-1850), American feminist **6** 150-151

FULTON, ROBERT (1765-1815), American inventor, engineer, and artist **6** 151-152

Fulton, Ruth
see Benedict, Ruth Fulton

FU MINGXIA (born 1978), Chinese diver **24** 149-151

FUNK, CASIMIR (1884-1967),
Polish-American biochemist **22** 187-189

FURPHY, JOSEPH (1843-1912), Australian
novelist **6** 152-153

FÜRÜZAN (Fürüzan Selçuk; born 1935),
Turkish author and director **22** 189-190

Fury (ship)
Parry, Sir William Edward **29**
311-313

FUSELI, HENRY (1741-1825), Swiss
painter **6** 153-155

FUSTEL DE COULANGES, NUMA DENIS
(1830-1889), French historian **6** 155

FUX, JOHANN JOSEPH (1660-1741),
Austrian composer, conductor, and
theoretician **6** 155-156

G

GABLE, WILLIAM CLARK (1901-1960),
American film actor **6** 157-158
Harlow, Jean **29** 182-184
Lombard, Carole **29** 249-251

GABO, NAUM (1890-1977), Russian
sculptor and designer **6** 158-159

GABOR, DENNIS (1900-1979),
Hungarian-British physicist who invented
holographic photography **6** 159-160

GABRIEL, ANGE JACQUES (1698-1782),
French architect **6** 160-161

GABRIELI, GIOVANNI (c. 1557-1612),
Italian composer **6** 161-162

Gabrielle (play)
Augier, Émile **29** 20-22

Gabrini, Niccola di Lorenzo
see Rienzi, Cola di

GADAMER, HANS-GEORG (1900-2002),
German philosopher, classicist, and interpretation theorist **6** 162-163

GADDAFI, MUAMMAR AL- (born 1942),
head of the revolution that set up the
Libyan Republic in 1969 **6** 163-165

GADSDEN, JAMES (1788-1858), American
soldier and diplomat **6** 165-166

GAGARIN, YURI ALEXEIVICH (1934-1968),
Russian cosmonaut **6** 166-167

GAGE, MATILDA JOSLYN (1826-1898),
American reformer and suffragist **6**
167-169

GAGE, THOMAS (1719/20-1787), English
general **6** 169-170

GAGNÉ, ROBERT MILLS (born 1916),
American educator **6** 170

Gaines, Clarence E., (1923-2005),
American basketball coach
Garber, Mary **29** 167-169

GAINSBOROUGH, THOMAS
(1727-1788), English painter **6** 170-172

GAINSBOURG, SERGE (Lucien
Gainsbourg; 1928-1991), French singer,
songwriter and actor **27** 138-141

GAISERIC (died 477), king of the Vandals
428-477 **6** 172

GAITÁN, JORGE ELIÉCER (1898-1948),
Colombian politician **6** 172-173

GAITSKELL, HUGH (1906-1963), British
chancellor of the exchequer
(1950-1951) and leader of the Labour
Party (1955-1963) **6** 173-174

Gaius Sallustius Crispus
see Sallust

GALAMB, JOSEPH (Jozsef Galamb;
1881-1955), Hungarian-American
engineer **24** 154-155

GALBRAITH, JOHN KENNETH
(1908-2006), economist and scholar of
the American Institutionalist school **6**
174-177

GALDÓS, BENITO PÉREZ (1843-1920),
Spanish novelist and dramatist **6**
177-178

GALEN (130-200), Roman physician **6**
178-180
influence of
Falloppio, Gabriele **29** 157-159

GALERIUS, EMPEROR OF ROME (Gaius
Galerius Valerius Maximianus; c.
250-311), Thracian emperor **28** 132-134

Galilei, Galileo
see Galileo Galilei

GALILEO GALILEI (1564-1642), Italian
astronomer and physicist **6** 180-183
influence of
Amontons, Guillaume **29** 3-5
influenced by
ibn Bajja, Abu Bakr Muhhamad **29**
207-209

Galileo in Prison (novel)
Brod, Max **29** 95-97

GALL, FRANZ JOSEPH (1758-1828),
German founder of phrenology **29**
165-167

GALLATIN, ALBERT (1761-1849),
Swiss-born American statesman, banker,
and diplomat **6** 183-184

GALLAUDET, THOMAS HOPKINS
(1787-1851), American educator **6** 185

GALLEGOS FREIRE, RÓMULO
(1884-1969), Venezuelan novelist,
president 1948 **6** 185-186

GALLO, ROBERT CHARLES (born 1937),
American virologist **22** 191-193

GALLOWAY, JOSEPH (c. 1731-1803),
American politician **6** 186-187

GALLUP, GEORGE (1901-1984), pioneer
in the field of public opinion polling and
a proponent of educational reform **6**
187-189

GALSWORTHY, JOHN (1867-1933),
English novelist and playwright **6** 189-190

GALT, SIR ALEXANDER TILLOCH
(1817-1893), Canadian politician **6**
190-191

GALT, JOHN (1779-1839), Scottish
novelist **18** 156-158

GALTIERI, LEOPOLDO FORTUNATO
(1926-2003), president of Argentina
(1981-1982) **6** 191-193

GALTON, SIR FRANCIS (1822-1911),
English scientist, biometrician, and
explorer **6** 193-194

Galton Society
Osborn, Henry Fairfield, Sr. **29**
306-308

GALVANI, LUIGI (1737-1798), Italian
physiologist **6** 194-195

GÁLVEZ, BERNARDO DE (1746-1786),
Spanish colonial administrator **6**
195-196

GÁLVEZ, JOSÉ DE (1720-1787), Spanish
statesman in Mexico **6** 196

GALWAY, JAMES (born 1939), Irish flutist
18 158-160

GAMA, VASCO DA (c. 1460-1524),
Portuguese navigator **6** 196-198
influence of
Borough, Stephen **29** 74-76

GAMBARO, GRISELDA (born 1928),
Argentine author **23** 115-117

GAMBETTA, LÉON (1838-1882), French
premier 1881-1882 **6** 198-199

GAMOW, GEORGE (1904-1968),
Russian-American nuclear physicist, as-
trophysicist, biologist, and author of
books popularizing science **6** 199-200

GAMZATOV, RASUL (Rasul Gamzatovitch
Gamzatov; 1923-2003), Pagestani poet
28 134-136

GANCE, ABEL (1889-1981), French film
director **25** 145-147

GANDHI, INDIRA PRIYADARSHINI
(1917-1984), Indian political leader **6**
200-201

GANDHI, MOHANDAS KARAMCHAND
(1869-1948), Indian political and
religious leader **6** 201-204

GANDHI, RAJIV (1944-1991), Indian
member of Parliament and prime
minister **6** 204-205

GANDHI, SONIA (née Sonia Maino; born
1946), Indian politician **25** 147-149

GREEN, WILLIAM R. (1872-1952), American labor union leader **6** 521

GREENAWAY, KATE (Catherine; 1846-1901), English author and illustrator **18** 168-169

GREENBERG, CLEMENT (1909-1994), American art critic **6** 521-523

GREENBERG, HENRY BENJAMIN (Hank; 1911-1986), American baseball player **25** 161-165

GREENBERG, URI ZVI (1898-1981), Israeli author and activist **24** 158-159

GREENE, CATHERINE LITTLEFIELD (1755-1814), American inventor **22** 200-203

GREENE, GRAHAM (born 1904), English novelist and dramatist **6** 523-524

GREENE, GRAHAM (born ca. 1952), Canadian-Native American actor **6** 524-525

GREENE, NATHANAEL (1742-1786), American Revolutionary War general **6** 525-526

Greenfield, Jerry, (born 1951)
see Ben & Jerry

GREENSPAN, ALAN (born 1926), American economist **6** 526-528

GREER, GERMAINE (born 1939), author and authoritative commentator on women's liberation and sexuality **6** 528-530

GREGG, JOHN ROBERT (1867-1948), American inventor of system of shorthand writing **21** 178-180

GREGG, WILLIAM (1800-1867), American manufacturer **6** 530-531

GREGORY I, SAINT (c. 540-604), pope 590-604 **6** 531-532

GREGORY VII (c. 1020-1085), pope 1073-85 **6** 532-534

GREGORY IX (Ugo [Ugolino] di Segni; 1145-1241), Roman Catholic pope (1227-1241) **21** 180-183

GREGORY XII (Angelo Corrario; c. 1327-1417), pope 1406-1415 **18** 169-171

GREGORY XIII (1502-1585), pope 1572-1585 **6** 534
    Baius, Michael **29** 31-33

GREGORY XVI (Bartolommeo Alberto Cappellari; Mauro; 1765-1846), Roman Catholic pope 1831-1846 **25** 165-166

GREGORY, LADY AUGUSTA (1852-1932), Irish dramatist **6** 535-536

GREGORY, DICK (Richard Claxton Gregory; born 1932), comedian and civil rights and world peace activist **6** 536-537

GREGORY OF TOURS, SAINT (538-594), Frankish bishop and historian **6** 534-535

Gregory the Great, Saint
see Gregory I, Saint

GRETZKY, WAYNE (born 1961), Canadian hockey star **6** 537-539

GREUZE, JEAN BAPTISTE (1725-1805), French painter **6** 539

GREVER, MARIA (nee Maria de la Portilla; 1894-1951), Mexican musician **24** 159-161

GREY, CHARLES (2nd Earl Grey; 1764-1845), English statesman, prime minister 1830-1834 **6** 539-540

GREY, SIR GEORGE (1812-1898), English explorer and colonial governor **6** 540-541
    Ballance, John **29** 42-44

GREY, ZANE (Pearl Zane Gray; 1872-1939), American author **20** 160-162

GRIBEAUVAL, JEAN BAPTISTE VAQUETTE DE (1715-1789), French army officer **20** 162-163

GRIEG, EDVARD HAGERUP (1843-1907), Norwegian composer **6** 541-542

GRIERSON, JOHN (1898-1972), Canadian and British filmmaker **6** 542-543

GRIFFES, CHARLES TOMLINSON (1884-1920), American composer **6** 543-544

GRIFFITH, DAVID WARK (1875-1948), American filmmaker **6** 544-545

GRIFFIN, MERV (Mervyn Edward Griffin, Jr.; 1925-2007), American television personality and producer **28** 146-149

GRIFFITH, SIR SAMUEL WALKER (1845-1920), Australian statesman and jurist **6** 545-546

GRIFFITH JOYNER, FLORENCE (1959-1998), American athlete **19** 130-133

Grillet, Alain Robbe
see Robbe-Grillet, Alain

GRILLPARZER, FRANZ (1791-1872), Austrian playwright **6** 546-547

Grimaldi, Rainier de
see Rainier III, Prince of Monaco

GRIMKÉ, ANGELINA EMILY (1805-1879) AND SARAH MOORE (1792-1873), American abolitionists and women's rights agitators **7** 1-2

GRIMKÉ, ARCHIBALD HENRY (1849-1930), American editor, author, and diplomat **7** 1-2

GRIMM, JAKOB KARL (1785-1863) AND WILHELM KARL (1786-1859), German scholars, linguists, and authors **7** 3-4

GRIMMELSHAUSEN, HANS JAKOB CHRISTOFFEL VON (1621/22-1676), German author **7** 4-5

GRIS, JUAN (1887-1927), Spanish painter **7** 5-6

GRISHAM, JOHN (born 1955), American author and attorney **7** 6-8

GRISSOM, VIRGIL IVAN (Gus Grissom; 1926-1967), American astronaut **25** 166-168

GROMYKO, ANDREI ANDREEVICH (1909-1988), minister of foreign affairs and president of the Union of Soviet Socialist Republic (1985-1988) **7** 9-11

GROOMS, RED (born 1937), American artist **7** 11-12

Groot, Huig de
see Grotius, Hugo

GROOTE, GERARD (1340-1384), Dutch evangelical preacher **7** 12-13

GROPIUS, WALTER (1883-1969), German-American architect, educator, and designer **7** 13-14
theatre projects
    Piscator, Erwin **29** 315-317

GROS, BARON (Antoine Jean Gros; 1771-1835), French romantic painter **7** 14-15

GROSS, AL (Alfred J. Gross; 1918-2000), Canadian inventor **28** 149-151

GROSS, SAMUEL DAVID (1805-1884), American surgeon, author, and educator **21** 183-185

GROSSETESTE, ROBERT (1175-1253), English bishop and statesman **7** 15

GROSSINGER, JENNIE (1892-1972), American hotel executive and philanthropist **7** 15-17

GROSZ, GEORGE (1893-1959), German-American painter and graphic artist **7** 17-18

GROTIUS, HUGO (1583-1645), Dutch jurist, statesman, and historian **7** 18-19

GROTOWSKI, JERZY (born 1933), founder of the experimental Laboratory Theatre in Wroclaw, Poland **7** 19-20

GROVE, ANDREW (András Gróf; born 1936), American businessman **18** 171-174

GROVE, FREDERICK PHILIP (c. 1871-1948), Canadian novelist and essayist **7** 20-21

GROVES, LESLIE (1896-1970), military director of the Manhattan Project (atom bomb) during World War II **7** 21-22

GRÜNEWALD, MATTHIAS (c. 1475-1528), German painter **7** 23-24

GUARDI, FRANCESCO (1712-1793), Italian painter **7** 24-25

H

HAGENS, GUNTHER VON (Guinther Gerhard Liebchen; born 1945), German anatomist **27** 157-159

HAGUE, FRANK (1876-1956), American politician **7** 63-64

Hague Court
see International Court of Justice; Permanent Court of Arbitration; Permanent Court of International Justice

HAHN, OTTO (1879-1968), German chemist **7** 64-65

HAHNEMANN, SAMUEL (Christian Friedrich Samuel Hahnemann; 1755-1843), German physician and chemist **21** 190-193

HAIDAR ALI (1721/22-1782), Indian prince, ruler of Mysore 1759-1782 **7** 65-66

HAIG, ALEXANDER M., JR. (born 1924), American military leader, diplomat, secretary of state, and presidential adviser **7** 66-67

HAIG, DOUGLAS (1st Earl Haig; 1861-1928), British field marshal **7** 67-68

HAIGNERE, CLAUDIE ANDRE-DESHAYS (born 1957), French astronaut and government official **25** 176-178

Haiku (haikai; literary form)
Arakida Moritake **29** 287-288

HAILE SELASSIE (1892-1975), emperor of Ethiopia **7** 68-70

HAKLUYT, RICHARD (1552/53-1616), English geographer and author **7** 70

HALBERSTAM, DAVID (1934-2007), American journalist, author and social historian **18** 180-183

HALDANE, JOHN BURDON SANDERSON (1892-1964), English biologist **7** 70-71

HALE, CLARA (nee Clara McBride; 1905-1992), American humanitarian and social reformer **20** 166-168

HALE, EDWARD EVERETT (1822-1909), American Unitarian minister and author **7** 71-72

HALE, GEORGE ELLERY (1868-1938), American astronomer **7** 72-74

HALE, SARAH JOSEPHA (née Buell; 1788-1879), American editor **7** 74-75

HALES, STEPHEN (1677-1761), English scientist and clergyman **7** 75

HALÉVY, ÉLIE (1870-1937), French philosopher and historian **7** 76

HALEY, ALEX (1921-1992), African American journalist and author **7** 76-78

HALEY, MARGARET A. (1861-1939), American educator and labor activist **7** 78-79

HALFFTER, CHRISTÓBAL (born 1930), Spanish composer **7** 79-80

HALIBURTON, THOMAS CHANDLER (1796-1865), Canadian judge and author **7** 80

HALIDE EDIP ADIVAR (1884-1964), Turkish woman writer, scholar, and public figure **7** 80-82

Halifax, 3rd Viscount
see Halifax, 1st Earl of

HALIFAX, 1ST EARL OF (Edward Frederick Lindley Wood; 1881-1959), English statesman **7** 82-83

HALL, ASAPH (1829-1907), American astronomer **7** 83-84

HALL, DONALD (born 1928), New England memoirist, short story writer, essayist, dramatist, critic, and anthologist as well as poet **7** 84-85

HALL, EDWARD MARSHALL (1858-1927), British attorney **22** 204-205

HALL, GRANVILLE STANLEY (1844-1924), American psychologist and educator **7** 85-86

HALL, LLOYD AUGUSTUS (1894-1971), American scientist and inventor **28** 154-156

HALL, PETER REGINALD FREDERICK (born 1930), English theater director **24** 162-165

HALL, PRINCE (c. 1735-1807), African American abolitionist and founder of the first black masonic lodge **26** 136-138

HALL, RADCLYFFE (Marguerite Radclyffe Hall; 1880-1943), British author **20** 168-170

HALLAJ, AL-HUSAYN IBN MANSUR AL (857-922), Persian Moslem mystic and martyr **7** 86-87

HALLAM, LEWIS, SR. AND JR. (Lewis Sr. ca. 1705-1755; Lewis Jr. 1740-1808), American actors and theatrical managers **7** 87

HALLECK, HENRY WAGER (1815-1872), American military strategist **22** 205-207

HALLER, ALBRECHT VON (1708-1777), Swiss physician **7** 87-88

HALLEY, EDMUND (1656-1742), English astronomer **7** 88-89

HALONEN, TARJA KAARINA (born 1943), Finnish president **25** 178-180

HALS, FRANS (1581/85-1666), Dutch painter **7** 89-91

HALSEY, WILLIAM FREDERICK (1882-1959), American admiral **7** 91-92

HALSTED, WILLIAM STEWART (1852-1922), American surgeon **22** 207-209

HAMADA, SHOJI (1894-1978), Japanese potter **26** 138-140

HAMANN, JOHANN GEORG (1730-1788), German philosopher **7** 92

HAMER, FANNIE LOU (born Townsend; 1917-1977), American civil rights activist **7** 93-94

HAMILCAR BARCA (c. 285-229/228 B.C.), Carthaginian general and statesman **7** 94-95

HAMILL, DOROTHY (born 1956), American figure skater **25** 180-183

HAMILTON, ALEXANDER (1755-1804), American statesman **7** 95-98

HAMILTON, ALICE (1869-1970), American physician **7** 98-99

HAMILTON, EDITH (1867-1963), American educator and author **22** 209-211

HAMILTON, SIR WILLIAM ROWAN (1805-1865), Irish mathematical physicist **7** 99-100

HAMMARSKJÖLD, DAG (1905-1961), Swedish diplomat **7** 100-101

HAMM-BRÜCHER, HILDEGARD (born 1921), Free Democratic Party's candidate for the German presidency in 1994 **7** 101-103

HAMMER, ARMAND (1898-1990), American entrepreneur and art collector **7** 103-104

HAMMERSTEIN, OSCAR CLENDENNING II (1895-1960), lyricist and librettist of the American theater **7** 104-106

HAMMETT, (SAMUEL) DASHIELL (1894-1961), American author **7** 106-108

HAMMOND, JAMES HENRY (1807-1864), American statesman **7** 108-109

HAMMOND, JOHN LAWRENCE LE BRETON (1872-1952), English historian **7** 108-109

HAMMOND, LUCY BARBARA (1873-1961), English historian **7** 109

HAMMURABI (1792-1750 B.C.), king of Babylonia **7** 109-110

HAMPDEN, JOHN (1594-1643), English statesman **7** 110-111

HAMPTON, LIONEL (1908-2002), African American jazz musician **22** 211-213

HAMPTON, WADE (c. 1751-1835), American planter **7** 111-112

HAMPTON, WADE III (1818-1902), American statesman and Confederate general **7** 112

HAMSUN, KNUT (1859-1952), Norwegian novelist **7** 113-114

HAN FEI TZU (c. 280-233 B.C.), Chinese statesman and philosopher **7** 124-125

Han Kao-tsu
see Liu Pang

HAN WU-TI (157-87 B.C.), Chinese emperor **7** 136

HAN YÜ (768-824), Chinese author **7** 136-137

HANAFI, HASSAN (born 1935), Egyptian philosopher **7** 114

HANCOCK, JOHN (1737-1793), American statesman **7** 114-116

HAND, BILLINGS LEARNED (1872-1961), American jurist **7** 116

Händel, Georg Friedrich
see Handel, George Frederick

HANDEL, GEORGE FREDERICK (1685-1759), German-born English composer and organist **7** 116-119
Cuzzoni, Francesca **29** 132-134

HANDKE, PETER (born 1942), Austrian playwright, novelist, screenwriter, essayist, and poet **7** 119-121

HANDLER, RUTH (Ruth Mosko; 1916-2002), American businesswoman **25** 183-185

HANDLIN, OSCAR (born 1915), American historian **7** 121-122

Handschuchsheim, Ritter von
see Meinong, Alexius

HANDSOME LAKE (a.k.a. Hadawa' Ko; ca. 1735-1815), Seneca spiritual leader **7** 122-123

HANDY, WILLIAM CHRISTOPHER (1873-1958), African American songwriter **7** 123-124

HANKS, NANCY (1927-1983), called the "mother of a million artists" for her work in building federal financial support for the arts and artists **7** 126-127

HANKS, TOM (Thomas Jeffrey Hanks; born 1956), American actor **23** 135-137

HANNA AND BARBERA (William Hanna, 1910-2001; Joseph Barbera, 1911-2006), American producers and directors of animated cartoons **28** 156-159

HANNA, MARCUS ALONZO (1837-1904), American businessman and politician **7** 127-128

Hanna, William
see Hanna and Barbera

HANNIBAL BARCA (247-183 B.C.), Carthaginian general **7** 128-130

Hanover dynasty (Great Britain)
see Great Britain–1714-1901 (Hanover)

HANSBERRY, LORRAINE VIVIAN (1930-1965), American writer and a major figure on Broadway **7** 130-131

HANSEN, ALVIN (1887-1975), American economist **7** 131-132

Hansen, Emil
see Nolde, Emil

HANSEN, JULIA BUTLER (1907-1988), American politician **7** 132-133

HANSON, DUANE (1925-1990), American super-realist sculptor **7** 133-135

HANSON, HOWARD (1896-1981), American composer and educator **7** 135-136

HAPGOOD, NORMAN (1868-1937), American author and editor **7** 137-138

HARA, KEI (1856-1921), Japanese statesman and prime minister 1918-1921 **7** 138

HARAND, IRENE (born Irene Wedl; 1900-1975), Austrian political and human rights activist **7** 139-145

HARAWI, ILYAS AL- (Elias Harawi; 1930-2006), president of Lebanon **7** 145-146

HARBURG, EDGAR YIPSEL (Irwin Hochberg; E.Y. Harburg; 1896-1981), American lyricist **26** 140-142

Hardenberg, Baron Friedrich Leopold von
see Novalis

HARDENBERG, PRINCE KARL AUGUST VON (1750-1822), Prussian statesman **7** 146-147

HARDIE, JAMES KEIR (1856-1915), Scottish politician **7** 147-148

HARDING, FLORENCE KLING (Florence Kling DeWolfe Harding; 1860-1924), American First Lady **28** 159-161

Harding, Stephen, Saint
see Stephen Harding, Saint

HARDING, WARREN GAMALIEL (1865-1923), American statesman, president 1921-1923 **7** 148-149
Cabinet
Hoover, Lou Henry **29** 195-197

Hardouin, Jules
see Mansart, Jules Hardouin

HARDY, HARRIET (1905-1993), American pathologist **7** 150

HARDY, THOMAS (1840-1928), English novelist, poet, and dramatist **7** 150-152

HARE, ROBERT (1781-1858), American chemist **7** 152-153

harem et les cousins, le (book)
Tillion, Germaine **29** 358-360

HARGRAVES, EDWARD HAMMOND (1816-1891), Australian publicist **7** 153-154

HARGREAVES, ALISON (1962-1995), British mountain climber **26** 142-144

HARING, KEITH (1958-1990), American artist tied to New York graffiti art of the 1980s **7** 154-155

HARINGTON, JOHN (1560-1612), English author and courtier **21** 193-195

HARIRI, RAFIC (1944-2005), politician and businessman **28** 161-163

HARJO, JOY (Born 1951), Native American author, musician, and artist **25** 185-187

HARJO, SUZAN SHOWN (born 1945), Native American activist **18** 183-185

HARKNESS, GEORGIA (1891-1974), American Methodist and ecumenical theologian **7** 155-156

HARLAN, JOHN MARSHALL (1833-1911), American jurist **7** 156-157

HARLAN, JOHN MARSHALL (1899-1971), U.S. Supreme Court justice **7** 157-159

Harlem renaissance (American literature)
Gilpin, Charles **29** 172-174

HARLEY, ROBERT (1st Earl of Oxford and Earl Mortimer; 1661-1724), English statesman **7** 159-160

HARLOW, JEAN (1911-1937), American film actress **29** 182-184

HARNACK, ADOLF VON (1851-1930), German theologian **7** 160

HARNETT, WILLIAM MICHAEL (1848-1892), American painter **7** 160-161

Harold "Fairhair"
see Harold I

Harold Haardraade
see Harold III

HAROLD I (c. 840-933), king of Norway 860-930 **7** 161-162

HAROLD II (Harold Godwinson; died 1066), Anglo-Saxon king of England of 1066 **7** 162

HAROLD III (1015-1066), king of Norway 1047-1066 **7** 163

Harold the Ruthless
see Harold III

HARPER, FRANCES (Frances Ellen Watkins Harper; 1825-1911), African American author, abolitionist and women's rights activist **18** 185-187

HARPER, JAMES (1795-1869), American publisher **22** 213-216

HARPER, STEPHEN (born 1959), Canadian prime minister **27** 159-161

HARPER, WILLIAM RAINEY (1856-1906), American educator and biblical scholar **7** 163-164

HARPUR, CHARLES (1813-1866), Australian poet and author **22** 216-218

HARRIMAN, EDWARD HENRY (1848-1909), American railroad executive **7** 164-165

HARRIMAN, PAMELA (1920-1997), American ambassador and patrician **18** 187-189

HARRIMAN, W. AVERELL (1891-1986), American industrialist, financier, and diplomat **7** 165-166

HARRINGTON, JAMES (1611-1677), English political theorist **7** 166-167

HARRINGTON, MICHAEL (1928-1989), American political activist and educator **7** 167-169

HARRIOT, THOMAS (1560-1621), English scientist and mathematician **23** 137-139

HARRIS, ABRAM LINCOLN, JR. (1899-1963), African American economist **7** 169-171

HARRIS, BARBARA CLEMENTINE (born 1930), African American activist and Anglican bishop **7** 171-172

HARRIS, FRANK (1856-1931), Irish-American author and editor **7** 172-173

HARRIS, JOEL CHANDLER (1848-1908), American writer **7** 173-174

HARRIS, LADONNA (born 1931), Native American activist **18** 189-191

HARRIS, PATRICIA ROBERTS (1924-1985), first African American woman in the U.S. Cabinet **7** 174-175

HARRIS, ROY (1898-1979), American composer **7** 175-176

HARRIS, TOWNSEND (1804-1878), American merchant and diplomat **7** 176-177

HARRIS, WILLIAM TORREY (1835-1909), American educator and philosopher **7** 177-178

HARRISON, BENJAMIN (1833-1901), American statesman, president 1889-1893 **7** 178-179
    Wanamaker, John **29** 372-375

HARRISON, GEORGE (1943-2005), English musician **25** 187-191

HARRISON, PETER (1716-1775), American architect and merchant **7** 179-180

HARRISON, WILLIAM HENRY (1773-1841), American statesman, president 1841 **7** 180-181

HARSHA (Harshavardhana; c. 590-647), king of Northern India 606-612 **7** 181-182

Hart, Emma
    see Hamilton, Lady; Willard, Emma Hart

HART, GARY W. (born 1936), American political campaign organizer, U.S. senator, and presidential candidate **7** 182-184

HART, HERBERT LIONEL ADOLPHUS (1907-1992), British legal philosopher **22** 218-219

HART, LORENZ (1895-1943), American lyricist **29** 184-186

Hart, Mickey, (born 1943), American musician
    Hussain, Zakir **29** 204-206

HARTE, FRANCIS BRET (1837-1902), American poet and fiction writer **7** 184-185

HARTLEY, DAVID (1705-1757), British physician and philosopher **7** 185

HARTLEY, MARSDEN (1877-1943), American painter **7** 186

HARTSHORNE, CHARLES (born 1897), American theologian **7** 186-187

HARUN AL-RASHID (766-809), Abbasid caliph of Baghdad 786-809 **7** 188

HARUNOBU, SUZUKI (ca. 1725-1770), Japanese painter and printmaker **7** 188-189

HARVARD, JOHN (1607-1638), English philanthropist **21** 195-197

Harvard College
    see Harvard University (Cambridge, Massachusetts)

Harvard University (Cambridge, Massachusetts)
    literature
        Baker, George Pierce **29** 33-35

HARVEY, WILLIAM (1578-1657), English physician **7** 189-190

Harwell, Ernie, American sports broadcaster
    Spink, J.G. Taylor **29** 347-349

HARWOOD, GWEN (nee Gwendoline Nessie Foster; 1920-1995), Australian poet **26** 144-146

HASAN, IBN AL-HAYTHAM (ca. 966-1039), Arab physicist, astronomer, and mathematician **7** 190-191

Hasan, Mansur ben
    see Firdausi

Hasan Ali Shah
    see Aga Khan

Hasan ibn-Hani, al-
    see Abu Nuwas

HASKINS, CHARLES HOMER (1870-1937), American historian **7** 191-192

Hasong, Prince
    see Sonjo

HASSAM, FREDERICK CHILDE (1859-1935), American impressionist painter **7** 192

HASSAN, MOULEY (King Hassan II; 1929-1999), inherited the throne of Morocco in 1961 **7** 194-195

HASSAN, MUHAMMAD ABDILLE (1864-1920), Somali politico-religious leader and poet **7** 194-195

HASTINGS, PATRICK GARDINER (1880-1952), British lawyer and politician **22** 219-221

HASTINGS, WARREN (1732-1818), English statesman **7** 195-196

HATCH, WILLIAM HENRY (1833-1896), American reformer and politician **7** 196

Hathorne, Nathaniel
    see Hawthorne, Nathaniel

HATSHEPSUT (ruled 1503-1482 B.C.), Egyptian queen **7** 196-197

HATTA, MOHAMMAD (1902-1980), a leader of the Indonesian nationalist movement (1920s-1945) and a champion of non-alignment and of socialism grounded in Islam **7** 197-199

HAUPTMAN, HERBERT AARON (born 1917), American mathematician **24** 165-167

HAUPTMANN, GERHART JOHANN ROBERT (1862-1946), German dramatist and novelist **7** 199-201

HAUSHOFER, KARL (1869-1946), German general and geopolitician **7** 201

HAUSSMANN, BARON GEORGES EUGÈNE (1809-1891), French prefect of the Seine **7** 201-202

Hauteclocque, Philippe Marie de
    see Leclerc, Jacques Philippe

HAVEL, VACLAV (born 1936), playwright and human rights activist who became the president of Czechoslovakia **7** 202-205

HAVEMEYER, HENRY OSBORNE (1847-1907), American businessman **22** 222-224

HEINZ, HENRY JOHN (H.J. Heinz; 1844-1919), American businessman **19** 136-138

HEISENBERG, WERNER KARL (born 1901), German physicist **7** 261-263
influence of
Berg, Moe **29** 50-52

HEISMAN, JOHN WILLIAM (Johann Wilhelm Heisman; 1869-1936), American football coach **24** 171-174

HELD, ANNA (c. 1870-1918), French comedienne **29** 186-188

Helicopter (aircraft)
Williams, Sunita **29** 376-379

HELLER, JOSEPH (1923-1999), American author **7** 263-265

HELLER, WALTER (1915-1987), chairman of the Council of Economic Advisors (1961-1964) and chief spokesman of the ''New Economics'' **7** 265-266

HELLMAN, LILLIAN FLORENCE (born 1905), American playwright **7** 267-268

Hell's Angels (film)
Harlow, Jean **29** 182-184

HELMHOLTZ, HERMANN LUDWIG FERDINAND VON (1821-1894), German physicist and physiologist **7** 268-269

HELMONT, JAN BAPTISTA VAN (1579-1644), Flemish chemist and physician **7** 269-271

HELMS, JESSE (born 1921), United States Senator from North Carolina **7** 271-272

HELOISE (c. 1098-c. 1163), French abbess **27** 167-169

HELPER, HINTON ROWAN (1829-1909), American author and railroad promoter **7** 272-273

HELVÉTIUS, CLAUDE ADRIEN (1715-1771), French philosopher **7** 273-274

HEMINGWAY, ERNEST MILLER (1898-1961), American novelist and journalist **7** 274-277

HÉMON, LOUIS (1880-1913), French-Canadian novelist **7** 277

HEMPHILL, JOHN (1803-1862), American jurist and statesman **22** 234-236

HENDERSON, ARTHUR (1863-1935), British statesman **7** 277-278

HENDERSON, DONALD AINSLIE (D.A.; born 1928), American public health official **22** 236-238

HENDERSON, FLETCHER (James Fletcher Henderson; 1897-1952), African American musician **26** 148-150

HENDERSON, RICHARD (1735-1785), American jurist and land speculator **7** 278-279

HENDERSON, ZELMA (1920-2008), American civil rights figure **29** 188-191

HENDRIX, JIMI (born Johnny Allen Hendrix; 1942-1970), African American guitarist, singer, and composer **7** 279-283

HENG, CHANG (Zhang Heng; Pingzhi; 78-139), Chinese scientist and author **24** 174-176

HENG SAMRIN (born 1934), Cambodian Communist leader who became president of the People's Republic of Kampuchea (PRK) in 1979 **7** 283-285

HENIE, SONJA (1912-1969), Norwegian figure skater **20** 172-173

Henri I (king of Haiti)
see Christophe, Henri

HENRI, ROBERT (Robert Henry Cozad; 1865-1929), American painter **22** 238-240

Henry (IV, count of Luxemburg)
see Henry VII (Holy Roman emperor)

Henry (prince, Portugal)
see Henry the Navigator

Henry I (Holy Roman emperor)
see Henry I (king of Germany)

HENRY I (876-936), king of Germany 919-936 **7** 285-286

HENRY I (1068-1135), king of England 1100-1135 **7** 286-287

HENRY II (1133-1189), king of England 1154-1189 **7** 287-289

Henry III (king of Navarre)
see Henry IV (king of France)

HENRY III (1017-1056), Holy Roman emperor and king of Germany 1039-1056 **7** 290

HENRY III (1207-1272), king of England 1216-1272 **7** 290-292

HENRY IV (1050-1106), Holy Roman emperor and king of Germany 1056-1106 **7** 292

HENRY IV (1367-1413), king of England 1399-1413 **7** 292-293

HENRY IV (1553-1610), king of France 1589-1610 **7** 293-295

HENRY V (1081-1125), Holy Roman emperor and king of Germany 1106-1125 **7** 295-296
Anacletus II **29** 7-9

HENRY V (1387-1422), king of England 1413-1422 **7** 296-297

HENRY VI (1421-1471), king of England 1422-61 and 1470-1471 **7** 298-299

HENRY VII (1274-1313), Holy Roman emperor and king of Germany 1308-1313 **7** 299-300

HENRY VII (1457-1509), king of England 1485-1509 **7** 300-302

HENRY VIII (1491-1547), king of England 1509-1547 **7** 302-305
divorce issue
Babington, Anthony **29** 27-29

HENRY, AARON (born 1922), African American civil rights activist **7** 306-307

HENRY, JOSEPH (1797-1878), American physicist and electrical experimenter **7** 307-308

HENRY, MARGUERITE (Margurite Breithaupt; 1902-1997), American author **19** 138-140

HENRY, O. (pseudonym of William Sydney Porter; 1862-1910), American short-story writer **7** 308-309

HENRY, PATRICK (1736-1799), American orator and revolutionary **7** 309-311

Henry of Anjou
see Henry II (king of England)

Henry of Bolingbroke
see Henry IV (king of England)

Henry of Bracton (Bratton)
see Bracton, Henry de

Henry of Derby
see Henry IV (king of England)

Henry of Lancaster
see Henry IV (king of England)

Henry of Navarre
see Henry IV (king of France)

Henry Plantagenet (duke of Normandy)
see Henry II (king of England)

Henry the Fowler
see Henry I (king of Germany)

HENRY THE NAVIGATOR (1394-1460), Portuguese prince **7** 305-306

HENSEL, FANNY MENDELSSOHN (Fanny Cäcilie Mendelssohn-Bartholdy; 1805-1847), German composer and pianist **26** 150-152

Henselt, Adolf von, (1814-1889), German pianist and composer
Lenz, Wilhelm von **29** 243-245

HENSON, JIM (James Maury Henson, 1936-1990), American puppeteer, screenwriter, and producer **19** 140-142

HENSON, JOSIAH (1789-1883), African American preacher and former slave **7** 311-312

HENSON, MATTHEW A. (1866-1955), African American Arctic explorer **7** 312-314

HOCKNEY, DAVID (born 1937), English photographer and artist **7** 429-431

HODGKIN, ALAN LLOYD (born 1914), English physiologist **7** 431-432

HODGKIN, DOROTHY CROWFOOT (1910-1964), English chemist **7** 432-434

HODLER, FERDINAND (1853-1918), Swiss painter **7** 434-435

HOE, RICHARD MARCH (1812-1886), American inventor and manufacturer **7** 435-436

HOFF, TED (Marcian Edward Hoff, Jr.; born 1937), American inventor **28** 176-178

HOFFA, JAMES R. ("JIMMY") (1913-1975), American union leader **7** 436-437

HOFFMAN, ABBIE (1936-1989), American writer, activist, and leader of the Youth International Party **7** 437-439

Hoffman, Dustin
Bernstein, Carl **29** 52-54

HOFFMANN, ERNST THEODOR AMADEUS (1776-1822), German author, composer, and artist **7** 439-440
Scudéry, Madeleine de **29** 341-343

HOFFMANN, FELIX (1868-1946), German chemist and inventor **28** 179-180

HOFFMANN, JOSEF (1870-1956), Austrian architect and decorator **7** 440-441

HOFFMAN, MALVINA CORNELL (1885-1966), American sculptor **23** 148-150

HOFHAIMER, PAUL (1459-1537), Austrian composer, and organist **7** 441

HOFMANN, AUGUST WILHELM VON (1818-1892), German organic chemist **7** 441-442

HOFMANN, HANS (1880-1966), German-American painter **7** 442-443

HOFMANNSTHAL, HUGO VON (1874-1929), Austrian poet and dramatist **7** 443-444

HOFSTADTER, RICHARD (1916-1970), American historian **7** 444-445

HOFSTADTER, ROBERT (1915-1990), American physicist **25** 199-202

HOGAN, BEN (1912-1997), American golfer **19** 148-150

HOGARTH, WILLIAM (1697-1764), English painter and engraver **7** 446-447

HOGG, HELEN BATTLES SAWYER (1905-1993), Canadian astronomer **22** 244-247

Hohenheim, Theophrastus Bombastus von
see Paracelsus, Philippus Aureolus

HOKINSON, HELEN ELNA (1893-1949), American cartoonist **23** 150-152

HOKUSAI, KATSUSHIKA (1760-1849), Japanese painter and printmaker **7** 447-448

HOLBACH, BARON D' (Paul Henri Thiry; 1723-1789), German-born French encyclopedist and philosopher **7** 448-449

HOLBEIN, HANS, THE YOUNGER (1497/98-1543), German painter and graphic artist **7** 449-450

HOLBERG, LUDVIG (Hans Mikkelsen; 1684-1754), Scandinavian author **23** 152-155

HOLBROOK, JOSIAH (1788-1854), American educator **7** 450-451

HÖLDERLIN, JOHANN CHRISTIAN FRIEDRICH (1770-1843), German poet **7** 451-452

HOLIDAY, BILLIE (1915-1959), American jazz vocalist **7** 452-453

HOLLAND, JOHN PHILIP (1840-1914), Irish-American inventor **7** 453-454

HOLLAR, WENCESLAUS (Wewzel Hollar; Václav Hollar; 1607-1677), Bohemian engraver **28** 180-183

HOLLERITH, HERMAN (1860-1929), American inventor and businessman **19** 151-152

HOLLEY, ROBERT W. (1922-1993), American scientist **29** 191-193

Hollweg, Theobald von Bethmann
see Bethmann Hollweg, Theobald von

HOLLY, BUDDY (Charles Hardin Holley; 1936-1959), American singer, songwriter, and bandleader **22** 247-249
Diddley, Bo **29** 144-146

HOLM, HANYA (née Johanna Eckert; born 1893), German-American dancer and teacher **7** 454-455

Holm, Saxe
see Jackson, Helen Hunt

HOLMES, ARTHUR (1890-1965), English geologist and petrologist **7** 455-456

HOLMES, JOHN HAYNES (1879-1964), American Unitarian clergyman **7** 456-457

HOLMES, OLIVER WENDELL (1809-1894), American physician and author **7** 457-458

HOLMES, OLIVER WENDELL, JR. (1841-1935), American jurist **7** 458-459

Holocaust
writers about
Massaquoi, Hans J. **29** 270-272

HOLST, GUSTAV (1874-1934), English composer **7** 459-460

Holy Roman Empire
1024-1125 (Franconian dynasty)
Anacletus II **29** 7-9

HOLYOAKE, KEITH JACKA (1904-1983), New Zealand prime minister and leader of the National Party **7** 460-462

HOLZER, JENNY (born 1950), American Neo-Conceptualist artist **7** 462-463

HOMANS, GEORGE CASPAR (1910-1989), American sociologist **7** 463-465

HOMER (ancient), Greek epic poet **7** 468-469

HOMER, WINSLOW (1836-1910), American painter **7** 468-469

HONDA, ISHIRO (Inoshiro Honda; 1911-1993), Japanese filmmaker **26** 158-160

HONDA, SOICHIRO (1906-1991), Japanese automaker **7** 469-470

HONECKER, ERICH (1912-1994), German Communist Party leader and head of the German Democratic Republic (1971-80s) **7** 471-472

HONEGGER, ARTHUR (1892-1955), Swiss composer identified with France **7** 472-473

HONEN (1133-1212), Japanese Buddhist monk **7** 473

Honorius II, (Lamberto Scannabecchi), pope 1124-1130
Anacletus II **29** 7-9

HOOCH, PIETER DE (1629-after 1684), Dutch artist **7** 473-474

HOOK, SIDNEY (1902-1989), American philosopher and exponent of classical American pragmatism **7** 474-475

HOOKE, ROBERT (1635-1703), English physicist **7** 475

HOOKER, HENRY CLAY (1828-1907), American rancher **29** 193-195

HOOKER, JOHN LEE (1917-2001), African American musician **23** 155-157

HOOKER, RICHARD (1554-1600), English theologian and Church of England clergyman **7** 475-476

HOOKER, THOMAS (1586-1647), English Puritan theologian, founder of Connecticut Colony **7** 476-477

HOOKS, BELL (BORN GLORIA JEAN WATKINS) (born 1952), African American social activist, feminist, and author **7** 477-481

HOOKS, BENJAMIN LAWSON (born 1925), executive director of the NAACP and first African American commissioner of the FCC **7** 481-483

Hsien-tze
see Shih Ko-fa

Hsin Shun Wang
see Li Tzu-ch'eng

Hsin-chien, Earl of
see Wang Yang-ming

HSÜAN TSANG (c. 602-664), Chinese Buddhist in India **8** 6-7

HSÜAN-TSUNG, T'ANG (685-762), Chinese emperor **8** 7-8

HSÜN-TZU (Hsün Ch'ing; c. 312-c. 235 B.C.), Chinese philosopher **8** 8

HU SHIH (1891-1962), Chinese philosopher **8** 63-65

HUANG CH'AO (died 884), Chinese rebel leader **8** 8-9

HUANG TSUNG-HSI (1610-1695), Chinese scholar and philosopher **8** 9-10

HUBBARD, L. RON (1911-1986), American author and founder of Scientology **18** 202-204

HUBBLE, EDWIN POWELL (1889-1953), American astronomer **8** 10-11

HUBLEY, JOHN (1914-1977), American animator and filmmaker **21** 208-210

HUCH, RICARDA (1864-1947), German novelist, poet, and historian **8** 11-12

HUDSON, HENRY (flourished 1607-1611), English navigator **8** 12-13

Hudson River school (American art)
Ames, Ezra **29** 1-3

Hueffer, Ford Madox
see Ford, Ford Madox

HUERTA, DOLORES (born 1930), Hispanic American labor activist **18** 204-207

HUERTA, VICTORIANO (1854-1916), Mexican general and politician **8** 13-14
political opponents and associates
de la Barra, Francisco León **29** 245-247

HUGGINS, SIR WILLIAM (1824-1910), English astronomer **8** 14-15

HUGHES, CHARLES EVANS (1862-1948), American jurist and statesman **8** 15-16

HUGHES, HOWARD ROBARD (1905-1976), flamboyant American entrepreneur **8** 16-17
Harlow, Jean **29** 182-184

HUGHES, JOHN JOSEPH (1797-1864), Irish-American Catholic archbishop **8** 17-18

HUGHES, LANGSTON (1902-1967), African American author **8** 18-19

HUGHES, RICHARD (1900-1976), English author **19** 158-160

HUGHES, TED (1930-1998), English poet laureate **8** 19-21

HUGHES, WILLIAM MORRIS (1864-1952), Australian prime minister 1915-1923 **8** 21-22

HUGO, VICOMTE VICTOR MARIE (1802-1885), French author **8** 22-25

HUI-TSUNG (1082-1135), Chinese emperor and artist **8** 25

HUI-YÜAN (334-416), Chinese Buddhist monk **8** 25-26

HUIZINGA, JOHAN (1872-1945), Dutch historian **8** 26-27

HULAGU KHAN (Hüle'ü; c. 1216-1265), Mongol ruler in Persia **8** 27-28

HULL, BOBBY (Robert Marvin Hull; born 1939), Canadian hockey player **20** 181-183

HULL, CLARK LEONARD (1884-1952), American psychologist **8** 28

HULL, CORDELL (1871-1955), American statesman **8** 28-29

HULL, WILLIAM (1753-1825), American military commander **8** 29-30

Human rights
activists for
Blackwell, Alice Stone **29** 61-63

HUMAYUN (1508-1556), Mogul emperor 1530-1556 **20** 183-185

HUMBOLDT, BARON FRIEDRICH HEINRICH ALEXANDER VON (1769-1859), German naturalist and explorer **8** 30-31

HUMBOLDT, BARON WILHELM VON (1767-1835), German statesman and philologist **8** 31

HUME, BASIL CARDINAL (George Haliburton Hume; 1923-1999), English clergyman and theologian **22** 249-250

HUME, DAVID (1711-1776), Scottish philosopher **8** 31-34

HUMMEL, JOHANN NEPOMUK (1778-1837), Austrian pianist and composer **25** 204-206

HUMPHREY, DORIS (Doris Batcheller Humphrey; 1895-1959), American dancer and choreographer **23** 157-159

HUMPHREY, HUBERT HORATIO, JR. (1911-1978), mayor of Minneapolis, U.S. senator from Minnesota, and vice-president of the U.S. **8** 34-36

HUN SEN (born 1951), Cambodian prime minister **8** 39-42

HUNDERTWASSER, FRIEDENSREICH (Friedrich Stowasser; 1928-2000), Austrian-born visionary painter and spiritualist **8** 36-37

HUNG HSIU-CH'ÜAN (1814-1864), Chinese religious leader, founder of Taiping sect **8** 37-38

Hungary (Hungarian People's Republic; nation, East-Central Europe)
culture
Curtiz, Michael **29** 130-132

Hung-li
see Qianlong

Hungson, Prince
see Taewon'gun, Hungson

HUNG-WU (1328-1398), Chinese Ming emperor 1368-98 **8** 38-39

HUNT, H. L. (1889-1974), American entrepreneur **8** 42-44

HUNT, RICHARD MORRIS (1827-1895), American architect **8** 44

HUNT, WALTER (1796-1859), American inventor **21** 210-212

HUNT, WILLIAM HOLMAN (1827-1910), English painter **8** 44-45

HUNTER, ALBERTA (1895-1984), African American blues singer **23** 160-162

HUNTER, FLOYD (born 1912), American social worker and administrator, community worker, professor, and author **8** 45-46

HUNTER, JOHN (1728-1793), Scottish surgeon **29** 202-204

HUNTER, MADELINE CHEEK (1916-1994), American educator **8** 47-48

HUNTER, WILLIAM (1718-1783), Scottish anatomist **8** 48-49
Hunter, John **29** 202-204

HUNTINGTON, ANNA HYATT (Anna Vaughn Hyatt; 1876-1973), American sculptor and philanthropist **23** 162-164

HUNTINGTON, COLLIS POTTER (1821-1900), American railroad builder **8** 49

HUNTLEY AND BRINKLEY (1956-1970), American journalists and radio and television news team **8** 49-51

Huntley, Chester Robert, (Chet; 1911-1974)
see Huntley and Brinkley

HUNYADI, JOHN (1385-1456), Hungarian military leader, regent 1446-1452 **8** 51-52

HURD, DOUGLAS (born 1930), English Conservative Party politician and foreign secretary **8** 52-55

HURSTON, ZORA NEALE (1903-1960), African American folklorist and novelist **8** 55-56

HUS, JAN (a.k.a. John Hus; ca.1369-1415), Bohemian religious reformer **8** 56-59

HUSÁK, GUSTÁV (1913-1991), president of the Czechoslovak Socialist Republic **8** 59-61
  Novotný, Antonín **29** 291-293

HUSAYN, TAHA (1889-1973), Egyptian author, educator, and statesman **8** 61-62

HUSAYNI, AL-HAJJ AMIN AL- (1895-1974), Moslem scholar/leader and mufti of Jerusalem (1922-1948) **8** 62-63

HUSEIN IBN ALI (c. 1854-1931), Arab nationalist, king of Hejaz 1916-1924 **8** 63

Huss, John
  see Hus, Jan

HUSSAIN, ZAKIR (born 1951), Indian singer and musician **29** 204-206

HUSSEIN IBN TALAL (1935-1999), king of the Hashemite Kingdom of Jordan (1953-80s) **8** 65-67

HUSSEIN, SADDAM (1937-2006), socialist president of the Iraqi Republic and strongman of the ruling Ba'th regime **13** 415-416

HUSSEINI, FAISAL (1940-2001), Palestinian political leader **19** 160-162

HUSSERL, EDMUND (1859-1938), German philosopher **8** 67-68

HUSTON, JOHN MARCELLUS (1906-1987), American film director, scriptwriter, and actor **22** 250-252

HUTCHINS, ROBERT MAYNARD (1899-1977), American educator **8** 68-69

HUTCHINSON, ANNE MARBURY (1591-1643), English-born American religious leader **8** 69-71

HUTCHINSON, THOMAS (1711-1780), American colonial governor **8** 71-72

Hu-t'ou
  see Ku K'ai-chih

HUTT, WILLIAM (William Ian DeWitt Hutt; 1920-2007), Canadian actor and director **27** 171-173

HUTTEN, ULRICH VON (1488-1523), German humanist **8** 72-73

HUTTON, JAMES (1726-1797), Scottish geologist **8** 73-74

HUXLEY, ALDOUS LEONARD (1894-1963), English novelist and essayist **8** 74-75

HUXLEY, JULIAN (1887-1975), English biologist and author **8** 75-77

HUXLEY, THOMAS HENRY (1825-1895), English biologist **8** 77-79

HUXTABLE, ADA LOUISE (nee Ada Louise Landman; born 1921), American journalist **26** 162-165

HUYGENS, CHRISTIAAN (1629-1695), Dutch mathematician, astronomer, and physicist **8** 79-81

Huysmans, Charles Marie Georges
  see Huysmans, Joris Karl

HUYSMANS, JORIS KARL (1848-1907), French novelist **8** 81-82

HVIEZDOSLAV (Pavol Országh; Pavol Országh Hviezdoslav; 1848-1921), Slovakian poet **24** 181-182

Hybridization
  see Plant breeding (botany)

HYDE, DOUGLAS (1860-1949), Irish author, president 1938-45 **8** 82-83

Hyde, Edward
  see Clarendon, 1st Earl of

HYDE, IDA HENRIETTA (1857-1945), American physiologist and educator **22** 252-254

HYMAN, FLO (Flora Jean Hyman; 1954-1986), American volleyball player **26** 165-167

HYMAN, LIBBIE HENRIETTA (1888-1969), American zoologist **8** 83-84

HYPATIA OF ALEXANDRIA (370-415), Greek mathematician and philosopher **8** 85

Hypochondriack
  see Boswell, James

I

IACOCCA, LIDO (LEE) ANTHONY (born 1924), American automobile magnate **8** 86-88

Iapassus, Potomac tribal leader
  Argall, Samuel **29** 18-20

Iatrophysics
  Borelli, Giovanni Alfonso **29** 69-72

IBÁÑEZ DEL CAMPO, CARLOS (1877-1960), Chilean general and president **8** 88

ÍBARRURI GÓMEZ, DOLORES (1895-1989), voice of the Republican cause in the Spanish Civil War **8** 88-90

IBERVILLE, SIEUR D' (Pierre le Moyne; 1661-1706), Canadian soldier, naval captain, and adventurer **8** 90-91

IBN AL-ARABI, MUHYI AL-DIN (1165-1240), Spanish-born Moslem poet, philosopher, and mystic **8** 91

IBN BAJJA, ABU BAKR MUHHAMAD (c. 1085-1139), Arab philosopher and scientist **29** 207-209

IBN BATTUTA, MUHAMMAD (1304-1368/69), Moslem traveler and author **8** 91-92

IBN GABIROL, SOLOMON BEN JUDAH (c. 1021-c. 1058), Spanish Hebrew poet and philosopher **8** 92

IBN HAZM, ABU MUHAMMAD ALI (994-1064), Spanish-born Arab theologian and jurist **8** 93

IBN KHALDUN, ABD AL-RAHMAN IBN MUHAMMAD (1332-1406), Arab historian, philosopher, and statesman **8** 93-94

Ibn Rushd
  see Averroës

IBN SAUD, ABD AL-AZIZ (1880-1953), Arab politician, founder of Saudi Arabia **8** 94-95

Ibn Sina
  see Avicenna

IBN TASHUFIN, YUSUF (died 1106), North African Almoravid ruler **8** 95-96

IBN TUFAYL, ABU BAKR MUHAMMAD (c. 1110-1185), Spanish Moslem philosopher and physician **8** 96

IBN TUMART, MUHAMMAD (c. 1080-1130), North African Islamic theologian **8** 96-97

Ibo (African people)
  Ojukwu, Chukwuemeka Odumegwu **29** 298-301

Ibrahim ou L'Illustre Bassa (Ibrahim or the Illustrious Bassa; novel)
  Scudéry, Madeleine de **29** 341-343

IBRAHIM PASHA (1789-1848), Turkish military and administrative leader **8** 97-98

IBSEN, HENRIK (1828-1906), Norwegian playwright **8** 98-100

IBUKA, MASARU (1908-1997), Japanese inventor and businessman **28** 184-186

ICHIKAWA, KON (1915-2008), Japanese filmmaker **29** 209-211

ICKES, HAROLD LECLAIRE (1874-1952), American statesman **8** 100-101

ICTINUS (flourished 2nd half of 5th century B.C.), Greek architect **8** 101

IDRIS I (1889-1983), king of Libya 1950-69 **8** 102

IDRISI, MUHAMMAD IBN MUHAMMAD AL- (1100-1165?), Arab geographer **8** 102-103

If I Had a Million (film)
  Mankiewicz, Joseph L. **29** 261-263

IG Farben (German company)
  Bosch, Carl **29** 76-78

Kuznetsov
see Litvinov, Maxim Maximovich

KWANGGAET'O (375-413), Korean statesman, king of Koguryo **9** 139-140

KWANGJONG (925-975), Korean statesman, king of Koryo **9** 140

KWASNIEWSKI, ALEKSANDER (born 1954), Polish politician **27** 220-222

KYD, THOMAS (1558-1594), English dramatist **9** 140-141

KYPRIANOU, SPYROS (born 1932), president of the Republic of Cyprus **9** 141-143

L

LA BRUYÈRE, JEAN DE (1645-1696), French man of letters and moralist **9** 145

LA FARGE, JOHN (1835-1910), American artist and writer **9** 149-150

LA FAYETTE, COMTESSE DE (Marie Madeleine Pioche de la Vergne; 1634-93), French novelist **9** 150-151

LA FLESCHE, FRANCIS (1857-1932), Native American ethnologist **9** 152-154

LA FLESCHE PICOTTE, SUSAN (1865-1915), Native American physician and activist **24** 223-225

LA FLESCHE, SUSETTE (1854-1903), Native American activist and reformer **9** 152-154

LA FOLLETTE, ROBERT MARION (1855-1925), American statesman **9** 155-156

LA FONTAINE, JEAN DE (1621-1695), French poet **9** 156-157

LA GUARDIA, FIORELLO HENRY (1882-1947), American politician, New York City mayor **9** 166-167

LA METTRIE, JULIEN OFFRAY DE (1709-1751), French physician and philosopher **9** 179-180

La Pasionaria
see Ibárruri Gomez, Dolores

LA ROCHEFOUCAULD, FRANÇOIS, DUC DE (1613-1680), French moralist **9** 208-209

LA SALLE, SIEUR DE (René Robert Cavelier; 1643-1687), French explorer and colonizer **9** 210-211

La Scala (opera house; Milan)
Salieri, Antonio **29** 333-335

LA TOUR, GEORGE DE (1593-1652), French painter **9** 222

LA VERENDRYE, SIEUR DE (Pierre Gaultier de Varennes; 1685-1749), French-Canadian soldier, explorer, and fur trader **9** 239-240

La Vergne, Marie Madeleine Pioche de
see La Fayette, Comtesse de

Labour party (Australia)
leaders
Lyons, Enid Muriel **29** 258-260

Labriolle
see Velasco Ibarra, José María

LABROUSTE, PIERRE FRANÇOIS HENRI (1801-1875), French architect-engineer **9** 144

Labrunie, Gérard
see Nerval, Gérard de

LACAN, JACQUES (1901-1981), French psychoanalyst **9** 145-147

LACHAISE, GASTON (1882-1935), French-born American sculptor **9** 147

LACHAPELLE, MARIE (1769-1821), French obstetrician and teacher **21** 245-247

Lackland, John
see John (king of England)

LACOMBE, ALBERT (1827-1916), Canadian missionary priest **9** 147-148

LACORDAIRE, JEAN BAPTISTE HENRI (1802-1861), French Dominican preacher **9** 148

LACY, SAM (Samuel Harold Lacy; 1903-2003), African American journalist **26** 207-209

LADD, WILLIAM (1778-1841), American pacifist **9** 149

LADD-FRANKLIN, CHRISTINE (1847-1930), American logician and psychologist **23** 202-204

Lady Is a Tramp, The (song)
Hart, Lorenz **29** 184-186

LAENNEC, RENÉ (René-Théophile-Hyacinthe Laënnec; 1781-1826), French physician and inventor **21** 247-249

LAFAYETTE, MARQUIS DE (Marie Joseph Paul Yves Roch Gilbert du Motier; 1757-1834), French general and statesman **9** 151-152

LAFONTAINE, SIR LOUIS-HIPPOLYTE (1807-1864), Canadian politician **9** 157-158

LAFONTAINE, OSKAR (born 1943), German politician **9** 158-160

LAFORGUE, JULES (1860-1887), French poet **9** 160-161

LAGERFELD, KARL (born 1938), German-French designer of high fashion **9** 161-162

LAGERKVIST, PÄR FABIAN (born 1891), Swedish author **9** 162-163

LAGERLÖF, SELMA OTTILIANA LOVISA (1858-1940), Swedish author **9** 163-164

Lagery, Otto de
see Urban II

LAGOS, RICARDO (born 1938), president of Chile **27** 223-225

LAGRANGE, JOSEPH LOUIS (1736-1813), Italian-born French mathematician **9** 164-166

LAHR, BERT (Irving Lahrheim; 1895-1967), performer and comedian in burlesque, vaudeville, musical comedy, film, and television **9** 167-168

LAING, R. D. (1927-1989), Scottish psychiatrist and author **26** 209-211

LAIRD, MELVIN R. (born 1922), U.S. congressman and secretary of defense **9** 168-170

LAKSHMIBAI (Laksmi Bai; Rani of Jhansi; c.1835-1857), Indian queen and national hero **22** 41-42

LALIBELA (ruled c. 1181-c. 1221), Ethiopian king and saint **9** 170

LALIQUE, RENÉ (1860-1945), French glass and jewelry designer **26** 211-213

LAMAR, LUCIUS QUINTUS CINCINNATUS (1825-1893), American politician and jurist **9** 170-171

LAMARCK, CHEVALIER DE (Jean Baptiste Pierre Antoine de Monet; 1744-1829), French naturalist **9** 171-173

LAMARQUE, LIBERTAD (Libertad Lamarque Bouza; 1908-2000), Argentine entertainer **26** 213-215

LAMARR, HEDY (Hedwig Eva Marie Kiesler; 1913-2000), American actress and inventor **27** 225-227

LAMARTINE, ALPHONSE MARIE LOUIS DE (1790-1869), French poet and diplomat **9** 173-175

LAMAS, CARLOS SAAVEDRA (1878-1959), Argentine scholar, statesman, and diplomat **9** 175-176

LAMB, CHARLES (1775-1834), English author, critic, and minor poet **9** 176-177
Lamb, Mary **29** 237-239

LAMB, MARY (1764-1847), English author **29** 237-239

Lamb, William
see Melbourne, 2nd Viscount

Lambert, Johann Heinrich, (1728-1777), German mathematician and philosopher
Amontons, Guillaume **29** 3-5

LAMBSDORFF, OTTO GRAF (born 1926), West German minister of economics **9** 177-179

Lambton, John George
see Durham, 1st Earl of

LINCOLN, BENJAMIN (1733-1810),
American military officer **9** 418-419

LIND, JAKOV (Heinz ''Henry'' Landwirth;
1927-2007), Austrian autobiographer,
short-story writer, novelist, and
playwright **9** 419-420

LIND, JENNY (Johanna Maria Lind;
1820-1887), Swedish coloratura soprano
26 233-235

LINDBERGH, ANNE MORROW (born
1906), American author and aviator **9**
420-421

LINDBERGH, CHARLES AUGUSTUS
(1902-1974), American aviator **9**
421-423

LINDGREN, ASTRID (Astrid Anna Emilia
Ericcson; 1907-2002), Swedish author
and editor **28** 219-221

LINDSAY, JOHN VLIET (born 1921), U.S.
congressman (1959-1965) and mayor of
New York (1966-1973) **9** 423-424

LINDSAY, VACHEL (1879-1931),
American folk poet **9** 424-425

LINDSEY, BENJAMIN BARR (1869-1943),
American jurist and reformer **9** 425-426

LINH, NGUYEN VAN (1915-1998), secretary-general of the Vietnamese
Communist Party (1986-1991) **9**
426-427

LINNAEUS, CARL (Carl von Linné;
1707-1778), Swedish naturalist **9**
427-429
    plant classification
        Colden, Jane **29** 118-119

LINTON, RALPH (1893-1953), American
anthropologist **9** 431

LIPCHITZ, JACQUES (1891-1973),
Lithuanian-born American sculptor **9**
432-433

LIPATTI, DINU (Constantin Lipatti;
1917-1950), Romanian musician and
composer **28** 222-223

LIPPI, FRA FILIPPO (c. 1406-1469), Italian
painter **9** 439

LIPPMANN, GABRIEL (1845-1921),
French physicist and inventor **25**
269-271

LIPPMANN, WALTER (1889-1974),
American journalist **9** 439-440

LIPPOLD, RICHARD (1915-2002),
American Constructivist sculptor **9**
440-442

Lisandrino
    see Magnasco, Alessandro

Lisbôa, Antônio Francisco
    see Aleijadinho, O

LIST, GEORG FRIEDRICH (1789-1846),
German economist **9** 443-444

LISTER, JOSEPH (1st Baron Lister of Lyme
Regis; 1827-1912), English surgeon **9**
444-445

LISZT, FRANZ (1811-1886), Hungarian
composer **9** 445-447
    students of
        Lenz, Wilhelm von **29** 243-245

Little, Malcolm
    see Malcolm X (film)

LITTLE MILTON (James Milton Campbell;
1934-2005), American blues musician
26 236-237

LITTLE, ROYAL (born 1896), American
textile tycoon **9** 449-451

Little Entente (1920-38;
Czechoslovakia-Romania-Yugoslavia)
    Beck, Józef **29** 48-50

LITTLE RICHARD (Richard Penniman;
born 1932), American rock 'n' roll
musician **9** 447-449

Littleton, Mark
    see Kennedy, John Pendleton

LITTLE WOLF (1818?-1904), Cheyenne
chief **18** 255-257

LITVINOV, MAXIM MAXIMOVICH
(1876-1951), Soviet diplomat **9** 451-452

Liu Ch'e
    see Han Wu-ti

Liu Chi
    see Liu Pang

LIU HSIEH (c. 465-522), Chinese literary
critic **9** 452-453

Liu Hsiu
    see Kuang-wu-ti

LIU PANG (Han Kao-tsu or Liu Chi; 256
B.C.-195 B.C.), Chinese emperor **9** 453

LIU SHAO-CH'I (born 1900), Chinese
Communist party leader **9** 453-455

LIU TSUNG-YÜAN (773-819), Chinese
poet and prose writer **9** 455-456

Liuzzi, Mondino de
    see Luzzi, Mondino de'

LIUZZO, VIOLA (1925-1965), American
civil rights activist **19** 203-205

LIVERIGHT, HORACE B. (1886-1933),
American publisher **23** 229-231

LIVERMORE, MARY (1820-1905),
American suffragette and reformer **29**
247-249

LIVERPOOL, 2ND EARL OF (Robert Barks
Jenkinson; 1770-1828), English
statesman, prime minister 1812-1827 **9**
456-457

Liverpool, University of (England)
    Barkla, Charles Glover **29** 46-48

Livestock
    see Cattle industry

LIVIA (ca. 58 B.C. - 29 A.D.), Roman
empress, wife of Augustus **9** 457-460

LIVINGSTON, EDWARD (1764-1836),
American jurist and statesman **9**
460-461

LIVINGSTON, ROBERT (1654-1728),
American colonial politician **9** 461-462

LIVINGSTON, ROBERT R. (1746-1813),
American jurist and diplomat **9** 462-463

LIVINGSTONE, DAVID (1813-1873),
Scottish missionary and explorer in
Africa **9** 463-465

LIVY (Titus Livius; c. 64 B.C.-c. 12 A.D.),
Roman historian **9** 465-467

Lizardi, José Joaquín Fernández de
    see Fernández de Lizardi, José Joaquín

LLERAS CAMARGO, ALBERTO
(1906-1990), Colombian statesman,
twice president **9** 467

LLEWELYN AP GRUFFYDD (died 1282),
Prince of Wales **9** 468

LLOYD, HENRY DEMAREST (1847-1903),
American social reformer **9** 468-469

LLOYD GEORGE, DAVID, (1st Earl of
Dwyfor; 1863-1945), English statesman,
prime minister 1916-1922 **9** 469-471

LLOYD, HAROLD (1893-1971), American
actor **20** 226-229

LLOYD-JONES, ESTHER MCDONALD
(born 1901), school personnel specialist
who focused on development of the
whole person **9** 471-472

LOBACHEVSKII, NIKOLAI IVANOVICH
(1792-1856), Russian mathematician **9**
472-474

LOBENGULA (died c. 1894), South African
Ndebele king **9** 474-475

Loch Ness Monster
    Scott, Sir Peter Markham **29**
        339-341

LOCHNER, STEPHAN (c. 1410-1451),
German painter **9** 475

LOCKE, ALAIN (1886-1954), African
American educator, editor, and author **9**
475-478

LOCKE, JOHN (1632-1704), English
philosopher and political theorist **9**
478-480

Lockheed Martin Corporation
    Martin, Glenn L. **29** 265-267

LOCKWOOD, BELVA (1830-1917),
American lawyer, suffragist, and
reformer **19** 205-207

LULA DA SILVA, LUIZ INÁCIO (Lula; born 1945), president of Brazil **27** 244-247

LULL, RAYMOND (1232/35-1316), Spanish theologian, poet, and missionary **10** 39-40

LULLY, JEAN BAPTISTE (1632-1687), Italian-born French composer **10** 40-41

Lully, Raymond
see Lull, Raymond

LUMET, SIDNEY (born 1924), American filmmaker and television director **22** 305-307

LUMIÈRE BROTHERS (Auguste Marie Louis, 1862-1954, and Louis Jean, 1864-1948), French inventors **10** 41-43

LUMUMBA, PATRICE EMERY (1925-1961), Congolese statesman **10** 43-45

LUNDY, BENJAMIN (1789-1839), American journalist **10** 45-46

LUNS, JOSEPH (1911-2002), West European political leader **10** 46-47

LURIA, ISAAC BEN SOLOMON ASHKENAZI (1534-1572), Jewish mystic **10** 47-48

LUTHER, MARTIN (1483-1546), German religious reformer **10** 48-51
family
    Bora, Katharina von **29** 256-258

LUTHULI, ALBERT JOHN (1898-1967), South African statesman **10** 51-52

LUTOSLAWSKI, WITOLD (1913-1994), Polish composer **10** 52-53

LUTYENS, EDWIN LANDSEER (1869-1944), English architect **10** 54-55

LUXEMBURG, ROSA (1870-1919), Polish revolutionary **10** 55-56

LUZ, ARTURO ROGERIO (born 1926), Philippine painter and sculptor **10** 56-57

LUZHKOV, YURI MIKHAYLOVICH (born 1936), mayor of Moscow **18** 266-268

LUZZATO, MOSES HAYYIM (1707-1747), Jewish mystic and poet **10** 57-58

LUZZI, MONDINO DE' (c. 1265-1326), Italian anatomist **10** 58
    Fallopio, Gabriele **29** 157-159

LWOFF, ANDRÉ (1902-1994), French microbiologist and geneticist **10** 58-59

LY, ABDOULAYE (born 1919), Senegalese politician and historian **10** 60

LYAUTEY, LOUIS HUBERT GONZALVE (1854-1934), French marshal and colonial administrator **10** 60-61

LYDGATE, JOHN (c. 1370-1449/50), English poet **10** 61-62

LYELL, SIR CHARLES (1797-1875), Scottish geologist **10** 62-63

LYND, HELEN MERRELL (1896-1982), American sociologist and educator **10** 63-64

LYND, ROBERT STAUGHTON (1892-1970), American sociologist **10** 64-65

LYND, STAUGHTON (born 1929), historian and peace militant **10** 65-66

LYNDSAY, SIR DAVID (c. 1485-1555), Scottish poet and courtier **10** 66-67

LYON, MARY (1797-1849), American educator, religious leader, and women's rights advocate **10** 67-69

LYONS, ENID MURIEL (1897-1981), Australian politician **29** 258-260

LYONS, JOSEPH ALOYSIUS (1879-1939), Australian statesman, prime minister 1932-39 **10** 69-70
    Lyons, Enid Muriel **29** 258-260

LYSANDER (died 395 B.C.), Spartan military commander and statesman **10** 70

LYSENKO, TROFIM DENISOVICH (1898-1976), Soviet agronomist and geneticist **10** 71

Lytton of Knebworth, 1st Baron
see Bulwer-Lytton, Edward

M

MA, YO-YO (born 1955), American cellist **20** 232-234

MAAS, PETER (1929-2001), American author **27** 248-251

MAATHAI, WANGARI MUTA (born 1940), Kenyan environmental activist **18** 269-271

MABILLON, JEAN (1632-1707), French monk and historian **10** 72

MABINI, APOLINARIO (1864-1903), Filipino political philosopher **10** 72-73

Mabovitch, Golda
see Meir, Golda

MABUCHI, KAMO (1697-1769), Japanese writer and scholar **10** 73-74

MACAPAGAL, DIOSDADO P. (born 1910), Filipino statesman **10** 74-76

MACAPAGAL-ARROYO, GLORIA (Gloria Arroyo; born 1947), presidnet of the Philippine islands **25** 278-280

MACARTHUR, DOUGLAS (1880-1964), American general **10** 76-78

MACARTHUR, JOHN (c. 1767-1834), Australian merchant, sheep breeder, and politician **10** 78

MACAULAY, CATHARINE (Catherine Sawbridge Macaulay Graham; 1731-1791), British author and feminist **25** 280-282

MACAULAY, HERBERT (1864-1945), Nigerian politician **10** 78-79

MACAULAY, THOMAS BABINGTON (1st Baron Macaulay of Rothley; 1800-1859), English essayist, historian, and politician **10** 79-80

MACBETH (died 1057), king of Scotland 1040-1057 **10** 81

MACBRIDE, SEAN (1904-1988), Irish statesman **19** 218-220

MACCREADY, PAUL (1925-2007), American aeronautical engineer **20** 234-237

MACDONALD, DWIGHT (1906-1982), American editor, journalist, essayist, and critic **10** 81-83

MACDONALD, ELEANOR JOSEPHINE (born 1906), American epidemiologist **10** 83-84

MACDONALD, JAMES RAMSAY (1866-1937), British politician **10** 84-85

MACDONALD, SIR JOHN ALEXANDER (1815-1891), Canadian statesman **10** 85-87

MACDOWELL, EDWARD ALEXANDER (1861-1908), American pianist and composer **10** 87-88

MACEO, ANTONIO (1845-1896), Cuban general and patriot **10** 88-90

MACH, ERNST (1838-1916), Austrian physicist **10** 90-91

MACHADO DE ASSIS, JOAQUIM MARIA (1839-1908), Brazilian novelist **10** 91-92

MACHADO Y MORALES, GERARDO (1871-1939), Cuban general and president **10** 92-93

MACHAUT, GUILLAUME DE (c. 1300-1377), French composer and poet **10** 93-94

MACHEL, SAMORA MOISES (1933-1986), socialist revolutionary and first president of Mozambique **10** 94-96

MACHIAVELLI, NICCOLÒ (1469-1527), Italian author and statesman **10** 97-99

Machine gun
see Weapons and explosives

MACINTYRE, ALASDAIR CHALMERS (born 1929), Scottish-born philosopher and ethicist **10** 99-100

MACIVER, ROBERT MORRISON (1882-1970), Scottish-American sociologist, political philosopher, and educator **10** 100-101

MERRILL, CHARLES E. (1885-1956), founder of the world's largest brokerage firm **10** 519-520

MERRILL, JAMES (1926-1995), American novelist, poet, and playwright **10** 521-522

Merrimack Manufacturing Co.
Moody, Paul **29** 283-284

MERTON, ROBERT K. (1910-2003), American sociologist and educator **10** 522-523

MERTON, THOMAS (1915-1968), Roman Catholic writer, social critic, and spiritual guide **10** 523-525

MERULO, CLAUDIO (1533-1604), Italian composer, organist, and teacher **10** 525-526

MESMER, FRANZ ANTON (1734-1815), German physician **10** 526-527

MESSALI HADJ (1898-1974), founder of the Algerian nationalist movement **10** 527-528

MESSERSCHMITT, WILLY (Wilhelm Emil Messerschmitt; 1898-1978), German aircraft designer and manufacturer **25** 291-293

MESSIAEN, OLIVIER (1908-1992), French composer and teacher **10** 528-529

MESSNER, REINHOLD (born 1944), Austrian mountain climber and author **22** 316-318

METACOM (a.k.a. King Philip; 1640-1676), Wampanoag cheiftain **10** 529-531

Metal (chemistry)
Roebuck, John **29** 326-328

Metallurgy (science)
Austin, Moses **29** 22-24

Metastasio, (Pietro Antonio Domenico Bonaventura Trapassi; 1698-1782), Italian dramatist
Salieri, Antonio **29** 333-335

METCALFE, CHARLES THEOPHILUS (1st Baron Metcalfe; 1785-1846), British colonial administrator **10** 531-532

METCHNIKOFF, ÉLIE (1845-1916), Russian physiologist and bacteriologist **10** 532-533

Meteorology (science)
Amontons, Guillaume **29** 3-5

METHODIUS, SAINT (825-885), Greek missionary and bishop **4** 362-363

Metro-Goldwyn-Mayer (film studio)
Harlow, Jean **29** 182-184
Minnelli, Vincente **29** 281-283
Shearer, Norma **29** 343-345

Metsys, Quentin
see Massys, Quentin

METTERNICH, KLEMENS VON (1773-1859), Austrian politician and diplomat **10** 533-536

Meun, Jean de
see Jean de Meun

Mexico (United Mexican States; republic, North America)
AZTEC EMPIRE
exploration
Córdoba, Francisco Hernández de **29** 126-128
REPUBLIC
border disputes
de la Barra, Francisco León **29** 245-247
Mexican Empire
Carlotta **29** 108-110
UNITED STATES RELATIONS
diplomatic relations
de la Barra, Francisco León **29** 245-247

MEYERBEER, GIACOMO (1791-1864), German composer **10** 536-537

MEYERHOF, OTTO FRITZ (1884-1951), German biochemist **10** 537-539

MEYERHOLD, VSEVOLOD EMILIEVICH (1874-1942?), Russian director **10** 539

MFUME, KWEISI (born Frizzell Gray; born 1948), African American civil rights activist and congressman **10** 539-542

MGM
see Metro-Goldwyn-Mayer (film studio)

MI FEI (1051-1107), Chinese painter, calligrapher, and critic **11** 12-13

MICAH (flourished 8th century B.C.), prophet of ancient Israel **10** 542-543

MICHAEL VIII (Palaeologus; 1224/25-1282), Byzantine emperor 1259-1282 **11** 1-2

Michel, Claude
see Clodion

MICHELANGELO BUONARROTI (1475-1564), Italian sculptor, painter, and architect **11** 2-5

MICHELET, JULES (1798-1874), French historian **11** 5-6

MICHELOZZO (c. 1396-1472), Italian architect and sculptor **11** 6-7

MICHELSON, ALBERT ABRAHAM (1852-1931), American physicist **11** 7-8

MICHENER, JAMES (1907-1997), American author **19** 245-247

MICKIEWICZ, ADAM BERNARD (1798-1855), Polish poet **27** 263-265

MIDDLETON, THOMAS (1580-1627), English playwright **11** 8-9

MIDGELY, MARY BURTON (born 1919), British philosopher who focused on the philosophy of human motivation and ethics **11** 9-10

MIES VAN DER ROHE, LUDWIG (1886-1969), German-born American architect **11** 10-12

MIKAN, GEORGE (1924-2005), American basketball player **21** 297-299

MIKULSKI, BARBARA (born 1936), United States senator from Maryland **11** 13-15

MILÁN, LUIS (c. 1500-after 1561), Spanish composer **11** 15-16

MILES, NELSON APPLETON (1839-1925), American general **11** 16-17
Masterson, Bat **29** 272-274

MILHAUD, DARIUS (born 1892), French composer and teacher **11** 17-18

Military dictatorships
see Dictatorships

Military leaders, Chilean
Carrera, Juan José **29** 110-112

Military leaders, Egyptian
Orabi, Ahmed **29** 304-306

Military leaders, Japanese
admirals
Okada, Keisuke **29** 301-302

Military leaders, Nigerian
Ojukwu, Chukwuemeka Odumegwu **29** 298-301

Military strategy
techniques
Chennault, Claire Lee **29** 114-116
Zeppelin, Count Ferdinand von **29** 387-389

MILIUKOV, PAVEL NIKOLAYEVICH (1859-1943), Russian historian and statesman **11** 18-19

MILK, HARVEY BERNARD (1930-1978), American politician and gay rights activist **11** 19-21

MILKEN, MICHAEL (born 1946), American businessman **19** 247-249

MILL, JAMES (1773-1836), Scottish philosopher and historian **11** 21

MILL, JOHN STUART (1806-1873), English philosopher and economist **11** 21-23

MILLAIS, SIR JOHN EVERETT (1829-1896), English painter **11** 23-24

MILLAY, EDNA ST. VINCENT (1892-1950), American lyric poet **11** 24-25

MILLER, ARTHUR (1915-2005), American playwright, novelist, and film writer **11** 25-26

MILLER, GLENN (Alton Glenn Miller; 1904-1944), American musician **19** 250-251

MILLER, HENRY (born 1891), American author **11** 26-27

MUGABE, ROBERT GABRIEL (born 1924), Zimbabwe's first elected black prime minister **11** 227-229

MUHAMMAD ALI PASHA (Mehmet Ali Pasha; Muhammad Ali; 1769-1849), Ottoman Turkish ruler of Egypt **27** 265-267

MUHAMMAD, ELIJAH (Poole; 1897-1975), leader of the Nation of Islam ("Black Muslims") **11** 230-231

MUHAMMAD BIN TUGHLUQ (ruled 1325-1351), Moslem sultan of Delhi **11** 229

Muhammad ibn Daud
see Alp Arslan

Muhammad Shah (1877-1957)
see Aga Khan III

MUHAMMAD TURE, ASKIA (c. 1443-1538), ruler of the West African Songhay empire **11** 231-232

Muhibbi
see Suleiman I

MÜHLENBERG, HEINRICH MELCHIOR (1711-1787), German-born American Lutheran clergyman **11** 232-233

MUHLENBERG, WILLIAM AUGUSTUS (1796-1877), American Episcopalian clergyman **11** 233-234

MUIR, JOHN (1838-1914), American naturalist **11** 234

MUJIBUR RAHMAN, SHEIK (1920-1975), Bengal leader who helped found Bangladesh **11** 234-236

MUKERJI, DHAN GOPAL (1890-1936), Indian author and Hindu priest **22** 328-330

MULDOWNEY, SHIRLEY (born ca. 1940), American race car driver **11** 236-238

MULLER, HERMANN JOSEPH (1890-1967), American geneticist **11** 238-239

Müller, Johann
see Regiomontanus

MÜLLER, JOHANNES PETER (1801-1858), German physiologist and anatomist **11** 239-240

MÜLLER, KARL ALEXANDER (born 1927), Swiss-born solid-state physicist **11** 240-241

MÜLLER, PAUL HERMANN (1899-1965), Swiss chemist **11** 241-242

MULRONEY, MARTIN BRIAN (born 1939), prime minister of Canada **11** 242-246

MUMFORD, LEWIS (1895-1990), American social philosopher and architectural critic **11** 246-247

Mun Sun
see Yi Hwang

MUNCH, EDVARD (1863-1944), Norwegian painter and graphic artist **11** 247-248

MUNDELEIN, GEORGE WILLIAM (1872-1939), American Roman Catholic cardinal **11** 248-249

Mundinus
see Luzzi, Mondino de'

Munich Conference (1938)
Beck, Józef **29** 48-50

Municipal government
Pendergast, Thomas J. **29** 313-315

Munitions
see Weapons and explosives

MUÑOZ MARÍN, JOSÉ LUÍS ALBERTO (1898-1980), Puerto Rican political leader **11** 249-250

MUÑOZ RIVERA, LUÍS (1859-1916), Puerto Rican political leader **11** 250

MUNSEY, FRANK ANDREW (1854-1925), American publisher **11** 251

MÜNZER, THOMAS (1489?-1525), German Protestant reformer **11** 251-252

Murabi-tun, al-
see Almoravids, (ruled 1062-1147)

MURASAKI SHIKIBU (c. 976-c. 1031), Japanese writer **11** 252-253

MURAT, JOACHIM (1767-1815), French marshal, king of Naples 1808-1815 **11** 253-254

MURATORI, LODOVICO ANTONIO (1672-1750), Italian historian and antiquary **11** 254-255

MURCHISON, SIR RODERICK IMPEY (1792-1871), British geologist **11** 255-256

Murder Must Advertise (novel)
Sayers, Dorothy L. **29** 335-337

MURDOCH, JEAN IRIS (1919-1999), British novelist **11** 256-257

MURDOCH, RUPERT (born 1931), Australian newspaper publisher **11** 257-258

MURILLO, BARTOLOMÉ ESTEBAN (1617-1682), Spanish painter **11** 258-259

Murjebi, Hamed bin Mohammed el
see Tippu Tip

MURNAU, F.W. (Friedrich Wilhelm Plumpe; 1888-1913), German film director **22** 330-332

Muromachi shogunate
see Japan—1338-1573 (Ashikaga shogunate)

MURPHY, AUDIE (1924-1971), American army officer and actor **18** 299-301

MURPHY, CHARLES FRANCIS (1858-1924), American politician **11** 259-260

MURPHY, FRANK (1890-1949), American jurist and diplomat **11** 260-261

MURRAY, ANNE (Morna Anne Murray; born 1945), Canadian singer **27** 267-269

MURRAY, ARTHUR (Arthur Murray Teichman; 1895-1991), American dance school founder **27** 269-271

MURRAY, GILBERT (George Gilbert Aime Murray; 1886-1957), English scholar **23** 250-253

MURRAY, JAMES (1721-1794), British general **11** 261-262

Murray, John (1732-1809)
see Dunmore, 4th Earl of

MURRAY, JOSEPH (born 1919), American physician **18** 301-303

MURRAY, LESLIE ALLAN (born 1938), Australian poet and literary critic **11** 262-263

MURRAY, PAULI (Anna Pauline Murray; 1910-1985), African American/Native American civil right activist and priest **23** 253-256

MURRAY, PHILIP (1886-1952), American labor leader **11** 264-265

MURRAY, WILLIAM (Lord Mansfield; 1705-1793), English judge **23** 256-258

MURROW, EDWARD ROSCOE (1908-1965), American radio and television news broadcaster **11** 265-266

MUSA MANSA (died 1337), king of the Mali empire in West Africa ca. 1312-1337 **11** 266

MUSGRAVE, THEA (born 1928), Scottish-born composer **11** 266-268

MUSHARRAF, PERVEZ (born 1943), Pakistani head of sate **22** 332-335

MUSIAL, STAN (Stanislaus Musial, Stanley Frank Musial; born 1920), American baseball **19** 260-262

Music
world music
Hussain, Zakir **29** 204-206

Musical comedy (United States)
Hart, Lorenz **29** 184-186
Minnelli, Vincente **29** 281-283

Musicals (United States)
librettists/lyricists
Hart, Lorenz **29** 184-186

Musicians, American
bandleaders
Oliver, Joseph "King" **29** 302-304

NERVI, PIER LUIGI (1891-1979), Italian architect and engineer **11** 346-348

NESBIT, E(DITH) (Edith Nesbit Bland; Fabian Bland; 1885-1924), English author and activist **23** 263-265

NESSELRODE, COUNT KARL ROBERT (1780-1862), Russian diplomat **11** 348-349

NESTOR, AGNES (1880-1948), American labor leader and lobbyist **26** 273-275

NESTORIUS (died c. 453), Syrian patriarch of Constantinople and heresiarch **11** 349-350

Netaji (führer)
see Bose, Subhas Chandra

NETANYAHU, BINYAMIN (born 1949), Israeli ambassador to the United Nations (1984-1988), head of the Likud Party, and prime minister **11** 350-351

NETO, ANTÓNIO AGOSTINHO (1922-1979), Angolan intellectual and nationalist and first president of the People's Republic of Angola **11** 351-352

Neuaegyptische Grammatik (New Egyptian Grammar)
Erman, Adolf **29** 154-156

NEUFELD, ELIZABETH F. (born 1928), American biochemist **11** 352-353

NEUMANN, BALTHASAR (1687-1753), German architect **11** 354-355

Neurospora (mold)
Tatum, Edward Lawrie **29** 356-358

NEUTRA, RICHARD JOSEPH (1892-1970), Austrian-born American architect **11** 355-356

NEVELSON, LOUISE (1900-1988), American abstract sculptor **11** 356-357

NEVERS, ERNIE (Ernest Alonzo Nevers; 1903-1976), American athlete **20** 281-283

Neville, Richard
see Warwick and Salisbury, Earl of

NEVIN, JOHN WILLIAMSON (1803-1886), American Protestant theologian **11** 357

NEVINS, ALLAN (1890-1971), American historian **11** 357-359

NEVSKY, ALEXANDER (ca. 1220-1262), Russian grand duke and prince **11** 359

New Amsterdam
see New York City (New York State)

New England Patriots (football team)
Berry, Raymond **29** 57-59

New France
see Canada (nation, North America)

New School for Social Research (New York City)
Dramatic Workshop and Studio Theater
Piscator, Erwin **29** 315-317

New York City (New York State)
MODERN PERIOD
architecture
Pokorny, Jan Hird **29** 320-321

New York Mets (baseball team)
Berra, Yogi **29** 54-57

New York Sun (newspaper)
Brisbane, Arthur **29** 93-95

New York World (newspaper)
contributors
Brisbane, Arthur **29** 93-95

New York Yankees (baseball team)
Berra, Yogi **29** 54-57

New Zealand (island nation; Southern Pacific Ocean)
administration
Ballance, John **29** 42-44
wars, Maori/foreigners
Ballance, John **29** 42-44

NEWBERY, JOHN (1713-1767), English publisher **11** 360-361

NEWCOMB, SIMON (1835-1909), American astronomer **11** 361-362

NEWCOMEN, THOMAS (1663-1729), English inventor and engineer **11** 362
Roebuck, John **29** 326-328

NEWHOUSE, SAMUEL IRVING (1895-1979), American media tycoon **11** 362-364

NEWMAN, BARNETT (1905-1970), American painter **11** 365

NEWMAN, JOHN HENRY (1801-1890), English cardinal and theologian **11** 365-367

NEWMAN, PAUL LEONARD (born 1925), American actor and humanitarian **18** 306-308

NEWTON, HUEY P. (born 1942), co-founder of the Black Panther Party **11** 367-369

NEWTON, SIR ISAAC (1642-1727), English scientist and mathematician **11** 369-372

NEXØ, MARTIN ANDERSON (1869-1954), Danish author **11** 372

NEY, MICHEL (1769-1815), French marshal **11** 372-373

Neyra, Álvaro de Mendaña de
see Mendaña de Neyra, Álvaro de

NEYMAN, JERZY (1894-1981), American statistician **21** 316-318

NGALA, RONALD GIDEON (1923-1972), Kenyan politician **11** 373-374

NGATA, SIR APIRANA TURUPA (1874-1950), Maori leader, politician, and scholar **11** 374-375

Ngengi, Johnstone Kamau
see Kenyatta, Jomo

NGOR, HAING S. (c. 1947-1996), Cambodian American actor and human rights activist **25** 310-312

NGOYI, LILLIAN (1911-1980), South African civil rights activist **20** 283-284

NGUGI WA THIONG'O (James Ngugi; born 1938), Kenyan writer **11** 375-376

Nguyen Ali Quoc (Nguyen That Thanh)
see Ho Chi Minh

NI TSAN (1301-1374), Chinese painter **11** 400

NICHIREN (1222-1282), Japanese Buddhist monk **11** 376-377

NICHOLAS I (1796-1855), czar of Russia 1825-1855 **11** 377-378

NICHOLAS II (1868-1918), czar of Russia 1894-1917 **11** 378-380
Andreyev, Leonid Nikolayevich **29** 11-13
Borodin, Mikhail Markovich **29** 72-74

NICHOLAS V (Tommaso Parentucelli; 1397-1455), Italian pope 1447-1455 **26** 299-300

Nicholas of Cusa
see Cusa, Nicholas of

NICHOLAS OF ORESME (c. 1320-1382), French bishop, writer and translator **11** 380

NICHOLAS, SAINT (Santa Claus; died 345), Lycian bishop **20** 284-285

NICHOLSON, BEN (1894-1982), English painter **11** 380-381

NICHOLSON, SIR FRANCIS (1655-1728), English colonial governor **11** 381-382

NICKLAUS, JACK (born 1940), American golfer **11** 382-383

Nicola Pisano
see Pisano, Nicola

NICHOLS, MIKE (Michael Igor Peschkowsky; born 1931), American film and theater director and producer **20** 285-288

NICOLSON, HAROLD GEORGE (1886-1968), British diplomat, historian, biographer, critic and journalist, and diarist **11** 383-384

NICOLSON, MARJORIE HOPE (1894-1981), American educator **11** 384-385

NICOMACHUS OF GERASA (c. 60-c. 100), Greek mathematician, philosopher, and musical theorist **25** 312-314

NIDETCH, JEAN (born 1927), founder of Weight Watchers **21** 318-320

OORT, JAN HENDRIK (1900-1992), Dutch astronomer **11** 523-524

Open-door policy (Liberia)
Barclay, Edwin **29** 44-45

Opera, Italian
18th century
Cuzzoni, Francesca **29** 132-134
Salieri, Antonio **29** 333-335

OPHÜLS, MAX (Max Oppenheimer; 1902-1957), German film director and screenwriter **23** 275-277

OPPENHEIM, MERET (1913-1985), Swiss Surrealist artist **11** 524-525

OPPENHEIMER, ERNEST (1880-1957), British South African businessman **24** 288-290

OPPENHEIMER, J. ROBERT (1904-1967), American physicist **11** 525-526

ORABI, AHMED (1841-1911), Egyptian military leader **29** 304-306

ORCAGNA (1308?-1368?), Italian painter, sculptor, and architect **11** 526-527

Ordóñez, José Battle y
see Batlle y Ordóñez, José

ORELLANA, FRANCISCO DE (c. 1511-1546), Spanish explorer **11** 527-528

ORFF, CARL (1895-1982), German musician **26** 276-278

Orford, 1st Earl of
see Walpole, Robert

Organization for Economic Cooperation and Development
Ikeda, Hayato **29** 211-213

ORIGEN (Origenes Adamantius; c. 185-c. 254), Early Christian theologian **11** 528-529

Origin of Species (book; Darwin)
editions and translations
Bronn, Heinrich Georg **29** 97-99
influence of
Biffen, Sir Rowland Harry **29** 59-61

Original sin (religion)
Baius, Michael **29** 31-33

ORLANDO, VITTORIO EMMANUELE (1860-1952), Italian statesman **11** 529-530

ORLÉANS, CHARLES (1394-1465), French prince and poet **11** 530

ORLÉANS, PHILIPPE II (1674-1723), French statesman, regent 1715-23 **11** 530-531

ORMANDY, EUGENE (Jenö Blau; Jenö B. Ormándy; 1899-1985), American conductor **28** 264-266

Ornithology (science)
Scott, Sir Peter Markham **29** 339-341

Oroetes (flourished 522), Persian governor of Sardis
Anacreon **29** 9-11

OROZCO, JOSÉ CLEMENTE (1883-1949), Mexican painter **12** 1-2

ORR, BOBBY (Robert Gordon Orr; born 1948), Canadian hockey player **12** 2-4

ORR, JOHN BOYD (1st Baron Orr of Brechin; 1880-1971), Scottish nutritionist and UN official **12** 4-5

ORTEGA, DANIEL (born 1945), leader of the Sandinista National Liberation Front and president of Nicaragua **12** 5-7

ORTEGA, KATHERINE DAVALOS (born 1934), Hispanic American government official **25** 319-321

ORTEGA Y GASSET, JOSÉ (1883-1955), Spanish philosopher and essayist **12** 7-8

ORTELIUS, ABRAHAM (Abraham, Ortels; 1527-1598), Flemish cartographer **12** 8-9

ORTIZ, ALFONSO ALEX (1939-1997), Native American anthropologist and activist **26** 278-280

ORTIZ, SIMON J. (born 1941), Native American author and storyteller **12** 9-12

ORTON, JOHN KINGSLEY ("Joe;" 1933-1967), British playwright **12** 12-14

ORWELL, GEORGE (1903-1950), British novelist and essayist **12** 14-15

Osagyefo
see Nkrumah, Kwame

OSBORN, HENRY FAIRFIELD, SR. (1857-1935), American paleontologist **29** 306-308

OSBORNE, JOHN (1929-1994), English playwright **12** 16-17

OSBORNE, THOMAS MOTT (1859-1926), American reformer **12** 17-18

OSCEOLA (c. 1800-1838), Seminole Indian war chief **12** 18

OSGOOD, HERBERT LEVI (1855-1918), American historian **12** 18-19

OSLER, SIR WILLIAM (1849-1919), Canadian physician **12** 19-20

OSMAN I (Othman; 1259-1326), Turkish warrior-leader who established the Ottoman state as an independent entity **12** 20-22

OSMEÑA, SERGIO (1878-1961), Philippine lawyer and statesman **12** 22-24

OSMOND, DONNY AND MARIE (Donald Clark Osmond; born 1957 and Olive Marie Osmond; born 1959), American singers **27** 283-285

Osorio, Mariano, (1777-1819), Chilean general
Carrera, Juan José **29** 110-112

OSTROVSKY, ALEXANDER (Alexander Nikolayevich Ostrocsky; 1823-1886), Russian playwright **26** 280-283

Oswald, F.
see Engels, F.

OSWALD, LEE HARVEY (1939-1963), presumed assassin of John F. Kennedy **21** 328-330

OTIS, ELISHA GRAVES (1811-1861), American manufacturer and inventor **12** 24

OTIS, HARRISON GRAY (1765-1848), American statesman **12** 25

OTIS, JAMES, JR. (1725-1783), American Revolutionary statesman **12** 25-27

OTTERBEIN, PHILIP WILLIAM (1726-1813), American clergyman **12** 27-28

OTTO I (912-973), Holy Roman emperor 936-973 **12** 28-29

OTTO III (980-1002), Holy Roman emperor 996-1002 and German king 983-1002 **12** 29-30

OTTO, LOUIS KARL RUDOLF (1869-1937), German interpreter of religion **12** 30-32

OTTO, NIKOLAUS AUGUST (1832-1891), German engineer and inventor **21** 331-333
Maybach, Wilhelm **29** 274-277

OTTO OF FREISING (c. 1114-1158), German historiographer and philosopher of history **12** 30

Otto the Great
see Otto I

OUD, JACOBUS JOHANNES PIETER (1890-1963), Dutch architect **12** 32

OUGHTRED, WILLIAM (1574-1660), English mathematician **23** 277-279

OUSMANE, SEMBENE (1923-2007), Senegalese novelist and filmmaker **12** 32-33

OU-YANG HSIU (1007-1072), Chinese author and statesman **12** 33-34

OVID (Publius Ovidius Naso; 43 B.C.-A.D. 18), Roman elegiac and epic poet **12** 34-36

OVINGTON, MARY WHITE (1865-1951), civil rights reformer and a founder of the National Association for the Advancement of Colored People **12** 36-37

Owain ap Gruffydd
see Glendower, O.

PERÓN, EVA (MARÍA) DUARTE DE
(1919-1952), the second wife and
political partner of President Juan Perón
of Argentina **12** 225-226

PERÓN, ISABEL MARTINEZ DE (born
1931), first woman president of
Argentina (1974-1976) **12** 226-228

PERÓN, JUAN DOMINGO (1895-1974),
Argentine statesman, president 1946-55
12 228-230

PEROT, HENRY ROSS (born 1930),
American businessman and activist **12**
230-231
Jordan, Hamilton **29** 220-222

PÉROTIN (Perotinus; flourished c.
1185-1205), French composer and
musician **12** 231-232

PERRAULT, CLAUDE (1613-1688), French
scientist and architect **12** 232-233

PERRET, AUGUSTE (1874-1954), French
architect **12** 233

Perreti, Felice
see Sixtus V

PERRIN, JEAN BAPTISTE (1870-1942),
French physicist **12** 233-236

Perry, Edgar A.
see Poe, Edgar Allan

PERRY, HAROLD ROBERT (1916-1991),
African American Roman Catholic
bishop **12** 236-237

PERRY, MATTHEW CALBRAITH
(1794-1858), American naval officer **12**
237-239
Tokugawa Yoshinobu **29** 382-384

PERRY, OLIVER HAZARD (1785-1819),
American naval officer **12** 239

PERRY, RALPH BARTON (1876-1957),
American philosopher **12** 239-240

PERRY, WILLIAM JAMES (born 1927),
President Clinton's secretary of defense
(1994-) **12** 240-242

PERSE, SAINT-JOHN (Alexis Saint-Léger
Léger; 1887-1975), French poet and
diplomat **12** 242-243

PERSHING, JOHN JOSEPH (1860-1948),
American general **12** 243-244

Perske, Betty Joan
see Bacall, Lauren

Persse, Isabella Augusta
see Gregory, Lady Augusta

PERTH, 16TH EARL OF (James Eric
Drummond; 1876-1951), English
statesman **12** 244-245

**Peru, Republic of (nation, Western South
America)**
Spanish conquest
Pizarro, Juan **29** 318-320

PERUGINO (c. 1450-1523), Italian painter
12 245-246
Aretino, Pietro **29** 16-18

PERUTZ, MAX (1914-2002), English crys-
tallographer and biochemist **12** 246-248

Peshkov, Aleksei Maximovich
see Gorky, Maxim

PESOTTA, ROSE (1896-1965), American
union organizer **12** 248-249

PESTALOZZI, JOHANN HEINRICH
(1746-1827), Swiss educator **12** 249-250

PÉTAIN, HENRI PHILIPPE (1856-1951),
French general and statesman **12**
250-252

Peter (emperor, Brazil)
see Pedro

Peter (king, Portugal)
see Pedro

PETER I (Peter the Great; 1672-1725), czar
of Russia 1682-1725 **12** 253-256

PETER I (1844-1921), king of Serbia
1903-18, and of the Serbs, Croats, and
Slovenes 1918-21 **12** 256

PETER III (Pedro; c. 1239-85), king of
Aragon 1276-85 **12** 256-257

PETER, SAINT (died c. 65), apostle and
bishop of Rome **12** 252-253

Peter Canisius, St.
see Canisius, St. Peter

Peter Claver, St.
see Claver, St. Peter

Peter Kanis
see Canisius, St. Peter

Peter Leopold
see Leopold II (emperor)

Peter Lombard
see Lombard, Peter

Peter the Great
see Peter I (czar, Russia)

PETERS, CARL (1856-1918), German
explorer and colonizer **12** 257-258

PETERSON, EDITH R. (born Edith Elizabeth
Runne; 1914-1992), American medical
researcher **12** 258-259

PETERSON, OSCAR (1925-2007),
Canadian pianist **23** 304-306

PETO, JOHN FREDERICK (1854-1907),
American painter **12** 259

PETŐFI, SÁNDOR (1823-1849),
Hungarian poet and revolutionary leader
23 306-308

PETRARCH (Francesco Petrarca; 1304-74),
Italian poet **12** 259-261

**PETRIE, SIR WILLIAM MATTHEW
FLINDERS** (1853-1942), English archeologist **12** 261-262

Petrograd (city; Russia)
see St. Petersburg (city; Russia)

PETRONIUS ARBITER (died c. 66), Roman
author **12** 262-263

PEVSNER, ANTOINE (1886-1962), Russian
sculptor and painter **12** 263-264

Pevsner, Naum Neemia
see Gabo, Naum

PEYO (Pierre Culliford; 1928-1992),
Belgian cartoonist **28** 280-282

PHAEDRUS (c. 15 BC-c. 50), Greek/
Roman fabulists **20** 296-297

Pharmaceutical industry
Merck, George Wilhelm **29** 279-281

PHIBUN SONGKHRAM, LUANG
(1897-1964), Thai statesman, prime
minister 1938-44 and 1948-57 **12** 264-265

PHIDIAS (flourished c. 475-425 B.C.),
Greek sculptor **12** 265-267

Philadelphia (city; Pennsylvania)
businesses
Wanamaker, John **29** 372-375

Philadelphos of Egypt
see Ptolemy II

Philanthropists, American
20th century
Merck, George Wilhelm **29**
279-281

PHILIDOR, FRANÇOIS-ANDRÉ
(François-André Danican-Philidor;
1726-1795), French composer and chess
player **21** 347-349

PHILIP (died 1676), American Wampanoag
Indian chief 1662-76 **12** 267-268

PHILIP (Prince Philip; Philip Mountbatten;
born 1921), Duke of Edinburgh and
husband of Queen Elizabeth II of the
United Kingdom **24** 308-310

Philip I (king of Portugal)
see Philip II (king of Spain)

PHILIP II (382-336 B.C.), king of Macedon
359-336 **12** 269-271

PHILIP II (Philip Augustus; 1165-1223),
king of France 1180-1223 **12** 268-269

PHILIP II (1527-1598), king of Spain
1556-1598 **12** 271-273

PHILIP III (1578-1621), king of Spain
1598-1621 **12** 273-274

PHILIP IV (the Fair; 1268-1314), king of
France 1285-1314 **12** 274

PHILIP IV (1605-1665), king of Spain
1621-65 **12** 275

PINKNEY, WILLIAM (1764-1822), American attorney, diplomat, and statesman **22** 355-357

Pinocchio (film)
Johnston, Ollie **29** 216-218

PINOCHET UGARTE, AUGUSTO (1915-2006), Chilean military leader and dictator **12** 315-317

PINTER, HAROLD (born 1930), English playwright **12** 317-318

PINTO, ISAAC (1720-1791), Jewish merchant and scholar **12** 318

PINZÓN, MARTIN ALONSO (1440?-1493), Spanish navigator **22** 358-360

PINZÓN, VICENTE YÁÑEZ (1460?-1524?), Spanish navigator **22** 360-361

PIO, PADRE (Francesco Forgione; 1887-1968), Italian priest **20** 297-299

PIPPIN, HORACE (1888-1946), African American painter **12** 318-319

PIRANDELLO, LUIGI (1867-1936), Italian playwright novelist, and critic **12** 319-321

PIRANESI, GIOVANNI BATTISTA (1720-1778), Italian engraver and architect **12** 321-322

Pirates
Morgan, Sir Henry **29** 284-287

PIRENNE, JEAN HENRI (Jean Henri Otto Lucien Marie Pirenne; 1862-1935), Belgian historian **12** 322-323

Pisa, University of
Borelli, Giovanni Alfonso **29** 69-72
Ferri, Enrico **29** 159-162

Pisan, Christine de
see Christine de Pisan

PISANELLO (Antonio Pisano; before 1395-1455), Italian painter and medalist **12** 323-324

Pisano
see Pisanello

PISANO, GIOVANNI (c. 1250-1314/17), Italian sculptor **12** 324-325

PISANO, NICOLA (Nicola d'Apulia; c. 1220/25-1278/84), Italian sculptor **12** 325

PISCATOR, ERWIN (1893-1966), German theatrical producer **29** 315-317

PISCOPIA, ELENA LUCREZIA CORNARO (1646-1684), Italian philosopher **26** 293-295

PISSARO, CAMILLE (1830-1903), French painter **12** 326-327

PISTON, WALTER (born 1894), American composer **12** 327-328

PITT, WILLIAM, THE ELDER (1708-1778), English statesman **12** 328-329

PITT, WILLIAM, THE YOUNGER (1759-1806), English statesman **12** 329-331

PIUS II (Enea Silvio de'Piccolomini; 1405-1464), pope 1458-64 **12** 331

PIUS IV (Giovanni Angelo de' Medici; 1499-1565), pope 1559-65 **12** 332

PIUS V (Antonio Ghislieri; 1504-1572), pope 1566-72 **12** 332-333
Baius, Michael **29** 31-33

PIUS VI (Gianangelo Braschi; 1717-99), pope 1775-99 **12** 333-334
Azara, José Nicolás de **29** 24-26

PIUS VII (Luigi Barnabà Chiaramonti; 1740-1823), pope 1880-23 **12** 334-335

PIUS IX (Giovanni Maria Mastai-Ferretti; 1792-1878), pope 1846-78 **12** 335-336

PIUS X (Giuseppe Melchiorre Sarto; 1835-1914), pope 1903-14 **12** 336-337

PIUS XI (Ambrogio Damiano Achille Ratti; 1857-1939), pope 1922-39 **12** 337-339

PIUS XII (Eugenio Maria Giuseppe Pacelli; 1876-1958), pope 1939-58 **12** 339-340

PIZARRO, FRANCISCO (c. 1474-1541), Spanish conquistador in Peru **12** 340-341
Pizarro, Juan **29** 318-320

Pizarro, Gonzalo, (1506-1548), Spanish colonial governor
Pizarro, Juan **29** 318-320

Pizarro, Hernando, (1475?-1578), Spanish explorer
Pizarro, Juan **29** 318-320

PIZARRO, JUAN (c. 1495-1536), Spanish conquistador **29** 318-320

PLAATJE, SOLOMON TSHEKISHO (1878-1932), South African writer **12** 341-342

Plaek
see Phibun Songkhram, Luang

Plague, bubonic
see Bubonic plague

PLANCK, MAX KARL ERNST LUDWIG (1858-1947), German physicist **12** 342-344
quantum theory
Bose, S.N. **29** 78-80

Plant breeding (botany)
Biffen, Sir Rowland Harry **29** 59-61

Plant classification (botany)
Colden, Jane **29** 118-119

PLATH, SYLVIA (1932-1963), American poet and novelist **12** 344-345

PLATO (428-347 B.C.), Greek philosopher **12** 345-347
influence on philosophers
ibn Bajja, Abu Bakr Muhhamad **29** 207-209

PLATT, THOMAS COLLIER (1833-1910), American politician **12** 347-348

PLAUTUS (c. 254-c. 184 B.C.), Roman writer **12** 348-350

PLAZA LASSO, GALO (1906-1987), Ecuadorian statesman **12** 350-351

PLEKHANOV, GEORGI VALENTINOVICH (1856-1918), Russian revolutionist and social philosopher **12** 351-352

PLENTY COUPS (c. 1848-1932), Native American tribal leader and Crow chief **12** 352-355

Plessis, Armand du
see Richelieu, Armand Jean Du Plessis De

Plessy v. Ferguson (legal case)
Henderson, Zelma **29** 188-191

PLINY THE ELDER (23/24-79), Roman encyclopedist **12** 355-356

PLINY THE YOUNGER (c. 61-c. 113), Roman author and administrator **12** 356

PLISETSKAYA, MAYA MIKHAILOVNA (born 1925), Russian ballet dancer **12** 356-358

PLOMER, WILLIAM (William Charles Franklyn Plomer; 1903-1973), South African/British author **24** 312-313

PLOTINUS (205-270), Greek philosopher, founder of Neoplatonism **12** 358-359

PLOTKIN, MARK (born 1955), American ethnobotanist and environmentalist **23** 308-310

PLUTARCH (c. 46-c. 120), Greek biographer **12** 359-360

PO CHÜ-I (772-846), Chinese poet **12** 362-363

POBEDONOSTSEV, KONSTANTIN PETROVICH (1827-1907), Russian statesman and jurist **12** 360-361

POCAHONTAS (c. 1595-1617), American Indian princess **12** 361-362
Argall, Samuel **29** 18-20

POE, EDGAR ALLAN (1809-1849), American writer **12** 363-365

POINCARÉ, JULES HENRI (1854-1912), French mathematician **12** 365-366

POINCARÉ, RAYMOND (1860-1934), French statesman **12** 366-368

POIRET, PAUL (1879-1944), French fashion designer **19** 291-293

POTTER, DENNIS (1935-1994), British essayist, playwright, screenwriter, and novelist 12 412-414

Pottery
Roebuck, John 29 326-328

POULENC, FRANCIS (1899-1963), French composer 12 414-415

POUND, EZRA LOOMIS (1885-1972), American poet, editor, and critic 12 415-417
influenced by
Arakida Moritake 29 287-288

POUND, ROSCOE (1870-1964), American jurist and botanist 12 417-418

POUSSAINT, ALVIN FRANCIS (born 1934), African American psychiatrist 24 313-316

POUSSIN, NICOLAS (1594-1665), French painter 12 418-420

POWDERLY, TERENCE VINCENT (1849-1924), American labor leader 12 420-421

POWELL, ADAM CLAYTON, JR. (1908-1972), African American political leader and Baptist minister 12 421-422

POWELL, ANTHONY (1905-2000), English novelist 12 422-423

POWELL, COLIN LUTHER (born 1937), African American chairman of the Joint Chiefs of Staff 12 424-425

POWELL, JOHN WESLEY (1834-1902), American geologist, anthropologist, and explorer 12 425-426

POWELL, LEWIS F., JR. (1907-1998), U.S. Supreme Court justice (1972-1987) 12 426-428

POWERS, HIRAM (1805-1873), American sculptor 12 428-429

POWHATAN (c. 1550-1618), Native American tribal chief 12 429-430
Argall, Samuel 29 18-20

POZZO, BROTHER ANDREA, S.J. (1642-1709), Italian artist and architect 25 341-342

PRADO UGARTECHE, MANUEL (1889-1967), Peruvian statesman 12 430-431

PRAETORIUS, MICHAEL (c. 1571-1621), German composer and theorist 12 431-432

Prague (city; Czech Republic)
Brod, Max 29 95-97
Novotný, Antonín 29 291-293

Prague Spring (1968)
Novotný, Antonín 29 291-293

PRAN, DITH (born 1942), Cambodian American journalist and activist 18 328-331

PRANDTAUER, JAKOB (1660-1726), Austrian baroque architect 12 432

PRASAD, RAJENDRA (1884-1963), Indian nationalist, first president of the Republic 12 433

PRAXITELES (flourished c. 370-330 B.C.), Greek sculptor 12 433-434

PREBISCH, RAÚL (1901-1986), Argentine economist active in the United Nations 12 434-436

PREGL, FRITZ (1869-1930), Austrian physiologist and medical chemist 12 436-437

PREM TINSULANONDA (born 1920), military leader and prime minister of Thailand (1979-1988) 12 437

PREMADASA, RANASINGHE (born 1924), president of Sri Lanka (1988-) 12 437-439

PREMCHAND (1880-1936), Indian novelist and short-story writer 12 439

PREMINGER, OTTO (1895-1986), Austrian filmmaker and theater producer/director 18 331-332

PRENDERGAST, MAURICE BRAZIL (1859-1924), American painter 12 440

PRESCOTT, WILLIAM HICKLING (1796-1859), American historian 12 440-441

Preservation architecture
Pokorny, Jan Hird 29 320-321

Presidential Medal of Freedom
Korematsu, Fred 29 234-236

PRESLEY, ELVIS ARON (1935-1977), American singer and actor 12 441-442

PRESTES, LUIZ CARLOS (1898-1990), Brazilian revolutionary and Communist leader 12 442-444

PRETORIUS, ANDRIES (1798-1853), South African politician and general 12 444-445

PRÉVERT, JACQUES (Jacques Henri Marie Prevert; 1900-1977), French poet and filmmaker 27 297-298

PREVIN, ANDRE (Andreas Ludwig Priwin; born 1929), German American composer and conductor 18 333-334

PRÉVOST, ABBÉ (1697-1763), French novelist, journalist, and cleric 12 445-446

Prévost d'Exiles, Antoine François
see Prévost, Abbé

PRICE, FLORENCE BEATRICE (nee Florence Beatrice Smith; 1887-1953), African American composer and music educator 26 306-308

PRICE, LEONTYNE (Mary Leontyne Price; born 1927), American prima donna soprano 12 446-447

PRICE, RICHARD (1723-1791), English Nonconformist minister and political philosopher 12 447-448

PRICHARD, DIANA GARCÍA (born 1949), Hispanic American chemical physicist 12 448-449

PRIDE, CHARLEY FRANK (born 1938), African American musician 23 317-319

PRIDI PHANOMYONG (1901-1983), Thai political leader 12 449

PRIEST, IVY MAUDE BAKER (1905-1975), treasurer of the United States (1953-1960) 12 450-451

PRIESTLEY, J(OHN) B(OYNTON) (1894-1984), English author of novels, essays, plays, and screenplays 12 451-452

PRIESTLEY, JOSEPH (1733-1804), English clergyman and chemist 12 452-453

Prignano, Bartolomeo
see Urban VI

PRIMATICCIO, FRANCESCO (1504-1570), Italian painter, sculptor, and architect 12 453-454

PRIMO DE RIVERA Y ORBANEJA, MIGUEL (1870-1930), Spanish general, dictator 1923-30 12 454-455

Primrose, Archibald Philip, (5th Earl of Rosebery; 1847-1929), British statesman
Douglas, Sir John Sholto 29 148-150

PRINCE, HAL (Harold Smith Prince; born 1928), American theatrical producer and director 19 295-298

PRINCIP, GAVRILO (1894-1918), Serbian nationalist and assassin 21 353-355
Franz Ferdinand 29 162-164

PRINGLE, THOMAS (1789-1834), Scottish author and abolitionist 23 319-320

Prison reform
see Penal reform

PRITCHETT, V(ICTOR) S(AWDON) (born 1900), English short story writer, novelist, literary critic, journalist, travel writer, biographer, and autobiographer 12 455-457

Privateers
see Pirates

Prizefighters
see Athletes, American

PROCLUS DIADOCHUS (born 410), Byzantine philosopher 12 457

PROCOPIUS OF CAESAREA (c. 500-c. 565), Byzantine historian 12 457-458

RICOEUR, PAUL (born 1913), French exponent of hermeneutical philosophy **13** 157-158

RIDE, SALLY (born 1951), American astronaut and physicist **13** 158-160

RIDGE, JOHN ROLLIN (Yellow Bird; 1827-1867), Native American author **22** 373-375

RIDGE, THOMAS JOSEPH (born 1946), American governor of Pennsylvania and first secretary of the Department of Homeland Security **24** 334-337

RIDGWAY, MATTHEW BUNKER (1895-1993), American general **13** 160-161

RIDGWAY, ROZANNE LEJEANNE (born 1935), American diplomat **24** 337-338

Ridolfi Plot
Babington, Anthony **29** 27-29

RIEFENSTAHL, LENI (born 1902), German film director **13** 161-163

RIEL, LOUIS (1844-1885), Canadian rebel **13** 163-164

RIEMANN, GEORG FRIEDRICH BERNARD (1826-1866), German mathematician **13** 164-165

RIEMENSCHNEIDER, TILMAN (1468-1531), German sculptor **13** 166

RIENZI, COLA DI (or Rienzo; 1313/14-1354), Italian patriot, tribune of Rome **13** 166-167

RIESMAN, DAVID (1909-2002), American sociologist, writer, and social critic **13** 167-168

RIETVELD, GERRIT THOMAS (1888-1964), Dutch architect and furniture designer **13** 169

Rigaud, Pierre François de
see Vaudreuil-Cavagnal, Marquis de

RIIS, JACOB AUGUST (1849-1914), Danish-born American journalist and reformer **13** 169-170

RILEY, JAMES WHITCOMB (1849-1916), American poet **13** 170-171

RILKE, RAINER MARIA (1875-1926), German lyric poet **13** 171-172

RILLIEUX, NORBERT (1806-1894), American inventor **20** 309-311

RIMBAUD, (JEAN NICOLAS) ARTHUR (1854-1891), French poet **13** 172-174

RIMMER, WILLIAM (1816-1879), American sculptor, painter, and physician **13** 174

RIMSKY-KORSAKOV, NIKOLAI ANDREEVICH (1844-1908), Russian composer and conductor **13** 174-175

RINGGOLD, FAITH (Faith Jones; born 1930), African American painter, sculptress, and performer **13** 175-177

RIO BRANCO, BARÃO DO (José Maria da Silva Paranhos; 1845-1912), Brazilian political leader **13** 177

RIORDAN, RICHARD JOSEPH (born 1930), American politician; mayor of Los Angeles **13** 177-179

RIPKEN, CAL, JR. (Calvin Edwin Ripken, Jr.; born 1960), American baseball player **18** 346-349

RIPLEY, GEORGE (1802-1880), American Unitarian minister and journalist **13** 179-180

Riqueti, H. G. V. de
see Mirabeau, Comte de

Rissho Daishi
see Nichiren

RITCHIE, DENNIS MACALISTAIR (born 1941), American computer programmer **27** 310-311

Rite of Spring (ballet music; Stravinsky)
Roerich, Nicholas **29** 328-330

RITSCHL, ALBRECHT BENJAMIN (1822-1889), German theologian **13** 180

RITTENHOUSE, DAVID (1732-1796), American astronomer and instrument maker **13** 180-181

RITTER, KARL (1779-1859), German geographer **13** 181-182

Ritter, Mary
see Beard, Mary Ritter

RITZ, CESAR (1850-1918), Swiss hotelier **29** 324-326

RIVADAVIA, BERNARDINO (1780-1845), Argentine independence leader, president 1826-27 **13** 182-183

RIVAS, DUQUE DE (Angel de Saavedra; 1791-1865), Spanish poet, dramatist, and statesman **13** 398

RIVERA, DIEGO (1886-1957), Mexican painter **13** 183-184

RIVERA, FRUCTUOSO (c. 1788-1854), Uruguayan statesman **13** 184-185

RIVERA, JOSÉ EUSTACIO (1888-1928), Colombian novelist **13** 185-186

Rivera, Luis Muñoz
see Muñoz Rivera, Luís

RIVERS, LARRY (Yitzroch Loiza Grossberg; 1923-2002), American artist **13** 186-187

RIVLIN, ALICE M. (born 1931), American economist and political advisor **18** 349-350

RIZAL, JOSÉ (1861-1896), Philippine national hero **13** 187-189

RNA
see Ribonucleic acid (biochemistry)

ROA BASTOS, AUGUSTO (born 1917), Paraguayan author **24** 338-341

ROACH, HAL (Harold Eugene Roach; 1892-1992), American filmmaker **28** 290-292

ROACH, MAX (Maxwell Lemuel Roach; 1924-2007), American jazz drummer, composer, and educator **28** 292-296

Roadrunner (cartoon character)
Jones, Chuck **29** 218-220

ROBARDS, JASON (Jason Nelson Robards, Jr.; 1922-2000), American actor **22** 375-378
Bacall, Lauren **29** 29-31

ROBBE-GRILLET, ALAIN (1922-2008), French novelist **13** 189-190

ROBBIA, LUCA DELLA (1400-1482), Italian sculptor **10** 19-20

ROBBINS, JEROME (Rabinowitz; 1918-1998), American director and choreographer **13** 190-192

ROBERT I (1274-1329), king of Scotland 1306-29 **13** 192-194

ROBERT II (1316-1390), king of Scotland 1371-90 **13** 194

ROBERT III (c. 1337-1406), king of Scotland 1390-1406 **13** 194-195

ROBERT, HENRY MARTYN (1837-1923), American engineer and parliamentarian **21** 367-370

ROBERT, SHAABAN (1909-1962), Tanzanian author who wrote in the Swahili language **14** 128-129

Robert Bruce
see Robert I (king, Scotland)

ROBERTS, FREDERICK SLEIGH (1st Earl Roberts of Kandhar, Pretoria, and Waterford; 1832-1914), British field marshal **13** 195-196

ROBERTS, JOHN GLOVER, JR. (born 1955), American jurist, chief justice of the United States Supreme Court 2005-**26** 320-322

Roberts of Kandahar, Pretoria, and Waterford, 1st Earl
see Roberts, Frederick Sleigh

ROBERTS, ORAL (Granville Oral Roberts; born 1918), American evangelist **28** 296-298

Roberts v. City of Boston (legal case)
Henderson, Zelma **29** 188-191

Robertson, Anna Mary
see Moses, Grandma

ROBERTSON, SIR DENNIS HOLME (1890-1963), English economist **13** 196

RUMFORD, COUNT (Benjamin Thompson; 1753-1814), American-born British physicist **13** 360-362

RUMI, JALAI ED-DIN (1207-1273), Persian poet and Sufi mystic **13** 362-363

RUMSFELD, DONALD HAROLD (born 1932), American statesman **23** 353-355

Rumsfeld v. Padilla (legal case)
Korematsu, Fred **29** 234-236

RUNDSTEDT, KARL RUDOLF GERD VON (1875-1953), German field marshal **13** 363-364

RUNEBERG, JOHAN LUDVIG (1804-1877), Finnish poet **25** 363-364

RURIK (died c. 873), Norman warrior **13** 364

RUSH, BENJAMIN (1745-1813), American physician **13** 364-365

RUSH, WILLIAM (1756-1833), American sculptor **13** 365-366

RUSHDIE, AHMED SALMAN (born 1947), Indian/British author **13** 366-368

RUSK, DAVID DEAN (1909-1994), American secretary of state (1961-1969) **13** 368-370

RUSKA, ERNST AUGUST FRIEDRICH (1906-1988), German engineer **13** 370-371

RUSKIN, JOHN (1819-1900), English critic and social theorist **13** 371-372

RUSSELL, ANNA (Anna Claudia Russell-Brown; 1911-2006), British born Canadian-American comedienne **28** 307-309

RUSSELL, BERTRAND ARTHUR WILLIAM (3rd Earl Russell; 1872-1970), British mathematician, philosopher, and social reformer **13** 373-374

RUSSELL, BILL (William Felton Russell; born 1934), African American basketball player and coach **20** 320-322

RUSSELL, CHARLES EDWARD (1860-1941), American journalist and reformer **13** 374-375

RUSSELL, CHARLES MARION (1864-1926), American painter **13** 375-376

RUSSELL, CHARLES TAZE (1852-1916), American religious leader **13** 376-377

RUSSELL, ELIZABETH SHULL (born 1913), American geneticist **13** 377-379

RUSSELL, JAMES EARL (1864-1945), educator and college dean who developed Teachers College **13** 379-380

RUSSELL, JOHN (1792-1878), English statesman, Prime minister 1846-52 **13** 380-381

Russell, 3d Earl
see Russell, Bertrand Arthur William

Russell of Kingston Russell, 1st Earl
see Russell, John

Russian art
Bakst, Leon **29** 35-37
Roerich, Nicholas **29** 328-330

Russian literature
literary criticism
Triolet, Elsa **29** 364-366

Russian Revolution (1905)
supporters
Andreyev, Leonid Nikolayevich **29** 11-13

Russian Revolution (1917; October)
Bolsheviks
Borodin, Mikhail Markovich **29** 72-74
opponents
Andreyev, Leonid Nikolayevich **29** 11-13

Russian Social-Democratic Labor Party
see Bolsheviks (Russian politics)

Russo-Japanese War (1904-1905)
Russia and
Andreyev, Leonid Nikolayevich **29** 11-13

RUSSWURM, JOHN BROWN (1799-1851), African American and Liberian journalist, educator, and governor **13** 381-382

RUSTIN, BAYARD (1910-1987), American social activist **13** 382-383

RUTAN, BURT (Elbert L. Rutan; born 1943), American aeronautical engineer **20** 322-325

RUTAN, DICK (Richard Glenn Rutan; born 1938), American aviator **20** 325-326

RUTH, GEORGE HERMAN, JR. (Babe Ruth; 1895-1948), American baseball player **13** 384

Ruth, Dr.
see Westheimer, Ruth Karola

RUTHERFORD, ERNEST (1st Baron Rutherford of Nelson; 1871-1937), British physicist **13** 384-387

RUTLEDGE, JOHN (1739-1800), American jurist and statesman **13** 387-388

RUYSBROECK, JAN VAN (1293-1381), Flemish mystic **13** 388-389

RUYSCH, RACHEL (1664-1750), Dutch artist **24** 341-343

RYAN, LYNN NOLAN (born 1947), American baseball player and author **13** 389-391

Ryan's Daughter (film)
Lean, David **29** 239-241

RYDER, ALBERT PINKHAM (1847-1917), American painter **13** 391-392

RYERSON, (ADOLPHUS) EGERTON (1803-1882), Canadian Methodist clergyman and educator **13** 392-393

RYLE, GILBERT (1900-1976), English philosopher **13** 393-394

RYLE, MARTIN (1918-1984), British radio astronomer **25** 365-367

S

SA
see Storm troopers, Nazi (SA)

SÁ, MEM DE (1504-1572), Portuguese jurist and governor general of Brazil **13** 395

Saadi
see Sa'di

Saadi, Yacef, Algerian National Liberation Front leader and statesman
Tillion, Germaine **29** 358-360

SAADIA BEN JOSEPH AL-FAYUMI (882-942), Jewish scholar **13** 396

SAARINEN, EERO (1910-1961), Finnish-American architect and industrial designer **13** 396-398

SAARINEN, ELIEL (1873-1950), Finnish-American architect and industrial designer **13** 396-398

Saavedra, Angel de
see Rivas, Duque de

Saavedra Lamas, Carlos
see Lamas, Carlos Saavedra

SABATIER, PAUL (1854-1941), French chemist **13** 398-399

SÁBATO, ERNESTO (born 1911), Argentine novelist and essayist **13** 399-400

SABBATAI ZEVI (1626-1676), Jewish mystic and pseudo-Messiah **13** 400-401

Sabbatius, Flavius Petrus
see Justinian I

SABIN, ALBERT BRUCE (1906-1993), Polish-American physician and virologist who developed polio vaccine **13** 401-402

SABIN, FLORENCE RENA (1871-1953), American anatomist **13** 402-405

Sablé, Treaty of
Anne of Brittany **29** 13-15

Sabotino, Marchese of
see Badoglio, Pietro

SACAJAWEA (c. 1784-c. 1812), Native American translator/interpreter, and guide **13** 405-408

STIEGEL, HENRY WILLIAM (1729-1785), German born American iron founder and glassmaker **14** 451

STIEGLITZ, ALFRED (1864-1946), American photographer, editor, and art gallery director **14** 451-452

STILICHO, FLAVIUS (died 408), Roman general **14** 452-453

STILL, CLYFFORD (1904-1980), American Abstract Expressionist artist **14** 453-454

STILL, WILLIAM (1821-1902), African American abolitionist, philanthropist, and businessman **14** 454-455

STILL, WILLIAM GRANT (born 1895), African American composer **14** 455-456

STILWELL, JOSEPH WARREN (1883-1946), American general **14** 456-457

STIMSON, HENRY LEWIS (1867-1950), American lawyer and statesman **14** 457-458

STIRLING, JAMES (1926-1992), British architect and city planner **14** 458-459

STIRNER, MAX (1806-1856), German philosopher **14** 459-460

STOCKHAUSEN, KARLHEINZ (1928-2007), German composer **14** 460-461

STOCKTON, ROBERT FIELD (1795-1866), American naval officer and politician **14** 461-462

STODDARD, SOLOMON (1643-1728/29), American colonial Congregational clergyman **14** 462-463

STOKER, BRAM (Abraham Stoker; 1847-1912), Irish author **14** 463-464

STOKES, CARL B. (1927-1996), African American politician **14** 464-465

STOLYPIN, PIOTR ARKADEVICH (1862-1911), Russian statesman and reformer **14** 465-466

STONE, EDWARD DURRELL (1902-1978), American architect, educator, and designer **14** 466-468

STONE, HARLAN FISKE (1872-1946), American jurist; chief justice of U.S. Supreme Court 1914-46 **14** 468-470

STONE, I. F. (Isador Feinstein; 1907-1989), American journalist **14** 470-471

STONE, LUCY (1818-1893), American abolitionist and women's suffrage leader **14** 471-472
Blackwell, Alice Stone **29** 61-63

Stone, Miriam
see Harwood, Gwen

STONE, OLIVER (born 1946), American filmmaker **14** 472-475

STONE, ROBERT ANTHONY (born 1937), American novelist **14** 475-476

STOPES, MARIE (1880-1958), British scientist and birth control advocate **14** 476-478

STOPPARD, THOMAS (Thomas Straussler; born 1937), English playwright **14** 478-479

STORM, THEODOR (1817-1888), German poet and novelist **14** 479-480

Storm troopers, Nazi (SA)
Röhm, Ernst **29** 330-332

STORY, JOSEPH (1779-1845), American jurist and statesman **14** 480-481

Story of My Life, The (autobiography; Keller)
Sullivan, Anne Mansfield **29** 352-353

Story of the Kelly Gang, The (film)
Kelly, Ned **29** 226-228

Storytellers
Londonderry, Annie **29** 253-256

STOSS, VEIT (c. 1445-1533), German sculptor **14** 481-482

STOUFFER, SAMUEL A. (1900-1960), American sociologist and statistician **14** 482-483

STOUT, JUANITA KIDD (1919-1998), African American judge **23** 382-384

STOVALL, LUTHER MCKINLEY (born 1937), American silkscreen artist **14** 483-484

STOWE, HARRIET ELIZABETH BEECHER (1811-1896), American writer **14** 484-485

STRABO (c. 64 B.C.-c. A.D. 23), Greek geographer and historian **14** 485-486

STRACHAN, JOHN (1778-1867), Canadian Anglican bishop **14** 486-487

STRACHEY, GILES LYTTON (1880-1932), English biographer and critic known for his satire of the Victorian era **14** 487-488

STRACHEY, JOHN (Evelyn John St. Loe Strachey; 1901-1963), British author and politician **20** 352-354

Strada, La (film)
Masina, Giulietta **29** 268-270

STRADIVARI, ANTONIO (c. 1644-1737), Italian violin maker **14** 488-490

STRAFFORD, 1ST EARL OF (Thomas Wentworth; 1593-1641), English statesman **14** 490-491

STRAND, MARK (born 1934), fourth Poet Laureate of the United States **14** 491-493

STRAND, PAUL (1890-1976), American photographer **19** 369-371

STRANG, RUTH MAY (1895-1971), American educator **14** 493-494

STRASBERG, LEE (Israel Strasberg; 1901-82), American acting instructor, director, and founding member of the Group Theatre **14** 494-495

Strathcona and Mount Royal, 1st Baron
see Smith, Donald Alexander

STRAUS, ISIDOR (1845-1912), American merchant **14** 496

STRAUSS, DAVID FRIEDRICH (1808-1874), German historian and Protestant theologian **14** 496-497

STRAUSS, FRANZ JOSEF (1915-1988), West German politician **14** 497-498

STRAUSS, JOHANN, JR. (1825-1899), Austrian composer **14** 498-499

STRAUSS, LEO (1899-1973), German Jewish Socratic political philosopher **14** 499-500

STRAUSS, LEVI (Loeb Strauss; 1829-1902), American businessman **20** 354-356

STRAUSS, RICHARD (1864-1949), German composer and conductor **14** 500-501

STRAUSS, ROBERT SCHWARZ (born 1918), Democratic fundraiser and strategist **14** 501-502

STRAVINSKY, IGOR FEDOROVICH (1882-1971), Russian-born composer **14** 502-506

STRAWSON, SIR PETER FREDRICK (1919-2006), English philosopher **14** 506-507

STREEP, MERYL LOUISE (born 1949), American actress **23** 384-387

STREETON, SIR ARTHUR ERNEST (1867-1943), Australian landscape painter **14** 507-508

STREISAND, BARBRA (Barbara Joan Streisand; born 1942), American entertainer **18** 386-388

STRESEMANN, GUSTAV (1878-1929), German statesman and diplomat **14** 508-509

Strickland, Susanna
see Moodie, Susanna

STRINDBERG, AUGUST (1849-1912), Swedish author **14** 509-511

STRINGER, HOWARD (born 1942), Welsh-American businessman **28** 338-340

STROESSNER, ALFREDO (1912-2006), Paraguayan statesman **14** 511-512

STRONG, JOSIAH (1847-1916), American clergyman and social activist **14** 512-513

TEBALDI, RENATA (Renata Ersila Clotilde Tebaldi; 1922-2004), Italian opera singer **26** 357-359

TECUMSEH (c. 1768-1813), American Shawnee Indian tribal chief **15** 133

TEDDER, ARTHUR (1890-1967), British military leader **19** 379-381

TEGGART, FREDERICK J. (1870-1946), comparative historian, librarian, sociologist, and educator who initiated sociology at the University of California **15** 133-134

TEILHARD DE CHARDIN, MARIE JOSEPH PIERRE (1881-1955), French theologian and paleontologist **15** 134-136

TEKAKWITHA, KATERI (Catherine Tegakovita; 1656-1680), Native American nun **23** 395-397

Telegraph (communications)
development
Gray, Elisha **29** 176-178
transatlantic cable
Bright, Charles Tilston **29** 91-93

TELEMANN, GEORG PHILIPP (1681-1767), German composer **15** 137-138

Telemanque
see Vesey, Denmark

Telephone (communications)
Gray, Elisha **29** 176-178

TELESIO, BERNARDINO (1509-1588), Italian philosopher of nature **15** 138-139

Television (United States)
police dramas
Webb, Jack **29** 375-376

TELKES, MARIA (Maria DeTelkes; 1900-1995), Hungarian American scientist **24** 407-409

TELLER, EDWARD (born 1908), Hungarian-American physicist **15** 139-141

Temperance movement (United States)
leaders
Livermore, Mary **29** 247-249

Temperature scales (physics)
Amontons, Guillaume **29** 3-5

Temple, Henry John
see Palmerston, 3d Viscount

TEMPLE, WILLIAM (1881-1944), ecumenicist and archbishop of Canterbury **15** 141-143

Temüjin
see Genghis Khan

TEN BOOM, CORRIE (Cornelia Ten Boom; 1892-1983), Dutch author **25** 411-413

Tenant of Wildfell Hall, The
Brontë, Anne **29** 99-101

Tendzin Gyatso
see Dalai Lama

TENGKU, ABDUL RAHMAN ("the Tengku"; born 1903), first prime minister of the Federation of Malaya and later of Malaysia **15** 340-341

TENNENT, GILBERT (1703-1764), American Presbyterian clergyman and evangelist **15** 143-144

TENNYSON, ALFRED (1st Baron Tennyson; 1809-92), English poet **15** 144-146

TENSKWATAWA (Lalewithaka; 1775-1836), Shawnee religious leader **20** 359-362

TENZING NORGAY (born 1914), Nepalese mountain climber **20** 362-364

TER BORCH, GERARD (1617-1681), Dutch painter **15** 146

TERENCE (Publius Terentius After; 195-159 B.C.), Roman comic playwright **15** 146-148

TERESA (Mother Teresa; Agnes Gonxha Bojaxhiu; 1910-1997), Catholic nun and missionary; Nobel Prize for Peace recipient **15** 148-151

TERESA OF AVILA (Teresa Sanchez de Cepeda y Ahumada; 1515-1582), Spanish nun **20** 364-366

TERESHKOVA, VALENTINA (born 1937), Russian cosmonaut **15** 151-152

TERKEL, LOUIS ("Studs"; born 1912), American radio personality and author **15** 152-153

TERMAN, LEWIS MADISON (1877-1956), American psychologist **15** 153-154

TERRA, GABRIEL (1873-1942), Uruguayan politician, president 1933-38 **15** 154-155
Baldomir, Alfredo **29** 39-41

TERRELL, MARY CHURCH (Mary Eliza Church Terrell; 1863-1954), African American activist and feminist **23** 397-399

Terror, Reign of
see French Revolution–1792-95 (Reign of Terror)

Terrorists
Europe
Keenan, Brian **29** 223-225
victims of
Corrigan, Mairead **29** 128-130

TERRY, ELLEN (Dame Ellen Alice [or Alicia] Terry; 1847-1928), English actress **24** 409-411

TERTULLIAN (Quintus Septimius Florens Tertullianus; c. 160-c. 220), North African theologian and apologist **15** 155-156

TESLA, NIKOLA (1856-1943), Croatian-American inventor and electrical engineer **15** 156-157

Tetanus (medicine)
Kitasato, Shibasabura **29** 230-232

TEWODROS II (1820-1868), emperor of Ethiopia **15** 158-159

Texas (state, United States)
settlement
Austin, Moses **29** 22-24

THACKERAY, WILLIAM MAKEPEACE (1811-1863), British novelist **15** 159-161

THALBERG, IRVING (1899-1936), American filmmaker **20** 366-368
Shearer, Norma **29** 343-345
von Stroheim, Erich **29** 367-369

THALES (c. 624-c. 545 B.C.), Greek natural philosopher **15** 161

THANT, U (1909-1974), Burmese statesman and UN secretary general **15** 161-162

THARP, MARIE (1920-2006), American geologist and oceanographic cartologist **15** 162-164

THARP, TWYLA (born 1941), American dancer and choreographer **15** 164-165

THARPE, ROSETTA NUBIN (1915-1973), African American musician **24** 411-413

THATCHER, MARGARET HILDA (born 1925), prime minister of Great Britain (1979-1990) **15** 165-168

Thayendanegea
see Brant, Joseph

THAYER, ELI (1819-1899), American reformer, agitator, and promoter **15** 168

THAYER, SYLVANUS (1785-1872), American educator and engineer **15** 168-169

THEANO (born c. 546 BC), Greek mathematician and physician **23** 399-401

Theater
directors
Piscator, Erwin **29** 315-317
experimental
Piscator, Erwin **29** 315-317
racial aspects
Gilpin, Charles **29** 172-174
staging
Bakst, Leon **29** 35-37

THEILER, MAX (1899-1972), American epidemiologist and microbiologist **15** 169-170

THEMISTOCLES (c. 528-462 B.C.), Athenian politician **15** 170-171

Themistogenes of Syracuse
see Xenophon

THEOCRITUS (c. 310-c. 245 B.C.), Greek poet **15** 171-172

TUTU, ARCHBISHOP DESMOND (born 1931), South African Anglican archbishop and opponent of apartheid **15** 360-361

TUTUOLA, AMOS (born 1920), Nigerian writer **15** 361-362

TWACHTMAN, JOHN HENRY (1853-1902), American painter **15** 362-363

TWAIN, MARK (Samuel Langhorne Clemens; 1835-1910), American humorist and novelist **15** 363-366

TWAIN, SHANIA (Eileen Regina Edwards; born 1965), Canadian singer-songwriter **26** 361-363

TWEED, WILLIAM MARCY (1823-1878), American politician and leader of Tammany Hall **15** 366-367

Twentieth Century (film)
Lombard, Carole **29** 249-251

Twentieth Century Fox (film company)
Lombard, Carole **29** 249-251

Twort, Frederick William, (1877-1950), English bacteriologist
d'Hérelle, Félix Hubert **29** 140-142

TYLER, ANNE (born 1941), American author **15** 367-368

TYLER, JOHN (1790-1862), American statesman, president 1841-45 **15** 368-369

TYLER, MOSES COIT (1835-1900), American historian **15** 369-370

TYLER, RALPH W. (born 1902), American educator/scholar **15** 370-371

TYLER, ROYALL (1757-1826), American playwright, novelist, and jurist **15** 371-372

Tyler's Insurrection
see Peasants' Revolt (England; 1381)

TYLOR, SIR EDWARD BURNETT (1832-1917), English anthropologist **15** 372-373

TYNDALE, WILLIAM (c. 1495-1536), English biblical scholar **15** 373-374

TYNDALL, JOHN (1820-1893), Irish physicist **15** 374

Typhoid Mary
see Mallon, Mary

TYRRELL, GEORGE (1861-1909), Irish-English Jesuit priest and theologian **15** 374-375

TYRRELL, JOSEPH BURR (J.B. Tyrrell; 1858-1957), Canadian geologist and explorer **23** 410-412

TZ'U-HSI (1835-1908), empress dowager of China 1860-1908 **15** 375-376

U

UAR
see Egypt (United Arab Republic; nation, North Africa)

UBICO Y CASTAÑEDA, GENERAL JORGE (1878-1946), president of Guatemala (1931-1944) **15** 377-378

UCCELLO, PAOLO (1397-1475), Italian painter **15** 378-379

UCHIDA, MITSUKO (born 1948), Japanese pianist **23** 413-415

UEBERROTH, PETER VICTOR (born 1937), Former baseball commissioner **15** 379-381

UELSMANN, JERRY (born 1934), American photographer **20** 384-385

UHLENBECK, KAREN (born 1942), American mathematician **15** 381-382

ULANOVA, GALINA (1910-1998), Russian ballerina **15** 382-383

ULBRICHT, WALTER (1893-1973), East German political leader **15** 383-384

ULFILAS (c. 311-c. 382), Arian bishop of the Visigoths **15** 384

ULPIAN, DOMITIUS (died 228), Roman jurist **15** 385-386

Umayado no Miko
see Shotoku Taishi

Umdabuli we Sizwe
see Mzilikazi

UNAMUNO Y JUGO, MIGUEL DE (1864-1936), Spanish philosopher and writer **15** 386-387

UNÁNUE, JOSÉ HIPÓLITO (1755-1833), Peruvian intellectual, educator, and scientist **15** 387-388

Underground Railroad
see African American history–Slavery and abolition (Underground Railroad)

UNDERHILL, JOHN (c. 1597-1672), American military leader and magistrate **15** 388

UNDSET, SIGRID (1882-1949), Norwegian novelist **15** 388-389

UNGARETTI, GIUSEPPE (1888-1970), Italian poet **15** 389-390

Union of Soviet Socialist Republics (former nation, Northern Eurasia)
SOVIET UNION (SINCE 1917)
and Afghanistan
Wilson, Charlie **29** 379-381
European policy
Novotný, Antonín **29** 291-293

Unitarianism (religion)
Livermore, Mary **29** 247-249

UNITAS, JOHNNY (John Constantine Unitas; 1933-2002), American football player **20** 385-387
Berry, Raymond **29** 57-59

United Arab Republic
see Egypt (United Arab Republic; nation, North Africa)

United Australia Party
Lyons, Enid Muriel **29** 258-260

United Kingdom
see Great Britain; Northern Ireland

United Nations
supporters
Koo, Wellington **29** 232-234

United Party of the Socialist Revolution
see Communist Party of Cuba

United States Air Force (U.S.A.F.)
Chennault, Claire Lee **29** 114-116

United States Sanitary Commission
Livermore, Mary **29** 247-249

U.S. Department of Agriculture
see Agriculture, U.S. Department of

U.S. Navy
aircraft and rocketry
Williams, Sunita **29** 376-379

University College (Dublin)
O'Faolain, Nuala **29** 294-296

UNSER, AL, SR. (born 1939), American race car driver **23** 415-417

UPDIKE, JOHN (born 1932), American author of poems, short stories, essays, and novels **15** 390-392

UPJOHN, RICHARD (1802-1878), English-born American architect **15** 392

Upper Egypt
see Egypt (United Arab Republic; nation, North Africa)

URBAN II (Otto de Lagery; 1042-99), pope 1088-99 **15** 393

URBAN VI (Bartolomeo Prignano; 1318-89), pope 1378-89 **15** 394

URBAN VIII (Maffeo Barberini; 1568-1644), Italian Roman Catholic pope (1623-1644) **26** 301-302

URBAN, MATT (1919-1995), American solider **19** 391-392

Urban government
see Municipal government

UREY, HAROLD CLAYTON (1893-1981), American chemical physicist and geochemist **15** 394-396

URQUIZA, JUSTO JOSÉ (1801-1870), Argentine dictator, general, and statesman **15** 396-397

URRACA (c. 1078-1126), Queen of Leon-Castilla **23** 417-418

Uruguay, Eastern Republic of (nation, South East South America)
20th century
Baldomir, Alfredo **29** 39-41

UTAMARO, KITAGAWA (1753-1806), Japanese printmaker **15** 397

UTHMAN DON FODIO (1755-1816), Moslem teacher and theologian **15** 397-398

Uticensus, Marcus Porcius Cato
see Cato the Younger

V

V-1 and 2 (rockets)
Stuhlinger, Ernst **29** 349-351

Vaca, Álvar Núñez Cabeza de
see Cabeza de Vaca, Álvar Núñez

VADIM, ROGER (Roger Vadim Plemiannikov; 1928-2000), Russian/French filmaker and author **22** 413-415

VAGANOVA, AGRIPPINA YAKOVLEVNA (1879-1951), Russian ballet dancer and teacher **24** 425-427

VAIL, THEODORE NEWTON (1845-1920), American businessman **23** 419-421

VAJPAYEE, ATAL BEHARI (born 1926), prime minister of India **19** 393-395

VALADON, SUZANNE (Marie Clémentine Valadon; 1865-1935), French artist and model **27** 354-356

VALDEZ, LUIS (born 1940), Hispanic American playwright and filmmaker **15** 399-400

VALDIVIA, PEDRO DE (c. 1502-53), Spanish conquistador and professional soldier **15** 400-401

VALENS, RITCHIE (Richard Steven Valenzuela; 1941-1959), Hispanic American musician **22** 415-417

VALENTI, JACK JOSEPH (1921-2007), presidential adviser and czar of the American film industry **15** 401-403

VALENTINO, RUDOLPH (Rodolfo Alfonso Raffaelo Pierre Filibert de Valentina d'Antonguolla Guglielmi; 1895-1926), Italian/American actor **20** 388-390

VALENZUELA, LUISA (born 1938), Argentine author **23** 421-423

VALERA Y ALCALÁ GALIANO, JUAN (1824-1905), Spanish novelist and diplomat **15** 403

VALERIAN (Publius Licinius Valerianus; c. 200-c. 260), Roman emperor 253-260 **15** 404-405

VALÉRY, PAUL AMBROISE (1871-1945), French poet, philosopher, and critic **15** 405-406

VALLA, LORENZO (c. 1407-57), Italian humanist **15** 406

VALLANDIGHAM, CLEMENT LAIRD (1820-1871), American politician **15** 406-407

VALLE INCLÁN, RAMÓN MARIA DEL (c. 1866-1936), Spanish novelist, playwright, and poet **15** 407-408

VALLEE, RUDY (Hubert Prior Vallee; 1901-1986), American vocalist **28** 359-361

VALLEJO, CÉSAR ABRAHAM (1892-1938), Peruvian poet **15** 408-409

VAN BUREN, MARTIN (1782-1862), American statesman, president 1837-41 **15** 410-411

VAN DER GOES, HUGO (flourished 1467-82), Flemish painter **15** 416-417

VAN DIEMEN, ANTHONY MEUZA (1593-1645), Dutch colonial official and merchant **15** 420

Van Diemen's Land
see Tasmania (state, Australia)

VAN DOESBURG, THEO (1883-1931), Dutch painter **15** 421

VAN DONGEN, KEES (Cornelis Theodorus Marie Van Dongen; 1877-1968), Fauvist painter, portraitist, and socialite **15** 421-422

VAN DUYN, MONA (1921-2004), first woman to be appointed poet laureate of the United States **15** 422-423

VAN DYCK, ANTHONY (1599-1641), Flemish painter **15** 423-425

VAN DYKE, DICK (Richard Wayne Van Dyke; born 1925), American actor, author, and producer **25** 416-418

VAN EEKELEN, WILLEM FREDERIK (born 1931), Dutch secretary-general of the Western European Union **15** 426-427

VAN GOGH, VINCENT (1853-1890), Dutch painter **15** 427-429

VAN HORNE, SIR WILLIAM CORNELIUS (1843-1915), American-born Canadian railroad entrepreneur **15** 429-430

VAN PEEBLES, MELVIN (Melvin Peebles; born 1932), American film director and producer, actor, author, and musician **21** 414-416

VAN RENSSELAER, KILIAEN (c. 1580-1643), Dutch merchant and colonial official in America **15** 430-431

VAN VECHTEN, CARL (1880-1964), American writer and photographer **18** 400-402

VAN VLECK, JOHN HASBROUCK (1899-1980), American physicist **25** 418-420

VANBRUGH, SIR JOHN (1664-1726), English architect and dramatist **15** 409-410

VANCE, CYRUS R. (1917-2002), American secretary of the army and secretary of state **15** 411-413

VANCE, ZEBULON BAIRD (1830-1894), American politician **15** 413-414

VANCOUVER, GEORGE (1758-1798), English explorer and navigator **15** 414-415

VANDER ZEE, JAMES (1886-1983), photographer of the people of Harlem **15** 418-419

VANDERBILT, CORNELIUS (1794-1877), American financier, steamship and railroad builder **15** 415-416

VANDERBILT, GLORIA (born 1924), American designer, artist, and author **19** 395-397

VANDERLYN, JOHN (1775-1852), American painter **15** 417

VANDROSS, LUTHER (1951-2005), American singer **26** 364-366

Vane, Harriet (literary character)
Sayers, Dorothy L. **29** 335-337

VANE, SIR HENRY (1613-1662), English statesman **15** 425-426

Vanguard I (satellite)
Stuhlinger, Ernst **29** 349-351

Vannucci, Pietro
see Perugino

VAN'T HOFF, JACOBUS HENDRICUS (1852-1911), Dutch physical chemist **15** 431-432

Vanzetti, Bartolomeo
see Sacco, Nicola and Vanzetti, Bartolomeo

VARDHAMANA MAHAVIRA (c. 540-470 B.C.), Indian ascetic philosopher **10** 135-137

Varennes, Pierre Gaultier de
see La Verendrye, Sieur de

VARÈSE, EDGARD (1883-1965), French-American composer **15** 432-433

VARGAS, GETULIO DORNELLES (1883-1954), Brazilian political leader **15** 433-434

VARGAS LLOSA, MARIO (born 1936), Peruvian novelist, critic, journalist, screenwriter, and essayist **15** 434-436

VARMUS, HAROLD ELIOT (born 1939), medical research expert and director of the National Institutes of Health (1993-) **15** 436-437